Dictionary of the Middle Ages

AMERICAN COUNCIL OF LEARNED SOCIETIES

The American Council of Learned Societies, organized in 1919 for the purpose of advancing the study of the humanities and of the humanistic aspects of the social sciences, is a nonprofit federation comprising forty-five national scholarly groups. The Council represents the humanities in the United States in the International Union of Academies, provides fellowships and grants-in-aid, supports research-and-planning conferences and symposia, and sponsors special projects and scholarly publications.

MEMBER ORGANIZATIONS

AMERICAN PHILOSOPHICAL SOCIETY, 1743
AMERICAN ACADEMY OF ARTS AND SCIENCES, 1780
AMERICAN ANTIQUARIAN SOCIETY, 1812
AMERICAN ORIENTAL SOCIETY, 1842
AMERICAN NUMISMATIC SOCIETY, 1858
AMERICAN PHILOLOGICAL ASSOCIATION, 1869
ARCHAEOLOGICAL INSTITUTE OF AMERICA, 1879
SOCIETY OF BIBLICAL LITERATURE, 1880
MODERN LANGUAGE ASSOCIATION OF AMERICA, 1883
AMERICAN HISTORICAL ASSOCIATION, 1884
AMERICAN ECONOMIC ASSOCIATION, 1885
AMERICAN FOLKLORE SOCIETY, 1888
AMERICAN DIALECT SOCIETY, 1889
AMERICAN PSYCHOLOGICAL ASSOCIATION, 1892
ASSOCIATION OF AMERICAN LAW SCHOOLS, 1900
AMERICAN PHILOSOPHICAL ASSOCIATION, 1901
AMERICAN ANTHROPOLOGICAL ASSOCIATION, 1902
AMERICAN POLITICAL SCIENCE ASSOCIATION, 1903
BIBLIOGRAPHICAL SOCIETY OF AMERICA, 1904
ASSOCIATION OF AMERICAN GEOGRAPHERS, 1904
HISPANIC SOCIETY OF AMERICA, 1904
AMERICAN SOCIOLOGICAL ASSOCIATION, 1905
AMERICAN SOCIETY OF INTERNATIONAL LAW, 1906
ORGANIZATION OF AMERICAN HISTORIANS, 1907
AMERICAN ACADEMY OF RELIGION, 1909
COLLEGE ART ASSOCIATION OF AMERICA, 1912
HISTORY OF SCIENCE SOCIETY, 1924
LINGUISTIC SOCIETY OF AMERICA, 1924
MEDIAEVAL ACADEMY OF AMERICA, 1925
AMERICAN MUSICOLOGICAL SOCIETY, 1934
SOCIETY OF ARCHITECTURAL HISTORIANS, 1940
ECONOMIC HISTORY ASSOCIATION, 1940
ASSOCIATION FOR ASIAN STUDIES, 1941
AMERICAN SOCIETY FOR AESTHETICS, 1942
AMERICAN ASSOCIATION FOR THE ADVANCEMENT OF SLAVIC STUDIES, 1948
METAPHYSICAL SOCIETY OF AMERICA, 1950
AMERICAN STUDIES ASSOCIATION, 1950
RENAISSANCE SOCIETY OF AMERICA, 1954
SOCIETY FOR ETHNOMUSICOLOGY, 1955
AMERICAN SOCIETY FOR LEGAL HISTORY, 1956
AMERICAN SOCIETY FOR THEATRE RESEARCH, 1956
SOCIETY FOR THE HISTORY OF TECHNOLOGY, 1958
AMERICAN COMPARATIVE LITERATURE ASSOCIATION, 1960
AMERICAN SOCIETY FOR EIGHTEENTH-CENTURY STUDIES, 1969
ASSOCIATION FOR JEWISH STUDIES, 1969

Dictionary of the Middle Ages

JOSEPH R. STRAYER, *EDITOR IN CHIEF*

Volume 11

SCANDINAVIAN LANGUAGES—TEXTILES, ISLAMIC

CHARLES SCRIBNER'S SONS • NEW YORK

Copyright © 1988 American Council of Learned Societies

Library of Congress Cataloging in Publication Data
Main entry under title:

Dictionary of the Middle Ages.

Includes bibliographies and index.
1. Middle Ages—Dictionaries.   1. Strayer,
Joseph Reese, 1904–1987

D114.D5   1982   909.07   82-5904
ISBN 0-684-16760-3 (v. 1)   ISBN 0-684-18274-2 (v. 8)
ISBN 0-684-17022-1 (v. 2)   ISBN 0-684-18275-0 (v. 9)
ISBN 0-684-17023-X (v. 3)   ISBN 0-684-18276-9 (v. 10)
ISBN 0-684-17024-8 (v. 4)   ISBN 0-684-18277-7 (v. 11)
ISBN 0-684-18161-4 (v. 5)
ISBN 0-684-18168-1 (v. 6)
ISBN 0-684-18169-X (v. 7)

Published simultaneously in Canada
by Collier Macmillan Canada, Inc.
Copyright under the Berne convention.

7 9 11 13 15 17 19   B/C   20 18 16 14 12 10 8

PRINTED IN THE UNITED STATES OF AMERICA.

The *Dictionary of the Middle Ages* has been produced with
support from the National Endowment for the Humanities.

The paper in this book meets the guidelines for
permanence and durability of the Committee on
Production Guidelines for Book Longevity of the
Council on Library Resources.

Maps prepared by Sylvia Lehrman.

Editorial Board

Advisory Committee

Editorial Staff

Contributors to Volume 11

F. R. P. AKEHURST
University of Minnesota
SIRVENTES

THEODORE M. ANDERSSON
Stanford University
SIGRDRÍFUMÁL; SIGURD; SIGURÐARKVIÐA IN FORNA; SIGURÐARKVIÐA IN MEIRI; SIGURÐARKVIÐA IN SKAMMA

SARAH ARENSON
Man and Sea Society, Tivon, Israel
SHIPS AND SHIPBUILDING, RED SEA AND PERSIAN GULF

S. G. ARMISTEAD
University of California, Davis
SPANISH LITERATURE: BALLADS

ANI P. ATAMIAN
SĪS; TARSUS

JÁNOS M. BAK
University of British Columbia
STEPHEN I OF HUNGARY, ST.; STEPHEN, CROWN OF ST.; SZÉKESFEHÉRVÁR

CARL F. BARNES, JR.
Oakland University, Rochester, Michigan
SONDERGOTIK; STRASBOURG CATHEDRAL

ROBERT BARRINGER
St. Michael's College, University of Toronto
SEVEN DEADLY SINS

MICHAEL L. BATES
American Numismatic Society
SEALS AND SIGILLOGRAPHY, ISLAMIC

ÜLKÜ Ü. BATES
Hunter College, City University of New York
SELĀMLIK; ŞEREFE

SILVIO A. BEDINI
SCIENTIFIC INSTRUMENTS; SYLVESTER II, POPE

ROBERT BEDROSIAN
SEBĒOS; SHADDĀDIDS; SPARAPET

ISAAC BENABU
Hebrew University of Jerusalem
SEPHARDIM

ANNA G. BENNETT
TAPESTRY, ART OF; TAPESTRY, MILLEFLEURS

LIONEL BIER
Brooklyn College, City University of New York
TAQ-I BOSTAN; TAXT-I SULEIMAN

A. J. BLISS
University College, Dublin
SIR ORFEO

JEROME BLUM
Princeton University
SERFS AND SERFDOM: RUSSIA

C. E. BOSWORTH
University of Manchester
SEBÜKTIGIN; SELJUKS OF RUM; ṬĀHIR IBN AL-ḤUSAYN; TAHIRIDS

WILLIAM M. BOWSKY
University of California, Davis
SIENA

DENIS G. BREARLEY
University of Ottawa
SEDULIUS SCOTTUS

SEBASTIAN P. BROCK
The Oriental Institute, Oxford
SYRIAN CHRISTIANITY

ROBERT BROWNING
Dumbarton Oaks Research Center
SCHOLARSHIP, BYZANTINE CLASSICAL

LESLIE BRUBAKER
Wheaton College, Norton, Massachusetts
SCREEN, CHANCEL; SCRINIUM; SCRIPTORIUM; SCROLL, INHABITED; SERAPH; STIKARION; SYNAXARY; TABULA ANSATA; TESSERA

LANCE W. BRUNNER
University of Kentucky
SEQUENCE (PROSA)

JAMES F. BURKE
University of Toronto
SPANISH LITERATURE: ROMANCES

ROBERT I. BURNS, S. J.
University of California, Los Angeles
SPAIN, CHRISTIAN-MUSLIM RELATIONS; SPAIN, MUSLIM KINGDOMS OF

JAMES E. CATHEY
University of Massachusetts, Amherst
SKAÐI; SURTR

A. C. CAWLEY
University of Leeds
SECOND SHEPHERDS' PLAY

FRED A. CAZEL, JR.
University of Connecticut
TAXATION, ENGLISH

CONTRIBUTORS TO VOLUME 11

YVES CHARTIER
University of Ottawa
SOLESMES

FREDERIC L. CHEYETTE
Dartmouth College
SIMON DE MONTFORT

STANLEY CHODOROW
University of California, San Diego
TANCRED (CANONIST)

MARLENE CIKLAMINI
Rutgers University
SNORRI STURLUSON

DOROTHY CLOTELLE CLARKE
SPANISH LITERATURE: VERSIFICATION AND PROSODY

JEROME W. CLINTON
Princeton University
SHĪRĀZ; TABRĪZ

SIDNEY L. COHEN
Louisiana State University
SUTTON HOO

LAWRENCE I. CONRAD
Wellcome Institute for the History of Medicine
SUYŪṬĪ, AL-

JOHN J. CONTRENI
Purdue University
SCHOOLS, CATHEDRAL; SCHOOLS, PALACE; SMARAGDUS OF ST. MIHIEL

ROBERT COOK
Newcomb College
STRENGLEIKAR

WILLIAM J. COURTENAY
University of Wisconsin, Madison
TERMINISM

SLOBODAN ĆURČIĆ
Princeton University
SERBIAN ART AND ARCHITECTURE

MICHAEL T. DAVIS
Mt. Holyoke College
SOUFFLET

FREDERICK A. DE ARMAS
Louisiana State University
SPANISH LITERATURE: SENTIMENTAL ROMANCES

LUCY DER MANUELIAN
SKEWṘA; T^c^ALIN; TAT^c^EW; TEKOR

HORACE W. DEWEY
University of Michigan
SLAVIC LANGUAGES AND LITERATURES

ALAN DEYERMOND
Westfield College, University of London
SPANISH LITERATURE; SPANISH LITERATURE: TRANSLATIONS

WACHTANG DJOBADZE
California State University, Los Angeles
SVETI CXOVELI

ANN DOOLEY
St. Michael's College, University of Toronto
TÁIN BÓ CUÁILNGE

WILLIAM DUNPHY
St. Michael's College, University of Toronto
SIGER OF BRABANT

WILLIAM EAMON
New Mexico State University
TECHNOLOGY, TREATISES ON

MARCIA J. EPSTEIN
University of Calgary
TENSO

JOHN H. ERICKSON
St. Vladimir's Seminary
SCHISMS, EASTERN-WESTERN CHURCH; SERDICA, COUNCIL OF; STUDIOS MONASTERY; SYNAXARY; SYNODIKON OF ORTHODOXY

ANN E. FARKAS
Brooklyn College, City University of New York
TEREM

MARGOT E. FASSLER
Yale University
SEQUENCE, LATE

CHARLES B. FAULHABER
University of California, Berkeley
SPANISH LATIN LITERATURE

PAULA SUTTER FICHTNER
Brooklyn College, City University of New York
SIGISMUND, EMPEROR

JOHN V. A. FINE, JR.
University of Michigan
SERBIA; STEFAN LAZAREVIĆ; STEFAN NEMANJA; STEFAN PRVOVENČANI; STEFAN TOMAŠ; STEFAN TOMAŠEVIĆ; STEFAN UROŠ II MILUTIN; STEFAN UROŠ IV DUŠAN; STEFAN VUKČIĆ KOSAČA; STJEPAN KOTROMANIĆ; SYMEON OF BULGARIA

DONALD F. FLEMING
SQUIRE

PATRICK K. FORD
University of California, Los Angeles
TALIESIN

CLIVE FOSS
University of Massachusetts, Boston
SEBASTE

GUY FOURQUIN
Université de Lille III
SERFS AND SERFDOM: WESTERN EUROPEAN

CHARLES F. FRAKER
University of Michigan
SPANISH LITERATURE: CHRONICLES

ROBERTA FRANK
Centre for Medieval Studies, University of Toronto
SKÁLDATAL; SKALDIC POETRY

GLADYS FRANTZ-MURPHY
Iona College, New Rochelle
TAXATION, ISLAMIC

JOHN B. FREED
Illinois State University
SWABIA

EDWARD FRUEH
Columbia University
SIGEHARD OF ST. MAXIMIN; SISEBUT

NINA G. GARSOÏAN
Columbia University
SEPUH; ŠINAKAN; TANUTĒR

CONTRIBUTORS TO VOLUME 11

ADELHEID M. GEALT
Indiana University
SEGNA DI BONAVENTURA; SEMITECOLO, NICOLETTO; SIMONE DA BOLOGNA; SIMONE MARTINI; SINOPIA; SPINELLO ARETINO; STIACCIATO; TADDEO DI BARTOLO; TEMPERA PAINTING

DOUGLAS GIFFORD
University of St. Andrews
SPANISH LITERATURE: POPULAR POETRY

THOMAS F. GLICK
Boston University
SEVILLE

PETER B. GOLDEN
Rutgers University
SELJUKS; SHAH-ARMAN; SULTAN; TAMERLANE

OLEG GRABAR
Fogg Art Museum, Harvard University
SŪQ

JORGE J. E. GRACIA
State University of New York at Buffalo
SCHOLASTICISM, SCHOLASTIC METHOD

VIVIAN H. H. GREEN
Lincoln College, Oxford
TAXATION, CHURCH

JAMES GRIER
Queen's University, Ontario
TE DEUM

KAAREN GRIMSTAD
University of Minnesota
SINFJQTLI; STARKAÐR; SVIPDAGSMÁL

MARY GRIZZARD
University of New Mexico
SERRA, PEDRO AND JAIME; SITULA; TERRA SIGILLATA

BJARNI GUÐNASON
Háskóli Íslands
SKJQLDUNGA SAGA

JOSEPH GUTMANN
Wayne State University
SYNAGOGUE

EMILY ALBU HANAWALT
Boston University
SUDA

WILLIAM LIPPINCOTT HANAWAY, JR.
University of Pennsylvania
SHĀHNĀMA

NATHALIE HANLET
TATWINE OF CANTERBURY

JOSEPH HARRIS
Harvard University
SKÍRNISMÁL

ARMAD Y. AL-HASSAN
TECHNOLOGY, ISLAMIC

RALPH S. HATTOX
Emory University
SELIM I

EINAR HAUGEN
SKRÆLINGS

JOHN BELL HENNEMAN
Princeton University
TAXATION, FRENCH

ROBERT H. HEWSEN
Glassboro State College
SEWAN, LAKE; SHIRVAN; ŠIRAK; SIWNIK^{c}; TARŌN; TAYK^{c}; TBILISI

JOHN HUGH HILL
TANCRED (CRUSADER)

RICHARD C. HOFFMANN
York University
TENURE OF LAND, WESTERN EUROPEAN

ANDREW HUGHES
University of Toronto
TENOR

ALFRED L. IVRY
Brandeis University
SOLOMON BEN JUDAH IBN GABIROL

MICHAEL JACOFF
Brooklyn College, City University of New York
TEGLIACCI, NICCOLÒ DI SER SOZZO

CHARLES W. JONES
SCHOOLS, MONASTIC

JENNIFER E. JONES
SEVEN SLEEPERS OF EPHESUS; SIGN OF THE CROSS; SPIERINC, CLAEYS; TETRAMORPH

WILLIAM CHESTER JORDAN
Princeton University
SENESCHAL; SERGEANT; SONG OF LEWES; SUMPTUARY LAWS, EUROPEAN

PETER A. JORGENSEN
University of Georgia
SIGURÐAR SAGA FÓTS; SIGURÐAR SAGA ÞÖGLA

JACQUES JOSET
Universitaire Instelling, Antwerpen
SHEM TOV

G. H. A. JUYNBOLL
SUNNA; SUNNITES

WALTER EMIL KAEGI, JR.
University of Chicago
SCHOLAE; SOLDIERS' PORTIONS; STRATEGOS; STRATIOTAI; TAGMATA

HOWARD KAMINSKY
Florida International University
SCHISM, GREAT

WILLIAM E. KAPELLE
Brandeis University
STRATHCLYDE, KINGDOM OF

ALEXANDER P. KAZHDAN
Dumbarton Oaks Research Center
SKYLITZES, JOHN; SYMEON METAPHRASTES

MAJID KHADDURI
The Johns Hopkins Foreign Policy Institute
TENURE OF LAND, ISLAMIC

DALE KINNEY
Bryn Mawr College
TALENTI, FRANCESCO

CHRISTOPHER KLEINHENZ
University of Wisconsin, Madison
SICILIAN POETRY

JAMES E. KNIRK
Universitetet i Oslo
SVERRIS SAGA

CONTRIBUTORS TO VOLUME 11

LINDA KOMAROFF
Hamilton College
SERDĀB

BARBARA M. KREUTZ
Bryn Mawr College
SHIPS AND SHIPBUILDING, MEDITERRANEAN

Y. TZVI LANGERMANN
Hebrew University of Jerusalem
SCIENCE, JEWISH

JACOB LASSNER
Wayne State University
ṬABARĪ, AL-

ROBERT E. LERNER
Northwestern University
STEPHEN II, POPE

ARTHUR D. LEVINE
University of Toronto
SOLMIZATION; STAFF; SUMER IS ICUMEN IN

JOHN LINDOW
University of California, Berkeley
SKÁLDSKAPARMÁL; SNORRA EDDA

FRANCES RANDALL LIPP
Colorado State University
SEX AETATES MUNDI

DONALD P. LITTLE
McGill University
TAYMĪYA, IBN

DEREK W. LOMAX
University of Birmingham
SPANISH LITERATURE: SERMONS

ERIK LÖNNROTH
Göteborgs Universitet
SWEDEN

JOSEPH H. LYNCH
Ohio State University
SIMONY

BRYCE LYON
Brown University
SCUTAGE; SIMON DE MONTFORT THE YOUNGER

MICHAEL McCORMICK
The Johns Hopkins University
SIGNATURES; STEPHEN OF TOURNAI; STICHOMETRY; STYLUS

JULIA H. McGREW
Vassar College
STURLUNGA SAGA

D. R. McLINTOCK
University of London
STRASBOURG OATHS; TATIAN

WILFERD MADELUNG
The Oriental Institute, Oxford
SECTS, ISLAMIC; SHĪᶜA

GEORGE MAKDISI
University of Pennsylvania
SCHOOLS, ISLAMIC

KRIKOR H. MAKSOUDIAN
SMBAT I THE MARTYR; SMBAT SPARAPET; STEPᶜANOS ASOŁIK TARŌNECᶜI

YAKOV MALKIEL
University of California, Berkeley
SPANISH LANGUAGE

MAHMOUD MANZALAOUI
University of British Columbia
SECRETUM SECRETORUM

IVAN G. MARCUS
Jewish Theological Seminary
SCHOOLS, JEWISH

J. Y. MARIOTTE
Archives de la Haute-Savoie
SWITZERLAND

SHAUN E. MARMON
The Johns Hopkins University
SLAVERY, ISLAMIC WORLD

JOAQUÍN MARTÍNEZ-PIZARRO
State University of New York at Stony Brook
SVEN AGGESEN

RALPH WHITNEY MATHISEN
University of South Carolina
SIDONIUS APOLLINARIS

BRIAN MERRILEES
University of Toronto
SEINTE RESURECCION, LA; SIMUND DE FREINE

JOHN MEYENDORFF
St. Vladimir's Seminary
SERGIUS OF RADONEZH, ST.; SYMEON THE NEW THEOLOGIAN, ST.; SYNKELLOS

THOMAS MONTGOMERY
Tulane University of Louisiana
SPANISH LITERATURE: BIBLE TRANSLATIONS

MICHAEL MORONY
University of California, Los Angeles
ṢIFFĪN

MARINA MUNDT
Universitetet i Bergen
STURLA ÞÓRÐARSON

JOHN H. MUNRO
University of Toronto
SCARLET; SILK; TEXTILE TECHNOLOGY; TEXTILE WORKERS

RHOADS MURPHEY
Columbia University
ṢINF

SEYYED HOSSEIN NASR
Temple University
SĪNĀ, IBN

COLBERT I. NEPAULSINGH
State University of New York at Albany
SPANISH LITERATURE: LYRIC POETRY

JOHN W. NESBITT
Dumbarton Oaks Research Center
SEALS AND SIGILLOGRAPHY, BYZANTINE; TECHNOLOGY, BYZANTINE

HELMUT NICKEL
Metropolitan Museum of Art
SWORDS AND DAGGERS

THOMAS S. NOONAN
University of Minnesota
SLAVS, ORIGINS OF

JOSEPH F. O'CALLAGHAN
Fordham University
SIETE PARTIDAS; SPANISH ERA

TOMÁS Ó CATHASAIGH
St. Michael's College, University of Toronto
TARA

CONTRIBUTORS TO VOLUME 11

BARBARA OEHLSCHLAEGER-GARVEY
University of Illinois
Tablion

NICOLAS OIKONOMIDES
Université de Montréal
Sebastokrator; Taxation, Byzantine

BERNARD O'KANE
American University in Cairo
Ṣuffa

DUANE J. OSHEIM
University of Virginia
Sutri, Synod of

ROBERT OUSTERHOUT
University of Illinois
Solea; Synthronon

HERMANN PÁLSSON
University of Edinburgh
Sörla Saga Sterka; Sturlaugs Saga Starfsama

ANGELO PAREDI
Biblioteca Ambrosiana, Milan
Sforza

OLAF PEDERSEN
University of Aarhus
Sundials

CAROL TALBERT PETERS
Squarcione, Francesco

NORMAN J. G. POUNDS
Cambridge University
Steelmaking

JAMES M. POWELL
Syracuse University
Sicilian Vespers; Sicily, Kingdom of

JOSÉ M. REGUEIRO
University of Pennsylvania
Spanish Literature: Drama

ROGER E. REYNOLDS
Pontifical Institute of Mediaeval Studies, Toronto
Stations of the Cross; Syrian Rites

BRIGITTE BEDOS REZAK
State University of New York at Stony Brook
Seals and Sigillography, Western European

THEODORE JOHN RIVERS
Schwabenspiegel

ELAINE GOLDEN ROBISON
Sigebert of Gembloux

LINDA C. ROSE
Serdica; Sergios I; Sirmium; Skanderbeg; Socrates Scholasticus; Sozomen; Tabula Peutingeriana; Tafur, Pero de; Tarasios

JOEL ROTH
Jewish Theological Seminary
Talmud, Exegesis and Study of

STEVEN ROWAN
University of Missouri, St. Louis
Syndic

JAMES R. RUSSELL
Columbia University
Seals and Sigillography, Sasanian; Škand-Gumānīg Wizār; Spāhbad

A. I. SABRA
Harvard University
Science, Islamic

ANTONIO SÁNCHEZ ROMERALO
University of California, Davis
Spanish Literature: Dawn and Spring Songs

T. A. SANDQUIST
University of Toronto
Statute

PAUL SCHACH
University of Nebraska
Svarfdæla Saga

NICOLAS SCHIDLOVSKY
Sticheron

KENNETH R. SCHOLBERG
Michigan State University
Spanish Literature: Satire

JAMES A. SCHULTZ
University of Illinois at Chicago
Solomon and Marcolf

DOROTHY SHERMAN SEVERIN
Westfield College, University of London
Spanish Literature: Troy Story

LARRY SILVER
Northwestern University
Stoss, Veit; Syfer, Hans

BARRIE SINGLETON
University of London
Stockton, Thomas; Stowell, John; Sutton, Robert

PAUL SOLON
Macalester College
Somnium Viridarii

PRISCILLA P. SOUCEK
New York University
Shadirvan

ERNEST H. SOUDEK
Suso, Heinrich; Tauler, Johannes

SUSAN SPECTORSKY
Queens College, City University of New York
Shāfi^{c}ī, al-

GABRIELLE M. SPIEGEL
University of Maryland
Suger of St. Denis

J. STEYAERT
University of Minnesota
Sluter, Claus

YEDIDA K. STILLMAN
State University of New York at Binghamton
Sumptuary Laws, Islamic; Ṭaylasān

KENNETH R. STOW
University of Haifa
Servi Camerae Nostrae

LARRY E. SULLIVAN
Lehman College, City University of New York
Textbooks

RONALD GRIGOR SUNY
University of Michigan
Tamar

CONTRIBUTORS TO VOLUME 11

DONALD W. SUTHERLAND
University of Iowa
Seisin, Disseisin; Sheriff

JUNE SWANN
Central Museum, Northamptonshire
Shoes and Shoemakers

EDITH DUDLEY SYLLA
North Carolina State University
Swineshead

GEORGE S. TATE
Brigham Young University
Sólarljóð

ROBERT B. TATE
University of Nottingham
Spanish Literature: Biography; Spanish Literature: Lost Works

J. WESLEY THOMAS
University of Kentucky
Steinmar; Tannhäuser

B. BUSSELL THOMPSON
Spanish Literature: Hagiography

DERICK S. THOMSON
University of Glasgow
Scottish Literature, Gaelic

R. W. THOMSON
Dumbarton Oaks Research Center
Shotʿa Rustʿaveli

WARREN T. TREADGOLD
Hillsdale College
Schism, Photian; Symeon the Logothete

A. L. UDOVITCH
Princeton University
Sicily, Islamic

RICHARD W. UNGER
University of British Columbia
Ships and Shipbuilding, Northern European

CHARLES VERLINDEN
Slavery, Slave Trade

ERICH VON RICHTHOFEN
University of Toronto
Spanish Literature: Epic Poetry

PETER VON SIVERS
University of Utah
Syria

STEPHEN L. WAILES
Indiana University
Schrätel und der Wasserbär, das; Sperber, der; Stricker, der

JOHN K. WALSH
University of California, Berkeley
Spanish Literature: Hagiography

EDWIN J. WEBBER
Northwestern University
Spanish Literature: Instructional Works

WILLIAM K. WEST
Surveying

ESTELLE WHELAN
Seljuk Art and Architecture; Textiles, Islamic

LYNN WHITE, jr.
University of California, Los Angeles
Technology, Western

GREGORY WHITTINGTON
New York University
Screen; Sedilia; Spandrel; Spolia; Squinch; Stringcourse; Tetraconch

DANIEL WILLIMAN
State University of New York at Binghamton
Schools, Grammar

MARTHA WOLFF
Art Institute of Chicago
Schongauer, Martin

JENNY WORMALD
St. Hilda's College, Oxford
Scotland: History

VICKIE ZIEGLER
Pennsylvania State University
Seifried Helbling; Spervogel and Herger

RONALD EDWARD ZUPKO
Marquette University
Setier; Shilling; Shire; Stone

Dictionary of the Middle Ages

Dictionary of the Middle Ages

SCANDINAVIAN LANGUAGES—TEXTILES, ISLAMIC

SCANDINAVIAN LANGUAGES. The Scandinavian languages (modern Danish, Faroese, Icelandic, Norwegian, and Swedish) derive from the base common to all Germanic languages, an Indo-European daughter dialect reconstructed as Proto-Germanic. (Finnish and Lapp, other languages in Scandinavia, are not Indo-European and therefore have no historical connection with Proto-Germanic or its later descendants other than the absorption of loanwords through cultural contacts.) Proto-Germanic split into several dialects, including North Germanic or Proto-Scandinavian.

The oldest surviving records in a Scandinavian language were written in the runic alphabet and date from about A.D. 200. In the period before about 550, the language still represented a stage close to the East (such as Gothic) and West (earliest Old High German, Old English) branches of Germanic, but with certain distinctly Nordic forms. The oldest form of the runic alphabet, named the futhark after its first six letters, contained twenty-four symbols. In Scandinavia, twenty-three symbols were used to represent five vowels (*i, e, a, o, u*), sixteen consonants, and two semivowels. The approximately 125 inscriptions extant in this "older futhark" were found on stones or loose metal or bone objects within the modern boundaries of Denmark, Norway, and Sweden, as well as Germany, Poland, and the Ukraine. The form of the symbols remained constant over several centuries, and the entire futhark, when it was written as such, was always in the same fixed order. This common Scandinavian cultural artifact was probably transmitted on carved sticks, and most of the runic inscriptions, now lost, were made on wooden items.

The period 600–800 yields fewer inscriptions, none of which are Danish. Toward the end of this interlude there emerged from Denmark a "younger futhark" based on the older one but having only sixteen symbols. There are 412 Danish inscriptions in the younger futhark, about 12 in Norway, more than 100 in the British Isles, 53 in Iceland, about 30 in Greenland, and 3 in the Faroes—and more than 2,500 in Sweden, some 2,000 of which were carved in the period 800–1100. Most inscriptions are found on memorial stones. (The younger futhark was further modified in southern Norway and Sweden to simplify the sixteen symbols.) The reduction in number of units led to ambiguities. The *i*-rune stood for both *i* and *e;* the *u*-rune for *u, o, y,* and *ø;* the *a*-rune for *a, æ* and *ǫ;* the *b*-rune for *b, p, mb,* and *mp;* the *t*-rune for *t, d, nd,* and *nt;* and the *k*-rune for *k, g, ng,* and *nk*. Diphthongs were not always written as such.

The emergence of the younger futhark coincides with a major restructuring of the phonology of Scandinavian languages. The semivowel *j* was lost initially, and the old *j*-rune became *a* (Proto-Scandinavian [PSc] **jāra* > *ār* [year]). The previous *a*-rune then came to be used for nasalized *ã*. The voiced and voiceless spirants became nondistinctive—that is, *ð* and *þ*, for instance, were then allophonic variants of each other. Prosodic relationships changed when unstressed short vowels were deleted—for example, PSc **dagaR* > Old Icelandic (OI) *dagr* (day), **horna* > OI *horn* (horn). Unstressed diphthongs became monophthongs—for instance, **sunauR* > **sunōR* > OI *sonar* (son; genitive singular), **kurnai* > **kornē* > OI *korni* (grain; dative singular). The stressed syllables reacted to the shortening by adding more vocalic distinctions. A following *i* or *j* caused stressed back vowels to be fronted, as in **dōmiðō* > OI *dǿmða* (I judged), **skiutiR* > OI *skýtr* (he shoots), **hauRjan* > OI *heyra* (hear). A following *a* lowered a stressed *i* or *u* to *e* or *o*, respectively, as in **wiraR* > **werR* > OI *verr* (man) or **hurna* > **horna* > OI *horn*

(horn). A following *u* or *w* caused rounding of stressed vowels, as with **barnu* > OI *bǫrn* (children), **trigguR* > OI *tryggr* (safe). The five short vowels of PSc were thus increased to possibly nineteen with the addition of *y, ø,* and *æ* by *i*-umlaut from *u, o,* and *a,* respectively; of *ǫ* from *a* through *u*-umlaut; of a combined product *ǿ* from both *i*- and *u*-umlaut of *a;* and of nasalized variants created with the loss of *a* following *n.* There were also long vowels and diphthongs of all types. This very complex array became simpler in time with the merger of the nasalized vowels with their non-nasal counterparts, and of short *æ* with *e* (in the west), for instance. The consonants were affected by various assimilations, such as **zn, *zð* > *nn, ðð* (**razna* > OI *rann* [house], **gazðaz* > **gaððR* > OI *gaddr* [point]); **Xt* > *tt* (**naXt-* > OI *nátt* [night]).

The radiation of phonological innovation in early medieval times has been traced from three areas: western Norway and its settlements in the Faroes and Iceland; the south, with Denmark as the major source; and northeastern Norway and central and northern Sweden. The oldest changes originated in the west, from which *a*-umlaut, *u*-umlaut, and *i*-umlaut spread during the period of the Atlantic settlements. These innovations show the strongest effects in the west, with decreasing application toward the east. OI thus has *holt* (woods) through *a*-umlaut from PSc **hulta,* whereas the Danish and Swedish form is *hult.* The effects of *u*-umlaut similarly decrease toward the east, as with OI *bǫrn,* Danish (Da) *børn,* but Swedish (Sw) *barn* (children) or OI *mǫnnum* (men; dative plural), but Old Danish (ODa) and Old Swedish (OSw) *mannum.* An example for *i*-umlaut is OI *skýtr* (he shoots) but OSw *skiūter.* The west was also the source of nasal assimilation during an early period—for instance, PSc **brant-* (steep) > OI *brattr,* Da *brat,* but Sw *brant;* of the loss of *v* before *r* (OI *reiðr* vs. Da *vred* [wroth]); and of later changes, the number and importance of which decreased as the southern area became more active.

In Denmark in the tenth century there started a process of monophthongization, whereby such contrasts as PSc **stain-* > OI *steinn* : Da *sten* (stone), OI *auga* : Da *øje* (eye), and PSc **raukiR* > **ræykr* > OI *reykr* : Da *røg* (smoke) were created. The monophthongization of these earlier diphthongs spread north into Sweden, giving the impression of an original and basic east–west dialect boundary. Two other major innovations began in Denmark but have remained restricted to the southern area. The continental Scandinavian system of secondary ("musical") accent was replaced in Danish dialects by no secondary accent in words of more than one syllable—where Swedish and Norwegian have it—and by a glottal stop in monosyllables—where Swedish and Norwegian have just the primary (dynamic) accent. (The loss of secondary accent in Faroese and Icelandic was probably an independent phenomenon.) The correspondence to monosyllables in the earlier forms of the language is shown by OI *akr* : Sw *åker* : Da *ager* [*a·ˀɣər*] (field), the latter with a glottal stop. The other major innovation in Danish, likely resulting from increased dynamic accent on the stem vowel, was the change of postvocalic *p, t, k* to *b, d* (modern [ð]), *g* (modern [ɣ] or Ø). Thus there are cognates like OI *gapa* : Da *gabe* (gape), OI *gata* : Da *gade* [*ga·ðə*] (street), and OI *bók* : Da *bog* [*bo·ˀɣ*] (book). The "softening" of *p, t, k* extends northward into the southern provinces of Sweden and Norway.

An important innovation, whose application was more consistent in East Scandinavian, was the "breaking" of *e* to *ea* (> *ja*) under the influence of a following *a* (or > *jǫ* with following *u* or *w*). As examples, PSc **helpan* > OI *hjálpa* : Da *hjælpe* : Sw *hjälpa* (help) (but PSc **stelan* > OI *stela* : Sw *stjäla* [steal], PSc **feta* > OI *fet* : Da *fjed* : Sw *fjät* [step]), and PSc **erþu* > OI *jǫrð* : Da, Sw *jord* can be cited. The east also innovated in the simplification of initial consonant clusters beginning with *h.* The loss of initial *h* can be seen in such examples as OI *hlaupa* : Sw *löpa* : Da *løbe* (leap, run), OI *hnot* : Da *nød* (nut), OI *hrafn* : Da *ravn* (raven), OI *hjálpa* : Sw *hjälpa* [*jælpa*] (help), and OI *hvítr* : Sw *vit* (white). The east also displays progressive *i*-umlaut (Sw *hjälpa*) and the development of *-fn-* to Da *-wn-* : Sw *-mn-*, as in Da *havn* [*hawˀn*] : Sw *hamn* vs. OI *hǫfn* (haven, harbor).

From around 1000 into the 1300's the term *dǫnsk tunga* (Danish tongue) was used for the still rather uniform Scandinavian languages, even for western dialects like Icelandic and Norwegian, and as late as 1340–1360 the term was used by Eysteinn Ásgrímsson in the poem *Lilja.* The various dialects certainly were mutually understood throughout the Middle Ages until morphological simplification of Danish, Swedish, and Dano-Norwegian, on the one hand, contrasting with the deep conservatism of Icelandic and Faroese, on the other hand, gradually formed an east–west barrier to comprehension. The specifically Danish innovations eventually erected a barrier at the Øresund.

BIBLIOGRAPHY
Kristján Árnason, *Quantity in Historical Phonology* (1980), 60–121; Oskar Bandle, *Die Gliederung des Nordgermanischen* (1973), 24–95; Einar I. Haugen, *The Scandinavian Languages* (1976), 97–223, and *Scandinavian Language Structures* (1982); Haugen and Thomas L. Markey, *The Scandinavian Languages* (1972); Finn Hødnebø, "Norsk språk," in *Kulturhistorisk leksikon for nordisk middelalder,* XII (1967); Peter Skautrup, "Hvorledes dansken blev til," in *Festskrift till Jöran Sahlgren,* Karl G. Ljunggren, ed. (1944), and "Dansk tunge," in *Kulturhistorisk leksikon for nordisk middelalder,* II (1957).

JAMES E. CATHEY

[See also **German Language; Indo-European Languages, Development of.**]

SCANDINAVIAN LITERATURE: BALLADS. In Scandinavia the ballad is defined much as it is in English and Scottish traditions: it is a folk song that tells a story. Even when this simple definition is amplified, Scandinavian and British traditions remain in close agreement: the ballad is a folk song whose origin is most likely to be traced back to the French dance songs of the Middle Ages; it employs a language rich in commonplaces and tells its story from an impersonal point of view, tending to focus its narrative on one or two key scenes; it is always sung to rounded melodies in strophes of two or four lines with end rhyme and is characteristically associated with a lyrical refrain. Scandinavian and British ballad traditions differ solely with regard to this last point—whereas in Great Britain only roughly half of all ballad types have been recorded with a refrain, in Scandinavia the refrain is almost always present.

Although ballads are considered to constitute a medieval genre in Scandinavia, most of what can be learned about them stems not from the Middle Ages but, rather, from songbooks of the nobility and antiquarian anthologies of the sixteenth and seventeenth centuries, and from the folk tradition of the nineteenth and twentieth centuries. Evidence that ballads were performed in Scandinavia as early as 1200, the date usually given for the beginnings of the ballad tradition there, is so slight that some scholars have suggested that the ballad might largely be a postmedieval phenomenon.

Sources from the Middle Ages have very little to say about the ballad dance, and in each case the information they give is equivocal. The Icelandic *Þorgils saga ok Hafliða* (*ca.* 1220) mentions that at a wedding held in 1119 at the farm of Reykjahólar, there were "dance amusements"; but it is impossible to determine whether these dances were performed to the singing of ballads or of some other songs—or, for that matter, whether they were a feature of twelfth-century Icelandic culture as reported in the saga or a later practice familiar to the thirteenth-century saga author and mistakenly attributed by him to an earlier age.

Similar questions are raised when we consider the thirteenth-century Danish chronicle *Rydårbogen,* which mentions the custom of dancing at court in the time of King Svend in 1157—are these indeed ballad dances or some other kind of dance, and has the author anachronistically attributed court dancing to the twelfth century? A fresco from about 1380 in Ørslev Church in Skælskør, Denmark, is often assumed to depict the ballad dance, but its testimony, too, is equivocal. On the fresco a row of dancers—women wearing crowns and holding hands with young men in harlequin dress—is stepping to the right; however, the inclusion in the fresco of an animal blowing a horn suggests that this dance was to instrumental music rather than to ballad song.

Even though none of the scattered medieval sources seems to bear certain evidence of ballad dance, the many references to dance in extant ballad texts make us confident that it was a universal feature of the medieval Scandinavian ballad performance. The refrain is especially rich in such references. The Danish ballad "Black Iver" (*The Types of the Scandinavian Medieval Ballad* [TSB], F23) has an internal refrain that goes: "You tread a dance!"; and the refrain to the Faroese "Guttorm in Hattarmot" (TSB E39) goes: "Let's stamp hard on the floor!/Let's not spare our shoes!/God will rule where we'll dance another Yule!" By the nineteenth century the practice of performing ballads in the dance had died out nearly everywhere except in the Faroe Islands, where it still survives. The Faroese dance as we know it probably resembles medieval practice quite closely: the dancers form a ring, taking three steps to the left, right foot brought against left and back again. They repeat this series of steps until the end of the ballad.

Only one melody that may have been used as a ballad tune has been preserved from the Middle Ages. It was recorded in the Danish Codex Runicus (*ca.* 1300) under a text fragment that reads like half of a four-line ballad strophe: "I dreamed a dream late last night/of silk and velvet fine." The melody is in the key of D with an ambitus of D to A. The next recordings of what may be ballad tunes are found in hymnals of the sixteenth century, in which ballad-like melodies were occasionally used to carry the words of the new Lutheran hymns. The first certain recording of a ballad melody—to "Oluf Strangeson's Jousting Match" (TSB D300)—was written into a ballad manuscript in the late sixteenth century by the Danish collector Anders Sørensen Vedel. Although medieval sources tell us nothing about the details of the performance of ballad melodies, modern Faroese practice again points the way—it suggests that ballads were not sung, but chanted by one or two lead singers, who rested their voices between stanzas while the rest of the dancers carried the metrically more complex refrain.

The earliest known ballad texts are extremely fragmentary. Preserved in medieval manuscripts are some eight or ten fragments no longer than a strophe that—like the verse from Codex Runicus—seem balladlike but cannot be associated with any known ballad. The Icelandic *Sturlunga saga* contains two of these: the often cited quatrain "Lopt is in the islands,/gnawing puffin bones!/Sæmund is on the heaths,/eating berries alone!" and the refrain-like "So are my sorrows heavy as lead." The first recordings of what must certainly be ballad texts are from the fifteenth century. The oldest of these is a garbled strophe from the Danish "Angelfyr and Helmer the Champion" (TSB E90), which was written by the cartographer Claudius Clavus on his map of Greenland from 1425. Two refrains have been preserved from this period: the one from "Holger the Dane and Burman" (TSB E133), which was written under the figure of Holger Danske in a fresco on the vaulted ceiling of Floda Church in Södermanland, Sweden, and one from a Marsk Stig ballad (TSB C14) used by a scribe as a pen test in a Danish manuscript from 1454. The longest text from the medieval period is a fragment of seven stanzas from "The Knight in Stag's Disguise" (TSB A43), in a Danish manuscript from the 1450's.

The first complete ballad texts from the sixteenth-century songbooks of Danish and Swedish noblemen reveal a number of different metrical forms. The two principal ones, the couplet and the quatrain, together dominate the corpus. The couplet, regarded as the older of the two, has four stresses per line: "Her ér en jómfru på vórt lánd,/og hún vil áldrig háve mánd!" (There is a maiden in our land, and she would never have a man!; from the Danish "The Knight in Bird's Disguise" [TSB A44]). In the quatrain stanza the rhymeless odd lines contain four stresses and the rhymed even ones, three: "Ébbe han tjéner i kóngens gård/både for gúld og fǽ;/Péder, hans bróder, lader býgge et skíb,/han réjser óp sejltrǽ" (Ebbe serves at the king's court for both gold and fee; Peter, his brother, has had a ship built, he raises up the mast tree; from the Danish "Ebbe Skammelson" [TSB D251]).

Here and there in the corpus of Scandinavian ballads there are strophic forms that vary somewhat from the predominant ones. Best known of these are the repetition stanza, the "Little Karin" stanza, and the "Proud Ellen" stanza. (The last two are named after exemplary Danish ballads—TSB B14 and D241—in which these strophic types were used.) The repetition stanza is a couplet, the last line or line and a half of which is repeated as a lead-in to the following couplet, as can be seen in the Icelandic "The Ballad of Gunnhild" (TSB D231):

> There I saw with my two eyes,
> the archbishop lying by her side.
> *Refrain:* I really did wish to depart from the world.
>
> My two eyes,
> the archbishop lying by her side.
> There I saw for a second time,
> by her lying five knights in a line.
> *Refrain:* I really . . .

The repetition stanza probably achieved its earliest popularity in Denmark, where 9 percent of ballad types utilize this strophic type, and from there spread to the Faroes and to Iceland, where it must have been especially favored—it is used in fully 20 percent of all ballad types.

Like the repetition stanza, the "Little Karin" stanza is a variation of the couplet, but in this case the four-stress line has been extended to six stresses: "Och kära mína hófmän, I stíllen édert låg,/mens jág får gå til kýrkan att väcka úpp min fár" (And my dearest gentlemen, please settle down your troop, while I to church do hasten to rouse my father up; from the Swedish "Duke Silverdale" [TSB A45]). The "Little Karin" stanza was particularly popular in later Swedish tradition but also found admirers in Denmark. The "Proud Ellen" stanza is a quatrain in which the even lines have been shortened from three stresses to two, and the rhyme is almost always masculine: "Óp da vågned den únge brúd,/

og véndte hun sig:/'Jeg béder dig fór den øverste Gúd,/du slå ikke mig'" (Up then woke the girlish bride, and she turned around: "I beg of you by the Highest Power, don't strike me down; from "Proud Ellen's Revenge" [TSB D241]). Like the repetition stanza, this strophic type seems to have attained some degree of popularity first in Denmark and then spread elsewhere, specifically to Iceland, where it was especially beloved as a ballad meter, and to Sweden.

The frequent inclusion of the refrain in ballad manuscripts is a hallmark of Scandinavian tradition and has readily led to the supposition that it was a rare ballad type that was performed without one. There are two types of refrain: the end refrain and the internal refrain. The end refrain—used with both couplet stanzas and quatrains—consists of a single verse line, usually of from three to eight stresses, that is sung at the close of each stanza to round it off—for example, "Do put your words well," from the Danish "King Valdemar and His Sister" (TSB D346), and "Yonder my sweetheart awakens under the linden tree," from the Danish "The Knight's Runic Spell" (TSB E37). Only in Faroese tradition is the end refrain regularly extended to a length of from two to five lines.

The internal refrain is found mainly in couplet ballads, in which it is sung following the first line of the stanza, with a supplementary end refrain following the second line. The Danish "The Maid at Court" (TSB D4) offers a good example: "There was great joy and even greater glee,/—*In the greenwood*—/Sir Ove and proud Ingelil will soon married be./—*To the maiden's bower riding*." Although, as in this example, the internal and end refrains need not be rhymed, many of them are linked by half rhyme or even whole rhyme. In a very small number of ballads, the wording of the refrain is varied somewhat from stanza to stanza as the story progresses, but this seems to reflect the singing style of the sixteenth and seventeenth centuries rather than medieval tradition.

The refrain can serve any one of a number of functions in any given ballad text. Often it echoes the major theme of the ballad, sometimes referring to the most important dramatic act—for example, in "Proud Ellen's Revenge": "She betrayed him while he slept." Sometimes the refrain helps to set the mood of the ballad: in the comic Danish "Sir Palle's Wedding" (TSB D153), the refrain is a merry one: "The leaves are coming out green"; whereas in the tragic "Hildebrand and Hilda" (TSB A42), also from Denmark, it strikes a sad note: "Sorrow is heavy when you bear it alone." Numerous refrains completely ignore the ballad story and refer to the occasion of the ballad performance—for example, the refrains noted above that mention the ballad dance.

In a number of older manuscripts, the texts of some ballads begin with one or more lyrical introductory strophes that have no connection with the ballad story itself and are often in some metrical form other than that of the song they introduce. One or several verse lines from these introductory strophes usually provide the refrain used with each stanza of the ballad. In the Icelandic "The Ballad of Alexander" (TSB D337), which is in quatrains, the last line of the opening three-line strophe is used in this way: "So it is in this world,/others you must always doubt./—*Alexander has his ship fitted out*." These lyric stanzas were once viewed as the scattered remnants of medieval dance strophes that, when combined with narrative song, gave rise to the ballad genre. Today, however, these introductory strophes are not thought to be the original source of the refrain; rather, they are seen as late embellishments, signature verses, usually incorporating and expanding upon the refrains of the ballads for which they were composed.

Ever since Svend Grundtvig's pioneering edition of Danish ballads, *Danmarks gamle folkeviser*, Scandinavian ballad types have customarily been grouped according to theme. In *The Types of the Scandinavian Medieval Ballad* (1978)—a systematic catalog of the entire Scandinavian corpus of 838 ballad types—the categories are six: (A) ballads of the supernatural, (B) legendary ballads, (C) historical ballads, (D) ballads of chivalry, (E) heroic ballads, and (F) jocular ballads.

Ballads of the supernatural, numbering seventy-five types, relate stories about witchcraft and runic charms, magic transformations, strange creatures in nature, and ghosts. The themes of these ballads are very widespread—found throughout the ballad literatures of Europe, for example, are variants of "The Elf-Shot" (TSB A63), about a young man who refuses to dance with an elf maid and dies from her curse. Popular throughout Scandinavia and with a close parallel in Scottish tradition is "The Two Sisters" (TSB A38; Child 10), about how the guilt of a woman who has drowned her beautiful younger sister is revealed by a musical instrument, usually a harp, made from the dead girl's bones. Widespread throughout Scandinavia are "Sir Stig's Runes" (TSB

A4), in which a nobleman casts a runic love spell on the wrong woman and must cope with the consequences, and "The Maid in Bird's Disguise" (TSB A16), about a hunter who breaks the spell cast by a woman who has transformed her stepdaughter first into a doe and then into a bird. "Aage and Else" (TSB A67) is less widespread but of interest because its story—about a young woman who so greatly mourns the death of her fiancé that he is disturbed in his grave and goes to her bower to tell her not to grieve—is an echo of the final episode of the Eddic poem *Helgakviða Hundingsbana II.*

Before the nineteenth century, ballads of the supernatural were condemned for the superstitions they contained, and it was not until the Romantic age that editors and scholars came to appreciate their archaic elements of belief. In his headnote to "The Elf-Shot" in *Danmarks gamle folkeviser,* Svend Grundtvig discussed the many European variants of this ballad type, concluding that it was very ancient and stemmed, as did perhaps the genre as a whole, from Brittany, the home of this ballad's fullest text. This theory was further developed by Francis Child and Paul Verrier. Axel Olrik has studied attitudes toward supernatural beings expressed in this group of ballads and has noted that they vary from what appear to be more archaic ones of dependence, fear, and resignation to later ones of freedom, sympathy, and optimism. Working with Olrik's ideas, Ernst Frandsen has divided these ballads into three chronological groupings: the first reflects pagan man's fear of nature's power; the second, the confidence of the Christian; and the third, the use of supernatural themes to achieve a sentimental or picturesque effect.

Legendary ballads, numbering thirty-seven types, deal primarily with Christian themes, such as the lives of the Virgin Mary and of Christ, the lives of saints and martyrs, miracles, and visions. This group is most richly represented in east Scandinavian tradition: Danish tradition contains thirty types and Swedish eighteen, whereas in the entire west Scandinavian area (Norway, Iceland, the Faroes) a total of only twenty-six types is found. Ballads about Mary and Christ are most popular in Danish tradition—one example is "The Flight to Egypt" (TSB B3), in which Mary instructs a farmer to harvest newly sown grain from a field that she and Jesus pass on their journey to Egypt. Popular throughout east Scandinavia are ballads about miracles, such as the restoration to life of lovers or the healing of cripples, although perhaps the most interesting of these types, "Men Lost at Sea" (TSB B26), is found in both eastern and western regions. In this ballad a crew of men lost at sea runs out of food and decides that someone must be sacrificed, but when they cannot bring themselves to eat him, they are saved by Mary in east Scandinavia and a dove in west Scandinavia.

Much more widespread throughout Scandinavia are ballads about saints and martyrs, some of which have parallels in British tradition—for example, "St. Stephen and Herod" (TSB B8; Child 22), in which Stephen tells Herod about portents of the birth of Christ and is subsequently punished, and "Maria Magdalena" (TSB B16; Child 21), in which Christ meets the Magdalene at a well (or stream) and assigns her a penance before shriving her. Found only in fragmentary texts from Norway is the most thoroughly studied of the legendary ballads, "The Dream Ballad" (TSB B31), in which a man sleeps from Christmas to Twelfth Day and then goes to church to tell about his dream visions of heaven and hell, and of Doomsday.

Because of their Catholicism, legendary ballads were suppressed in the sixteenth-century songbooks of the nobility. However, that they must have continued to exist in oral tradition for a long time after that is attested by the fact that the bulk of our extant texts stems from broadside prints and nineteenth-century oral tradition. Sverker Ek has argued that these ballads were of strictly popular origin and that they were performed in association with religious celebrations at local cult centers.

Historical ballads have been characterized differently in the two major works that have sought to catalog entire corpora. In the first of these, *Danmarks gamle folkeviser,* all ballads containing references to historically known persons were grouped under this rubric. In *The Types of the Scandinavian Medieval Ballad,* however, the editors have chosen to restrict this category in two ways: (1) the events related must be historical, with external corroborative evidence of this historicity; and (2) the events treated must be of national rather than regional or local significance. These more restrictive criteria have reduced the number of historical ballads by nearly two-fifths, from sixty-eight to forty-one, with most of those removed reclassified as ballads of chivalry.

Historical ballads were especially popular in Denmark: over half of the types in *The Types of the Scandinavian Medieval Ballad* concern events in Danish history or give a Danish view of conflicts between Denmark and Sweden. The earliest events commemorated in ballad are found in two examples from the twelfth century—the killing of the Danish king Erik II Emune in 1137 (TSB C1) and the struggle in 1157 among three pretenders to the Danish throne (TSB C2).

In the thirteenth century, memorable people and events were celebrated in no fewer than nineteen different ballads. In Danish tradition the figure of Queen Dagmar inspired four ballads: two about her arrival in Denmark to meet her future husband ("Queen Dagmar and Sir Strange," TSB C3, and "Sir Strange and Dagmar's Lady-in-Waiting," TSB D277); the third, about her efforts to help the poor and oppressed ("Queen Dagmar in Denmark," TSB C4); and the fourth, about her death in childbirth ("Queen Dagmar's Death," TSB C6). In Swedish tradition the Folkung family inspired three ballads, all telling about the abduction of brides: "The Abduction from Vreta Convent" (TSB C8), "Sir Lavrents and Bengta Sunesdatter" (TSB C10), and "Folke Algotsson" (TSB C16). In Norwegian tradition three ballads relate the deeds of the pirate Alv Erlingsson: in "Little Alv's Viking Adventures" (TSB C12) and "Little Alv in Øresund" (TSB C13), he is successful against the Hansa fleet; and in "The End of Little Alv" (TSB C17), he is captured by a man who recognizes him and is taken to the queen and then executed.

Only six ballads were composed about happenings in fourteenth-century Scandinavia, the most noteworthy of which are the Norwegian ballad (preserved only in Faroese tradition) "Maid Margaret" (TSB C22) and the Danish "Niels Ebbesen" (TSB C25). In "Maid Margaret" Princess Margaret of Norway is sold by two treacherous companions into marriage with a foreign count, and later is burned at the stake when no one recognizes her upon her return to Norway. In "Niels Ebbesen" a count from Holstein, who has conquered northern Jutland, accuses a local Danish patriot of treason and is later slain by that patriot and his followers.

Almost all of the twelve ballads composed about events of the fifteenth century and the first two decades of the sixteenth treat the political conflicts that raged within the disintegrating Scandinavian union: "Sten Sture the Elder and the Dalecarlians" (TSB C35) tells of a Swedish victory in 1501/1502 over King Hans of Denmark, and "King Christian II in Sweden" (TSB C39) relates the story of King Christian's taking of Stockholm in 1520.

In Svend Grundtvig's view, ballads giving an accurate account of an event were probably composed soon afterward, whereas ballads that were inaccurate were likely to have been composed after some time had elapsed. Grundtvig's ideas have been challenged by later generations of scholars, who have pointed out flaws in his reasoning: for example, ballads seeming to give a very accurate report of an event may in fact have been composed much later with the aid of written sources; and, on the other hand, ballads deemed inaccurate may nonetheless be quite early, reflecting a partisan view of events not found in other sources. There is today reluctance to make sweeping generalizations about the relationship of historical ballads to the events they describe, although there is widespread agreement that historical ballads should be treated like any other historical documents as far as dating is concerned—one must have compelling reasons to regard a ballad as much older than its earliest written text.

Ballads of chivalry constitute the largest and most varied group, numbering 440 in all. Erotic themes predominate: successful and unsuccessful courtship, seduction, rape, abduction, incest, adultery, jealousy, and crimes of passion. Among the most popular ballads of chivalry are "Esbern Snare" (TSB D16), "Proud Ellensborg" (TSB D72), "Sir Palle's Wedding" (TSB D153), and "Valdemar and Tove" (TSB D258). In "Esbern Snare" a knight tests the skill at needlework of the girl he wants to marry, is delighted with the results, and proposes to her. In "Proud Ellensborg" an enterprising woman fetches her dilatory fiancé from abroad, where he is about to marry another. An equally enterprising woman in "Sir Palle's Wedding" tricks the man who wants to rape her by substituting for herself her carriage boy dressed as a woman. In "Valdemar and Tove" the queen is jealous of King Valdemar's mistress, Tove, and decides to kill her by locking her in a steam bath (in the Danish, Icelandic, and Norwegian versions).

Other themes frequently treated in ballads of chivalry are death and escape from death, combat, revenge and punishment, murder, and execution. Of ballads dealing with these themes, the following were sung throughout most of Scandinavia: "Svend in Rosengård" (TSB D320), "The Hasty Answers" (TSB D324), and "King Valdemar and His Sister" (TSB D346). Like the Scottish ballad "Edward" (Child 13), "Svend in Rosengård" consists of a conversation between a mother and her son, in which she asks where he has been and why there is blood on his sword (or foot), and he confesses to the murder of his brother. In "The Hasty Answers" a girl is accused by her father of having taken a lover, but she denies having done so until she is shown his severed hand; in some versions she then commits suicide out of grief and remorse, but in others she takes revenge on her father by setting fire to his house and burning him to death. In "King Valdemar and His Sister" the queen plots the seduction of the king's sister, then tells the king and encourages him to punish her.

Included among the ballads of chivalry in *The Types of the Scandinavian Medieval Ballad* are the "novelistic ballads," a term coined by Grundtvig for long, multi-episodic ballads often containing international epic and folktale motifs. "Paris and Queen Ellen" (TSB D381), for example, tells the story of the love affair between Paris and Helen, and the siege of Troy. The tragic love story of Tristan and Isolde is found in varying forms in ballads sung in Denmark, Iceland, and the Faroes (TSB D383–D386).

The category of heroic ballads is the second largest, numbering 167 types, and consists primarily of ballads of west Scandinavian origin. They are very similar to the legendary sagas (*fornaldarsögur*) composed in thirteenth- and fourteenth-century Iceland—their stories are told loosely, in a broadly epic manner that is quite distinct from the concentrated dramatic style of other ballad categories (except for novelistic ballads, which are thought to have been modeled on the style of the heroic ballads); and they, too, relate the adventures of great champions pitted against both human and supernatural rivals. Best known of the heroic ballads are those composed in close agreement with *Vǫlsunga saga* and *Þiðreks saga af Bern,* about the adventures of Sigurd the Dragon Slayer and his fatal involvement with Gudrun and Brynhild: the Norwegian "Sigurd Svein" (TSB E50); the Danish "Sivard Snarensvend" (TSB E49) and "Sivard and Brynhild" (TSB E101); the Swedish "Sivert Snarensven" (TSB E49); and the sprawling Faroese cycle "The Ballad of Sigurd," consisting of four parts—"Regin the Smith" (TSB E51), "Brynhild's Ballad" (TSB E100), "Hogni's Ballad (TSB E55), and "Aldrias' Ballad" (TSB E38). Also typical of this category is the burlesque "Thor of Havsgård" (TSB E126), which is a recasting of an Eddic poem, *Þrymskviða* (The lay of Thrym), about how Thor dressed as a bride in order to retrieve his stolen hammer from an amorous giant.

The last category, jocular ballads (seventy-seven types), is a new one—scholars have customarily regarded these not as ballads but as vulgar folk songs belonging to a later age. But even though many individual types may be ephemeral because of their topicality, the category itself is probably as old as the rest of the genre. One of the oldest and most widespread of the jocular ballads is "Lave and Jon" (TSB F11), which tells how an unsuccessful suitor manages to trick his rival and sleeps with the bride on her wedding night. Equally widespread is "The Domesticated Farmer" (TSB F33), in which a farmer does all the housework for his lazy wife and is scolded for his trouble.

Ballad collecting in Scandinavia began in Denmark with Anders Sørensen Vedel's work, which led to the publication in 1591 of his *Et hundrede udvalgte danske viser* (One hundred selected Danish ballads), based on the songbooks of the Danish nobility, the oldest of which was *Hjertebog* (The heart book), from the 1550's. Vedel's edition of ballads of principally historical or at least pseudo-historical content was supplemented in 1657 by Mette Gjøe's anonymously published *Tragica,* which favored ballads with erotic themes. In 1695 the academician Peder Syv reprinted Vedel's work, adding to it a second 100 ballads from both written and oral sources. Vedel's and Syv's editions gained considerable currency throughout the far-flung Danish kingdom, especially in the provinces of Norway, Iceland, and the Faroes, where ballads from them were sung both in the original Danish and in translation.

During the Enlightenment of the early eighteenth century, ballads were despised by the educated as a vulgar display of superstition and ignorance, but their continued popularity among the rural and urban working classes is attested by the printings of broadside texts and the reprintings of Syv's edition. In the latter part of the eighteenth century, interest in medieval traditions was reawakened; symptomatic of the times was the appearance in two parts (1780–1784) of B. K. Sandvik and Rasmus Nyerup's collection *Levninger af middel-Alderens digtekunst* (Relics of medieval poetry), which was clearly inspired by Thomas Percy's *Reliques of Ancient English Poetry* (1765). Nyerup immersed himself in new ballad projects, among them assisting Wilhelm Karl Grimm with his translation *Altdänische Heldenlieder, Balladen und Märchen* (1811) and collaborating with W. H. F. Abrahamson and Knud Rahbek in a re-edition of Syv's collection with a music supplement, which appeared as *Udvalgte danske viser fra middelalderen* (Selected Danish ballads from the Middle Ages; 5 vols., 1812–1814).

Meanwhile, in Sweden, Arvid August Afzelius and the poet Erik Gustav Geijer, inspired by the national Romanticism of the times, were preparing their somewhat flawed edition of Swedish ballads with a music supplement, *Svenska folk-visor från forntiden* (Swedish ballads from the old days; 3 vols., 1814–1816). In Norway it was not until the mid 1800's that there was any interest in recording ballad texts; in 1853 M. B. Landstad published *Norske Folkeviser* (Norwegian folksongs), which, like Geijer and Afzelius' work, was more distinguished by patriotic fervor than by good editorial practice. A small selection of Faroese ballads, *Færöiske Kvæder,* was edited by Venceslaus Ulricus Hammershaimb (2 vols., 1851–1855).

The 1830's and 1840's saw the beginnings of Scandinavian ballad scholarship and the development of critical editorial principles, chief among which was faithfulness to the source text. The first critical edition of ballads with commentary and notes was Adolf Iwar Arwidsson's three-volume *Svenska fornsånger* (Old Swedish songs; 1834–1842). However, it was not until the 1840's that the work of the Danish comparatist Svend Grundtvig catalyzed the study of ballads in Scandinavia. His most important contribution was his exemplary twelve-volume edition of *Danmarks gamle folkeviser* (Denmark's old ballads), volume I of which was published in 1853; it was continued by Axel Olrik, Hakon Grüner Nielsen, and others until its completion in 1976. Grundtvig is also responsible for the editing of both the Icelandic and the Faroese corpora: his collaboration with the Icelander Jón Sigurðsson resulted in the publication of the two-volume *Íslenzk fornkvæði* (Old Icelandic ballads; 1854–1885); and with Jørgen Bloch he edited the Faroese corpus (1871–1876), although their manuscript, *Corpus carminum Færoensium,* remained unpublished until Christian Matras undertook the task in 1941. In 1934 Otto Andersson published his edition of the corpus of Swedish ballads sung in the ethnically Swedish districts of Finland *Folkvisor* (Ballads), which is volume V.1 of the series Finlands Svenska Folkdiktning.

Since the late nineteenth century there have been a number of efforts to collect ballads from oral tradition. Most remarkable is that of Evald Tang Kristensen, a teacher from Jutland, whose varied collection of folklore includes about 3,000 ballad texts, a few of them never before attested in Denmark. His texts were published in the series Jydske Folkeminder (Jutish folklore, 1868–1891) and in later volumes of *Danmarks gamle folkeviser.* In 1902 a Danish musicologist, Hjalmar Thuren, traveled to the Faroe Islands to transcribe from oral tradition melodies of native Faroese and Danish ballads by way of preparation for his monograph study *Folkesangen paa Færøerne* (Folk songs in the Faroes; 1908). His student Grüner Nielsen followed him there in 1921, and again in 1927 and 1928, when he made wax phonograph recordings of ballad excerpts. In 1958 the modern tape recorder was used in a collecting effort sponsored by the Swedish Broadcasting Corporation, in which all of Sweden and Swedish-speaking parts of Finland were canvassed, with particularly rich results from the Finnish Ahvenanmaa (Åland Islands). A similar expedition was sponsored to the Faroe Islands in 1959, and at that time approximately forty hours of recordings, mostly of ballads, were made. Although since Kristensen's day collectors have not expected to discover previously unknown ballad types, Mortan Nolsøe did just that when recording the repertoires of several Faroese singers in the late 1960's and early 1970's. But these new ballads—"Gislar's Ballad" (TSB E112) and "Ilint's Songs" (TSB E127)—must be seen as the last gleanings after a very rich harvest.

BIBLIOGRAPHY

Erik Dal, *Nordisk folkeviseforskning siden 1800* (1956), and, as editor, *Danish Ballads and Folk Songs,* Henry Meyer, trans. (1967); Sverker Ek, *Norsk kämpavisa i östnordisk tradition: Ett försök till tudelning av det nordiska folkvise-materialet* (1921); *Four-and-Forty: A Selection of Danish Ballads,* Alexander Gray, ed. and trans. (1954); Ernst Frandsen, *Folkevisen: Studier i middelalderens poetiske litteratur* (1935); Otto Holzapfel, *Bibliographie zur mittelalterlichen skandinavischen Volksballade* (1975); Sigurd Bernhard Hustvedt, *Ballad Criticism in Scandinavia and Great Britain During the Eighteenth Century* (1916, repr. 1971), and *Ballad Books and Ballad Men: Raids and Rescues in Britain, America, and the Scandinavian North Since 1800* (1930); Bengt R. Jonsson, Svale Solheim, and Eva Danielson, eds., *The Types of the Scandinavian Medieval Ballad* (1978); Knut Liestøl, ed., *Folkevisor* (1931); Axel Olrik, ed., *A Book of Danish Ballads,* E. M. Smith-Dampier, trans. (1939); Richard C. A. Prior, trans., *Ancient Danish Ballads* (1860); Johannes C. H. R. Steenstrup, *The Medieval Popular Ballad,* Edward G. Cox, trans. (1914, repr. 1968); Rosa Warrens, trans., *Schwedische Volkslieder*

der Vorzeit (1857), *Dänische Volkslieder der Vorzeit* (1858), and *Norwegische, isländische, färöische Volkslieder der Vorzeit* (1866); Peter Johann Willatzen, trans., *Alt-isländische Volks-Balladen und Heldenlieder der Färinger* (1865).

PATRICIA CONROY

[See also **Dance; Denmark; Eddic Poetry; Faroese Ballads; Iceland; Sturlunga Saga; Sweden; Þiðreks Saga; Vǫlsunga Saga.**]

SCANDINAVIAN LITERATURE: GRAMMATICAL. Grammar teaching came to Scandinavia in the eleventh century along with Christianity. Grammar, as the first course in the trivium, was a key to the student's entry into the learning of the Roman church. Only Latin grammar was taught in the schools established in connection with the cathedral chapters, and later the monasteries. The standard textbooks were the *Ars grammatica* of Aelius Donatus (*ca.* 350), especially the *Ars minor* and book III of the *Ars maior,* and the *Institutiones grammaticae* of Priscian (*ca.* 520). These were pedagogical, descriptive-normative grammars and had to be supplemented by some use of the vernacular of the pupils. In England, Aelfric had composed his *Donatus Angliae* (commonly referred to as *Grammar, ca.* 1000), in which English glosses accompanied the Latin text. A single leaf is preserved of an Icelandic parallel, in which the conjugation of *amo* is presented with native translations of the forms as well as the grammatical terminology: "AMABIT hann skal elska; ET PLURALITER ok margfalldliga, AMABIMUS ver skulum elska . . ." (AM 921, 4°; reprinted in Ólsen, pp. 156–158).

Beginning with Abelard (*ca.* 1079–1142) and Petrus Helias (*fl.* 1142–1166), European familiarity with Aristotle's speculative logic led to the rise of a new, philosophical grammar. It reached its greatest development in the work of the thirteenth-century *modistae* at the University of Paris, so called because they were concerned with the *modi significandi* (modes of signifying), a first step toward a universal grammar of human language. Four of the most renowned *modistae*—Martinus, Boethius, Johannes, and Simon—are given the byname Dacus, suggesting that (by a medieval confusion) they may have been Danes. Roman Jakobson has called Boethius "one of the greatest Danish contributors to the theory of language, and we do not forget that it was Denmark which throughout many centuries gave to international linguistics a long list of supreme thinkers" (p. 295). These men were, however, active in Paris, and we know nothing of their possible influence on work in Scandinavia. That Latin grammatical teaching was effective there is reflected in the Latin of such historians as the Dane Saxo Grammaticus (*fl. ca.* 1200), but no native grammatical literature is preserved outside of Iceland.

The Icelanders early made themselves famous as recorders of native lore. Parallel with the writing of religious and secular (even pagan) matter in Old Icelandic went an active interest in the language itself. The framework was that of contemporary Latin grammar, but the effort of applying its categories to a very different language led to original solutions that in some cases foreshadowed much later, even modern, linguistic thinking. Four grammatical treatises are preserved, thanks to their being appended to manuscripts of Snorri Sturluson's *Edda* (*ca.* 1220; known also as the *Prose Edda* or *Younger Edda*). The association is appropriate in the light of Snorri's purpose: to describe the content and form of skaldic poetry, which involved close attention to metrics and poetic figures, then regarded as a part of grammar. The treatises immediately precede or follow the section entitled *Skaldskaparmál* (The language of poetry), in which Snorri expounds and exemplifies the forms and metaphors of skaldic poetry.

But the treatises are not by Snorri. Except for the third, they are anonymous; scholars have dated the first to about 1150 and the last to about 1340. Explicit attribution in one manuscript and internal evidence have permitted the *Third Grammatical Treatise* to be identified as the work of Snorri's nephew, Ólafr Þórðarson "Hvítaskald" (the white poet; 1210–1259).

FIRST GRAMMATICAL TREATISE

Preserved only in the Codex Wormianus (W; *ca.* 1360) and without any separate heading, the First Grammatical Treatise (FGT) must have been copied at least twice, leaving us on many points in doubt as to the wording of the original. This is particularly disturbing in regard to the examples used to illustrate the discussion. The FGT is not only the oldest, but also by far the most original and interesting of the treatises. Only seven folio pages long, it provides the materials for a phonemic analysis of spoken Icelandic in the first half of the twelfth century. The analysis is an incidental result of the author's dissatisfaction with the current adaptations of the Latin alphabet to Icelandic. Knowing that the English had added and subtracted letters in writing their language, he proposed to do the same for Icelandic, "in order that it might become easier to write and read, as is now customary in this country as well, laws, genealogies or sacred writings, and also that historical lore which Ari Thorgilsson has recorded in his books with such understanding wit" (Haugen ed., 1972, p. 13).

This treatise is roughly contemporary with the earliest preserved Icelandic manuscripts, and it reflects a well-established tradition of writing. The First Grammarian (FG), as we shall call him, then treats successively the vowels, diphthongs, and consonants, with the goal of composing an adequate alphabet for Icelandic. Accepting the five Latin vowels—*a, e, i, o, u*—he proposes to add four more. These he defines as phonetically intermediate and suggests corresponding complex symbols to reflect their positions: *ǫ* between *a* and *o*, *ę* between *a* and *e*, *ø* between *e* and *o*, and *y* between *i* and *u*. His phonetics is one-dimensional: in each triad the new vowel is spoken with the mouth either more or less "open" than are the other two. The result is nevertheless correct in placing what we now know as the "umlaut" vowels in relation to the standard five-vowel system of Latin (and Proto-Nordic):

less open	o	e	o	u		i	→	y	→	u	high
	↑	↑	↑	↑							
	ǫ	ę	ø	y	=	e	→	ø	→	o	mid
	↑	↑	↑	↑		↑				↑	
more open	a	a	e	i		ę				ǫ	
							↖		↗		low
								a			

Having propounded his system, the FG replies to possible objections by producing what now are called "minimal pairs," embedded in sentences to show that every change of a vowel produces meaningful differences: "A man inflicted a wound (*sar*) on me; I inflicted many wounds (*sǫr*) on him."

He then uses the same method of commutation to establish that each of the nine vowels can be "spoken in the nose" (nasalized). He proposes to mark the nasals with a superscript dot, and again he produces a minimal pair for each vowel contrast. In view of the absence of manuscript evidence and of nasal vowels in modern Icelandic, this part of his argument has been questioned. Yet each of his examples is confirmed by the known etymology of the words he cites. What he could not know was that a following nasal consonant had been lost before the turning of the vowels into nasals (a process similar to that which produced the nasal vowels of French). Finally, he proves that each vowel, oral or nasal, can be either long or short, and he proposes marking the long vowels with an acute accent. Accordingly, each of his nine vowels can appear in four guises—V, V̇, V́, V̇́—giving him an alphabet with thirty-six vowels. The feature of length is well attested and remains unquestioned. It has been noted, however, that the short nasals are not strictly phonemic, since they occur only in the vicinity of nasal consonants. The FG may also have been confused about the distinction of short *e* and *ę*, which may already have merged, according to Hreinn Benediktsson (p. 141).

The treatment of diphthongs is more problematic. The FG proposes six, three falling (*ei, ey, au*) and three rising (*ia, io, ui*). The falling ones are well attested, though later developments show that the first element must have fluctuated considerably. The rising ones caused him difficulty (being neither convincingly diphthongal nor completely enumerated), especially *ia* (later *ja*). He chose to write it *ea* (and *io* presumably as *eo*) on the authority of a century-old skaldic verse in which *ia* had (exceptionally) been disyllabic.

In adapting the consonants, the FG needed fewer changes: *þ* was added (as it already had been in Old English); *k* and *q* were replaced by *c* as being redundant; *y* to represent the semivowel *u* and *z* for the cluster *ds* (or *ts*) could be dispensed with. To save "time and parchment" he would allow ǥ for *ng*, *x* for *ks* (*gs*), and capitals for geminates (including *K* for *cc*). His only linguistic contribution here was to identify consonant length as distinctive, again with minimal pairs: *sękr* (outlawed)—*sękkr* (sack); *fús* (eager; neuter plural)—*fúss* (masculine singular).

In these analyses the FG demonstrated his mastery of the Latin grammatical tradition without once referring to a specific textbook source. He went beyond it by applying its principles to his native tongue in ways that were not completely clarified until the twentieth century. His medieval *littera* (Old Icelandic: *stafr*) foreshadowed the modern phoneme, while his minimal pairs showed an understanding of the principle of contrast. He has enabled modern linguists to identify with great assurance the phonological units and the overall system of the earliest Icelandic, even prior to the oldest preserved manuscripts. Earlier scholars have made valiant efforts to break through his veil of anonymity, concentrating on one Hallr Teitsson (1085–1150), of whom it was said that on an expedition to Rome in his sixty-fifth year "he spoke everywhere he went the language of the people as if he were born there." However, Hreinn Benediktsson (pp. 201–203) regards the problem as uninteresting; and the latest critic, Federico Leoni, is inclined to consider the essay as a compilation "einer isländischen gelehrten oder halbgelehrten Gemeinschaft" (of an Icelandic learned or half-learned group). In his new edition (1975) Leoni has expanded the European framework of the FGT, but his cavalier dismissal neglects the FG's skill, so rare in the Middle Ages, in applying grammatical theory to vernacular practice.

SECOND GRAMMATICAL TREATISE

The Second Grammatical Treatise (SGT) is preserved in Codex Wormianus and, more fully, in Codex Upsaliensis (U; de la Gardie 11) of the *Edda* (*ca.* 1300). Its editors, Verner Dahlerup and Finnur Jónsson, dismiss it not only as poorly preserved but also as an insignificant contribution (but see the new edition by Raschella). The SGT has not been as intensively studied as the FGT in terms of its sources; so far none has been found. It is premature to reject its contents as mere scholastic learning. While the FGT is a phonemic analysis intended to establish an alphabet, the SGT takes the alphabet for granted and provides what would now be called a study of Icelandic phonotactics, the distribution in context of its phonemes. The author presents his analysis in two different, but structurally congruent, diagrams, one circular and one tabular. The letters are divided into those that occur only initially (*þ, v, h, q*), before and after vowels (*b, d, f, g, k, l, m, n, p, r, s, t*), by themselves (*a, e, i, o, u, y; æ, ao, av; ey, ei;* nonsyllabic *i*), geminated (capitalized: *B, D, F, G, K, L, M, N, P, R, S, T*), and only finally (*ð, z, x, c*). He seems to be at least aware of the FGT (length mark, capitals for geminates, merged vowels). He makes an interesting if obscure comparison of his diagram to the keyboard of a musical instrument. In his essay he provides some of the information about distribution that the FGT regretted he did not have the space to include. The dating is uncertain: 1200 to 1250 has been suggested.

THIRD GRAMMATICAL TREATISE

The Third Grammatical Treatise is preserved in three main manuscripts: Codex Wormianus and two manuscripts from the Arnamagnaean collection, AM 748 4° (which contains fragments of the *Poetic Edda*) and AM 757 4°, both from the fourteenth century. The latest available edition, by Björn Ólsen (1884), is based on AM 748, though the Wormianus text is also printed in full. Its supposed author, the above-mentioned Ólafr, traveled to the courts of Denmark and Norway (1239–1241) and followed in his uncle's footsteps both as a skald and as a collector of native lore. Trained as a cleric, he is known to have conducted a Latin school from about 1250, which may be when he wrote his treatise (and his reason for writing it).

The text is based mostly on Priscian and Donatus, both of whom are mentioned frequently. After an introduction on the nature of human language, he goes on to apply (or misapply) their doctrines to Icelandic phonology. He (or a later redactor) interpolates a section on the runic alphabet (which he calls the *stafróf,* after the Old English *stæfrōf* or *-ræw*); here we learn of his discussion of runes with King Waldemar II of Denmark. Attribution by Ólsen (pp. xxiv–xxv) to a lost work on runes by one Thórodd Rúnameistari is firmly rejected by Finnur Jónsson (1901, pp. 934–935). The phonetic classification of the vowels is based not on the aperture of the lips, but on their presumed place of production in the oral channel. The syllable is defined, as are the parts of speech, in slavish dependence on Priscian. The interest of this section is in the vivid translations of the grammatical terms: *participium* as *hluttekning* (part-taking), *interjectio* as *meðalorpning* (between-throwing). These were not adopted into modern Icelandic, but others were—for instance, *fornafn* (pronoun) and *samtenging* (conjunction).

A second section restates for Icelandic pupils parts of Donatus' *Ars maior* III, known as the "Barbarismus." This is rhetoric, a listing of the many "barbarisms" and "solecisms" of which the poets had been guilty, as well as the "tropes" and "metaphors" with which they had ornamented their style. But no attempt is made to translate the Latin (really Greek) terms, except for throwing in an occasional Icelandic equivalent. The author's contribution is to provide Icelandic examples from skaldic poetry to replace the Latin ones. In all, thirty-four named skalds are represented, plus many anonymous verses that may be by the author.

FOURTH GRAMMATICAL TREATISE

The Fourth Grammatical Treatise is a self-declared continuation of the preceding treatise, but by a different author. It closely follows Alexander of Villa Dei's *Doctrinale* and Eberhardus Bethuniensis' *Graecismus* (both *ca.* 1200) in listing the *colores rhetorici* of the classical poets. One pities the Icelandic schoolboys who were faced with such terms as *ephexegesis* and *antipophora,* even if they were exemplified and explained in Icelandic. On internal evidence the author must have worked in the 1340's. He has been identified with one Bergr Sokkason (*d.* 1350), who may also have written the prologue that joins the four treatises to Snorri's *Edda* (Jónsson, p. 938).

Aside from the treatises there are only fragmentary Icelandic materials, including a few glosses. The first and second treatises are precious contributions to phonology; the third and fourth are more nearly allied to the school of poetic analysis exemplified by Snorri. Here the old native skaldic tradition joins hands with the newly learned rhetoric of the classics.

BIBLIOGRAPHY

Sources. Manuscript facsimiles include *Codex Wormianus (The Younger Edda): MS no. 242 fol. in the Arnemagnaean Collection in the University Library of Copenhagen,* intro. by Sigurður Nordal (1931); *Fragments of the Elder and the Younger Edda, AM 748 I and II 4:0,* intro. by Elias Wessén (1945); *Snorre Sturlasons Edda: Uppsala-handskriften DG 11,* intro. by Anders Grape (1962).

Editions and commentaries include, chronologically: Rasmus Rask, ed., *Snorra Edda* (1818), 297–353 (based only on Wormianus); Sveinbjörn Egilsson, ed., *Edda Snorra Sturlusonar* (1848), 159–212 (based on all the codices and MSS mentioned); [Sveinbjörn Egilsson and Jón Sigurðsson], *Edda Snorra Sturlusonar: Edda Snorronis Sturlæi,* 3 vols. (1848–1887), translation and commentary in Latin, II (1852), 1–248; Björn M. Ólsen, *Den tredje og fjærde grammatiske afhandling i Snorres Edda* (1884); Verner Dahlerup and Finnur Jónsson, *Den første og anden grammatiske afhandling i Snorres Edda* (1886); Gustav Neckel and Felix Niedner, trans., *Die jüngere Edda mit dem sogenannten ersten grammatischen Traktat* (1925, repr. 1966); Einar I. Haugen, *First Grammatical Treatise: The Earliest Germanic Phonology* (1950, 2nd rev. ed. with bibliography 1972); Hreinn Benediktsson, ed., *The First Grammatical Treatise* (1972); Federico Albano Leoni, ed., *Il primo trattato grammaticale islandese* (1975); Fabrizio D. Raschella, *The So-called Second Grammatical Treatise: An Orthographic Pattern of Late-Thirteenth-century Icelandic* (1982).

Studies. Michael Barnes, "Notes on the First Grammatical Treatise," in *Arkiv för nordisk filologi,* **86** (1971); H[einrich] Be[ck], "Grammatischer Traktat," in *Kindlers Litteratur Lexikon,* III (1967); Hreinn Benediktsson, *Early Icelandic Script* (1965); Sveinn Bergsveinsson, "Wie alt ist die 'phonologische Opposition' in sprachwissenschaftlicher Anwendung?" in *Archiv für vergleichende Phonetik,* **6** (1942); Geoffrey L. Bursill-Hall, "The Middle Ages," in *Historiography of Linguistics,* Thomas A. Sebeok, ed. (1975); Lucy Grace Collings, "The 'Málskrúðsfræði' and the Latin Tradition in Iceland" (M.A. thesis, Cornell, 1967), contains an English translation of part 2 of the *Third Grammatical Treatise; Corpus philosophorum Danicorum medii aevi,* 8 vols. (1955–1979); Tryggvi Gíslason, "Språkvitenskap," in *Kulturhistorisk leksikon for nordisk middelalder,* XVI (1971); Anne Holtsmark, *En islandsk scholasticus fra det 12. århundre* (1936), and "Grammatisk litteratur: Om modersmålet," in *Kulturhistorisk leksikon for nordisk middelalder,* V (1960); Roman Jakobson, "Glosses on the Medieval Insight into the Science of Language," in *Mélanges linguistiques offerts à Émile Benveniste* (1975); Finnur Jónsson, *Den oldnorske og oldislandske litteraturs historie,* II.2 (1901), 921–939; Heinrich Keil, ed., *Grammatici Latini,* 8 vols. (1857–1880); Federico Albano Leoni, "Beiträge zur Deutung der isländischen 'Ersten grammatischen Abhandlung,'" in *Arkiv för nordisk filologi,* **92** (1977); K. J. Lyngby, "Den oldnordiske udtale oplyst ved den ældste afhandling om retskrivningen i Snorra-Edda," in *Tidskrift for philologi og pædagogik,* **2** (1861); James W. Marchand, "Two Christian Skaldic Fragments," in *Arkiv för nordisk filologi,* **91** (1976); Adolf Noréen, "De nordiska språkens nasalerade vokaler," in *Arkiv för nordisk filologi,* **3** (1886); Björn M. Ólsen, *Runerne i den oldislandske litteratur* (1883); Magnus Olsen, "Den förste grammatiske avhandling: Til kommentaren og om forfatteren," in *Arkiv för nordisk filologi,* **53** (1937); Hermann Pálsson, "Fyrsta málfræðiritgerðin og upphaf íslenzkrar sagnaritunar," in *Skírnir,* **139** (1965); Robert H. Robins, *Ancient and Medieval Grammatical Theory in Europe* (1951), 69–90. Heinrich Roos, "Grammatisk litteratur: Vedrørende latin," in *Kulturhistorisk leksikon for nordisk middelalder,* V (1960); Didrik Arup Seip, review of Holtsmark, *En islandsk scholasticus fra det 12. århundre,* in *Norsk tidsskrift for sprogvidenskap,* **9** (1938); Bjarne Ulvestad, "'Grein sú er máli skiptir': Tools and Tradition in the First Grammatical Treatise," in *Historiographia linguistica,* **3** (1976); Julius Zupitza, ed., *Ælfrics Grammatik und Glossar* (1880).

EINAR HAUGEN

[See also **Aelfric; Alphabets; Aristotle in the Middle Ages; Classical Literary Studies; Donatus of Fiesole; Grammar; Priscian; Saxo Grammaticus; Snorri Sturluson.**]

SCANDINAVIAN LITERATURE: RELIGIOUS. The medieval ecclesiastical literature of Scandinavia and Iceland in the vernacular is best divided into three categories: (1) epic literature such as apocryphal writings, saints' lives, revelations, and visions; (2) homiletic literature, sermons, biblical commentaries and translations; (3) theological handbooks or books of instruction and schoolbooks of various kinds, prayerbooks and other writings connected with private devotion. Much of this literature has close affinities with similar literature in Latin, foreign or native, and must be seen on a background of teaching and preaching. Not many of these works can be classed as original in content, but striking examples of successful adaptations of foreign writing can be found that show how this branch of Scandinavian literature influenced native, secular writing in form and style. It illustrates the reception of Christian (and mostly Latin) culture in countries that became members of the universal church fairly late.

Christianity was introduced in the North from the ninth century onward, first in Denmark and Sweden, and later in Norway and Iceland and the other North Atlantic communities (the Faroes and Greenland). It cannot be known when exactly the area had become totally christianized, especially not Sweden and Norway, but the end of the missionary period proper can be conveniently put at the time of the establishment of an archdiocese for the countries at Lund in 1104. No ecclesiastical literature in the vernacular has survived in contemporary manuscripts from the missionary period. Our understanding of the founding years of the Scandinavian church is built on foreign sources or gleaned from nonliterary sources.

The oldest extant manuscripts of ecclesiastical literature in the vernacular are from Norway and Iceland about 1150, and from Sweden and Denmark not much earlier than about 1300.

Until the archdiocese of Lund was established, the countries of the North had belonged to the metropolitan province of Hamburg-Bremen, and it would be reasonable to assume that all foreign influence came from the Continent and through the archsee, the more so as the first archbishop of Hamburg, St. Ansgar, was credited with bringing Christianity to Denmark and Sweden around 830. However, a strong direct influence from the British Isles can also be discovered in all the countries, and the early use of the vernacular in writing in Norway and Iceland was most probably inspired from England. In 1152 Niðarós in Norway (present-day Trondheim) became the archsee for Norway and the North Atlantic countries, followed by Uppsala for Sweden in 1164. This threefold administrative division of the Scandinavian church (Lund, Niðarós, Uppsala) lasted until the end of the Middle Ages.

There is no doubt that the vernacular was used in teaching and preaching from the missionary period on, and it is possible to acquire some understanding of the character of the earliest Scandinavian church literature—a period that properly belongs to literary prehistory—from a close scrutiny of the homilies and saints' lives written in Norway and Iceland already in the twelfth century or of contemporary Latin literature from Denmark, Sweden, and Norway. Most works in the earliest period of writing and probably also in the pre-literary period belong to categories 1 and 2 and are translations or adaptations of traditional church literature, such as Gregory the Great's homilies and dialogues or age-old saints' lives. If it were possible to describe the character of the Scandinavian church literature of the twelfth century in one word, that word should be Carolingian, for most of the inspiration seems to have been drawn from the works of Charlemagne's scholars, Alcuin, Paul the Deacon, and their circle.

As the centuries passed, new inspiration was sought in somewhat younger centers of learning, such as Bologna, Paris, the English or German universities, or various religious houses outside Scandinavia and Iceland. In Scandinavia the oldest monasteries were the Benedictine houses in Lund, Odense, and Nidarholm, established about 1100, soon followed by other monasteries and nunneries, and by numerous Dominican and Franciscan houses from the thirteenth century on. From the end of the fourteenth century and to the end of the Middle Ages the many cloisters of the order of St. Birgitta (1303–1373) in Scandinavia and Finland were prominent centers of literary activity. The Scandinavian church reflected current European fashions very closely in its vernacular literature, and it was only rarely to the fore in theological or spiritual matters; in such areas the Scandinavian contributions to Latin learning and literature carried more weight.

EPIC LITERATURE

Legends of the saints were an important part of church life, and it is not surprising that a very full repertoire of saints' lives is among the earliest writings. One of the earliest layers of Old Norse-

Icelandic prose epic is hagiography, and the genre continued to be popular and alive until the end of the Middle Ages. Several collections of saints' lives are extant (for instance, AM 645,4°, Cod. Holm. 2 fol., *Codex Scardensis, Reykjahólabók*). In Sweden an effort to make available in translation lives of the most commonly venerated saints began about 1300 and resulted in a number of fine legendaries (*Fornsvenska legendariet* and others). In comparison the Danish repertoire is quite modest, although in Denmark the hagiographic legend was also the most important category of epic prose in the Middle Ages. The importance of European hagiographic writing is reflected in the fact that legends about local Scandinavian saints are modeled, sometimes very closely, on foreign lives of popular saints, such as St. Martin in the case of confessors.

All categories of hagiographic epic are found in Scandinavian literature, from the genres of the primitive church—biblical apocrypha, acts of the apostles, and passions of the martyrs—to the full-scale vita, which could encompass the life of any martyr or confessor in the threefold composition *vita, passio* (or *mors*), and *miracula*. More than 100 saints (or groups of saints, for instance the Seven Sleepers of Ephesus) have had their story told in the so-called *heilagra manna sögur,* sagas from the 400-year period of active interest in hagiographic literature in Iceland (and Norway). Some of the lives are found in more than one version, such as the *postola sögur* (sagas of the apostles), the *biskupa sögur* (bishops' sagas), and sagas about the most popular saints of the North, such as St. Óláfr of Norway, or favorite saints from other countries, such as St. Thomas of Canterbury (*Tómas saga erkibyskups*) and Sts. Martin and Nicholas.

Toward the end of the Middle Ages a new wave of interest in hagiography swept Scandinavia. In Iceland and Sweden this resulted in an updating of the repertoire, which came to include saints who can best be described as saints of fashion, such as the Fourteen Holy Helpers, St. Anna, mother of the Blessed Virgin, and Gregory on the Stone. Most of these new lives are based on printed sources in Low German from about 1500, and they reflect the close connection at the end of the Middle Ages between northern Germany and the Scandinavian countries. Hagiography as serious entertainment in the German-Scandinavian area survived the introduction of printing, and a fair number of Low German prints from before and after 1500 belong to this category. However, the Lutheran Reformation that followed a few decades later put an end to the lively interest in saints' legends in the North.

As in Latin hagiography and elsewhere the corpus of saints' lives was constantly revised in order to make the legends fuller or better. One result of such revisions is a series of long, some would say overlong, Icelandic legends of the fourteenth century, such as *Tveggja postola saga Jóns ok Jacobs* (Saga of the two apostles John and James) or version II of the *Nikolaus saga erkibyskups,* padded with additional material and re-edited in an elaborate, florid style. But revision of the corpus could also take another course toward the relative brevity found in the legends of *Legenda aurea,* the widely used and much-admired legendary by Jacobus de Voragine (*d.* 1298). *Legenda aurea* is the source of many legends in Scandinavian literature, and a number of miracles of Mary found in the rich Icelandic-Norse tradition can only have come from this work.

An important section of this category is the vast Marian literature in the Scandinavian vernaculars. The growing veneration of the Blessed Virgin from the twelfth century on throughout the Latin church is mirrored closely in the liturgy and the literature of the Nordic countries. The apocryphal stories of her life, the Gospel of Pseudo-Matthew and the Gospel of the Birth of Mary (*Evangelium de nativitate Mariae*), were known in Iceland already in the twelfth century and became the chief sources of *Maríu saga,* a compilation of the thirteenth century. Pseudo-Matthew was also used in Danish and Swedish writings of the fourteenth century and later.

The Assumption of Mary is told several times, either based on some version of *Transitus Mariae* or taken from St. Elizabeth of Schönau's vision, in Old Norse from the twelfth century on, in Swedish and Danish in the fourteenth century and later. Mary's laments under the Cross are given in various versions (Danish: *Mariaklager;* German: *Marienklagen*): three Icelandic ones, four Danish (the oldest of them found in a runic manuscript from the first half of the fourteenth century: Stockholm, Royal Library, MS A 120), and two Swedish versions. They are based directly or indirectly on Godfrey of St. Victor's *Planctus ante nescia* or the so-called *Tractatus S. Bernardi,* attributed to Ogerius of Trino (*d.* 1214).

The most copious section of Marian literature, regarded by some as a special genre, is the corpus of miracles. Some of them have ancient sources, but most of them have been recorded from the eleventh century on, attesting to the increasing popularity of Our Lady. The Icelandic collections are probably the largest in any European vernacular, and long series of miracles are also found in Swedish. During the last hundred years or so before the Lutheran Reformation this class appears to have been by far the most popular epic church literature in prose in the north. In Iceland several miracles have been recorded in metrical versions.

Hagiographic poems in the vernacular seem to be known only from Iceland, with the exception of a few Marian poems from the late Middle Ages in Sweden and Denmark. The oldest known poem of this type is *Geisli* (or *Óláfs drápa*) about St. Óláfr of Norway, composed by Einarr Skúlason about 1152 and recited by the poet himself in the cathedral of Niðarós, shortly after the archdiocese had been founded. *Plácítus drápa* is another early hagiographic poem, about the Roman martyr St. Placid, or St. Eustace. *Guðmundar drápa*, in honor of Guðmundr Arason, from the fourteenth century, was written by his biographer Arngrímr Brandsson (see *Guðmundar saga biskups*). There are numerous other poems, mainly from the later Middle Ages, which tell about saints otherwise known from Icelandic-Norse prose legends, and are often, but not always, based on the prose versions.

A specific Icelandic genre of epic poetry, *rímur,* originated in the fourteenth century and has been popular in Iceland ever since. Among the oldest rímur is a poem about the death of St. Óláfr of Norway, *Óláfs ríma,* attributed to Einarr Gilsson (*fl.* 1367–1369); it is one of very few poems in this genre with a hagiographic theme.

Visions constitute an important class of epic church literature whose origins are to be found in the apocryphal apocalypses, such as that of St. Paul or the Descent into Hell (*Descensus Christi ad inferos*). Through Latin versions these and similar works became known in Norway and Iceland already in the twelfth century, in the rest of Scandinavia probably somewhat later.

In the early Middle Ages it was mainly through the works of Gregory the Great that visions of or journeys to the other world became popular elements in pious stories. A complete translation of Gregory's four books of dialogues into Old Norse was made in the twelfth century (much of this translation is still extant). Later on one of the most popular visions was that of Tundalus (*Visio Tnugdali*), composed in the twelfth century and soon translated into many languages; an Old Norse translation was made perhaps as early as the mid thirteenth century (*Duggals leizla*), two Swedish versions from the fifteenth century are known, and although no Danish versions exist, the story was known in Denmark in Latin versions from the thirteenth century on. These and other versions, such as that of Gundelin (also known from Icelandic versions), Gottskalk or Thurcill, have often been claimed as sources of or direct inspiration for the visions found in Norse-Icelandic prose (such as *Óláfs saga Tryggvasonar* and two versions of the *Guðmundar saga,* with *Rannveigarleizla*) or poetry (such as *Sólarljóð*). The Norwegian poem *Draumkvæde,* of uncertain, but much disputed, date (recorded in the 1840's), has sometimes been thought to belong to the medieval tradition.

Revelations have more or less the same background as visions, or at least they belong to the same literary category or subcategory, and it is perhaps not worthwhile in a survey to distinguish the two genres. Mystics of the twelfth century and later became well known in Scandinavia: Elizabeth of Schönau, Mechthild of Hackeborn, Bonaventura, Heinrich Suso, and others. The Swedish Dominican Petrus de Dacia (*d.* 1289) wrote about Kristina of Stommeln, but the most original contribution to the genre in the north came from St. Birgitta of Vadstena, whose *revelationes* were recorded and edited in Latin by her confessors. Her revelations were first printed in Lübeck in 1492, but well before that they had become extremely well known in Scandinavia and elsewhere in Europe. The Latin revelations were translated into various vernaculars in the fifteenth century. They exist in early Swedish translations, some perhaps even in St. Birgitta's original draft, and the Swedish version, or part thereof, could therefore well represent a more original text than the Latin standard edition. In her field of literature St. Birgitta's contribution to late medieval literature is by far the most important from Scandinavia.

HOMILIES AND SERMONS

Homilies and sermons were very much part of the missionary activity, and there is good reason to believe that the most popular homiliaries in the Latin church, such as Paul the Deacon's, were known in the North, wholly or in part, in the early years of the missionary period. It appears likely that some texts of this category were translated as early as the eleventh century in Norway and Iceland,

and the oldest extant manuscript in Icelandic (AM 237a, fol.), from about 1150, consists of two fragments of homiletic texts.

There was no obvious reason why the Norwegian-Icelandic church should cultivate a homiletic literature in the vernacular, since it was almost a rule elsewhere in the Latin church that homiliaries or source-books for the preachers were in Latin, while the delivery of course was in the vernacular. Once again it has been suspected that the inspiration to use the vernacular may have come from England (Aelfric and others).

The early Norse manuscripts show clearly that the taste in homiletic literature in the far North was quite Catholic and conservative. Most of the texts found in translation or adaptation in Old Norse manuscripts are such as can be found in any great Latin homiliary of the day (Alanus' or Paul the Deacon's), as always with a preference for the Carolingian repertoire. The great masters were Gregory the Great, whose forty Gospel homilies were translated already in the twelfth century, Augustine, Bede, Caesarius of Arles, Maximus, and a few more. Two almost complete manuscripts from about 1200 are our main source for a close study of the early homiletic tradition in the archdiocese of Niðarós: the Icelandic book of homilies (Cod. Holm. 15,4°) and the Norwegian book of homilies (AM 619,4°).

No single source for either of the two Old Norse homiliaries has been found. They are compiled from several sources, mostly Latin but in a few cases possibly Old English. It is moreover reasonable to suppose that some of the sermons or homilies are original compositions inspired by contemporary preaching elsewhere in the church, for which no written sources exist. The most illuminating example of what has been called "personal authorship, in a framework of ecclesiastical tradition" (Fredrik Paasche), is the Dedication Homily.

In the Dedication Homily the anonymous homilist interprets the various parts of a timber church (hence the popular, but somewhat misleading, name of the text, the Stave-church Homily, often found in scholarly literature) in two series of symbolic meanings. His spiritual outlook resembles closely that found so often in twelfth-century exegesis, when architectural symbolism was immensely popular. Whether the homilist was an Icelander or a Norwegian will never be known. The Dedication Homily is found in both books of homilies (in AM 237a, fol., and in an Icelandic manuscript of the fifteenth century).

The Norwegian book of homilies is organized very neatly after the church year, whereas the composition of the Icelandic one is much less tidy. In the Norwegian book there are two parts that cannot be classified as homilies or sermons: a translation of Alcuin's tract *De virtutibus et vitiis* and a translation of an Old French poem, a debate of the body and the soul erroneously called *Visio Pauli* in the manuscript. The debate is probably the oldest surviving Norse translation from Old French; it is two or three decades earlier than the first French-influenced courtly romances written in Norway. Both Alcuin's tract and the debate could have been, and probably were, used from the pulpit.

Very little is known about the homiletic repertoire in the Norwegian church province from about 1200 on. Only few and scattered texts have survived. In Denmark and Sweden, where no early sermons or homilies in the vernacular are known, a good number of texts can be found from about 1400 on. They are mostly inspired by the new style in pulpit eloquence introduced by the mendicant orders.

The best-known late medieval collection of sermons in Danish is Christiern Pedersen's, printed in Paris in 1515 and again in Leipzig in 1518, commonly called the *Jærtegnspostil.* Christiern Pedersen, who later became one of the leaders of the Protestant movement, was an industrious bookman—editor, printer, author, translator—and has been called the father of the Danish language.

Knowledge of the Scriptures was mostly transmitted to a wider audience through preaching and the liturgy, and there seems to have been no single early translation made in any of the Scandinavian languages of either the whole Bible or a substantial part of it. In the books of homilies and similar texts where considerable numbers of biblical quotations are found, it is easily detected that most quotations are ad hoc translations from Latin.

An Old Norse translation of the first books of the Old Testament (up to 2 Kings), *Stjórn,* has various layers from the thirteenth and early fourteenth centuries. The first part (Genesis and eighteen chapters of Exodus) of the corpus, as we know it today, is copiously annotated with material from Petrus Comestor's *Historia scholastica,* Vincent of Beauvais's *Speculum historiale,* and various other sources. This, the youngest part of *Stjórn,* was written at the instigation of the Norwegian king Håkon Magnusson (*d.* 1319).

A Swedish translation with commentary from a

slightly younger date than *Stjórn* is the so-called paraphrase of the Pentateuch, which was perhaps composed by Mattias of Linköping (*d. ca.* 1350), St. Birgitta's confessor and the foremost northern biblical scholar of his day. Other books of the Bible were translated in the Bridgetine houses of Vadstena and Nådendal. A Danish translation of the beginning of the Old Testament (up to 2 Kings) dates from the latter half of the fifteenth century. It is the least important of the biblical translations in medieval Scandinavia.

A few poems in Old Norse should perhaps be classified as sermons in verse: *Leiðarvísan* (twelfth century), whose subject is the observance of Sunday, *Harmsól* (twelfth century) and *Líknarbraut* (thirteenth century), about the Passion of Christ, and *Lilja,* the most important and best-loved religious poem from medieval Iceland. *Lilja* depicts the Christian drama from Creation to Judgment, with the Passion of Christ as the center of attention and also as the center of the elaborate composition of this 100-stanza poem.

HANDBOOKS

Theological handbooks and schoolbooks of various kinds were mostly in Latin. The most popular of the translated books seems to have been *Elucidarius,* sometimes attributed to Honorius Augustodunensis. An early Old Norse translation is still extant in a manuscript from about 1200, and a closely related version is found in *Hauksbók* (*ca.* 1300). Sweden had two versions of the book, one from 1430–1450, somewhat abbreviated, and a complete translation by Jöns Budde from 1487–1491. The Danish version of the book, *Lucidarius,* is a translation of the German *Volksbuch* (*ca.* 1200) and was most likely written in the fourteenth century.

The dialogue form found in *Konungs skuggsjá* (King's mirror), a Norwegian *speculum* from the mid thirteenth century, also containing a good deal of theological learning, was probably taken from models such as *Elucidarius* and other instructional books current in the North.

Prosper's epigrams, translated into Old Norse in the twelfth century, and various excerpts of Bernard of Clairvaux's and Hugh of St. Victor's writings were most likely intended for classroom use.

Calendars, manuals for priests, liturgical tracts, and legal texts, all intended for practical pastoral use among the clergy, exist in fair numbers in Old Norse, but these texts in the vernacular are outnumbered by Latin texts of the same kind known to have existed in the North.

In all the Scandinavian languages a fair number of books connected with private devotion, prayerbooks and the like, are extant from the last century or two before the Lutheran Reformation. As in the other categories of Scandinavian church literature, the inspiration has come from abroad, and most sources are Latin, although a growing German influence is felt. The numerous manuscripts of this category from Sweden and Denmark deserve a closer bibliographical study.

BIBLIOGRAPHY

Editions. Michael Barnes, ed., *Draumkvæde* (1974); Hreinn Benediktsson, ed., *The Life of St. Gregory and His Dialogues* (1963); Þorvaldur Bjarnarson, ed., *Leifar fornra kristinna fræða islenzkra* (1878); Peter Cahill, ed., *Duggals leiðsla* (1983); Peter G. Foote, ed., *Lives of Saints, Perg. fol. nr. 2 in the Royal Library, Stockholm* (1962); Ludvig Holm-Olsen, ed., *Konungs skuggsjá* (1945, rev. ed. 1983); Gustav Indrebø, ed., *Gamal norsk homiliebok* (1931); Gustaf E. Klemming *et al.*, eds., *Svenska medeltids-postillor,* 7 pts. (1879–1974); Agnete Loth, ed., *Reykjahólabók,* 2 vols. (1969–1970); Christiern Pedersen, *Danske skrifter,* C. J. Brandt and R. Th. Fenger, eds., I, II (1850–1851), containing *Jærtegnspostillen*; George Stephens, ed., *Ett forn-svenskt legendarium,* 3 vols. (1847–1874); Carl Rikard Unger, ed., *Heilagra manna sögur,* 2 vols. (1877), *Maríu saga* (1871), *Postola sögur* (1874), and *Stjórn* (1862); Ole Widding, ed., *Alkuin i norsk-islandsk overlevering* (1960); Theodor Wisén, ed., *Homiliu-Bók* (1872).

Bibliographies. Hans Bekker-Nielsen, *Old Norse-Icelandic Studies: A Select Bibliography* (1967); Ole Widding, Hans Bekker-Nielsen, and L. K. Shook, C. S. B., "The Lives of the Saints in Old Norse Prose: A Handlist," in *Mediaeval Studies,* **25** (1963). See also the copious references in *Kulturhistorisk leksikon for nordisk middelalder,* 22 vols. (1956–1978).

Studies. Hans Bekker-Nielsen, Thorkil Damsgaard Olsen, and Ole Widding, *Norron Fortællekunst* (1965); Oluf Friis, *Den danske Litteraturs Historie,* I (1945); Ludvig Holm-Olsen, "Middelalderens litteratur i Norge," in Edvard Beyer, ed., *Norges litteraturhistorie,* I (1974); Hans Schottmann, *Die isländische Mariendichtung* (1973); Eugène Napoleon Tigerstedt, ed., *Ny illustrerad svensk litteraturhistoria,* 2nd ed., I (1967); E. O. G. Turville-Petre, *Origins of Icelandic Literature* (1953, repr. 1967).

HANS BEKKER-NIELSEN

[See also **Birgitta, St.; Birka; Bishops' Sagas; Denmark; Einar Skúlason; Eysteinn Ásgrímsson; Gamli Kanóki; Guðmundar Saga Biskups; Hagiography, Western Euro-**

pean; Leiðarvísan; Líknarbraut; Missions and Missionaries; Norway; Preaching and Sermon Literature, Western European; Rímur; Sólarljóð; Sweden.]

SCANDINAVIAN LITERATURE: RHYMED CHRONICLES. A rhymed chronicle, be it Scandinavian, continental, or of any other origin, is an account in verse, typically doggerel, of an event or series of events that can, by and large, be viewed as historical, or at least were regarded as historical at the time of composition. The events of such metrical reportage are ordered chronologically and are thematically unified by association with a member or members of an aristocratic family (kings, dukes, counts, masters of orders) who affected those events. A necessary condition for the composition, continued practice, and further evolution of the genre was interest in both the immediate and the distant historical past among dominant aristocrats. They assured the genre's popularity and favored good working relations between chronicler and court. A further definitional aspect of the rhymed chronicle, particularly of its Scandinavian representatives, is its typically propagandistic intent: it seeks to enhance, condone, or even sanctify history as shaped by a particular aristocratic individual or lineage. Programmatically, the Scandinavian rhymed chronicle is devoted to the elevation of individual or regional purpose, and this devotion orchestrates its sympathies. With Scandinavian rhymed chronicles thus defined, universal chronicles, monastic histories, and biographical accounts of individuals, whether in verse or in prose, are excluded from consideration.

Runic inscriptions, sagas of families and kings, provincial laws, and skaldic verse—all of which are largely indigenous genres and antedate the advent of the rhymed chronicle in Scandinavia—bear witness to an early and pervasive interest in individualistic history in Scandinavia. Such interest may well have set the stage for importation of the rhymed chronicle from the Continent, but the decisive factors giving impetus to the genre's diffusion in the North were surely political. The bitter controversies surrounding problems of succession in early-fourteenth-century Sweden and selection of a forceful leader in that country during dissolution of the Kalmar Union in the fifteenth century certainly prompted composition of chronicles to popularize individuals, specifically Duke Erik Magnusson and Karl Knutsson in *Erikskrönikan* (The chronicle of Erik, sometimes called The Elder Chronicle), and *Nyakrönikan* (The new chronicle) or *Karlskrönikan* (Karl's chronicle), respectively. These are the finest representatives of the historical chronicle in verse produced in Scandinavia, and together they cover virtually the entire sequence of historical events in Sweden from the early fourteenth century down to the conclusion of the fifteenth. They remain our best and most vivid sources for depicting the history of the period whose events they relate.

The rhymed chronicle had its initial period of florescence on the Continent during the latter half of the twelfth century. Its earliest representative is Geffrei Gaimar's *Estoire des Engleis* (just prior to 1140), followed by the *Kaiserchronik* (*ca.* 1150), Wace's *Geste des Bretons* (*Roman de Brut, ca.* 1155) and *Geste des Normans* (*Roman de Rou,* 1174), Benoît de Sainte-Maure's *Chronique des ducs de Normandie* (*ca.* 1180), and Layamon's *Brut* (*ca.* 1204/1205 or 1189/1199). It was not until a century later that the rhymed chronicle was to flourish again, though there is the occasional exception to this general rule, such as Philippe Mousket's *Chronique rimée* (*ca.* 1243–1245). It was the continental renaissance of the rhymed chronicle in the late thirteenth and early fourteenth centuries that was to have its effect on the North, for the twelfth-century Anglo-Norman chronicles passed unnoticed in Scandinavia, or at least failed to inspire imitation.

By the early fourteenth century, the now revived rhymed chronicle had been extended far beyond the confines of Angevin Britain, and we note, for example, Melis Stoke's *Rijmkroniek van Holland* (*ca.* 1305), Ottokar's *Österreichische Reimchronik* (before 1320), Jan van Boendale's *Brabantsche yeesten* (*ca.* 1316), the *Braunschweigische Reimchronik* (1279–1280, with additions to 1298), and the *Livländische Reimchronik* (*ca.* 1290). The tradition of the rhymed chronicle had thus reached the Netherlands, northern Germany, and the Baltic provinces, and was thence transported to Scandinavia, one of the many results of increased commercial and cultural exchange with the Hanseatic League.

The first and perhaps finest of the Scandinavian rhymed chronicles, *Erikskrönikan,* is one of the progeny of this renaissance and increased contact with the Continent, and it set the pattern for all successive Scandinavian chronicles. Consisting of 4,545 lines in its most extensive version, it was composed by an anonymous chronicler sometime between 1322 and 1332 in *knittelvers,* a doggerel in rhymed couplets with a line that usually contains four stressed and a varying number of unstressed syllables. It was use of this meter in the courtly tales of the *Eufemiavisor* (1303–1312) that assured its dominance as the leading form for "expository" verse in late medieval Scandinavia, and there is every reason to believe that the *Eufemiavisor* was known to the author of *Erikskrönikan* (*EK*). The first two stanzas of *EK* are illustrative:

gud hawe heder äro ok looff
han er til alskons dygd vphooff
all jorderikis frygd ok hymmerikis nade
thz han er welduger ouer them bade

May God grant you honor and praise.
He is the source of all comely virtue,
All earthly pleasure and heavenly grace,
For he reigns over them both.

The format, meter, style, rhetorical devices, and organization (prologue, body, concluding prayer of intercession) of the chronicles are clearly derivative from continental, particularly German, models, and identification of probable sources for the Scandinavian chronicles has long been a matter of scholarly debate. Both the *Braunschweigische Reimchronik* and the *Livländische Reimchronik* were thought to have served as models for *EK* (for instance, by von der Ropp). More recently, however, Sven-Bertil Jansson has convincingly demonstrated that this is not the case. Though derivative in form, the Scandinavian chronicles are highly independent in content and setting. While they seldom achieve the splendor of earlier, indigenous forms of literary expression, they are remarkable for their characterizations and remain our best sources for knowledge of a critical period in the "Europeanization" of Scandinavia (1250–1350) and an era of political transition that charts a course from the Union of Kalmar (1397–1457) to regional fragmentation.

With the exception of the brief *Eirik og Hugaljo,* Norway lacks rhymed chronicles, as do Iceland and the Faroe Islands; Denmark can claim only the relatively late *Danske Rimkrønike* (Danish rhymed chronicle); and Sweden holds title to the first and most representative of the genre. Thus, diffusion of the rhymed chronicle follows the same lines as those established for importation of other linguistic materials in the later Middle Ages: southeastern Scandinavia encompassing Denmark and southern Sweden, below a diagonal defined by a line extended from Kalmar in the south to Örebro in central Sweden and thence to Oslo, the "Lindqvist diagonal."

The ranges of borrowed units of expression, such as Swedish *håsa* (stockings) from Middle Low German *hose(n),* and of the derivative format in which those units were employed, coincide to define a sphere of cultural influence. The emergence within this sphere of Sweden, as the area in which the rhymed chronicle as a specific genre first attracted the greatest number of practitioners, is certainly due in part to the fact that the chronicle was an effective vehicle for communicating the political turbulence that raged more violently there than elsewhere in the Scandinavia of the time. Historical events of sufficient importance were few in Norway and Denmark after 1300. In Denmark the rather bland recitation of historical fact in chronicle format could hardly compete with the celebration of a mythologized past as accomplished in its *Kjæmpeviser;* approximately 500 of these lyrical and epic poems from the period 1300 to 1500 have survived.

To be sure, Denmark had not been without historical writing in the twelfth and thirteenth centuries, as witnessed by the notable achievements of Anders Suneson (*d.* 1228), Sven(d) Aggeson's *Compendiosa historia regum Daniae* (1185), and Saxo's *Gesta Danorum,* but it lacked vernacular accounts of history until the advent of *Kjæmpeviser* and the *Rimkrønike.* However, as popular ballads, the *Kjæmpeviser* lack the aura of political urgency and the note of didacticism so typical of rhymed chronicles.

The *Rimkrønike* was the most ambitious literary undertaking in late medieval Denmark. It appeared as an incunabulum in 1495, printed at Copenhagen by a Dutch immigrant, Gotfred of Ghemen. Together with Johannes Frabri's printing at Stockholm the same year of Gerson's *Om djävulens frestelse* (On the devil's temptation), it is the oldest known incunabulum in a Nordic tongue. The chronicle is the work of monks at Sorø Monastery, perhaps a certain Niels Clementsen (*d.* 1444), who appears to be the person referred to in the introduction to the Low German translation of 1477. The chronicle may have been composed at the behest of Queen Margaret as a *speculum regale* for the young King Erik.

In any event, the *Rimkrønike* relates the history of Denmark from Humle and the eponymous Dan to the time of Christian I in a series of first-person monologues in which each ruler describes his life and reign. In format, then, it is identical to the

Swedish *Lilla rimkrönikan* (Lesser rhymed chronicle), compiled some two decades earlier. The work was circulated in various manuscript versions, numerous fragments of which have been preserved, prior to its translation into Low German and subsequent appearance in Danish at the hands of Gotfred of Ghemen. One fragment was discovered at Ericsberg in Södermanland, Sweden, a property in the possession of the family of King Karl Knutsson, the subject of *Karlskrönikan* (after 1452).

Throughout the *Rimkrønike* there are appeals to support preservation of the Scandinavian union, and the chronicle long remained a topical book. Copies of the printings from 1501 and 1504 have been lost, but an edition from 1508 has been preserved. A lengthy poem about King Hans that contains statements in support of the union has been added to the edition of 1533, and there are further printings from 1534, 1555, 1573, and 1613, after which the chronicle fell into oblivion until Grundtvig introduced it in his periodical, *Danne-Virke,* in 1816, and Christian Molbech edited it for the first time in 1825.

With its view of reality as paradigmatic generality, medieval historical writing assumed that, in addition to cataloging and describing events of the past, it was the task of the historian to provide practical instruction, to supply a handbook for statesmen and a mirror of morality as reflected in the lives of distinguished persons. Didactic emphasis comes to the fore in the Anglo-Norman chronicles, as well as the chronicles from the period of wide continental florescence in the thirteenth century; but this emphasis is generally lacking in Scandinavian rhymed chronicles, whose authors are not particularly well schooled in the theory of medieval rhetoric. Then, too, they rarely indulge in the often superfluous or repetitive descriptions so prevalent in Romance or continental chronicles. Chronological detail is held to a minimum, and Scandinavian chronicles are typified by an adherence to the immediate issue; there are no extensive asides on manner of presentation, and there is frequent reference to oral sources and eyewitness reports. Then, too, though in *knittelvers,* alliteration is often employed, perhaps as a linguistic appeal to established authority. But there are also appeals to textual authority, particularly to the Dietrich von Bern cycle.

All of these traits are manifested in *EK,* which details Sweden's history from the rule of Erik Eriksson (1249) to the selection of Magnus Eriksson as king in 1319, and is the subject of the most detailed of any commentary on a medieval Scandinavian text. *EK* contains no reference to Charlemagne or Arthur, but to Dietrich von Bern alone (line 20) of all epic heroes, and the unknown author, possibly from Uppland, gives no evidence of learning or of clerical training or influence. He was obviously well schooled in martial arts, was presumably a soldier in the service of Duke Erik Magnusson or his brother Waldemar, and reveals considerable awareness of the interconnections between the political scene in contemporary Sweden and feudal practices abroad. His avowed duty is to provide *fagher ord ok skämptan* (beautiful words and pleasure) while advancing the cause of his patron, Duke Erik, of the ducal party, and of its leader, Mats Kättilmundsson, after the deaths of Erik and Waldemar at the hands of their brother Birger.

After the prologue (lines 1–28), events are chronicled to the fall of Landskrona (lines 29–1,804) in 1301. The bulk of this section is occupied with Birger Jarl's expedition to Finland, a campaign against the Finns that is regarded as a crusade against heathens (lines 1,324–1,385). We then visit Queen Eufemia's court in Oslo and are told of her maternal grandfather's death (lines 1,894–1,899). Geographical and genealogical horizons are constantly expanded to embrace numerous generations and all of the lands surrounding the Baltic. Lines 1,832–3,623 relate events of the years 1317–1319, including Duke Erik's sea battle with King Håkon of Norway in 1309. Then (lines 3,624–4,071) follows the feast at Nyköping Castle, to which Erik and Waldemar are invited by King Birger, who promptly incarcerates them and has them slain. The description of the feast is similar to that at Attila's Susa, and it has been proposed that this central episode alone formed the original chronicle, to which the preceding and following sections were later added for wider interest.

Whatever the validity of this thesis, the scene of the Nyköping feast and its tragic outcome provide the nucleus of dramatic tension for the chronicle; all that precedes and all that follows seems to focus on this event, and all of the narrative's political energies lead up to and subsequently derive from this episode. It is here that *EK* approaches the quality of a true epic, the only one of the rhymed chronicles to do so. Throughout, its narrative force is punctuated by the stereotypical expressions and formulaic phrases of epic.

From the relatively high artistic attainment that *EK* represents, it is a distinct fall to its descendants: *Karlskrönikan* (*KK*; *ca.* 1452); the stanzas inserted to link *EK* and *KK*, which describe events between 1319 and 1389, whereupon *KK* begins; the three *Sturekrönikor* (1452–1470, 1470–1487, and 1488–1496). The composite chronicle composed of *EK*, *KK*, and the three Sture Chronicles has been termed *Stora rimkrönikan* (The great rhymed chronicle) in contrast with *Lilla rimkrönikan*.

Lilla rimkrönikan (*LRK*), an anonymous chronicle of 450 lines, was, according to its final lines, completed in 1448. In first-person monologues, Swedish kings from the legendary Erik to Christopher (1441) step forth to give brief accounts of their reigns. *LRK* derives from *Stora rimkrönikan*, *Prosaiska krönikan* (*ca.* 1450), and *Þiðreks saga*. It originally ended with Karl Knutsson, but in later redactions was continued with the Sture kings.

Finally, there is *Om konung Albrekt* (The chronicle of King Albrekt), Sweden's first political allegory, which consists of 225 lines in *knittelvers*. Lines 1–116 are in Codex Holm. D4 (1430–1450); the remaining lines, derived from a manuscript other than D4, are in the Messinius copybook (1616). This chronicle must have been composed shortly after the deposition of Albrekt of Mecklenburg in 1388. Its mirthful language and wordplay provide a veneer for an underlying bitterness in the face of foreign intervention. Hardly courtly in tone, this brief "chronicle" approaches the form of the popular ballad.

Of the chronicles composed after *EK*, only *KK* merits serious attention—not as a work of literature but as a source of historical information. *KK*, which consists of 9,628 lines, is the longest of the rhymed chronicles. Completed in 1452, it depicts Sweden's history from 1390 to 1452 and is contained in twelve manuscripts. It is usually interpreted as being two distinct chronicles, presumably by two different, anonymous authors: lines 1–2,765, the *Engelbrektskrönikan* (The Engelbrekt chronicle), and lines 2,766–9,628, the *Karlskrönikan* proper. The first portion details the rise of the popular hero Engelbrekt Engelbrektsson, who opposed the ambitions of Erik of Pomerania. He led his rebellion from about 1430 until he was murdered by Magnus Bengtsson Nat och Dag on 4 May 1436, whereupon the first portion of the chronicle ends. The second portion is concerned with consolidation of the realm under Karl Knutsson, Engelbrekt's ruthless former co-commander. It paints Karl's enemies (such as Erik Puke and Jöns Bengtsson) in the darkest of colors and breaks off rather inconclusively with the slaying of Magnus Gren at Möre in 1452. *KK* was thus ripe for the extensions it soon attracted, but all lack even the slight narrative control of *KK* and certainly have none of the artistry of *EK*.

Completion of the *Stora rimkrönikan* signaled the demise of the rhymed chronicle in Scandinavia and opened the door for the professional historian, who emerged in Sweden in the person of Ericus Olai (*d.* 1486), author of the *Chronica regni Gothorum* and professor of theology at the newly founded University of Uppsala.

BIBLIOGRAPHY

Editions include *Svenska medeltidens Rim-Krönikor*, Gustaf E. Klemming, ed., 3 vols. (1865–1868); *Erikskrönikan*, Rolf Pipping, ed. (1921, repr. 1963); *Karlskrönikan*, intro. by Oscar Wieselgren (1938); *Den Danske Rimkrønike*, Helge Toldberg, ed., 3 vols. (1958–1961); *Didrikskrönikan*, Bengt Henning, ed. (1970).

Studies include Ingvar Andersson, *Källstudier till Sveriges historia 1230–1436* (1928), and *Erikskrönikans författare* (1958); Gustaf Cederschiöld, *Om Erikskrönikan* (1899); Björn Hagström, review of Henning's *Didrikskrönikan*, in *Arkiv för nordisk filologi*, **88** (1973); Karl Ivar Hildeman, *Medeltid på vers* (1958); Sven-Bertil Jansson, *Medeltidens rimkrönikor* (1971); Natan Lindqvist, *Sydväst-Sverige i språkgeografisk belysning*, 2 vols. (1947); Erik Lönnroth, *Medeltidskrönikornas värld* (1941); Erik Neuman, "Karlskrönikans proveniens och sanningsvärde," in *Samlaren*, **8** (1927), **12** (1931), and **15** (1934); Erik Noreen, "Författarfrågor i 'Nya eller Karlskrönikan' (RK2)," in *Arkiv för nordisk filologi*, **55** (1939–1940); Rolf Pipping, *Kommentar till Erikskrönikan* (1926); Goswin, Freiherr von der Ropp, *Zur deutsch-skandinavischen Geschichte des XV. Jahrhunderts* (1876); Helge Toldberg, "Erikskrönikans omarbejdelse og fortsættelse," in *Arkiv för nordisk filologi*, 77 (1962).

T. L. Markey

[See also **Anglo-Norman Literature; Benoît de Sainte-Maure; Brut, The; Chronicles; Denmark; Dutch Literature; Erikskrönikan; Eufemiavisor; Gaimar, Geffrei; Karlskrönikan; Philippe Mousket; Saxo Grammaticus; Sweden; Þiðreks Saga; Wace.**]

SCANDINAVIAN MYTHOLOGY. Scandinavian mythology is that portion of Germanic religion preserved in Scandinavian narratives of the Middle Ages. It has, therefore, a diachronic aspect, namely the development of the material from Indo-European origins through Scandinavian recordings, and a synchronic aspect, namely the interpretation of the texts themselves in their medieval Norse context. Strictly speaking, the study of mythology should encompass only analysis of narrative, but in practice Scandinavian mythology has regularly included the study of the religious practices of the Scandinavians and other early Germanic peoples.

But for the *Gesta Danorum* of Saxo Grammaticus and a few other exceptions, it would be possible to refer to Scandinavian mythology as Old Norse mythology or, more accurately, Old Icelandic mythology, since virtually all the material is retained in Icelandic texts of the thirteenth century and later. As the conversion of Iceland to Christianity occurred in or around the year 1000, one of the first tasks of the student of Scandinavian mythology is distinguishing Christian from pagan within the extant material.

THE SOURCES OF SCANDINAVIAN MYTHOLOGY

One group of texts may with assurance be dated to the pagan period before the conversion: the poetry of the early skalds. It begins with Bragi Boddason the Old, who lived sometime between the late eighth and early tenth centuries, almost certainly in Norway. His work, like that of many other skalds, recounts myths and heroic legends as they were depicted in such artifacts as shield decorations or carvings in a hall. Myths of Thor figure most prominently in this early poetry, with Eilífr Goðrúnarson's *Þórsdrápa* providing the most elaborate example. Thor's duel with the Midgard serpent is frequently mentioned, not least by Bragi himself; and two Icelandic poets of the conversion period addressed verse directly to Thor, praising him for his slaying of giants and cataloging his victims, some of whom are now unknown. Skaldic poetry was transmitted orally, in some cases for centuries, before its recording in manuscripts began during the thirteenth century.

A second important source, heterogeneous like the skaldic poems and also anchored in the pagan period, is Eddic poetry. Although the date and origin of each single poem are obscure and often a matter of dispute, many scholars would now agree that Eddic poetry as a genre originated during the pagan period and that the poems as we have them now reflect also the medieval Icelandic milieu in which they were recorded after oral transmission. Although a few poems may possibly have been composed by Christians, most are considered to be faithful sources of Scandinavian mythology. Nearly all the relevant poems are found in the first half of the Codex Regius of the *Poetic Edda;* a few other manuscripts also contain mythological poems in Eddic style. Thor is again widely represented, playing a major role in four Eddic poems (*Hárbarðsljóð, Hymiskviða, Þrymskviða, Alvíssmál*), although sometimes the treatment of him does not seem very reverent. Odin too figures in four poems (*Hávamál, Vafþrúðnismál, Grímnismál, Hárbarðsljóð*), and Freyr and Loki are the subject of one poem each (*Fǫr Skírnis*—also known as *Skírnismál*—and *Lokasenna,* respectively). There may have been other mythological Eddic poems, now lost.

The most consistent picture of Scandinavian mythology is contained in Snorri Sturluson's *Prose Edda.* Of this remarkable handbook of poetics, all the *Gylfaginning* and about one-third of the *Skáldskaparmál* consist of myth as retold by Snorri. Opinion on Snorri's faithfulness to pagan myth has varied, but most scholars have seemed willing to accept his word, despite the two centuries separating him from the conversion. His accounts of the mythology agree with those of the Eddic poems, which he clearly knew well. More important, the myths and heroic legends were needed to explain the elaborate system of kennings and *kend heiti* of skaldic diction described in the *Skáldskaparmál.* In general, the tradition of skaldic diction stretches unbroken from the pagan to the Christian period. As this poetry can be neither understood nor composed without knowledge of the mythic and heroic narrative keys to the diction, the narratives must have been passed down continuously in tradition. All the myth and heroic legend recounted in the *Skáldskaparmál* is directly motivated as explanation of the origin of poetic diction, although sometimes the explanation proceeds beyond what is needed to comprehend a given kenning. In the *Gylfaginning,* on the other hand, the myth is recounted seemingly for its own sake, and heroic legend is ignored. Much of the material in *Gylfaginning* is concerned with the structure of the universe, a subject treated only by implication in *Skáldskaparmál,* in the various lists of kennings or *kend heiti* for this topic.

Snorri also delves into mythic prehistory in a euhemerized form, in the prologue to his *Edda* and in *Ynglinga saga,* the first saga of his *Heimskringla.* Mythic and religious material is to be found at yet a further remove in some of the *fornaldarsögur,* as a written genre primarily a product of the fourteenth and fifteenth centuries but probably descended from a much older oral genre; in the *Íslendingasögur,* or family sagas (for example, the description of a pagan temple in *Eyrbyggja saga*); and in certain kings' sagas (*konungasögur*) and the *þættir* (short narratives) embedded in them.

Almost no myth was recorded elsewhere in Scandinavia, with the exception of the *Gesta Danorum* of Saxo Grammaticus (*fl.* 1185–1208). A cleric writing the history of his people from their origins to his own time, Saxo had very different motives from his near-contemporary Snorri, but, like Bede (672/673–735) and Paul the Deacon (*ca.* 720–*ca.* 799), he used material pertaining to the pagan period, and thus he sometimes retells Scandinavian myth in Danish guise. As a source of Scandinavian mythology, however, Saxo poses difficult problems. Perhaps the most important is the extent to which he deviates from his sources in his euhemerism or is faithful to otherwise unknown eastern Scandinavian mythic variants. Among the most important myths recast into Saxo's pompous Latin are the death of Baldr and Odin's vengeance, and Thor's visit to the giant Geirrøðr.

Although myths were not, except for Saxo, recorded outside Iceland, they must have been known, and for the most part probably in the forms they take in Iceland. One may hazard this assumption on the basis of representations in art, primarily stone carving, of scenes from myth. By far the most popular scene among extant carvings is Thor's battle with the Midgard serpent, echoing the popularity of the story in skaldic poetry. Other scenes are also known. Some scholars have been less than cautious in their identification of myth in plastic art, however, and the uncertainty in aligning an artifact with a text will always preclude certain identification.

Religious practice, as opposed to myth, may be equally well reconstructed throughout Scandinavia. Here the major source, besides archaeology, is the study of place-names, a strong scholarly tradition in Scandinavia. Theophoric place-names offer information on the age, distribution, and cults of the various gods, and etymology and other philological tools permit conclusions about forms of worship and similar problems. Most but not all of the gods cited in the mythology are found in place-names; a few deities are limited to place-names and hence remain obscure.

The Germanic religion reflected in Scandinavian mythology is also found described in material relating to other Germanic areas. As the Germanic peoples seldom used their runic writing system for religious purposes and never for recording myth, however, religious and mythic material is quite limited in the vernacular Germanic languages, which came to be written down on parchment only as a result of the influence of the church. Examples of vernacular texts that have been used in the study of Germanic religion and Scandinavian mythology include the Merseburg charms, the Wessobrunn prayer, and the poem *Muspilli.*

Far more important are accounts, in Latin, of the period before the conversion. Although these may be said to begin with Julius Caesar (*De bello gallico,* 6), the most important classical source is without question the *Germania* of Tacitus. It is rich in description of religious practice, much of which may be directly related to myth recorded more than a millennium later in Scandinavia. Other important sources are the Gothic history of Jordanes (*ca.* 550), the various lives of the missionaries, including especially Rimbert's *Vita Anskarii* (after 865), and Adam of Bremen's *Gesta Hammaburgensis ecclesiae pontificum* (1073–1076). The Arab traveler Ibn Fadlan described Viking funeral practice of the tenth century, and many other chroniclers and historians of the Middle Ages made at least passing reference to religious beliefs and rites of Germanic peoples.

GODS AND GODDESSES

In the prologue to his *Edda,* Snorri offers a euhemeristic view of the origin of the Norse pantheon. "The great majority of mankind, loving the pursuit of money and power, left off paying homage to God. . . . In the end they lost the very name of God" (Young trans., 23). Even so, says Snorri, they continued religious speculation concerning the identity of the One who ruled the cosmos, but in a material rather than a spiritual way. In Troy, he continues, there grew up a great chieftain named Trór, now known as Thor. One of his descendants was Vóden or Odin, "a man famed for his wisdom and every kind of accomplishment" (26). With his second sight, Odin knew that his future greatness lay in the North, and so he set off with his followers. "Through whatever lands they went such glorious exploits were related of them that they were looked on as gods rather than men" (26). Odin settled in Sigtuna, Sweden, and appointed his family and followers to the various surrounding kingdoms.

Snorri tells essentially the same story in the

opening chapters of *Ynglinga saga,* but without the expressly religious connotation. In both sources he stresses that twelve chieftains presided over the temples in Troy (which is equated with Asgard), a pattern which Odin followed in Scandinavia. Although the learned speculations of the prologue and *Ynglinga saga* are quite distant from the mythic world of *Gylfaginning,* it is still not surprising that in the latter Snorri has the three demons who answer Gylfi's questions report that there is one chief god, called All-father (ON: *Alfǫðr*), at the head of a pantheon of twelve gods. In Troy this All-father had twelve names, all of which are recognizable Odin names; later he is explicitly equated with Odin. All-father was the eternal ruler over all things, and the creator of the cosmos and man, whom he endowed with life. The righteous will be with him after death, but the wicked shall go to Hel and thence down to Niflhel. The portrait of this figure seems to point to the unnamed deity postulated by Snorri in the prologue as the object of speculation of men who had forgotten God. The similarities to the Christian God, however, are probably also intended to be ironic.

Odin is called All-father because he is "the highest and oldest of the gods" (Snorri, Young trans., 48), ruler of all things, including the gods, and father of all the gods. He is also known by a great many other names. The name Odin (ON: *Óðinn,* cognate with Old English *Wōden,* Old Saxon *Woden,* and Old High German *Wuotan*) probably derives from a common Germanic form meaning "leader of the possessed." In the transfer of the Roman calendar to Germanic areas, Odin was equated with Mercury, and so Wednesday (*Mercurii dies*) bears his name; it derives from Old English *Wodnes dæʒ* (Odin's day). Within the mythology Odin plays a principal role in the myths of creation and ordering of the cosmos, the war between the Æsir and Vanir, the acquisition of the mead of poetry, the death of Baldr, and Ragnarǫk (the end of the world). He contested in wisdom in a verbal exchange with the giant Vafþrúðnir, spouted divine lore while being tortured by the human king Geirrøðr, and taunted his son Thor in an exchange of insults and boasts. He sacrificed his eye for wisdom and apparently sacrificed himself to himself. Odin has usually been interpreted as lord of hosts, of magic, wisdom, and poetry, or war and of death.

The other twelve gods, according to Snorri, are as follows:

Thor. The son of Odin and Earth, Thor is the strongest of gods and men. Besides his hammer, Mjǫllnir, which he uses to slay giants, he possesses a belt of strength and iron gauntlets. He has two goats who pull his chariot. Important myths in which Thor figures center on battles with giants and other enemies of the gods; of these the most important is the Midgard serpent, who lies in the sea coiled about the entire earth. Giants with whom Thor contended were Geirrøðr, Hymir, Hrungnir, Þrymr, and Utgarða-Loki. Thor slew the first four but was outwitted by the last (according to Snorri, the only source of the tale). Thor is generally regarded as a personification of the positive power of might to make the world safe from the forces of chaos. He was also involved in fertility, probably through his association with lightning; Mjǫllnir has been seen as the bolt of lightning that Thor uses as his weapon. His name (ON: *Þórr,* cognate with OE *Þunor,* OS *Thunar,* and OHG *Donar*) probably means "thunderer." *Jovis dies,* the day of Jupiter, became Thursday, the day of Thor.

Baldr. The fairest and best of the gods is Baldr, the son of Odin and his wife, Frigg. In the one myth about him, Baldr is made nearly invulnerable by his mother and then slain by his blind half-brother, Hǫðr, according to Snorri and the Eddic poem *Lokasenna,* at the instigation of Loki. Baldr and Hǫðr are to be reunited after Ragnarǫk—the "doom of the gods." This tale has, perhaps more than any other, attracted scholars and poets. Although agreement has still not been reached, a possible explanation for the myth is that it explains the origin of death and funerary custom. Other explanations generally regard the Baldr story as some sort of loan from the Orient, perhaps reflecting ritual.

Njǫrðr. "He controls the path of the wind, stills sea and fire, and is to be invoked for seafaring and fishing. He is so wealthy and prosperous that he is able to bestow abundance of land and property on those who call on him for this" (Snorri, p. 51). Njǫrðr has two major moments in the mythology. In the first, he was exchanged as a hostage during the great war between the Æsir and the Vanir, a war which resulted in the integration of these groups. In the second, he was married to the giantess Skaði, who chose Njǫrðr as her husband in compensation for the slaying of her father, Þjazi. Thus Njǫrðr functions as a mediator between two important oppositions within the mythological system, Æsir–Vanir and gods–giants. As the masculine

Silver image presumed to be a heathen symbol (Thor's hammer?) but apparently influenced by the Christian cross. Iceland, 10th century. NATIONAL MUSEUM OF ICELAND

counterpart of the goddess Nerthus (the names may be derived from the same linguistic form), whose cult is described by Tacitus, Njǫrðr would also seem to be involved with fertility. His children, Freyr and Freyja, are clearly figures of fertility.

Freyr. Apparently the son of Njǫrðr and his sister, Freyr, like his sister Freyja, was very beautiful. According to Snorri, "He decides when the sun shall shine or the rain come down, and along with that the fruitfulness of the earth, and he is good to invoke for peace and plenty. He also brings about the prosperity of men" (pp. 52–53). Freyr has one important moment in the mythology, involving his marriage to the giantess Gerðr, for whom he conceived a terrible passion when he spied her from the vantage point of Odin's high seat. Freyr sent his servant Skírnir to woo her. Skírnir won Gerðr for Freyr when he threatened her with curses addressed toward her sexuality and marriageability. Unlike his father, Freyr is the active suitor in the god-giant courtship, and he seems to have enjoyed better success than his father did. Freyr is universally regarded as a fertility god.

Týr. The boldest and most courageous of the gods, Týr is to be invoked by brave men and has power over victory in battle. Like many of the other gods, he too figures prominently in only one myth, the binding of the wolf Fenrir (or Fenris). As this wicked beast grew up, only Týr had the courage to feed it. When the gods foresaw that Fenrir was to do them terrible harm, they commissioned dwarfs to make them increasingly strong fetters, which they placed about the wolf as if in sport. Fenrir balked at the last fetter; it was so slender that he thought it must be made with guile, and little fame could result in breaking loose from it. As a pledge of good faith Týr put his hand in the wolf's mouth as the binding proceeded. When the wolf struggled furiously against the unbreakable bond, all the gods laughed except Týr; he lost his hand. Týr gave his name to Tuesday, a rendering of *Martis dies,* thus equating Týr with the warlike Mars. Further, *Týr* is the only one of the gods' names that derives from the divine sphere within the Indo-European parent language. It is cognate with such forms as Sanskrit *deva-,* Old Irish *día,* Lithuanian *diẽvas,* and Latin *deus,* all of which mean "god." Since other forms derived from the same root have to do with such concepts as "heaven" or "day," many scholars have assumed that Týr is a pale reflection of the Indo-European sky god, perhaps replaced in the course of time by Odin. Georges Dumézil, however, has argued that Týr represents the judicial aspects of sovereignty.

Bragi. Probably the deification of Bragi Boddason the Old, first of the skalds, the god Bragi is a minor figure. He is called the god of poetry, a role he would have to share with Odin.

Heimdallr. This enigmatic figure functions as the warden of the gods. He is stationed at the end of their territory, near the bridge leading to the rest of the universe. Endowed with preternatural hearing and keen sight, he is ever awake, and at the onset of Ragnarǫk he will blow his horn to warn the gods of the impending arrival of the forces of chaos.

Hǫðr. The slayer of Baldr.

Víðarr. When Odin falls to the wolf Fenrir at Ragnarǫk, his son Víðarr will avenge him.

Váli. According to certain poetic sources, including *Vǫluspá* 33–34, Váli is the avenger of Baldr.

Ullr. The stepson of Thor and his wife, Sif, Ullr is all but unknown in the extant mythology. To judge from the extensive place-names in which his name figures, he was once a popular god, particularly in eastern Scandinavia.

Forseti. The son of Baldr and his wife, Nanna, Forseti is apparently involved in the settling of lawsuits. Virtually nothing else is known of him.

After listing these twelve gods—the last few of whom seem to be included merely to reach the number twelve—Snorri mentions another figure "also reckoned among the Æsir." This is Loki, fair of face but mercurial of disposition, usually evil. He is the instigator of much trouble for the gods, but often he helps to put things right. In so doing, he frequently bestows some treasure on the gods; these include the stronghold at Asgard, Odin's horse, Sleipnir, Thor's hammer, Mjǫllnir, Sif's golden hair, and so forth. On at least two occasions he accompanied Thor on his journeys to Giantland; but both these stories, telling of Thor's encounters with Þrymr and Útgarða-Loki, are regarded as late and untrustworthy. More palpable is Loki's role as opponent of the gods. He apparently arranged Baldr's death, he once reviled all the gods at a banquet, and—most important—he will help lead the forces of evil at Ragnarǫk, battling with and slaying Heimdallr at the final battle. As a result of these basic contradictions and oppositions, scholars have tended to interpret Loki as a trickster figure, parallel to the trickster in many other mythologies. A trickster typically possesses a volatile, impetuous character, which causes him to act for the moment only. Although he often suffers for his actions, frequently these actions are creative, and mankind is the beneficiary.

Snorri goes on to list the goddesses, according to him fourteen in number, not including others who are reckoned among them. Only a few, however, are of any real significance. The foremost is Frigg, wife of Odin. Like Odin she has knowledge of the future, but she apparently chooses not to exercise it. In myth she is seen acting as wife by giving counsel to Odin before he goes off to visit Vafþrúðnir and contending with him before he goes off to visit Geirrøðr. Her greatest moment, however, occurs in the Baldr story. She takes oaths from all creatures and things not to harm Baldr and then reveals to Loki that she has not taken an oath from mistletoe. After Loki encourages Hǫðr to cast the fatal mistletoe at Baldr, Frigg arranges for Hermóðr to descend to Hel in an attempt to bring Baldr back to the world of the living. In summary, it seems that Frigg represents the connubial and maternal functions of woman within the mythology. Her name is found as the first component of "Friday," which renders *Veneris dies,* the Latin day of Venus. The Indo-European root from which the name *Frigg* derives means "love."

Frigg may be contrasted with the other major goddess, Freyja, the sister of Freyr. Freyja's role is largely passive. She is desired by the giants and sometimes promised to them, although the promise is never fulfilled. Like Freyr she seems to be primarily a fertility figure.

The other goddesses listed by Snorri are pale figures, some just names. When Snorri indicates a function for one of these goddesses, it usually is a transparent application of the meaning of her name. Eir, for example, whose name means "mercy," is the best of physicians; and from Vǫr, whose name means "aware," nothing may be concealed. Strangely, Snorri omits from this list Iðunn, the wife of Bragi; she is one of the few minor goddesses to play even a small role in mythic narrative. As guardian of the golden apples of the gods, she maintains the secret of their eternal youth. Loki betrayed her to the giant Þjazi, and the gods began to age. Loki changed himself into a falcon and rescued her, and Þjazi was killed in pursuit. (Thereafter his daughter Skaði was given one of the gods in marriage as compensation. As will be recalled, she chose Njǫrðr.)

Other important female figures include the Norns, who attend at birth and "choose the fates for men." Following Vǫluspá, Snorri names the three principal Norns Urð, Verðandi, and Skuld, that is, "Became," "Becoming," and "Is to be," thus stressing their role in past, present, and future. A second group is the Valkyries. As the etymology of the term *valkyrja* suggests, they are choosers of the slain (*valr,* "carrion," and *kyrja,* an agent-noun from *kjósa,* "choose"). Snorri reports that they serve in Valhǫll, Odin's hall, and are sent by Odin to determine the outcome of battle. There were also the *dísir,* female figures not described by Snorri but mentioned in many poetic sources. Perhaps fertility figures, they seem to have been more important to religious practices than to myth.

The counterparts of the gods and goddesses are the forces of evil, manifested as giants, frost giants, trolls, wolves, and other creatures. The giants should probably not be regarded as very much larger in stature than the gods, as the two groups intermarry and sometimes exchange hospitality. The etymology of the Old Norse word for "giant," *jǫtun,* remains uncertain, but one guess associates the word with the verb "to eat," thereby placing evil devouring at the center of the conception of the giants. There is little real evidence for this assumption. In practice, the frost giants and trolls are not separated from other giants; the name of the frost giants associates them with cold, which frequently bears negative connotations in the mythology. Wolves have long had similarly negative connotations, as attested by certain Germanic legal formulas. Snorri tells of wolves who pursue and will ultimately swallow the sun and the moon at Ragnarǫk.

The worst wolf, of course, is Fenrir, who was bound by Týr but will slay Odin at Ragnarǫk. He is one of three monster siblings sired by Loki on a giantess. The others are the Midgard serpent and Hel. When the gods realized the evil inherent in these creatures, they bound Fenrir; Odin cast the serpent into the sea, where he lies coiled about the entire earth; and Hel he sent down to Niflheim, the "misty world," and gave her charge of the world of the dead. Loki's offspring are therefore the greatest enemies of Odin and Týr (Fenrir), Thor (the serpent), and all men (death).

CREATION AND COLLABORATION OF THE GODS

The basic theme of Scandinavian mythology involves the struggle between the forces of good (the gods) and the forces of evil (the giants and their kin) for the creation and maintenance of order. This struggle and the opposition on which it is based are found from the time of creation and extend to Ragnarǫk. They make up the subject of the Eddic poem *Vǫluspá,* a mythic history of the universe, and are inherent in the other myths.

In the beginning, as both *Vǫluspá* and Snorri explain, there was nothing except a yawning void called Ginnungagap. Then (here Snorri alone preserves a fuller account) a world grew up to the south. Called Múspell (similar to the German *Muspilli*), it was hot and fiery. Its role in the world drama is indicated by its guardian figure, Surtr (perhaps "the dark one"), who will harry the world with flames at Ragnarǫk. In a cold environment where frost giants join the forces of evil, one might expect fire to be a positive rather than a negative force; it heats dwellings and converts dead fish and animals into food. The explanation for this seeming discrepancy is probably to be sought in the potential dangers involved in using fires indoors in an area where most buildings were of wood. That fire could also be used as a weapon of destruction is certainly borne out by the accounts in contemporary sagas of thirteenth-century Iceland, telling of the burning of enemies within their houses in fires deliberately set by assailants. The artistic reflection of this practice is to be seen in the family sagas, most notably in *Njáls saga,* where Njáll's enemies burn him and his family in his farm.

The creation story then sets up a basic opposition, within Ginnungagap, between the light and heat of Múspell and the dark and cold to the north, in part materialized from rivers called Élivágar (perhaps "storm waves," which some observers have equated with the icy polar sea). At the point where hot and cold neutralized each other, drops of liquid grew in the form of a man. That was Ymir or Aurgelmir, the first of the giants and progenitor of the frost giants, via a hermaphroditic conception; as he sweated while he slept, a man and woman grew under his arms, and one of his legs conceived a son with the other. Thus the forces of chaos are the first to emerge from the primal void.

Ymir was suckled by the cow Auðumla, who in turn licked frosty salt blocks. From the salt emerged Búri, first of the race of the gods. His son was Borr. Borr married Bestla, the daughter of a giant, and they had three sons: Odin, Vili, and Vé (at an earlier linguistic stage the three names were linked by alliteration). Thus the gods and giants are joined from the start through their association with the cow and through Bestla.

Borr's sons carry out the creation of the cosmos. As in many other mythologies, the first creative act is a killing, in this case of the giant Ymir. The mythic significance of this killing can probably not be overstated; the cosmos is created by the slaying of the first of the forces of chaos. Order is created from chaos by the dismemberment and distribution of his body, when Borr's sons make the earth from Ymir's body, the sea from his blood, the mountains from his bones, and so forth. As a side effect of the killing, all but one of the race of giants perish in the flood of Ymir's blood, an interesting parallel to the Old Testament flood story. In that one giant escaped, however, the gods' creation was imperfect, and so they must continue to renew it by overcoming giants whenever they have the chance.

The creation of order involved more than just the physical landscape. Time was ordered when the sun, moon, and stars were assigned their stations, and the gods gave names to the times of day.

Finally the gods created man, by granting life to two trees, Askr and Embla (perhaps "Ash" and "Elm"). They were the first man and woman. Thus, by their slaying of a giant, the sons of Borr created an ordered cosmos for man.

That cosmos may be envisioned as a series of concentric circles. Near the middle is Midgard (ON: Miðgarðr, central enclosure), made by the gods for man. Around Midgard stretches the uninhabited earth, covered by forests and mountains and cut by rivers. What separates Midgard from this part of the world is that Midgard has been made sacred for man. The unsacred part of the world is dangerous for man (and god); it is inhabited by the forces of chaos, including the giants, who are said to live to the east in Utgard (ON: *Útgarðr,* outer enclosure). It is in this unsettled, dangerous area that the gods have their encounters with the giants, reaffirming order against chaos with each victory. Finally, the earth is encircled by the sea, the most unknown and dangerous area of all. Here the Midgard serpent lies in wait for Thor, the greatest adversary of the giants.

This is "the" world. There are, however, other worlds. Sometimes the sources seem to regard these spatially, sometimes symbolically. The most important of these is no doubt the world of the dead, sometimes located under the earth.

Reflecting Midgard and man's struggle against chaos is Asgard (ON: *Ásgarðr,* the enclosure of the Æsir), the realm of the gods. It is located at the very center of the universe (sometimes set in the heavens), where the world tree (the ash Yggdrasill, perhaps "steed of Odin") stands. The tree symbolizes the cohesive structure of the universe; its roots join the various worlds. The precarious status of the universe is embodied in the tree, which is being gnawed from above by four harts and below, at the roots, by serpents led by a certain Níðhǫgg; the tree itself is rotting. Words of insult between Níðhǫgg and an eagle who sits in the branches of the tree are conveyed by a squirrel. When Ragnarǫk comes, the tree will tremble and shake.

Asgard is connected to the earth by the bridge Bifrǫst, which some have equated with the Milky Way. In Asgard the gods have their halls, and judgments are made daily near the foot of the tree. There is the well of wisdom, in which Odin pledges his eye, and whence fates are issued.

Many of these conceptions of creation are to be found elsewhere, particularly in Iranian and Manichaean tradition, and the notion of a world tree is also widespread, perhaps most in Central Asian traditions. Hypotheses of borrowing have therefore often been advanced. It must be noted, however, that these notions are well integrated within the mythology and identifiable within other Germanic traditions. If borrowing occurred, it happened long ago; and the possibility of Indo-European inheritance must always be kept open.

The first major event in mythic history was a war—not, strangely enough, between gods and giants, but between gods and another group, the Vanir. Treated allusively in *Vǫluspá,* the war is associated in *Skáldskaparmál* with the acquisition of the mead of poetry; more details are given in the euhemerized context of the opening chapters of *Ynglinga saga* in Snorri's *Heimskringla.* Apparently the Vanir infiltrated Asgard with some sort of female figure, Gullveig or Heiðr (equated by some with Freyja), powerful in magic. The ordinary gods or Æsir fought more conventionally, with Odin casting a spear over the opposing host. This act ordinarily caused his opponents to be seized with panic. When the war was fought to a standstill, the two sides exchanged hostages. Njǫrðr and Freyr left the Vanir and joined the Æsir, who in turn sent two figures, called Hœnir and Mímir, to the Vanir. When it turned out that Hœnir's counsels were purely a product of Mímir's advice, the Vanir killed Mímir and returned his head to the Æsir. Odin had it pickled and uses it as a source of wisdom.

The truce was made concrete by the mingling of spittle from the two warring parties. The Æsir made a man of the spittle, Kvasir, the wisest in the world. He was soon killed by some dwarfs, however, and his blood was fermented with honey into the mead of poetry. After the dwarfs had slain a giant and his wife, the giant's son, Suttungr, seized the mead from them and gave it for safekeeping to his daughter Gunnlǫð. Later Odin, calling himself Bǫlverkr (evildoer), got himself hired by Suttungr's brother Baugi; his wages were to be one drink of the mead. To get it, Baugi bored through the mountain protecting Gunnlǫð, and Bǫlverkr changed himself into a serpent and slithered through the hole. (*Hávamál* 106 may suggest that Odin bored the hole himself). Bǫlverkr then slept with Gunnlǫð for three nights and was rewarded with three swallows of the mead, which sufficed for him to drink it all. Changing himself into an eagle, he flew back to Asgard with Suttungr in hot pursuit, also in the form of an eagle. Although he spilled a bit—the "poetaster's share"—Odin got most of the mead home safely. That is the origin of the mead of poetry, the working metaphor for skaldic poetry.

The war between the Æsir and Vanir has often been regarded as the reflection of an actual religious war between adherents of a battle-oriented cult (the Æsir) and adherents of a fertility cult (the Vanir). Various scenarios and venues have been proposed, ranging from prehistory to the Viking Age. However, even if one accepts that a religious war would provide a likely basis for such a myth (the overrunning of an indigenous, agrarian population by the mobile, warlike Indo-European culture would offer one model), the impact in the Norse sources is exclusively mythic. Details of battle are few. The presence of Gullveig among the Æsir serves as the etiology for the kind of magic called *seiðr,* and the Æsir's strategy seems to have been wholly based on Odin's magic powers of binding. Indeed, most of the emphasis of the story is on the truce and its aftermath, the acquisition of the mead of poetry by the Æsir. It thus seems likely that the war and reconciliation represent a continuation of the origin myth, reconciling the inclusion of gods of might and of fertility in the pantheon.

Georges Dumézil has adduced several striking parallels from other traditions. In Indic tradition the Nasatya join the gods led by Indra, and in Irish tradition the Tuatha Dé Danann draw on the secrets of the gods led by Bres; the Sabine war from early Roman history offers a third parallel. Dumézil suggests that these narratives all derive from a common Indo-European myth explaining how the aspects of fertility were mythically integrated with other elements of society. Furthermore, Dumézil sees the myth as a direct reflection of the reality of proto–Indo-European social structure, where the estates of the priesthood, the military, and farmers were forced to coexist. The reflections of these three estates in myth Dumézil terms the three "functions" of sovereignty, military might, and fertility. The functions are, according to Dumézil, fulfilled by various deities within the various Indo-European daughter mythologies: Mithra and Varuna, Indra, and the Nasatya in Indic tradition; Jupiter, Mars, and Quirinus in Rome; and so forth. Within Norse mythology the equation places Odin and Týr in the first function, Thor in the second function, and the Vanir—of whom only Njǫrðr, Freyr, and Freyja are named—in the third function.

In assigning two gods to the first function, Dumézil argues that sovereignty had two separate aspects within Indo-European society. One, typified by the Indic god Mithra, for example, dealt with law and contract; the other, typified by Mithra's alternate or opposite, Varuna, dealt with the awesome aspects of sovereignty. The Scandinavian counterparts of these gods are, according to Dumézil, Týr, sovereign god of law, and Odin, sovereign god of magic. Týr's one act, the sacrifice of his hand for the binding of the wolf Fenrir, coupled with the ancient form of his name, lends credence to this equation, as does Odin's obsession with all forms of knowledge. The parallel to Týr's sacrifice of his hand is Odin's sacrifice of his eye to the well of knowledge in order to attain wisdom. Odin's binding is of an awesome, magic sort (as typified by the result of his flinging a spear over an enemy army), Týr's of a contractual sort (the binding of Fenrir). Many more parallels might be adduced.

Deriving Thor from the Indo-European second function explains many of the similarities he shares with such other second-function figures as Indra (for example, large appetite, red hair, association with the atmosphere and rain), especially the battle with a great monster.

Third-function figures tend to be doubled, like the Indic Nasatya or Aśvins. Here one thinks not only of Freyr and Freyja but also of the male Njǫrðr and his linguistic double, Nerthus, the goddess described by Tacitus.

An Old Norse mythic text which may reflect the Indo-European social structure is the Eddic poem *Rígsþula.* It tells how Rígr, actually the god Heimdallr, made his way among men and sired various social groups. Although the poem appears to be incomplete, and some details are problematic, in general a good case may be made. If so, the social structure, which according to Dumézil informs the mythology, is here assigned a divine origin.

The myth of the war and reconciliation is integrally associated with that of the acquisition of the mead of poetry. Thus, at the moment when the race of gods was unified, one of the most important aspects of wisdom was created and subsequently ordained for gods and men. The significance of this is plain. The god of magic is also the god of poetry, in which was embedded the wisdom needed to ensure the safety of the entire community of gods. Its reflex in the world of men is skaldic poetry, which could be used for magic (*níð*) or, more generally, for the passing of history and other cultural information, in addition to encomium.

The role of the mead seems to be that of an intoxicating agent used to trigger an ecstatic wisdom performance. This is explicit in *Grímnismál,* when Agnarr gives Odin a drink at the onset of Odin's monologue, and implicit in many other contests of wisdom. The obverse seems to occur in *Lokasenna,* where Loki disrupts a feast of the gods (brought about by Thor's gaining of a cauldron for brewing—here the mead is symbolic of the unity of the family of gods). As Loki assails each of the gods with wisdom of the wrong sort, Heimdallr accuses him of being drunk.

Thus the universe and its basic premises are established. A united family of gods, representing all the essential functions of proto–Indo-European social structure, and led by a god armed with the wisdom resulting from their unification, must fight for order against the forces of chaos. Most of the rest of the mythology tells of this struggle.

DESTRUCTION AND REBIRTH OF THE GODS

Odin's primary contribution to the struggle is his contest of wisdom with Vafþrúðnir, the wisest of the giants, as recounted in the Eddic poem *Vafþrúðnismál.* Assuming a disguise, as he usually does, Odin wagers his head against that of the giant. Vafþrúðnir begins the exchange with a series of four questions. They concern, significantly, the names of the elements of the cosmos: day, night, the river separating the territory of the gods from that of the giants, and the field where the last battle is to take place. Naturally Odin possesses this knowledge; it is, presumably, just the sort of thing he has gone to such trouble to learn. Odin then poses a series of questions on similar topics: the origin of the universe and its parts, leading up to Ragnarǫk. Odin wins the exchange and the giant's head by asking what Odin himself spoke into the ear of his dead son Baldr—the ultimate piece of wisdom.

Besides establishing his superiority in wisdom over the wisest giant, and therefore presumably over all the giants, Odin also overcomes the two other major groups, men and gods. His encounter with men, told in *Grímnismál,* involves not an exchange but a demonstration of his superiority. When King Geirrøðr has Odin, who calls himself Grímnir, strapped between the flames of two fires, Odin spews forth a series of stanzas full of cosmic wisdom. Where *Vafþrúðnismál* dealt more with cosmic history, *Grímnismál* deals with cosmic order. Odin speaks, naming the holy places of the gods and then, in a terrifying epiphany, revealing his own godhead. Geirrøðr falls on his sword, and one infers that Odin's superiority is duly established.

On the level of the gods, Odin, this time disguised as the ferryman Hárbarðr, humiliates Thor in a verbal duel described in the Eddic poem *Hárbarðsljóð.* Although the poem is rightly regarded as farce, its mythic significance is surely that even the mighty Thor stands no chance in such an exchange. Thor boasts of his own prowess in slaying giants, but Odin clearly comes away the winner, stressing acts of deceit and magic.

One other major Odin myth is also concerned with his acquisition of wisdom. According to the Eddic poem *Hávamál* he spent nine nights hanging on a windy tree—which few have hesitated to identify with the world tree—wounded with a spear, sacrificed "myself to myself." For this he won the runes, nine mighty songs, and a drink of the mead of poetry. The similarities to the Christ story have long been noted, but the story seems equally rooted in Germanic traditions of sacrifice. The myth provides a bridge to Odin's role as god of the dead, whom he sometimes rouses in his quest for wisdom.

Odin entertains the dead, usually understood as dead warriors (ON: *einherjar*), in *Valhǫll* (hall of the dead). As described in *Grímnismál* and *Gylfaginning,* it is a splendid palace, with six hundred forty doors, through each of which nine hundred sixty warriors will march abreast to Ragnarǫk. Until Ragnarǫk the *einherhjar* amuse themselves by fighting all day; at night their wounds are healed and the fallen arise to join in the feasting. Foreign influence is evident in the picture of the palace, but the conception of the ever-fighting warriors is mythically consistent.

As Odin uses his wisdom against giants, Thor uses his strength. His role is that of the conventional hero who slays monsters and thus keeps the forces of evil at bay. Of his many battles, several especially stand out. One is his ritual duel with Hrungnir. It is significant because, as Vafþrúðnir was the wisest of the giants, so Hrungnir is the strongest. Thus superiority is established on two fronts. Certain aspects of the story, particularly in Snorri's version, seem reminiscent of initiation ritual. Thor is accompanied by the boy Þjálfi, who tricks Hrungnir into standing on his shield and himself kills the clay giant who accompanies Hrungnir.

Thor's journey to, and slaying of, the giant Geirrøðr and his daughters still await convincing interpretation, largely because the principal source, Eilífr's *Þórsdrápa,* remains obscure. Thor's journey to, and killing of, the giant Þrymr, the subject of the Eddic poem *Þrymskviða* (and not mentioned by Snorri), is burlesque in tone but conventional in effect; Thor kills giants and regains his hammer, the symbol of his physical superiority over them, and here used expressly for fertility. Thor's visit to, and outwitting by, the giant Skrýmir or Útgarða-Loki, hardly known outside Snorri, seems to be based on medieval adaptation of the patterns of folktale. Its significance is perhaps to be sought in the circumstances of Snorri's *Edda* itself and not in myth.

One of the most widespread of the myths of Thor, and perhaps the most significant, tells of the time when he hooked the Midgard serpent on a fishing line, hauled it up, and nearly killed it. The serpent, perhaps a symbol of what Carl Jung and Erich Neumann term the *uroboros,* is located at the farthest distance from the sacred center of the earth and therefore represents the greatest level of danger of the unknown. Although some poetic sources seem to indicate that Thor killed the serpent after hauling it up, Bragi Boddason and Snorri, who begin and end the historical procession of sources, agree that the serpent escaped. Indeed, given the overall structure of the mythology, it is appropriate that Thor's great enemy, the strongest symbol of chaos, should escape him until the end of the world.

A curious myth, told in the Eddic poem *Alvíssmál,* describes how Thor outwitted a dwarf who had sued for the hand of Thor's daughter. Thor continued to put questions until daybreak, when the sun's rays apparently turned the dwarf to stone. The story seems late and anachronistic, but it is at least consistent in showing the power of the gods over other creatures in contests of wit.

Despite their demonstrations of superiority over the forces of chaos, the gods suffer two ghastly setbacks. The first is Baldr's death. A major point of the story seems to be that Baldr stays dead. After he falls and Frigg sends Hermóðr off to try to bring him back, Hel agrees to release Baldr if all creation will weep for him. Upon Hermóðr's return the gods set about fulfilling the condition, but one old giantess, thought to be Loki in disguise, refuses, and Baldr must stay with Hel until Ragnarǫk. Thus death and the elaborate funeral prepared for Baldr have come to the Æsir, and Ragnarǫk, when the entire order of the gods will fall, is made possible and brought closer.

Ragnarǫk (fate of the gods) is described in detail by the *Vǫluspá* poet and Snorri. In both sources it seems to follow hard on the binding of Loki, the punishment for his role in the death of Baldr. Loki's career has thus come full circle. He began as a giant but joined the Æsir despite his three evil children. The mechanism of his joining the Æsir, mentioned in *Lokasenna,* is an oath of blood brotherhood he swore with Odin. Perhaps this was a deliberate attempt by Odin to divert Loki's evil intentions elsewhere; or Odin may have known through prophecy that Loki was to provide the gods with such treasures as Sleipnir and Mjǫllnir. In either case, the failure of the strategy is foreshadowed in *Lokasenna* and made explicit by Baldr's death, when Loki acts to dissolve the order prevailing within the family, between brother and brother.

The breakdown of this order is one of the prime ingredients of Ragnarǫk. As *Vǫluspá* puts it, in a stanza cited by Snorri: "Brothers will fight / and kill each other, / siblings do incest; / men will know misery, / adulteries be multiplied, / an axe-age, a sword-age, / shields will be cloven, / a wind-age, a wolf-age, / before the world's ruin" (Snorri, p. 86). As the ties binding men are broken, so is the ordered conception of time, which the gods established at the creation. The breakdown of time, perhaps indicated by the various "ages" the poet cites, is made explicit at the very onset of Ragnarǫk. It begins with three terrible winters, with no intervening summer; these seasons were a basic unit of time reckoning. Day and night are also lost, as wolves swallow the sun and moon.

As all the distinctions of the world are lost, as the universe dissolves into chaos, the bonds that hold the forces of evil in check are broken. Surtr leads the sons of Múspell from the south; the giants attack on the terrible ship Naglfar, with Loki at the helm, and all the denizens of Hel break loose. These forces are joined by Fenrir and the Midgard serpent, both now free at last.

As they approach Bifrǫst and prepare to violate the last spatial distinction, that separating Asgard from Utgard, the sacred from the profane, Heimdallr sounds his horn. Even the world tree, the very center of the universe and symbol of its order, shakes with terror.

The final battle is envisioned as a series of individual combats. Odin is devoured by the wolf Fenrir but avenged by Víðarr. Thor meets the Midgard serpent and this time realizes his goal of slaying it, but at the cost of his own life. However, he manages to stagger back nine paces before falling, which indicates a kind of symbolic victory. Freyr meets death at the hand of Surtr. To these combats mentioned in *Vǫluspá,* Snorri adds that Týr falls before the hound Garmr (perhaps a double of Fenrir). Finally the entire earth is consumed by Surtr's fire, the flames of Múspell, the first world to exist. Chaos has seemingly returned to chaos.

Yet order still reigns. After the crisis, Æsir will again inhabit the sacred plain. Order is set and bonds reestablished as Baldr and his brother and slayer Hǫðr live together in harmony. Although *Vǫluspá* alludes to Hœnir, according to some sources one of the gods involved in the original creation, Snorri follows *Vafþrúðnismál* and limits himself exclusively to gods of the younger generation. Besides Baldr and Hǫðr, he peoples the new world with Odin's sons Víðarr and Váli and Thor's sons Móði and Magni, who still possess the hammer Mjǫllnir. In this new world, fertility is renewed as unsown fields grow. Two humans who survived the flames will repopulate the earth, and the sun will leave a daughter even fairer than herself; thus will order be reestablished. This new world seems to be a paradise where elements of chaos are wholly lacking.

The significance of Ragnarǫk is the significance of the entire body of myth. As an example we may cite the heroic legend of the battle of Hjaðningar, known to many poets and spelled out by Snorri. The story dooms two armies to eternal battle—rather like Odin's dead warriors, the *einherjar*—which only Ragnarǫk can check. Ragnarǫk breaks the eternal circle of strife and conflict.

Many parallels, pagan and Christian, have been adduced to Ragnarǫk, as to so many other Norse myths. In the context of the entire mythology, however, Ragnarǫk and its aftermath make good sense. The cyclic universe is a widespread religious phenomenon, and the seeds of disaster were planted from the very start. Although there are certain discrepancies within the sources, the story as a whole is quite well integrated.

This essay has attempted a sketch of Scandinavian mythology, regarding the many disparate texts as a unified body of myth, and seeking a consistent reading of that entire body, primarily by relating each myth to a larger context. The approach has entailed special reliance on Snorri and *Vǫluspá*. The other side of the coin involves detailed study of each myth for itself, a sifting of probable sources and what is known of religious practice. Such an approach is amply described in the handbooks cited in the bibliography.

BIBLIOGRAPHY

The complete corpus of skaldic poetry, with manuscript readings, reconstituted texts, and Danish translations, is to be found in Finnur Jónsson, ed., *Den norsk-islandske skjaldedigtning,* 2 vols. in 4 (1912–1915). Lee M. Hollander, *The Skalds: A Selection of Their Poems* (1945, repr. 1947), contains select translations. A convenient edition of Eddic poetry is Gustav Neckel and Hans Kuhn, eds., *Edda: Die Lieder des Codex Regius nebst verwandten Denkmälern,* I, 4th ed. (1962). Henry Adams Bellows, *The Poetic Edda* (1923, repr. 1957), provides translations. The best edition of Snorri's *Edda* is Finnur Jónsson, ed., *Edda Snorra Sturlusonar: Udgivet efter håndskrifterne* (1931). Arthur G. Brodeur, *The Prose Edda* (1916, repr. 1960), is a complete translation, and *The Prose Edda of Snorri Sturluson: Tales from Norse Mythology,* Jean I. Young, trans. (1964), offers translations of the pertinent mythological sections. The standard edition of Saxo is Jørgen Olrik and H. Ræder, eds., *Saxonis Gesta Danorum,* 2 vols. (1931–1957). Oliver Elton, *The First Nine Books of the Danish History of Saxo Grammaticus* (1894, repr. 1967), contains an English translation of all the mythological material. On theophoric place-names see first Magnus B. Olsen, *Farms and Fanes of Ancient Norway,* Th. Gleditsch, trans. (1928). More cautious is Jöran Sahlgren, "Hednisk gudalära och nordiska ortnamn," in *Namn och Bygd,* 38 (1950). A recent study of Snorri's mythology is Anne Holtsmark, *Studier i Snorres mytologi* (1964).

Virtually complete bibliographic coverage is included in Jan de Vries, *Altgermanische Religionsgeschichte,* 2 vols., 3rd ed. (1970), which is the most complete handbook. More accessible are the bibliographic notes in Edward O. G. Turville-Petre, *Myth and Religion of the North: The Religion of Ancient Scandinavia* (1964), certainly the best handbook in English. The bibliography of the entire Old Norse area, including mythology and religion, has been annually noted since 1963 by Hans

Bekker-Nielsen, *Bibliography of Old Norse-Icelandic Studies* (1964–). See also J. A. B. Townsend, "Old Norse Bibliography," in the 1967 *Bibliography of Old Norse-Icelandic Studies* (1968), 7–34, and Peter Buchholz, "A Bibliographic Introduction to Mediaeval Scandinavia," in the 1971 *Bibliography of Old Norse-Icelandic Studies* (1972), 9–87. Peter Buchholz, *Bibliographie zur alteuropäischen Religionsgeschichte: 1954–1964* (1967), and Jürgen Ahrendts, *Bibliographie zur alteuropäischen Religionsgeschichte: 1965–1969* (1974), provide exhaustive coverage of early European religion.

Besides the invaluable works of de Vries and Turville-Petre, mentioned above, general coverage of the overall mythology begins with Jacob Grimm's massive *Teutonic Mythology,* 4 vols., translated from the 4th ed. by James Steven Stallybrass (1883–1888, repr. 1976), and extends to Brian Branston, *Gods of the North* (1955), and Hilda R. Ellis Davidson, *Gods and Myths of Northern Europe* (1964, repr. 1973). Davidson, *Scandinavian Mythology* (1969), contains many useful photographs of relevant artifacts. Georges Dumézil offers his reading of the mythology in *Gods of the Ancient Northmen,* Einar Haugen, ed. (1973), which also contains some of his papers on Scandinavian mythology. Dumézil's large scholarly production, much of which is concerned with Scandinavian mythology, is surveyed by C. Scott Littleton, *The New Comparative Mythology: An Anthropological Assessment of the Theories of Georges Dumézil,* 3rd ed. (1982). Objections to Dumézil's theories are voiced by Ernest A. Philippson, "Phänomenologie, vergleichende Mythologie und germanische Religionsgeschichte," in *PMLA,* 77 (1962).

Much stimulating recent work on myth is applicable to Scandinavian mythology. Useful collections are Thomas A. Sebeok, ed., *Myth: A Symposium* (1955, repr. 1958, 1965), which contains a seminal essay by Claude Lévi-Strauss, "The Structural Study of Myth," 81–106; John Middleton, ed., *Myth and Cosmos: Readings in Mythology and Symbolism* (1967); Pierre Maranda, *Mythology: Selected Readings* (1972, repr. 1973). An example of the psychological approach is Erich Neumann, *The Origins and History of Consciousness,* R. F. C. Hull, trans. (1954, rev. ed. 1969, repr. 1970). Mircea Eliade approaches myth from the field of comparative religion; his two relevant works are *The Sacred and the Profane: The Nature of Religion,* Willard R. Trask, trans. (1959), and *Shamanism: Archaic Techniques of Ecstasy,* Trask, trans. (1964, repr. 1970, 1972), with comments on Germanic religion, 379–387.

JOHN LINDOW

[See also **Adam of Bremen; Æsir; Alvíssmál; Baldr; Bragi Boddason the Old; Charms, Old High German; Eddic Poetry; Eilífr Goðrúnarson; Eyrbyggia Saga; Family Sagas, Icelandic; Fenris Wolf; Fornaldarsögur; Freyr; Frigg; Grímnismál; Gylfaginning; Hárbarðsljóð; Hávamál; Heimdallr; Hel; Hœnir; Jordanes; Kenning; Lokasenna; Loki; Midgard Serpent; Mímir; Njǫrðr; Norns; Norse Flyting; Odin; Ragnarǫk; Rigsþula; Rimbert; Runes; Saga; Saxo Grammaticus; Skaldic Poetry; Snorra Edda; Snorri Sturluson; Surtr; Þættir; Thor; Þrymskviða; Ullr; Vafþrúðnismál; Valhalla; Valkyrie; Vanir; Viking Art; Vǫluspá; Wessobrunner Gebet.**]

SCANDINAVIAN TEMPLES. A number of sources, mainly in the *Poetic Edda,* provide a fairly full picture of the myths of pre-Christian religion in Scandinavia. However, these sources contain very little information about sanctuaries and cult practices in pagan time. In this respect the Icelandic sagas of the thirteenth and fourteenth centuries are much richer in words. According to *Eyrbyggja saga,* the pagan sanctuary was a special building, named *hof,* with an altar (*stallr*) for sacrifices, and idols in a smaller room (*afhús*). The pagan worshipers met in the *hof* for ritual sacrifices and meals. The same impression is conveyed by Snorri Sturluson's *Heimskringla* and by the *Landnámabók,* a learned work from the thirteenth century, recording in detail the habitation of Iceland in the ninth century and further development in the following period.

These sources have been considered very trustworthy, even in questions of pagan belief and cult, and until very recently most descriptions of Scandinavian temples and pagan worship have used them as their firm point of departure. But Iceland turned to Christianity more than 200 years before these narratives were written, and modern historical criticism is inclined to dismiss them as almost completely fictitious. This leaves us with scattered and unsatisfactory source material: a number of place names with traces of pagan cult; a few dim passages in the *Edda* and in authentic skaldic poetry from the pre-Christian period; provisions of bans on heathen cults in some law texts of the early Christian time; plus a number of archaeological sites, most of these inexplicable or at least difficult to interpret.

When studying pagan cult in Scandinavia it is important to remember that there is no evidence of any vocational heathen priesthood. It seems to have been the duty of the chieftains to effect communion of man and the divine powers. The king acted as supreme servant of the cult, safeguarding it at the principal places of worship in his country, but he was evidently not supported in this by a sacerdotal organization that watched over the religious life of the people. Because of this lack of central control, the cult rituals might have developed differently in the Scandinavian provinces; we cannot arbitrarily transfer information about cult activity from one region to another.

As in many other religions, the sacrifice (*blót*) was a dominant feature. It is revealed in both private and communal worship and both for supplication and for thanksgiving. We meet two essentially different forms: the votive sacrifice and the convivial sacrifice, the latter presupposing a communal act of worshiping and some kind of religious site for the celebration of the mutual convivial meal. Heathen poetry conveys the impression that the slaughter of sacrificial animals was in itself a ritual, and that the meat was possibly "baked" in earth-covered pits, lined with hot stones. In addition to the feast, the ceremony may have included singing, dancing, and the enactment of mythological scenes.

The heathen cult of the south Germanic peoples, Christianized centuries before the Scandinavians, seems to have been centered on open-air worship (in groves and woods, by springs). Even the convivial sacrifice could be celebrated at holy places in the open. The same tendency is found in the written sources relating cult practice among Scandinavians. An Arab traveler, Ibn Fadlan, describes a cult site with crude idols at the beginning of the tenth century, raised by Nordic merchants in Russia. Early Christian legislation in the Danelaw, Norway, and Sweden contain articles prohibiting the performance of pagan rituals on mounds of earth and stone (*hǫrgr*), in groves, by wells, in sanctuaries in the open (*vé*), and in palisade enclosures (*stafgarðr*). However, this definitely does not reflect the full amount of heathen cult practice. When Christianity had won, pagan religious buildings would surely have disappeared very quickly, and pagan worship would have become clandestine acts in remote places; therefore, the introduction of Christianity could very well have caused a revival of nature sanctuaries far away from the farms and villages.

The conception of the heathen Scandinavian temple is primarily connected to the appellative *hof.* But it is doubtful whether the *hof* was in fact a building exclusively used for religious purposes. At least it seems certain that it was neither a "temple" in the classical sense of this word nor a counterpart to the Christian church, such as the sagas tend to indicate.

In three *Edda* poems (*Vǫluspá, Vafþrúðnismál,* and *Hymiskviða*) the term *hof* is used for the gods' own dwellings. In pagan and conversion-era skaldic poetry, there is only one proper reference to the *hof.* The Christian skald Sigvatr Þórðarson visited Sweden about 1020 and describes in *Austrfararvísur* how he came to a *hof* but was turned away because they were celebrating *alfablót* (sacrifice to elves) on the farmstead. Sigvatr's way of expressing this seems to show that the *hof* was a part of the farmstead or perhaps just an appellative used for a farm, where people met for pagan worship. The latter possibility is strengthened by the frequent occurrence of *hof* in place-names in Norway, Sweden, and Iceland. In Norway twenty-two farm names begin with a god's name, followed by *-hof,* and no less than eighty-five farms are simply called *Hof.* Correspondingly, Iceland had twenty-four farms with the name *Hof.* It seems unlikely that so many farmsteads should have adopted their names from a temple building standing on their ground. The very nature of the name indicates that the term *hof* incorporates the farm itself as a center for convivial sacrifices. *Hof* might have been the usual term for major farmsteads, where the owners celebrated ritual meals for the people in the region. This does not necessarily imply the presence of separate temple buildings. The spacious *veizluskáli,* the feast hall, so typical of the chieftains' farms in the Viking Age, would provide ample room for such celebrations.

Local legends in Iceland attach the term *hof* to nearly one hundred different archaeological sites. These *hoftóftir* (temple sites) have received much scholarly attention, and some authors have even attempted to arrange chronological and typological tables of the development of the *hof.* But the great majority of these legends are products of nineteenth-century national Romanticism, and most of the sites are in fact remains of medieval farms, chapels, byres, and pens. However, one site is of considerable interest. At Hofstaðir in Mývatnssveit there are remains of an impressive longhouse, consisting of a thirty-six-meter- (118-ft) long hall with three additions, one at the north gable and two on the western side. Because of the place name, "*hof*-stead," and of features reminiscent of the *hof* described in *Eyrbyggja saga,* this site has kept its reputation as a proper *hoftóft,* and although our present archaeological knowledge of Viking Age farms in Iceland compels us to identify the site as a dwelling house of a chieftain, it can at the same time very well have served as a *hof* for the people in the area, who came to the chieftain (*goði*) for major religious celebrations. This assumption is confirmed by a unique feature at the site: the oval structure south of the gable front seems to contain a large pit for "baking" meat. The size and position in the open would make this pit unsuitable for daily cooking but well suited for the ritual preparation of sacrificial animals for a convivial meal attended by a large crowd.

A religious building of a completely different type—though unjustly classified as a *hof* in Norse medieval writings—was the temple at the important sanctuary at Uppsala in Sweden. This temple was still in use about 1100, and about 1075 it was described (from a distance) by the German historian Adam of Bremen in his *Gesta Hammaburgensis ecclesiae pontificum*. Adam's account is pieced together from sources of varying reliability, but it leaves no doubt as to the existence of a temple building, in which there were idols, allegedly of the gods Thor, Odin, and Freyr. The keynote of the account is the description of the gruesome sacrificial ceremonies that took place in the holy grove of the precinct. The role of the temple in the cult is not explained. Very large crowds gathered for the religious festivities in Uppsala, and the temple can hardly have housed the participants of convivial meals. Perhaps its primary function was to shelter the idols. Images might have stood there and had offerings brought to them for centuries, and the erection of a building over them may be due to influence from Christian practice at the end of the heathen time.

The same development might have happened elsewhere, and the author of this article has (reluctantly) offered the idea that this could explain why the term *hǫrgr*, which generally stands for simple stone heaps and other open-air sanctuaries, appears in a few sources from the late pagan period with the meaning "(small) houses."

Traces of earlier human activity have been found below the floor of the Romanesque church in Gamla Uppsala. The excavator suggested that these are remains of the famous temple, and imaginative scholars have ventured into a wide variety of reconstructions of the temple on the basis of very slight and dubious evidence. It is not advisable to take any of these reconstructions seriously.

A widespread hypothesis claims that medieval churches in Scandinavia were often placed on sites once used for heathen cults. This is, however, not the case. Apart from the possible traces in Uppsala and from a find of amulets in Mære, Norway, no indications of continuity from pagan to Christian sanctuaries has been found in any of the numerous Scandinavian churches where excavations have been carried out since World War II. Another suggestion, according to which many churches should stand within the premises of large triangular pagan sanctuaries, has proved to be an archaeological fallacy.

BIBLIOGRAPHY

A full bibliography until 1965 is found in Olaf Olsen, *Hørg, Hov og Kirke* (1966), with an English summary, 277–288, also printed as *Årbøger for nordisk Old-kyndighed og Historie, 1965* (1966). Works of major interest are: Daniels Bruun and Finnur Jónsson, "Om hove og hovudgravninger på Island," in *Aarbøger för nordisk Oldkyndighed og Historie,* **24** (1909); Ejnar Dyggve, "Three Sanctuaries of Jelling Type," in *Scripta Minora* of Studier utg. av Kungl. Humanistiska Vetenskapssamfundet i Lund (1959–1960); Hans-Emil Lidén, "From Pagan Sanctuary to Christian Church: The Excavation of Mære Church in Trøndelag," in *Norwegian Archaeological Review,* **2** (1969), with comments from Wilhelm Holmqvist and Olaf Olsen; Sune Lindqvist, "Uppsala hednatempel: Gamla och nya Spekulationer," in *Ord och Bild,* **36** (1927); Magnus Olsen, *Hedenske kultminder i norske stedsnavne* (1915); Olaf Olsen, "Vorchristliche Heiligtümer in Nordeuropa," in *Vorgeschichtliche Heiligtümer und Opferplätze in Mittel- und Nordeuropa,* Herbert Jankuhn, ed. (1970), 259–278, "The 'Sanctuary' at Jelling, with Some Observations on Jelling's Significance in the Viking Age," in *Mediaeval Scandinavia,* **4** (1974), and "Is There a Relationship Between Pagan and Christian Places of Worship in Scandinavia?" Council for British Archaeology, Report no. 60 (1986); Thede Palm, "Uppsalalunden och Uppsalatemplet," in *Vetenskaps societeten i Lunds. Årsbok* (1941), 79–109; Allan Rostvik, *Har och harg* (1967); Herm. M. Schirmer, "Horg og hov," in *Foreningen til norske fortidsminnemærkers bevaring, Aarsberetning for 1906;* Albert Thümmel, "Der germanische Tempel," in *Beiträge zur Geschichte der deutschen Sprache und Literatur,* **35** (1909); Jan de Vries, *Altgermanische Religionsgeschichte,* I (1956), 372–393.

OLAF OLSEN

[See also **Adam of Bremen; Eddic Poetry; Eyrbygga Saga; Skaldic Poetry; Snorri Sturluson.**]

SCARLET, a fine woolen broadcloth dyed partially or wholly in that peculiar, vivid red color whose name was ultimately borrowed from the textile itself. It was the most expensive woolen manufactured in medieval Europe, rivaling the better silks in price and luxury appeal. Those features were determined essentially by dyestuffs extracted from two related Mediterranean female shield lice: *Coccus ilicis* and *Kermococcus vermilio,* now called kermes (from Arabic *qīrmiz,* worm), but known to the ancient world as *cocci* (berries) and to medieval Europe as *grana* (grains). Two other insects producing similar if less popular vermilion dyes were *Porphyrophora hamelii* and *Coccus polonicus* (St. John's blood). From the sixteenth century they were largely displaced by the more powerful Mexican insect dye cochineal (*Grana cochinilla*); and that in turn, from the 1880's, by aniline (polyazo) dyes.

While all medieval scarlets were dyed "in grain" with kermes, some also contained additional dyes, especially woad (blue), affixed first to the wools, and weld (yellow). Such mixed dyeing explains why the colors of some medieval scarlets were said to be purple, brown, black, sanguine, or even green; a "white scarlet" was one made of undyed "white" wools, subsequently dyed "in the piece" with kermes. In later medieval England and France, the term "scarlet" came to be reserved exclusively for those broadcloths dyed uniquely in kermes.

The etymology of the term "scarlet" remains uncertain. The word is documented only from the early eleventh century as Old High German *scarlachen* and then as Latin *scarlatum,* with its derivatives, French *escarlate* and Italian *scarlatto.* The common explanation that these words were derived from the Persian *saqirlāt* or *saqalāṭ* is undoubtedly false. The Persian terms cannot be documented before about 1300 and were themselves influenced by *scarlatto,* but borrowed ultimately from the Arabic *siqlātūn,* a costly brocaded silk. Nevertheless, since such silks were the most aristocratic textiles of the Islamic world, and since those of Muslim Spain were dyed from the tenth century in locally produced kermes, *siqlātūn* may have influenced the formation of the European terms, especially the Romance variants. But "scarlet," especially in Germanic variants, was evidently also influenced by the Old High German *scarlachen* (shear cloth), originally meaning a fine, felted, shorn woolen, which, in its eleventh-century northern reappearance, was a much more luxurious fabric than the patterned-weave worsteds it largely displaced.

BIBLIOGRAPHY

Wolfgang Born, "Scarlet," in *Ciba Review,* no. 7 (1938); J. and Charles Cotte, "Le kermès dans l'antiquité," in *Revue archéologique,* 5th ser., 7 (1918); Robert James Forbes, "Dyes and Dyeing," in *Studies in Ancient Technology,* IV, 2nd ed., rev. (1964), esp. 114–122; Judith Hofenk-De Graaff, "The Chemistry of Red Dyestuffs in Medieval and Early Modern Europe," in N. B. Harte and K. G. Ponting, eds., *Cloth and Clothing in Medieval Europe: Essays in Memory of Professor E. M. Carus-Wilson* (1983), esp. 71–79; John J. Hummel, *The Dyeing of Textile Fabrics,* 2nd ed. (1898); John H. Munro, "The Medieval Scarlet and the Economics of Sartorial Splendour," in N. B. Harte and K. G. Ponting, eds., *Cloth and Clothing in Medieval Europe: Essays in Memory of Professor E. M. Carus-Wilson* (1983), esp. 13–70; Guy de Poerck, *La draperie médiévale en Flandre et en Artois: Technique et terminologie,* 3 vols. in 2 (1951); J.-B. Weckerlin, *Le drap "escarlate" au moyen âge: Essai sur l'étymologie et la signification du mot écarlate* (1905); Kurt Zangger, *Contribution à la terminologie de tissus en ancien français attestés dans les textes français, provençaux, italiens, espagnols, allemands, et latins* (1945).

JOHN H. MUNRO

[See also **Dyes and Dyeing; Qirmiz; Textiles; Wool.**]

SCHAMPIFLOR, or *Alten Weibes List* (The old woman's ruse), a fourteenth-century Middle High German verse tale (*Märe*) of 462 lines written in the Thuringian dialect, survives in one manuscript only. A synopsis of the tale follows.

Against the wiles of clever women there is no defense! Rupart, a brother of the king of England, is a student in Paris. Standing on the Peripont one day, he is overcome by the beauty of a lady. He follows her and learns that she is Schampiflor, wife of the very rich and handsome Bilamor. Rupart engages an old matchmaker, instructing her to spare no expense for a secret rendezvous. Schampiflor, impressed with costly presents, finally consents to a meeting in the matchmaker's house. But Rupart is detained elsewhere that day, so the desperate matchmaker invites a very good-looking passerby, who, unfortunately, happens to be Bilamor. But Schampiflor shows presence of mind; she pounces on her husband, accusing him of infidelity, but is finally mollified with the promise of expensive jewelry. The Englishman's investment was in vain.

Clever extrication from impending disaster is a favorite theme of farcical tales (*Schwankmären*) and Shrovetide plays, as is love purchased with money or presents. Andreas Capellanus treats the theme repeatedly (*De amore per pecuniam acquisito* 1.9). The proper names used suggest a French source, but they are interchangeable. In a closely related story by "der arme Konrad" (now titled *Frau Metze die Käuflerin*) the action takes place in Würzburg and the detained suitor is a high-ranking cleric (*tuomprobst*). Because of the old woman matchmaker, both stories were titled *Alten Weibes List* by different editors, which caused confusion. While the occurrence of students and clerics in this type of story is high, the use of a matchmaker, according to Hermann Tiemann, was a current literary device. It followed classical models transmitted through medieval Latin *comoedia,* such as *Baucis et Thraso, Pamphilus de Amore,* and *Lidia.*

BIBLIOGRAPHY

Hanns Fischer, *Studien zur deutschen Märendictung* (1968), 352; Karl Heinz Schirmer, *Stil- und Motivuntersuchungen zur mittelhochdeutschen Versnovelle* (1969); Wolfgang Stammler, ed., *Die deutsche Literatur des Mittelalters: Verfasserlexikon,* IV (1953), 43, and V (1955), 534; Hermann Tiemann, "Bemerkungen zu einer Entstehungsgeschichte der Fabliaux," in *Romanische Forschungen,* 72 (1960).

KLAUS WOLLENWEBER

[See also **Capellanus, Andreas; Konrad von Würzburg; Mären; Middle High German Literature.**]

SCHISM, GREAT (Western Schism, Great Schism of the West). From 1378 to 1409 the papacy was divided into two "obediences," one centered in Avignon and the other in Rome. The former continued the Avignon papacy that had enjoyed universal European obedience in the previous three quarters of a century; now, however, it was recognized only by France, the Spanish realms of Navarre, Aragon, and Castile, Scotland, the island of Sicily, and some of the western territories of the empire. The Roman line was recognized by England, Ireland, most of the empire, Poland, Hungary, the Teutonic Order, the Scandinavian realms, and almost all of Italy; Portugal moved back and forth but eventually ended in this camp. A few borderlands of the empire in the northwest remained neutral. In 1409 the Council of Pisa declared both the Avignon and the Roman contender deposed and elected a new pope. Even though this solution was supported by most European polities, both of the deposed popes retained significant obediences and the Pisan solution had to be repeated and revised by the Council of Constance. This body deposed the Avignon and Pisan popes, and accepted the abdication of the Roman one; on 11 November 1417 it elected Pope Martin V, who quickly secured recognition from all polities except the county of Armagnac (which held out for several years) and Hussite Bohemia.

There had been many schisms before this in the Western church, but none had lasted so long or had raised such profound problems of legitimacy. Even today, although subsequent popes reused the papal styles of one Pisan and both Avignon contenders (John XXIII, Benedict XIII, Clement VII), and the papacy has approved their listing as antipopes, their lines have not been formally declared illegitimate, and the issue remains a subject of scholarly debate. The reasons for this indeterminacy lie in the peculiarities of the schism itself—its background, immediate causes, beginnings, structures, and eventual solution.

BACKGROUND

The Avignon popes before the schism had developed a strong, centralized government of the church based not on absolutism but on collaboration with the upper estates of Christendom. The cardinals, legally mere creatures of the pope, in fact enjoyed many privileges of wealth and status, shared with the pope in the governance of the church, and were consulted by him on all important matters. The kings and princes of Europe recognized the pope's right to bestow all major and many minor benefices in their lands and to impose substantial fiscal burdens on church property; in return the pope usually appointed candidates desired by the lay powers and shared some of his revenues with them. The residence of the popes in Avignon—far more convenient than Rome for dealings with most of Europe—and the French nationality of the popes and a majority of the cardinals and curial officials were further marks of a European rather than predominantly Italian papacy. At the same time, even while constructing palaces and government buildings, the popes from about 1350 on put much of their wealth into reestablishing papal authority in the Papal States in central Italy, partly because the revenues from these lands were important and partly because a secure territorial base in Italy would allow the papacy to overcome the most serious defects of their Avignon residence—undue dependence on French power and separation from their proper see of Rome. Pope Urban V moved to Rome in 1367 in the belief that the work of pacification had been completed; in fact it had not been, and he felt forced to return to Avignon in 1370. His successor, Gregory XI, resolved on the same course, even though in 1375 there had been a general rising in the Papal States against the pope's authority, with Florence, fearful of papal encroachments on Tuscany, acting as a prime instigator. Gregory nevertheless left Avignon on 13 September 1376 and arrived in Rome on 17 January 1377, along with a cadre of government officials and all but six of the cardinals. His return marked the end of the old Avignon system.

Rome itself was turbulent and the Papal States were pacified in name only. The papal presence was felt everywhere as domination by the French, a sentiment that Florence encouraged by manifestos and by a corps of agents agitating in Rome. Long-growing Italian resentment over the loss of the papal residence and the consequent impoverishment of Rome was now focused on a determination to keep the papacy for good. Gregory realized, but too late, that his hope for a peaceful implantation of the Avignon papacy in Rome had been mistaken; long an invalid, he could do nothing during his final months of life, and his death in Rome on 26 March 1378 was the signal for the Romans to act. Of the sixteen cardinals in the city, four were Italian, seven were "Limousin" (the southern French group), and five were "French" (including the Aragonese Pedro de Luna); a common anti-Limousin sentiment united the French and Italian groups. The Roman magistrates urged the cardinals to choose a Roman as pope and observed that the failure to do so would put the cardinals in mortal danger. When they entered their conclave, which was not duly sealed off, on 7 April 1378, there were Roman troops in the rooms below, bells tolled during the night, and large numbers of people outside shouted demands for a Roman, or at least an Italian—"Otherwise we'll kill them all!" In these circumstances the various factions seem to have agreed on the advisability of choosing an Italian. On 8 April they elected Bartolomeo Prignano, archbishop of Bari and veteran official of the papal court, as Pope Urban VI. The election was repeated the next day, and Urban was enthroned and quickly accepted as pope by both the Romans and papal officials. The cardinals formally announced their choice to their six colleagues in Avignon and to the princes of Europe; they asked for and received the usual papal grants of privileges and benefices; they attended Urban's consistories and in general gave him every sign of recognition.

POPE AND ANTIPOPE

The new pope's behavior, however, soon caused the cardinals to regret their choice. Unable or unwilling to fit himself into the Avignon system and preside over the papacy as the cardinals' chief, Urban declared his intention of reforming the church and began by attacking the cardinals' luxurious way of life, their greed, nepotism, and moral weaknesses. His behavior toward them became increasingly abusive; when faced with their objections, he proclaimed his papal omnipotence against them. His behavior at this time and subsequently led modern historians of otherwise different views to agree that Urban was mentally disturbed, a conclusion the cardinals themselves also reached. As early as the beginning of May, the French cardinals and high members of the papal court began to leave Rome for Anagni; by the end of June all but the Italians were there, and these latter were summoned on 20 July to join their colleagues in resolving the problem posed by Urban's alleged lack of right to the papacy. Meanwhile, letters were sent to Paris warning the king of France that all was not well. On 2 August the cardinals publicly declared Urban's election invalid because of intimidation, and on 9 August they declared him no pope and anathematized him for holding his office illegally. Moving to Fondi, where the three Italian cardinals joined the main body, the college chose one of themselves, Robert of Geneva, a relative of Charles V of France, as Pope Clement VII (1378–1394), on 20 September. Although the three Italian cardinals did not participate in the election, their tacit consent can be inferred by their acceptance of it.

The three Italian cardinals, who abandoned Urban, had first proposed that the issue be resolved by a general council of the universal church, which in the legal thought of the time was generally considered competent to take cognizance of accusations of papal malfeasance. Others also proposed this remedy, and it was the way favored by leading theologians and lawyers at the University of Paris, most notably Henry of Langenstein and Conrad of Gelnhausen. But the French cardinals rejected the proposal, chiefly because they insisted that only the cardinals could judge the crucial point: whether

Urban had been elected under legally impermissible duress. In any case the princes of Europe did not press for a council but, rather, established the schism by choosing sides, some at once, others only after hesitations and inquiries that gave rise to a large mass of evidence about the events of 1378 and a powerful battery of legal treatises on both sides. The central issues, unresolved to this day, were whether the cardinals' choice of Urban had been determined by intimidation (the objectively menacing circumstances were not in doubt), and whether in any case they had not remedied any defect in the elections by their subsequent recognition of Urban as pope. Their own argument was that even this recognition had been due to the continuing danger of death to which they were subjected in Rome.

While Clement VII hoped to establish himself in Rome by force of French arms, he soon had to withdraw, first to Naples, which he left for Sperlonga on 13 May, and then, on 22 May 1379, to Avignon, arriving 20 June. His hopes remained, however; Duke Louis of Anjou, brother of King Charles V of France, was chosen to lead the fight. After Louis's death in southern Italy in 1384, this way of ending the schism by force (the *via facti*) became increasingly unrealistic. Europe was settling into an acceptance of the schism, which reflected the French system of alliances as well as the hostility to France of England, some of the western German territories, and much of Italy. Furthermore, the princes of Europe profited from the weakness of the divided papacy by getting concessions in return for their respective adherences. The king of Castile recognized Clement VII in 1381 in return for a limit on the pope's right of appointment to Castilian benefices, his capacity to raise money from the Castilian clergy, and his jurisdiction over the clergy. England, on the other hand, had already developed numerous limitations on papal power; the schism simply prevented the popes from effectively protesting. The schism also reversed the gains of the Avignon period and permanently reduced the papal share of the revenues of church property all over Europe. Apart from the University of Paris, which had to be silenced by royal decree in 1381, there were few voices in the first decade to urge that the interest of the church universal required not the determination of which papacy was the true one but, rather, the collaboration of both sides to end the schism.

Such voices were, however, raised in the 1390's, first in France, and then in Europe at large. The prime movers were the dukes of Berry and Burgundy, uncles of King Charles VI and real rulers of France from 1392 on, after Charles had been struck by insanity. The dukes considered the advantages of the Avignon papacy to be outweighed by that papacy's cost (the French church provided almost all of its income) and by the schism's frustration of peace negotiations with the English. After Clement VII died (September 1394) and was succeeded by the Spaniard Pedro de Luna, as Benedict XIII (1394–1423), the French pushed openly to end the schism. The only feasible solution, by this time, was a nonjudicial one that would not leave one party branded as schismatic. The ideal form of such a solution would have been the voluntary abdication of both papal contenders (the *via cessionis*). It was the duke of Berry's chief ecclesiastical agent, Simon de Cramaud, titular patriarch of Alexandria, who formulated the rationale of such a solution and secured its approval by the first Paris council of the French clergy in February 1395. The University of Paris, acting under leaders willing to collaborate in the Berry-Burgundy program (John Gerson and Pierre d'Ailly, the two most distinguished theologians, were not among them), not only promoted the *via cessionis* in writings and diplomatic action but also developed the idea of "partial subtraction of obedience" as a means of imposing the *via cessionis* on the reluctant contenders: they were to be deprived of their power to appoint to benefices and to impose fiscal exactions on the clergy. As far as France was concerned, partial subtraction encapsulated a whole century's cultivation by the university of the program of the "Liberties of the Gallican church"—a reaction to both thirteenth-century and Avignonese papalism.

The new French policy was rejected by both papal contenders. Benedict XIII, who as Cardinal Pedro de Luna had taken part in the events of 1378, had at first regarded Urban VI's election as valid, but had then joined his colleagues in believing it to have been vitiated by duress. He saw the *via cessionis* with its political sine qua non of nonjudgment as a guarantee that the true papal line (that of Clement VII and himself) would never be recognized by the church at large and as a threat that the false (Urbanist) line might in fact prevail. In any case he refused to be dictated to by the Paris forces headed by Simon de Cramaud. Urban's successor, Boniface IX (1389–1404), expressed the general conviction of the Urbanist obedience that the current Avignon line had originated in an arbitrary schism from the pope—Urban VI—who had been universally recognized after his election; if the French and their allies now wished to end the schism, let them recognize Boniface.

This conviction of rectitude on the part of the Urbanist papacy was reinforced by its structure as a new institution, different from the preceding and current Avignon papacies in significant ways. Not only the cardinals had deserted Urban VI, but almost all the trained personnel of the papal financial office (the *camera apostolica*) and many other French bureaucrats as well. The new pope could replace them only with men whose lack of technical qualification was balanced by loyalty. He naturally turned to the leading families of his own Naples (he belonged to the Brancacci family), who in a short time secured effective control of the Roman papacy, from the cardinalate on down. Under Boniface IX this group held eight of eleven cardinalates as well as all the places of authority in the Papal States. Their "papacy" was a supremely desirable possession even in the curtailed dimensions imposed by the schism; it would be some time before they could understand that reunion by means of the *via cessionis* might not only preserve but also enhance what they had won. While the Avignon cardinals were in a rather different situation, in which the power of the French government was a decisive factor, they too approached the problem of union with calculations of future advantage. While both contending popes rejected the *via cessionis* as a degradation of papal supremacy, their cardinals could be less rigid.

CONFLICT AND RESOLUTION: CONCILIARISM

French policy pursued two great aims after 1395. Embassies from the crown as well as the University of Paris were sent to all the major powers of both obediences, asking adherence to the *via cessionis* in its most attractive form: a voluntary double abdication. At the same time the possibility of a coerced abdication was broached; Simon de Cramaud along with some other Parisians, began to speak of deposing both contenders if they should prove obdurate. The canonistic argument to justify this most extreme action was developed by Simon in his treatise "On the Subtraction of Obedience" (*De substraccione obediencie*) of 1396/1397. He argued that the "status" of the universal church was the church's supreme interest, to which even the pope was subject, and that the contenders' refusal to abdicate was destroying that status. In the Paris council of 1398, at which Simon served as the crown's chief spokesman, his program was accepted in the form of "total" subtraction: not just the removal of papal powers noted above, but the determination that a pope who refused to abdicate—specifically Benedict XIII—was objectively a schismatic, therefore a heretic, and hence ipso facto disqualified from being pope. France subtracted its obedience from Benedict on 27 July 1398, and was followed by the college of Avignon cardinals, except for five cardinals who remained loyal to Benedict, and the kingdom of Castile.

Efforts were now made to persuade Europe's rulers to join France in subtraction. Like the previous efforts in behalf of the *via cessionis,* these did not lead to immediate results, but they did project the images of the French program onto the public stage. The vicissitudes of French politics made steadfast adherence to so demanding a policy very difficult, and from 1403 to 1406 obedience was restored to Benedict. The agitation continued, however, with the University of Paris keeping the union program alive. Eventually the ideal of union by the *via cessionis* secured widespread recognition, and both successors of Boniface IX, Innocent VII (1404–1406) and Gregory XII (1406–1415), were elected under the condition of swearing an oath to abdicate if their opposite number in Avignon would do so as well. Benedict XIII had in fact been forced to accept the *via cessionis* as the price of France's restoration of obedience in 1403, and although he did not intend to follow through, his pledge was on record.

A large French embassy led by Simon de Cramaud went to both popes in 1407–1408 in order to arrange their simultaneous abdication; when both popes resisted, the embassy worked directly with the cardinals and secured the fusion of the two colleges on 29 June 1408. The cardinals issued a call for a general council of the European church to meet at Pisa in March 1409 so as to implement the *via cessionis,* if necessary by deposition. The Council of Pisa duly assembled, with representatives from both obediences (the Spanish and west German polities, as well as Naples, were the chief absentees). Under the presidency of Simon of Cramaud, it declared both Benedict XIII and Gregory XII deposed as schismatics and therefore heretics; a new pope, Alexander V, was chosen to head the united church. The French had secured this victory by renouncing any ambition to obtain their own pope; the real power in the papal court was held by the Neapolitan cardinal Baldassare Cossa, who in 1410 succeeded Alexander V as John XXIII.

Although the Pisan line secured the adherence of all but a few rulers, Benedict retained the allegiance of the Spanish realms and Scotland, and Gregory had some support in Italy. John XXIII, unfortunately, did not have the traits of character to overcome these holdouts. Pressed by Emperor Sigismund, he summoned a new council to meet at Constance, to end the schism once and for all. It did so, in the way described above.

While the French action for union aimed only at restoring a single papacy, the program of action by general councils evoked very strong, long-accumulating sentiments for a comprehensive reform of the church "in head and members." Both Pisa and Constance saw much agitation on this matter, and at the latter council the doctrine of "conciliarism" was officially proclaimed: that a general council representing the whole church was the supreme ecclesiastical authority to which even popes had to submit. In fact much limitation of papal power, in the sense of the "Gallican Liberties," was achieved at Constance by concordats between the rulers of Europe and the new pope, Martin V (1417–1431), and even the constitutional principles of conciliarism were accepted by the new pope in modified form.

BIBLIOGRAPHY

Étienne Delaruelle *et al., L'église au temps du Grand Schisme et de la crise conciliaire (1378–1449),* 2 vols. (1962–1964); Arnold Esch, "Das Papsttum unter der Herrschaft der Neapolitaner," in *Festschrift für Hermann Heimpel*, pt. 2 (1972), which analyzes the inner structure of the Urbanist papacy; Jean Favier, *Les finances pontificales à l'époque du Grand Schisme d'Occident, 1378–1409* (1966); Johannes Haller, *Papsttum und Kirchenreform* (1903); Howard Kaminsky, *Simon de Cramaud and the Great Schism* (1983); John J. N. Palmer, *England, France, and Christendom, 1377–1399* (1972); Édouard Perroy, *L'Angleterre et le Grand Schisme d'Occident* (1933); Michael Seidlmayer, *Die Anfänge des grossen abendländischen Schismas* (1940); Richard Trexler, "Rome on the Eve of the Great Schism," in *Speculum,* **42** (1967); Walter Ullmann, *The Origins of the Great Schism* (1948, repr. 1972), detailed and sound, but strongly Urbanist; Walter Brandmüller, "Zur Frage nach der Gültigkeit der Wahl Urbans VI.," in *Annuarium historiae conciliorum,* **6** (1974), covers the literature since Ullmann's work.

The only general works in English are outdated: Alexander Flick, *The Decline of the Medieval Church,* 2 vols. (1930, repr. 1967); George J. Jordan, *The Inner History of the Great Schism of the West* (1930); up-to-date references are in Robert W. Swanson, *Universities, Academics, and the Great Schism* (1979).

Howard Kaminsky

[See also **Ailly, Pierre d'; Alexander V, Antipope; Antipope; Babylonian Captivity; Church, Latin: 1305–1500; Conciliar Theory; Conclave, Papal; Councils, Western; Gerson, John; Henry of Langenstein; Hus, John; Hussites; Papacy, Origins and Development; Wyclif, John.**]

SCHISM, PHOTIAN. The schism that began as a division within the Byzantine church over the right of Photios (*ca.* 810–*ca.* 893) to be recognized as patriarch of Constantinople soon became a wider dispute when Pope Nicholas I (*r.* 858–867) asserted his right to judge the question and then decided against Photios.

The origins of the controversy went back to the final condemnation of iconoclasm in the Byzantine church in 843, which brought with it reunion of the Eastern and Western churches. The new iconophile patriarch of Constantinople, Methodios, clashed with a group led by the monks of the monastery of the Studios, who objected to his allegedly careless ordinations of replacements for iconoclast priests and bishops. After Methodios' death in 847, his successor as patriarch, Ignatios, drew criticism for his condemnation of Gregory Asbestas, archbishop of Syracuse and a partisan of Methodios. Gregory appealed his case (which remains very obscure) to Rome. Though Methodios and his supporters have often been considered as "moderates" in dealing with repentant iconoclasts, and Ignatios and his followers as "extremists," the evidence actually indicates that Methodios was the more rigorous of the two. Methodios' party, however, does seem to have been more open to government control and more favorable to secular learning than Ignatios' group.

Ignatios had been nominated by the empress Theodora II, and after her fall in 856 he quarreled with Bardas, then the main adviser of Emperor Michael III (*r.* 842–867) over Bardas' liaison with his own daughter-in-law. In 858 Bardas forced Ignatios to abdicate and arranged the election to the patriarchate of Photios, a strict iconophile, a defender of Gregory Asbestas, and a layman. Photios was rushed through holy orders and consecrated patriarch by Gregory, whose case was still being considered at Rome. An attempted compromise between Photios and Ignatios quickly broke down, and a number of bishops and monks, including the Studites, refused to accept Photios as patriarch on the grounds that Ignatios' abdication was involuntary and therefore void, that Photios' hurried elevation from layman to patriarch was uncanonical, and that Gregory's position rendered his consecration of Photios invalid. These dissidents and Ignatios were then condemned at a synod summoned by Photios.

In 860 Photios sent word of his accession and the deposition of Ignatios to Pope Nicholas, who asserted his right to judge the matter and sent two legates to investigate. At the same time Nicholas requested the return to Roman jurisdiction of the ecclesiastical provinces of Calabria, Sicily, and Illyricum (the Balkans except for Thrace), annexed to the patriarchate of Constantinople by the iconoclast emperor Leo III (*r.* 717–741). The pope's legates took part in a council held at Constantinople in 861, which found Ignatios' deposition and Photios' consecration valid, declared Gregory Asbestas innocent, and took no action on the disputed provinces. Nicholas, however, refused to accept the decisions of this council on the ground that his legates had exceeded their authority. In 863, after an unsuccessful attempt at negotiations with Constantinople, the pope, persuaded by refugee partisans of Ignatios led by the abbot Theognostos, held a synod at Rome that declared Photios deposed and Ignatios restored.

Tensions heightened in 866, when the khan of Bulgaria, Boris (renamed Michael), who had accepted Christianity from Byzantium only two years before, transferred his allegiance to Rome in anger at being denied a separate patriarch for the Bulgarian church. Further, between 865 and 867 the Byzantines were negotiating with the Carolingian emperor Louis II, who had been in intermittent conflict with Nicholas, with the aim of having the pope excommunicated by Photios and expelled from Rome by Louis, whose imperial title would in return be recognized at Constantinople. In 867 Photios convoked a general council of the Eastern church, which condemned Pope Nicholas and proclaimed Louis emperor. Photios' case against Nicholas rested partly on Nicholas' supposed tyranny in the West and partly on the activities of the papal missionaries to Bulgaria, who had followed the usual Western practice in various matters of discipline (such as clerical celibacy) and in using the Creed with the *Filioque,* which stated that the Holy Spirit had proceeded not only from the Father but from the Son. The *Filioque* was the principal basis for the council's declaring the pope a heretic.

Almost immediately after the end of the council, however, Michael III was overthrown and killed, and Basil I (*r.* 867–886) became emperor. Basil repudiated the ecclesiastical policy of Michael, including the recent council, compelled Photios to abdicate, and reinstated Ignatios as patriarch. The schism with the West was formally ended with the condemnation of Photios at the Fourth Council of Constantinople (869–870).

Photios, however, still had partisans in Byzantium. When Ignatios died in 877, Basil appointed Photios as his successor and petitioned Pope John VIII (*r.* 872–882) for recognition of Photios and for a new council at Constantinople. John agreed and sent legates to the council with a statement of his conditions for recognizing Photios. This council, held in 879–880, was presided over by Photios, who presented the pope's statement to the council in a substantially altered Greek translation and so obtained agreement on more favorable terms than John had intended. Expressing annoyance at what had been done, John approved the council only with reservations, and relations between Rome and Constantinople remained strained until Photios' deposition by Emperor Leo VI (*r.* 886–912) in 886. Nevertheless, it seems to be true that there was no "Second Photian Schism" during Photios' second term as patriarch, as was believed earlier. Tension between former partisans of Photios and Ignatios continued into the tenth century in Byzantium, and the issues raised during the Photian Schism, particularly the *Filioque,* contributed to the lasting schism between East and West that began in 1054.

BIBLIOGRAPHY

Joseph Hergenröther, *Photius: Patriarch von Konstantinopel,* 3 vols. (1867–1869), is still the fundamental study, not sympathetic to Photios. John B. Bury, *History of the Eastern Roman Empire* (1912, repr. 1965), 180–209, offers a clear and dispassionate statement of the facts. Francis Dvornik, *The Photian Schism* (1948), is a carefully documented defense of Photios. Daniel Stiernon, *Constantinople IV* (1967), treats the whole schism; it is not pro-Photian. Richard Haugh, *Photius and the Carolingians* (1975), is a theological analysis sympathetic to Photios. John A. Meijer, *A Successful Council of Union* (1975), is a thorough but uncritically pro-Photian analysis of the council of 879–880. Cyril Mango, "The Liquidation of Iconoclasm and the Patriarch Photios," and P. Karlin-Hayter, "Gregory of Syracuse, Ignatios, and Photios," in Anthony Bryer and Judith Herrin, eds., *Iconoclasm* (1977), are complementary studies refuting the characterizations of Photios as "moderate" and Ignatios as "extremist."

WARREN T. TREADGOLD

[See also **Bardas, Caesar; Basil I the Macedonian; Boris I of Bulgaria; Bulgaria; Byzantine Church; Byzantine Empire: History; Councils, Byzantine; Councils, Western; Cyril and Methodios, Sts.; Filioque; Ignatios, Patriarch; Nicholas I, Pope; Philosophy and Theology, Byzantine; Photios; Schisms, Eastern-Western Church; Theodora II, Empress; Trinitarian Doctrine.**]

SCHISMS, EASTERN-WESTERN CHURCH. The separation of the Eastern and Western churches in the course of the Middle Ages differs from most schisms in that it cannot be dated with precision nor can its immediate causes, whether doctrinal or disciplinary, be easily specified. Serious theological and ecclesiological differences were not always pressed, and when interruptions in official recognition and communion did occur, few if any regarded them as absolute or irreversible. Yet by the end of the fifteenth century the separation of the churches was in effect complete, with each regarding the other as alien, estranged from right belief and practice.

Already in the fourth century, controversy over trinitarian doctrine divided the churches of the Roman Empire along East-West lines. Following the First Ecumenical Council (Nicaea, 325), Rome insisted on the letter of Nicene orthodoxy and actively supported Easterners exiled for their opposition to Arianism. In the East, churchmen often questioned or challenged the Nicene formula, though not always out of Arian convictions, and resented Western interference in Eastern disciplinary matters. Gradually a "neo-Nicene" party emerged in the East under the leadership of Basil of Caesarea. Despite mistrust on the part of the Westerners and other "Old Nicenes," a united theological stand against the Arian menace was achieved. Yet ecclesiastical tensions remained. The Second Ecumenical Council (I Constantinople, 381) marked the defeat not only of Arianism but also of Old Nicene efforts to wrest control of Eastern ecclesiastical affairs from the neo-Nicenes. Particularly portentous was its third canon, which gave the bishop of Constantinople "primacy of honor after the bishop of Rome, because Constantinople is New Rome." Though the canon was directed chiefly against Alexandria's efforts to dominate Eastern affairs, it also implied a concept of church order fundamentally different from that held in Rome. For the Easterners, differences in rank arise not from any essential inequality of the churches but rather from the secular importance of their cities. The Roman church, on the other hand, insisted that its primacy was God-given, based not on secular importance or even conciliar decision but rather on Christ's promise to Peter (Matt. 16:18).

Disagreement over disciplinary matters, such as the deposition of John Chrysostom, continued in the following decades. The outbreak of Christological controversy further complicated matters. The Fourth Ecumenical Council (Chalcedon, 451) sparked the revolt of Monophysites (adherents of a one-nature Christology) in Egypt and Syria. The delicate task of restoring the unity of the imperial church fell largely to the emperors and patriarchs in Constantinople. Their task was not made easier by Rome. From the doctrinal point of view Chalcedon had been a great triumph for Pope Leo I and his *Tome;* therefore Rome was suspicious of any move to compromise its authority. At the same time the council's twenty-eighth canon, approved despite the protests of the Roman legates, had expanded upon the understanding of primacy earlier put forward at I Constantinople: just as "Old Rome" was honored because it was the imperial capital, so now Constantinople, the "New Rome," was to be honored—and given a greatly expanded patriarchal jurisdiction.

Such is the background of the Akakian schism, which divided Rome and Constantinople from 484 (the year of the formal condemnation of Akakios) to 519 (the year Patriarch John II signed the *libellus* demanded by Pope Hormisdas). Guided by Patriarch Akakios of Constantinople, Emperor Zeno in 482 issued the *Henotikon* (formula of union), which tried to ignore Chalcedon and Leo's *Tome* in an effort to placate the Monophysites. While this policy enjoyed moderate success in the East, it led to the excommunication of Akakios by Pope Simplicius. Relations were restored only after a reorientation of imperial policy under Justin I (518–527) and Justinian (527–565). Latin in culture, they were eager to restore imperial authority in the West, which since the mid fifth century had been abandoned to invading barbarians, and they recognized that ecclesiastical unity was a prerequisite for this. The names of Akakios and his successors therefore were expunged from the dyptichs of Constantinople, even though some of them had been ardent supporters of Chalcedon, and Patriarch John was able to tell Pope Hormisdas that Old Rome and the New were now as one.

The emperors had not abandoned hope of reconciling the Monophysites, however. Justinian's efforts to meet their objections to Chalcedon culminated in a new ecumenical council (II Constantinople, 553) and the condemnation of the "Three Chapters." The council's decisions were forced upon Pope Vigilius, then resident in Constantinople, and only reluctantly accepted in the West, where they prompted several local schisms; but the unity of the two Romes within one imperial church was maintained.

Under Heraklios (*r.* 610–641) a new union formula was devised, this one proclaiming one divine energy or operation in Christ. This Monenergist doctrine was attacked by Chalcedonians in the East. In the West Pope Honorius I (625–638) also objected but in passing suggested that the true unity in Christ was one of will. This Monothelite (one-will) formula was quickly seized upon by Patriarch Sergios of Constantinople as an ideal instrument for reuniting everyone, and in 638 it was embodied in an imperial *Ekthesis*. Repudiated in Rome, the *Ekthesis* was withdrawn by Heraklios in 640, but his successor, Constans (641–668), still cherished hopes of general reunion. His *Typos* (648), which forbade any further debate on the subject of wills, did not end the controversy, however. A Byzantine archimandrite, Maximus, carried his opposition to Monotheletism to Rome, where a council under Pope Martin in 649 condemned the *Typos* and broke off communion with Constantinople. Arrested for treason, Martin and Maximus died in miserable exile, but their doctrine eventually triumphed, if only because Arab conquests throughout the East were making Monotheletism politically irrelevant. In 657 pope and patriarch quietly began to exchange credentials, and in 663 the emperor made an impressive state visit to Rome; however, final resolution of the controversy was delayed until 680–681, when a new ecumenical council met in Constantinople. A *Tome* by Pope Agatho was enthusiastically received, Monenergism and Monotheletism were condemned, and their adherents—including four patriarchs of Constantinople and the hapless Pope Honorius—were anathematized.

If anything, loss of the ancient patriarchates of Alexandria, Antioch, and Jerusalem to the Arabs drew Rome and Constantinople closer. Constantinople was no longer tempted to compromise with the heretical and culturally alien elements of Syria and Egypt. At the same time a flood of Eastern refugees made Rome more cosmopolitan than ever before. To be sure, cultural differences were beginning to cause friction. The so-called Synod in Trullo (Constantinople, 692) criticized a number of Latin practices; Pope Sergius I refused to sign its canons and was spared the fate of Pope Martin only when Roman resistance foiled an imperial attempt to arrest him. Yet cordial relations were quickly restored when Pope Constantine I made a grand visit to Constantinople in 710. All parties remained loyal to the ideal of one Christian Roman Empire.

The iconoclastic and Filioque controversies. In the eighth century this common allegiance weakened. From 726 onward Byzantium was rent by controversy over an imperially initiated program of iconoclasm. Popes Gregory II and III refused to cooperate with the imperial policy and gave assistance to Eastern iconodules. Emperor Leo III (717–741) retaliated by transferring jurisdiction over Illyricum and southern Italy from Rome to Constantinople, a move that was to complicate ecclesiastical relations long after the defeat of iconoclasm. The political situation in central Italy posed a more immediate problem for the papacy, however. Byzantine might was on the wane; the last imperial stronghold, Ravenna, fell to the Lombards in 752. A new protector was found in the person of the Frankish king Pepin, who in 754 entered Italy to "restore" to the popes the "patrimony of St. Peter"—the territories which they hitherto had governed on behalf of the emperor in Constantinople. This new papal-Frankish alliance culminated in 800, when Pope Leo III crowned Pepin's son Charlemagne "emperor of the Romans." The political unity that had facilitated amicable relations between the two Romes was effectively at an end.

The papacy now was in an independent but delicate position between Byzantium and the Franks. Communion with Constantinople was restored with the condemnation of iconoclasm at the Seventh Ecumenical Council (II Nicaea, 787); but Charlemagne's Frankish bishops, misled by a faulty translation of the council's acts and eager to assert their own superiority, castigated its teaching on images at the Synod of Frankfurt (794) and in the *Libri Carolini*. Pope Adrian I was left with the difficult task of soothing their ruffled feelings. Another point of discord focused on the wording of the Nicene-Constantinopolitan Creed. In its original form, preserved unaltered in the East, the creed spoke of the Holy Spirit as proceeding "from the Father." In Spain the phrase "and from the Son" (*Filioque*) was added in the seventh century as a safeguard against Arianism. From Spain the phrase spread to France and Germany, where Charlemagne's theologians accused the Greeks of heresy for omitting it from the creed! For the time being, at least, Rome tactfully but firmly rejected the interpolation, and Pope Leo III (795–816) had the creed without *Filioque* set up on silver plaques in St. Peter's.

The Photian schism raised a number of earlier differences to the level of open controversy. In the East a new wave of iconoclasm (815–843) had left a legacy of party strife. When Patriarch Ignatios (847–858; 867–877) was pressured into resignation and replaced by a learned layman, Photios (858–867; 877–886), his supporters persuaded Pope Nicholas I (858–867) to intervene. Nicholas already had done much to advance papal authority in the disintegrating Carolingian Empire, and he was not reluctant to extend this authority to the East. His legates acquitted Photios at a council in Constantinople in 861, but he repudiated their action on the grounds that they had exceeded their mandate, and in 863 he declared the patriarch a usurper. The dispute was embittered by renewed controversy over jurisdiction over Illyricum. There the nascent Bulgar state was at the point of converting to Christianity, and competiton between Byzantine and Frankish missionaries was calling attention not only to cultural differences but also to the *Filioque* issue. A council convoked by Photios in Constantinople in 867 denounced Rome's intervention in Byzantine internal affairs, its intrusions in Bulgaria, and the *Filioque,* and excommunicated Nicholas. The situation was suddenly reversed by a palace revolution in Constantinople. A new emperor, Basil I (867–886), reinstated Ignatios; and at a new council in Constantinople in 869–870 legates of Pope Adrian II (867–872) secured the condemnation of Photios. Both Basil and Rome had underestimated support for Photios, however, and on Ignatios' death he was quietly restored to the patriarchal throne. A union council in Constantinople in 879–880 under Photios and legates of Pope John VIII (872–882) finally healed the schism: on the level of discipline each church recognized the other as supreme in its sphere, and on the level of doctrine additions to the creed were explicitly condemned.

In the tenth century the prestige of the papacy, now under the degrading domination of the Roman nobility, was at its nadir in Constantinople. The revival of imperial aspirations in Ottonian Germany did little to improve matters. Early in the eleventh century the *Filioque* was introduced in Rome, and, perhaps as a consequence, the names of the popes ceased to be included in the dyptichs in Constantinople. Yet on the whole apathy rather than hostility characterized relations between the churches. This situation changed in the mid eleventh century with the appearance of the Normans in southern Italy and the Seljuk Turks in Asia Minor. Collaboration against the common enemy now became highly desirable, but certain developments in the Western church made the prerequisite for collaboration—theological and ecclesiastical agreement—difficult to attain. A powerful reform movement was seeking to free the church from abuses like lay investiture, which had arisen because of the feudal system; and it was doing so by stressing the universal authority of the pope in a matter quite unknown in the East.

Mutual excommunications of 1054. In 1054 a serious quarrel erupted. Certain Greek practices in southern Italy had been condemned at the reforming Council of Siponto (1050). In retaliation Patriarch Michael Keroularios had ordered the Latin churches in Constantinople to adopt the Greek rite and encouraged his associates to write against Latin practices, above all the use of unleavened bread (azymes) in the Eucharist. Humbert of Silva Candida, leading theoretician of the reform, drafted a vitriolic response on behalf of Pope Leo IX (1048–1054), but before it was published a conciliatory letter arrived from Keroularios. For the moment the patriarch had deferred to the wishes of Emperor Constantine IX, who sought a renewed alliance with the papacy against the Normans. Humbert therefore was sent to Constantinople as head of a legation charged with negotiating a comprehensive agreement. His initial approach—conciliating the emperor while treating the patriarch as a contumacious rebel—badly miscalculated sentiment in the capital, and when he made public his earlier treatise on liturgical differences and charged the Greeks with heresy for omitting the *Filioque* from the creed, support for Keroularios only increased. The irate Humbert finally deposited a bull of excommunication on the altar of Hagia Sophia and departed;

a synod under Keroularios in turn excommunicated the legates.

The events of 1054 suggest how far apart the churches had drifted, above all in their understanding of authority, but they hardly mark the consummation of the schism, as historians like Gibbon once claimed. Almost at once new negotiations began, in which differences were diplomatically ignored in order to facilitate alliance against the Turks. The ensuing crusades brought closer contact between Latins and Greeks but did little to resolve religious differences. The Greeks were alarmed by the crusaders' violence and resented the establishment of a Latin hierarchy in the crusader principalities. The Latins in turn blamed Greek treachery for the crusades' lack of success. Hostility culminated in the Fourth Crusade (1204), which sacked Constantinople and made it the capital of a Latin empire. New efforts at reconciliation followed the recovery of Constantinople by Michael VIII Palaiologos (1258–1282). A union negotiated at the Council of Lyons (1274) served Michael's political interests but gained little support in the East and did not survive his death. Yet despite the animosity engendered by such events as the Fourth Crusade, many Eastern churchmen still viewed the schism as a temporary estrangement which free discussion of doctrinal issues at a true union council could easily resvolve. Such optimism was dashed by the Council of Ferrara-Florence (1438–1439). After months of debate all but one of the weary Greek delegates signed the council's decree of union, which conformed to the Latin doctrinal position, but in the East the union was generally regarded as a betrayal of the faith. Many believed submission to the sultan would be preferable to submission to the pope. The council in fact had revealed less the underlying unity of the churches than their underlying disunity.

BIBLIOGRAPHY

Yves Congar, *After Nine Hundred Years: The Background of the Schism Between the Eastern and Western Churches* (1959); Francis Dvornik, *The Photian Schism* (1948), *The Idea of Apostolicity in Byzantium and the Legend of the Apostle Andrew* (1958), and *Byzantium and Roman Primacy* (1966); George Every, *The Byzantine Patriarchate, 451–1204* (1962); J. M. Hussey, *The Orthodox Church in the Byzantine Empire* (1986); John Meyendorff, *Byzantine Theology: Historical Trends and Doctrinal Themes,* 2nd ed. (1979); Steven Runciman, *The Eastern Schism* (1955).

JOHN H. ERICKSON

[See also **Arianism; Byzantine Church; Byzantine History; Christology; Church, Latin; Councils, Ecumenical; Councils, Western; Constans II, Emperor; Ekthesis; Filioque; Henotikon; Heresies, Byzantine; Ignatios; Maximus the Confessor, St.; Michael Keroularios; Monophysitism; Monothelitism; Nicholas I, Pope; Philosophy and Theology, Byzantine; Photios.**]

SCHISMS, ISLAMIC. See **Sects, Islamic.**

SCHOLAE (BYZANTINE), important Byzantine military units that formed an imperial palace bodyguard in the fifth and sixth centuries. Each schola included about 500 men, originally recruited from barbarians but later from indigenous sources. The number of scholae varied from five to eleven. The soldiers of the scholae, who were called *scholarioi* or *scholarii,* lost military effectiveness in the reign of Justinian I and their posts became purchasable, but they were reorganized into an efficient *tagma* in the second half of the eighth century by Constantine V. He created the domestic of the scholae as the commander of the newly reformed and militarily effective *tagma* of scholae. This domestic was a linear descendant of the earlier *protectores domestici.* The *magister officiorum* had been the de jure commander of the earlier scholae, although from the late sixth century the actual commander appears—until the reforms of Constantine V—to have been the *comes domesticorum.*

In the reign of Romanos II (959–963) the scholae were divided into scholae of the East and West under their respective domestics, of whom the domestic of the scholae of the East became, for a few decades, the most powerful military commander within the Byzantine Empire.

BIBLIOGRAPHY

J. B. Bury, *The Imperial Administrative System in the Ninth Century* (1911, repr. 1958), 49–57; John F. Haldon, *Byzantine Praetorians: An Administrative, Institutional, and Social Survey of the Opsikion and Tagmata, c. 580–900* (1984); Nicholas Oikonomides, *Les listes de préséance byzantines des IXe et Xe siècles* (1972), 329–330.

WALTER EMIL KAEGI, JR.

[See also **Byzantine Empire: Bureaucracy; Domestic; Justinian I; Romanos II; Tagmata.**]

SCHOLAE (LATIN). See **Schools, Palace.**

SCHOLARS' PRIMER. See **Auraicept na nÉces.**

SCHOLARSHIP, BYZANTINE CLASSICAL. The Byzantines inherited from the Hellenistic and Roman worlds a system of education based upon the study and imitation of a limited body of Greek literature that furnished authoritative models of style. This classical literature comprised in the main the poems of Homer and Hesiod, the Greek lyric poets, Attic tragedy and comedy, some Hellenistic poetry, the Attic orators and historians, and Plato's dialogues. Since the third century B.C. scholars had busied themselves with establishing and preserving the texts of these works, providing them with explanatory and critical commentaries, and writing systematic treatises on their language, meter, and style. At the same time schoolmasters had used them as teaching material and drawn on the work of scholars to provide the more elementary textbooks which they required. The grammarian taught his youthful pupils how to read with understanding and critical appreciation the literature of the classical world, and in particular its poetry; the rhetorician taught adolescents how to express themselves by imitating classical models. The Atticist movement of the early centuries A.D., which laid increasing emphasis on the use of classicizing language in contradistinction to the slowly changing living tongue, encouraged the detailed study of classical texts and the preparation of normative grammars and lexica of classical Greek. Command of an archaizing literary language became a mark of status and an aim—sometimes the principal aim—of education.

Such was the heritage which the Byzantines received from their Greek past. The Christianization of late antique society scarcely affected educational and scholarly practice. Classical Greek texts, in spite of their pagan background, were not replaced either as subjects of study or as models for imitation. Hence the body of commentaries, lexica, grammars, and the like compiled by pagan scholars was, insofar as it survived, fully available and acceptable to Byzantine educators. The only significant exceptions to this general rule were that certain works of the fourth-century church fathers were sometimes used as models for imitation side by side with the works of the Attic orators, and that a simple grammatical commentary on the Psalms was sometimes used in teaching the elements of Greek grammar.

The late sixth and early seventh centuries—from the death of Justinian (565) to the Arab conquests (*ca.* 640)—saw a gradual decline in the level and range of Byzantine high culture. The Academy of Athens, itself a distant descendant of Plato's Academy, had been closed in 529, and Athens soon ceased to play any significant role as a center of higher education and scholarship. Antioch had been devastated by invasions and earthquakes. In the cities of western Asia Minor cultural decline accompanied economic decline. Only Constantinople and Alexandria, with its outlier in Gaza, remained centers in which the classical heritage was actively preserved and transmitted. The Arab conquests turned decline into catastrophe. Alexandria was cut off from Constantinople. The new rulers did not suppress Greek learning, but it lost much of its prestige and ceased to be a means of upward social mobility. In those regions which remained under Byzantine rule the strain of endless warfare led to the virtual disappearance of the leisured urban upper class for whom classical culture was a symbol of status. Grammarians and rhetoricians were no longer in demand. Only in Constantinople does there seem to have been a slender continuity of educational and scholarly tradition, supported by a dwindling class of officials. The iconoclast disputes, which lasted with interruptions from the 720's to the middle of the ninth century, broke up the unity of these defenders of traditional culture but did not cause their disappearance. And here and there, in monasteries and elsewhere, we hear of isolated men who possessed and studied the work of the scholars of antiquity.

In the early ninth century the military threat to the Byzantine Empire diminished and the economy improved. In their new mood of confidence ruling groups in the capital and elsewhere sought to revive the study and teaching of classical Greek literature as part of their re-identification of themselves as the heirs of the Christian Roman Empire. New textbooks of grammar and rhetoric began to be written. A new cursive book hand, which had probably been developed in the course of the religious disputes of the end of the eighth century, enabled texts to be copied more quickly and in smaller compass. In the course of the ninth and early tenth centuries most surviving classical literature was transcribed from the old, cumbersome majuscule hand into the new minuscule. This transcription was no mechanical act of copying. The best available old mauscripts were sought out, variant readings were compared, what could be found of ancient commentaries was entered in the margin of the text, and explanations of rare words were copied from lexica. What was not transcribed into the new hand at this period was generally doomed to disappear. The patriarch Photios (*ca.* 820–*ca.* 892) could still in his youth read many works of literature and scholarship which were soon afterward lost. Along with this deliberate preservation of ancient literature went the compilation of aids to its reading, such as lexica of rare words, and of manuals of rhetoric designed to improve the style and effectiveness of speakers and writers whose aim was more and more to imitate ancient models.

The Byzantine Empire in the tenth century was the superpower of Europe and the Near East. Its self-assured and self-assertive ruling groups looked for an ideology of grandeur and found it in the revived culture of late antiquity. Familiarity with classical literature, thought, and science was now a requisite for a successful official career and a badge of status. Encyclopedic works of compilation made this culture more readily accessible than it had been for centuries. Many of these were produced under the patronage of the learned emperor Constantine VII (*r.* 913–959), who was able to command resources in men and books to which no private patron could aspire. Among the products of his patronage were a great historical encyclopedia, compilatory treatises on agriculture and medicine, and works on imperial ceremonial and on foreign policy. But other similar compilations seem to have depended on private initiative, in particular the voluminous literary encyclopedia known as the *Suda.*

In the eleventh and twelfth centuries knowledge of classical literature and imitation of certain of its genres played an even more important part in Byzantine intellectual and social life. Some of the literature of the period displays a slavish imitation of Attic language and style that probably cramped the author's self-expression. Other writers wrote pastiches successful enough to deceive later classical scholars. Others again wrote Atticizing Greek but innovated freely in vocabulary and style. All this betokens long and systematic study of classical models. We know, too, of very many treatises on grammar, meter, and style, handbooks of rhetoric, lexica, and the like composed during the period. In particular there survive a number of the model exercises in composition from which pupils learned not only the principles of style but also the details of morphology, syntax, and semantics of classicizing Greek.

Scholars of this period copied and compiled the surviving remnants of ancient commentaries, as their predecessors had done. But they also often show a new independence of judgment which enabled them on occasion to challenge ancient authority or to cite contemporary material to elucidate classical texts. The commentaries of John Tzetzes (*ca.* 1180) or Eustathios (*fl. ca.* 1160–1192) are independent works of scholarship rather than faithful compilations. At the same time the interest of scholars and men of letters was extended from the form of ancient literature to its content. Ancient philosophy was once again studied for its own sake and not as a mere propaedeutic to the study of theology. Interest moved from Aristotle's *Logic* and Porphyry's commentary upon it to the dialogues of Plato and the *Physics, Metaphysics,* and *Ethics* of Aristotle. Michael Psellos (1019–1078) was deeply involved with Plato, whom he approached with the aid of the commentaries of the Neoplatonists of late antiquity, and regarded himself as a Christian Platonist. His pupil John Italos was condemned by the church for his Platonist views and his devotion to pagan, that is, classical, literature. The late eleventh and early twelfth centuries saw a number of scholars take up again, after a gap of six centuries, the tradition of writing philosophical commentaries on Aristotle. Notable among these were Eustratios, bishop of Nicaea, and Michael, bishop of Ephesus. Later in the century there is evidence of serious study of the works of the fifth-century Neoplatonist philosopher Proclus. Some of the theological disputes of the period concern essentially philosophical questions and bear witness to the widespread interest in the philosophical tradition of antiquity.

The capture of Constantinople by the Fourth Crusade in 1204 and the ensuing breakup of the Byzantine Empire put an end to the institutions which had fostered classical education. But it did not destroy the prestige or the attraction of classical Greek culture. On the contrary, the scattered Byzantine intellectuals realized all the more clearly that their possession and understanding of a body of literature and thought, Christian as well as pagan, which the West knew only fragmentarily and in translation, made them the superiors of their hated and despised conquerors. The word "Hellene," from being a pejorative term equivalent to "pagan," came to be a term of praise with both a cultural and an ethnic connotation. The Greek classics were even more than before models to be imitated and therefore to be studied.

Teachers, men of letters, and prelates who had survived the sack of Constantinople drifted to one or other of the centers of Greek power which sprang up in the former provinces, and in particular to Nicaea and Epiros. Nicaea, as the seat of the patriarch and hence of an emperor with some claims to legitimacy, proved the more attractive. Schools were set up in Nicaean territory in which men who had studied and taught in Constantinople passed on their tradition of learning to the following generation. Twelfth-century works of learning and scholarly treatises were carefully collected and copied. When in 1261 the Nicaean emperor Michael VIII recaptured Constantinople, the men and the books were available to ensure the maintenance of Byzantine classical studies after the interruption of two generations.

The restored empire of the Palaiologoi was but a pale shadow of its predecessor. Much territory had been lost forever; more was soon to be taken from it. Power and prestige were no longer concentrated in Constantinople. Thessaloniki and Mistra developed a cultural life of their own. Ioannina, for a time capital of an independent principality, and Trebizond, center of a mini-empire which remained outside of Byzantine control, became lesser centers of learning. But it was first and foremost in Constantinople that classical literature was studiously copied, commented on, and imitated.

The scholars who set the tone at the end of the thirteenth century were polymaths. Mathematics, astronomy, musical theory, and medicine interested them no less than literature in the narrow sense. They knew the importance of finding and copying rare or unknown texts, like the geography of Ptolemy or the epic poetry of Nonnus. They knew, too, how to compare the readings of several manuscripts and construct a rudimentary critical text.

In Thessaloniki other scholars pursued similar studies at about the same time. It was there that in the early fourteenth century Demetrios Triklinios (*ca.* 1280–1340), by studying the surviving works of the ancient metrical writers, attained an understanding of ancient Greek quantitative meter which often enabled him to emend on metrical grounds the texts he found in manuscripts. He has been called the first of modern philologists. Other early-fourteenth-century scholars busied themselves with ancient mathematical, astronomical, and musical writings, collecting, emending, studying, and commenting on difficult texts long neglected. The Attic dramatists, tragic and comic, were the objects of particular study, and many Byzantine scholars of the late thirteenth and early fourteenth centuries produced their own version of the texts accompanied by commentary, partly based on older exegetic material, partly consisting of fairly elementary grammatical explanation. The large number of late Byzantine manuscripts of classical texts with some kind of scholarly apparatus is an indication of the number of persons who sought a more than superficial acquaintance with classical tradition and sought to conserve it. This widespread interest in and esteem for classical literature is reflected in the often slavish imitation of classical models which is typical of much late Byzantine literature in the learned tongue. Moreover, this archaizing taste was catered to by the lexica which several late Byzantine scholars compiled, and which carefully distinguished classical forms and meanings from those of the living language of the age.

The civil wars which racked the Byzantine Empire in the mid fourteenth century not only caused widespread devastation and loss of territory but also undermined the authority and prestige of that official class to which so many men of learning belonged. The classicizing renaissance of the age of Michael VIII (*r.* 1259–1282) and Andronikos II (*r.* 1282–1328) ended abruptly. Along with social degradation went a kind of loss of nerve. The indigent, begging schoolmaster replaced the erudite scholar, sure of his intellectual and social standing. The number of classical texts studied in schools diminished and the quality of commentaries upon them sank. But the decline must not be overestimated. Right up to the capture of Constantinople by the Ottoman Turks in 1453 many continued to study, appreciate, and imitate classical Greek literature, and a pedagogical tradition that went back to Alexandria, if not to the Athens of Isocrates and Plato, was maintained.

By the end of the fourteenth and beginning of the fifteenth centuries the cultural relations between Greek East and Latin West were changing drastically. Westerners were now eager to learn from the Greeks, who in their turn recognized that the Latins had a respectable intellectual tradition of their own. When in 1396 Coluccio Salutati, chancellor of Florence, invited the Byzantine scholar and diplomat Manuel Chrysoloras (*ca.* 1355–1415) to teach Greek in Florence, a new epoch began. Chrysoloras brought with him not only manuscript books, carefully selected, but a tradition of critical study without parallel in the West. Many notables of Florence and other cities became his pupils, and his influence on the first generation of Italian humanists was considerable. In the first half of the fifteenth century other Byzantine scholars followed Chrysoloras' example and came to Italy to teach. At the same time Italians sometimes spent years in Constantinople studying Greek; the Sicilian Giovanni Aurispa and Francesco Filelfo of Tolentino were the most noteworthy. These men brought back with them not only their knowledge of the language and literature of Greece but also a stock of manuscript books, which were avidly read, copied, and studied by their fellow countrymen.

The fall of Constantinople in 1453 brought many refugee Greek intellectuals to the West. Some earned a humble living as copyists of Greek in regions as distant as England. Others held chairs at the universities of Italy, which by this time numbered among their students men from Spain, France, England, Germany, and Poland. Such a man was Demetrios Chalkokondyles (1425–1511), an Athenian who taught at Perugia, Rome, Padua, Florence, and Milan. He numbered among his pupils the German Johann Reuchlin (1455–1522) and the Englishmen Thomas Linacre (1460?–1524), Henry VIII's personal physician, and William Grocyn (1446?–1519), the first scholar to teach Greek in Oxford. Chalkokondyles also prepared for the press the first printed editions of Homer (1488), Isocrates (1493), and the *Suda* (1499). Another refugee scholar was Bessarion (*ca.* 1403–1472), a native of Trebizond and a former pupil in Mistra of Georgios Gemistos Plethon (*ca.* 1355–1452). He became a cardinal of the Roman church and used his wealth and influence not only to assist less fortunate Greek refugees, but also to acquire a magnificent library of Greek manuscript books, which he bequeathed to the Marcian library in Venice. In these and other ways Byzantine classical scholarship became a part of the great intellectual movement of the Renaissance.

GRAMMAR

Byzantine textbooks of orthography, prosody, morphology, syntax, and meter were all derivative from the works of the Alexandrian grammarians of the Hellenistic period, and in particular from those of Dionysios Thrax (*fl.* 100 B.C.), Apollonios Dyskolos (second century), and Herodian (second century). Byzantine scholars made no fresh description or codification of the Greek language. Such innovations as they made lay in the form in which the material was presented.

The brief *Technē grammatikē* (Art of grammar) of Dionysios Thrax continued in use throughout the Byzantine period. A vast body of schoolmasterly commentary grew up around it, providing illustrations, explanations, and discussions of its terse rules, and so adapting Dionysios' scientific work to pedagogical purposes. The commentaries are generally anonymous, derivative, and difficult to date. Many certainly belong to the Byzantine period.

Theodosios (probably fifth century) reduced the immense and detailed morphological work of Herodian of Alexandria to a work titled *Introductory Rules on Inflection of Nouns and Verbs.* This treatise, which was for centuries in use in Byzantine schools, gathered an accretion of commentaries around itself, notably by John Charax (probably eighth century) and by George Choiroboskos (*ca.* 800). The commentaries are many times longer than the text they seek to explain. An epitome of Herodian's huge *Universal Prosody* is probably also the work of Theodosios. It deals with accents, quantities, breathings, punctuation, elision, and the like, and it was used as a source by many usually anonymous treatises on these topics designed for school use, some of which were arranged alphabetically as lexica for reference; others were composed in verse for easy memorizing.

Few grammatical handbooks can be plausibly dated to the later seventh and eighth centuries, a period of decline in Byzantine education and culture. Such as do exist are derivative in character.

In the early ninth century Theognostos composed a textbook of orthography and grammar arranged as 1,003 brief rules and based on Herodian. By the twelfth century a new method of presentation made its appearance. Grammar was now taught by a catechism-like series of questions and answers to be learned by heart. Several anonymous grammatical questionnaires survive in manuscripts of the twelfth and thirteenth century. The *Questionnaire* (*Erōtēmata*) of Manuel Moschopulos (*ca.* 1265–1315) was a standard textbook in the fourteenth century; those of Manuel Chrysoloras, Manuel Kalekas (*d.* 1410), and Demetrios

Chalkokondyles were dominant in the fifteenth; and that of Constantine Laskaris (1434–1501) was the first book to be printed in Greek, at Milan in 1476. Maximos Planudes (*ca.* 1255–1305) wrote a grammar in the form of a dialogue.

Elementary grammar could also be taught through a detailed grammatical commentary on a literary text, in which the words were parsed one after another. Such a commentary on Homer's *Iliad* existed in antiquity. A similar commentary (*Epimerismi*) on the *Psalms* was composed by George Choiroboskos in order that pupils could learn grammar without being exposed to the baneful influence of pagan literature. It may have been mainly used for the teaching of novices in monasteries. But in the mid tenth century we find a schoolmaster in Constantinople using Theognostos' rules and Choiroboskos' *Epimerismi* to teach lay pupils.

Byzantine treatises on syntax were all derivative from the *Syntax* of Apollonios Dyskolos of Alexandria. Apollonios began his syntactical analysis with words, not with sentences, and his epitomators and imitators all followed his example. Michael Synkellos of Jerusalem wrote a manual of syntax in the early ninth century. Niketas of Herakleia (*ca.* 1100) composed a syntax in verse. Gregory Pardos, metropolitan of Corinth (mid twelfth century), wrote a handbook of syntax which remained authoritative in the later Byzantine period, in spite of its loose structure and conceptual confusion. Maximos Planudes appended a short treatise on syntax to his grammar. John Glykys, patriarch of Constantinople (1305–1319), wrote a manual of syntax illustrated by copious quotations from classical authors.

METER

The loss of the distinction between long and short vowels in living speech made the quantitative meter of ancient Greek poetry difficult for the Byzantines to understand. The handbooks of meter which they composed and the metrical observations in Byzantine commentaries on classical texts are almost exclusively based, directly or indirectly, on the lost *Universal Prosody* of Herodian or on the surviving *Manual* (*Encheiridion*) of Hephaistion (second century). George Choiroboskos wrote a long commentary on Hephaistion's book, drawing on a fuller version than that now surviving. A number of shorter anonymous commentaries display no originality. School textbooks on meter of a very elementary kind are numerous, especially from the later Byzantine period, some of them being themselves in verse, notably that of John Tzetzes. The varieties of the hexameter are the subject of several treatises. Michael Psellos and John Botaneiates wrote on the iambic trimeter. Isaac Tzetzes (*d.* 1138) wrote a lengthy introduction to the lyric meters of Pindar. But it was by turning from these Byzantine compilations to the study of Hephaistion himself that a few fourteenth-century scholars like Demetrios Triklinios gained an understanding of ancient meter more thorough and profound than any of their predecessors for a thousand years and used that knowledge to detect and emend corruptions in the texts of lyric poets and dramatists.

LEXICA

The numerous surviving Byzantine lexica belong mainly to one of three classes: (1) those providing explanations of difficult words encountered in reading classical texts, (2) those prescribing the words to be used in literary composition, and (3) those setting out the supposed origin—and hence the original meaning—of words. All three types had forerunners in classical antiquity. One major lexicon, the *Suda,* by its structure and content falls outside this classification.

Alexandrian scholars and their successors had already compiled extensive dictionaries of rare and difficult words in literary texts. Those of Didymus, Tryphon, and Pamphilos did not survive into the Byzantine period. That of Diogenianos (second century) was the main source, though probably in an abbreviated form, of the lexicon of Hesychios of Alexandria (early sixth century), who also drew on a short rhetorical lexicon for Christian schools wrongly attributed to Cyril of Alexandria, as well as on particular vocabularies. Hesychios preserves, often in garbled form, a vast number of rare literary or dialect words with brief explanations. About the same period Stephanos of Byzantium compiled a lexicon of geographical and ethnographical names, each accompanied by brief historical and mythological notes and detailed information on points of orthography and morphology. Stephanos' lengthy work was soon abbreviated, and it is the shortened version (*Ethnica*) which survived and was widely used in the Byzantine period.

The revived interest in classical literature in the ninth century created a need for new lexica. The future patriarch Photios compiled a lexicon of 7,000 to 8,000 words, each accompanied by a brief explanation and sometimes by an illustrative quotation from classical literature. His purpose was both to facilitate reading and to prescribe the language to be used in writing. His principal sources were an epitome of the Cyril lexicon, some of the Atticist lexica of antiquity, Platonic glossaries, and his own extensive reading. It was probably in the circle of Photios, if not under his immediate direction, that the first Byzantine etymological lexica were compiled. These were based on the assumption that language was not an arbitrary system of signs but that there was a direct correspondence between the structure of language—or at any rate of the Greek language—and that of the universe. All words, if properly analyzed, provided an insight into the nature of that which they denoted. This doctrine, alluded to in the half-serious etymologies proposed by Plato in the *Cratylus* (for example, *anthropos* [man] from *ano* [upwards] and *thro* [I look]), was systematized by the Stoics, who compiled the first lists of words with their supposed etymologies.

In the fifth century Orion of Thebes and Oros composed lengthy etymological lexica; their work survives only in epitomes and excerpts. It was on the basis of such works as these that in the ninth century an immense etymological lexicon, the so-called *Etymologicum genuinum,* was compiled in Constantinople; it has not yet been published in full. A similar lexicon, the *Etymologicum gudianum,* belongs to the same period and draws on similar sources. These works were abbreviated, combined, and fused with material from the Cyril lexicon and other sources by different scholars in subsequent centuries. The most important of the resulting etymological dictionaries, the *Etymologicum magnum,* was compiled in the mid twelfth century. Its author handles his heterogeneous material freely and imaginatively, often proposing four or five possible etymologies for a single word. Apart from the insight which they provide into medieval views of language, these lexica occasionally preserve citations from lost authors and snippets of ancient scholarship.

Byzantine men of letters felt the need of a lexicon both to understand ancient authors and to compose their own works in literary Greek. Several short works of this latter kind survive from the middle Byzantine period, usually with a title such as *Collection of Useful Words.* All owe much to versions of the Cyril lexicon. In the later Byzantine period, when imitation of classical models was highly valued, several longer lexica were compiled on the basis of earlier lexica, commentaries on texts, grammatical works, and the like. Their purpose was primarily prescriptive rather than descriptive. The longest, that of Pseudo-Zonaras, was compiled, perhaps in Nicaea, in the early years after the Fourth Crusade. It contains about 19,000 entries. The number of surviving manuscripts—more than fifty—testifies to the widespread use of this lexicon. Teachers sometimes compiled lexica for the use of their students, and several of these were widely copied and used, in particular the *Collection of Attic Words* of Manuel Moschopulos, the *Selection of Attic Words and Expressions* of Thomas Magister (*ca.* 1270–1325), and the so-called *Lexicon Vindobonense* of Andreas Lopadiotes (fourteenth century). These works are repetitive and uncritical. Yet they reveal how the continuity of literary Greek was maintained; and occasionally they preserve a fragment of a lost work of antiquity.

The *Suda,* often referred to in older works as *Suidas,* is a very lengthy mid-tenth-century compilation of more encyclopedic character than the foregoing lexica. Most of the entries are brief and lexical. But there are a number of long factual articles on topics of philosophy, science, history, and geography, and in particular a series of biographies of ancient writers with lists of their works and sometimes short critical judgments. The sources of the *Suda* are many and complex—lexica, grammatical works, commentaries, theological treatises, and an epitome of the *Onomatologos* of Hesychios of Miletos (sixth century), a kind of biographical dictionary of Greek literature. The *Suda* is a striking example of the encyclopedic learning of the tenth century.

COMMENTARIES ON ANCIENT AUTHORS

From Hellenistic times classical Greek literature, and particularly poetry, had been the subject of scholarly commentary. The great Alexandrian philologists, such as Aristophanes of Byzantium and Aristarchus, discussed problems of textual criticism, semantics, historical and mythological allusion, and literary structure in a multitude of treatises addressed to learned readers. Their work was soon epitomized, simplified, and often trivialized by successors who had in mind the needs of schoolmasters, and who added much elementary grammatical and metrical explanation and sometimes a prose paraphrase of the more difficult poetical texts, such as the odes of Pindar. These commentaries were separate books, and only incidentally were passages from them copied by readers in the margin of the text which they explained. The compilation of such commentaries on Homer, the school text par excellence, was still being practiced in the sixth century.

In the ninth and early tenth centuries the revival of interest in classical literature led scholars to seek out and copy what they could find of ancient commentaries on literary texts. What they found was mainly derivative material for school use and was often fragmentary, since schoolbooks get hard wear. On some writers, like Homer, they found a wealth of exegetic material, on others very little. When they transcribed literary texts from the old majuscule hand into the more compendious minuscule, they often copied such explanatory notes as were available in the margins of the text, frequently adding further explanatory material from lexica, grammars, or from their own reading. These marginal commentaries are known as scholia. They are particularly rich for Homer, for whom a learned commentary of late antiquity seems to have survived into the Middle Ages, Pindar, the Attic tragedians, Aristophanes, and some Hellenistic poets. For prose writers in general—who were the concern of the rhetorician rather than the grammarian—less ancient explanatory material survived. There are, however, fairly extensive scholia on Demosthenes, Thucydides, and Plato.

Until the end of the eleventh century, Byzantine scholars limited themselves to reproducing the commentaries which they had inherited from antiquity, occasionally padding them with elementary matter. By the twelfth century a new spirit of independence showed itself. Men like John Tzetzes, his brother Isaac, and Eustathios felt themselves the intellectual equals of the scholars of antiquity and treated their surviving work, the so-called ancient scholia, no longer as a heritage to be conserved but rather as a quarry to be exploited. They handled such work critically, frequently expressed disagreement with it, and put forward their own opinions on matters with which the ancients had not dealt. John Tzetzes wrote commentaries on a great variety of authors, from Homer to Lykophron. His commentaries on the comedies of Aristophanes display considerable independence and a fair measure of wrongheadedness. One of Tzetzes' more bizarre productions is the commentary on his own collected letters in 12,674 lines of verse, a farrago of learning and polemic. Eustathios composed extremely long commentaries on the *Iliad* and the *Odyssey* and on Pindar (of which only the preface survives), in which he often used events and customs of his own day to illustrate points in the text. Tzetzes' and Eustathios' commentaries are separate books, not marginal appendages to the text.

The production of commentaries continued unabated in the late Byzantine period. In Constantinople, Maximos Planudes wrote commentaries on many poetical texts from Hesiod to Aratos as well as on the treatise on the theory of numbers of Diophantos. His pupil Manuel Moschopulos wrote on Pindar, on the dramatists, and on the *Eikones* of Philostratos. In Thessaloniki, Thomas Magister and Demetrios Triklinios wrote on the dramatists and on Hellenistic poetry. These scholars used the ancient scholia, often in abbreviated form, for questions of mythology, history, and antiquities. Their own interest lay rather in grammar, meter, and textual criticism. They were philologists, not antiquarians, and their work in some ways foreshadows that of the Renaissance humanists. Not all late Byzantine scholars showed their originality and learning. Many manuscripts of this period survive in which classical poetry—often in a selection reflecting the teaching program of a school—is accompanied by an elementary commentary in which grammatical explanations are embedded in a running paraphrase, while unfamiliar words are explained by interlinear glosses. Teachers of rhetoric prepared elementary grammatical and stylistic commentaries on prose texts of antiquity or on their own model compositions. The level of scholarship is not high; but the frequency of such manuscripts suggests that some acquaintance with classical literature was more widespread than in earlier periods.

PHILOSOPHY

The Neoplatonist scholars of late antiquity, men like Proclus, Damaskios, Simplikios, and John Philoponos, commented extensively on the works of Plato and Aristotle in the fifth and early sixth centuries. The closure of the School of Athens by Justinian in 529, though it did not put an end to the study and teaching of philosophy in Athens, diminished the resources and undermined the prestige of the largely pagan scholars who taught there. Many of the Alexandrian Neoplatonists were Christians, and there the study of philosophy lingered on until after the Arab conquest of Egypt. Stephen of Alexandria wrote learned commentaries on many of Aristotle's works in the middle years of the seventh century.

Thereafter there was a break in the tradition. The years of desperate struggle against Arabs and Bulgarians and of fierce internal disputes over the adoration of images did not favor the study of a philosophy whose origins were entirely pagan. Only the most jejune handbooks of logic were copied and studied. It was not until the late eleventh century that serious study and teaching of the central texts of Greek philosophy began again. Michael Psellos probably wrote a commentary on Aristotle's *Physics,* though his authorship has been disputed. His pupil John Italos commented on other works of Aristotle. Theodore of Smyrna (*ca.* 1100) wrote a survey of Aristotle's physical writings. In the early twelfth century the tradition of detailed critical and analytical commentary on Aristotle was taken up again by Eustratios of Nicaea and Michael of Ephesos, who wrote on the *Nicomachean Ethics,* on the *Rhetoric,* and on the logical and biological works.

The serious study of philosophy, and particularly of Neoplatonist philosophy, could easily lead to accusations of heresy. The theologian Nicholas of Methone wrote a refutation of Proclus' *Elements of Theology* in which he accused some of his contemporaries of cryptopaganism. Yet the late Byzantines did not abandon Plato and Aristotle. George Pachymeres (1242–*ca.* 1310) wrote a lengthy exposition of their doctrines. Commentaries on particular works were written by Leo Magentinos, Theodore Metochites, and John Pediasimos in the first half of the fourteenth century, as well as by several anonymous and undatable scholars. George Scholarios, who after the Turkish conquest in 1453 became patriarch of Constantinople under the name Gennadios II, copied and commented on many of Aristotle's works, and translated into Greek Thomas Aquinas' commentary on the *De anima.* Georgios Gemistos Plethon, as well as commenting on several works of Aristotle, wrote an important work, *On the Differences Between Aristotle and Plato.* His *Laws,* a project for an ideal city in which Christianity would be replaced by a purified and philosophical Greek paganism, was modeled on the *Laws* of Plato. All copies of the lengthy work were burned by order of Patriarch Gennadios after 1453. In the meantime men like Bessarion and the Italian Marsilio Ficino had begun to arouse passionate interest in Greek philosophy in Renaissance Italy.

BIBLIOGRAPHY

Robert Browning, "Byzantine Scholarship," in *Past and Present,* **28** (1964), "Enlightenment and Repression in Byzantium in the Eleventh and Twelfth Centuries," in *Past and Present,* **69** (1975), and "Homer in Byzantium," in *Viator,* **6** (1975); Guglielmo Carallo, "Conservazione e perdi dei testi greci: Fattori materiali, sociali, culturali," in A. Giardina, ed., *Tradizione dei classici: Trasformazioni della cultura* (1986), 83–172, 246–272; C. N. Constantinides, *Higher Education in Byzantium in the Thirteenth and Early Fourteenth Centuries* (1982); Alphonse Dain, "La transmission des texts littéraires classiques de Photius à Constantin Porphyrogénète," in *Dumbarton Oaks Papers,* **8** (1954); Herbert Hunger, *Die hochsprachliche profane Literatur der Byzantiner,* II (1978), 3–83; Salvatore Impellizzeri, "L'umanesimo bizantino del IX secolo e la genesi della 'Biblioteca' di Fozio," in *Rivista di studi bizantini e neoellenici,* n.s. **6–7** (1969–1970); Paul Lemerle, *Le premier humanisme byzantin* (1971), *Byzantine Humanism* (1986); Richard Reitzenstein, *Geschichte der griechischen Etymologika* (1897, repr. 1964); Leighton D. Reynolds and N. G. Wilson, *Scribes and Scholars: A Guide to the Transmission of Greek and Latin Literature,* 2nd ed. (1974); Steven Runciman, *The Last Byzantine Renaissance* (1970); John E. Sandys, *A History of Classical Scholarship,* I (1903); Kenneth M. Setton, "The Byzantine Background to the Italian Renaissance," in *Proceedings of the American Philosophical Society,* **100** (1956); Alexander Turyn, "The Sophocles Recension of Manuel Moschopoulos," in *Transactions of the American Philological Association,* **80** (1949), *Studies in the Manuscript Tradition of the Tragedies of Sophocles* (1952), and *The Byzantine Manuscript Tradition of the Tragedies of Euripides* (1957); Nigel A. Wilson, *Scholars of Byzantium* (1983).

ROBERT BROWNING

[See also **Andronikos II Palaeologos; Bessarion; Byzantine Empire; Byzantine Literature; Byzantine Poetic Forms; Classical Literary Studies; Constantinople; Epiros, Despotate of; Gemistos Plethon, Georgios; George Scholarios; Grammar; Greek Language, Byzantine; Iconoclasm, Christian; Islam, Conquests of; Manuel Chrysoloras; Michael VIII Palaiologos; Mistra; Neoplatonism; Nicaea, Empire of; Palaiologoi; Philosophy and Theology, Byzantine; Photios; Plato in the Middle Ages; Psellos, Michael; Rhetoric: Byzantine; Scriptorium; Suda; Thessaloniki; Translation and Translators; Trebizond.**]

SCHOLASTICISM, SCHOLASTIC METHOD.

The term "Scholasticism" comes from the Latin *schola,* which originally meant a learned conversation, debate, or dissertation, but later came to refer to a school or place of learning. In the nineteenth century the term "Scholasticism" was used almost exclusively as a synonym for "medieval philosophy," but it has also been used to denote an attitude, a state of belief, a movement or the system of thought bequeathed by that movement, or even a teaching and learning method not necessarily associated with the medieval period. These uses of the term, however, are too broad, for there are many medieval philosophers who are clearly not Scholastics. And, although "Scholasticism" has been used in connection with other historical periods, its origin is found in the Middle Ages, where a lecturer, particularly one who taught the liberal arts (trivium and quadrivium) in a recognized school, was called *scholasticus*.

The most widely accepted use of the term today refers to the common method of teaching and learning used in various disciplines, particularly in philosophy and theology, in medieval schools after the twelfth century. This method arose as a by-product of the attempt to achieve knowledge of the various disciplines. This knowledge was supposed to be concordant with both human reason and the Christian faith, and for this reason it was necessary to bring about a *concordia discordantium*, that is, a harmony among apparently differing opinions that medieval scholars regarded as authoritative. Scholastics considered themselves, as Bonaventure (*ca.* 1217–1274) explicitly points out, not fabricators of new doctrines, but "compilers and weavers of approved opinions" (*Sentences* II, Man. 2, p. 1, *Praelocutio*). It was assumed that this *concordia* was possible because the authorities who seemed to disagree among themselves had been sanctioned by posterity and/or by the church, which implied (1) that the basic principles to which they adhered were true and, therefore, (2) that they could not contradict each other on fundamental matters.

The process used to bring about this *concordia* was textually oriented and often involved introducing distinctions showing that texts purported to be in disagreement in fact discussed different aspects of an issue and, therefore, could still be in fundamental agreement. When this procedure was not successful, Scholastics did not hesitate to engage in noncontextual and metaphorical interpretations of the conflicting texts to bring them into line with each other, even though they were aware of the dangers of such a procedure. The use of levels of interpretation based on levels of meaning first occurred in connection with scriptural passages, but the technique was freely extended first to legal and theological texts and later to others.

This procedure gives the Scholastic method two of its basic characteristics, a textual orientation and a concern with detail; only through careful textual analysis and the introduction of subtle distinctions could apparent conflicts be brought into harmony. An important tool of the procedure was Aristotelian logic. Discussions were supposed to adhere to the syllogistic rules worked out by Aristotle and his followers and passed on to the medievals by Boethius (*ca.* 480–524/526) and others. As early as the twelfth century, John of Salisbury pointed out the importance of Aristotle's *Topics* for conducting any kind of disputation (*Metalogicon* 2.4 and 3.5). Before the second half of that century, medievals depended only on the *logica vetus* (the introductory works) for their logic, but after 1150 they had the complete Aristotelian *Organon*. It should also be noted that it became common among Scholastics to use Aristotelian concepts and nomenclature, even if they disagreed with particular Aristotelian doctrines.

In spite of the importance given to Aristotle, the Scholastic attitude toward him was not servile. Scholastics considered his work authoritative in natural philosophy, logic, and related fields, but they did not refrain from disagreement with his ideas when they thought his views contradicted a higher authority (for example, Scripture) or reason. Indeed, even authors very sympathetic to his views, such as Albertus Magnus (*ca.* 1200–1280), Thomas Aquinas (1224–1274), and Francisco Suárez (1548–1617), introduced substantial modifications into his philosophy. The textual orientation, the emphasis on detail, the introduction of subtle distinctions, the juxtaposition of contrary opinions, and the use of technical Aristotelian terminology carried to extremes in the later part of the period were largely responsible for the deprecating connotations given to the term "Scholastic" by Renaissance humanists.

Not all texts were regarded as having the same degree of authority. Above all were the Scriptures, followed by the opinions of the Fathers, the writings of the masters, and finally the work of the philosophers. This gave the method its peculiarly religious orientation; ultimately, as Leff has accurately pointed out, "faith still had the last word." The overall aim of the enterprise was Christian, and the fundamental authoritative sources were scriptural and ecclesiastical. Thus the accepted view was that philosophy was to be considered a servant of theology (*ancilla theologiae*).

The locus of this enterprise was the medieval university. As a result, the literary genres used by Scholastics reflect university activities and settings. The most important of these genres are the commentary, the question, and the summa. All of them have prototypes and ancestors among ancient and Islamic writings, but the immediate sources of the particular structures they developed and of their popularity after 1200 are found in the university classroom. For the commentary the key element was the textual analysis carried out by masters in the university. As early as the twelfth century, Hugh of St. Victor (*d.* 1141) had identified two conditions required for the acquisition of knowledge: the *lectio* and the *meditatio* (*Didascalion,* Preface). This monastic structure was carried into the university, where the *lectio* became the reading of an authoritative text in the classroom, while the *meditatio,* having to do with the understanding of the text, involved exposition and explication. This procedure contributed decisively to the development and popularity of the commentary.

As with the commentary, precedents of the Scholastic question (*quaestio*) can be found in the early Middle Ages as well as in ancient and Islamic writings. But the classroom discussion in the twelfth and thirteenth centuries and the later university disputation are its immediate sources. In contrast with lectures, disputations (*disputationes*) involved the discussion of issues rather than of texts, even if most often they were prompted by problems raised by texts. Apart from the discussions that took place in the classroom, usually in the afternoon (mornings were reserved for *lectiones*), public disputations were held during Advent and Lent, and gave a master the opportunity to present his views on various subjects and his colleagues the opportunity to challenge them. When the subject matter of the disputation was predetermined, the result was called a *quaestio disputata,* and when there were no restrictions in this respect, the written result was called a *quaestio de quolibet.* In either case the *quaestio* posed a problem in the form of a question (*aporia*) that could be answered affirmatively or negatively. After authorities in favor and against the issue under dispute were presented, the master gave a carefully worked-out answer (*responsio* or *determinatio*) and addressed any objections raised.

Summae developed out of the need for systematic expositions to be used by beginners, who often required a general introduction to the subject matter. They were usually large compilations of established opinion on a particular subject, such as theology, philosophy, logic, or morals. The summae were generally organized according to accepted structures. For example, theological summae usually followed the structure of the Creed.

In spite of the differences among the commentary, the question, and the summa, these literary genres were not necessarily incompatible. After the second half of the thirteenth century, for example, many commentaries and summae adopted the question format. In the commentary, questions were raised on particular texts, while in the summa they were raised on a particular topic. Moreover, partial introductory expositions abounded within both commentaries and questions, and the exposition of texts was not restricted to commentaries by any means, although only in commentaries are there comprehensive textual expositions (*ad litteram*).

The structure, principles, and literary genres of the Scholastic method became standard in the thirteenth century and continued in use until the sixteenth. There are prime examples in the work of every major Scholastic of the period. But the origin of the method is found in the eleventh and twelfth centuries, in the work of the theologians and canon lawyers who prepared collections of often conflicting authoritative texts on various topics. In these collections they either tried to harmonize the texts by using Aristotelian logic and concepts or gave rules whereby they could be harmonized. A good example of a theological work of this sort that does not attempt to harmonize the texts it contains, but which gives rules to that effect, is the *Sic et non* of Peter Abelard (*ca.* 1079–*ca.* 1142). The most influential theological work that attempts harmonization is the collection *Quattuor libri sententiarum* of Peter Lombard (*ca.* 1100–1160). This work became enormously popular and was sanctioned as an official textbook to be used in the theological faculties of medieval universities. It is in commentaries on the *Sentences* of Peter Lombard, arising from the lectures of masters of theology, that a considerable amount of Scholastic philosophy and theological thought is found.

Canon lawyers faced a similar task in a different context. For them the problem was to reconcile the apparently conflicting statements from church councils, papal decrees, and other pronouncements with legal implications. Although there were several famous compilers who attempted to carry out this task, or at least to develop rules whereby it might be carried out, such as Bernold of Constance (*d.* 1100) and Ivo of Chartres (*d.* 1115), the most successful was Gratian (*fl. ca.* 1140), whose work, entitled *Concordantia discordantium canonum* and known as the *Decretum,* established itself as the basic source of canon law for the later Middle Ages. In that capacity, it had an influence on almost every major theologian of the later medieval period.

After the sixteenth century the Scholastic method changed considerably, preparing the way for the manuals used in seminaries and other Catholic religious institutions until the nineteenth century. Both the commentary and the question were neglected in favor of a systematic organization that involved theses and proofs. This new format resembled the deductive method modeled on the mathematical sciences made popular by Descartes and others. Unfortunately, although perhaps as rigorous as the method used by medieval Scholastics, the new method introduced a rigidity in the process of learning that discouraged free inquiry and discussion, the marks of the earlier procedure.

BIBLIOGRAPHY

Marie D. Chenu, *Toward Understanding Saint Thomas,* A. M. Landry and D. Hughes, trans. (1964), 58–69, 77–99; Alan B. Cobban, *The Medieval Universities: Their Development and Organization* (1975); Frederick C. Copleston, *A History of Philosophy,* II, pt. 1 (1963), 241–246; Étienne Gilson, *History of Christian Philosophy in the Middle Ages* (1955), 246–250; Martin Grabmann, *Die Geschichte der scholastischen Methode,* 2 vols. (1909–1911, repr. 1961); Jozef IJsewijn and Jacques Paquet, eds., *The Universities in the Late Middle Ages* (1978); Norman Kretzmann *et al.,* eds., *The Cambridge History of Later Medieval Philosophy* (1982), 11–34, 80–98, 101–104; Paul Oskar Kristeller, "Humanism and Scholasticism in the Italian Renaissance," in *Byzantion,* **17** (1944–1945); Gordon Leff, *Medieval Thought: St. Augustine to Ockham* (1958).

George Makdisi, "The Scholastic Method in Medieval Education: An Inquiry into Its Origins in Law and Theology," in *Speculum,* **49** (1974); Désiré J. Mercier, *A Manual of Modern Scholastic Philosophy,* T. L. Parker and S. A. Parker, trans., 2 vols. (1928); John Murdoch and Edith Sylla, eds. *The Cultural Context of Medieval Learning* (1975); Josef Pieper, *Scholasticism,* Richard Winston and Clara Winston, trans., sec. I, chap. 2 (1964), 37–44; Hastings Rashdall, *The Universities of Europe in the Middle Ages,* F. M. Powicke and A. B. Emden, eds., 3 vols. (1936); James A. Weisheipl, "Curriculum of the Faculty of Arts at Oxford in the Early Fourteenth Century," in *Mediaeval Studies,* **26** (1964), and "The Evolution of Scientific Method," in Vincent E. Smith, ed., *The Logic of Science* (1964); and Maurice de Wulf, *History of Mediaeval Philosophy,* Ernest C. Messenger, trans., I–II (1925–1926, rev. ed. 1952).

JORGE J. E. GRACIA

[See also **Abelard, Peter; Albertus Magnus; Aquinas, St. Thomas: Aristotle in the Middle Ages; Arts, Seven Liberal; Bernold of Constance; Boethius; Bonaventure, St.; Gratian; Hugh of St. Victor; Ivo of Chartres, St.; John of Salisbury; Law, Canon; Peter Lombard; Philosophy and Theology, Western European; Quaestiones; Quodlibet; Universities.**]

SCHONGAUER, MARTIN (*ca.* 1450–1491), the most accomplished northern European engraver before Albrecht Dürer, was born in Colmar, the son of a goldsmith. Trained as a painter in Colmar, he probably traveled to the Netherlands, as his work shows familiarity with that of the great fifteenth-century Flemish painters, particularly Rogier van der Weyden. Although Schongauer was famed as a painter in his own day, very few paintings from his hand survive. The splendid *Madonna in a Rose Arbor* (1473) in St. Martin's, Colmar, gives an indication of his stature as a painter. In contrast, the 116 engravings that survive in numerous impressions represent his entire oeuvre in that medium. His engravings are characterized by an increasing tendency toward balanced and uncluttered compositions and by the brilliant use of a crisp, economical hatching line permitting a controlled range of effects of shadow and texture. In his avoidance of late Gothic mannerism, Schongauer prepared the way for the next generation of German artists. His graphic technique exerted a decisive influence on Dürer.

BIBLIOGRAPHY

Julius Baum, *Martin Schongauer* (1948); Ernst Buchner, *Martin Schongauer als Maler* (1941); Eduard Flechsig, *Martin Schongauer* (1951); Max Lehrs, *Geschichte und kritischer Katalog des deutschen, niederländischen und französischen Kupferstichs im XV. Jahrhundert,* V (1924); Ulrich Middeldorf, "Martin Schongauers klassischer Stil," in Arnold Bergsträsser, ed., *Deutsche Beiträge zur geistigen Überlieferung,* I (1947); Charles I. Minott, *Martin Schongauer* (1971); Jakob Rosenberg, ed., *Martin Schongauer Handzeichnungen* (1923); Alan Shestack, ed., *The Complete Engravings of Martin*

Madonna in a Rose Arbor. Painting (heavily restored) by Martin Schongauer, 1473. Collegiate Church of St. Martin, Colmar. FOTO MARBURG/ART RESOURCE

Schongauer (1969); Franz Winziger, *Die Zeichnungen Martin Schongauers* (1962).

MARTHA WOLFF

[See also **Engraving; Weyden, Rogier van der.**]

SCHOOLS, BYZANTINE. See **Universities, Byzantine.**

SCHOOLS, CATHEDRAL. The cathedral schools, along with the parish, monastic, and palace schools, and later the universities, developed gradually and fitfully in the Middle Ages. Each type of school trained its students to assume a particular role in medieval society. They never undertook the task of public education, nor did they attempt to give their students a general education. Parish schools tried to transmit the fundamentals of Christianity to young children. Monastic schools sought to provide young monks with the experience necessary for contemplation and for an intimate knowledge of God. The universities trained specialists in law, medicine, philosophy, and theology.

Cathedral schools existed to train clergy in their professional duties as ministers of the Christian people. The bishop in whose cathedral complex the school was located needed a group of trained priests to administer the various needs of his diocese. Thus, the education dispensed in cathedral schools was largely practical and emphasized effective reading, pleasing singing of hymns, knowledge of church law, preparation of documents, the performance of the liturgy, and the administration of the sacraments. The priest also had to know the Bible. These practical and professional concerns necessitated a broad range of ancillary studies in literature, the liberal arts, and, in some cases, theology and philosophy. Although the purpose of study in literature and the arts was to serve the higher study of Scripture and the cult of God, it often happened that a particular cathedral school and its masters gained a reputation for excellence in a certain field, such as logic, medicine, philosophy, or grammar.

The beginnings of the cathedral schools date from the decline of the Roman educational system. Clergy in the early church received their general education as laymen in the municipal schools of the empire. When they "converted" to the service of the church, they learned their ecclesiastical skills by practice and imitation. As the Roman schools began to close, however, bishops could not be assured of the educational level of their priests. They began to establish schools of their own. The first bishops' schools in the fourth and fifth centuries clearly imitated the monastic schools. St. Augustine's school for young clergy who lived together in Hippo, North Africa, was called a *monasterium clericorum.* In the sixth century Fulgentius of Ruspe and Caesarius of Arles established schools for their clergy. Bishop Caesarius, a former monk, even taught his clergy and daily quizzed them on what they had learned. In 527 the Council of Toledo created a system of cathedral schools and established guidelines for them. Young men destined for an ecclesiastical career would be tonsured and would reside together in the *domus ecclesiae.* The bishop would designate a master (*praepositus*) to teach them. When they reached eighteen years of age, the young students were free to choose between marriage and the priesthood. In northern Italy and in Rome, where urban life persisted, the cathedral schools were important centers of instruction in the seventh and eighth centuries. North of the Alps, at least twenty cathedrals had active schools during this time. The curriculum of the schools was influenced by the monastic example. Many bishops had earlier been monks and tried to organize their clergy along monastic lines. The program of reading and meditation at the heart of monastic education supplemented the more technical and professional program of studies in the bishop's school.

Monastic and cathedral schools were given a prominent role in the Carolingian reform movement. The leaders of the Carolingian renaissance, especially Charlemagne and Alcuin, believed that society should be modeled on the values of the Scriptures, an ideal that required learning and education. In a series of important decrees that were repeated and imitated by bishops throughout the ninth century, Charlemagne ordered all cathedrals and monasteries to provide schools for training the ecclesiastical leaders of Christian society. What had been accomplished by the initiative of this or that bishop now was expected of every bishop. Furthermore, discipline and cohesiveness among the cathedral clergy were enhanced when cathedral life was reorganized along canonical, quasi-monastic lines shortly after Charlemagne's death. The records of scores of cathedral schools survive and bear witness to the new prominence they enjoyed—a position in European society that would only increase as the cathedral towns became vital urban centers of population, business, and government.

The revival of the towns was not the only reason cathedral schools began to dominate educational and intellectual life late in the tenth century. The destruction and disruption inflicted on many monasteries by the Norse and Magyar raids of the tenth century also played a role. Even more significant were the monastic reform movements that began in the tenth century and continued through the twelfth century. These reforms, associated with the Cluniac order, Peter Damian, and Bernard of Clairvaux, sought to enhance the spiritual atmosphere of monastic life through additional prayer, adherence to the word of the Scriptures, and less involvement in the world external to the monastic cloister. Almost by default, the cathedral schools took on the double burden of accommodating dialectic and other aspects of Greek learning to the Western Christian tradition and of providing trained men for ecclesiastical and political administration. The cathedral schools at Rheims, Laon, Chartres, Orléans, Liège, Toledo, Cologne, Canterbury, and especially Paris became leading centers of European intellectual life in the eleventh and twelfth centuries. Many of the most important twelfth-century writers and masters active in the decades just before the establishment of the universities were either trained in or taught in cathedral schools.

The intellectual climate of the cathedral school depended entirely on the master. Schools could be famous in one generation only to disappear from view after the demise of a gifted master. Until the twelfth century, when a license to teach was required of masters, no explicit standards governed the choice and conduct of the master. The bishop, as in the case of Caesarius of Arles in the sixth century or Fulbert of Chartres in the eleventh, could personally supervise the education of the cathedral clergy. Generally, the archdeacon of the cathedral was charged with selecting and supervising the master, who appears in the sources under many different titles: *magister, scholasticus, didascalcus,* and *nutritor* are among the most common. In theory the master had to be old enough to be a deacon, that is twenty-five, although younger masters are known. His classroom could be anywhere in the episcopal complex—in the cathedral itself, in a special little building, or in a room of the episcopal palace. The master had only a handful of students at any one time, perhaps around twenty. In addition to instructing his charges, the master sought to prepare a new teacher to take his place. Many masters left teaching behind to mount the ladder of ecclesiastical success. Gerbert of Aurillac (Pope Sylvester II) became pope at the behest of his former pupil at Rheims, Otto III, emperor of the Holy Roman Empire. A school's reputation might last for several decades if a successful, new teacher could be prepared. Masters were sensitive to tradition and freely acknowledged their debts to their predecessors. Several medieval texts contain lists of masters in a kind of genealogy of learning. Fees for instruction became a matter for concern in the eleventh and twelfth centuries. There is some indication that masters were remunerated for their work in the cathedral, but not much is known about teachers' salaries and student fees.

Curriculum varied from school to school, depending on resources and the special interests of the master. All students who came to the cathedral school around seven years of age could be guaranteed a course of elementary instruction that would teach them to read and write elementary Latin, to sing, and to calculate.

Instruction in reading began with recognition of the letters of the alphabet and then syllables. Reading instruction went hand in hand with writing. Students learned to copy out on parchment or wax tablets the letters they were beginning to master. The next stage was to begin reading a text. The psalter served as the medieval primer in both monastic and cathedral schools. Students were introduced to words and phrases through continual study of the Psalms. This early and repeated exposure to the psalter affected lifelong intellectual habits. In the masters' own writings, the psalter often is the most frequently cited biblical book. Psalms were meant to be sung. While learning to read the text of the Psalms, young students were introduced to the technical requirements of chant, a discipline they would use throughout their careers when participating in the Christian liturgy or in the canonical offices. Masters devised a system of notation based on the use of neumes to guide their students' voices. Bits and pieces of neumic notation occur in many nonmusical manuscripts, indicating that students used random moments to practice the techniques of chant. Calculation, or the *computus,* was another elementary skill the young student had to master. In addition to being able to perform the basic arithmetical functions (made quite complicated by the use of Roman numerals), students had to be able to reckon time and to follow the annual and liturgical calendars. Fixing the date of important holy days, given the various calendars and the movement of heavenly bodies, required mastery of complicated formulas. Among other calculations, students had to know how to measure fields, tally harvests, disburse and divide payments, and determine the amount of wax needed to make a certain number of candles. Masters used a variety of arithmetical puzzles to sharpen their students' minds and to give them practical experience in dealing with numbers. Finger counting, or digital reckoning, was widely taught as a means of handling a large series of numbers rapidly.

As the student acquired these basic skills, he was also introduced to a more sophisticated study of the Latin language, the language of the Christian religion and thus the language of the clergy and of educated laymen. Intense study of Latin began in earnest after reading, writing, calculation, and chant were mastered. For students who came from a Celtic or Germanic background, Latin was especially difficult to learn. Only a few of them ever mastered this foreign language. Masters used many of the same grammars that circulated in the Roman schools to teach their students about the parts of speech and to drill them in syntax, orthography, and word usage. Several glossaries, both Latin–Latin and bilingual, helped to build up the student's Latin vocabulary. Students were expected not only to be able to read Latin but also to write and to speak it with ease. Dialogues, puzzles, jokes, and set speeches complemented the technical grammatical manuals. Learning Latin was a lifelong task. Masters argued among themselves about the proper pronunciation of a Latin word or criticized a colleague for an apparently improper usage of a declension.

Knowledge of Latin prepared the young man for further studies that would lead eventually to the priesthood. The intensity and duration of study depended on the talents the student demonstrated in his earlier years. To become a parish priest required knowledge of the Bible, certain hymns and prayers, canon law, and the ability to perform correctly the ceremonies of the faith. Standards of competency in these areas varied from place to place and from century to century. Maintaining the level of training of the parish clergy was a perennial problem for conscientious bishops. Students who demonstrated particular talent in reading, singing, or writing prepared for lives as lectors, cantors, scribes, or notaries. Their gifted voices and talented hands destined them for careers as specialists charged with reading or singing the divine words in the choir or during the Mass, writing and decorating manuscripts in the scriptorium, or copying and preserving the diocese's important adminstrative documents in the cathedral archives.

Intellectually gifted students went on to a rigorous study of grammar, that is, Roman and early medieval poets and prose authors, and the other arts. The master guided students through the major texts and manuals word by word, line by line, explicating the grammatical and literary significance of the text at hand. In the process the student would acquire information and ideas from different ages and different cultures. History and geography were read. Law, rhetoric, and dialectic were the other liberal arts in the program. Reading and discussion of the sciences, geometry, arithmetic, astronomy, music, and medicine could also be pursued at this stage. Several schools gave their students a smattering of Greek. Which fields of study were pursued and how deeply they were studied, again, varied. Grammar was preeminent among the arts in the ninth century, dialectic in the twelfth century. The concept of the seven liberal arts existed only in the manuals, and even there the definitions of the arts and even their number differed.

Masters from Augustine at Hippo to Abelard in France agreed that the purpose of advanced training was to illuminate further the Christian faith. Certainly the masters and their more advanced pupils were aware of the prestige attached to their position as intellectuals and derived great personal pleasure from their studies. Those studies, however, were justified (after some debate in the sixth, seventh, and eighth centuries) by their subservience to the sacred science, the study of Scripture. The same techniques of textual analysis the student used in his literary studies were also applied to the sacred text. Master and student explicated the Bible to uncover its multiple meanings. Everything in the Bible was meaningful, no matter how inconsequential or trivial it might seem. Since God was believed to be the author of the Bible, inconsistencies and contradictions could be only apparent and had to be explained to defend the integrity and authenticity of the divine word. In these higher studies, student and master drew upon their knowledge of language, history, number, geography, astronomy, logic, and the other disciplines mastered earlier. They also had on their library shelves guidebooks to biblical vocabulary and problems. Commentaries on the Bible written by renowned masters helped to guide the way and formed an important part of study. Sometimes medieval masters wrote their own commentaries for the use of their friends and colleagues elsewhere or for the use of an educated layman such as a king or emperor.

In the eleventh and twelfth centuries, as masters wrestled with the problems posed by the new translations of Greek works, the fame of a cathedral's master or of its library could attract students from beyond the limits of the diocese. Some twelfth-century cathedral schools attracted an international student body. At the same time, the growth of the towns in which the schools were located and the simultaneous institutional growth of the monarchies in the medieval West opened up new opportunities for clergy trained in the cathedral schools. Schools were crowded with students, many of whom sought bureaucractic rather than ecclesiastical positions. Masters competed, sometimes bitterly, among each other for teaching positions and for students. Bishops complained that they were losing authority over their own schools. Concerned moral leaders decried what they perceived to be overspecialization and the ousting of wisdom and service as the purposes of education by the drive for prestige, renown, and profit. In this turbulent atmosphere, in circumstances that are not precisely clear, several towns developed a new educational institution—corporations of masters or of students, which determined their own administrative structures, academic requirements, and curricula. The first universities were better suited than the cathedral cloisters to provide the new education in the new circumstances of the twelfth and thirteenth centuries.

BIBLIOGRAPHY

Sources. Peter Abelard, *The Story of Abelard's Adversities,* J. T. Muckle, trans. (1964); Gerbert of Aurillac, *The Letters of Gerbert, with His Papal Privileges as Sylvester II,* Harriet P. Lattin, trans. (1961); John of Salisbury, *The Metalogicon of John of Salisbury: A Twelfth-century Defense of the Verbal and Logical Arts of the Trivium,* Daniel D. McGarry, trans. (1955).

Studies. John W. Baldwin, *Masters, Princes, and Merchants: The Social Views of Peter the Chanter and His Circle,* 2 vols. (1970), and *The Scholastic Culture of the Middle Ages, 1000–1300* (1971); Georges Bourbon, "La license d'enseigner et le role de l'écolatre au moyen âge," in *Revue des questions historiques,* **19** (1876); Donald Bullough, "Le scuole cattedrali e la cultura dell'Italia settentrionale prima dei communi," in *Vescovi et diocesi in Italia nel medioevo* (sec. IX–XIII) (1964), 111–143; John J. Contreni, *The Cathedral School of Laon from 850 to 930: Its Manuscripts and Masters* (1978); Philippe Delhaye, "L'organisation scolaire au XIIe siècle," in *Traditio,* **5** (1947); Peter Dronke, "New Approaches to the School of Chartres," in *Anuario de estudios medievales,* **6** (1969); Roberto Giacone, "Masters, Books, and Library at Chartres According to the Cartularies of Notre-Dame and Saint-Père," in *Vivarium,* **12** (1974); Nikolaus M. Häring, *Life and Works of Clarembald of Arras, a Twelfth-century Master of the School of Chartres* (1965); Jacques Le Goff, *Les intellectuels au moyen âge* (1955); Émile Lesne, *Les écoles de la fin du VIIIe siècle à la fin du XIIe* (1940); Loren C. MacKinney, *Bishop Fulbert and Education at the School of Chartres* (1957); Rosamond McKitterick, *The Frankish Church* *and the Carolingian Reforms, 789–895* (1977); Gérard Paré, Adrien Brunet, and Pierre Tremblay, *La renaissance du XIIe siècle: Les écoles et l'enseignement* (1933); Gaines Post, "Alexander III, the *licentia docendi,* and the Rise of the Universities," in Charles H. Taylor and John La Monte, eds., *Anniversary Essays in Mediaeval History by Students of Charles Homer Haskins* (1929, repr. 1967), and "Masters' Salaries and Student-Fees in the Mediaeval Universities," in *Speculum,* 7 (1932); Pierre Riché, *Education and Culture in the Barbarian West, Sixth Through Eighth Centuries,* John J. Contreni, trans. (1976), and *Les écoles et l'enseignement dans l'occident chrétien de la fin du Ve siècle au milieu du XIe siècle* (1979); John R. Williams, "The Cathedral School of Rheims in the Eleventh Century," in *Speculum,* 29 (1954), and "The Cathedral School of Reims in the Time of Master Alberic, 1118–1136," in *Traditio,* 20 (1964).

JOHN J. CONTRENI

[See also **Abelard, Peter; Alcuin of York; Arts, Seven Liberal; Augustine of Hippo, St.; Bernard of Clairvaux, St.; Calendars and Reckoning of Time; Carolingians and the Carolingian Empire; Charlemagne; Cluny, Order of; Dialectic; Doctor; Fulbert of Chartres; Grammar; Latin Language; Medicine, Schools of; Monastery; Otto III, Emperor; Peter Damian, St.; Reform, Idea of; Scholasticism, Scholastic Method; Scriptorium; Sylvester II, Pope; Universities.**]

Schoolmaster, with birch, examining students. Woodcut from *Exposito hymnorum secundum usum Saru,* 1497. From Edward Hodnett, *English Woodcuts 1480–1535.* © 1935 OXFORD UNIVERSITY PRESS. THE NEW YORK PUBLIC LIBRARY, ASTOR, LENOX, AND TILDEN FOUNDATIONS

SCHOOLS, GRAMMAR. The Jewish religious culture and its offshoots Christianity and Islam are characterized together as religions of the book; a written revelation of the divine is central to each of them. They also share the advantage of an alphabetic script that makes reading and writing possible even for children and novices after a very short training period. Consequently, an education designed to prepare young men for religious study is found in each tradition, and even in the darkest moments of general educational decline, religious oppression, or economic stagnation there have been religious schools to keep elementary literacy alive. The medieval grammar schools, Jewish, Muslim, Byzantine, and Latin, all served to teach young scholars the crafts of writing and reading their own versions of the alphabet. Handwriting and phonology, the translation of the letters into sounds and vice versa, are the minimal skills indicated by the Latin phrase *ars grammatica.*

Because an alphabetic script is so easy for young children to learn, as long as it is reasonably consistent in its representations of sounds by symbols, this minimal grammar school could be a very simple, casual meeting between a child and any literate person, the classical slave-pedagogue, for example, or the medieval parish priest. In the Jewish and Muslim traditions, introductory grammar was followed by intensive study of Scripture and religious law, texts that controlled and taught the meaning of the language. The problem of language training had other complications in the Greek and Latin traditions: more inflected languages and larger and more varied corpora of literature.

Children in ancient Greece and then in the Byzantine Empire were trained in urban schools by professional teachers (*sophistai*) for public service, beginning with grammar but passing as rapidly as possible into a study of the classics and later of the fathers of the church as well, a study designed to give them a rhetorical treasury to draw on in their public or ecclesiastical oratory. In Roman classical education too, the grammar school had been a preparatory stage, kept as short as possible, for rhetorical training; and the program included Greek. The Roman teachers needed to explain the peculiarities of this foreign language, and to do so they adopted the formal analysis of language, apparently invented by the Greek sophists for the sake of rhetorical display, which also goes by the name of *grammatica*.

The method was adapted to Latin by late classical authors, then reduced to systematic manuals, notably by Donatus (who taught grammar at Rome in the middle of the fourth century, and one of whose pupils, Jerome, was largely responsible for the Vulgate translation of the Bible, the work that secured Latin as the clerical, written language of Europe in the Middle Ages), and Priscian (who wrote a Latin grammar at the end of the fifth century for the Greek-speaking functionaries of the Roman imperial capital at Constantinople). Latin was a necessary, but after the sixth century a second, language in Europe, and the books of Donatus and Priscian were the major primers of analytic Latin grammar for generations of scholars, mostly male and clerical or religious by profession, who needed Latin literacy to pursue any learned career in the fields of philosophy, theology, the law, and medicine. Training in elementary grammar was provided by several different institutions; the graded, standardized grammar school or gymnasium did not appear until the late Renaissance.

Following the provisions of the Rule of St. Benedict and the well-publicized example of Cassiodorus' house of Vivarium (both from the sixth century), any sizable monastery needed a scriptorium and a grammar school to teach its own young oblates, and many also offered the education to outsiders. The first book of the *Etymologies* of Isidore of Seville, the leading encyclopedia of the early Middle Ages, is a treatment of grammar based on Donatus. The most far-reaching effect of the Carolingian renaissance early in the ninth century was the grammar school and Latin reform mobilized by Charlemagne's brilliant "minister of education," Alcuin of York. Cathedrals and large collegiate churches developed their own grammar schools in imitation of the monastic schools, each governed by its *scholasticus* and typically using Donatus' *Ars minor* as its core curriculum. To ensure a supply of literate boys for the clergy, the Fourth Lateran Council in 1215 made grammar schools mandatory for all cathedrals. The mendicant orders offered urban grammar schools as a pious service and as recruiting centers. Few of the medieval *scholastici* were so inventive at teaching as to have their schools noticed; a great exception was the twelfth-century cathedral school of Chartres, where a holistic grammar-and-authors course was available to an international student body, including John of Salisbury, one of the most polished Latinists of the Middle Ages, who left a description of the program at Chartres. The collegiate or chapter schools, and the later urban chantry and friars' schools, were the originals of the English public and grammar schools, the elementary preparation of choice for university students.

Grammar was the first liberal art of the trivium, in the Latin tradition of education adopted in the universities; every faculty of arts therefore taught grammar, usually by adding the polish of lectures on Donatus and Priscian to a practical reading knowledge that the students had acquired before matriculating. At the beginning of the thirteenth century, to meet the challenge of an expanding student population, two novel grammar primers appeared, the *Graecismus* of Eberhard of Béthune (*d.* 1212) and the *Doctrinale* of Alexander of Villedieu (*d.* 1240), which made the rules of classical grammar easier to memorize in their hexameter verses. Both works entered the curricula of the university arts faculties and stayed there until the Renaissance humanists convicted them of barbarism and drove them out in the sixteenth century.

BIBLIOGRAPHY

William Boyd and Edmund J. King, *The History of Western Education*, 10th ed. (1972); James J. Murphy, *Medieval Rhetoric: A Select Bibliography* (1971); Louis John Paetow, *The Arts Course at Medieval Universities, with Special Reference to Grammar and Rhetoric* (1910); Pierre Riché, *Education and Culture in the Barbarian West*, John J. Contreni, trans. (1976).

DANIEL WILLIMAN

[See also **Alcuin of York; Arts, Seven Liberal; Carolingians and the Carolingian Empire; Charlemagne; Grammar; John of Salisbury; Latin Language; Priscian; Trivium; Vulgate.**]

SCHOOLS, ISLAMIC. By the second half of the twelfth century the Latin West had two new institutions of higher learning: the university and the college. They were based on the juridical principles of legal personality and the charitable trust, respectively. The university had not been known before. It was as unknown to Greek and Roman antiquity as it was to Byzantium and Islam; and it owed nothing to the cathedral and monastic schools that it eventually replaced. It was strictly a product of the Latin West. The college, however, developed in Islam during its first century, that is, during the seventh and eighth centuries, as an eleemosynary institution. From the eighth to the tenth centuries it went through three stages of development. Before it appeared in Paris in the last quarter of the twelfth century, the college had been unknown to Greece, Rome, Byzantium, and the Latin West. It was strictly a product of Islam.

THE MUSLIM COLLEGE AND ITS CURRICULUM

Knowledge in Islam was classified under three divisions: the Islamic sciences, the "ancient sciences," and the Arabic or literary sciences. The Islamic sciences, *al-ᶜulūm ash-sharᶜīya* (sciences of the revealed law), consisted mainly of the Koran and its science, the *ḥadīth* and its sciences, and the legal sciences, eventually including legal dialectic. The "ancient sciences," *ᶜulūm al-awāʾil,* consisted especially of the philsophical, natural, and mathematical sciences translated from the Greek. The Arabic or literary arts, *al-ᶜArabīya, ᶜulūm al-adab,* usually grouped under the all-embracing designation *naḥw,* consisted of grammar and the rhetorical arts. Of these three divisions the first and third alone were institutionalized, while the "ancient sciences" were not admissible in the collegiate system. The reason for this exclusion was the principle that nothing could be a subject of the religiously authoritative oral transmission of knowledge from master to disciple that would contravene the tenets of Islam. As Greek thought was in opposition to that of Islam on such basic doctrine as the existence of a unique, personal, and almighty God, the non-eternity of the world, and the resurrection of the body, it was excluded from the established curriculum. Not only were these sciences excluded, but also all others that were held to be tainted with such sciences, as for example the science of *kalām,* rationalist or philosophical theology. The exclusory principle was based on the law of *waqf* (charitable trust), whose interpreters were the jurisconsults, the *fuqahāʾ,* always a conservative force in Islam.

The Muᶜtazilite inquisition. The Muslim college, as it finally emerged in the tenth century, resulted from the struggle between the traditionalist jurisconsults and the rationalist theologians, particularly the Muᶜtazila. The turning point in that struggle was the great inquisition, the *miḥna*. Begun in 832, the penultimate year of al-Maʾmūn's caliphate, it spanned the Abbasid caliphates of al-Muᶜtasim and al-Wāthiq, and ended in 848, the second year of the caliphate of al-Mutawakkil (*r.* 847–861). During that decade and a half, many doctors of the law, jurisconsults, qadis, and witness notaries were imprisoned, flogged, or beaten to death. The question put to these men of law was a theological one; it concerned the nature of the Koran, since the Koran was considered to be the actual, not the inspired, word of God: "Is the Koran created or uncreated (al-Qurʾān Makhlūq)?" If the answer went against the Muᶜtazilite doctrine of the created character of the Koran, the jurist was condemned. The inquisition eventually exhausted itself against the stubborn resistance of the traditionalist jurisconsults, who were led by the heroic figure of Aḥmad ibn Ḥanbal (780–855). Legal traditionalism emerged triumphant over the theological rationalism of the Muᶜtazila, who lost their political power, never again to regain it.

As a result, the Muslim college became and remained strictly conservative, organized on the basis of the charitable trust, with law as the queen of the sciences in its curriculum, while the other subjects were ancillary. Because the one indispensable chair of the college was the chair of law, one chair to each college, all other members of the staff were subordinate to the professor of law, who was, more often than not, the director of the college.

The masjid-khan complex. Islam had then—and still has—two kinds of mosques: the masjid, the simple everyday mosque found in great numbers in the various quarters of the city, and the Friday mosque, or great mosque, called *al-masjid al-jāmiᶜ*, or simply *al-jāmiᶜ*. The college originated in the masjid type of mosque. In the early Islamic era, the masjid was used for the teaching of one or more of the Islamic sciences and literary arts. After the mid ninth century, more and more masjids came to be devoted to the legal sciences. In the tenth century there was a flourishing of a new type of college, combining the masjid with a khan or inn to lodge law students from out of town. The great patron of this second stage in the development of the college was Badr ibn Ḥasanawaih (*d.* 1014/1015), governor of several provinces under the Buyids, and to whose name 3,000 masjid-khan complexes were credited over the thirty-year period of his governorship.

The reason for the masjid-khan complex was that the student of law had to pursue his studies over a protracted period of time, usually four years for undergraduate studies alone, and an indeterminate period for graduate studies, often as many as twenty years, during which the graduate disciple assisted the master in teaching. The masjid could not be used for lodging, except in special cases, such as that of the wayfarer for a few days or the destitute ascetic who had given up worldly pursuits and withdrawn from the society of men to devote himself to prayer and meditation. The inn or khan thus became the lodging place of the staff and students and was founded in proximity to the masjid.

The madrasa. The final stage in the development of the Muslim college was the madrasa, which combined the teaching function of the masjid with the lodging function of the khan. The madrasa, known in small numbers in the tenth century, began to flourish in the eleventh. The great patron of this period was Niẓām al-Mulk (1018–1092), prime minister under the Seljuks, who founded a network of madrasas throughout the lands of the eastern caliphate, those of Baghdad and Nishapur being the better known among them.

Early scholarship maintained that the madrasa was a development from a private to a public state institution; that it became a state institution in the eleventh century under Niẓām al-Mulk, who introduced the study of Ashᶜarism (based on al-Ashᶜari's theories) as the official orthodoxy of Islam. On the contrary, the madrasa at no time became an official institution. It was, by the very nature of its legal basis, a private foundation instituted for a public purpose. The sultan Nūr al-Dīn (1118–1174) made it quite clear that he had never used any moneys from the public treasury (*bait al-māl*) to found his madrasas. This boast points to two things: (1) that founders of *waqf*s, according to *waqf* law, were supposed to use their own privately owned wealth to institute their *waqf*s, and (2) that there were founders who used public funds and whose foundations were therefore invalid, being based on misappropriated (*maghṣūb*) property.

The madrasas of Niẓām al-Mulk could not be regarded as official state institutions, since, like all madrasas, they were exclusive in character. Niẓām's madrasas were founded by him as Shafiᶜi madrasas, where only Shafiᶜi students were admitted, to the exclusion of members of the three other schools of Sunni law. Furthermore, the chair in each of the Nizamīya madrasas was for the Shafiᶜi professor of law. The latter may have also been an Ashᶜarite theologian, as in the case of some professors, but they were hired in their capacity as professors of law. There was no chair of theology as such, whether of the Ashᶜarite or Muᶜtazilite variety.

The curriculum of the madrasa was essentially that of the masjid-khan of the previous stage of development. The difference between the masjid college and the madrasa college was that the former, once instituted, became free of its founder, whereas the latter could be administered by its founder and his progeny to the end of his line. He was thus able to keep the administration of his endowment under his own and his posterity's direction.

In all its three stages the Muslim college was a charitable trust, administered by the law of *waqf*. The peculiar needs of law students guided its development into an institution that provided, first, tuition, then lodging, then stipends and food. With the masjid as a college of law, students were the beneficiaries of tuition when the endowment provided for the salary of the professor of law, who often was the imam of the masjid—its leader of prayer. With the masjid-khan complex, the student became the beneficiary of at least tuition and lodging. With the madrasa he became, in addition, the beneficiary of a stipend and food. The amounts differed from college to college according to the importance of the endowment and the fluctuations in revenue from rents and harvests.

OTHER MUSLIM PLACES OF LEARNING

The typology of Islamic institutions of learning usually included, besides the masjid and the madrasa, the great mosque (*jāmiᶜ*) with its study circles (*ḥalqa*; plural: *ḥalaqāt*); the *dār al-hadīth* and the *dār al-qur'ān,* primarily for the study of the sciences of the Koran and *ḥadīth;* the various monastery colleges (*ribat, khānqāh, zāwiya*); and a variety of combinations of two or three of these institutions administered by a single charitable trust. The *madrasa-jāmiᶜ* developed later in many parts of the Islamic world, especially in Cairo.

Home and library studies. The Greek sciences were studied in private, in the homes of scholars, and particularly in the hospitals (*māristān,* from the Persian *bīmāristān*), where medicine played the role of Trojan horse for those sciences considered inadmissible in institutionalized learning. While the Greek sciences were excluded from the regular curricula of the religious institutions by the law of *waqf,* the manuscript books treating them were admitted into the libraries. These institutions, also based on the law of *waqf,* nevertheless helped to preserve for posterity the books whose subjects were excluded from the curricula. The reason for this apparent paradox may be sought in the fact that the prohibition applied only to the religiously authoritative oral transmission of their contents from master to disciple. The prohibition did not in principle extend to their being read privately, copied, or even discussed in disputations or, less formally, outside of the regular curricula of the teaching institutions.

These libraries existed early in Islam, up to the middle of the eleventh century, during which century they began to be annexed to the teaching institutions. Others had an ephemeral existence beyond that period. The terms used to designate these libraries consisted of a combination of any of the following set of three terms—*dār* (house), *khizāna* (repository), and *bait* (house)—with any of the following set of three—*ḥikma* (wisdom), *ᶜilm* (learning, knowledge), and *kutub* (books). The resulting nine combinations have all been documented.

THE METHODOLOGY OF LEARNING

Memorization. The methodology of learning in medieval Islam relied heavily on memorization. The cultivation of memory and its aids, repetition (*iᶜāda*), discussion (*mudhākara*), and notebooks, served both the Koran and *ḥadīth.* From the emphasis on memory and its aids, cultivated to ensure the correct transmission (*riwāya*) of the sacred Scripture, emphasis came to be placed also on understanding (*dirāya*). Besides the Koran and *ḥadīth,* a vast repertoire of poetry from pre-Islamic and early Islamic times was committed to memory for its lexical value in clarifying the sacred Scripture.

Scholastic method. With the advent of legal studies, the scholastic method (*tarīqat an-naẓar,* the method of disputation) was developed, based on the conflicting opinions of jurisconsults (*khilāf,* similar to Peter Abelard's *sic et non*); disputation (*munāẓara*), practiced from early times by the grammarians and jurisconsults; and dialectic (*jadal*), to which the jurisconsults were attracted for its value in strengthening disputation and raising it to the level of an art.

This scholastic method was essential to Islam in that it was the method used in order to define orthodoxy. Unlike Christianity, Islam had no councils or synods for this purpose. Its orthodoxy was based on the consensus (*ijmā*) of the doctors of the law. This consensus, which had to be unanimous, resulted from the confrontation of the conflicting opinions (*fatwā*; plural: *fatāwā*) of the jurisconsults in the arena of disputation. The opinion surviving through the process, and against which there were no objections worthy of being taken into account (silence was tantamount to tacit approval), eventually passed into the realm of orthodoxy.

One of the most prolific genres of legal literature in Islam is that of *khilāf.* Conflicting opinions were compiled, either simply as pro-and-con opinions, or including the solutions that the compilers offered as worthy of preference. What produced this literature was the fact that the *mustaftī,* the layman who solicited a legal opinion, was entitled to solicit from as many muftis (jurisconsults) as he desired and then follow the opinion of his choice. This practice was sanctioned because all opinions before consensus were equally valid; so also were conflicting opinions unresolved by consensus.

The work that, in Islam, best illustrates the scholastic method which appeared later at the height of its perfection in the West in the *Summa theologiae* of St. Thomas Aquinas (1224–1274) is that of Ibn ᶜAqīl (1040–1119), jurisconsult and theologian of Baghdad, in his *Wāḍiḥ* on the sources, theory, and methodology of the law. The main structural difference between the two books is that the thesis in the articles of the *Summa* is found after the objections and before the replies to the objections, whereas in the *Wāḍiḥ* it is at the beginning of the article, preceding both the objections and the replies to them.

LEGAL STUDIES AND THE LICENSE TO TEACH

Legal studies were responsible for the development of the *taᶜliqa,* or compilation of lecture notes, which was then adopted by the grammarians, and in one instance at least by the *kalām* theologians. The *taᶜliqa* was an integral part of the education of the graduate student of law; it was one of the requirements for the license to teach.

The term for license or authorization is *ijāza,* and for the license to teach law, *al-ijāza bi 't-tadrīs,* or, more specifically, the license to teach law and issue legal opinions, *al-ijāza bi 't-tadrīs wa 'l-fatwā.* This license to teach was distinct from the simple *ijāza,* which was a license to transmit authoritatively a *ḥadīth,* or a collection of *ḥadīths*, and, by extension, any other book in the fields of the Islamic sciences or literary arts. Thus, the only license required for the authoritative teaching of a field of knowledge was that for the teaching of law. The professor of law was singled out for the designation of *mudarris,* though he shared with all other professors the title of *shaikh* (*magister*).

STUDENTS IN THE MUSLIM COLLEGE

There were two levels of students in the college of law, whether masjid or madrasa: the undergraduate student, *mutafaqqih,* and the graduate fellow, *ṣāḥib* or *faqīh.* The term *faqīh* was also applied to the accomplished doctor of the law, as well as to the jurisconsult who issued solicited legal opinions, though, in this last function, he was specifically designated by the term *muftī,* he who issues *fatāwā.* The *faqīh,* as graduate student, was also designated by the term *ṣāḥib,* or fellow of the master jurisconsult. The latter chose his fellows or disciples (*aṣḥāb*) from among the most successful of his own graduate students, or from those of others who came to him for their graduate studies.

Undergraduate students. The undergraduate student of law began his studies at the approximate age of fifteen, having already completed his primary studies in the *kuttāb,* and/or *maktab,* the elementary schools, where he learned the rudiments of reading, writing, and grammar, and where he memorized the Koran and *ḥadīth,* or parts thereof. The college of law had, besides the professor of law, a teaching staff that usually included a *muḥaddith,* who taught the sciences of *ḥadīth,* a *naḥwī* (grammarian), who taught the literary arts, and a *muqriʾ,* a Koranic scholar who taught the Koranic sciences, including exegesis and the canonical variant readings. The undergraduate law course was usually divided into four quarters (*rubʿ*), taught in four years, after which the *mutaffaqqih,* if chosen by his master for higher studies, became a *faqīh* and *ṣāḥib* (fellow) of the *mudarris,* or professor of law.

Graduate students. Once the law student finished his basic law course, he began in earnest his graduate studies, which included the study of *khilāf* and *jadal,* and attended the disputations of his elders in preparation for his eventual participation in them. The emphasis of the graduate period was placed on the student becoming an expert disputant; and to this end, he was required to learn vast repertoires of disputed questions (*masāʾ il khilāfīya*). The most successful disputant was one who had the most extensive repertoire of objections and replies to these objections on the disputed points of law. Such a repertoire was memorized and kept in fresh rehearsal, as more and more disputed questions were added to expand the repertoire with a view to achieving excellence and leadership in one's field.

Riyāsa, or leadership, was the aim of the jurisconsult. For it was this leadership that, over and above the license to teach, brought the scholar fame and fortune, since he was then sought from far and wide for his legal opinions, and offered posts for the professorship of law (*tadrīs*). The competition among disputants was very stiff indeed, and matters developed to such a point that all else was set aside in the pursuit of excellence in disputation.

The final ordeal of the graduate law student came with the disputation that led to the license to teach. This was held in class. The most advanced student defended a thesis or theses against the professor.

Besides the professorship of law, not always available, the jurisconsult with a license could always issue legal opinions to those soliciting them from him. He could stay on, in some of the madrasas, as assistant to his professor, in the post of *muʿīd* (*repetitor*), or *mufīd,* a sort of scholar in residence who helped students by imparting "useful information" (*fāʾida,* plural: *fawāʾid*) in answer to their questions. The *faqīh* also became the elementary school teacher.

BIBLIOGRAPHY

See Arthur S. Tritton, *Materials on Muslim Education in the Middle Ages* (1957), including the bibliography on pages ix–xii. See also the following works by George Makdisi: "Muslim Institutions of Learning in Eleventh-century Baghdad," in *Bulletin of the School of Oriental and African Studies University of London,* **24** (1961), "Madrasa and University in the Middle Ages," in *Studia islamica,* **32** (1970), "The Madrasa as a Charitable Trust and the University as a Corporation in the Middle Ages," in *Correspondance d'Orient,* **11** (Actes du Ve Congrès International d'Arabisants et d'Islamisants) (1970), "Law and Traditionalism in the Institutions of Learning of Medieval Islam," in Gustave E. von Grunebaum, ed., *Theology and Law in Islam* (1971), 75–88, "The Madrasa in Spain: Some Remarks," in *Revue de l'occident musulman et de la Méditerranée* **15/16** (1973), "The Scholastic Method in Medieval Education: An Inquiry into Its Origins in Law and Theology," in *Speculum,* **49** (1974), "Interaction Between Islam and the West," in *idem*, Dominique Sourdel, and Janine Sourdel-Thomine, eds., *Medieval Education in Islam and the West* (1977), "*Ṣuḥba* et *riyāsa* dans l'enseignement médiéval," in *Recherches d'islamologie: Receuil d'articles offert à Georges C. Anawati et Louis Gardet par leurs collègues et amis* (1977), 207–221, "An Islamic Element in the Early Spanish University," in Alford T. Welch and Pierre Cachia, eds., *Islam: Past Influence and Present Challenge* (1979), 126–137, "On the Origin and Development of the College in Islam and the West," in Khalil I. Semaan, ed., *Islam and the Medieval West: Aspects of Intercultural Relations* (1980), 26–49, and *The Rise of Colleges: Institutions of Learning in Islam and the West* (1981).

GEORGE MAKDISI

[See also **Arabic Language; Arabic Literature; Arabic Numerals; Ashᶜarī, al-; Damascus; Egypt, Islamic; Fatwā; Ḥadīth; Ḥanbal, Aḥmad ibn Muḥammad Ibn; Khan; Koran; Law, Islamic; Madrasa; Mosque; Mutawakkil, al-; Muᶜtazila, al-; Niẓām al-Mulk; Philosophy and Theology, Islamic; Waqf.**]

SCHOOLS, JEWISH. Among the norms of Judaism is the father's religious duty to instruct his children in the basic requirements of God's will as formulated in the Torah, that is, in the Hebrew Bible and its continuing rabbinic interpretations (Deut. 6:7). This ancient religious mandate resulted in widespread Jewish literacy, especially among sons. It applied to children of the poor as well as of the wealthy, to those from ordinary households as well as from famous families. Usually implemented by private instructors who acted as the father's agent or surrogate, various forms of private and community-sponsored elementary and more advanced instruction developed in the self-governing Jewish communities of medieval Europe. Although technically under parental supervision, educational institutions were also regulated by the elders of the community, especially in the case of the orphaned and the indigent.

As mediators of culture, Jewish schools reflected and fostered the major cultural differences that were obtained between the Rhenish and northern French Jewish society (Ashkenazic Jewry), on the one hand, and the communities of Spain (Sephardic Jewry), which were influenced by the earlier Muslim-Jewish encounter in southern Spain, on the other. Although they shared the same sacred Scriptures and most of the same rabbinic canon, such as the Babylonian Talmud, Ashkenazic and Sephardic communities adopted different attitudes toward the relative importance of those texts as well as sharply divided attitudes toward non-Jewish studies.

Despite the local autonomy that was characteristic of most medieval European Jewish communities, distinctive Ashkenazic and Sephardic educational patterns existed. Fostered in the Rhineland towns of Mainz, Worms, and Speyer, and in the Jewish communities in Champagne of Troyes and Ramerupt, the Ashkenazic educational ideal combined concentration on dialectical talmudic study with the religious ethos of ascetic pietism. That ideal shaped the religious educational norms of Jewish communities in medieval England, northern Italy, Bohemia, and Moravia, and eventually in Poland, Lithuania, and Russia. For its part, the Sephardic ideal placed special emphasis on the separate study of the Bible, Hebrew grammar, and the law codes as well as on the Talmud. Above all, it differed from the Ashkenazic curriculum by including not only Jewish texts but also scientific and philosophical subjects as dealt with in works by non-Jews. The Sephardic agenda directly influenced Italian Jewish schooling in the late Middle Ages as well as Jewish communities in such places as Thessaloniki and Safad in the Ottoman Empire.

It is known from several French and German Jewish texts from the twelfth through fourteenth centuries that a boy of five or six was introduced to formal learning in a special ceremony that functioned as a cultural rite of passage. On the late spring holiday of Shavuot (Pentecost), which traditionally denotes the giving of the Torah on Mount Sinai, the boy was wrapped in a coat or prayer shawl and brought by his father to the teacher, who awaited him either in the synagogue schoolroom or in the teacher's house. The teacher sat the child on his lap and showed him a slate on which was written the Hebrew alphabet, verses from the Bible, and the sentence "May the Torah be my occupation." The teacher read each letter and the child repeated it. Then the slate was covered with honey and the child licked it. The child was then given honey cakes and peeled hard-boiled eggs on which were written additional biblical verses. After reading them aloud after the teacher, the child ate the inscribed cakes and eggs, thereby symbolically incorporating the words of the Torah.

The model of this ceremony apparently was an ancient Jewish magical initiation ceremony for adult memory retention associated with a supernatural power called "Prince of the Torah" (*sar ha-torah*). It is found in early Jewish mystical texts (*Heikhalot* literature) that Jews brought from Palestine to Italy. From there it was transmitted by Italian Jews who immigrated to the medieval Rhenish and northern French Jewish communities as part of the initiation ceremony for boys. Evidence from late antiquity of a child's eating inscribed cakes when starting school is found in Syriac Christian texts, probably under Jewish influence. Various versions of this ceremony were retained for centuries as a formal rite by which Ashkenazic boys were introduced to Hebrew literacy, and traces of related springtime customs can be found even among some Mediterranean Jewish communities.

Once begun, formal instruction proceeded rapidly. The child first learned the Hebrew consonants, sometimes with the aid of didactic maxims: "*alef, bet* (=A, B) (means) learn (*'alef*) two (*bet* also stands for 2) torahs, the written one (Scripture) and the oral one (rabbinic lore)," and so on throughout the alphabet. In an account from twelfth-century northern France, a father tells his son's tutor to teach the letters the first month, the vowel points the second month, combine letters into words the third month, and afterward begin to study the Pentateuch with the first verses of the book of Leviticus. The latter was an ancient Jewish custom derived from the idea that the pure ones (children) should study purity (the laws of ritual purity and animal sacrifices described in Leviticus). It may have been preferred for magical associative reasons as well: the first word of the book may be translated, "and he read." After learning the basic reading skills, the child would study the weekly section of the Pentateuch that was read publicly in the synagogue and the liturgy. This initial training in minimal literacy was to be followed by some study of the Mishnah (edited *ca.* 200) and the Talmud (edited *ca.* 500).

In Spain, a late-fourteenth-century account emphasizes that the father should teach his son biblical verses from the time he starts speaking (Deut. 6:7; 33:4) and should start to teach him the alphabet when he is three. When he is a little older, the father should hire a tutor. Under Muslim curricular influence, Jewish children in Spain learned grammar when they studied Bible, as Muslims did when they learned the Koran. Some Jewish youngsters also studied the Arabic vernacular with special instructors. In northern Europe, however, instruction was often conducted in the French or German vernacular, but these languages, not to speak of Latin, were not studied formally.

As time went on, the Bible was studied less and less in the north as a subject in its own right. The great Bible and Talmud commentator, Rabbi Solomon ben Isaac of Troyes (called Rashi, *d.* 1105), advised his readers not to spend too much time studying the Bible because its stories are more enjoyable to read than the difficult legal texts that require concentrated study. His grandson, the brilliant jurist Rabbi Jacob ben Meir (Rabbenu Tam, *d.* 1171) made clear what was at stake. He counseled Jews to study only the Talmud because in it could also be found quotations from the Bible and the Mishnah. Similarly, in the early fourteenth century, Rabbi Judah ben Asher, who had grown up in Germany with his distinguished father, Rabbi Asher ben Jehiel, but had migrated to Spain, advised his own son to study the Spanish curriculum of Bible and grammar, which he had not done in his own youth in Germany.

Although the picture is still not clear, some attention was paid to a girl's education as well. Except in a few cases of the daughters of learned rabbinic figures, such as those of Rabbi Eleazar of Worms (*d. ca.* 1230), girls in northern Europe received instruction only in the laws that directly affected them, not in advanced talmudic dialectical study for its own sake or for intellectual and religious ends. Thus, Rabbi Judah ben Samuel, the Pietist (*d.* 1217), the author of *Sefer Ḥasidim* (The book of the pietists), advises that fathers should teach their daughters the codified laws about the sabbath, dietary norms, and ritual purity laws involving menstruation, but not legal reasoning itself by which to derive new decisions. Under Muslim influence, the education of girls in Spain was even more restricted than it was in the north, but in the more open atmosphere of Renaissance Italy, significant advances were made.

The cultural ideal of northern European Jewry put special value on higher religious study, which increasingly became synonymous with the study of the Talmud. In the tenth and eleventh centuries, the Talmud teacher taught the text orally to the relatively passive student, who relied on the teacher for the correct reading of the text. After the introduction of Rashi's comprehensive commentary on the Talmud, which, in part, established the text, a new approach developed in the academies of the Rhineland and Champagne. Now a master sat among advanced students each of whom had studied one section of the talmudic corpus. Collectively, the students could draw upon any part of the Talmud that seemed to contradict or present difficulties to a correct understanding of the passage under examination in class. The master then considered and resolved contradictions posed by passages in different sections of the Talmud. Students, in turn, raised other questions for the master.

As a result of the new dialectical approach to the study of the Talmud, some masters earned reputations for logical prowess in proportion to their ability to resolve the logical contradictions they and their students raised. A premium was now placed on *ḥiddushim* (*novellae*), not simply on a clear understanding of the text, as before; and a mystique developed around individual rabbinic masters, similar to the academic reputations of schoolmen such as Abelard. Masters competed for attention on the basis of their new solutions to difficult scholastic problems in the talmudic corpus, and students built their own careers by copying and adding to their masters' glosses, which became known as *tosafot* ("additions" to Rashi's *kunteres,* that is, his *commentarius*).

This new educational ethos was further nurtured by the close social and religious ties that students developed with their mentors. In thirteenth-century Germany, for example, students lived with Rabbi Eleazar of Worms: the master eulogizes his murdered wife for providing for his students' every need. A little later in the century, Rabbi Meir ben Baruch of Rothenburg (*d.* 1293) also housed and fed many students in his home. Behavior as well as intellectual fare was internalized as evidenced by a book written by one of Rabbi Meir's students about his daily habits. The cultural ideal was one of piety as well as of intellectual growth.

In the Spanish schools, three levels of academic achievement were noted in the twelfth century: beginners studied the Pentateuch and the liturgy; advanced students studied in addition the rest of Scripture and the law in codified form; and sages were the very few who progressed to the study of the Mishnah and the Talmud and its commentaries. In their approach to Talmud study as well, the Spanish masters differed from their northern coreligionists. At first, the rabbis in the Muslim centers of Andalusia were heavily dependent on the oral tradition that had been transmitted to Spain from the Jewish talmudic academies of Baghdad. The approach there was conservative, not innovative: the student was supposed to become another link in the oral chain of interpretation derived from Babylonia, where the Talmud had been edited. Spanish rabbis did not assume, in contrast to the dialecticians of northern France and the Rhineland, that a bright student should solve apparent difficulties in the text based on the text itself. Rather, he should rely solely on earlier tradition.

With the Almohad invasion of Andalusia in the twelfth century, talmudic study in Spain moved northward into Christian kingdoms, first of Aragon and then, after the riots of 1391, of Castile. The methods of the Rhenish and northern French Talmud glossators were introduced in the thirteenth century in Barcelona. And after 1391, the academies of Castile combined the more conservative earlier approach with the newer and more daring scholastic modes of study. Even after the Spanish expulsion in 1492, Castilian masters perpetuated distinctive curricular emphases in communities of the Iberian exiles, for instance in Thessaloniki and farther east.

In addition to the religious curriculum of Bible, codes, and some Talmud, the Spanish Jewish elite was encouraged to spend time in the study of the natural sciences and philosophy; logic and mathematics (algebra, geometry); optics, music, and medicine; botany and metallurgy; and eventually, metaphysics. This emphasis in the Sephardic curriculum was introduced in the Muslim south and continued after the Jewish communities in Christian Spain grew to prominence from the twelfth century onward. A major cultural struggle over the allegedly destructive influence of philosophy led to its proscription by the chief rabbi of Barcelona, Rabbi Solomon ben Adret. In 1305, he issued a fifty-year ban against Jews studying natural science (excepting medicine) and philosophy before their twenty-fifth birthday and against anyone teaching it to someone below that age.

This event nearly coincided with the introduction in Toledo by Rabbi Asher ben Jehiel, from Germany, of the northern methods of talmudic study with special emphasis on the Talmud as the apex of the Jewish curriculum. His position as religious judge of Castilian Jewry gave his academy additional prestige. Together, these events served to temper the cultural uniqueness of the Sephardic curriculum and modify it in the direction of the Ashkenazic one. Still, authorities loyal to the Sephardic approach were not completely silenced, and there was criticism in the fourteenth century about the neglect of the Bible and Hebrew grammar.

Despite these changes, the Spanish émigrés to Italy and Holland, for example, preserved much of the special quality of their earlier educational ideal.

When it came to implementing a given curriculum and supervising instruction, fathers and community officials could be involved, depending on circumstances. In the north, many fathers hired tutors for their sons, who were taught on a private basis in their own homes or in the teacher's home. In other cases, the synagogue building would serve as the schoolroom. As early as the thirteenth century, the use of a special room in the synagogue led to the designation of a primary school as a *ḥeder* (room). Teachers there were paid directly by parents or by the community, which sponsored classes, for example for orphans or indigent children.

Regardless of who paid the teacher, the community leaders were involved with teaching arrangements whenever conflicts arose. Teachers were contracted for varying lengths of time, from a few months to a year or more, and problems arose over breach of contract. One way of handling areas of conflict was to place teachers under the supervision of an educational administrator, as in eleventh-century Champagne. The more common solution was for the aggrieved party to appeal for a ruling from recognized rabbinic or communal authorities.

For example, a father appealed to Rabbi Meir of Rothenburg regarding a teacher who had violated a proviso in his contract prohibiting him from gambling. The rabbi decided that the teacher was entitled to his wages up to the time of his dismissal for cause. Another decision was designed to protect a child in a dispute between his father and his tutor. A father hired a tutor for a year and dismissed him before the year was over. Subsequently, the father changed his mind and wanted the teacher to resume his work, but the teacher refused on the grounds that he had been dismissed and thereby released from his contract. Rabbi Meir ruled that the contract was still binding, first because a contract cannot be terminated by verbal means. And even more importantly, the teacher could not be released from his obligation, since a father may not cancel the obligation owed to his son. A father may act as his son's agent to the son's betterment but not, as in this case, to his detriment.

In addition to rulings on Jewish educational matters made by individual rabbinic authorities, Jewish communities held synods from time to time to deal with issues of religious discipline and public welfare. Among the decisions of the joint Rhenish synods of the communities of Mainz, Worms, and Speyer held in the 1220's was a provision that every Jewish male should set aside time for study and that if he could not study Talmud he should study Scripture or classical rabbinic homilies (midrash) according to his ability. More dramatic was the major synod held in Valladolid in 1432 in the wake of the disruptive consequences of the 1391 riots. Additional taxation on the Jewish community was decreed to support Jewish education.

In addition to legal and communal decisions that sought to resolve conflicts or crises arising out of educational issues, some religious leaders also tried to offer practical moral guidance for parents. Thus Rabbi Judah the Pietist counseled parents that a tutor should not be irascible and, even more important, should be God-fearing. The stakes were very high because, as Rabbi Judah put it, children's minds are like the minds of adults when dreaming: they believe that anything can be true.

BIBLIOGRAPHY

Israel Abrahams, *Jewish Life in the Middle Ages* (1896, repr. and rev. 1975); Eliahu Ashtor, "On Jewish Education in Medieval Spain" (in Hebrew), in *Ensyklopedia ḥinukhit,* IV (1964), 241–251; Simḥah Assaf, ed., *Mekorot le-toledot ha-ḥinukh be-yisraʾel,* 4 vols. (1925–1948); Salo W. Baron, *The Jewish Community,* 3 vols. (1948); Moritz Güdemann, *Geschichte des Erziehungswesens und der Kultur der abendländischen Juden während des Mittelalters und der neueren Zeit,* 3 vols. (1880–1888, repr. 1966); Louis I. Rabinowitz, *The Social Life of the Jews of Northern France in the Twelfth Through Fourteenth Centuries* (1938, 2nd ed. 1972); Cecil Roth, *The Jews in the Renaissance* (1959); Isadore Twersky, *Studies in Jewish Law and Philosophy* (1982), 69–75 (Hebrew section).

IVAN G. MARCUS

[See also **Ḥasidei Ashkenaz; Jacob ben Meir; Jewish Communal Self-Government: Europe; Jews in Europe: After 900; Law, Jewish; Maimonidean Controversy; Rabbinate; Rashi (Rabbi Solomon ben Isaac); Talmud, Exegesis and Study of; Thessaloniki.**]

SCHOOLS, MONASTIC. The term "monastic schools" suggests precise definitions that seldom hold up. Tensions resulting from a combination of the words "monk" (solitary) and "school" (group or class) persist. The contributions of monasticism to education are pragmatic compromises between regular and secular, personal salvation and communal evangelism, vocational service and liberal arts. Clerical and monastic are even antagonistic offices, though often filled by the same individuals. Consequently, this article does not treat a culture or a system, but rather pedagogical acts of medieval monks and monastic communities that have advanced education. As Dom Edward C. Butler wrote, "All the services of Benedictines to civilization and education and letters have been but by-products."

Inherent in Christ's life and teaching was a balance between the academic and scriptural. The first, Hellenic, was rhetorical and dialectical, characterized by institutionalism—of master and disciples, of schools and education: Paul schooled Titus and Luke; Peter schooled Mark and Silas; some claim that John schooled Polycarp and Papias. With the admission of gentiles, catechumenate instruction began. The second, Hebraic, centered on the memorized word, on law and prophecy, on fatherhood and brotherhood. During the Nicene period the clergy cultivated Hellenism in metropolitan centers recognized as apostolic sees, accepting classical schooling based on encyclopedic or liberal arts curriculum as fundamental to the verbalized and ritualized Christianity that they regarded as the new philosophy.

Many lay Christians, offended by the arrogance of the imperial clergy and cultivating a puritan asceticism, took the Law, Prophets, Psalms, and Gospels as their guide and ruled themselves as recluses within their own walls or in retreats and deserts, rejecting not only paganism but also the church that had inherited pagan culture. When tolerance ended martyrdom in the fourth century, ascetics took the martyrs' places as "God's athletes," contrasting spiritual regimens with academic disciplines.

Such ascetics formed the monastic wave of the post-Nicene period. They rejected Hellenic science as "learned ignorance" and practiced scriptural "unlearned wisdom." Since "to ruminate" on Scripture, a favorite phrase, required literacy, the anchorites and hermits soon found a need to gather as cenobites for communal study and hours of prayer. Pachomius (*d.* 346), who headed Egyptian communities totaling thousands, established vocational apprenticeships; his regulations included corporate prayer, chant and history, bookmaking, and regular garb. In Cappadocia, Basil's Rule, which determined the course of Eastern monasticism, was a vocational catechism based on poverty, chastity, and obedience; it included prescriptions for training children precedent to vocation. At Bethlehem, Jerome developed a monastery of biblical scholarship. The sweep of public interest in the new monasticism inspired an abundant literature of history and hagiography, such as the *Apophthegmata patrum,* the *Verba seniorum,* Palladius' *Lausiac History,* and Rufinus' *History of the Monks.*

In general, Byzantine and Oriental monks simply Christianized secular learning. But beginning with the Montanist Tertullian, Western ascetics grew increasingly anti-philosophical and inveighed against the pagan arts and sciences; for example, the council of Carthage in 398 prohibited the reading of secular works. Nevertheless, during the fourth and fifth centuries the Roman clergy, largely drawn from the aristocratic class, expected to provide their laity and clergy with disciplined ritual only, in addition to the traditionally pagan public education.

The cenobites, who were settling the wastelands, found it necessary to require postulants to show an elementary literacy before admission. Most frequently their test was recital of the Psalter and Creed. The novice then was apprenticed to an elder who guided his mental and spiritual growth. The poverty, chastity, and obedience that evolved as monastic ideals clearly required physical, verbal, and musical development as the path to salvation, the *opus Dei.*

John Cassian at Marseilles composed his *Institutes* and *Conferences,* and Honoratus began a tradition of learning at Lérins. These and many other founders traveled and observed the centers in Egypt and the Levant. Bishops like Eusebius of Vercelli and Augustine of Hippo organized their clergy into disciplined canonries, partly to impose the celibate life and partly to provide Christian instruction. Augustine's *Confessions* and pedagogical writings, his Neoplatonism and emphasis on the chronology of history at the expense of Greek, free speculation, mathematics, and science, determined an idiom of monastic instruction for subsequent centuries. His exemplar, Archbishop Ambrose of Milan, an ardent sponsor of monasticism, popularized hymnology, which became central to the *opus Dei.* He is the first authenticated practitioner of silent reading, an art apparently unpracticed in antiquity, which became the conventual mode of Benedictines: "They shall rest in their beds with all silence, or he that wishes to read may so read to himself that he do not disturb another" (rule 48).

Scriptural study made writing and bookmaking necessary. As indicated in the earliest monastic literature and regulations, monks thought scribal art the preeminent form of labor. His biographers report that Martin of Tours, the first monk in Gaul, permitted writing as the only art for his brothers because it occupied mind, eye, and hand and aided concentration. Monks determined Western writing practice. They did not invent the vellum codex but popularized it. Pagan Romans disliked animal skins as a writing surface because it was hard on the eyes and possibly because it suggested the barnyard. And the codex form did not appeal because they did not read themselves but were read to. Conversely the monks' basic study was typology, comparing Old and New Testament passages as types. For them, the quick turning of pages was convenient. Leather was durable, indeed everlasting, as compared with fragile papyrus; it matched the scriptural *verbum aeternum.* Monks also popularized minuscule letters, which expressed monastic humility; Carolingian minuscule, which has proved the most popular of all typefaces, was born in abbeys like Corbie and Tours.

As the Roman legions withdrew from Western Europe, public education declined. German rulers generally condemned literacy as a mark of Roman degeneracy. Theodoric, king of the Goths and Romans, was exceptional in supporting grammatical schooling. His master of offices, the Roman Boethius, tried to fill the vacuum left by the dissipation of Greek knowledge, composing tracts and translations that would become the staple of cathedral schools from the late ninth century on. And his successor, Cassiodorus, founded on his Calabrian estates two monasteries for the study of pious and secular learning. Bishops Fulgentius of Ruspe and Caesarius of Arles followed Augustine's model of imposing communal rule on their clergy, providing an education no longer readily available in public schools.

Caesarius was present at the council of Vaison in 529, which decreed: "All priests in the parishes must, as is already the very wholesome custom in all Italy, receive the younger unmarried lectors into their homes and instruct them in the singing of psalms, in the church lessons, and in the law of the Lord, so that they may have able successors." In 527 the Council of Toledo created an episcopal school with a responsible master. Such acts, periodically confirmed throughout the Middle Ages, established the secular clergy as agents responsible for Western education. The "liberal arts" that they inherited tended to follow the sevenfold formula of Capella, Augustine, Cassiodorus, and Isidore (grammar, rhetoric, dialectic, music, arithmetic, geometry, astronomy), but the last three, never important in Latin Rome, evaporated.

Monks as such (increasingly some doubled as priests) had no such responsibility. Their vocation called for schooling for oblates, novices, and religious only. Benedict of Nursia specified disciplined learning of Scripture, exegesis, ritual, and tradition, together with labor enough to make each community economically self-sufficient: three hours of reading a day in winter, two in summer, and a good part of every Lord's day; each monk to receive a volume at the beginning of Lent to be read in extenso, and on permitted journeys a single small volume; at all meals an appointed reader to be heard in silence; the abbot to dispense stylus and wax tablets. The hours of common prayer were seven, with nocturnal vigils and Mass in addition. Every artisan must avoid taking pride in his skill. Oblates (customarily received at age seven) and even adolescents could be corrected by a whipping and the deprivation of food.

Before the sixth century ended, the secular clergy could no longer fulfill the social responsibilities inherited from the empire; suffice to recall the ignominious papacy of Vigilius (*d.* 555). The monks took over. They had trained themselves to the ideal and practice of poverty; often they had settled in virgin land, whereas the secular clergy were enclosed in starving cities. In Isidore's Seville the seculars received at least some of their training in monasteries. The Irish, newly converted by the fifth-century missions of Palladius and Patrick, for the next century and more turned to Gallican and Visigothic models rather than to Roman in forming their clannish church, more monastic than clerical. The Irish missions of the monk Columba to Scotland (*ca.* 563) and the monk Columbanus to Burgundy, Swabia, and Lombardy (*ca.* 590–*ca.* 615) reveal a vocational training that included a smattering of Greek-Christian writings and some pagan Latin, especially grammars, transmitted by apprenticeship, not schools.

In 590 Gregory the Great became the first monk to be elected pope. He had to draw brothers from the cloisters to staff his needs. His mission of Augustine, prior of Gregory's own monastery in

Rome, with monkish companions and successors, established latinate and vocational education at Canterbury. For more than sixty years this English church survived precariously until Pope Vitalian sent the Greek monk Theodore of Tarsus as archbishop and the African Hadrian, then an abbot near Monte Cassino. The two developed a school at Canterbury that became the center of education for all England, admitting not only oblates and novices but clergy and laity as well. A remarkable instance of the new schooling occurred when Pope Agatho sent John, archcantor of St. Peter's and abbot of the monastery of St. Martin in Rome, to Benedict Biscop's monastery in Northumbria in 680. John not only taught the Roman rite throughout the annual cycle, but spread his oral and written lessons to all communities of the province, and left texts behind him when he returned from Britain to Rome.

This Gregorian model of monastic missions, which interchanged with the Irish, circled the Continent with foundations that not only Christianized the Low Countries and Germany but modified existing practices of the Gallican and Gothic clergy. The Merovingians had abetted the decline and disappearance of schools, but their successors, the Carolingians, based in Austrasia, enthusiastically patronized the missionary monks. Lesne and others have shown that although parish and episcopal schools disappeared in each separate province for one generation or several during Merovingian rule, there were always some few schools operating somewhere. King Sigebert of East Anglia returned from schooling in France to establish *paedagogos et magistros iuxta morem Cantuariorum* (instructors and masters according to the Kentish pattern) in his kingdom.

Byzantium experienced no serious breaks in its Hellenic tradition, though under Abbot Theodore (798–826) Studion in Constantinople was a center of learning and book publishing. But "Christendom" was developing as a new Germanized Roman culture that needed schooling. Despite themselves the monks had developed a skill and pedagogy based on values culled from dying Rome suitable for their vocation, which embraced not only worship but domestic economy, *conversatio*. Monasteries, now fast adopting the Benedictine Rule and modifying the Antonian tradition of pure spirituality, readily spread their vocational culture to the public. Bede and Boniface did not regard it as remarkable that kings were schooled by monks.

The large abbeys and canonries began to designate qualified brothers as schoolmasters. Theodore and Hadrian interspersed pious learning with the art of meter, astronomy, and "ecclesiastical arithmetic." "Even today," wrote Bede a generation later, "disciples of theirs remain who know Latin and Greek as well as their native tongue." Except in very special instances Greek knowledge disappeared, but though the monks spoke their several vernaculars in hours of labor, all ritual and instruction continued in patristic Latin, a by-product of the Gregorian missions that extended to the secular church. It dominated all writing. True, Bede and presumably other monks translated Scripture into the vernacular, though his translations have disappeared. Vernacular writing was common in the East (for example, Ulfilas). The oldest Western instance is Cædmon's hymn (*ca.* 680); it was Whitby monks who put in writing all his oral verse. On the Continent vernacular glosses, prayers, verse, translations, colloquies, and even the earliest epics and dramas were nurtured by monks and nuns, for they were the active scribes. The abbeys were virtually the only safe repositories of writing, not only because ascetics were contemplative but because enclosed brotherhoods exercised constant vigilance against fire and rapine. Fires were especially common in Carolingian times because poverty and rulers' fears of revolt discouraged stone building. Though St. Gall is recorded to have burned down five times, its present library contains books written on the spot in the eighth century. Obviously the regulars saved the books.

Charlemagne imposed a catholic uniformity throughout his empire, including the Roman ritual and the Benedictine Rule, but not a common school system. He begged, borrowed, or stole literate masters wherever he could find them to teach in three kinds of schools: palatine, episcopal, and monastic. Into the Germanic system of courtly apprenticeship, consisting essentially of training in chivalry and warfare under the master of equitation, and oral rhetoric and law under the chamberlain, his father, Pepin, and he introduced masters of letters, mainly borrowed or converted monks. Recovering from Merovingian neglect, the priesthood revived training in the liberal arts; but of the formulated seven arts only grammar received much attention. Of professions, medicine disappeared with the disappearance of Greek texts and migrants. Charlemagne treated clerical and monastic schools as one; to the church schools he brought vocational training and to the monasteries lay students: "Et ut scholae, legentium puerorum fiant, psalmos, notas, cantus, compotum, grammaticam, per monasteria vel episcopia et libros catholicos bene emendate" (And that there should be, in monasteries or cathedrals, schools of boys studying psalms, writing, singing, computus, grammar, and well-edited Catholic books; *Admonitio generalis, a.* 789, *c.* 72). Those six subjects were a graded vocational curriculum, inherited primarily from Willibrord, Boniface, and other Insular missionaries.

Psalmi denoted the literacy required of *pulsantes* (petitioners) or knockers (in other words, those who had not yet passed examination in *psalmos*). In addition to psalms it could include primers like the *Distichs of Cato* or the *Liber scintillarum* of Defensor of Ligugé; also Benedict's and other claustral rules, from which evolved the medieval genre of Mirrors for Princes. *Notae* denoted penmanship, required of novices as soon as they acquired elementary literacy. *Notae* were also required for nuns, as indicated by the rules from Caesarius on. The tradition of textbooks *notarum* includes the *De orthographia* of Cassiodorus, of Bede, and of Alcuin. From this study branched the later medieval discipline of letter writing, *ars dictaminis,* evolved from ancient and medieval collections of model letters. Certain episcopal centers like the *Schola cantorum* of Rome and the diocesan school of Chrodegang of Metz (*d.* 766) intensively cultivated *cantus* (chant), but the monastic ritual demanded an equally intense discipline. Hellenic liberal "music" completely disappeared before cantoral oral tradition, except for the verbal texts of hymnody, which began to acquire some written signs (neumes) in the Carolingian period. *Computus* (counting) began as the study of time, because time in all its aspects, from verbal metrics and hours of prayer to the Augustinian Six Ages of the World and Eternity, was essential to the regulated life. The study became extremely complex not only because of the divergences ("paschal controversies") between the Hebraic lunar calendar (source of the movable feasts) and the Roman solar calendar (fixed feasts), but also because every converted people had its own conventions of time that had to be reconciled; for example, there were more than a score of conflicting New Years. The monks, because of their stability and because of insoluable rivalries among apostolic bishops, included in *computus* searching studies of astronomy, arithmetic, general science *(natura rerum)*, history, and hagiography.

Monastic histories consisted of two genres: (1) chronicles and annals, which were extensions of Eusebius' *Chronicon,* which evolved from annotated calendars, and (2) tribal histories inspired by the notion of a chosen people, such as the Gothic histories of Cassiodorus and Jordanes, the Visigothic history of Isidore, the Frankish history of Gregory of Tours, the English history of Bede, and the Lombard history of Paul. The monks did not produce secular histories of the classic type, such as Orosius' *Universal History* or Einhard's *Life of Charlemagne.* Their hagiography, closely bound to the liturgical calendar, was normally composed in prose for lections and sermons, but both masters and students incessantly composed metrical saints' lives as grammatical exercises; they pointed the way to both drama and epic. *Grammatica* was not the elementary study of letters embraced in *psalmi,* but an advanced study of figured language (for example, Bede's *De schematibus et tropis*) and metered verse (his *De arte metrica*), largely derived from Jerome and drawing upon the Christian Latin poets. Some rigidly selected pagan literature (Vergil, Cicero, Horace, Terence, Sallust), usually excerpts or florilegia, was sometimes studied. To these should be added Theodore and Hadrian's "ecclesiastical arithmetic," that is, number symbolism, so intensively promulgated by Augustine as a key to the scriptural life.

Rhetoric in the ancient sense was avoided. Alcuin, who was not a monk until his retirement as abbot of Tours, tried to revive classical rhetoric for the palace school, and his pupil Hrabanus was among the first to describe it and dialectic as liberal arts; but only after Boethius' writings began to penetrate the cathedral schools did they become part of the curriculum. *Libri catholici bene emendate* was the final study, continued by the masterful all their lives. They rigorously re-edited and preserved canonical scriptures and patristic commentary (exegesis), homilies, lexicons, and glossaries. The latter gave rise to lapidaries, bestiaries, and herbals. The most sacred writings were assigned only to the most able scribes.

Charlemagne blurred distinctions among his three types of schools, but his successor, Louis the Pious, under the influence of Benedict, abbot of Aniane (*d.* 821), summoned reforming councils to Aachen in 816 and 817 with the purpose of returning monasticism to the practice of the desert Fathers, removing all secularity from the cloisters as disruptive to spirituality: "No school shall be kept in a monastery except for oblates." Such reforms, continued through the Middle Ages, tended to limited responsibility for public education to secular clergy and palatine schools. Those abbeys that continued to teach seculars separated them from the oblates and novices, sending their masters to classrooms in town or, as in the "Plan of St. Gall," establishing a schoolroom outside the cloister but within the abbatial community; so, apparently, Notker Balbulus (*d.* 912) became master of the external school and Ratpert the internal. By the middle of the century the important masters were transferring from abbeys to cathedrals (Heiric and Remigius, for example), and even to palaces (John Scottus at Laon). With the development of the Cluniac order the influence of monasteries in Frankish education waned. A last important abbatial school was Lanfranc and Anselm's at Bec.

The Saxon emperors of the tenth century in Lotharingia and the east revived monasticism as a social arm, however, and used episcopal, collegiate, and monastic personnel interchangeably. Thus, scholars such as Gerbert at Rheims (later Pope Sylvester II), Eracle of Liège, whose disciple Dunstan spread Lotharingian monks and ideas through England, and Godehard of Hildesheim greatly influenced education. The Byzantine princess Theophano traveled the length of the empire in company with abbots and bishops, absorbing and spreading Greek and Italian lore, if not language, that modified the Carolingian curricula, especially with Boethian dialectic and the fresh study of natural science, as in the case of Hermannus Contractus of Reichenau.

Pre-Reformation complaints that cloistered monks of the later Middle Ages had so neglected their internal schools as to tolerate illiteracy are borne out by many documents, such as the edict of Pope Benedict XII in 1336 that all convents of Black Monks "of sufficient means" keep a master to teach the monks *sciencias primitivas,* that is, grammar, logic, and philosophy. Each convent was to send one-twentieth of its number to the universities; but that quota apparently was seldom if ever filled.

As towns and commerce expanded, diocesan cloisters of canons regular and collegiate churches, now adopting updated Augustinian rules, dominated higher education. Whether they should properly be considered monastic schools is doubtful. An exemplary instance is the abbey of St. Victor, founded by William of Champeaux (1113) and endowed by Louis VI. Hugh of that house composed numerous didactic works that marked the path to the university age. It is paradoxical that such contemplatives should make the twelfth century a great age of historiography (Orderic, Guibert, Suger, Otto of Freising). Likewise guesthouses of convents on "the pilgrim roads" became informal schools for admixing monks with crusaders, wandering knights, traders, and singers sacred and profane in Latin and the vernacular.

Even more questionable is the role played by the mendicant friars, regarded as regular but uncloistered ascetics. Though they founded, taught in, and patronized schools of every persuasion and dominated the universities, the cleavage between Franciscan Conventuals and Spirituals indicates how ambiguous was the relation of friars to the field of education. One should recall the story of Francis' refusal to allow possession of a single work of learning: "After you have a psalter, you will covet a breviary. And after you have a breviary you will sit like a great prelate and say to your brother, 'Fetch me the breviary.'" So, too, with the wide variety of later schools fostered by ascetics of benevolent aims, from the almonry schools and Brethren of the Common Life of the fourteenth century to the communities of "flower children" of the twentieth. Though monasticism has left permanent marks on Western education, its role has been ancillary.

BIBLIOGRAPHY

Sources. Bede, *Bedae Venerabilis Opera Didascalica,* 3 vols., in *Corpus Christianorum Series Latina,* CXXIII (1975–1980); Benedict of Nursia, *The Rule of Saint Benedict, in Latin and English,* Justin McCann, ed. and trans (1952); Cassiodorus, *Cassiodori Senatoris Institutiones,* R. A. B. Mynors, ed. (1937); Hugo of St. Victor, *Didascalicon,* Jerome Taylor, trans. (1961).

Studies. Gustave Bardy, "Les origines des écoles monastiques en Occident," in *Sacris erudiri,* 5 (1953); Ursmer Berlière, "Écoles claustrales au moyen âge," in *Bulletin de la classe des lettres de l'Académie Royal de Belgique* (1921); James Bowen, *A History of Western Education,* I (1972) and II (1975); Dom Edward Cuthbert Butler, *Benedictine Monachism,* 2nd ed. (1924, repr. 1962); Solange Corbin, *L'église à la conquête de sa musique* (1960); Jacques Fontaine, *Isidore de Seville et la culture classique dans l'Espagne wisigothique,* 2 vols. (1959); Werner Jaeger, *Early Christianity and Greek Paideia* (1961); David Knowles, *The Monastic Order in England,* 2nd ed. (1963); Jean Leclercq, *The Love of Learning and the Desire for God: A Study of Monastic Culture,* Catherine Misrahi, trans., 2nd rev. ed. (1974);

Emile Lesne, *Histoire de la propriété ecclésiastique en France,* V: *Les écoles de la fin du VIIIe siècle à la fin du XIIe siècle* (1940); Wilhelm Levison, *England and the Continent in the Eighth Century* (1946); Aimée Lorcin, "La vie scolaire dans les monastères d'Irlande aux Ve–VIIe siècles," in *Revue du moyen âge latin,* 1 (1945); Henri Marrou, *A History of Education in Antiquity,* George Lamb, trans. (1956), and *Saint Augustin et la fin de la culture antique,* 4th ed. (1958); Gerard Paré *et al., La renaissance du XIIe siècle: Les écoles et l'enseignement* (1933); Friedrich Prinz, *Mönchtum und Gesellschaft im Frühmittelalter* (1976); Pierre Riché, *Education and Culture in the Barbarian West,* John J. Contreni, trans. (1976).

CHARLES W. JONES

[See also **Anchorites; Arts, Seven Liberal; Brethren of the Common Life; Calendars and Reckoning of Time; Canterbury; Carolingians and the Carolingian Empire; Cato's Distichs; Chivalry; Church, Latin; Clergy; Computus; Dictamen; Franciscans; Hermits, Eremitism; Historiography, Western European; Medicine, History of; Mendicant Orders; Merovingians; Mirror of Princes; Monasticism, Byzantine; Monasticism, Origins; Pepin III and the Donation of Pepin; Quadrivium; Rhetoric; Sex Aetates Mundi; Trivium;** and individual personalities.]

SCHOOLS, PALACE. Schools (*scholae*) were a prominent feature of court life in many barbarian monarchies during the early Middle Ages. *Schola* seems not to have had a precise, fixed meaning. Most historians prefer to translate *schola* as "the group or corporation of young people at court." Many ecclesiastical and secular officials received their early training at court. Children usually joined the palace entourage shortly after puberty. To judge from some of the school texts created by the masters, instruction was quite elementary. Riddles, jokes, and question-and-answer dialogues between masters and students seem to have been the chief pedagogical methods employed.

The training dispensed at the palace was essentially vocational. Young princes and the sons of nobles who were sent to court for instruction and to cement the ties of their families to the king were schooled in the military and bureaucratic duties they would later assume. In the early Frankish courts, supervision of the young people was entrusted to the mayor of the palace. The atmosphere in the palace schools was quite informal. There was no fixed curriculum. Instruction could take place anywhere in the palace, including in the baths, and at any time. Relationships among students and their mentors was quite convivial. Some texts complain of excessive drinking. Some parents worried about the immorality at court.

The best-known palace school was that of the Carolingians, particularly during the reign of Charlemagne (768–814), when masters such as Alcuin and Einhard were among those who directed the school. Royal patronage made the palace a magnet that attracted poets, grammarians, and liturgists from Ireland, Anglo-Saxon England, Spain, and Italy. It was the most literary of the early court schools. The notaries in the royal chancery, the manuscript illuminators, the scribes responsible for disseminating Carolingian minuscule, and medical practitioners were all linked to the school. Later Carolingian kings continued to draw scholars to their courts. In the Carolingian view, the school served a sharply defined function: to establish norms of behavior and practice and to produce individuals capable of realizing the ideal of a Christian society.

Later in the ninth century, the Anglo-Saxon Alfred the Great established a school at his court, while on the Continent some tenth-century nobles in France and Germany continued the tradition of the palace school. By the eleventh and twelfth centuries, the academic functions of the palace school had been taken over by the monastic, cathedral, and municipal schools, and, later, by the universities. The courts continued to remain centers of artistic and literary patronage.

BIBLIOGRAPHY

Franz Brunhölzl, "Der Bildungsauftrag der Hofschule," in Bernhard Bischoff, ed., *Karl der Grosse: Lebenswerk und Nachleben,* II: *Das geistige Leben* (1965); Donald Bullough, *The Age of Charlemagne,* 2nd ed. (1973); John J. Contreni, *The Cathedral School of Laon from 850 to 930: Its Manuscripts and Masters* (1978); Heinrich Fichtenau, *The Carolingian Empire,* Peter Munz, trans. (1957); Pierre Riché, *Education and Culture in the Barbarian West,* John J. Contreni, trans. (1976), and *Les écoles et l'enseignement dans l'Occident chrétien de la fin du Ve siècle au milieu du XIe siècle* (1979); Richard E. Sullivan, *Aix-la-Chapelle in the Age of Charlemagne* (1963).

JOHN J. CONTRENI

[See also **Alcuin of York; Alfred the Great; Carolingians and the Carolingian Empire; Charlemagne; Einhard; Mayor of the Palace; Universities.**]

SCHRÄTEL UND DER WASSERBÄR, DAS. The Heidelberg manuscript Cpg. 341 preserves a 352-line *Märe* known as *Das Schrätel und der Wasserbär* (following the superscription in the manuscript) or, in standard German, *Kobold und Eisbär.* It was earlier attributed to Heinrich von Freiberg, author of minor religious and chivalric poems as well as a conclusion to Gottfried von Strassburg's *Tristan und Isolde.* This attribution is, however, rejected in more recent scholarship, and the tale is judged anonymous. Probably written around 1300, it tells the following story.

The king of Norway decides to send a tame polar bear to the king of Denmark. Upon landing in Denmark, the man entrusted with the beast seeks shelter for the night at a prosperous farm. His host welcomes him courteously but warns him that a goblin has taken over the premises; no one can match its strength and fury, the house is a wreck, and the farmer and his family are living in the fields. Trusting to God, the visitor goes inside nonetheless; he and the bear eat a hearty meal, then fall asleep by the fire. The goblin appears and begins to roast meat on a spit. He notices the unfamiliar animal and decides to drive it away. Hit three times with the spit, the bear attacks; a fierce battle ensues for hours, and the goblin finally flees, defeated. In the morning the visitors depart. As the farmer goes to work in his fields, the battered goblin appears and asks if the "great big cat" still lives. The farmer says it does indeed, and that it has given birth to five kittens. Aghast at the prospect of five more foes as powerful as the first, the goblin flees and leaves the farm in peace.

Based on a folktale, this story is set on a farm but told in the manner of a chivalric adventure. There is droll juxtaposition of rural detail, such as foodstuffs and furnishings, with phraseology and motifs drawn from courtly literature. The author, well versed in the latter, brought its style to his humble subject with amusing results.

BIBLIOGRAPHY

The text is in Friedrich Heinrich von der Hagen, ed., *Gesammtabenteuer,* III (1850, repr. 1961), 261–270. See also Hanns Fischer, *Studien zur deutschen Märendichtung* (1983), 362–363; Stephen L. Wailes, "Social Humor in Middle High German Mären," in *Amsterdamer Beiträge zur älteren Germanistik,* **10** (1976).

STEPHEN L. WAILES

[See also **Heinrich von Freiberg; Mären; Middle High German Literature.**]

Christ carrying the cross. Panel painting by Hans Schüchlein from the high altar at Tiefenbronn (1469). ART RESOURCE/FOTO MARBURG

SCHÜCHLEIN, HANS (Schüchlin), Swabian painter of the last third of the fifteenth century. His high altar at Tiefenbronn (1469) shows the powerful influence of contemporary Flemish art. He is documented in Ulm from 1468 to 1503. Schüchlein's work features stiff, slender figures and grimacing henchmen scattered throughout flat, richly described landscapes. His son-in-law was the painter Bartholomäus Zeitblom (*d.* 1518/1522).

BIBLIOGRAPHY

Alfred Stange, *German Painting: XIV–XVI Centuries* (1950) and *Deutsche Malerei der Gotik,* VIII (1957, repr. 1969), 13–16.

LARRY SILVER

[See also **Gothic Art: Painting and Manuscript Illumination.**]

SCHÜLER VON PARIS, DER (The student of Paris), an anonymous Middle High German verse tale extant in three very different versions. The basic plot is as follows: A young nobleman, as a student (*schuolere*) in Paris, falls in love with the daughter of a rich and very protective burgher. The lovers find a way to meet, but in their passionate embrace the youth suddenly dies. At the funeral mass the broken-hearted girl expires. The true lovers are buried together.

Version *C* of about 1300 (now in Munich, 702 lines) is the simplest and seems closest to the original. The student is the son of a baron, and 322 lines are given to his introduction, parentage, and upbringing. He dies and is found in the garden. The writer is from Thuringia, his style influenced by Konrad von Würzburg.

In version *B* of the early fourteenth century (now in Vienna, 704 lines), the hero is a count, and the young lady is kept locked up in a tower. This added fairy-tale element increases the difficulty of the lovers' meeting and of removing the corpse. The writer is from northern Bohemia, and he knows the *C* version.

The *A* version comes in two redactions: one of 1,116 lines preserved in a manuscript now in Heidelberg, and one of 792 lines preserved in three manuscripts. Of these three manuscripts, the one now in Pommersfelden, late thirteenth century, written in East Thuringian dialect, is the oldest. Here the student, an English nobleman, dies from a hemorrhage resulting from a bloodletting earlier that day. The girl's lengthy lament is laced with scholarly ornament borrowed from the *Physiologus,* and farcical elements are added: a monk as go-between, and a friend dressed up as a maid who removes the corpse. The poet's style is much influenced by Wolfram von Eschenbach, Konrad von Würzburg, Heinrich von Morungen, and Hartmann von Aue. In turn, the *A* version seems to have influenced version *C*.

The courtly sentimental love story is strongly erotic and, in part, reminiscent of the Tristan legend. Comparison with later treatments of the theme (Boccaccio's *Decameron,* IV, 6 and 8) leaves little doubt that the ultimate source is a French fabliau. Classical models can be found in the stories of Hero and Leander and Pyramus and Thisbe.

BIBLIOGRAPHY

Hanns Fischer, *Studien zur deutschen Märendichtung,* 2nd ed. (1983); Hans-Friedrich Rosenfeld, *Mittelhochdeutsche Novellenstudien* (1927, repr. 1967) and "Der Schüler von Paris," in *Die deutsche Literatur des Mittelalters: Verfasserlexikon,* IV (1953); Karl-Heinz Schirmir, *Stil- und Motivuntersuchungen zur mittelhochdeutschen Versnovelle* (1969).

KLAUS WOLLENWEBER

[See also **Fabliau and Comic Tale; Hartmann von Aue; Heinrich von Morungen; Konrad von Würzburg; Middle High German Literature; Wolfram von Eschenbach.**]

SCHWABENSPIEGEL. The name *Schwabenspiegel* (Swabian mirror) was assigned in the seventeenth century to an anonymous German legal work dating from 1275/1276. It draws on the *Deutschenspiegel,* a lawbook whose principal component is a thirteenth-century High German adaptation of the *Sachsenspiegel* (Saxon mirror), and additional material from Roman and canon law and from other sources.

Thus, the *Schwabenspiegel,* which originated in Augsburg, contains the same customary and feudal laws as the *Sachsenspiegel,* plus references from Bavarian law *(Lex Baiuvariorum),* Carolingian capitularies, German imperial law, and Roman and canon law. References to works of various authors are also included, such as those of Isidore of Seville, Berthold von Regensburg (*d.* 1272), and David of Augsburg (*d.* 1271). The laws enumerated in the *Schwabenspiegel,* divided into both articles and chapters, concern inheritance and the family, as well as criminal and public, law. Its sections on private and civil law and legal procedure are the same as those sections in the *Deutschenspiegel.* The popularity of the *Schwabenspiegel* is demonstrated in the fact that it was subsequently translated into Latin, French, and Czech.

The *Schwabenspiegel* also reflects the politics of the interregnum (1254–1273) in Germany. It indicates how weak the German monarchy became after the death of Frederick II (1250) by demonstrating that the German princes and the papacy gained control of the elective powers governing the choice of the German king.

Much like the *Sachsenspiegel,* the *Schwabenspiegel* influenced many other lawbooks, especially that of Ruprecht von Freising, whose work (1328) comprises the laws and institutions of fourteenth-century Holland. Many of the laws in Ruprecht's book are taken directly from the *Schwabenspiegel,* particularly those regarding theft, Jews, and inheritance. The *Schwabenspiegel* also had an influence on the laws of Louis IV the Bavarian and on the fourteenth-century municipal laws of Munich. Furthermore, it served as the basis for one other lawbook, known as the *Frankenspiegel,* which originated in Hesse between 1328 and 1338. The *Frankenspiegel* is divided into four parts: court procedures; civil, criminal, and public law; feudal law; and municipal law. It shows the influence of Louis IV the Bavarian (1314–1346) and reveals his strong and continued opposition to Pope John XXII. Because of Louis' influence, the *Frankenspiegel* is also known as *Das kleine Kaiserrecht.*

BIBLIOGRAPHY

Sources. Heinrich Gengler, ed., *Des Schwabenspiegels Landrechtsbuch,* 2nd ed. (1875); Karl A. Eckhardt and Alfred Hübner, eds., *Deutschenspiegel,* in *Monumenta Germaniae historica: Fontes iuris germanici antiqui,* n.s. III (1933); Karl A. Eckhardt and Rudolf Grosse, eds., *Schwabenspiegel,* in *Monumenta Germaniae historica: Fontes iuris germanici antiqui,* n.s. IV and V (1960–1964).

Studies. Karl A. Echkardt, *Der Deutschenspiegel: Seine Entstehungsgeschichte und sein Verhältnis zum Schwabenspiegel* (1924), "Heimat und Alter des Deutschenspiegels," in *Zeitschrift der Savigny-Stiftung für Rechtsgeschichte,* **45** (1925), *Rechtsbucherstudien,* I (1927), and "Zur Schulausgabe des Deutschenspiegels," in *Zeitschrift der Savigny-Stiftung für Rechtsgeschichte,* **50** (1930); Lutz Hatzfeld, "Frankenspiegel oder Kaiserrecht?" in *Tijdschrift voor Rechtsgeschiedenis,* **26** (1958); Ernst Klebel, "Studien zu den Fassungen und Handschriften des Schwabenspiegels," in *Mitteilungen des Instituts für österreichische Geschichtsforschung,* **44** (1930); Hans Lentze, *Die Kurzform des Schwabenspiegels* (1938); Claudius F. von Schwerin, "Zum Problem des Deutschenspiegels," in *Zeitschrift der Savigny-Stiftung für Rechtsgeschichte,* **52** (1932).

THEODORE JOHN RIVERS

[See also **Berthold von Regensburg; Law Codes: 1000–1500; Law, German: Post-Carolingian; Sachsenspiegel; Two Swords, Doctrine of.**]

SCIENCE, ISLAMIC. The term "Islamic science," like the alternative term "Arabic science," refers to the scientific endeavors of individuals and institutions in the medieval world of Islam. These endeavors began in the middle of the eighth century, in the form of a vigorous translation effort centered in Baghdad, which continued throughout the ninth and into the tenth century. They reached their highest levels of achievement at different times and places over a period extending to the beginning of the fifteenth century. Afterward came a period of stagnation and even impoverishment, though faint traces of this tradition were still to be seen in the Middle East when Napoleon led his expedition to Egypt in 1798, bringing with it some of the early seeds of a new scientific awakening.

Some of the products of Islamic science—Arabic translations of Greek scientific, philosophical, and medical works, and treatises originally written in Arabic and in which ideas and techniques from different ancient sources had been amalgamated, systematized, and expanded—played an important part in bringing about a renaissance of learning in Europe when these works became available in Latin translations made in Sicily and Spain in the twelfth and thirteenth centuries. This Arabo-Latin transmission of scientific knowledge took place when Islamic science was still to make further progress in its own habitat for some two hundred years, and it fell far short of being a wholesale transfer of Islamic accomplishments in the preceding centuries. While a few of the Arabic translations and treatises now survive only in Latin versions (such as works by al-Khwārizmī, al-Kindī, and Ptolemy), the full record of the Islamic achievement in the sciences is now to be found in manuscripts that, despite the hazards of history, have been preserved in large numbers in libraries scattered over the Middle East, Asia, Europe, and the United States, where the great majority of them await study.

Those who carried on this tradition were, throughout its duration, individuals of different ethnic origins who came from various parts of the vast Muslim world; many were Christians and, in the initial period, some were pagans, and some were Jews. The use of the terms "Arabic" and "Islamic" to characterize their work is meant to signal two facts without which we can hardly understand their activities as a single, continuous tradition. The first is the predominance of Arabic as the language of scientific expression and communication. It was through the vehicle of Arabic that a non-Arab scholar in eleventh-century Nīshāpūr or fifteenth-century Samarkand had access to the results arrived at in ninth- or tenth-century Baghdad, and an astronomer working in fourteenth-century Damascus became acquainted with writings produced in eleventh-century Cairo, twelfth-century Spain, or thirteenth-century Maragheh (Marāgha). And while some scientific treatises began to be composed in languages other than Arabic (mostly Persian but sometimes also Turkish) from the eleventh century onward, Arabic remained the language mostly preferred by Arabs and non-Arabs writing on scientific matters. The second fact is the centrality of Islamic religion to the civilization that gave birth and nourishment to the new scientific tradition—a centrality that makes Islam the point of reference (though not always the premise) for all cultural activities, however heterogeneous they may be in origin or character. "Arabic" and "Islamic" are consequently used here interchangeably, in the sense just indicated, to denote one and the same entity, though sometimes with different emphases. (The reader should know, however, that by "the Arabic sciences" [*ᶜulūm al-ᶜarabīya*] medieval scholars themselves understood those disciplines, such as grammar and philology, which were concerned with the Arabic language, and they referred to such sciences as mathematics and astronomy as "the sciences of the ancients" [*ᶜulūm al-awāᵓil*], a designation correctly indicating their origin, while reserving the expression "Islamic sciences" to the newly developed branches of religious studies, such as the study of law or theology.)

THE ANCIENT HERITAGE

The Greco-Arabic transmission of science and philosophy has been described as a "continuation" of the Greek tradition or as a "reception" of the ancient legacy into the new civilization. Neither description is correct without serious qualification. "Reception" might imply a passive attitude on the part of the recipient, which certainly was not the attitude of the Muslims who urged, supported, and participated in the transmission process. As for the continuity of Hellenism, it is known that Greek science, after a golden age during the Hellenistic period, had begun to decline sharply in the third century A.D. and had ceased to show any signs of real vigor after the murder of the Neoplatonic philosopher Hypatia by a Christian mob in Alexandria in 415. To be sure, the ninth and tenth centuries witnessed a spectacular revival of Hellenism in the arabized Middle East; but this important event is better described as an act of appropriation that can be understood only in terms of the motivations, ideals, and interests of the appropriators, and not merely as a consequence of the circumstances left behind in the same area by the earlier penetration of Greek culture.

It is important for appreciating the extent and the consequences of the translation effort in the eighth and ninth centuries to realize that it was almost entirely a patronized activity that received full support and encouragement from the rulers and elites of the Islamic society. Some translations (particularly of alchemical writings) are said to have been made already under the Umayyads at Damascus. But it was not until the accession of the Abbasids to the caliphate in the middle of the eighth century, with Baghdad as the new capital, that the translation effort grew into an enterprise of enormous dimensions. At first the scientific texts rendered into Arabic were astronomical works originally written in Sanskrit and Middle Persian (Pahlavi). But before the end of the reign of Hārūn al-Rashīd (786–809), and at his court, masterpieces of Greek science such as the *Elements* of Euclid and the *Almagest* of Ptolemy had already been made available to readers of Arabic. During al-Maᵓmūn's caliphate (813–833), the Library of Philosophical Sciences (Khizānat al-Ḥikma), already in existence during al-Rashīd's reign, was transformed into an important institute, known as Bayt al-Ḥikma (House of Wisdom), for the translation of Greek scientific works and the promotion of their study. This work was urged on by the caliph himself or by people closely associated with his court and dependent upon it. Stories tell of al-Maᵓmūn's personal interest in the scholars he employed as astonomers, astrologers, mathematicians, and translators. One story even ascribed the whole translation project to a dream in which al-Maᵓmūn took advice from none other than Aristotle. Historical sources associate Yaḥyā ibn Khālid al-Barmakids, the powerful and enlightened Iranian vizier who served al-Rashīd from 786 to 803, with the first translations of Euclid's *Elements* and Ptolemy's *Almagest,* as well as with translations of literary works from Pahlavi. Three intellectually talented individuals, the Banū Mūsā or Sons of Mūsā ibn Shākir, who during al-Maᵓmūn's life had studied at Bayt al-Ḥikma, patronized distinguished translators, such as Ḥunayn ibn Isḥāq (809/810–877) and Thābit ibn Qurra (836–901), and were also personally active in procuring Greek manuscripts from Byzantium.

The agents of transmission—the individuals without whose expertise and readiness to make the ancient texts available in the language of their patrons there would have been no Arabic science as we know it—belonged to various ethnic groups and professed different faiths. The majority of them were Christians, mostly members of the Nestorian sect founded in the fifth century who had carried on a tradition of learning in medicine, philosophy, and theology in schools and monasteries dispersed over the Near East and Central Asia. The greatest among them was Ḥunayn ibn Isḥāq, of the Arab tribe of al-ᶜIbādi from al-Ḥīra in southern Iraq. He trained and led a number of translators, including his son Isḥāq, who were responsible for putting into Arabic (and Syriac) a very considerable portion of Greek medical, philosophical, and mathematical writings. Many of the Arabic translations were made through the intermediary of Syriac, but Ḥunayn himself and his son were able to translate directly from Greek.

The Sabaeans (Mandaeans) of Ḥarrān in northern Mesopotamia, remnants of an ancient, Semitic, pagan community that had retained a strongly Hellenized culture, contributed another important translator, especially of Greek mathematical works, in the person of Thābit ibn Qurra. Astrology had played a central role in Sabaean religious lore, and this was connected with an interest in astronomy and mathematics. The Sabaeans' knowledge of Greek and Syriac (the latter being their native tongue and the language of their liturgy and religious literature) obviously qualified the learned among them for the translation work that was in great demand in ninth-century Baghdad.

The result of these efforts over a period of roughly 150 years was that the Arabic language came to acquire a scientific legacy never before equaled in richness and variety. Through the early translations from Sanskrit and Pahlavi, Islamic scholars became acquainted with distinctive Indian astronomical concepts and methods of numerical computation. After the deluge of translations from Greek and Syriac they gained possession of the bulk of Hellenistic science and a very considerable amount of Greek philosophy. Thus, to give just a very few examples, in medicine they came to know most of the Hippocratic and Galenic writings and their derivatives; in philosophy, the works of Aristotle, some of Plato's dialogues, and a substantial number of the Greek commentaries on the Aristotelian corpus; and in the exact sciences, practically every classic of elementary and higher mathematics—by Euclid, Archimedes, Apollonius of Perga, Ptolemy, Diophantus, and others. Scientific translations had of course been made earlier in the Middle East and Central Asia—from Greek into Sanskrit and Pahlavi, or from Sanskrit into Pahlavi, or, most important, from Greek into Syriac. But never before had there been so many translations from so many sources into one language. This fact is important for understanding not only the role of Islamic civilization as a transmitter of scientific knowledge, but also some of the distinctive features of Arabic science.

It is not difficult to think of practical motives behind the interest of the early caliphs in the "ancient sciences." Alchemy, one of the earliest of these sciences to attract their attention, was full of the promise of untold riches. Astronomy and astrology were closely related, and belief in the use of astrology was widespread among the learned as well as the ignorant. Knowledge of mathematics was essential for certain engineering projects, and medicine was obviously beneficial. A fuller and more satisfactory explanation would, however, have to view the translation movement as part of the intellectual ferment that gripped Islamic society in the centuries following the Arab conquests. Nor would it be farfetched to seek a large part of the explanation in the genuine curiosity and intellectual ambition of those, like the ninth-century Muslim philosopher al-Kindī, who found Greek thought inherently attractive and who worked hard to make it a permanent possession of Islamic society.

With the decline of Abbasid power and the eventual breakup of the Abbasid empire, centers of learning multiplied across the Islamic world following the proliferation of dynastic rules that vied with one another for cultural and intellectual eminence as well as for political power. Court patronage, now multiple and dispersed, continued to be the predominant form of support under which scientific activities flourished. In Cairo the Fatimid caliph al-Ḥākim (996–1021) founded in 1004 a large public library, Dār al-ᶜIlm (House of Science), which continued to exist as a center of Ismaili propaganda until 1171, when it was closed by the Ayyubids. The library was said to contain a large number of books on all branches of knowledge, many of which came from the caliph's own renowned collection. Al-Ḥākim's interest in astrology must have had something to do with his patronage of the astronomer Ibn Yūnus (*d.* 1009), who had previously served his father, and he was able to attract another famous mathematician, al-Ḥasan ibn al-Haytham (*d. ca.* 1040), from Iraq to work on a project for regulating the flow of the Nile. During roughly the same period of time (first half of the eleventh century), the vicissitudes of political life in Central Asia forced the great al-Bīrūnī (*d. ca.* 1050) to seek support from one dynastic rule after another—Samanid, Ziyarid, Ghaznavid. Later in the same century the algebraist al-Khayyāmī (Omar Khayyām) for many years enjoyed the support of the Seljuk sultan Jalāl al-Dīn Malikshāh (*r.* 1072–1092) at Isfahan, working on a solar-calendrical reform, having been patronized for some time earlier by the chief judge at Samarkand, Abū Ṭāhir, to whom he had dedicated his treatise on cubic equations. Under the rule of the Almohads, and somehow in harmony with their expressed ideology, twelfth-century Spain witnessed a flowering of philosophical, medical, and astronomical thought associated with the names of Ibn Rushd (Averroës), Abū Marwān ibn Zuhr (Avenzoar, *ca.* 1092–1162), and al-Biṭrūjī (Alpetragius, *fl. ca.* 1190), respectively. In the thirteenth century the Mongols founded an observatory at Maragheh (Marāgha) in Azerbaijan, where the Persian mathematician Naṣīr al-Dīn al-Ṭūsī (1201–1274) assembled a distinguished and active group of scholars from various parts of the Islamic world. And, in fifteenth-century Samarkand, it was in the college-cum-observatory institution (madrasa) founded and supervised by the scientist-prince Ulugh Beg (*d.* 1449), grandson of Tamerlane, that Ghiyāth al-Dīn Jamshīd al-Kāshī (*d.* 1429), as the most distinguished member of the group of scientists gathered there, did his remarkably original work in numerical analysis.

In the early period, not only were important scholars such as Ḥunayn (a Nestorian Christian) and Thābit (a Mandaean, Sabian "pagan") non-Muslims, but they owed their knowledge of Greek language and thought to pre-Islamic institutions that had survived under Islam. By contrast, the majority of scientists patronized in later centuries across the Muslim world were Muslims who knew no Greek, who sought no means of learning it, and who gained their education (scientific and otherwise) mainly through Arabic. It is certain that a strong scientific tradition continued to exist under these circumstances for a long time, and that individuals who distinguished themselves in the sciences often enjoyed the support of rulers and rich notables. But we are still far from clear as to how these individuals managed to master and convey difficult scientific matters in a large variety of fields. One important favorable condition for what appears to have been a remarkably fast and easy diffusion of scientific knowledge was undoubtedly the wide use of paper (as distinguished from papyrus or parchment) and the consequent availability of manuscripts at a relatively cheap cost. The Muslims had learned the technique of papermaking from Chinese prisoners of war in the middle of the eighth century; soon thereafter the manufacture of various types of paper had quickly spread westward from Samarkand, where the Chinese art had been first introduced, to Baghdad, Cairo, Yemen, and Spain. Already in the ninth and tenth centuries papermaking was a flourishing business in Iran and Iraq, and urban cultural centers like Basra and Baghdad contained special quarters in which manuscripts were sold, bought, and copied. Thus, while well-known scholars enjoyed the rich resources provided by their patrons, others were able to obtain literary, philosophical, and scientific works in the marketplace. Early in the ninth century, to buy a copy of the *Almagest* in Baghdad, the young Sanad ibn ᶜAlī, the son of a Jewish astrologer, who later became a mathematician and astronomer of note, sold his father's donkey to raise enough money. In eleventh-century Bukhara the young Ibn Sīnā was able to obtain a commentary by al-Fārābī on Aristotle's *Metaphysics* for only three dirhams (admittedly an exceptionally low price). And in the same century Ibn al-Haytham, who spent the later part of his life in Cairo living on what he earned from copying mathematical texts, wrote a commentary on the *Almagest* in a style that expressly assumed the easy availability of Ptolemy's book.

INSTITUTIONS OF ISLAMIC SCIENCE

Another factor following from the widespread use of paper and the abundance of manuscripts was the proliferation of libraries throughout the Islamic world. Some of these, for example palace libraries like Bayt al-Ḥikma, were not public in the proper sense, but they were available at least to the scholars employed by the caliph. And the large library established by the Fatimids in Cairo is said to have been for public use and to have also functioned as a place for instruction. Private libraries existed in very large numbers, and they must have played a part in the dissemination of scientific knowledge. As for the libraries attached to mosques and madrasas, they were for all to use, being charitable endowments for the benefit of all Muslims.

The observatory, as a full-fledged scientific institution that was furnished with a building, a permanent staff, a library, and an assortment of astronomical instruments, was a creation of Islamic civilization. It, too, contributed to the promotion of the mathematical sciences. But being dependent on the fortunes or the whims of the royal patron, and undoubtedly also because of its usual association with astrology, it had a precarious existence and tended to be short lived. One of the most important observatories in Islam, that built by the Mongol *il-khan* at Maragheh in 1259, was exceptional in having enjoyed a long life of fifty-seven years. The observatory built in the sixteenth century by the Ottoman sultan Murād III for the Damascene astronomer-engineer Taqī al-Dīn ibn Ma^{c}rūf (*d.* 1585), was demolished by order of the sultan only three years after it was started.

In the eleventh century a number of schools of higher learning, called madrasas, were established under the Seljuks in Iraq and Iran. In legal terms these were endowed institutions, and to that extent they should perhaps not be regarded as state establishments. Nevertheless, the man who endowed them was the highest official in the Seljuk administration, the energetic vizier Niẓām al-Mulk (*fl.* 1063–1092), who alone had the power to appoint professors and whose name was attached to the system he initiated. It would be unreasonable to dissociate the founding of the Niẓāmīya madrasas from the political affairs at a time when the Sunni Seljuks were gravely concerned about Ismaili subversive propaganda emanating from the Fatimids in Egypt. (Niẓām al-Mulk was assassinated by an Ismaili in 1092.) Ostensibly, the madrasas were schools of religious law, and their professors were appointed as professors of law. This emphasis on religious education came to characterize all madrasas to be founded later in other parts of the Muslim world, for example in Egypt and Syria, more or less on the Niẓāmīya model. And insofar as the madrasas had anything like what we might call a curriculum, the study of the "ancient sciences" was not part of it. The situation was obviously relevant to the fortunes of the rational sciences in medieval Islam, and the implications of this situation are still to be studied in depth.

It will be enough to remark here that, despite the preponderance of religious teaching, there were good reasons for at least some aspects of the mathematical sciences to enter the madrasa. The *fuqahā*$^{\supset}$, or legal experts, had developed an interest in arithmetic and algebra as tools of calculating the exact apportioning of legacies according to the sometimes complicated rules of inheritance. Indeed a whole branch of Islamic law, called ^{c}*ilm al-farā*$^{\supset}$*iḍ*, had come into existence to take care of this problem. Astronomical knowledge also came to be perceived as of use in determining the direction in which the Muslims faced while praying, and in regulating the astronomically defined times of prayer (such as sunrise, sunset, and noontime). In the later period some of the scholars who worked on these problems (essentially problems of spherical astronomy), and on related problems in numerical computation, algebra, or geometry, were in fact attached to madrasas or, as timekeepers, to mosques (the two institutions were often closely connected or identical). And we have to add the important, though usually ignored, fact that teaching activities within the madrasa frequently reflected the personal interests of the teacher, which sometimes extended to abstract problems in the sciences rather than to the requirements of a rigid curriculum, if such existed.

Samarkand observatory, built by Sultan Ulugh Beg, *ca.* 1430. RICHARD HARRINGTON—CAMERA PRESS FROM PHOTO TRENDS

All things considered, the general picture that emerges is that scientific education in medieval Islam was largely an individual affair in which individual students made special arrangments with individual teachers. As the student moved from one teacher to another, and sometimes even from one country to another, he was driven by his own interests and attracted by the fame of the teacher with whom he sought to study. A certain order, handed down from Hellenistic times, was followed in the study of the mathematical sciences (Euclid preceded the minor astronomical works, and the *Almagest* came last), and the emphasis was on the major texts in a given field—a practice also followed in religious and philological studies. It was only in the period of decline that short abstracts and summaries came to replace the classics. That this only partly structured and only partly institutionalized system of education worked is proved by the long-lasting scientific tradition in Islam, though we do not yet know the full details of how it worked. It was, however, a precarious sytem and it was eventually allowed to falter and fade.

ACHIEVEMENTS

A tradition of scientific investigation that consumed the energies of so many able individuals over such a long period of time was bound to bear fruit; indeed, interesting and often important results have been identified in the extant works of these individuals, and some of these results are known to have been assimilated in Western science. There is space here only to describe some outstanding achievements in general terms.

In the domain of mathematics, Islamic scholars devised and successfully applied new and elaborate techniques of computations. In some cases, their work in this field led them to construct sophisticated mechanical computers. Having been early introduced to the Indian decimal place-value system of numeration and, through Greek astronomy, to the old Babylonian sexagesimal system, they went on to devise methods for calculating with decimal fractions. They took significant steps toward extending the concept of number, inherited from the Greeks, so as to include irrational magnitudes as well as natural numbers and common fractions. They added to the limited, ad hoc trigonometric methods they learned from the Greeks (Ptolemy's chord function) and from the Indians (the sine and tangent functions) and eventually developed them into an independent discipline no longer subservient to astronomy. They recast the algebraic modes of solving numerical problems found among the Greeks and the Indians, thereby creating a new form of algebraic discourse and setting the science of algebra on a new course (but without introducing a symbolic calculus), and they went a long way in exploiting the use of higher geometry (conic sections) in the solution of higher-than-quadratic equations. Starting already in the ninth century and continuing into the fifteenth, Islamic geometricians persistently probed the foundations of Euclidean geometry, in particular Euclid's theory of parallels, and in doing so were led to prove a number of non-Euclidean theorems, though they did not go so far as to suggest alternatives to the Euclidean system. They studied the properties of numbers, in the tradition of the Pythagorean "science of number," and discovered some new theorems and problems.

Of all the mathematical disciplines, astronomy was the one that attracted more attention than any other. Islamic astronomers performed a large number of observations, mainly but not exclusively for improving parameters of the Ptolemaic models for planetary motions. This work was suggested in part by the variety of numerical values derived from the various sources, but was principally inspired by an early and clear recognition of the role of testing in astronomical research. Ultimately guided by the same idea, they constructed ever more sophisticated and reliable observation instruments—sundials, armillary spheres, astrolabes, quadrants, equatoria. Disturbed by a contradiction between Ptolemy's principle of uniform motion and certain features that he introduced into his planetary theory to maintain correspondence with observational results, they set about devising new models that successfully saved the avowed principle as well as the phenomena. This was not a case of philosophy encroaching upon astronomy proper (as has been sometimes suggested), but a medieval example of what T. S. Kuhn has called "normal science": the aim was simply to remove a puzzle generated by the perceived contradiction.

In antiquity, optics was a science conceptually related to geometry and practically allied to astronomy. In the eleventh century an Arab mathematician living in Egypt, Ibn al-Haytham, produced a large treatise, *Kitāb al-Manāẓir* (Book on optics), the purpose of which was to put the science of optics on a new basis and which in fact superseded the treatise attributed to Ptolemy, itself the most advanced treatment of light and vision that has come down from antiquity. In the beginning of the fourteenth century, a Persian mathematician working in Tabrīz, Kamāl al-Dīn al-Fārisī (*d.* 1320), produced the first correct explanation of the shape and order of the primary and secondary rainbows.

Islamic engineers, supported by rich patrons, described and executed mechanical devices (clocks, water-lifting machines, fountains, and so on) that can be said to have illustrated certain mechanical principles in an empirical and nonmathematical way; but mathematics was essentially involved in their extension of the Archimedean investigation of floating bodies, and in their study of weights, of various types of balances, of the determination of specific gravities, and of the proportion of metals in alloys. Alchemy was a complex field in which a large number of properties of various materials were gathered, investigated, and applied.

Under the name of natural philosophy there were acute speculations about space, time, motion, and force, in which concepts akin to the early modern ideas of impetus and *conatus* appear. Some mathematicians went so far as to apply the parallelogram of motion to "dynamical" concepts (pressure and resistance) borrowed from the Islamic dialectical theologians.

Throughout the period from the ninth to the fourteenth century, mathematicians included in their works discussions of the problem of how to determine the direction of Mecca (or the *qibla*) at a given locality. This was an attempt on their part to be of service to the community of Muslims who were enjoined to face toward Mecca while performing their five daily prayers. The *qibla* problem was a problem in mathematical geography for which Islamic astronomers devised various solutions. At first these solutions were based on already available Greek methods, but they gradually grew in complexity, finally culminating in the construction of tables displaying the *qibla* for all latitudes and longitudes.

Also of use to religious practice was the work done by astronomers on timekeeping by the sun and the stars and the compilation of tables for regulating the times of prayers—work that reached its highest point of perfection in Egypt and Syria under the Mamluks (1250–1517). Here again, the problems involved were problems in spherical astronomy, and already in the thirteenth century universal solutions, applicable in all localities, were discovered. An important institutional development in the same period was the establishment of the office of *muwaqqit,* or timekeeper, in the major mosques, and the office was filled by scholars trained in astronomy. Thus, for the first time in medieval Islam, the astronomer was admitted into a permanent, religious institution, and from the thirteenth to the nineteenth century most astronomers in Egypt and Syria were *muwaqqits*. One consequence of this new development was the shrinking in number of astrological writings and the proliferation of works on timekeeping and on prayer tables. Thus, it has been said that the science of timekeeping was the major branch of astronomy cultivated under the Mamluks. The mosque, unlike the observatory, was not a scientific institution, and the *muwaqqit* was not employed to carry on scientific research for its own sake. But that did not prevent some *muwaqqits* from allowing their interests to take their investigations well beyond the requirements of their office. One of the great astronomers of medieval Islam, Ibn al-Shāṭir (*d. ca.* 1375), was a *muwaqqit* at the Umayyad mosque in Damascus. Besides his work on observational astronomy and the construction of highly imaginative instruments, he was able to bring to completion the research in planetary theory already begun by the astronomers of thirteenth-century Maragheh.

THE CHARACTER OF ISLAMIC SCIENCE

Even while this schematic and incomplete picture is being pieced together by historians, difficult questions continue to be asked about the originality and specific character of Islamic science. Originality is a relative as well as a vague concept, and if defined arbitrarily or anachronistically it ceases to be of value in the assessment of past achievements. For example, the ninth-century translation movement, though immediately concerned with transmission rather than invention, was a highly imaginative and in some respects unprecedented enterprise, and as such it constituted an initiative of great originality that turned out to be of critical importance not only for Islam but for the history of civilization. Furthermore, as the above examples show, one would not be at a loss to enumerate a large number of innovations in the work of Islamic scientists in several fields of inquiry. But it would be a vain undertaking to look for an Archimedes or a Newton in the Middle Ages.

Much more interesting is the question of characterization: what features, if any, distinguish the scientific work in medieval Islam? But this question too has been dominated by essentialism, an attitude still manifest in attempts to deduce characteristics of Islamic science from alleged inseparable attributes of Islamic civilization. Some scholars, for example, have detected in Islamic mathematics an "arithmetizing" tendency essentially connected with certain features of the Arabic language. Others have seen in the physicalistic models proposed by Islamic astronomers a symptom of a propensity of the "Semitic mind" to gravitate toward the sensible and away from the abstract. Others still have appealed to something called an atomistic mode of thinking. And again others have looked for mystical visions as expressions of the motifs underlying scientific concepts and trends.

Such essentialist explanations are worthless substitutes for genuine historical inquiries. The arithmetizing tendency (if by this is meant the emphasis on algebra) can be accounted for in terms of elements in the Greek and Indian legacies, and it must be balanced with the considerable attention given to geometry and geometrical methods. As for the physicalistic models of Islamic astronomers, they are best understood as representing solutions to problems suggested by juxtaposing two books, both of which were written by Ptolemy: the abstract *Almagest* and the not-so-abstract *Planetary Hypotheses*. Mysticism was deeply involved in alchemy, but there is no evidence of its influence on other scientific endeavors.

G. J. Toomer, a classicist who works on Arabic science, has remarked that a characteristic passage from an Arabic mathematician, if translated into classical Greek, would be "indistinguishable in form, style, and terminology from the kind of work which was read in Alexandria in the 4th century." One must agree. But even with regard to the uniquely Greek legacy, peculiar circumstances of transmission have brought about significant differences. It is known that after the death of Alexander the Great, mathematics migrated to Alexandria, and the philosophy that remained in Athens was distinctly innocent of mathematics. It so happened that Baghdad became heir to both the Alexandrian and Athenian traditions, and in consequence the science and philosophy that originated there differed in character from their immediate parents—Hellenistic science and philosophy. Thus, the great Islamic scientists were imbued with a Greek philosophical outlook, and all major philosophers in Islam (al-Kindī, al-Fārābī, Ibn Sīnā, and Ibn Rushd, among others) wrote extensively and competently on the sciences, including mathematics and astronomy. In this respect, a great deal of Arabic science and philosophy appears to be closer in character to their counterparts in the classical rather than in the Hellenistic period.

It is precisely the high quality and sophisticated content of Islamic science that give poignancy to the problem of decline. The question is not why the efforts of Islamic scientists did not produce "the scientific revolution" (probably a meaningless question), but why their work declined and eventually ceased to develop after the impressive flowering of the earlier centuries. Why, for instance, did algebra fail to make significant progress after the twelfth century? Why was the work of Ibn al-Haytham and Kamāl al-Dīn in experimental optics not continued along lines already drawn by these two mathematicians? Why did the observatory, once conceived and established as a specialized scientific institution, fail to gain a permanent footing? And why did the long-standing interest in astronomical observations not develop into more sophisticated programs? These and similar questions are forced upon us by the fact that what we have in the extant works of Arabic scientists is not protoscience but science in the proper sense of the word. Underlying these questions are component questions about motives, attitudes, institutions, and cultural circumstances that necessarily affected the rise and decline of Islamic science—questions for which we are to seek answers only by means of historical, empirical methods.

BIBLIOGRAPHY

For accounts of the state of research on Islamic science in the 1980's, see David A. King, "The Exact Sciences in Medieval Islam," in *Middle East Studies Association of North America, Bulletin,* **14** (1980); and J. L. Berggren, "History of Mathematics in the Islamic World," *ibid.,* **19** (1985).

On the Greek influence and the career of Hellenism in Islam, see Ignaz Goldziher, "The Attitude of Orthodox Islam to the 'Ancient Sciences,'" in M. L. Swartz, ed. and trans., *Studies on Islam* (1981), 185–215; Joel L. Kraemer, *Humanism in the Renaissance of Islam* (1986); David Pingree, "The Greek Influence on Early Islamic Mathematical Astronomy," in *Journal of the American Oriental Society,* **93** (1973); Franz Rosenthal, *The Classical Heritage in Islam,* Emile and Jenny Marmorstein, trans. (1975); A. I. Sabra, "The Appropriation and Subsequent Naturalization of Greek Science in Medieval Islam," in *History of Science,* **25** (1987); G. J. Toomer, "The Mathematical Sciences: The Role of the Islamic

World in the Development and Transmission of the Ancient Heritage" (1984, unpublished).

Reliable surveys are Roger Arnaldez and L. Massignon, "Arabic Science," in René Taton, ed., *History of Science: Ancient and Medieval Science from the Beginning to 1450,* A. J. Pomerans, trans. (1964–1965), 385–521; Pierre M. M. Duhem, *To Save the Phenomena: An Essay on the Idea of Physical Theory from Plato to Galileo,* Edmund Donald and Chaninah Maschler, trans. (1969); Edward S. Kennedy, "The Arabic Heritage in the Exact Sciences," in *al-Abḥāth,* **23** (1970), "The Exact Sciences," in *The Cambridge History of Iran,* IV (1975), "The Exact Sciences in Iran Under the Saljuqs and Mongols," *ibid.,* V (1968), and "The Exact Sciences in Timurid Iran," *ibid.,* VI (1986); A. I. Sabra, "The Scientific Enterprise," in Bernard Lewis, ed., *The World of Islam* (1976), 181–200; Joseph Schact and Clifford E. Bosworth, eds., *The Legacy of Islam* (1974).

Accounts of developments in individual sciences or periods are Adel Anbouba, "L'algèbre arabe aux IXe et Xe siècles: Aperçu général," in *Journal for the History of Arabic Science,* **2** (1978); J. L. Berggren, *Episodes in the Mathematics of Medieval Islam* (1986), a good introduction to concepts and techniques; B. G. Goldstein, "The Making of Astronomy in Early Islam," in *Nuncius,* **1** (1986); A. P. Juschkewitsch, *Geschichte der Mathematick im Mittelalter* (1964); David A. King, "The Astronomy of the Mamluks," in *Isis,* **74** (1983); Roshdi Rashed, *Entre arithmétiques et algèbre: Recherches sur l'histoire des mathématiques arabes* (1984); George A. Saliba, "The Development of Astronomy in Medieval Islamic Society," in *Arabic Studies Quarterly,* **4** (1982).

For individual scientists, see the *Dictionary of Scientific Biography.*

Three substantial studies of Islamic institutions of learning are Youssef Eche (al-Ishsh), *Les bibliothèques arabes* (1967); George Makdisi, *The Rise of Colleges: Institutions of Learning in Islam and the West* (1981); Aydin Sayılı, *The Observatory in Islam and Its Place in the General History of the Observatory* (1960, repr. 1981). See also Sami Hamarneh, "Medical Education and Practice in Medieval Islam," in Charles D. O'Malley, ed., *The History of Medical Education* (1970), 39–71.

On the transmission of Arabic science to Europe, see Charles Homer Haskins, *Studies in the History of Mediaeval Science* (1924, 2nd ed. 1927, repr. 1960), 278–302; David C. Lindberg, "The Transmission of Greek and Arabic Learning to the West," in *idem,* ed., *Science in the Middle Ages* (1978), 52–90. For a discussion of the translations into European languages, see Marie-Thérèse d'Alverny, "Translations and Translators," in Robert L. Benson and Giles Constable, eds., *Renaissance and Renewal in the Twelfth Century* (1982, repr. 1985), 421–462.

A. I. Sabra

[See also **Arabic Numerals; Astrology/Astronomy, Islamic; Barmakids; Bīrūnī, Muḥammad ibn Ahmad Abū'l-Rayḥān al-; Caliphate; Clocks and Reckoning of Time; Fatimids; Hārūn al-Rashid; Inheritance, Islamic; Madrasa; Maʾmūn, al-; Niẓām al-Mulk; Optics, Islamic; Philosophy and Theology, Islamic; Qibla; Schools, Islamic; Technology, Islamic; Translation and Translators, Islamic.**]

SCIENCE, JEWISH. Because Judaism is a system of laws and principles for guiding human conduct and not a method for doing science, we must first make clear that by "Jewish science" we refer to the scientific activities undertaken by Jews. This science was perforce part and parcel of the science pursued by non-Jews in the given place and time. When speaking in particular of "Jewish science" in the Middle Ages, we have in mind three rather distinct types of activity: (1) research and writing undertaken by Jews within the various branches of science, completely within the scientific traditions of their non-Jewish neighbors; (2) scientific investigations carried out by Jews in response to problems of specifically Jewish interest, such as the various astronomical problems associated with the Jewish calendar; and (3) the translations of scientific works, mainly from Arabic, into Hebrew.

The translations are very important for the modern scholar, who uses them to establish both the texts themselves and the pattern of their transmission. From the point of view of the medieval Jews, they were undertaken, it seems, primarily to answer the internal needs—indeed, cravings—of the various Jewish communities for scientific knowledge, thus serving much the same purpose as many of the scientific books written originally in Hebrew. Some Jews were active in translation projects, usually into Latin, at the specific request of Christian patrons.

The other two types of activity were not limited to the Hebrew language, and much important material is in Arabic, usually written in Hebrew characters. Though most of this material is found in treatises composed on the various branches and problems of science, many important discussions found their place in works on philosophy and religious law.

EARLY WORKS

The bulk of the activity with which we will be concerned began around the tenth century. However, there are a few earlier medieval texts that are quite significant not only in terms of their content but also because they show that Jewish scholars were familiar with material of Greek and Near Eastern origin before the efflorescence of science under the Abbasid caliphs. We shall first scan this earlier literature.

The *Mishnat ha-Middot* is a short treatise on practical geometry giving, without proof, rules for the mensuration of the important figures in plane and solid geometry. Though there has been some controversy as to the date of the treatise, recent scholarship has fixed it well before the Arab period. Its closest relative in the Greek tradition seems to be the work of Hero of Alexandria. The *Mishnah* is quoted a number of times in medieval religious texts. It was also an important source for the geometry of al-Khwārizmī, who was perhaps the first to write significant mathematical texts in Arabic.

The *Baraita di-Shemuel* and *Baraita di-Mazalot* are primarily concerned with astrology. Both contain parameters for the planetary motions, and both make use of the Greek term *stirigmos* for station; this word is not found in Hebrew works written after the rise of Arab astronomy. The first treatise contains a discussion of the planetary distances as well. Interest in planetary motions may not have been connected solely with astrological questions; it may, rather, have been a natural expansion of the interest in astronomy generated by the problems of the lunisolar Jewish calendar. For example, there are several sets of planetary positions appended to the very early work on the Jewish calendar (823–824) by the Muslim al-Khwārizmī, *Istikhrāi taʾrīkh ai-yahūd*.

The medical compendium associated with the name of Asaph the Physician was written somewhere in the Near East before the Arab conquests. This Hebrew material furnishes material on prognosis, diagnosis, hygiene, and pharmacy drawn from a range of sources, including both known and unknown Greek works. The approach is for the most part Hippocratic. Early Hebrew terminology, such as *gidim* (sinews), is employed, and some medical remarks from the Talmud are brought forth. Great emphasis is placed on medical ethics, especially caring for the needy. This work was cited by later physicians, both Jewish and non-Jewish.

ASTRONOMY

In surveying Jewish science in the period after the rise of Arab science, we shall concentrate on astronomy, the most developed and most esteemed of the sciences during the Middle Ages, and the most thoroughly studied by modern scholars.

Fixing the calendar entailed the study of the motions of the sun and the moon. These were espoused in great detail by Isaac Israeli of Toledo in his *Yesod ᶜOlam* (Foundation of the world; *ca.* 1310), which provided all the necessary mathematical and astronomical background, as well as much valuable ancillary material, such as information on observations related to the compilation of the Alfonsine Tables. Israeli's book superseded the efforts of such earlier writers on the calendar as Abraham bar Ḥiyya (twelfth century), known to the Latins as Savasorda, and Abraham ibn Ezra (*d.* 1167). Related to the Jewish calendar was perhaps the most difficult problem in medieval astronomy, the determination of the visibility of the lunar crescent. A very thorough exposition of this subject is found in the *Treatise on the Sanctification of the New Moon* of Moses Maimonides (*d.* 1204). Though the basic theory is that of Ptolemy and most of the parameters can be traced to al-Battānī, several details of Maimonides' theory are not known elsewhere.

Because it deals with the motions of the heavenly bodies, astronomy was, in the medieval world view, a stepping stone to theological speculations. Astronomical discussions of varying quality are found in many philosophical works; most valuable in this regard is Maimonides' *Guide of the Perplexed.* Maimonides goes into detail on several points. For example, in part II, chapter 24, he draws some striking conclusions on the basis of deductions he has made from al-Qabīṣī's *Treatise on the Distances and Sizes of the Planets*.

Apart from these issues, which had some religious motivation, Jews were active in the other branches of astronomy. They acquainted themselves with the basic works of the Greeks in Arabic translation and with many of the contributions of the Arabs. For Jews in Arabic-speaking countries, this could be done by transcribing Arabic texts, whether translations or originals, into Hebrew characters. The Hebrew translations that were made were not limited to such basic works as the *Almagest* of Ptolemy, the *Sphaerica* of Menelaus, the very popular astronomical summary of al-Farghānī, and *On the Configuration of the World* of Ibn al-Haytham. Many specialized treatises, including those offering criticism of accepted models, were also translated—the works of Jābir ibn Aflaḥ and al-Zarqālī, for example. The translations were undertaken primarily in the border regions between the Islamic and Christian worlds, especially Spain, southern France, and Italy. To the Ibn Tibbon and Kalonymus families belong many of the most prominent translators; Jacob Anatoli should also be mentioned. Several very popular handbooks were written in Hebrew by Abraham bar Ḥiyya, who was familiar with Arab astronomy.

Accurate tables to be used in conjunction with standard texts were indispensable to the practicing astronomer. Again, we know of Arabic tables transcribed into Hebrew characters, such as the *zīj* of al-Fārisī, popular in Yemen, and of other tables written in Hebrew. Both the very popular tables of bar Ḥiyya and the equally popular *Six Wings* of Immanuel Bonfils of Tarascon (*ca.* 1365), which was translated into Byzantine Greek, were based upon the *al-zīj al-ṣābi* of al-Battānī. On the other hand, the tables of Levi ben Gerson (1288–1344) represent an original contribution. Many other sets of tables are known to exist and await scholarly analysis.

Although the calculation of planetary positions was the main preoccupation of the working astronomer—and the precision of his results a major factor in the high esteem enjoyed by the science—there was also a great deal of concern with the physical workings of the heavens. This concern was deepened by the incompatibility of the epicycles and eccenters of Ptolemaic theory with the fundamental principles of the Aristotelian world view. This concern was shared by Jewish thinkers. Al-Biṭrūjī's *Astronomy,* which offered an alternative, albeit unsatisfactory, model, was translated; al-Biṭrūjī's proposals were discussed by Isaac Israeli; they also influenced Levi ben Gershom's search for better models. In his *Guide of the Perplexed,* Maimonides referred to this problem as the "true perplexity," and even his later followers, such as Rabbi Joseph Albo (early fifteenth century), continued to raise the subject. Joseph Naḥmias (early fourteenth century) wrote a detailed treatise on the subject in Arabic, which was translated into Hebrew; the models that he proposed remain unstudied.

Jewish astronomers also wrote on astronomical instruments. Perhaps the most popular of these treatises was the *Kli ha-Niḥoshet* (Brass instrument) of Abraham ibn Ezra, which describes the astrolabe. Isaac al-Ḥadīb (Sicily, fifteenth century), among others, wrote on the construction of the equatorium, a type of analog computer for planetary positions. Levi ben Gerson invented a simple but effective device for measuring angular distances, the Jacob's staff. This tool had a transversal scale developed by Levi to eliminate errors in reading the smaller subdivisions of the degree. Jacob ben Machir's quadrant achieved renown among both Jews and non-Jews. Yet despite the existence of a good number of treatises, only a very few instruments with Hebrew writing have survived.

The most important and original astronomer of the medieval period was Levi ben Gershom. He worked in southern France, possibly in the service of the Avignon papacy, and his astronomical works were translated into Latin. Among his significant achievements were a determination of the planetary distances greater by several orders of magnitude than the small values accepted in the Middle Ages; the attempt at matching his theory to his own observations; the concern with atmospheric refraction; and the attempt to anticipate experimental errors.

ASTROLOGY

Throughout the Middle Ages astrology was popular in Jewish circles. A number of works on astrology were written by Abraham ibn Ezra; these works were influential in the spread of astrological techniques among Christians as well as among Jews. Astrological references are found in mystical works—for instance, in many of the commentaries to the *Sefer Yetzira* (Book of creation). A number of actual horoscopes have been preserved among the documents of the Cairo genizah, and these yield information of interest, such as the continued popularity of the *Sindhind* among astrologers long after astronomers had switched to more modern tables.

Strong opposition to the belief in and practice of astrology was expressed by some thinkers. Maimonides voiced scientific doubts similar to those found in Islamic writings, for example regarding the impossibility that one part of the ecliptic was beneficent and another maleficent. However, Maimonides' main objections were theological. Free will is a cornerstone of the Jewish outlook, and any belief that challenges the notion of man's absolute freedom to do right or wrong threatens the very basis of the religion. Moreover, astrology remained intrinsically and inextricably tied up with star worship. Those who, like Abraham bar Ḥiyya, nevertheless defended astrology were forced to come face to face with these accusations. Various compromises were suggested, most of which recognized man's vulnerability to the astral forces but allowed the righteous to escape the "decrees of the stars."

MATHEMATICS

In mathematics Jewish scholars were familiar with many Greek texts through their Arabic versions. Euclid's *Elements,* Nicomachus' *Arithmetic,* and Archimedes' *On the Sphere and the Cylinder* were translated; only a few Arabic works were rendered into Hebrew. These translations have been a boon to modern scholars. The Hebrew version of the *Algebra* of Abū Kāmil ibn Shujā^c^ is clearer than either the original Arabic or the Latin translation. The writer of this article has recently discovered some important Hebrew texts on dealing with regular polyhedra.

Other basic works were not translated, and thus were studied only by Arabic-speaking Jews, sometimes with interesting results. For example, there is no Hebrew version of Apollonius' *Conics.* Maimonides studied the Arabic version along with Ibn al-Haytham's restoration of book VIII, commented on both, and referred to the theorem on the asymptotes to the hyperbola in part I, chapter 73, of his *Guide.* Some later Jewish scholars, not knowing the *Conics,* offered interesting constructions of their own for this.

It is not surprising that the Jews most famous for their work in astronomy are by and large the same people who contributed to mathematics. The *Liber embadorum* of bar Ḥiyya is the earliest European exposition of Arab algebra, and it was also one of the first books to introduce trigonometry to that continent. Its influence is seen in the work of Fibonacci. This same bar Ḥiyya made methodological advances, which he put forth in his encyclopedic *Tower of Faith.* Abraham ibn Ezra wrote several works on mathematics; he was particularly instrumental in introducing to Jewish readers the decimal positional system of arithmetic. Levi ben Gershom contributed to trigonometry, mathematical induction, the summation of series, and combinatorial analysis. Immanuel Bonfils advanced the exponential calculus by recognizing that the integers from one to nine should be given the value zero (that is, $a \cdot 10^0$).

Material of great mathematical interest can be found in the halakhic literature as well. Religious problems led to interesting observations on the theory of probability. For example, Isaac Arama (Spain, *ca.* 1420–1494), in his discussion of a lottery system used to divide priestly duties, may have anticipated Bernoulli's "law of large numbers." Particularly intriguing is Maimonides' unequivocal statement of the transcendental character of π, found in his commentary to the fifth mishnah in *^c^Eruvin,* chapter 1: "You must realize that the ratio of the diameter of the circle to its circumference is not known and can never be expressed exactly. This is [due to] no lack of our achievement, as the ignorant claim, but rather the matter is by its nature inscrutable."

MEDICINE

In contrast with astronomy and mathematics, medicine, particularly medical theory, did not profit from much independent thinking in the Middle Ages; at present one cannot point to many original contributions of Jewish medicine. Maimonides, however, was one of the few medieval critics of Galen. Moreover, this same sage has been rightly praised for his emphasis on the social and environmental conditions necessary for the recovery of the patient. Some medieval works do contain noteworthy clinical observations. New material can be found in some of the pharmacological compendia.

Historians of Jewish medicine in the medieval period have concentrated on biographical and social investigations. A medical career held the promise not only of a good livelihood but also of political influence. At various times Jewish physicians held high posts at the courts of both Christian and Muslim rulers. Maimonides served at the court in Cairo. Jewish physicians, particularly several members of the illustrious Ibn Waqqār family, held high posts at several Christian Spanish courts. Of course, such offices had their dangers as well; we have records of Jewish physicians who were executed for failing to cure the ruler.

Several Jews were among the most famous and most frequently cited medical authorities. Māsarjuwayh (eighth century), a very early writer, is known to us through the frequent references to him by al-Rāzī. Perhaps the most influential of all was Isaac Israeli of Qayrawān (ninth century). Charles Singer has called his *On Fevers* "perhaps the best clinical treatise of the Middle Ages." His works were translated into Latin in the eleventh century and remained in use until the seventeenth century.

Multilingual drug glossaries were compiled. Particularly noteworthy is that of the Spaniard Jonah ibn Biklarish (late eleventh century), which gave names in Syriac, Persian, Greek, Latin, and Spanish.

Jews are known to have been active in government hospitals in Cairo and Damascus. We learn from a responsum of Rabbi Joseph Colon (Italy, *ca.* 1420–1480) of a group of Jewish physicians who formed a sort of consortium. Although our sources often indicate harmony between Jewish and non-Jewish physicians, particularly in the Islamic world, numerous records of religious discrimination also exist.

More so than with the other sciences, one must emphasize the role of the Hebrew language in medical literature. Works were translated from Arabic and several European languages. Most esteemed was the *Canon* of Avicenna (Ibn Sīnā). Translated by Nathan ha-Me'ati in 1279 and published in 1491, it is the only Hebrew scientific incunabulum. Roger Bacon, and later Petrus Mosellanus, acknowledged the importance of Hebrew for the serious student of medicine. The great work of Vesalius (sixteenth century) includes Hebrew terminology.

OTHER SCIENCES

Those who wrote on biology, both human and animal, depended for the most part on earlier authorities, primarily Greek. The *Shaᶜar ha-Shamayim* (Gate of heaven) of Gershon ben Solomon (thirteenth century) is perhaps the most comprehensive such compilation in Hebrew. Meir Aldabi (*ca.* 1360) was one of the few who added remarks and observations of their own. The halakhic literature is a potential source of valuable material on this subject. For example, Moses Naḥmanides (Spain, 1194–1270), in his novellae to the tractate *Ḥullin,* records original investigations in ornithology.

Jewish scientists do not seem to have been particularly interested in technology. However, the religious literature of necessity contains some fairly detailed descriptions of devices, manufacturing procedures, and the like, drawn from daily life. This potentially rich source has hardly been explored.

END OF THE MIDDLE AGES

We know of several Jewish scientists who were active as the Middle Ages drew to a close. Most famous of all is Abraham Zacuto (1452–*ca.* 1515), the astronomer whose work figured prominently in the exploratory voyages of the Portuguese. Jewish science was affected, mainly for the worse, by several factors. Jews were expelled from Spain and southern France, their most important scientific centers during the Middle Ages. Nonetheless, recent research has shown that the scientific tradition, particularly in astronomy, remained surprisingly vigorous in several areas along the Mediterranean littoral for several centuries. Jews living in Islamic lands shared with their Muslim neighbors the relative decline in Arab science, though medieval texts continued to be studied for a long time; in fact, there is a nineteenth-century copy (Arabic, in Hebrew characters) of the tables of Ibn al-Shāṭir (fourteenth century). The exclusion of Jews from European universities must also have had an adverse effect. Factors within the Jewish community probably played a part as well; this whole chapter of Jewish history has not been investigated sufficiently.

BIBLIOGRAPHY

Sources. Al-Biṭrūjī, *On the Principles of Astronomy,* Bernard R. Goldstein, ed., 2 vols. (1971); Friedrich S. Bodenheimer, trans., *Gate of Heaven* (1953); Judah D. Eisenstein, ed., *Otsar Midrashim,* II (1915, repr. 1956), 280–285, 542–548, for *Baraita di-Shemuel* and *Baraita de-Mazalot;* Solomon Gandz, ed. and trans., *The Mishnat ha-Middot,* in his *Studies in Hebrew Astronomy and Mathematics,* Shlomo Sternberg, ed. (1970); Abraham ibn Ezra, *The Beginning of Wisdom,* Raphael Levy, ed. and trans. (1939); Isaac Israeli, *Liber Yesod Olam,* B. Goldberg and L. Rosenkranz, eds. (1846, 1848), and *Tratado de las fiebres,* José Llamas, ed. (1945); Martin Levey, *The Algebra of Abū Kāmil* (1966); Moses Maimonides, *Treatise on the Sanctification of the New Moon,* Solomon Gandz, trans. (1956), and *The Guide of the Perplexed,* Shlomo Pines, trans. (1963); Moses Naḥmanides, *Ḥiddushei ha-Ramban,* pt. 2 (1961–1962), 75b–76a.

General. Salo W. Baron, *A Social and Religious History of the Jews,* VIII, 2nd ed. (1958); Ben-zion Dinur, *Yisraᵓel ba-Golah,* II, bk. 4 (1969), esp. chap. 15; Alexander Marx, "The Scientific Work of Some Outstanding Mediaeval Jewish Scholars," in Israel Davidson, ed., *Essays and Studies in Memory of Linda R. Miller* (1938); Charles Singer, "Science and Judaism," in Louis Finkelstein, ed., *The Jews,* II (1949) (for names of scientists; otherwise filled with inaccuracies); Harry A. Wolfson, "The Classification of Sciences in Mediaeval Jewish Philosophy," in *Hebrew Union College Jubilee Volume* (1925), and "Additional Notes," in *Hebrew Union College Annual,* 3 (1926).

Translations. L. V. Berman, "Greek into Hebrew: Samuel ben Judah of Marseilles," in Alexander Altmann, ed., *Jewish Medieval and Renaissance Studies* (1967); Moritz Steinschneider, *Die hebräischen Übersetzungen des Mittelalters und die Juden als Dolmetscher* (1893, repr. 1956); J. L. Teicher, "The Latin-Hebrew School of

Translators in Spain in the Twelfth Century," in *Homenaje a Millás-Vallicrosa,* II (1956).

Astronomy. Arthur Beer, "Astronomy," in *Encyclopedia judaica,* III (1971), good for names and treatises but contains a number of errors; Solomon Gandz, "The Astronomy of Maimonides and Its Sources," in *Archives internationales d'histoire des sciences,* **3** (1950); Bernard R. Goldstein, "The Medieval Hebrew Tradition in Astronomy," in *Journal of the American Oriental Society,* **85** (1965); *The Astronomical Tables of Levi ben Gerson* (1974), "The Hebrew Astrolabe in the Adler Planetarium," in *Journal of Near Eastern Studies,* **35** (1976), "Levi ben Gerson: On Instrumental Errors and the Transversal Scale," in *Journal for the History of Astronomy,* **8** (1977), "The Survival of Arabic Astronomy in Hebrew," in *Journal for the History of Arabic Science,* **3** (1979), "The Status of Models in Ancient and Medieval Astronomy," in *Centaurus,* **24** (1980), a review of *Geschichte des arabischen Schrifttums* (vol. VI), in *Isis,* **71** (1980), "The Hebrew Astronomical Tradition: New Sources," *ibid.,* **72** (1981), *The Astronomy of Levi ben Gerson* (1985), and "Scientific Traditions in Late Medieval Jewish Communities," in Gilbert Dahan, ed., *Les Juifs au regard de l'histoire* (1985); Otto Neugebauer, "The Astronomy of Maimonides and Its Sources," in *Hebrew Union College Annual,* **22** (1949); Peter Solon, "The *Six Wings* of Immanuel Bonfils and Michael Chrysokokkes," in *Centaurus,* **15** (1970).

Astrology. Alexander Altmann, "Astrology," in *Encyclopaedia judaica,* III (1971); Bernard R. Goldstein and David Pingree, "Horoscopes from the Cairo Geniza," in *Journal of Near Eastern Studies,* **36** (1977); Abraham Halkin, ed., *Igeret teiman* (1952), introduction; Alexander Marx, "The Correspondence Between the Rabbis of Southern France and Maimonides About Astrology," in *Hebrew Union College Annual,* **3** (1926).

Mathematics. Marshall Clagett, ed., *Archimedes in the Middle Ages,* IV, pt. 1 (1980), 335–341; Pamela H. Espenshade, "A Text on Trigonometry by Levi ben Gerson," in *Mathematics Teacher,* **60** (1967); Solomon Gandz, "The Invention of the Decimal Fractions and the Application of the Exponential Calculus by Immanuel Bonfils of Tarascon (*ca.* 1350)," in *Isis,* **25** (1936), and *Studies in Hebrew Astronomy and Mathematics,* Shlomo Sternberg, ed. (1970); Jekuthiel Ginsburg, "Rabbi ben Ezra on Permutations and Combinations," in *Mathematics Teacher,* **15** (1922); E. S. Kennedy, "Al-Khwārizmī on the Jewish Calendar," in *Scripta mathematica,* **27** (1964); Y. Tzvi Langermann, "An Anonymous *Book of Euclid*" (in Hebrew), in *Kiryat Sefer,* **59** (1984), and "The Mathematical Writings of Maimonides," in *Jewish Quarterly Review,* 75 (1984); Y. Tzvi Langermann and J. P. Hogendijk, "A Hitherto Unknown Hellenistic Treatise on the Regular Polyhedra," in *Historia mathematica,* **11** (1984); Martin Levey, "The Encyclopedia of Abraham Savasorda: A Departure in Mathematical Methodology," in *Isis,* **43** (1952), and "Abraham Savasorda and His Algorism: A Study in Early European Logistic," in *Osiris,* **11** (1954); Nachum L. Rabinovitch, *Probability and Statistical Inference in Ancient and Medieval Jewish Literature* (1973); David E. Smith and Jekuthiel Ginsburg, "Rabbi ben Ezra and the Hindu-Arabic Problem," in *American Mathematical Monthly,* **25** (1918).

Medicine. Isaac Alteras, "Jewish Physicians in Southern France During the Thirteenth and Fourteenth Centuries," in *Jewish Quarterly Review,* **68** (1978); Friedrich S. Bodenheimer, "The Biology of Abraham ben David Halevi of Toledo," in *Archives internationales d'histoire des sciences,* **4** (1951); R. Y. Ebied, *Bibliography of Mediaeval Arabic and Jewish Medicine and Allied Sciences* (1971); Mordecai Etziony, "Nathan ben Joel and His *Zori Haguf,*" in *Bulletin for the History of Medicine,* **37** (1963); Harry Friedenwald, *The Jews and Medicine: Essays,* 2 vols. (1944, repr. 1967); Shelomo D. Goitein, "The Medical Profession in the Light of the Cairo Geniza Documents," in *Hebrew Union College Annual,* **34** (1963); Saul Jarcho, "Guide for Physicians (*Musar harofim*) by Isaac Judaeus," in *Bulletin for the History of Medicine,* **15** (1944); J. Leibowitz, "Maimonides on Medical Practice," *ibid.,* **31** (1957); Max Meyerhof, "Mediaeval Jewish Physicians in the Near East from Arabic Sources," in *Isis,* **28** (1938), and "The Medical Works of Maimonides," in Salo W. Baron, ed., *Essays on Maimonides* (1941); David Romano, "Judíos escribanos y trujamanes de árabe en la Corona de Aragón (reinados de Jaime I a Jaime II)," in *Sefarad,* **38** (1978), esp. 73–77; Fred Rosner, "Maimonides the Physician: A Bibliography," in *Bulletin for the History of Medicine,* **43** (1969); Cecil Roth, "The Qualification of Jewish Physicians in the Middle Ages," in *Speculum,* **28** (1953); Moritz Steinschneider, "Jüdische Ärtze," in *Zeitschrift für hebräische Bibliographie,* **17** (1914) and **18** (1915).

Technology. S. M. Passamaneck, "Rashi and Marine Architecture," in *Jewish Quarterly Review,* **67** (1976–1977); Esra Shereshevsky, "Some Aspects of Everyday Life in Rashi's Times," *ibid.,* **65** (1974–1975).

Bibliographies of modern scholars. Fielding H. Garrison, "Bibliographie der Arbeiten Moritz Steinschneiders zur Geschichte der Medizin und der Naturwissenschaften," in *Sudhoffs Archiv für Geschichte der Medizin,* **25** (1932); José L. Lacave, "Bibliografía del Professor Francisco Cantera Burgos," in *Sefarad,* **37** (1977); David Romano, Juan Vernet, and Francisco Cantera, "Bibliografía del Dr. Millás," *ibid.,* **30** (1970); J. Schacht, "Max Meyerhof," in *Osiris,* **9** (1950).

Y. Tzvi Langermann

[See also **Abraham bar Ḥiyya; Abraham ben Meïr ibn Ezra; Archimedes in the Middle Ages; Astrolabe; Astrology; Astronomy; Calendars and Reckoning of Time; Levi ben Gershom; Maimonides, Moses; Mathematics; Medicine, History of; Naḥmanides, Moses; Pharmacopeia; Translation and Translators, Jewish.**]

SCIENTIFIC INSTRUMENTS. Little of the ancient learning, including knowledge of scientific instrumentation, was retained in the West following the fall of the Roman Empire, much of the highly developed Hellenistic science and technology having been lost along with the Greek language that was its vehicle. It continued to flourish in the East for a time, however. The closing of many schools as a consequence of religious and political problems caused scholars to flee to Iran and Syria, taking with them their knowledge of Hellenistic culture. From the Islamic world it was dispersed once more, particularly from Baghdad, which had become the new center of cultural and scientific development.

SURVIVAL OF GRECO-ROMAN INSTRUMENTS

Ptolemy's Almagest. Following the translation of Ptolemy's *Almagest* into Arabic (*ca.* 800), many advances were made in the development of scientific instrumentation. New types of computational devices were produced, as reflected in the work of al-Bīrūnī (*ca.* 1000), in which he described such items as a special gear train for demonstrating the revolutions of the sun and moon at their relative rates. It could be applied to an astrolabe and appeared to have a strong affinity with the *antikythera* machine of the Greeks.

The Greco-Roman traditions nurtured in the Islamic world were transmitted to the West through Sicily in the tenth and eleventh centuries, and again through Spain in the twelfth and thirteenth centuries. With scholarship developing chiefly at Paris and Oxford, a slow but constant growth in mathematics, alchemy, astrology, and navigation took place, culminating with the emergence of the artisan toward the end of the fifteenth century. Several factors were responsible for this growth, particularly the fall of Constantinople, which directed trade to the West; the gradual transition from feudal suzerainty to nation-states; and the persisting depression that encompassed most of Europe.

The development of the sciences brought with it a need for instrumentation, some of which was fulfilled with instruments of the Greco-Roman tradition that were transmitted through the Arabs, notably the armillary sphere, the globe, and the astrolabe.

Armillary sphere. The armillary sphere probably evolved from the equinoctial ring used by the Greeks to determine the time of the equinox. It was primarily a representation of the universe featuring the principal circles of the celestial sphere: the horizon, the meridian, the equator, the tropics, the arctic and antarctic circles, as well as the earth, and often the sun, moon, planets, and certain stars. It was used to demonstrate the apparent motions of the heavenly bodies and to determine their positions at any time or place. The sphere became increasingly popular and was constructed according to one of the theories of the universe.

Subsequently, a teaching version was devised that was often depicted in miniature paintings of thirteenth- and fourteenth-century manuscipts. It was a miniaturization of the larger instrument equipped with a handle so that it could be held by a lecturer. The teaching armillary became particularly popular in the Middle Ages and was often used as an adjunct to John of Sacrobosco's *Sphaera* in the presentation of elementary astronomy. By the sixteenth century the teaching armillary had been elaborated to include movable figures of the planets, pointers, and other embellishments to denote the positions of stars.

Another portable type of armillary was derived in 1534 by Reiner Gemma Frisius in the form of an astronomical ring that enabled the time to be determined at night as well as in the daytime.

Globe. The globe, which also had its origins in Greek culture, was known as early as the third century B.C. Crates of Mallos was credited by Strabo (64/63 B.C.–*ca.* A.D. 25) in the latter's *Geographica* as having exhibited at Pergamum about 150 B.C. a terrestrial globe that he had made to demonstrate the sphericity of the earth. The earliest detailed description of a celestial globe was provided by Ptolemy in his *Almagest* (second century A.D.). He presented methods for making, marking, and mounting a globe on an axis so that it revolved to follow the diurnal motion of the stars, inclining the axis to the latitude so that the visible celestial hemisphere could be seen above the plane of the horizon. The earliest existing example of a globe is the Atlante Farnese at Naples, generally dated in the first century and believed to have been a copy of an earlier one.

The construction of a celestial globe was described in the Sūrya Siddhānta texts of the first half of the fifth century, which contained assimilated Hellenistic astronomical knowledge. These texts were introduced into the Islamic world by Iranian astronomers and translated into Arabic. The first

Arabic treatise on the subject was produced more than half a century later, and apparently provided the earliest knowledge of the globe in the Islamic world.

The globe was not unfamiliar to the Romans; it is depicted on coins and in a fresco in a villa near Pompeii, for instance. A treatise on globemaking was produced by Leontios Mechanikos of Byzantium in the seventh or eighth century, and his skills in globemaking were carried to Syria, where by the third century native craftsmen had learned to construct globes for astrological purposes. By the ninth century, then, globemaking in the Islamic world had been firmly established.

The earliest surviving celestial globes made in the Islamic world date from 1080. Nearly all of them are cast from brass or bronze and spun on a lathe, with the outlines of the constellations, great circles, divisions of the ecliptic, names of the stars, and other information engraved with a burin. A few later examples consisted of wooden cores covered with paper gores. Sometimes on the metal globes the stars were represented with inlaid silver points; on more elaborate examples, lines and inscriptions were damascened in gold or silver.

An extensive account of globemaking was included in the *Libros del saber de astronomía* of King Alfonso X of Castile, compiled in 1297 and based on Arabic texts. A variety of materials were listed, with a preference stated for the use of wood covered with parchment layers, thin leather, or plaster, in that order. In addition to the constellations and their constituent stars, stellar magnitudes, great circles, and other features, the band of the ecliptic was featured, divided according to the signs of the zodiac to indicate the position of the sun in relation to the stars on any date of the year. When the globe was placed within a circle representing the horizon, with the polar axis fixed in a meridian ring at an angle corresponding to the latitude of the place where it would be used, and was allowed to turn, it demonstrated the rising and setting of the stars and the sun, and the stellar appearance of the sky.

The oldest European globes date from the late fifteenth century, when globemaking was revived by German makers of mathematical instruments. The terrestrial globe did not fulfill any practical purpose, however, until after Martin Behaim had produced his *erdapfel* in 1492, after which the terrestrial globe became a necessary tool for cartographers and navigators in the age of exploration and discovery that expanded the boundaries of the known world during the next century.

Astrolabe. Also derived from Greek culture was the planispheric astrolabe, the invention of which was attributed to Hipparchus in the second century B.C. The first unquestionable description of the instrument, however, occurred in the writings of John Philoponos of Alexandria about 500. The astrolabe is basically a flattened armillary sphere, or a celestial sphere in a stereographic projection upon a plane, by means of which all circles of the sphere are represented. It consists of a base plate, called the *umm* or *mater,* over which is pivoted a rete or celestial map marked with the principal stars and the annual path of the sun. It is possible to reproduce the appearance of the sky at any moment by turning the rete over the *mater* to determine the time, the rising and setting of a star, the length of day or night, the time of astronomically defined ritual prayer, and to make astrological predictions.

The *mater* of the astrolabe was usually made of a thick, circular plate of brass hollowed at the center to accommodate several plates engraved on both sides with a number of circles and intersecting arcs, each side of each plate calculated for a different latitude. The reverse side of the *mater* varied in its components but generally included graphs for meridian altitudes of the sun from a number of latitudes, a sine graph for trigonometrical calculations and azimuths of the direction of Mecca from other cities, cotangent tables, a shadow square for altitude measurements, and astrological tables. Western astrolabes often included degree scales, zodiac and calendar scales, the arcs of the unequal hours, and a shadow square.

Three types of astrolabes were developed in the sixteenth and seventeenth centuries: the *saphea Arzachelis,* which was revived as the *astrolabium catholicum;* the Rojas projection; and a form of universal astrolabe devised by Philippe de La Hire in the late seventeenth century.

The earliest surviving example of the astrolabe is Iranian, made in the tenth century. The earliest European examples that have survived are from the twelfth century.

The astrolabe was probably transmitted to the Islamic world from Hellenistic sources in the seventh century, shortly after the conquest of Syria by the Sabians of Harran. The instrument was much improved by the Muslims and was introduced into Europe through Muslim Spain in the tenth or eleventh century. Its use spread through Europe,

Astrolabe, front view, showing animal forms on the rete. Brass, 12.75 cm (5 in) in diameter, *ca.* 1325–*ca.* 1425. SMITHSONIAN INSTITUTION, PHOTO NUMBER 49,918

and it continued to be employed for astronomical observation, surveying, and astrological divination until the mid seventeenth century.

INSTRUMENTS OF INDIAN AND ISLAMIC ORIGIN

Quadrant. An instrument that had no Hellenistic predecessor and that derived from Sanskrit sources was the quadrant. The name has been given to several instruments, all of which have the same general characteristics but not always the same application. Generally, a quadrant consists of a flat plate of wood or metal in the shape of one-quarter of a circle and is used for astronomical purposes.

The simplest form was inscribed with a scale of ninety degrees along its curved edge and equipped with sights attached to each end of the straight edge; it had a plumb line and bob suspended from the apex of the right angle. The radii were divided sexagesimally, and crossed parallel lines were drawn from these divisions to the scale of ninety degrees to create a nomogram of sines and cosines of the angles marked on the arc. Other lines generally included were the arcs of sines and "versed sines" and "the arc of the obliquity of the ecliptic." This form was known as a sinecal quadrant (*rub' al-mujayyub*) or quadrant of the canon (*rub' al-dastur*). It was developed in early Islam and based on trigonometrical knowledge derived from India.

In the form of the quadrant of the canon, the instrument passed into Europe in the tenth century, as the *quadrans canonis* or *quadrans vetustissimus*. Another form, called the *quadrans vetus* and designed by Robertus Anglicus about 1276, was engraved with a diagram of the unequal hours above the scale of degrees and was used for telling time by means of a sliding bead on a plumb line. Later it was provided with a zodiacal scale of solar declinations so that the sun's declination could be readily ascertained. Later still, it was made useful

Quadrant for measuring altitudes. Brass, 25.5 cm (10 in) high, 1364. SMITHSONIAN INSTITUTION, PHOTO NUMBER 64,198

for any latitude by engraving the zodiacal scale on a sliding cursor alongside the scale of degrees.

The astrolabe-quadrant was another form, invented by Ya^{c}aqob ben Mahir ibn Tibbon Mahir, also called Prophatius Judaeus (*ca.* 1236–*ca.* 1304), of Marseilles, Lunel, and Montpellier. He called the instrument *roba*^{c} *Yisreal* (quadrant of Israel), and it became known as the *quadrans novus* to distinguish it from earlier forms. It was based on the principle of the astrolabe and fulfilled many of the functions of that instrument. In it the essential lines of the stereographic projection of the rete and plates of the astrolabe were ingeniously reduced to one-quarter of a circle, and it became at the same time an observational instrument and a true slide rule.

Equatorium. Another instrument that came to the West from the Islamic world, through translations of two Arabic texts included in the *Libros del saber de astronomía,* was the equatorium, an instrument designed to find the positions of the planets according to the Ptolemaic theory without the need for calculations. One of these texts, by Albulcacim Abnacahm of Granada, provided for brass plates engraved with graduated circles for each of the planets; the other text, *Tratado de la azafea* (dedicated to al-Mu^{c}tamid ibn ^{c}Abbād), by Abū Isḥāq Ibrāhīm ibn Yaḥyā al-Naqqash, also known as al-Zarqālī or Azarquiel, considerably simplified it by combining all the planets on the two sides of a single plate. An early attempt to devise such an instrument had been made by Proclus about 450. Although equatoria were undoubtedly made in the Islamic world, no example has survived.

The first Western astronomer known to have described the equatorium was Campanus of Novara, who explained its use in his *Theorica planetarum* (second half of the thirteenth century). He modified and improved the instrument, but it remained difficult to use until Peter Nightingale described an equatorium of a much more practical form in his *Tractatus de semissis* (1293). Nightingale's instrument consisted of eight graduated half circles combined in a single instrument to represent all the planets. The equatorium was again modified and made more convenient about 1340 by John of Lignères. It became a companion instrument to the astrolabe for the astronomers of Merton College. A little earlier (1326/1327) Richard of Wallingford, abbot of St. Albans Abbey, invented an instrument he named the Albion. In it Richard returned to the original concept of using a separate plate for each planet but having all of them incorporated within a *mater* somewhat in the form of an astrolabe.

The ultimate improvement of the equatorium was described in the Middle English *Treatise on the Astrolabe* (1391/1392) generally attributed to Geoffrey Chaucer, in which two inscribed circles were utilized to provide maximum economy and efficiency. However, the instrument was modified and further simplified again and again by mathematicians and astronomers during the fifteenth and sixteenth centuries. One of these later versions was accommodated on the face of a one-sided astrolabe, described by Franciscus Sarzosius of Aragon in a publication on the equatorium in 1526.

Torquetum. The torquetum, which may be considered an antecedent of the modern astrocompass, was introduced before the end of the thirteenth century and was used for measuring the heights of stars, celestial latitudes, or angles along the horizon. Its invention is generally attributed to Jābir ibn Aflah, called Geber, who lived in or near Seville, or to Naṣīr al-Dīn al-Ṭūsī, who lived during the same period. Others attribute its invention to Bernard of Verdun or to Franco of Polonia, whose treatise of 1284 did much to introduce the torquetum to medieval astronomers and was responsible for Regiomontanus' interest in it.

The torquetum consisted of several brass plates engraved with divided circles and an alidade. It could be adjusted to the latitude from which observations are being made, and was used to calculate the time of observation, to establish the pairs of coordinates of a star in the horizontal, equatorial, and ecliptic systems, and to demonstrate the basic concepts of spherical astronomy. The assembly was supported on a horizontal plate that, when oriented, made it possible to take measurements of the azimuth or angles measured along the horizon. It was a complicated instrument and difficult to use, and much more adaptable as a demonstrational device than for observational practice. The earliest known example, dated 1444, is part of the library of the convent at Cusa.

Observatory. The astronomical observatory as an institution, staffed with professional astronomers engaged in ordered duties and a program of observations with scientific instrumentation, seems to have arisen in the Islamic world. Little is known of the earliest systematic observations, which were conducted under Caliph al-Maʾmūn about 830/831, but it is known that the instruments with which they were made were constructed according to the descriptions provided in Ptolemy's *Almagest.*

A permanent site or building was used for the Shammasīya observatory at Baghdad and for the Qasilynn observatory at Damascus, which served as prototypes for later observatories in the Islamic world. It is probable that some of them consisted primarily of a group of astronomical instruments used by the astronomer himself, who may have had other employment at the same time, and possibly several assistants. Others probably consisted of an informal group of scholars supported by a wealthy patron who jointly used instruments maintained in a permanent location. Later observatories were built, following special designs and at great expense, to house very large instruments in a permanent installation with a salaried staff. One of the best known of these was established at Marāgha (Maraghen), Azerbaijan, in 1259 by Hulagu, possibly inspired by a request from his brother Möngke to build an observatory at Qaraqorum. It was established by al-Ṭūsī and was furnished with instruments made in the tradition of Ptolemy's *Almagest.*

Arab astronomers were well aware of the observatory instruments described by Ptolemy, and proceeded to make and improve similar ones. These included a meridian armillary consisting of a graduated bronze ring having the form of an alidade set upon the meridian for measuring solar altitudes in zenith distance; the plinth, a large stone sundial accurately aligned to the meridian and used only for determining the obliquity of the ecliptic; an equatorial armillary made in the form of a bronze ring set firmly parallel to the plane of the equator; and a parallactic instrument known as "Ptolemy's rulers," a type of transit used to measure the zenith distance of a star or the moon at culmination. This last consisted of an alidade pivoted at the summit of an upright pole equipped with a plumb line and a bar hinged lower on the post and used to measure the chord of the angle formed between the alidade and the post.

Another of Ptolemy's instruments was the observational armillary astrolabe with concentric pivoted rings, the inner one made with sights and the others being rotatable around the axis of the poles of the ecliptic and the north-south polar axis, set within an adjustable meridian ring. This enabled a variety of observations to be made, including the determination of coordinates of stars. Part of Ptolemy's standard observatory equipment was a water clock used for timing observations at night, when a sundial could not be used.

The Ptolemaic instruments were of medium size, not too small to graduate with a fair degree of precision, yet not so large as to become cumbersome. To obtain the necessary rigidity, instruments were constructed of masonry when the foundations of the structure could be made secure, as at the observatories built for the Mughul maharaja Sawāʾī Jai Singh II (*r.* 1699–1743) at Jaipur, Delhi, and Ujjain in India.

INSTRUMENTS OF POSSIBLE EUROPEAN ORIGIN OR DEVELOPMENT

Polar sighting tube. An instrument that was prevalent in the medieval period was the polar sighting tube. Its function has never been fully ascertained, and it has generally been assumed that it was used to identify the polestar. It may also have been used to tell time in relation to the stars in the same manner that the nocturnal was used in a later period. Some believe that the polar sighting tube was merely part of the furniture of the astrologer and had no scientific function.

The polar sighting tube appears in at least five drawings or miniatures ranging in date from the eleventh through the fourteenth century. The earliest is a drawing from a manuscript of the *Senten-*

tiae astrolabi de Gerbert (930/1003; St. Gall, Stiftsbibliothek), a work by Gerbert of Aurillac, who later became Pope Sylvester II. In the course of his scientific studies, Gerbert constructed an armillary sphere fixed in position and properly oriented with its axis parallel to that of the earth and directed toward the celestial pole. In order to achieve this, Gerbert wrote, it was necessary to place a tube in such a manner that it remained fixed for the course of the night and one could observe the star believed to be at the pole; if this was the polestar, it could be observed all through the night, but if it was another, it would change position and it could not be seen through the tube for more than several moments. A miniature in the St. Gall manuscript depicts Ptolemy looking with one eye through a long tube supported on a spiral column terminating in a Corinthian capital that maintains the tube at a fixed angle. The tube is painted green, suggesting that it may have been a hollow reed or wooden tube, oriented by means of a graduated circle. The manuscript is a palimpsest, and the erased portion of the text is no longer recoverable.

A manuscript of the twelfth century provides a representation of Gerbert sighting through a polar tube. The explanatory text says: "According to this method one makes a semicircle, in which one fixes a tube by means of which it is possible to observe the pole and the last star of the Little Bear in order to determine the time at night. All of this can be verified by means of the astrolabe. Thus the pole and the last [star] of the Chariot indicate the hours of the night. The tube is fixed thus upon the cut-out disk. . . ." In the miniature the head and shoulders of the future pope are encompassed within a circle of four rings, with Gerbert looking through a long tube, not at the actual polestar but at a small star of the Giraffe (probably XII 230 Piazzi), which in the tenth century was near the pole. The manuscript was destroyed in World War II, and only a photograph of the miniature has survived.

Further confirmation of Gerbert's use of the polar sighting tube occurs in the chronicle of Bishop Thietmar von Merseburg, in which he notes that while Gerbert was at Madgeburg, he had made a clock, "setting it up by night, having sighted through a tube a certain star serving as guide to navigators [the polestar]." The text then goes on to state that such tubes were permanently fixed at a right angle upon a base or pedestal and used for sighting the polestar, and that if the tube's diameter was of sufficient width, it would be possible to see the polestar circling the rim of the field of vision while the center of the tube marked the true north pole.

The instruments illustrated in the two miniatures relating to Gerbert are the only two representations that may be construed as of polar sighting tubes. Several other depictions of a later period appear to be astrological furniture. A thirteenth-century manuscript of Peter Comestor's *Historia scholastica,* belonging to Conradus Philosophus (now in Munich), and a fifteenth-century encyclopedia in Latin have representations of Ptolemy or Pythagoras observing the skies through a hollowed elderberry branch, presumably to identify him as an astrologer. The magician Nectanebo is shown searching the stars with a sighting tube to determine the fate of King Alexander in a thirteenth-century manuscript of *La vraie ystoire dou bon Roi Alexandre,* and a miniature of slightly earlier date represents the sage Hermannus Contractus holding an astrolabe, Euclid at his left with an armillary sphere in one hand while observing through a sighting tube. A more elaborate, later copy of the latter has Euclid using a shorter tube. In a thirteenth-century manuscript now in Munich, Ptolemy is depicted observing a star through a tube of four sections, which appear to be collapsible, with one tube fitting into another as in the modern spyglass.

In an epistle to his friend Constantine of Fleury, Gerbert noted that he had constructed an armillary sphere, to the main circles of which he had fastened the symbols of the most important stars and constellations. Gerbert also built a celestial sphere consisting of two hemispheres of metal joined together and pierced at both poles. Through these openings a polar tube was inserted and fixed in such a manner that the observer could sight the polestar by means of it. The celestial globe could be oriented by turning it upon its axis. The globe with its axial tube trained on the polestar would probably have been mounted upon a columnar support similar to the one depicted in the St. Gall miniature.

Compass. By the eleventh or twelfth century, instruments were required for navigation; until then, sailing depended almost totally on the mariner's knowledge of the winds and on soundings. The magnetic compass was well known to mariners of the north by the twelfth century, for it was described in a treatise of 1187, entitled *De naturis rerum,* by Alexander Neckham, an English scholar and mariner studying in Paris, and in *La bible*

Guyot, of Guiot of Provins (composed between 1203 and 1208). Neckham described the compass as consisting of a needle transfixed in a reed floating on water. He then described a pivoted needle that whirled around to point consistently in a northerly direction. In 1218 Jacques de Vitry wrote that the compass was a necessity at sea, and that it was used to determine the wind direction in inclement weather.

The first extant reference to the dry compass occurred in the *Epistola de magnete* (1269) by the French soldier Peter Peregrinus of Maricourt. He described a magnetized needle on a vertical axis in a wooden bowl having a graduated verge ring. In time the compass card, also called the fly, was attached to the needle and able to rotate independently for finding directions. It was enclosed in a wooden box having a glass cover sealed in resin to protect it from moisture and the elements. The compass needle was formed of soft iron wire bent double into a loop equal to the circumference of the fly and then attached to the underside of the fly with strips of glued paper.

The origin of the magnetic compass or how it came to Europe is not known. There is evidence that the magnetic needle was used in China in antiquity, and it has been speculated that it may have been brought overland to Europe prior to Marco Polo's voyage. It has also been proposed that it originated in Scandinavia, passed to the Normans, and through them reached the Mediterranean region in the eleventh century.

The compass's magnetic needle lost its magnetization after a time, and it had to be restored by means of a lodestone. This consisted of magnetite, a natural oxide of iron that exhibits magnetic properties in its native state. A piece of this mineral was shaped and provided with an armature consisting of plates of soft iron placed at each pole and then bound in a casing of brass. It was provided with a "keeper" or "keeping plate" of soft iron to maintain its strength or "virtue." The magnetic properties of the needle were restored and reinforced by periodically stroking it with the lodestone, which became a required item for the mariner at sea. It was not until about 1750 that artificial magnets were first produced and replaced the lodestone.

Eventually, navigation was achieved by the compass instead of reliance upon the wind, and a lubber's point was added to the instrument to show the fore and aft lines of the vessel.

By the time of Columbus, mariners had noted the phenomenon described as the variation of the compass, which was recorded on charts and used as a guide to longitude. This led Flemish instrument makers to realign the fly over the needle so that when the needle indicated magnetic north, the fly pointed true north. This resulted in confusion until a variant compass was devised that had an alidade attached over the compass box to enable a bearing to be taken with the polestar to verify the azimuth of the compass.

Cross-staff. Another basic navigational instrument that came into being in the Middle Ages was the cross-staff, also called the fore-staff or Jacob's staff. In various countries it was also known as the *balestriglia, balestilha, arbalista,* or *baculus,* because of its resemblance to the crossbow. Traditionally claimed to have been invented by the Chaldeans, it was first described by Levi ben Gershom, a Languedoc-born Jewish scholar, in 1342.

The cross-staff was first used by astronomers to measure the distance between two stars and by mariners to measure the angular elevation of the sun or a star above the horizon. It consisted of a squared rod of hardwood approximately thirty inches (about 76 cm) in length with scales calibrated on all four sides, and equipped with three or four "transoms" or crosspieces that fitted friction-tight on the shaft. They were used one at a time and could be moved forward and backward along the rod. In use, the observer fitted a transom on the rod and pointed the instrument toward the sun while resting one end against his eye socket. The bottom edge of the transom was aligned so that it rested upon the horizon. It was then moved backward or forward until its upper edge appeared to rest on the sun. The observer was forced to look directly into the sun, which placed him at a disadvantage. Eventually a piece of colored glass was added to reduce the glare. When the top and bottom edges of the transom touched the sun and the horizon, the sun's altitude could be read from the appropriate scale engraved along the rod at the point at which the transom rested. When it was used with a table of solar declinations, the latitude of a ship could be determined.

Glasses. Three types of glasses were used at sea for measuring periods of time. The "watch glass" measured four hours, the "half-watch glass" measured two hours, and the third measured the half hour. Each time a glass was turned after the sand had run its course, the ship's bell was struck; thus the time of each "watch" was announced by the

Instruments for measuring distances at sea: armillary sphere, compass, etc. (on table); globe, hourglass, dividers, and dry compass (?) (at desk); lodestone compass (in foreground). Engraving by J. Galle based on the drawings of Stradanus, 1560. NEW YORK PUBLIC LIBRARY

number of bells recording the half hours that had elapsed, from one to eight. A time glass of thirty seconds' duration was also used to measure the speed of a ship in conjunction with the log. It was later modified to a glass of twenty-eight seconds' duration, and the length of the log line was reduced by half.

The history of the time glass is not well known. Reference to "dyolls" as part of the equipment of European ships in the late thirteenth century are thought to have been to time glasses, but the first certain reference is from the fourteenth century. The invention depended upon the ability to blow glass vials of sufficient accuracy and transparency. Time glasses are not mentioned in the *Libros del saber de astronomía* of the late thirteenth century, a work that relied heavily on Muslim sources, and it is believed that they probably came into use in Europe in the late thirteenth century, as a navigational aid.

THE RISE OF INSTRUMENT MAKING

It was not until the advent of the printed book, the development of engraving, and the consequent revival of Greek mathematics and astronomy during the last quarter of the fifteenth century that instrument making developed as an art. Prior to that time the instruments available to men of science were such common devices as drafting compasses, dividers, and the balance. More specialized instruments, such as astronomical observational instruments—the astrolabe, calculating devices, and the sundial—depended on scholarly appreciation of a manuscript tradition. While craftsmen were available for rough preparation of instruments by such means as metal casting, the graduation and engraving had to be done by the men of science.

The dissemination of the newly discovered learning brought with it an increased demand for the traditional instruments. As texts describing their construction and use became more available, mechanicians and craftsmen were sought who were capable of producing them. As a consequence, two categories of instrument makers emerged by the beginning of the sixteenth century. One consisted of the astronomers and other men of science who designed and actually constructed instruments for observation and for their own use. The greater number of artisans specialized in certain types of instruments, which they produced in large numbers. In time both categories became centered in Nuremberg and Augsburg and their environs; guilds became extremely well developed and their members had great skill in their specialties.

It was not until the end of the sixteenth century that both types of makers had spread to England, France, Italy, and the Low Countries as well as Germany, where new centers developed. In Augsburg a center developed as a consequence of the high prices paid for instruments by the Danish astronomer Tycho Brahe (1546–1601). At Prague, Erasmus Habermehl produced a great number of original instruments for Emperor Rudolf II; for his physician, Francesco Paduani of Forli; and possibly for Tycho Brahe. Thomas Geminus (*ca.* 1510–1562), who may have been connected with the instrument-making center established by Gualterius Arsenius at Louvain, migrated to England in 1540 and brought with him his engraving talents at the time when sheet brass was first being produced in England.

Toward the end of the Middle Ages, astronomy began to cater more to the practical needs of a changing society, as evidenced by the treatises that have survived. The period of discovery and colonization made new demands on astronomical science to respond to the needs of navigation and cartography. Meanwhile, knowledge and teaching of the sciences spread, resulting in the founding of important schools at Paris in France, at Merton College in England, at Vienna and at Nuremberg during the fourteenth and fifteenth centuries. John of Gmunden taught Georg Peuerbach, who in turn taught Johann Müller (Regiomontanus). The old *Theorica planetarum* was replaced (1472/1473) with Peuerbach's *Theoricae novae planetarum,* which had an important impact on the study of astronomy.

Johannes Regiomontanus (1436–1476) brought a new understanding to the relationship between theory and observation in the study of astronomy by his belief that the subject could be reformed by a better knowledge of celestial phenomena. In the early 1470's he founded an atelier for the production of scientific instruments, an astronomical observatory, and a press for the publishing of books on navigation and surveying as well as astronomy. The art of the engraver was used in the illustration of his publications, and in the graduation and decoration of the instruments produced by the atelier. He constructed new instruments for astronomical observations that he conducted at regular intervals as part of a long-range program and were continued after his death by his assistant, Bernhard Walther. The observations made at Nuremberg provided the foundation for the sixteenth-century astronomy of Nicholas Copernicus and Tycho Brahe.

During the late Middle Ages the making of scientific instruments was often the work of the clockmaker, and it may be said that the craft of the clockmaker and that of the instrument maker were closely linked. Several important clockmakers of the late medieval period were also makers of scientific instruments. Jean Fusoris (*ca.* 1365–1436) of Giraumont produced both clocks and instruments for a number of distinguished patrons. Lorenzo della Volpaia of Florence (1446–1512) founded a dynasty of distinguished clock- and instrument-makers who worked until the end of the sixteenth century, like himself producing public clocks and a variety of mathematical instruments.

It was not until the end of the medieval period and the early Renaissance, however, that instrument making became a separate craft, and that specialized instruments for specific needs, such as the simplified astrolabe for the navigator, appeared; and it was not until the early seventeenth century that optical instruments came into being.

BIBLIOGRAPHY

Albert Anthiaume and Jules Sottas, *L'astrolabe-quadrant du Musée des antiquités de Rouen* (1910); A. C. Crombie, *Medieval and Early Modern Science,* 2 vols. (1959, repr. 1963); Marcel Destombes, "Globes célestes et catalogues d'étoiles orientaux du moyen-âge," in *Actes du VIIIe Congrès international d'histoire des sciences* (1957); Robert Eisler, "The Polar Sighting-Tube," in *Archives internationales d'histoire des sciences,* no. 6 (1949); Willy Hartner, "The Principle and Use of the Astrolabe," in Arthur U. Pope, ed., *A Survey of Persian Art* (1930), III, 2,530–2,554 and figs. 844–852, and VI, pls. 1,397–1,402; G. R. Kaye, *The Astronomical Observatories of Jai Singh* (1918); Francis R. Maddison, "A 15th Century Islamic Spherical Astrolabe," in *Physis* (1962), fasc. 2; Leo A. Mayer, *Islamic Astrolabists and Their Works* (1956); Henri Michel, *Traité de l'astrolabe* (1947) and "Les tubes optiques avant le telescope," in *Ciel et terre,* **70,** nos. 5 and 6 (1954); John D. North, *Richard of Wallingford: An Edition of His Writings,* 3 vols. (1976); Emmanuel Poulle, *Un constructeur d'instruments astronomiques au XVe siècle, Jean Fusoris* (1963); Derek J. de Solla Price, "Precision Instruments to 1500," in Charles Singer *et al.,* eds., *A History of Technology,* III (1957), "On the Origin of Clockwork, Perpetual Motion Devices, and the Compass," in *Contributions from the Museum of History and Technology,* U.S. Museum Bulletin no. 218 (1959), and, as editor, *The Equatorie of the Planetis* (1955); George Sarton, *Introduction to the History of Science,* 3 vols. in 5 (1927–1947); Aydin Sayili, *The Observatory in Islam* (1960); Ernst Zimmer, *Leben und Wirken des Johannes Muller von Königsberg genannt Regiomontanus,* 2nd ed., rev. and enl. (1968).

SILVIO A. BEDINI

[See also **Armillary Sphere; Astrolabe; Astrology/As-**

tronomy; Biruni, al-; Calendars and Reckoning of Time; Clocks and Reckoning of Time; Compass, Magnetic; Cross-Staff; Equatorium; Fusoris, Jean; Geography and Cartography, Western European; Levi ben Gershom; Navigation: Western European; Peter Peregrinus of Maricourt; Richard of Wallingford; Science, Islamic; Sylvester II, Pope.]

SCOTLAND: HISTORY. By the mid eleventh century the disparate Celtic and Anglian kingdoms of northern Britain had become a single political unit, the kingdom of Scotland. It was a country whose geography suggests immense problems. The great mountain ranges of Drumalban in the west and the Mount in the east made access to the western and northern parts of the kingdom notably difficult, while the hills of the southern border region made it not much less cut off. To problems of political control were added economic problems, for there was comparatively little good land, this being concentrated mainly on the east coast and the central belt dividing highlands from borders, although even that was partly marshland. Its position in relation to the outside world was hardly more favorable. Within the landmass of Britain, it was, like Wales, vulnerable to domination by the powerful and wealthy kingdom of England. Its northern position and economic poverty gave it little appeal to the major powers of Europe. Yet its geographic, political, and economic weaknesses were recognized far less by contemporaries than by later historians. The dominant theme of the history of the independent Scottish kingdom before 1603 is the remarkable extent to which it established a place for itself in relation to England and to northern Europe.

That history falls into three phases: the period of friendship with England, until 1290; then the wars of independence, which abruptly destroyed that friendship, and lasted until the mid fourteenth century; and finally two centuries when war with England gave way to more passive hostility and Scotland could expand her contacts with Europe.

FRIENDSHIP WITH ENGLAND

The first phase set the scene for the structure of society that lasted throughout the Middle Ages. Twelfth-century Scotland, at least on the surface, was transformed almost beyond recognition, as a line of highly able kings introduced new people and new ways of life, both secular and ecclesiastical, and did so largely from England. As the Normans who came to England in the second great influx under Henry I (1100–1135) pushed north in search of land, along with younger sons and relatives of those who had come with William the Conqueror in 1066, they were welcomed into Scotland, especially by David I (1124–1153), Malcolm IV (1153–1165), and William the Lion (1165–1214). Initially in Lothian and later in Galloway and Clydesdale in the southwest, and even in the semi-independent province of Moray, lying beyond the Mounth, the Anglo-French friends of the king and their hangers-on were given estates. English monasteries supplied monks for the new religious foundations endowed by the crown; close contacts between the English and Scottish monarachies made this natural enough. David I, one of the greatest Scottish kings, and brother-in-law of Henry I, held the important English earldom of Huntingdon and had spent his youth at the English court.

But David's greatness did not lie in his ability to

make Scotland look like a mirror image of England. Even in this period of close contact, the point was not so much enthusiasm for England as enthusiasm for the world outside Scotland and the desire to model itself on and be noticed by that world. European influence, distilled largely through England, created the vision of an admittedly small-scale but authentic example of an up-to-date European kingdom, which David and his successors did much to realize. Not every settler came from England. The earliest of David's many monastic foundations, made in 1113, was the Tironensian monastery at Selkirk, established with Benedictines from Tiron in France. Beauvais canons were brought to Scotland for the Augustinian house at Jedburgh, founded about 1138. Behind such foundations lay the inspirations that created an upsurge of interest in England and Scotland alike: the revival of the monastic ideal in late-eleventh- and twelfth-century Europe and the towering figure of St. Bernard of Clairvaux. Similarly, in secular life, some of the settlers came directly from France. Flemings also were given land, especially in Clydesdale, Moray, and Aberdeenshire; and in the drive to encourage urban development kings founded burghs for both economic and sociopolitical reasons. It was the Flemings, noted for new technology in wool production and for trading, who were sought as the nucleus of the urban populations.

A country with few recognizable charters before the late eleventh century, whose towns and money economy were a new feature in the twelfth century, may be seen as coming into line with European society somewhat belatedly. But not everything was a matter of catching up. The early medieval church in Scotland may be termed "Celtic," but it was certainly not wholly isolated, in view of the parallels detectable with the churches of Ireland, Gaul, and Spain. The largely ineffective criticisms of its religious customs leveled by Margaret, the Anglo-Saxon wife of Malcolm Canmore (1058–1093), and the highly effective impact of David I were less a matter of bringing it into line than, as with the monasteries, a reflection of current trends in Europe. By 1200 the eleven dioceses within the boundaries of the kingdom represented the final resolution of the gradual and uncertain move toward a system of territorial dioceses going on since the eighth century. The vast *paruchiae* of the past were now broken down into small, manageable units; these parishes defined the areas from which churches were entitled to tithes. This new level of organization was much in keeping with the new mood of the church, emanating from the reformed papacy of the late eleventh and twelfth centuries.

Economically, Scotland shared in the European boom; as population increased so did the demand for food, and thus the need for more ploughed land. Small as the new burghs were, they nevertheless represented a marked advance on earlier settlements, like Perth, Edinburgh, and Glasgow, existing on trade routes and river crossings. Now there were flourishing commercial centers, underwritten with privileges granted by kings. The merchants, already before 1200 asserting their exclusive right to trade, and the prominent craftsmen, together produced a new level of economic activity. On the land, the Anglo-Norman settlers had a large share in the opening up of new land; the monks of the new border abbeys, Melrose, Jedburgh, and others, grew rich on sheep farming. The wool trade became the basis of commercial life, as it was to remain throughout the Middle Ages, supported by the export of hides and fish. Indeed, Scottish wool originally had a high reputation and was in demand abroad. Only at the end of the thirteenth century, when Scotland, like England, was afflicted by sheep scab, did the quality of wool decline. By then the era of prosperity was coming to an end in Scotland, as in Europe as a whole, forcing spendthrift landowners to retrench. Economic expansion as well as social adventuring was becoming a thing of the past, as the source of land, which had formed the basis of it, began to dry up.

In the twelfth century, the availability of land had provided the attraction for the king's new Anglo-Norman barons and knights. If the peaceful mode of their coming makes it inappropriate to speak of "conquest," their expectations and understanding of the conditions on which they held their land do make it possible to speak of the feudalization of Scotland. The crown and its foreign feudatories imposed, at least on the top level of society, a considerable change; and when Anglo-Norman clerks wrote their charters, they created a corpus of evidence that makes twelfth-century Scotland look profoundly different.

The extent of real change is impossible to pinpoint. Lordship was now defined, and, to an extent, limited. The rights of the lord over the fief he granted were carefully preserved in the rules governing the succession of his vassal's heirs, but at the same time his power to summon his vassal for military service was restricted to twenty or forty days; and only on specific occasions—the knighting of his eldest son, for example, or the ransoming of himself, once—could he demand financial aid. In late medieval Scotland, lords and their followers began to describe their mutual obligations in a new kind of document, the bond of manrent (allegiance) and maintenance. This agreement shows that the limitations recorded by the feudal charter had been swept away; men conceived of their obligations in very general terms, and one may suspect that it had always been so, for behind the definitions associated with lordship of land lay the personal lordship over men, which could not be so readily defined. Moreover, peaceful settlement in Scotland brought out the Norman genius for assimilation, unlike in England, where the dominant note was their genius for imposing control over a conquered state. In Scotland, kinship, as the basis of social obligations, survived into the early modern period, along with a system of justice that was a sophisticated form of the blood feud. The army remained, as it had earlier been, a "common army," summoned on a territorial basis, even if it was supplemented by the "mailed and mounted knight." The cheeses that the early-thirteenth-century feudal vassals of the earl of Lennox were required to provide for the king's army are an undoubted reminder of a nonfeudal past. It is indeed possible that the sheer speed with which new language and new modes were introduced to Scotland, at a time when they were already highly developed and even beginning to decline elsewhere, meant that they never fully took root.

SOCIAL REORGANIZATION

Yet behind the question of the fashionable terms on which men now held their land lay changes more profound and long-lasting. The great Scottish families of later centuries, Grahams, Montgomeries, Hays, Flemings, and many others, were all the descendants of the new settlers. By 1286, when the last of a line of highly effective kings, Alexander III, died, Scotland had a flourishing commercial life, based on the new towns.

The lingering remnants of the ethos of a warrior society were now refined and domesticated. The activities of Malcolm Canmore in the late eleventh century reflect attitudes of the past, contrasting sharply with the eagerness with which the young Malcolm IV sought knighthood at the hands of the English king Henry II, accompanying him to Toulouse on campaign in 1159 as the inducement that finally brought him the desired prize. Eagerness was not weakness, nor an indication of dependence on England. Malcolm IV's kingship was "European" rather than "Celtic"; that stirred up native resentment, and he returned from Toulouse to face a rising of six Celtic earls, which foundered on the fortifications of Perth and the king's Norman vassals. Already one earl had accepted the new trend: Duncan, earl of Fife, received his earldom anew from David I, as a feudal fief. Old and new sensationally came together in 1215, when the Celtic earl of Ross, Farquhar Maccintsacairt, finally defeated the MacWilliams, a Moray family who had threatened the security of an innovating monarchy for almost a century. The Celtic magnate sent the Normanized king, Alexander II, the heads of his enemies "as new gifts to the new king"; in gratitude, the king made him a knight.

The monarchy began to assert its control over larger tracts of its disunited and disparate kingdom, and did so through the medium of its new men. The general significance of Farquhar's gift was that the formerly semi-independent province of Moray had been brought within the orbit of the crown. Already, the rising power of the crown was seen in tangible form in the line of new burghs along the Moray Firth, established by Alexander II's father, William the Lion, for administrative as well as economic purposes. These burghs, growing up around royal castles, became the caput of the new sheriffdoms and provided friendly enclaves within hostile areas. In the northeast, as in the southwest, (Dumfries, Galloway, and Clydesdale) the creation of a few great lordships and numerous smaller fiefs brought into native society men of power and military experience who were in a personal as well as a "feudal" sense wholly dependent on the king. For the Anglo-French and Flemish settlers, the kinless men, only the king could offer protection, and their success was inevitably tied to the success of the crown itself. Thus both the adventurers who came north, and the more obvious allies of the monarchy, those friends from the south whom it invited in, together produced a royal affinity of considerable reliance. It was all the more impressive because it extended beyond the greatest families (Bruces, de Morevilles, and others) to lesser men who created the basis of a gentry class and who began to find their way into the service not only of the Anglo-Normans but also of native landowners like the earls of Atholl and Lennox.

Desire to minimize resentment no doubt lay

behind the fact that until just after 1200, no immigrant reached the highest rank of earl; and the earls' responsibility for summoning the common army remained unchallenged. Beyond that, the king's support was given to his Norman barons and knights. His justice became more pervasive in their interests, and those who wished to join the favored circle were left without doubt that the price was conformity to the new style of continental kingship. Not all conformed. In the twelfth century, the rebellions of the six earls, of Somerled in the west, and the Macheths and MacWilliams in the north, were motivated, even if not wholly, by hostility to new methods and new people. The powerful earls of the provinces of Scotland were too isolated and localized to withstand a bloc of men gradually established throughout the whole of non-Highland Scotland, linked by common ambition, common interest, and a common focal point, the crown. Two of the rebels of 1160 were Fergus of Galloway and Ferteth of Strathearn. Fergus' grandson, Lachlan according to some of his charters and Roland in others, turned up in Inverness in July 1187 to defeat Donald MacWilliam; Gilbert, son of Ferteth, was one of the few nonroyal founders of a monastery, Inchaffray in Perthshire, established in 1200 after the death of his son Gillechrist. Support for the ruling house, emulation of its enthusiasms, the combination of Gaelic and French names, all suggest an inevitable acceptance, however grudging, of change that could not be stopped.

The power of the crown at home was paralleled by its confident attitude abroad. Close relations with England never undermined the insistence of the leaders of Scottish society that their country was not simply an adjunct of the wealthier southern kingdom. Kings and churchmen united in the long struggle, throughout the twelfth century, to resist the claims of the archbishops of York over the Scottish church, entering with enthusiasm into the new world of bureaucratic processes and political machination to invoke the aid of the papacy. They did not get all they wanted; counterpressure from England persuaded the papacy to refuse the demand for metropolitan status for the bishops of St. Andrews, and Scotland remained until the late fifteenth century a unique phenomenon, a province of the church without an archbishop. But its place as an independent province was recognized when in 1192 Pope Celestine III finally declared Scotland a "special daughter" of the church of Rome, subject to none save the pope. A century later most Scottish churchmen were to add a spiritual dimension to the fight for political independence, to the point of backing an excommunicate king, Robert Bruce, against the English.

Political and, on occasion, military conflict arose from two sources: the attempts of the Scots to push their border farther south, and the claims of overlordship advanced by the English crown. The dramatic assertion of that overlordship by Edward I in 1291 has sent modern historians, as much as English and Scottish clerks of the day, scurrying to the records of the earlier claims, to discover the extent of their validity. It has proved an inconclusive search. But one scholar has advanced the convincing thesis that these claims tended to be raised most vociferously in answer to Scottish aggression. For David I, Malcolm IV, and William the Lion, the northern counties of England proved an irresistible temptation to an expansionist monarchy. Repeated and tedious demands were sometimes backed up by force. On one such occasion, in 1174, William the Lion led an army into Northumbria, losing both it and himself in the fog near Alnwick and falling captive to the English. That led to the only undoubted instance of formal English overlordship, the price exacted by Henry II under the Treaty of Falaise for William's release. It was not an overlordship that sat heavily on the shoulders of the Scots. It was, however, a sharp reminder that demands for English territory could be countered by the greater demand for overlordship. It lasted only until 1189, when Richard I willingly gave it up in return for Scottish cash to help finance his crusade. More generally, the triangular structure of the diplomatic and military pursuits of England, Scotland, and France, that familiar feature of the later Middle Ages, was already in existence in the thirteenth century, exemplified by the fact that both Alexander II and III married first English and then French brides. The Angevin kings had as much interest in their French territories as their English kingdom; the disposition of their northern neighbor was therefore a matter of concern to them and of potential usefulness to the French. Thus, in 1209, negotiations between Philip Augustus and William the Lion, which possibly included plans for a marriage alliance, brought King John up to the border with a large army, and with considerably more success than he had had in Normandy five years earlier.

The claim to the English northern counties effectively died with William in 1214, although it was not until 1237, with the Treaty of York, that it was finally buried. As in later centuries, possession of the important border burgh of Berwick was a greater source of trouble than it was probably worth; so it was with the northern counties. In neither case were the English prepared to let the Scots get away with it, and the solution came only when the Scots acknowledged that fact. They did so more readily in the case of Berwick. The long obsession with the northern counties demonstrates their independent ambitions, but it was a sterile obsession. When it was dropped, the thirteenth-century kings, Alexander II and III, turned to a much more fruitful pursuit, the expansion of the border on the west. The Western Isles, part of the mainland, and the Isle of Man were under the sovereignty of the Norwegian crown. Two expeditions by Alexander II, in 1221–1222 and 1249, began the process of annexation. A disastrous and cumbersome expedition by the great fleet of Haakon IV in 1263 was finally driven by autumnal gales onto the shore at Largs, where the tattered descendants of the Vikings were defeated by Scottish local levies. This completed the process, and by the Treaty of Perth of 1266 the western seaboard was formally recognized as part of the Scottish kingdom. It was not a complete victory. Politically but not socially assimilated, this area, the Macdonald lordship of the Isles in the later Middle Ages, remained relatively beyond the control of the crown. The last of the semi-independent provinces of Scotland, the lordship was finally suppressed by James IV in the 1490's. Nevertheless, apart from the northern islands of Orkney and Shetland, eventually acquired by the crown in 1468–1469, when they were pledged as the dowry of Margaret of Denmark in her marriage to James III, the kingdom of Scotland had reached its final form.

WARS OF INDEPENDENCE

Two centuries of comparative peace were savagely and abruptly ended when, in 1286, Alexander III died without male heirs, leaving only a four-year-old granddaughter to succeed him. The next ten years were marked by the attempts of Edward I of England to bring Scotland under English control, first by proposing to marry his heir, Edward, to the child-queen, Margaret, and then, after her death in 1290, by asserting English overlordship and extracting homage from the claimants to the vacant throne so that, when the issue was decided in favor of John Balliol in 1292, there was no doubt that Balliol was a vassal king. The collapse of that policy in the face of Scottish resistance in 1295–1296 brought the two countries to war—the wars of independence, which lasted, in a more or less virulent form, until the mid 1350's.

By the 1290's, only a few families—Bruces, Balliols, and Comyns—were major landowners in England and Scotland, and they did not doubt that their main interests lay in the north. It may be difficult now to understand the profound psychological shock that was produced when two centuries of strong kingship ended literally overnight, with the smashed body of the king at the foot of the cliffs of Kinghorn and the prospect of rule by a female child. (The Scots were to become familiar with the problems of minority and even of female rule, but that was in the future.) The eruption of rival claims to the throne by Robert Bruce and John Balliol in 1286 left no doubt of the maelstrom that dramatically threatened to engulf the nation. The proposed marriage alliance with England, a country with which there were close ties—particularly when planned with due attention to maintaining Scotland's independence—had a great attraction; the former ally Edward I could be seen as the present protector. It was equally reasonable for the Scots to turn to Edward when thirteen claimants made their bids for the throne in 1290. Inviting a foreign ruler with a reputation for justice to arbitrate in an internal dispute was not a novel idea; it had happened recently, when Louis IX of France was called in to arbitrate between Edward's father, Henry III, and his barons, without any question of admission of overlordship. To that extent, Edward I—scarcely unaware of the precedent—changed the rules when he insisted on such an admission. The ability of this king's right and left hand not to know what the other was doing was marked, and was seen again when he made the same demands of his vassal John Balliol while strenuously resisting similar demands made of him by the king of France.

Social structure and attitudes militated against a ready upsurge of national reaction to Edward. Avoiding civil war and settling the succession were initially much more pressing issues than the question of suzerainty, particularly when there was no reason to suppose that it would be more forcefully imposed than it had been by Henry II. While Bruce, Balliol, and others fought for high stakes in the court that Edward established to judge the competing claims, between 1290 and 1292, those outside the circle of men involved were scarcely aware of or troubled by the fact that behind the competitors stood Edward I. For most of the population—the people who would have to fight if resistance was to be offered—the outcome was of little importance. Their vision was local; their leader in society was not the remote figure of the king, but the local lord.

Edward's ambition was to outweigh his political judgment and evoke a reaction that went beyond such considerations. His interpretation of suzerainty was strictly legal, but it was a political affront. Appeals from the court of a lesser to a greater lord were one thing; appeals from the king's court to the court of another king were quite another, as Edward, vassal of the king of France, knew very well. The number of appeals from Balliol's court to Edward's after 1292 was small but more than enough for King John, or rather his greatest subjects, who pushed him into resistance in 1295. King John not only refused to answer Edward's summons for aid in his war against France but also concluded a treaty with France in 1296, the "Auld Alliance," which lasted until 1560. This brought swift and savage reprisal. Edward came north with an army, deposed John, and publicly humiliated him, stripping him of the insignia of royalty (hence the nickname wrongly believed to be a comment on his weak personality, "Toom Tabard" [the empty coat]). Edward's progress into northern Scotland as far as the Moray Firth and his establishment of direct English rule, with English officials in the Scottish localities, brought the reality of his claim home for the first time to a wide section of the population. The initiative, lost by a defeated aristocracy, passed to lesser men, to Andrew de Moray, and to one of the rare spirits of the age, the Renfrewshire knight William Wallace.

A spectacular victory over the English at Stirling Bridge in 1297, followed in 1298 by the crushing defeat of the Scots at Falkirk, gives Wallace's career a meteoric flavor, combining the stuff of legend with the dismal inevitability of Anglo-Scottish military history. But the significance of the short period in which Wallace became "guardian of Scotland," backed by the "middling folk" who rose against Edward's local officials in northern and southern Scotland, was far greater than this. It was not that an unpatriotic nobility now added snobbery to their other vices and stood aloof from the lesser-born leader of a nationalist rising; rather, extraordinary circumstances produced an extraordinary departure from the hierarchical norm. The "middling folk" are the unnamed and too often neglected group whose support for the enterprises of their superiors was the crucial determining factor. Now they acted for themselves, and in doing so enhanced their power to claim a voice in the affairs of the great; it was not something which the aristocracy of the later Middle Ages forgot. Nevertheless, neither they nor Wallace himself saw their position in 1297–1298 as a permanent shift of power in their favor.

It was, however, easier for the "middling folk" than for the aristocracy to appear as single-minded champions of freedom. Attention has rightly been drawn to the fact that the future King Robert, the second great nationalist hero of the wars of independence, pursued a tortuous path of shifting allegiances before seizing the throne in 1306 and thus committing himself to the fight for independence. But his failure to support Wallace, guardian in the name of King John, and his changes of front after the reemergence, in late 1298, of aristocratic opposition to Edward, have much to do with the fact that the Bruce family never gave up their own claim to the throne and denied the validity of Balliol's claim. To see this as selfish ambition triumphing over noble patriotism is too simple. Succession to the throne by primogeniture was not, in the 1290's, a long-accepted principle, making Balliol's claim clear-cut. Even in England, the principle was laid down only by Edward I, in 1290, and it was not firmly established in Scotland. The rights and honor of a magnate's family were as proper a concern as the liberties of his country. The period after 1298 therefore saw internal dissension between Bruce and the great family of Comyn, principal supporters of Balliol. It also saw continuing attempts by Edward to impose English rule, culminating in 1305 with a moderate and statesmanlike plan to associate English and Scots in government under the English king. It might have worked nine years earlier, but it was now too late for compromise. Bruce declared himself king in 1306; the following year brought the death of Edward I.

The significance of that death is not that Edward I would have in the end succeeded where his dismal son failed. Beyond the human opposition to Edward lay an enemy much more implacable: the geography of Scotland. For seven years after Falkirk, Edward had moved his government north to York. But there was no solution to the problem of permanent control of a country that stretched far north, where the geography became ever more inhospitable. The mountain ranges offered no opportunity for a would-be conqueror to ring them with mighty castles as Edward had done in Wales. Scotland north of Forth, as the Romans had discovered and as Edward died trying not to recognize—indeed, as the Scottish monarchy itself realized—was an area hard to control even from Edinburgh, and impossible from the south.

What was crucial was the breathing space which Edward's death gave the new king. In the last year of Edward's life, Bruce had been on the run, defeated in three battles. Now he could turn against his other enemies, those within Scotland who did not accept him as king. For the next two years, the Comyns in the north and the Macdougalls of Lorn in the west were the targets for savage attacks. Defeated, and their lands ravaged, they fled to England, leaving Bruce unchallenged by anyone of sufficient power—although by no means wholly accepted—and free to begin the recapture of the principal castles: Edinburgh, Perth, Roxburgh, and others. It was to regain the last great castle, Stirling, that he was forced to take the appalling risk of a pitched battle against the English in 1314. The Battle of Bannockburn brought him Stirling and immense prestige, but it did not bring admission of English defeat. Only in 1328 did the weak minority government of Edward III recognize Bruce, by the treaty of Edinburgh-Northampton, as the independent king of an independent kingdom. In practice, however, there was no real doubt after 1314 that Scotland was free of English domination. That lasted just as long as Bruce lived.

He was succeeded in 1329 by his five-year-old son David. Five years later David was sent to France for safety, remaining there until 1341, when southern Scotland was again overrun by English armies, those of Edward III and Edward Balliol, son of John and inheritor of both his father's claim and his father's willingness to rule as vassal of the English king. The pattern was repeated. Scottish independence wavered and then collapsed in the face of superior English military strength south of the Forth. The north could not be held, and that, combined with the appeal to Edward III of a greater prize, the French crown, brought the annual appearance of English armies to an end in 1337. It was not quite over. King David was captured by the English at Neville's Cross, near Durham, in 1346. His inept attempt to invade northern England on behalf of France kept him out of Scotland for another eleven years. The last great English attack came in 1356, with the "Burnt Candlemass," when Edward laid waste southeast Scotland. In 1357 David was released, and although the language of overlordship continued in diplomatic negotiations as long as Edward lived, and was occasionally revived thereafter up until the reign of Henry VIII, the real threat and the period of concentrated warfare were over.

If the basic pattern of society had been established in the twelfth and thirteenth centuries, the wars of independence had also left their mark. It was not only the "middling folk" who had new prominence. At the request of the French, the leading burghs had been represented in the 1295 treaty; thereafter, they were present at a number of parliaments when money was required. The ransom of 100,000 marks demanded for David II's release in 1357 made raising money a matter of urgency; from that time, the burgesses' place in parliament was permanent. Scotland now had a parliament of three estates. It never was a bicameral parliament, as in England; it was, on a small scale, similar to the national assemblies of Europe, in France, Spain, the empire, and elsewhere. This was not simply because the wars of independence meant that Scotland would no more model itself on England. It was the result of the fact that, compared to other countries, late medieval Scotland was rarely involved in war. Scotsmen did go abroad in search of military adventure, mainly to France, where their reputation as soldiers was high, and where the Hundred Years War gave them plenty of opportunity to exercise their talents against the English. But apart from the successful ambition of the southern landowners to drive the English out of their territory in the last quarter of the fourteenth century, with the taking of the last English outpost, Roxburgh, in 1460, and the dramatic reversal of 150 years of neutrality at Flodden Hill in 1513, the Scots were almost never called on to fight at home.

EXPANDING CONTACT WITH EUROPE

After David II's death in 1371 and the end of the move toward what has rightly been called "intensive government," dictated by war and the need to pay a massive ransom, the history of Scotland takes on a new character. There were to be no more spectacular events, victories, and defeats. The Battle of Flodden Hill was the only real break in the pattern of relative calm which was to last until the Reformation of 1560. At first sight, it appears a dismal and stagnant period, enlivened only by failures of kings and aggression of magnates, when central government looked increasingly undeveloped, and the localities slumbered in ungoverned isolation or tore themselves to pieces with uncontrolled feuds, while economically nothing was done to improve the country's position as an exporter of a few poor-quality raw materials.

Stagnation, however, is the wrong word for the incalculable benefits, for a small country, of the cessation of continuous war. As the pressure at home subsided, Scotland became able (to an extent it had never been before and would not be again once the links with England were renewed after the Reformation and with the union of the crowns in 1603) to look beyond its immediate neighbor and allow free rein to that earlier vision of the monarchy as a European kingdom. The essential context for that was stability at home. This stability was created by the fact that Scotland was not subjected to the tensions produced in other countries by government demands. There was no substantial unrest—no peasant revolts or town uprisings, no development even of a vocal lower house of shire gentry and burgesses—because the monarchy was not caught in the spiral of needing to raise taxes and thus increasing the number of collectors, all of which would make the costs of government and warfare heavier. The lairds and burgesses of late medieval Scotland were not particularly interested in central government because it impinged on them so little; even the magnates were left comparatively free to pursue local rather than national interests.

The continuing acceptance of the role of the magnate in dealing informally with crime and civil dispute on the basis of compensation to the victims of crime rather than retribution, and the general ability of the localities to manage their own affairs, does much to explain the astonishing paradox of a monarchy with serious disadvantages that was yet profoundly strong. David II's nineteen years in Scotland, out of a nominal reign of forty-two years, set the pattern for the future. The first two Stewart kings, Robert II (1371–1390) and Robert III (1390–1406), were weak men. Their successors, the first four Jameses, all succeeded as minors, so that their rule had to be maintained by others. In an age when the person of the king was fundamental to government, this was generally and rightly regarded as a problem of massive and destructive proportions; Scotland suffered from it to a unique degree. Yet comparative absence of the need for a lead from the center substantially minimized that problem. The monarchy was the focal point for the kingdom, not the direct ruler. Its prestige was immense, all the more so because it was not tarnished by resentment. There were, in this quiescent period, a few sensational events. James I was murdered in 1437 by a small group of aggrieved kinsmen who had suffered at the hands of a ruthless and avaricious king, and James III was killed in 1488 at the Battle of Sauchieburn, fighting unsuccessfully against a small army of rebels. On the other hand the crisis with the mighty earls of Douglas was resolved in the 1450's in favor of James II.

Prestige at home enabled the monarchy to reassert its role as a European power. No king of this period thought of himself as other than a European monarch of importance. All were conspicuous spenders, building palaces, acquiring that often useless but certainly expensive status symbol, artillery, spending money on ships, and maintaining courts that, if again on a small scale, nevertheless had a style and dignity modeled on the most fashionable center, the court of Burgundy. They made their voices heard abroad. James II, III, and IV all played a part in French affairs, the latter two stage-managing treaties between France and Denmark; and James IV went even further, with his long-term and wholly unrealistic effort to reunite Christendom in a crusade against the Turks.

No doubt this voice from the north was not taken altogether seriously, although Scotland's potential, to both France and Spain, as a makeweight against England made it impossible for it to be ignored, and its own self-confidence brought it greater recognition than its position and comparative poverty merited. Certainly the crown's insistence on its place abroad further enhanced its prestige at home, and where it led, others followed. Politically, Scotland's main tie was with France, but economic and cultural contact went far beyond the political ally.

It is true that Scotland was poor, and that the decline of her wool trade, beginning at the end of the thirteenth century and continuing until the mid fifteenth century, did not encourage the development of cloth-making, as in England. But it did encourage the development of other exports, particularly fish. The fifteenth century also saw the final assertion by the merchants of the royal burghs of their complete dominance of burgh affairs and stranglehold on foreign trade to the exclusion of the nonroyal burghs. It also saw the expansion of that trade, especially to the Low Countries, France, the

Baltic, Spain, and even England, to the extent that permanent communities were set up in the Low Countries and Scandinavia.

In this field, as in others, it was to Burgundy and Flanders that the Scots looked, rather than to France. In music and the visual arts, Flanders led the world of northern Europe, and it was there that the Scots turned for inspiration. Late-fifteenth-century churchmen had their tombstones made in Bruges, and at least one, William Scheves, archbishop of St. Andrews, had his portrait painted by one of the leading Flemish miniaturists, Quentin Massys. For the Church of Holy Trinity, Edinburgh, the provost, Edward Bonkil, commissioned a magnificent set of panels from the artist Hugo van der Goes. Scots musicians went to the Low Countries to be trained and returned to transmit their skills in the song schools that provided choristers and music for the church. In education also it was an age of expansion. The universities of Oxford and Cambridge were now effectively closed to Scottish students. The gap was filled in a way that exemplifies the new confidence, at home and abroad; three universities were founded, at St. Andrews (1411), Glasgow (1451), and Aberdeen (1495), serving mainly as first-degree colleges from which scholars went to pursue further study at the great centers of learning abroad. Some of them, notably John Major (*ca.* 1469–1550) and Hector Boece (1465–1536), were scholars of distinction in the cosmopolitan world of the academy. By then, the exchange of intellectual ideas was being subsumed into the world of religious debate. In the 1530's, Major, who first introduced John Calvin to the ideas of Luther when he attacked these ideas in Paris, and Boece, the friend and ally of Erasmus, were fighting out their academic rivalries in the context of the growing fear of heresy. It was not only among churchmen, however, that attitudes were changing. The early signs of that revolutionary change in attitude among the laity, no more explicable in fifteenth-century Scotland than in any other society, when educated laymen began to read for themselves, are clearly evident by the end of the fifteenth century and were to have a profound effect, not only on education but on the hitherto clerical preserves of law and administration.

In the reign of the attractive and highly cultured James IV (*r.* 1488–1513), all these trends reached their highest—and lowest—points. Whether it is accurate to speak of "Renaissance Scotland" is an open and not wholly helpful question. What is important is the existence of a court of dazzling quality, in which men of towering individual talent, even genius (William Dunbar, Gavin Douglas), along with other, lesser men, wrote poetry of a very high order. Already, the previous reign had seen the even more remarkable Robert Henryson, perhaps the greatest of them all; remarkable because he was not a court poet but a Dunfermline schoolmaster, writing for an audience outside the court. Politically, James tried to continue the new and understandably unpopular policy of his father, the revival of friendship with England, strengthened by his marriage in 1503 to Margaret Tudor. That, and his attempt at the same time to maintain the Auld Alliance and influence other European rulers, including the papacy, provided the spectacle of the Scottish monarchy at its most assertive. It was an attractive soap bubble. The complexities and shifts in European relations, the ambitions of pope and secular rulers, were far beyond the abilities of a Scottish king to deal with. Reality came in 1513 with the death of the king and most of the governing elite of Scotland in the rain and mud of Flodden Hill, the battle fought because James could no longer resolve the conflict between France and England. It was a terrible reversal of a long period of advance and flourishing such as Scotland had never before experienced. But it was no more than a temporary reversal, a personal rather than a national disaster.

BIBLIOGRAPHY

Evan W. M. Balfour-Melville, *James I, King of Scots, 1406–1437* (1936); Geoffrey W. S. Barrow, *Regesta regum Scottorum*, 2 vols. (1960), *Robert Bruce and the Community of the Realm of Scotland* (1965), *The Kingdom of the Scots* (1973), and *The Anglo-Norman Era in Scottish History* (1980); Jennifer M. Brown, ed., *Scottish Society in the Fifteenth Century* (1977); Annie I. Cameron, *The Life and Times of James Kennedy, Bishop of St. Andrews* (1950); Ronald G. Cant, *The University of St. Andrews* (1970); Ian B. Cowan, *The Parishes of Medieval Scotland* (1967); *idem* and David E. Easson, eds., *Medieval Religious Houses in Scotland* (1976); William C. Dickinson, *Scotland from the Earliest Times to 1603*, Archibald A. M. Duncan, ed., 3rd rev. ed. (1977); John G. Dunbar, *The Historic Architecture of Scotland* (1966); Archibald A. M. Duncan, *The Nation of the Scots and the Declaration of Arbroath, 1320* (1970), and *Scotland: The Making of the Kingdom* (1975); John Durkan and James Kirk, *The University of Glasgow, 1451–1577* (1977); *idem* and Anthony Ross, *Early Scottish Libraries* (1961).

H. G. Farmer, *A History of Music in Scotland* (1947); W. Ferguson, *Scotland's Relations with England* (1977); Isabel F. Grant, *Social and Economic Developments of Scotland Before 1603* (1930); Alexander M. Kinghorn, *The Chorus of History* (1971); Robert L. Mackie, *King James IV of Scotland* (1958); Peter McNeill and Ranald G. Nicholson, *An Historical Atlas of Scotland* (1975); John MacQueen, *Robert Henryson* (1967); Ranald G. Nicholson, *Edward III and the Scots* (1965) and *Scotland: The Later Middle Ages* (1974); Robert S. Rait, *The Parliaments of Scotland* (1924); Grant G. Simpson, *Scottish Handwriting, 1150–1650* (1973); Edward L. G. Stones, ed., *Anglo-Scottish Relations, 1174–1328* (1965); *idem* and Grant G. Simpson, eds., *Edward I and the Throne of Scotland, 1290–1296* (1978); Bruce Webster, *Scotland from the Eleventh Century to 1603* (1930).

JENNY WORMALD

[See also **Barons' War; Cnut the Great; David I of Scotland; David II of Scotland; Douglas, Gavin; Dunbar, William; Duncan I of Scotland; Edward I of England; Edward II of England; Edward III of England; England: Norman-Angevin; Feudalism; Hugo van der Goes; Henryson, Robert; Macbeth; Malcolm IV of Scotland; Robert I of Scotland; Robert II of Scotland; Strathclyde, Kingdom of; William I of England.**]

SCOTTISH LANGUAGE. See **Celtic Languages.**

SCOTTISH LITERATURE, GAELIC. Gaelic-speaking people settled in Scotland on a significant scale from about A.D. 500, although there were earlier groups of Gaelic visitors and colonists. Columba came from Ireland to join his fellow Gaels and extend the Christian church's influence to neighboring peoples, such as the Picts, about 563. Thus Gaelic has been used in Scotland since before the time of what we call Old Irish (better described as Old Gaelic).

Through conquest, political and religious prestige, intermarriage, trade, and the arts, Gaelic spread from its original western base in Dál Riata (Argyll and the southern Inner Hebrides), eventually supplanting British (which we know as Welsh in later times) and Pictish. It reached its peak of expansion and prestige about the twelfth century, and then gradually gave way to Anglian (later to be called Scots and English).

There are very sparse records in Gaelic from these centuries before 1200: occasional verses, such as those by Adamnan (*ca.* 624–704), Columba's biographer; an account of the early colony of Dál Riata (entitled *Senchas Fer nAlban*), perhaps dating originally from the seventh century; annalistic entries about Scotland incorporated in the Irish annals; a piece of legend, history, and propaganda for the Gaelic royal line, called the *Duan Albanach* or Scottish Lay, dating from about 1093; and a short series of prose notitiae, dating from about 1130–1150, in the Book of Deer.

We cannot claim to have examples of Gaelic literature in the conventional sense before the thirteenth century. But since we have sufficient evidence of a Gaelic society with its normal appurtenances (laws and judges, poetry and historians, churchmen, sculptors, manuscript illuminators, craftsmen working in precious metals, musicians), it is reasonable to suppose that various forms of literature flourished in these early centuries. The evidence of quite late medieval times seems to argue continuous literary links with the early centuries, and it is usual to postulate roughly parallel developments in Scotland to those we have so fully attested from Irish evidence.

Scottish Gaelic manuscript sources are very late, and probably the most illuminating manuscript is the Book of the Dean of Lismore, compiled for the most part between 1512 and 1526. Mainly a verse anthology, it provides evidence of the deeply entrenched practice of courtly panegyric by professional poets as well as other types of verse, such as religious verse, satire, love poetry, sententious and aphoristic verse, and bawdry. It includes also a large collection of heroic ballads, a few of them of Scottish origin (see Meek). This anthology shows us that the work of Irish poets in these modes was also known and prized. The Scottish authors are in the main connected with Perthshire and Argyllshire (to use more modern geographical labels), since these were the parts of Scotland most familiar to the compilers of the manuscripts. And the political and military spheres of influence of the MacDonalds and the Campbells probably represented, in the fifteenth and sixteenth centuries, the most fertile ground for such literary activity.

HEREDITARY BARDIC POETS

From other manuscript sources, mainly of the sixteenth and seventeenth centuries but drawing on earlier sources, we see that there were several clearly defined and long-lasting lines of hereditary poets and *seanchaidhean* (traditional historians) associated particularly with certain ruling families. Thus we discern a succession of poets of the surname MacEwen serving at one time the MacDougalls of Dunollie in Argyll and later the Campbell chiefs (including the earls of Argyll). A succession of seven MacEwen poets can be distinguished between about 1400 and 1650, but it is not possible to pinpoint verse by each of them. The earliest identifiable poem is a lament for MacDougall of Dunollie, a fifteenth-century chief (found in Watson, *Scottish Verse from the Book of the Dean of Lismore*). It uses the literary convention of pathetic fallacy to great effect, as in:

> A flood tide covers the hillocks after John's death—that is one of the visible signs of it; there is no foam on the sea on the surface of the bays around Connel. [The name "Connel" refers to a sea cataract producing turbulence and foam.]

The later members of this dynasty were involved in the translation of John Calvin's catechism into Gaelic.

Again, we find a slightly shorter succession of poets of the name of Ó Muirgheasáin, associated with the Macleans of Mull (probably) and the MacLeods of Harris and Dunvegan. Other similar successions can be detected in Perthshire and Skye. The most famous, and the longest-lived, of these dynasties was that of the MacMhuirichs, who traced their descent from Muireadhach (or Muiredach) Albanach Ó Dálaigh (Scottish: Muireadhach Ó Dálaigh), an Irish professional poet who is thought to have fled to Scotland about 1215. Muireadhach addressed two poems to the earls of Lennox, and these are the earliest surviving courtly panegyrics composed in Gaelic in Scotland or addressed to a Scottish patron. The succession of poets claiming descent from him extends to the mid eighteenth century, over 500 years later, and Lachlan MacMhuirich in 1800 claimed to be eighteenth in descent from Muireadhach. Our record of this long-surviving dynasty is very patchy, but we can distinguish members of it in 1411, 1485–1541 (four individuals), and in the seventeenth and eighteenth centuries. The two poets whose work survives best are Cathal and Niall MacMhuirich. Cathal's poetry spans the period from before 1618 to about 1651(?), and Niall's from about 1660 to about 1719.

Gaelic verse composed by trained professional poets from the thirteenth to the eighteenth century in Scotland has close links with similar Irish verse of the same period (though the tradition lasted a little longer in Scotland). It draws on a common body of metrical and linguistic conventions, and a common store of thematic motifs, historical and legendary learning, and stylistic devices, although there are variants of many of these models unique to Scotland. Central to the verse is the concept of the poet as custodian of legendary, historical, and literary learning and as both servant and mentor to his patron. Clearly he allowed himself some freedom and relaxation from these binding obligations, and these issue in occasional love poems, satires, or literary exercises on the fringes of his central oeuvre. Sometimes his work is dedicated to a divine patron, and so we get a good deal of religious verse, including Mary-cult poems. There were elaborate training routines for these poets, requiring many years of study in bardic schools, and a huge program of memorization of meters, linguistic rules, poems, tales, and perhaps genealogical tables and other esoterics.

Thus we find Muireadhach addressing an earl of Lennox probably between 1215 and 1220, reminding him of his ancestry (actual and legendary) and of his obligations to poets who praise him. These obligations are expressed in terms of goods: "It were fitting for me to have twenty milch cows, swift Scottish foals, the choice of all kindly fresh-hazelled lands, from you, Amhlaoíbh who are young and gentle-eyed" (see Carney and Greene, *Celtic Studies,* 94–97, for the Gaelic text). Early in the fourteenth century a poem by the blind poet MacGurcaigh (Watson, *Scottish Verse*) describes the galleys of John MacSween of Knapdale, and we can see in the lines quoted here the strong Norse influence on the style of decking out the ships:

> The prows of the ships are arrayed
> with quilted hauberks as with jewels,
> with warriors wearing brown belts;
> Norsemen—nobles at that.
> The prows of the brown-sailed ships
> are decked with swords which have gold and ivory
>   settings;
> . . . .
> shields hang from the long sides of the ships.
> (Thomson, *An Introduction to Gaelic Poetry,* p. 28)

In 1411 another MacMhuirich poet made a battle incitement before the Battle of Harlaw. Late in the fifteenth century we have a series of MacMhuirich poems lamenting the death of the MacDonald leader Aonghas Óg and the forfeiture of the lordship of the Isles about 1493. From the early years of the sixteenth century there survive a number of courtly, satiric, and bawdy poems, especially by Sir Duncan Campbell of Glenorchy, who mourns in one the loss of his virility and finds that his wife no longer lavishes culinary and other attentions on him.

The number of surviving poems in the courtly love tradition is small; the best-known examples are those by a fifteenth-century countess of Argyll and by Niall Mór MacMhuirich (dating from about 1600). In both cases there may well be strong elements of personal experience present, and probably Eóin MacMuireadhaigh's *Námha dhomh an dán* (Dean of Lismore's MS, 61) represents the more central fictional tradition. The tradition spills over into the semibardic and vernacular verse of the sixteenth century and later. The theme of religion is a recurring one, sometimes forming the central subject of a poem, and often appearing as a biographical confessional element in poems on other topics.

There is no doubt, however, that the staple product of the professional classical poets was praise poetry, and this is prominent in all periods and in all poetic dynasties. Examples of such poetry were created when Fionnlagh Ruadh addressed a succession of poems to the MacGregor chief who died in 1519 (Watson, *Scottish Verse*), or the MacEwens made poems for the chiefs of clan Campbell (Watson, "Unpublished Gaelic Poetry"); and Eoin Óg Ó Muirgheasáin recounted the life and military exploits of Ruairi Mór MacLeod of Dunvegan (*d.* 1626). Common thematic conventions include description of the chief's or patron's demesne, residence, and household; the relation of the country's prosperity to the ruler's health or survival; the recounting of genealogical and legendary information; the application of an apologue to link the patron's case with one in history or story; description of the chief's appearance and his moral attributes and character; and a concluding courtly address to the lady of the house.

Certain stanzas from the Book of the Dean illustrate these themes:

> Surety of the folk of song is MacGregor who bestows cattle; patron of poet-bands and famed in the hunt, his white hand that reddens spears.
>
> Harps are played in harmony in the hands [of minstrels] in the hero's stronghold; the members of his household move from their games of backgammon to walk in the shade of the garden.
>
> A lovely hand, long and decked with rings, is that of Caitilín of the white palms; red are her lips, luscious and noble, and the rosy gleaming nails of her hands.
>
> In the van of Clan Donald learning was commanded, and in their rear were service and honor and self-respect.
>
> Remember Colin your own father; remember again Archibald; remember Duncan after them, the friendly man who loved hounds.
>
> Glen Lyon's prince of sword blades, a mighty shield unstinting to poets, a hand like Oscar in every fight—that is the one the prince resembles.

The succession of professional poets continued until the second quarter of the eighteenth century, Donald MacMhuirich in South Uist being the last, but it had become clear to them by the middle of the seventeenth century that the days of their class were numbered, as Highland chiefs began to turn to other styles of living. This realization gives rise to a series of statements of the ideal that they saw being evaded:

> Clearly it is a loss to your family when it comes to enumerating their battles or their original rights, that they should lack gracious knowledge—which produces clear information—or the searching out of their genealogy that leads to clarity.
>
> The race of Colla did not make a practice of having no men of knowledge among them until now—an inescapable circumstance; their nobles take the wrong turning and go astray.

These examples take us well beyond the normal chronological bounds of medieval literature, but it is in the Middle Ages that they belong in tone and sentiment. And much of that tone was transferred to the vernacular poetic tradition in Gaelic also. (For more detailed accounts of the classical bardic verse, see bibliography: Watson [1922]; Thomson [1974, 1977, 1983].)

The Book of the Dean of Lismore is the main source of surviving bardic verse, but examples occur in the Books of Clanranald, and in a number of manuscripts in the National Library of Scotland, Edinburgh; the Royal Irish Academy, Dublin; and elsewhere.

GAELIC PROSE

Although prose, in the Scottish Gaelic context, was less prestigious than verse, it was cultivated for certain forms and purposes, most notably for the telling of tales, but also for chronicles and histories, lives of saints and religious writings, and medical treatises. The rich accumulation of surviving tales—in medieval manuscripts and especially in the manuscript and tape archives assembled by nineteenth- and twentieth-century collectors such as John F. Campbell, John L. Campbell, Calum Maclean, and the collectors from the School of Scottish Studies—point to a widespread and long-lasting cultivation of prose for saga and tale. It is fairly generally agreed now that many, or perhaps most, of these tales had written or literary originals, and occasionally the links between modern oral versions and earlier manuscript ones can be demonstrated. The contemporary story of Conall Gulbann is thought to be a sixteenth-century romance; *Cath Fionntrágha* (The battle of Ventry), which has roots in the Middle Ages, was still being copied in the eighteenth century; and a fragmentary version of the *Táin,* the Old Irish epic, was recorded from oral tradition as late as a quarter of a century ago. Although the scribal involvement of literary families (such as the MacMhuirichs) in such tales is known, there is little by way of strict demonstration that particular versions of such tales were composed by identifiable individuals in medieval Scotland. (For some general discussion of this point, see Bruford.)

The medical manuscripts (of which twenty-nine survive) are of fifteenth-to-seventeenth-century provenance, written and preserved by the members of hereditary medical dynasties such as the Beatons, O'Conachers, and MacLachlans, and drawing mainly on the medical sources (such as Greek and Arabic) current at the time, with some addition of local herbal lore and clinical observation. One of the best-known examples of these manuscripts is the *Lilium Medicinae,* fundamentally the work of the early-fourteenth-century Bernard of Gordon, but in its Gaelic version written at Montpelier in 1415 (see Mackinnon and "Manuscripts, Medical," in Thomson, *The Companion to Gaelic Scotland*).

The main surviving example of historical prose is that written by members of the MacMhuirich family in the Black and Red Books of Clanranald (see Cameron, II, 138–309). This represents a compilation of chronicle and genealogical data, with a final section of recent and contemporary history compiled by Niall MacMhuirich, probably shortly after 1700. It must be in considerable part derived from earlier family manuscripts. Parts of the manuscripts consist of genealogy and chronicle surrounding praise poetry, some of this material being of fifteenth-century origin and perhaps earlier, while legend, pseudohistory, and pseudogenealogy set the patrons in a framework that extends before the Middle Ages and in some instances before the start of the Christian era. In another instance we find a MacPhail scribe inserting genealogies of West Highland clans (the "1467 genealogies") into a collection of mainly religious writings (National Library of Scotland, Edinburgh, MS 72.1.1.). Presumably the seventeenth-century MacEwen poet who traces the Argyll chief back to Adam (see Watson, "Unpublished Gaelic Poetry") had access to Campbell Gaelic manuscripts of a similar kind, and we can assume that such miscellanies were common. The late medieval Scottish chronicles, such as that of John of Fordun (*ca.* 1320–1384), and the further elaborative work of Hector Boece (*ca.* 1465–1536), draw on the legendary and spurious elements of the story of the Gaels' origins, rather than on more sober annals, which seem also to have existed for certain periods. For example, the Iona chronicle is deduced as underlying the account of early Scottish events in the Irish annals.

POPULAR VERSE (FOLK SONG)

It is right at the end of the medieval period that we can distinguish the earliest surviving popular, as opposed to classical or professional, Gaelic verse. This verse, often referred to as folk song, is concerned with personal feelings and local incidents, with early battles, heroes, violent deaths, imprisonments, and praise and laments for individuals. Some of the earliest examples relate to members of the MacGregor clan, harried by encroaching Campbells, sometimes killed or executed, as Gregor MacGregor was in 1570. These songs generally use a different range of meters from those favored by the professional bards, and there are strong indications that these meters are themselves very ancient and were probably used throughout the Middle Ages. Examples are the strophic stanza, which probably derives from the *ochtfhoclach* stanza, and the four-stress, eight-syllable line, which may go back to very ancient four-stress alliterative verse. (See Thomson, "The Poetic Tradition in Gaelic Scotland.") Many of these later songs (especially ones of seventeenth-century dating) survived in the repertoire of tweed waulkers (those who "fulled" or thickened woven cloth by beating it, keeping time by singing), and finally came to rest in the Outer Hebrides, though they had earlier originated in various parts of Gaelic Scotland (see Thomson, *op. cit.*, and Collinson and Campbell). Another example of detritus from medieval times is the, collection of hymns, incantations, and charms made by Alexander Carmichael in the second half of the nineteenth century and published under the title of *Carmina gadelica*. Few of these verses are either ascribed to authors or dated, and they come from widely separated periods, but a significant core of them are pre-Reformation.

The intermingling of Scottish and Irish writings and their haphazard preservation in a variety of traditions produce severe difficulties for scholars, and these are only gradually being resolved. The isolation and conservatism of Gaelic society in Scotland led, furthermore, to an unusually late survival of modes and attitudes that are essentially medieval. These considerations have dictated an extension of the dating limit of 1500 generally used in this Dictionary, and in isolated instances such an extension could even impinge on the twentieth century.

BIBLIOGRAPHY

John W. M. Bannerman, *Studies in the History of Dalriada* (1974), and *The Beatons* (1986); Alan Bruford, *Gaelic Folk-tales and Mediaeval Romances* (1969); Alexander Cameron, *Reliquiae celticae*, 2 vols. (1892–1894); Alexander Carmichael, *Carmina gadelica*, 6 vols. (1900–1971); James Carney and David Greene, eds., *Celtic Studies* (1968); Francis Collinson and John L. Campbell, *Hebridean Folksongs*, 3 vols. (1969–1981); William Gillies, "Courtly and Satiric Poems in the Book of the Dean of Lismore," in *Scottish Studies*, **21** (1977), and "The Gaelic Poems of Sir Duncan Campbell of Glenorchy," in *Scottish Gaelic Studies*, **13** (1978–1981); Kenneth H. Jackson, "The Poem 'A Eolcha Alban Vile,'" in *Celtica*, **3** (1956), and "The Duan Albanach," in *Scottish Historical Review*, **36** (1957); John MacDonald, "An Elegy for Ruaidhrí Mór," in *Scottish Gaelic Studies*, **8** (1955–1958); Donald MacKinnon, *A Descriptive Catalogue of Gaelic Manuscripts . . . in Scotland* (1912); Donald E. Meek, "The Corpus of Heroic Verse in the Book of the Dean of Lismore" (diss., Univ. of Glasgow, 1982); Edmund C. Quiggin, *Poems from the Book of the Dean of Lismore* (1937); Neil Ross, *Heroic Poetry from the Book of the Dean of Lismore* (1939); Derick S. Thomson, "The MacMhuirich Bardic Family," in *Transactions of the Gaelic Society of Inverness*, **43** (1960–1963), "The Harlaw Brosnachadh: An Early Fifteenth-century Literary Curio," in James Carney and David Greene, eds., *Celtic Studies* (1968), *An Introduction to Gaelic Poetry* (1974), "Three Seventeenth-century Bardic Poets: Niall Mór, Cathal, and Niall MacMhuirich," in Adam J. Aitken, Matthew P. McDiarmid, and Derick S. Thomson, *Bards and Makars* (1977), *The Companion to Gaelic Scotland* (1983), and "The Poetic Tradition in Gaelic Scotland," in *Proceedings of the Oxford (1983) International Conference on Celtic Studies* (1984); William J. Watson, "Classic Gaelic Poetry of Panegyric in Scotland," in *Transactions of the Gaelic Society of Inverness*, **29** (1914–1919), "Unpublished Gaelic Poetry," in *Scottish Gaelic Studies*, **3** (1931), and *Scottish Verse from the Book of the Dean of Lismore* (1937).

DERICK S. THOMSON

[See also **Adamnan; Bard; Bardic Grammars; Celtic Languages; Dál Riata; Irish Literature; Ó Dálaigh, Muireadhach Albanach.**]

SCREEN, a structure of wood, metal, stone, or other material whose function is to separate, seclude, protect, or conceal one person, place, or thing from another. In this sense a screen facade is a building front that extends vertically or laterally so as to hide the edifice behind it.

The word "screen" is normally used to describe an interior partition that separates one part of a church, hall, or room from the rest. A screen chamber is an apartment thus divided from a larger interior, especially when it is enclosed by a solid rather than an openwork screen. Such a partition is called a screen wall, particularly when built of stone.

Screens of a wide variety of materials and uses were employed in the Middle Ages, most notably in ecclesiastical settings. Although the term is sufficiently broad to embrace any and all partitions short of load-bearing walls, the main types listed below deserve mention.

An *altar screen* (or reredos) is a partition, higher than an altar rail, that separates the main altar of a church from the area behind it, such as a presbytery or a retrochoir.

A *chancel screen* separates the chancel from the body of a church. The word "chancel" denotes either the entire area set apart for the clergy or, less broadly, the sanctuary alone. In the latter sense a chancel screen may divide the sanctuary from the choir in front of it. (See following article.)

A *chapel screen*, a partition between a chapel and the aisle, nave, or transept of a church, is more substantial than a chapel rail.

A *choir screen* encloses the choir of a church (and often the sanctuary as well), dividing it from the aisles or ambulatory along its sides and back. Strictly speaking, a choir screen is distinct from the chancel screen or rood screen that separates the front of the chancel or choir from the nave, but the terms are used synonymously as often as not.

An *iconostasis* is a screen dividing the sanctuary from the rest of the interior in churches of the Greek rite. Its function is largely identical with that of a rood screen.

A *pardon screen* shields the penitent in a confessional from the view of the priest.

A *rood screen* separates the choir or chancel from the nave of a church, hiding the clergy from view; it is so called because it supports a rood (a large cross or crucifix). In the later Middle Ages rood screens acquired architectural proportions, often consisting of two screen walls connected by vaulting and sometimes housing stairs leading up to a rood loft (an upper platform used as a pulpit for reading the Epistles and Gospels, or for sermons). Rood screens were frequently adorned with sculpture and other ornament, and the largest of them might house altars or small chapels. As a result of subsequent changes in the liturgy, few rood screens have survived; the finest Gothic example (*ca.* 1500) is at Albi Cathedral. In France a rood screen is called a *jubé*; in Italy, a *tramezzo*.

A *sanctuary screen* separates the sanctuary proper from the larger chancel or choir, or from the nave in a small church, oratory, or chapel; it is synonymous with "chancel screen" in the most limited sense of that term.

A *screens passage* is the space between the service screen and the end wall of a medieval hall, giving access to the kitchens and other service facilities.

BIBLIOGRAPHY

Banister Fletcher, *A History of Architecture on the Comparative Method,* 19th ed., rev. by R. A. Cordingley (1986).

GREGORY WHITTINGTON

[See also **Altar–Altar Apparatus; Architecture, Liturgical Aspects; Iconostasis; Transenna.**]

SCREEN, CHANCEL (from Latin *cancellus,* "rail" or "latticed barrier"), a barrier separating the eastern end of a church, which was reserved for the altar and clergy, from the main part of the building, or nave. Known as templons in the Byzantine East, chancel screens usually consisted of a low colonnade supporting a railing. Almost always carved in marble, sometimes in exceptional cases a chancel barrier was sheathed in precious metal (for example, silver at Hagia Sophia in Constantinople). The barrier became increasingly high in Byzantine churches after the ninth century and frequently was replaced by an iconostasis, as is still seen in Russian Orthodox churches.

Rood screen in Albi Cathedral, *ca.* 1500. PHOTO: WIM SWAAN

BIBLIOGRAPHY

Ann Wharton Epstein, "The Middle Byzantine Sanctuary Barrier: Templon or Iconostasis?" in *Journal of the British Archaeological Association,* **134** (1981): Richard Krautheimer, *Early Christian and Byzantine Architecture* (1975), 157, 212–213; Thomas Mathews, *The Early Churches of Constantinople: Architecture and Liturgy* (1970), 109–110, 122–125.

LESLIE BRUBAKER

[See also **Chancel; Iconostasis.**]

SCRINIUM, a Latin term describing a box, case, or chest used to hold scrolls, books, or other documents. Such a container, pictured in numerous medieval author portraits, for example those in the *Vergilius romanus* (Vat. lat. 3867), is also called a capsa.

LESLIE BRUBAKER

SCRIPTORIUM, a place where manuscripts were written and copied. In the West, most scriptoria seem to have been housed in monasteries until the late Middle Àges. Orders such as the Cistercians regulated the production of books in their scriptoria. Hence, characteristic palaeographical and codicological patterns sometimes allow scholars to group together isolated manuscripts and hypothesize their place of origin. The existence of permanent scriptoria in Byzantium is less certain. Scholars have linked small groups of manuscripts to imperial or monastic centers—both types are documented. But private enterprise also produced manuscripts, perhaps on an ad hoc basis.

BIBLIOGRAPHY

Walter Cahn, "The Rule and the Book: Cistercian Book Illumination in Burgundy and Champagne," in Timothy G. Verdon, ed., *Monasticism and the Arts* (1984), 139–172; Jean Irigoin, "Centres de copie et bibliothèques," in *Byzantine Books and Bookmen* (Dumbarton Oaks Colloquium, 1971) (1975), 17–27.

LESLIE BRUBAKER

[See also **Manuscript Books, Production of; Monastery.**]

SCRIPTUARIES. See **People of the Book.**

SCROLL, INHABITED, a continuous foliate band, usually composed of alternating spirals, with small animals, insects, or birds perched within the foliage. The running acanthus scroll (rinceau), a popular Hellenistic motif, was widely diffused throughout the Greco-Roman world. Animal and bird insertions became widespread only in the eleventh century, even though they were known earlier (tenth-century Anglo-Saxon manuscript of Bede's *Life of St. Cuthbert:* "Aethelstan Offering a Book of St. Cuthbert," in Cambridge, Corpus Christi College, MS 183, f. 1v). In the twelfth and thirteenth centuries, Anglo-Norman illuminators enriched the foliage spirals with an increasing variety of figures, animals, and grotesques (twelfth-century Bible, Oxford, Bodleian Library, MS Auct. E inf 1).

Aethelstan offering a Book of St. Cuthbert, 937. The miniature is surrounded by a frame of leafy scrolls inhabited by birds and lions with candelabralike ornaments. Cambridge, Corpus Christi College, MS 183, f. 1v. BY COURTESY OF THE MASTER AND FELLOWS OF CORPUS CHRISTI COLLEGE, CAMBRIDGE

BIBLIOGRAPHY

Claus M. Kauffmann, *Romanesque Manuscripts, 1066–1190* (1975); Elżbieta Temple, *Anglo-Saxon Manuscripts, 900–1066* (1976); George Zarnecki *et al.*, eds., *English Romanesque Art, 1066–1200* (1984), 82–133.

LESLIE BRUBAKER

[See also **Anglo-Norman Art; Anglo-Saxon Art; Manuscript Illumination, European.**]

SCULPTURE. See nationalities and individual artists.

SCUTAGE (from Latin *scutum,* "shield"), sometimes known as escuage, appeared in contemporary records as *scutagium, scuagium,* or *escuagium,* that is, shield money. Scutage was the commutation of the knightly service a vassal owed his lord into a payment of money. With the money received, the lord normally hired mercenary knights. This practice, which developed only after the economic revival of Western Europe made money available, began in England during the reign of Henry I (1100–1135). Already in 1100 the church was paying scutage on lands held, in lieu of quotas of knights owed. Soon lay vassals also began to pay scutage, generally at the rate of one mark (13*s.* 4*d.*) and occasionally of two marks. A scutage higher than one pound was considered exorbitant. Levied scutages often took the names of the campaigns that they financed. The scutage levied in 1159, for example, was referred to as the "scutage of Toulouse" because it was used for Henry II's campaign in the county of Toulouse. At first scutages were levied only for military operations, with the provision that each vassal could decide whether he would serve with his quota of knights or pay the scutage. As the twelfth century progressed, however, vassals increasingly commuted all their military service, thereby permitting Henry II, Richard I, and John to hire large mercenary armies for their campaigns on the Continent.

Until Henry II's reign, scutages were levied upon the quotas of knights due from the fiefs granted to royal vassals by William the Conqueror. These vassals had meanwhile subenfeoffed land to other knights, with the result that they could make a profit. They collected scutage from all their vassals but paid the king only the amount on the old quota or enfeoffment. In 1166, to ensure collection of scutage on all the knights' fees enfeoffed since the time of William the Conqueror, Henry II held the inquest of knight service, which required each royal vassal to declare how many additional knights' fees had been enfeoffed. Thereafter, Henry II collected scutages on the new figure.

As long as the number and rates of the scutages levied were not excessive, the system worked well. Protest arose under Richard I (*r.* 1189–1199) when he began demanding a lump sum from each vassal rather than levying a scutage at a fixed rate. These lump sums were invariably higher than the amount a scutage would have produced. Richard justified this innovation by arguing that he deserved more pecuniary compensation because, when a royal vassal chose not to serve, he deprived the king not only of a knight but also of a commander in the field. Under John, baronial discontent mounted. He levied seven scutages between 1199 and 1206 and at least four more in the period to 1214. Sometimes he exacted scutages with no intention of fighting and often he increased the rate, at times to two and a half marks and occasionally to three marks, as in 1214. This move, added to all his other unpopular policies and acts, triggered the events that culminated in Magna Carta, article XII of which ordered that henceforth no extraordinary aid or scutage could be levied except by the "common counsel of the realm," that is, by the consent of the great council.

Between 1218 and 1258, Henry III (*r.* 1216–1272) levied at least twelve scutages at varying rates; these were generally supplemented by lump sums to help defray mounting military expenses. After the constitutional crisis and civil war between 1258 and 1265, Henry levied no scutage for the rest of his reign. Under his son Edward I (*r.* 1272–1307) only three scutages were collected. With the decline of feudalism in the thirteenth century, levies dependent upon the feudal system depreciated in value. To finance their military operations, Edward I and his successors in the fourteenth century turned increasingly to parliamentary taxation. In the spring of 1340 parliament enacted a statute that abolished all unparliamentary levies, including that of scutage. For a Scottish military expedition in 1385 Richard II unsuccessfully attempted to collect a scutage and in a parliament the same year explicitly renounced any claim to a scutage.

Although the levying of scutages developed first in England, a similar practice arose on the Continent. French kings introduced scutages effectively in the early thirteenth century, and throughout the century commutation of military service became common in the other feudal states of France and of the Low Countries.

BIBLIOGRAPHY

James F. Baldwin, *The Scutage and Knight Service in England* (1897), remains the most comprehensive treatment of scutage. Valuable also are Sydney K. Mitchell, *Studies in Taxation Under John and Henry III* (1914); John H. Round, *Feudal England* (1895, repr. 1964); Helena M. Chew, "Scutage Under Edward I," in *English Historical Review,* 37 (1922), and "Scutage in the Fourteenth Century," *ibid.,* 38 (1923). For scutage on the Continent see Ferdinand Lot, *L'art militaire et les armées au moyen âge en Europe et dans le Proche Orient,* 2 vols. (1946).

BRYCE LYON

[See also **Edward I of England; England; Feudalism; Fief; France; Henry I of England; Henry II of England; Henry III of England; Inquest, English; John, King of England; Knights and Knight Service; Magna Carta; Mints and Money; Richard I of England; Taxation, Church; Taxation, England; Toulouse.**]

SEAFARING. See **Navigation.**

SEAL OF FAITH. See **Knik^{c} Hawatoy.**

SEALS AND SIGILLOGRAPHY, BYZANTINE. It was common practice in the Byzantine Empire, from the sixth century to 1453, for lead seals (*bullae*) to be attached to official documents and private letters. Sigillography (the study of seals) involves their transcription and dating. Usually a seal bears, in linear inscription or monogrammatic form, one or more of the following: a name, a dignity, a title, a representation of the Virgin or a saint. Seals, which survive in the tens of thousands, provide valuable information concerning prosopography, geography, and civil and ecclesiastical administration. Because of the scarcity of source materials, they are of particular importance for the study of the seventh and eighth centuries.

BIBLIOGRAPHY

Werner Seibt, *Die byzantinischen Bleisiegel in Österreich,* I (1978), 33–40; G. Zacos and A. Veglery, *Byzantine Lead Seals,* I, pt. 1 (1972), ix–xiii.

JOHN W. NESBITT

Lead seal of Patriarch Leo of Constantinople, 1134–1143. BYZANTINE VISUAL RESOURCES © 1987, Dumbarton Oaks, Washington, D.C.

Islamic hematite seal of uncertain date and provenance. The inscription reads, "Yathiqu Farīd billāh" (Farid relies on God). COLLECTION OF THE AMERICAN NUMISMATIC SOCIETY, 1958.67.1

SEALS AND SIGILLOGRAPHY, ISLAMIC. In the Islamic world, seals (Arabic: *khātam*) were used for validating documents, marking property, and securing parcels. Every individual with affairs to transact had a seal, usually worn as a ring or on a neck cord, or carried in a small bag. Personal seals were engraved only with the owner's name and, often, a short pious motto; official seals were more elaborate. Seals were impressed into bullae of clay, lead, or wax, or inked for direct stamping.

BIBLIOGRAPHY

"Khātam," in *Encyclopaedia of Islam,* new ed., III (1971), provides a full discussion of the history and use of seals in the Islamic world, and has a good bibliography. For the only catalog, see Ludvik Kalus, *Catalogue des cachets, bulles et talismans islamiques* (1981).

MICHAEL L. BATES

SEALS AND SIGILLOGRAPHY, SASANIAN. Seals were used extensively on legal and commercial documents by members of the Sasanian middle and upper classes and, together with coins, are the most numerous type of cultural artifact to survive from Sasanian Iran and Mesopotamia. The *ḥtmh dᵓyqrᵓ* (Syriac, "seal of honor/value") was a status symbol. Cylinder and stamp seals were used by the Achaemenids, and a number of sealings of the Parthian dynasty have been found, particularly at the old capital of Nisa.

Sasanian seals were used as talismans, to identify ownership, to serve as a signature, or to verify the authenticity of a document or the integrity of a shipment. For documents, sealings were generally small, on a delicate piece of fine clay, and were attached to the parchment or papyrus by a thin leather strip or a thread. Some sealings bear the curvature of a rolled document or of its glass container. On merchandise, a number of seal impressions were made on a single lump of clay of lesser quality; the bottom of the lump often bears the marks of the crossing of the ropes with which a parcel was tied. There were officially licensed trade companies in the Sasanian Empire with offices close to the gates of cities; large numbers of sealings have been found at these ruined sites.

All known Sasanian seals are of the stamp, rather than the cylinder, type. The styles and periods of their predominance are ring bezel (third–fourth centuries), pierced and decorated ellipsoid (fourth–fifth centuries), hemispherical dome (fifth–sixth centuries), and deep cabochon (sixth–seventh centuries). The stone of which the seal was made had significance; glass seals were rare. According to the Islamic historian al-Masᶜūdī, Xusrō I Anōšarwān (*r.* 531–579) used four seals with four devices: three of ruby, with devices of Justice (for the taxes), Temporization (for the council), and Fidelity (for the post), and one of turquoise, with the device of Agriculture, for the royal estates.

Titles found on seals reflect the range of Sasanian administration: *mog* (*mgw*) and *mowbed (mgwpt)*—Zoroastrian "priest" and "high priest" respectively—are the titles most frequently found, attesting to the important role of the priesthood at every level of government: *šahriyār* (king), *framādār* (commander), *andarzbed* (councillor), *amārgar* (financial official), and *šahrab* (satrap). In the *Mādiyān ī hazār dādistān* (Book of a thousand judgments) official seals are described as *muhr ī pad kār framān dāštan* (seal with executive command). A title of the magi frequently encountered is *driyōšān ǰadagōw ud dādwar* (intercessor for the poor and judge); *driyōš* (New Persian: *darvīš;* poor [standing in need of God]) is a term for the Zoroastrian faithful; the office was borrowed by the Christian Armenians in the fourth or fifth century. Seals provide proper names, toponyms, and the names of fire temples.

Formulas expressed religious values. *Abastān ō yazdān* (reliance upon the gods), *abastān ō yazad* (reliance upon [the] god), or *abastān ō rōz* (reliance upon the day; compare the formula *rōz weh,* good day) is frequent. Another slogan, found especially on later seals, is *abzōn* (increase; the Pahlavi adjective *abzōnīg* translates the Avestan *spənta* [incremental, holy]). Formulas such as *weh* (good) and *xwarrah ud huram* (glory and joy) similarly reflect the life-affirming values of the Mazdean faith. The word *rāst* (true, correct) on seals (compare Arabic *saḥḥa,* with the same meanings, on later Islamic seals) is used for verification. There are also pious injuctions, such as *Mihrak ī Frahādān wēn wahišt ī rōšn* (Mihrak, son of Frahād, behold the Paradise of Light) or *tan ī was-kāmag, ruwān wēn* (O covetous body, regard the soul).

A number of seals have been identified as Christian on the basis of their iconography. The inscriptions, where in Middle Persian rather than Syriac, are not of specifically Christian content, and even have Zoroastrian formulas such as "Reliance on the god(s)"; but representations of the cross, of the sacrifice of Isaac, and of Daniel in the lion's den are clear. At Dwin, the capital of the marzpanate of Persarmenia, a number of Sasanian and Armenian sealings have been found together.

The Zoroastrian seals of the period have a wide variety of motifs. The fire altar, flanked by guards, is found also on coins. Ibexes, gazelles, and rams are found; the latter is a Mithraid symbol, on a medallion of the early Islamic period from Iran. The ram there seems to symbolize death, and the seal is most likely an apotropaic amulet.

Another seal apparently depicts Frēdōn (Avestan: Thraētaona; New Persian: Farīdūn), a mythical hero associated in the *Avesta* and in later *nirangs* (incantations) with healing, drawing a youth out of the maw of a monster. The latter is most likely Aždahāk (Avestan: Aži Dahāka; New Persian: Ẓaḥḥāk), a dragon described in the *Avesta* as wishing to empty the world of men. Thraētaona imprisons him. Here, Aždahāk seems to represent disease, against which the seal is to afford amuletic protection. So close is the association between Farīdūn and the dragon he fights that a recent Parsi amulet against disease, in Gujarati script (in the writer's possession), mistakenly invokes the dragon: *Ažīm Dahākəm yazamaide* (We worship Aži Dahāka).

A number of seals show a wolf suckling two children. This is probably an image borrowed from the Roman myth of Romulus and Remus. Perhaps Iranians associated it with the legend that Cyrus was suckled by a bitch after being abandoned. The wolf may also have been a totemic symbol of ancient Hyrcania (New Persian: Gorgān, "of the wolves").

Portraiture on the seals corresponds to Sasanian conventions in other media. Married couples are shown, sometimes holding a ring between them, as on Parthian examples. There are naked dancing girls, and courtly ladies holding tulips. The quality of the seals varies from crudely incised stick figures to portraits of exquisite detail on precious stones.

Sasanian jadeite seal, 6th century. METROPOLITAN MUSEUM OF ART, GIFT OF CHARLES K. WILKINSON, 1937, 37.32

BIBLIOGRAPHY

Phyllis Ackerman, "Sāsānian Seals," in Arthur U. Pope, ed., *A Survey of Persian Art,* 3rd ed. (1977); A. D. H. Bivar, *Corpus inscriptionum iranicarum,* pt. III, *Pahlavi Inscriptions,* vol. VI, *Kushan and Kushano-Sasanian Coins; Sasanian Seals . . .* (1968), a portfolio of plates, and *Catalogue of the Western Asiatic Seals in the British Museum, Stamp Seals,* II, *The Sasanian Dynasty* (1969); Christopher S. Brunner, *Sasanian Stamp Seals in the Metropolitan Museum of Art* (1978); Arthur E. Christensen, *L'Iran sous les Sassanides,* 2nd ed. (1944, repr. 1971); Malcolm Colledge, *Parthian Art* (1977); Margaret E. Frazer, "Hades Stabbed by the Cross of Christ," in *Metropolitan Museum Journal,* 9 (1974); Richard N. Frye, "Sasanian Clay Sealings in the Collection of Mohsen Foroughi," in *Iranica antiqua,* 8 (1968), "Inscribed Sasanian Seals from the Nayeri Collection," in *Forschungen zur Kunst Asiens: In Memoriam Kurt Erdmann* (1970), "Sasanian Seals and Sealings," in Philippe Gignoux and A. Tafazzeli, eds., *Mémorial Jean de Menasce* (1974), and "The Use of Clay Sealings in Sasanian Iran," in *Acta iranica,* 3rd ser., *Textes et mémoires,* V, *Varia 1976* (1977); Richard N. Frye, ed., *Sasanian Seals in the Collection of Mohsen Foroughi, Corpus inscriptionum iranicarum,* pt. III, *Pahlavi Inscriptions,* vol. VI (1971), and *Sasanian Remains from Qasr-i Abu Nasr* (1973).

Philippe Gignoux, "Les collections de sceaux et de bulles sassanides de la Bibliothèque Nationale de Paris," in *La Persia nel medioevo* (1971), "Intailles sassanides de la collection Pirouzan," in *Acta iranica,* VI, *Monumentum H. S. Nyberg,* III (1975); "Cachets sassanides du British Museum," in *Acta iranica,* 3rd ser., *Textes et mémoires,* V, *Varia 1976* (1977), *Catalogue des sceaux, camées et bulles sasanides de la Bibliothèque nationale et du Musée du Louvre,* I and II (1978), and "Sceaux chrétiens d'époque sassanide," in *Acta iranica,* XV, *In memoriam R. Ghirshman,* I (1980); Philippe Gignoux and R. Gyselen, "Nouveaux cachets sasanides de la collection Pirouzan," in *Studia iranica,* 7 (1978); Robert Göbl, *Der sāsānidische Siegelkanon* (1973), and *Die Tonbullen vom Tacht-e Suleiman* (1976); Gerd Gropp, "Some Sasanian Clay Bullae and Seal Stones," in *American Numismatic Society, Museum Notes,* **19** (1974); M. F. Kanga, "Abzon," in *Encyclopaedia iranica,* I, fasc. 4 (1985); Judith A. Lerner, *Christian Seals of the Sasanian Period* (1977).

J. R. RUSSELL

[See also **Ardešīr I; Avesta; Naqsh-i Rustam; Sasanian Art and Architecture; Sasanians; Xusrō I Anošarwān; Zoroastrianism.**]

SEALS AND SIGILLOGRAPHY, WESTERN EUROPEAN. A seal (German: *Siegel;* Italian: *sigillo;* French: *sceau;* Spanish: *sello*) is a mark of authority and/or ownership, pressed in relief upon a plastic material by the impact of a matrix or die-engraved intaglio.

The medieval terminology concerning seals varied. In ancient Rome, *signum* (more rarely *signaculum* or *sigillum*) was used to designate the impression; the matrix was described as *annulus*. By the end of the fifth century *signum* tended to designate the handwritten signature rather than the signet ring's impression, which came to be called *annulus* or *sigillum*. In the Occident, from the twelfth to the sixteenth century, *sigillum* was the definitive designation for both the wax impression and its matrix, while the term *bulla* was reserved for impressions in metal. The matrix was also at times called *typarium, sigillatorium,* or *cunei*. From the thirteenth century on, the term "signet" indicates a wax impression of a small module. In the fifteenth century the term "cachet" appears, meaning a small seal impression in low relief, applied directly to letters in order to fasten and secure them.

THE HISTORY OF MEDIEVAL SEAL USAGE

The practice of sealing answers two ancient and continuing needs, the marking of personal property and the assertion of individuality, and it has been in use without interruption from the dawn of Mesopotamian civilization until the present day. Over the entire period of its usage, the seal has recurrently served three functions: closure and guarantee of the integrity of contents or texts; claim and proof of ownership; and authentication of documents, converting them into executory instruments by affirming that the text represents the sealer's will.

The earliest stone matrices (*ca.* fourth millennium B.C.) found at Susa were used to stamp the clay stoppers of store jars as a sign of ownership. By the third millennium, the Babylonians impressed cylinder seals upon clay cuneiform tablets to express the authority of the sealer. The Egyptians likewise used the cylinder seal as a legal signature and, by the second millennium, had introduced the flat scarab seal ring with swivel mount, possibly in connection with their adoption of papyrus. The typical seal form in classical Greece consisted of an engraved semiprecious stone matrix set into the bezel of a ring. Despite the preceding Etruscan usage of Egyptian-type scarabs, the Romans generally followed the Greek example of ring-set intaglio gems. A category of two-sided lead disks with Roman imperial effigies has survived, but their function is disputed. Some diplomatists infer that these detached objects served as seals. Other interpreters note the absence of specific textual reference to these "seals" in comprehensive Roman diplomatic treatises. Nevertheless, it is possible that the leaden seals (*bullae*) routinely used in the Byzantine Empire were imitations of this form. The papal use of *bullae* from the sixth century on appears to be a reintroduction into the West of the standard Byzantine practice. By the seventh century, the bishops of Ravenna and Benevento had copied this usage of the papal chancery.

Whether seals were ever used for documentary validation in classical Rome is unclear. Extant acts of the imperial chancery are not sealed, but some surviving public acts of provincial imperial officials, such as registered deeds, safe-conducts, and city-gate passes, display in their lower margins clay impressions bearing the effigy of the emperor. In the private sector, polyptych wax tablets constituted the medium for contracts, and seals functioned primarily as a means to ensure the integrity of the inner duplicate text by securing the laces that bound the folded tablets (*obsignatio*). In some instances, however, seals were placed at the bottom of the inner text and therefore could not have been used for closure of the tablets; this seems to indicate a validating function similar to that of the autograph signature (*subscriptio*). In any case, the use of seals was widespread throughout Roman society, since each contracting party and witness affixed his seal to written transactions. The mounted intaglio gem came to be replaced by a signet ring of silver, gold, bronze, or iron directly engraved with the owner's name and a pious invocation, symbol, or human figure. In the late Roman Empire (fourth century on), documentary sealing became restricted to wills as autograph signatures alone came to validate contracts. By the end of the fifth century, illiterate persons signed by making a cross in the presence of a capable witness who in turn wrote the full name of the incapacitated person, together with a statement certifying his own participation. The cross, one of the commonest symbols on signet rings, was in its handwritten form called *signum,* and by the seventh century preceded all subscriptions, autograph or not. Seal rings of private individuals, which survive in large number from the Merovingian period, were used to produce impressions that served as a means of guaranteeing the closure of letters, as tokens of credence, and/or as marks of office. Testaments continued, far into the sixth century, to be the only documents regularly sealed.

The use of seal rings therefore passed from the Roman Empire to the new kingdoms of the migration period. The golden ring of Childeric, king of the Salian Franks (*d.* 481), was unearthed in 1653, and a similar ring of his son Clovis (*d.* 511) is reliably described in an eighth-century text. Lombard texts, also of the eighth century, indicate that Lombard kings sealed their documents. Preserved to this day are the sapphire of Alaric II, king of the Visigoths (*d.* 507), and the amethyst of Theodoric the Great, king of the Ostrogoths (*d.* 526). All of these signet rings were engraved intaglio, with a facing portrait of the ruler and a reversed inscription of his name. The oldest surviving seal impression in wax is that of the Frankish king Thierry III attached to a document of 679. Sealings of this period were not recorded in the body of the documents, which already bore signs of validation, such as the royal subscription (the monogram). Such seals do not appear to have had legal standing as means of authentication, but they likely contributed to the legitimacy of royal decrees by investing them with the authority implicit in the earlier practice of Roman imperial officials. This usage of the royal Merovingian chancery is of signal importance because the systematic sealing of diplomas fostered the evolution of the seals into the primary means of medieval documentary authentication.

From the time of this initial appearance (*ca.* sixth century), the affixation of wax impressions to the lower margin of documents stood as an exclusive royal practice. Carolingian kings and emperors carefully continued to exercise this prerogative and in turn were imitated by neighboring rulers, possibly Grimoald of Benevent (*ca.* 810) and Erispoë of Brittany (852); surely Boson of Provence (879), Beranger of Italy (888), Eudes of France (888), and Zwentebold of Burgundy (895); and by the dukes of Franconia and Saxony upon their ascension to the throne of Germany (Conrad, 911; Henry I, 919). The sealed charters of the kings of Mercia (Offa, 790), of Wessex (Aethelwulf, 857), and of England (Edgar, 960) have been recognized as forgeries.

Sealing for documentary validation in this period, a mark of sovereign authority, soon paralleled the diffusion of that authority. The Carolingian administration delegated power to counts and bishops, who, as royal or imperial representatives, assumed local legal, military, and financial responsibilities, and thus came to assume substantial elements of public authority. Bishops were the first nonroyal individuals to validate acts with their personal seals (Rouen, 872; Paderborn, 862/887; Mainz, 888; Toul, 898; Cologne, 953/965; Trier, 959; Strasbourg, 961). This precedence of bishops may best be explained by the observations that from late Roman times they had, at the pope's request, used a seal to close their letters, had maintained writing offices to which private individuals turned for the drawing up of their transactions, and could enforce the execution of private deeds issued under their aegis at a time when such documents lacked other potent guarantors of executory validity.

A further spread of documentary sealing that occurred during the tenth century involved the lay aristocracy: Arnulf, duke of Bavaria (927), and Otto, duke of Worms (987). However, when the fake seals of Arnulf (941) and Baldwin (988–1035), counts of Flanders, and of Geoffrey Greymantle, count of Anjou (977), are excluded from the sequence, these instances appear isolated; it was only in the second half of the eleventh century that magnates undertook to seal systematically, with their successors maintaining the usage. Between 1050 and 1090 the seals of the dukes of Aquitaine, Lorraine, and Normandy, and of the counts of Anhalt, Anjou, Blois-Champagne, Burgundy, Brabant, Chiny, Hainaut, Flanders, Luxembourg, Nevers, and possibly Toulouse, first appeared. The initial seal usage by nonroyal rulers in France, occurring late relative to their assumption and exercise of other regalian rights, was associated with the weakening of central authority under King Philip I (1060–1108) and the diffusion of public responsibilities to smaller territories (duchy, county, later castellany). The princely sealed charter developed as the royal diploma lost its public character, when the king could no longer guarantee justice and protection, and as new requirements for peace and order required irrefutable executory charters. The potentates came to rule effectively within their principalities, controlling judicial institutions and police powers, directing the Peace of God, and developing an administrative structure that soon included a chancery. Their use of seals constituted a system of documentary control, a tool of administration and government, and an imitation of the royal model.

Once established, seal usage continued with the successors (bishops) or heirs (potentates) of the first sealers. By the early twelfth century, the range of seal usage had expanded to include lord castellans, who after 1180 were followed by simple knights. This diffusion of sealing to the lesser nobility followed the disintegration of the larger political units, though this alone cannot fully account for the dissemination that reached even women and cities.

The first known female sealer (1002) is the German empress Kunegund, but her example was not imitated until a century later. Other queens—Matilda, wife of Henry I of England (*ca.* 1100), and Bertrada of Montfort, widow of Philip I of France (1115)—then began to seal, and during the second half of the twelfth century the wives of magnates sealed in turn. A similar chronology applies to cities: Cologne (1114–1119), Mainz (1150), Pisa (1160), Trier (1171), Arras (1175), Arles and Metz (1180), Cambrai (1185), Avignon (1189), Pontoise (1190), Meulan (1195), Valenciennes (1197), and St. Omer (1199).

Clearly, as it spread from royal and imperial chanceries, documentary sealing underwent a fundamental change. The manifestation of authority and the authoritative guarantee previously deriving from the incumbent's personal power, whether royal, episcopal, or feudal, now became increasingly associated with the seal itself, which soon evolved into a legally binding general technique of commitment. Given the simultaneous revival of written records and of economic activity, the seal proved an ideal instrument for validation of the former and control and guarantee of the latter. By the mid-thirteenth century, religious communities, parishes, universities, the lower clergy, local officials, bourgeois, craftsmen, Jews, guilds, and nonnoble landowners all sealed routinely. In medieval Western Europe, sealing had become so widespread and mandatory that an unnotarized document lacking a seal or displaying a damaged one was suspected of inauthenticity. Although in the Middle Ages seals came to be used primarily for documentary validation, they also served to guarantee contents (reliquaries, bandages on wounds from an ordeal, containers, and merchandise) and to assert ownership (bells, pottery, ceramics).

The social extension and diversification of seal usage were soon accompanied by a specialization according to function. Seals were originally the personal marks of their owners. When the owner, private or corporate, became invested with recognized legal authority, the personal seal acquired the character of a *sigillum authenticum.* This represented an official guarantee, and was therefore sought by private persons of a lower social status whose seals could carry only the limited guarantee of their own personal commitment. Initially, within royal chanceries, there appeared a new category of administrative seals, distinct from the great seal of the king but partaking of his deputed authority, such as the royal seal for the Jews (*ca.* 1203–1206, suppressed in 1223) and the seal of the *Châtelet* (1238) in France, and the seal of the English Exchequer (early thirteenth century). New seals of jurisdiction, distinct from their personal (great) seals, were adopted by secular and ecclesiastical authorities. Subsequently, these official seals were further differentiated according to the specific purpose of the documents they were to guarantee: *sigillum ad causas* (lawsuits), *sigillum ad contractus* (contracts), *sigillum obligationum* (debts), *sigillum hereditagiorum* (inheritances), and *sigillum pro mundinis* (fairs).

Also appearing by the thirteenth century were the royal private seal (*sigillum secreti* or *secretum,* or privy seal)—in England, about 1206; in the Empire, about 1272; in Castile, 1293; in France, about 1312—and its papal equivalent, the *annulus piscatoris* (1265). At first used only in intimate connection with the personal affairs of the ruler, such as the closing of private warrants, by the early years of the fourteenth century the private seal had evolved into an official object validating the acts of an administrative department. In consequence, rulers developed the signet to seal in personal and household matters.

Private seals and signets were likewise adopted by the church, the nobility, and cities for sealing letters, instructions, and warrants, and were used in preference to appending their great seals. The gradual replacement of parchment by more fragile paper for missives and documents during the second half of the fourteenth century helps to explain the disappearance of hanging seals, in favor of the lighter affixed signet impressions, from all but major state documents.

Despite the overwhelming use of seals, other means of authentication never completely disappeared during the Middle Ages. In southern France, in Spain, and in Italy, the revival of Roman law in the twelfth century involved the reintroduction of the personal subscription and the handwritten signature as a means of documentary validation. It also reinforced the practice of public notaries, who as a group had survived the collapse of the Roman Empire and had continued, in southwestern Europe, to offer the guarantee of their publicly registered handwritten signature. By the end of the fifteenth century, the notarial signature was recognized throughout northern and central Europe as validating deeds, and the sealing of contracts became unnecessary. By the dawn of the sixteenth century (seventeenth century in the Holy Roman Empire), seal usage had become confined to royal chanceries and official courts; private individuals authenticated their transactions with their own autograph signatures or that of a notary. The usage of the signet, though widespread, was thereafter reserved to closing correspondence and had lost all legal status.

SEAL TECHNIQUE

The matrix, engraved intaglio, is a unique object, in contrast with the multiple impressions that are issued from it in relief. A tangible sign of the identity and authority of its owner, the matrix might not be lost, stolen, or misused without serious consequences for its owner and, in these circumstances, would be publicly disclaimed. Matrices were routinely changed upon modification of the owner's social status, title, or function; and at the owner's death the matrix was defaced, destroyed, or buried with him. The silver matrices of the French queens Constance of Castile and Isabella of Hainaut have been found in their tombs. By the fourteenth century, custom called for the destruction of royal, imperial, and papal matrices at the death of the owner.

Most medieval matrices were metallic. Engraved gemstones were used; more rarely, matrices were made of ivory, bone, and even wood. The usually employed metals were copper alloys, principally latten and bronze, though lead was often adopted by poorer sealers. Kings and occasionally potentates might use gold for their signets. Queens, cities, and religious communities usually chose silver for their great seal matrices. A pair of iron or steel dies in the form of pincers used to impress leaden *bullae* was termed *boulotirion.*

Ordinary matrices either were flat or had an integral appendix. Flat matrices constitute the earlier type, in use from the late eleventh century to the beginning of the fourteenth century, at which time the second type became predominant. In France and England, flat matrices frequently had the form of disks with projecting lugs to allow for the impression of two-sided seals with a constant die axis.

Medieval seal impressions that authenticate a document may be of wax or of metal. The ancients had used clay, which upon drying was brittle. By Roman times, a small amount of wax was customarily added to the clay to make it more resilient. Ultimately the wax replaced clay as the plastic material. The composition of the waxes used in medieval seals has not been established with certainty. The general mixture is of about two-thirds beeswax and one-third various other substances, such as resins, pitch, chalk, and ashes, intended to harden and/or color the final impression. The addition of specific coloring agents began in the eleventh century and continued to evolve thereafter; white (plaster), red (lead tetroxide and vermilion), green (verdigris), and brown (pitch) became regularly used. Exceptional colors include pink, black, and blue; bicolored seals are a Central European phenomenon. A few royal chanceries ascribed specific significance to particular colors. In France, Philip Augustus and his successors reserved green wax for solemn grants in perpetuity and natural yellow wax for temporary grants; the English royal chancery followed this practice. In the Holy Roman Empire red wax had by the fifteenth century become an imperial prerogative.

The size of seal impressions varies from one to five and a half inches. The shape is also variable, including such forms as square, oval, rectangular, triangular, lozenge, pear-shaped, trefoil, and scutiform. The majority of seals, however, are round or pointed-oval, the latter generally associated with the depiction of standing figures (prelates, women, saints).

Metallic impressions (*bullae*), always round, are found in northern Italy, southern France, Spain, and Germany, though in all these areas they coexisted with wax impressions. In central and southern Italy, *bullae* were used exclusively; they are entirely unknown in England and Flanders. Most *bullae* are leaden; gold *bullae,* however, were appended to solemn diplomas by the Carolingian and German emperors, the Norman kings in Sicily, the Angevins in Naples, and the kings of Aragon and Hungary.

The method of attaching seals to documents varied according to the nature of the seal impression and the period. *Bullae* were always pendant, while wax impressions might be either applied or appended. Until the eleventh century, waxen seals were invariably applied by pouring and impressing the wax through a cruciform incision in the document. The seal of Edward the Confessor (1057) appears to be the first to have been appended in Western Europe. In France, Louis VI irregularly adopted this usage (1113), which became the standard method under Louis VII (1137). In Germany this practice was introduced by Conrad III (1138–

Seal of Richard the Lionhearted, 1195. ARCHIVES NATIONALES, PARIS. D 1307 et bis

Seal of Bayonne, 1298. ARCHIVES NATIONALES, PARIS. F 3867

Seal of Mary of Burgundy, 15th century. ARCHIVES NATIONALES, PARIS. F 108

1152). From the twelfth to the fifteenth century, wax seals were pendant for all ranks of society throughout Europe. Initially the technique of appendage involved the insertion of leather and parchment tags through a pair of cuts made in the folded lower margin of the parchment document, following which the waxen impression was affixed to the free ends. Alternatively, and more simply, a tongue of the lower margin of the document could be cut horizontally and then receive the wax impression(s) at its tip. A third method involved laces of braided flax, wool, or silk inserted through holes made in the lower margin of the document, the color of the fabric occasionally having an administrative or heraldic significance.

Pendant seals resulted from the enlargement of impressions at a time of growing scarcity of parchment, on which the applied seals took too much space. They imitate *bullae,* which both hung and could be impressed recto-verso. Pendant wax seals allowing for two-sided impressions were introduced in direct imitation of Byzantine *bullae* by Edward the Confessor. Edward's successor, William the Conqueror, used the reverse of his royal great seal to display his title and image as duke of Normandy. Louis VII of France, upon his accession to the duchy of Aquitaine, imitated the English two-sided seal with the obverse of majesty and ducal reverse. After Louis' divorce from Eleanor of Aquitaine (1152), the ducal reverse became inappropriate. His chancery retained the concept of a reverse impression, albeit one smaller than the obverse, the counterseal. The use of counterseals spread to all categories of sealers, as a means of endowing their seals with greater authenticity and as security against forgery.

Applied seals, however, never completely disappeared. Signet impressions closed missives and authenticated minor deeds throughout the Middle Ages. From the fourteenth century on, they were at times made by embossing a square of paper with wax interposed between it and the document.

SEAL ICONOGRAPHY

A manifest sign of identity, the seal reflects graphically the status of its owner. The legend, usually inscribed around the circumference of the seal, starts at the top and continues around from right to left on the impressions. Beginning with a cross and immediately followed by a word indicating the seal's nature (*sigillum, secretum, contrasigillum*), the inscription next gives the name of its owner in the genitive form. The legends of royal great seals are exceptional in that, as on the coinage, the name of the king and his title, not preceded by *sigillum,* appear in the nominative so as to express the concept that royal power is not derivative. This formulation was used first by the Frankish king Dagobert (629–638), and with rare exceptions remained a royal prerogative throughout Europe. Latin was the predominant language of legends, though by the thirteenth century the vernacular began to appear.

Depictions on seals relate less to the sealer's self-perception than to his status and function within society. Seal iconography is thus role-oriented and articulated around group (social and/or familial), rather than individual, identity. Indeed, medieval society may be said to have differentiated itself, expressing and defining the degrees of its hierarchy, through the medium of its seals. The royal seal underwent an iconographic evolution sensitive to the then recognized symbols of power. Merovingian kings are shown as half figures with long hair (a sign of rulership among Germanic tribes) and clad in a Roman military tunic. The Carolingians adopted an antique profile in imitation of the Roman emperors. Otto I, emperor of Germany, imitating contemporary Byzantine models, introduced a facing crowned bust bearing orb and scepter (962). This type was immediately copied by Lothair (*ca.* 966) and by his Capetian successors Hugh (987–996) and Robert II (996–1031). With Emperor Otto III (997) there appeared the type of majesty: the enthroned, frontally facing crowned emperor bearing orb and scepter. This program for seal iconography, inspired by the images of seated sovereigns in Carolingian manuscripts, became the prototype for royal great seals throughout Europe and during the entire medieval period. In 1031, Henry I of France adopted the enthroned figure with regalia, as did Edward the Confessor (1057) and Coloman of Hungary (1111).

Eleventh- and twelfth-century seals of the aristocracy virtually always display a single representative image, the equestrian in arms, which matched the military function of their owners. With the spread of sealing to the minor nobility (*ca.* 1180), a cleavage appeared between the older aristocracy, which retained the equestrian type, and the knights, who engraved their seals with coats of arms. The knights thus asserted a nobility based on a specific pattern of kinship, the lineage, rather than focusing on the function of military leadership, in which they played a subordinate role.

It is generally agreed that heraldic devices appeared first on the battlefield to identify warriors rendered indistinguishable by helmets and heavy armor, but the oldest extant illustrations of heraldry are documented on seals. Conceivably the earliest known heraldic seal is that of William, count of Luxembourg (1123), although the design that decorates his lance flag likelier represents a pattern of leatherwork than the barruly of the Luxembourg family. The seals of Raoul, count of Vermandois (*ca.* 1135); of Gilbert of Clare, count of Pembroke (1138–1148); of Waleran, count of Meulan and Worcester (*ca.* 1142); and of Henry, duke of Saxe and Bavaria (1144), however, depict on banners or shields those devices that were to remain for generations the heraldic emblems of their families. The shield rapidly became the characteristic template for the display of heraldic figures on seals. Removed from its military context and thus abstracted, it came to serve all categories of sealers (clergy, women, bourgeois, nonnoble landowners, corporations) as the basic locus for a sigillographic heraldic device. In this way the seal, intrinsically a sign of identity, offered a natural medium for, and contributed greatly to the spread of, this newer expression of identity, the heraldic system. Despite the fact that the heraldic seal constitutes half of all extant items from the twelfth to the fifteenth century, seals nevertheless display a remarkable diversified iconography: women in current fashion; lords in jousting, hunting, or hawking attire; ecclesiastics in sacerdotal costume; armed mayors; walled cities; crenellated castles; monuments and buildings of all kinds; scenes and objects of daily life. On seals medieval culture is richly staged.

SIGILLOGRAPHY

Sigillography encompasses the preservation and study of seals. Born in the seventeenth century with the pioneering works of Benedictines, chief among them Jean Mabillon, sigillography incorporates elements of diplomatics, law, and archaeology; of art; of social, political, and cultural history. The conservation of some 50,000 extant matrices, and of 2 to 3 million seal impressions for all of Western Europe (fifth to fifteenth centuries), is a principal goal of sigillographic collections and their curators. France holds the largest number of preserved seal impressions, the most important groupings being located at the Bibliothèque Nationale and the Archives Nationales in Paris, and in the departmental archives at Lille, Rouen, Strasbourg, and Mulhouse. In England, the two premier public collections are those of the Public Record Office and the British Library, both in London. The main collections of Switzerland are in the State Archives of Basel and the Swiss National Museum at Zurich. The Royal Archives in Madrid and the Archives of the Crown of Aragon in Barcelona hold the chief Spanish resources. The main Austrian collections can be found at the National Archives and the Kunsthistorisches Museum in Vienna. In Belgium, the Netherlands, and the Scandinavian countries, the main holdings are preserved in the General or National Archives. In Germany and in Italy, seal collections are widely scattered, but an overview is available in the works of Erich Kittel and Giacomo Bascape. Most national collections maintain, in addition to original seals, series of cast copies reproducing originals that may be housed locally and/or at a distance, or that may no longer survive. Such concentrations enable easy consultation of otherwise scattered material while protecting the fragile originals from excessive manipulation. Further access to sigillographic sources is provided by inventories. Catalogs of seals are of two types: those describing the seals and casts of a particular archive or collection, and those treating seals referable to a specific geographical region or other theme. The arrangement of contents in these catalogs is not uniform and there is as yet no generally accepted standard. The French school, following Louis Douët d'Arcq, has adopted an arrangement based upon the social class and identity of the sealer; this rests upon an arbitrary and perhaps too theoretical vision of medieval society. Until 1918 the German school, following F. K. von Hohenlohe-Waldenburg, used a typological arrangement based on iconographic devices. This proved ineffective for the study of social and legal aspects of seals, and was replaced after 1918 by the Douët d'Arcq classification. A proper catalog must take into account the question of authenticity, for forgeries are not uncommon. From the seventeenth century on, fake matrices were produced for collectors, but assessment techniques should allow an easy discrimination of these from the genuine. Medieval forgeries present somewhat greater difficulties; genuine seals may have been appended to forged documents, and aftercast impressions, though legally fakes, may yet provide the only evidence for no longer extant originals.

Seals are personalized objects and ubiquitous survivors of civilization. Being precisely dated and localized by the documents to which they were affixed, and possessing in addition their own text and iconography, they rank as precise and illuminating sources for medieval culture and society.

BIBLIOGRAPHY

Bibliographies include S. Trehearne Cope, "Heraldry, Flags, and Seals: A Select Bibliography . . . 1920 to 1945," in *Journal of Documentation,* 4 (1948/1949); René Gandilhon and Michel Pastoureau, *Bibliographie de la sigillographie française* (1982); Poul B. Grandjean, *Sigilligrafisk litteratur* (1941). Further information is in Giacomo C. Bascapè, *Sigillografia: Il sigillo nella diplomatica, nel diritto, nella storia, nell'arte,* I: *Sigillografia generale* (1969), with bibliography at the end, II: *Sigillografia ecclesiastica* (1975), III: *I sigilli nella storia del diritto medievale italiano,* by Mariano Welber (1984); Erich Kittel, *Siegel* (1970).

Manuals and treatises include Wilhelm Ewald, *Siegelkunde* (1914, repr. 1975); Arthur Giry, *Manuel de diplomatique* (1895, 2nd ed. 1925, repr. 1969); Walter de Gray Birch, *Seals* (1907); Hilary Jenkinson, *A Guide to Seals in the Public Record Office,* 2nd ed. (1968); Hugh S. Kingsford, *Seals* (1920); René Laurent, *Sigillographie* (1985); Dom Jean Mabillon, *De re diplomatica libri VI* . . . (1681), II, 126–152; Michel Pastoureau, *Les sceaux,* Typologie des Sources du Moyen Âge Occidental, fasc. 36 (1981); Joseph Roman, *Manuel de sigillographie française* (1912); Thomas F. Tout, *Chapters in the Administrative History of Medieval England,* V (1930).

Catalogs are Brigitte Bedos [Rezak], *Corpus des sceaux français du moyen âge,* I, *Les sceaux des villes* (1980); Louis Douët d'Arcq, *Collection de sceaux,* 3 vols. (1863–1868); Roger H. Ellis, *Catalogue of Seals in the*

Public Record Office: Personal Seals, 2 vols. (1978–1981); Wilhelm Ewald *et al., Rheinische Siegel,* 7 vols. (1906–1972); Donald L. Galbraith, *Inventaire des sceaux vaudois* (1937); Walter de Gray Birch, *Catalogue of Seals in the Department of Manuscripts in the British Museum,* 6 vols. (1887–1900); Araceli Guglieri Navarro, *Catálogo de sellos de la Sección de sigilografía del Archivo histórico nacional,* 3 vols. (1974); Bror E. Hildebrand, *Svenska sigiller från medeltiden,* 2 vols. (1862–1867); Lewis C. Loyd and Doris M. Stenton, eds., *Sir Christopher Hatton's Book of Seals* (1950); Henry Petersen, *Danske adelige sigiller fra det 13. i 14. aarhundrede* (1897); Faustino Menéndez Pidal and Elena Gómez Pérez, *Matrices de sellos españoles (siglo XII al XVI)* (1987); Johann-Theodor de Raadt, *Sceaux armoriés des Pays-Bas et des pays avoisinants,* 4 vols. (1898–1903); Gustave Schlumberger, Ferdinand Chalandon, and Adrien Blanchet, *Sigillographie de l'orient latin* (1943); Pietro Sella, *Inventari dell'Archivio segreto vaticano. I sigilli dell'Archivio vaticano,* 6 vols. (1937–1964); John H. Stevenson and Marguerite Wood, *Scottish Heraldic Seals,* 3 vols. (1940); Alec B. Tonnochy, *Catalogue of British Seal-dies in the British Museum* (1954).

Studies on seal history, iconography, and usage include Robert Henri Bautier, "Échanges d'influence dans les chancelleries sourveraines du moyen âge, d'après les types de sceaux de majesté," in *Comptes-rendus de l'Académie des inscriptions et belles-lettres* (1968), and "Origine et diffusion du sceau de juridiction," *ibid.* (1971); Brigitte Bedos [Rezak], "Les sceaux juifs français," in Bernard Blumenkranz, ed., *Art et archéologie des juifs en France médiévale* (1980), "The King Enthroned: A New Theme in Anglo-Saxon Iconography . . . ," in Joel T. Rosenthal, ed., *Kings and Kingship* (1986), "The Social Implications of the Art of Chivalry: The Sigillographic Evidence (France, 1050–1250)," in Edward R. Haymes, ed., *The Medieval Court in Europe* (1986), and "Suger and the Symbolism of Royal Power: The Seal of Louis VII," in Paula L. Gerson, ed., *Abbot Suger and Saint-Denis* (1986); Charles H. Blair, "Armorials upon English Seals from the Twelfth to the Sixteenth Centuries," in *Archaeologia,* **89** (1943); Michael T. Clanchy, *From Memory to Written Record* (1979); Maximin Deloche, *Étude historique et archéologique sur les anneaux sigillaires et autres des premiers siècles du moyen âge* (1900); Germain Demay, *Le costume au moyen âge d'après les sceaux* (1880, repr. 1978); Toni Diederich, *Die alten Siegel der Stadt Köln* (1980); Herbert Ewe, *Schiffe auf Siegeln* (1972); Julian Gardner, "Some Cardinals' Seals of the Thirteenth Century," in *Journal of the Warburg and Courtauld Institutes,* **38** (1975); Timothy A. Heslop, "English Seals from the Mid Ninth Century to 1100," in *Journal of the British Archaeological Association,* **113** (1980), "The Virgin Mary's Regalia and 12th Century English Seals," in Alan Borg and Andrew Martindale, eds., *The Vanishing Past* (1981), and "Seals," in George Zarnecki, Janet Holt, and Tristram Holland, eds., *English Romanesque Art* (1984).

George Henderson, "Romance and Politics on Some Medieval English Seals," in *Art History* (1978); Thomas E. S.-E. Howard de Walden, *Some Feudal Lords and Their Seals* (1904, repr. 1984); Benito F. Isla, "La imagen de la Virgen en los sellos," in *Revista de archivos, bibliotecas y museos* (1922 and 1923); Michael Jones, "The Seals of John IV, Duke of Brittany," in *Antiquaries Journal,* **55** (1975); Henry C. Maxwell-Lyte, *Historical Notes on the Use of the Great Seal of England* (1926); Gale Pedrick, *Monastic Seals of the XIIIth Century* (1902), and *Borough Seals of the Gothic Period* (1904); Reginald Lane Poole, "Seals and Documents," in his *Studies in Chronology and History,* Austin Lane Poole, comp. and ed. (1969); Otto Posse, *Die Siegel der deutschen Kaiser und Könige von 751 bis 1913, 5* vols. (1909–1913, repr. 1981); Helen Rosenau, "Notes on Some Qualities of Architectural Seals During the Middle Ages," in *Gazette des beaux-arts,* 6th ser., **90** (1977); Hans Wentzel, "Portraits à l'antique on French Medieval Gems and Seals," in *Journal of the Warburg and Courtauld Institutes,* **16** (1953); David H. Williams, *Welsh History Through Seals* (1982); Alfred B. Wyon and Allan Wyon, *The Great Seals of England* (1887), completed by Terence A. M. Bishop and Pierre Chaplais, eds., *Facsimiles of English Royal Writs to A.D. 1100* (1957), and Hilary Jenkinson, "The Great Seal of England," in *Antiquaries Journal,* **16** (1936).

BRIGITTE BEDOS REZAK

[See also **Archives; Bull, Papal; Chancery; Charter; Châtelet; Diptych; Heraldry; Parchment.**]

SEBASTE (modern Sivas), a city in Turkey (39° 44′ N × 37°01′ E), near the headwaters of the Kızıl Irmak (ancient Halys). Founded by Pompey and named for Augustus, it has always flourished from its location on the routes that lead through Anatolia to the Middle East. In late antiquity, it became the seat of an archbishop and a capital of Armenia. Restored by Justinian and burned by Xusrō I in 575, it resisted the attacks of the Arabs and long remained under Byzantine rule. After 911 it was the capital of a theme and an increasingly important center for Armenians as the seat of a bishop and of nobles resettled from the East. First captured by the Turks in 1059, it was strengthened by the Byzantine emperor Romanos IV a decade later at a time of increasing Turkish raids and dissension between the Greek and Armenian populations. After the battle of Manazkert (Manzikert), it was ruled by Armenians until, in about 1090, the Danishmendids made it their capital; it fell to the Seljuks in 1174 and the Mongols in 1243. In the early fourteenth century, when it was the residence of the Mongol governor of Anatolia, Sivas reached the height of its prosperity as a great commercial city, the largest in Anatolia, and the seat of a Genoese consul. Subsequently, it became the capital of an independent state and briefly fell to the Ottomans before Tamerlane captured it in 1400. The accompanying massacre and destruction provoked an irrevocable decline. Under continuous Ottoman rule from 1407, the city retained considerable strategic and commercial importance but never regained its earlier prosperity. Late antique and Byzantine Sebaste has virtually disappeared, but Turkish Sivas is noted for its splendid monuments, images of its greatness, among them the Ulu Cami (Danishmendid), the hospital of Qayqāwūs I (Seljuk, 1217), and three magnificent theological schools, richly decorated with stonework of the Mongol period.

BIBLIOGRAPHY

Claude Cahen, *Pre-Ottoman Turkey,* J. Jones-Williams, trans. (1968); Albert Gabriel, *Monuments turcs d'Anatolie,* II (1934), esp. 131–164; F. Hild and M. Restle, *Tabula Imperii Byzantini,* II: *Kappadokien* (1981).

CLIVE FOSS

[See also **Anatolia; Arcrunis; Armenian Geography; Danishmendids; Manazkert; Mongol Empire; Pontus; Seljuks of Rum; Tamerlane.**]

SEBASTOKRATOR, a Byzantine title created in 1081 by Alexios I Komnenos and bestowed upon his brother Isaac, who thus obtained the second hierarchical rank after the emperor. After the creation of the new title of *despotes* in the late twelfth century, the *sebastokrator* held the third rank until the fourteenth century, after which the title disappeared. Initially reserved for close relatives of the emperor, it was later bestowed upon distant relatives and even upon independent neighboring rulers. The title of *sebastokrator* also appeared in the fourteenth-century Serbian empire of Stefan Dušan.

BIBLIOGRAPHY

Božidar Ferjančić, "Sevastokratori u Vizantiji," in *Zbornik Radova Vizantološkog Instituta* (of Belgrade), **11** (1968), 141–192, and "Sevastokratori i kesari u Srpskom carstvu," in *Zbornik Filozofskog Fakulteta* (of Belgrade), **11,** pt. 1 (1970), 255–269, both in Serbo-Croatian with French summary; A. P. Każdan, "Sevastokratory i despoty v Vizantii XII v.," in *Zbornik Radova Vizantološkog Instituta,* **14/15** (1973), with a reply by Ferjančić; George Ostrogorsky, *History of the Byzantine State,* Joan M. Hussey, trans., 3rd ed. (1969).

NICOLAS OIKONOMIDES

[See also **Alexios I Komnenos; Caesar; Despot.**]

SEBĒOS is the presumed author of an Armenian history that deals with the sixth and seventh centuries. Precisely who this individual was and when he wrote remains a matter of dispute among specialists. Such confusion, however, in no way diminishes the value of the *History,* which is a major primary source for the history of Byzantium, Armenia, Iberia, and Iran. The work opens with a brief account of late-fifth-century events, then passes to a description of divided Armenia's condition in the late sixth century: the effects of Byzantine rule in historical western Armenia and of Iranian rule in the eastern section. The reigns of Byzantine emperors from Maurice (582–602) through Constans II (641–648) are described, with special emphasis on the reign of Heraklios I (610–641).

In the absence of contemporary extant Iranian sources, the *History* takes on added importance as a source on the later Sasanians. Some Iranists, such as A. Christensen, made prodigious use of "Sebēos"; others, such as Theodor Nöldeke, all but ignored this very important work. In addition to commenting on religious issues involving Armenia and Byzantium, the author provides information unavailable from other sources on religious events in Iran. The author concludes with the events of 661, after describing the Arab invasions and early domination of the Caucasus, early Byzantine-Arab relations, and the fall of Sasanian Iran to Arab troops.

Presently only one archetypal manuscript of this *History* exists (a seventeenth-century copy of a now-lost sixteenth-century manuscript). Discovered in 1842 by Hovhannes Shahxatᶜunyan, the untitled work was titled (perhaps incorrectly) the *History of Heraclius* and attributed by its discoverer to a seventh-century Armenian bishop named Sebēos, mentioned by medieval Armenian authors as the writer of a history. Shahxatᶜunyan's suggested title and author have been challenged repeatedly over the years, and the various Armenian editions and their translations have borne different titles. The situation is complicated further by the fact that in Shahxatᶜunyan's manuscript the *History* was preceded by one (or possibly two separate) shorter chronographical work(s), apparently not the work of "Sebēos," presently known to Armenists as "pseudo-Sebēos," or the *Primary History of Armenia.* Shahxatᶜunyan believed that the chronographies were also the work of "Sebēos." Consequently, in early Armenian editions and translations of "Sebēos" the seventh-century historical work appears as the third "book," though neither stylistically nor thematically related to what precedes it.

BIBLIOGRAPHY

For a concise account of the manuscript, editions, and an Armenian bibliography, see George Bournoutian, "Sebēos: A Historical Controversy," in *The Armenian Review,* **28** (1975). The classical Armenian text of Sebēos (including the *Primary History*) was published by Kerope P. Patkanian, *Patmutᶜiwn Sebeosi episkoposi i Herakln* (Bishop Sebēos' History of Heraclius) (1879). The French edition, Frédéric Macler, trans., is *Histoire d'Héraclius par l'évêque Sébéos* (1904). The English edition, Robert Bedrosian, trans., is *Sebēos' History* (1985). An English translation of the *Primary History* is found in Moses Khorenatsᶜi, *History of the Armenians,* Robert W. Thomson, trans. (1978), 357–368.

ROBERT BEDROSIAN

[See also **Armenian Literature; Historiography, Armenian.**]

SEBÜKTIGIN (Turkish, "beloved prince") (*d.* 997), founder of the Ghaznavid dynasty in Afghanistan, eastern Iran, and northern India (977–1186). The special significance of the Ghaznavid dynasty in medieval Islamic history was its role in exploiting the wealth and slave manpower of northern India and in beginning the process of Islamization there.

Like various other founders of provincial dynasties in eastern Islam, Sebüktigin was of Turkish slave origin. We have an account of his early life in a testament attributed to him and addressed to his son and successor, the great sultan Maḥmūd of Ghazna (*r.* 998–1030). It seems that he came from Barskhān on the shores of the Issyk-Kul, the lake in Central Asia lying in the eastern part of what is now the Kirghiz SSR. Brought into the Samanid emirate of Transoxiana and Khorāsān at an early age, he was sold there as a slave and eventually rose to eminence through his military abilities in the service of the Turkish general Alptigin, commander of the Samanid forces in eastern Iran. After involvement on the losing side in a succession dispute, Alptigin in 961 was compelled to withdraw to the far periphery of the Samanid Empire, to what is now eastern Afghanistan, taking with him Sebüktigin. Thus it was that in Ghazna a body of Turkish military slaves assumed power, with Sebüktigin becoming their chief in 977 and beginning a twenty-year reign.

From his base at Ghazna, Sebüktigin began a policy of aggrandizement both southward through Afghanistan into Baluchistan and eastward toward the Indus Valley and the plains of India. A rival group of Turkish soldiers in Bust were subdued and Quṣdār (northeastern Baluchistan) was added to his dominions (977–978). Most significant for the future pattern of Ghaznavid expansion was the drive down the Kabul River Valley to the Indus. Here Sebüktigin's Turkish troops came up against the powerful Indian dynasty of the Hindūshāhīs under Rājā Jaipāl, but in 986/987 he defeated the latter and a coalition of Indian princes, annexing the lands along the Kabul River as far as Peshawar, which was to provide the base for his son's career of conquest in India. Finally, Sebüktigin was also active in the West, intervening in the Samanid province of Khorāsān, together with Maḥmūd, to help Emin Nūh ibn Mansūr against the rebellious generals Abū ᶜAlī Sīmjūrī and Fā'iq Khāṣṣa (994–995), being himself rewarded with the governorship of Balkh and his son with command of the army in Khorāsān. Thus, as Samanid power palpably declined and the emirs were unable to control their powerful commanders, Sebüktigin and Maḥmūd were well placed to seize a substantial share of the spoils when the Samanid Empire finally collapsed at the end of the tenth century.

Sebüktigin died in 997, appointing a younger son, Ismāᶜīl, as his successor; but it was the abler and militarily more experienced Maḥmūd who in 998 was able to set Ismāᶜīl aside and seize complete control of the Ghaznavid emirate, making it within a few years one of the mightiest military empires ever known in eastern Islam.

BIBLIOGRAPHY

Vasily V. Bartol'd, *Turkestan down to the Mongol Invasion,* 4th ed. (1977), 261–265; Clifford E. Bosworth,

The Ghaznavids: Their Empire in Afghanistan and Eastern Iran 994–1040, 2nd ed. (1973), 39–45, and, in *Cambridge History of Iran,* IV (1975), 165–168; Muḥammad Nāẓim, *The Life and Times of Sulṭān Maḥmūd of Ghazna* (1931, repr. 1973), 28–33, and "The Pand-Nāmah of Subuktigīn," in *Journal of the Royal Asiatic Society* (1933).

C. E. BOSWORTH

[See also **Afghanistan; Alptigin; Ghaznavids; Samanids.**]

SECOND COMING. See **Millennialism; Parousia.**

SECOND SHEPHERDS' PLAY. The Towneley (Wakefield) cycle of medieval biblical pageants from the first half of the fifteenth century has two shepherds' plays, which are the twelfth and thirteenth of the series. In the manuscript these plays are entitled *Pagina pastorum* (Pageant of the shepherds) and *Alia eorundem* (Another of the same), but they are often referred to as the First and Second Shepherds' Plays or as *Prima pastorum* and *Secunda pastorum.* They are clearly by the same dramatist, the anonymous "Wakefield Master," who used a characteristic nine-line stanza rhyming $a a a a^4 b^1$ $c c c^3 b^2$ (the superscript figures indicate the usual number of stresses in each line), with central rhymes in the first four lines. (If each of the central rhymes is placed at the end of a line, the first four lines become eight and the stanza may be regarded as a thirteener.) Both plays are localized in the Wakefield area: "Hely" in the first play (v. 244) points to Healey in West Yorkshire, and "Horbery" in the second play (v. 455) is Horbury, near Wakefield. There may even be an allusion in the second play to the first: Mak's mention of Gybon Waller and of John Horne, who "made all the garray" (v. 564), seems to refer to John Horne of the First Shepherds' Play and his quarrel with Gyb over an imaginary flock of sheep. This allusion, if such it is, may also be evidence that the first play continued to be performed after the second was written. No one has satisfactorily explained why the Towneley cycle should have two shepherds' plays. But it is reasonable to suppose that the author of the first play realized he could improve on his own handiwork, and did so in the second.

The First Shepherds' Play has 502 lines; the second has 754 lines. In the second play the Wakefield dramatist unfolds a comic plot involving Mak the sheep stealer and his wife, Gyll (Jill). His theft of a sheep and the trick to conceal it is a folktale motif found, with variations of detail, in more than one European literature. The best-known of the analogues in English is *Archie Armstrang's Aith,* a ballad by the Rev. John Marriott, printed in Sir Walter Scott's *Minstrelsy of the Scottish Border* (1802–1803). But the detection and punishment of the thief are not in the analogues; this difference may be due to the Wakefield author's original treatment of the traditional tale.

One of the most interesting aspects of this pageant is the art with which the comic, secular plot is linked to the Adoration scene at the end, so that the play has an essential unity and preserves its religious identity. Charles M. Gayley observed that the "pastoral atmosphere is already shot with a prophetic gleam; the fulfilment is, therefore, no shock or contrast, but a transformation—an epiphany." Homer A. Watt and others have pointed out the parallels and contrasts between the comic theme of Gyll's false childbirth and the serious theme of the Nativity, and have shown how in several details the Mak and Gyll episode is "a perfect burlesque of the charming Christ-child scene that concludes the play."

Furthermore, the characterization of Mak, Gyll, and the shepherds, the skillful handling of the nine-line stanza (divided among five or six speakers in rapid exchanges of dialogue), and the Wakefield Master's genius for finding the right words and rhythms to express many different moods all help to make the Second Shepherds' Play an outstanding achievement.

The play ends with the shepherds, their earthly cares forgotten, taking joyful leave of Mary and the Christ Child (vv. 746–754):

1 Pastor. Fare well, lady so fare to beholde,
With thy childe on thi kne.
2 Pastor. Bot he lygys full cold.
Lord, well is me! Now we go, thou behold.
3 Pastor. Forsothe, allredy it semys to be told
Full oft.
1 Pastor. What grace we have fun!
2 Pastor. Com furth; now ar we won!
3 Pastor. To syng are we bun—
Let take on loft!

The story of the shepherds and the Nativity has indeed been "told / Full oft" but never in a livelier manner than in this play.

BIBLIOGRAPHY
A. C. Cawley, ed., *The Wakefield Pageants in the Towneley Cycle* (1958); Robert C. Cosbey, "The Mak Story and Its Folklore Analogues," in *Speculum,* **20** (1945); Charles Mills Gayley, *Plays of Our Forefathers* (1907), 146–147; Jeffrey Helterman, *Symbolic Action in the Plays of the Wakefield Master* (1981), 73–114; V. A. Kolve, *The Play Called Corpus Christi* (1966), 112–113; T. M. Parrott, "Mak and Archie Armstrang," in *Modern Language Notes,* **59** (1944); Carl J. Stratman, *Bibliography of Medieval Drama,* 2nd ed., 2 vols. (1972), esp. I, 4,513–4,566; Homer A. Watt, "The Dramatic Unity of the 'Secunda Pastorum,'" in *Essays and Studies in Honor of Carleton Brown* (1940, repr. 1969), 161–162; Rosemary Woolf, *The English Mystery Plays* (1972), 188–193.

A. C. CAWLEY

[See also **Drama, Western European; Mystery Plays; Towneley Plays.**]

SECRETUM SECRETORUM (Secret of secrets; Arabic: *Sirr al-asrār*), a widely disseminated, frequently translated pseudo-Aristotelian mirror for princes containing, besides gnomic, moral, and pragmatic advice, sections on hygiene, astronomy, physiognomy, onomancy, military tactics, talismans, alchemy, and lapidary and herbal lore. It purports to be a translation into Arabic, by the ninth-century translator Yaḥyā ibn al-Biṭrīq, of an epistle sent to Alexander the Great by Aristotle. One passage seems in fact to derive from an eighth-century Arabic translation of a pseudo-Aristotelian *General Epistle.* Various sections echo teachings and anecdotes connected elsewhere with Greek, Hellenistic, Byzantine, and Asian authorities. A short form was expanded into a long form, in which the arcane and the pseudosciences predominate, and in which passages of Plotinian emanationary doctrine have been inserted from the encyclopedia of the universalist-minded Sincere Brethren (*Ikhwān al-ṣafāᵓ*).

A Latin version of the hygiene section is the work of the twelfth-century Johannes Hispalensis; the full Latin translation was made in crusading lands in the thirteenth century by Philippus Tripolitanus. From Philippus' version, directly or indirectly, come many translations in the vernaculars of medieval and early modern Europe, mostly undertaken for secular notables; in them, passages are modified or inserted to suit local circumstances and interests. Philippus' text influenced thinkers such as Roger Bacon, Bradwardine, and Wyclif. The *Secretum* preserved and transmitted the middle range of Hellenistic knowledge and intellectual attitudes, in modified form, to early modern times.

There are fourteen known separate English prose versions, partial or complete, translated between 1400 and 1702. There are also Middle English verse versions by Gower (book VII of the *Confessio Amantis*), Hoccleve, and Lydgate, and early modern verse versions by Sir William Forrest and Patric Scot. These versions illustrate the late medieval and sixteenth-century effort to develop an expository style and a quasitechnical vocabulary.

BIBLIOGRAPHY
Sources. ᶜAbd al-Raḥman Badawi, ed., *Al-uṣūl al-yūnāniyyā lil-naẓariyāt as-siyāsiyyā fi al-Islām* (1954); Mahmoud Manzalaoui, *Secretum Secretorum: Nine English Versions* (1977); Robert Steele, ed., *Secretum secretorum* (1920), and *Three Prose Versions of the Secreta Secretorum* (1898).
Studies. Mario Grignaschi, "L'origine et les métamorphoses du 'Sirr-al-asrār,'" in *Archives d'histoire doctrinale et littéraire du moyen âge,* **43** (1976); Mahmoud Manzalaoui, "The Pseudo-Aristotelian *Kitāb Sirr al-asrār:* Facts and Problems," in *Oriens,* **23–24** (1974); W. F. Ryan and Charles B. Schmitt, *Pseudo-Aristotle, the "Secret of Secrets": Sources and Influences* (1982).

MAHMOUD MANZALAOUI

[See also **Aristotle in the Middle Ages: Bacon, Roger; Bradwardine, Thomas; Gower, John; Hoccleve (Occleve), Thomas; Lydgate, John; Mirror of Princes; Neoplatonism; Wyclif, John.**]

SECTS, CHRISTIAN. See **Heresies, Western European.**

SECTS, ISLAMIC. The great schism of Islam, out of which most later sectarian movements grew, occurred in the First Civil War (656–661). This war pitted the fourth caliph, ᶜAlī ibn Abī Ṭālib, who was a cousin and son-in-law of the prophet Muḥammad, against Muᶜāwiya ibn Abī Sufyān, who was a remote cousin of the third caliph, ᶜUthmān, and who became the fifth caliph. The supporters of ᶜAlī were known as his *shīᶜa,* or party. A group of his early supporters who turned against him, after he agreed to an arbitration of his conflict with Muʿāwiya, became known as the Kharijites (*khawārij,* or seceders). Shīʿa and Kharijites survived the end of the First Civil War and came to constitute politico-religious opposition parties to the Umayyad caliphate, which commenced with Muʿāwiya. The Umayyads were supported by the majority of the faithful, later known as the Sunnites.

SHIISM

The early Shīʿa, concentrated in Al-Kufa in Mesopotamia, continued to uphold the right of the family of the Prophet, most often descendants of ʿAlī, to the supreme leadership of the Muslim community, called the caliphate or imamate. The death of Ḥusayn, son of ʿAlī and grandson of the Prophet, while fighting for his family's right at Karbalāʾ in 680, added a passionate element of tragedy and martyrdom to the religious outlook of the Shīʿa.

Soon a division into a moderate and a radical wing became apparent. The more radical elements came to view the imam not only as the legitimate head of the Muslim community, but also as a divinely chosen and guided leader in religion. They held that ʿAlī, as such a leader, had been entitled to the immediate succession of Muḥammad and had been wrongfully pushed aside by the first three caliphs.

The Kaysānīya. In 685 a radical Shiite movement gained control of Al-Kufa and proclaimed another son of ʿAlī, Muḥammad ibn al-Ḥanafīya, the imam and Mahdi, or messianic restorer of Islam. After the suppression of the revolt and the death of Ibn al-Ḥanafīya, many of the sectarians, known as the Kaysānīya, claimed that he was alive in hiding and expected his return in glory.

One of the subsects issuing from the Kaysānīya formed the nucleus of the revolutionary movement that brought the Abbasid dynasty to power in 750. The Abbasids, however, soon shook off their Shiite supporters and ruled with broad Sunni backing.

Jaʿfar and the role of the imam. As the Kaysānīya disintegrated, their radical Shiite views were adopted and developed by the supporters of a grandson of Ḥusayn, Muḥammad al-Bāqir (*d. ca.* 735), and the latter's son, Jaʿfar al-Ṣādiq (*d.* 765). These two imams were contemporary to the development of the early Sunni schools of religious law and were accepted by their followers as authoritative teachers of law and religion. Jaʿfar also taught an esoteric mysticism that was widely influential.

As the role of the imams as teachers of religion grew in importance, the radical Shīʿa adopted the doctrine of their impeccability and infallibility (*ʿiṣma*). They held that after the closing of the age of prophethood with the prophet Muḥammad there must exist at all times a divinely guided imam, without whom the earth could not last even for a moment. After ʿAlī and his two sons Ḥasan and Ḥusayn, the imamate was to continue to be handed down from father to son among the descendants of Ḥusayn. Although the divinely guided imam was entitled to the supreme political leadership, Imam Jaʿfar strictly forbade his followers to engage in revolutionary activity on his behalf and taught that the rightful imams would not regain political power until the appearance of the Qāʾim (riser) imam in the distant future. The movement thus remained for the most part politically quietist.

The Imāmīya, or Twelvers. After the deaths of Imam Jaʿfar and some of the later imams, splits occurred in the radical Shiite movement. Most successful in the long run was the group developing into the Twelver Shīʿa or Imāmīya. Twelvers traced the imamate through their eleventh imam, who died in 874, to a hidden son they attributed to him. This twelfth imam was identified with the Mahdi and Qāʾim who would appear and rule before the end of the world. During the early time of his absence (*ghayba*), four successive representatives were held to be in touch with him to convey his orders and instructions to his community. After the death of the fourth one in 941, no one could claim to have regular access to the imam, who was, however, held to be alive on earth and might occasionally show himself to some of his followers. His teaching authority fell to the scholars (*ʿulamāʾ*) learned in the doctrine of the imams.

Twelver Shiism spread early from Al-Kufa throughout southern Iraq, to Baghdad, and to some regions of Iran. It flourished under the Shiite Buyid dynasty in the eleventh and twelfth centuries, and much of its basic religious literature was produced then. Baghdad was the main center of Twelver Shiite scholarship at first. Later, as the situation of Shiism in the capital deteriorated, it was replaced by Hilla (Al-Hilla), about fifty-eight miles (ninety-three kilometers) south of Baghdad. Hilla remained the seat of learning during the Mongol era (thirteenth and fourteenth centuries), which brought a new resurgence of Twelver Shiism in eastern Islam.

Only in the sixteenth century, however, did it become the official and predominant religion of Iran. To the west, Twelver Shiite communities arose in the Jabal ᶜĀmila region of southern Lebanon and in Aleppo in northern Syria. The latter community grew in particular during the reign of the Twelver Shiite Hamdanid dynasty in the tenth century.

Twelver Shiism failed to spread to Egypt and the Maghrib. However, an early offshoot that considered the line of imams to have ended with the seventh, Mūsā al-Kāẓim, and expected his return as the Mahdi gained a foothold among the Berber tribes of the Sūs region in southwestern Morocco in the ninth century and lasted there for about 300 years.

At the fringe of the early Imāmīya, various sects arose that were considered extremists (*ghulāt*) and were commonly expelled by the main community. They tended to view the imams as manifestations of the divine spirit and to repudiate the validity of the religious law for those able to grasp the true nature of the imams. While most of these sects were ephemeral, the Nuṣayrīs (known in modern times as ᶜAlawids) greatly expanded under the reign of the Hamdanids in northern Syria, especially in the Jabal al-Anṣārīya, which has since remained their stronghold.

The Ismailis. Politically the most important Shiite movement in medieval Islam was the Ismāᶜīlīya. This sect was named after Ismāᶜīl, the eldest son of Imam Jaᶜfar. Ismāᶜīl predeceased his father but was recognized by the Ismailis as the transmitter of the imamate to his own son Muḥammad. The Ismailis promised the imminent appearance of Muḥammad ibn Ismāᶜīl as the Mahdi, and they were active in many parts of the Islamic world by the second half of the ninth century.

A prominent early wing of the Ismailis was known as the Qarmatians after its early leader, Ḥamdān Qarmat. The most spectacular success of the Qarmatians was in setting up a state in Bahrain, in eastern Arabia (899), from which they invaded the heartland of the Abbasid caliphate and threatened Baghdad itself. In 930 Qarmatians sacked Mecca and carried off the Black Stone of the Kaaba as a symbolic gesture signifying the end of the era of Islam. Though the stone was returned two decades later as the movement lost its vigor, the Qarmatian state survived until 1078.

Another branch of the Ismaili movement was the Fatimids, who established their own caliphate in Tunisia in 909. The Fatimid caliphs, who later founded Cairo and ruled in Egypt, claimed to be descendants of Muḥammad ibn Ismāᶜīl and were recognized by many Ismailis as their imams. The mass of the population of the Fatimid Empire, however, was never converted to Ismaili Shiism, so that religious support for the dynasty was confined to small communities inside and outside its borders.

Fatimid Ismailism was further weakened by several schisms. Under the caliph al-Ḥākim (*d.* 1021) an extremist group, later known as the Druzes (*Durūz*), proclaimed his divinity. Though the sect was suppressed in Egypt after al-Ḥākim's death, it gained followers in the mountains of Syria and Palestine, where it has survived to the present.

After the death of the caliph al-Mustanṣir in 1094, the Persian Ismaili communities under their leader, Ḥasan-i Ṣabbāḥ, recognized al-Mustanṣir's eldest son and appointed successor, Nizār, as their imam. Nizār was, however, pushed aside and eventually killed by a powerful vizier, who put another son of al-Mustanṣir, al-Mustaᶜlī, on the throne. The Nizārīs thus did not recognize the later Fatimid caliphs as their imams.

The Nizārī leaders resided in the mountain stronghold of Alamūt in the Elburz Mountains in northern Persia. After the fourth successive Nizārī leader, these leaders came to be recognized as imams and descendants of Nizār. In open revolt against the Seljuk rulers of Iran, the Nizārīs pursued a policy of seizing impregnable mountain fortresses and of spectacular political murder of prominent enemies for the purpose of intimidation. They were accused by their enemies of employing hashish to condition young converts for their suicidal missions of murder and were therefore sometimes called *ḥashīshīya*. From this word derived their name Assassins, used by the crusaders, which then entered European languages.

Nizārīs were also active in Syria, especially in the mountain area west of Hama, where they occupied Maṣyāf and other strongholds in the twelfth century. They were ruled there by agents sent from Alamūt. The most famous of these was Rāshid al-Dīn Sinān (1162–1192), known among the crusaders as the Old Man of the Mountain.

Alamūt was surrendered to the Mongol conquerors in 1256, and its last imam, Rukn al-Dīn Khūrshāh, was put to death by them. The Nizārī imams, descendants of Khūrshāh, lived thereafter mostly in hiding though in contact with their communities. The line of imams soon split in two, with one branch leading to the agha khans in modern times, and the other disappearing in the eighteenth century.

Al-Mustaᶜlī was recognized as the imam by most Ismailis in the Fatimid Empire and by the sizable community in Yemen. A further split occurred, however, after the assassination of the Fatimid caliph al-Āmir in 1130. After some confusion, a cousin of the caliph, al-Ḥāfiẓ, was put on the throne in Cairo and gained general recognition there as the imam. The majority of the community in Yemen, however, recognized an infant son of al-Āmir, al-Ṭayyib, in spite of the disappearance of the child after the father's death. Considering him to be alive in hiding, they broke with the Fatimid caliphs.

After the overthrow of the Fatimid caliphate by Saladin in 1171, the Ismaili community in Egypt disintegrated until it disappeared altogether in the fourteenth century. The community in the Maghrib had been extinguished already in the eleventh century by Sunni massacres. The Tayyibi branch has lasted to the present, however, chiefly in Yemen and India.

The religious teaching of the Ismailis has been fundamentally characterized by the search for an esoteric, hidden meaning in religious scripture and law. This esoteric aspect was kept secret from outsiders and made accessible to neophytes only upon an oath of initiation. In substance it consisted of a cosmology of Neoplatonic origin, adopted in the early tenth century, and a cyclical history of revelation through seven prophetic eras. The emphasis on this esoteric doctrine led in some instances to a repudiation of the religious law of Islam. Official Fatimid Ismailism, however, always insisted on the equal validity of the esoteric and the exoteric aspects of religion, and identified the latter with the law. Nizārī Ismailism tended to exalt the rank of the imams above prophethood. On 8 August 1164 the Nizārī imam Ḥasan formally proclaimed the resurrection and with it the abrogation of the religious law. By its opponents, Sunnis and Shiites alike, Ismailism was commonly described as a plot to destroy Islam, and its adherents were more ruthlessly persecuted than most other heretics.

The Zaydis. The moderate wing of the early Shīᶜa crystallized in the Zaydi movement, named after Zayd ibn ᶜAlī, a brother of Muḥammad al-Bāqir, who was killed in a revolt in Al-Kufa in 740. The Zaydis did not recognize a line of divinely appointed imams, nor did they consider their imams impeccable and infallible. Rather they were prepared to support any descendant of Ḥasan or Ḥusayn learned in religion who would rise against the illegitimate caliphate. They supported a series of abortive revolts during the eighth and early ninth centuries in Iraq, Arabia, and Iran. In 864 they succeeded in founding a Zaydi state in the coastal area and mountains south of the Caspian Sea. Zaydi communities maintaining their independence under Alid rulers lasted there until the sixteenth century. In northern Yemen a Zaydi imamate was established in 897. The Zaydi community there has survived to the present. In its religious and legal doctrine, Zaydism differed from Sunnism less than other branches of the Shīᶜa.

KHARIJISM

While the Shīᶜa supported the principle of legitimism, basing the right to the imamate on close blood relationship with the Prophet, the Kharijites stressed the principle of accountability of the imam for his acts and held that any violation of Koranic rules and the law must cause the forfeiture of his title. They thus repudiated the caliphate of ᶜUthmān after the first six years of his reign and that of ᶜAlī after his agreement to the arbitration, since they considered their acts thereafter in violation of divine orders. They also excommunicated all those who did not accept their principles and thus repudiated the later Sunni caliphate. They chose their own imams while rejecting the Sunni restriction of the imamate to members of the tribe of Quraysh.

Radicals and moderates. The early Kharijite movement, centered in Basra, soon split into several sects differing mainly in the degree of their militancy toward the Muslim community at large. Most extreme were the Azraqīs, followers of Nāfiᶜ ibn al-Azraq, who considered all other Muslims, even other Kharijites, to be polytheists. These other Muslims, in the Azraqī view, were to be fought relentlessly and even murdered. Even women and children were to be shown no mercy.

The Najadāt, followers of Najda ibn ᶜĀmir, broke away from the Azraqīs and adopted less extreme views. They considered the quietist Kharijites merely hypocrites (*munāfiqūn*) and did not allow the murder of Muslims of differing persuasion.

These and other radical Kharijite groups staged revolts in Iraq, Arabia, and southern Persia in the Umayyad period and were ultimately extinguished because of their uncompromising militancy. Only the more moderate groups, the ʿAjāride, an offshoot of the Najādat, the Ṣufrīya, and especially the Ibāḍīya (also Abāḍīya), who developed doctrines that permitted them to live in peace with the Muslim community, at least in times of relative weakness, were able to propagate their views widely outside Basra and to gain a lasting following in many parts of the Muslim world. The Ṣufrīya were heavily involved in revolts in Iraq, and the ʿAjārida were in revolt in southeastern Iran from the end of the Umayyad age to the tenth century. In Oman a numerous Ibāḍī community established itself during the Umayyad age. In the Maghrib, Ṣufrī missionaries were active apparently from the same time as those of the Ibāḍīya, the early eighth century. While the Ibāḍī doctrine spread initially among the Berbers of Tripolitania, the Ṣufrīya found support in the western Maghrib and in Tunisia. The great Berber revolt, which effectively removed the Maghrib west of Qayrawān from the caliph's control in the late Umayyad and early Abbasīd periods, was led by Ṣufrī chiefs. In 757 Ṣufrīs occupied the town of Sijilmāsa, which became the center of the movement in the Maghrib under the Berber dynasty of the Banū Midrār, who ruled until the tenth century.

Most successful, however, in expanding throughout the Muslim world were the Ibāḍīya, the only Kharijite sect that has survived to the present and whose literature is extant. A great missionary effort was made by the leadership in Basra in the late Umayyad age. Ibāḍī communities in Yemen and in Ḥaḍramawt lasted at least until the twelfth century. In Oman an Ibāḍī imamate was first established in 750 and has lasted, with interruptions, until the present. From Oman, the Ibāḍī sect spread also to the east coast of Africa.

In the Maghrib, Ibāḍī missionary activity first bore fruit in Tripolitania, especially among the Hawwāra Berbers and the Nafūsa. Here the first, short-lived attempts to establish an Ibāḍī imamate in the Maghrib were made in the late Umayyad and early Abbasid ages. As the coastal regions of the eastern Maghrib as far as Qayrawān came firmly under Abbasid control after 761, many Ibāḍīs moved to the central Maghrib, where Ibāḍism also spread widely among the local tribes. Tāhart, in the west of present-day Algeria, became the center of Ibāḍī activity, and it was here that ʿAbd al-Raḥmān ibn Rustam was elected imam about 777. The Rustamid dynasty of Ibāḍī imams at its peak controlled territories stretching from Meknes in Morocco to Tripoli. After a steady decline, the dynasty was overthrown and Tāhart occupied by the Fatimid army in 908.

A fierce revolt, which nearly succeeded in overthrowing the Fatimid caliphate, was led by Abū Yazīd (*d.* 947), chief of the schismatic Ibāḍī sect of the Nukkār. This was the last major military effort of the Ibāḍīs in the Maghrib, and their influence among the Berber tribes receded. However, the Jabal Nafūsa in Tripolitania, the home of the Nafūsa tribe, remained a center of Ibāḍī learning. The remnants of the Ibāḍī community in the central Maghrib first moved to the oasis of Wargla and later to the Mzāb. Controlling the hinterland of the Maghrib and the Sahara for several centuries, the Ibāḍīs played an important role in the trans-Saharan trade and the spread of Islam south of the desert.

OTHER SECTS

While the schism of the Shīʿa and the Kharijites was fundamentally concerned with the question of the supreme leadership of the Muslim community, there were other conflicts around theological questions that sometimes gave rise to sectarian movements, though more often merely to theological schools considered heretical by the majority.

Free will and the Qadarīya. The question of human free will versus predestination arose early in Islam, and with it appeared the Qadarīya, who, against the predominant doctrine of divine determinism, upheld free will. Many religious scholars in the main centers of learning in Iraq, Arabia, and Syria in the Umayyad age were counted as Qadarīs. In the surroundings of Damascus, the Qadarīya constituted a sectarian movement that played a role in late Umayyad political history.

The Muʿtazila. The Qadarīs were soon largely absorbed by the theological school of the Muʿtazila, who sent propagandists to many provinces of the Islamic empire in the late Umayyad period from their center in Basra. In the Maghrib, some Berber tribes accepted their teaching and are mentioned there, until the tenth century, under the name of Wāṣilīya (after Wāṣil ibn ʿAṭāʾ, one of the Basran founders of the movement). In southern Iraq and southwestern Persia the Muʿtazila also gained a numerous following and took on the character of a sectarian movement.

The Murjiʾa. The Murjiʾa arose initially, in the later seventh century, as a movement seeking a compromise between the Shīʿa and the Umayyad caliphate. They suspended judgment concerning the ᶜAlī versus ᶜUthmān question. Opposed to the practice, adopted by the warring religious parties, of excommunicating political opponents from Islam, the Murjiᵓa held that no Muslims, however wrong their acts, should be deprived of the status of believers. This aspect of their teaching took on new significance in the struggle of the non-Arab converts to Islam in Khorāsān and Transoxiana for full recognition as Muslims. As the Umayyad authorities tried to continue taxing them as non-Muslims on the grounds that they did not practice Islam fully, a powerful insurrection erupted among them, led by the Murjiᵓa, who maintained that faith consisted only in belief in God and the message of Muḥammad in general, to the exclusion of works. Converts confessing Islam must thus be accorded the status of believers even though they might not know and practice any details of the ritual and law.

This view was espoused in Al-Kufa by the contemporary Abū Ḥanīfa. Murjiᵓī doctrine, understood as the exclusion of works from the definition of faith, later remained a characteristic of the Ḥanafī legal school, except for those who adopted Muᶜtazilite theology, while Sunnism in general upheld the view that works form a part of faith.

Almoravids and Almohads. Sunni reform movements sometimes also took on sectarian form. To be noted here are the two successive movements that swept the western Maghrib in the eleventh and twelfth centuries and expanded into the Iberian Peninsula to confront the Christian reconquest: the Almoravids and the Almohads.

The Almoravids (*al-Murābiṭūn*) were named after their fortified convent (*ribāṭ*), located on an island either in the river Senegal or off the Atlantic coast, from which the movement started. It was supported by Berber clans belonging to the Saharan Ṣanhāja "confederation." Their spiritual leader and teacher, ᶜAbd Allāh ibn Yāsīn al-Jazūlī, was a scholar of the legal school of Mālik prevalent in the towns of the Maghrib and a Sufi adhering to the tradition of the conservative mystic al-Junayd. The Almoravids suppressed heresies in Morocco, espoused the strict application of Maliki law, and strengthened the authority of the Maliki scholars throughout their empire. They recognized the Abbasid caliphate and assumed merely the title *amīr al-muslimīn* (commander of the Muslims). The movement thus represented Sunni orthodoxy without deviation. Its narrow legalistic outlook was reflected in the public burning of several works of al-Ghazālī.

A sharp, partly heretical reaction against the Almoravids arose in the movement of the Almohads (*al-Muwaḥḥidūn,* "those who proclaim the Oneness of God"). The movement arose among the Berber Maṣmūda of southwestern Morocco. Its founder, Muḥammad ibn Tūmart (*d.* 1130), claimed to be the Mahdi and as such to be infallible. His theological doctrine of the unity of God (*tawḥīd*), which gave the movement its name, was essentially derived from Ashᶜarī theology with some Muᶜtazilī influence. In the law he advocated a return to the sources (Koran, *ḥadīth,* and consensus) and rejected the authority of the legal schools, including that of Mālik. With his unrestricted religious authority, he excommunicated all his opponents as infidels, especially the Almoravids and the Maliki scholars of the law.

BIBLIOGRAPHY

A. J. Arberry, ed., *Religion in the Middle East,* II (1969), 96–118, 171–186, 285–348; Ignaz Goldziher, *Introduction to Islamic Theology and Law,* Andras and Ruth Hamori, trans. (1981); Henri Laoust, *Les schismes dans l'Islam* (1965); Shahrastani, *Livre des religions et des sects,* D. Gimaret and G. Monnot, trans. (1986); W. Montgomery Watt, *The Formative Period of Islamic Thought* (1973); Julius Wellhausen, *The Religio-political Factions in Early Islam,* R. C. Ostle, ed., R. C. Ostle and S. M. Walzer, trans. (1975).

WILFERD MADELUNG

[See also **Alamūt; ᶜAlī ibn Abī Ṭālib; Almoravids; Assassins; Atlas Mountains; Berbers; Buyids; Caliphate; Druzes; Emir; Fatimids; Ḥadīth; Ḥākim bi-Amr Allāh, al-; Ḥallāj, al-; Heresy, Islamic; Historiography, Islamic; Ifrīqiya; Imam; Islam, Religion; Ismāᶜīlīya; Kufa, Al-; Law, Islamic; Millennialism, Islamic; Muᶜtazila, al-; Mysticism, Islamic; Philosophy and Theology, Islamic; Qāᵓim, al-; Shiᶜa; Sunna; ᶜUlamāᵓ; Zaydis.**]

SECTS, JEWISH. See **Karaites.**

SEDILIA (sing., sedile), a group of seats for the clergy, usually three in number (for the priest, deacon, and subdeacon). The sedilia may be movable but usually consist of a series of arched niches in the south wall of the chancel, near the altar.

Sedilia are often vaulted and enriched with gables, pinnacles, and other ornaments. They are especially common in England.

BIBLIOGRAPHY
Illustrations are in Banister Fletcher, *A History of Architecture,* 19th ed. (1986); Cyril M. Harris, *Historic Architecture Sourcebook* (1977), 484.

GREGORY WHITTINGTON

[See also **Furniture, Liturgical.**]

SEDULIUS SCOTTUS (Scotus) (*fl.* 848–858 or 874), Irish poet and scholar whose Irish name was Siadhal or Shiel. He is important for the understanding of Irish and Continental learning of the time. After moving to Liège he came under the patronage of Bishop Hartgar and subsequently Emperor Lothair I. His works include poems skillfully written in classical Latin meters, a treatise on the art of government entitled *On Christian Rulers,* and grammatical and theological commentaries that testify to extensive learning and judicious use of earlier manuscripts, compilations, and florilegia, some of which are no longer extant. He probably had some knowledge of Greek.

BIBLIOGRAPHY
Bibliographies. J. F. Kenney, *The Sources for the Early History of Ireland,* I (1929, 2nd ed. 1966), 553–569; Michael Lapidge and Richard Sharpe, *A Bibliography of Celtic-Latin Literature 400–1200* (1985), 672–686.

Life. For the life of Sedulius and the work of his circle, see Max Manitius, *Geschichte der lateinischen Literatur des Mittelalters,* I (1911, repr. 1974), 315–323, II (1923, repr. 1976), 802, III (1931, repr. 1973), 1062. For a more recent biography, see Franz Brunhölzl, *Geschichte der lateinischen Literatur des Mittelalters,* I (1975), 449–466, 568. See also Frederic J. E. Raby, *A History of Secular Latin Poetry in the Middle Ages,* I (1934, rev. ed. 1957), 242–247.

Studies. For his contribution to Western European culture, see M. L. Laistner, *Thought and Letters in Western Europe* A.D. *500 to 900,* 2nd ed. (1957), 251–252, 300, 315–320, 335–336, 347–349. Concerning his political treatise and poetry, see Sedulius Scottus, *On Christian Rulers and the Poems,* Edward G. Doyle, trans. (1983). Concerning his theological commentaries, see R. E. McNally, *The Bible in the Early Middle Ages* (1959), esp. 93, 107–115. For the importance of his grammatical works, see M. Louis Holtz, "Grammairiens irlandais au temps de Jean Scot: Quelques aspects de leur pédagogie," in *Jean Scot Érigène et l'histoire de la philosophie* (1977), 69–78.

DENIS G. BREARLEY

[See also **Carolingian Latin Poetry; Exegesis, Latin; Grammar; Rhetoric.**]

SEGMENTAL ARCH. See **Arch.**

SEGNA DI BONAVENTURA (*fl.* 1298–1331), Sienese painter. A pupil of Duccio, he was the father of Niccolò di Segna. A number of his signed works survive, including four panels depicting the Mourning Virgin, St. John the Evangelist, St. Paul, and St. Bernard in half length (Siena, Pinacoteca); a large *Madonna Enthroned with Saints* (Collegiata di S. Giuliano, Castiglione Fiorentino); and a *Madonna and Child with Sts. Sylvester Gozzolini and Benedict* (New York, Metropolitan Museum).

BIBLIOGRAPHY
Bernard Berenson, *Italian Pictures of the Renaissance: Central Italian and North Italian Schools,* I (1968), 392–394; James H. Stubblebine, *Duccio di Buoninsegna and His School,* I (1979), 130–137; John White, *Duccio: Tuscan Art and the Medieval Workshop* (1979).

ADELHEID M. GEALT

[See also **Duccio di Buoninsegna; Maestà;** and illustration overleaf.]

SEIFRIED HELBLING. An unknown Austrian knight, writing in the thirteenth century, left fifteen poems dealing generally with political and social questions and, to a much smaller extent, with religious life. The only surviving manuscript is from the sixteenth century; there is also an early-fourteenth-century fragment. Because Seifried Helbling appears in poem XIII as a *Spielmann* of low birth, the first editor of the texts, Theodor von Karajan, mistakenly believed that that was the poet's name. Given the author's generally critical remarks about this kind of writer and his defense of knights, subsequent critics have rejected *Helbling,* a word meaning a coin equivalent to a halfpenny, as the name of the author.

It is highly likely that the writer preferred to remain anonymous, at least in larger circles, since

Madonna Enthroned with Saints. Panel painting by Segna di Bonaventura showing Sts. Gregory and John the Baptist with angels and donors, mid 1320's. CASTIGLIONE FIORENTINO, COLLEGIATA DI SAN GIULIANO, SGF 26397

his attacks on prominent public figures are often quite sharp. Critics such as Ursula Liebertz-Grün and Dieter Vogt question the supposition of earlier scholars that he belonged to the lower nobility. The writer was active in Lower Austria between approximately 1280 and 1300, when he was already an older man. His education was quite broad; he uses Latin phrases often, and he is familiar with the works of the classical period of Middle High German. His work reflects knowledge of Walther von der Vogelweide, Wolfram von Eschenbach, Der Stricker, and Wernher der Gartenære, among others.

Until the late twentieth century, when a revival of scholarly interest took place, most Helbling research had been done in the mid and late nineteenth century, when scholars established the chronology of the texts. Karajan's order was first rejected by Ernst Martin and then by the major Helbling critic, Joseph Seemüller. Poems I–IV, VIII–X, and XV form the *Lucidarius* group, a series characterized by the dialogue between a knight and his servant about contemporary life and mores. The writer himself calls his work the little *Lucidarius,* referring to a well-known prose dialogue of that name written in the last decade of the twelfth century. It presented theological and general knowledge that seems to have directly influenced this poet.

Although the earlier poems, XIV, V, and XIII, which attack the Habsburgs, deal more directly with current events, history serves more as a background to the poetry than as a theme. Generally, the movements of the great princes and nobles concern him not from a political point of view, but from a moral and social one. Even when he is most politically engaged, as in V, his thrust is still toward ethical and decent behavior, as when he attacks the greed of the *ministeriales* who rob the land and monasteries. He is not so much concerned with foreigners, noting their failings only in passing; in the best tradition of Austrian patriots, he castigates those he loves best. For example, in the first *Lucidarius* poem, the servant wants to know how he can recognize a genuine Austrian. He describes various extravagantly dressed types, some of them of peasant origin, reminiscent of young Helmbrecht. These the older knight criticizes sharply. While those peasants who lead lives unseemly to peasants come in for their share of scorn, the degeneration of the knights' conduct does not escape the laconic but devastating tongue of the poet, as in his description of the knight who is most heroic in the tavern (I). The description of the true Austrian (I, 11. 479–530) is very reminiscent of the ideal knight of the classical Middle High German period, as Hartmann von Aue might have described him.

In many of the poems we catch glimpses of daily life, as in III, which takes place in a public bath, or in II, which begins after dinner as the knight and the servant converse. Unlike the high nobility, the knight does not eat luxurious foods, such as game.

Criticism of mores occasionally takes the form of allegory, as in II and VII, with the struggles between virtue and vice. His purely religious poetry, XI and

XII, a paraphrase of the Ave Maria and the *Vokalspiel,* a religious counterpart of Walther's *Vokalspiel,* are put at the end of his work, just after the spiritual poems that close the *Lucidarius* collection.

BIBLIOGRAPHY

Editions. Theodore von Karajan, "Siefried Helbling," in *Zeitschrift für deutsches Altertum,* **4** (1844); Joseph Seemüller, *Seifried Helbling* (1886).

General studies. Standard literary histories are Helmut de Boor, *Die deutsche Literatur im späten Mittelalters: Zerfall und Neubeginn* (1962), 398–403; Gustav Ehrismann, *Geschichte der deutschen Literatur bis zum Ausgang des Mittelalters,* II, pt. 3 (1935, repr. 1959), 335–337.

Specific studies. Ursula Liebertz-Grün, *Seifried Helbling: Satiren kontra Habsburg* (1981); Ernst Martin, "Zu Seifried Helbling," in *Zeitschrift für deutsches Altertum,* **13** (1866), and "Ein östreichischer [sic] Satiriker aus dem Ende des 13. Jahrhunderts (der sogenannte Seifried Helbling)," in *Die Grenzboten: Zeitschrift für Politik und Literatur,* **27** (1868); Walther Mitzka, "Seifried Helbling," in Wolfgang Stammler *et al.*, eds., *Die deutsche Literatur des Mittelalters: Verfasserlexikon,* II (1977), 372–373; Roderick Schmidt, "Aeiou: Die mittelalterlichen 'Vokalspiele' und das Salomon-Zitat des Reinbot von Durne," in Karl Heinz Schirmer and Bernhard Sowinski, eds., *Zeiten und Formen in Sprache und Dichtung: Festschrift für Fritz Tschirch* (1972), 113–133, esp. 114–120; Joseph Seemüller, "Studien zum kleinen Lucidarius," in *Sitzungsberichte der österreichischen Akademie der Wissenschaften,* **102** (1882); Dieter Vogt, *Ritterbild und Ritterlehre in der lehrhaften Kleindichtung des Stricker und im sogennanten Seifried Helbling* (1985); Anton Wallner, "Seifried Helbling," in *Zeitschrift für deutsches Altertum,* **72** (1935); Gerhard Wolf, *Die Kunst zu Lehren: Studien zu den Dialoggedichten ("Kleiner Lucidarius") der "Seifried-Helbling" Sammlungen* (1985).

VICKIE ZIEGLER

[See also **Elucidarium and Spanish Lucidario; Hartmann von Aue; Middle High German Literature; Stricker, Der; Walther von der Vogelweide; Wernher der Gartenære; Wolfram von Eschenbach.**]

SEINTE RESURECCION, LA, a late-twelfth-century Anglo-Norman Resurrection play surviving in incomplete form in two versions: Paris, Bibliothèque Nationale, MS fr. 902, and London, British Library, MS Add. 45103 (the Canterbury version). The extant scenes portray Joseph of Arimathea obtaining and burying Christ's body, and events surrounding the entombment.

BIBLIOGRAPHY

The edition is T. Atkinson Jenkins, John M. Manly, Mildred K. Pope, and Jean G. Wright, eds., *La Seinte Resureccion from the Paris and Canterbury MSS* (1943). See also Grace Frank, *The Medieval French Drama* (1954), 86–92; Mary Dominica Legge, *Anglo-Norman Literature and Its Background* (1963), 321–328.

BRIAN MERRILEES

[See also **Anglo-Norman Literature; Drama, Western European.**]

SEISIN, DISSEISIN. *Saisine* and *dessaisine* were words formed in French in the early 1100's, new nouns derived from the old verb *saisir.* The verb meant "to place (someone) in possession" or "to take possession." Its past participle, *saisi,* might mean simply "in possession." *Saisine* thus had several senses: "a placing (of someone) in possession," "a taking of possession," and "possession" simply. *Dessaisine* was narrower. It meant "a displacing" of one in possession, an ejectment, a taking away.

The words migrated into English, and *saisine* into Scots as *sasine.* In the twelfth century the concepts they denoted became important in the allied systems of French customary law, English common law, and Scottish feudal law, and the words were much caught up in legal speech. Their legal importance lay in two areas. First, the laws were reluctant to recognize any purely conventional rights in real property—rights, that is, which rested merely on resolve and agreement. To own an interest in land or the like one must have seisin too. So, a sale of land was not effective until the seller placed the purchaser in seisin, and a claim to inherit was empty unless some ancestor had been in seisin. Second, the laws developed special procedures, like the English assize of novel disseisin, to afford recovery where men had been deprived of their property just lately. Plaintiffs in these procedures had to tell of recent seisin recently upset. Since the defense was limited to denial or to readily demonstrable justifications, the plaintiffs might not have to tell of much else. The recent seisin commonly was, or seemed to be, the very basis for recovery.

In legal usage the words were altered a little in

meaning in order to express these doctrines most conveniently. Thus the Scots *sasine* meant a transfer of possession that effected a conveyance of lands. In France and England, when seisin meant possession it always denoted possession that expressed an interest, possession "shot through with elements of right" (Joüon des Longrais).

In later times the relevant legal doctrines changed vastly, and they carried with them the senses of the terms, which accordingly came to have different meanings in the three countries and everywhere moved far from the original significations. In Scotland and again in England the law eventually decided to recognize purely conventional rights in real property. So by 1500 a Scotsman had received *sasine* if he had a notarized document in hand, and from 1535 seisin of English property shifted from seller to buyer in the instant when they struck their bargain. In France in the thirteenth century it was found to serve justice if in many cases seisin was simply attributed to men. Hence, for example, the doctrine "le mort saisit le vif" (the deceased passes seisin to the living), in which seisin passed automatically from the ancestor when he died to his lawful heir.

In all three countries there grew great forests of these technical usages. In the end these technical usages drove "seisin" and "disseisin" out of the general vocabulary. Even the lawyers eventually had to adopt the word "possession" when they needed to speak of actual control of property.

BIBLIOGRAPHY

For the origin of the words, see Walther von Wartburg, *Französisches etymologisches Wörterbuch,* XVII (1966), 19–22, under **sazjan;* Adolf Tobler and Erhard Lommatzsch, *Altfranzösisches Wörterbuch,* IX (1973), under *saisine, saisir;* and R. C. Van Caenegem, *Royal Writs in England from the Conquest to Glanvill* (1959), 313–314, 465. *Saisine* is attested in its Latin reflex *saisina* from *ca.* 1130 and in French from the late 1150's, but already in 1114–1118 *saisine* and *dessaisine* probably underlay the Latin *inuestitura* and *dissaisiatione* of the *Leges Henrici Primi,* L. J. Downer, ed. (1972), 63.1 (including note) and 53.5.

The several senses of *saisir* and *seisi* are attested from 1135–1140 in Geffrei Gaimar, *L'estoire des Engleis,* Alexander Bell, ed. (1960), where, however, the early occurrence of *saisine,* cited in *Französisches etymologisches Wörterbuch,* is a corrupt reading in line 2,179. See also *Leges Henrici Primi,* 43.4. In its Latin reflex *saisitus, saisi* occurs with the meaning "in possession" as early as 1096—see Ordericus Vitalis, *Historia Ecclesiastica* 9.3.

For the early legal use of the terms, see Frederick Pollock and Frederic W. Maitland, *The History of English Law,* 2nd ed. II (1898), 29–80. Maitland's interpretation has raised great controversy, which is summarized with references to the literature by S. F. C. Milsom in the reissue of Pollock and Maitland, *The History of English Law,* I (1968), lxxxvi–lxxxviii. See especially F. Joüon des Longrais, *La conception anglaise de la saisine* (1925), and, since 1968, Donald W. Sutherland, *The Assize of Novel Disseisin* (1973), 1–42, and S. F. C. Milsom, *The Legal Framework of English Feudalism* (1976), 24, 36–64, 154–186. Maitland's critics may have erred by not considering, as he did, the use of *saisine* and *dessaisine* in the general vocabulary of French. The views expressed in the present article accordingly lie closer to Maitland's than to those of his critics'.

For the development of legal meaning in the 1200's and after, see François Olivier-Martin, *Histoire de la coutume de la prévôté et vicomté de Paris,* II, pt. 1 (1926), 45–72; Sutherland, *Assize of Novel Disseisin,* 144–166; A. W. B. Simpson, *A History of the Land Law,* 2nd ed. (1986), 173–188; and H. H. Monteath, "Heritable Rights," in The Stair Society, *An Introduction to Scottish Legal History* (1958), 156–170.

DONALD W. SUTHERLAND

[See also **Assize, English; Bracton, Henry de; Gaimar, Geffrei; Glanville, Ranulf de; Henry II of England; Law, English Common; Law, Scots; Ordericus Vitalis; Tenure of Land, Western European; Trespass.**]

SELĀMLIK (from *selam,* to greet), the term used in Ottoman Turkish for the part of a residence that was reserved for male visitors. This reception area, according to the size of the residence and importance of the owner, varied from a single room to a number of structures around a common yard. The *selāmlık,* being the semipublic area, reflected in its size, decoration, and construction the status and wealth of its owner. Young women were not allowed in this area when male visitors were present.

ÜLKÜ Ü. BATES

[See also **Harem.**]

SELEUCIA. See **Ctesiphon.**

SELIM I (*r.* 1512–1520), ninth Ottoman sultan, also referred to as Yavuz (the Grim, the Resolute). The son of Bāyazīd II, Selim initially faced a problem common to heirs to the Ottoman throne: warfare with his brothers to determine the eventual successor. Selim's problem was compounded because his eldest brother, Ahmet, enjoyed his father's favor and Korkud, a young man inclined more toward scholarly reflection than political intrigue, was the favorite of the religious elements at court. Selim, aware of his precarious position, had a valuable ally in the Janissary corps, and this support allowed him to consider unexpected, unprecedented preemptive action: Rather than allow Ahmet an opportunity to seize the throne by waiting for his father to die, with Janissary backing he forced the old man to abdicate in April 1512 and was proclaimed sultan. Korkud and Ahmet were pursued and murdered, while Bāyazīd survived his ouster by only a few months, perhaps poisoned at Selim's instigation.

A great part of Selim's support by the Janissary corps can be traced to their dissatisfaction with the way Bāyazīd (and Ahmet) handled seditious elements in eastern Anatolia. The *kızılbaş,* Shiite supporters of the charismatic Safawid ruler of Iran, Shah Ismāᶜīl I (*r.* 1501–1524), had come to pose a grave threat to Ottoman interests in the east, a threat that had been dealt with ineffectively by the old regime. As soon as his throne was secure, Selim struck against the heart of the problem: marching east with a large army, he engaged and soundly defeated Shah Ismāᶜīl's forces at Çaldıran in eastern Anatolia in August 1514. Selim eliminated the rebellious elements with ruthless efficiency and occupied Tabriz, while the defeated Ismāᶜīl fled eastward into Iran. Selim had successfully protected Ottoman interests in Anatolia, although he failed to follow up his victory by eliminating Ismāᶜīl's forces altogether, no doubt partly because of the hardship of the winter in the east, and of Ismāᶜīl's success in reconsolidating his forces and recapturing his capital of Tabriz. More important, Selim's attention at this point was drawn in a completely different direction.

In 1513, anticipating an Ottoman drive eastward, Ismāᶜīl had concluded a pact with the Mamluk rulers of Egypt and Syria, and the perceived threat this posed to his rear is generally given as Selim's primary motive for launching hostilities against the Mamluks in the summer of 1516. Relations between the two giants had long been deteriorating, however, since Ottoman advances eastward in the mid fifteenth century had given them an ever-lengthening common border with the Mamluks. Open hostilities had broken out in 1485, and a number of outstanding grievances (among which were the Mamluks' giving asylum to political refugees from the Ottomans and disputes concerning hegemony over small principalities on the border) had continued to mar their relations. A final, cataclysmic confrontation was inevitable. The warrior aristocracy of the Mamluks proved no match for Ottoman tactical superiority and use of field artillery. In August 1516 Selim's army routed the Mamluks at Marj Dābiq, north of Aleppo. The Mamluk sultan Qānṣūh al Ghawrī died on the field, and the retreating Mamluks found themselves shut out of Aleppo by a population weary of their misrule. By early 1517, the Ottomans had occupied Egypt. Selim I now set about eliminating what remained of the Mamluk hierarchy.

With the defeat of the Mamluks, the Ottomans came into possession not only of Syria and Egypt, but also of the Hejaz and the holy cities of Mecca and Medina. During the reign of Selim I the Ottoman state was transformed from one solely dedicated to conquest in Europe, with only limited designs on Muslim lands in central Anatolia, to one that encompassed many of the most important centers of Islam. Selim completed the conquest, but not the consolidation, of these new holdings. This job was left to his son Süleyman the Magnificent (*r.* 1520–1566), for Selim I, while on campaign in Europe, died after a short illness in September 1520.

BIBLIOGRAPHY

Although many exist in Turkish, there is no major monograph in a Western language dealing solely with the reign of Selim I. Good accounts of his reign can be found in Halil Inalcik, *The Ottoman Empire: The Classical Age, 1300–1600,* Norman Itzkowitz and Colin Imber, trans. (1973); and Stanford J. Shaw, *History of the Ottoman Empire and Modern Turkey,* I (1976). Readers particularly concerned with the Ottoman conquest of the Arab East will profit from consulting Peter M. Holt, *Egypt and the Fertile Crescent, 1516–1922* (1966).

RALPH S. HATTOX

[See also **Aleppo; Anatolia; Arabia; Bāyazīd II; Crimea, Khanate of; Egypt, Islamic; Hejaz; Janissary; Mamluk Dynasty; Ottomans; Qānṣūh al-Ghawrī.**]

Great Mosque of Isfahan, north dome chamber, 1088–1099. COURTESY OF ELECTA EDITRICE, MILANO

SELJUK ART AND ARCHITECTURE were produced primarily under the two main ruling branches of the Turkish Seljuk (more properly Saljūqid) clan, in Iran (1038–1157) and in Anatolia (1077–1307).

THE GREAT SELJUKS

In Iran the Great Seljuks had a major impact on religious architecture and on the diffusion of previously localized artistic traditions. As for the former, most of the significant innovations can be traced to the reign of Sultan Malikshāh I (1072–1092) and his powerful vizier Niẓām al-Mulk. For example, at Isfahan, the Seljuk capital, Niẓām al-Mulk inserted a domed chamber in the sanctuary of the Great Mosque, enclosing the area in front of the miḥrāb (prayer niche), where the imam customarily stood to lead the communal prayers, as well as the minbar, or pulpit, from which the sermon was preached. Although his purpose was probably to ensure that the sultan and his entourage might worship without fear of assassination, one important effect was to exclude most of the congregation from the Friday prayer service. Of more permanent significance was the insertion of four *eyvān*s on the axes of the courtyard. (An *eyvān* is a vaulted hall closed at one end.) The two on the longitudinal axis served respectively as the main entrance to the mosque and as a kind of ceremonial passage to the domed chamber; the function of the two side *eyvān*s is unclear. It is not certain that this plan was established during the reign of Malikshāh, but a four-*eyvān* mosque was built at the small city of Zavāra (Zavāreh) in 1136, suggesting that the type had already been introduced in the capital. Thenceforth, the four-*eyvān* mosque remained canonical in Iran, though it occurred only very rarely elsewhere.

Niẓām al-Mulk also actively promoted the development of a new institution—the madrasa, a school of orthodox theology and law—as a means of countering the successes of Shiite propagandists trained in Fatimid Egypt. Although no surviving Seljuk building in Iran can be identified with certainty as a madrasa, the institution itself quickly took root throughout the Islamic world, its characteristic form being determined in each region by customary architectural practice and materials.

Unified Turkish control of the vast Iranian territory, however, led to a mingling of previously distinct provincial traditions, as in the rapid spread across northern Iran of private mausolea in forms originating in the northeast, in Khorāsān and Transoxiana; eventually they reached as far west as Azerbaijan and even into neighboring Anatolia. Such a mausoleum might be centralized in plan, like the circular Chihil Dukhtarān (*ca.* 1054) at Damghan and the octagonal "towers" at Kharraqān (1067–1068 and 1093), or it might be a domed square like the Gunbad-i Surkh (1148) at Maragha.

Not only were old traditions mingled, but also, under the patronage of the new ruling class, they were raised to new heights, particularly in architectural decoration. Exterior walls were usually faced with bricks laid in intricate patterns (called *hazār bāf*), probably also originally a northeastern tradition. In the course of the Turkish period the patterns became ever more varied and intricate, the mortar-filled spaces between bricks came to play an increasing role in the two-dimensional designs, and often a third dimension was added as well—in the form of networks of projecting bricks that cast shadows over sun-baked surfaces. It was in this period, too, that turquoise-glazed bricks and tiles were introduced, first as accents to the brick surface, then as major elements in *hazār bāf* designs.

Aside from architecture and its decoration, little Iranian art survives from the Seljuk period proper. Most of what is commonly labeled "Seljuk" was actually produced under small Turkish successor dynasties like the Salghurids of Fārs and the Ildegizids of Azerbaijan. Only one illustrated manuscript is known, a long Persian poem of love and war entitled *Varqeh va Gulshāh* (İstanbul, Topkapi Sarayi, MS Hazine 841). Its seventy-one miniatures were probably painted in Azerbaijan near the border with eastern Anatolia at the beginning of the thirteenth century. The strip compositions without spatial depth, the vivid colors, and the rendering of vegetation and architectural details reveal close affinities with painting in nearby northern Mesopotamia.

Among other small arts of twelfth- and thirteenth-century Iran, ceramics stand out, particularly those painted in metallic luster. In this technique the glazed tile or vessel was first fired at a high temperature. Then its surface was painted with designs in a metallic oxide, and it was fired again, at a lower temperature and in a smoky kiln receiving a minimum of air; the fire thus could burn only by drawing the oxygen from the oxide, leaving a metallic residue on the glazed surface. Once polished, this metallic film lent a shimmering luster to the designs. The luster-painting technique had been known in Islam since the ninth century, when it was practiced in Mesopotamia, Egypt, and perhaps Syria, but the earliest-known Iranian pieces are dated 1179 (London, British Museum) and 1191 (Chicago, Art Institute).

Although a number of cities have been suggested as sources for Iranian lusterware, only Kashan has been convincingly connected with an identifiable stylistic group. Its hallmarks include tiny overall patterning scratched through the lustered expanses, multipetaled floral forms, standing birds with long legs and flying birds showing both wings, and precisely arranged groups of dots on various elements of the design. Aside from vessels and tile revetments, the Kashan workshops were especially noted for large *miḥrāb*s composed of several large panels that combine decoration in luster and cobalt blue with several levels of relief. These *miḥrāb*s are among the masterpieces of medieval Iranian art.

Other works in the same technique but with different stylistic features, though frequently labeled "Rayy," "Sāva," or "Gurgan," cannot yet be associated with specific centers. The same is true of so-called minai (*mīnāʾī*) ware, a type of polychrome-painted pottery developed in Iran. (See frontispiece to volume 6.) Like lusterware, minai pieces had to be fired twice at different temperatures, in order to accommodate the properties of the different pigments. Minai vessels in particular are frequently decorated with recognizable scenes from the *Shāhnāma,* the great Persian epic, and thus help to fill some gaps in present-day knowledge of Iranian manuscript painting. Ceramics in other techniques, as well as glass, textiles, and silver-inlaid bronzes, also flourished in Iran in this period.

Although during the lifetime of Malikshāh the Seljuk ruling family directly controlled large parts of the Islamic world outside Iran, the surviving

Persian lusterware bowl with flared sides, 1191.

works commissioned by its members and their deputies—for example, at the Great Mosques of Damascus and Aleppo and on the city walls at Āmid—do not reflect Iranian styles. The impact of Seljuk patronage was indirect, showing itself in more elaborate and monumental public display, which was carried still farther by the Turkish successor dynasties, thus raising regional artistic traditions to new levels of brilliance.

THE SELJUKS OF RUM

In previously Christian Anatolia (Rum) a collateral branch of the Seljuk clan established itself in 1077; a separate chapter of Islamic art and architecture unfolded there. Until about the middle of the twelfth century, the Seljuks of Rum were simply one of the more powerful of several Turkish dynasties controlling Anatolian provinces. Only after about 1140 did they become clearly dominant, gradually gaining control, directly or through vassal relations, of most of the peninsula. Seljuk architecture and art flourished from then through the thirteenth century. Although, in the absence of preexisting Islamic artistic traditions, craftsmen in twelfth- and thirteenth-century Anatolia drew heavily upon those of neighboring Iran, northern Mesopotamia, and northern Syria, a strong component of originality was always present in their works.

Asia Minor is rich in timber and stone, and its Islamic architects, like those before them, built in these materials, as well as in brick. Although few Seljuk congregational mosques survive in their original forms, it appears that, in place of the large courtyards typical of other Islamic regions, central bays with open roofs often sufficed. Madrasa complexes and round or polygonal mausolea were also lavishly sponsored by members of the Seljuk family and their followers. An outstanding example is the Khwand Khātūn complex at Kayseri, founded by the wife of ᶜAlāᵓ al-Dīn Kayqubād I (*r.* 1219–1237) and finished in 1238; it incorporates a mosque, a madrasa, and an octagonal domed mausoleum.

Perhaps the most striking architectural contribution of the Seljuks of Rum, however, was a series of caravansarais, called "khans," along the main roads. Remains of approximately 100 are known, 8 of which are still relatively well-preserved "sultan khans," or royal caravansarais, constructed of stone and often richly decorated. These buildings were intended as hotels for travelers, particularly merchants with their caravans of goods. All were protected by strong, fortified walls and could be entered only by single main portals, which were easily defensible. Inside were arrayed stables; dormitories; private bedrooms, often equipped with fireplaces and other comforts; storerooms; mosques; baths; and occasionally even libraries. Among the services commonly available were medical and veterinary treatment, blacksmithing and other kinds of repair work, and free meals—sometimes with musical accompaniment. Almost all the sultan khans were built in the first half of the thirteenth century. Among the best-preserved examples is that at Palas on the road between Kayseri and Sivas, built by Kayqubād I in 1232–1236.

In view of the natural resources available, it is not surprising that carving in wood, stone, and stucco became a major mode of Turkish architectural decoration in Anatolia. The earliest Seljuk monument known is the carved wooden minbar now in the ᶜAlāᵓ al-Dīn mosque at Konya (Ikonion), the Seljuk capital; it is dated 1155. The interlocking geometric motifs that constitute its designs are strongly reminiscent of some of the brick and tile patterns of Iran.

The elegant Anatolian stone carving was particularly concentrated on portals; in this focus and in many of the motifs chosen—like the double-headed birds carved in relief on the city walls of Konya (now destroyed) and elsewhere—a relationship with neighboring northern Mesopotamia is discernible.

An example of the distinctive approach of the Anatolian stone carver to portal design is to be found at the Ince Minare madrasa in Konya (*ca.* 1258). There, the sculptor played imaginatively with "classical" structural members. The capitals of engaged colonnettes support nothing or are missing altogether; the colonnette shafts sometimes taper downward to points above their bases; inscription bands intertwine and flow over curving and projecting surfaces, like elastic ribbons around a knobby bundle. And, applied to the surface—arbitrarily but symmetrically—are lushly plastic vegetal forms, knots, bosses, and isolated bits of geometric interlace.

Polychrome pottery was produced in Anatolia, but the most impressive ceramic products were faience-mosaic revetments like those on the interior walls and dome surface of the Karatay madrasa at Konya (1251). There turquoise, dark blue, and white pieces are laid in an intricate pattern of radial stars, with knotted inscriptions in Kufic script set against floral scrolls; geometric inscriptions fill the "Turkish triangles," or faceted pendentives, below the dome.

Little survives of metalwork and other small arts from Seljuk Anatolia, but a red silk textile, woven with gold thread and inscribed with the name of Sultan Kayqubād I, now in the Musée des Tissus, Lyons, suggests the richness of what has been lost. It is also from thirteenth-century Anatolia that the earliest surviving Islamic woven carpets are known. The "Konya carpets," as they are called, are usually woven in continuous geometric designs, with geometric or pseudo-Kufic borders. Most of them were found in Seljuk mosques and are now kept in the Museum of Turkish and Islamic Art in İstanbul.

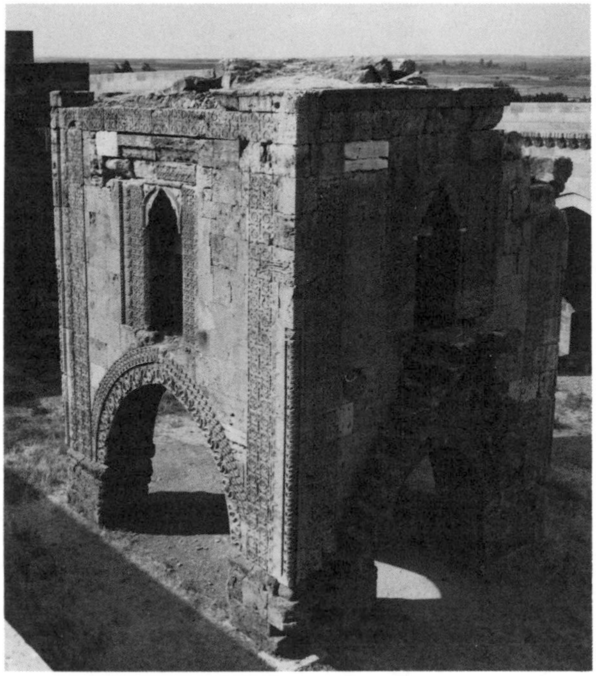

Sultan khan at Palas. Constructed by Kayqubād I in 1232–1236. COURTESY OF ELECTA EDITRICE, MILANO

BIBLIOGRAPHY

Oktay Aslanapa, *Turkish Art and Architecture* (1971); Claude Cahen, *Pre-Ottoman Turkey* (1968); Kurt Erdmann, *Das anatolische Karavansaray des 13. Jahrhunderts,* 3 vols. (1961–1976), and *Seven Hundred Years of Oriental Carpets,* Hanna Erdmann, ed., May H. Beattie and Hildegard Herzog, trans. (1970), 41–46; Richard Ettinghausen, "Evidence for the Identification of Kāshān Pottery," in *Ars islamica,* 3 (1936), and "The 'Wade Cup' in the Cleveland Museum of Art: Its Origin and Decorations," in *Ars orientalis,* 2 (1957); André Godard, "Ardistān et Zawārè," in *Athār-é Īrān,* 1 (1936); Oleg Grabar, "The Visual Arts, 1050–1350," in *Cambridge History of Iran,* V, J. A. Boyle, ed. (1968), 626–658; Robert Hillenbrand, "The Development of Saljuq Mausolea in Iran," in *The Art of Iran and Anatolia from the 11th to the 13th Century A.D.,* William Watson, ed. (1974), 40–59; Arthur Lane, *Early Islamic*

Karatay madrasa at Konya showing a portion of the dome on "Turkish triangle" pendentives, 1251. COURTESY OF ELECTA EDITRICE, MILANO

Pottery (1947, 4th rev. ed. 1958); Assadullah S. Melikian-Chirvani, "Le roman de Varqe et Golšâh," in *Arts asiatiques,* 22 (1970); Julian Raby, ed., *The Art of Syria and the Jazira, 1100–1250* (1985); D. S. Rice, *The Wade Cup in the Cleveland Museum of Art* (1955); Tamara Talbot Rice, *The Seljuks in Asia Minor* (1961).

ESTELLE WHELAN

[See also **Calligraphy, Islamic; Ceramics, Islamic; Eyvān; Glass, Islamic; Gunbadh; Iconology, Islamic; Ikonion; Ildegizids; Isfahan; Islamic Art and Architecture; Kashi; Khan; Madrasa; Malikshāh; Manuscript Illumination, Islamic; Miḥrab; Minai Ware; Minbar; Mosque; Niẓam al-Mulk; Qubba; Rugs and Carpets, Islamic; Textiles; Transoxiana.**]

SELJUKS, a Turko-Muslim dynasty that ruled over much of Iran, Iraq, Syria, Asia Minor, and parts of Central Asia from the mid eleventh to the mid thirteenth century. The dynasty is subdivided into the following branches: Great Seljuks (1038–1194), Seljuks of Rum (*ca.* 1077–*ca.* 1307), Seljuks of Syria (1078–1117), and Seljuks of Kirmān (1041–1186).

ORIGINS

The Seljuks traced their descent to the Qınıq, a subdivision of the Oghuz confederation that had formed east of the Caspian Sea in the Kazakhstan steppes, in the late eighth century. Elements of this tribal union originated in the Eastern Türk qaghanate in Mongolia (552–630, 680–741), to whose downfall they had contributed. Hemmed in by their Turkic neighbors on the steppe and by the Samanids in the south, the Oghuz were unstable and a source of regional instability.

According to tradition, Seljuk ibn Doqaq (known as Timür Yalıgh, "Iron Bow"), the eponymous founder of the dynasty, held the position of *sü-bashi* (warlord) in either the Oghuz or the Khazar state. About 985, after a falling out with his overlord, the *yabghu* of the Oghuz, he fled with his family and retainers to Jand, across the Syr Darya from Transoxiana. In this Islamic environment, Seljuk became a Muslim. Earlier, the family may have been under Khazar Judaic influence (indicated, for instance, by the names of Seljuk's sons: Mīkāʾīl, Isrāʾīl, Mūsā, Yūnus).

Oghuz groupings, including the Seljuks, functioned as mercenaries in the struggle among the Samanids (removed from the scene in 1005), the Ghaznavids, and the Qarakhanids for hegemony in Transoxiana. Although the details of their involvement are not entirely clear, Seljuk forces were found in both the Samanid and the Qarakhanid armies. Eventually the bands led by Arslan/Isrāʾīl, his brother Mūsā, and their nephews Toghrıl and Chaghrı ibn Mīkāʾīl, occasionally at odds with one another, took service with the maverick Qarakhanid ruler of Transoxiana, ʿAlī Tegin. The latter opposed the Qarakhanid supreme ruler, Yūsuf Qadır Khan, and the Ghaznavid sultan, Maḥmūd.

When ʿAlī Tegin suffered a defeat in 1025–1026, Arslan/Isrāʾīl's band shifted its nominal allegiance to the Ghaznavids and settled in northern Khorāsān. (Arslan/Isrāʾīl remained a hostage with the Ghaznavids and died in captivity. His leaderless forces became little more than marauding bands.) In 1028/1029 the Ghaznavids struck against them to curtail their brigandage, but this move was counterproductive. In response, some Seljuks moved on to Azerbaijan and made their way to the "*ghāzī* line" against Christian Transcaucasia and Byzantium (Seljuk raids here may have begun a decade earlier). Others dispersed, creating chaos in their wake. They soon returned to western Khorāsān, however, and resumed their depredations.

About 1034, Mūsā, Toghrıl, and Chaghrı, who had remained with their forces in Central Asia, sought refuge in Khwārizmian service. But the Khwārizmshāh, Hārūn ibn Altuntash, died shortly thereafter, the victim of Ghaznavid intrigues, and much of Khwārizm passed into the hands of the Oghuz leader Shāhmalik, who proceeded to expel the Seljuks. In desperation Toghrıl and Chagrı migrated to troubled Khorāsān, access to which had been officially denied them by the Ghaznavid ruler Masʿūd (1031–1041). In 1035, the Seljuks defeated a Ghaznavid force at Nasā. Masʿūd now tried to coopt them into his administration of the region and thereby lessen—he hoped—their destructive impact on this, his most prosperous province. Thus, Nasā, Farāva, and Dohistān were given to Chagrı, Toghrıl, and Mūsā Beyghu, respectively. They would now be Ghaznavid servitors. The Seljuks, however, paid little attention to these agreements. Moreover, however well the Seljuks per se may have been doing, fresh bands of impoverished Turkoman nomads continued to enter Khorāsān from Central Asia. These bands were barely under Seljuk control. Many went further west, to the frontier, to Azerbaijan, even to Iraq, seeking booty and as little supervision as possible. Ghaznavid attempts to check their raiding (largely induced by the threat of starvation, to which their depredations and disruptions surely contributed) failed. By 1040, after the Seljuks had taken important cities, such as Merv and Nıshapur, Masʿūd decided to crush them. It was the Ghaznavid army, however, that was destroyed at Dandānqān (May 1040) by the Seljuks. Iran and the lands to the west lay open before these tribesmen who so recently had been homeless and hungry.

THE SULTANATE OF THE GREAT SELJUKS

Following the victory at Dandānqān, Seljuk forces moved against the declining Ghaznavids and the Oghuz state. Shāhmalik was defeated (1042) and subsequently captured. Khwārizm now fell under Seljuk control. In keeping with Turkic traditions of bipartite rule, Chaghrı emerged as the principal Seljukid in the east, his capital at Merv; Toghrıl, who had already declared himself sultan when he took Nishapur in 1038, was ruler of the west and the acknowledged head of the Seljuk clan. Qavurd Qara Arslan, a son of Chaghrı, established himself in Kirmān about 1041, giving rise to the Seljuk dynasty of Kirmān.

As more Central Asian Oghuz, seeking food and plunder, flocked to their banner, the Seljuk leaders were faced with the problem of directing their energies to the service of the dynasty. This and subsequent migrations of Oghuz resulted in the large-scale introduction into the Middle East of a new ethnic element, the Turks, who would, in time, turkize northwestern and northeastern Iran and Asia Minor.

Aided by the collapse of an effective opposition from the strife-torn Iranian petty dynasts, Toghrıl conquered the Iranian plateau. By 1042, from his center at Rayy, he had organized campaigns against Iraq, Transcaucasia, and Anatolia. The most troublesome tribal elements were directed to the Christian frontiers. In 1055, at the invitation of the caliph, al-Qaʾīm (1031–1075), Toghrıl entered Baghdad and quickly deposed the Buyids, who had controlled Baghdad and the caliphs since 945. Al-Qaʾīm hoped to use the Sunni Seljuks not only against the Shiite Buyids but also against the Shiite Fatimids, whose domains were centered in Egypt.

As the ruler of Iran and the protector of the caliph in Baghdad, Toghrıl could claim to be the preeminent political leader of the Islamic world. This did not prevent a number of his kinsmen and their tribal followers from revolting against him, however. Toghrıl suppressed this revolt, and also an attempt by the last Buyid governor of Baghdad to reestablish himself in the city. By 1062, Toghrıl's authority was so great that he felt free to demand one of the caliph's daughters in marriage, and al-Qaʾīm felt obliged to comply.

Meanwhile, Toghrıl's brother Chagrı (*d.* 1060) had been succeeded in his domains by his son Alp Arslan ("Brave Lion"). When Toghrıl died without a male heir in 1063, Alp Arslan succeeded his uncle as sultan. Alp Arslan's rise to supreme power was not uncontested. Indeed, Toghrıl may have designated Alp Arslan's younger half brother, Sulaymān, who was backed by Toghrıl's powerful minister, Kundurī, as his successor. However, aided by his brilliant vizier, Niẓām al-Mulk, and by his strong power base in the rich eastern territories, Alp Arslan was able to secure the throne and, in doing so, to unite the whole of the Seljuk realm.

Alp Arslan's claim to supreme rule was disputed by his kinsman Qutlumush (or Qutalmısh) ibn Isrāʾīl/Arslan, who revolted in 1064. Relying on his professional army commanded by *ghilmān* (slave-soldiers, largely of Turkic origin; sing., *ghulām*), Alp Arslan defeated Qutlumush. In 1067 he was faced with a rebellion by his older brother Qavurd, whom he also defeated. These revolts pointed to the growing gulf between the imperial sultanate, with its *ghulām* army, Persian bureaucracy, and Near Eastern monarchic traditions (which Alp Arslan was cultivating), and the older Turkic conceptions of the state as the shared property of the ruling, charismatic clan. Both of these traditions often conflicted with the egalitarian and even anarchic instincts of the tribesmen. The resultant tensions were never alleviated.

Alp Arslan, seeking employment for the troublesome Turkomans, encouraged them to raid the Byzantine borderlands, Fatimid Syria, and Transcaucasia (he himself campaigned there, taking Ani in 1064 and extending his sway to Georgia and northern Azerbaijan in 1067–1068). In fact, his real interest lay in Syria, as its conquest would further enhance his standing as the premier figure in the Islamic world. The Turkoman raids on Byzantium, however, largely beyond his immediate control, provoked a response from Constantinople. Although some kind of understanding appears to have been worked out between Emperor Romanos IV Diogenes and the sultan in 1070, it fell apart when Romanos launched a campaign into Armenia. Alp Arslan, who was planning the conquest of Fatimid Syria and Egypt, was forced to face the Byzantines. At the Battle of Manazkert (Malazgirt), 19 August 1071, the Byzantines were badly defeated and Romanos captured. Alp Arslan, still more interested in Syrian and Muslim affairs, gave Romanos remarkably easy terms (ransom, alliance, tribute, and border adjustments) and sent him home. The deposition of Romanos in 1072 nullified these arrangements, which were probably unworkable as the uncontrolled Turkoman raids against Byzantium continued. In time, these raids led to the conquest of much of Anatolia, which would be organized into the sultanate of Rum.

Following Manazkert, Alp Arslan turned to the east and launched a campaign against Qarakhanid Central Asia, where previously he had demonstrated Seljuk power. The campaign was interrupted by his assassination.

Malikshāh (1072–1092), the official heir, succeeded his father. Once again, Qavurd, who had the sympathy of the Turkoman tribes and tribal elements in the army, made a bid for the throne. It failed and he was strangled, according to Turkic custom, with a bowstring (January 1074). There were also revolts by the young ruler's brother Tekish (Tökish), which ended in the latter's blinding (1084/1085). The sons of the erstwhile rebel Qutlumush also showed little inclination to accept Malikshāh's overlordship. One of them, Sulaymān, by 1080 had laid the foundation for the sultanate of Rum.

The Seljuk sultanate reached the zenith of its power under Malikshāh and the brilliant vizier Niẓām al-Mulk. It had under its authority a vast expanse from the Mediterranean to Central Asia and from Arabia to the Caucasus. The caliphate, which held its own political agenda, was compelled to coexist with the Seljuks as an unequal partner. The Anatolian Seljuks, however, were largely independent and often hostile toward the central government.

From his capital at Isfahan, Malikshāh was active on all fronts. He completed his father's military objectives against Qarakhanid Central Asia and thwarted Ghaznavid thrusts as well (1073). In 1089, in response to appeals from local religious leaders, he was again active in Turkistan against the Qarakhanids. The latter were forced to accept his overlordship. In Transcaucasia, unrelenting Seljuk pressure not only secured Azerbaijan (an important concentration point for the Turkomans who were pouring into Anatolia), but also brought Georgia more fully under Seljuk control (1075–1086). At the same time, Seljuk forces under Tutush ibn Alp Arslan and Artuq Beg were strengthening and expanding Seljuk positions in northern Iraq, southern Syria, and Palestine and penetrating eastern Arabia, the Hejaz, and Yemen.

Malikshāh's death brought the long-brewing domestic crisis to the fore. Twelve-year-old Berkyaruq (1092–1105), his son and eventual successor, was immediately faced with rebellious relatives who sought either the sultanate or their own autonomous domains. In the midst of this turmoil, the First Crusade was barely noticed. The most serious threat, posed by Tutush, who from his power base in Syria had seized much of western Iran and Iraq, ended with the latter's death in battle in 1095. Nonetheless, a combination of Berkyaruq's youth, factional divisions within the bureaucracy, and the force of Turkic tradition led to the de facto dismemberment of the sultanate. Some formal recognition of this was given in the modus vivendi worked out between Berkyaruq and his brothers in 1104. Muḥammad Tapar, who had waged continuous war with him, was recognized as a sultan in his own right with authority in Syria, northwestern Iran, the Anatolian borderlands, and upper Mesopotamia. Sanjar ibn Malikshāh was confirmed as the *malik* of Khorāsān and Transoxiana. Berkyaruq, who died of exhaustion shortly afterward, was to be master of central and southern Iran, Iraq, Mecca, and Medina. In addition, local atabegs and tribal chiefs (for instance, the Artuqids, Zangids, and Sökmenids) had begun to—or were about to—create their own states.

Muḥammad Tapar (1105–1118), who ruled as supreme sultan (although Sanjar was largely autonomous in the east), temporarily retarded these centrifugal tendencies. With his death, they fully surfaced. Sanjar (1118–1157), "king of the east," was recognized as the senior Seljukid by Maḥmūd II (1118–1131) and the other sons of Muḥammad Tapar, but he remained in, and primarily concerned himself with, the affairs of Khorāsān and Transoxiana. In the west, in what became the "Iraqi sultanate," further fragmentation and discord were the norm. Thus, during the rule of Masᶜud (1134–1152) the more enterprising emirs and atabegs, such as Shams al-Dīn El-digüz and ᶜImād al-Dīn Zangi, established states of more than local significance. Serious threats would come from the now independent and expansionist Georgian kingdom, from a revived caliphate, and, in the last quarter of the twelfth century, from the Khwārizmshāhs, who had begun to expand, via Azerbaijan, into the Iraqi sultanate. The last Seljuk of any note, Toghrıl III (1161–1176), who fought to free himself from the great Turkish emirs, perished at the hands of the Khwārizmshāh Tekish.

In the eastern sultanate, Sanjar, whose power had been unequaled in the Seljuk realm, was fatally undermined by the invasion of the Qara Khitai, a people of Mongol origin who had ruled northern China as the Liao dynasty (947–1125) and had been driven thence into Central Asia by the Jürchen. The Qara Khitai defeated Sanjar in battle in 1141 and took over Transoxiana, but they did not attempt to conquer Iran. Shortly after this time, Sanjar suppressed challenges to his authority by rebellious vassals (the Khwārizmshāhs and the Ghurids), but his hold was shaky. The mortal blow to the eastern sultanate was struck by Oghuz tribesmen who were being driven westward by the Kipchaks and other nomads. Sanjar, while attempting to subdue them, was defeated and captured (1153), a misfortune that completely undermined Seljuk prestige. Sanjar escaped in 1156 but died in 1157, and the eastern sultanate perished with him.

THE SELJUKS OF RUM

The Seljuk dynasty in Anatolia, known as the Seljuks of Rum, was founded by Sulaymān ibn Qutlumush ibn Isrāᵓīl/Arslan. Following his father's death (in a revolt against Alp Arslan in 1064), he and his brothers moved westward. After Manazkert (1071), he placed himself at the head of the Turkoman bands operating in Anatolia. Sometime between 1075 and 1081, Sulaymān took Konya (Ikonion) and İznik (Nicaea), the latter becoming the Rum Seljuk capital until the crusaders displaced the Seljuks in 1097. Thereafter, Konya became the primary center. Sulaymān took the title of sultan, much to the displeasure of Malikshāh. Sulaymān's attempted expansion into Syria, governed by Tutush, ended in his defeat and death in 1086.

In 1092, Sulaymān's son Qılıj Arslan I (1092–1107), a hostage for his father's sins during the lifetime of Malikshāh, escaped and returned to Anatolia. Although aided by the decline of the Great Seljuks, he faced difficult competition from various Turkish begs (especially the Danishmendids), not to mention the Byzantines (his occasional allies) and the Crusaders. Taking advantage of Great Seljuk discord, he seized Mosul but then fell in battle against Muḥammad Tapar. His sons Shāhanshāh (or Malikshāh, *r.* 1107–1116) and Masᶜūd (*r.* 1116–1155) were hard pressed by Byzantium and the Danishmendids. Masᶜūd succeeded in reasserting his family's paramountcy in the last decade of his rule. Qılıj Arslan II (*r.* 1155/1156–1192), after initial difficulties, extended his authority over much of Turko-Muslim Anatolia, including the Zangid-protected Danishmendids (1174). Emperor Manuel I attempted to contain him, but this effort ended in the Byzantine disaster at Myriokephalon in 1176.

Some years later an aging Qılıj Arslan attempted to abdicate, dividing his holdings among his eleven heirs. The result was chaos. Resuming the sultanate in the face of a Byzantine-Ayyubid alliance partly directed at him, he came to an uneasy understanding with Frederick I Barbarossa, leader of the Third Crusade. Misunderstandings, however, led to a brief crusader occupation and sacking of Konya.

Kaykhusraw I (1192–1210), the designated heir, found his authority everywhere contested by his brothers, and was finally forced to take refuge in Byzantium. He eventually returned to the sultanate, but he found that Byzantium, which had been shorn of Constantinople in 1204, was much more interested in Asia Minor. Kaykhusraw died in 1210 at Alashehir, a battle in which his army defeated the Byzantines.

Kaykhusraw's son Kayqāwūs I (*r.* 1210–1219), like his father, sought to secure maritime trade outlets and extend his power to the southeast (Cilicia, Syria, upper Mesopotamia). In 1214, he took Sinop, a port of northern Anatolia, and made the neighboring Greek state of Trebizond his vassal. In 1217–1218 he achieved limited successes in Cilician Armenia and Ayyubid lands in northern Syria.

These activities paved the way for Kayqubād I (1219–1237), whose reign marked the apogee of Seljuk rule in Anatolia. He continued Seljuk expansion in the north (Sughdāq in the Crimea was taken in 1225) and the southeast, where there was conflict with the Ayyubids. Cilician Armenia in the south, Trebizond in the north, and Georgia in the east recognized his overlordship to varying degrees. His regional paramountcy was demonstrated in 1230, when, at the head of a Seljuk-Ayyubid coalition, he defeated the Khwārizmian Jalāl al-Dīn, ending the latter's attempt to expand westward.

A greater threat, however, loomed on the horizon: the Mongols. The disaster came during the reign of Kaykhusraw II (1237–1245/1246), whose self-indulgent rule left the sultanate ill-prepared. A massive rebellion of disgruntled Turkomans, led by a popular preacher, Bābā Isḥāq, which the government suppressed only with great difficulty (*ca.* 1240–1243), sapped its strength. The Mongols arrived in 1242. At the Mongol-Seljuk confrontation at Kösedagh (26 June 1243), the Seljuks were badly trounced. Kaykhusraw's minister, Muhadhdhab al-Dīn, managed to persuade the Mongols that the complete conquest of Rum would be too costly and that they should accept it as a tribute-paying vassal.

Even distant Mongol overlordship proved to be onerous. After a bungled attempt by the *parwāna* Muᶜīn al-Dīn, minister of Kaykhusraw III (1265–1282), to conspire with the Mamluks, the administration was placed in the hands of Mongol governors with puppet Seljuks on the throne. The last Seljuk died probably in 1308.

THE SELJUKS OF SYRIA

A peripheral vassal of the Great Seljuks, the short-lived Syrian line was founded by Tutush (1077–1095), Malikshāh's brother. In 1086 he defeated the Rum Seljukid Sulaymān, but was never able to control all of Syria. After Malikshāh's death, Tutush took northern Syria, eastern Anatolia, and Mesopotamia, and declared himself sultan. Defeated by Berkyaruq in 1095, he died at the hands of a disgruntled *ghulām.*

Tutush's sons Riḍwān (*r.* 1095–1113 in Aleppo) and Doqaq (*r.* 1095–1104 in Damascus) fought for supremacy in Syria, which allowed the Fatimids to regain Palestine. Riḍwān acknowledged Fatimid suzerainty in exchange for aid against his brother, who was defeated in 1097. Both brothers joined the struggle against the crusaders, with mixed results. After their deaths, the line, under Alp Arslan (1113–1114) and Sulṭānshāh (1114–1117), lost the little importance it had. Various atabegs, including the Artuqids and the Zangids, eventually came to dominate the region.

THE SELJUKS OF KIRMĀN

The Seljuk state in Kirmān was founded during the 1040's by Qavurd (*r.* 1043–1073), elder brother of Alp Arslan. It remained a relatively untroubled provincial backwater for most of its history. Its rulers, with few exceptions, were noted for their devotion to public works, education, and other pacific pursuits. The reign of Qavurd's grandson, Arslanshāh I (1101–1142), was particularly distinguished for its peace and prosperity. By the late twelfth century, however, dynastic strife among the sons of Toghrılshāh (1156–1170) led to a period of internal anarchy (1170–1187), which ended with the occupation of the region by the same rebellious Oghuz tribes (led by Dinar Beg) that had humbled Sanjar.

CONCLUSION

The Great Seljuk sultanate, and to varying degrees the other Seljuk states, were marked by two sharply contrasting structural features. On the one hand, there was the Iranian tradition of absolute monarchy directly modeled on the Turko-Iranian Ghaznavid state (Niẓām al-Mulk began his career in Ghaznavid service) and on the powerful Muslim legal tradition. On the other hand, there was the egalitarian and anarchic spirit of the Turkish tribesmen, along with their tribal tradition and customary law that extended even to the ruling house.

As the Great Seljuk state, with its Persian bureaucracy and *ghulām* army, moved further from its roots, the discontent of the tribesmen, who were always difficult to control, mounted. The dynasty, never able to reconcile these contradictory elements within both the royal clan and the state at large, succumbed to the divisive forces it had unleashed. The constant internecine strife contributed to the initial military successes of the crusaders against the Seljuks. It was also a major factor in the relatively easy Mongol conquest of Iran.

It should be noted that it was the Seljuk movement that first introduced a large, coherent mass of Turks to the Near and Middle East. During the Seljuk and Ilkhanid periods more tribes (predominantly Oghuz) entered the region, thereby changing the ethno-linguistic complexion of Anatolia and northwestern and northeastern Iran, which became and has since remained Turkic.

BIBLIOGRAPHY

For a general survey, see Claude Cahen, "The Historiography of the Seljuqid Period," in Bernard Lewis and P. M. Holt, eds. *Historians of the Middle East* (1962); M. F. Köprülü, "Anadolu Selçukluları tarihinin yerli kaynakları," in *Belleten,* 27 (1943), for the Islamic sources; J. Moravcsik, *Byzantinoturcica,* II (1958), for the Byzantine sources.

Islamic sources. Muḥammad Aqsarāyī, *Musāmarat al-Akhbār va Musāyarat al-Akhyār,* O. Turan, ed. (1944); Abu'l-Faḍl Baihaqī, *Tārīkh-i Baihaqī,* ᶜAlī A. Fayyāḍ, ed. (1971); Fatḥ ibn ᶜAlī al-Bundārī al-Iṣfahānī, *Zubdat al-Nuṣra wa Nukhbat al-ᶜUṣra,* an abridgment of ᶜImād al-Dīn al-Iṣfahānī's *Nuṣrat al-Fatra wa ᶜUṣrat al-Fitra,* M. Th. Houtsma, ed., in *Recueil de textes relatifs a l'histoire des seldjoucides* (1889); ᶜAlī ibn Naṣir al-Ḥusainī, *Akhbār Dawlat al-Saljuqiyya,* M. Iqbal, ed. (1933); Kamāl al-Dīn ibn al-ᶜAdīm, *Biyografilerle Selçuklular Tarihi. Ibnü'l-Adîm Bugyetü't-taleb fi Tarihi Haleb,* A. Sevim, trans. (1982); ᶜIzz ad-Dīn ibn al-Athīr, *Al-Kamil fī al-taᵓrikh,* C. J. Tornberg, ed., 15 vols. (1851–1876); H. W. Duda, *Die Seltschukengeschichte des Ibn Bibi* (1959); Abu'l-Faraj ibn al-Jawzī, *Al-Muntaẓam fī Ta'rīkh al-Mulūk wa'l-Umam,* F. Krenkow, ed. (1939–1941); Minhāj ibn Siraj Jūzjānī, *Ṭabaqāt-i Nāṣirī,* ᶜAbd al-Ḥayy Habībī, ed. (1963–1964), with an English edition, *A General History of the Muhammadan Dynasties of Asia . . . ,* Ṭabakāt-i Nāṣirī, trans., 2 vols. (1970); Afḍal al-Dīn Kirmānī, *Badā'iᶜ al-Azmān fī Waqā'i' Kirmān,* M. Bayānī, ed. (1947); Ẓahīr al-Dīn Nīshāpūrī, *Seljuqnāma,* I. Afshār, ed. (1953); Niẓām al-Mulk, *Siyār al-Mulūk* (*Siyāsat-nāma*), M. Qazvīnī and M. Chahārdihī, eds. (1956), with an English edition, *The Book of Government or Rules for Kings,* Hubert Darke, trans. (1960, 2nd ed. 1978); Abu Bakr Muḥammad al-Rāvandī, *Raḥat aṣ-Ṣudūr va Āyat as-Surūr,* M. Iqbāl, ed. (1921); Abu'l-Naṣr Muhammad al-^{c}Utbī, *Ta'rīkh al-Yamīnī* (1869).

Transcaucasian sources. Samuel Anec^{c}i, *Hawak^{c}-munk^{c} i groc^{c} patmagrac^{c},* A. Tēr-Mik'elean, ed. (1893), with French translation by Marie Brosset, in *Collection d'historiens arméniens,* II (1876); Vardan Barjraberdec^{c}i, *Mecin Vardanay Barjrberdeçwoy Patmut^{c}iwn tiezera-kan,* M. Ēmin, ed. (1861); Kirakos Ganjagec^{c}i, Pat-mut^{c}iwn Hayoc^{c}, K. A. Melik-Ohanǰanyan, ed. (1961), with a Russian edition, *Kirakos Gandzaketsi: Istoriia Armenii,* L. A. Khanlarian, trans. (1976); Aristakēs Lastivertc^{c}i, *Patmut^{c}iwn,* K. N. Yuzbašyan, ed. (1963); S. Qauxč^{c}išvili, ed., *K^{c}art^{c}lis C^{c}xovreba,* I–II (1955, 1959), with French edition, *Histoire de la Géorgie,* M. F. Brosset, trans. (1849–1850).

Syriac source. Bar Hebraeus, *The Chronography of Gregory Abu'l Faraj,* E. A. Wallis Budge, trans. and ed. (1932).

Studies. Wilhelm Barthold, *Turkestan Down to the Mongol Invasion,* 4th ed. (1977); C[lifford] E. Bosworth, *The Ghaznavids* (1963), and "The Political and Dynastic History of the Iranian World (A.D. 1000–1217)," in *Cambridge History of Iran,* V (1968); Claude Cahen, "Le Malik-nāmeh et l'histoire des origines Seljukides," in *Oriens,* 2 (1949); Peter B. Golden, "The Migrations of the Oğuz," in *Archivum ottomanicum,* 4 (1972); Vladimir Gordlevskii, *Gosudarstvo Sel'dzhukidov Maloi Azii* (1941); Ibrahim Kafesoğlu, *Sultan Melikşah devrinde Büyük Selçuklu imparatorluğu* (1953), and *Harezmşah-lar devleti tarihi* (1956); Carla L. Klausner, *The Seljuq Vezirate* (1973); Mehmet Altay Köymen, *Selçuklu devri Türk tarihi* (1963); A. K. S. Lambton, "The Internal Structure of the Saljuq Empire," in *Cambridge History of Iran,* V (1968); Vladimir Minorsky, *Studies in Caucasian History* (1953); M. Sanaullah, *The Decline of the Saljūqid Empire* (1938); Martin Strohmeier, *Seldschukische Geschichte und türkische Geschichtswissenschaft* (1984).

PETER B. GOLDEN

[See also **Aleppo; Alp Arslan; Atabeg; Azerbaijan; Buyids; Damascus; Ghazi; Ghaznavids; Ghurids; Iran; Isfahan; Khazars; Khwārizmshāhs; Malikshāh; Nishapur; Niẓām al-Mulk; Qarakhanids; Qaykhosraw (Kaykhusraw) I; Samanids; Sultan; Transoxiana; Toghrıl Beg; Turkomans; ^{c}Ulamā$^{\supset}$**.]

SELJUKS OF RUM, a Turkish dynasty of Anatolia (*ca.* 1077–*ca.* 1307). The warriors of the Oghuz tribe of Turkomans, who started infiltrating across the northeastern borders of the Iranian world from Transoxiana and the Central Asian steppes in the early decades of the eleventh century, speedily overran most of Iran, and penetrated into Armenia and Transcaucasia. The two leaders of the Seljuk family of the Oghuz, Toghrıl and Chaghrı, soon seized power in Iran and Iraq, and by 1055 Toghrıl had entered Baghdad as the ostensible protector of the Abbasid caliphs. Thus was founded the Great Seljuk sultanate, centered in Iran.

Others of the Turkomans had, however, already moved into Byzantine Asia Minor, often as *ghāzīs,* enthusiastic warriors for their newly found faith of Islam. In part they aimed at fulfilling the religious duty of jihad, in part at finding plunder and good pasture for their herds. And increasingly, after the establishment of the Great Seljuk sultanate, these raiders wished to escape from the central control of the sultans. It is improbable that these bands ever envisaged the actual overthrow of the mighty Byzantine Empire.

The real weakness of the Byzantine Empire was nevertheless demonstrated by the victory of the Great Seljuk sultan Alp Arslan (1063–1072) at Manazkert in 1071, after a series of campaigns had weakened the Armenian princes who guarded the routes through eastern Anatolia. Soon after this, we first hear of the four sons of Qutlumush ibn Isrā$^{\supset}$īl/Arslan, one of whom, Sulaymān, was to found the Seljuk sultanate of Rum (from the *Bilād al-Rūm* of the Islamic geographers, that is, the "land of the Greeks, Rhomaioi"). The sons of Qutlumush no doubt led only some of many Turkoman bands that were making lightning raids across Anatolia as far as the Aegean Sea around Latrus and also raiding through Syria and Palestine, where they came up against the Fatimids of Egypt. Sulaymān seems to have achieved a certain primacy among the leaders of these bands, for Byzantine sources accord him the title of "sultan," which must have been either self-assumed or else awarded by consensus of the Turkomans. One of the Turkoman raids penetrated as far west as Nicaea, where in 1081 Sulaymān established a principality that endured for sixteen years until in 1097 a joint crusader-Byzantine force recovered it for Christendom. The security of the Bosporus was threatened, but the strong rule of Alexios I Komnenos (1081–1118) managed to deflect Sulaymān's activities toward the Taurus region, where a Byzantine general, the Armenian Philaretos, had set up a virtually independent principality. Sulaymān was killed in 1086, but his son Qılıj Arslan I (1092–1107) managed to get himself recognized by the Turkoman chiefs who had followed Sulaymān after his own release from captivity under Malikshāh on the latter's death in 1092. After the sultan's demise, the Great Seljuk sultanate was for several years racked by internecine strife; this fact allowed the Seljuks of Rum to consolidate their position in Anatolia with minimal interference from the east.

While the Seljuks were controlling the more southerly routes across Anatolia, those across the center and north through Cappadocia to Ankara (Ancyra) and beyond were dominated by rival groups of Turkomans, above all by the Danishmendids. Emir Dānishmend (*d.* 1104), though the hero of a later epic glorifying the family's exploits, is a shadowy figure; but there is no gainsaying the forcefulness of the line he founded, which controlled Sivas, Amasya, Tokat, Kayseri, and Ankara, and which disputed Maraş and Malatya with the Seljuks, only temporarily showing a united Turkoman front against the First Crusade.

The Seljuks' base was the town of Konya (Ikonion), which was to remain their capital for two centuries and which they beautified and turned into a center of art and learning. Their power was at this time essentially an inland one, on the Anatolian plateau, for the crusader states of Antioch and Edessa and the Rubenid kingdom of Cilician Armenia, which emerged in the later twelfth century, cut them off to the south, and on the north and west they faced the Byzantines and the Danishmendids.

The middle decades of the twelfth century saw the Seljuks, plagued by succession disputes, temporarily overshadowed by the Danishmendids until the latter fell into dissension; Seljuk fortunes revived under Qılıj Arslan II (1155/1156–1192). An agreement with Manuel I Komnenos in 1161 at Constantinople gave Qılıj Arlsan II a free hand against rivals in Anatolia, and his decisive victory over the emperor at Myriokephalon in 1176 allowed him to consolidate his position.

About 1186 or 1187 the aged sultan decided to divide his territories among his numerous sons, keeping for himself only the capital, Konya. The inevitable disputes after his abdication reduced the sultanate to near anarchy, a condition to which the passage of the Third Crusade through southern Anatolia in 1190 and the crusaders' pillaging of Konya contributed.

The slow task of rebuilding the sultanate fell to the brothers Sulaymān II and Kaykhusraw I (1192–1210). Their success was such that the first forty years of the thirteenth century were the sultanate's apogee.

A prerequisite for the strengthening of the state was the acquisition of outlets to the sea. There had been tentative movements through Lycia in the southwest, and in the north Samsun had been seized about 1194 but then lost to the Byzantine princes of Trebizond. In 1207, Kaykhusraw I acquired the southern port of Antalya, important as an outlet for trade from the Black Sea region, above all trade in slaves, that crossed Anatolia en route to Egypt. His successor, Kayqāwūs I (1210–1219), seized the northern port of Sinop from the Greeks in 1214.

Kayqāwūs was succeeded by Kayqubād I (1219–1237), who undertook naval operations as far as the Crimea. A Turkish garrison was installed at Sughdāq, in the Crimea, in 1225. In eastern Anatolia, Kayqubād annexed Erzinjan, and in northern Syria and Iraq he fended off the Khwārizmian adventurer Jalāl al-Dīn Mangubirti in 1230. He was now the dominant figure in Anatolia, with the Armeno-Cilician, Greek, and Georgian princes acknowledging his suzerainty. It was about this time that the first rumblings of the Mongol menace were heard. An envoy of the Great Khan Ögedey appeared in Rum in 1236, demanding tribute. There was also discontent among the Turkomans of eastern Anatolia, which resulted in the rebellion led by a charismatic popular religious leader, Bābā Isḥāq (*ca.* 1240–1242). The Mongols appeared in 1242 in eastern Anatolia and decisively defeated the Seljuk army at Kösedagh, to the east of Sivas, in 1243. Kayqubād's successor, Kaykhusraw II (1237–1245/1246), fled before the Mongols, who advanced as far as Kayseri before a settlement could be negotiated. In the settlement, the Seljuks of Rum agreed to become tributaries of the Mongols, thereby ending the unfettered independence of the sultanate.

The last sixty years of the sultanate were spent under what was, in effect, a Mongol protectorate, with the sultan's power progressively reduced. Kaykhusraw II died in 1246, leaving only minors as heirs. Through Mongol favor, the Armenian princes of the east enjoyed a revival of power, while the Turkoman chiefs and high officials of state became increasingly insubordinate and intrigued with the Mongols. Against these centrifugal tendencies, Kayqāwūs II and his tutor (or atabeg), the Greek Qaratay, endeavored to preserve the unity of the sultanate and to regularize the extortionate demands of the Mongols for the upkeep of their troops in Anatolia. At one point the sultan had to flee, and control of the crumbling sultanate passed to the *parwāna* (agent for the Mongols) Muᶜīn al-

Dīn Sulaymān; before this, the sultanate had been in effect partitioned between Kayqāwūs II in the west and his brother Qılıj Arslan IV in the east. Much of their efforts were devoted to preserving the formal structure of Islam in Anatolia against Mongol pressure.

An attempt to bring about intervention by the Mamluk sultan of Egypt, Baybars, who had acquired the reputation of an Islamic hero from his victories against the Mongols in Syria and against the crusader states, proved in the end disastrous. Although Baybars defeated the Mongols at Elbistan in 1277, he died soon afterward, and a general rising in Anatolia against the Mongols failed to materialize. Muᶜīn al-Dīn Sulaymān was executed by the Ilkhan Abaqa, and the Mongol protectorate was, after 1277, succeeded by the imposition of direct Mongol rule.

The Seljuk sultans remained as puppets under viziers loyal to the real masters of the state, and their names survived on coins until the beginning of the fourteenth century. Kayqubād III seems to have been executed by Ghāzān Khan in 1303, and his successor, Masᶜūd II, lingered for only a few more years. The end of the dynasty was so obscure that contemporary chroniclers do not mention it; the last members of the family seem to have lingered on in Sinop and perhaps in Alanya.

Out of the ruins of the sultanate, and the slightly later collapse of the Ilkhan Mongols, there arose in the fourteenth century a network of Turkoman beyliks (principalities) in Turkey, as it may now be called (the term *Turchia* is widespread in Western sources of the thirteenth century). From these competing principalities the Ottomans were eventually to emerge victorious.

Obvious long-term historical trends of the Seljuk rule in Rum include the gradual turkization of Anatolia. This was, however, an uneven process, leaving large groups of Greeks in the west and Armenians in the east. Concurrent with turkization was islamization, not only through the settlement of Turkomans but also through some conversions among the indigenous peoples, a process that continued until the fifteenth century, when a rough equilibrium seems to have been reached. Islamization undoubtedly included the expropriation of Christian church endowments and their reconstitution as Muslim *awqāf* (sing., *waqf*) trusts for charitable and religious purposes.

As for the economy, the frequent warfare does not seem to have prevented a high degree of agricultural prosperity, attested by travelers, together with the widespread exploitation of mineral resources—for instance, alum, which was exported by the Genoese to Western Europe. There was also a flourishing textile industry, including carpet weaving. Urban life was vigorous, with a notable part played in the towns by confraternities of craftsmen—with mystical religious elements—headed by the *akhi*s. Later, Seljuk Anatolia was to be the birthplace of two highly influential dervish orders, the Mevlevīs and the Bektashīs.

The splendor of Seljuk art and architecture can be seen in the many surviving mosques, madrasas, dervish monasteries (*tekkes*), and caravanserais in the Anatolian towns and countryside, above all in Konya, Sivas, and Kayseri; there are also remains of royal palaces in Konya and at Qubādābād on the shores of Beysehir Lake. In all these, and in the expressions of religious feeling in literature, continuing influences from Iran are apparent. These influences were given an added impetus in the thirteenth century by the flight westward, before the advancing Mongols, of many Persian artists, craftsmen, scholars, and religious leaders. Among the latter were the mystics Shams al-Dīn Muḥammad Tabrīzī and Bahāᵓ al-Dīn Walad, father of Jalāl al-Dīn Rūmī, who inspired the development of the Mevlevī order of dervishes and became its leader.

BIBLIOGRAPHY

The sources, primary and secondary, Christian and Islamic, are very thoroughly surveyed in Claude Cahen, *Pre-Ottoman Turkey,* J. Jones-Williams, trans. (1968).

Many important studies come from Turkish scholars. Two of particular interest are by Osman Turan: *Selçuklular tarihi ve Türk-İslâm medeniyeti* (1965, 2nd ed. 1969) and *Selçuklular zamaninda Türkiye* (1971).

A number of important studies have appeared in Western languages. In addition to Cahen's *Pre-Ottoman Turkey,* see J. M. Hussey, ed., *The Cambridge Medieval History,* IV, pt. I (1966), esp. chap. 18; Tamara Talbot Rice, *The Seljuks in Asia Minor* (1961); Speros Vryonis, Jr., *The Decline of Medieval Hellenism in Asia Minor and the Process of Islamization from the Eleventh Through the Fifteenth Century* (1971).

For the chronology of the rulers, see C[lifford] E. Bosworth, *The Islamic Dynasties: A Chronological and Genealogical Handbook* (1967). For Seljuk art, see Oktay Aslanapa, *Turkish Art and Architecture* (1971); Rice, *op. cit.*; Behçet Ünsal, *Turkish Islamic Architecture in Seljuk and Ottoman Times* (1959, repr. 1973).

C. E. Bosworth

The Martyrdom of St. Sebastian. Panel from the St. Sebastian altarpiece of Nicoletto Semitecolo, 1367, Biblioteca Capitolare, Padua. ALINARI/ART RESOURCE

[See also **Alexios I Komnenos; Anatolia; Ancyra; Aq Qoyunlu; Byzantine Empire: History; Cilician Kingdom; Crusades and Crusader States; Danishmendids; Dervish; Ghāzī; Ikonion; Ilkhanids; Karamania; Manazkert; Manuel I Komnenos; Mints and Money, Islamic; Mongol Empire; Myriokephalon; Ottomans; Qara Qoyunlu; Qaykhosraw (Kaykhusraw) I; Qılıj Arslan II; Romanos IV Diogenes; Rubenids; Rum; Trebizond; Turkomans.**]

ŠEM TOB. See **Shem Ṭov.**

SEMITECOLO, NICOLETTO (*fl.* 1353–1370), Venetian painter. Among other signed and dated works is his altarpiece depicting the life of St. Sebastian now in the Biblioteca Capitolare, Padua (1367; his name is here spelled Nicholeto Semitecholo). The four panels of this painting are stylistically related to works by Paolo Veneziano and Guariento, and some of their naturalistic tendencies were inspired by the paintings of Giotto and Tommaso da Modena, the latter a contemporary of Nicoletto's (an outstanding work by Tommaso being the frescoes of prominent Dominicans, in the chapter house of S. Niccolò in Treviso, dated 1352).

BIBLIOGRAPHY

Bernard Berenson, *Italian Pictures of the Renaissance: The Venetian School,* I (1957), 165; Rodolfo Pallucchini, *La pittura veneziana del trecento* (1964), 120–124; John White, *Art and Architecture in Italy: 1250–1400* (1966), 378–379. An interesting treatment of the artistic milieu from which Nicoletto came is Michelangelo Muraro, *Paolo da Venezia* (1969).

ADELHEID M. GEALT

[See also **Gothic Art: Painting and Manuscript Illumination; Guariento di Arpo; Paolo Veneziano.**]

SENESCHAL, etymologically "old servant," was used in the Middle Ages to describe two types of senior official: (1) the household official who advised his lord and managed his estates, and (2) the provincial administrator in southern France, the counterpart of the northern bailli.

The phrase "household official" when applied to the early Middle Ages can be misleading. In order to rule effectively, great lords needed to travel, and the household officials traveled with them. Only as administrative systems became more elaborate in the late eleventh and, especially, the twelfth century was there a pronounced tendency for the household officials to remain in one place and to supervise from there the judicial and financial affairs of their lords.

The household official known as the royal seneschal in France was originally the senior servant in the king's entourage, whose primary duty was to see to the provisioning of the itinerant court. This position gave the seneschal an important role in finance and in court ceremonial, and it furnished him with a wide network of contacts and patronage. Gradually he emerged as the most important political administrator after the king himself, his power extending not simply to a general supervisory role but also to administration of justice and (with the constable) to command of the feudal army. The Capetian seneschal has been compared to the Carolingian mayor of the palace in terms of influence, power, and danger to the dynasty. In the early twelfth century the office fell to the Garlande family, whose overweening ambition finally erupted into a crisis in which they were stripped of the office by Louis VI. Thereafter, the powers of the seneschal were steadily reduced. From the beginning of the thirteenth century, the office was usually kept vacant except on ceremonial occasions.

In Normandy the seneschal was one of the three most important household officials in the time of Duke William I the Bastard (mid eleventh century). With the chamberlain and the butler, the seneschal oversaw all parts of the duke's administration. He was particularly active in the administration of justice during the period of Angevin rule (*ca.* 1150–1204). The most famous of the men who occupied the position was William Fitz Ralph (*d.* 1200), a former itinerant justice, who was the duke's vicegerent when he was in other of his domains (England, for example). The seneschal corresponded to the English justiciar. The office of seneschal in Normandy was suppressed after the conquest of Philip II Augustus.

Seneschals with similar characteristics—ceremonial, political, and judicial—existed in the administrative hierarchies of other great fiefs, such as Flanders and Champagne. In the latter, the office was hereditary in the Joinville family. In England and Germany, however, the word "seneschal," when it was used, was normally applied to the estate managers of the monarchs or of rural lords. There was no great similarity between these men and the French household seneschal either in power or in danger to the throne. In Germany the seneschals tended to be chosen from among serfs.

The seneschals in royal administration in the south of France trace their origins to noble estate managers and advisers. The terminology was simply retained after the incorporation of the south into the royal domain in the early and middle thirteenth century. The office of royal seneschal was the counterpart of that of the royal bailli in the north, with certain important differences. The unsettled conditions in the south encouraged the government, through at least the mid thirteenth century, to choose northerners for the post. The seneschals, once chosen, were considerably more active in military affairs than were the baillis. This may partly explain a slight tendency to name rather more substantial nobles to the post in the south than in the north.

The procedural Roman law used in the south required more expertise and feeling for southern culture than the early royal seneschals ordinarily possessed. Consequently, they called in and depended on legal advisers trained in judicial administration. As a secondary consequence, the administration of justice in the south was more sophisticated and became a model for later northern developments.

The most successful seneschals were much more than military governors who had delegated their judicial function. As conditions in the south improved after the mid thirteenth century, the administrative dimensions of the seneschal's office began to be emphasized and rewarded. Though some men, such as Henri de Courances, in the later period of their careers became military commanders per se, the majority of those "promoted" (of whom interesting examples are Guillaume d'Authon, Arnoul de Courferaud, and Guillaume de Cohardon) found their appropriate place as counselors and special investigators for the Parlement of Paris. Perhaps the most famous of the royal seneschals and an administrator of first-rate ability by any standard was Eustache de Beaumarchais, who, in various capacities, served St. Louis, his brother Alphonse of Poitiers, Philip III, and Philip IV. His main work was in the seneschalsy of Toulouse, and he may be credited with much of the success in maintaining effective royal authority in the sometimes hostile region.

BIBLIOGRAPHY

On the grand seneschal as well as the territorial administrator in France, see Ferdinand Lot and Robert Fawtier, *Histoire des institutions françaises au moyen âge,* 3 vols. (1957–1962). See also Charles Haskins, *Norman Institutions* (1918), and Henri F. Delaborde, *Jean de Joinville et les seigneurs de Joinville* (1894), on the household official in two important provinces. A good summary of information on the territorial administrator is James W. Fesler, "French Field Administration: The Beginnings," in *Comparative Studies in Society and History,* 5 (1962–1963). This must be supplemented by Léopold Delisle's study in *Recueil des historiens des Gaules et de la France,* XXIV (1904). An intensive study of the administration of one seneschalsy is Robert Michel, *L'administration royale dans la sénéchaussée de Beaucaire au temps de saint Louis* (1910). Intensive scholarly studies of the infrastructure of administration in the seneschalsies are Joseph R. Strayer, *Les gens de justice du Languedoc sous Philippe le Bel* (1970); and Jan Rogozinski, "The Counsellors of the Seneschal of Beaucaire and Nîmes, 1250–1350," in *Speculum,* **44** (1969). Additional valuable information is available in good local histories, such as Léon Ménard, *Histoire civile, ecclésiastique, et littéraire de la ville de Nismes,* 7 vols. (1744–1758); and Claude de Vic and Joseph Vaisette, *Histoire générale de Languedoc,* 16 vols., 2nd ed., with additions by Auguste Molinier (1872–1904).

William Chester Jordan

[See also **Bailli; Butler; Castellan; Chamberlain; Constable of the Realm; Joinville, John of; Justiciar; Law, French: In the South; Louis IX of France; Mayor of the Palace; Normans and Normandy; Philip II Augustus.**]

SENTENCES. See **Proverbs and Sententiae.**

SEPHARDIM (from Hebrew: *sepharad,* Spain), those Jews who lived in Spain during the Middle Ages and their descendants, expelled from Spain and Portugal at the end of the fifteenth century. Jews settled in Spain at a very early date, and by the end of the fourth century the number was significant enough to warrant the issue of special regulations regarding their status. (The Council of Elvira, for example, decreed among other things that Jews and Christians were not allowed to mix freely.) Under the Visigothic kings their presence was favored at first, but with the Visigoths' conversion to Christianity, Jewish observance was strictly forbidden. It was only after the Muslim conquest of Spain in 711 that Jews began to enjoy the cultural freedom and prosperity that culminated in the golden age of Spanish Jewry. The great figures of the period distinguished themselves for their wide spectrum of activity: avid study of the Torah and Talmud combined with excellence in medicine, astronomy, philosophy, mathematics, and poetry.

During the Almohad persecutions of the mid twelfth century, Jews sought refuge in the Christian kingdoms of the north, where, despite being viewed with hostility for their contact with Muslim Spain, they succeeded as diplomats, financiers, and physicians. Their expertise in Arabic made them instrumental in conveying Arab learning to Christian Spain and, through it, to the rest of Europe. The court of Alfonso X of Castile (*r.* 1252–1284) became a prominent center of Jewish scientific activity, and Jews played a significant role in his Toledo school of translators. Among the earliest Bible translations into Spanish are some based on the Masoretic text, and the first printed Spanish Bible (Biblia del Oso, 1569) alludes to the importance of these traditional translations.

The year 1391 saw the rise of a wave of persecutions (due, in part, to the ambivalent attitude of the crown toward Jews) that swept the country and culminated in the promulgation of the Edict of Expulsion in March 1492. Many Jews fled to Portugal, from which they were expelled in 1497; others converted. Some Jews crossed the Mediterranean to North Africa, and many more headed for the Ottoman Empire; both groups preserved their native language, Judeo-Spanish. Thus was created the Sephardic diaspora.

Important communities were established in Italy, Venice and Ferrara being prominent centers in the sixteenth and seventeenth centuries. In Spain discrimination broke out anew, this time against "New Christians" (Marranos), resulting in more emigration by those who sought to return to the faith of their forefathers. New communities arose in Western Europe, Amsterdam becoming a flourishing center of Sephardic culture in the seventeenth and eighteenth centuries, with learned academies and schools for teaching Hebrew to the new exiles.

Other communities were established in England and in the Americas.

Apart from their history and language, Sephardim distinguish themselves from their fellow Jews in Central and Eastern Europe (Ashkenazim) by their pronunciation of Hebrew, by their rabbinical schools, and by their traditions both in the synagogue and in the home. A Sephardic prayer rite evolved in medieval Spain that was adopted by North African and Middle Eastern communities, so that the term "Sephardic" is mistakenly extended to these communities as well.

BIBLIOGRAPHY

Eliyahu Ashtor, *The Jews of Moslem Spain,* 3 vols. (1973); Yitzhak F. Baer, *A History of the Jews in Christian Spain,* Louis Schoffman and H. Halkin, trans., 2 vols. (1961); R. D. Barnett, ed., *The Sephardi Heritage,* I (1971); Haim Beinart, *Conversos on Trial* (1981); Mercedes J. Benardete, *Hispanic Culture and Character of the Sephardic Jews* (1953); Cecil Roth, *A History of the Marranos* (1932); Hirsch J. Zimmels, *Ashkenazim and Sephardim* (1958).

ISAAC BENABU

[See also **Anti-Semitism; Bible; Converso; Expulsion of the Jews; Inquisition; Jews in Christian Spain; Jews in Muslim Spain; New Christians.**]

SEPUH (Avestan: *vīsō-puθra;* Middle Iranian: *vispuhr, vāspuhr*), the name given to all the members of an Armenian medieval noble family with the exception of its head (*tanutēr*). On occasion a "senior" (*mec* or *awag*) *sepuh* is mentioned by the sources (he was probably the heir apparent of the *tanutēr*), but in the early Middle Ages all the *sepuh*s seem to have been equal and joint holders of their family's patrimony. In the Bagratid period, however, the *sepuh*s were gradually emancipated and obtained personal appanages.

BIBLIOGRAPHY

Nicholas Adonts, *Armenia in the Period of Justinian,* Nina G. Garsoïan, ed. and trans. (1970), 357–359, 486–487, n. 26, 521, n. 77, 522, nn. 80–84; Émile Benveniste, *Titres et noms propres en iranien ancien* (1966), 22–26; Hakob Manandyan, *Feodalizme hin Hayastanum* (1934), 50–52, 192–195.

NINA G. GARSOÏAN

[See also **Armenia, Social Structure; Tanutēr.**]

SEQUENCE (Prosa), a chant that followed the Alleluia of the Latin Mass. It became, along with the trope, one of the most important musico-poetic accretions to the medieval liturgy. The production of new sequences was most intense from the mid ninth to the twelfth century, but sequences continued to be written well into the sixteenth century. The repertory of surviving sequences is enormous: around 5,000 sequence texts have been edited in the thirteen volumes devoted to the genre in *Analecta hymnica medii aevi.* These texts were "proper" in the sense that they were appropriate for a specific liturgical day or season. All but four sequences were removed from the liturgy through the reforms of the Council of Trent (1545–1563). (A fifth, the *Stabat Mater,* was reinstated by Pope Benedict XIII in 1727.)

The sequence underwent significant stylistic change, yet retained two fundamental, genre-defining characteristics: syllabic text setting and couplet structure (or progressive parallelism)—a structure based on pairs of isosyllabic lines, with each pair sharing the same melody, thus musically *aa bb cc.* The most significant stylistic changes involved the gradual shift from unequal prose lines to regular, rhymed verse. This shift, which was widespread by the late eleventh century, divides surviving sequences into two broadly defined stylistic types, referred to either simply as early and late or as sequences from the first and second epoch.

Although a wealth of scholarly literature has been devoted to the sequence, fundamental aspects concerning its origin and early development remain uncertain. Two basic problems have inhibited a clear understanding: lack of early documentation and assumptions by modern scholars about the morphology of the genre that cannot be reconciled with the surviving sources. An overview of these sources is a necessary preliminary to any study of the early sequence.

EARLIEST SEQUENCES

The earliest surviving manuscripts containing sequences are from the end of the ninth or beginning of the tenth century. These are, for the most part, small collections or fragments without musical notation from various centers in France or northern Italy. Among surviving sources, larger collections with musical notation of up to 140 sequences (Paris, Bibliothèque Nationale, fonds lat. 1118 [*ca.* 987–*ca.* 996]), from southern France, begin to appear by the second half of the tenth century. By the eleventh century, large collections from centers widely dispersed throughout the Latin West become increasingly more numerous. Sequences are usually included in manuscripts that contain tropes and other medieval accretions to the liturgy but are also found in a number of graduals and, less often, in collections of miscellaneous liturgical items.

Two distinct sequence traditions, each with its own repertory, existed by the late ninth century. The geographical distribution of the traditions essentially corresponded to the partition of the Carolingian Empire into East and West Francia, established in the Treaty of Mersen (870). In each tradition, one center assumed particular prominence: the monasteries of St. Gall, in East Francia, and St. Martial of Limoges, in the West. St. Gall's stature is due in particular to Notker Balbulus' *Liber hymnorum,* a collection of sequences that formed the basis of the remarkably stable East Frankish repertory. Important sequence manuscripts were also produced in other East Frankish centers, but their repertories essentially reflected that of St. Gall.

St. Martial's stature now rests more on the strength of its library than on any identifiable creative figures like Notker. The library preserved the richest collection of Frankish chant (especially sequences and tropes) to have come down to us. The manuscripts, however, reflect a broader southern French tradition, rather than exclusively the practice at St. Martial: only about one-quarter of the sixteen sequence manuscripts from the library cataloged and inventoried by Richard Crocker were probably copied at the monastery; the remaining manuscripts were acquired from other centers in the region during the Middle Ages by zealous librarians. Scarcity of early source material, particularly in northern France, a region of fundamental importance to the early history of the genre, has made it impossible either to identify composers or to locate the most important ninth-century centers in the West.

Although the East and West Frankish repertories have a number of melodies in common, differences with respect to texts, manuscript format, and terminology bespeak essentially independent traditions. Only rarely were the same texts transmitted in both East and West Frankish sources; preference for certain stylistic features kept their textual traditions sharply defined and separate.

West Frankish sources generally transmitted pieces in two ways: (1) melismatically, that is, music without the text, and (2) syllabically, that is, music and text together with a neume above each syllable. The melodic transmission without text was called a *sequentia,* while the complete piece (text and music) was called a *prosa,* or *prosa ad sequentiam.* In a West Frankish manuscript, the *prosae* and *sequentiae* were generally grouped together in separate sections called, respectively, a *prosarium* and a *sequentiarium;* both transmitted, in different ways, the same repertory. East Frankish manuscripts, with one notable exception (St. Gall, Stiftsbibliothek, MS 484, which contains melodies without text), transmitted pieces with both text and music together; the music was usually written as melismas in the margins, and the entire piece was called a *sequentia.*

Sequence melodies in both traditions were often identified by colorful titles, many of which are enigmatic: "Puella turbata," "Duo tres," and "Occidentana" are three examples. Since the medieval use of the term "sequence" was not consistent in East and West Frankish sources, terminology should be carefully clarified in any discussion of the genre. Although scholars have pressed to have the West Frankish use of the term "prose" adopted in modern writings, late-twentieth-century trends, followed here, have been to use "sequence" to refer to the whole piece (that is, text with music), while reserving the Latin form, *sequentia,* for the textless version.

The *Liber hymnorum* is of the utmost importance to the history of the sequence, providing information relevant to the dissemination of the genre, the date and extent of the early repertories of both East and West Francias, and the relationship between the two traditions. This impressive collection, containing forty sequences with texts by Notker set to thirty-three melodies, was presumably complete by around 880. Notker provided a dedicatory preface, which includes the well-known account of how, as a youth, he first came into contact with the genre: a monk from Jumièges, fleeing after the Norman sack of his monastery, arrived at St. Gall with an antiphonary containing some sequences (that is, *versus ad sequentias*); Notker was taken with the idea, but found the quality of the texts so poor that he set out to write his own texts. Notker's tale reflects what must have been typical of early patterns of dissemination. From its origin in northern France, sequences were carried to new centers throughout the Frankish kingdom and eventually well beyond its borders. Imported works were absorbed into the newly forming repertories or supplied with new texts as tastes or local liturgies demanded. To a lesser degree, the creation of entirely new works—text and music—was stimulated by contact with the rapidly spreading genre. Regional and local traditions thus show a much greater diversity in style and repertory than the pre-Carolingian or Gregorian chant of the Mass propers, imposed throughout the kingdom by Pepin and, more vigorously, by Charlemagne.

The *Liber hymnorum* has been reconstructed by Wolfram von den Steinen. It was used by Richard Crocker as a means of establishing an important segment of the first-generation West Frankish repertory (*ca.* 850–880). By determining which sequences from the western tradition Notker must have known and used as models, Crocker was able to confirm their existence by 880, even though the earliest preserved versions of many of these works are found in manuscripts copied over a century later.

ORIGINS OF SEQUENCES

The early history of the sequence is closely linked to the Alleluia of the Mass. Before 830, Amalarius of Metz provided in his *Liber officialis* a clear account of the connection between the two when he reported the practice of replacing the jubilus of the Alleluia after the verse with a melisma (*jubilatio*) that the singers called a *sequentia.* It has been assumed that the first sequences developed from these jubilus-replacements through the addition of a text. Nevertheless, the relationship between sequence and Alleluia is complex and fraught with controversy. Many of the large-scale sequences, for example, share little, if any, relationship to an Alleluia, from which they are stylistically far removed. Furthermore, although these sequences—like the early jubilus-replacements—are transmitted in melismatic form as sequentias, it is not likely that they were conceived as independent melismas, to which texts were subsequently added.

To account for the wide gulf between the modest *sequentiae* Amalarius must have had in mind and the ambitious *versus ad sequentias* that Notker used as models, Richard Crocker advanced the notion that some type of "creative leap" must have taken place between 830 and 850. According to Crocker, if the aparallel sequences provided the idea for the more ambitious efforts, then it seems more likely that that idea came quickly to fruition through a bold creative gesture rather than a drawn-out process of organic growth and adaptation.

Study of the early sequence reveals a varied stylistic world, where exceptions to commonly held notions about the genre are frequent. Crocker's systematic exploration of this world in *The Early Medieval Sequence* has produced a much clearer understanding of style and structure in the sequence and the implications these hold for its early history.

STRUCTURE AND PERFORMANCE

The most distinctive characteristic of the large-scale sequence is the couplet structure, which brings pairs of isosyllabic lines of text, syllabically set, into a musical relationship through a shared melodic phrase. The effects of this structure and possible reasons for its adoption must be studied in terms of both text and music. Musical repetition serves as both a powerful organizing force and a means of expansion. It gives emphasis to the musical phrases and thereby helps clarify the large-scale structures built from these phrases. Clarity of phrases is further sharpened by standard and distinctive cadences and a bold new melodic style focused around the final or secondary tonal centers. Sequence melodies are often organized around flexible but clearly recognizable motives or melodic gestures and a controlled exploration of register. The discipline and tight organization of these melodies stand in sharp contrast to the rhapsodically ornamental flights of the Gregorian Graduals and Alleluias.

The elevated prose of the texts, or "art-prose," as it has been called, provides continuity and a sense of progression within the repetitive melodic structure. The text—through its properties of syntax, sonority, prose rhythm, and rhetoric—has a critical role in determining the shape of the piece. The interaction of textual and musical structure—the way the syntax is aligned with and reinforces the musical phrases or, on occasion, reinterprets them into larger groupings in the overall design—is an important aspect of the early sequence. Couplets, or doubles, are characteristic, but their use was not an invariable structural prerequisite: single lines are the norm at the beginnings and ends of pieces (thus, musically, *a bb cc . . . xx y*) but also occur internally. Of the sixteen melodies common to the *Liber hymnorum* and the West Frankish repertory, all but two show some departure from regular couplet structure. Concern for consistent parallelism was apparently not as great in the ninth century as it became subsequently, when departures were "corrected" to produce regular doubles.

Another important structural feature of the early sequence is phrase length, which varies from one couplet to the next. Each group of sequence texts set to the same melody displays a unique plan or pattern. Although sequences are highly individual in their profiles, etched by varying phrase lengths and melodic contour, Crocker observed that a number of pieces share a basic shape or, at least, a general strategy integrating text and music to create emphatic climactic moments within the overall form. The skill with which this was accomplished marks the early sequence as a lofty Frankish creation—one of the finest artistic achievements of the Carolingian period.

Since East and West Frankish traditions held many melodies in common, the most pronounced stylistic distinctions between them occur in the approach to the texts. Notker preferred the elegant diction and vocabulary of classical Latin prose, often expressed in complex and sophisticated syntax. West Frankish composers, on the other hand, seemed to value a more exuberant diction, rich in assonance (especially end-assonance on *-a* or *-ia*) and alliteration, often at the expense of smooth, or even coherent, syntax. Notker's texts seem to read better, while West Frankish texts seem more singable.

Contiguous repertories generally relied heavily on East or West Frankish texts and melodies. West Frankish pieces, for example, comprised the bulk of the early repertory at Winchester, while varying combinations of East and West Frankish works were adopted in Italian centers. Regional and local repertories, however, developed their own character, revealed both in the way imported pieces were transmitted and in the new works created there.

Documentation concerning performance of the early sequence is almost completely lacking. Numerous theories have been advanced, but it seems highly unlikely that unequivocal solutions to the problems of performance can be reached. The crucial problem has been in determining whether the textless *sequentiae* were sung as well as the syllabic versions, and, if so, in what relationship to one another they were performed. Instrumental participation in performance has been suggested, particularly in West Frankish sequences, on the basis of the use of names of instruments as titles to the *sequentiae,* or the frequent mention of instruments in the texts themselves. Polyphonic performance is documented by around 1000 in the Winchester Troper, or in the ninth century if one accepts *Rex caeli Domine* (which is used as an example in Musica Enchiriadis) as a sequence. Crocker has suggested that a direct performance, where the texted version is sung straight through, should now be the norm; this approach can then be modified to explore the numerous other performance possibilities.

During the eleventh century stylistic features indigenous to the early sequence gradually gave way to new ideals. Phrase lengths purposefully varied to create large-scale design in the earlier works turned increasingly more symmetrical with the influx of rhyme and scansion: the prose texts of the ninth and tenth centuries were transformed into verse by the twelfth, and the sequence became a different type of song. The transitional sequences of the eleventh century often show a fascinating combination of the earlier ideals of varied phrase lengths and the new principles of regular versification. The repertory awaits systematic study.

BIBLIOGRAPHY

Lance W. Brunner, "The Sequences of Verona, Biblioteca Capitolare, CVII and the Italian Sequence Tradition," 2 vols. (diss., Univ. of North Carolina at Chapel Hill, 1977), with collections of complete pieces in II, and "A Perspective on the Southern Italian Sequence: The Second Tonary of the Manuscript Monte Cassino 318," in *Early Music History,* **1** (1981); Richard L. Crocker, "The Repertoire of Proses at Saint Martial de Limoges" (diss., Yale, 1957), "The Troping Hypothesis," in *Musical Quarterly,* **52** (1966), *The Early Medieval Sequence* (1977), and, with John Caldwell, "Sequence (i)," in *The New Grove Dictionary of Music and Musicians,* XVII (1980), 141–156; N. de Goede, ed., *The Utrecht Prosarium* (Monumenta musica Nederlandica, VI) (1965); Guido M. Dreves and Clemens Blume, eds., *Analecta hymnica medii aevi,* 55 vols. (1886–1922), esp. VII–X, XXXIV, XXXVII, XXXIX–XL, XLII, XLIV, LIII–LV, for principal editions of the texts; Otto Drinkwelder, *Ein deutsches Sequentiar aus dem Ende des 12. Jahrhunderts* (1914); Lars Elfving, *Étude lexicographique sur les sequences limousines* (Studia latina Stockholmiensa, VII) (1962); Jacques Handschin, "Trope, Sequence, and Conductus," in *Early Medieval Music up to 1300,* Anselm Hughes, ed. (New Oxford History of Music, II) (1954), 128–174; René-Jean Hesbert, *Le Prosaire de la Sainte-Chapelle: Manuscrit du Chapitre de Saint-Nicolas de Bari,* in *Monumenta musicae sacrae,* I (1952), *Les Manuscrits Musicaux de Jumièges, ibid.,* II (1954), *Le Prosaire d'Aix-la-Chapelle: Manuscrit 13 du Chapitre d'Aix-la-Chapelle, ibid.,* III (1961), and *Le Tropaire-Prosaire de*

Dublin: Manuscrit Add. 710 de l'Université de Cambridge, ibid., IV (1966); David Hiley, ed., *Eight Sequences for St. Benedict and St. Scholastica* (1980), and "The Norman Chant Traditions—Normandy, Britain, Sicily," in *Proceedings of the Royal Musical Association,* **107** (1980–1981); Andreas Holschneider, *Die Organa von Winchester* (1968), and "Instrumental Titles to the Sequentiae of the Winchester Tropers," in *Essays on Opera and English Music in Honour of Sir Jack Westrup,* Frederick W. Sternfeld, Nigel Fortune, and Edward Olleson, eds. (1975), 8–18; Anselm Hughes, ed., *Anglo-French Sequelae, Edited from the Papers of the Late Dr. Henry Marriott Bannister* (1934); Heinrich Husmann, *Tropenund Sequenzenhandschriften* (1964); Klaus Heinrich Kohrs, *Die aparellelen Sequenzen* (1978); Frank Labhardt, *Das Sequentiar Cod. 546 der Stiftsbibliothek von St. Gallen und seine Quellen,* 2 vols. (1959–1963); Kenneth Levy, "*Lux de luce:* The Origin of an Italian Sequence," in *Musical Quarterly,* **57** (1971); Carl Allan Moberg, *Über die schwedischen Sequenzen,* 2 vols. (1927); Anselm Schubiger, *Die Sängerschule St. Gallens vom achten bis zwölften Jahrhundert* (1859, repr. 1966); Hans Spanke, "Rhythmen- und Sequenzenstudien," in *Studi medievali,* n.s. **4** (1931); Bruno Stäblein, "Zur Frühgeschichte der Sequenz," in *Archiv für Musikwissenschaft,* **18** (1961), "Die Sequenzmelodie 'Concordia' und ihre geschichtlicher Hintergrund," in *Festschrift Hans Engel zum siebzigsten Geburtstag,* Horst Heussner, ed. (1964), and *Notker der Dichter und seine geistige Welt,* 2 vols. (1948).

LANCE W. BRUNNER

[See also **Amalarius of Metz; Gregorian Chant; Jubilus; Latin Meter; Mass, Liturgy of; Melisma; Notker Balbulus; Sequence, Late.**]

SEQUENCE, LATE, also known as late-style or second-epoch sequence, was, like its antecedents from earlier centuries, a long chant sung after the Alleluia and before the Gospel at Mass. Because these sequences were part of the great surge of interest in rhythmic verse that emerged in the late eleventh and early twelfth centuries, late sequences were written in regular, rhymed, accentual Latin verse, rather than in the prose couplets characteristic of earlier sequences.

Twelfth-century poets developed many verse patterns for sequences and other comparable liturgical poetry, and these are systematically described in twelfth- and thirteenth-century treatises on the art of rhythmic poetry. The most popular verse form for late sequence poetry is that employed in the strophe from the famous twelfth-century sequence "Laudes crucis attolamus," for feasts of the Cross, which is given here with an English translation. The meter is trochaic dimeter, with missing syllables at the ends of the third and sixth lines. Even though the poetry is strophic, individual half strophes were usually set to the same music, thus suggesting the paired couplet structure characteristic of early sequences. The bipartite structure of individual strophes was emphasized not only by setting half strophes to the same music, but also by rhyming the cadences of final lines of paired half strophes. Also present in the example are techniques commonly used by late sequence poets: alliteration, rhymes within lines as well as at the ends of lines, and assonance.

Dulce melos tangat celos
dulce lignum dulci dignum
credimus melodia.
Voce uita non discordet
cum uox uitam non remordet
dulcis est symphonia.

Let the sweet melody touch heaven.
We believe the sweet wood [of the Cross]
Is worthy of sweet melody.
Let not life be in discord with voice:
When the voice does not disquiet life,
The consonance is sweet.

Because many late sequence texts conform to a small number of popular verse patterns, new texts could readily be set to preexisting melodies. Indeed, all large late sequence repertories contain one or more groups of texts, each of which is set to one melody (contrafacta). This technique of writing several new texts for one melody, most highly developed at the abbey of St. Victor in Paris during the twelfth century, actually provided a way of linking texts that were related in theme.

Late sequence melodies themselves are simple in their directness, organized around the finals and reciting tones of the modes, most often the modes on "d" and "g." Each sequence melody is made up of a series of double phrases, each doublet serving for a strophe of poetry. The phrases are usually punctuated by cadential formulas that serve to emphasize the accentual, rhymed cadences of the poetry, and to form a kind of musical refrain throughout a given piece. Many of the most popular late sequence melodies are made up of interrelated musical phrases that develop melodic ideas in a variety of ways. In addition to writing original melodies, late sequence composers also employed the techniques of adaptation and centonization to generate new melodies.

The sources containing the first large repertories (over fifty late sequences) demonstrate that Paris was a leading center for late sequence production in the twelfth century. The first surviving witnesses with large collections date from the first quarter of the thirteenth century and slightly later, yet the venerable age of their contents is demonstrated by the fact that they contain two distinct traditions of late sequences: one from the cathedral of Notre Dame and the other from the Augustinian abbey of St. Victor. The earlier of these was that of the cathedral of Notre Dame, the repertory of texts and music created in the first half of the twelfth century by Adam Precentor and his school. Sometime in the 1130's, Adam left the cathedral for the abbey of St. Victor; thus he is probably one and the same with the famous poet called Magister Adam of St. Victor by Thomas of Cantimpré in the thirteenth century, and mentioned by both Richard of St. Victor and Alan of Lille in the twelfth century.

The large repertory of late sequences created by Adam and his school served as a foundation for the second Parisian repertory created by Victorine composers in the second half of the twelfth century. In the second Parisian repertory, the Victorines developed a unique system of musical symbolism that grew out of the writings of Hugh of St. Victor and his particular notions of the purposes of religious art.

Late sequences continued to be written in large numbers during the thirteenth through the fifteenth century. However, Italian humanists wearied of both their medieval Latin style and their themes. The reformed missal of Pope Pius V (1570) retained but four sequences, three of which are late-style.

BIBLIOGRAPHY

Analecta hymnica medii aevi, Clemens Blume, Guido Dreves, and Henry M. Bannister, eds., XLIV, XLV (1915–1922); John F. Benton, "Nicholas of Clairvaux and the Twelfth-century Sequence, with Special Reference to Adam of St. Victor," in *Traditio,* **18** (1962); Margot E. Fassler, "Who Was Adam of St. Victor: The Evidence of the Sequence Manuscripts," in *Journal of the American Musicological Society,* **38** (1984), "Accent, Meter, and Rhythm in Medieval Treatises 'De rithmis,'" in *Journal of Musicology,* **5** (1987), "The Role of the Parisian Sequence in the Evolution of Notre-Dame Polyphony," in *Speculum,* **62** (1987), and *The Twelfth-century Parisian Sequence Repertories: Liturgical Poetry and Music in the Service of Reform Theology,* 2 vols. (forthcoming); Michel Huglo, "Un nouveau prosaire Nivernaise," in *Ephemerides liturgicae,* **71** (1957); Eckhard Hegener, *Studien zur "zweiten Sprache" in der religiösen Lyrik des zwölften Jahrhunderts: Adam von St. Viktor, Walter von Chatillon* (1971); Jean-René Hesbert, *Le prosaire de la Sainte-Chapelle: Manuscrit du Chapître de Saint Nicholas de Bari (vers 1250)* (1952); Henrich Husmann, "Notre Dame und Saint-Victor: Repertoire-Studien zur Geschichte der gereimten Prosen," in *Acta musicologica,* **36** (1964); Traugott Lawler, ed., *The Parisiana Poetria of John of Garland* (1974); Giovanni Mari, *I trattati medievali di rithmica latina* (1899); *Les Proses d'Adam de Saint-Victor: Texte et Musique,* Eugène Misset and Pierre Aubry, eds. (1901); Hans Spanke, "Die Kompositionkunst der Sequenzen Adams von St. Viktor," in *Studi medievali,* n.s. **14** (1941).

MARGOT E. FASSLER

[See also **Adam of St. Victor; Hugh of St. Victor; Jubilus; Mass, Liturgy of; Melisma; St. Victor MS.**]

SÉQUENCE DE STE. EULALIE, LA. See **Eulalie, La Séquence de Ste.**

SERAPH, a six-winged creature, highest of the nine orders of angels; seraphim are first described surrounding the Lord in Isaiah 6:2–3. The seraphic cry, "Holy, holy, holy is the Lord of Hosts, the whole earth is full of his glory" (Isa. 6:3), was incorporated into the liturgy at an early date. Images of seraphim appeared by the sixth century. They are usually depicted with three pairs of wings emerging from a central head. Two wings folded together rise upward, while another pair, also folded, descend downward; two feet often protrude from the tips of the lower wings. The fifth and sixth wings extend laterally in flight.

In addition, seraphim are often shown with some of the characteristics of cherubim, such as being covered with eyes (*polyommata*) or having the heads of a man, lion, ox, and eagle (tetramorphic), but they are normally distinguishable by inscription or by content. The bottom illustration on page 298 of volume 3 shows such conflated images of seraphim and cherubim.

Seraphim occur by themselves in liturgical contexts, but most often accompany Christ when an indication of his divine nature is appropriate. Hence, they frequently appear in works depicting

Christ in Majesty, the Ascension, the Crucifixion, and Visions of the Lord.

BIBLIOGRAPHY

D. I. Pallas, "Eine Differenzierungen unter den himmlischen Ordnungen (ikonographische Analyse)," in *Byzantinische Zeitschrift,* **64** (1971); Oskar K. Wulff, *Cherubim, Throne und Seraphim* (1894).

LESLIE BRUBAKER

[See also **Angel; Angel/Angelology; Cherub.**]

SERBIA. In the middle of the sixth century the Balkans—including what is now Yugoslavia—were Byzantine. In about 550 Slavs, who had been living north of the Danube and occasionally raiding the Balkans, began settling in its central and eastern parts, particularly along the Timok and Morava rivers. The Avars appeared in Pannonia in the late 560's, subjugating many Slavs there. Many others fled into the Balkans. By the 580's various Slavs under Avar command were invading the Balkans as well. The Byzantines were too weak to stop them. By the mid 580's most of what is now Serbia and Macedonia was occupied by Slavs, and Byzantium had lost control of most of this territory. Between 591 and 602 the campaigns of Emperor Maurice regained control of the main centers and routes, but large-scale Slavic settlement remained. Maurice's gains were wiped out in the chaos that followed his murder in 602 by Phokas, which set off a major war with Persia. By about 620 the regions that were to be Serbian (except certain southern Dalmatian ports) were occupied by Slavs.

THE BEGINNINGS

During the reign of the Byzantine emperor Heraklios (610–641), if we can believe Constantine VII Porphyrogenitos (*De administrando imperio, ca.* 950), the Serbs arrived from north of the Carpathians. After settling briefly in Macedonia, they departed. Then, deciding to return, they made themselves masters of Raška (the southern part of what is now Serbia, centered between the Lim and Ibar rivers), Pagania (to the south of the lower Neretva), Zahumlje (roughly modern Hercegovina), Trebinje, Konavli, southern Dalmatia, and probably Dioclea (Duklja, roughly modern Montenegro), northern Macedonia, and eastern Bosnia. The Serbs seem to have been Iranians; however, some scholars have considered them Slavs. Their numbers were relatively small; their success resulted from tight military organization. Instead of establishing a single state, they set up smaller, county-size units called *župa*s under *župan*s. Relatively quickly (surely by the late eighth century) most, if not all, Serbs had been assimilated by the Slavs who had preceded them into this region and whom the Serbs had subjugated. However, the Serbian name survived to denote the Slavic people whom they conquered and the language of these Slavs. In this article the term "Serb" refers to the Slavic people that resulted. The Slavic component was probably identical to that which settled the western and northwestern Balkans and became the Croatians. These Slavs who became the Serbs and Croatians were probably already distinguishable from the Bulgaro-Macedonians, dwelling to the east and south of the Serbs.

THE NINTH CENTURY

Because they lived far from Italy and Byzantium, whence come our early sources, we know very little about the early history of the Serbs. In the ninth century the Bulgarians pressed westward, subjugating the Slavs of the Timok River. This danger seems to have proved a catalyst in uniting various Serbian tribes to oppose them. The Byzantines, also, seeking to check the Bulgarians, were interested in building up a stronger Serbia in Bulgaria's rear, and seem to have played a part, through diplomacy and gold, in creating some Serbian unity. In the 840's the Bulgarians invaded Serbia. The Serbs, after several years of fighting, drove them out.

The Serb ruler, Vlastimir, who defeated the Bulgarians, also expanded his state to the west. He married his daughter to the *župan* of Trebinje and raised his son-in-law's title to prince. Vlastimir was overlord of Trebinje, and this relationship continued throughout the next century, for, Constantine Porphyrogenitos reports, "The princes of Terbounia [Trebinje] have always been at the command of the prince of Serbia." When Vlastimir died, his realm was divided among this three sons, Mutimir, Strojimir, and Gojnik.

In 853 or 854 Boris of Bulgaria sent an army led by his son Vladimir against the Serbs. The Serbs again defeated the Bulgarians, capturing Vladimir and twelve leading Bulgar boyars. Boris ransomed them back and made peace. Good relations between the two peoples followed for the rest of Boris' reign. Shortly thereafter Mutimir seized the Serbian

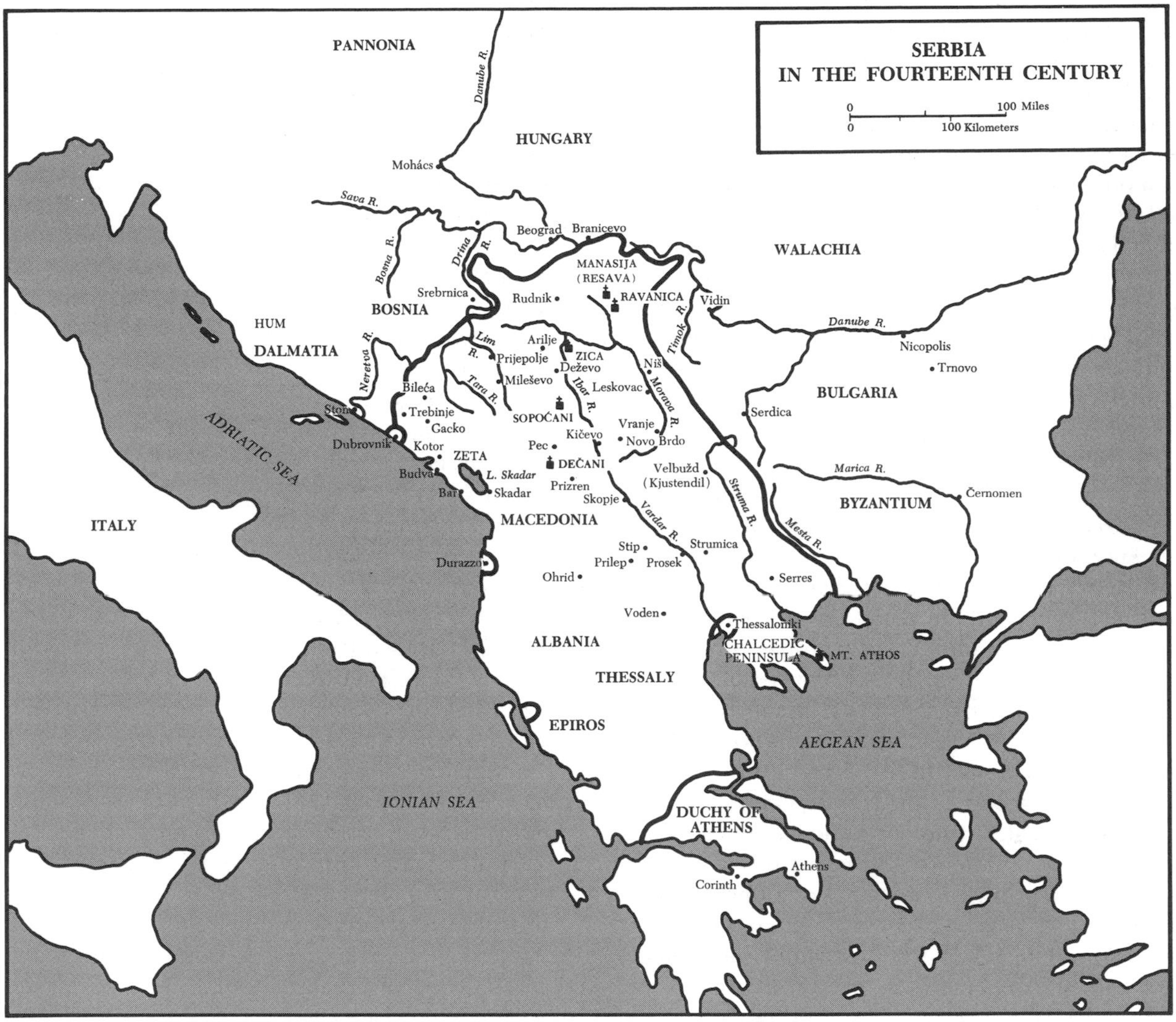

throne, exiling his two brothers to the Bulgarian court. Gojnik's son, Peter, fled to Croatia. Mutimir ruled until about 891, when he died, leaving the throne to his sons, led by the eldest, Prvoslav.

Within a year Peter overthrew them and took over in Serbia. The Bulgarians, unhappy with this change, participated in an attempt to overthrow Peter. When this failed, Symeon of Bulgaria (893–927) agreed to recognize Peter, who placed himself under Symeon's protection. This resulted in a twenty-year peace within Serbia and between it and Bulgaria, enabling Peter to concentrate on his western border. He defeated Tišemir of Bosnia, annexing the territory up to and including the Bosna River Valley. He then expanded along the Neretva, where he clashed with Michael of Zahumlje, who also ruled Trebinje and most of Duklja (modern Montenegro). Christianity presumably was spreading gradually at this time within Serbia. Unfortunately no sources touch on this process. Peter's name shows him to have been a Christian, and possibly during his long reign he encouraged the spread of that religion. Since Serbia bordered on Bulgaria, with which it was allied, presumably

Christian influences and missionaries came from there.

THE TENTH CENTURY

In 917 Byzantium, fighting a major war against Symeon, sought allies; possibly Peter by then sought greater independence from Bulgaria. In any case, Peter accepted Byzantine money and joined the Byzantine coalition against Bulgaria. The same year Symeon, having first defeated the Byzantines at Anchialo, invaded Serbia. He captured Peter, who died in a Bulgarian prison, and installed Mutimir's grandson Paul (Pavel), who had long lived in Bulgaria, on the throne. The Byzantines tried to replace Paul with Prvoslav's son, Zaharije. However, Symeon managed to capture Zaharije, leading the Byzantines to woo Paul, which they did successfully. Paul planned a surprise attack on Bulgaria, whose troops were in the east besieging Adrianople. Warned, Symeon in about 922 sent a Bulgarian army against Serbia, which defeated Paul and placed Zaharije, who by then had agreed to support Symeon, on the Serbian throne. Zaharije, however, was not truly converted to the Bulgarian side. It was, after all, natural for a Serb to be pro-Byzantine and anti-Bulgarian because the former, a distant state, offered Serbia greater independence from the latter, a powerful, interfering neighbor. Furthermore, Zaharije had long lived in Constantinople. Zaharije incited various Slavic tribes along their common border to rebel against Symeon. Symeon sent an insufficient force to quell these disturbances; some Bulgarian generals were killed and their heads and weapons were sent to Constantinople. So, in 924, Symeon sent a large army against Serbia which included Strojimir's grandson Časlav, who had long been a hostage in Bulgaria. The Bulgarian armies ravaged much of Serbia, forcing Zaharije to flee to Croatia. Symeon then summoned the Serbian *župan*s to pay homage to Časlav. When they appeared, he took them all prisoner, arresting Časlav as well, and sent them to Bulgaria as captives. He thus annexed Serbia directly, a move he believed necessary because the Serbs had proved unreliable allies.

After Symeon's death in 927, Časlav escaped to Serbia (probably in 927/928, perhaps as late as 931), found popular support, and restored a Serbian state. He submitted to Byzantine overlordship, gaining Byzantine financial and diplomatic support. Throughout his reign, which lasted until about 960, he maintained close ties with Byzantium. Most scholars believe that under him Byzantine influence (including that of the Byzantine church) greatly increased in Serbia. Unfortunately, the sources are silent on the subject. The borders of Časlav's state are unknown, though eventually he extended them well into Bosnia. He was killed in about 960 while fighting the Hungarians in that region. The other prominent Serbian state at this time was that of Michael of Zahumlje, an ally of Symeon. After Symeon's death he improved relations with the empire, accepting the court rank of proconsul. He also was on good terms with the papacy, under whose jurisdiction his church lay. He ruled Zahumlje into the 940's.

After Časlav's death Serbia disintegrated and Duklja annexed part of it. Duklja also gained control of Zahumlje and Trebinje. Duklja's ruler was John Vladimir. In the 990's Emperor Basil II, during his war with Samuil of Bulgaria, made an alliance with John Vladimir, causing Samuil to attack Duklja. Defeating and imprisoning John Vladimir, Samuil gained control of both Raška and Duklja. John Vladimir then made peace with Samuil, married his daughter Kosara, and returned to rule Duklja as Samuil's vassal. He gave Samuil little support, however, remaining neutral during Basil's great counteroffensive, which by 1018 had conquered Samuil's state. In the final year of the Byzantine-Bulgarian war, Samuil's successor, John Vladislav, murdered John Vladimir in a church after violating a safe-conduct, making John Vladimir a martyr. Miracles occurred at his grave, and he soon was considered a saint.

THE ELEVENTH CENTURY

After John Vladimir's murder Duklja's history becomes obscure. Since John Vladislav was fighting for survival against Basil, it is unlikely that he could have annexed Duklja. The last known member of John Vladimir's family was his uncle, Dragimir, whom Samuil had placed over Trebinje and Zahumlje. He was murdered in Kotor by local citizens in 1018, the year Basil destroyed the last remnants of Samuil's state. Many scholars believe that about this time Duklja fell under direct Byzantine rule. Others believe it remained under a prince of its ruling family who accepted Byzantine suzerainty.

In any case, sources are silent about Duklja until the 1030's, when a certain Stefan Vojislav is found ruling there. How he acquired power and how long he had ruled Duklja is not known, but he was a Byzantine vassal. Between 1034 and 1036 he refused homage to the empire. Byzantine troops captured him and placed Duklja under the military governor of Durazzo (Dyrrachium). By 1038/1039 Vojislav had escaped from Byzantium; returning to Duklja, he took to the mountains with an evergrowing following. Soon he had liberated most of Duklja; subsequent Byzantine expeditions against him failed. He carried out a guerrilla war, making hit-and-run attacks from the mountains against the larger, better-equipped Byzantine forces. When the Byzantines became occupied in suppressing Peter Deljan's rebellion in the early 1040's, Vojislav achieved full independence and established his capital at Skadar (Italian: Scutari; modern Shkodër), maintaining other courts at Trebinje, Kotor, and Bar. His territory stretched along the coast as far north as Ston, thus including part of Zahumlje. In the 1040's further Byzantine campaigns against Vojislav failed. The empire enlisted on its side Ljutovid, ruler of Zahumlje, giving Vojislav an excuse to expel Ljutovid and annex even more—possibly all—of Zahumlje. Vojislav died (probably 1043) having achieved Duklja's independence and greatly expanded its borders. Duklja was to be the leading Serbian state until Raška supplanted it in the following century.

After Vojislav's death his lands were divided among his widow and five sons. Local nobles (particularly in Trebinje) tried to take advantage of the new situation to secede, and Byzantium tried through intrigues within the family to regain its influence in Duklja. These threats led to peace among the brothers, enabling them to reassert control over Trebinje. Shortly thereafter (about 1046) one brother, Michael, emerged as king. Whether his brothers agreed to this or whether Michael forced this upon them is not known. Thereafter Michael ruled all Duklja. At most, his brothers ruled appanages, which were allowed no independent foreign policy and owed tribute and service to the king.

The greatest threat to Duklja remained Byzantium. To reduce this danger and probably also to avoid giving his brothers the opportunity to utilize a Byzantine-Dukljan war to assert themselves against him, Michael made peace with the empire. A widower with, according to the unreliable Chronicle of the Priest of Dioclea, seven sons, he married a relative of Emperor Constantine IX and received the court rank of protostrator. He retained his independence but restored to Byzantium some of Durazzo's hinterland, which had been seized by Vojislav in 1042 or 1043. After this agreement, Michael asserted himself against his brother Radoslav, seizing part of the *župa* of Zeta and assigning it to one of his own sons. Subsequently he regularly awarded conquered territory to his own sons; for example, between 1060 and 1074 he conquered Raška and assigned it to another son, Petrislav. In 1072 George Vojteh in Macedonia, then part of the empire, rebelled. He sought aid from Michael, who sent the rebels an army under his son Constantine Bodin and a second army under a general named Petrilo. En route to join the rebels, Bodin was crowned tsar of the Bulgarians at Prizren. Both armies were soon defeated, Bodin being captured and Petrilo returning to Duklja, and the revolt died out. Bodin remained a prisoner until about 1078.

Michael, by sending Bodin to aid the rebels, was departing from his Byzantine alliance. He was soon in communication with the pope, from whom he received a crown in 1077. In 1081 the Normans attacked the Byzantine city of Durazzo. The Dukljans, still officially imperial allies, sent an army under Bodin. However, earlier that year Bodin had married an Italian lady from Bari, whose father headed the Norman party in that city. At the key battle (October 1081) the Dukljans sat on the sidelines; their nonparticipation contributed to the Norman conquest of Durazzo. Whether their inactivity was owing to an agreement with the Normans or whether they felt it best to keep their army intact to defend Duklja against the victor is unknown. However, Duklja now could expect a Byzantine attack whenever the Byzantines managed to defeat the Normans.

In 1081 or 1082 Michael died. Bodin probably succeeded him immediately. However, his position was not secure until he had suppressed a revolt in Zeta on behalf of Michael's brother Radoslav. While this was occurring, it seems that Raška broke away from Duklja. Though no source mentions a revolt there, we are told that Bodin, having secured his own position in Duklja, marched successfully against Bosnia and Raška. Since Raška had already been annexed by Michael, a conquest by Bodin would have been necessary only if it had seceded. Bodin (*ca.* 1084) put two *župan*s—Vukan and Marko—over Raška. They were probably sons of Petrislav, whom Michael had placed over Raška between 1060 and 1074. They swore oaths of loyalty to Bodin. Marko immediately disappears from the sources, but Vukan remained in power in

Raška for many years and was to become a prominent figure in Serbian history. Neither Raška nor the part of Bosnia that Bodin gained was incorporated into an integrated state with Duklja. Each region retained its own nobility and institutions, and simply acquired a member of the Dukljan royal family to head the local structure. In 1089 the pope raised the bishop of Bar to archbishop and subordinated Bodin's whole state to him. In the long run this was to affect only some of Duklja's coastal territory, as most of the interior of Duklja as well as Bodin's other territories remained under the jurisdiction of Orthodox bishops. There is no evidence that Vukan ever tried to subject the churches in Raška to Rome. The list of the archbishop's theoretical suffragan bishoprics does not include Zahumlje, suggesting that it may already have seceded from Duklja.

In 1085, after the Norman leader, Robert Guiscard, died, Byzantium regained Durazzo. Able now to act against Duklja, it launched its long-expected attack between 1089 and 1091. The Byzantines not only defeated Bodin's army but also, it seems, took him prisoner again. A civil war soon erupted in Duklja among Bodin's many relatives, which greatly weakened Duklja and gave the Serbs of Raška a chance to assert their independence; Bosnia and, if it was not already separate, Zahumlje also seceded. The leader of Raška in this venture was Vukan, who, as noted, was a Dukljan—possibly a nephew of Bodin—placed over Raška by Bodin. Up to this point—through the eleventh century—the leading Serbian center had been Duklja. But now, because of Duklja's defeat by the Byzantines and the long civil war that followed, accompanied by the loss of its peripheral territories, leadership passed to the Serbs of Raška. In the twelfth century Serbs based in Raška (rather than Duklja) became the leading opponents of Byzantium. In fact, when the Dukljan civil war ended in about 1146, the Dukljan victor, Radoslav, bore the title "prince" (*knez*) rather than "king" and was a Byzantine vassal. Raška was to remain the leading Serbian center from then until the end of the Middle Ages. Thus, henceforth in this article the terms Raška and Serbia are used as synonyms.

In the early 1090's Vukan of Raška took the title "grand (*veliki*) *župan*." His state was centered near modern Novi Pazar. Under him were various local *župans*, each over a county, who seem to have been more or less autonomous as far as their internal affairs were concerned, but who were obliged to support the grand *župan* in battle. It seems the *župans* were hereditary rulers of their counties—local Raškans with their own local supporters who had had authority there before the Dukljans annexed Raška. In about 1090 Vukan began raiding into imperial territory, first in the vicinity of Kosovo and later along the Vardar. Initially the Byzantines, occupied elsewhere, could not take action against him, but by 1095 they had obtained his submission. Vukan's son Uroš went to Constantinople as a hostage. When Byzantium became involved with the First Crusade, Vukan pressed south into Macedonia again; the empire could do nothing about it until 1106, when once again Vukan submitted. This Serbian drive south into Macedonia remained steady over the next two and a half centuries.

THE TWELFTH CENTURY

Vukan was succeeded by his son Uroš I in about 1125. The Serbs revolted for full independence from Byzantium in about 1126. The empire defeated them, settling many Serbian prisoners around Nicomedia. In 1130 Uroš' daughter Jelena (Helena) married Béla II the Blind, king of Hungary (1131–1141), who, owing to his blindness, relied heavily on others, including his wife and her brother Beloš, who had come to Hungary. Close relations were thus established between Serbia and Hungary. These continued under Béla's successor, his minor son, Géza II (1141–1162), for whom Beloš was regent, and Uroš I's successor, his son Uroš II, who was Beloš's brother.

In 1149 the Byzantine emperor Manuel I Komnenos (1143-1180) moved his army to Avlona (modern Vlorë, Albania) in order to attack Norman Italy. Meanwhile the Serbs, Normans, and Hungarians exchanged envoys, which led to another Serbian revolt. This uprising went beyond renouncing allegiance to Byzantium. First, the Serbs posed a threat to Byzantium's Adriatic supply base during its attack on Italy. Second, the Serbs attacked a loyal Byzantine vassal, Radoslav of Duklja, whom they forced to take refuge in Kotor. The Serbs under Uroš II occupied much of the Dukljan interior and Trebinje, leaving Radoslav only part of his coast. Radoslav sought aid from Manuel, while Uroš received Hungarian support. After various minor skirmishes, during which it captured Serbia's major fortresses while the Serbian armies took to the mountains as guerrillas, the Byzantine army decisively defeated the Serbs and Hungarians on the

River Tara (1150); much devastation of Serbia followed and Serbian prisoners were resettled on Byzantine territory. The Byzantines replaced the defeated Uroš with his brother Desa. However, Uroš, having sought mercy from Manuel, was restored as grand *župan* of Serbia. Reassuming its ties of vassalage, Serbia promised military aid for Byzantium's wars, owing 2,000 men for western campaigns and 500 men for eastern campaigns. Radoslav was restored as ruler of all Duklja. Peace with Byzantium seems to have been unpopular with the pro-Hungarian faction at the Raškan court. In 1155 that group ousted Uroš for Desa. Byzantine troops then deposed Desa and restored Uroš, who reaffirmed his Byzantine alliance. Desa was granted Dendra (near Niš) as an appanage. Various Serbian hostages were taken to Constantinople. Around 1161–1162 the Byzantines placed Desa on the Serbian throne. Presumably Uroš II (or possibly a fourth brother, Primislav, who may have briefly held Raška) had shown too much independence. In 1163 or 1164 Desa provided troops for Manuel's campaign against Hungary. The Byzantines by now had suppressed many Serbian uprisings, but Serbia never remained pacified. Even when the Byzantines changed rulers in Serbia—as they did upon occasion—they could not prevent new revolts from erupting.

Between 1166 and 1168 a new dynasty appeared in Raška, headed at first by a certain Tihomir, who was soon ousted by his brother Stefan Nemanja. This dynasty (the Nemanjíci) was to rule Serbia until 1371. Where its founders came from and what—if any—connection they had to the preceding dynasty is unknown. Tihomir possibly was installed by Manuel. A Byzantine oration, referring to events of about 1166, states that Manuel easily reduced the Serbs to submission; they repented and accepted the ruler Manuel appointed over them. Since the time is right, it is tempting to see this as referring to Tihomir's installation. In any case, by 1168 Serbian territory was divided among four brothers: Tihomir, the eldest, who bore the title grand *župan,* Miroslav, Stracimir, and Stefan Nemanja. Nemanja soon drove Tihomir from Serbia. When Tihomir tried to return in about 1171, he was killed in battle. The three remaining brothers divided the Serbian territory, and Nemanja became grand *župan.* A Byzantine attack in 1172 forced Nemanja into submission. He underwent a humiliating ceremony at the imperial camp and then was taken to Constantinople for another degrading ceremony featuring long orations. Then, as a sworn vassal, Nemanja was allowed to return to Serbia as its ruler. He remained loyal to his oath until Manuel died in 1180. While Nemanja held Raška, his brother Miroslav became ensconced in Hum (formerly Zahumlje). Stracimir held an appanage to the north of Raška on the West Morava River.

When Byzantium declined after Manuel's death, Nemanja expanded south into northern Macedonia and Kosovo. He also acquired Duklja, which by then was coming to be called Zeta (after one *župa* within it), and reached the southern Dalmatian coast. He assigned Zeta to his eldest son, Vukan; no Zetan territory remained under its former dynasty. He also acquired Niš and the territory east of it as far as Serdica (modern Sofia, Bulgaria). In 1189 he received the crusading Western emperor Frederick I Barbarossa at Niš and tried unsuccessfully to create a coalition against Byzantium. In 1190 the Byzantines finally invaded and defeated Nemanja in battle; however, they could not have won a resounding victory because they recognized Serbia's independence and allowed Nemanja to retain his acquisitions of Leskovac, Vranje, Zeta, and parts of Kosovo and of northern Albania. Niš and the territory along the Sardica-Beograd route reverted to the empire. Probably at this time Nemanja's second son, Stefan, married Eudokia, the niece of Emperor Isaac II Angelos and daughter of Alexios III Angelos, who was to depose Isaac in 1195. In 1196 Nemanja abdicated and became a monk, taking the name Simeon. He first resided at the magnificent monastery he built, Studenica. Then he moved to Mt. Athos, where his youngest son, Sava, was already a monk. Emperor Alexios III granted him the dilapidated monastery of Hilandar (Khilendar) for the Serbs. Nemanja and Sava repaired it, making it a major institution that throughout the Middle Ages remained a leading Serbian cultural center. Soon after his death Nemanja was canonized.

THE THIRTEENTH CENTURY

Nemanja's second son, Stefan, succeeded; some believe Stefan's succession resulted from his being son-in-law to the new Byzantine emperor, Alexios III. Vukan, the eldest son, who already held Zeta (which some scholars believe indicates he had been the heir to the throne of Raška), continued to hold Zeta and Trebinje. Displeased with Stefan's succession, Vukan proclaimed himself king, deriving his right to the title from the former kings of Zeta.

Thus, despite Nemanja's wish for cooperation between his sons, Vukan established himself as an independent ruler. He negotiated with Rome and Hungary, becoming a vassal of the Hungarian king, Imre, who added "Serbia" to his title. In 1202, with Hungarian aid, Vukan attacked Raška and deposed Stefan, who fled. Soon, Stefan, possibly with Bulgarian aid, regained Raška. War continued sporadically between the two brothers until 1207 or 1208, when Sava, returning from Athos with their father's body, mediated a peace, leaving the status quo. Vukan died shortly thereafter, but the struggle was continued by his son King George, who accepted Venetian suzerainty. In about 1216 Stefan conquered Zeta, ending its separatism and independent kingship. He eventually assigned Zeta, it seems, to his own son Radoslav. Recently, however, this assignment has been questioned by scholars who believe Stefan retained Zeta himself. In either case, he successfully made Zeta the patrimony of his own family rather than of Vukan's heirs. Until Dušan's death (1355) Zeta remained part of Raška with no special privileges. Frequently it was administered by the heir to the Raškan throne, who bore a title connected not with Zeta but with his position at the Raškan court. Agreements made by the young holder of Zeta generally had to be confirmed by the ruler of Raška. However, though Zeta retained no special legal position, its nobles tended to be unruly. They frequently revolted or supported revolts by the holders of Zeta against the rulers of Raška.

In this period Stefan supported a certain Strez, who had a small principality centered at Prosek (Greek: Prosakon) on the Vardar, in his struggle to wrest Macedonia from Boril's declining Bulgarian state. As a result, in 1214 Boril, allied with the Latin Empire (established in Constantinople in 1204), attacked Serbia. Stefan repelled this attack as well as a second one that year by Michael I of Epiros. The resistance to Epiros seems to have made a strong impression, for Epiros was not to attack Serbian territory again. In fact, after Michael's death in 1215, his successor, Theodore, concluded peace with Serbia and his daughter married Stefan's heir, Radoslav.

In 1217 Stefan was crowned king of Serbia by a papal legate, and from his coronation became known as Stefan Prvovenčani (The First-crowned). This flirtation with Rome was unpopular with many of his subjects and especially with the church organization. Sava, who had become abbot of Studenica, returned to Mt. Athos in protest. These ties with Rome proved short-lasting; Sava went to Nicaea, the residence of the displaced "Byzantine" emperor, and recognized the patriarch in Nicaea as the ecumenical patriarch (his ecumenical claims had been rejected by the archbishop of Ohrid [Ochrid], the chief bishop in Epiros and Serbia's suzerain archbishop). In exchange the patriarch recognized Serbia as an autocephalous archbishopric. Sava became Serbia's first archbishop (1219–1233). He established about ten suffragan bishoprics under himself, uniting under his jurisdiction the Serbian lands of Hum and Zeta; this contributed to the centralization of the Serbian state. Ohrid's protests about this hierarchical change were ignored. Sava directed the translation of a Byzantine Nomocanon that became Serbia's first canon law code; he promulgated it at a council held in 1221 at the archbishop's seat of Žiča, a monastery Stefan built.

Stefan died in 1227; his eldest son, Radoslav, was crowned king at Žiča by Archbishop Sava. The younger sons, Vladislav and Uroš, received appanages. Stefan's youngest son had become a monk, also taking the name Sava. He shortly thereafter was appointed bishop of Hum and from 1263 to 1270 was to be archbishop of Serbia. Thus the close ties between dynasty and church and the dynasty's role within the church continued. The church strongly supported the dynasty, and each ruler gave the church large tracts of land and built at least one major monastery. Radoslav, married to Theodore of Epiros' daughter, maintained ties with Epiros and sought to improve relations with the archbishop of Ohrid. This may have seemed to some a threat to the newly won independence of the Serbian church. In any case, after Theodore's defeat and capture by John Asen II of Bulgaria in 1230, opposition increased against Radoslav, who was forced to flee to Dubrovnik in 1234. He was succeeded by his brother Vladislav, who, it seems after his coronation, married a daughter of the powerful John Asen. (Radoslav eventually returned to Serbia to become a monk.) Archbishop Sava I, upset by the dissensions among his nephews, abdicated, going on pilgrimage to Palestine. On his return journey, Sava died at the Bulgarian court in Trnovo (1235); his body was returned and buried in the monastery of Mileševo, built by Vladislav. Sava was soon canonized and his relics worked many miracles; his cult was important throughout the rest of the medieval and Turkish periods.

When Asen died in 1241, Bulgaria entered a

decline. Many scholars associate Vladislav's deposition and the succession of the third brother, Uroš (1243–1276), with this. It is impossible to prove that Radoslav and Vladislav were representatives of pro-Epiros and pro-Bulgarian parties, respectively, in Serbia. But at least Asen's death removed a prop that might have aided Vladislav and prevented Uroš's successful coup. Uroš seems to have been the ablest of the three brothers, though he had the advantage over them of having his reign coincide with the decline of Serbia's two formerly powerful neighbors, Epiros and Bulgaria. Under Uroš, Serbia became a significant Balkan power. Serbia's rise is attributable not only to the weakening of its neighbors but also to its rapid economic development, associated with the opening of its mines. The mines were developed primarily by the Sasi (Saxons from Hungary), whose communities were granted many privileges. The first mine referred to in the sources is Brskovo on the Tara, mentioned in 1254. It was soon followed by mines at Rudnik, Kopaonik, and Novo Brdo. The silver, gold, lead, copper, and iron extracted attracted more coastal merchants to Serbia. Merchants from Dubrovnik and Kotor established privileged colonies in economic and mining centers in Serbia. These foreign colonies—Saxon and Dalmatian—enjoyed freedom for their Catholic religion (provided they did not proselytize among Serbs) and the right to live under their own officials and laws. Quarrels with local Serbs were resolved by mixed courts. These Dalmatian merchants, particularly those from Kotor, soon took over the high financial offices at the Serbian court. They also bought the right to collect taxes and tolls within Serbia. The mines and increased trade improved the Serbian ruler's economic position greatly, giving him cash to hire mercenaries. This provided a means to control his nobles, for he now had available a military force independent of them.

Uroš, seeking to centralize his state, did not create appanages for any son. Dragutin, his eldest son, lived at court. A Byzantine envoy who visited Serbia to negotiate a marriage that did not materialize (owing to Serbian opposition)—and whose account may thus be somewhat biased—described the Serbian court as follows: "The Great King, as he is called [Uroš], lives a simple life in a way that would be a disgrace for a middling official in Constantinople; the king's Hungarian daughter-in-law [Dragutin's wife] works at her spinning wheel in a cheap dress; the household eats like a pack of hunters or sheep stealers." The envoy also stressed the insecurity of the highways. Dragutin wanted an appanage, and his Hungarian in-laws exerted pressure for this too. Uroš resisted, and some scholars believe he even considered replacing Dragutin as heir with his younger son, Milutin. Dragutin finally in 1276 demanded to share power. Uroš refused and Dragutin rebelled, receiving military help from his Hungarian father-in-law. Their joint armies defeated Uroš in battle near Gacko (in modern Hercegovina). Uroš became a monk, dying in about 1278 at Sopoćani, the beautiful monastery he had founded.

Dragutin immediately gave his mother an appanage, including Zeta, Trebinje, and part of western Serbia. His younger brother, Milutin, took up residence there. Dragutin seems to have maintained a pro-Hungarian policy, which may not have been appreciated by his nobility. In any case, in 1282 Dragutin fell from a horse and broke his leg. The sources imply that his injury was serious enough for his future to be in doubt; therefore a council was convoked at Deževo at which Dragutin abdicated in favor of his brother Milutin. The sources seem to leave much unsaid; for if his health was the problem, why did the council not create a temporary regency? Thus many scholars consider the leg an excuse for the nobles to depose Dragutin, a deposition they wanted for political reasons. Milutin seems not to have been present; thus, probably the nobility, rather than he, were the moving force at Deževo. Milutin became king for life; Dragutin, giving up the royal title, received an appanage in western Serbia, including the mining town of Rudnik, Arilje, and Dabar (seat of a bishop residing in the monastery of St. Nicholas at Banja). Most scholars believe the council also decreed that Dragutin's son, Vladislav, should succeed Milutin. In 1284 the Hungarian king granted Dragutin a second appanage north of Serbia and south of the Sava and Danube that included Mačva, Usora, possibly Sol (Tuzla), and Srem ulterior (on the south bank of the Sava). He retained his Serbian lands as well. The two regions were not integrated into one state; each remained under the suzerainty of a different overlord.

As we shall see, relations between Dragutin and Milutin seem to have been friendly at first. The Serbian nobles desired to press south against Byzantium; possibly Dragutin's failure to carry out this policy caused his overthrow. In any case, Milutin immediately in 1282 joined Charles of Anjou's coalition against Byzantium and conquered Skopje, which became his main residence. The Byzantines summoned the Nogaj Tatars to raid Serbia. The Serbs repelled their attack, and then in 1283 Milutin, supported by Dragutin, pressed further into Macedonia, occupying more territory.

At about this time two brothers (Drman and Kudelin) rebelled against the Hungarians and established an independent principality centered at Braničevo and Kučevo. Dragutin's and the Hungarians' joint action in 1285 failed to dislodge them; they retaliated, ravaging Dragutin's lands. Dragutin then received help from Milutin and in roughly 1291 defeated them and annexed Braničevo. Shortly thereafter Šišman of Vidin attacked Serbia, possibly in retaliation for some action against him by Dragutin. The attackers took no territory but burned the monastery of Žiča. Milutin, angry, marched against Šišman and captured Vidin. Peace soon followed, restoring Šišman to Vidin under Serbian suzerainty. However, Šišman's Nogaj overlords disliked this turn of events and threatened to attack Serbia. Milutin preserved peace by sending the Nogajs many gifts and his eldest son, Stefan Dečanski, as a hostage. He remained there several years until in 1299 the Golden Horde destroyed the Nogajs; in the chaos that followed, Dečanski escaped and returned home.

THE FOURTEENTH CENTURY

Milutin gave Zeta to Dečanski as an appanage. Until this time Dragutin's relations with Milutin appear to have been good, with Dragutin contributing to Milutin's expansion in Macedonia and Milutin to Dragutin's expansion along the Danube. However, Dragutin, perhaps correctly, saw Dečanski's receiving Zeta as a sign that Milutin intended Dečanski, not Dragutin's son Vladislav, to succeed. Relations worsened. As a result Milutin concluded peace with Byzantium. In a 1299 treaty Byzantium recognized Milutin's conquests down to Ohrid, Štip, and Strumica, which were defined as the Byzantine border fortresses. Milutin also married Simonis (Serbian: Simonida), the daughter of Andronikos II; it was his fourth marriage. Tensions continued between the two brothers, and many Serbian nobles, probably unhappy about peace with Byzantium, supported Dragutin. War broke out between them in 1301 or 1302, for Milutin is then found holding Dragutin's town of Rudnik; war lasted, presumably sporadically, until a treaty was signed in 1312 restoring matters to prewar conditions. Relations remained tense thereafter; when their mother died in 1314, Dragutin did not attend the funeral. Milutin absorbed her appanage, which included Trebinje, Konavli, additional coastal territory, and probably the region of the upper Lim.

In 1314 Dečanski, probably incited by the nobles of Zeta, rebelled; Milutin defeated him, allegedly blinded him, and exiled him to Constantinople. He was allowed to return, probably in 1320. In 1316 Dragutin died and Milutin absorbed his Serbian lands; he was unable to prevent the Hungarians from eventually regaining Dragutin's Mačva-Srem lands in 1319. However, Milutin retained Braničevo. He took advantage of Dragutin's death to imprison Vladislav. However, his state did not become tranquil; various nobles in his northern Albanian lands revolted in 1318. Disorders continued until Milutin died (without a will) in October 1321. At that time sources mention bands of roving armed men plaguing Serbia. Civil war immediately erupted among his sons Dečanski and Constantine and his nephew Vladislav.

Throughout his reign Milutin actively developed Serbia's mines; under him Novo Brdo became the richest silver mine in the Balkans. From them Milutin derived much wealth, which among other things supported mercenaries to balance the independent-minded nobility and carry on his war with Dragutin, and enabled him to do considerable church-building. One source says he fulfilled a vow to build one church for every year he reigned. Not surprisingly, the church actively supported him in his war against Dragutin. Milutin was the first Serbian ruler to coin money extensively. Simonida's arrival led to increased byzantinization at the Serbian court. Milutin also initiated *pronoias*—Byzantine service estates—in Serbia.

Constantine probably was Milutin's intended heir. He was proclaimed king immediately and started coining money. Vladislav, freed from jail, established himself with an army in Dragutin's former lands in the north. Dečanski, claiming, "Look and be amazed, I was blind and now I see," became the third claimant. The miracle of his regained sight is described in his saint's life, written long after his death. Hostile sources claim that he had not been totally blinded but had hidden the fact he could see until then. Interestingly, no Byzantine source mentioning his exile in Constantinople comments on his being blind. The church supported Dečanski, and, according to church sources, the populace, because of the miracle, flocked to him; in January 1322 the archbishop of Serbia crowned him king and his son, Stefan Dušan, "young king." This was the first coronation of a "young king" (*mladi kralj*). Was it done to create a co-ruler because of Dečanski's blindness? For Constantine claimed, in the Byzantine tradition, that the blind had no right to rule. Or was that coronation an attempt to assure Dušan's subsequent succession?

Soon thereafter Constantine was defeated and killed in Zeta, which was given to Dušan as an appanage. Vladislav, having revived Dragutin's state in the north with local support, called himself king and coined money. He seems also to have been supported by the Hungarians. Soon war broke out between the two cousins. Defeated, probably late in 1324, Vladislav fled to Hungary, where he eventually died. Thus, by 1325 Dečanski had established his rule in Serbia. However, internal squabbles continued among various Serbian nobles, particularly in Serbian Hum. In 1326 Stjepan Kotromanić of Bosnia took advantage of them to annex a great part of Hum. Dečanski seems to have been powerless to stop him. Bosnia's success was aided by the fact that the family which emerged as the most powerful in Hum—the Draživojevići—supported Kotromanić.

Soon civil war erupted in Byzantium. Serbia, with longtime ties to the elderly Emperor Andronikos II, father of Milutin's wife Simonida (who had returned to Constantinople and become a nun when Milutin died), supported him. His rival and grandson, Andronikos III, received help from Michael Šišman of Bulgaria. Michael had repudiated his Serbian wife, Anna, Dečanski's sister, and married Andronikos III's sister. Serbian aid did not prevent Andronikos III's triumph in 1328. However, it did cause him and Michael to dislike Serbia, whose rising power disturbed both rulers. They planned joint action against Serbia, which, however, was poorly coordinated; the Bulgarian army arrived alone on 28 July 1330 to face the Serbian army at Velbužd (modern Kjustendil). In the ensuing battle the Bulgarian army was annihilated and Michael Šišman was killed. Dečanski agreed to peace on the condition that his sister Anna (with her and Michael's minor son) return to rule in Trnovo. Serbian troops accompanied her to Trnovo, where some remained to guard her. Bulgaria never regained its former position; the victory guaranteed Serbian hegemony over it for the rest of the century and also Serbian dominance over Macedonia for the next half-century.

The Serbs now had an excuse to go against Michael's Byzantine allies, but Dečanski chose not to do so, thereby alienating many nobles. Dečanski and Dušan soon quarreled. The pro-Dušan sources claim evil advisers turned Dečanski against his son; Dečanski decided to seize Dušan and exclude him from his inheritance. He sent an army into Zeta against Dušan. Peace was negotiated in the early spring of 1331. Shortly thereafter Dečanski summoned Dušan. Dušan feared for his life. His advisers persuaded him to resist. In the ensuing battle in August 1331, Dušan's troops triumphed and captured Dečanski. Dušan was crowned king in September. Byzantine sources stress the support of Dušan by the leading Serbian nobles; they wanted to campaign against Byzantium for lands and booty, but Dečanski had not approved. These nobles, according to Byzantine sources, were regularly a pressure group for Serbian expansion south, and no ruler who opposed them was safe. Seeking a king to carry out their wishes, they were the moving force behind Dušan's revolt; at first Dušan was more or less their puppet, powerless to resist their throwing his father into prison in chains and then murdering him that November. Dečanski, buried at Visoki Dečani, the beautiful monastery he built, was soon canonized and his cult became popular.

The Bulgarians took advantage of these disorders to depose Anna and establish a nephew of Michael Šišman, John Alexander, as their tsar. Dušan and the Serbian nobles, wanting their hands free to move against Byzantium, agreed to the change. In December 1331 an alliance was concluded, sealed by Dušan's marrying John Alexander's sister, Jelena (Helena). Good relations with Bulgaria continued throughout his reign. In 1332 Dušan suppressed a revolt in Zeta when some nobles seem to have tried to secede and form their own principality. This suggests that Zetan feeling still was strong, and possibly explains why a member of the Raškan dynasty was so frequently installed to rule Zeta. It also suggests that the seeds for the splintering of Serbia that occurred after Dušan's death were already present during his reign.

In 1334 a leading Byzantine general, Syrgiannes, revolted and sought Dušan's help. This was granted. Under Syrgiannes' command Serbian armies invaded Macedonia. The Byzantines soon assassinated Syrgiannes, and the Serbs, faced with a Hungarian attack, agreed to a peace recognizing considerable Serbian gains, including Ohrid, Prilep, Strumica, and Prosek (the last captured by Dečanski previously), making the Byzantine-Serbian frontier very close to the present Greek-Yugoslav border. The Serbs then successfully repelled the Hungarians.

In 1341 Andronikos III died, leaving a minor son, John V. Immediately the regency for the young emperor split; civil war broke out between John Kantakuzenos and the other regents who were based in Constantinople. Kantakuzenos came to Serbia for help; Dušan hesitated, but his council of twenty-four nobles was unanimous for action, showing the nobles were still exerting pressure to go south against Byzantium. The sources do not agree on what Kantakuzenos promised them, but clearly the Serbs were offered some imperial territory. The Serbs then attacked the empire, gaining during 1342–1343 more of Macedonia (including Kastoria) and most of Albania. In 1343, after Kantakuzenos won the support of the magnates of Thessaly, Dušan switched sides and declared for the regency. While the Byzantines fought one another in Thrace, he, the regency's ally, fought for himself. Wiping out the stain of earlier failures, in September 1345 he finally took Serres (Serrai). He then took Drama and occupied the rest of Macedonia and the Chalcidic Peninsula, including Mt. Athos.

In late 1345 Dušan began calling himself tsar. Then, in April 1346, he held a huge assembly at Skopje attended by the archbishop of Ohrid, the Bulgarian patriarch of Trnovo, and various leading representatives from Mt. Athos. They raised the rank of the Serbian archbishop to patriarch. The new patriarch (whose seat was to be in Peć) then crowned Dušan emperor (tsar) of the Serbs and Greeks. Dušan's minor son, Uroš, was crowned king and nominally given the Serbian lands to rule. Dušan, the "emperor," though in fact he ruled the whole state, had particular responsibility for "Romania," the Greek lands. He allowed the Greek lands to retain Greek as their official language and keep most of their existing laws and institutions. He even left many Greeks as local officials while others continued to retain their *pronoia*s, simply swearing fealty to Dušan. He was particularly generous to Mt. Athos, confirming or extending the monasteries' immunities (many becoming totally tax-free) and granting them many new estates. Thus the Greek population was able to continue living much as it had. The Serbian lands received their first public law code (*Zakonik*), which Dušan promulgated in an assembly in 1349. Further articles were decreed at a second council (1353/1354).

Kantakuzenos won Constantinople in February 1347, but Dušan took advantage of his various difficulties, including a plague epidemic, to annex Epiros and Thessaly in 1348. He assigned these newly conquered regions to relatives or commanders to administer: his brother-in-law John Komnenos Asen received most of Albania; his half brother Symeon received Epiros, and his general Preljub, Thessaly. In 1350 he attacked Bosnian Hum to try to recover it. Kantakuzenos took advantage of this to launch an attack to regain Thessaly. To support this effort, the Constantinopolitan patriarch excommunicated the new Serbian patriarch and emperor, accusing them of usurping titles, deposing Greek bishops for Serbs, and reassigning Greek bishoprics to the jurisdiction of the Serbian church. Dušan, giving up his Bosnian campaign, hurried back to repel the Byzantine invaders.

He soon began dreaming of conquering Constantinople and becoming *the* emperor. Realizing he needed a fleet, he tried to make arrangements with Venice; but Venice, fearing a decline in its position in the Levant if a strong Dušan obtained Constantinople, politely refused. After Dušan repelled a Hungarian attack in 1354, he died in December 1355 (aged about forty-seven), before arranging any plan against Constantinople.

Dušan is considered one of the greatest of medieval Balkan conquerors, for he doubled Serbia's size (winning the parts of Macedonia his predecessors had not conquered, Albania, Thessaly, Epiros, and the Chalcidic Peninsula). However, his strength should not be exaggerated. He acquired these lands during a Byzantine civil war when few troops could defend them, and he won cities entirely by sieges without a single open-field battle. He rose from a semi-puppet of his nobles to become their master; however, he never changed the structure of his state. He won the obedience of many nobles by offering them lands and booty from his campaigns. Those whose loyalty he thus won and his foreign mercenaries then provided the muscle to cow any who remained recalcitrant. But his failure to establish centralized institutions and his permitting the nobles to retain great authority in their counties meant that the basis for separatism remained. His empire disintegrated piecemeal during and after the reign of his son and successor, Uroš V (1356–1371).

At Dušan's death disintegration began. Certain Greek magnates revolted, liberating Kavalla and the coastal territory between the Struma and Mesta rivers. In the north, along the Danube's southern bank, the Rastislalići, supported by Hungary, seceded. By 1361, as Hungarian vassals, they held Braničevo. Dušan's half brother, Symeon, declared himself tsar, and, supported by John Komnenos Asen of Valona, moved against Zeta. However, having held a council in April 1357 declaring support for Uroš, the Serbian nobles repelled Symeon's attack. He never tried to take Serbia again; instead, he established by 1359 an independent principality in Thessaly and Epiros. There he founded the famous Meteora monasteries. John Komnenos Asen established his own independence in Albania. But while these southern conquests of Dušan seceded, the core of his state, including most of Macedonia and the Chalcidic Peninsula, held.

This core can be divided into three parts: the south (including part of Macedonia with Serres its capital), the central Serbian lands of Uroš, and the western territories, including Zeta. Under Uroš these western lands loosened their ties with the center. But since the leading nobles there usually expressed loyalty to Uroš, no legal separation occurred. The leading western nobles were Vojislav Vojinović, the strongest—holding lands along Zeta's borders between the Drina and the coast, including Gacko, Popovo Polje, Konavli, and Trebinje—and the Balšić brothers in Zeta. The latter started Uroš' reign with a small holding. By 1360, as a result of a marriage, supporting Uroš against Symeon, and perhaps land-grabbing, they had acquired much of the territory between Lake Skadar and the coast, including probably the port of Bar.

In 1361 these two leading nobles split. When Vojislav, supported by Uroš, attacked Dubrovnik, the Balšići defended Dubrovnik. Their ability to act independently illustrates the weakness of Uroš' control over his state. The war was indecisive, and Dubrovnik was spared further trouble when Vojislav died in September 1363. His lands went to his widow, who was soon attacked by Vojislav's nephew Nikola Altomanović.

The death of Vojislav, who, though active in his own interests, had remained loyal to Uroš, weakened Uroš' position and encouraged more separatist activity. Needing a new protector, Uroš decided, or was persuaded, to turn to Vukašin Mrnjavčević, a high courtier under Dušan and holder of considerable territory around Prilep. Having in 1364 crowned Vukašin "despot," Tsar Uroš in 1365 crowned him king, re-creating in theory the situation existing when Dušan was tsar and Uroš king. However, in fact Vukašin became the dominant figure. Scholars often depict Vukašin as a usurper. However, though Vukašin may have pressured Uroš into crowning him, at first Uroš' rights were respected; there are joint coins and joint wall paintings portraying Uroš in the senior position on the right. Moreover, since Uroš was weak, possibly even feeble-minded, he clearly needed support. The epics depict Vukašin as Uroš' *kum* (godfather). Though no contemporary source confirms this, it offers a plausible explanation for Uroš' action. One in trouble would naturally turn to his *kum*. Thus, quite possibly Vukašin's coronation was a mutually convenient act, executed voluntarily by Uroš. Though in time Vukašin came to act increasingly on his own—by the late 1360's he was issuing charters and carrying out diplomatic relations by himself—he never ousted Uroš. He may have planned to establish his own dynasty. He crowned his son Marko "young king." But, since Uroš was childless, a desire to secure Marko's succession need not have threatened Uroš' position. Only Orbini, a late author (1601), on the basis of an unknown source, suggests friction between them, stating that in 1368/1369 Uroš joined a coalition against Vukašin, causing his brief imprisonment by Vukašin. Vukašin, however, did take advantage of his position to expand his personal holdings much farther into Macedonia and Kosovo, acquiring Prizren and Skopje.

Meanwhile, the southern lands that Serbia retained, including the Greek lands, with Serres the leading city, went to Dušan's widow. Though she had become a nun, she continued an active political role. She never quarreled with Uroš; in fact, he frequently resided at her court, being recognized as Serres' overlord. His name appears first in her charters, though he probably had no actual authority there. In 1365 Vukašin's brother, John Uglješa, who had previously been active in Serres, was crowned despot. By 1366 he was de facto ruler of Serres. Uroš' name soon disappeared from official documents there, but no secession of Serres occurred, for Uglješa and Vukašin maintained close cooperation. Thus the core of Dušan's state remained united. And, as under Dušan, under Uglješa the Greek language and laws were used in Serres, and ethnic Greeks held major positions in church and state.

In this period, besides the military activity in the borderlands, skirmishes occurred inside Serbia, in particular as part of the struggle for Vojislav's former lands among his widow, his nephew Nikola Altomanović, Lazar Hrebeljanović, the Balšići, Vukašin, and Tvrtko I of Bosnia. An element in the varying alliances in this struggle was the resentment certain nobles felt against the Mrnjavčevići and the position they had achieved.

A more serious problem, however, was the appearance in Europe of the Ottoman Turks, followed by their expansion. In 1354 they acquired Gallipoli, on the European side of the Dardanelles. From there they, or Turkish tribes loyal to them, expanded into Thrace, acquiring Philippopolis (1363) and Adrianople (1369). They became a threat to Uglješa, who had pressed beyond Dušan's Mesta River border into the Rhodope Mountains. The borders here between his holdings and those of various Turkish groups were unclear, but the Turkish threat to the security of Serres was clear. Uglješa attempted to create a coalition against the Turks. To obtain Byzantine support, he tried to improve relations with the Byzantine church, which had excommunicated the Serbs in 1350. But when he felt ready for action in 1371, he had enrolled only his brother Vukašin. The leading Serbian nobles were independent enough to avoid having to participate, and either failed to realize the extent of the Turkish danger or feared to leave their regions lest hostile neighbors seize their lands.

Thus, Uglješa and Vukašin set out against the Turks alone. Their armies engaged the Turks at Černomen on the Marica River on 26 September 1371 and were annihilated. Both Vukašin and Uglješa were killed. The Battle of the Marica was the Ottomans' greatest success to that time, and far more significant in opening up the Balkans to the Turks and weakening Serbian resistance than the more famous Battle of Kosovo (1389). Owing to its vast losses at Marica and the increasing separatism that followed, Serbia became ripe for the picking. Uroš, who had not gone to the battle, died childless in December 1371, ending the Nemanjić dynasty on the male side. No subsequent ruler of Serbia bore the title tsar. (Lazar, though called tsar in the epics, actually was entitled prince.) Vukašin's son Marko, already young king, was crowned king after Vukašin's death; but, being neither from the recognized dynasty nor more powerful than other leading nobles, he could not assert his authority over Uroš' state. In fact, after Marica the Brankovići and Balšići seized part of Marko's family's holdings. Thus, since no figure of national unity existed, separatism increased, further reducing Serbian unity and potential resistance to the Turks, and causing the Serbs to lose further manpower in the warfare among the various nobles. The nobles, hostile to one another and involved in enriching themselves at the expense of their neighbors, were blind to the seriousness of the Ottoman danger and unwilling to cooperate against it.

After the Battle of the Marica, Uglješa's territory was lost: Manuel Palaiologos, the Byzantine governor of Thessaloniki, recovered Serres and the Chalcidic Peninsula, while the region between the Vardar and Struma rivers seceded under John and Constantine Dejanović of Kumanovo. Vukašin's state also broke up. His son Marko retained part of Macedonia, including Prilep, and part of the Kosovo region. The Balšići in Zeta and the Brankovići in western Macedonia (with Ohrid) made themselves independent. The lands north of the West Morava River seceded under Lazar Hrebeljanović (residing in Kruševac), and Nikola Altomanović—who was coining his own money prior to Marica—remained independent at Rudnik. Beyond the separatism and weakening of Serbian resistance following the battle, Marica led to Byzantium's, Bulgaria's, Marko's, and the Dejanovići's accepting Ottoman suzerainty by 1373.

After Marica the Balšići of Zeta expanded to the east, where they clashed with the Brankovići; they also continued fighting in Albania against the Topia family. Lazar allied himself with Tvrtko I of Bosnia against Altomanović, whom they eliminated, dividing his lands. Tvrtko obtained his western lands, the Upper Drina, the Lim region, and Prijepolje (including Mileševo, with Sava's relics). The Balšići grabbed some of Altomanović's territory near the coast. Tvrtko acquired these coastal lands in 1377, after various local nobles revolted against the Balšići and submitted to Tvrtko. In 1377 Tvrtko, descended from Nemanja through his mother (Dragutin's daughter), was crowned king of Serbia and Bosnia, his kingship rights being derived from Serbia's. But he never obtained a role in Serbia and no Serbian nobleman outside Tvrtko's realm regarded him as overlord.

Lazar took Altomanović's eastern lands, including Užice and the mining town of Rudnik. Since he also held Novo Brdo, which he probably had seized after Marica, Lazar held the richest mines in Serbia, giving him wealth and contributing to his rapid rise to become the major lord in Serbia. His becoming a Hungarian vassal during his war with Altomanović probably helped his subsequent campaigns to the north that brought him to the Danube. In 1379 he defeated the Rastislalići and acquired their holdings, including Braničevo. Then, stronger, when King Louis I of Hungary died in 1382, he shed his vassalage. Lazar also benefited because his territory lay farthest from Turkish centers, sparing his lands their ravages in the early years and also attracting to his region immigrants from Turkish-threatened areas.

Lazar built churches (including the Ravanica Monastery), granted the church much land, and helped spread Christianity in the northern regions, where, except for certain towns on the Danube, little evidence of earlier Christian penetration exists. In 1375 he made peace with the Constantinopolitan patriarch by renouncing the right of the Serbs to hold the tsarist title and received Byzantine recognition for the Serbian patriarch's title. With this recognition, church peace, and other services to the church, the church strongly supported Lazar, giving him in about 1378 a church coronation as prince. He entitled himself "Lord of the Serbs and the Danube, Stefan [the Serbian royal name] Prince Lazar, Autocrat of All Serbs." Until the late 1380's Lazar maintained close ties with Vuk Branković, who had married his daughter and recognized Lazar as his suzerain. Relations between them cooled somewhat after 1386/1387, when Lazar married a second daughter to George II Balšić, a rival of Vuk's. This probably explains why Vuk dropped Lazar's name from his coins at this time. In 1387, right after the Balšić marriage, Lazar added "and the Coast" to his title and Balšić recognized Lazar as his suzerain.

In the mid 1380's the Turks began raiding Lazar's region. In 1386 they took Niš, and possibly forced Lazar to accept their suzerainty. In 1388 a Turkish raiding party penetrated into Hum, but at Bileća it was wiped out by Vlatko Vuković's forces. In 1388 Lazar, if he had accepted vassalage in 1386, repudiated it; otherwise he refused an initial Turkish demand that he accept their suzerainty. His repudiation or refusal caused the Turks to invade Serbia. Lazar headed a coalition, including Vuk Branković and a Bosnian contingent under Vlatko Vuković. The two armies met on Kosovo Polje 28 June 1389. Lazar and Sultan Murad I were killed, and both armies took heavy losses. The Turks' losses were so extensive they could not continue their campaign; their remnants returned east so the new sultan, Bāyazīd I, could secure his throne. Thus the battle was a draw—in fact, the Bosnians announced it was a Christian victory—but its long-range effects were a Turkish victory; for the Serbs, in losing a large number of the roughly 15,000 soldiers they had amassed, had lost a large percentage of their overall manpower, whereas the Turks had many more troops in the east who returned in the following years to face little serious Serbian opposition.

Vuk Branković, though depicted in the epics as a traitor, in fact fought well. Lazar's state was left to his widow, Milica, and minor son, Stefan Lazarević. The Hungarians took advantage of Milica's difficulties to attack in November. Faced with this threat, Milica accepted Ottoman suzerainty. Vuk Branković also tried to take advantage of Milica's weakness and allied with the Hungarians. The church supported Milica. However, Vuk's independence was soon eliminated by the Turks. In January 1392 they took his town of Skopje. Soon Vuk too had to accept vassal obligations. These are documented from a November 1392 charter but surely they date from earlier that year. Thus, by the end of 1392 all the Serbian lands except Zeta under the Balšići—most of which within a year also accepted Ottoman suzerainty—and Hum under Tvrtko had become tributary to the Ottomans. However, the quarrel between Vuk and Milica, though short-lasting and insignificant—no battle was fought between them—seems to have caused a campaign of slander against Vuk that affected the epics and eventually the written historical tradition. Orbini's *History of the Slavs* (1601) claims Vuk betrayed Lazar at Kosovo. Since the early epics do too, most scholars believe Orbini's source was oral. No earlier written source accuses Vuk. One can conclude that Vuk became a scapegoat because after Kosovo he opposed the sainted Lazar's widow, while Lazar, canonized by the Serbian church in the 1390's, became the hero of the Kosovo epics, whose contents were made to parallel the New Testament, with Vuk cast in the role of Judas.

The Serbian vassal states owed the sultan tribute and soldiers who were to be led by the vassal lord in person. Bulgaria fell to the Turks in 1393. In 1395 the Ottomans attacked Walachia. At the Battle of Rovine, on the Turkish side against the Vlachs were Marko Kraljević ("the king's son," as the epics call him) and Constantine Dejanović, both of whom were killed. After their deaths, the Turks annexed their lands. Despite this role that history forced upon him, Marko became the greatest Serbian opponent of the Turks in the epics. In 1398 the

Turks, angry at Vuk Branković for allying with Venice and possibly for his absence from the Wallachian campaign, drove him from his lands. Accounts of his fate differ, though he seems not to have lived long thereafter; his widow and sons retained only a small portion of his Macedonian lands, while Stefan Lazarević, a loyal Ottoman vassal, acquired most of his Kosovo-area holdings. Stefan was by far the strongest Serbian lord. His loyalty, gaining him the sultan's support, enabled him to expand his lands and acquire greater control over the remaining, much-weakened Serbian nobles. Stefan led effective Serbian units in the Ottoman armies at Rovine (1395), Nicopolis (1396), and Ankara (1402).

THE FIFTEENTH CENTURY

After Timur (Tamerlane) defeated and captured Bāyazīd I at Ankara (1402), Stefan shed his vassalage. He visited Constantinople en route home. The emperor granted him the title despot, which was held thereafter by all Serbia's rulers. Opposed by his nephew George Branković, the son of Vuk and Stefan's sister, and having tense relations with Bāyazīd's son Suleyman, who controlled Ottoman Europe in the Ottoman civil war that followed the Ankara defeat, Stefan became a vassal of Hungary's King Sigismund, who awarded Stefan the Mačva banate and Beograd for life. He refortified Beograd and made it his capital, making it for the first time a Serbian capital. Sigismund in 1411 awarded to Stefan the rich mining town of Srebrnica, on the Bosnian side of the Drina, which Sigismund had recently conquered. This town was to be a frequent source of conflict between Bosnia and Serbia for the next fifty years, weakening both to the Ottomans' advantage. Both needed the income from its mine, particularly later, when both again faced Ottoman tribute demands. Stefan established good relations with Sultan Mehmed I, who triumphed in the Ottoman civil war in 1413. In 1421 Balša Balšić of Zeta died without sons, leaving his lands to Stefan. Owing to Venetian action, however, Stefan, obtained only part of Zeta. But he did acquire Bar and Budva. In 1426 a council at Srebrnica declared that because Stefan had no sons, his nephew George Branković was to be his heir. Stefan died in July 1427.

Besides his political role, Stefan was active culturally. He built several monasteries (including Manasija). During his reign Serbia enjoyed a literary revival consisting of both translations from the Greek and original works, spurred on by various Bulgarian and Greek émigrés who fled their homelands after Ottoman occupation. Stefan was both a participant in and a patron of literature. That Marko and the Brankovići were rivals of Lazar's dynasty, and that the literary figures who produced the surviving chronicles were affiliated with Stefan's court, probably explain the chronicle tradition's slighting Marko's and the Brankovići's careers. The literati's and the church's support of Lazar's dynasty in building Lazar's cult also created the tradition making Kosovo more significant than Marica.

George (Djuradj) Branković succeeded in 1427. He retained vassal ties to Hungary and received the title despot from Byzantium. Beograd, according to prior agreement, reverted to Hungary. In 1428 the Ottomans launched a major attack against him, taking Niš and Kruševac. Branković had to accept Ottoman suzerainty. He erected the great fortress of Smederevo at the junction of the Morava and the Danube; it became Serbia's last capital. Many Greeks, associates of George's Greek wife, Irina (Serbian: Jerina) Kantakuzena, and her brother, Thomas, who also lived at court, came thither and had considerable impact on Serbian court life and culture. In 1439 the Ottomans took Smederevo. When Novo Brdo fell in 1441, Branković fled to Hungary; Serbia, annexed by the Ottomans, disappeared as a state.

In 1443 the papacy mobilized a crusade led by János Hunyadi. Branković participated, leading an army of Serbian exiles. The crusaders drove the Ottomans (that is, garrison troops) from Serbia, which reappeared as a state under Branković. Murad II, by treaty in 1444, recognized Serbia's independence. When the crusaders broke their treaty and continued the war later in 1444, Branković, who had the most to lose, refused to participate; indeed, it seems he warned the Turks of the forthcoming attack, which Murad and the main Ottoman army annihilated at Varna in November 1444. Branković then reaffirmed his status as an Ottoman vassal, remaining on good terms with the sultan at the expense of bad relations with the Hungarians, whose attempts to send armies through Serbia to engage the Turks were resisted. In fact, after Hunyadi was defeated by the Ottomans at Kosovo in 1448, Branković seized him on his way home and briefly held him for ransom.

The Ottomans launched a major assault against Serbia in 1455. Southern Serbia (the Kosovo region and Novo Brdo) fell. Branković retained only the territory north of the West Morava River. In 1456, in the midst of a second Ottoman campaign against Serbia and Hungarian-held Beograd, Branković died. His heir, his son, Lazar, died two years later. Lazar's daughter then married Stefan Tomašević, son of the king of Bosnia, who received the title despot and the last remaining Serbian fortress, Smederevo, as her dowry. In 1459 the Ottomans took Smederevo and Serbia again disappeared as a state. This time Ottoman control was to last until the nineteenth century.

BIBLIOGRAPHY

Mihailo J. Dinić, *Srpske zemlje u srednjem veku* (1978); John V. A. Fine, Jr., *The Early Medieval Balkans* (1983), and *The Late Medieval Balkans* (1987); *Istorija srpskog naroda* [Dragoslav Srejović *et al.*, eds.], I–II (1981, 1982), publ. by Srpska književna zadruga, Beograd; Josef Konstantin Jireček, *Istorija Srba*, 2 vols., trans. and rev. by Jovan Radonić (1952); Rade Mihaljčić, *Kraj srpskog carstva* (1975); Evgenii P. Naumov, *Gospodstvuyushchii klass i gosudarstvennaya vlast v Serbii XIII–XV vv.* (1975).

JOHN V. A. FINE, JR.

[See also **Adrianople; Avars; Bayazīd I, Yildirim; Boris; Bosnia; Bulgaria; Byzantine Empire: History; Croatia; Dyrrachium; Epiros, Despotate of; Heraklios; Hungary; Hunyadi, János; John VI Kantakouzenos; Lazar Hrebeljanović; Macedonians; Manuel I Komnenos; Marica River; Maurice, Emperor; Murad I; Murad II; Ochrid; Ottomans; Philippopolis; Pronoia; Samuil of Bulgaria; Sava, St.; Slavic Languages and Literature; Slavs; Stefan Lazarević; Stefan Nemanja; Stefan Prvovenčani; Stefan Tomašević; Stefan Uroš IV Dušan; Stefan Uroš II Milutin; Symeon of Bulgaria; Tvrtko I.**]

SERBIAN ART AND ARCHITECTURE. Serbia, an independent state between the twelfth and fifteenth centuries, occupies the central portion of the Balkan Peninsula. The Serbs, a pagan Slavic tribe, moved into the general area during the Slavic migrations of the sixth century, disrupting the existing urban civilization. Once settled, the Serbs were Christianized, eventually becoming Orthodox (in the hinterlands) and Catholic (along the Adriatic coast). The religious division reinforced the centuries-old cultural divide found in this area.

THE BEGINNINGS

The emergence of architectural and artistic production among the Serbs was slow to appear, and can be safely associated only with the period after the conversion to Christianity. The oldest known building of this period is the church of St. Peter at Ras (near Novi Pazar), generally thought to date from the tenth century. Built of rough stone, the church features an unusual centralized plan surmounted by a dome elevated on a tall drum and supported by squinches. Externally, it displays a modest repertoire of crudely executed corbeled table friezes that link it to the pre-Romanesque church architecture which flourished along the Adriatic littoral between the ninth and eleventh centuries. The best-preserved example of that architecture is the church of St. Michael near Ston, dating probably from 1077–1081. In the hinterlands of Serbia, this architectural genre is represented by the church of St. Peter at Bijelo Polje, probably built in the eleventh century and enlarged by the addition of two giant Romanesque bell towers, one of which survives.

TWELFTH CENTURY

The establishment of Serbia's political independence under Stefan Nemanja (1166/1168–1196) signaled the beginning of monumental church architecture in Serbia. Three major churches from this period survive: the church of St. Nicholas at Kuršumlija (before 1170); St. George, better known as Djurdjevi stupovi (Towers of St. George), near Novi Pazar (1170–1171); and the church of the Virgin at Studenica Monastery (begun about 1183; frescoed about 1208/1209). The three churches, though clearly related in their plans and spatial articulation, are quite different in execution. The church of St. Nicholas was built by Byzantine builders (probably before Nemanja) in a manner typical of twelfth-century Constantinopolitan architecture. Its twin-tower west facade with a large, open, barrel-vaulted porch between the towers was probably built by Nemanja, and may have been inspired by the roughly contemporary cathedral of Kotor. The next church to be built by Nemanja—Djurdjevi stupovi—took into account both the Byzantine plan of St. Nicholas and its Romanesque twin-tower facade. The crude execution of the building suggests that it was the work of local artisans. Especially revealing is the lopsided dome, which, though conceptually Byzantine, is the antithesis of typical Byzantine domes in terms of its execution.

The church of the Virgin at Studenica, built as

Nemanja's mausoleum, though related in plan, differs from its two predecessors in building technique, revealing the presence of yet another group of builders in Serbia at that time. The main part of the church was executed by highly skilled craftsmen trained in a Romanesque workshop of some coastal city (possibly Kotor). Its architectural details and decorative sculpture display the highest level of quality, comparable with the best Romanesque works of southern Italy, to which it is closely related. The dome of Studenica, on the other hand, is a genuine Byzantine work. Its large size, low twelve-sided drum, and interior scalloping suggest that its builders may have come from Constantinople.

An entirely different situation is evident in the realm of monumental painting of this period. While Romanesque painting flourished along the Adriatic coast (for instance, St. Michael near Ston), Byzantine painting appears to have predominated in the hinterlands. The best example of twelfth-century Byzantine painting in Serbia is the church of Djurdjevi stupovi. What is known of its monumental fresco program reveals that it was carefully integrated into the architectural framework and that its stylistic mannerisms generally coincided with those of other known Byzantine works of the second half of the twelfth century. Figures were elongated and at times distorted; movements were agitated and expressed through linear highlighting of hair and drapery against a background of generally somber colors. The frescoes of Djurdjevi stupovi belong to the mainstream of so-called Komnenian painting, a style widespread in the twelfth century from Russia to Bulgaria, Palestine, and Italy.

Architectural links with the Adriatic littoral continued throughout this period, with the flow of influences proceeding in both directions. While Romanesque architecture left a lasting imprint in the hinterlands, church architecture of the coast echoed certain Byzantine characteristics. Most notable among these is the dome, which dominates the interior as well as the exterior of these buildings. The most significant monuments of this group are the church of the Virgin in a monastery of the same name on the island of Mljet (second half of the twelfth century), St. Luke (1195) and St. Mary (1221) in Kotor, and the church of Sts. Sergius and Bacchus at Podi (date unknown), which illustrate the proliferation of "Romano-Byzantine" church architecture along the Adriatic coast.

THIRTEENTH CENTURY

Serbia's independence was consolidated after the death of Byzantine Emperor Manuel I Komnenos (1180). Internal difficulties that subsequently plagued the empire and eventually led to the fall of Constantinople to the Latins in 1204 benefited the young Serbian state. The years 1217 and 1219 witnessed the proclamation of the kingdom and the establishment of the independent Serbian Orthodox Church, respectively. Favorable external circumstances, combined with rapid economic growth largely owing to the development of gold and silver mines, fostered a steady expansion of Serbia throughout the thirteenth and the first half of the fourteenth century.

Serbian architecture and art of the thirteenth century display a curious parting of the ways. Architecture remained largely conservative and in the hands of local builders. Painting, on the other hand, was inundated with Byzantine artists, generally assumed to have fled from Constantinople and other important Byzantine centers under Latin control.

Church planning, in a most general sense, continued along the lines established during Nemanja's reign, although the size of church domes was substantially reduced and the lateral porches replaced by low transept wings (possibly under the influence of Mt. Athos). The building technique, revealing virtually exclusive use of stone and crude detailing, shows no signs of change compared with such older local works as the church of St. Peter at Ras. Throughout the thirteenth century Serbian architecture remained remarkably free of any Byzantine influence. The best examples of Serbian architecture of this period are the churches of Žiča (1207–1215), the Holy Apostles at Peć (1225–1260), Mileševa (1222–1228), Sopoćani (after 1260), Gradac (*ca.* 1275), and Arilje (1296). All reveal a stubborn adherence to earlier conventions in which the rigors of Romanesque architecture were never fully understood.

Quite a different picture is presented by Serbian painting of this period. Unlike architecture, which was characterized by provincial conservatism, Serbian painting was distinguished by the highest level of quality and was strictly Byzantine in character. It is generally believed that during the Latin occupation of Constantinople, the best Byzantine painters were employed by the Serbian kings. Regardless of the specific ethnic backgrounds of these painters, which we may never know, it is safe to say that to understand the mainstream of Byzantine monu-

Sopoćani Monastery, after 1260. YUGOSLAV PRESS AND CULTURAL CENTER, NEW YORK

The Crucifixion. Fresco in the church of the Virgin, Studenica, 1209. YUGOSLAV PRESS AND CULTURAL CENTER, NEW YORK

mental painting of the thirteenth century, one must turn to Serbian painting of this period first. The presence of Greek painters in Serbia, occasionally mentioned in written sources, was no doubt a crucial element in the development of Serbian painting. Yet the strong regional input must not be overlooked. The appearance of national saints, rulers' portraits, and iconographic themes with specific local flavor attest to major modifications stemming from the roles played by local patrons and artists alike.

From the very beginning of the thirteenth century, painting in Serbia was marked by a break with the highly mannered style of late Komnenian painting. A new sense of monumentality emerged in the compositional structure and in the handling of individual figures. These characteristics are abundantly evident in the surviving frescoes in the church of the Virgin at Studenica. The grand Crucifixion on the west wall of the naos stands as one of the masterpieces of Byzantine art while displaying certain traits of Italian dugento painting. More emphatically Byzantine are the frescoes of Mileševa, painted sometime between 1222 and 1228. They are distinguished by a greater sense of plasticity and by the fact that they were mostly painted on yellow backgrounds. In some of the frescoes, scored gold leaf was applied to this background, emulating mosaic. The frescoes of the church of the Holy Apostles at Peć share certain iconographic archaisms with Mileševa, but are distinguished from them in style and character. The church, intended to be the mausoleum of Serbian archbishops, is dominated by a large Deesis in the main apse, an unusual subject for such a location but understandable in the context of the building's intended function. Links with Palestine through the first Serbian archbishop, Sava I, have been suggested.

The high point of thirteenth-century Serbian

painting was reached with the frescoes of Sopoćani. The masters of Sopoćani carried on the tradition initiated by the painters of Mileševa, but they exceeded the achievements of the latter on several levels. The monumentality and classical spirit of the Sopoćani frescoes have no parallels in either Byzantine or Western art of the period, though the artist(s) who painted them undoubtedly came from a major Byzantine workshop. Sopočani frescoes, most notably the Dormition of the Virgin on the west wall of the naos, are large in size and monumental in content. They are inhabited by figures carefully balanced against a background of credible architecture. The figures display a volumetric fullness going beyond that of Mileševa frescoes. This quality was extended into the handling of draperies, which ceased to be decorative surface patterns and acquired a three-dimensionality of their own.

The decades immediately following the reconquest of Constantinople by the Byzantines in 1261 were marked by the emergence of a new style referred to as Palaiologan art. Eventually this new art took root in Serbia, reaching its apogee there during the second decade of the fourteenth century.

FOURTEENTH CENTURY

Political turmoil in Serbia during the last quarter of the thirteenth century was partially settled by King Milutin after his marriage to Simonis (Serbian: Simonida), the youngest daughter of the Byzantine emperor Andronikos II in 1299. As dowry, the Serbian king acquired Byzantine territories that he had previously conquered. Having gained the upper hand in Balkan politics, Milutin began to challenge the Byzantine emperor in more subtle ways. He started a cultural "byzantinization" of Serbia, which soon yielded startling results. Economically stronger than the Byzantine emperor, Milutin initiated a vast building program extending well beyond the frontiers of his state—Jerusalem, Constantinople, Thessaloniki, Mt. Athos—and employing numerous builders and artists. His demand far outpaced Serbia's supply of such craftsmen, resulting in the influx of Byzantine builders and painters. Within a decade Serbia assumed the leading role in Byzantine architecture and painting.

Serbian architecture after 1300 reveals that Milutin had acquired the best Byzantine builders from the main centers of the time—Constantinople, Thessaloniki, and Arta. The main church of the Serbian monastery of Hilandar (Chilandari) on Mt. Athos, rebuilt in 1303, displays unmistakable links with the architecture of Constantinople. The churches of the Virgin of Ljeviša in Prizren (1307–1309) and of St. George at Staro Nagoričino (1312–1313), on the other hand, are more akin to those of Arta and its environs. Finally, the church of the Gračanica Monastery (begun probably in 1311–1312) displays links with Thessaloniki but moves beyond any of the contemporary achievements in that city.

Serbian painting of this period, much like architecture, was in the mainstream of Byzantine development, for a while representing its best. Recognizing the role of King Milutin as a major patron of art, modern scholars have labeled his contribution "the King Milutin school," but the term is no better suited to painting than it would be to Serbian architecture of this period. The sheer quantity of what was painted within a decade suggests that a substantial number of painters must have been in the service of King Milutin. In the churches of the Virgin of Ljeviša at Prizren (*ca.* 1310–1313) and St. Nichetas at Čučer, near Skopje (before 1316), the King's Church at Studenica (1314), and the churches at Staro Nagoričino (1313–1318), Hilandar (finished *ca.* 1318–1320), and Gračanica (finished *ca.* 1320) are preserved extensive fresco programs that reveal the character of this art with considerable clarity. This art differs from that of the preceding century. Large-scale compositions gave way to small-scale, combined with a relative increase in the number of figures. New cycles were introduced with almost encyclopedic compulsion. Classicism became confined to isolated, often misunderstood details. Political propaganda became an important component of church art of this period. Glorification of the king, the royal dynasty, and its saintly ancestry replaced the humbler royal and monastic processions of the previous century.

The church of St. Stephen at Banjska Monastery, built as the king's mausoleum (*ca.* 1312–1313), stands out as a unique achievement among King Milutin's churches. Built in the Romanesque style, it was deliberately modeled after Studenica (Nemanja's mausoleum church), as we are told by Milutin's biographer, Danilo. The choice was colored by political considerations. The builders were brought from Pomorje, on the Adriatic littoral. Pomorje was given particular attention by King Milutin with the help of his mother, Dowager Queen Jelena (Helena), whose Catholic background and ties made her particularly suitable as a regent for the area. Jelena, occasionally with Milutin, patronized Catholic monasteries within her domain

Christ turning water into wine. Fresco in the church of the Holy Savior, Dečani Monastery, 1335–1350. YUGOSLAV PRESS AND CULTURAL CENTER, NEW YORK

and sent generous gifts to churches on the other side of the Adriatic (for instance, St. Nicholas in Bari).

Architectural and artistic links with the coast continued under King Milutin's successors. His son, Stefan Dečanski, appointed a Franciscan monk, Vita of Kotor, as the master builder of his mausoleum church at Dečani Monastery (1327–1335). The large domed building perpetuated the established tradition of royal mausoleums. In part this continued under Stefan Dušan, whose mausoleum church of the Holy Archangels near Prizren (1343–1349; destroyed) was erected by coastal builders but was distinguished by its Byzantine five-domed silhouette. The reign of Dušan, who proclaimed himself emperor of the Serbs and the Greeks (1346), marked the apogee of the Serbian medieval state. Territorially expanded and economically strong, Serbia became the most immediate threat to the weakened Byzantine Empire. The real beneficiaries of this confrontation ultimately proved to be the Turks, whose role in Balkan affairs during the second half of the fourteenth century became major.

Few churches of this period could be strictly labeled Byzantine, despite the strong Byzantine influence on Serbian architecture. A new blend of Byzantine and Romanesque architecture dominated the scene, as may be observed in a number of churches in the vicinity of Dušan's capital, Skoplje: for instance, Matejić (*ca.* 1350) and Markov Manastir (begun *ca.* 1346–1347).

The principal monument of Serbian painting from the reign of Stefan Dušan is Dečani. The painting of its twenty major cycles, hundreds of compositions, and thousands of figures took fifteen years to complete (1335–1348) and was accomplished by scores of artists distinguished by their skills as well as background. The frescoes of Lesnovo (*ca.* 1346, and 1349) illustrate both subtle theological concepts and political propaganda for Dušan's empire. The traditional Byzantine linking of the church and the state in the common sacred mission is illustrated here with singular eloquence.

LAST PHASE

The last important phase of Serbian medieval art began about 1371 and continued until 1459 (the final fall of Serbia to the Turks). Territorially shrunken, Serbia changed its political and cultural configuration. Architectural and artistic activity flourished in its northern parts, within the plain of the Morava River and its tributaries (hence the term "Morava school," commonly employed in scholarly literature). Despite the increasing Turkish pressure, this period was characterized by a large volume of construction ranging from new fortified

Ravanica Monastery, 1375–1377. ART RESOURCE

towns—Kruševac, Stalać, Golubac, and above all Smederevo, the last capital of medieval Serbia—to large fortified monasteries—Ravanica, Manasija—and scores of churches. By that time Serbia had become the last Orthodox Christian state in the Balkans that had not been overrun by the Turks, and thus the last haven in which artistic production continued to flourish.

The churches of Lazarica at Kruševac (after 1370–1371) and Ravanica (1375–1377) illustrate the beginning of a new trend in architecture. In addition to revealing a blend of Byzantine and Romanesque characteristics in a unique, national style, these churches also demonstrate that the influence of Mt. Athos, particularly in planning, had become strong. One of the hallmarks of this architecture is its exuberant exterior decoration, including large amounts of relief sculpture. Links with Armenia and Georgia have been explored, as have those with late Gothic developments in Italy, particularly Venice. The later churches, such as Kalenić (1407) and Manasija (1407–1418), illustrate the perpetuation of this trend, as well as the survival of the centuries-old local building tradition that maintained affinities with Romanesque architecture of the Adriatic littoral (Manasija).

Serbian painting of this period is also characterized by a new stylistic development: Ravanica (1377–1387), Kalenić (*ca.* 1413), and Manasija (1406–1418). The new style is distinguished from the preceding on almost all levels. Compositions became bigger and less confusing in spatial terms; figures regained the sense of plasticity rendered in a realistic mode; and colors became brighter and richer. The art of this era was distinguished by poignancy and elegance. This brief and intense flash of artistic greatness was brought to an abrupt end by the Turkish conquest in 1459. Although the medieval tradition came to a halt at that time, it should be noted that much of the artistic production in Serbia under the Turkish occupation, and as late as the eighteenth century, continued to display a strong conservative adherence to the medieval heritage.

BIBLIOGRAPHY

Gordana Babić, V. Korać, and S. Ćirković, *Studenica* (1986); Dimitrije Bogdanović, V. J. Djurić, and D. Medaković, *Chilandar* (1978); Milka Čanak-Medić and Dj. Bošković, *L'architecture de l'époque de Nemanja,* I (1986); Slobodan Ćurčić, *Gračanica: King Milutin's Church . . .* (1979) and *Art and Architecture in the Balkans: An Annotated Bibliography* (1984); Aleksandar Deroko, *Srednjevekovni gradovi u Srbiji* (1950), and *Monumentalna i dekorativna arhitektura u srednjevekovnoj Srbiji* (1953, 3rd ed. 1985); Vojislav J. Djurić, *Icônes de Yougoslavie* (1961), an exhibition catalog, *Sopoćani* (1967), in German, and *Byzantinische Fresken in Jugoslawien* (1976); Horst Hallensleben, *Die Malerschule des Königs Milutin* (1963); Richard H. L. Hamman-MacLean, *Die Monumentalmalerei in Serbien und Makedonien von 11. bis zum frühen 14. Jahrhundert,* 2 vols. (1963–1976); Vojislav Korać, *Graditeljska škola Pomorja* (1965); Jovanka Maksimović, *Srpska srednjovekovna skulptura* (1971), and *Srpske srednjovekovne minijature* (1983); Pavle Mijović and Mirko Kovačević, *Gradovi i utvrdjenja u Crnoj Gori* (1975); Gabriel Millet, *L'ancien art serbe. Les églises* (1919); Gabriel Millet and A. Frolow, *La peinture du moyen âge en Yougoslavie,* 4 vols. (1954–1969); André Mohorovičić, ed., *Enciklopedija likovnih umjetnosti,* 4 vols. (1959–1966), for basic information on individual monuments; Milorad Panić-Surep, *Yugoslavia: Cultural Monuments of Serbia,* Madge Phillips-Tomašević, trans. (1965); Vladimir R. Petković, *La peinture serbe du moyen âge,* II (1934), and *Pregled crkvenih spomenika kroz povesnicu srpskog naroda* (1950); Svetozar Radojčić, *Portreti srpskih vladara u srednjem veku* (1934), *Staro srpsko slikarstvo* (1966), and *Geschichte der serbischen Kunst* (1969); Bojana Radojković, ed., *Istorija primenjene umetnosti kod Srba,* I (1977).

SLOBODAN ĆURČIĆ

[See also **Byzantine Art; Byzantine History; Early Christian and Byzantine Architecture; Stefan Nemanja; Stefan Uroš IV Dušan; Stefan Uroš II Milutin; Vita of Kotor.**]

SERDĀB (Persian, "cold water"), a vaulted underground area intended to provide a refuge from the summer's heat. Such subterranean chambers are especially common in Iraq and Iran, in both palace and domestic architecture, as, for example, in the ninth-century buildings at Samarra. Ground-level windows or a kind of chimney facing the north provide ventilation.

BIBLIOGRAPHY

Keppel A. C. Creswell, *Early Muslim Architecture,* 2nd ed., II (1969), 81–82; George Michell, ed., *Architecture of the Islamic World* (1978), 202.

LINDA KOMAROFF

[See also **Islamic Art and Architecture.**]

SERDICA (Sardica, modern Sofia), an important Balkan city (42° 41′ north, 23° 19′ east) that occupied a strategic position on the routes to Constantinople, Belgrade, Macedonia, and the Danube. In 343 a church council was held at Serdica in an effort to reconcile the conflict between Arian and Nicene views. It was a favorite residence of the emperor Constantine the Great. Burned by the Huns in 447, captured by the Slavs and Avars during their invasions of the Balkans in the early seventh century, Serdica became an important border fortress against the Bulgars when the Byzantines recaptured it. In 809, the Bulgar chief Krum took the city, destroyed the fortress, and massacred the garrison. In 986 the Byzantine emperor Basil II failed in an effort to retake it, but at the beginning of the eleventh century he succeeded, and it again became a Byzantine border fortress. Subsequent emperors settled Pechenegs and Serbians around Serdica. The Turks captured the city in 1382, and it remained Turkish except for a brief Hungarian occupation in 1443.

BIBLIOGRAPHY

John V. A. Fine, Jr., *The Early Medieval Balkans* (1983); Petur D. Peev, Spas Muleshkov, and K. Marinov, *Sofia* (1965); George Ostrogorsky, *History of the Byzantine State,* Joan Hussey, trans. (1956, rev. ed. 1969).

LINDA C. ROSE

[See also **Avars; Bulgaria; Constantine I, the Great; Huns; Krum; Slavs.**]

SERDICA, COUNCIL OF. In 342/343 coemperors Constans I (Western, sympathetic to the Nicene party) and Constantius II (Eastern, sympathetic to the Arians) convened a council in Serdica (modern Sofia) in a vain effort to resolve the doctrinal and disciplinary issues dividing their churches. The Eastern bishops objected to the seating of Athanasius of Alexandria, who had been deposed at Tyre in 335, and withdrew. The Westerners, under the presidency of Hosius of Córdoba, then excommunicated the leading Eastern bishops and proceeded to confirm the restoration of Athanasius and to acquit Marcellus of Ancyra of heresy. The council also enacted twenty-one disciplinary canons, of which canons 3, 4, and 5, establishing the bishop of Rome as a court of appeal in certain instances, are of particular significance for subsequent ecclesiastical developments.

BIBLIOGRAPHY

Sources. Giovanni D. Mansi, *Sacrorum conciliorum collectio,* III (1759), 1–140; Cuthbert H. Turner, *Ecclesiae Occidentalis Monumenta iuris antiquissima,* I (1930).

Studies. Hamilton Hess, *The Canons of the Council of Sardica, A.D. 343* (1958); W. Schneemelcher, "Sardika," in *Lexikon für Theologie und Kirche,* IX (1964).

JOHN H. ERICKSON

[See also **Arians; Athanasius of Alexandria, St.**]

ŞEREFE, the external gallery surrounding the upper part of a minaret, placed about two-thirds toward the finial of the shaft. An internal staircase provides the access to the *şerefe.* The muezzin calls the faithful to communal prayers from the *şerefe.* The *şerefe* itself, and its console or brackets, are traditionally the area of a Turkish minaret where decorative elements occur.

ÜLKÜ Ü. BATES

[See also **Minaret; Muezzin.**]

SERFS AND SERFDOM: RUSSIAN. The origins and evolution of serfdom in Russia have long been among the most disputed topics of Russian historiography. The debate began in the nineteenth century and still continues as new hypotheses are advanced and old ones discarded. In prerevolutionary times two competing theses emerged. The first, called the "decree" interpretation, held that the Russian peasant had been a freeman until a ukase of the tsar enserfed him. That decree was never found but the decree school surmised that it was promulgated around 1592. In the second half of the nineteenth century a "nondecree" interpretation appeared. Its adherents denied that the state had the initiating role. The explanations they advanced included the theory that serfdom established itself through the long-term residence of peasants on a given manor, that it rose out of the indebtedness of peasants to their seigniors, and that it grew out of the use of tax rolls by landlords to bring back peasants who had run away from their estates. Further study and new archival finds have discredited or at least diminished the significance of these factors. Soviet historians have turned their attentions to the social and economic origins of the enserfment and view it as the final step in a long process that began centuries before in the Kievan era. Their contributions have provided valuable information about the early history of the Russian peasantry and have shown that the roots of the enserfment reach far back into Russian history.

During the Kievan period (ninth through thirteenth centuries) the status of many peasants declined when large-scale private landownership began to develop. Land that had belonged to independent peasant communes was absorbed into estates owned by princes and by church and lay lords, and the peasants were reduced to renters or landless laborers. As time went on a distinction began to be drawn between these peasants and those who still lived in their own free communes, with the former considered to be of an inferior and dependent status although they had not lost their personal freedom. There were two other groups in Kievan rural society who had lost their freedom: slaves and indentured laborers. The indentured laborers were borrowers who were held in debt servitude until they had paid back their loans.

MONGOL DOMINATION

The Kievan federation, weakened by nomad invasions, internal strife, declining trade, and the dwindling prestige of Kiev itself, was unable to survive the onslaught of the Mongols who rode into Russia in 1237 and in a few short years swept all before them. Many who lived in the Dnieper basin migrated to the northeast, to Suzdal, the forested colonial land that lay between the Oka and upper Volga rivers and was to become the heartland of Russian national life. The decline of the Kievan federation and the colonization of the northeast reversed the trend toward deterioration in the status of the peasantry. The princes who ruled in the northeast needed settlers to clear the forests and to expand the ill-defined frontiers of their princedoms. The need was intensified by calamities that nearly overwhelmed them. The Mongols demanded heavy tribute and all too frequently invaded in force. There were scores of wars with neighboring peoples, almost ceaseless civil war among the princedoms into which Suzdal was divided, devastating visitations of the Black Death, forest fires that swept across the tilled clearings, and frequent famines. These misfortunes pushed Suzdal into a long era of political and economic decline, marked by depopulation and empty villages. To populate their princedoms rulers invited peasants in other princedoms to settle as free renters on land owned by the prince, offering them long exemptions from all obligations, light dues when the exemptions ended, communal autonomy, and freedom of movement. Lay and church lords made similar offers, willingly advanced loans and subsidies to prospective tenants, and were given charters by the princes that allowed them to offer settlers freedom from certain governmental obligations.

Most of the land held by members of the upper orders was their free private possession, which they could dispose of as they wished. Princes also distributed land on condition of service to the donor. Usually these conditional land grants went to the lesser servitors of the prince, free and unfree, who made up his court. Wealthy boyars and monasteries also granted land on condition of service to their free and unfree servitors, and sometimes small landowners put themselves and their property under the protection of a lay or church magnate, voluntarily transforming themselves into servitors holding land on condition of service. The practice became increasingly common but did not become widespread until the sixteenth century, when it played a significant role in the enserfment of the Russian peasant. In time, land held on condition of service came to be called a *pomeste* and its holder a *pomeshchik*.

Another development of these centuries of Mongol domination that was to prove important to the peasantry was the grant by princes of charters to landlords. These charters gave the landlords governmental powers over the people who lived on their lands and immunity from interference by the prince's officials. The extent of the immunities varied, with great monasteries and powerful lay proprietors given wider powers than lesser lords, but for the most part peasants who lived on privately owned land became more the subjects of the landlord than of the prince. There are indications that during the Kievan period some landowners had been granted public rights over their renters, but during the era of the Mongol domination the granting of seignorial immunities became common. By the middle of the sixteenth century, with Russia free of the Mongol yoke and united under the house of Moscow, the judicial and police power of lords over their peasant renters had become an established institution, so that the throne no longer found it necessary to issue charters that confirmed this power.

LORD AND PEASANT

Although private landowning continued to advance in the northeast there was still a vast area into which it had not yet been introduced. This was known as the "black land," and the people who lived on it were known as the "black people." The black people recognized the prince as the superior owner of the land and paid him a regular quitrent. The prince felt free to give away black land. When that happened, as it increasingly did from the late fifteenth century on, the peasants who lived on the land became the renters of the individual or monastery to whom the land had been given. By the end of the sixteenth century the black land had disappeared nearly everywhere except in frontier regions.

Early in the fifteenth century the seignorial peasantry began to be divided into separate categories, each with its own obligations. The first group were called the "old inhabitants" (*starozhiltsy*). They were the people who had lived on the manor for a certain number of years. They had to meet all of the obligations demanded by seignior and state. Then there were the "newcomers" (*novoprikhodtsy*), who were given exemptions from some or all of their obligations to attract them to settle on the manor and possibly also because they lacked the means to pay full obligations. A third group were sharecroppers (*polovniki*), who paid from one-fifth to as much as one-half of their crops to the seigniors. Usually on arrival they received a loan of cash or grain from the landlord to get started, and as a rule they were exempted from all or part of their obligations to the prince.

The peasants' dues in cash and kind that they owed to their seigniors were known collectively as *obrok* and the labor services as *barshchina,* with the former being far more important in the peasants' total obligations than the latter. The peasant (unless he was exempted) also owed obligations to the state. The government made its levies upon the village commune as a whole rather than upon the individual household, and the commune's own officials divided the obligation to the government among the individual taxpayers, presumably, according to their ability to meet them or according to their status as "old inhabitant," "newcomer," or sharecropper. Obligations demanded by the government of seignorial and black peasants alike included such things as providing goods and cash for the maintenance of the prince's local officials, building and repairing fortifications, and carting and messenger services.

Peasants still had the right of freedom of movement, and treaties between princes often affirmed that right by agreeing to allow peasants to move freely between their realms. At the same time each ruler wanted to keep peasants from leaving his territory, and so from at least as early as the mid thirteenth century some rulers agreed in treaties not to accept peasants from one another's princedoms. They also sometimes included in charters they granted to lords clauses that limited or forbade the grantee to offer inducements to prospective peasant settlers who lived in the prince's realm. These and similar restrictions curbed the peasant's freedom of movement by reducing the number of choices the peasant had in selecting a new place of residence.

A more direct restraint on peasant freedom of movement was imposed by prohibiting them from leaving except during a certain specified period and after giving their seignior due notice of their intention to depart. In the course of the fifteenth century this became the norm and was given the sanction of law in the Law Code (*Sudebnik*) of Tsar Ivan III in 1497. The code ordered that the peasant could leave only one week before or one week after St. George's Day in autumn (26 November) and had to pay his seignior an exit fee.

In addition to the black and seignorial peasants there were some who, as in the Kievan era, were slaves or were held in debt servitude. Apparently some slave owners, especially monasteries, settled their slaves on holdings in return for payments in cash, kind, and labor, and in time these slaves were fused with the free peasant renters. As for peasant borrowers, not all of them were required to work for their creditors, and until the mid fifteenth century the lender could not compel his peasant debtor to remain on his land. Thereafter, however, princely charters forbade their departure except during the St. George's period and then only if they had repaid their debts.

During the fifteenth century, and possibly even as early as the late fourteenth century, signs of economic recovery were evident. Technological innovations, a slow revival of domestic and foreign trade, and the resumption of the minting of coins were among the developments that prepared the way for economic revival in the late fifteenth and first half of the sixteenth centuries. So, too, did the creation of a unified realm that provided still more scope for the growth of trade and agriculture. By his triumph in the civil wars that filled most of his reign, Vasilii II (1425–1462) established the supremacy of Moscow over the other princedoms, and in 1480 his son Ivan III freed Russia of the Mongol hegemony.

These developments were the prelude to a revolution in the status of the landlords, in their tenures, in their relationship to the peasants who lived on their manors, and in the status of the peasants themselves. In 1556 Ivan IV (1533–1584) decreed that all landholders other than churchmen had to perform military service for him and had to provide additional mounted warriors in proportion to the amount of land they held. Those unable to perform that service had to make a money payment, and those who failed to meet the obligation were to have their land taken from them. Though there were some minor exceptions, landholding by laymen became a monopoly of a single class of Russia society—the servitors of the tsar. These men held their land either as allods or as benefices, that is, *pomestia*. The introduction of the service requirement inevitably tended to reduce the alodial proprietor to the status of *pomeshchik* since he, like the *pomeshchik,* now held his land on condition of service to the throne. Meanwhile, the *pomeste* became the dominant form of lay seignorial tenure. That happened because the nearly ceaseless military activities of the newly unified state created an ever-increasing demand for servitors who were given *pomestia* carved out of state-owned land. The great increase in the number of *pomeshchiki* made it necessary to introduce regularization into the serving relationship to ensure that it would function effectively. A special governmental agency was established to supervise the operation of the system and standards were set for the size of the *pomeste,* scaled according to the rank of the servitor. This increase in the numbers of the *pomeshchiki,* the reliance of the government on them for its military strength, and Ivan IV's growing distrust of the great nobility gave the *pomeshchiki* more and more influence in the political and economic life of Russia. That growing influence and the military dependence of the state upon the *pomeshchiki* was to have a disastrous effect upon the status of the peasantry.

RISING PEASANT OBLIGATIONS

The economic upswing created a new situation to which landlords had to adjust. Most adopted the traditional expedient of seigniors in every European land in a time of transition—they borrowed, and many of them went heavily into debt. Of much more importance for the evolution of the lord-peasant relationship, they sought to adjust to the changing conditions by making greater demands on their peasants.

As could be expected, there was great variety in the amounts and in the types of dues and services that seigniors demanded. But they exhibited a common pattern of development. Many dues in kind were converted into cash payments, reflecting the growth of the money economy; labor services were increased; and the government demanded more. The available sources do not allow exact comparisons between the total amount of obligations paid by peasants at different times during the sixteenth and first half of the seventeenth centuries, but clearly the burden of dues and services required of the individual peasant household mounted during these years. The rise in obligations apparently began in the early sixteenth century. The increase in the amount of money dues was especially striking. Scattered data from different parts of the realm indicate that the cash payment per holding or per peasant increased several times over between the early years of the sixteenth century and the first half of the seventeenth century. The decline in the value of money that marked these years accounted for a large part, and perhaps in some cases all, of the increase. The scarcity of price data makes it impossible to measure accurately the amount of the inflation, but estimates indicate that the increase in money dues kept pace with the fall in the purchasing power of the currency. Apparently in the seventeenth century the continued drop in the value of money did not cancel out all of the increase in money dues, so that there was probably a real increase in them. Typically, lords did not commute into cash all of the dues the peasants had to pay in kind. Payments in kind allowed the seignior to achieve a certain measure of self-sufficiency and he could sell any surplus. Also, seigniors must have realized that the peasants on their land could not raise enough money to pay all of their dues in cash. Indeed, they had trouble enough in meeting the cash payments that were demanded of them. A writer of the mid sixteenth century reported that money dues were the most difficult obligation that the peasants had, and he urged that they be converted into payments in kind.

The other major change in peasant obligations was the increase in the *barshchina,* the labor services. In the era of the Mongol domination, as was pointed out earlier, labor services were exceptional. When lords had demesnes, slaves usually tilled them. In the sixteenth century some lords decided to take advantage of the increased demand for farm goods and the mounting prices by creating or enlarging their demesnes and producing for market on their own account. That led to an increase in their demand for labor services from their peasant renters. Soviet historians, hemmed in by remarks, even incidental ones, of Marx and Lenin, tend to put much emphasis upon the use of *barshchina* in this period and imply that it became the principal form of peasant obligation. Actually, although evidence points clearly to the increased use of the labor obligation, payments in cash and kind continued to be the predominant form of peasant dues. In large parts of Russia the labor service was unknown, especially in the north. In the steppe, where small *pomestia* prevailed, there was a considerable amount of demesne, but often it was worked by slaves or by the *pomeshchik* himself and his family. Only in the central region, the Oka-Volga triangle, and in the east in the Kama River basin, where there were estates with large demesnes, did labor services assume major importance in the obligations of the peasants.

Usually, agreements between lords and peasants did not specify the nature of the work to be done nor the amount. Instead, the peasant was required to do what other peasants did, and sometimes the stipulation was that the peasant had to do as much as the seignior wanted. In practice the labor service, usually one day a week at the end of the fifteenth century, was often, though not always, increased to two and three days.

The payments demanded of the peasants by the state increased, too, and rose even more than did seignorial obligations. The emergence of the unified state, its policy of territorial expansion, its frequent wars, and the increased use of money created a much greater need for cash than had hitherto existed. In the later decades of the fifteenth century taxes paid in labor and kind began to be converted into cash levies, and in the sixteenth century the changeover was completed. The payments in kind made to support the local administrative officials of the tsar also began to be commuted into money. Meanwhile the amount of taxes increased many times over. The conversion of dues in kind into cash, and the depreciation in the value of money, accounted for a large part of the increase, but there was a very considerable real increase. The biggest rise in the taxes came in the latter decades of the sixteenth century, when devastation and depopulation of much of the land drastically reduced the state's revenues so that the government taxed even more heavily the peasants who had not fled. Even this sharp rise was dwarfed by the increase in taxes in the first half of the seventeenth century. The nominal rise outpaced the real one, but after discounting the effects of inflation the absolute increase was apparently enormous.

DECLINING CONDITION OF THE PEASANTRY

The additional burdens imposed upon the peasantry were not offset by major increases in their productivity. Instead, there was regression in the last decades of the sixteenth and first two decades of the seventeenth centuries. Consequently the economic position of the peasantry steadily worsened, evidenced by a decline in their incomes, a decrease in the size of their holdings, a rise in the numbers of landless or nearly landless villagers, and a great increase in their indebtedness. Data for thousands of peasant holdings listed in the tax registers show the decline in the average size of holdings. The increase in population that began in the latter part of the fifteenth century undoubtedly accounted for much of the decline in size of holdings in the first half of the sixteenth century. But the decline was most severe in the last three decades of that century, when crisis overwhelmed the realm and people fled by the thousands from the old regions of settlement. Those who remained had no incentive to farm more land, or even as much as they formerly had, because the mounting taxes and seignorial obligations would mean that they would be working only for state and seignior. The growth in the numbers of landless or nearly landless peasants, called *bobyli,* also gave evidence of the deterioration in the condition of the peasantry. The *bobyli* had increased during the course of the sixteenth century, but they formed only a small part of the peasantry until the last years of that century and the first decades of the seventeenth century, when their numbers rose to record heights.

The most striking evidence of the decline in the condition of the peasantry was the rise in peasant indebtedness to their seigniors. Peasant borrowing from their lords was an old story, but the practice became far more common in the sixteenth century than it had ever before been. The increase in their obligations and then the economic downturn of the late sixteenth and early seventeenth centuries made it very difficult for peasants to avoid borrowing. The loan contracts specified various ways for the borrower to pay back his debt, but increasingly from the late fifteenth century peasants agreed to pay the interest on their loans by working for their creditors. Often they found it impossible to pay back the principal and so became lifelong peons of their creditors with a status not much different from that of slaves.

The deteriorating economic position of the peasantry was paralleled by a decline in their legal status and above all in their freedom to come and go as they pleased. The restrictions on their freedom of movement imposed by their seigniors, and more importantly by the state, became progressively more severe, with each step leading farther down the road to enserfment. The limitation on peasant departure to the two weeks around St. George's Day in autumn, prescribed in the Code of 1497, was reaffirmed in Ivan IV's code of 1550, but with some new provisions, including an increase in the exit fee. In theory the peasant still was free to leave if he met the prescribed conditions; and the records show that there were people who were able to leave legally and of their own choice. But seigniors, anxious to keep their peasants, took measures that severely restricted the freedom of movement for many. These seigniors illegally raised the exit fee to sums that the peasant could not afford; they refused to allow peasants to leave who owed them money or who were delinquent in their taxes. And there were lords who beat, tortured, and chained peasants to prevent their departure. The peasant had no effective legal remedy against these acts, for he was under the jurisdiction of his seignior, who sat in judgment in disputes between his renters and himself. The peasant's only recourse was the illegal act of running away, and many thousands did just that. Some found the freedom they sought in frontier areas, but most settled on land that belonged to some other seignior who had the same authority over them that their old landlord had. Their only gain was that they were starting afresh.

There was, however, a legal way by which peasants, seemingly without a chance of meeting the requirements for departure, could move: by having their exit fee, debts, and tax arrears paid for them by another lord on whose property they settled and to whom they were now in debt. This was known as "exportation" (*vyvoz*) of peasants. The peasants often gained by it because the new lord offered them freedom from certain obligations to persuade them to accept his offer. The old lord had to give his permission for the exportation; if he refused his action was subject to legal review. The luring of peasants by offers of easier terms was not a new practice. Already in the fifteenth century landlords had asked their rulers to take action against it. The sovereigns, however, did nothing except limit departures to the St. George's Day period. They continued in this inaction until the last decades of the sixteenth century. By that time the desperate situation in which the country found itself and the pressures from landlords, who saw more and more of their peasants taken from them, finally convinced the government that it had to take positive measures.

THE *OPRICHNINA*

The crisis that engulfed Russia in the latter sixteenth and first decades of the seventeenth centuries rose out of a concatenation of catastrophes that in largest part could be traced back to the insane drive of Ivan IV to wipe out all opposition, real or imagined, to his absolute rule. In 1560 Ivan, who until then had been intimate with the high nobility, turned completely against them. At first he employed various forms of harassment; then in 1565 he embarked upon a program of wholesale confiscation of their estates, resettlement, and brutal extermination. To carry through this policy he created the organization called the *Oprichnina* that divided his realm into two parts. In one part the existing governmental machinery continued to operate and the landowners remained undisturbed. In the part called the *Oprichnina,* which ultimately covered half of the state, Ivan created a new administration and confiscated all private property, much of it the land of the high nobility. He kept about one-fourth of the land for himself and gave the rest to the men of the *Oprichnina* organization on condition of military service to the tsar. He executed many of the former proprietors and settled the rest on the frontiers, far from their old homes, on service tenure. He also used the *Oprichnina* as an instrument of senseless terror against the common people as well as against the high nobility, torturing and murdering many thousands of his innocent subjects. In 1572 he disbanded the *Oprichnina,* declaring that it had accomplished its purpose, and some of the confiscated properties were returned to their former owners or their descendants.

The senseless and reckless violence of the *Oprichnina* upset social and economic life and left a legacy of suffering and discontent that lingered for many years. The damage done to the social fabric by the *Oprichnina* was compounded by the long and unsuccessful Livonian War, which dragged on from 1558 to 1583 and brought much sacrifice and suffering to the Russian people. To make matters worse, there were at least two major plague epidemics, several years of crop failure and famine, five major and many minor Tatar raids between 1556 and 1576, and, not surprisingly, a catastrophic economic depression. The central feature of the crisis was a mass flight from the central and northwestern parts of the realm. The movement began on a small scale around the middle of the century. At first those who fled were of the lowest rungs of society, but then more solid members of the rural community, such as village elders, joined the exodus. By the 1570's the movement had become a mass migration. By the early 1580's the old regions of settlement were so depopulated that Ivan could not raise the soldiers he needed to continue the Livonian War and so had to withdraw from it. The extent of the flight reached astonishing proportions. Entire districts were emptied of their inhabitants; in some districts as many as 97 percent of the farm homesteads were vacant.

Nor was the flight limited to the countryside. City populations plummeted, too. Most of the migrants fled east and south into regions that Ivan IV's conquests had opened to Russian settlement. Others went to the far less hospitable reaches of northern Russia; some fled into the "untamed steppe" to join the cossacks; and still others probably went no farther than the forests and marshes that abounded in the old regions of settlement. Slavery, which had been on its way out as landlords gained greater powers over their renters, revived under the pressure of the crisis when many peasants sold themselves into slavery. A quirk in the law code of 1550 allowed them to leave their old seignior without paying him fees, gaining them the protection of the powerful lord to whom they sold themselves and freeing them from the burden of taxation since slaves, not being legal individuals, were not taxed.

THE TIME OF TROUBLES

As could be expected, the depopulation had a disastrous impact upon economic life. Agriculture suffered by the flight of so large a part of its labor force and by the withdrawal of so much land from cultivation. Commerce suffered from the decline in both supply and demand. In the late 1580's signs of recovery began to appear, the old regions of settlement began to fill up as people drifted back to their old homesteads, deserted fields were once more taken under the plow, and agriculture and trade began to revive. The recovery continued until the first years of the seventeenth century, when a series of crop failures brought on famine, pestilence, and widespread unrest. Then a pretender to the throne, called the False Dmitrii, invaded, and Russia in 1605 entered into the years of wars, chaos, and calamity known as the Time of Troubles. Once again people fled from their homes, with depopulation and devastation even greater than they had been in the 1570's and 1580's, and economic life came to a standstill. The Time of Troubles ended in 1613 with the election of Michael Romanov to the imperial throne, but the economic difficulties continued until the 1620's, when a very gradual recovery got under way. The old regions of settlement were recolonized. The government offered exemptions from its taxes for certain periods to those who settled on abandoned land or cleared hitherto untilled land. It sold state and court land at low prices. And it promoted settlement on the frontiers by granting land there to servitors and monasteries and by building fortified frontier posts to protect against raids by the nomads who roamed the lands beyond the frontiers.

The last acts in the enserfment of the peasantry were played out against this background of terrorism, foreign and civil wars, political chaos, and economic disaster and slow recovery. As mentioned earlier, the ever-mounting need of the absolutist regime for servitors had resulted in a great increase in the number of *pomeshchiki,* the men who held their land on condition of service to the tsar. Their importance and value to the throne became even greater in the political and economic crises of the last four decades of the sixteenth century. Their needs and their demands became serious concerns of the government, and they were demanding further restrictions on the peasants' freedom of movement. During the years when so many peasants ran away, wealthy lords and monasteries were better able than most other seigniors to attract peasants to their lands and to hold them. They were better able, too, to "export" peasants, whether legally or illegally, from the manors of lesser servitors. The loss of so many of their peasants through flight or through "exportation" threatened many servitors with economic ruin. That would mean that they would be unable to meet their obligations to serve the throne at the very time when the state's needs were the greatest, thereby endangering the very existence of the state. Ivan IV's wars had emptied the treasury, and so he could not offer financial help to his servitors. The state also faced the grave consequences of the loss of much of its tax revenues because of the departure of so many peasants from the lands of the servitors. The plain fact was that the peasants' right of free movement, even as limited as it was, offered a serious threat to the power and well-being not only of the servitors but of the state itself.

The solution the state adopted to solve this dilemma was to end the peasants' freedom of movement. The first steps were taken in the 1570's, when restrictions were put on the right of wealthy monasteries to acquire more land. This limitation was made at least in part to satisfy the demands of the servitors, who saw the monasteries as enemies of their own interests—the monasteries, with their greater wealth and their exemptions, were able to buy valuable land and attract peasant settlers. In 1580 the state made a direct attack upon the peasants' right of departure. Ivan IV issued a decree that has not been preserved but whose contents have been made known by other contemporary materials. The decree ordered that the peasants could not leave their present place of residence, wherever it might be, until such time as the tsar lifted the ban. The period of the ban was known as the "forbidden years" (*zapovednye gody*). During these years the provisions of the law that guaranteed peasants the right of free movement were suspended. The first nationwide forbidden year was in 1581. Thereafter they became the rule, with more than half of the 1580's and 1590's, and every year from 1603 on, declared a forbidden year. Despite this, people still regarded them as temporary expedients, so that on into the seventeenth century rental agreements between seigniors and peasants specified that the peasant would remain until the tsar's decree that would end the forbidden years.

Though evidence indicates that the legislation checked peasant departures, it was not as effective as had been hoped. The necessary condition for its successful operation was that lord and peasant abide by the terms of the decree. Instead, peasants continued to run off. And seigniors continued to lure them away by offers of better terms than those under which they presently lived, or they raided the villages of other lords and forcibly abducted their peasants. The government found that it was unable to enforce legislation that was being evaded so generally and on so wide a scale. The servitors who lost peasants could not protect themselves: either they were away from their manors in the tsar's service, or they lacked the means to check the flight or kidnapping of their peasants.

The government realized that it would have to adopt more stringent measures. It found the vehicle by which to carry out its intentions in a cadastral survey that Ivan IV had ordered in 1581 to get accurate information for the levy of taxes. The registers that were drawn up contained the name of each male adult peasant and his place of residence. The survey was apparently completed in 1592. Five years later, on 24 November 1597, the throne issued a decree ordering that all peasants who had left their residences within the preceding five years were to be sought out and returned with their families and personal possessions to their former place of residence. Peasants who had left more than five years before could not be compelled to return if their old landlord had not complained to the authorities. Hitherto the courts had found it difficult if not impossible to decide whether a peasant was a legal resident of a manor or whether he was a runaway or had been abducted. Now the land registers provided irrefutable evidence of a peasant's legal residence, which became the legal basis for his permanent attachment to a specific manor. By setting the five-year limit the decree legalized illegal departures before 1592 and so accepted violations of the forbidden years made before that date. But the decree gave all landlords protection against further departures and in effect bound the peasant to the manor on which he had lived in 1592. Those peasants who had left before 1592 were entered in the land register as residents of the manor of their new seignior, and so they too were subject to the decree of 1597. These restrictions applied only to those peasants listed in the land registers as the head of the household. The other peasants who lived with him still had the right to come and go as they pleased. They could freely make an agreement with any seignior on whose land they wished to settle as a renter. In their contracts, however, they agreed that they would never leave their landlord, or that they could depart only at his death, or only if they paid the seignior a large exit fee.

Apparently, however, the provisions of the 1597 decree were not enough to satisfy the servitors. The crop failures of 1601 and succeeding years severely affected their economic situation and brought many of them to ruin. To help them Tsar Boris Godunov in 1601, and again in 1602, ordered that all lesser servitors, except those of the Moscow district, could "export" up to two peasants from any one estate during the St. George's period. That was the last time that the ban on peasant departures was lifted. It seems unlikely that Boris' actions ever actually helped the lesser servitors, because of the onset of the Time of Troubles. In 1607, in the midst of the Troubles, the then tsar, Vasilii Shuiskii, pushed back the time of recovery of departed peasants from five to fifteen years, that is, back to 1592. The law ordered that peasants living in a place other than their place of residence in 1592 were to be returned to that earlier residence if a complaint had been entered with the authorities that they had left illegally. Shuiskii tried to add teeth to his decree by ordering that fines be levied on seigniors who received peasants who had departed their old place of residence illegally.

Shuiskii's ukase was an attempt to bind the peasant more closely to his seignior at a time when society was near anarchy and when peasants were openly evading their obligations and disregarding the prohibition upon their freedom of movement. Peasant evasion of the laws and open resistance reached far back into Russia history and had increased with the decline in their personal freedom that began in the fifteenth century. Their most common form of protest had been flight, but, as mentioned earlier, this usually meant merely the exchange of one seignior for another. Sometimes their discontent crested into violence, but these remained local outbreaks. During the Time of Troubles, however, many peasants, and particularly those who had run away to the frontiers and tasted freedom, saw an opportunity to carry through a social revolution that would free them forever from their dependence upon the seigniors. In 1606 serious uprisings erupted in many parts of the realm. In the south a major revolt broke out, led by Ivan Bolotnikov, a runaway slave. After many adventures in foreign lands Bolotnikov returned to Russia and roused peasants and slaves by promising the abolition of all restrictions upon their freedom, the execution of Tsar Vasilii Shuiskii and of all rich people, and the division of their wealth and their women among his followers. He won many adherents, but the class nature of his movement was diluted when it was joined by servitors who wanted to overthrow the boyar-dominated government of Shuiskii. Bolotnikov got as far as Moscow. Then some of his gentry supporters deserted him, he was pushed back, and in 1607 his forces were routed and he was probably executed. Some of his peasant followers then threw in with a new pretender to the throne, called the Second False Dmitrii, who appeared in 1607, but that movement, too, came to naught. And so when the Time of Troubles ended in 1613 the status of the peasantry was the same as it had been when they began. Their right of free movement had been taken from them, though it was still regarded as being in temporary abeyance.

THE ROMANOVS

In contrast to the unchanged condition of the peasantry, the servitor class emerged from the Time of Troubles in a stronger position. The machinations of the great noble families who survived the repressions of Ivan IV and Boris Godunov had discredited their caste and had led to the death of many of them. A national army led by servitors and burghers had driven out the foreign invaders and ended the Time of Troubles, and an assembly controlled by the servitors elected Michael Romanov to the imperial throne and turned over to him the absolute power that Ivan IV had possessed. Only a few of the great noble families managed to retain their wealth and their prestige, either because they were kinsmen of the Romanovs or because they had given undisputed evidence of their loyalty to the new dynasty. Many of the gentry, too, had suffered during the long years of crisis, especially during the Time of Troubles. Many had perished, and others had been pushed down into the peasantry by economic pressures. But as a class they had triumphed along with the restored absolutism; the coronation of Michael was the symbol of their victory.

As part of the price for their loyalty and continued support they demanded stronger legislation to restrict the peasant, and they wanted the government to issue a definitive statement affirming the attachment of the seignorial peasantry. For peasants continued to run away, and wealthy lords and monasteries continued to pirate peasants from lesser men. The servitors wanted especially to extend the period for the recovery of illegally departed peasants, which had been restored to five years at the end of the Time of Troubles. They complained that five years did not give them enough time to locate and get back their peasants, that they were unable to recover their peasants from powerful men who had taken them, and that these powerful men took back peasants who had been living on the land of the lesser seigniors for longer than five years. In response to their protests the government extended the period of recovery to nine years, and then, in 1642, to ten years for peasants who had run away and fifteen years for those taken illegally by other lords. These measures apparently still did not prevent the pirating of peasants by powerful seigniors, and in any event the lesser servitors lacked the means to recover their peasants, unlike wealthy lords, who could hire agents to track down runaways and bring them back. Finally, the government promised that it would abolish the recovery period as soon as it compiled new land registers. Once the registers were drawn up runaway or pirated peasants would have to be returned to the seigniors on whose land they lived when the register was made, no matter how long the peasants had been away. The government also promised that it would bind to the seignior not only the head of the peasant household but all the other members of the household, who, as explained above, still enjoyed the right of free movement.

Before the promise could be kept Tsar Michael died and was succeeded by his sixteen-year-old son Alexis. The young tsar turned over the direction of his government to his tutor, B. I. Morozov. Morozov was of that group of great lords about whom the lesser servitors had been complaining. Now he took advantage of his position to gain more wealth and more peasants for himself, his family, and his friends. His abuses led to unrest and riots and, in 1648, to his dismissal. A chief source of dissatisfaction had been the chaos into which legislation and court procedure had fallen, and the new administration decided to appoint a commission to codify the laws. The commission turned over its codification for approval to the National Assembly (*Zemskii sobor*), which had been convened. The Assembly, dominated by lesser servitors, approved the code with amendments and additions. It was called the *Sobornoe ulozhenie,* the Assembly Code.

The purpose of the codification was not so much to introduce innovations as it was to provide an orderly arrangement of existing law and custom. Nonetheless, chapter 11 of the code, which was concerned with the peasantry, completed the long process of enserfment. It marked, too, the victory of the lesser servitors over the magnates as well as over the peasants, for the code met nearly all of their wishes. Most of the thirty-four sections of chapter 11 dealt with the recovery of peasants who had run away or who had been taken away by other lords. The two major innovations of the chapter carried out the promises the government had made a few years earlier: these abolished the time limit for the recovery of peasants and took away the freedom of movement of those members of the household who had possessed that right until then. The peasant and his family, including the spouses of his married children and their children, and all his property, including grain that the household had raised, had to be returned if the lord from whom he had departed demanded it, no matter how long it had been since he had left. The code stipulated that the new registers were to be used as proof of residence to bind all the members of the household. The code confirmed the seignior's nearly unlimited authority to move his peasants from one place to another as if they were movable property, thereby attaching the peasant to the person of his seignior rather than to a piece of land. The law considered that all goods belonged ultimately to the seignior, thereby depriving the peasant of his right of full ownership of his personal property. The peasant also lost most of his legal competence. As before he continued under the jurisdiction of his lord in all except the most serious cases arising within the boundaries of the manor. Now, in addition, the code ordered that in all cases involving the peasant with persons outside the manor he was to be represented in court by his lord, except for certain specified major crimes.

These confirmations and extensions of the powers of the seignior over his peasants were not accompanied by any precise definition of the rights of the peasants nor of the exact nature of their relationship to the seignior. That meant that there were no legally recognized norms to protect the peasant against the arbitrary actions of his seignior. This led almost immediately to a further deterioration in the status and condition of the peasantry. Seigniors took peasants off the land and made household servants of them, they tried cases in their own courts that were supposed to be tried in government courts, and they imposed cruel punishments and even death upon their peasants. They disregarded the law's few restrictions on their power to move their peasants about, and in time they bought and sold their peasants as if they were cattle.

By the middle of the seventeenth century, then, the long process of clipping away at the freedom of the Russian peasantry finally led to their enserfment. The once free peasant had been bound to the will of his seignior. Theoretically, the law recognized him as a legal individual and not as a slave, but about the only significant consequence of that distinction was that the serf had to pay taxes and the slave did not. For all practical purposes the only rights that the peasant possessed were those allowed him by his seignior, who literally owned him. His only recourse against the oppression of his seignior was the illegal expedient of flight, sabotage, and violence.

The seignorial peasants constituted the majority of the Russian peasantry in the seventeenth century. The black peasants, now much reduced in number, escaped enserfment but not without some loss of their freedom. Their payments to the state, the supreme owner of the black land, which they made through their communes formed an important part of the state's revenues. To ensure that the peasant would not leave and so escape his share of the commune's obligation, the state gradually bound the peasant to his commune. He could leave only if he provided a substitute to take over his holding and pay his dues.

BIBLIOGRAPHY

Seminal works of the pre-Soviet period include Mikhail A. Diakonov, *Ocherki iz istorii selskago naseleniya v moskovskom gosudarstve XVI–XVII vv.* (1898), and *Ocherki obshchestvennago i gosudarstvennago stroya drevnei Rusi,* 4th ed. (1912); Yurii V. Gote, *Zamoskovnyi krai v XVII veke* (1906); V. O. Klyuchevskii, "Proiskhozdenie krepostnogo prava v Rossii," in *Opyty i issledovannia,* I (1918); Nikolai Pavlov-Silvanskii, *Feodalizm v drevnei Rusi* (1907); N. Rozhkov, *Selskoe khozyaistvo Moskovskoi Rusi v XVI veke* (1899); Vasilii I. Sergeevich, *Drevnosti russkogo prava,* 3 vols. (1909–1911); Mikhail Vladimirskii-Budanov, *Obzor istorii russkogo prava,* 6th ed. (1909).

The "classic" Soviet study is Boris D. Grekov, *Krestyane na Rusi s drevneishikh vremen do XVII veka* (1946). See also L. V. Cherepnin, "Iz istorii drevnerusskikh feodalnykh otnoshenii XIV–XVI vv.," "Iz istorii formirovaniya klassa feodalno-zavisimogo krestyanstva na Rusi," in *Istoricheskie zapiski,* **9** (1940) and **56** (1956), and *Obrazovanie russkogo tsentralizovannogo gosudarstva v XIV–XV vekakh* (1960); Evgeniya I. Kolycheva, *Kholopstvo i krepostnichestvo (konets XV–XVI v.)* (1971); Vadim I. Koretskii, *Zakreposhchenie krestyan i klassovaya borba v Rossii vo vtoroi polovine XVI v.* (1970), and *Formirovanie krepostnogo prava i pervaya krestyanskaya voina v Rossii* (1975); Daniil P. Makovskii, *Razvitie tovarno-denezhnykh otnoshenii v selskom khozyaistve russkogo gosudarstva v XVI veke* (1963); A. G. Mankov, *Razvitie krepostnogo prava v Rossii vo vtoroi polovine XVII veka* (1962); Viktor M. Paneiakh, *Kabalnoe kholopstvo na Rusi v XVI veke* (1967); R. G. Skrynnikov, *Rossiia posle Oprichniny* (1975); Stepan B. Veselovskii, *Feodalnoe zemlevladenie v severo-vostochnoi Rusi,* I (1947).

Works by non-Russian authors include Jerome Blum, *Lord and Peasant in Russia from the Ninth to the Nineteenth Century* (1961); Alexandre Eck, *Le moyen âge russe,* 2nd ed. (1968); Richard Hellie, *Enserfment and Military Change in Muscovy* (1971); D. Odinetz, "Les origines du servage en Russie," in *Revue historique de droit français et étranger,* 4th ser., **10** (1931); Robert E. F. Smith, *The Enserfment of the Russian Peasantry* (1968).

JEROME BLUM

[See also **Agriculture and Nutrition; Allod; Benefice; Black Death; Boyar; Ivan III of Muscovy; Kievan Rus; Mints and Money, Russian; Mongol Empire; Muscovy, Rise of; Vladimir-Suzdal.**]

SERFS AND SERFDOM: WESTERN EUROPEAN. In the feudal West, a large number of laborers were dependents of rural lords whose large domains required a great deal of manpower. Human labor was absolutely essential for agricultural production because technological advances were minimal. But the serfs had some interest in economic development; they could raise their children in their own home, thus removing an obstacle that slavery had posed to demographic expansion in the ancient world.

Serfdom had replaced slavery by about 1000, although this transformation had been foreshadowed several centuries earlier by the weakening or even the disappearance of public authority and the growth of the power of the aristocracy.

Serfdom was one of the factors in the economic expansion of Western Europe, and this expansion in turn led to a weakening of serfdom before the fourteenth century. By the end of the Middle Ages there were only traces of serfdom in most of the Western European countries. On the other hand, in Central and Eastern Europe, a second form of serfdom, almost unknown in the West, was firmly established. This type of serfdom remained one of the fundamental elements of the Eastern economy and society until very recently.

FROM SLAVERY TO SERFDOM

In both the Roman Empire and the Germanic world there was a basic distinction between two categories of people; even as late as the time of Charlemagne, the emperor could write to one of his *missi* (delegates): "There are only two classes: that of the free and that of the slave." The free man was subject only to the public authorities, and in principle was protected by them. The slave was the property of his master and had no rights of his own. He was subject to the whims of his owner, who could treat him as he pleased, as if he were a chattel or a domestic animal. The slave was not classified as a person.

But the great mass of slaves cultivating the vast domains of the wealthy Romans little by little dwindled in numbers. This resulted in part from the spread of Christianity, which asserted that since every human being has a soul, they are all equal in the sight of God, who created them, free or slave, in his own image and who considers all humans bound by the same rules of morality. Thus, in contrast with pagan antiquity, a slave now had certain rights; for example, his family could no longer be considered the offspring of the master's animals. Also, the freeing of slaves became a pious act pleasing to God. But Christianity could not attack slavery directly, as it was such an important part of the Roman and barbarian worlds. All it could do was to encourage its slow decline and gradual transformation.

In the sixth century there were still a large number of slave markets. The works of Gregory of Tours, for example, show that the social order of Merovingian Gaul was still largely based on slavery. But the number of slaves began to dwindle. Slave groups had never reproduced themselves adequately, and new sources of slaves had always been necessary. Both in the Roman Empire and in the barbarian societies, the slave market had been supplied from the victims of wars and raids. In the sixth century, however, the church forbade the enslavement of Christians. Even if this prohibition was respected only little by little, as religious beliefs became more important to the Roman and romanized people and to the German tribes who had occupied the lands of the western part of the Roman Empire, the source of slaves declined with the decline in tribal warfare (in spite of the disorders in the Merovingian kingdoms). The only people who could then be captured as slaves were the pagans on the northern and eastern frontiers of the Christian Germanic kingdoms. The intake diminished and slaves became more expensive. A few centers, such as Verdun in the sixth century, had rich businessmen who profited from the slave trade. Also, on the Atlantic coast of Gaul, there were imports of Anglo-Saxon slaves who were reexported to the Mediterranean. The Anglo-Saxons had long had the custom of selling their compatriots abroad. Pope Gregory the Great found Anglo-Saxons in the Roman slave market, and was thus inspired to undertake the conversion of England.

During the eighth century, the demand for slaves increased in the rich Mediterranean lands that had been conquered by the Muslims. This led to a new increase in the price of slaves. Most of them were Slavs (hence the French "esclave" and the English "slave"). These slaves were taken through the French river valleys to Muslim Spain, or through the Alpine passes to Venice, where they were shipped to Syria or Egypt. The merchants of Verdun, up to the tenth century, organized these caravans, both those to Spain and those to Italy. Christians, however, were still exported, although not in very great numbers. In the reign of Louis the Pious, Bishop Agobard of Lyons denounced the Jews who carried on the slave trade, noting that they were not bound by the church's prohibition of the trade. However, while the slave trade through Frankish lands continued into the tenth century, it declined somewhat because Charlemagne had forbidden the sale of slaves outside the boundaries of his empire.

By the seventh and eighth centuries, competition of Muslim markets and the increasing irregularity of the food supply had brought about a fundamental change in the situation of the unfree. Gangs of slaves gradually disappeared, both because the West was going through a centuries-long economic depression and because the administrative system of rural estates collapsed. This situation encouraged landlords to get rid of the gangs of slaves, which were difficult to oversee, and to settle slave families on small individual holdings. This policy of setting up large numbers of small households was widespread in eighth-century Gaul, and had as a secondary result the diminution of the "reserve" (the part of the domain cultivated directly for the benefit of the lord). The lord could require the services of a slave who had become a tenant at certain times in the agricultural year (plowing, harvesting), while at other periods the tenant could work his own holding. This dispersion of slaves among individual households resembles, at a lower level, the practice of giving vassals a benefice (fief) instead of having them live in or near the lord's dwelling.

From this time on, the slave and his wife subsisted on the products of the bit of land granted by the lord, to whom they owed annual payments, usually in kind. As far as the lord was concerned, they were part-time farmhands. They raised their children, which solved the problem of preventing a decrease in the number of unfree workers, and also provided a reserve of young slaves (or servants) for the lord. Thus the relationship between slave and master had been profoundly changed. The rights of the slave over his own family were recognized, and he had gained a certain degree of economic independence. He could sell his surplus products and keep his small savings. The legal vocabulary had not changed, but little by little the slave had become a serf.

THE RESIDUE OF SLAVERY

If, in the period before 1000, one is uncertain as to whether to translate *servus* as "slave" or as "serf," there is no possible doubt by the eleventh century. From then on, we are discussing serfs, many of whom were descendants of Carolingian slaves.

The status of a serf, like that of a slave, was marked by a complete absence of personal liberty. He could enter the ranks of free men only through a formal ceremony of manumission. This hereditary taint was transmitted through the mother, a reminder of the period when marriages of slaves were not recognized as real marriages. If both husband and wife were unfree, the children were serfs; and if a free man married a serf, the same rule applied. More and more it became the custom to say that a serf was an *homme de corps,* that is, the property of his lord. A bond between man and man (at this level and all other levels of society) united the serf to his owner. The owner could sell him, bequeath him like any other piece of property, ask for his service whenever he desired, even take back the land he held and reduce him to his former status of domestic servant. But the lord also had the duty of protecting and defending the serf against any and all dangers. In return, the master could have a fugitive serf pursued and returned; the bond between man and man could not be broken by the flight of one who was unfree. This rule created a problem in the case of *formariage,* in which a female serf married the serf of another lord and went to live on the lands of the latter. The husband's lord would acquire additional dependents (the female serf and her offspring), but the woman and her children still belonged to her lord. This problem could be settled only by a compromise between the two lords. Usually they agreed to divide the children between them or one bought out the other's claim. In order to control this migration of laborers and the resulting division between ownership and rights to labor services, masters exercised their right to approve or disapprove a marriage outside their domains. The payment for *formariage,* often a heavy one, was made to the lord who had lost a serf, but only if he agreed to accept it.

Since the serf was the property of his master, it is not surprising that, on the death of a serf, the inheritance legally went to his lord (right of mainmort). In practice this right was reduced to a claim to some or all of the serf's chattels (the best cow, for example). The land generally went to the heirs of the deceased serf.

Even when he had a landholding, the serf was not a full member of a peasant community. He suffered serious disabilities. He could not become a member of the clergy or a monk; he was excluded from all public institutions, such as the courts, where he could not even testify because he was not allowed to take an oath. His master still had full power to punish him for misdeeds or crimes. The granting of hereditary holdings to the serfs, even though they were smaller than those of freemen, did improve their position. If the master sold a serf, he sold him with his holdings, so the life of an unfree man was not greatly altered by the sale. The church had managed to make a very insensitive society accept the idea that a serf was not to be treated as a beast. And while the serf owed more rent and more labor services for his land than did the free peasant, custom was gradually limiting arbitrary demands of the master by fixing the amount to be given and the work to be done.

The political developments that led to the appearance of feudalism around 1000 (earlier in France than in the Middle Kingdom or in Germany) had important effects on legal and social class distinctions. Public institutions were decaying everywhere. In turn it became impossible to prove one's liberty in the courts. The legal barrier that separated the unfree from the free was weakened; the old concepts of liberty and servitude were destroyed. Thus, during the period from 1000 to 1200 there was a slow but steady elimination of the social and legal distinctions that had set the serf apart from other peasants.

THE GROWTH OF SERFDOM

From the eleventh century on, the serfs were no longer only the descendants of men who had been slaves. As one reads the documents that became more and more numerous during the late eleventh and twelfth centuries, one finds increasing uniformity in peasant society almost everywhere in the West. In fact, the process had begun earlier, but it grew more rapidly in the feudal period.

Merovingian Gaul was, as Ganshof said, "an ideal milieu for the formation of clientage" at all levels of society. The movement began in the late empire but reached full development only later. People sought protection against violence, disorder, and anarchy. The village communities were too isolated, too distant from each other to form pockets of defense. Almost always it was necessary to find a protector, who in turn was often protected by someone even more powerful. By the fourth century the weak had sought the protection of the great landlords who had accepted high office to escape the demands of the Roman treasury and to protect themselves against growing insecurity. The clients of these great men were largely small rural landholders who entered the relationship of clientage either as individuals or as part of a village community. The patron of a village did not always hold a neighboring estate; he might be an army officer whose protection seemed more helpful to the villagers. At times there was even some rivalry, the soldier placing himself between the lord of an estate and the peasants. This foreshadowed later conflicts in the feudal period between the landlord and the lord who controlled the local courts and government. At times an important personage combined both military power and the possession of a great domain; this made his control even more oppressive. Marc Bloch was correct when he saw, even in this early period, the figure of the soldier-landlord beginning to overshadow the countryside.

Bonds between man and man already existed at all social levels. From the fourth century on, entrance into the clientage of another man was expressed by the verb *se commendare* (to commend oneself). But while there was a community of interests between commended men of high rank and their very powerful protectors, such a community did not exist between peasants who commended themselves and the great man of the region. His "protection" was so oppressive that it diminished their liberty. Even this affliction, however, might seem preferable to accepting a long and economically ruinous period of military service. For these dependents of humble origin, the former small landowners, even if they continued to farm and live on their land, lost their basic right of property to their protector, who thus built up a great estate.

Thus the legal distinction between free and unfree started to break down in the period from 500 to 1000. The authority of the great landlord, who would become a seignior about the year 1000, fell more and more heavily on the poorer people of the countryside. The barrier placed by the great landholder between the king and the world of the peasants was continually strengthened and heightened. Charlemagne contributed to this change. The kings for a long time had left all of the lesser rural population to the discretion of the aristocrats, who could thus easily diminish the number of free small landholders. In reading the *Polyptyque* of Irminon (a survey of the lands of a monastery prepared between 806 and 829), one can see that the old division between coloni (free men) and the unfree was disappearing and that all the villagers are simply called the "men," that is, the dependents of the abbey of St. Germain-des-Prés. The Carolingians played an unfortunate role in diminishing the freedom of the coloni. They thought that they could control the free peasants by using the aristocracy as their agent, but all that they did was to strengthen the bonds of dependence. And by granting privileges of "immunity" to the great ecclesiastical landholders they also conceded public powers, especially the right to hold a court. The master was thereafter the judge of his dependents, free as well as unfree. And lay lords soon gained rights of justice, with or without privileges of immunity. Moreover, many free peasants were led to the army by the lord and not by the count. The barrier between poor free men and public institutions continued to grow higher as the lords put pressure on the "free" to keep them from attending the courts. The master was bound to bring criminals who were free to the court of the count, but in practice this did not last long. Otherwise, all peasants came under the judicial power of the lords. Finally, the lords bought off the obligation to military service of their "free" men. Since the mark of a free man was to be a judge and a soldier of the king, there was nothing left of the status of a *franc* (free man) by the ninth century. In a warlike society, which scorned those who did not serve in the army, these men could hardly avoid being considered unfree. In spite of repeated assertion of his supposed liberty as late as the ninth century, the colonus wound up being treated almost as a slave. The status of the colonus and that of the slave had gradually become so close that "liberty" was only a slighly higher status than slavery.

Initially, feudalism weighed heavily on the peasantry. After 1000 and up to the middle of the twelfth century, feudalism was changing and becoming more uniform. This growing uniformity was connected with the growing powers of the lords, which, if not entirely new, became more precise. Even if they could be shifting and contradictory, the terms used to describe social status show the tendency toward uniformity. To describe the peasants, words such as *manentes* (inhabitants in general) or *villani* (villeins, inhabitants of a village) were used, at least in France. In England *villani* designated only the unfree, but in both countries "villein" had a pejorative overtone (as did *manant* in France). Moreover, did *servus* and its feminine equivalent *ancilla* still always mean unfree? About 1030 the monastery of Cluny received the gift of an estate "with serfs, male and female whether free or unfree." Thus considerations were not only ancestry, which made some free and others unfree, but also varying degrees of subjection to the lord. The benefactor of Cluny was a lord, and, to the monk who drew up the act, all the dependents of a lay master were unfree, were serfs, even if they were of free ancestry, because on a lay estate they had heavier obligations than those who had an abbot as a master and who were considered to be free. In fact, liberty could be considered a matter of degree; one man could have "a very small degree of liberty," while another could have a little more or a little less. The exactions of the lords could differ greatly, depending on the character of the master and local and regional customs.

DEGREES OF DEPENDENCY

At the very bottom of these various grades of dependence were persons who did not have the slightest degree of liberty. These were often called the men of the property (*hommes propres*) or the *hommes des corps;* they were serfs in the full sense of the word. Since, however, contemporaries applied this last term loosely, jurists were reluctant to use it. All this makes it difficult to find an exact definition of serfdom, and scholars have disagreed on the meaning of the term. The dispute is of some importance since, depending on the definition used, the status of the group in the population as a whole can vary widely. According to Marc Bloch, beginning with the tenth century, former free coloni, freedmen, and slaves who had been granted their own bits of land had merged into one social class. This class could be recognized by three signs of subjection: chevage (head tax), *formariage,* and mainmort. Chevage was a small annual payment in recognition of the state of servitude. As for *formariage* and mainmort, only serfs were burdened by them. These serfs now formed the vast majority of the peasant population. There were only a few free men, dependents of the lord only because of their place of residence, as twelfth-century texts prove. Finally, from the thirteenth century on, the number of serfs gradually declined as a great movement of manumission set in. The documents on which Marc Bloch based this theory came from several estates of the abbey of St. Germain-des-Prés (south of Paris), which were described in the *Polyptyque* of Irminon and were given charters of freedom in the middle of the thirteenth century. Bloch concluded that all "men" had been bound to pay mainmort; therefore they had all been serfs.

Leo Verriest argued against Bloch that "man" is a very vague word with many meanings, and that it could include all the inhabitants of the lands in question, as some of the phrases in the charters

A German serf from Mainz Cathedral, 1235–1239. CATHEDRAL AND DIOCESAN MUSEUM, MAINZ

seem to indicate. Two of the charters of freedom (those of Thiais and Villeneuve St. Georges) make a clear distinction between serfs and the other inhabitants. The serfs, whose names are given and who were only a small group, were freed from the duties connected with their personal servitude. On the other hand, all the inhabitants, in return for a large payment, received franchises—the abolition of mainmort, payments for *formariage,* and tallage at the will of the lord. Thus, by 1250 mainmort and *formariage* were not yet specifically servile dues, as they would become in areas where serfdom continued to exist. As for the head tax, it is not mentioned in the St. Germain charters; it was a levy that did not exist everywhere.

It seems certain that in the Île-de-France, the chosen area for these two opposing historians, by 1200 serfs were only a minority of the rural population—about 20 percent by my calculations. One could say the same of the region around Orléans, where serfs were far less numerous than the *villani.* Verriest was not wrong when he said that the region around Paris was not the only one where the growth of serfdom had been limited.

Elsewhere, if the definition of serfdom was equally vague, were the serfs also a minority of the rural population? In France there were provinces at the beginning of the thirteenth century where serfs were still a majority of the population: Champagne, Nivernais, northern Burgundy—in short, a good part of central France. On the other hand, in the south (for example, in Aquitaine) they were only a minority. Along the coast of Provence, as along all the shores of the Mediterranean, slaves (in the old sense of the word) were becoming more numerous. As for Germany, one must distinguish the eastern provinces, a region of colonization where serfdom appeared only at the end of the Middle Ages, and the old Germany of the west, where serfdom was much more common than to the west of the Rhine and the Meuse. There were two forms of serfdom in this region. As Perrin put it: "The tenants who tilled or worked on the lands of rural lordships had been grouped at an early date into a single class of *hörig,* a class formed largely of the *servi casati* [slaves who had been settled on small holdings]. As to the 'hommes de corps,' or *leibeigen,* they were in part, descendants of the *mancipia* [slaves] of the reserve-domain. . . ." The latter had cultivated the land directly for the lord and had passed through an intermediate stage somewhat like that of the *censuales* (rent-payer). After the thirteenth century, modifications and ameliorations in the status of the serfs were not the work of the lord, but were determined by local custom.

Other countries saw rapid progress at first. In Spain, where the granting of privileges was essential to sustain the colonization and resettlement of lands conquered from the Moors, the kings encouraged the decline of serfdom. The same was true in Lombardy and Tuscany, where the great Italian towns led the movement. For many reasons—to weaken the power of the nobles in the countryside, to put pressure on those who refused to accept the rule of urban governments, to gain adherents to a democratic faction, to acquire more taxpayers, and also because of sincere moral and religious convictions—many towns abolished all forms of personal subjection, and then control over landholdings. They got rid of obstacles to liberty and suppressed or diminished the financial demands of the lords. These advances, however, were neither universal nor lasting. On the one hand, the Italian princes did not follow the example of the city-states. On the other, the cities were often more oppressive than the lords; they offered a lower standard of living for the peasants while admitting their complete liberty under the law.

This leaves the case of England, which we will discuss later. In England the number of villeins—the English term for the unfree—was very large, and it remained at a high level for a long time. Norman law (which did not recognize serfdom) had no lasting influence.

It became increasingly difficult to distinguish between serf and freeman because both were almost always peasants at the same economic level. Marc Bloch wrote that "the serf was a villager (*vilain*) and something more" (and worse); Georges Duby answered that in the region of Mâcon about 1300, "the serf was a villager like all the others." By the second half of the eleventh century, in many regions nothing distinguished the serf from the "free" peasant except the name. Often enough, however, this name no longer had any real significance. Juridical distinctions among commoners had become empty phrases. Sometimes, as in the Île-de-France, one could not go so far, but the personal subjection of the serf nevertheless scarcely distinguished him from the others. The burdens imposed by the lord were only slightly heavier for the serfs, and most serfs were simply smallholders like many of the other villagers. Custom protected the tenures of groups, and since, at least in France, these tenures were in fact hereditary, there was no new form of typically servile possession before the thirteenth century. However, as Perrin has shown, the lord had an interest in allowing only his serfs to hold lands in his seigniory. It would have been impossible, or at least difficult, to exercise the right of mainmort over a free man or the serf of another lord. Thus, in places such as Lorraine, the lord or his agent had to ratify through the ceremony of investiture any change in the possession of a holding. He could thus bar anyone except one of his own serfs from his land. By the eleventh century there is evidence of a system that favored the servile group, over whom the lord had the fullest rights, when it was a matter of transferring land. Moreover, following the example of their predecessors in dealing with slaves, the lords reserved the *fiefs de service,* minor but profitable offices, for their serfs. These offices were administrative jobs such as mayor, policeman, provost, bailiff, judge, miller, keeper of the oven, and operator of the winepress. These positions, then, would be held by men whom the lords knew best and whose state of servitude made it unlikely that they would become too independent. In possession of a fief (a bit of land for which no payment was owed) and receiving a percentage of fines and payments for their services, these petty officers rose far above even free peasants, and in the end formed what Duby called "a little rural aristocracy."

One can see, then, the difference between serfdom and slavery. Serfdom did not thwart an individual who had initiative, especially in economic matters, nor did it prevent the growth of population from the eleventh through the thirteenth century. It was certainly a factor in the growth in the economy of Western Europe during these centuries. And the serfs who were given administrative and judicial functions by their lords were among the most active agents of economic growth. By increasing the wealth of their lord, they also increased their own. Some of them became village leaders, and ranked among the richest peasants; others managed to slip into the nobility. This was especially true in Germany, where the "ministerials" (estate managers) became serf-knights (and in a few cases, nobles) who rendered homage like any other knight. The economic and social success of this group wiped out the strain of servitude that it had carried.

The distinction, which was becoming more and more unclear, between the serfs and men who were more or less free was being supplanted by another, based on the different size of peasant holdings. A serf could have more land than a free man. No longer was it the rule, as it had been in the Carolingian period, that the allotment given to an unfree man should be smaller than that of a free man. In spite of the growth of the power of the lords, from the eleventh century on there was a distinction based on the size of the holding and not on legal status. There were two groups (the relative size varied from village to village): those who had a plow and a plow team (plowmen or farmers), and those we would call laborers or farmhands. Both groups, however, profited from the expansion in the amount of cultivated land after 1100.

THE SECOND SERFDOM

Faced by the exactions of the lords, the peasants had not been inactive. More and more they had learned to form a united front that the lord could not ignore. The clearing of new farmland on a large scale gave all peasants, free or not, an opportunity either to improve their lot rapidly or to put pressure on their lord.

Between 1050 and 1100, just when the great clearings began, "franchises" or "liberties" were granted to new settlements or to old villages. These were privileges that went beyond problems of personal status to grant general exemptions from existing rules and to give legal, economic, and social benefits. These grants helped to create in twelfth-century France a new concept of personal liberty. Under the Carolingians liberty meant participation in public institutions (the courts and the army); later liberty was to be free from any taint of personal dependence. Now it was the status of being a man who enjoyed the franchises that protected him against the arbitrary exercise of the lord's power.

Thus the clearings and the grant of "liberties" led to the decline of serfdom in many parts of the West. If the lords wanted to have new lands, they had to give inducements to their *hôtes* ("guests," the name given to the peasants who came to do the work of clearing). Thus the charters founding new settlements (*villeneuves*) had to guarantee personal freedom and the renunciation of arbitrary taxation (from which the serfs more than the "free" had long suffered). And since it was necessary to keep the inhabitants of old villages from seeking better conditions of life in the new "towns," charters for the old settlements, modeled on the franchises of the new, had to be granted.

Thus, in the twelfth century, the serfs, who felt more and more that their status was humiliating and a bar to economic advancement, were more anxious than before to acquire liberty. They felt this earlier in the rapidly growing towns, peopled by peasants from the region, many of whom must have been of servile origin, than in purely rural villages. It is certain that many of them gained their freedom by migrating to towns or lands that were being cleared, far enough away from their master so that they could call themselves, and be accepted as, free men. To be sure, there were agreements among lords by which they promised to return each other's runaway serfs, but this danger could be avoided by fleeing some distance from one's native lordship. Moreover, the lord who received the serf had no reason to ask too many questions about the former residence and status of the laborer who offered to work for him. Other serfs, especially toward the end of the twelfth century, profited from the negligence of the lord or his agents and the increasing use of money to pay for service, and hired themselves out as farmhands. Here again, time and distance would eventually wipe out their origin.

In many regions villeinage swallowed up serfdom because, fairly early, burdens that seemed incompatible with liberty were abolished or lightened for all peasants, including the serfs. Thus serfdom disappeared. In Normandy, in all of western France, and in the region of Mâcon, there were no serfs by the beginning of the twelfth century. In Picardy (except for Vermandois) the same thing had happened by 1180 (and even at the beginning of the eleventh century, there were no serfs in the lands between Montreuil and Bapaume).

Elsewhere serfdom disappeared a little later, not as the result of a slow decline, but through the process of manumission, usually of a group rather than an individual. In the Île-de-France many serfs became rich enough to buy their freedom, either individually or, more often, as a village or urban association. This was done elsewhere as well, but the Paris region was unusually rich and populous, and the percentage of serfs who were well off and even wealthy was unusually high. Around 1250 Louis IX (St. Louis), religious houses, and lay lords freed all their serfs in return for large payments. At the same time they exempted all their dependents—the free and those who had just been freed—from mainmort and *formariage.* They also changed payments that had been taken at the discretion of the lord (such as tallage) into fixed rents, because they seemed a mark of servitude. Lay lords, who were usually short of money, were more willing to make these concessions than were the clergy, who often acted only on orders from the king. In the Paris region, as in some of the other provinces, it was a strong lay authority (royal or princely) that struck the final blow against serfdom.

Other peasants were less fortunate, and in some regions serfdom contaminated villeinage. This happened in Vermandois, Champagne, and central and southwestern France. In these areas mainmort, *formariage,* and arbitrary tallage, which had formerly been paid by the free as well as the unfree, were now considered signs of servitude. This development took place between 1250 and 1300, for example, in a section of Champagne, even though it bordered on the Paris region, where serfdom was being abolished.

We can thus speak of a second serfdom. When this appeared, the basis of servitude was not personal but, rather, the possession of certain landholdings. We can then use a phrase that is inaccurate for the first kind of serfdom—the serf "attached to the soil." This could be a mild form of serfdom, as in the Mâcon region, where it applied to an economic, not a juridical, group. The serf was to pay tallage and give labor service at the will of the lord; he had to stay day and night on his land; but his condition was not hereditary. In the region of Lyons one can learn a great deal by noticing the areas in which the second serfdom could be found. It existed only in the mountainous areas, the last to be cleared in the thirteenth century. In that period of overpopulation men would take land under any conditions because it was scarce, and it was easier to accept serfdom because the holdings that were granted were quite large. The new serfdom did not always affect a large part of the peasantry; in the southwest, where the condition was hereditary, the *questals* (tallage-payers) were a minority. Overall, the new serfdom was generally limited to very poor peasants, who were forced by misery to accept their status. In France, at least, this new serfdom had almost vanished before it was abolished by Louis XVI and the Revolution.

The rapid growth in population, beginning a little before 1000 and continuing a little past 1300, was a blessing for the unfree in France, but it was not always beneficial elsewhere. In England, overpopulation during the twelfth century caused the condition of those called villeins to deteriorate. This was the second serfdom. Bound to the soil, the villeins, who were one-fourth to three-fourths of the population, depending on the region, could not leave their holding, or transfer it to another, without the consent of their lord. Tallage and labor service were due at the will of the lord. Even free tenants had to protect themselves against attempts to make them perform servile labor. Some free men had to admit that they were villeins in order to obtain land in this period of overpopulation.

By the middle of the fourteenth century, and for a century or more after, the situation changed everywhere in the West. Repeated outbreaks of the Black Death, rebellions, urban and rural uprisings, and the difficulties of the lords in this period of war, disorder, and economic depression, diminished the number of serfs in many regions. But the change was neither complete nor rapid. One of the objects of the Peasants' Revolt of 1381 in England was to obtain charters of freedom from the lords, especially ecclesiastical lords, like those that had been gained, without violence, by French peasants in the thirteenth century. Richard II, threatened by the rebels, promised to abolish serfdom, but the final defeat of the uprising made it easy to annul this promise. Only gradually did economic pressures, such as scarcity of labor, lead to a withering away of English serfdom during the next century.

It was on the eastern borders of Europe that the new serfdom became deep-rooted: in Brandenburg, Hungary, Romania, and the Slavic countries. In Brandenburg, for example, as population declined during the last part of the fourteenth century, vacant land was plentiful and the lords added these deserted fields to their domains. But how could they profit from these enlarged holdings when there were fewer and fewer workmen to be hired? The aristocrats profited from the collapse of high authority, just as the Frankish lords had profited from the decline of the Carolingians. The princes allowed the lords to usurp royal rights, and this led to the imposition of new "rights" over peasants and the appearance of the new serfdom. The peasants of eastern Germany, formerly the most free of all peasants in the West, found themselves bound to the lords' estates and forced to accept heavy labor services. This new serfdom remained typical in most of the Eastern European countries down to the nineteenth century and even into the twentieth century.

BIBLIOGRAPHY

Marc Bloch, *Feudal Society,* L. A. Manyon, trans., 2 vols. (1961), and *French Rural History,* Janet Sondheimer, trans. (1966); R. Boutruche, *Seigneurie et féodalité,* 2 vols. (1968–1970); Frederic L. Cheyette, ed., *Lordship and Community in Medieval Europe* (1968); Richard B. Dobson, *The Peasants' Revolt of 1381,* 2nd ed. (1983); Georges Duby, *Rural Economy and Country Life in the Medieval West,* C. Postan, trans. (1968), and *The Early Growth of the European Economy,* Howard B. Clarke, trans. (1974); Charles E. Dufourcq and J. Gautier-Dalché, *Histoire économique et sociale de l'Espagne chrétienne au moyen âge* (1976); Guy Fourquin, "Le premier moyen âge," "Le temps de la croissance," and "Au seuil du XIVe siècle," in Georges Duby, ed., *Histoire de la France rurale,* I (1975), *Lordship and Feudalism in the Middle Ages,* Iris Sells and A. L. Lytton Sells, trans. (1976), "La chrétienté latine occidentale désenclavante," in Pierre Léon, ed., *Histoire économique et sociale du monde,* I (1977), *The Anatomy of Popular Rebellion in the Middle Ages,* Anne Chesters, trans. (1978), and *Histoire économique de l'occident médiéval,* 3rd ed. (1979); John B. Freed, "The Origins of the European Nobility: The Problem of the Ministerials," and "The Formation of the Salzburg Ministerialage in the Tenth and Eleventh Centuries: An Example of Upward Social Mobility in the Early Middle Ages," in *Viator,* 7 (1976) and 9 (1978).

François L. Ganshof, *Feudalism,* Philip Grierson, trans., 2nd ed. (1964); John Hatcher, *Rural Economy and Society in the Duchy of Cornwall, 1300–1500* (1970); Rodney Hilton, *Bond Men Made Free: Medieval Peasant Movements and the English Rising of 1381* (1973); Archibald R. Lewis, *The Development of Southern French and Catalan Society* (1965); *Les libertés urbaines et rurales du XIe au XIVe siècle* (1968); Edward Miller and John Hatcher, *Medieval England: Rural Society and Economic Change, 1036–1348* (1978); Hugues Neveux, "Déclin et reprise: La fluctuation biséculaire (1330–1560)," in Emmanuel Le Roy Ladurie, ed., *Histoire de la France rurale,* II (1975); Charles E. Perrin, "Le servage en France et en Allemagne," in *Storia del medioevo* (1955), and *Seigneurie rurale en France et en Allemagne du début du IXe à la fin du XIIe siècle,* 3 vols. in 1 (1966); M. M. Postan, ed., *The Cambridge Economic History of Europe,* I, 2nd ed. (1966); *Recueils de la Société Jean Bodin,* II, *Le servage,* 2nd ed. (1959); Doris M. Stenton, *English Society in the Early Middle Ages,* 2nd ed. (1952); Sylvia Thrupp, ed., *Early Medieval Society* (1967); Léo Verriest, *Institutions médiévales* (1946); Lynn T. White, *Medieval Technology and Social Change* (1962).

GUY FOURQUIN

[See also **Benefice; Blacks; Class Structure, Western; Colonus; Commendation; Feudalism; Fief; Gregory of Tours, St.; Gregory I the Great, Pope; Mainmort; Ministerials; Slavery, Islamic World; Slavery, Slave Trade; Tenure of Land.**]

SERGEANT. In medieval languages, the word "sergeant," or "serjeant," always carried the connotation of service: a sergeant was a servant. The two words are simply variants, both deriving from the Latin verb *servire,* "to serve." But unlike modern "servant," which usually implies menial labor, the term "sergeant" in the Middle Ages could be applied to many distinct kinds of persons, some quite elevated in the contemporary social hierarchy. The commonest meaning given the word was that of a soldier below a knight in rank and equipment. The variety of such sergeants was remarkable. Both lightly armed foot soldiers and heavily armed mounted soldiers bore the title. In France it was a fiscal convenience to assess the tax liability of communities in terms of their obligation to provide the money for a certain number of military sergeants.

"Sergeant" was also used in England for a category of tenant. Men were said to hold their land "by sergeanty" if the land was technically to provide a reward or income for furnishing (1) the services of a military sergeant, (2) part of the services or equipment of a military sergeant, (3) ceremonial services at the coronation, or (4) certain humorous or trivial services otherwise unclassifiable. Such tenures were not liable, ordinarily, to scutage. Eventually they were divided, according to their service, into grand sergeanties and petty sergeanties. Lower-level functionaries who enforced the peace, made arrests, and protected jails and other property were routinely called sergeants (though words from other roots were employed synonymously: custodian, guard, beadle, even janitor, in the sense of doorkeeper).

Two final peculiar English usages of the word should be noted. Serjeant at law was the highest rank of the common lawyer, from whom, most often, royal judges were drawn. Those serjeants retained by the crown were designated king's (or queen's) serjeants. "Sergeant," spelled usually with the letter *g,* was also used as the title of an officer of the Corporation of London.

BIBLIOGRAPHY

England. Frederick Pollock and Frederic Maitland, *The History of English Law,* 2nd ed., reiss. (1968), I, 214–217, 282–290, 323, 334, 355, 520, and II, 268, 275, 620. J. Round, *The King's Serjeants and Officers of State* (1911), a learned but erratic book, must be balanced by Elisabeth Kimball, *Serjeanty Tenure in Medieval England* (1936). See also Bryce Lyon, *A Constitutional and Legal History of Medieval England,* 2nd ed. (1980), 132, 439, 628.

France. William Chester Jordan, *Louis IX and the Challenge of the Crusade* (1979), 168–170, 178–180.

WILLIAM CHESTER JORDAN

[See also **Banneret; Baron; Class Structure, Western; Estate Management; Feudalism; Fief; Frankalmoin; Knights and Knight Service; Law, English Common; Ministerials; Sac and Soc; Scutage; Squire; Taxation, French; Tenure of Land; Warfare.**]

SERGIOS I was patriarch of Constantinople from 610 to 638. He attempted to effect a reconciliation with the Eastern churches in the provinces reconquered by Emperor Heraklios. However, the resultant Monothelite doctrine, embodied in the *Ekthesis* (of which he was the main author), proved unacceptable to many, particularly Patriarch Sophronios of Jerusalem (634–638), who strongly opposed it. The university at Constantinople was reopened during the patriarchate of Sergios.

BIBLIOGRAPHY

George Ostrogorsky, *History of the Byzantine State,* Joan Hussey, trans., 2nd ed. (1968); Andreas N. Stratos, *Byzantium in the Seventh Century,* I and II (1968–1972).

LINDA C. ROSE

[See also **Byzantine Church; Councils (Ecumenical, 325–787); Ekthesis; Heraklios; Heresies, Byzantine; Monothelitism.**]

SERGIUS OF RADONEZH, ST. (*ca.* 1314–1392), founder of the monastery of the Holy Trinity and the major leader of a monastic revival during which numerous communities were founded in the forests of northern Russia. After leaving his native city of Radonezh to become a hermit, Sergius was eventually forced by circumstances to accept the company of other monks and proved himself as an organizer and social leader. His life was marked by the traditional monastic virtues of simplicity, humility, and dedication to manual labor, which led historians to establish a parallel between Russian monasticism, of which he was a model, and the Cistercian movement in the West. His biographers note in his life only a few examples of mystical and miraculous events, but these include a vision of divine light during the celebration of the Eucharist—a direct spiritual link with fourteenth-century Byzantine hesychasm. Sergius was closely connected with the Muscovite princely family but refused to be consecrated bishop in 1378. In 1380 he bestowed his blessing on Grand Prince Dmitrii for military resistance to the Mongols. The veneration of his relics within the monastery he founded (now known as Zagorsk) remains popular in Russia.

BIBLIOGRAPHY

Epiphanius, a disciple and contemporary of Sergius, is the principal source. For his *Life,* see Nikolai S. Tikhonravov, *Drevniya Zhitiya Sergiya Radonezhskago* (1892, repr. 1967). In English see Pierre Kovalevsky, *Saint Sergius and Russian Spirituality,* W. Elias Jones, trans. (1976); Serge A. Zenkovsky, ed. and trans., *Medieval Russia's Epics, Chronicles, and Tales* (1974).

Studies include Georgii Petrovich Fedotov, *The Russian Religious Mind,* II, *The Middle Ages,* John Meyendorff, ed. (1966), esp. 195–229; Nicolas Zernov, *St. Sergius—Builder of Russia,* Adeline Delafield, trans. (1939, 2nd ed. 1945).

JOHN MEYENDORFF

[See also **Alexis of Moscow; Cistercian Order; Dmitrii Ivanovich Donskoi; Hesychasm; Muscovy, Rise of; Russian Orthodox Church.**]

SERMENTS DE STRASBOURG. See **Strasbourg Oaths.**

SERMONS. See **Preaching and Sermons.**

SERRA, PEDRO AND JAIME (*fl. ca.* 1363–1399, *ca.* 1361–1375, respectively), Spanish painters. The brothers had a similar style, Sienese-derived Italo-Gothic. They produced decorative panels with compositions set in symmetrical designs and gentle, flowing lines against gold backgrounds. Best-known among their works is Pedro's Holy Spirit altarpiece (documented 1394), for a chapel in S. María, Manresa (illustration overleaf).

BIBLIOGRAPHY

Mary Grizzard, *Bernardo Martorell* (1985), chap. 7; Chandler R. Post, *A History of Spanish Painting,* II (1930), chaps. 22, 23.

MARY GRIZZARD

[See also **Gothic, International Style.**]

SERVATUS. See **Lupus of Ferrières.**

SERVI CAMERAE NOSTRAE. The Latin phrase *Servi camerae nostrae* (servants of our [imperial] chamber), describing the status of the Jews under

SERVI CAMERAE NOSTRAE

Pentecost. Central panel of the Holy Spirit altarpiece by Pedro Serra, 1394. S. María, Manresa. FOTO MAS

his rule, first appeared in a charter of privileges granted by Emperor Frederick II in 1234 (Aronius *Regesten,* 468). From this time the term became standard in imperial texts. Commentaries on Roman and canon law and theological texts like Thomas Aquinas' *Summa theologiae* (IIa–IIae, 10–12) also refer to the Jews as the *servi* of princes. Related terms are from France (*Judaei nostri* and *Tanquam proprii servi,* twelfth to mid thirteenth centuries), as well as England (*quasi catallum nostrum,* late twelfth century) and Spain (*servi regis,* later twelfth century). However, as Gavin Langmuir has stressed, the imperial *Servi camerae nostrae* (*SCN*), with its intimations of actual servitude, is unique.

Langmuir has also corrected earlier thinking, principally that of Salo Baron, by stressing the difference and lack of conflict between *SCN* and *perpetua servitudo* (perpetual servitude). This latter term—introduced by Pope Innocent III in 1205, although its origins are in letters issued by Alexander II in 1063—refers only to the status assigned the Jews in canon law, the function of which was to force them into a passive and submissive mold by means of discriminatory legislation.

In contrast, and as the commentators on both Roman and canon law emphasize, *SCN,* like its related terms, refers neither to a body of legislation nor, despite intimations, to true servitude. The initial invocation of *SCN* is clear on this point, saying of the Jews, *Servi sunt nostrae camerae speciales,* that is, "They have a distinct and irregular form of attachment to the imperial chamber." According to Guido Kisch, Frederick II created the term *SCN* because he believed he could protect the Jews only by assigning them a *ius singulare* (unique constitutional/legal status) making them directly dependent on the emperor.

This attribution of motives is debatable, as is Kisch's argument that Frederick II drew on the term "perpetual servitude," present in the *Decretals* of Gregory IX (X.5, 6, 13), issued in 1234, to fashion *SCN.* The emperor may equally have had a term like *Tanquam proprii servi* in mind.

The meaning of *SCN* is best understood by following its development in royal and imperial charters of privilege and protection from the ninth century on. In the charters of Frederick II, *SCN* appears as a qualification in the central clause stating that the emperor is taking the Jews under his royal *tuitio* (protection). In the 826 charter of Louis I the Pious, no such qualification appears; it is assumed, as was the case in all early medieval *tuitio* charters, that Jews are permanent residents and subjects of the realm who are acquiring special rights and protections (*ius speciale*). However, by 1157 Frederick I added *Ad cameram nostram pertinent* (They are specially related to our chamber) to his texts. The constitutional status of the Jews clearly required redefinition, and to accomplish this Frederick I instituted a special relationship between the Jews and the chamber (or fisc), one of the first permanent institutions of the medieval kingdom. Like the chamber itself, the Jews were to be considered an integral and indivisible component of the kingdom (empire). Thus, while they had lost any status they may have once possessed in the imperial-feudal legal nexus, a constitutional rationale for their presence still existed.

This solution, nevertheless, was artificial; it did not hold up under pressure. Accordingly, in 1234 Frederick II substituted *servi* for *pertinent,* expressing de jure what had existed de facto since 1157. The Jews had become constitutionally déclassé. Their presence in the empire was justifiable only by asserting their total dependence on the emperor. This dependence was the common denominator linking the conceptions underlying not only *SCN* but also terms like *Tanquam proprii servi.* All of them indicate the Jews' lack of normal status and their vulnerability to royal (ducal, or other) arbitrariness and manipulation. In this sense, *SCN* measures the increasing stages of Jewish isolation and ultimate legal and constitutional "outlawry" from all of (lay) medieval society.

The Jews themselves, as seen in the *Milhemet Mitzvah* of Meir ben Simeon of Narbonne (mid thirteenth century), correctly perceived the dependency and instability their special status created. For, with reference to King Louis IX of France and with apparent obliviousness to the theoretical arguments of the legists that the Jews were not slaves in fact, Meir said: "We are his slaves [*'Avadim*] . . . and our property is his to do with as he pleases" (Parma, Biblioteca Palatina, MS 2749, fols. 226b, 228a). Perhaps intentionally, Meir was accurately paraphrasing the justifications given by the chronicler Guillaume Le Breton for King Philip II Augustus of France's 1180 confiscation and expulsion of the Jews from the Île-de-France.

BIBLIOGRAPHY

Salo W. Baron, "'Plenitude of Apostolic Powers' and Medieval 'Jewish Serfdom,'" in his *Ancient and Medieval Jewish History,* Leon A. Feldman, ed. (1972); Vittore Colorni, *Legge ebraica e leggi locali* (1945); Guido Kisch, *The Jews in Medieval Germany* (1949, 2nd ed. 1970); Gavin Langmuir, "*Tanquam servi:* The Change in Jewish Status in French Law About 1200," in *Les juifs dans l'histoire de France,* Myriam Yardeni, ed. (1980), which lists nearly all important previous discussions of *servi camerae nostri.*

KENNETH R. STOW

[See also **Jews and the Catholic Church; Jews in Europe; Law, Jewish.**]

SETIER (from the Latin *sextarius,* a measure of capacity, the "sixth part" of the *congius,* from *sex,* "six"), a measure of capacity employed throughout most of France for liquids and dry products. The Parisian standard wine setier (also known as a *velte*) contained 375.6 cubic *pouces* (7.45 liters), or 4 *quartes* or 8 *pintes* or 16 *chopines* equal to 1/36 muid. For most dry products the Parisian standard contained 2 *mines* (156.10 liters), or 4 minots or 12 *boisseaux* equal to 1/12 *muid.* As a measure of superficial area it was originally the extent of land that could be sown with a setier of seed. There were numerous variations and specialized uses for the setier, however, both in Paris and in the provinces.

BIBLIOGRAPHY

Ronald E. Zupko, *French Weights and Measures Before the Revolution* (1978).

RONALD EDWARD ZUPKO

[See also **Boisseau; Muid; Weights and Measures, Western European.**]

SEVEN DEADLY SINS. From the writings of Evagrius Ponticus, John Cassian, and Gregory the Great, medieval Christendom came to accept certain sins as headings under which all evil actions and tendencies could be ranged. Never completely standardized in order, number (originally eight, later seven), or name, these sins were most commonly listed as: pride (*superbia*), envy (*invidia*), anger (*ira*), sloth (*acedia*), avarice (*avaritia*), gluttony (*gula*), and lust (*luxuria*).

Scripture taught that some acts (the later "mortal" sins) produced spiritual death (1 John 5:16; 1 Cor. 6:9–10), but new to the medieval period was the attempt to understand the relationships among these various acts that made them a coherent group: the deadly or capital or cardinal sins. Theological investigation into these relationships flourished during the twelfth and thirteenth centuries, using models drawn from human psychology (Jean de la Rochelle, Albertus Magnus) and cosmological symbolism (Peraldus, Grosseteste). In popular works, however, the deadly sins were frequently confused with vices or with demons of temptation, and this imprecision led theologians from the time of Aquinas to adopt other organizing principles in their moral analysis. After 1500 the scheme of the deadly sins played little part in formal theology and church teaching.

Popular delight in numerological correspondence and analogy continued, nevertheless, to multiply links between the sins and other septenary models both natural and religious, such as planets, powers of soul and elements of body, sacraments, gifts of the Holy Spirit, and petitions of the Our Father. Preaching handbooks, penitentials, and pastoral summae widely incorporated the scheme of the deadly sins, and from Carolingian times ecclesiastical synods first urged and later required its use in catechesis, preaching, and hearing of confessions. By 1215 the deadly sins had thus become for Western Christendom a fundamental part of daily life, "as real as the parish church itself" (Bloomfield). In Byzantine popular piety and culture, however, the older, more tangible image of demons given charge over distinct spheres of temptation was never successfully dislodged by this developed notion of the deadly sins.

As structural elements and as vehicles for satire the sins appeared from the beginning in the vernacular literatures, both in great works (Dante, Langland, Chaucer, Spenser) and in numerous minor genres (itineraries, "mirrors," devotional tracts). It is widely accepted that such works reflected important changes in the nature of medieval life through the way they gave primacy among the sins at different periods to pride or sloth or avarice.

The complex iconography of the deadly sins began from motifs in the allegorical battle between virtues and vices illuminated in the manuscripts of the *Psychomachia* of Prudentius. Illustration developed in sculpture, fresco, and the minor arts, using at first examples taken from everyday life or from classical and scriptural sources, and then more elaborate images (tree, wheel, the human body) representing the organic relationships observed among the sins. True personification of the sins themselves emerged only in fourteenth-century art, often in connection with representations of purgatory and hell. Throughout the medieval period in both art and literature the sins were associated with a rich variety of attendant animal and planetary motifs.

BIBLIOGRAPHY

The fundamental study is Morton W. Bloomfield, *The Seven Deadly Sins* (1952). Also, Siegfried Wenzel, "The Seven Deadly Sins: Some Problems of Research," in *Speculum,* **43** (1968), "The Sources of Chaucer's Seven Deadly Sins," in *Traditio,* **30** (1974), and "Vices, Virtues, and Popular Preaching," in *Medieval and Renaissance Studies,* **6** (1976); Lester K. Little, "Pride Goes Before Avarice: Social Change and the Vices in Latin Christendom," in *American Historical Review,* **76** (1971).

For Eastern tradition see P. Mijović, "Personnification des sept péchés mortels dans le jugement dernier à Sopoćani," in *L'art byzantin du XIIIe siècle,* V. Djurić, ed. (1967), esp. 239–248; and G. Every, "Toll Gates on the Air Way," in *Eastern Churches Review,* **8** (1976).

For the iconography: Adolf Katzenellenbogen, *Allegories of the Virtues and Vices in Mediaeval Art* (1939); Rosemond Tuve, *Allegorical Imagery* (1966), 57–143.

ROBERT BARRINGER

[See also **Confession; Iconography; Penance, Penitentials; Preaching and Sermon Literature, Western European; Virtues and Vices.**]

SEVEN LIBERAL ARTS. See **Quadrivium; Trivium.**

SEVEN SLEEPERS OF EPHESUS, a legend of seven Christian young men of Ephesus who fell asleep during the reign of the Roman emperor Decius (249–251) and awoke 200 years later, under the rule of Theodosius II (408–450). After the assassination of Philip the Arab in 249, Decius, his successor, attempted to enforce the state religion amid much political instability and moral upheaval. Each citizen was ordered to appear in public before a special commission to make a sacrifice to the gods and receive a document (*libellus*) identify-

The Seven Sleepers of Ephesus, depicted in the *Stuttgarter Passionale, ca.* 1130. Stuttgarter Landesbibliothek, cod. bibl. 2°57, fol. 109v. FOTO MARBURG / ART RESOURCE

ing the holder as pagan. Those Christians who refused became martyrs. Under this affliction, known as the Decian Persecution, legend has it that seven young Christian men escaped to a cave, where they fell asleep, awakening two centuries later, in the time of a Christian state.

The legend is thought to have been set down first in Syriac or Greek. However, it was known in both the Eastern and the Western church by the sixth century. Both Jacob of Serugh and Gregory of Tours recorded it. The legend has also been related in Arabic, Persian, Coptic, Armenian, Latin, and the Romance languages. One of the most popular accounts of the Seven Sleepers is the prose version by the early-thirteenth-century French poet Chardri. The pervasive dissemination of the tale was undoubtedly enhanced through its adoption by Muslim tradition as an illustration of points of faith and the resurrection of the dead. Some scholars, such as F. L. Cross, suggest that the legend arose in Syriac-speaking churches in connection with Origenist controversies over the resurrection of the body.

In the 1930's German archaeologists headed by Franz Miltner discovered the Seven Sleepers' Church and a burial site presumed to have been their place of refuge. Evidence found in situ suggests that both church and tomb were destinations of well-established pilgrimages. Honigmann concludes that it is incontestable that about the middle of the fifth century, a group of men really believed or tried to make others believe this tale. The story received ecclesiastical support and was used to refute certain heresies, such as that of the "Origenist heresy." The feast of the Seven Sleepers of Ephesus is 27 July.

BIBLIOGRAPHY

Clive Foss, *Ephesus After Antiquity* (1979); Ernst Honigmann, "Stephen of Ephesus and the Legend of the Seven Sleepers," in his *Patristic Studies* (1953); Michael Huber, *Beitrag zur Visionsliteratur und Siebenschläferlegende des Mittelalters,* 3 vols. (1902–1908), and *Die Wanderlegende von den Siebenschläfern* (1910); John Koch, *Die Siebenschläferlegende, ihr Ursprung und ihre Verbreitung* (1883); Louis Massignon, *Les sept dormants d'Ephèse . . . en Islam et en chrétienté,* 2 vols. (1955–1961); Brian S. Merrilees, ed., *La vie des set dormanz by Chardri* (1977); Franz Miltner, "Das Cömeterium der sieben Schläfer," in *Forschungen in Ephesos,* IV, pt. 2 (1937).

JENNIFER E. JONES

[See also **Chardri; Ephesus; Gregory of Tours, St.; Origen.**]

SEVILLE, Spanish city located on a meander of the Guadalquivir River, ninety-seven kilometers (sixty miles) from the Atlantic coast at Cádiz. Known as Ishbilīya in Arabic, Seville was second to Córdoba in size and importance throughout most of the Islamic period, reaching its maximum extension of 187 hectares (462 acres) and its greatest population (83,000) in the mid twelfth century, when the city was favored by Almohad dynasts.

Until the ninth century, the city was confined to the limits of the primitive Roman *oppidum* (town). After the sack of the city by Norman pirates in 844, the Umayyad emir ᶜAbd al-Rahmān II ordered the reconstruction of the walls to include both the old city and the newer suburbs to its east and north. The walls were rebuilt in the early tenth century and again a century later. Finally, in 1170–1171 the Almohad caliph Abū Yaᶜqūb Yūsuf, who made Seville his capital, rebuilt the portion of the wall adjacent to the river, after a calamitous flood. The Alcázar, or citadel, originally built by ᶜAbd al-Raḥmān II, was restored by the Almohads, who were likewise responsible for building a new main mosque (1172–1176), of which only the minaret, now called the Giralda, still remains. At the time of the conquest of the city by Ferdinand III of Castile (1248), Seville boasted seventy-two mosques.

After the fall of the Umayyad caliphate in Seville (1013), the chief religious judge (qadi), Abū'l-Qāsim ibn ᶜAbbād, proclaimed himself ruler (*ḥājib*) of an independent Sevillian principality that lasted until the Almoravid conquest of 1091. Its greatest ruler, al-Muᶜtaḍid (*r.* 1042–1069), both enlarged the kingdom and wrote poems praising the city's undoubted grandeur during this period.

The Almohads, in building a new main mosque near the river, to the south of the old urban center, created a dual economic zonation whereby the export and local economic activities were each confined to specific areas. The Alcaicería, or covered market, where expensive silks were sold for export, was located near the riverine port. The Alhóndiga, or flour exchange, supplying the needs of the townspeople was in the center of town, near the previous main mosque. Islamic Seville was a center for the trade, both domestic and overseas, of the olive oil produced in the nearby Aljarafe region. A picture of the economic life of Almohad Seville is preserved in the market regulation, or *ḥisba,* treatise of ibn ᶜAbdūn, which describes not only a great variety of alimentary trades but also construction, textile, and iron industries.

The city had received its domestic water supply from an arched aqueduct of Roman construction, known in the later Middle Ages as the Caños de Carmona. By the twelfth century this system had fallen into disrepair, but it was restored by the Almohad rulers in 1172. The Castilians encountered the system still functioning, and in 1254 Alfonso X ordered a "Master Caxico" (probably a resident Genoese) to "make the water [of the Carmona aqueduct] flow to two fountains in Seville as it used to flow in the time of the Moors." The Almohads, when building their new main mosque, uncovered the Roman sewer system and altered and enlarged its course.

When the Castilian army captured the city in 1248, most of the Muslim population fled and was replaced by settlers of predominantly Castilian origin. The mosques were granted as churches or houses, with three reserved as synagogues for the Jewish population.

The Christian conquest resulted in a severe depopulation of the city, as the displacement of the Muslim residents created many open spaces separating Christian neighborhoods with relatively low population densities. Low-density areas on the urban periphery, adjacent to the walls, tended to attract monastic establishments. The Jewish quarter occupied approximately 11 percent of the walled city; hence the density of Jewish settlement, up to the pogrom of 1391, must have been substantially greater than that of the Christian population. A small Muslim quarter, housing mainly artisans (masons, weavers, and smiths, in particular), also subsisted after the Christian conquest.

Postconquest society was characterized by an urban aristocracy whose wealth was based in rural properties, particularly in the Aljarafe district, and by a large number of free burghers, or *francos,* who were prominent in the textile industry and in local commerce. Overseas trade was in the hands of Genoese (who had been established in the city since Almohad times as merchants, armorers, and bankers), Florentines, and Castilians. These groups dominated the export trade in wheat, olive oil, hides, and other agricultural products, which in turn dominated the overseas commerce.

The functional separation of the city into two distinct economic zones survived unchanged from Almohad times. International trade was centered near the river in the Barrio de la Mar (in fact, a separate jurisdictional entity) and in the so-called Genoese and Castilian quarters, where the Genoese and textile exchanges (Lonja de Genova, Lonja de los Paños) were located, along with the covered market and olive-oil warehouses. The economic life of the city proper continued to be located nearer the city's center.

BIBLIOGRAPHY

Ramón Carande, *Sevilla, fortaleza y mercado,* 2nd ed. (1975); Antonio Collantes de Terán Sánchez, *Sevilla en la baja edad media: La ciudad y sus hombres* (1977); Julio González, *Repartimiento de Sevilla,* 2 vols. (1951); Manuel González Jiménez, *La repoblación de la zona de Sevilla* (1975); Eváriste Lévi-Provençal, *Seville musulmane au debut du XIIe siècle: Le traité d'Ibn ᶜAbdūn* (1947); Leopoldo Torres Balbás, "Crónica arqueológica de la españa musulmana," in *Al-Andalus,* **10** (1945).

THOMAS F. GLICK

[See also **Almohad Art; Almohads; Almoravids; Blacks; Castile; Exploration by Western Europeans; Hispano-Mauresque Art; Jews in Muslim Spain; Mudéjar Art; Rushd, Ibn; Spain, Christian-Muslim Relations; Spain, Muslim Kingdoms of: Umayyad Art; Umayyads of Córdoba.**]

SEWAN, LAKE (Classical Armenian: Gełam; Medieval Armenian: Gełarkᶜuni; Greek: Lychnitis; Turkish: Gökça). The smallest of the three great lakes of the Armenian plateau, Lake Sewan (Sevan) occupies a high basin surrounded by the Pambak and Shakhdag Mountains in what is now the east-central Armenian SSR. The lake lies at an elevation of about 6,279 feet (1,914 meters) and is about 45 miles (72 kilometers) long and 23 miles (37 kilometers) wide. About twenty-eight permanent streams enter the lake, which is drained by one small river, the Zanga (Armenian: Hrazdan; Russian: Razdan), which has been harnessed for hydroelectric power since World War II. This has led to a gradual reduction of the lake whereby Sewan Island, with its two ninth-century churches, St. Karapet and Arakelocᶜ (Apostles), built by Princess Mariam of Siwnikᶜ, has become a peninsula. Numerous fish are caught in Lake Sewan, especially the *išχan* (prince), a kind of trout.

BIBLIOGRAPHY

S. T. Eremyan, "Gelakuneacᶜ cov," in *Hayastanĕ ĕst "Ašxarhacoycᶜ"-i* (1963), 47; *Nagel's Encyclopedia-Guide: U.S.S.R.* (1978), 725–728, 745–746; Ferdinand C. F. Lehmann-Haupt, *Armenien, einst und jetzt,* 2 vols.

SEX AETATES MUNDI

in 3 (1910–1931), I, 158–164; "Sevan," in *Great Soviet Encyclopedia,* XXXI (1982); Marietta Sergeevna Shaginyan, *Journey Through Soviet Armenia* (1954), 183–185; A. Surkhatyan, ed., *Guide-book Through Transcaucasia* (1932).

ROBERT H. HEWSEN

[See also **Armenia, Geography.**]

SEX AETATES MUNDI, the six ages of the world, is a commonplace of medieval historical thought; the ages are the traditional divisions of history from Creation to Doomsday. The first age extends from Adam to Noah; the second age, from Noah to Abraham; the third age, from Abraham to David; the fourth age, from David to the Babylonian Captivity; the fifth age, from the Babylonian Captivity to Jesus; and the sixth age, from Jesus to Doomsday. With a few minor variations and an occasional occurrence of a system of five ages, this division into six ages is repeated again and again in histories and in summaries of history in other types of writings. We find it, for example, in Orosius, in Gregory I the Great, in Isidore of Seville, in Bede, in Aelfric, and in the fourteenth-century *Cursor mundi* and *Polychronicon.* It is even represented in the border scenes of the stained-glass window in Canterbury Cathedral that portrays the wedding at Cana. Medieval historians frequently included estimates of the lengths of the ages, with or without a reminder of the biblical warning against predicting Doomsday. Each of the five ages already past was thought to have lasted roughly 1,000 years. The idea of the six ages was sufficiently entrenched in eighth-century England for Bede to be charged with heresy for departing radically from the usual dating of the beginning of the sixth age.

The six ages of the world doubtless provided a convenient formula for organizing and remembering scriptural history. The concept was not, however, merely a convenience for historians and their readers. It was also Christian doctrine, an important part of the typology linking history, liturgy, and the spiritual life of the individual.

The concept originated in Jewish apocalyptic writings as one of many ways of conceiving the span of history preceding the messianic age, the last phase of man's earthly history, to be followed—according to the later apocalypses—by an eternity of bliss in heaven for the righteous. Early Christian writers shared the eschatological interests of Jewish apocalyptic, but they also sought specifically Christian interpretations of history. The six ages proved readily adaptable to eschatology and Christian apologetic. The six ages, followed by a seventh messianic age, constituted a "world week" parallel to Creation week. As Adam was created on the sixth day, so Jesus, the second Adam, came in the sixth age. As the six days of creation were followed by a seventh day of rest, later sanctified and commemorated in weekly sabbath observances, so the six ages would be followed by a seventh in which man would enjoy the life for which he was created and would be free from evil. In the idea of an eternity to follow the messianic age, the Christian writers found support for their view that Christianity had superseded Judaism and had made Sunday, not Saturday, the proper day for worship. For the Christians, the eternity to follow the seventh age was the eighth age, comparable to Sunday, which can be considered both as an eighth day following the seventh and as the first day of the following week.

In the fifth century St. Augustine fell heir to the eschatology of the world week, and out of it he formulated the interpretation of the ages of the world that subsequently entered the mainstream of medieval thought. First of all, he treats the six ages as useful divisions of history, not just as a symbolically conceived prelude to the ages to come. He reinterprets the seventh age, eliminating the millenarian emphasis and seeing it in part as a symbol for the spiritual peace enjoyed by the faithful of the sixth age rather than as an age in its own right. Insofar as it is an actual age, it is a mysterious prelude to the eighth age of eternity. As the seventh day of Creation week lacks an evening, so will the seventh age give place to the eighth without a break. Augustine fully develops the idea of the eighth age, which he sees foreshadowed in the Resurrection and the descent of the Holy Spirit at Pentecost, and in the liturgy commemorating these events. To the parallel between history and liturgy, Augustine adds that of the stages of human life, the seven ages of man.

Augustine, then, gave the six ages of the world sufficient significance as history that they could be used independently of the theology of the world week. He also, however, made them inseparable from that theology, for the message of salvation is implicit in his view of history as an octave of ages.

BIBLIOGRAPHY
Bedae Opera de temporibus, Charles W. Jones, ed. (1943), esp. 130–138, 345; Peter Hunter Blair, *The World of Bede* (1970), 265–271; Fernand Cabrol and Henri Leclercq, *Dictionnaire d'archéologie chrétienne et de liturgie,* IV, 1 (1920), 858–994; Jean Daniélou, "La typologie de la semaine du IVe siècle," in *Recherches de science religieuse,* 35 (1948), and *The Bible and the Liturgy* (1956, repr. 1961, 1964), chaps. 14–16; David C. Fowler, *The Bible in Early English Literature* (1976), chaps. 5, 6; Milton McC. Gatch, *Preaching and Theology in Anglo-Saxon England: Aelfric and Wulfstan* (1977), chap. 7; Charles W. Jones, "Some Introductory Remarks on Bede's Commentary on Genesis," in *Sacris Erudiri,* 19 (1969–1970); Auguste Laneau, *L'histoire du salut chez les Pères de l'Église: La doctrine des âges du monde* (1964); Émile Mâle, *The Gothic Image: Religious Art in France of the Thirteenth Century,* Dora Nussey, trans. (1972), 194–195; C. A. Patrides, *The Grand Design of God: The Literary Form of the Christian View of History* (1972), chaps. 2, 3; David Syme Russell, *The Method and Message of Jewish Apocalyptic: 200 B.C.–A.D. 100* (1964), chaps. 8, 11.

FRANCES RANDALL LIPP

[See also **Aelfric; Apocalyptic Literature and Movement, Jewish; Augustine of Hippo, St.; Bede; Gregory I the Great, Pope; Historiography, Western European; Isidore of Seville, St.; Orosius.**]

SEXPARTITE VAULT. See **Vault.**

SFORZA, a powerful Milanese family. The Attendoli were farmers who cultivated lands at Cotignola, near Ravenna. Muzio Attendolo (1369–1424) left the fields to follow the condottiere Alberico da Barbiano. In admiration for his bravery Muzio was given the nickname of "Sforza" (the powerful). The sons of Muzio Attendolo Sforza founded the various branches of the family: the Sforza of Milan, of Pesaro, and of Santafiora.

Francesco I Sforza (1401–1466) was a condottiere, first in the pay of the Visconti, then of the pope, then of the Venetians, and finally of Filippo Maria Visconti, duke of Milan. In 1441 Filippo Maria married his illegitimate daughter, Bianca Maria, to Francesco Sforza. The Ambrosian Republic (1447–1450), set up on the death of Filippo Maria, was soon politically bankrupt. Attacked by the Venetians, the Genoese, and the French, Milan was forced to entrust its defense to Francesco Sforza. After years of war Francesco, at the Peace of Lodi (1454), persuaded Venice, Florence, Rome, and Naples to form the Italian League, which made possible forty years of relative peace.

Sforza reorganized the army and the government, encouraged industry and commerce, especially with the countries beyond the Alps, and brought expert Tuscan bankers to Milan. He also fostered work on the construction of the cathedral, founded by Gian Galeazzo Visconti in 1386, and on the Certosa of Pavia. Scholars, writers, musicians, and artists came to his court.

When Francesco Sforza died in 1466, his widow secured the succession for their son Galeazzo Maria (*r.* 1466–1476). In 1468 Galeazzo married Bona of Savoy, a cousin of Louis XI of France. Despotic and vicious, Galeazzo promoted policies that were confused and ended by isolating Milan. He increased agricultural production by constructing new canals, and he encouraged the growing of rice and the production of silk. He was killed by three conspirators on 26 December 1476. His widow acted as regent for their minor son, Gian Galeazzo II Maria, aided by the chancellor, Cicco Simonetta. In 1478, when Genoa rebelled against the Sforza and the Swiss occupied the Ticino Valley, Ludivoci il Moro, brother of the murdered Galeazzo Maria, offered to return to Milan to assist the regent, threatening to attack the city if he were rebuffed. By 1479 he had persuaded Bona to surrender the regency and had become master of the Sforza state.

In 1489 Ludovico married his nephew Gian Galeazzo to Isabella, daughter of the king of Naples. When Gian Galeazzo died in 1494, Ludovico, hoping to ward off Neapolitan influence, encouraged Charles VIII of France to intervene in Italy. A large number of Italian states formed a coalition against Charles. On his death in April 1498, Louis XII became king. Louis, the grandson of Valentina Visconti, claimed that he had a better right to hold Milan than did Ludovico. In the summer of 1499, Louis entered Italy and Ludovico had to flee. Early in 1500 he tried to regain Milan but was captured by the French and taken to France, where he died in 1508.

The years of Ludovico's rule were a splendid period in the history of Milan. Industry and commerce flourished. The court was thronged with architects (Donato Bramante), painters (Leonardo da Vinci), musicians, writers, and printers. Ludovico's son Massimiliano, with the help of the Swiss, succeeded in regaining control of Milan for a few years (1512–1515), but the victory of Francis I at Melegnano in 1515 put Milan again under French rule. France lost Milan in 1524 when the imperial army won the Battle of Pavia and captured the king of France. At the Peace of Cambrai in 1529, Emperor Charles V recognized Francesco II Sforza, the younger son of Ludovico, as duke of Milan. When Francesco died in 1535, Charles V took over the duchy and sent a Spanish governor to Milan. For the next two centuries Milan was to remain a dependency of Madrid.

BIBLIOGRAPHY

Cecilia M. Ady, *A History of Milan Under the Sforza,* Edward Armstrong, ed. (1907); Julia Cartwright, *Beatrice d'Este, Duchess of Milan (1475–1497),* 2nd ed. (1903); Lacy Collison-Morley, *The Story of the Sforzas* (1934); Christopher Hare, *Isabella of Milan* (1911); Francesco Malaguzzi-Valeri, *La corte di Lodovico il Moro,* 4 vols. (1913–1923); Caterina Santoro, *Gli Sforza* (1968); Klaus Schelle, *Die Sforza: Bauern, Condottieri, Herzöge* (1980); *Storia di Milano,* VII and VIII (1956–1957).

ANGELO PAREDI

[See also **Condottieri; Italy, Fourteenth and Fifteenth Centuries; Louis XI; Milan; Visconti.**]

SHADDADIDS. The Shaddadids were an important Muslim dynasty ruling in eastern Transcaucasia in the tenth and eleventh centuries. Their main centers were Ganjak in Caucasian Armenia (later Azerbaijan), Dwin in eastern Armenia, and, later, the Bagratid capital of Ani in northern Armenia (twelfth century). The numerous references to the Shaddadids found in Armenian, Georgian, Arabic, and Persian sources were collected and analyzed by Vladimir Minorsky in his *Studies in Caucasian History.* According to these sources, the founder of the dynasty, Muḥammad ibn Shaddād, took power from the ruling Musafirids at Dwin in the mid tenth century, but the position of the family was not firmly established at Dwin until 971. Muḥammad's son Faḍl secured power in Albania, where he ruled from 986 to 1031, waging successful battles against the Armenian and Georgian Bagratids, and perhaps engaging the Rawwadids in Caucasian Armenia. During the next decade Faḍl's descendants were on the defensive against Byzantines, Georgians, Caucasian mountaineers, Russians, Rawwadids, and Oghuz Turks.

The Shaddadids were most powerful under Abu 'l-Aswār Shāwur, who ruled Dwin from 1022 to 1049 and Ganjak from 1049 until 1067. In alliance with the Byzantine Empire, which was attacking western Armenia, Abu 'l Aswār invaded Ani in the early 1040's. He was appointed governor of Ani in 1065 by Toghrıl, to whom he had submitted in 1054–1055. Subsequently the city of Ani was purchased from the Seljuks (1072), and a secondary branch of the Shaddadids, descended from Abu 'l Aswār's son Manūchihr (Minučihr), ruled there, with interruptions, from 1072 until 1199.

Following his appointment as governor of Ani in 1065, Abu 'l Aswār allied with the Turkomans and continued offensive military operations against the petty princes of eastern Asia Minor. He also invaded the holdings of his relatives, the Shīrwan-Shahs, from 1063 until after 1094. Eventually the expansion of Seljuk power ended the main line of the Shaddadids. After Abu 'l Aswār's son Faḍl II was captured by the Georgians, the Shīrwān-Shāh invaded Albania. This was followed by two invasions of the Seljuk general Sawtegin, to whom Faḍl III yielded his lands in 1075.

The Shaddadids appear to have been of Kurdish origin, though they often adopted Daylamite and Armenian names, peoples with whom they had marriage and trade alliances. Shaddadid rule over Ganjak and Dwin, cities with important Muslim populations, differed considerably from their rule in Ani, whose population was predominantly Christian. Despite Christian-Muslim friction there, the period of Shaddadid rule over Ani was one of important cultural and economic development.

BIBLIOGRAPHY

The main source on the Shaddadids of Dwin and Ganjak is Münejjim Bashi, *Jamiᶜ al-duwal.* For the Shaddadids of Ani, the thirteenth-century Armenian historian Vardan Arewelcᶜi is the main source: see his *Hawakᶜumn patmutᶜean Vardanay vardapeti Lusabaneal* (1862).

Studies include *Cambridge History of Iran,* J. A. Boyle, ed., V (1968), 34–35; Hakob Manandyan, *The Trade and Cities of Armenia in Relation to Ancient World Trade,* Nina G. Garsoïan, trans. (1965), 176–177, 180–182; Vladimir Minorsky, *Studies in Caucasian History* (1953), which contains a translation of the *Jamiᶜ al-duwal* and detailed comparative studies of the Shaddadids of Ganjak (1–76) and of Ani (79–103); E. Denison Ross, "Shaddād, Banū," in *Encyclopaedia of*

Islam, 1st ed., IV (1934); Aram Ter Ghevondian, "Munaǰǰim Bašin Dvini ev Ganjaki Šaddadyanneri masin" (Müneǰǰim Bashī on the Shaddadids of Dwin and Ganjak), in *Banber matenadarani,* **6** (1962), and "Anin Šaddadyanneri tiryutʿ," in *Hay žołovdri patmutʿyun* (History of the Armenian people), III (1976).

ROBERT BEDROSIAN

[See also **Albania (Caucasian); Ani in Širak; Armenia, Geography; Armenia: History of; Armenian Muslim Emirates; Azerbaijan; Dwin; Ganjak; Kurds.**]

SHADIRVAN is a Persian term also used in Arabic and Turkish for "water channel" or "fountain." In Iran a section of a streambed paved with stones to control and channel the flow of water is known as a *shadirvan.* In the Mediterranean Islamic world this term was applied to watercourses and fountain basins in homes, gardens, and mosques. Sometimes the water fell over an inclined plane, and sometimes it was sprayed in a jet from a spout. In homes and gardens it was popular to have a zoomorphic spout, often a sculpture in the form of a lion, rabbit, or bird. In Turkish mosques the basin holding water for ritual ablutions is known as a *shadirvan.* Usually this basin's outer walls are provided with spigots for the convenience of worshipers.

BIBLIOGRAPHY

Celal E. Arseven, *Türk sanati tarihi* (*ca.* 1956), 511–515; ʿAli Akbar Dihkhuda, *Loghat-nama* (1969); Reinhart Dozy, *Supplement aux dictionnaires arabes,* I (1881, repr. 1927, 1968), 715; Godfrey Goodwin, *A History of Ottoman Architecture* (1979).

PRISCILLA P. SOUCEK

[See also **Irrigation; Technology, Islamic.**]

SHĀFIʿĪ, AL- (Muḥammad ibn Idrīs al-Shāfiʿī, 767–820), famous legal theorist of Sunni Islam and founder of the Shāfiʿī school, or rite, of Islamic law. Through his teaching and writing, Shāfiʿī altered the course of the development of jurisprudence by his persuasive systematic presentation of its methodology.

Shāfiʿī was born in Palestine, either in Gaza or in Ascalon. He was a member of the prophet Muḥammad's tribe (Quraysh) on his father's side; his mother was from the ʿAzd tribe. Shāfiʿī's father died when he was very young; his mother then brought him to Mecca, where he grew up in relatively poor circumstances. Shāfiʿī early on showed a scholarly bent and as a boy devoted time to studying Arabic literature, jurisprudence, and the traditions of Islam (*ḥadīth*)—oral and written reports about the prophet Muḥammad's life and the lives of his family and close associates.

When he was about twenty, Shāfiʿī went to Medina to study with the famous legal scholar Mālik ibn Anas (*d.* 795). He remained there until Mālik's death. After that he spent some time in the Yemen and then in Iraq, but his activities in each place and the length of time he stayed cannot be established with certainty from the available sources. In 814, he went to Egypt, and he lived and taught in Cairo until his death.

The importance of Shāfiʿī's thinking can best be understood in the context of the development of Sunni jurisprudence during the first two centuries of Islam. The prophet Muḥammad tried to organize the early Muslims into a community based on belief in Islam rather than one based on a tribal system. To a certain extent he succeeded, and he thereby created the beginnings of Islamic law—a sacred law that describes the total life of the Muslim in relation to God. While the Prophet was alive, he was available to provide the early Muslims with guidance, to act as a model for them, and to explain the Koran. However, the Koran is not a code of laws, nor does it set out a theory of law as a framework for further legal development. Therefore, after Muḥammad's death, people turned for advice to groups of pious individuals who thought about and discussed with each other the most Muslim way of conducting all aspects of daily life. These men became Islam's first lawyers, consulted by rulers and government officials on the proper implementation of Islam and by individual Muslims on particular issues. As each of them gained a reputation for knowledge, he acquired a circle of pupils who wished to listen to his lectures, ask him questions, and write down his teaching.

These lawyers surveyed existing legal institutions and practices with a view to introducing religious and moral ideas into both public and private life. They based their doctrines on the Koran and on their own considered opinion (*raʾy*) of what was correct.

In addition to the lawyers, there was another group of early specialists who discussed, collected, and wrote down information about the Prophet's life. They informed themselves and others of what was done, said, or decided by the Prophet, his family, and his close associates on all possible subjects. These men were the traditionists of Islam. They too gained reputations for knowledge and acquired pupils. By the end of the first century of Islam, traditionists had felt it necessary to quote their authorities, and thus each tradition came to consist of a text (*matn*) and a chain of transmitters (*isnād*), a list of names, in chronological order, of people who had known the Prophet or were themselves reputed religious scholars. A major activity of the traditionists was differentiating between genuine and false traditions, usually by considering the reliability of the transmitters in the *isnād*.

It was not unusual for a scholar to be both a traditionist and a lawyer. Shāfiᶜī's teacher, Mālik, for example, combined these two branches of scholarly activity and often used traditions to support legal doctrine. He did not do so regularly, and he often preferred the local doctrines of Medina to those expressed in the traditions. Nevertheless, after Mālik, incorporating traditions into legal reasoning became one of the most characteristic features of Islamic jurisprudence.

Although Shāfiᶜī always considered himself a disciple of Mālik and a member of the school of law that was growing up around Mālik's teaching, once he had created his own legal theory, he attempted to convert the Medinese scholars as well as the scholars of other areas to his point of view. Shāfiᶜī's major systematic innovation was to insist upon a formal role for traditions in legal theory. In his polemical writings, Shāfiᶜī attacked his predecessors for their inconsistent use of legal source material in general and in particular for their failure to systematically integrate traditions into the theoretical thinking upon which they based their doctrines. However, by Shāfiᶜī's time, thousands of traditions had been collected; many of them were doubtless genuine, but some had certainly been made up in support of various partisan doctrines. Shāfiᶜī saw that unless a consistent method was effected for sifting them, traditions could be found to support almost any doctrine.

In developing criteria for discriminating among traditions and establishing their value as evidence for doctrine, Shāfiᶜī elaborated *uṣūl al-fiqh,* the discipline dealing with the sources or theoretical bases of law. They are the Koran, the sunna (model behavior of the Prophet), *ijmāᶜ* (the consensus of the community), and *qiyās* (a method of analogical reasoning). The classical theory of Sunni Muslim law bases the whole legal system on these four sources, and Shāfiᶜī is considered the author of this theory. First and foremost, the Koran is consulted, but since it is not a complete legal document the next source consulted is the sunna of the Prophet, which is to be ascertained by reference to traditions. The traditions that document the sunna reliably are those with chains of transmitters that go directly back to the Prophet himself. This is a point that Shāfiᶜī insisted upon repeatedly. He declared himself anxious at any time to change his doctrines if he learned of traditions from the Prophet supporting different ones. Shāfiᶜī was also willing to admit traditions with *isnāds* from the Prophet's family or close associates as subsidiary arguments, but these traditions could be superseded by the use of *qiyās* based on traditions from the Prophet. *Qiyās,* the use of analogical reasoning to reach a conclusion on a matter about which there is neither a statement in the Koran nor a tradition from the Prophet, is, in fact, *raᵓy,* the considered opinion of the early lawyers, with specific rules for its use. *Ijmāᶜ* is the consensus of the Muslim community on doctrines sanctioned by local practice and scholarly approval.

Shāfiᶜī presented his thinking in numerous treatises, most of which have survived. They were collected by his pupils and are available today in one large compendium, the *kitāb al-umm* (published in Cairo in 1903–1908 in seven volumes, and again in 1961 in eight volumes). Only a small portion of *kitāb al-umm* has been translated into English.

In the process of collecting, disseminating, and commenting upon his work, Shāfiᶜī's pupils created a school of law. Today, the Shāfiᶜī school is prominent in lower Egypt, certain parts of the Arabian peninsula, Malaya, Indonesia, East Africa, and parts of Central Asia.

BIBLIOGRAPHY

Majid Khadduri, *Islamic Jurisprudence: Shāfiᶜī's Risāla* (1961); Joseph Schacht, *The Origins of Muhammadan Jurisprudence* (1950), and "On Shāfiᶜī's Life and Personality," in *Studia Orientalia Joanni Pederson* (1953); Fuat Sezgin, *Geschichte des arabischen Schriftums,* I (1967).

SUSAN SPECTORSKY

[See also **Cairo; Ḥadīth; Koran; Law, Islamic; Malīk ibn Anas; Sunna.**]

SHAHANSHAH. See **Šāhan-šāh.**

SHĀH-ARMAN (*shāh-i Arman, Arman-shāh*), a Persian term meaning "king of the Armenians" and often applied to the Turko-Muslim rulers of the Xlat^c (Akhlāṭ or Khilāṭ or Khlat^c) region near the northwestern corner of Lake Van in eastern Anatolia, hence, sometimes *Akhlāṭ-shah.* Prior to the Seljuk conquest about 1084–1085, this border region, with a mixed Kurdish and Armenian population, had been ruled (since 983) by the Kurdish Marwanids. The Marwanids submitted to the Seljuks but in 1100 were replaced, at the request of the populace, by a Seljuk *ghulām* (military slave), Sökmen al-Quṭbī. The latter founded the Shāh-Arman statelet, associated primarily with his family, which lasted until 1207. Sökmen, an important figure in the anti-crusader Muslim coalitions of the Syro-Anatolian borderlands, was considered a just ruler by his Armenian subjects. His support of Muḥammad Tapar against Barkiyāruq in the intra-Seljuk struggles for the throne following the death of Malikshāh in 1092 ultimately strengthened his position. At the time of his death in 1112, Sökmen's realm included Manazkert, Arčēš, Mayyāfāriqīn (Martyropolis), and other regions of eastern Anatolia. His son Ibrāhīm (*r.* 1112–1128), mired in domestic difficulties, lost much of this territory. Recovery came under Sökmen II (*r.* 1128–1185), who became one of the leading participants in the Turko-Muslim struggle against the expanding Georgian kingdom. The contest for Ani and the Armenian lands (1161–1175), from which the Georgians ultimately emerged victorious, diverted Sökmen II from the steady encroachments of the Ayyubids. Thus, when he died without a male heir, an Ayyubid bid for the Shāh-Arman realm was checked only by the intervention of the Ildegizid atabeg Jahān Pahlawān. Begtimur (*r.* 1185–1193), one of Sökmen II's servitors, now took the throne. He barely survived an attempted Ayyubid takeover, only to be murdered by his son-in-law and fellow *ghulām* Aq Sunqur (*r.* 1193–1197). Begtimur's son Muḥammad (*r.* 1198–1206) regained the throne but was largely a figurehead for the Kipchak *ghulām* Quṭlugh, who ran the government. This internal chaos, exacerbated by Georgian inroads, allowed yet another *ghulām,* Balaban (*r.* 1206–1207), to seize power. He was toppled by the Seljuk Toghrıl-Shāh, but the bulk of the Shāh-Arman realm, including Xlat^c, fell to the Ayyubids in 1207.

BIBLIOGRAPHY

Sources. Muslim sources include Abū 'l Fida, *Kitāb al-Mukhṭasar fī Akhbār al-bashar,* 2 vols. (1956–1961); Ibn al-Athīr, *Ta$^⊃$rīkh al-bahīr fī al-dawla al-aṭabakiyya,* A. A. Tolaymat, ed. (1963); Ibn al-Azraq al-Fāriqī, *Ta$^⊃$rīkh Mayyāfāriqīn,* in Ibn al-Qalānisī, *Dhayl Ta$^⊃$rīkh Dimashq,* Henry F. Amedroz, ed. (1903); al-Ḥusaynī, *Akhbār Dawlah al-Saljūqīyah,* Muḥammad Iqbāl, ed. (1933); Hamd Allāh Mustaufī al-Kazwīnī, *The Ta$^⊃$rīkh-i guzīda; or "Select History" of Hamdu$^⊃$llah Mustawfī-i Qazwīnī,* Edward G. Browne, ed., 2 vols. (1910–1913); Fuad Köprülü, "Anadolu Selçukluları tarihinin yerli kaynaakları," in *Türk tarih kurumu belleten,* **27** (1943).

Armenian sources include Matthew of Edessa, *Patmut^{c}iwn Matt^{c}ēosi Uṙhayec^{c}woy* (1869), extracts translated into French by William McGucken, Baron de Slane, along with the continuation of the chronicle by Grigor the Priest, in *Recueil des historiens des Croisades: Historiens orientaux,* 5 vols. (1872–1906), I; Samuel of Ani, *Hawak^c munk^{c}i groc^{c}patmagrac^c,* A. Ter Mik^{c}elean, ed. (1893), translated by Marie F. Brosset as "Chronique," in *Collection d'historiens arméniens,* II (1876).

Syriac sources include Bar Hebraeus, *The Chronography of Gregory Abu l-Faraj . . . ,* Ernest A. Wallis Budge, trans. (1932); Michael the Syrian, *Chronique de Michel le syrien, patriache jacobite d'Antioche . . . ,* Jean B. Chabot, ed. and trans., 3 vols. (1899–1910, repr. 1963).

Studies. Claude Cahen, "Le diyār Bakr au temps des premiers Urṭukides," in *Journal asiatique,* **22** (1935); Vladimir F. Minorsky, "Caucasia in the History of Mayyāfāriqīn," in *Bulletin of the School of Oriental and African Studies,* **13** (1949), and *Studies in Caucasian History* (1953); Osman Turan, *Doğu Anadolu Türk devletleri tarihi* (1973).

PETER B. GOLDEN

[See also **Arčēš; Armenia, Geography; Armenia: History of; Armenian Muslim Emirates; Ayyubids; Ildegizids; Malikshāh; Manazkert; Seljuks; Xlat^c.**]

SHĀHNĀMA. The *Shāhnāma* (Book of kings) is an epic poem in Persian embodying a large part of the Iranian national legend. It was completed in about 1010 by Abū 'l-Qāsim Firdawsī (940/941–1020/1025). Almost nothing is known about Firdawsī's life, and no other works can be attributed to him with certainty. Internal evidence in the

Shāhnāma indicates that Firdawsī was born into the *dehqān* (provincial landowning class) in Ṭūs, a city in the eastern Iranian province of Khorāsān. This class had existed since the Sasanian period, and in Firdawsī's time it preserved the older Iranian traditions, values, and way of life.

In the late tenth century there was a well-developed tradition of writing works titled *Shāhnāma*. The pattern had been set in the late Sasanian period when a lengthy chronicle was compiled by the court and called *Khwadāy* (*Xwadāy*) *Nāmag* (Book of kings). This chronicle and succeeding versions in the early Islamic period formed the basis of a great deal of Firdawsī's *Shāhnāma*. When Firdawsī began writing his epic (probably around 975), he had available to him several prose and verse versions of the chronicle of the kings of Iran, but it appears that he actually worked from a prose *Shāhnāma* that had been compiled in 957 by four experts at the order of the governor of Ṭūs. This text, like the preceding works titled *Shāhnāma* and the Sasanian chronicle (except for fragments), has perished, but the introduction to it has survived. Much of the material in Firdawsī's *Shāhnāma* derives directly from this prose version, but Firdawsī must have used orally transmitted stories and other books as well.

The poetic meters used in Persia from the tenth century on were quantitative, being based on regularly recurring patterns of long and short syllables. The meter that Firdawsī chose for his *Shāhnāma* consisted of eight metrical units corresponding to the classical bacchius in two hemistichs, called *motaqāreb* (*mutaqārib*). The hemistichs of each line have end rhyme, but successive lines do not rhyme with each other. There is a regular caesura between hemistichs, but no regular one within each hemistich. This form, which resembles rhyming couplets, is the most suitable Persian form for extended narrative poetry.

Firdawsī's *Shāhnāma* is a vast epic in terms both of its size and of the time span and variety of material encompassed by it. The critical edition published in Moscow (1960–1971) runs to something over 45,000 lines. It is a history of the Iranian people from the creation of the world until the conquest of the Sasanian dynasty by the Arabs in the seventh century. The existing chronicle and *Shāhnāma* tradition provided Firdawsī with the basic format for his epic, and he used the unifying theme of Iranian kingship and legitimate succession to tie his material together.

The narrative of the *Shāhnāma* is a chronological account of four successive dynasties: the Pishdadian, the Kayanian, the Ashkanian or Parthian (*ca.* 150 B.C.–A.D. 224), and the Sasanian (224–651). Each of these dynasties is subdivided into the reigns of its kings, totaling fifty in all, and it is the stories of these kings that form the basic narrative units of the text. Woven into this sequence of reigns from the latter days of the Pishdadians through the Kayanians is an extensive cycle of heroic tales centered on an eastern Iranian dynasty from Sīstān that forms a counterpoint to the succession of kings. Rustam, the mighty hero of Sīstān, was a Saka or Scythian hero, and tales of him were probably brought to Sīstān (from Sakastan, land of the Sakas) when the Sakas invaded and settled the area in the second century B.C. Over the centuries these tales of the Saka heroes were "nationalized" by the Iranians, and the genealogies of these heroes were integrated with those of the Iranian royal house.

The Pishdadian dynasty is mythical; the Kayanian is probably legendary; and the Parthian and Sasanian dynasties are historical. The greater part of the narrative concerns the historical dynasties, but the Parthians are dealt with only briefly, whereas the Sasanians are treated at great length. Not all the material in this part is "historical" in the strict sense, for Firdawsī weaves into his narrative legends and romances such as that of Xusrō and Shirin. The epic spirit that imbues the mythical and legendary parts of the *Shāhnāma* is to some extent lacking in the historical sections. Here the poet had more detailed historical records to work from and consequently less scope within which to exercise his imagination. Firdawsī says that he tried to remain faithful to his sources, and the result is that in the latter portions of his text he becomes more a versifier of history than an epic poet. The present-day audiences for oral recitations of the *Shāhnāma* (like the audiences of the past, so far as we can tell) prefer listening to the mythical and legendary parts of the epic, and show little interest in the historical parts.

Iranian literature since pre-Islamic times has always had a strong didactic aspect, and the *Shāhnāma* is squarely within this tradition. Scattered through the text are passages that point out morals; uphold the social order; preach the virtues of wisdom, justice, and honesty; and stress the value of honor, manliness, patriotism, and freedom. At the same time there are many passages empha-

The Battle of Pashan begins. Safavid miniature from a *Shāhnāma* MS of *ca.* 1530–1535. THE METROPOLITAN MUSEUM OF ART, NEW YORK, GIFT OF ARTHUR A. HOUGHTON, JR., 1970 (1970.301.37)

sizing the transitory nature of earthly existence and the fickleness of fortune. A sense of fatalism and the vanity of human desires is strong in the legendary parts of the *Shāhnāma,* but less so in the historical sections, where the stress is on ethical values.

The world of the *Shāhnāma* is centered in Iran and extends outward in all directions. The geographical scope of the action in the poem is vast. War and hunting expeditions carry the Persian heroes far beyond the boundaries of Iran to Arabia, Byzantium, Central Asia, China, India, and elsewhere. Despite this variety of terrain, local color is not used by Firdawsī; and whether the action be in Arabia or in China, the only variable is the enemy.

This outward-looking quality of the *Shāhnāma* can be accounted for by the varied sources of the Iranian epic and the broad extent of the Iranian cultural area. When the Iranian people entered the plateau that is now Iran in the second millennium B.C., they brought with them tales and legends predating the time when they began to form a separate nation. Long after the plateau was settled, the Iranian world remained broad. Iranians were found from the Caucasus and the steppes north of the Black Sea to the borders of China and Tibet. As groups became isolated, variations of older legends must have developed, along with stories and tales peculiar to each group and locality. All these formed tributaries that fed into the mainstream of the national legend.

As the Iranians made their way onto the plateau, over a period of time many of them began shifting from a nomadic to a sedentary way of life. Conflicts undoubtedly developed between the pastoralists and the agriculturalists. From these transitional times and later, one of the major themes of Iranian epic poetry began to emerge: Iran against Turan. Religious and national traditions in Iran hold that the Iranians and the Turanians were of one race, but that the Iranians became settled and developed urban life before the Turanians. The Oxus River (Amu Darya) traditionally formed the boundary between these hostile nations. Various traditions must have come together to form Firdawsī's version, for in the *Shāhnāma* the Turanians are identified as Central Asian Turks and sometimes as Chinese.

To the basic conflict between settled peoples and nomads, Zoroastrianism, the religion prevalent in Iran from the beginning of Sasanian times to the coming of Islam, added a moral dimension of good against evil, so that in the *Shāhnāma* we find the theme of this conflict in its various dimensions objectified as a long-continuing war between Iran and Turan, beginning during the Pishdadian dynasty and continuing well into the age of the Kayanians. Rustam, the greatest hero in the *Shāhnāma,* spends most of his long fighting career contending with the Turanians, who are Iran's most bitter enemy throughout the national legend.

The language of the *Shāhnāma* is relatively simple, with no glaring discontinuities of style. Its simplicity is due to the low number of Arabic loanwords in it and the restrained use of rhetorical devices. There is no great difference between the language of the narrative and that spoken by the characters. Social levels are equalized by this language, in that friends and enemies, kings and generals all speak at the same stylistic level. This is also true of the language used by the poet himself when he enters the narrative to comment on the action or to draw a moral.

Until very recently the lack of an adequate critical edition of the *Shāhnāma* had impeded up-to-date critical studies of the work in the manner of contemporary works on such epics as the *Iliad* and the *Chanson de Roland.* The *Shāhnāma* has been translated—in full and in part—into English and other languages, but again the lack of a critical edition from which to work renders these translations somewhat unrepresentative of Firdawsī's original.

BIBLIOGRAPHY

A critical edition is *Shāhnāma,* Evgeny A. Bartels, ed., 9 vols. (1960–1971).

Translations include *Sháhnáma,* Arthur G. Warner and Edmond Warner, trans., 9 vols. (1905–1925); *Das iranische Nationalepos,* Theodor Nöldeke, trans., 2nd ed. (1920), translated by Leonid Bogdanov as *The Iranian National Legend* (1930, repr. 1979); *The Epic of the Kings,* Reuben Levy, trans. (1967).

Studies include Īraj Afshār, *Bibliography on Firdawsī* (1968), in Persian; W. Barthold, "Zur Geschichte des persischen Epos," in *Zeitschrift der Deutschen morgenländischen Gesellschaft,* **98** (1944); William L. Hanaway, Jr., "The Iranian Epics," in Felix J. Oinas, ed., *Heroic Epic and Saga* (1978); Henri Massé, *Les épopées persanes* (1935).

WILLIAM LIPPINCOTT HANAWAY, JR.

[See also **Bahrām VI Čōbēn; Iranian Literature; Pahlavi Literature; Parthians; Sasanians; Xwadāy Nāmag.**]

SHAMS AL-DĪN MUḤAMMAD. See Ḥāfiẓ.

SHAPUR. See Šābuhr.

SHEM TOV (Šem Ṭob, Santo, Santob de Carrión) (*fl.* mid fourteenth century), Hebrew and Spanish poet. His complete Jewish name is Rab (Rabbi) Shem Tov ben Yitzhak Ardutiel, and the forms Santo or Santob de Carrión appeared in his most remarkable work, written in Castilian around 1350, the *Proverbios morales,* a series of poems on ethical and intellectual questions. He lived during the reigns of Alfonso XI (1312–1350) and his son Pedro I (1350–1369). The few biographical facts we have are deduced from the work itself, which has been transmitted in five manuscripts. Shem Tov also wrote, in Hebrew, a liturgical hymn (*Vidui,* confession), a *ma*ᶜ*ase* (*magāma,* narrative in rhymed prose), and a *bakkashah* (liturgical supplication).

Shem Tov embodies perfectly the Judeo-Spanish cultural symbiosis of his social class in fourteenth-century Spain. The *Proverbios morales* remain one of the enigmatic texts of the Middle Ages in Spain, partly because the philological reconstitution of these approximately 725 heptasyllabic quatrains, *a b a b* (with the possibility of homoeoteleuton) involves asking complex questions. At the same time, not only their literal meaning but also their philosophical and religious interpretation have been and are still discussed.

Shem Tov's system of thought in *Proverbios morales* is characterized by skepticism. In contrast to the dominant ideology of the hierarchy of concepts and values, he unequivocally espoused relativism and the inherent subjectivity of any judgment on any being or any thing (with a few essential exceptions—God, the king, the law). The starting point of his philosophy, like its ending point, is the *I,* who confesses his limits, and the *other,* who is as limited as the former, but perhaps in a different way. The presupposed of this discourse is the observed contemplator, the judge denuded by the accused. The *I* and the *other* continue to metamorphose themselves until they exchange their criteria of appreciation and of course their first opinions.

The *Proverbios morales* is a philosophical work heralding the Renaissance, although it leads to a paralysis of the will. This system of thought tries to integrate movement, change, and dynamism but in fact undercuts its own foundation. The work is thus an aborted attempt. Yet a step forward has been made, and the author rightly deserves a place in the history of Western thought, if only because the philosophy of the poet of Carrión is antidogmatic and open. This characteristic is unusual enough in the Middle Ages, even in the late medieval period, to justify its being included here.

BIBLIOGRAPHY

Sources. Editions of the *Proverbios morales* include Augustín García Calvo, *Don Sem Tob: Glosas de Sabiduría o Proverbios morales y otras Rimas* (1974); Ig. González Llubera, *Santob de Carrión: Proverbios morales* (1947); Theodore A. Perry, ed., *Santob de Carrión: Proverbios morales* (1986), and an English translation, *Santob: The Moral Proverbs of Santob de Carrión* (1987).

Studies. E. Alarcos Llorach, "La lengua de los 'Proverbios morales' de don Sem Tob," in *Revista de filología española,* **35** (1951); Yitzhak Fritz Baer, "Poetic Remains from 14th Century Castile" (in Hebrew), in *Minha le-David* (1935), 197–214, and *A History of the Jews in Christian Spain,* Louis Schoffman, trans., I (1961), 358, 447, note 43; Clark Colahan and Alfred Rodriguez, "Traditional Semitic Forms of Reversibility in Sem Tob's *Proverbios morales,*" in *Journal of Medieval and Renaissance Studies,* **13** (1983); Ig. González Llubera, "The Text and Language of Santob de Carrión's *Proverbios morales,*" in *Hispanic Review,* **8** (1940), and "A Transcription of MS. C of Santob de Carrión's *Proverbios morales,*" in *Romance Philology,* **4** (1950–1951); Jacques Joset, "Opposition et réversibilité des valeurs dans les *Proverbios morales:* Approche du système de pensée de Santob de Carrión," in *Hommage au professeur Maurice Delbouille: Marche Romane* (1973), 171–189, and "Quelques modalités du YO dans les *Proverbios morales* de Santob de Carrion," in *Mélanges Jules Horrent* (1980), 193–204; L. López Grigera, "Un nuevo códice de los *Proverbios morales* de Sem Tob," in *Boletín de la real academia española,* **56** (1976); Theodore A. Perry, "The Present State of Shem Tov Studies," in *La corónica,* **7** (1978); Carlos Polit, "La originalidad expresiva de Sem Tob," in *Revista de estudios hispánicos,* **12** (1978); J. Amador de los Ríos, *Historia crítica de la literatura española,* IV (1863), 461–515; Claudio Sánchez-Albornoz, *España: Un enigma histórico,* I (4th ed. 1973), 535–556, and the English edition, *Spain: A Historical Enigma,* C. J. Dees and D. S. Reher, trans. I (1975), 477–491; Leopold Stein, *Untersuchungen über die "Proverbios morales" von Santob de Carrión, mit* *besonderem hinweis auf die Quellen und Parallelen* (1900); S. M. Stern, review of González Llubera's edition, in *Romance Philology,* 5 (1952), 242–247.

JACQUES JOSET

[See also **Jews in Christian Spain; Spanish Literature.**]

SHEPHERDS' PLAYS. See **Second Shepherds' Play; Towneley Plays.**

SHERIFF. In medieval England each county had as its head an appointed agent of the king called the sheriff. The Anglo-Saxon term was *scírgeréfa* (shire reeve, agent for the county). Its first use occurred just after 1000. Sheriffs were apparently established by then in all the existing counties, except in the still-unshired north, but the office must have been new. When the north was divided into counties in the eleventh and twelfth centuries, sheriffs were appointed there too.

The traditional head of the county was its noble ealdorman, later called the earl. He was supposed to preside in the county court along with the bishop and the sheriff. But earls and bishops could not attend closely to county affairs, and it seems likely, therefore, that all through the eleventh century this level of government was ordinarily directed by the sheriff. His leadership became entirely clear soon after the Norman conquest in 1066. Earldoms were turned into titles of dignity without essential links to the counties after which they were named, and the bishops' courts were separated from secular institutions. Thus the sheriff emerged as the general ruler of the county, president of its court, leader of its military levies with charge of defense and police, and collector of revenues.

Although he was always in principle the king's appointed official, the sheriff often tended to escape royal control. After the Norman conquest the office was commonly given to earls and important barons. In a few counties it became hereditary in such hands, and remained so. London gained the permanent right to elect sheriffs for itself and Middlesex. In sharp reaction to the dangers of these arrangements, Henry II (*r.* 1154–1189) inaugurated a period when appointments went to career men in the king's service. But this was disliked in the counties. By way of concession, it became the practice during the thirteenth century to appoint local residents of the knightly class, and this prevailed as the rule for the rest of the Middle Ages. In the meantime royal control had been strengthened by the development of institutions for supervision. From 1109 the Exchequer held semiannual audits of the sheriffs' accounts. From 1166 justices "in eyre," and later "of assize," were commissioned by the central administration to visit the counties and review their government.

Through these centuries, however, the central government's most effective way of tightening its control in the localities was by the creation of specialized officers and organizations that would operate throughout the kingdom for assigned purposes and answer directly to the center. As the policy was pursued, one function after another was taken away from the sheriff. For example, "escheators" were given charge, from the 1230's, of lands that escheated to the king. Royal manors were leased to parties who accounted at the Exchequer. Special taxes were handled by collectors of subsidies. From as early as the twelfth century the sheriff was forbidden to dispose of the most serious charges of crime, the pleas of the crown, which were reserved for the king's commissioned justices; and after 1194 the pleas of the crown were in many respects "kept"—prepared for the justices—by county coroners and not by the sheriffs. By about 1200 the royal justices had also taken over whatever business the sheriff's county courts had had in disputes over land ownership. In the 1300's the hearing of other civil cases mostly flowed to the Common Pleas in Westminster, and in the 1400's jurisdiction over minor crimes was assigned to the justices of the peace. These last were groups of gentry resident in each county who held continuing royal commissions to "keep the peace." Established in the early fourteenth century as a regular part of local government, they had power to direct the sheriff; and their group, not the sheriff, was thenceforth the true head of the county. The sheriff, however, remained important. He was the executive agent of the justices of the peace and all other justices, and he had residual responsibility for police. He collected the king's debts, bailed prisoners or denied them bail, and impaneled juries. His county court chose the representatives in parliament. But he was one among many officials.

Outside the counties proper, the office of sheriff was imitated in the "palatine" areas of Chester and Durham. Beginning with Bristol in 1373, several boroughs had their own sheriffs. By imitation or imposition the office spread to Wales (especially with the Statute of Wales of 1284) and Ireland. It was also taken up in Scotland, but there it developed far differently.

The first few Scottish sheriffs were appointed by King David I (1124–1153) as his agents in several areas to which he assigned them. David's successors amplified the practice, so that by the early thirteenth century there were sheriffs as far afield as Dumbarton and Inverness. The sheriff's responsibility might extend over a former thanage, but more often it was over an area newly defined, and afterward alterable, for administrative convenience. For Scotland it is proper, therefore, to speak not of counties but of sheriffdoms. The sheriff's influence might fade away in farther parts of his sheriffdom, especially if this extended through the Highlands. There were also many "regalities" where the sheriff had no important authority.

In Scotland the office escaped the whittling away of duties that characterized the later English development. As in England, sheriffs were prohibited from holding the pleas of the crown, but they always retained a comprehensive civil jurisdiction, both of first instance and upon appeal from the baronial courts. The sheriff had charge of police and military affairs, and he collected the bulk of the king's revenues from the land, including escheats and proceeds of taxation. The continued integrity of the office is a sign of the relative weakness of central royal administration. So is the fact that magnates were often appointed as sheriffs, and that after about 1300 many of them held the office by hereditary right.

BIBLIOGRAPHY

William Croft Dickinson, *The Sheriff Court Book of Fife* (1928); William A. Morris, *The Medieval English Sheriff to 1300* (1927, repr. 1968), and, with Joseph R. Strayer, eds., *The English Government at Work; 1327–1336,* II (1947), 41–108; Annette J. Otway-Ruthven, *A History of Medieval Ireland* (1968), 173–181.

DONALD W. SUTHERLAND

[See also **Escheat, Escheator; Justices, Itinerant; Justices of Common Pleas; Justices of the King's Bench; Justices of the Peace; Law, English Common; Parliament, English; Westminster, Statutes of.**]

SHĪᶜA, a major schismatic movement in Islam that subsequently divided into numerous branches. The name means party and referred first to the partisans of ᶜAlī, cousin and son-in-law of the prophet Muḥammad, whose claim to the caliphate they supported in the First Civil War following the murder of the third caliph, ᶜUthmān, in 656.

After the assassination of ᶜAli in 661 and the triumph of his opponent Muᶜāwiya, the founder of the Umayyad caliphate, the Shīᶜa remained active as an opposition movement espousing the rights of the "Family of the Prophet," in particular the sons and descendants of ᶜAlī, to the supreme leadership of the Muslim community. Centered in Al-Kufa, the former capital of ᶜAli, it partly reflected local Iraqi patriotism and resentment of the Syrian ascendancy under the Umayyads. Soon, however, religious aspects came to the fore and deepened the gulf between the Shīᶜa and the Sunnite majority of Muslims.

The violent death of ᶜAlī's son Ḥusayn, grandson of the prophet through his daughter Fāṭima, at the hands of a Kufan army sent by their Umayyad governor near Karbalāᵓ in 680 profoundly shaped the religious outlook of the Shīᶜa and provided it with a powerful and passion-filled motive for revolt. Karbalāᵓ became one of its holy cities. Among the Kufan Shīᶜa, who had first encouraged Ḥusayn to seek the caliphate and then failed to support him, a movement of radical penitents arose seeking revenge on those responsible for his death. Soon they backed a Kufan revolt in favor of another son of ᶜAlī, Muḥammad Ibn al-Ḥanafīya (by a wife other than Fāṭima).

The revolt ended in failure, but the movement supporting his cause, known as the Kaysānīya, survived. They espoused several of the beliefs that remained fundamental for the later radical Shīᶜa. Thus they repudiated the legitimacy of the caliphate of the three predecessors of ᶜAlī: Abū Bakr, ᶜUmar, and ᶜUthmān. They taught that ᶜAlī had been the legatee of the Prophet and was thus solely entitled to the succession as supreme leader (imam) of the Muslim community. ᶜAli was succeeded as the divinely guided imam by his three sons, Ḥasan, Ḥusayn, and Muḥammad. They called the latter the Mahdi, the Restorer of Islam, and denied his death, claiming that he was alive in concealment and would reappear to lead the cause of the Shīᶜa and the cause of justice to victory.

A branch of the Kaysānīya that continued the line of imams through Muḥammad ibn al-Ḥanafiya's son Abū Hāshim formed the core of the revolutionary movement that overthrew the Umayyad dynasty and established the Abbasid caliphate in 750. They held that Abū Hāshim had appointed Muḥammad ibn ᶜAlī, who became father of the first Abbasid caliph, as his successor. The Abbasids thus came to power with Shiite backing as representatives of the Family of the Prophet (their ancestor al-ᶜAbbās was an uncle of Muḥammad) and as avengers of ᶜAli and his martyred descendants. They soon cut loose, however, from their ties with the Shīᶜa and identified with the Sunnite majority.

With the rise of legal and theological schools in Islam in the late Umayyad age, imams among the Shīᶜa took on a new role as authoritative teachers in matters of religion. A grandson of Ḥusayn, Muḥammad al-Bāqir, gained great prestige among the radicals through his teaching, which was continued and elaborated by his son Jaᶜfar al-Ṣādiq (*d.* 765). Al-Bāqir and al-Ṣadiq established a school of doctrine and thus became the founders of a branch of the Shīᶜa, the Imāmīs, which developed into the major radical wing, with its own ritual, law, and theology. The Imāmīs recognized al-Bāqir and al-Ṣādiq as their fifth and sixth imams. The moderate wing constituted itself about the same time, after the failure of a revolt of Muḥammad al-Bāqir's brother Zayd in 740; it was a sectarian movement known as the Zaydis, with its own doctrinal school.

The Imāmī Shīᶜa taught that there must at all times be a divinely appointed and guided leader and religious teacher of mankind. After the age of the prophets, the imams were these leaders and teachers, protected by God from sin and error. Their knowledge in religion was perfect, equal to that of the prophet Muḥammad, and thus their authority was absolute, just as his had been. This belief generally did not imply the expectation that the imams might in any way change or add to the religious message of Muḥammad. Rather, they were the guarantors of its purity and correct interpretation. Failure to recognize the rightful imams or to obey them was equally as grave an offense before God as repudiation or disobedience of the Prophet. For the Imāmī Shīᶜa, the great majority of the Muslim community had virtually become apostate from the true faith by its support of the illegitimate caliphate of the predecessors of ᶜAlī and by its continued denial of the rights and authority of the imams. The Imāmī believed that after ᶜAlī, Ḥasan, and Ḥusayn, the imamate would continue among the descendants of the latter, handed down from father to son, until the end of the world.

Although they considered the imams entitled to the rule of the Muslim community and repudiated the legitimacy of the historic caliphate, the Imāmī Shiites were at this stage politically quietist. Imam Jaᶜfar al-Ṣādiq refused any involvement in revolutionary activity and strictly forbade his followers to take up arms against the unjust rulers, a policy also followed by his successors. The imams were not expected to gain their rightful position until the advent of their *Qaᵓim,* usually identified with the Mahdi, who would rise with the sword and rule the world.

Various splits occurred in the Imāmī Shīᶜa regarding the succession of some of the imams. Historically important was the schism of those Shiites who traced the imamate through Jaᶜfar al-Ṣādiq's son Ismaᶜil, even though the latter had died before his father. This faction, known as the Ismailis, developed into a widespread revolutionary movement in the ninth century, establishing and supporting the Fatimid caliphate (909–1171) in Tunisia and Egypt. Later offshoots of the Ismaili movement were the Druzes in Palestine and Lebanon and the Nizārīs, known to the crusaders as the "assassins," in Syria and Iran. The main Imāmī group, which developed into the Twelver Shīᶜa, traced the imamate through Ismaᶜil's brother Mūsā al-Kāẓim (*d.* 799). After the death of their eleventh imam, Ḥasan al-ᶜAskari, in 874, they came to recognize a son who was believed to have been secretly born to Ḥasan as the twelfth and last imam. The Twelver Shiites identified this son with the *Qaᵓim* and the Mahdi expected to appear before the end of the world and establish universal justice on earth. In the meantime, they believed, he was living on earth in a state of absence or occultation. According to Twelver doctrine, during the so-called lesser occultation four successive agents claimed to be in direct communication with the hidden imam and conveyed his orders and instructions to the community. In the greater occultation, after the death of the fourth agent, no one could claim regular contact with the imam, though he might occasionally reveal himself to one of his followers in real life or in a dream. The teaching authority of the imams and some of their functions in the execution of the law were now held to have fallen to the Shiite *ᶜulamāᵓ,* the scholars who preserved and transmitted their message.

Originating in Al-Kufa, Imāmī Shiism spread early throughout southern Iraq. In the Abbasid capital, Baghdad, the quarter of Karkh on the west bank of the Tigris was inhabited by Shiites and became the main center of Twelver Shiite learning during the age of the Buyids (945–1055), a Shiite dynasty. In Persia, the towns of Qum, Rayy, and Nishapur housed large Shiite communities from the ninth century. The country as a whole, however, did not become predominantly Shiite until the sixteenth century, when the Safavid dynasty adopted Twelver Shiism as the official religion.

In Syria, Aleppo was the home of some early Shiite scholars and of a sizable Twelver Shiite community from the reign of the Shiite Hamdanid dynasty (944–1015). The Jabal ᶜAmīl region in southern Lebanon was another early Twelver Shiite site. In the late Mamluk age it developed into an important center of Shiite learning and then produced a number of scholars who played a leading role in the propagation and establishment of Shiism in Safavid Persia. Related to the Twelver Shīᶜa is the Nusayrī community, in modern times often called Alawīs, which was established in Syria in the tenth century, especially in the Jabal Ansariye region east of Latakia. It sprang from the extremist fringe of the early Imāmī Shīᶜa, which was condemned as heretical and excommunicated by the mainstream Shīᶜa. While adhering to the line of imams recognized by the Twelver Shīᶜa, the Nusayrīs embraced an esoteric teaching that viewed the imams as manifestations of the divine and supported antinomianism and belief in metempsychosis. Twelver Shiism was never significant in Egypt, North Africa, or Muslim Spain.

In spite of the Shiite repudiation of the legitimacy of the caliphate and other Sunnite governments, Imāmī Shiites have often held influential positions in them, including the vizierate, and Shiites commonly made up a disproportionately large share of the secretarial class in eastern Islam. This was facilitated partly by the fact that Shiite law specifically allowed the practice of precautionary dissimulation of religious beliefs and encouraged the holding of office under illegitimate rulers if the holder was able to protect and benefit the imams or the Shiite community. Sunnites in turn frequently accused, justly or injustly, Shiite officials of disloyalty and sabotage, down to the charge against Naṣīr al-Dīn al-Ṭūsī, the Shiite philosopher and counselor of the Mongol conqueror Hulagu, that he was responsible for the overthrow of the Abbasid caliphate by the Mongols in 1258. The Shīᶜa did benefit from the disestablishment of Sunnism as the official religion following the Mongol conquest and witnessed, after the Buyid age, a second period of expansion and efflorescence of religious scholarship.

Shiite religious life differs markedly from the Sunnite by its emphasis on martyrdom, which in more radical doctrine gave rise to the claim that every imam had been murdered in one way or another by the enemies of God. The public lamentations carried out annually on the death day of the martyred Ḥusayn frequently provoked clashes with the Sunnites. Pilgrimages to the shrines of the imams in Medina and the holy cites of Iraq and Persia were an integral part of Shiite religiosity at a time when comparable manifestations of popular worship of Sufi saints were commonly condemned by orthodox Sunnite *ᶜulamāᵓ*. Shiite religious law deviated in a few points from Sunnite law, such as in its more generous treatment of women and cognates in inheritance and in permitting a kind of marriage on term. In theology, the Shīᶜa came to adopt the doctrine of the Muᶜtazila, a school eventually suppressed by the Sunnites as heretical, which espouses human free will—against the Sunnite dogma of predestination—and a radically anti-anthropomorphist concept of God.

BIBLIOGRAPHY

Dwight M. Donaldson, *The Shiᶜite Religion* (1933, repr. 1984); S. Husain M. Jafri, *Origins and Early Development of Shiᶜa Islam* (1979); Henri Laoust, *Les schismes dans l'Islam* (1965); *Le Shīᶜisme Imāmite* (Colloque de Strasbourg: 6–9 Mai 1968) (1970); Moojam Momen, *An Introduction to Shiᶜi Islam* (1985); Muḥammad H. Ṭabāṭabāᵓī, *Shiᶜite Islam,* S. Hossein Nasr, ed. and trans. (1975, 2nd ed. 1977).

WILFERD MADELUNG

[See also **Abbasids; ᶜAlī, Ibn Abī Ṭālib; Alids; Assassins; Caliphate; Druzes; Fatimids; Hamdanids; Ḥasan, Ibn ᶜAlī Ibn Abī Ṭālib, al-; Heresy, Islamic; Ḥusayn Ibn ᶜAlī, al-; Idrisids; Imam; Iran; Ismaᶜiliya; Islam, Religion; Millennialism, Islamic; Muᶜtazila, al-; Mysticism, Islamic; Philosophy and Theology, Islamic; Pilgrimage, Islamic; Sects, Islamic; Zaydis.**]

SHILLING. In the early Middle Ages the shilling—also scilling and solidus—was a small gold weight of about .05 ounces or 1.3 grams, employed as a measure of value among various Germanic peoples. In the early wergild codes of England, the shilling was a gold coin akin perhaps to the Merovingian tremissis (gold triens). In the later codes the Kentish shilling was worth twenty silver sceattas (sing., sceat, once considered to be the predecessor of the penny), or the equivalent of twenty silver pennies, while elsewhere in England the normal legal equation was four or five pennies, with four being traditional in Mercia and five in Wessex. The same codes also show that the differences lay not in the values of the different sceattas, but in the values of the different shillings.

After the penny became the principal circulating coin in England during the eighth century, the shilling became a money of account (as did the monetary pound), equal to twelve silver pennies (pence, denarius, *deniers,* and other names), or 1/20 pound of silver. It continued as a money of account throughout the Middle Ages until minted as a silver coin by Henry VII in 1504.

The relationship of twelve pennies to the shilling may have been regulated by English dealings with the Franks. After the Conquest, William I brought with him from Normandy the Roman weight scale, and he divided his pound into twelve ounces. Preferring the shilling of twelve pennies to the shilling of four or five pence that continued to linger on in certain areas late into the Anglo-Saxon period, he brought about the valuation of the pound at twenty shillings and the shilling at twelve pence. These units of account became the official ones for governmental purposes.

The Middle English word *shilling* comes from the Old English *scilling,* a form akin to Old High German *skillink* (a gold coin), Old Norse *skillingr,* and Gothic *skillings,* all of which derive from a prehistoric Germanic compound whose first constituent is represented by the English word shield (Old English *sceld*). At various times the shilling was thought to come from the Latin *scilicus,* a quarter-ounce or 1/48 of the Roman libra or pound, or from a Saxon word, *scilling,* meaning a "piece cut off" and referring either to pieces of broken silver that were thrown into a scale pan to make up for the loss of weight of light coins when payment was made by weight, or else, perhaps, to portions of a coil of gold or silver clipped off and employed as small change.

RONALD EDWARD ZUPKO

[See also **Mints and Money, Western European; Penny; Pound; Trade, European.**]

SHIPS AND SHIPBUILDING, MEDITERRANEAN. The history of Mediterranean ships and shipbuilding in the ten centuries from 500 to 1500 may be divided into three successive stages. The first, long stage, to about 1100, is the least documented, but we know that it included two developments of great importance for the future, involving the abandonment of traditional Mediterranean practices in favor of new approaches better suited to the radically changed conditions of the Middle Ages. The second stage, the twelfth and thirteenth centuries, saw a marked increase in the volume of commercial shipping, which stimulated some notable advances in nautical technology and maritime institutions. Then the last stage, in the fourteenth and fifteenth centuries, saw the continuing expansion of shipping that opened the Mediterranean to nautical influences from the north; this merging of maritime traditions led to the definitive breakthrough in the design of the sailing ship.

FROM THE CLASSICAL ERA TO 1100

To put the medieval changes in proper perspective, one must begin with the situation at the close of the classical era. The aristocrat of Greco-Roman shipping was the galley, employed for warfare and official business, and seemingly an ideal ship type for a sea like the Mediterranean, which is relatively calm during the traditional six-month sailing season. The classical Mediterranean also had many varieties of ships entirely dependent on sail power: Roman sailing ships ranged from small fishing boats to huge imperial grain freighters, and at least the large ships routinely made trans-Mediterranean voyages. Yet galleys were the primary focus for experimentation and improvement. They mounted sails for cruising but derived their combat effectiveness from their oar power. In the Roman era, oar power was enhanced by adding a second and later a third bank of oarsmen above the original single bank, and at the height of the Roman Empire more than one oarsman to an oar seems to have been tried.

At the end of the Middle Ages, galleys still retained their special aura, and were still thought to be the Mediterranean's prime combat vessel. In fact, however, their days were already numbered due to the transformation of the sailing ship over the Middle Ages. Appropriately, the first change associated with the medieval Mediterranean seagoing vessel involved sail type.

The square sail had been preeminent in the classical Mediterranean ship; centered on a mast with an equal proportion of its area extending on either side at right angles to the ship's hull, it is a highly effective sail if routes can be designed to take advantage of a following wind. We cannot be sure exactly when the square sail began to fade in importance, since we have no contemporary ship depictions from the late sixth to the late ninth century. However, from the late ninth to the fourteenth century, all Mediterranean ship depictions show triangular lateen sails, a form of fore-and-aft rig. Fore-and-aft sails, as their name implies, function best when stretched out more or less parallel with the length of the ship. All modern yachts use fore-and-aft sails, since they can be slanted to permit adequate forward progress in a variety of wind conditions. Medieval lateen-rigged ships could not come nearly so close to heading into the wind as do modern yachts; also, in order to change tack or direction, they apparently had to "fall off the wind," loose the sail, and then hoist the great yardarm on end in order to set the sail on the opposite side—an awkward process. Nonetheless, the medieval lateen rig did offer some increase in directional flexibility, and its emerging popularity represented significant change.

It was once believed that the Arabs, after reaching the Mediterranean in the late seventh century, introduced the lateen sail from waters further east. However, as Lynn White noted, there is no hard evidence for the lateen in the East until at least the thirteenth century. Moreover, Lionel Casson discovered several Greco-Roman depictions of variations on the fore-and-aft rig, proving that at least the concept was known to the classical Mediterranean. It is noteworthy that Casson's classical examples all show fore-and-aft rigs on small boats. With the disappearance of official trans-Mediterranean shipping runs after the collapse of the western Roman Empire, small boats and local shipping assumed new importance. Their rigs would thus have had increased prominence. Also, a passage in Procopius suggests that something like the lateen was used in the sixth century on the *dromon,* a new galley type. Altogether, it is now generally accepted that increased use of the lateen began to spread across the Mediterranean very early in the medieval period, building on Greco-Roman experience with various forms of fore-and-aft rig.

A more flexible sail type must have proved a distinct asset in the early medieval Mediterranean, given the Arab conquest of half the perimeter and most major islands in the seventh and eighth centuries. These Arabs had lacked maritime experience when they first reached the Mediterranean, but after a brief hesitation they took enthusiastically to the sea, and from the seventh to the eleventh century there were recurrent Arab-Byzantine naval encounters and sea raids on each other's territory, frequently involving hundreds of ships (if not the thousands reported by contemporary chroniclers). Maurice Lombard believed that much of the deforestation around the Mediterranean basin should be attributed to the frenzied shipbuilding on both sides during this period.

Arab-Byzantine confrontations were not the only threat to shipping. Piracy represented a more constant danger, with no one power in a position to police Mediterranean waters. As a sideline or full-time occupation, piracy became endemic all over the Mediterranean. Indeed, throughout the entire medieval period there was to be no firm dividing line between piracy and "legitimate" naval operations. At Genoa in the thirteenth and fourteenth centuries, for example, corsairing expeditions constituted a popular and openly acknowledged opportunity for investment. By the late fourteenth century, most Mediterranean governments had adopted strict regulations concerning such ventures, but the need for convoys and armed guards on shipboard persisted, and new designs in merchant ships were judged as much on ability to withstand attack as on carrying capacity.

In the early medieval period, before the development of convoy systems, the unsettled conditions surely meant a shorter average lifespan for ships. This may have influenced the evolution of a new method of ship construction, the second major maritime development associated with the early medieval Mediterranean, and one of crucial significance. In the Mediterranean until the medieval period, all ships had been constructed from the outside in, "shell-first." Immediately after laying the keel (putting down a long, solid timber to constitute the base), the Greco-Roman shipwright began to form the hull by edge-joining planking out and up into the desired hull shape, fastening each plank to the one below with mortise-and-tenon joinery in the manner of a cabinetmaker. The internal framework was largely added after the fact; the basic shape of the ship, and most of its strength, derived from the exterior shell and its tenoning. By the later Middle Ages, however, all Mediterranean ships apparently were constructed "skeleton-first," with hull planking nailed onto a basic framework

Construction of a round ship. Fragment of a polyptych by Paolo Veneziano (or school), Venice, *ca.* 1340. MUSEO STORICO NAVALE, VENICE

already in place. The framework had become the key element, as it is today.

The shift to skeleton-first technique clearly represented savings in time and labor, since the laborious cutting of mortises and the meticulous edge-joining of planks could be eliminated. But even more important for the future, the skeleton-first approach would permit ship design to become, over time, much more ambitious. For this reason, maritime historians have long hoped to establish how and when the change took place. Today, thanks largely to excavations and reconstructions undertaken by the Institute of Nautical Archaeology at Texas A & M University, the transition is becoming clear. A Byzantine merchant ship of the seventh century, known as the Yassi Ada ship, shows the change already under way; compared with Roman ships, it exhibits less reliance on mortise-and-tenon joints and greater reliance on the framework, with stout floor frames inserted after only a few strakes of hull planking had been built up from the keel. An eleventh-century merchant ship excavated off the coast of Turkey (the Serçe Liman ship) has proved to be almost completely skeleton-built. The change thus seems to have been a gradual evolution, representing expediency rather than any sudden conceptual leap forward. One likely contributing factor was an increased scarcity of wood. The shell-first technique demanded ample supplies of good lumber with specific characteristics for shaping the hull. Skeleton-first construction, with hull planking nailed onto an existing framework, could adapt more easily to whatever lumber was available.

Few ship depictions have survived from the early medieval period, and the nomenclature of ship types can be misleading, for a name may persist long after the ship type has been substantially altered. Nonetheless, certain early medieval trends can be discerned. The Byzantine Empire seems to have remained loyal to Roman naval traditions longer than the rest of the Mediterranean world. Although Byzantine emperors varied in their interest in naval matters, Byzantium did retain the concept of a separate, official fleet, over and above any merchant ships pressed into service in a crisis. Moreover, galleys (*dromon, ousiakos, pamphylos, chelandion*) continued to constitute the prime element in the Byzantine navy until at least the tenth century, and were never completely displaced.

Early medieval Arab ships, such as the *koumbarion,* the Byzantine term for the Arab ship type most frequently encountered in naval battles, are described as slower and heavier than Byzantine galleys. This suggests that the Arabs favored sailing ships, or perhaps a hybrid design incorporating some of the sturdy characteristics of merchant ships. This is not surprising, since Arab territory ran from Syria to Spain, and with Arab raiders ranging all over the Mediterranean, their vessels had to be roomy enough for the spoils of raids, which might include hundreds of captives. Furthermore, we know that Arab ships sometimes carried horses for use on land raids.

This is not to say that all Mediterranean Arabs employed the same ship type, any more than all Byzantine ships were galleys. Indeed, no two ships in the early medieval centuries would likely have been identical. But hybrids—sailing ships with supplementary oar power—apparently were particularly popular in this period. We find such ships all over the Mediterranean later in the Middle Ages, known by various names (such as *tarida, tarette, sagena, sagitta, gripo, linys*), sometimes counted in contemporary records as galleys, sometimes as sailing ships, but always characterized by a combination of fixed sails with a small complement of oars. Presumably valued in the early medieval period as all-purpose vessels, ideal for combining corsairing and commerce, such hybrids were employed in the later Middle Ages for coastal trading and sometimes the transport of military supplies, including horses.

If hybrid ship types were indeed particularly popular in the early Middle Ages, this would accord with other indications that most Mediterranean ships then were comparatively small and also comparatively simple in design. We have only a few crude depictions of pre-twelfth-century ships, no adequate written descriptions, and no construction plans. (Naval architecture in the modern sense only developed later in the Middle Ages, made possible by the widespread adoption of skeleton-first construction and stimulated by the increasing economic significance of the ship.) However, the seventh- and eleventh-century merchant vessels excavated in the eastern Mediterranean by the Institute o Nautical Archaeology, the Yassi Ada and Serçe Liman ships, were relatively small (roughly 67 feet/20.5 meters and 49 feet/15 meters respectively) and seemingly single-decked. The evidence of cooking facilities and the remains of personal possessions suggest a small crew living on board, perhaps sleeping on deck. We cannot be sure that these two ships were typical, but they do bear out long-held assumptions concerning this period.

TWELFTH AND THIRTEENTH CENTURIES

In the twelfth century, the Mediterranean experienced a dramatic surge in maritime commerce, and both the number and the size of ships increased markedly. The crusades were a key factor. In the First Crusade, most participants made their way east overland, but ships of the Italian maritime cities were employed to supply the armies, to rescue trapped forces, and to keep the crusaders in communication with Western Europe. In the three later crusades of the twelfth century, Italian ships were increasingly hired to transport entire armies. There was also incidental business, as when Richard the Lionhearted, too impatient to wait for the English fleet at Marseilles, hired Genoese ships to take his personal entourage to Sicily. And in between the crusades there was steady traffic back and forth to the newly won territories.

The overall effect on the Genoese, Pisan, and Venetian economies is well known, but there was also a general stimulation of shipping and shipbuilding throughout almost all of the Christian Mediterranean, from Barcelona to Ragusa (Dubrovnik). In the thirteenth century, Louis IX's ship purchases and charterings for his crusading expeditions transferred huge sums to Genoese shipowners and shipbuilders, but Benjamin Kedar has noted that ships from lesser ports also benefited, transporting miscellaneous followers of the crusading armies, sometimes on ships capable of carrying 500 to 1,000 passengers. Only in Arab shipping do we sense a relative decline in importance. S. D. Goitein found evidence in the Cairo genizah documents that Muslim ships carrying up to 500 passengers were not exceptional at Cairo in the late eleventh century, and Muslim maritime traffic was then wide-ranging. Yet in the twelfth and thirteenth centuries, while Muslim maritime activity certainly did not cease entirely, it is noteworthy that an Arab traveler such as Ibn Jubayr had to make his trans-Mediterranean voyages on Genoese ships.

Not surprisingly, the marked increase in maritime activity in Christian Mediterranean ports led to changes in the capitalization and management of shipping, which in turn led to changes in shipbuilding practice and nautical technology. In the first half of the twelfth century, the owner of a ship tended to be an experienced mariner who contracted with merchants on a voyage-by-voyage basis and was himself the ship's *patronus* or captain. (In the earlier maritime codes, the term *patronus* is used virtually interchangeably with *nauclerus,* which later came exclusively to mean sailing master or pilot.) Crew members were then likely to be involved in all the affairs of the ship, sometimes taking a share of the profits in lieu of wages. This approach continued throughout the Middle Ages on smaller ships and on ships operating out of the smaller ports. However, by the later twelfth century the great demand for shipping gave rise to a new, quasi-corporate system in the major ports, with several investors banding together to lease or even to finance the construction of a ship (often through selling shares to the public) and then to manage its ventures. Also, at Genoa, for example, by the middle of the thirteenth century, we find the larger merchant houses building their own vessels. Such ships, presumably incorporating any innovations in design that might enhance profits, then sailed under the command of a *patronus* whose prime function was to represent management's interests; the *nauclerus* or sailing master was now a salaried subordinate, and the crew members were hired hands.

In the twelfth and thirteenth centuries, the now-plentiful ship depictions show only lateen sails in the Mediterranean, on both galleys and sailing ships. Since in the Renaissance the Tyrrhenian port of Amalfi was credited with the "invention" of the lateen sail, we can surmise that the Amalfitans had perhaps made some definitive improvement in that rig in the early medieval period, or perhaps their early trading ventures had popularized that sail in portions of the Mediterranean unfamiliar with it. In any case, while the placement or angling of the mast or masts might vary, Mediterranean ships by now seem universally to have been lateeners; as Auguste Jal long ago observed, from the twelfth century on the Mediterranean was a notably homogeneous maritime world.

Increased attention to record-keeping in the twelfth and thirteenth centuries means that we know a good deal about that period's ships and shipping practices. Clearly, galleys were employed more in the eastern than in the western Mediterranean. Not only was Byzantine influence stronger in eastern waters, but the distances across open water were shorter. Yet even in the eastern Mediterranean, galleys never constituted more than a fraction of the total number of ships in this period. They were used principally for battle and guard duty, for carrying important passengers or dispatches, and only to a very limited extent for transporting goods. In style, one notable change from late Roman galleys was the abandonment of the underwater ram at the bow. (Boarding and capturing, not sinking, the enemy were now the objectives in battle.) Otherwise, there doubtless was considerably local variation in the configuration of galleys. Byzantium, after all, had had several different galley types in the early medieval period, and the conflicting evidence concerning the disposition of oarsmen in the twelfth and thirteenth centuries suggests that variations persisted. Some galleys appear to have had two tiers of rowing banks, with as many as 100 oarsmen distributed, one man to an oar, along the upper and lower benches on either side. Other galleys in this period seemingly paired their oarsmen two to an oar, and had all of their rowing benches on the same level. In either case, some of the men could abandon their oars for combat during a naval engagement; this was one of the advantages of the fact that oarsmen then were hired freemen, not convicts or slaves. But galleys often carried a complement of marines as well. There are records of galleys ranging up to 130 feet (39.5 meters) long in this period, but the conditions on board must have been very cramped. The galleys were shallow, and typically the length-to-breadth ratio was eight or ten to one, permitting only a narrow platform down the center between the rowing benches. Thus, even though large lateen sails were carried for cruising, these galleys were not designed for long periods at sea. As frequently as possible, they would make port at night.

We know less than we would like about the dimensions of the sailing ships that mainly comprised the merchant fleets of this period. We can be sure that the vast majority were relatively small; even in the fifteenth century, 3,000 of Venice's roughly 3,300 sailing ships seem to have had a deadweight rating (maximum cargo weight) of 100 tons or less. (In other words, the seventh-century Yassi Ada ship, with an estimated deadweight rating of 60 tons, would not have seemed out of place even in the late Middle Ages.) Nonetheless, many sailing ships of the twelfth and thirteenth centuries were a very respectable size. Frederic Lane speculated that for the trans-Mediterranean trade of the major port cities in this period, a typical *navis*

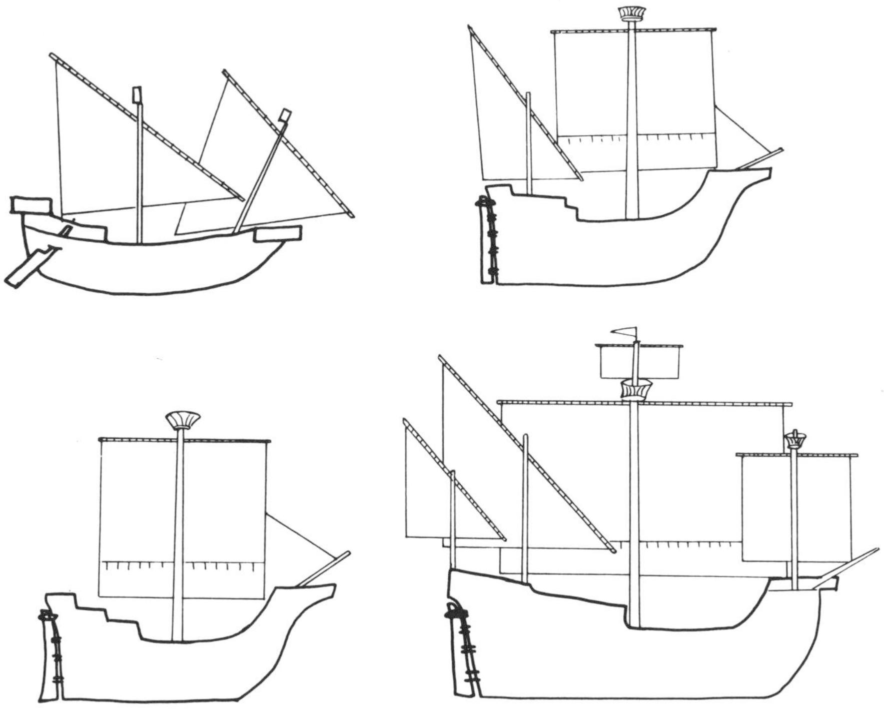

The evolution of the full-rigged ship: (*a*) two-masted lateener with steering oars, typical of the 13th century; (*b*) single-masted, cog-style ship with square sail and stern rudder, reflecting the influence of northern merchant ships in the 14th century; (*c*) cog-style ship with lateen mizzen added, typical of late-14th-century merchant ships; (*d*) full-rigged ship, a four-masted carrack of the 15th century. Reproduced from Frederic C. Lane, *Venice: A Maritime Republic* © 1973 THE JOHNS HOPKINS UNIVERSITY PRESS

or *nef* would have been a two-masted, two-decked lateener, with sizable superstructures (forecastle and sterncastle) and a deadweight rating of about 200 tons. Lane, who made a thorough study of medieval tonnages, compared this with the estimated deadweight rating of 100 tons for the *Santa Maria* and 180 tons for the *Mayflower*. Moreover, a few sailing ships in the thirteenth century, particularly some built for crusading or pilgrim passenger service, were very big indeed. The exact dimensions remain somewhat controversial because of gaps in the sources and the variability of medieval measurements. However, Lane calculated a deadweight rating of 500 tons for the *Roccafortis*, built at Venice and roughly 120 feet (36.5 meters) from stem to stern. John Pryor's study of thirteenth century crusading transports postulates for an archtypical three-decker a deadweight rating of about 800 metric tons and an overall length of about 115 feet (35 meters). Genoa's *Oliva* was said to have carried 1,000 passengers, and its *Paradisus Magnus* to have been even larger. Some of these huge ships, designed to accommodate both passengers and cargo, had as many as four decks. Undoubtedly heavy and awkward to maneuver, these vessels did nonetheless benefit from an improvement in sail material. Cotton, introduced from the Arab east, had come to replace linen in sailcloth by the thirteenth century, and thus the big lateen sails were now quicker-drying and somewhat less susceptible to sagging.

By the end of the thirteenth century, keen competition and the new style in management had begun to affect maritime technology as well as ship size. We find growing interest in navigational aids. There is literary evidence that a crude form of compass, a magnetized needle floating in a bowl of water, had come into use by the late twelfth century. Within another 100 years, a more sophisticated compass, a self-contained instrument with its needle pivoting dry, was apparently available in the Mediterranean, together with carefully drawn sea charts, and tables for calculating distances and a ship's locations on its route. (Presumably the sea charts that ships carried were simpler versions of the elaborate portolan charts that still survive.) As Frederic Lane observed, the adoption of navigational aids coincided with pressures to dispatch trans-Mediterranean shipping even in the winter months of worst visibility. But surely another influential factor was the vastly increased volume of shipping, which meant that not all ships could be manned by seasoned mariners. Not surprisingly, the latter tended at first to resist the new navigational aids. However, by the late Middle Ages at least the simpler sorts of aids were commonly employed. True navigational accuracy would not become possible until the eighteenth century, when a secure method for determining longitude was finally achieved with the perfection (in England) of the marine chronometer and the sextant. However, the developments of the thirteenth century did at least begin to change attitudes and expectations. Particularly in the Mediterranean, mariners began to take control of the sea in a new way.

There were two late-thirteenth-century developments involving galley design. Around 1290, Venice began building galleys with enhanced oar power, achieved in a new manner. Instead of adding yet another tier of oarsmen or putting several men to an oar, which the Romans had tried, the Venetians extended and slanted the individual rowing benches of their single-bank galleys so that every bench could accommodate three men, each with his own oar; the oars, now necessarily much longer, were pivoted over an external frame or outrigger. This *a zenzile* or *a terzaruolo* system was harder on oarsmen; for adequate leverage, they had to rise and fall, in unison, with each stroke. It became more difficult to recruit men for galley service. Yet the system unquestionably resulted in streamlined galleys with enhanced power and speed.

Almost simultaneously, Venice (later followed by Genoa and Barcelona, and still later by Florence) began to build "great galleys" to carry a larger volume of goods or passengers. At least initially, these were no longer than traditional galleys, but they were roughly two feet broader of beam and had deeper hulls. For rowing, they too employed the *a zenzile* system, but because of their greater bulk they used oar power as little as possible, usually relying instead on their huge lateen sails. They were thus really hybrids—and a good example of the inappropriateness of "long" ship and "round" ship as absolute terms of differentiation between warships and merchant ships. In the long-distance trade for which they were primarily designed, and especially on the regular runs to England and Flanders that began in the mid fourteenth century, these great galleys flourished for some time. There were never a great many in service, but they ceased to be cost-effective only in the changed commercial climate of the latter fifteenth century. While they could not carry nearly as much as the bigger sailing ships, their coupling of size with maneuverability, and their large, well-armed crews, made them relatively impregnable. Moreover, their combination of huge sails with oar power meant that they could be scheduled precisely. Venice, for example, used them not only for fast freight but also to carry great numbers of pilgrims to the Holy Land.

Most of the great galleys were built with government subsidy. In this respect, they represented something of a new development in Mediterranean commercial shipping, which had typically relied on private enterprise. Increasingly now, however, private shipowners and shipbuilders were concentrating on the sailing ship. This meant that by the fourteenth century, governments were finding that they also had to take extraordinary measures if they wanted adequate numbers of traditional galleys for defensive purposes. In Venice, therefore, the Arsenal was greatly expanded, principally to build and maintain, at government expense, an official fleet of "regular" galleys. Genoa took a more indirect approach. It promulgated a rule largely restricting Genoese traffic to the Levant to "subtiles," the traditional slender galleys, thus providing a sure incentive for their continued construction. The kingdom of Aragon adopted neither of these approaches, seemingly resigned to doing without; when in 1325 the sultan of Tlemcen proposed chartering some Catalan light galleys, he was told there no longer were any.

FOURTEENTH AND FIFTEENTH CENTURIES

The fourteenth century was characterized by increasing government intervention in all manner of shipping matters. Mercantile interests had come to be viewed as communal interests. Already in the thirteenth century, safety issues had begun to be addressed, with the establishment, for example, of loading limits; a stipulated maximum waterline mark was required on every hull. By the fourteenth century, all of the major ports seem to have had boards or commissions inspecting ships and shipyards, and enforcing increasing numbers of rules concerning ship design and shipping practices. This certainly represented a change from the eleventh and twelfth centuries, when Mediterranean shippers and shipowners had been on their own, and the only protective device was the *conserva* system, whereby pairs or groups of ships would agree to function as a unit on a voyage, helping each other in emergencies and sharing any profits with the survivors of any ship that was wrecked. At least insofar as the major ports were concerned, the fourteenth century, with its elaborate regulations and its highly organized insurance systems and convoys, presented a very different picture.

Long-term, the most significant fourteenth-century development in Mediterranean ship design was not the great galley but the adoption of northern characteristics for the sailing ship. Northern ships had been coming into the Mediterranean occasionally ever since the crusades, but routine northern merchant-ship ventures are not documented until the mid fourteenth century, roughly the same time as the first regular Genoese runs to England. By then, the typical northern merchant ship was a cog, high in the water, blunt-ended, rigged only with one very large square sail, and steered by means of a fixed sternpost rudder. The cog offered a marked contrast to the typical Mediterranean merchant ship, with its rounded ends, lower profile amidships, lateen sails, and Roman-style lateral steering oars. We do not know exactly when or how the cog caught on in the Mediterranean. There are references to Catalan and Venetian *cocas* or *coche* as early as 1310 or 1315, and it has been suggested that ships from Bayonne, by then coming into the Mediterranean, had perhaps inspired the earliest cog-style designs. Or perhaps the occasional Mediterranean ship venturing north in the late thirteenth century had brought word home of the cog's good features. In any case, by the latter part of the fourteenth century, both records and depictions reveal at least some Mediterranean ships with all of the characteristics of the cog. Of course, many small Mediterranean ships continued to be built along traditional lines, and some ships exhibited only a partial change. (Some, for example, adopted the hull configuration of the cog but retained two masts, one lateen-rigged and the other with a square sail.) But from this point on, the Mediterranean was no longer a closed sea in relation to ship design.

For major shipowners, the new northern elements had some compelling advantages. The cog's sturdiness and greater carrying capacity were desirable for the long voyages now undertaken by many Mediterranean ships, not only to the English Channel but also to the ports of the Black Sea. The cog's overall configuration also made it more resistant to attack, since the high sides provided protection for the crossbowmen now carried on most large merchant ships. Then, too, with ever-bigger ships, the cog's square sail had considerable appeal. Yardarms bearing huge lateen sails were heavy to raise and lower, and difficult to handle when changing course, requiring big crews; with a square rig, on the other hand, the yardarm with its sail attached stayed in place, and one only had to let the sail drop or brail it up. (That crew size influenced the change in sail type seems borne out by the fact that galleys, with many oarsmen available to work the sails, continued to use the lateen.) Crew-related issues probably also influenced the adoption of the sternpost rudder. Steering oars seem to have worked well; Joinville, crossing the Mediterranean with Louis IX, had remarked at the ease with which large ships were maneuvered with them. But steering oars called for more skill in handling than did the sternpost rudder, and such expertise may now have been harder to come by. Lane noted the declining status of seamen between the thirteenth and fifteenth centuries, and more and more one heard of difficulty in recruiting and retaining competent crews.

By the late fourteenth century, Mediterranean shipping had become a highly specialized business. The superpowers were Venice, Genoa, Barcelona, Majorca, and Valencia. Big ships from these ports dominated long-distance trade, developing specializations in cargo and sophisticated differential freight rates. Meanwhile, cabotage and the routine trade in everyday necessities, including foodstuffs, were left largely to ships from the lesser Mediterranean ports, or to the smaller, owner-captained ships that all major ports still had. Ships from Portugal and the Bay of Biscay now also circulated in the Mediterranean, competing for the short-haul trade.

The ultimate refinement of the sailing ship took place in the fifteenth century. By then, maritime commerce was so thoroughly internationalized that it is hard to tell which region deserves credit. However, either as a local Mediterranean advance or under the influence of Bayonne or the Portuguese, in the course of the fifteenth century the carrack, the first true full-rigged ship, appeared. The carrack's stubby lines were reminiscent of the cog, although most carracks were notably larger. They also had more elaborate and massive superstructures, particularly a much enhanced quarterdeck dominating the stern. But the carrack's most important characteristic was its combination of sails, a major breakthrough, coupling the propelling power of the square sail with the directive thrust of the lateen. Typically, carracks carried a huge square mainsail and a small square topsail on the mainmast, a square foresail over the forecastle, and in the stern one or two additional sails (the mizzen and bonaventure mizzen), which were lateens. All of these sails were also controlled in new and better ways. Overall, the full-rigged carrack represented the achievement, at last, of truly flexible and effective sail power. There would, of course, continue to be further refinements, but in principle the possibilities inherent in sail power had now been mastered.

The carrack was obviously the result of continuous experimentation with sail types after the reintroduction of the square sail, as Mediterranean shipowners and shipbuilders strove to improve their ships' speed and handling. The carrack also answered the continuing need for a more defensible sailing ship. Not only did its impressive size make it more than a match for low-slung galleys, but also its enlarged quarterdeck made possible the effective mounting of cannons, which had first been used in naval combat in the Mediterranean in the mid fourteenth century. In other words, the carrack was the perfect all-purpose ship for the maritime world of the late Middle Ages, where on the whole there was still no marked differentation between fighting ships and merchant ships.

In the sixteenth century, as governments began to create genuinely separate navies, there would be further work on galley design. The Mediterranean was reluctant to abandon what had always been its preeminent combat ship and the traditional aristocrat of that sea. However, the future now clearly belonged to the sailing ship, even if this was not yet fully understood at the close of the Middle Ages. Moreover, the future lay beyond the Mediterranean; solidly built ships with flexible sail power had true oceangoing potential. Coasting Africa, the lively little lateen-rigged caravels of Portugal continued for a time to recall the old days, but the great period of maritime growth and innovation in the Mediterranean had come to an end.

BIBLIOGRAPHY

Scholarly inquiry into the history of European ships and shipbuilding essentially began with Auguste Jal, whose monumental *Archéologie navale* (1840) was followed by his *Glossaire nautique* (1848). While Jal can no longer be considered reliable on details such as the measurements of medieval ships, maritime historians still value his perceptive and encyclopedic grasp of the subject; a multivolume version of the *Glossaire* is *Nouveau glossaire nautique d'Augustine Jal* (1970–). The most important English-language periodical for maritime history is *The Mariner's Mirror* (1911–), published in Great Britain. Reports on Mediterranean underwater archaeology, significant for the history of ship construction, appear in the *International Journal of Nautical Archaeology and Underwater Exploration* (1972–), also a British publication. Also valuable for this topic are the newsletters and excavation reports of the Institute of Nautical Archaeology, directed by George Bass and based at Texas A & M University, College Station, Texas. The volumes of papers delivered at the Colloques Internationals d'Histoire Maritime organized by Michel Mollat in the 1950's and 1960's are important for medieval Mediterranean maritime history in general; see especially Jacques Heers on late medieval maritime specialization and Genoese shipping, and Maurice Lombard on shipbuilding and deforestation in *Le navire et l'économie maritime du moyen âge au XVIIIe siècle en Méditerranée principalement: Travaux du Deuxième colloque . . . , Paris 1957* (1958). See also *Les sources de l'histoire maritime en Europe, du moyên âge au XVIII siècle: Actes du Quatrième colloque . . . , Paris 1959* (1962); and Paul Adam on the origins of the lateen sail, and Federigo Melis on economic factors in fourteenth-century maritime developments, in *Océan Indien et Méditerranée: Travaux du Sixième collogue . . . , Venice 1962* (1970). Several papers of interest, including Abraham L. Udovitch on the duration and routes of commercial voyages from Muslim Egypt in the eleventh century, appear in *La navigazione mediterranea nell'alto medioevo: XXV* (Centro Italiano di Studi sull'Alto Medioevo, Settimane di studio), 2 vols. (1978). A number of Frederic C. Lane's studies in his collected papers, *Venice and History* (1966), discuss issues important for medieval Mediterranean shipping as a whole, such as tonnage and the maritime compass. For illustrations of medieval Mediterranean ships, and brief but sound overviews, see George F. Bass, ed., *A History of Seafaring Based on Underwater Archaeology* (1972); and Lionel Casson, *Illustrated History of Ships and Boats* (1964).

Sources. In addition to archaeological findings (so far, only for the early period) and ship depictions (always to be used with caution), there are written records concerning ships and shipbuilding. But these, too, must be used with caution. For an excellent discussion of (and listing) of key documents concerning thirteenth-century ships, and of the problems such records present, see René Bastard de Péré, "Navires méditerranéens du temps de Saint Louis," in *Revue d'histoire économique et sociale,* 50 (1972).

Specialized studies, 500–1100. Hélène Ahrweiler, *Byzance et la mer* (1966); Walter Ashburner, ed., *The Rhodian Sea Law* (1909); George F. Bass and Frederick H. Van Doorninck, Jr., *Yassi Ada* (1982); Aly Mohammed Fahmy, *Muslim Naval Organization in the Eastern Mediterranean from the Seventh to the Tenth Century A.D.,* 2nd ed. (1966), and *Muslim Sea-Power in the Eastern Mediterranean from the Seventh to the Tenth Century A.D.* (1966); S. D. Goitein, *A Mediterranean Society,* I (1967), 301–352; Barbara M. Kreutz, "Ships, Shipping, and the Implications of Change in the Early Medieval Mediterranean," in *Viator,* 7 (1976); J. Richard Steffy, "Reconstruction of the 11th Century Serçe Liman Vessel: A Preliminary Report," in *International Journal of Nautical Archaeology,* **11** (1982); Lynn T. White, jr., "The Diffusion of the Lateen Sail," in his *Medieval Religion and Technology: Collected Essays* (1978).

Specialized studies, 1100–1500. R. C. Anderson, *Oared Fighting Ships* (1962); Eugene H. Byrne, *Genoese Shipping in the Twelfth and Thirteenth Centuries* (1930); Fredric L. Cheyette, "The Sovereign and the Pirates, 1332," in *Speculum,* **45** (1970); John E. Dotson, "Jal's *Nef X* and Genoese Naval Architecture in the 13th Century," in *The Mariner's Mirror,* **59** (1973); Charles-Emmanuel Dufourcq, *L'Espagne catalane et le Maghrib aux XIIIe et XIVe siècles* (1966), 28–98; Giovanni Forcheri, *Navi e navigazione a Genova nel trecento: Il "Liber Gazarie"* (1974); Benjamin Z. Kedar, "The Passenger List of a Crusader Ship, 1250," in *Studi medievali,* 3rd ser., **13** (1972); Barbara M. Kreutz, "Mediterranean Contributions to the Medieval Mariner's Compass," in *Technology and Culture,* **14** (1973); Frederic C. Lane, *Venetian Ships and Shipbuilders of the Renaissance* (1934); Michael E. Mallett, *The Florentine Galleys in the Fifteenth Century* (1967); Michel Mollat, "Problèmes navals de l'histoire des croisades," in *Cahiers de civilisation médiévale,* **10** (1967); John H. Pryor, "The Naval Architecture of Crusader Transport Ships," in *The Mariner's Mirror,* **70** (1984); E[va] G. R. Taylor, *The Haven-finding Art* (1956); Alberto Tenenti, "Venezia e la pirateria nel Levante: 1300 C.–1460 C.," in *Convegno internazionale di storia della civiltà veneziana, 1st, Venice* (1968), *Venezia e il Levante fino al secolo XV,* I, pt. 2 (1973).

BARBARA M. KREUTZ

[See also **Barcelona; Compass, Magnetic; Genoa; Lateen Sail; Navies; Navigation, Western European; Portolan Chart; Technology, Western; Valencia; Venice; Warfare, Byzantine; Warfare, Western European.**]

SHIPS AND SHIPBUILDING, NORTHERN EUROPEAN. Ships were essential to most transportation and personal travel in medieval Europe. Trading connections depend on the ability to move goods at low enough cost, and in the great majority of cases in the Middle Ages that meant moving them by water. Although people could afford to travel on land more often than goods could be sent that way, individuals often relied on travel in ships to maintain contact with other Europeans.

In the course of the Middle Ages, shipbuilding in northern Europe changed from a simple industry carried on by men with little training and located anywhere those men happened to be to an industry with fixed locations, sizable investment, and a system for the training of skilled personnel. Shipbuilding also showed significant technical progress both in the methods of construction and in the design of the vessels. Innovation was not limited to any single period but stretched over the entire Middle Ages. Shipbuilding is another example of the lively technical advance and of the great inventiveness that took place in the Middle Ages, a period traditionally and incorrectly thought to be one of stagnation.

The Roman presence in Gaul and Britain apparently had little effect on shipbuilding in northern Europe. The Romans had a unique method of building ships: strength came from the external planks, which were held together by mortise-and-tenon joints. In a few cases, Mediterranean shipbuilders did construct vessels with that type of hull in northern Europe, but native Celtic shipwrights continued to use their own proven designs. The Romans accepted this traditional practice and used the native knowledge and skill to deal with problems presented by northern seas. One distinguishing feature of Celtic shipbuilding was the variety of ship types that could be and were produced, each type suited to certain waters or tasks. While the list of ship designs is lengthy, a few were more commonly used and formed the basis for the shipbuilding traditions of northern Europe in the Middle Ages.

SHIP TYPES

The curragh was a skin boat with wickerwork filling the spaces between the heavy wooden ribs. Hides were stretched over the hull to make it watertight. The stern was drawn up a bit more sharply than the bow. Curraghs are usually associated with the Irish coast and apparently were in common use there and along the Atlantic coast throughout the Middle Ages. Curraghs could reach twelve meters in length and could carry a sail, though they were often rowed. The relatively long and rounded hull allowed the curragh to bob like a cork in the water and to bend and twist, riding on top of the waves so it could survive in the open ocean.

The cog may be related to the seagoing sailing ships that so impressed Julius Caesar when he saw Celts using them in heavy seas off the north coast of Gaul. Caesar mentioned a relatively flat bottom, planking placed end-to-end, no keel, high freeboard, and a mast with a single sail carried about one-third of the way back from the bow. At the beginning of the Middle Ages the cog had no keel. The bottom was flat, with planks there placed end-to-end. Planking on the sides, on the other hand, was overlapping or clinkered. Strength presumably came from that external skeleton. There were heavy ribs to which the hull planks were nailed. The posts at bow and stern were straight and at a sharp angle to the bottom. There was high freeboard, so the carrying capacity was relatively large. The cog was a sailing ship, carrying one square sail on a mast stepped about in the middle of the vessel. It was primarily a cargo ship, used presumably by Frisian traders in the early Middle Ages. The flat bottom made it ideal for service along the coast of Frisia and to Scandinavia through coastal shallows and inlets. The boat could be set on a sandbank as the tide went out, unloaded and loaded, then refloated with the tide. The cog was the ideal boat for the trading network of Frisian merchants built up in the seventh through ninth centuries. There was even a special harbor set aside for cogs at Birka, Sweden.

The pram or punt was one of the simplest of Celtic boats. The side formed a right angle with the flat bottom, which was made of planks placed edge-to-edge. The last bottom plank was L-shaped, making it also the first plank of the side. The sides were made of planks, each overlapping the one below. Such vessels were very long relative to the width but could still carry sizable quantities for their dimensions. They were pulled along rivers or poled across lakes and shallows, not sailed. Vessels of the pram design appear often throughout the Middle Ages as fishing boats, riverboats, or ferries. They were especially important in early medieval Europe, where rivers were the major avenues for the carriage of goods and of people.

Hulks also were used on rivers but had the added capacity of being able to sail on the open seas. Their hulls were strongly built with heavy planking. The shape was that of half an eggshell or a hollowed-out banana. There were no posts and no keel but a thick center plank. The ends were rounded, with the planks characteristically only coming together without connecting pieces to hold them together. The planks overlapped. For further watertightness and lateral strength, the seams were covered with heavy timbers. Control, as on many early medieval ships, was given by two side rudders set near the stern. Hulks carried masts that were not very strong, so they may have been towed along rivers more often than sailed. The shape of the hull made hulks effective in tidal estuaries and rivers. They were therefore especially popular in the Low Countries, where they were in widespread use in the ninth century and earlier.

While the pram and curragh found and kept their own specific places, both the cog and the hulk were to be transformed in the course of the High and late Middle Ages. Those two were joined in the eighth century by a third type, which for some three centuries dominated the seas of northern Europe, the Viking ship.

This ship was descended from the Scandinavian and north German rowing barge, which was the relatively long, low type used for carrying immigrants from the Continent to Britain in the sixth and seventh centuries. The barge was typically an open boat with a very high ratio of length to breadth. In the eighth century it got a real keel, which set it apart from boats of Celtic design. It already had a single mast with a single square sail, introduced soon after the migration period. The sail was made of leather or cloth reinforced with leather strips. More important, though, were the changes in the internal structure. The overlapping planks of the hull supplied strength. They were scarfed where necessary, so no single hull plank was very long. Shipbuilders added internal ribs to give lateral strength and stability, but these were all below the waterline. The planks above the waterline were there only to keep out the water and made no structural contribution. The Scandinavian ship rode high in the water and made little wake, and because of the low resistance, it was relatively fast, especially with a following breeze. Altogether, it was a highly flexible ship with good maneuverability, great potential range, good stability, and excellent handling characteristics. In addition, it could be adapted to different tasks.

Viking ship of *ca.* 800, believed to have been a pleasure craft used in protected waters. ART RESOURCE

The Viking ship was the greatest accomplishment of early medieval shipbuilding. Without that unique type, the great Viking expansion, trading, exploration, and colonization of the ninth and tenth centuries would not have been possible. There were two basic types of Viking ship by 800, one for carrying people and the other for carrying goods. The *karv* belonged to the first category. While it carried a square sail on a mast, the mast was easily retracted. There were places for oarsmen along the entire length of both sides of the vessel. With its large crew, the *karv* was usually a warship but could also carry goods. It had a length-to-breadth ratio of from 4.5:1 to more than 7:1.

The cargo ship, the *knarr* (*knorr, knörr*), typically had a ratio of from 2.3:1 up to 5:1. Both had the same fine curving lines and double-ended, pointed hull. For control they both relied on a single, balanced side rudder attached near the stern. Since the ship was perfectly symmetrical, the slightest movement of the rudder directed the vessel. Both types were easily beached and the warship was especially effective for raiding because it could be quickly run up on a shore. The cargo ship had high freeboard. That limited the effectiveness of the two or three pairs of oars at the bow, but they were rarely used, so the gain in carrying capacity from having a large, deep, open space around the mast was well worth it. The *knarr* was a sailing ship, the mast being permanently fixed. While it could not match a hulk of the same dimensions in capacity, it could easily carry a Viking, his family, and his possessions from Norway to Iceland. It was these cargo ships that made voyages across the North Atlantic to Iceland, Greenland, and Canada, and that maintained trading connections between Scandinavia and the Atlantic islands throughout the Middle Ages.

In the eleventh and twelfth centuries Scandinavian builders further changed Viking ships, making them larger but less flexible. The warship became even longer, increasing the number of rowers per side from the fifteen to twenty on the *karv* to twenty-five to thirty and even more. The largest may have reached more than sixty oarsmen per side. While the extremely long ships did carry large crews, a great advantage in battle, the warship of twenty-five oarsmen to a side and about 24 meters (78/79 feet) in length was most commonly used because of its maneuverability. All these longships had much greater freeboard than their ninth-century predecessors, which made rowing even more an auxiliary mode of power. Cargo ships also became larger, as well as more squared off. The fine curving lines were partially abandoned for greater carrying capacity. The general tendency after about 1000 was for the crosstimbers (the crosspieces that sat on the frames and gave lateral strengthening at the waterline) to be placed more toward the bottom of the hull. As that happened, the frames became flatter, as did the bottom of the ship. More crossbeams had to be added above. The result was a simpler form of construction and greater space in the hold. Cargo ships were commonly about 25 meters long, but even larger ships were built to carry bulk cargoes, such as grain, across the North Sea.

In the central Middle Ages the Scandinavian cargo ship—the buss, as it was often called—remained in use for a broad range of tasks. The keel, a related type built mostly in England and western France, was also widely used as a cargo carrier. The name presumably came from the true keel, one of the distinguishing features of early Viking ships. The rig was the same—a single square sail on a single mast—but with the addition of a number of lines to various parts of the sail to give better control. The keel also proved an effective warship, at least for patrol work in the English Channel and for amphibious operations in the British Isles and along the French coast. The Cinque

Ports, those towns on the English south coast required to supply naval forces to the king, typically fulfilled their responsibility by sending keels until the end of the thirteenth century. The hulk did not disappear but held its place as a carrier of bulk goods along rivers and tidal estuaries. It also appears to have been built along the Atlantic front and probably used as a coaster. The hulk, like the keel, remained small compared with the dominant cargo ship of the twelfth and thirteenth centuries, the cog.

THE DEVELOPMENT OF THE COG

Around 1100 the simple flat-bottomed cog was transformed by the addition of a keel, perhaps inspired by the success of Scandinavian shipwrights. The keel gave the vessel sharply increased stability and made it a much better sailer, especially in a crosswind. That and some improvements to the rig combined to make the cog a truly effective seagoing ship. The flat bottom remained, so there was no sacrifice in carrying capacity. The cog was always tubby, and that did not change either. The ratio of length to breadth stayed at about 2.5–3.0:1. The sharp angle of the posts remained, as did that of bottom to sides. Over time both would be decreased slightly. Another advantage of the improved cog was that it could be built bigger. By the late thirteenth century cogs were as much as 30 meters (98 feet) long and no more than 9.5 meters (31 feet) broad, and had a draught of from 3 to 4 meters (about 10 to 13 feet). Compared with the typical Viking cargo ship of about 1000, the thirteenth-century cog could carry more than five times as much. There was little change in crew size, so over those years sailors became much more productive. The adoption of the cog meant a significant saving, especially for the carriage of bulk goods—for instance, grain from newly developed farms in the Baltic basin to the growing towns in Western Europe. That trade was made possible by development of the new and larger cog.

The big ship needed a larger sail to move its greater weight. The simple rig of a single square sail on a single mast remained. Sail area ranged from 82 to 175 square meters (882–1,884 square feet). That could be raised to as much as 335 square meters (3,602 square feet) with the addition of bonnets: strips of cloth sewed to the bottom of the sail. If the wind freshened, they could easily be removed. Bonnets made it possible to adjust total sail area without having to hoist or lower the heavy yard and sail. Even with all bonnets, there was still much less sail area per ton on a thirteenth-century cog than on a Viking ship. The cog was slow. Sails on cogs were heavier and less flexible than those on Viking ships. All those features made cogs far from easy to handle.

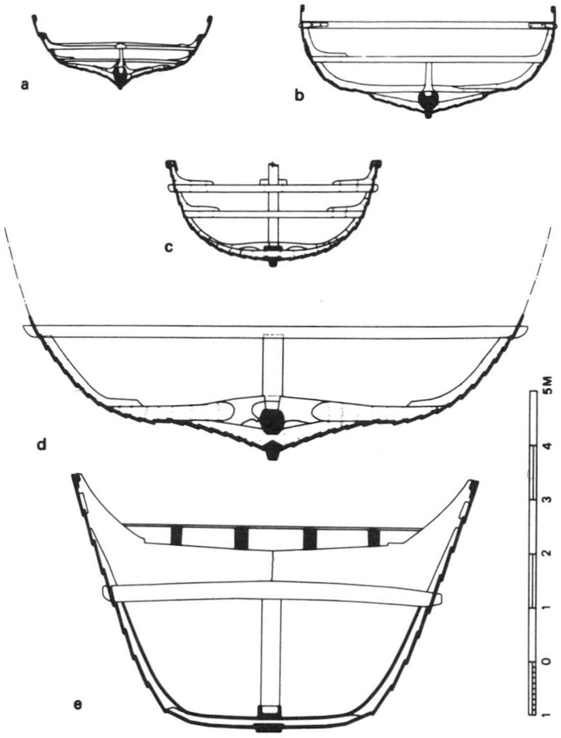

Cross-sections of Scandinavian ship-finds: (*a*) small trading ship, *ca.* 1000; (*b*) large deep-sea trader, *ca.* 1000; (*c*) trader, *ca.* 1100; (*d*) deep-sea trader, a buss, *ca.* 1200; (*e*) cog, *ca.* 1380. © OLE CRUMLIN-PEDERSEN

A major improvement in controlling big ships came with the introduction of the sternpost rudder in the late twelfth century. The advance came first in northern Europe, long before it was taken over in the Mediterranean. The straight sternpost made it easy to attach a rudder there. Side rudders were excellent steering devices, but as cogs got bigger, the size of the side rudder grew as well. It became difficult to find a single piece of wood long enough and strong enough for the rudder. It also became difficult to fit the much heavier rudder so as to minimize friction in its operation. Attaching the rudder to the sternpost took care of the problem of minimizing friction, but weight remained a difficulty. Ropes had to be added to the tiller to move the heavy sternpost rudder. It proved especially effective on long reaches—for example, in sailing around the northern end of Jutland on the way in and out of the Baltic. By the thirteenth century the sternpost rudder was typical equipment on all cogs.

The new big cogs with keels could not sit on sandbanks, as had their predecessors. Rather, while being loaded and unloaded, they rode in the water alongside a quay. Builders therefore added reinforcing protective planks along the sides to act as bumpers. Before that, shipwrights were interested only in extra protection for the bottoms of ships. Quays and docks had disappeared from northern Europe with the Romans, and ports became just pieces of beach where vessels could easily be brought up out of the water. That simple form continued to exist in the twelfth and thirteenth centuries for keels and busses, types of essentially Scandinavian design, but from the eleventh century on, those simple facilities were increasingly joined by quays, typically small ones built of wood. The new quays were common in larger ports and handled the great majority of cargo. Over time they grew in number and in size to accommodate the bigger cargo ships.

The cog was the dominant warship of northern Europe in the High Middle Ages as well. The high freeboard increased the overall size and carrying capacity of the cog but also put it much higher in the water than any other contemporary type. Small superstructures were added both fore and aft. Perhaps borrowed from Mediterranean practice, these castles were mostly for defense. They put archers and other soldiers well above any potential opponent and gave them a great advantage in hurling missiles.

Scandinavian shipbuilders added castles to their warships, but that could not overcome the advantage of the cog. In fact, the Scandinavian kingdoms abandoned longships, using cogs instead for their navies. The king of England came more and more to rely on cogs, rented from merchants, for his navy. Cogs could carry more men for each meter of length than any other type of ship. They were therefore highly defensible and ideal transports, and in battle offered the best available platform for launching an attack onto an enemy's decks. Battles at sea were still like land battles, fought hand-to-hand, so the greatest number of men and the largest deck area were critical to victory. Maneuverability counted for little, and therefore the greatest shortcoming of the cog was not a handicap.

Cogs stood out to sea instead of hugging the coast because their deeper draft made it impossible for them to pass through many of the streams and fjords that had been avenues for earlier types. The bigger cog then dictated a change in trade routes in the North and Baltic seas. Cogs were the principal carriers of men, supplies, and animals from northern European ports to the eastern Mediterranean for the crusades of the twelfth and thirteenth centuries. They made the vogages along the Atlantic front, stopping in Iberia and then going through the Straits of Gibraltar into the Mediterranean. Apparently, though cogs could make that trip and carry a relatively large payload doing it, their sailing qualities made it impossible for them to sail back out into the Atlantic. It was not until late in the thirteenth or early in the fourteenth century that modification in hull design and especially in the lines used to control the sails made the cog a practical sailing ship both for use in the Mediterranean and for going in and out of that sea.

Long before the cog became a common vessel in southern European waters, it had made possible major shifts in both economic and naval power in the north. Just as the Viking ship was necessary to the raids and the trading and colonizing ventures of Scandinavians in the ninth and tenth centuries, so the dominant position of the cog in northern European waters lay behind the development of towns along the north coast of Germany and the political power of their alliance, the Hanseatic League. The cog was the dominant carrier of goods in northern Europe in the High Middle Ages. Other types continued to be built and were widely used, but the cog was technically superior, particularly for rapidly growing trades and also for naval uses.

Shipbuilders continued to construct oared vessels in northern Europe, but their uses became increasingly specialized. Many smaller ships shed their auxiliary oars to rely exclusively on sail. Increasingly, if a ship had oars, they were the principal form of propulsion. Galleys were powerful and effective warships in the Mediterranean, but they could never match that performance in the north. The high seas could easily swamp a vessel with such low freeboard. Galleys of Mediterranean design might have length-to-breadth ratios similar to those of Viking longships, but without the system of ribs and heavy overlapping planking they could not survive voyages on the open sea. Nevertheless, some galleys were built in the north. They found use as patrol vessels along the coasts, for amphibious operations, and for attacking other galleys. The galleys carried supplementary sails, modeled on either the older Scandinavian longships or contemporary Mediterranean galleys. Since the galleys had no economic function, the decision to build them was a political one. The French government at the end of the thirteenth century even went to far as to import Genoese shipwrights to a royal shipyard at Rouen modeled on Spanish examples. Those Italian craftsmen built and maintained galleys of Mediterranean design. The English government was quick to respond by constructing its own galleys, perhaps of similar design. Those reached seventy oars per side, much greater than the maximum for northern European oared vessels such as the barge or balinger. The need to import shipbuilders from the Mediterranean to construct galleys suggests that northern European shipwrights could do a good job only when dealing with their own straightforward designs. Moreover, in the High Middle Ages, ships native to northern Europe appear to have become easier to build, of simpler construction. That may have made it harder for the northerners to deal with new problems or to make adaptations of the designs they knew well. The success of the High Middle Ages may have bred a certain conservatism and willingness to adhere to past practice. If so, that complacency was first shaken, and then totally altered, in the fourteenth and fifteenth centuries.

FOURTEENTH AND FIFTEENTH CENTURIES

The changes in the late Middle Ages were not limited to rapid development in the design of ships. There were also significant improvements in the techniques of building ships and breaks with past practice in the organization of the shipbuilding operation itself. Northern European shipbuilders were exposed more frequently to the designs of their southern European counterparts. More ships of different sizes and types made voyages from the Mediterranean to the North Sea and, later, to the Baltic. More shipwrights from southern Europe found their way to shipyards in the north. Craftsmen in the industry, like their ships, moved more easily over long distances. The result was much easier access to technical information of all kinds. The process did not guarantee greater experimentation in the design of ships, but it at least increased the likelihood of innovation.

New tools had come into use, making shipwrights more effective. Builders of Viking ships had not cut their logs but had split them with axes and then dressed the wood with adzes. The frame saw, a blade in the middle of an open rectangular frame, was used in the Mediterranean basin throughout the Middle Ages, but in northern Europe, even by 1250, the conversion from axes and adzes to saws for preparing ships' timbers was not complete. Saws had the advantage of saving wood. They were also much more accurate and even led to the separation of the tasks of ship carpenter and sawyer. The introduction of the breast auger also made the work of the shipbuilder easier. Augers were used to make the many holes in the planking so that nails or treenails could be put through them. By putting a pad at the top of the auger, the carpenter could put his weight behind the stock and increase the power of the cutting edge. This was especially effective for making the bigger holes in the main ribs and planks. Breast augers were already in use by the eleventh century, and their use increased through the later Middle Ages. In the fifteenth century breast augers were joined by a new tool for making holes, the brace, which was much more efficient than an auger, especially for making the hundreds of small holes in a ship. It was a great saver of time and energy for the ship carpenter and so came into widespread use on shipbuilding wharves.

In the eleventh century, shipbuilders had been itinerants moving from place to place to practice their trade on any convenient piece of beach or shore. In the High Middle Ages they increasingly became established in a single location, because of the larger size of the ships being built and the channeling of trade through specific and growing towns. They also became increasingly specialized, dropping other part-time occupations. The process accelerated rapidly in the fourteenth and fifteenth centuries. Towns in the Low Countries, and more commonly in Germany, set apart a certain part of town for shipbuilding wharves. The land was sold to shipbuilders or leased to them. The goal in part was to quarantine the fire danger that always existed in shipbuilding yards. It had the additional effect of improving the status of the men who built ships and making it easier for them to work and to trade ideas.

Shipbuilding was subjected to increasing legislation. Governments recognized the growing importance of shipbuilding to the economy and to supplies of important goods. They had long appreciated its role in naval affairs. Regulations tended in direct and indirect ways to limit the transfer of technology, a trend that became more pronounced in the years after the Middle Ages. Legislation extended to the shipbuilders themselves. The fourteenth and fifteenth centuries saw the formation of guilds of ship carpenters in many northern European ports. The guilds were chartered and sanctioned by local regional governments, which often retained the right to decide what rules would apply in the guilds. These organizations, set up to perform religious and social as well as economic functions, also served to promote the development of new knowledge in shipbuilding and to promote the spread of that knowledge. Above all, they served as training institutions. There was no strict progression from apprentice through journeyman to master even by the end of the fifteenth century, but there was a formalized program for teaching young men how to build ships. The institutional changes and the improvements in the status and income of ship carpenters grew out of their ability to produce more effective ships.

For the carriage of bulk goods the cog was superseded in the fifteenth century in the Baltic by a composite type that drew from the designs of both the cog and the hulk. The hulk grew progressively larger through the thirteenth and fourteenth centuries as shipbuilders slowly solved the problem of how to make a bigger and still seaworthy vessel of that design. The final solution to the problem was to borrow certain features from the cog. The resulting composite was called by both names, some ships being called cog in one port and hulk in the next. The average size of the cog in the late fourteenth century was probably around 100 tons, and that did not change with the introduction of the composite type. What did change was the sailing qualities and the potential carrying capacity per meter of length. The new type was still clinker-built, with strength coming from the overlapping of the hull planks. The generally rounded form of the hulk was retained but a broad, flat bottom, a strong keel and stem, and sternposts like those of the cog were added. The bow continued to be brought up, as in earlier hulks, while the stern owed more to the cog. There was no change in rig or in length-to-breadth ratio. The new type was better at riding in tides and estuaries than the old cog and had more carrying capacity than the old hulk. Draft was the same as or less than in a comparable cog, so more harbors were accessible. It was faster than the earlier hulk. All these improvements created a more productive bulk carrier, one ideally suited for voyages from Prussia and the east Baltic to the cities of northwestern Europe.

The most important innovation in the design of European sailing ships took place in the fifteenth century. The first full-rigged ship was probably built on the western coast of Europe, perhaps on the shores of the Bay of Biscay. The full-rigged ship combined some features of northern European designs with southern building methods. First built around 1400, the type did not come into use in the North and Baltic seas until the second half of the fifteenth century. The new type had three masts, the fore- and mainmasts carrying square sails and the mizzenmast having a triangular or lateen sail. The addition of the lateen, long in use in the Mediterranean, made it possible to sail closer to the wind. Square sails gave more driving force per square meter of sail and the possibility of dividing the sail area among a number of pieces of canvas. That gave captains greater flexibility and thus increased the safety as well as speed. Northern builders were familiar with true fore-and-aft sails such as the spritsail, which had all the advantages of the lateen and was easier to handle. In the fifteenth century both the spritsail and the staysail came into use on small craft, especially boats used on inland waterways. The combination of staysail and spritsail proved to be a very efficient rig for small boats but was too light for big ships. It was two centuries before these sails were transferred to large cargo carriers.

The full-rigged ship of the fifteenth century had a system of planking previously unknown in northern Europe, a system that was truly revolutionary. Strength came not from the external planking but from an internal frame. Ships were built from the inside out, the hull planks pinned to the frame and placed edge-to-edge. The well-established northern system of overlapping planks remained in use, however, primarily for the largest sailing ships. Henry V of England had such a ship of 1,400 tons built for him in the second decade of the fifteenth century, and a number of other ships of 1,000 tons and more were clinker-built and proved to be adequate sailers. But during the course of the fifteenth century the Mediterranean method of skeleton construction came to dominate shipbuilding in the north. Less wood was needed in this type of construction, and it was easier to repair a ship with the new planking system. In addition, damage to the hull did not mean a threat to the structural integrity of the vessel, so the new building system meant a more durable ship. It was possible to build ships larger without more than a proportional increase in weight. The hull design and the sail plan combined to make the full-rigged ship more efficient, faster, and safer. Northern shipbuilders were slow to learn how to build the new type of hull, but the success in northern waters of vessels from the Mediterranean, such as Genoese carracks, and from the Biscay coast convinced local shippers of the value of the new design. They began by importing ships of the new type directly from the south, and then slowly developed the technique for building skeletal hulls for relatively large cargo ships. By the end of the fifteenth century they were beginning to transfer that skill to other types, such as fishing boats.

By the end of the Middle Ages, northern European shipbuilders were able to construct a new type of vessel that was a better sailing ship than any of its predecessors. They had established the essential features of the design of big wooden sailing ships for the next three centuries. The full-rigged ship produced in northern European yards was capable of maintaining and expanding trading contacts within Europe.

The fifteenth century had put an end to the isolation of the major shipbuilding traditions in Europe, and from then on there was a single technology in European shipbuilding. There remained, of course, local and regional variations in response to local conditions, but increasing contact between different parts of the Continent during the second half of the Middle Ages produced an exchange of information and ultimately a common and much more efficient design for Europe's sailing ships. From the fifteenth century on, the contacts between different parts of Europe became ever more intense and progress in ship design continued. The greater effectiveness of shipbuilders in producing vessels to carry goods more safely and at lower costs was reflected in their improved status. Their incomes, their legal status within guilds, their houses with accompanying shipbuilding wharves in the growing towns of Renaissance Europe came as a result of their ability to master the new techniques of shipbuilding slowly developed by their predecessors through the Middle Ages.

BIBLIOGRAPHY

George Bass, ed., *A History of Seafaring Based on Underwater Archaeology* (1972), 159–204; A. W. Brøgger and Haakon Shetelig, *The Viking Ships: Their Ancestry and Evolution,* Katherine John, trans. (1951, repr. 1971); Detlev Ellmers, *Frühmittelalterliche Handelsschif fahrt in Mittel- und Nord Europa* (1972); Paul Heinsius, *Das Schiff de Hansischen Frühzeit* (1956); Friedrich Moll, *Das Schiff in der bildenden Kunst* (1929); R. Morton Nance, "The Ship of the Renaissance," in *The Mariner's Mirror,* **41** (1955); Richard W. Unger, *The Ship in the Medieval Economy: 600–1600* (1980).

RICHARD W. UNGER

[See also **Hanseatic League; Navies, Western; Navigation, Western European; Ships and Shipbuilding, Mediterranean; Technology, Western; Trade, European; Viking Navigation; Warfare, Western European.**]

SHIPS AND SHIPBUILDING, RED SEA AND PERSIAN GULF. The Red Sea and Persian Gulf are the two western outlets of the Indian Ocean, which bathes the shores of East Africa, the Arabian Peninsula, southern Iran, the Indian Subcontinent, the southeastern Asiatic lands, and the Malay Archipelago. These two bodies of water should be considered on three levels: as a means of communication between the lands bordering on them, as the extension of the western part of the Indian Ocean, and as the far western outlet of the main seaway connecting the Mediterranean with the Far East.

NATURAL CONDITIONS

The natural geographical features of these waters are essential to understanding the shipping system. In the open Indian Ocean, the monsoon (Arabic: *mawsin,* season) winds are a decisive factor. They blow regularly in a southwesterly direction from March to October, and in a northeasterly direction the other half of the year. As a rule, only the latter season is used for navigation, as the southwesterly monsoon is usually accompanied by rain and storms. It is possible to navigate independently of the monsoons, a method employed mainly for a southern crossing of the ocean with the eastern current going from Sumatra to Madagascar, or for close coastal navigation. In the Red Sea, treacherous alternating winds blow irregularly most of the year, and the same is true, to a lesser degree, of the Persian Gulf. There is a strong current going south along the East African shore, which affects routes and navigation. In the period of sails, the long calms characteristic of this region impeded navigation, while it was eased considerably by the fact that skies are seldom overcast and storms are quite infrequent. The shores are usually lined with coral reefs and are difficult to approach.

Many islands stud the waters, and navigation among them is quite dangerous. The few good natural harbors are backed either by relatively high mountain ranges or by extensive arid deserts. Others, especially in India, could not be used during the Middle Ages because of the extensive swamps created by the big rivers. The countries bordering on the Red Sea and Persian Gulf totally lack the two basic raw materials needed for ship construction, wood and iron. Wood was imported from as far as today's Burma and Kenya, while the Maldive and Laccadive islands, where coconut trees were abundant, served as a center for a light shipbuilding industry.

Land routes were another important factor in the localization of ports and their development. The main routes were: (1) the roads connecting the Red Sea and the Gulf of Suez with the Nile system and the Mediterranean, which consisted of the southern road, leading from Adulis or Suakin in Ethiopia, to ᶜAydhāb, Berenice, or Quṣayr, to Quṣ, north of Aswan, and the northern road, leading from Qulzum (Suez), al-Ṭūr, or Yothabe, to Pelusium (al-Faramāᵓ), Damietta, or Cairo; (2) the Gulf of Eilat, connected to the Egyptian complex by roads crossing the Sinai Peninsula, and to the Syrian coast by the Jordan Valley road; (3) a major caravan route leading north from the southern tip of the Arabian Peninsula (Aden, Zabīd), through the Hejaz and around the Gulf of Eilat; Jidda and al-Jār served only Mecca and Medina, respectively; (4) the main road on the western side of the Persian Gulf, leading from a series of alternative ports—Qalhāt, Moskat, Ṣuḥār, Bahrain (al-Bahrayn), al-Qaṭīf—north into Mesopotamia; (5) on the east, two main roads into the Persian mainland, one through Sīrāf and Fārs, the other through Hormuz and Kermān; and (6) the most important route in the whole area since ancient times, the inner waterway leading from Ubulla and Basra up the Euphrates, to a lesser degree through the Tigris, too, into Mesopotamia, and thence, following the Fertile Crescent, to northern Syria and Anatolia.

The Gulf of Kutch and the Bay of Bengal had the best access to the Indian mainland, while the ports of the Malabar coast, above all Quilon (Koulan), and those of Ceylon were the traditional emporia for Far Eastern goods. The great Asiatic land routes, such as the one passing through Baluchistan and the others south and north of the Caspian Sea, almost never connected with the Indian Ocean shipping system and constituted an alternative to it. The shifts in ports and routes during the medieval period are mainly a consequence of economic and political developments.

HISTORICAL SURVEY

Islamic poetry and the Koran itself contain many references to maritime activity. A few southern and eastern Arabian tribes were mainly seamen, while some of the merchants of the north also used maritime transports. But the rise of Islam marked the decline of south Arabia and its maritime tradition. The Umayyads tried hard to establish a navy in the eastern Mediterranean, but trade seems to have been practiced mostly by non-Muslim Iranians and Indians, even Chinese, in the East, Jews, Syrians, and Greeks in the West. For the first two centuries after the Islamic conquest our sources are quite meager. The papyri dealing with Egypt of the period hardly mention the Red Sea at all.

With the rise of the Abbasids and the establishment of Baghdad as their capital, Arabs and New Muslims started trading extensively with the East. The old Byzantine-Sasanian system, based mainly on Alexandria, Aden, and Ubulla, was gone, and with it the ports of Qulzum, Berenice, Yothabe, and Fārs. The old canal connecting Qulzum with the Nile system was abandoned definitively, as was also the port of al-Jār. Most of the traffic now passed through the ports of Sīrāf and Basra.

During the reign of the Chinese Tang dynasty, important Muslim merchant colonies were established along the Indian coast, southeast Asia, and China. Muslim merchants pushed further into Korea and Japan. This era was the apogee of trade in the Persian Gulf. Nevertheless, the old rivalry between the Persian Gulf and the Red Sea as two competing trade routes continued and intensified. This period is well known to us from Arabic sources, as, from the second half of the ninth century on, many chronicles, histories, geographies, and various manuals survive. Chinese sources add another aspect to the lively picture.

In the tenth century there was a thorough change. After the fall of the Tang dynasty, new powers rose also in India (the Chola Empire) and the Malay Archipelago (the Shrivijaya). Arabs, Persians, and even western Indians were no longer welcome east of Ceylon and lost their colonies in the East. The Abbasid Empire was crumbling too—

first Bedouins and Qarmatians, later Seljuks and crusaders, interfered with the land routes leading from the Persian Gulf to the eastern Mediterranean and the Black Sea.

Contemporaneously, the Fatimids, having conquered Egypt, encouraged trade in the Red Sea by effective protection, lower taxes, and broad international relations. This effort was their economic front in the war against the Abbasids. The period is well documented by the material of the Cairo genizah. In the Red Sea, Aden rose to importance again, and with it ᶜAydhāb and Quṣayr as intermediary ports. The Frankish presence around the Gulf of Eilat seems to have increased the importance of this more southern seaway as compared to the old caravan routes. The Fatimids were succeeded by the Ayyubids, who tried to continue their economic policies but faced a financial and political crisis that caused the loss of their hegemony in the maritime commerce of the East.

By the middle of the thirteenth century, the pendulum had turned again in favor of the Persian Gulf system. The commercial revival that started under the caliph al-Naṣīr (*r.* 1180–1225), with the active cooperation of the Seljuks of Rūm, reached its height under Mongol rule and the Yuan dynasty of China. This was also the period of the establishment of many Muslim merchant colonies in East Africa. Land routes were open, safe, and free, all the way from Peking to Layazzo in Lesser Armenia. At the center of the parallel maritime activity, Gujarat flourished. The main port of the Persian Gulf was no longer Sīrāf but Kīsh (Qays) in the thirteenth century, and Hormuz from then on. The thirteenth and fourteenth centuries were a period of intensive trade and free traffic in the Indian Ocean. Again there were Arabs in China, Chinese in the Persian Gulf, Europeans in the Far East, and Indians in all parts of the ocean. From the middle of the thirteenth century, European and Chinese sources add to our knowledge of these seas.

The last phase covers the period of the Circassian Mamluks of Egypt, who pulled trade back into the Red Sea by armed protection, direct contact with India, and harassment of the western outlets of international trade through the Persian Gulf, Lesser Armenia, and Cyprus. Al-Ṭūr took the place of Quṣar, and Aden surpassed its former glory. To this period (end of the fifteenth century) belong an important customs manual from Aden as well as another from Hormuz. These add much information to that given by a previous, similar Mediterranean manual. From the second half of the fifteenth century dates also the source of our knowledge regarding navigation in these seas, ascribed to the captain Aḥmad ibn Mājid. It gives invaluable information regarding ships, harbors, routes, navigational aides, and astronomy. Some of this information may be valid for previous centuries and is certainly based on a long seagoing tradition.

This tradition came to an abrupt end by the appearance and sudden predominance of the Portuguese. After the discovery of the Cape of Good Hope in 1487 and a reconnaissance tour of the East made the same year through Egypt, Vasco da Gama arrived easily in Calicut in 1498. About ten years later, Albuquerque got a hold on all the main western Indian ports, as well as Hormuz. The Red Sea and the Persian Gulf became enclosed and neglected waterways, with Portuguese bases all around them from India to East Africa. The main traffic avoided them on its direct route to the West. Neither the Mamluks with their Venetian allies, nor the Ottoman Turks, could reverse these facts. A new era had begun.

THE SHIPS

The ships plying the southern seas are known to us mostly from literary sources. No actual ships have been excavated, and known illustrations are few. For these reasons, scientific research relies heavily on the study of the present-day designs, which are thought to reflect older models. Indeed, the rate of development and change has been rather slow, and outside influences minimal.

It should first be emphasized that there is no trace of a tradition of rowed warships for this area. There were a few campaigns in the Red Sea, the Gulfs of Suez and Eilat, and along the northwestern shores of India, but it seems that for military purposes, warships of the Mediterranean type were launched into the southern seas. Another tradition of warships existed east of Bengal, but neither of these traditions ever penetrated firmly the western basin of the Indian Ocean and its gulfs. Even the ubiquitous pirates of these seas must have used a small version of the sailing ships common there, but we know very little of its characteristics.

In the late Umayyad and early Abbasid periods, wide use was made by Muslim fleets of Greek fire. The "destroyer" using this weapon was called a *harrāqa,* but it seems that outside the Mediterranean this name denoted mainly a pleasure riverboat. It is noteworthy that many of the existing

Arabic names of boats in the eastern seas derived from those of Abbasid rivercraft on the Tigris and Euphrates.

The typical ship of the western Indian Ocean may be described as a sailing cargo vessel. Its main features are still present in the type called a dhow by the Europeans. Some of these dhows still preserve what seems to be the original form—a sleek, double-ended hull—while others are characterized by a long overhanging bow and a raking stern. The features most peculiar to these ships are known from the literature and are indeed still observed today. The hull is mostly teak, imported from Burma, India, or East Africa. It is a hard and lasting material, which can withstand the reefs and devastating seaworms. In the Middle Ages, the shell was made first, in carvel fashion (planks edge-to-edge), using no nails; the planks were sewn together with palm- or coconut-tree fiber. Finishing was usually accomplished, not by painting, but by coating with shark oil and bitumen.

The rig consisted of fore-and-aft sails called by the Europeans the Arab lateen. They were quadrilateral, with the fore arm clipped off. The yard was very long, sometimes longer than the mast or even the ship itself. There was often a second mast, a mizzen (perhaps from the Arabic *mizan* [balance]), stepped just before the poop, both raking forward heavily. The sails were probably woven originally from palm leaves or papyrus, later from cotton, linen, or hemp, all found abundantly and in high quality all over the Middle East. This rig was very important in the general development of shipping, and its origin is highly controversial.

Steering was originally done by one or two oars at the quarters, but as early as the thirteenth century there is evidence of a stern rudder, possibly derived from Chinese influence. The anchors were probably made of stone, due to the lack of iron in the region, but in the thirteenth century we find an iron anchor of the grapnel type, common in the Mediterranean at that time. As for accommodation and inner arrangement, we know little of the number of decks and other utilities. Travelers tell us of inhumanly cramped conditions on board. On the other hand, there is evidence of cabins and inner compartments, unknown in the Mediterranean at the time, probably another Chinese influence.

In size and tonnage, the ships of the western Indian Ocean were probably equal to the average medieval Mediterranean ship—some 100 to 200 tons, with a proportion of 4:1:0.5, being about 100 feet (30 meters) in length, 25 feet (7.6 meters) beam, and 12 feet (3.7 meters) draught. Inside the gulfs, smaller ships were usually used.

THE PORTS

We know very little of the physical aspects of medieval ports in general. Even for the more sophisticated shipping in the Mediterranean, Muslim rule did not offer special facilities. According to a respectable source, the Muslims forgot the art of building underwater. It seems we should not expect any special harbor installations in Indian Ocean ports, except for a crude breakwater and perhaps a lighthouse, a customs house, and a caravanserai. There were no chains at the harbor entrance, but rulers used to strip the ships of their rig in order to control their departure.

Anchorage was mainly in the open; boats and barges brought the passengers and cargo in. In the gulfs, smaller boats were frequently beached. Although there were many ports that served local and regional commerce, international trade was usually concentrated in a few major ports, for reasons of convenience to both the foreign merchants and the local governments. These ports had their customs office or *minhāj*, which was enforced usually by a bureaucracy heavy with overseers, mediators, translators, and the like. The goods were classified according to several criteria—export or import, the size of the ship, state-monopoly or free-market merchandise. In Egypt, the former passed through a controlled, fixed-price market—the *matjar*. The latter were sold by auction (*halqa*) or in the open retail market (the suq or bazaar).

THE GOODS

It is customary to think of trade in the Indian Ocean in the Middle Ages as consisting mainly of transit trade in "spices" from the East to the Mediterranean lands. This was not the case. India itself was a great emporium. It imported copper and silver from the Middle East (also from the Far East) and exported gold, iron, and timber. The Persian Gulf exported salt to India and got back elephants, among other heavy commodities.

From the thirteenth century on, India became an important importer of horses from Arabia and Syria. There was a lively trade in finished goods—colored cotton textiles from India, heavy silks and brocades from the Middle East, home and war metal implements, highly finished furniture, and leather goods. Precious and semiprecious stones from south Arabia, coral from the Red Sea, pearls of the Persian Gulf, African ivory—all these were important trade items in the area, as well as in transit to the West. Chinese porcelain became a staple from the ninth century on. Foodstuffs were another vital bulk commodity—luxury items like sugar, candy, and special oils. Wine, a staple of maritime Mediterranean commerce, was lacking here, but of special importance was the Egyptian grain supply to Mecca, an economic fact of enormous religious and political consequence. Regular foodstuffs were very common in local trade, since the ports were often located in arid or swampy areas, unfit for agriculture, and had to be provided for (as well as mainland urban centers).

There was a vast passenger traffic, mostly pilgrims traveling to and returning from Mecca, but also those visiting Shiite shrines in Iraq and Iran, and even pilgrims to Buddhist temples. Slaves in large numbers were brought from East Africa to Iraq, Iran, and even China. Later, Indian and Malay eunuchs became the fashion in Turkish and Mongol courts in the Middle East. The famous spices themselves may be classified as follows: real spices, intended for food amelioration and preservation; dyes for coloring and fastening the colors of the extensive textile industries; pharmaceutical goods; and liturgical elements (for example, anointing oils).

MERCHANTS AND MARINERS

Compared with our knowledge of the Mediterranean merchant from the twelfth century on—his origin, methods, even scope—our information concerning the merchants of the Indian Ocean is indeed scant. There is no doubt that in the Persian Gulf and Red Sea most shipping was in Arab hands, although the Persians were very active too; the Indians were present in both these seas and even Chinese junks got to Sīrāf and Aden periodically. The controversy as to the ethnic identity of international merchants and open-sea shipowners is still open. Contrary to the traditional opinion, holding that in the western Indian Ocean they were mainly Muslim, and in the eastern Chinese, recent research tends to point out that in the east they were mainly south Asians (from such regions as the Malay Peninsula), and in the west Indians.

The famous Muslim examples of Indian Ocean merchants and shipowners, like Sindbad and Suleiman, were individual adventurers more than the representatives of a solid social class or group. The best-known group of Indian Ocean merchants are the Karimis, who appeared in the twelfth century and flourished in the thirteenth under the Ayyubids and Mamluks. Their position deteriorated badly in the fifteenth century. The Karimis were great merchants. They guaranteed the quality of the goods they carried and sold, made tremendous profits, and financed the rulers, who gave them protection on sea and land. The Karimi merchants were usually also owners of their ships (*nākhodā*), but not their captains (*rāhbān*). The sailors were free men, as in the West, but belonged to a different social class, with less mobility than in the West. A sailor could become a captain, but very seldom would he hope to own a seagoing ship or become a large-scale merchant.

The Jews played an important role in this field during the whole period. In the ninth century the "Rhadanites" were the only ones allowed or able to carry on trade in both shipping systems, the Mediterranean and the Indian Ocean. This situation still existed in Fatimid Egypt, with its Maghribian Jewish communities. There was an important Jewish community in Aden and others in several Indian ports.

TRADE ORGANIZATION

Turnover was much slower than in the Mediterranean, especially in the thirteenth and fourteenth centuries. A round trip to the east and back usually took two winters, with the summer spent there. If it included East Africa, it would take up to three years and more, and the same is true for the continuation farther east, to China or the East Indies. The ships were usually unarmed but sailed in convoys to spread the risk and augment security. There were no armed escorts, but the Red Sea was patrolled by government ships in Fatimid and Mamluk times.

Piracy was a major problem, with perpetual nests in nearly all the strategically located islands, like Shadwan, Socotra, Bahrain, Kīsh, and the Maldives, as well as the unavoidable coasts, like Oman, Gujarat, and Ceylon. Most coastal rulers practiced piracy as their legitimate right; only special treaties or armed protection could keep them off.

Because of the reefs, the pirates, and possibly overloading, shipwreck was quite frequent. Sometimes divers were used for cargo salvage, even of iron! This is not surprising, taking into consideration the lucidity of the water, the prevalent practice of pearl and coral diving, and the high price of the goods lost.

As in the medieval Mediterranean ports, merchants preferred or were pushed into more or less homogeneous quarters, but we do not hear of merchants' guilds or foreigners' "ghettos." There were many interreligious deals and partnerships among them. Each trading community was represented by a head, usually paid by the authorities, the *wakīl-al-Tujjar*. This institution was second in importance only to the main customs house. The *wakīl,* ordinarily a rich and influential merchant with some juridical background, managed his own or the community's warehouse as some kind of local bank and communication center. He cooperated with the authorities in supervising international and transit trade, collecting and in some places levying taxes and dues, and acting against offenders. The origin of this post and its influence on the ubiquitous late medieval consul are still unclear. The Jewish *wakīls* were usually negidim or rabbis, the Muslim ones qadis. Their office tended to become hereditary. The Indian merchants constituted a caste, like the Banians of Malabar or the Soulis of Chola.

Compared to the West, credit was quite restricted, banking rudimentary, and there were no insurance arrangements. Associations were short-term and based on "formal friendship" rather than on real and lasting contracts between parties.

Many of the payments were in cash, a fact that pertains to the general topic of the balance of payments between East and West in the Middle Ages and the alleged flow of gold to the East. The trade between the Muslim countries and the Far East seems balanced, however, although it had its secular changes, with the dynamics of trade deeply influenced by political and social developments.

CONCLUSION

From pre-Islamic times to the coming of the Portuguese, that is, roughly through the whole of the Middle Ages, the Indian Ocean, together with the Red Sea and Persian Gulf, constituted an enclosed shipping system, separated from that of the Mediterranean by a thin land barrier only, but differing from it thoroughly by the type of ships used, the modes of navigation, and the organization of shipping. Unlike the Atlantic and Pacific oceans, the Indian Ocean served as a bridge spanning the different cultures bordering on it, not as a barrier separating them. It should be regarded as a whole, although here only its northwestern quarter has been treated. Although visited by, and known to, Mediterranean people, the Indian Ocean constituted another ecumene, where Arabs, Persians, Indians, and other south Asian peoples came into contact, both materially and culturally.

BIBLIOGRAPHY

General histories of the Indian Ocean in English include Radha K. Mookerji, *Indian Shipping: A History of the Sea-borne Trade and Maritime Activity of the Indians* (1912, repr. 1962); Colin Simkin, *The Traditional Trade of Asia* (1968); and Auguste Toussaint, *History of the Indian Ocean* (1966). However, their medieval chapters are unsatisfactory. More useful are recent conferences dedicated especially or largely to medieval commerce in the Indian Ocean. See, for example, Donald S. Richards, ed., *Islam and the Trade of Asia: A Colloquium* (1970). Most important are the proceedings of the two sessions of the sixth International Colloquium on Maritime History (Colloque international d'histoire maritime): *Océan Indien et Méditerranée* (1964) and *Méditerranée et Océan Indien* (1970). Essential, too, is *Mare Luso-Indicum,* 2 vols. (1971–1973). For a comprehensive treatment of Chinese shipping, see Joseph Needham, *Science and Civilization in China,* IV, pt. 3 (1971), 379–699.

For basic information on navigational conditions in these waters, see Maḥmūd A. Amin ᶜAbd Allāh, *Al-jughrāfiyā al-tārīkhīyah li-ḥawḍ al-Baḥr al-Aḥmar* (1971); Husain Fauzī, *Hadīth al-sindibād al-qadīm* (1943); Albert Kammerer, *La mer rouge, l'Abyssinie et l'Arabie depuis l'antiquité* (1929); Alan J. Villiers, *Monsoon Seas* (1952) and *Sons of Sinbad* (1940, repr. 1969).

The main sources for the early medieval period are Aly Mohamed Fahmy, *Muslim Naval Organization in the Eastern Mediterranean from the Seventh to the Tenth Centuries* (1966); S. Qudratullah Fatimi, "In Search of a Methodology for the History of Muslim Navigation in the Indian Ocean," in *Islamic Quarterly,* **20** (1978); George F. Hourani, *Arab Seafaring in the Indian Ocean in Ancient and Early Medieval Times* (1951, repr. 1963); Archibald R. Lewis, *Naval Power and Trade in the Mediterranean, A.D. 500–1100* (1951, repr. 1970) and "Les marchands dans l'Océan Indien," in *Revue d'histoire economique et sociale,* **54** (1976); Syed Sulaiman Nadvi, *Arab Navigation,* Syed Ṣabāhuddīn ᶜAbdur Raḥmān, trans. (1966), which originally appeared in *Islamic Culture,* **20** and **28** (1942, 1951).

The rise of Arab trade in these waters during the Abbasid period is covered in Charles Pellat, *Le milieu baṣrien et la formation de Ǧaḥiẓ* (1953), chaps. 2 and 6. The main sources are listed in the Lewis article already cited and in Gerald R. Tibbetts, *Arab Navigation in the Indian Ocean Before the Coming of the Portuguese* (1971, repr. 1981). Still useful are the old collections by Gabriel Ferrand: *Relations de voyages et textes géographiques arabes, persans, et turcs, relatifs a l'extrème-orient du VIIe au XVIIIe siècles,* 2 vols. (1913–1914), and

Instructions nautiques et routiers arabes et portugais des XVe et XVIe siècles, 3 vols. (1921–1928); and Joseph T. Reinaud, *Fragments arabes et persans inédits, relatifs à l'Inde antérieurement au XIe siècle de l'ère chrétienne* (1845, repr. 1974). The Chinese sources are treated in Friedrich Hirth and W. Rockhill, eds. and trans., *Chau Ju-kua: His Work on the Chinese and Arab Trade in the 12th and 13th Centuries* (1911, repr. 1966); and Ma Huan, *Ying-yai sheng-lan: "The Overall Survey of the Ocean's Shores,"* J. V. G. Mills, trans. (1970).

For the maritime trade in the middle medieval period, to 1300, see the following: Jean Aubin, "La ruine de Sīrāf et les routes du Golfe Persique aux XIe et XIIe siècles," in *Cahiers de civilizations médiévales,* **2** (1959), and "Y'a-t'il eu interruption du commerce par mer entre le Golfe Persique et l'Inde du XIe au XIVe siècle?" in *Océan Indien et Méditerranée* (1964); Claude Cahen, "Un traité fatimide inédit d'époque fatimide-ayyubide," in *Journal of the Economic and Social History of the Orient,* **5** (1962); Neville Chittick, "East African Trade with the Orient," in Donald S. Richards, ed., *Islam and the Trade of Asia* (1970), 97–104; Solomon D. Goitein, "From the Mediterranean to India," in *Speculum,* **29** (1954), and "Letters and Documents on the India Trade in Medieval Times," in *Islamic Culture,* **37** (1963), both published as one article in his *Studies in Islamic History and Institutions* (1966), 329–350; Jung-Pang Lo, "Maritime Commerce and Its Relation to the Sung Navy," in *Journal of the Economic and Social History of the Orient,* **12** (1969); Jacques Le Goff, "L'occident medieval et l'Océan Indien: Un horizon onirique," in *Méditerranée et Océan Indien* (1970), 243–263; Bernard Lewis, "The Fatimids and the Route to India," in *Revue de la Faculté des sciences économiques de l'Université d'Istanbul,* **11** (1949–1950); Robert S. Lopez, "European Merchants in the Medieval Indies," in *Journal of Economic History,* **3** (1943); Marco Polo, *The Book of Ser Marco Polo,* Henry Yule, ed. and trans., enl. and rev. by Henri Cordier, 2 vols. (3rd rev. ed., 1903, repr. 1967, 1975); Leonardo Olschki, *Marco Polo's Precursors* (1943, repr. 1972).

For the late medieval period, from 1300 to the Portuguese conquests of the early sixteenth century, see Jean Aubin, "Les princes d'Ormuz du XIIIe au XVe siècle," in *Journal asiatique,* **241** (1953); Charles R. Boxer, *Four Centuries of Portuguese Expansion, 1415–1825* (1969); Claude Cahen and Robert B. Sergeant, "A Fiscal Survey of the Medieval Yemen," in *Arabica,* **4** (1957); Paul Kunitzsch, "Die arabischen Sternbilder des Südhimmels," in *Der Islam,* **51** (1974); Subhi Y. Labib, *Handelsgeschichte Ägyptens im Spätmittelalter (1171–1517)* (1965), 441ff.; Frederic C. Lane, *Venice, A Maritime Republic* (1973), esp. chap. 20.

For the ships and their fittings, see Paul Adam, "À propos des origines de la voile latine," in *Méditerranée et Océan Indien* (1970), 203–228; Lionel Casson, *Illustrated History of Ships and Boats* (1964), 161–168; Fahmy, *op. cit.,* 134–136; James Hornell, "A Tentative Classification of Arab Sea-craft," in *The Mariner's Mirror,* **28** (1942), and "The Sailing Craft of Western India," *ibid.,* **32** (1946); Hourani, *op. cit.,* chap. 3; Ibn Jubayr, *Voyages,* Maurice Gaudefroy-Demombynes, ed. and trans. (1949), I, 78–85; Hans Kindermann, *Schiff im Arabischen* (1934); Su^c^ad Mahir, *Al-baḥriyah fi Miṣr al-islamiyah* (1967); Alan Moore, "Craft of the Red Sea and the Gulf of Aden," in *The Mariner's Mirror,* **6** (1920); Jean Poujade, *La route des Indes et ses navires* (1946); Alan J. Villiers, *Sons of Sinbad* (1940, repr. 1969); A. Zayyat, *Mu^c^gam almarākib wa-lasfār fi-l-Islām* (1950).

Information on the ports and customs can be found in Claude Cahen, "Les escales dans le monde musulman mediéval," in *Recueils de la societé Jean Bodin pour l'histoire comparative de institutions,* **32** (1974); and Guy Le Strange, *Palestine Under the Moslems* (1890, repr. 1965), 328–334. Merchandise carried is treated in Eliyahu Ashtor, *Histoire des prix et des salaires dans l'orient mediéval* (1969), 73f.; Francesco Balducci Pegolotti, *La pratica della mercatura,* Allan Evans, ed. (1936), 411f.; Solomon D. Goitein, *A Mediterranean Society,* I (1967), 99–116 and 149–160; Wilhelm Heyd, *Histoire du commerce du Levant au moyen âge,* II (1886, repr. 1959), supplement I, 2; Maurice Lombard, *The Golden Age of Islam,* Joan Spencer, trans. (1975), 163–164.

For information on merchants and mariners, see the following: Sulaiman al-Mahri, *Al-Umda Al-Mahriya,* Ibrāhīm Khūrī, ed. (1970); Eliyahu Ashtor, "The Kārimī Merchants," in *Journal of the Royal Asiatic Society* (1956); Moshe Gil, "The Rādhānite Merchants and the Land of Rādhān," in *Journal of the Economic and Social History of the Orient,* **17** (1974); Solomon D. Goitein, "New Light on the Beginnings of the Kārim Merchants," *ibid.,* **1**, pt. 2 (1957), and *Letters of Medieval Jewish Traders* (1973).

For various aspects of trade organization, see Marc Bloch, "Le problème de l'or au moyen âge," in *Annales d'histoire économique et sociale,* **5** (1933); Solomon D. Goitein, *A Mediterranean Society* (1967), I, chap. 3 and 327–332, and *Letters of Medieval Jewish Traders,* (1973), 189; Frederic C. Lane, *Venice and History* (1966), 109–127; Maurice Lombard, "L'or musulman du VIIe au XIe siècles," in *Annales: E. S. C.,* **2** (1947); Rajaram N. Saletore, *Early Indian Economic History* (1973), chap. 9; Abraham L. Udovitch, "Commercial Techniques in Early Medieval Islam," in Donald S. Richards, ed., *Islam and the Trade of Asia* (1970), 37–62, and *Partnership and Profit in Medieval Islam* (1970).

SARAH ARENSON

[See also **Lateen Sail; Navies, Islamic; Navigation: Indian Ocean, Red Sea; Trade, Islamic.**]

SHĪRĀZ is the capital of Fārs (Pārs), the central southern province of Iran, which provided both the name of the official language of the country (*fārsī, pārsī,* "Persian"), and the name (Persia) by which the whole country was first known in the West. Ibn Baṭṭūṭa (*d.* 1368/1377) said of the Persian capital: "There is no city in the East that approaches Damascus in the beauty either of its markets, orchards, and streams or of its inhabitants, except Shīrāz."

Shīrāz is located in a fertile valley at the southern edge of Iran's central plateau. To the northeast lie the ruins of the great Achaemenid capital, Persepolis (near the site of the Sasanian capital Istakhr), and to the south the plateau breaks against a spur of the Zagros Mountains whose southern face descends sharply to the Persian Gulf and the plain of Khuzistan. Situated as it is, Shīrāz has served since the Islamic conquest as a major entrepôt on trade routes linking the ports of the Persian Gulf with the cities of western Iran—Isfahan, Qum, Hamadan, and Rayy (Tehran)—and, to a lesser extent, those in eastern Iran as well—Yazd, Kerman, Zāhidān.

The early history of Shīrāz is obscure. Like Baghdad, it appears to have been only a small city, although possibly of great antiquity, prior to the Islamic period. A settlement called *shira-its-tsi-ish* in Elamite provided workmen for the construction of the palace of Darius I at Persepolis in the early fifth century B.C. In the course of the Islamic conquest of Fārs, completed in 649, Shīrāz served first as the base of military operations and then replaced the ancient capital, Istakhr, as the administrative center of the province. (Istakhr remained a major city, and a center of opposition, until 1044, when it was leveled and its population dispersed by the Buyid ruler Abu Kālījār.) By 684 Shīrāz had prospered to the point that it was refounded on a much larger plan at the order of the Umayyad governor at Basra, Ḥajjāj ibn Yūsuf. This fact led later Islamic geographers to claim that the city was originally of Arab foundation.

With the decline of the authority of the caliphate in the ninth century, and the rise of semi-independent states in Iran and Central Asia, Shīrāz twice became the capital of rulers who exercised control over much of the region. Yaᶜqūb ibn Layth al-Ṣaffār (*d.* 879), founder of the Saffarid dynasty, moved his capital there from Sistan in order to have a base of operations closer to his ultimate, but unrealized, goal, Baghdad. Yaᶜqūb's brother and successor, ᶜAmr, retained Shīrāz as his capital throughout his reign. He built the first great congregational mosque (*masjid-i jāmiᶜ*) there in 894, portions of which still survive.

With ᶜAmr's defeat and death in 900/901, Shīrāz lost its status as a center of rule. It regained it some fifty years later, however, during the reign of the Buyid sultan ᶜAḍud al-Dawla (*d.* 983), whose family controlled not only Iran but also Baghdad and the caliphate for more than a century (932–1055). It was during the Buyid period that the walls of the city were built, a new channel was dug to supply the city with fresh water, and the city was expanded and much of it rebuilt.

The importance of Shīrāz declined after the Buyids for about eight centuries, but it remained a provincial capital of importance in the Islamic empire. It escaped the devastation of the Mongol invasions of the thirteenth century and those of Tamerlane in the fourteenth. In the late eighteenth century, Shīrāz saw the beginning of its last period of greatness, when Karim Khan Zand made it the capital of all Iran. He surrounded it with new walls and ditches, paved its streets, and constructed many fine buildings and a magnificent bazaar. In fact, most of the buildings that distinguish present-day Shīrāz were built in the Zandid period.

Shīrāz is famous in Iran as a city that has nurtured fine poets and saintly men. It was the home of two of the truly great poets of the Persian language: Saᶜdī (*d.* 1292), whose *Gulistān* (Rose garden) is the most widely read book in the language, and Ḥāfiẓ (*d.* 1389/1390), whose lyric *ghazals* set the standard by which all others are judged. A number of other fine poets, such as Ahli Shīrāzī, Būs'hāq, ᶜUrfī Shīrāzī, and Bābā Fighānī, were natives of the city.

Similarly, Shīrāz was the home of—and its citizens venerated—spiritually "perfect" men, Sunni (orthodox), Shiite, and Sufi (mystical), throughout its history. Its many tombs of saints, from that of Aḥmad ibn Mūsā (*d. ca.* 835), the brother of the eighth imam, to that of Molla Sadra, the great mystic teacher (*d.* 1630), have made Shīrāz an important place of pilgrimage for centuries.

Ibn Baṭṭūta was drawn there both to visit the tombs of its saints and to pay his respects to the aged Shaikh Majd al-Dīn Ismaᶜīl, whom he called "the marvel of the age." He was struck by the piety of the Shīrāzīs as well as by their handsome appearance.

BIBLIOGRAPHY

The best introduction to the history of Shīrāz in the Islamic period is John W. Limbert, *Shiraz in the Age of Hafez* (1973). Arthur J. Arberry, *Shiraz: Persian City of Saints and Poets* (1960), is more readily accessible. John I. Clarke, *The Iranian City of Shiraz* (1963), contains excellent maps and photographs of both the old and the new city. There are several evocative chapters on Shīrāz at the beginning of the modern period in Edward G. Browne, *A Year Amongst the Persians* (1893, 3rd ed. 1950, repr. 1959).

JEROME W. CLINTON

[See also **Baṭṭūṭa, Ibn; Buyids; Fārs; Ḥāfiẓ; Ḥajjāj ibn Yūsuf; Saᶜdī; Saffarids; Yaᶜqūb ibn Layth.**]

SHIRE. Sometime during the ninth century, districts called shires emerged in southern England as governmental units of judicial and military administration. King Alfred the Great of Wessex (871–899) rearranged these existing shires along standard patterns before his successors began organizing them in the north during the next century. Meaning literally a share or division of a larger whole, the Middle English forms *shir* and *shire* came from Old English *scir,* which signified an office, administrative area, appointment, or district, *scir* being akin to the Old High German word *scīra,* which denoted an official care or charge.

Evidence for the existence of shires before the ninth century is entirely conjectual. Even though Ine's Law mentioned ealdormen who held *scirs,* the latter cannot be accepted as proof of West Saxon shires by the late seventh century, since *scir* was used in the documents to denote any administrative area or office, irrespective of its nature.

The ealdormen (modern "aldermen") of the shires by Alfred's time were royal officials or representatives who either were members of royal families who had ruled over earlier territorial jurisdictions or were relatives of the king appointed to new posts. They mustered and led fyrdsmen (warriors) into combat, presided over shire moots (courts or government assemblies), and executed royal decrees. They usually were rewarded with land grants, hospitality and maintenance, and shares of the fines of justice, tolls, and duties collected.

The origins of the shires were diverse. In Wessex, they were organized around early settlements and their medieval boundaries were roughly similar to those existing today: Somerset, for example, coalesced around Somerton; Dorset, around Dorchester; and Wiltshire, around Wilton. It appears that the Wessex kings slowly established hegemony over various Anglo-Saxon chieftains whose lands traditionally had been separated by such topographical features as rivers and forests.

In other parts of England, shires were formed from independent states, from districts surrounding boroughs that were based mainly upon fiscal assessments, from recently conquered territories given to members of royal families, or from the unification of provinces. Among the earliest of the shires, Kent, Sussex, Essex, Middlesex, and Surrey were originally kingdoms. Norfolk and Suffolk were formed probably from tribal divisions within East Anglia. Northumbria and Mercia were not organized into shires until they were conquered by the Danes. Prior to these invasions, Northumbria was divided into districts that eventually became Yorkshire and Lancashire, while Mercia was formed from five large districts that may have been the original settlements.

Whatever their origins, territorial units as large as shires (eventually there were thirty-seven in England) were too difficult to administer for many governmental purposes, and more convenient local units were needed for tax collection, raising of fyrds (armies), and determination of legal disputes. Hence, by the middle of the tenth century the existing shires were subdivided into hundreds in the Anglo-Saxon areas and wapentakes in those regions controlled by the Danes. For even more accurate assessments, the latter were further subdivided into hides. Since the shires of the Midlands and the north were creations of Alfred and his West Saxon successors, and since they bore no relationship to earlier territorial arrangements, it is probable that their sudivision into hundreds and wapentakes was also due to the creativity of the Wessex monarchs.

After the Norman Conquest the shire's name was changed to "county," since the French district most analogous to it was the *comitatus* (county), a district subject to the *comes* (count).

BIBLIOGRAPHY

Hector M. Chadwick, *Studies on Anglo-Saxon Institutions,* rev. ed. (1963); Bryce D. Lyon, *A Constitutional and Legal History of Medieval England,* 2nd ed. (1980);

Frederic W. Maitland, *Domesday Book and Beyond,* rev. ed. (1987).

RONALD EDWARD ZUPKO

[See also **England, Anglo-Saxon; Hide; Jury; Law, English Common.**]

SHIRVAN (**Širvan**) (Persian: Shīrvān; Armenian: Šruan; Arabic: Shirwan, Shīrwān, or Sharwān), originally a tribal territory lying between the Sabran-chai and the Gilgil-chai in southeastern Caucasia between the foothills of the Caucasus and the river Kura, and during medieval times occupying about 598 square miles (1,550 square kilometers). Originally a part of Caucasian Albania, Shirvan became an important feudal principality in late Sasanian times (sixth century); the title of its ruler, Sharvanshah (shah of Shirvan), possibly dates from this period. It was overrun by the Arabs in the mid seventh century. The governorship of the region became hereditary (the title remained Sharvanshah), and the governors are said to have been independent as early as 861.

Under the rule of the Kasranid Sharvanshahs, Shirvan was united with neighboring Derbent and Xoruan; its capital was moved from Shirvan, on the Bardhaʿa-Derbent trade route, to Shamākhī, on the same road but further east. The Kasranids became subject to the Seljuk Turks in the eleventh century, and, although the Turks occupied Shirvan in 1131, the Kasranids continued to rule as their vassals until 1194, when Shirvan passed under Georgian suzerainty. With Georgian aid the Sharvanshahs reconquered Shirvan and Derbent, but ceded the important districts of Shakki, Kabala, and Mūkan to the Georgian kings.

In the thirteenth century the Kasranids became vassals of the Mongols, and then of the Mongol successor states, vacillating between the Ilkhanids of Iran and the Golden Horde of the Volga basin. In the fourteenth century the Kasranids became independent, then submitted successively to the Jalāyirids, Derbent (1383), Tamerlane (1386), again to Derbent, and, finally, in the early sixteenth century, became a vassal of Iran, which ended the rule of the Sharvanshahs.

BIBLIOGRAPHY

W. Barthold, "Shīrwān," in *Encyclopaedia of Islam,* 1st ed., IV (1934); D. M. Dunlop, *The History of the Jewish Khazars* (1954), and "Bākū," in *Enclyclopaedia of Islam,* new ed., I (1960); Guy Le Strange, *Lands of the Eastern Caliphate* (1905, 2nd ed. 1930, repr. 1966), 179–181; Vladimir Minorsky, ed. and trans., *A History of Sharvān and Darband* (1958).

ROBERT H. HEWSEN

[See also **Albania (Caucasian); Caucasia; Derbent; Georgia; Geography; Golden Horde; Ilkhanids; Tamerlane.**]

SHOES AND SHOEMAKERS. At first, shoes followed classical Roman styles based on the antique sandal, but as the civilization that succeeded it moved away from the Mediterranean, the sandal was gradually relegated to ceremonial use, to royalty and the clergy, the traditional heirs of the attitudes of the Roman Empire. By the twelfth century it was modified into mere appliqué straps on current footwear. In the northern climes, the sandal was replaced for general wear by closed footwear.

Eventually regional styles developed. Ravenna and parts of Italy retained classical styles, as did Constantinople, although the Byzantine Empire was quickly influenced by exotic styles from farther east. In the ninth century Charlemagne is said to have hated the clothes of other countries; after entreaties from the pope, however, he consented to wear shoes made in the Roman fashion while in Rome.

In the Byzantine Empire Oriental influence predominated with closed shoes and pointed toes, probably derived ultimately from ancient Hittite styles developed for mountainous terrain. For the upper classes, these were highly decorated with geometric designs, gilding, and inlays in bright, jewel-like contrasting colors.

The styles were copied and adapted in the turmoil of Europe, and, although decoration was generally restricted to a band up the center of the vamp, the workmanship was exquisite. Throughout the first half of the period the shoe was generally designed with a practical blunt pointed toe, becoming more oval in the ninth century. All footwear was without heels, apart from repair patches. Some of the Coptic shoes and the Irish shoes, which closely resembled them (though with curvilinear decoration), were made as straights (not shaped to right and left) to fit either foot. Styles were frequently slip-on, occasionally with a tab front, particularly in the eighth century. For more practical wear, there were higher-cut ankle shoes kept on by a lace threaded around the ankle through pairs of slots.

A change in construction occurred with the end of the Roman riveted method using hobnails, which were rendered unnecessary as metaled roads fell into disuse. Apart from some shoes of northern Europe that retained the prehistoric moccasin construction, closed shoes were now made turnshoe, with a separate sole. The method seems to have originated in the Middle East and was certainly used on the Coptic shoes. Fine gut was used for sewing; thongs were used for the coarser work, a primitive survival. They were both replaced around 1000 by thread of flax or hair wool. The welted construction, as still used, was introduced in the 1490's: the upper is attached to a narrow welt and then the welt is sewn to the sole. The upper seam was generally at the side throughout the period, although some of the Mediterranean styles retained the Roman back seam.

In the cities shoemakers continued to live and work close together, as they had in classical times, a practice that would persist until the Renaissance. From the twelfth century there were guilds of shoemakers, which gradually spread to the smaller towns. By the fourteenth and fifteenth centuries, the guilds reached their greatest power, protecting the shoemakers from outside competition and regulating standards. Shoemakers were found in all market towns, regardless of large supplies of raw material, though small tanners always used hides from local slaughterhouses. Cattlehide was always tanned for leather in northern Europe; and goatskin was more common around the Mediterranean.

In the early Middle Ages the most highly prized material was cordovan: alum-tanned goatskin. The industry had originated among the Moors of North Africa, the early center being Ghadames in modern Libya, though it seems likely it originated farther east. It was taken by the Moors to Spain, to their great city of Córdoba—hence its name. After the expulsion of the Moors in 1236 and with the move of culture north from the Mediterranean, the local raw material, cattlehide, replaced goatskin.

From about 1100, with a more settled civilization and the development of Gothic art and architecture, more sophisticated and impractical shoe styles came into fashion. The toe became unnaturally pointed and long, a style first seen briefly in the tenth century. Variations on the point persisted to the beginning of Renaissance styles in the late fifteenth century, with extreme lengths in the second half of the fourteenth and again in the mid fifteenth century and patten overshoes developed to protect them. The pointed shapes for both architecture and footwear appear to have originated with the Seljuks, and the styles spread to Europe via travelers and crusaders.

The typical shoe of the later Middle Ages was a side-laced ankle shoe that dipped low under the ankle bone. For work there were calf-length boots with lace or button fastenings. In the fifteenth century increasing wealth permitted long boots to replace the footed hose of cordwain leather.

Decoration on the shoes of the upper class followed Gothic styles and colors, with elaborate tracery cutouts or embossing on the uppers, styles especially popular in the mid fourteenth and mid fifteenth centuries.

In the East, Constantinople fell to the Turks in 1453 (the slain emperor identified on the battlefield only by the gold eagles on his shoes), while in Italy the beginnings of the Renaissance were modifying styles. Antonio Pisano (called Pisanello, *d. ca.* 1455), who made a medal of John VIII Palaiologos of Constantinople (*r.* 1425–1448), painted the Oriental-style heel on the horseman in his *The Vision of St. Eustace* of 1438. Heels first appear in Armenian manuscripts of the second decade of the fifteenth century and may have originated on riding boots, forming a useful anchor in the stirrup. They were quickly adopted in the Islamic world for all types of footwear. But heels were not of any significance in Europe itself until the sixteenth century, possibly developing from overshoes. Carpaccio (*d. ca.* 1425/1426) shows them in a Venetian scene of 1495, with platforms higher at the heel and sloping down to the toe.

By the 1450's, dress styles in Italy took on a softer, more comfortable line, and the toe was rounded off, a fashion that was gradually adopted throughout Europe, reaching Britain about 1490. For decoration, slashed and dagged styles, which had appeared in the last quarter of the fourteenth century, were again adopted, to become high fashion in the next century.

BIBLIOGRAPHY

Ruth Matilda Anderson, "The Chopine and Related Shoes," in *Cuadernos de la Alhambra,* 5 (1969); R. Blomquist, "Medeltiden skor i Lund," in *Kulturen* (1938); Eline Canter Cremers-van der Does, *Van Schoen-*

en en Schoenmakers (1960); C. Willett and Phillis Cunnington, *Handbook of English Medieval Costume* (1969); Robert Forrer, *Archäologisches zur Geschichte des Schuhes aller Zeiten* (1942); A. V. Goodfellow and J. H. Thornton, "Leather Shoe Parts and Other Leather Fragments," in *The Yorkshire Archaeological Journal,* **44** (1972); Willy Groenman-van Waateringe, *Society . . . Rests on Leather* (1975); Margrethe Hald, *Primitive Shoes* (1972); Susan Thomas, *Medieval Footwear from Coventry* (1980); J. H. Thornton, June M. Swann, *et al.,* "Excavated Shoes to 1600," in *Transactions of the Museum Assistants Group,* **12** (1975); Ruth Turner Wilcox, *The Mode in Footwear* (1948).

JUNE SWANN

[See also **Córdoba; Costume; Guilds and Métiers; Leather and Leatherworking; Technology, Islamic.**]

SHOT^{c}A RUSTA^{c}VELI (*fl. ca.* 1200) is the most renowned poet of Georgia, whose epic *Vep^{c}khistqaosani* is a national treasure. *Vep^{c}khi* is variously rendered as "tiger" or "panther"; the title thus means "The [man] in the panther's skin." Nothing is known for certain about Shot^{c}a. Rustaveli means "from Rustavi," but there are several towns so named in Georgia. Tradition has made him a courtier of Queen Tamar (T^{c}amar, *r.* 1184–1212), who was consumed with love for her and who ended his days in a monastery. Since the seventeenth century a portrait in the monastery of the Holy Cross in Jerusalem (founded *ca.* 1035 by a Georgian named Prochorus, disciple of Euthymios the Athonite) has been said to be of him. The poem is dedicated to Tamar, and Georgian scholars generally date its composition to the very beginning of the thirteenth century.

The Man in the Panther's Skin is set in a fantasy world of Arabia, India, and China. The hero, Tariel, falls in love with Nestan-Darejan, daughter of a king of India. She returns his love but is affianced to the prince of Khwarizm. Tariel kills him, but Nestan-Darejan is carried away to an inaccessible fortress in the land of the K^{c}ajis. Tariel wanders over the world in search of his beloved, dressed in a panther's skin and keeping apart from the rest of mankind. One day, while out hunting, Avt^{c}andil, lover of the Arabian king's daughter, T^{c}inat^{c}in, sees Tariel. After a long search at T^{c}inat^{c}in's request, he finds him; they become close friends and eventually succeed in rescuing Nestan-Darejan.

The poem delights in heroic action and is basically concerned with the intertwined themes of love, friendship, and devotion to the courtly service of women. In form it is cast as a complicated story within a story. It shows the influence of earlier Georgian texts: the *Amiran Darejaniani,* and the versions from the Persian of Gurganī's *Visramiani* and Niẓāmī's *Laylā and Majnūn.* Given the strongly Christian character of most earlier Georgian literature, it is surprising that the poem does not reflect a Christian ethos; there are no references to Christ, and only a few passing allusions to biblical persons or expressions. Hence, Rusta^{c}veli was frequently attacked in later Georgian clerical circles. But the influence of Neoplatonic philosophy is marked, and there are references to the works of Proclus, Nemesius, and Dionysius the Areopagite, which were available in Georgian by the twelfth century. The poem, however, is not an elaborate allegory, nor is it based on a foreign or earlier Georgian tale. In its essentials it is the product of Shot^{c}a's individual genius.

The oldest surviving manuscript of the poem dates to 1646, but some short quotations survive from the fifteenth century in inscriptions or on the margins of manuscripts. It was first printed in 1712 by Vakhtang (Waχtang) VI at the first Georgian press, which he founded in Tiflis. The hold of this great epic on the Georgian people is illustrated by the tradition, observed until the nineteenth century, that brides would bring a copy of it in their dowries. The literature on Rusta^{c}veli and his poem is immense, and today there are journals devoted to "Rustvelology" in the Georgian SSR.

BIBLIOGRAPHY

A bibliographical source is A. M. Babaian, *Shota Rustaveli: Bibliographicheskiĭ sprabochnik: 1712–1970* (1975). The best-known translation is that by Marjory S. Wardrop, *The Man in the Panther's Skin* (1912), reprinted as the *Knight in the Tiger's Skin* (1966), also reprinted under the latter title, supplemented and revised by E. Orbelyani and S. Jordanishvili (1938, 1939), the latter (published at Tbilisi) with an introduction by Pavlé Ingorokva. Other English renderings include Venera Urushadze, *The Knight in the Panther's Skin* (1968, 1971), in unrhymed quatrains; and R. H. Stevenson, *The Lord of the Panther-Skin* (1977). There is a French rendering by S. Tsouladzé, *Chota Roustaveli: Le chevalier à la peau de tigre* (1964).

R. W. THOMSON

[See also **Georgian Literature.**]

SHURFA. See **Şerefe.**

SIBYLLINE ORACLES is the name given to a collection of writings on various religious and historical topics attributed to the ten sibyls (listed by Vincent of Beauvais, based on the writings of Lactantius, Augustine, and others, as Cumana, Cymeria, Delphica, Erythraea, Hellespontia, Libyca, Persica, Phrygia, Samia, and Tiburtina). The early material was assembled in Hellenistic times and supplemented from Jewish, Latin, and early Christian sources. Cited by Christian apologists and church fathers as having foretold the coming of Christ and the Last Judgment, the writings also had an important if indirect effect on such medieval stories as that of the career of the Antichrist. The earliest extant manuscripts, in Greek, date from the fourteenth century.

Representations of individual sibyls appear in medieval art, especially the figure of the Erythraean sibyl, thought to be the most important and prophetic, as, for example, the headless figure holding two tablets in her right hand on the facade of Laon Cathedral (thirteenth century).

BIBLIOGRAPHY

Sources. Johannes Geffcken, ed., *Oracula sibyllina* (1902). See also Lactantius, *Patrologia latina,* VI (1844), 141–148; Augustine, *De civitate Dei,* in *Patrologia latina,* XLI (1841), 579–581; Vincent Bellovacensis (Vincent of Beauvais), *Speculum historiale* (1965), 2.100–102.

Studies. John J. Collins, *The Sibylline Oracles of Egyptian Judaism* (1972); Ernst Sackur, *Sibyllinische Texte und Forschungen* (1898, repr. 1963). For discussions of the sibyls in medieval art, see Émile Mâle, *L'art religieux du XIIIe siècle en France* (6th ed. 1925, new ed. 1958), 339–342, and *L'art religieux de la fin du moyen âge en France* (5th ed. 1949), 255–277.

SICILIAN POETRY. In his discussion of the various Italian dialects in the first book of *De vulgari eloquentia,* Dante gives special prominence to the Sicilian vernacular, which, he says, "claims for itself greater renown than any of the others, both because of the fact that whatever poetry has been written by Italians has been called Sicilian, and because of the fact that we find a great many of its native experts have written poetry in a grand manner" (I, xii, 2; R. S. Haller, trans.). Half a century later Petrarch, in the enumeration of love poets in the *Trionfo d'amore,* alludes to the former preeminence of the Sicilian poets: "i Ciciliani/che fur già primi" (iv, 35f; the Sicilians / who once were first). The Sicilian school of poets has a special place in the history of the Italian language and literature, for it was the first time in Italy that a group of writers had made a conscious effort to compose a unified body of artistic literature in the vernacular. By using Italian—and not Latin—for the elegant expression of sentiments, they essentially confirmed both its intrinsic worth and its viability as a literary language, one able to stand comparison with the older and more highly developed Romance vernaculars, especially Old French and Provençal.

The dawning of the Italian literary consciousness occurred at the court of Emperor Frederick II in Sicily between 1220 and 1250. Sicily—and Palermo in particular—was the crossroads, the hub, of the Mediterranean world; pilgrims and crusaders, merchants and traders, itinerant minstrels, notaries, scholars and teachers, doctors and scientists—in short, individuals of virtually all professions and religious persuasions from the diverse civilizations bordering on the Mediterranean—gathered and mingled in that unique court. Life in the imperial court until Frederick's death (1250) was characterized primarily by its open, cosmopolitan nature and its vibrant air of intellectual curiosity and activity. Among those present at the court were the astrologer Michael Scot (whose translations helped to introduce Arabo-Aristotelian philosophy to the West), the philosopher Theodore of Antioch, the noted mathematician Leonardo Fibonacci of Pisa, numerous notaries and jurists trained in law, grammar, and rhetoric at the University of Bologna, and many other men of learning from both East and West.

In addition to his intellectual imprint, Frederick II left his imperial mark on Sicily and the whole of southern Italy through his bureaucratically oriented central government and his promulgation of a royal law code, the *Liber Augustalis* (Constitutions of Melfi, 1231). The diversity and liberal character of the Sicilian court are also reflected in Frederick's own interests: in his scientific treatise on falconry (*De arte venandi cum avibus*); in his establishment of the University of Naples (1224); and in his continued patronage of the arts and learning, which followed the example set by his precursors in Sicily, the twelfth-century Norman kings.

In this extraordinary ambiance a group of some fifteen to twenty individuals, most of whom were civil servants, not poets, by profession and about whom we possess very little biographical information, began to compose lyrics in the Sicilian dialect, adhering to the established models of poetic excellence furnished by the Provençal troubadours and, to a lesser degree, by the northern French trouvères and German minnesingers. The subject of their poetry was love, usually termed *fin'amors* (courtly love), and their descriptions of the lady, the role of the lover, and the effects of passion generally follow conventional patterns. Their imitation and absorption of Provençal models and culture were so complete that in the distinctly nonfeudal society of Frederician Sicily they re-created in their lyrics the feudal setting, replete with the trappings of *fin'amors,* in which the lady became *midons* (my lord) and the poet her faithful vassal who served her in order to win her affection or some token thereof.

The Sicilians not only imitated the metrical forms (canso, tenso, descort) and the main themes, but also borrowed—and italianized—specific words from the amorous lexicon of the troubadours: *intendanza* (love), *amanza* (love), *drudo* (lover), *sollazzo* (pleasure), *gioia* (joy), *coraggio* (courage, heart), *dottanza* (fear), *ballia* (power), *talento* (desire). From the rich Provençal heritage they also drew many images and poetic devices (*coblas capfinidas, coblas unissonans,* the use of the *senhal* [a code name for the lady], the authorial "signing" of the poem). Despite these borrowings the Sicilian poets demonstrated their independent artistic sense in many and diverse ways. However, it is one thing to alter the course of literature by introducing new forms and new concepts, and another to modify it from within by revivifying the old by means of the new. Thus, alongside the servile and essentially sterile imitations of earlier models, there gradually emerged new forms, new images, and new concepts that, at first sharing many traits with the older modes, later attained a state of predominance and self-sufficiency. Indeed, the complementary principles of imitation and innovation operate in and characterize the poetic production of the Sicilian school.

One of the better-known Sicilian poets is Piero della Vigna (1180–1249), Frederick's faithful counselor, secretary, and logothete, who committed suicide while imprisoned on a false charge of treason. His literary reputation is based largely on his ornate Latin epistolary style, the *ars dictaminis,* learned at Bologna and influenced by the French Latin style. It was this stylistic attribute that Dante undoubtedly was imitating in his presentation of the poet's words in *Inferno* XIII:

La meretrice che mai da l'ospizio
di Cesare non torse li occhi putti,
morte comune e de le corti vizio,
infiammò contra me li animi tutti;
e li 'nfiammati infiammar sì Augusto,
che ' lieti onor tornaro in tristi lutti.
(vv. 64–69)

The harlot that never turned her whorish eyes from Caesar's household—the common death and vice of courts—inflamed all minds against me; and they, inflamed, did so inflame Augustus that my glad honors were changed to dismal woes. (C. S. Singleton, trans.)

Piero's poems in the vernacular, although generally traditional in subject matter, contain rhetorical flourishes and wordplay, as is shown in the following lines from the canzone "Amando con fin core e con speranza":

La morte m'este amara, che l'amore
mutaomi in amarore;
crudele, ché punio senza penzare
la sublimata stella de l'albore
senza colpa a tuttore
per cui servire mi credea salvare.
(vv. 13–18)

Death who changed my amorous desire to bitterness is bitter to me; Death is cruel, for he without consideration took the blameless and exalted morning star in whose service I found my happiness.

In *De vulgari eloquentia* Dante reserves high praise for the lyrics of Guido delle Colonne (*b. ca.* 1210), who was a judge at the imperial court and the presumed author of the *Historia destructionis Troiae* (1272–1287), a Latin prose translation of Benoît de Sainte-Maure's *Roman de Troie* (*ca.* 1165). Of particular interest and importance is Guido's use of scientific images and metaphors, which add a naturalistic dimension to the description of the phenomenology of love (see especially the canzone "Ancor che l'aigua per lo foco lassi").

Another poet meriting Dante's esteem is Rinaldo d'Aquino, who was perhaps the brother of St. Thomas Aquinas and who may have been falconer at Frederick's court. While his lyrics generally evoke the Provençal courtly ethos, he is best known for his popularly inspired poem "Già mai non mi conforto," in which a woman, lamenting the departure of her lover for the Holy Land, blames her anguish on the cross, the symbol of the crusades:

La croce salva la gente
e me face disviare.
La croce mi fa dolente,
e non mi val Dio pregare.
Oi croce pellegrina,
perchè m'ài sì distrutta?
Oimè, lassa, tapina,
chi ardo e 'ncendo tutta.
(vv. 25–32)

The cross saves humanity / and makes me lose the way. / The cross fills me with grief, / I get no help praying to God. / O pilgrim cross, / why have you destroyed me? / Alas, weary, wretched, / I burn and am all consumed. (Frederick Goldin, trans.)

The poetic production of Giacomino Pugliese is characterized by a popular or realistic quality. With one exception (the hauntingly beautiful canzone on the death of his lady, "Morte, perchè m'ài fatta sì gran guerra"), his lyrics are all composed in shorter meters and often contain dialogue (for instance, the sprightly *contrasto* "Donna, di voi mi lamento"). His is a poetry of memory, a remembrance of and a memorial to the alternate joy and anguish of a vibrant and real sensual passion; as such, his poetry represents a dramatic departure from the impersonal, artificial, and highly stylized conventions of the troubadour manner.

Among the other poets of the Sicilian school were Emperor Frederick II himself and his illegitimate son Enzo, Mazzeo di Ricco, Iacopo Mostacci, Odo delle Colonne, Ruggerone da Palermo, and Ruggieri (Ugieri) Apugliese. Of special interest is the canzone "Pir meu cori allegrari" by Stefano Protonotaro, which provides the only extensive example of the language actually used by the Sicilian poets. This poem was copied in the sixteenth century by the philologist Giovanni Maria Barbieri from a subsequently lost manuscript, the *Libro siciliano*. The remainder of the Sicilian lyrics are contained in manuscripts that were compiled and written by Tuscan scribes who transformed the original Sicilian dialect into a variety of Tuscan, and it is in this "tuscanized" form that the poems have come down to us.

In contrast with the generally refined and noble courtly lyrics of the Sicilian poets are the compositions of two contemporary rhymers, Compagnetto da Prato and Cielo d'Alcamo; nevertheless, their lyrics are found with those of the aulic poets in the major collection of early Italian poetry, Codex Vatican latini 3793. Compagnetto's two poems, although belonging to the popular genres of the complaint of the *chanson de malmariée* ("Per lo marito c'ò rio") and the *chanson de femme* ("L'amor fa una donna amare"), demonstrate a high degree of originality and artistic sophistication. As one of the few Italian examples of the pastourelle genre, Cielo's well-known *contrasto*, "Rosa fresca aulentissima," presents, in a mixture of courtly and rustic language, a realistic dialogue between a woman of the bourgeoisie and an itinerant jongleur. Thus, while the general situation is that of the pastourelle, in which a knight attempts to seduce a peasant woman, the characters here are vastly different, reflecting the Sicilian social and cultural milieu. Perhaps the major points of interest in this lively poem are the psychological interplay and development of the two interlocutors and the use of language to convey and/or mask inner feelings.

The generally acknowledged leader of the Sicilian school, as well as its most prolific, influential, and inventive member, is Iacopo (or Giacomo) da Lentini, a notary attached to the imperial court. While the subject matter of his extensive poetic corpus (between twelve and twenty-two canzoni, one *discordo,* and at least nineteen and possibly as many as twenty-five sonnets) depends on the troubadour tradition, Giacomo nevertheless reveals his originality through his use of natural and scholastic images, local allusions, and concern with the condition, function, and craft of the poet. The excellence of his canzone "Madonna, dir vi voglio" secures Dante's admiration in *De vulgari eloquentia.* His dissatisfaction with the limitations of troubadour modes lies at the heart of the canzone "Amor non vole ch'io clami," in which he expresses his double desire to avoid stylized amorous conventions and to shape his poetry along more original lines.

The problem of poetic virtuosity and originality was a very real one for the Sicilians, and Iacopo perrhaps met the challenge best, for it was he who, in the face of the fully developed troubadour tradition and in protest against its pervasive, stifling influence, invented the sonnet and demonstrated that its unique metrical form was the ideal mode for the presentation of his intellectually refined amorous and ethical sentiments. His sonnet "Io m'aggio posto in core a Dio servire" reveals his attempt to harmonize courtly sentiments with religious ideals and to reconcile profane and sacred love:

Io m'aggio posto in core a Dio servire,
com'io potesse gire in paradiso,
al santo loco, c'aggio audito dire,
'l si mantien sollazo, gioco e riso.
Sanza mia donna non vi voria gire,
quella c'ha blonda testa e claro viso,
chè sanza lei non poteria gaudere,
estando da la mia donna diviso.
Ma no lo dico a tale intendimento,
perch'io peccato ci volesse fare;
se non veder lo suo bel portamento
e lo bel viso e 'l morbido sguardare:
chè lo mi teria in gran consolamento,
veggendo la mia donna in ghoria stare.

I have set my heart to serving God / that I may go to Paradise, / the holy place, where, as I have heard, / there is always sweet conversation, play, and laughter. / I would not want to go without my lady, / without my lady of the fair hair and clear brow, / for without her I could know no joy, / being cut off from my lady. / But I do not say this in the sense / that I would want to commit a sin; / but only to see her beautiful bearing, / that beautiful face and soft gaze turned on me: / for I would stay eternally content / to behold my lady standing there in glory. (Frederick Goldin, trans.)

Despite much critical investigation and theorizing, the precise origin of the sonnet remains controversial. To arrive at his final fourteen-line creation, Iacopa da Lentini may have incorporated the eight-line *strambotto* (in the popular Sicilian form of the *canzuna*), or he may have based his metrical invention directly on the stanza of the canzone (Provençal: *canso*). However that may be, the earliest sonnets all have fourteen hendecasyllabic lines organized in a rigid alternating rhyme scheme for the quatrains (*abababab*) and in a much freer pattern for the tercets (usually either *cdecde* or *cdcdcd*). In creating the sonnet, Giacomo endowed it with qualities that would enable it to compete for preeminence with the Provençal literary tradition and particularly with the *canso* form.

The two most important criteria for the *canso* were newness and/or difficulty of form, on the one hand, and virtuosity in the use of technical and rhetorical devices, on the other. Thus, much of the success or failure of the sonnet, both in its competition with the *canso* and in its survival as a poetic mode, would depend on how well it conformed to these established standards of excellence. The sonnet was de facto a new poetic form, and the varying rhyme schemes of the tercets may be viewed as internal modifications that evidence the influence of the ever-changing structure of the *canso*. Furthermore, the sonnets of the Sicilian school demonstrate a thorough integration of the technical and rhetorical devices of the earlier tradition. The sonnet, then, as the only distinctive Italian verse form produced by the Sicilians, crowns the movement away from strict adherence to Provençal models by harmonizing traditional and original elements. Indeed, the general cultural significance of Frederick's court is enhanced by the invention of the sonnet, which, by attaining a high level of formal elegance and by demonstrating thematic richness and diversity, contributed in a major way to the beginnings of the Italian literary tradition.

The importance of the Sicilian poets lies in their being the first to use an Italian dialect as the medium for artistic expression, in their innovative imitation of earlier models to create a body of literature that would both mark the beginning of the Italian literary tradition and influence subsequent generations of poets, and in their invention and development of the sonnet, which in time would become the poetic vehicle par excellence in Italy and in the rest of Europe.

BIBLIOGRAPHY

Sources. Literary Criticism of Dante Alighieri, Robert S. Haller, ed. and trans. (1973); Roberto Antonelli, ed., *Giacomo da Lentini: Poesie* (1979); Guido delle Colonne, *Historia destructionis Troiae,* Mary Elizabeth Meek, trans. (1974); Frede Jensen, ed. and trans., *The Poetry of the Sicilian School* (1986).

Studies. Atti del Convegno internazionale di studi federiciani (1952); Giovanni A. Cesareo, *Le origini della poesia lirica e la poesia siciliana sotto gli Svevi* (1924); Gianfranco Contini, ed., *Poeti del duecento,* I (1960), 45–185; *Dai trovatori arabo-siculi alla poesia d'oggi* (1953); Peter Dronke, *The Medieval Lyric* (1968, 2nd ed. 1977), 151–156; Gianfranco Folena, "Cultura e poesia dei siciliani," in Emilio Cecchi and Natalino Sapegno, eds., *Storia della letteratura italiana,* I (1965), 271–347; Frederick Goldin, ed. and trans., *German and Italian Lyrics of the Middle Ages* (1973), 209–253; Anna Granville Hatcher, "Compagnetto da Prato: A Sophisticated Jongleur," in *Cultura neolatina,* **19** (1959); Christopher Kleinhenz, *The Early Italian Sonnet: The First Century (1220–1321)* (1986); Daniele Mattalía, "La scuola siciliana," in *Letteratura italiana: I minori,* I (1969); Bruno Panvini, ed., *Le rime della scuola siciliana,* 2 vols. (1962–1964); Emilio Pasquini and Antonio Enzo Quaglio, *Le origini e la scuola siciliana* (1971, 2nd ed. 1975), 171–240; Maurice J. Valency, *In Praise of Love:*

An Introduction to the Love-poetry of the Renaissance (1958), 195–204; Thomas C. Van Cleve, *The Emperor Frederick II of Hohenstaufen* (1972), 283–346; Ernest Hatch Wilkins, "The Invention of the Sonnet," in his *The Invention of the Sonnet and Other Studies in Italian Literature* (1959).

CHRISTOPHER KLEINHENZ

[See also **Canso; Courtly Love; Dante Alighieri; Descort; Frederick II; Iacopo da Lentini; Italian Literature: Lyric; Piero della Vigna; Provençal Literature; Tenso.**]

SICILIAN VESPERS, so called from the riot that broke out in Palermo on Easter Monday in 1282 and triggered the overthrow of the Angevin government of Sicily. Opposition to the rule of Charles I of Anjou was particularly strong on the island, where memory of its position as the center of the Kingdom of Sicily under the Normans and the Hohenstaufen was fresh. This opposition was fanned by the Byzantine emperor Michael VIII Palaiologos as part of his effort to prevent Charles from mounting an invasion of the Byzantine Empire. Pedro III of Aragon, whose wife, Constance, was the daughter of King Manfred of Sicily, worked to promote unrest. In addition to these factors, the strong dissatisfaction with the heavy tax burdens levied by Charles to support his foreign policy made his government unpopular.

On Easter Monday, 30 March 1282, following an incident in which a Sicilian lady was insulted by a French soldier outside the Church of S. Spirito in Palermo, there was widespread rioting against all of the French in the city. This quickly spread across the island. With some reluctance the cities, especially Messina, and a portion of the aristocracy threw their support against the French. What had begun as a popular rising was quickly channeled to the purposes of the nobility and of Pedro of Aragon. Pedro sent his ships to take advantage of the rebellion and entered into negotiations that resulted in his acclamation as king of Sicily by a parliament in Palermo on 4 December 1282.

BIBLIOGRAPHY

Michele Amari, *La guerra del vespro siciliano,* 3 vols. (1969); Léon Cadier, *Essai sur l'administration du royaume de Sicile sous Charles Ier et Charles II d'Anjou* (1891); Deno J. Geanakoplos, *Emperor Michael Palaeologus and the West, 1258–1282* (1959); Steven Runciman, *The Sicilian Vespers* (1958).

JAMES M. POWELL

[See also **Byzantine Empire: History; Crusades, Political; Michael VIII Palaiologos; Sicily, Kingdom of.**]

SICILY, ISLAMIC. Geographically the island of Sicily divides the Mediterranean into two parts. In the Middle Ages its location as an extension of the Italian Peninsula and its proximity to the coast of Tunisia accorded Sicily great strategic importance in war, in trade, and in cultural communication. One could not traverse the Mediterranean without stopping at Sicily or sailing very close to its coastline; thus the control of the island and its ports afforded its masters considerable military and commercial advantages. Control of Sicily implied a major role in the affairs of the Mediterranean world, and it is thus no wonder that during the Middle Ages possession of the island was a prize contested among the major Mediterranean powers.

At the time of the Islamic conquests in the mid seventh century, Sicily (together with the southern and eastern portions of the Italian Peninsula) was a province of the Byzantine Empire. The victorious westward progress of Arab armies across North Africa occurred in several stages, and it was not until the very end of the seventh century that the North African coastline came under permanent Muslim control.

Muslim raids on Sicily—mostly to acquire booty—began in the early eighth century and continued intermittently for well over a century. In 827 Ziyādat Allāh I (817–838), the semi-independent Aghlabid ruler of Ifrīqiya (comprising eastern Algeria, Tunisia, and Tripolitania), mounted a serious expedition that succeeded in establishing a long-term foothold on the island. From their base in Mazara, taken in 827, the Muslim forces slowly and at irregular intervals over a period of seventy-five years expanded their rule over the island, taking Palermo in 831, Castrogiovanni (the Byzantine capital of Sicily) in 859, Syracuse in 878, and Taormina in 902. Thus, by 902 most of Sicily was in their hands.

Throughout the two and a half centuries of Muslim hegemony, Sicily was administratively a province of Ifrīqiya. It was ruled by a series of governors (variously called walis or emirs) who were appointed, or at least approved, by the succession of dynasties controlling Ifrīqiya—the Aghlabids until

909, followed by the Fatimids until about 1050, and finally the semi-independent Zirids until the Norman conquest.

The governors generally had a free hand in the administration of the island. The Muslim population was neither homogeneous nor unified. It was composed of Arab groupings of varied provenance and tribal loyalty, of North African Berber tribesmen in the military service of a succession of princes from various dynasties, and of indigenous converts to Islam. Political and military power on the island was fragmented, and a good deal of the time and energy of its governors was taken up in trying to keep some semblance of order in the face of feuding factions and frequent localized rebellions. The incessant internal warfare among local warlords was certainly a factor in the comparatively easy and rapid Norman conquest in the 1070's.

While Muslim rule inevitably brought in its wake a degree of conversion to Islam among the indigenous population, conversion was numerically limited and geographically uneven. Islamization was most successful in the western part of the island (the Val di Mazara), much less so in the southern areas (the Val di Noto), and made hardly any headway in the northeastern corner of Sicily (the Val Demone), which remained staunchly Christian. Immigration from North Africa continually augmented the Muslim population of the island. There are no reliable population figures for this period, but some have estimated that at its height the Muslim population of Sicily reached as much as half a million—a figure that is probably on the high side.

Ethnic and religious diversity characterized the population of the island during the 250 years of Muslim domination. A majority of the inhabitants retained their Christian religious allegiance and were, in line with Islamic practice, accorded the status of protected minorities (dhimmis). In return for the payment of a poll tax (*jizya*) and adherence to certain other restrictive regulations, they were guaranteed the safety of their persons and property, and the freedom to follow the precepts of their own religion and maintain the institutions of their religious community. The same status was accorded to the small Jewish community of the island, which seems to have been concentrated mainly in the coastal towns.

For almost a century, beginning in 947, Sicily was ruled by the Kalbites, a semi-independent, hereditary dynasty of governors. The dynasty was founded by Ḥasan ibn ᶜAlī al-Kalbī, a military chieftain sent by the Fatimids to Sicily to quell a local rebellion. The independence of this dynasty was enhanced by the transfer of the Fatimid capital from Ifrīqiya to Egypt in the latter decades of the tenth century. Under the Kalbites, Sicily was virtually independent not only of the more distant Fatimids but also of their lieutenants, the Zirids of Ifrīqiya.

The period of Muslim rule in Sicily coincided with the early phases of the commercial revolution of the Middle Ages and was an era of brilliant economic prosperity for the island. During the late tenth and early eleventh centuries, Sicily was at the very hub of the expanding commercial activity in the Mediterranean world. Together with Tunisia, Sicily during this period was at the intersection of a number of major trade routes. Caravans from Sijilmāsa in southern Morocco, carrying African and Moroccan commodities, made their way to Tunisia, and from there these goods found their way to the markets of Palermo and Mazara. Sicily served as a commercial intermediary between Muslim Spain and the Muslim East, and ships traveling between the two ends of the Mediterranean regularly called at its ports. For European (mostly Italian) merchants in search of Eastern goods (flax, sugar, textiles of Egyptian provenance, pepper, spices, medical herbs, and so forth), the markets of Palermo and Mazara (as well as those of the Tunisian coastal towns) were closer and more accessible than those of the eastern Mediterranean. Even after the middle of the eleventh century, when Egypt replaced Sicily and Tunisia as the hub of East-West trade, Sicily remained an important center of international commerce, and reports on the activity and price levels of its markets were a regular part of the commercial correspondence of the eleventh century.

From at least the late tenth century, Sicily was a major producer of both raw and woven silk, which was actively traded in Mediterranean commerce. Its gold coin, the *rubāᶜīya,* or quarter dinar, was highly esteemed, much in demand in Egypt and in the trading towns of Syria and Palestine.

The Norman conquest of Sicily between 1060 and 1090 should be seen against the background of Christian Europe's energetic reassertion in the Mediterranean basin. The impetus that spurred the tremendous expansion of commercial exchange during the eleventh century brought in its wake a wave of naval and military activity against Islamic targets in the Mediterranean, stretching from Spain to Syria and Palestine. By the end of the century the Reconquest was well under way, crusading knights were in control of large parts of the Levant, and European powers had established a naval domination of the Mediterranean that was to last for several centuries.

Signs of the slow retreat of Muslim power in Sicily were already visible in the first half of the eleventh century. By the 1030's the Byzantines began to reassert themselves in the central Mediterranean with attacks on the northeast corner of the island at and around Messina. This coincided with raids by various Italian powers, such as the Amalfitans and the Pisans, on Sicily and the coastal towns of North Africa. By 1050 the Islamic states of the central Mediterranean were militarily (although not commercially) on the defensive. From their base in southern Italy the Normans first attacked Sicily in 1060. In 1061 Roger I succeeded in capturing Messina, in 1072 Palermo fell, and in the course of the next twenty years the entire island came under secure Norman control.

Arabic-speaking Muslim communities survived in Sicily for more than two centuries after the Norman conquest. The roots put down by Arab-Islamic culture during the Muslim period continued to bear fruit well into the twelfth century. The most famous and most important Arabic work produced in Sicily was the universal geography of al-Idrīsī, completed in 1154 and written at the behest and under the patronage of Roger II. During the twelfth and thirteenth centuries Sicily was an important center for the translation from Arabic of works on Aristotelian philosophy, astronomy, and medicine, which then passed into the mainstream of European intellectual life. The Islamic legacy is visible to this day in the architectural and decorative style of early Norman churches, as well as in the minor decorative arts of the Norman period. In 1246 the last Muslim community disappeared from the island, victim of both assimilation and persecution.

BIBLIOGRAPHY

The most authoritative study of the Muslim period of Sicilian history is Michele Amari, *Storia dei musulmani di Sicilia,* 2nd ed., 3 vols. (1933–1939). Amari also collected and translated many of the Arabic sources on Islamic Sicily in *Biblioteca arabo-sicula,* Arabic texts (1857) and Italian translations, 2 vols. (1881–1882). In English, Aziz Ahmad, *A History of Islamic Sicily* (1975), is the most useful summary of the subject and has an extensive bibliography. For the role of Sicily in the expanding commerce of the tenth through twelfth centuries, see Robert S. Lopez, *The Commercial Revolution of the Middle Ages, 950–1350* (1971); and especially S. D. Goitein, *A Mediterranean Society,* I, *Economic Foundations* (1967). Denis Mack Smith, *A History of Sicily,* I, *Medieval Sicily 800–1713* (1968), may also be consulted.

A. L. UDOVITCH

[See also **Aghlabids; Fatimids; Idrīsī, al-; Ifrīqiya; Silk; Trade, Islamic; Zirids.**]

SICILY, KINGDOM OF. The Kingdom of Sicily, founded by the Norman count of Sicily, Roger II, between 1101 and 1139, resulted from the conquest of the south Italian mainland and the island of Sicily by various bands of Norman adventurers in the eleventh century. The Neapolitan historian-philosopher Benedetto Croce viewed the establishment of this kingdom as an intrusion on the land of Sicily and the Italian south, never assimilated by the disparate native populations—Lombard, Greek, and Arab. He argued that they found in it "no stimulus to local pride, no comfort in examples of patriotic virtue." Not many have gone so far as Croce. His sense of frustration and disillusionment seems to be born more of post-Risorgimento southern Italy than of the *Regno,* as so many Italian historians call the Kingdom of the Normans and their successors. Most historians have dwelt on the achievements of this kingdom, celebrating its uniqueness and seeing in it the culmination of the Sicilian role in the Mediterranean. Yet it would not be wise to ignore the pessimistic note injected by Croce, for the problems he saw in the history of the south were real and enduring. Their shadows lend depth and substance to the brilliant hues employed by most others in writing the history of the *Regno.*

THE NORMAN CONQUEST

Those same Normans who had founded the duchy of Normandy in the tenth century and whose duke would conquer England in 1066 had ranged widely in the Mediterranean as well. The dates and the explanations of their first arrival in southern Italy belong partly to legend and partly to history. There are two main traditions in the sources. The one best attested tells how a certain Rodolph, very possibly Rodolph of Tosny, arrived at the court of Pope Benedict VIII (*r.* 1012–1034) to seek papal support and mediation in his dispute with Duke

Richard II of Normandy. Benedict, however, was concerned at this time about Byzantine expansion into the duchy of Benevento, and he turned to the Normans for their help. Very possibly, he put them in touch with a Lombard, Meles of Bari, who was leading a revolt against the Byzantine governor in southern Italy. With Norman aid, Meles raided Apulia in 1017 only to suffer a major defeat in the following year. Alongside this tradition is the story of a group of Norman pilgrims returning from the Holy Land and stopping in southern Italy at the shrine of St. Michael on Monte Gargano. While there, they came in contact with the Lombards and threw in their lot with them. If, however, there is confusion regarding the circumstances of these early contacts, it is clear that by the 1020's news of the opportunities to be had in southern Italy had marked it as a primary destination for Normans in search of adventure.

The land to which these Normans came had been part of the heartland of the Roman Empire but had fallen to the barbarian Ostrogoths in 491. Reconquered by the forces of the emperor Justinian in the early sixth century, it found itself hard-pressed by the southward expansion of the Lombards after 565. The Lombards established important centers of power at Benevento, Capua, and Salerno, while Naples and Amalfi maintained their independence. The Romans, or Byzantines, maintained control chiefly in Apulia and Calabria, centering their administration at Bari and on the island of Sicily. But in the seventh and early eighth centuries, the Aghlabid Muslim rulers of Tunis began raiding in Sicily. As a result of an internal dispute among the Byzantines, they were able to mount a full invasion resulting in the complete conquest of the island in the tenth century. By the eleventh century, despite the overthrow of the Aghlabids and the subsequent fragmentation of political power on the island, a flourishing Islamic culture had developed in Sicily.

The underlying stratum of population in southern Italy and Sicily was Romano-Byzantine. In some areas Latin prevailed, and in others, Greek. But Lombards formed a numerous minority on the mainland and Arab colonists predominated in western Sicily. The implications of these patterns of settlement for the development of political institutions and socio-legal structures are quite important, but not easy to trace in detail. Generally, throughout the south and in Muslim Sicily, there was acceptance of the view that each people had a right to its own law. While on the mainland this "personality of law" had a customary basis, in Muslim Sicily it rested on the division of the population into Muslims and dhimmis, those non-Muslims—Christians and Jews—subject to a special tax but allowed the practice of their religion. There is scant evidence in this period for any process of integration among these different populations. Thus, with the coming of the Normans, yet another group, this one bringing with it the feudal customs of northwestern Europe, entered on the south Italian scene.

The Normans were not long content with the role of mercenaries in the armies of native rulers. In 1030, Sergius, duke of Naples, rewarded the Norman Rainulf with the county of Aversa in return for his support against the Lombard prince, Pandulf of Capua. By the time that Rainulf died in 1045, he was also duke of Gaeta. His nephew, Richard, who succeeded to Aversa in 1049, became prince of Capua in 1058. In this way, the Normans began gradually to displace the Lombards. At the same time, the sons of Tancred of Hauteville, a lesser Norman noble, began to arrive in Italy and to carve out domains for themselves in Apulia at Byzantine expense. With the arrival of Robert Guiscard in

1047, the Hautevilles began to gain ascendancy over the Normans in Italy.

With his blond hair and ruddy complexion, Robert Guiscard cut a figure of the legendary Viking warrior across the face of Calabria. Together with his younger brother, Roger, who arrived in 1056, and with Richard of Capua, he shared the dominance of southern Italy. The two brothers also began to look toward Muslim Sicily. But the rapid expansion and consolidation of power in the hands of Robert Guiscard aroused concern both of the Byzantines and of the papacy at Rome. The popes of the early eleventh century had relied largely on the Byzantines to oppose Norman expansion in the south, devoting themselves chiefly to the internal politics of Rome and the interests of their families. Caught up in a web of aristocratic factionalism, the papacy had become ineffective not only in southern Italy but also, and more importantly, in its role of spiritual leadership of the church.

In the mid eleventh century, however, those movements of reform which had spearheaded monastic revitalization in Lorraine and Burgundy in the tenth and early eleventh centuries found considerable support in Italy as well. Moreover, the German king, Henry III, who was deeply committed to the movement to reform the church, used the occasion of his imperial coronation in 1046 to end a schism in the papacy and to secure the election of a series of German reformer popes, most notably Bruno of Toul, who took the name Leo IX. The reformed papacy could not ignore the growth of Norman power in Italy. In 1053, Leo proclaimed a holy war against them and led a papal army of Germans and northern Italians to Benevento. On 23 June, the combined Norman forces defeated the papal army at Civitate and took Leo prisoner (although the pope was released almost immediately). The papal effort to check Norman expansion had failed.

With the death of Leo IX in 1054 and of Henry III in 1056, imperial influence at Rome waned. In addition, relations with the Byzantine Empire were disrupted by the schism of 1054, which had brought to a head the theological and ecclesiastical tensions long existing between Rome and the patriarchate of Constantinople. Thus isolated, Pope Nicholas II brought about a diplomatic revolution in 1059 by recognizing Richard and Robert Guiscard as vassals of St. Peter: Richard as prince of Capua; Robert as duke of Apulia and Calabria, and as future duke of Sicily. This agreement, which pledged the Normans to defend the possessions of St. Peter, paved the way for the final overthrow of Byzantine power in southern Italy, culminating in the Norman conquest of Bari in April 1071. Perhaps, too, the allusion to the future conquest of Sicily indicated a major reason why Pope Nicholas was willing to enter this alliance with the Normans. Their preoccupation with Sicily would provide an outlet for expansionist efforts that might otherwise be directed toward papal lands around Rome.

As it was, the Norman conquest of Sicily consumed most of the second half of the eleventh century but by no means all Norman energies. Although it was a joint effort of Robert Guiscard and Roger, most of the fighting fell to the latter, for Robert increasingly turned his attention across the Adriatic. The opportunity for Roger to intervene in Sicily was provided by factionalism among the Muslims. In conjunction with the sultan of Syracuse, Roger took Messina in 1061 but failed in his effort to capture Palermo in 1068. In 1072, however, following Robert's victory at Bari, and supported by a fleet of fifty-eight ships, the brothers combined to capture Catania and Palermo. Still, it was not until 1091 that Norman control of the island was secure. Even in the first decades of the thirteenth century, the power of Muslim princes in the interior of the island posed a threat to the monarchy.

The last third of the eleventh century also witnessed the consolidation of Norman power on the mainland. The papacy continued to view this development with concern. Pope Gregory VII entered an alliance with Richard of Capua in 1074 aimed at protecting the papacy from Robert Guiscard. However, as Gregory became more deeply enmeshed in controversy with the young emperor Henry IV over the investiture of German bishops by the crown, he turned away from Richard. Abbot Desiderius of Monte Cassino brought Richard and Robert together once more, and they cooperated on the conquest of Salerno in December 1076. The Byzantines, in the person of the emperor Michael VII, also came to terms, but when Michael was deposed in 1078 Robert seized the opportunity to launch an attack on Corfu and Durazzo. Increasingly, the Normans were becoming a third force in relations between the papacy and the Holy Roman Empire as Gregory's conflict with Henry IV intensified. In 1084, Robert hastened from his siege of Durazzo to raise Henry IV's siege of Rome. Having rescued the pope and sacked the city, Robert withdrew southward; Gregory went with the Normans and died in Salerno on 25 May 1085. Robert resumed his war with the Byzantines only to succumb on 17 July on the island of Cephalonia. He was succeeded by his son Roger Borsa. The first generation of the Hautevilles had achieved much. On the eve of the launching of the First Crusade by Pope Urban II in 1095, they had breached the major barrier to European expansion into the eastern Mediteranean.

Historians are by no means certain about the impact of the Norman conquest on southern Italy and Sicily. It seems clear, however, that the conquerors did not rigidly impose their own social and political structures on the diverse fabrics of this society. At the same time, there is evidence that they attempted to integrate native institutions with their own. They adapted the feudal structures of Normandy to the task of organizing and administering their conquered lands. Given the nature of their conquest of the mainland, particularly the slow emergence of a central authority, the exercise of local power was fragmented. In the north and west, some large baronies, such as Molise, the Principate, Capua, and Avellino, formed virtually independent power bases through much of the later eleventh century. On the island of Sicily, Roger I was able to avoid the creation of great feudal lordships in rewarding his followers, retaining the major cities and large holdings as part of his demesne. Although the conquest involved the displacement of the privileged classes among their Lombard, Latin, Byzantine, and Arab predecessors, the effects on the great mass of the rural and urban population were most probably minimal during the eleventh century.

One area of major impact was religion. Byzantine Italy had looked to Constantinople. The conquest opened the south and the island of Sicily to Latin influence from Rome. One agency of the spread of Latin and papal power lay in the Norman patronage of Western monasticism. The Normans enjoyed close relations with Monte Cassino and La Cava in this period and played an important role in the spread of Latin monasticism in Sicily in the twelfth century. In the reorganization of the Sicilian church, the so-called Sicilian legateship shows a close working relationship developing between Roger I and Pope Urban II. Urban agreed in 1098 that during Roger's lifetime and that of his immediate heir, he would send no papal legate except with the advice and consent of the count and would permit the count to exercise legatine powers on the island of Sicily. This privilege also allowed Roger to control the selection and number of bishops to be sent to councils. Though some scholars have tried to stress the radical nature of this privilege, granted at a time when the papacy was endeavoring to restrict lay control of clerical offices, it seems better to read it in connection with the recent conquest of Sicily from the Muslims and the need for emergency powers to promote the interests of the Latin church on the island. Whatever tensions later developed between the papacy and the Norman rulers of Sicily over the meaning of this privilege, there is no question that it eased the task of establishing a Latin hierarchy in Sicily.

There is little evidence of Norman influence on the cultural life of southern Italy and Sicily in the eleventh century. Rather, we may assume that the Normans were themselves stimulated by their new environment. In the period before the establishment of the monarchy, the chief intellectual centers were in the Latin and Greek monasteries and in the cities. On the mainland, Monte Cassino under the vigorous leadership of Abbot Desiderius spread its influence as far as Salerno. The monastery was the major center of Campanian culture and letters. The *scripta Beneventana,* or Lombard script, achieved its greatest perfection there. Monte Cassino also came to serve as a mediator between the papacy and the Normans and was therefore in close contact with the Norman leaders. The earliest historians of the Norman conquest of Italy, Amatus and Leo of Ostia, were monks of Monte Cassino. The monastery was a focal point for the reform movement in southern Italy. The construction of the basilica (long since destroyed) begun by Desiderius was symbolic of this position. If we may accept the arguments of Ernst Kitzinger, the mosaics of this church, viewed from the perspective and evidence furnished by those in the cathedral of Salerno, show the paramount character of an eleventh-century revival of interest in the Roman basilican art of the post-Constantinian age. This art served to confirm Monte Cassino's leadership of Latin ecclesiastical forces in the south.

Among the cities, Salerno was especially notable for its medical school; Naples and Bari had a substantial group of educated laity; and Palermo was the center of Islamic culture, though that influence declined sharply following the conquest. In Sicily and Calabria, the Greco-Byzantine population was substantial and ties with Constantinople remained close. The long history of Byzantine rule in southern Italy also affected the cultural idiom of a large part of the non-Greek population as well, a dominance that would be long apparent in art.

But while the Normans promoted the interests of Latin Christianity, the existence of Orthodox Christian, Moslem, and Jewish minorities imposed realistic limits to their efforts. The Latinization of Greek Christians in Calabria and Sicily made little headway in this period, although eventually they were absorbed by the Latins. Many Muslims emigrated from Sicily at the time of the conquest and were replaced by Lombard (Latin) colonists from the mainland. Those who remained lived apart. Some were converted, but a substantial remnant were allowed the continued practice of their religion. There is also some evidence of increased efforts to convert the Jews of Sicily to Christianity under Roger I. Nevertheless, practical considerations of government strongly affected Norman religious policy with the result that elements of all these communities worked closely with their conquerors.

ROGER II AND HIS SUCCESSORS

On 22 June 1101, Roger I, the great count of Sicily, died. During the approximately fifteen years since the death of Robert Guiscard, Roger had taken advantage of the weakness of Robert's heir, Roger Borsa, to expand his own interests on the mainland. Thus it was not surprising that his son, Roger II, continued to pursue his father's claims to the duchy of Apulia. After the death of Roger Borsa's son William in 1127, Roger II moved quickly to claim the heritage of Robert Guiscard. On 23 August 1128, Pope Honorius II reluctantly invested Roger as duke of Apulia. Shortly after, Roger forced Robert of Capua to cede his principality to him. Having secured his power both in Sicily and on the mainland, he summoned an assembly to Salerno and obtained from it a declaration of his right to be king. On Christmas Day 1130 a representative of the antipope, Anacletus II, crowned him in the cathedral of Palermo. Roger was now a king, but recognition by Anacletus had the effect of isolating him from the other crowned heads of Europe. It was not until 1139 that he won from Pope Innocent II, in the Treaty of Mignano, an acknowledgement of his royal title.

The Kingdom of Sicily drew its name from the island conquered by the Normans from the Muslims rather than from the mainland provinces they had wrested from the Lombards, Byzantines, and native rulers. Moreover, there was in that title a recognition that the island was the base of Roger's power and that from it he had extended his rule to the mainland. This title, however, represented also a concession to the papacy and the Roman curia, who wanted to prevent the exercise of direct royal authority in those areas closest to the lands of St. Peter. Thus, on the mainland Roger was to be, as his title specified, prince of Capua and duke of Apulia. Yet this distinction had no long-range historical import. Roger integrated his mainland holdings into his new royal administration. Interestingly, however, the use of the island's name for the whole kingdom caused people to consider the mainland, too, as Sicily. In the fifteenth century, when, after a long separation, the mainland and the island were rejoined as a single kingdom, it was to be known as the Kingdom of the Two Sicilies.

Confronting Roger II was the task of welding the disparate lands and peoples of southern Italy and Sicily into a kingdom. The problem was difficult. The region had no monarchical tradition save that from the Byzantine *basileus*. The Normans themselves were accustomed to the ties of homage and vassalage that had, in Normandy, united them firmly to their duke, but they had little direct experience of feudal monarchy as it was developing in England under Henry I or in France under Louis VI. The Lombard populations of southern Italy had had only rare contacts with the Lombard kingdom of Pavia in northern Italy. In order for Roger to rule, he had to communicate his power effectively to all of these groups, but this was clearly not possible through any single royal idiom. The studies made by historians of the Norman monarchy reveal the difficulty of conforming it to existing patterns of European monarchy. At one and the same time, they have found it to be fundamentally feudal in character and Byzantine in spirit. They have stressed its development of a bureaucracy drawn from Greek and Arab elements and its evolution of a curia regis along lines similar to those of England and France.

In his penetrating studies of royal iconography in the reign of Roger II, Ernst Kitzinger has reached behind the Byzantine stylistic elements in the mosaics of the royal chapel and the Martorana at Palermo to their inner meaning. In both cases, he has suggested that Byzantine form cloaked Western conceptions of monarchy. He argues that the mosaic of Christ crowning King Roger found in the Martorana reveals a striking resemblance between the visage of Roger and that of Christ in a kind of declaration of the sacral character of kingship and suggests that the inspiration for this can best be traced to Ottonian Germany rather than to the Byzantine Empire. In accounting for this conflict of style and underlying meaning, he concludes: "Roger's Sicily was a medley of cultures, languages, and religions and lacked the objective norm of a dogma binding for all. The only normative element was the king himself."

Contemporaries also sensed that the Rogerian monarchy did not conform to their experiences. Otto of Freising (*d.* 1158), perhaps the most learned historian of the age, tells us that Roger's cruelties to the Apulians were patterned upon the deeds of the ancient Sicilian tyrants. Indeed, this theme of Roger's tyranny was fairly common and referred not only to his treatment of his subjects but also to the illegitimacy of his path to kingship. Yet, those in a position to observe closely remarked on his initiatives as a lawgiver and his abilities as a good ruler. Arab writers were struck by his tolerance of their religion. The sources seem to confirm that the monarchy had different faces, depending on the perspective from which one looked at it.

Erich Caspar, in discussing Roger's work in creating a royal government, speaks of the "feeling of belonging together" that bound the king to his officials. Certainly, Roger had to build such a spirit if he was to have an effective government. But the essence of his government rested on his personal success in imposing strong rule on the *Regno*. The diversity of titles enjoyed by royal officials on various levels under Roger—emir of emirs, archon of archons, logothetes, strategoi, catapans, justiciars, and chamberlains—reveals the function of monarchy in drawing together existing institutions to serve the needs of the crown. This process of adaptation also promoted a certain fluidity of meaning, perhaps best illustrated by the evolution of the office and title of emir from a rather general one to one referring to the admiral of a fleet. Further, some titles lost status rather quickly in this period while others gained. Roger created the justiciarate around 1136 for the administration of royal justice. Gradually this office was to assume a major role in the administration of the kingdom.

One might say that Roger based the unity of his kingdom on a principle of heterogeneity. The crown was the focal point for a gradual process of centralization that bound the diverse elements of this society to itself. The curia regis evolved to provide the crown the network it needed for this purpose. The development of the royal fiscal administration is a case in point. Roger preserved the Arabic *dīwān,* which was responsible chiefly for the collection of port duties. But he also created administrative structures to ensure the collection of feudal dues. The effectiveness of this aspect of his government may be measured to some extent in the so-called *Catalogus baronum,* listing fiefs and their obligations, the first section of which dates from about 1156. Roger also developed a firm policy aimed at protecting the integrity of the royal demesne. He centralized this fiscal administration in the curia regis under the chamberlain. It is impossible to detect in the "design" of Roger's government whether its feudal character or its Byzantine absolutism predominated. The weight of the evidence seems to argue that Roger was primarily a Westerner in his conception of royal power but that he employed the various idioms and institutions already existing in southern Italy and Sicily to make his power a reality to his subjects.

It was also necessary for Roger to impress the neighbors of his newly founded kingdom. He had done this first in his relations with the papacy and had thereby attained recognition of his royal title. But this had not satisfied the claims of the Byzantines or of the sultanate of Mahdia. Most scholars who have examined Roger's foreign policy have stressed its expansionist aspects. However, we ought not overlook the insecurity of his position in the *Regno,* which made his invasions of the Dalmatian coast and of North Africa essential elements in the building of a strong monarchy in an area contested by major powers. In shifting the balance of existing power in the central Mediterranean, Roger's policies fit generally into those of the northern Italian maritime cities—Pisa, Genoa, and Venice. Though Roger did not participate in the crusade movement against the Muslims of Syria and Palestine, he was the heir to the liberator of Sicily, and his war against the Muslims of Mahdia provided indirect aid to the crusade cause.

When Roger II died in 1154, the Kingdom of Sicily was the chief European power in the Mediterranean west of Greece. His son, William I (*r.* 1154–1166), came to power at the head of a strong and well-administered government. His chief minister, Maio of Bari, seems to have been dedicated to carrying on the Rogerian traditions of monarchy. Despite the conspiracies that weakened the monarchy under William, the overthrow of Maio, and the anarchy that continued into the period of the regency for the young William II (*r.* 1172–1189), there is ample evidence that royal government continued to function. Under William I, the offices of master justiciar and master constable appear on the mainland outside Calabria. In this period, however, the degree of control of the feudal aristocracy over crown functions is indicated by the fact that counts normally exercised the office of royal justiciar on their own lands, enabling them to dispense "high" justice to their subjects in the king's name. Some of the chief cities of the kingdom endeavored to throw off the tight rein imposed on them by Roger II. Some, like Messina, wanted to choose their own officials and to be ruled according to their own customs. But, as William II assumed personal control, he shifted the balance in favor of the monarchy once again. He achieved brilliant successes with his fleet against the Byzantines and the Muslims of North Africa. However, his major adversary was the Holy Roman Emperor, Frederick I Barbarossa, who was determined to achieve dominance in Italy. In 1184, William concluded a treaty whereby his heir and aunt, Constance, daughter of Roger II, would marry Frederick's son, Henry. This marriage laid the foundation for the passage of the Kingdom of Sicily into the hands of the Hohenstaufen.

After the death of William II (1189), Constance laid claim to her inheritance, but many of the barons of the *Regno* preferred Tancred of Lecce, an illegitimate son of William. There was broad support for Tancred, especially from those groups who saw advantage to themselves in dealing with a king who needed them more than they needed him. Tancred was forced to alienate lands from the royal demesne to the feudal aristocracy and to make concessions to the cities and to the local churches and monasteries. The papacy secured a restriction of the Sicilian legateship to the island of Sicily (1192), limiting the claims that had been made under William II. Tancred was also forced to make concessions to the English king, Richard the Lionhearted, who stopped in Sicily on his way to the Holy Land. Despite these efforts, Tancred's position was perilous. Henry, having secured his election as Emperor Henry VI following the death of his father, hastened to Rome for his coronation in 1191. He invaded the *Regno* but was repulsed. Nevertheless, after the death of Tancred in 1194, Henry was able to overthrow the regency for the infant William III and to have himself crowned king in Palermo.

Henry's reign (1194–1197) was short-lived but momentous. His accession brought the kingdom of Sicily into the orbit of the Holy Roman Empire. There it would remain for two generations. His goal was the creation of strong imperial power in Italy; he had small concern for his Sicilian subjects save for the support they could provide to his plans to spread his power across the Adriatic to Byzantium and eastward to the Holy Land. His wife, Constance, on the other hand, had as her primary concern the preservation of her inheritance. Following Henry's death she expelled the Germans and shortly before her death (1198) sought the protection of Pope Innocent III (1198–1216) for her four-year-old son, Frederick Roger.

EMPEROR FREDERICK II

The minority of Frederick Roger continued the "Time of Trouble" for the *Regno*. Markward of Anweiler, who claimed to represent the will of Henry VI, posed a serious threat to the papal guardianship, since he was backed by the remnant of Henry's troops in the kingdom. Innocent was forced to rely on the support of royal officials, led by Walter of Palear, the bishop of Troina, the local churches, and the barons. He and Frederick also had to make major concessions to the northern Italian maritime cities—Genoa, Pisa, and Venice—for their aid. Even after the death of Markward in 1202, various factions attempted to control the young monarch. In 1208, Frederick married Constance of Aragon. With the support of the Aragonese, he was in a more secure position.

Meanwhile, events in the Holy Roman Empire had moved to a critical stage. Innocent III had opposed the election of Frederick's uncle Philip of Swabia as German king and emperor-elect. Instead, he had supported the candidacy of Otto of Brunswick, the leader of the Welf cause in Germany. When Philip was murdered in a private quarrel in 1208, the road seemed open for Otto. But Otto, who had conceded to Innocent his acceptance of papal rights in Italy and Germany even as late as March 1209 at Speyer, began to abandon this position even before his coronation. When Otto moved on the Kingdom of Sicily in November 1210, Innocent III excommunicated him. The papacy, with French support, worked to undermine Otto's position in Germany. In November 1211, a German embassy informed the young Frederick

Roger in Palermo of his election to the German kingship. Aided by the pope and the Genoese, Frederick rushed to Germany, where the princes and bishops flocked to the Hohenstaufen eagle. There Frederick remained for the next eight years. Otto IV, beaten at Bouvines by Frederick's ally, Philip II Augustus of France, gradually yielded to the force of the young emperor-elect and finally died in 1218.

From 1197, and perhaps we should say 1189, to 1220, the Kingdom of Sicily was largely without effective government. Even in those years after Frederick had attained the position of emperor-elect (1215–1220), he continued to barter away the rights of the Sicilian crown for the support of the aristocracy, the Pisans, and the Genoese. Throughout this "Time of Trouble" Frederick followed the same policies that had been forced on Tancred and Constance by their exigencies, alienating crown lands to both churches and the feudal aristocracy, granting extensive freedoms to the major cities, and allowing northern merchants virtually free rein in the commerce of the kingdom. For much of this period, considerable portions of the Norman machinery of government were under local control, and crown revenues suffered from the alienations made by Constance, Tancred, and Frederick himself.

The return of Frederick to Italy for his imperial coronation was marked by intensive negotiations with the papacy regarding the status of the Kingdom of Sicily, imperial claims in central Italy, and Frederick's vow to go on crusade. The papacy insisted on the maintenance of the separation of Sicily from the empire. Frederick worked to keep Sicily under his personal control. In the end, it was Frederick who won; his concession of the German crown to his young son Henry was a small price to pay for the Kingdom of Sicily. In central Italy and Tuscany, Frederick recognized existing papal claims. Finally, he committed himself to a definite date for departure on the crusade. While this agreement was a compromise, its faithful implementation by Frederick would have relieved the papacy of most of its concerns about the threat from the unification of the *Regno* to imperial Italy. It was on this assumption that the way was paved for Frederick's coronation in November 1220. In the aftermath of his coronation, however, the new emperor's first thoughts were of his Kingdom of Sicily rather than his promises to the pope.

Reentering the *Regno* via Capua, Frederick promulgated a series of laws aimed at restoring the tradition of strong monarchy in the kingdom (December 1220). He demanded the resignation of all privileges issued between 1197 and 1220 into the hands of the crown. This measure particularly affected the status of the Genoese merchants in Sicily as well as the lay aristocracy. It had a major impact, also, on many bishoprics and monasteries. Frederick was soon confronted with a rebellion of the Muslims of Sicily and strong oppositions from the nobility and the churches. But there was no effective united front of his enemies. The Genoese were forced to trade without their special privileges. The Muslims were beaten and their remnant transferred to Lucera in Abbruzzi. The churches were staved off by protracted negotiations while Frederick dealt with the lay aristocracy forcefully. All the while, he put off the insistent demands of Pope Honorius III that he fulfill his crusade vow. Especially after the crusaders' loss of Damietta in Egypt in August 1221, and his failure to depart in 1225, Frederick's relations with the papacy deteriorated.

Despite his marriage to the heiress of the kingdom of Jerusalem, Frederick continued to focus his attention on Italy. After 1225, the papacy, recognizing that its plans were in serious jeopardy and that it was losing control in southern Italy, adopted a harder line. When Frederick failed to carry out his planned departure for the East in August 1227, the new pope, Gregory IX, put the excommunication required by the agreement of 1225 into effect.

Frederick's miscalculation of the papal reaction to his claim that illness had forced him to turn back from the crusade and his decision to go on crusade in 1228 while still under the ban exacerbated relations with Gregory. In 1229, the pope, probably provoked (in a technical sense at least) by incursions from the *Regno* into the duchy of Spoleto, invaded the Kingdom of Sicily. Very clearly, it was his intention to force a full renegotiation of the agreements reached with Frederick almost ten years earlier. But along with his success in securing the return of Jerusalem from the Muslims and obtaining a truce with Egypt, Frederick was able to return from the East and defeat the papal army. The resulting Treaty of Ceprano (1230) ostensibly maintained the status quo, but actually freed Frederick to pursue his chief objectives in Italy.

The promulgation of the Constitution of Melfi in 1231 was the fruition of the emperor's efforts at reestablishing royal power in the *Regno* in the 1220's, and the foundation of a much more systematic rationalization of state authority developed in the next two decades. With the aid of legal experts such as Archbishop James of Capua, Roffredus de Epiphaniis of Benevento, and above all Piero della Vigna, Frederick enunciated in fact what later lawyers would proclaim in theory: the concept of a king as *imperator in regno suo*. Drawing on Roman law, canon law, and the various legal traditions of the *Regno,* the Constitutions of Melfi set forth a program for a highly centralized monarchy, a "model state" of the Middle Ages. The three books of *Liber Augustalis,* as these laws are often called by modern scholars, range in detail over the origins of royal authority, the administration of justice, the functions of royal officials, and relations of the crown with various classes of subjects. Frederick was not content with the Norman approach to government through traditional structures. The Constitutions of Melfi greatly strengthened the effectiveness of the curia regis by detailing the administrative responsibilities of crown officials at each level to the central bureaucracy. Most importantly, Frederick attempted to break through the network of local authorities impeding effective royal administration. He provided that no count, baron, or prelate could serve as justiciar in his own lands. He also continued those policies initiated at Capua in 1220 to ensure the integrity of the royal demesne. The absence of evidence of large alienations of crown lands under Frederick confirms the importance of this policy to his concept of government.

Scholars seeking reference points by which to understand better the Sicilian monarchy of Frederick II have often pointed to the citation of Roman legal formulations in the Constitutions of Melfi or to Byzantine influences on the trappings of the Sicilian monarchy. Some have argued that Byzantine elements were important in structuring royal monopolies and crafts in the kingdom. Frederick's relations with the nobility have drawn the label "antifeudal." Special stress has been placed on the "modernity" of his state. As is often the case, none of these suggestions is without foundation, yet they seem to miss essential elements of the Frederician monarchy.

Frederick's work rests on a firm Norman foundation but marks a considerable advance on the goals of even a Roger II. Moreover, that Norman foundation, as we have seen, was certainly no replication of feudal Normandy in the south. The problem for Frederick, as for Roger, was one of unifying heterogeneity. Moving beyond his Norman grandfather, Frederick appealed to both Roman law and divine authority to justify his rule. But he did not stop there. Throughout his legislation, he appealed also to the authority of his Norman predecessors. All in all, *Liber augustalis* aimed at presenting a compelling case for strong monarchy to all the varied groups in the kingdom. The presence of arguments drawn from such varied sources reflects the greater sophistication of legal studies in Frederick's age. Yet, as in Roger's day, the crown was still searching for an effective idiom by which to communicate the basis of its authority to its subjects. With Frederick, the element that emerged as central stemmed immediately from his imperial status. The whole machinery of his government was harnessed to the task of identifying his kingly power in Sicily with his imperial role. The symbols of this effort are multiple. In art, his image as heir of the Romans appeared on the triumphal arch at Capua and adorned his coinage, especially the beautiful gold *augustalis,* whose very name conjured up its imperial meaning. The Constitutions themselves were termed *augustales* in early manuscripts. The concept of imperial authority, more particularly, of antique Roman power, was grafted onto the Norman monarchy of the south. During the later 1230's and the 1240's, Frederick's imperial vision came to dominate the interests of his Sicilian monarchy.

The Kingdom of Sicily provided the resources in men and money to enable him to launch his imperial program. It was there that he possessed the power that might lead to victory over the Lombard communes of northern Italy and a restoration of the *regnum italicum* of Charlemagne. This was the message of the Diet of Piacenza in 1236. In the words of Ernesto Pontieri, Frederick's policy was directed "not from the empire, . . . towards the *Regno* . . . but from the *Regno* towards the empire." But even with the financial and military resources of the Kingdom of Sicily behind him, Frederick was unable to deal a decisive blow to the aspirations of the Lombards. Following his victories at Vicenza and Cortenuova in 1236 and 1237, Frederick had to secure additional support from the *Regno* in the form of an unusually large *collecta,* the extraordinary aid (tax) that he had turned into a virtually annual levy ever since 1229. Flushed with victory, he rejected Milanese terms for a favorable peace and as a result consolidated his opposition, culminating in a renewal of the Lombard League and the entry of Genoa, Venice, and the papacy into the conflict. In 1239, Gregory IX excommunicated Frederick. The ensuing propaganda campaign both drew on and fed the intense divisions within Latin Christendom in the early thirteenth century. Following Gregory's death in 1241, Frederick worked to secure the election of a more sympathetic pope. It was not until 2 June 1243 that the cardinals were able finally to bring the vacancy to an end with the election of Sinibaldo Fieschi of Genoa as Pope Innocent IV. An eminent jurist, Innocent continued the policies of Gregory IX, especially the effort, aborted by Frederick's capture of some of the prelates, to hold a council of the church. Forced to flee Italy because of the threat from Frederick, Innocent summoned the council to meet in Lyons in the summer of 1245. There he condemned and deposed the emperor, who complained bitterly that he had not received a fair hearing. In 1248, Frederick suffered a major defeat outside Parma. Confronted with conspiracies even in his own court—he accused Piero della Vigna of treason—he was unable to launch a major offensive prior to his death on 13 December 1250 at Ferentino in Apulia.

ANGEVIN SICILY

Following the death of Frederick II, the papacy worked to ensure that the Kingdom of Sicily would no longer remain in the hands of the Hohenstaufen. The popes sought first the support of Henry III of England by naming his son Edmund to take the throne and, when that failed, turned to Charles of Anjou, the brother of King Louis IX of France. The heirs of Frederick II fought to maintain their hold on the Kingdom of Sicily. After the death of Frederick's son Conrad IV (1254), his natural son, Manfred, claimed the Sicilian crown and by 1257 was in complete control. He was crowned in Palermo on 10 August 1258. During the next few years, Manfred pursued an aggressive foreign policy, aimed chiefly against the Guelfs of northern Italy. But, in 1265, Charles of Anjou embarked for Italy. Soon Manfred's support in the *Regno* began to melt away. Manfred himself fell in battle at Benevento on 26 February 1266. The triumph of Charles of Anjou meant the end of Hohenstaufen rule in Italy, to which the execution of Frederick's grandson, Conradin, at Naples in 1268 was mere postscript.

Charles of Anjou became king of Sicily chiefly because of the determination of the papacy to prevent any future recurrence of a Sicilian-imperial nexus. The impact of this policy on the future of Italy was revolutionary in that it greatly increased French influence in Italy at the expense of the empire. Although Charles had reassured the papacy that he would not pursue the policies of Frederick II, he quickly became the leader of the Guelfs in central and northern Italy and set out to achieve a position of dominance in Mediterranean affairs. He soon realized the value and importance of the administrative, fiscal, and judicial machinery of Frederick's government in the *Regno* and, while he played down those claims offensive to the church, preserved intact the legislation of the Hohenstaufen. But he faced the problem of rewarding his followers. Since the barons of the kingdom had in considerable numbers abandoned the cause of Manfred, Charles had little choice but to carve new fiefs out of the royal demesne, even alienating some of the principal towns of the kingdom to his supporters in a major break with Norman-Swabian policy. Charles also exempted the churches from the *collecta,* which, despite his promise to the papacy, he maintained as a regular source of taxes. He also preferred the mainland to Sicily and made his base of operations Naples rather than Palermo. On balance, Charles was a strong and effective ruler, though his alienations of royal demesne strengthened the aristocracy at the expense of the monarchy.

Charles's position in southern Italy made him a logical figure to revive the flagging interests of the Latins in the Byzantine Empire. The Latin Empire of Constantinople, created as a result of the Fourth Crusade in 1204, had lost out to the Byzantines under Emperor Michael VIII Palaiologos in 1261. But Charles's efforts to dominate Mediterranean politics were continually frustrated. In 1270 he joined his brother Louis IX of France in a crusade against Tunis, but Louis died and Charles gained little. With the accession of Pope Gregory X and the official reunion of the Latin and Greek churches at the Second Council of Lyons in 1274, he was temporarily checked in his Byzantine policy. Finally, when the reunion of the churches broke down, Charles gained the support of Pope Martin IV for his invasion of Byzantium. He was thwarted, however, by the overwhelming disaster of the loss of the island of Sicily following the Sicilian Vespers of 1282.

The Vespers, which took its name from an incident on 30 March 1282 in which a Sicilian woman was insulted by a French soldier outside the church of S. Spirito in Palermo, was fueled by conspiracies hatched by Michael Palaiologos and Pedro III of Aragon. Michael furnished financial aid to Sicilian dissidents, while Pedro, whose wife, Constance, was the daughter of Manfred, put himself forth as the heir of the Hohenstaufen. As a result of the Vespers, the Sicilians drove the Angevins from the island and ultimately invited Pedro to be king.

Charles I died in 1285, leaving his son Charles II (*r.* 1285–1309) the task of recovering the island of Sicily. His efforts failed, and for more than a century thereafter the mainland and island kingdom remained separate, the former under Angevin and the latter under Aragonese rule.

The Angevins of Naples became deeply enmeshed in the affairs of Hungary through the marriage of Charles II to Maria, daughter of King Stephen V, and of Charles's sister to the heir to the throne. This Hungarian connection led to serious conflicts between the Neapolitan and Hungarian branches of the family in the fourteenth and early fifteenth centuries and certainly contributed to the eventual overthrow of the dynasty by Alfonso of Aragon in 1443. However, under Charles II and his son Robert (1309–1343), the Angevins flourished in Naples, creating there a royal capital with palaces and churches to reflect the new status of the city. Although Charles II was forced to recognize Frederick II of Aragon as king of Sicily (Trinacria) by the Treaty of Caltabellota in August 1302, Robert renewed the war in 1312 and managed to maintain a foothold in Sicily throughout his reign. But under Robert's successor and granddaughter, Joanna I (1343–1382), the conflict between the Hungarian and Neapolitan branches of the Angevins became a blood feud, ending in the murder of the queen. Charles III (1382–1386) and Ladislas (1386–1414) continued to pursue the dynastic ambitions of their family in Hungary, but the growing weakness of the crown gave an opportunity to the Neapolitan barons to assert their considerable power. Ladislas' sister, Joanna II (1414–1435), was for a time held captive by some of her nobles and even turned to Alfonso of Aragon for aid against her numerous opponents. In 1443 Alfonso succeeded in joining Naples to his island kingdom.

SICILY AND THE ARAGONESE

Sicily also had a turbulent history under the successors of Pedro of Aragon. The Aragonese succession had received overwhelming support from influential segments of the Sicilian nobility, but this did not long endure. Pedro's successor, James the Conqueror of Aragon, ruled Sicily through a viceroy in the person of his younger brother, Frederick. James had little concern for his Sicilian possession and even indicated his willingness to return the island to the Angevins if he received recompense. But Frederick was enamoured with Sicily and its Hohenstaufen heritage. He summoned a parliament in 1295 to support his bid for the crown. Crowned in 1926, Frederick II of Aragon had to face not merely the Angevins but also his brother James. However, he obtained the Peace of Caltabellota (1302), which acknowledged him as "king of Trinacria." This truce lasted only until 1312, when the war was renewed and continued under his successor, Frederick III, to 1373.

The Sicilian crown was forced to make large concessions to the nobility under Frederick II and his son. When Frederick III died in 1377, he was succeeded by his son-in-law, Martín of Aragon, who made good his claim to the throne with support from Spain. This reliance on Spain and on Spanish nobles for support not only drew Sicily more closely into the Spanish orbit but also led to the increased intrusion of the Spanish nobles into Sicily. Under Alfonso of Aragon, this dominance was completed. During his reign, the government of Sicily was thoroughly reformed. In 1443 he annexed the kingdom of Naples, restoring the two Sicilies to a united Aragonese rule. Alfonso represented the vigorous energies of the emerging power of Spain, harnessing the fiscal and military resources of Naples and Sicily to his Mediterranean vision.

CULTURAL ACHIEVEMENTS

The cultural life of the Kingdom of Sicily in the Middle Ages draws special meaning from its location on the southern frontier of Europe. Only the most superficial observer would view the emergence of the kingdom in the twelfth century, contemporary with the intellectual revival of Western Europe, as a mere coincidence. While the *Regno* did not play so prominent a role as Spain in the transmission of Greek and Arabic learning to the West, its contribution should not be minimized. From the foundation of the monarchy, the royal court served as the focal point of intellectual life and attracted Arab and Greek, as well as Latin, scholars. As early as 1109, the Englishman Adelard of Bath, the translator of Euclid and of the astronomical tables of al-Khwārizmī, visited Sicily. Under Roger II, al-Idrīsī composed his geography and dedicated it to that king. During the 1150's, there were translations of Euclid's *Optics* and Aristotle's treatises on logic. The emir Eugenius and Henricus Aristippus were responsible for a number of translations from Greek and Arabic, including the *Meno* and *Phaedo* of Plato and Ptolemy's *Almagest.*

The court of Emperor Frederick II benefited from his personal intellectual interests. He supported the work of Michael Scot, whose translation of Aristotle's *History of Animals* served his own interest in falconry, which found expression in his famous work, *De arte venandi cum avibus* (On the art of hunting with birds), a scientific treatise that drew on experience and observation as well as the works of earlier authorities. He was also interested in mathematics and had personal contacts with Leonardo Fibonacci of Pisa, author of a treatise on the abacus. He addressed philosophical questions to Muslim scholars, receiving a reply from the learned Ibn Sabin. His Constitutions of Melfi were translated into Greek in his lifetime. The leading figure in the Aristotelian revival of the thirteenth century, the Dominican Thomas Aquinas, was a subject of Frederick and received part of his education at Naples. In the fourteenth century, however, this aspect of the cultural role of the *Regno* waned. Moreover, the south played only a minor role in the humanistic and literary movements of the fifteenth century and their efforts to recover the classics of antiquity.

In 1224, Frederick II founded the University of Naples for the specific purpose of meeting the need of the *Regno* for an educated class. The early years of the university were troubled, especially due to Frederick's wars. The university may have received students as a result of Frederick's summoning of his subjects from Bologna to study at Naples, but it did not firmly establish its position as the intellectual center of the kingdom until the Angevin period. Frederick had been concerned to promote Naples as a center for legal studies, but he also favored the study of medicine. It was in these areas that the university made its reputation.

Frederick's interest in law, so evident in his own legislation, caused him to attract such figures as Piero della Vigna and Roffredus de Epiphaniis of Benevento to his court. Under the Angevins, a strong tradition of legal commentary developed in the work of Marinus da Caramanica, Andreas de Isernia, and Bartolomeo di Capua. In Lucas de Penna, Naples produced one of the leading postglossators of the fourteenth century, ranking with Bartolo da Sassoferrato among the legal scholars of that age. It is a mark of Neapolitan legal studies that they were deeply involved with the laws and customs of the *Regno*.

Medical education in the south of Italy had achieved an international reputation at Salerno even before the founding of the Kingdom of Sicily. Already in the eleventh century, Constantine the African, later a monk at Monte Cassino, was working in Salerno. In the twelfth century, Salerno was the chief center of medical education in Europe, and numerous translations of Greek and Arabic medical writings were made there. The Constitutions of Melfi reveal a special concern of the monarchy with the problems of public health. A law of Roger II, based on a Byzantine model, regulated the licensing and examination of physicians. Legislation of Frederick II established Naples and Salerno as centers for the study of medicine and put control of examinations into the hands of medical experts. Other laws of Frederick dealt with air and water pollution and regulated the preparation of medicines and the sale of foodstuffs. Later commentators lamented the ineffectiveness of this farsighted legislation. In the fourteenth century, Naples remained the center of medical study in the kingdom after the decline of Salerno.

The *Regno* produced no single literary figure of international repute in our period, though Boccaccio did spend some time in Naples, but it did make notable contributions to various branches of literature. Dante was the first to point to the importance of the Sicilian style of poetry in the development of the *dolce stil nuovo*. Likewise, the writing of Greek poetry continued well into the thirteenth century. Historical writing in both Latin and the vernacular flourished, especially under the Normans and in the early thirteenth century. But it is probably stating the obvious to say that the major cultural achievements of the *Regno* were in the realm of art and architecture. In these fields, no later works can really surpass the magnificent works of the Norman period, the *capella regia* and the Martorana from the period of Roger II, the royal monastery of Monreale, and the cathedrals of Palermo and Cefalù. These reveal the fusion of Byzantine and Western elements characteristic of the Norman age. Aside from the strong classical elements in the art of Frederick II, we should mention his building of castles, especially in Apulia. The Angevin period witnessed the making of the royal capital at Naples. Under Robert I, especially, the influence of Tuscan art was most pronounced, notably in Giotto's frescoes for the royal convent church of S. Chiara. As northern Italy became more and more the center of art and humanism, the Neapolitan court took on the luster of many of the princely courts of that region. This development was encouraged under Alfonso I of Aragon and his successors at Naples in the fifteenth century.

SOCIAL AND ECONOMIC DEVELOPMENTS

The social and economic development of southern Italy and Sicily in the Middle Ages presents the picture of a primarily agrarian region closely tied to the commercial and industrial growth of other areas. Although reasonably well-endowed with seaports, the Kingdom of Sicily lacked access to European markets available to northern Italian cities or those of the western Mediterranean. While cities like Amalfi and Bari had prospered in the pre-Norman period, they were outdistanced and even deprived of their position by the more aggressive northerners. Likewise, whatever commercial value had been attached to Messina, Palermo, and Syracuse under Muslim rule underwent drastic changes in the course of the twelfth century. The real wealth of the *Regno* was in its lands and the seas around them, and it was these, along with its important geographical location, that attracted conquerors.

The demographic history of the kingdom between the twelfth and the fifteenth century has been but little studied. Denis Mack Smith suggests that the population of Sicily around 1500, that is, in the aftermath of the plagues of the fourteenth century, was less than one million. It is possible that the total population of the mainland was about twice that figure. Previous to the Black Death (1347), there is no solid evidence for the size of the population. In all probability, however, and this receives some confirmation from the sources, there was constant growth down to the late thirteenth or early fourteenth century. True, some parts of Sicily were depopulated following the Norman conquest, but these were colonized from the mainland through the efforts of the crown. It was not until the disasters of the fourteenth century that we meet evidence of severe population decline. Thereafter, it would appear that the recovery was sluggish for a considerable period of time but had commenced before 1500.

The dominant class in the kingdom was the nobility. Under the Normans and Hohenstaufen, the crown worked assiduously to ensure that the feudal aristocracy rendered those services they owed for their fiefs. Although baronial rebellions occurred under most of the rulers of this period, the balance of power remained with the monarchy throughout the thirteenth century. On both the mainland and the island, however, the nobility emerged in dominant roles during the second half of the fourteenth century. Sharing this position of dominance with the nobility were the churches and monasteries of the kingdom. The Normans had been generous in their endowments and these were increased under the Angevins. By the end of our period, these groups rather than the crown were the largest landholders of the kingdom. The royal demesne, jealously guarded by the Normans and Hohenstaufen, had been alienated to successive waves of foreign aristocrats. There can be little doubt that demographic changes induced by the plagues of the fourteenth century also stimulated increased concentration of wealth in the hands of the aristocracy.

The history of southern Italian agriculture is bound in its beginnings to the practices of the Byzantines, Moslems, and Lombards who were settled on the land. From the time of the Norman conquest, the *Catalogus baronum* confirms the tendency of the Normans to concentrate their numbers in the richest agricultural areas. Certain crops, especially grain, were important export commodities. Wine, cheese, and oil were sent northward to feed the growing urban populations of Venice, Pisa, and Genoa. Much agricultural produce also went to Muslim North Africa in return for gold. But control of the sale of agrarian surpluses of the south was largely in foreign hands. During the twelfth century, Genoa, Pisa, and Venice held most of this trade. During the "Time of Trouble" the Genoese controlled a large part of eastern Sicily along with the port of Syracuse. The wars of Emperor Frederick II interrupted this trade, and Charles of Anjou transferred his favor to the merchants of Tuscany, who in the fourteenth century dominated the fiscal and commercial life of the Neapolitan kingdom. Sicily was drawn into the orbit of the Catalan merchants after the Vespers.

The major industry of the kingdom was the production of cloth, though mostly for domestic consumption. The famed silkworks of Palermo, founded under Roger II, was a palace industry. Some especially fine woolens were exported and gained an international reputation, but the quantity was small. On a much larger scale was the mining of alum, partially to meet the needs of the domestic cloth industry, but more for export to the north as well as to Africa. Other minerals and ores, such as iron, did not provide for the needs of the kingdom.

Urban life was bound up more with the court, the landed aristocracy in search of good living, foreign merchants, and the poor, than with a thriving class of native traders. The *Regno* produced a middle class of lawyers and bureaucrats but insufficient numbers of businessmen and merchants. The cities were unable to mount a significant enough pressure to gain much in the way of political autonomy. Messina took the lead, but few followed. As the fifteenth century dawned, aristocratic dominance of the land was finding its expression in the Renaissance at the royal court in Naples and at lesser courts in other cities of the kingdom.

BIBLIOGRAPHY

General works. Ferdinand Chalandon, *Histoire de la domination normande en Italie et en Sicile,* 2 vols. (1907, repr. 1960); Willy Cohn, *Das Zeitalter der Hohenstaufen in Sizilien* (1971); Benedetto Croce, *History of the Kingdom of Naples* (1970); David C. Douglas, *The Norman Achievement: 1050–1100* (1969), and *The Norman Fate: 1100–1154* (1976); Karl Hampe, *Germany under the Salian and Hohenstaufen Emperors,* Ralph Bennett, trans. (1974); Édouard Jordan, *Les origines de la domination angevine en Italie,* 2 vols. (1909, repr. 1960); Émile G. Léonard, *Les Angevins de Naples* (1954); Raffaello Morghen, *L'età degli svevi in Italia* (1974); Denis Mack Smith, *A History of Sicily,* 2 vols. (1968); Francesco de Stefano, *Storia della Sicilia dal secolo XI al XIX* (1948); Salvatore Tramontana, *Mezzogiorno normanno e svevo* (1972).

Special studies. David Abulafia, *The Two Italies: Economic Relations Between the Norman Kingdom of Sicily and the Northern Communes* (1977); Michele Amari, *La guerra del Vespro Siciliano,* 2 vols. in 3 (1969); Erich Caspar, *Roger II. (1101–1154) und die Gründung der normannisch-sicilischen Monarchie* (1963); H. E. J. Cowdrey, *The Age of Abbot Desiderius: Monte Cassino, the Papacy, and the Normans in the Eleventh and Early Twelfth Centuries* (1983); Jozsef Deér, *Papsttum und Normannen* (1972); Hermann Dilcher, *Die sizilische Gesetzgebung Kaiser Friedrichs II: Quellen der Konstitutionen von Melfi und Ihrer Novellen* (1975); Deno J. Geanakoplos, *Emperor Michael Palaeologus and the West: 1258–1282* (1959); Charles H. Haskins, *Studies in the History of Mediaeval Science* (1924), and *Studies in Mediaeval Culture* (1958); Wilhelm E. Heupel, *Der sizilische Grosshof unter Kaiser Friedrich II* (1940, repr. 1952); Jean A. Huillard-Bréholles, *Vie et correspondance de Pierre de la Vigne* (1865, repr. 1966); Evelyn Jamison, "The Norman Administration of Apulia and Capua," in *Papers of the British School at Rome,* **6** (1913), and *Admiral Eugenius of Sicily* (1957); Norbert Kamp, *Kirche and Monarchie im staufischen Konigreiche Sizilien,* 4 vols. (1973–); Ernst Kantorowicz, *Frederick the Second,* E. O. Lorimer, trans. (1957), *The King's Two Bodies* (1957), and *Selected Studies* (1965); Ernst Kitzinger, *The Art of Byzantium and the Medieval West* (1976); G. A. Loud, *Church and Society in the Norman Principality of Capua: 1058–1197* (1985); Erich Maschke, "Die Wirtschaftspolitik Kaiser Friedrichs II. im Königreich Sizilien," in *Vierteljahrschrift für Sozial- und Wirtschaftsgeschichte,* **53** (1966); Enrico Mazzarese Fardella, *I feudi comitali di Sicilia dai normanni agli Aragones* (1974); Léon-Robert Ménager, "L'institution monarchique dans les états normands d'Italie: Contribution à l'étude du pouvoir royal dans les principautés occidentales: aux XIe–XIIe siècles," in *Cahiers de civilisation médiévale,* **2** (1959), and "La législation sud-italienne sous la domination normande," in *Centro italiano di studi sull'alto medioevo* (1969); Ernesto Pontieri, *Ricerche sulla crisi della monarchia siciliana nel secolo XIII,* 3rd ed. (1958); James M. Powell, "Medieval Monarchy and Trade: The Economic Policy of Frederick II in the Kingdom of Sicily," in *Studi medievali,* 3rd ser., **2** (1962), "Honorius III and the Leadership of the Crusade," in *Catholic Historical Review,* **63** (1967), "Greco-Arabic Influences on the Public Health Legislation in the Constitutions of Melfi," in *Archivio storico Pugliese,* **31** (1978), and *idem,* trans. and ed., *The Liber Augustalis; or, Constitutions of Melfi* (1971); Alan Ryder, *The Kingdom of Naples Under Alfonso the Magnanimous* (1976); Antonio de Stefano, *L'idea imperiale di Federico II* (1927), and *La cultura alla corte di Federico II imperatore* (1950); Hiroshi Takayama, "The Financial and Administrative Organization of the Norman Kingdom of Sicily," in *Viator,* **16** (1985); Theodor Toeche-Mittler, *Kaiser Heinrich VI* (1867); Thomas C. Van Cleve, *Markward of Anweiler and the Sicilian Regency* (1937), and *The Emperor Frederick II of Hohenstaufen* (1972); Giovanni de Vergottini, *Studi sulla legislazione imperiale di Federico II in Italia* (1952); Helene Wieruszowski, *Politics and Culture in Medieval Spain and Italy* (1971); Lynn T. White, *Latin Monasticism in Norman Sicily* (1938); Georges Yver, *Le commerce et les marchands dans l'Italie meridionale au XIIIe et au XIVe siècle* (1903).

JAMES M. POWELL

[See also **Angevins; Bari; Germany, 1137-1254; Guelfs and Ghibellines; Hohenstaufen Dynasty; Italian Literature: Lyric Poetry; Italy, Byzantine Areas of; Latin Empire of Constantinople; Lombard League; Melfi, Con-**

stitutions of; Medicine, Schools of; Monte Cassino; Naples; Normans and Normandy; Palermo; Papal States; Sicilian Vespers; and individual personalities.]

SIDONIUS APOLLINARIS (*ca.* 432–*ca.* 485), Gallic writer and bishop of Clermont-Ferrand. Born to one of the most noble families in Gaul, his full name was Gaius Sollius Apollinaris Sidonius. Both his grandfather, also named Apollinaris, and his father had held the office of praetorian prefect of Gaul. In 452, Sidonius married Papianilla, daughter of the Arvernian senator Eparchius Avitus, the Roman emperor of 455–456. Sidonius began his public career as a tribune and notary under Avitus and then was made a count by the emperor Majorian (457–461). In 468, after a period of retirement, he was named prefect of Rome by the emperor Anthemius. After his return to Gaul, about a year later, Sidonius was chosen as bishop of Clermont-Ferrand and was faced immediately with the responsibility of defending the city against the Visigoths. He did this successfully, with the aid of his brother-in-law Ecdicius, until 475, when the emperor Nepos ceded the Auvergne to the Goths. For most of the next two years he was in exile as punishment for his pro-Roman activities, but ultimately the Visigothic king Euric allowed him to return to Clermont, where he died around 485 and soon after was included among the saints.

Sidonius was the most famous Gallic litterateur of his time. His twenty-four extant poems, published in 468, include three panegyrics, honoring the emperors Avitus, Majorian, and Anthemius, which are as noteworthy for their displays of schoolboy erudition as for their worth as historical sources. More valuable is his collection of 148 extant letters, modeled on those of Pliny and Symmachus, in nine books. His correspondents include his relatives, high-ranking laymen, and bishops from throughout Gaul. Published from around 470, the letters provide a reliable eyewitness account of the political developments and, in particular, of the state of Gallo-Roman aristocratic society and culture at the time when Gaul was undergoing the final phase of its transition from Roman to barbarian rule. They portray the continuing sense of a shared cultural heritage felt by educated Gauls at the very time they were coming under Germanic rule.

Sidonius' literary style, characterized by extensive use of sometimes strained antithesis, alliteration, and neat turns of phrase, was the usual product of the rhetorical schools of the day and was extremely popular. He was especially skilled at description, such as that of his estate, Avitacum, and of the court of the Visigothic king Theodoric, and at the telling of anecdotes, such as his account of a banquet given by the emperor Majorian at Arles in 461. Works of Sidonius that no longer survive include collections of his masses and epigrams and an unfinished biography of St. Anianus of Orléans.

Sidonius left a son, Apollinaris, and three daughters, Alcima, Severiana, and Roscia. Apollinaris fought on the side of the Visigoths against the Franks at Vouillé in 507 and in 515 was chosen as bishop of Clermont, although he died a few months later. By the end of the sixth century the family had vanished, providing a striking example of the inability of the most important fifth-century Gallo-Roman families to survive in barbarian Gaul.

BIBLIOGRAPHY

William B. Anderson, trans., *Sidonius Apollinaris: Poems and Letters,* 2 vols. (1936, 1965); *Clavis patrum latinorum,* 2nd ed. (1962), nos. 986–987a; Ormonde Dalton, ed. and trans., *The Letters of Sidonius,* 2 vols. (1915); Eleanor S. Duckett, *Latin Writers of the Fifth Century* (1930), 296–327; André Loyen, *Sidoine Apollinaire et l'esprit précieux en Gaule aux derniers jours de l'empire* (1943), and *idem,* ed., *Sidoine Apollinaire,* I, *Poemes* (1960), and *Sidoine Apollinaire,* II, III, *Lettres* (1970); M. Schanz, Carl Hosius, and Gustav Krüger, *Geschichte der römischen Litteratur,* IV, pt. 2 (1920), 43–55; Sidonius Apollinaris, "Carmina" and "Epistulae," in *Monumenta Germaniae historica: Auctores antiquissimi,* VIII (1887), 1–264; Courtenay E. Stevens, *Sidonius Apollinaris and His Age* (1933).

RALPH WHITNEY MATHISEN

[See also **Latin Literature.**]

SIEGFRIED. See **Sigurd.**

SIENA is a Tuscan hill town located about 1,000 feet (305 meters) above sea level on a westward spur of the Chiana mountain range. This beautiful site was flawed by a water supply inadequate for industry or navigation. The city itself stretches along three ridges and is shaped in the form of an inverted Y. The earliest settlement probably was in the southwestern portion of the town that came to be known as the *Terzo* (third) of Città (of the city).

Some thirty miles (48 kilometers) north the great commune of Florence bestrides the Arno River. Northeast beyond the Valdichiana lies Siena's age-old rival, Arezzo. Cortona, Chiusi, and Orvieto stretch across a north-south line at Siena's eastern border. To the west is the hill town of Volterra, and beyond, some forty miles (64 kilometers) from Siena, is the Tyrrhenian coast. The great expanse of the Tuscan Maremma lies toward the south and west, rich in minerals and pasturelands, but during the Middle Ages underpopulated and plagued by malaria.

EARLY HISTORY

Little is known of Siena's early history. Records are woefully scarce until the twelfth century. There may have been an Etruscan community in the vicinity of the medieval town. There was a Roman Siena, but even its precise location is in doubt.

When Roman Siena became Christian is uncertain. Medieval legend would trace it to the preaching of a Roman noble, Ansano, martyred during the persecution of Diocletian (*r.* 284–305). No written record of St. Ansano exists prior to the thirteenth century; but what is significant is that the medieval Sienese believed firmly in his ministry and martyrdom. Similarly, more important than any possible historical roots tying medieval to Roman Siena is the medieval Sienese belief in legends that linked them to the greatness of ancient Rome. Some Sienese traced their city's foundation to Senius and Ascius, sons of Remus, allowing Siena to share in the tradition of the she-wolf and her cubs. They also tied the emblem of the medieval commune, a black and white shield called the *balzana,* to these Roman legends.

Sienese devotion to St. Ansano has been used to explain a bitter dispute over the diocesan boundaries of Siena and Arezzo that raged from about the eighth to the twelfth century. Allegedly, the Aretine bishop had claimed the territory wherein the revered saint lay buried.

The poorly recorded controversy does highlight the prominent role played by the bishop of Siena in the political development of the early medieval town. In the ninth and tenth centuries he was far more influential in the town's affairs than were the imperial Carolingian counts. Even in the early twelfth century the nascent Sienese commune acted through the instrumentality of its bishop.

DEVELOPMENT OF THE COMMUNE

The Sienese succeeded in maintaining their loyalty to both their bishop and their emperor during the investiture controversy and throughout much of the late eleventh and early twelfth centuries. Only in 1167, during the lengthy struggles between the Hohenstaufen emperor Frederick I Barbarossa and the Sienese pope Alexander III, did the commune of Siena, like many others, avail itself of that conflict to oust its bishop and move rapidly toward the creation of a purely lay commune headed by its consuls, a magistracy that can be dated from at least 1156. Although Siena was not consistently loyal to the emperor, in 1185 it profited from his need for stability to obtain an imperial diploma that granted it important privileges, including the rights to elect communal consuls and to coin money.

Podestarile government. By the end of the twelfth century, like neighboring communes, Siena began to move from a consular to a podestarile regime. At first the podesta served alongside of or alternated with the consuls as the commune's highest magistrate, and he served as its chief military commander. Until the position became regularized and restricted to non-Sienese, citizens of Siena alternated in office with foreign podestas, men chosen because they would not be party to internal factionalism and family rivalries.

The twelfth- and early-thirteenth-century commune was led by urbanized members of the middle and lower ranks of the Tuscan nobility, men whose roots were to be found in the Sienese countryside. These urban nobles still maintained connections with their rural origins and continued to hold lands, castles, and villages in the dependent Sienese state, or *contado.* Gradually they came to be distinguished from the nonurbanized nobility by their slightly less bellicose style and by their involvement in commerce, banking, and industry. Those business activities also rapidly produced a number of wealthy burgers of non-noble origin who came to share political power with the urbanized nobility during the course of the thirteenth century. This arrangement is most clearly seen in the establishment of the government of the so-called Twenty-four Priors (*ca.* 1236–1271).

During these years of Ghibelline (or pro-imperial) domination, the organization of the *Popolo,* headed by the "captain of the people," succeeded in fusing with the commune and in gaining temporary ascendancy over it. That *Popolo,* largely a middle class of artisans whose strength lay in the force of numbers and in their compact and disciplined organization, gradually was taken over and replaced by the *popolo grasso* (fat people) of later years, the merchants, bankers, and industrialists, who during the course of the late thirteenth century would gain control of the commune itself.

Commerce and banking. The success of the Sienese in commerce and banking was already evident in the 1220's, as the new company of the Bonsignori became major bankers for the papacy. In ensuing decades Sienese, noble and nonnoble both, were prominent throughout Western Europe, whether at the French fairs of Champagne or the English court and countryside of Henry III (*r.* 1216–1272). The reasons for this rapid ascendancy remain largely unknown. Historians have long given much weight to Siena's location on the Via Francigena or Romea, a principal route from France to Rome. But the question arises as to why companies formed by citizens of other towns along the route, towns such as Viterbo, were not equally successful.

Guelf and Ghibelline rivalry. At least a century prior to this period of Sienese economic greatness, the city already had become embroiled in a rivalry that would have a major impact on all aspects of its foreign policy and would end only in the mid sixteenth century: the struggle with Florence. The generally Guelf, or pro-papal, diplomatic and military stance of its northern neighbor contributed to Siena's Ghibellinism. The rapid hegemony that Florence obtained over much of northern Tuscany, together with the presence of Volterra to the west and Arezzo to the east of Siena, early made Siena's southern regions and the Maremma the major object of Sienese expansion. These lands were wilder and less populated than the economically and politically more valuable portions of Tuscany open to Florentine control, and Siena's lack of a major source of water condemned it to lag industrially behind the increasingly populous and industrialized "city of the lily."

The rivalry with Florence lent impetus to the first major expansion of Siena into the Maremma in the 1140's. A seesaw struggle between the two cities continued, with interruptions, truces, and temporary alliances, for more than a century until 1260. That year Ghibelline Siena, with the aid of imperial troops then in the city, won what would be its greatest military victory over Florence: the Battle of Montaperti. On the eve of that conflict the Sienese first dedicated their city to the Virgin. They added the words "city of the Virgin" to a new silver coinage. This was to remain the one loyalty from which the Sienese never swerved, regardless of changes of regime or of political and diplomatic alliances.

The Ghibelline victory was short-lived, however. Manfred, natural son and heir of the Hohenstaufen emperor Frederick II (*d.* 1250), met defeat and death at Benevento in 1266. The papal champion Charles of Anjou was victorious at Tagliacozzo in 1268, and he executed the young Conradin, grandson of the late emperor. In 1269 Siena itself bowed to Florence at Colle di Val d'Elsa.

The Ghibelline epoch drew to a close. Papal enmity was added to Florentine military and economic pressure: the excommunication of Sienese public officials, loss of papal banking business, and withdrawal of ecclesiastical support against the recalcitrant debtors of Sienese companies. Major noble families deeply engaged in banking and commerce converted to Guelfism, among them the Tolomei, the Piccolomini, the immensely wealthy Salimbeni, and the Bonsignori (Buonsignori), whose bank of the *Gran Tavola* ("great table") still ranked among the greatest in Europe. Gradually, Guelfs gained the upper hand within the city, as they headed a changing group of signories or highest magistracies. But unlike Florence, where Guelfism coincided with some of the commune's greatest military and diplomatic successes, in Siena Guelfism never became a consuming internal political attachment. Nor did the "city of the Virgin" witness the creation of an independent Guelf party of any political significance. Siena's Guelfism, increasingly evident from the 1280's on, was imposed by external necessities and essentially consisted of the commune's new policy of alliance with, though not subservience to, Florence—by then the self-proclaimed champion of Guelfism par excellence.

Government of the Nine. The new state of affairs became embodied in a political regime that guided Siena's destinies for nearly seven decades (1287–1355): the Nine Governors and Defenders of the Commune and the People of Siena, or simply the Nine. A mixed burgher and noble oligarchy, it included many bankers and international merchants and required at least a pro forma Guelf allegiance. The Nine weathered numerous storms, including invading imperial armies of Henry VII

(1310–1313), the troops of the lord of Lucca, Gastruccio Castracani (*d.* 1328), financial crises, famines, onslaughts by some of the first of the *condottieri* (mercenary military commanders), especially the Provençal Fra Moriale (1354), and the horrors of the Black Death (1348). Only in 1355 did the regime collapse in a revolution that broke out during a visit to the city by the emperor-elect Charles IV.

Like other communes, from 1277 Siena had listed by name and excluded from its highest magistracy the most factious and bellicose of the urban noble families: the magnates. Statutory exclusion from the Nine, never completely enforced, did not prevent Sienese magnates from exercising great political power. Their ability to do so in part restrained them from making many serious attempts to overthrow the regime. Magnates headed diplomatic missions and military contingents and held key posts in every major communal office other than the Nine. That they did not take over the city also was due to the vigilance of others and to jealousies among the magnate families.

The governmental style of the Nine focused less on conscious innovation than on hard work, dedication to the essential functioning and details of public administration, and pragmatic experimentation. The regime developed, stabilized, and regularized many of Siena's most important governmental institutions and policies. These included expansion into and development of the *contado* (the rural area), land reclamation, the provisioning of the city, and reprisal and bankruptcy legislation. The last was necessitated particularly by the failure of the Bonsignori bank at the turn of the fourteenth century, a collapse made certain by pressures exerted by King Philip IV the Fair of France (*d.* 1314).

Urban planning and building under the Nine. If banking and commercial successes and the victory of Montaperti marked thirteenth-century Siena, the commune itself attained much of its greatness and the city acquired its basic structure and essential qualities under the aegis of the Nine, as they guided the destinies of an urban population that approximated 50,000 during the pre-plague decades of the fourteenth century. The Nine supervised serious and conscientious town planning. They intensified earlier efforts to widen and straighten streets and pave major arteries, and they imposed certain patterns of architectural uniformity. New building needed the approval of planning commissioners.

The commune now challenged the preeminence of the cathedral (dating from the mid 1200's) and its plaza, flanked by the great Hospital of Santa Maria della Scala. The ruling regime enthusiastically sponsored and supervised the construction of the Communal Palace (Palazzo Pubblico, begun 1298), with its slender, magnificent tower, Torre del Mangia (1338–1348), located on the edge of the Campo, a beautiful, new, shell-shaped plaza. This civic complex became the central focus of town life, and remains so today.

The Communal Palace, the home of the principal urban councils and magistracies, rapidly was decorated at public expense by Sienese artists who ranked among the finest masters of the International Gothic style. By about 1330 Simone Martini had completed a magnificent fresco of a Sienese war captain on his way to a successful siege. This equestrian figure, long identified as Guidoriccio da Fogliani of Reggio, and in 1944 described by Helene Wieruszowski as the earliest "portrait of a layman independent of religious significance," is located at one end of the meeting hall of the City Council (Palazzo Pubblico). In the adjoining chamber of the Nine Ambrogio Lorenzetti depicted the most famous artistic political allegory of the fourteenth century, the so-called allegory of Good and Bad Government, or the allegory of Justice, the Common Good, and Tyranny (*ca.* 1337–1340). The side walls portray the effects of good and bad government in the city and countryside, while the entire fresco depicts the political program that the Nine held as their ideal of rule.

Sienese art under the Nine. This period of the regime of the Nine coincides with the greatest epoch of Sienese art. While many artistic themes demonstrate clearly that Sienese religious piety and devotion to the Virgin had not abated, increasingly those characteristics were placed in the service of the lay commune and served to strengthen civic bonds and attachments. In 1315 Simone Martini adorned the City Council chamber with a *Maestà*. This Madonna exorted her subjects to rule with justice, give good counsel, avoid deceit, and not allow the powerful to oppress the weak. In 1308 the Sienese commissioned Duccio di Buoninsegna to replace an older portrait of the Madonna that they believed had aided them at the Battle of Montaperti. In 1311 his newly painted *Maestà* was borne through the streets in a public procession to the cathedral, where it was installed. The joyous festivities lasted three days.

Religion under the Nine. Civic attachments did

not preclude piety. Siena has been called the Tuscan home par excellence of the disciplinant (flagellant) confraternities. This religious spirit was far more prevalent and representative of the Sienese than the earthy and delightful cynicism of their best-known poet, Cecco Angiolieri (*ca.* 1260–*ca.* 1312). It was, moreover, Siena of the Nine that projected construction of what would have been the largest cathedral in Western Christendom—a project doomed to failure by a combination of poor architecture, faulty construction, the ravages of the Black Death, and enormous costs that a commune of Siena's relatively modest stature could not bear.

LATER SIENESE GOVERNMENTS

A series of unstable political regimes followed the collapse of the Nine. The Twelve Governors and Defenders of the Republic, a regime that especially represented both lower-middle-class and magnate interests, ruled uneasily for thirteen years. Its demise was followed by no less than four regimes in the single year 1368. Various mixed signories were attempted, including among them members of the Nine, magnates, and so-called reformers. Men whose forebears had served in one or another regime now were said to pertain to that particular group or *Monte*. The members of these various *Monti* shared in the political domination of Sienese governments throughout much of the remainder of the life of the independent republic.

The commune's political instability partially accounts for the thrust of the mission of St. Catherine of Siena (1347–1380), though not for her appearance in this city that so abounded in blessed and saints from many levels of society that it has been labeled the "antechamber of Paradise." The daughter of a dyer who lived near Fontebranda, the town's greatest fountain, and the church of St. Dominic, Catherine became a Dominican tertiary. Although she tended the ill, the poor, and prisoners, Catherine especially labored to end the factional disputes that rent her native city and to bring about a general pacification. Her letters also reveal her preoccupation with the general condition of the church during the latter stages of the Avignon papacy, as she strove to bring about yet another crusade to the Holy Land and to effect the return of the papacy to Italy.

The year of Catherine's death marked the birth of the other great saint whom Siena gave to the church. Though born in the subject commune of Massa Marittima, S. Bernardino (1380–1444) studied in Siena and considered himself a Sienese. He urged the Sienese to abandon the insignia of their factions and instead to adopt the monogram of Christ that was, in fact, installed on the facade of the Communal Palace. This Franciscan observant inveighed against contemporary morals and vanities in a fiery style that presaged the Florentine Dominican Girolamo Savonarola (1452–1498).

Siena's political instability after the fall of the Nine in 1355, its increasing subordination to Florence, and the eventual loss of independence did not preclude Siena from a modest though significant participation in the cultural developments of late medieval and early Renaissance Italy. The marble mosaics with which the Sienese began to decorate their cathedral in the late fourteenth century became a unique masterpiece. In the opening decades of the fifteenth century the city was further beautified by the sculpture of Jacopo della Quercia, whose fountain, the Fonte Gaia, adorned the Campo. While perhaps not of the caliber of the masters of the first half of the fourteenth century, Sassetta (originally from Cortona), Sano di Pietro, and Vecchietta were prominent artists. The noble Sienese bishop Enea Silvio Piccolomini, author of the *Commentaries,* became the scholarly humanist Pope Pius II (1458–1464). Siena had her share of storytellers, among them Fra Filippo degli Agazzari, author of the *Ensamples,* and Gentile Sermini, who wrote his *Novelle* about 1425. But the best of them was Gentile's contemporary, the imaginative preacher S. Bernardino.

Fifteenth-century Siena clearly was secondary to Florence and, if not a satellite community, was proportionately weaker than it had been during the preceding century. Opposition to Florentine hegemony, and Florentine designs on the community of Montepulciano, largely determined Siena's submission to the lordship of Gian Galeazzo Visconti (1399), as the duke of Milan attempted to extend his rule into Tuscany. Siena made other vain efforts to thwart or overthrow Florentine power. Between 1478 and 1480, for example, Siena joined Pope Sixtus IV and the Neapolitans in the war that resulted from the failure of the Pazzi conspiracy to oust the Medici from Florence. The diplomatic as well as military loss of 1480 occasioned the collapse of still another Sienese political regime, that of the Reformers, and in 1482 yet another *Monte*, the *Aggregati,* was added to the existing ones. Continued instability opened the way for the first native Sienese signory, that of Pandolfo Petrucci.

SIETE PARTIDAS

He came to power in 1488 and gradually developed a lordship similar to that of the Medici. But he did not build nearly so well: in 1525 his son Fabio was driven from the city.

The end of Sienese independence already was in sight. Rather than follow the tortuous turns of Sienese diplomacy, we should recognize that at this point Siena was soon to become a pawn in the far larger Habsburg-Valois conflicts of the sixteenth century. By 1530 the town was a satellite of Emperor Charles V and housed a Spanish garrison. In 1550 the horrified Sienese learned that the Spaniards planned to construct a fortress in their city as a protection against a possible French incursion into Tuscany. The Sienese then turned to King Henry II of France, whose commander, Blaise de Monluc (1502–1577), was to defend the beleaguered town against Spanish forces and the allied soldiery of the Florentine duke Cosimo de' Medici. Sienese historians linger patriotically over the details of the heroic but futile resistance to the siege of 1554–1555, the capitulation of 21 April 1555, and the retreat of some 2,000 Sienese to nearby Montalcino, where they established a short-lived government in exile. But the inevitable end of the story is quickly told: After some two years of Habsburg rule, Siena was sold to Cosimo de' Medici in 1557. Two years later, as a result of the Treaty of Câteau-Cambrésis, once-independent Siena at last became a portion of the Grand Duchy of Tuscany.

BIBLIOGRAPHY

William M. Bowsky, *The Finance of the Commune of Siena, 1287–1355* (1970), and *A Medieval Italian Commune: Siena under the Nine (1287–1355)* (1981); Robert Langton Douglas, *A History of Siena* (1902); Iris Origo, *The World of San Bernardino* (1962); Nicolai Rubinstein, "Political Ideas in Sienese Art: The Frescoes by Ambrogio Lorenzetti and Taddeo di Bartolo in the Palazzo Pubblico," in *Journal of the Warburg and Courtauld Institutes,* **21** (1958); Helene Wieruszowski, "Art and the Commune in the Time of Dante," in *Speculum,* **19** (1944).

WILLIAM M. BOWSKY

[See also **Banking, European; Bernardino of Siena, St.; Commune; Florence; Guelphs and Ghibellines; Italy; Tuscany; Urbanism: Western European.**]

SIETE PARTIDAS, a law code in the Castilian language attributed to Alfonso X, *el Sabio* (the Learned), king of León-Castile (1252–1284). It takes its name from its division into seven parts. The diversity of laws prevailing in the kingdom of León-Castile in the early thirteenth century prompted Ferdinand III (1217–1252) to project the development of a royal law common to all his dominions. During the reign of his son, Alfonso X, the project reached fruition with the publication probably in 1255 of the *Libro del fuero,* or, as it is better known today, the *Espéculo de las leyes,* of which five of seven books are now extant.

Including the principal themes of public and private law and heavily influenced by Roman law, the application of the *Libro del fuero* aroused strong protests in the cortes of 1272, compelling Alfonso X to limit its application and to confirm the older *fueros,* or customary laws, of the nobility and the towns. Thereafter, the jurists of the royal court reworked, refined, and expanded the *Libro del fuero,* transforming it, in the process, into the code known today as the *Siete partidas.* No critical edition exists, although J. A. Arías Bonet has published a modern edition of the *Primera partida.* The collation and dating of the manuscripts remains a matter of high priority, and, until it has been finished, statements concerning the formation of the *Partidas* can only be provisional.

Alfonso García Gallo has undertaken the most extensive studies of the work, modifying, in the course of doing so, many of his earlier opinions. In his judgment, the *Libro del fuero* served as the basis for the revision that was carried out probably after the death of Alfonso X and completed around 1290. As the *Siete partidas* was not given the force of law or promulgated, it was subject to further revision by private persons, so that today there is considerable variation among the several codices that survive. Alfonso XI, in the cortes of 1348, declared that he had not been able to discover that the *Partidas* had ever been promulgated, but he gave it legal force as supplementary to the other laws of the land. Two copies of the text were kept in his court for the use of royal judges. In the course of the late Middle Ages the *Partidas* came to supplant other sources of law in the kingdom of León-Castile, and it was also translated into Portuguese during the reign of King Denis (1279–1325) and into Catalan under King Pedro IV (1336–1387).

The *Siete partidas,* as elaborated by the royal jurists, is both comprehensive and systematic. Not only does it contain public and private, civil and criminal law, but it also draws upon philosophy and theology to provide the principles that serve as the foundation and justification for each law. Thus, the text has a distinct doctrinal content that sets it apart from other legal compilations of medieval Europe. The divergence of the *Siete partidas* from the laws then in vigor in the kingdom of León-Castile was also sharp, as it utilized the essential sources of Roman and canon law, namely, Justinian's *Code,* the *Digest,* and the *Decretals* of Gregory IX, as well as the *Libri feudorum,* the *Roles of Oléron,* and the writings of Aristotle, Seneca, and Thomas Aquinas.

The prologue attributes the work to Alfonso X, but, unlike the *Libro del fuero,* it does not state that he sought the counsel of the prelates and magnates of his court, nor does it state that he promulgated it. The *Libro de las leyes,* as the *Siete partidas* probably was called originally, was justified on the grounds that it was beneficial to both kings and their people to know and understand the law and their reciprocal rights and duties; the desirability of a uniform law was also emphasized. Each of the seven parts is divided into titles and each title into laws.

The first *partida* begins with an explanation of what law is and how it differs from custom. The legislator is admonished to seek the common good and to acknowledge his own obligation to obey the laws, just as his people do. The most substantial part of the first *partida,* however, concerns the doctrine and discipline of the Christian church and is a summation of canon law. The Trinity, the sacraments, the hierarchy, monastic life, excommunication, church property, clerical revenues, and pilgrimage are among the topics treated.

The second *partida* speaks of the rights and duties of kings and the obligation of their people to honor and obey them. Military organization and discipline and a title on universities are also included. The administration of justice, the functions of judges, attorneys, witnesses, judicial procedure, the proofs acceptable in court, judgments, and appeals are the subject matter of the third *partida.* In the fourth *partida,* the private law regulating betrothal, marriage, the rights of legitimate and illegitimate children, adoption, slaves and freemen, and the relationship between lords and vassals are discussed.

Commercial law is taken up in the fifth *partida:* loans, gifts, buying and selling, exchanges, the rights of merchants, markets, fairs, commercial companies, shipping, contracts, debts, and sureties are all considered. Wills, inheritances, and the guardianship of orphans and minor children form the substance of the sixth *partida.* The seventh and last *partida* is given over to criminal law: treason, falsehood, homicide, assault, torts, robbery, theft, rape, adultery, homosexuality, sorcery, imprisonment, torture, punishments, and pardons. Laws concerning Jews, Moors, and heretics are also included, and the last title deals with the meaning of words and the rules of law.

Integrating legal, philosophical, and theological learning, the *Siete partidas* is a unique monument in the legal history of medieval Europe, vaster than any code developed elsewhere but limited in its general utility by reason of its being written in Castilian rather than in Latin, the common tongue of scholars throughout the Continent. Even so, the *Siete partidas,* with the pervasive characteristics of Roman law, profoundly influenced both legal education and the development of the legal structure in the entire Iberian Peninsula.

BIBLIOGRAPHY

Juan Antonio Arías Bonet, ed., *Primera partida Alfonso X el Sabio según el manuscrito ADD. 20.787 del British Museum* (1975); Jerry R. Craddock, *The Legislative Works of Alfonso X, el Sabio: A Critical Bibliography* (1986); Alfonso García Gallo, "El 'Libro de las leyes' de Alfonso el Sabio: Del espéculo a las Partidas," in *Anuario de historia del derecho español,* **21–22** (1951–1952), and "Nuevas observaciones sobre la obra legislativa de Alfonso X," *ibid.,* **46** (1976); Antonio de San Martín, ed., *Las "Siete partidas,"* in *Los códigos españoles,* II–V (1872–1875); *Las "Siete partidas" del rey don Alfonso el Sabio,* 3 vols. (1807, repr. 1972).

JOSEPH F. O'CALLAGHAN

[See also **Alfonso X; Cortes; Corpus Iuris Civilis; Fuero; Law, Spanish.**]

ṢIFFĪN is the location of the battle between ᶜAlī and Muᶜāwiya that took place in July 657 near the right bank of the Euphrates, west of Raqqah. Muᶜāwiya's cousin, the commander of the faithful, ᶜUthmān, had been assassinated in Medina in 656 and the regicides had acclaimed ᶜAlī as his successor. Muᶜāwiya withheld his allegiance but, at first, left ᶜAlī to his enemies, who began to demand that the murderers be punished. After ᶜAlī defeated them at Basra in 656 and demanded Muᶜāwiya's recognition, Muᶜāwiya broke with him openly, became the leader of the movement to avenge ᶜUthmān as his next of kin by punishing his murderers, called for a council to choose a new commander of the faithful, attracted the support of ᶜAmr ibn al-ᶜĀṣ, and received the oath of allegiance as an independent governor in Jerusalem backed by the Syrian army.

ᶜAlī prepared to march against Syria with an Iraqi army. He met Muᶜāwiya with the Syrian army at Ṣiffīn in Jū l-Ḥijja May/June 657. The Syrians at first controlled access to the river and prevented the Iraqis from getting water until the Iraqis drove them away. The two armies confronted each other for the next two months. Neither side really wanted to fight. There were members of the same family or tribe on both sides, and all shared a general desire to avoid a full-scale engagement because of the potential for continuing revenge that bloodshed might cause; indeed, there were many who wanted a peaceful solution. The Kufan notable al-Ashᶜath ibn Qays al-Kindī is said to have feared that the Byzantines and Persians would attack the Arabs if they fought among themselves. Negotiations led to an impasse. ᶜAlī appealed to Muᶜāwiya to give him his allegiance, but Muᶜāwiya demanded vengeance for the death of ᶜUthmān and the holding of a council. ᶜAlī was unable to punish the regicides because some of them were among his most ardent supporters. There was a truce during June/July 657, when fraternization at the river led to discussions about who was responsible for the conflict and who was in the right. The Syrians justified Muᶜāwiya's right to revenge as ᶜUthmān's kinsman by appealing to the Koran (Sura 17:32–35). Some Iraqis argued that ᶜUthmān's murder was justified because he had been arbitrary and considered Muᶜāwiya to be a rebel who should be fought "until he reverts to obedience to God" (Sura 49:8–9).

The battle at Ṣiffīn began on 19 July 657 and lasted ten days. The traditional accounts are thoroughly embellished and tendentious, and it is impossible to determine the tactical course of the battle because it is represented as a series of confrontations between individuals and tribal units. Casualties were heavy, and one account claims that 70,000 were killed. The fighting was stopped when several men on the Syrian side, either voluntarily or on the instructions of Muᶜāwiya, parted the combatants by displaying copies or pages of the Koran and appealing to it to judge the issue. ᶜAlī and the core of his supporters wanted to continue fighting, but the Kufan clan leaders favored a truce, and the Koran reciters (*qurrāᵓ*) supported the appeal to the Koran. Together they forced ᶜAlī to agree to arbitration and insisted that Abū Mūsā al-Ashᶜāri, a neutralist who represented Kufan interests more than ᶜAlī's, be their arbiter. The arbitration agreement, which was concluded on 31 July 657, required that both arbiters, Abū Mūsā and ᶜAmr ibn al-ᶜĀṣ, decide the issue according to the Book of God and if necessary resort to common, agreed, and just custom (*sunna*). The Syrians claimed that the issue to be decided by the Koran was the legality of ᶜUthmān's murder, and when the agreement was announced, many Iraqis raised a great cry of "judgment belongs only to God," rejecting the inclusion of human judgment along with the Book of God. Some 4,000 *qurrāᵓ*, now favoring continued fighting, wanted ᶜAlī to repent of agreeing to arbitration, then left his army and returned to Kufa. Their break with ᶜAlī at Ṣiffīn was the starting point for the Khariji movement that preoccupied ᶜAlī for the remaining two and one-half years of his life and resulted in his death at the hands of a Kharijite assassin. Muᶜāwiya was able to return to Syria unopposed and to use Syria as a base to secure the empire for himself.

BIBLIOGRAPHY

Martin Hinds, "The Siffin Arbitration Agreement," in *Journal of Semitic Studies,* 17 (1972); Naṣr ibn Muẓāhim, *Waqᶜat Ṣiffīn* (1945–1946, 2nd ed. 1962–1963); Erling Petersen, *ᶜAli and Muᶜāwiya in Early Arabic Tradition* (1964); al-Ṭabarī, *Taᵓrīkh al-rusul waᵓl-mulūk*, M. J. de Goeje *et al.*, eds., I (1879), 3,265–3,333.

MICHAEL MORONY

[See also **ᶜAlī ibn Abī Ṭālib; Caliphate; Islam, Religion; Kufa, Al-; Muᶜāwiya; Syria.**]

SIGEBERT OF GEMBLOUX (*ca.* 1030–1112) was one of the most prolific, multifaceted, and important authors of the eleventh century. Raised in the abbey of Gembloux (diocese of Liège), which had an exceptionally fine school and library, he later spent twenty years as a teacher at the monastic school of St. Vincent in Metz. He returned to Gembloux around 1070, and there spent the rest of his long life.

His literary output may be divided into five main categories. He was from his youth a prolific hagiographer. He also wrote important histories (especially the *Chronica* and the *Gesta abbatum Gemblaciensium* [Deeds of the abbots of Gembloux]), which provide significant details concerning the dramatic events that constituted the investiture crisis of the eleventh century. Third, he himself participated in that conflict as an anti-Gregorian polemicist, defending royal and imperial investiture and also the validity of sacraments dispensed by married priests. He also argued movingly against Pope Paschal II's endorsement of secular military attacks against papal opponents. (A presumably significant epistle refuting one of Pope Gregory VII's two letters to Herman of Metz has not survived.) Fourth, he attempted to reconstruct the exact chronology of historical events between 381 and 1111, although he was unsuccessful in this pursuit. Finally, he wrote *De viris illustribus,* a catalog of 172 medieval authors, starting with Marcellus (a disciple of St. Peter) and ending with himself. Although he frequently provides only superficial information, many works and authors of the Middle Ages would be completely unknown were it not for Sigebert's compendium.

BIBLIOGRAPHY

A nearly complete *opera omnia* (notably excluding the anti-Gregorian tractates) is found in *Patrologia latina,* CLX (1880). Major works should be consulted in superior editions: *Chronica,* Ludowicus C. Bethmann, ed., in *Monumenta Germaniae historica: Scriptores,* VI (1844); *Epistola cuiusdam adversus laicorum in presbyteros coniugatos contumeliam,* and *Leodicensium epistola adversus Paschalem papum,* Ernest Sackur, ed., in *Monumenta Germaniae historica: Libelli de lite,* II (1892, repr. 1956); Robert Witte, *Catalogus Sigeberti Gemblacensis monachi de viris illustibus* (1974). See also M. De Waha, "Sigebert de Gembloux faussaire?" in *Revue belge de philologie et d'histoire,* 55 (1977).

ELAINE GOLDEN ROBISON

[See also **Biography, Secular; Gregory VII, Pope; Investiture and Investiture Conflict; Paschal II, Pope.**]

SIGEHARD OF ST. MAXIMIN (*d. ca.* 963). Born in the region of Aquitaine, Sigehard was a monk at the monastery of St. Maximin at Trier (Trèves). At the request of his abbot, Wiker, he wrote *De miraculis sancti Maximini,* describing the miracles attributed to St. Maximinus of Trier. The work was intended as a companion to an earlier vita of St. Maximinus, which had been revised by Lupus of Ferrières. Sigehard's writing, marked by a plain, unadorned style, belongs among the finest of the period.

BIBLIOGRAPHY

Max Manitius, *Geschichte der lateinischen Literatur des Mittelalters,* II (1923), 416, 420–422, 462; *Patrologia latina,* CXXXIII (1853), 965–978.

EDWARD FRUEH

[See also **Lupus of Ferrières.**]

SIGER OF BRABANT (*ca.* 1240–1281/1284). Mentioned as a protagonist in two university crises that were settled finally by the papal legate, cited to appear before the inquisitor of France, and identified in one source as a main target of an episcopal condemnation, Siger is placed by Dante along with Aquinas, Albertus Magnus, Boethius, and King Solomon, among others, in the fourth heaven of his *Paradiso* (canto X, 133–138).

In spite of having written twenty-two philosophical works, and having played a leading role in the major intellectual crisis of the thirteenth century, not to mention being immortalized by Dante, Siger was virtually unknown to historians of philosophy until the twentieth century.

He was born in the duchy of Brabant about 1240 and probably began his schooling in Liège, enrolling in the Faculty of Arts of the University of Paris about 1255/1257. His turbulent teaching career there dates from about 1263/1265. The papal legate, Simon of Brion, named Siger as the ringleader of a faction within the Faculty of Arts in 1266. Siger's early writings reveal similar headstrong traits, for he managed to profess such philosophical positions as an eternal world and a single intellect for all men, without seeming to be aware of their incompatibility with his Christian faith.

This radical departure from an eight-centuries-old Christian tradition of regarding philosophy as the handmaiden of theology was occasioned by a mammoth increase in available philosophical source material coupled with the curricular requirement of the University of Paris that it be taught and studied. The works of Aristotle and some Neoplatonists, together with interpretations of them by Islamic philosophers, achieved positions of predominant influence at Paris. The Aristotelian conception of science as a systematic body of knowledge, whose conclusions necessarily flowed from principles through strict demonstrations, was extended even to theology.

The exclusive pursuit of philosophy without regard for nonphilosophical consequences quickly aroused opposition from among the theologians, however. They noted that philosophical affirmations that the world had no beginning in time, that there was but a single intellect for all men, that the highest Being knew only itself, and that the world was ruled by a strict causal necessity imperiled Christian belief in a world created in time, personal immortality, Divine Providence, and human freedom. They were led by Bonaventure, who identified as the root cause of these errors the audacity of the Parisian professors in their philosophical inquiries. Even the mild-mannered Aquinas angrily challenged one of the philosophers, some say Siger himself, to attempt, "if he dared," a public rebuttal of Thomas' refutation of the Averroistic doctrine of a single intellect for all men.

The subsequent condemnation in 1270 of some of these philosophical positions by Étienne Tempier, the bishop of Paris, had its effect on Siger. He did not change any of his philosophical judgments, for he had always maintained that there was no truth superior to that of the Christian faith, but now, when dealing with philosophical positions of theological sensitivity, he took greater care to make clear that he was merely setting forth the views of the philosophers and not affirming them as true. Indeed, in his 1272/1273 *Questions on the "Metaphysics,"* Siger insisted that those charged with responsibility for expounding the works of the philosophers ought not to conceal their contents even if they were contrary to the truth.

Perhaps it was the influence of Aquinas and Albertus Magnus, whom Siger called the "outstanding men in philosophy," that led him to declare that the arguments proving that the world was eternal and that there was but a single intellect for all men were not, strictly speaking, demonstrative at all. At the conclusion of his *On the Intellective Soul* (1273/1274), Siger confessed not to know "according to the way of natural reason" what position ought to be held on the question of man's intellect. By 1275/1276, in his *Questions on the "Liber de Causis,"* Siger did not hesitate to call the Averroistic doctrine on man's intellect irrational, and, if it was held by Aristotle, well, after all, "he was human and capable of error."

Other masters in the Faculty of Arts were evidently less balanced in their philosophical arguments on theologically sensitive issues. Their consequent disclaimers that, of course, the contrary was true according to the faith appeared to many theologians and ecclesial authorities as tantamount to claiming that something could be true in philosophy and not true according to revelation, and vice versa. This so-called doctrine of a "double truth" was denounced by some theologians and ecclesial authorities. University decrees of 1272 and 1276 sought to circumscribe severely both the content and manner of teaching in philosophy. Unfortunately for Siger, his position was lumped in with the others, and, within a four-month period, he was called before Simon du Val, the inquisitor of France (23 November 1276); Pope John XXI asked the bishop of Paris for a written report on the errors being taught (18 January 1277); and Bishop Tempier issued a new solemn condemnation of 219 philosophical propositions (7 March 1277).

From available records we know that Siger had already fled Paris when summoned by the inquisitor, and that, sometime between 1281 and 1284, he met a tragic end at the papal court in Orvieto, stabbed to death by his demented secretary. Siger had likely decided to plead his own case at the Curia, a plea that must have been partly successful, because there is no record of any papal condemnation of his works.

Now that the bulk of his works have been published, his place in the history of Western philosophy can be assessed. He appears as a forceful teacher and an independent thinker, committed to the goal of a philosophical wisdom. Siger's sources included Aristotle, his commentator Ibn Rushd (Averroës), and sometimes Ibn Sīnā (Avicenna) and Proclus, and even Aquinas. He did not hesitate to criticize their arguments if he felt they were weak. Perhaps the time has come to speak of Siger's thought not as a "Latin Averroism" or a "heterodox Aristotelianism," but simply as "Sigerian."

BIBLIOGRAPHY

Étienne H. Gilson, *History of Christian Philosophy in the Middle Ages* (1955); Armand A. Maurer, *Medieval Philosophy,* 2nd ed. (1982); Fernand van Steenberghen, *Maître Sigre de Brabant* (1977).

WILLIAM DUNPHY

[See also **Albertus Magnus; Aquinas, St. Thomas; Aristotle in the Middle Ages; Boethius; Bonaventure, St.;**

Dante Alighieri; Paris, University of; Peter of Spain; Philosophy and Theology, Western European; Rushd, Ibn.]

SIGILLOGRAPHY. See **Seals and Sigillography.**

SIGISMUND, EMPEROR (1368–1437). Sigismund I was elected German emperor in 1410. He had already been chosen king of Hungary in 1387 and would be crowned king of Bohemia in 1420. A man of outsize ambitions and energy, who often described himself as a second Charlemagne, Sigismund was the second son of the Luxembourg emperor Charles IV (Charles I of Bohemia). His life was a long series of conflicts and half-realized enterprises that ranged the length and breadth of Europe and beyond.

Sigismund became king of Hungary only after raising an army to persuade his fiancée, Mary, the daughter of King Louis the Great of Hungary, to honor her promised marriage with him. He also had to combat French and Neapolitan claims to the crown of St. Stephen. It was only in the latter half of his reign that he enjoyed any real support among his subjects. One of his lifelong concerns both as emperor and king of Hungary was the ever-expanding power of the Ottoman Turks. He was the organizer of an international crusade that ended in disaster for the Christian forces at Nicopolis in 1396. The defeat persuaded Sigismund that only a united Christendom could end the Islamic threat to Europe, and he spent much of his life working toward this goal. Either through force or diplomacy, he tried to heal both the schism in the church of Rome and the split between the Latin and Eastern rites and to bring to an end the Hundred Years War, as well as conflicts between Hungary and Venice, and between Poland and the Teutonic Order and the Tatars. It was a staggering program, which came to all but naught.

Both as emperor and as king of Hungary, Sigismund was alert to the role bourgeois economic enterprise could play in enhancing royal and imperial power. In Hungary, where he moved to curb the influence of the landed magnates, he expended much effort on wresting control of the market towns from their feudal overlords. He strengthened the position of these centers by giving them independent legal jurisdiction. With tactics such as uniform export prohibitions (on such commodities as gold and silver) for the kingdom, he tried to give Hungary some approximation of economic unity. Under the influence of the Nuremberg mercantile houses, he sought to block the import of Venetian merchandise into Europe. In such a way did he hope to further the trade of the merchants of Central Europe in the Near East and around the Black Sea.

Sigismund was a major figure at the Council of Constance (1414–1418), which restored unity to the church in the West. He was also anxious to see genuine reform in ecclesiastical administration. His particular concerns were the number and nationality of cardinals, payment of annates, regulation of benefices, and the role of the curia in the church's legal affairs.

It was at Constance as well that Sigismund also became embroiled in the Hussite controversy. Having given the Bohemian reformer a safe-conduct to appear before the gathering, Sigismund nevertheless allowed Jan Hus's martyrdom at the stake in 1415 to go forward. The emperor's apparent deception made it very difficult for him to realize his claims to the Bohemian crown, though a coronation took place as early as 1420. Such formalities meant little, however, to Hus's more radical partisans. Sigismund used his position in the empire to organize the anti-Hussite crusades against his own subjects, but he was not able to lead a single successful battle against them. For their part, they branded him "the red demon," a reference, among other things, to the color of his beard. It was only in 1436, following his acceptance of the Compacts of Basel, which granted the chalice to the laity and permitted the free preaching of Hussite doctrine in Bohemia, that Sigismund was reluctantly accepted as the ruler of that kingdom.

BIBLIOGRAPHY

Aziz Suryal Atiya, *The Crusade of Nikopolos* (1934, repr. 1978); Frederick G. Heymann, *John Žižka and the Hussite Revolution* (1955, repr. 1969); Heinrich Koller, "Sigismund 1410–1437," in Helmut Beumann, ed., *Kaisergestalten des Mittelalters* (1985); Peter of Mladoňovice, "An Account of the Trial and Condemnation of Master John Hus in Constance," in Matthew Spinka, *John Hus at the Council of Constance* (1965); Denis Sinor, *History of Hungary* (1959).

PAULA SUTTER FICHTNER

[See also **Bohemia-Moravia; Councils, Western; Germany; Hungary; Hus, John; Hussites.**]

SIGN OF THE CROSS. From the time of Tertullian, Christian writers made reference to the use of the "sign of the Lord" to bless acts in daily life, to strengthen Christians during times of temptation and tribulation, and to recognize other Christians during times of persecution. The sign of the cross is also used in the liturgy, in baptisms and ordinations, and as a sign of the conclusion of the Mass. In the early centuries, the sign was drawn on the forehead by the thumb or finger of the right hand. The more popular method of drawing the right hand from forehead to breast, shoulder to shoulder, and then returning to the center was in practice by the sixth century. In the Western church, the cross is made as a stroke from left to right, whereas, in the Eastern church, the cross is made from right to left.

BIBLIOGRAPHY

F. L. Cross, ed., "Sign of the Cross," in *Oxford Dictionary of the Christian Church,* 2nd ed. (1966); Herbert Thurston, "The Sign of the Cross," in *The Month,* **118** (1911), and *Familiar Prayers: Their Origin and History,* Paul Grosjean, ed. (1953), 1–21.

JENNIFER E. JONES

[See also **Mass, Liturgy of; Ordination, Clerical.**]

SIGNATURES (also called "quire marks"), letters, numbers, or marks written in the margins of a manuscript book's quires and indicating the order in which the quires were to be assembled for binding. The signatures of Greek manuscripts typically appear on the recto of each quire's first folio; those of Latin manuscripts usually occur on the verso of each quire's last folio. This divergence may reflect different traditions of bookbinding in East and West.

BIBLIOGRAPHY

Bernhard Bischoff, *Paläographie des römischen Altertums und des abendländischen Mittelalters* (1979), 37–38.

MICHAEL MCCORMICK

[See also **Codex; Manuscript Books, Binding of; Quire; Writing Materials, Western European.**]

SIGRDRÍFUMÁL (The words of Sigrdrífa), the title assigned to a group of twenty-nine stanzas, mostly in *ljóðaháttr* (chant meter), found at the end of the fourth folio of the Eddic collection in Codex Regius 2365,4°. The conclusion was lost with the disappearance of the fifth folio. Eight additional stanzas survive in paper manuscripts. A prose preface and the opening stanzas describe how Sigurd rides onto a mountain called Hindarfjall and finds a mail-clad maiden asleep in a circle of shields. He awakens her by splitting the armor with his sword and she identifies herself as the valkyrie Sigrdrífa. She explains that she was condemned to a magic slumber by Odin after killing his favorite Hjálm-Gunnarr in battle. She then imparts a series of runic remedies (stanzas 5–19) and general gnomic precepts (stanzas 22–37). Sixteen of these stanzas are also preserved in the retelling of *Vǫlsunga saga* in a differing order.

The version of the episode related in *Vǫlsunga saga* contains two important additions to Codex Regius: Sigrdrífa is identified as Brynhild and at the conclusion of the episode she is betrothed to Sigurd. In all probability these additions represent a later speculation. Sigrdrífa was originally a distinct figure and the encounter with her a distinct adventure in Sigurd's career. Andreas Heusler assumed that this episode was the subject of a narrative *Erweckungslied* (awakening), of which the only remnants in the extant *Sigrdrífumál* are stanzas 1–5 and 20–21. The original sense of the encounter may have been to communicate wisdom to the youthful Sigurd. Only later was it developed into a romantic interlude and equated with Sigurd's betrothal to Brynhild.

Sigrdrífa's runic charms are designed to gain victory, guard against a woman's deceit, counteract poison, ease birth, avert shipwreck, heal wounds, ward off enemies, and promote wisdom. The gnomes are for the most part cast in negative terms. Men should avoid faithlessness, dealings with foolish men or witches, seduction, and drunkenness. They should fight openly rather than be burned in their houses, give a corpse a good burial, and be on their guard against potential avengers. The closest parallels to the charms and gnomes in *Sigrdrífumál* may be found in the Eddic poem *Hávamál.* Such historically detached and universal sentiments cannot be dated even approximately. Sigurd's encounter with a valkyrie may have taken shape at any time during the development of his legend, but there is no reason to think that it is a particularly old episode.

BIBLIOGRAPHY

Sources. The standard edition is Gustav Neckel, ed., *Edda: Die Lieder des Codex Regius nebst verwandten Denkmälern,* 4th ed. rev. by Hans Kuhn, I (1962). Translations are Henry Adams Bellows, ed. and trans., *The Poetic Edda* (1923, repr. 1969); Lee M. Hollander, ed. and trans., *The Poetic Edda,* 2nd ed. (1962, repr. 1977).

Studies. Theodore M. Andersson, *The Legend of Brynhild* (1980); Andreas Heusler, *Kleine Schriften,* Stefan Sonderegger, ed., II (1969), 223–291; Einar G. Pétursson, "Hvenær týndist kverið úr Konungsbók eddukvæða," in *Gripla,* 6 (1984); Hermann Reichert, "Zum Sigrdrífa-Brünhild-Problem," in *Antiquitates Indogermanicae: Studien zur indogermanischen Altertumskunde und zur Sprach- und Kulturgeschichte der indogermanischen Völker: Gedenkschrift für Hermann Güntert zur 25. Wiederkehr seines Todestages am 23. April 1973,* Manfred Mayrhofer *et al.*, eds. (1974); Hermann Schneider, "Verlorene Sigurddichtung," in *Arkiv för nordisk filologi,* 45 (1929).

Theodore M. Andersson

[See also **Brynhild; Eddic Meters; Eddic Poetry; Hávamál; Helreið Brynhildar; Vǫlsunga Saga.**]

SIGURD (Siegfried in German) is the preeminent male figure in Germanic heroic legend. His story is told in a variety of Norse and German texts, chiefly the *Poetic Edda, Vǫlsunga saga, Þiðreks saga,* and the *Nibelungenlied.* The name is Frankish, and efforts have been made to trace the legend to historical events in the Merovingian period. These efforts are purely speculative, and the earliest clear references to the story of Sigurd are from Norse skaldic poetry and British and Scandinavian rock carvings of the late Viking Age. Full details emerge only from the medieval texts. No Eddic poem about Sigurd can be dated with certainty before the twelfth century, and the mass of evidence dates from the very end of that century and the first part of the thirteenth.

The story, told in various forms, includes an account of Sigurd's birth and youthful adventures, his betrothal to Brynhild and marriage to Gudrun (Kriemhilt), and his murder. As a child he is fostered by the smith Reginn, whose brother Fáfnir, in the form of a dragon, broods on a treasure. After first avenging his father Sigmund, Sigurd kills the dragon and seizes the treasure. He next has an encounter with the valkyrie Sigrdrífa, secondarily identified as Brynhild by some texts. This episode is followed by his betrothal to Brynhild, which is broken when he comes to the court of Gjúki and is given a potion of forgetfulness to open the way for his marriage to Gjúki's daughter Gudrun. He subsequently impersonates his sworn brother Gunnarr and wins Brynhild for him. The deception is revealed in a quarrel between Brynhild and Gudrun, and Brynhild takes her revenge by contriving Sigurd's murder.

The oldest form of the legend is represented by the Eddic poem *Sigurðarkviða in forna,* only about half of which is preserved. In this earliest form it appears that there was no prior betrothal between Sigurd and Brynhild; her anger is motivated by her oath to have the greatest man and the thwarting of her desire by Sigurd's and Gunnarr's deception. The story is elaborated by the poet of *Sigurðarkviða in skamma,* parts of which are so allusive that the legendary form is uncertain. Sigurd's prior betrothal to Brynhild was fully developed only in the lost poem *Sigurðarkviða in meiri,* from which it passed into the prose harmonization of *Vǫlsunga saga.* The story of Sigurd's youth was told in two or more poems amalgamated in the Eddic *Reginsmál-Fáfnismál* and the episode with Sigrdrífa in the Eddic *Sigrdrífumál.* In addition there seems to have existed a "Sigurðar saga" composed around 1200 and used by the compilers of the *Poetic Edda* and *Vǫlsunga saga.* It is now lost.

The German versions of the story in *Þiðreks saga* and the *Nibelungenlied* go back to a common oral source from the late twelfth century (Andreas Heusler's "Brünhildenlied"). This German "Brünhildenlied" may also have influenced the Norse poets of *Sigurðarkviða in skamma* and *Sigurðarkviða in meiri.* It appears to have included the prior betrothal, which is referred to in *Þiðreks saga* but was suppressed by the *Nibelungenlied* poet, presumably in the interest of removing the onus of a broken commitment from Siegfried's character. The most conspicuous deviations from the Norse versions are that Siegfried overcomes Brynhild by force in Gunther's bed (the *Nibelungenlied* inserts a conquest in martial games in addition) and is murdered by Hagen in the forest, not in bed by the youngest of the Gjukungs (Gotþormr) as in most of the Norse texts. The story of Sigurd/Siegfried remained alive in medieval Scandinavian ballads and as late as the sixteenth century in *Das Lied vom hürnen Seyfrid* and Hans Sachs's *Der hörnen*

Seyfrid (1557). It survived in oral tradition into modern times in the ballad romances of the Faeroe Islands.

BIBLIOGRAPHY

For editions and translations consult the entries on the individual texts.

Studies. Theodore M. Andersson, *The Legend of Brynhild* (1980); Hilda R. Ellis, "Sigurd in the Art of the Viking Age," in *Antiquity,* **16** (1942); Andreas Heusler, *Nibelungensage und Nibelungenlied: Die Stoffgeschichte des deutschen Heldenepos* (3rd ed. 1929, repr. 1946, 1955, 1965); Heinz Hungerland, "Zeugnisse zur Vǫlsungen- und Niflungensage aus der Skaldendichtung," in *Arkiv för nordisk filologi,* **20** (1904); Friedrich Panzer, *Studien zur germanischen Sagengeschichte,* II (1912); Hermann Schneider, *Germanische Heldensage,* I (1928, repr. 1962), 73–210.

THEODORE M. ANDERSSON

[See also **Brynhild; Eddic Poetry; Nibelungenlied; Reginsmál and Fáfnismál; Þiðreks Saga; Vǫlsunga Saga.**]

SIGURÐAR SAGA FÓTS (Ásmundar Húnakóngs) is preserved in only one vellum manuscript, which dates from the latter half of the fifteenth century and in some thirty-five paper manuscripts. The saga, which was probably written in its present form around 1400, has been edited on three occasions.

This short story, which the narrator claims was found on the stone wall in Cologne, concerns the wooing of the wise and beautiful Princess Signý by King Ásmundr of Húnaland. However, the absent father promises her to King Sigurðr Foot, so named because of his jumping prowess. At the wedding festivities for Sigurðr and the unwilling Signý, Ásmundr appears with his retainer, Ólafr, "shoeboy," and extinguishes all the lights in the hall with the gust of air caused by one swing of his mighty spear. When the lights are lit, the bride has disappeared and Sigurðr returns home disgruntled. Generous offers of compensation by Ásmundr are refused by Sigurðr, and the former is compelled to defeat the latter in single combat. Ásmundr then asks Signý to decide between them. In an ambiguous passage she says that she has never intended to marry anyone other than Sigurðr, and the two men become sworn brothers.

Ásmundr then woos Elena, daughter of King Hrólfr of Ireland. Refused by the father, he attacks with his outnumbered force until only he and Ólafr remain, and they are thrown into a deep, dank dungeon. Signý then dreams of Ásmundr's plight and interprets the dream for Sigurðr, who subsequently scatters Hrólfr's army and captures the king. Ásmundr, whom Elena has previously released and royally entertained in her bower, intercedes on Hrólfr's behalf and is finally granted Elena's hand in marriage.

The saga, which uses many motifs common to the Hilde-Gudrun legend, is also possibly indebted to *Knýtlinga saga.* The material has been treated in one *rímur* version of sixteen stanzaic divisions prior to 1600 and in three unedited *rímur* from the eighteenth and nineteenth centuries.

BIBLIOGRAPHY

J. H. Jackson, ed., "Sigurthar saga fóts ok Ásmundar Húnakongs," in *PMLA,* **46** (1931); Finnur Jónsson, *Den oldnorske og oldislandske litteraturs historie,* III (2nd ed., 1924), 51, 114, and *idem,* ed., "Rímur af Sigurði fót," in his *Rímnasafn,* II (1922), 288–325; Agnete Loth, ed., *Late Medieval Icelandic Romances,* III (1963), 231–254; Finnur Sigmundsson, *Rímnatal,* 2 vols. in 1 (1966), esp. 423–424; Jón Thorkelsson, *Om digtningen på Island i det 15. og 16. århundrede* (1888), 163; Björn K. Thórólfsson, *Rímur fyrir 1600* (1934), 338; Bjarni Vilhjálmsson, ed., *Riddarasögur,* VI (1961), 63–84.

PETER A. JORGENSEN

[See also **Knýtlinga Saga; Riddarasögur.**]

SIGURÐAR SAGA ÞÖGLA is a native Icelandic combination of numerous mythical-heroic and romance motifs. It was evidently quite popular, being preserved in six vellum manuscripts from the mid fourteenth to the seventeenth century and in some fifty paper manuscripts. Of the two main recensions, only the longer has been edited (on three occasions). Although disagreement exists as to which of the versions is older, the original version of the tale probably goes back to the beginning of the fourteenth century. There has evidently been borrowing from *Klára saga,* and a link to *Viktors saga ok Blávus* is possible.

After a prologue in defense of the fantastic elements in some stories of the time, the saga follows the exploits of two brothers, Hálfdan and Vilhjálmr, in defeating the "Viking" Garðr the Greek and fighting cyclopses from their ships before being humiliated by the maiden "king," Sedentiana, and having their army decimated by a flying dragon. Their younger brother, Sigurðr the Silent (a male Cinderella), fostered by Count Lafranz of Lixion, sets off alone, saves a lion from a flying dragon, and wins magic-making treasure from two ogresses. In each case the grateful creatures later grant aid to the hero.

In rapid succession Sigurðr acquires four sworn brothers, and a suitable princess is found for each, as well as for the surviving older brother Vilhjálmr (Hálfdan's death at the hands of a giant is due to the curse of a dwarf whose child Hálfdan had mistreated years earlier). Sigurðr uses a magic ring to cause Sedentiana to fall in love with him and humbles her by having her chase him through the forest and by having her lie with a dwarf, a swineherd, and a hideous giant (really manifestations of Sigurðr, obtained by his looking into different parts of a magic mirror). After being publicly ridiculed, she introduces Sigurðr to their four-year-old son, Flores, and the wedding is finally celebrated with great splendor, singing, and the telling of stories.

The material has also been treated in one *rímur* version prior to 1600 (fifteen stanzaic divisions) and in five *rímur* redactions from the seventeenth to nineteenth centuries.

BIBLIOGRAPHY

Otto Jiriczek, "Zur mittelisländischen Volkskunde," in *Zeitschrift für deutsche Philologie,* **26** (1894, repr. 1966), 10–11, 23–25; Finnur Jónsson, *Den oldnorske og oldislandske litteraturs historie,* III (2nd ed. 1924), 114–115; Peter A. Jorgensen, "The Icelandic Translations from Middle English," in *Studies for Einar Haugen* (1972), 316; Eugen Kölbing, "Die Sigurdar saga Þǫgla und die Bevis saga," in *Zeitschrift für vergleichende Litteraturgeschichte,* **10** (1896); Agnete Loth, ed., *Late Medieval Icelandic Romances,* II (1963), 93–264; Finnur Sigmundsson, *Rímnatal,* 2 vols. in 1 (1966), esp. 427–430; Einar Ól. Sveinsson, "Viktors saga ok Blávus: Sources and Characteristics," in Jónas Kristjánsson, ed., *Viktors saga ok Blávus* (1964), cxviii–cxxvi, cxxxvii; Einar Thórðarson, ed., *Sagan af Sigurði þögula* (1883); Jón Thorkelsson, *Om digtningen på Island i det 15. og 16. århundrede* (1888), 163–164; Björn K. Thórólfsson, *Rímur fyrir 1600* (1934), 440–443; Bjarni Vilhjálmsson, ed., *Riddarasögur,* III (1954), 95–267.

PETER A. JORGENSEN

[See also **Klára Saga; Riddarasögur.**]

SIGURÐARKVIÐA IN FORNA (Old lay of Sigurd) is a Norse heroic poem containing the earliest version of the story of Sigurd and Brynhild. It is partially preserved in the Codex Regius (Gml. kgl. saml. 2365,4°) of the *Poetic Edda,* dating from about 1270. Approximately half the poem was lost with the disappearance of the fifth gathering in the Codex Regius, and only eighteen-and-a-half stanzas survive at the beginning of the sixth gathering. The poem is consequently also known as *Brot af Sigurðarkviðu* (Fragment of the lay of Sigurd). It has been dated as early as the tenth century and as late as the twelfth. The complete poem was available to the author of *Vǫlsunga saga,* who combined it with the narrative of two other Eddic poems (*Sigurðarkviða in skamma* and *Sigurðarkviða in meiri*). From this synthetic retelling Heusler reconstructed the following narrative for *Forna.*

Sigurd comes to the court of the Gjukungs, becomes the sworn brother of Gunnarr and Hǫgni, and marries their sister Gudrun. He then wins Brynhild, who has sworn to marry only the greatest man, for his sworn brother Gunnarr by deception; he crosses the flame wall that encircles her, impersonating Gunnarr, and shares her bed for three nights, with his sword separating them. He departs, and she is wed to Gunnarr. Sometime later Brynhild and Gudrun quarrel, and Gudrun reveals the deception. Brynhild incites Gunnarr against Sigurd by claiming that he abused Gunnarr's trust and slept with her. (Here the extant portion of the text begins.) Gunnarr consults with his brothers Hǫgni and Gotþormr, and the three of them kill Sigurd in the forest. Brynhild at first exults, then awakens a little before day and weeps over Sigurd's death. She reminds the brothers of their broken oaths of brotherhood and divulges that Sigurd was faithful to his oath since he placed his sword between them during the proxy nuptials.

The thrust of the poem is slightly ambiguous. To some extent it is a tale of deception and revenge in a harsh heroic tradition, but in Brynhild's grief over Sigurd's death there is also a suggestion of the erotic attachment that is fully developed in the later Sigurd poems. The competition of heroic and romantic themes is one of the underlying tensions. A second important theme is the variety of oaths. Sigurd swears an oath with Gunnarr and Hǫgni, but they break the oath and kill him. Brynhild has sworn to have only the greatest man but is cheated of her oath. She takes revenge by claiming that Sigurd broke his oath to Gunnarr and slept with her, but at the end of the poem she proclaims that he was faithful to his oath. These oaths are so many bonds guaranteeing orderly relationships; their perversion leads to tragedy. The poem may be understood to deal with the strains placed on a normal order by irrational factors such as Brynhild's ambition, the guile of the Gjukungs, and Sigurd's unthinking collaboration. A fundamental dilemma is suggested by the collision of personal passions with social contracts. The strength of the poem lies in the intimation of this larger theme and the stark brevity with which the poet projects the emotions of the characters, especially that of Brynhild.

BIBLIOGRAPHY

Edition. Gustav Neckel, ed., *Edda: Die Lieder des Codex Regius nebst verwandten Denkmälern,* rev. by Hans Kuhn (1962), 198–201.

Translations: Henry Adams Bellows, trans., *The Poetic Edda* (1923, repr. 1957, 1969), 404–409; Lee M. Hollander, trans., *The Poetic Edda* (2nd rev. ed., 1962, repr. 1977), 243–246.

Studies. Theodore M. Andersson, *The Legend of Brynhild* (1980); Andreas Heusler, "Die Lieder der Lücke im Codex Regius der Edda," in *Germanistische Abhandlungen Hermann Paul dargebracht* (1902), 1–98, repr. in his *Kleine Schriften,* II, Stefan Sonderegger, ed. (1969), 223–291.

THEODORE M. ANDERSSON

[See also **Brynhild; Eddic Poetry; Sigurd.**]

SIGURÐARKVIÐA IN MEIRI (The long lay of Sigurd), so titled by modern scholars in contrast to *Sigurðarkviða in skamma* (The short lay of Sigurd), was lost with the disappearance of the fifth gathering in the only complete manuscript of the *Poetic Edda* (Reykjavik, Arnamagnæn Manuscript Institute, Codex Regius 2365, 4°) and must be reconstructed from the prose paraphrase in *Vǫlsunga saga.* Details of the reconstruction are disputed, but the following outline is generally agreed on. Sigurd visits Brynhild in her remote residence, and they plight their troth. He then rides to the court of the Gjukungs (Gunnarr, Hǫgni, and Gotþormr) and is drugged by their mother, Grimhild, so that he forgets his pledge to Brynhild and is free to marry their sister Gudrun. Grimhild proposes Brynhild as a match for Gunnarr, and Sigurd wins her for his companion by crossing the flame wall that encircles her and presenting himself disguised as Gunnarr. Both marriages are celebrated. Sometime later Brynhild and Gudrun quarrel in the hall over a matter of precedence, and Gudrun reveals the deception practiced on her rival. Brynhild retires to her bed in shock and anguish, and Gunnarr tries to rouse her without success. Sigurd then seeks to reconcile her to her fate, and a passionate dialogue ensues in which he finally confesses that he shares her love and offers to abandon Gudrun. But Brynhild's love has turned to hate, and she rejects any accommodation. She incites Gunnarr to murder Sigurd, claiming that he had sexual intercourse with her during the proxy wooing. The conclusion is unclear from the retelling in *Vǫlsunga saga,* but the murder is carried out, and in all probability Brynhild commits suicide, as in *Sigurðarkviða in skamma.*

Meiri is likely to be the latest of the Eddic Sigurd poems and presupposes both *Sigurðarkviða in forna* and *Sigurðarkviða in skamma.* A date around 1200 is the best guess. The most important innovations are a fully developed prior betrothal between Sigurd and Brynhild (canceled by Grimhild's potion of forgetfulness) and the psychologically probing dialogues that precede Sigurd's murder. The older heroic story of Brynhild's wrath and revenge is systematically transformed into a story of thwarted passion. *Meiri* is the only version in which Brynhild and Sigurd love one another and declare themselves openly. The poet's preoccupation with the erotic dimension of the story shows clearly that he participated in the transition from epic to romance in the late twelfth and early thirteenth centuries. His example may have inspired some of the Icelandic sagas that deal with romantic themes, most notably *Laxdœla saga.*

The romantic version of the legend may have originated in Germany. *Þiðreks saga* (translated from a German original) makes reference to the prior betrothal between Sigurd and Brynhild, and the *Nibelungenlied* contains a variety of hints suggesting such a relationship. Perhaps the prior betrothal was a feature peculiar to the German form of the story, and *Sigurðarkviða in meiri* is to be understood as a late attempt on the part of an Icelandic poet to reconcile the Norse and German versions.

BIBLIOGRAPHY

Edition and translation. R. G. Finch, ed. and trans., *The Saga of the Volsungs* (1965).

Studies. Theodore M. Andersson, "The Lays in the Lacuna of Codex Regius," in Ursula Dronke *et al.,* eds., *Speculum Norrœnum: Norse Studies in Memory of Gabriel Turville-Petre* (1979), 6–26, *The Legend of Brynhild* (1980), and "Beyond Epic and Romance: Sigurðarkviða in meiri," in Rudolf Simek *et al.,* eds., *Sag-*

naskemmtun: Studies in Honour of Hermann Pálsson (1986), 1–11; Andreas Heusler, "Die Lieder der Lücke im Codex Regius der Edda," in *Germanistische Abhandlungen Hermann Paul dargebracht* (1902), 1–98, repr. in his *Kleine Schriften,* II, Stefan Sonderegger, ed. (1969), 223–291.

THEODORE M. ANDERSSON

[See also **Brynhild; Eddic Poetry; Sigurd.**]

SIGURÐARKVIÐA IN SKAMMA (The short lay of Sigurd), so titled in the manuscript Codex Regius 2365, 4°, is the only complete Eddic poem of Sigurd and Brynhild still extant, but in some ways it is the most difficult to understand because of its allusiveness. It may be described as an elegiac elaboration of *Sigurðarkviða in forna* (The old lay of Sigurd) from a late date in the twelfth century or from the early thirteenth century. Sigurd wins Brynhild for Gunnarr under circumstances that are not fully divulged. The quarrel of the queens is omitted, but Brynhild seethes with jealousy that her rival Gudrun should possess Sigurd and threatens to leave Gunnarr unless he arranges Sigurd's death. The deed is assigned to the younger brother Gotþormr, who is not bound to Sigurd by oath, and is carried out in Sigurd's bedchamber as he lies asleep next to Gudrun. Brynhild laughs when she hears Gudrun's lament, but Gunnarr sees through her mask and perceives her grief. Brynhild replies in a long monologue recalling the family pressure exerted on her to wed Gunnarr. She then stabs herself with a sword, but before dying she prophesies the fate of the family (told in the Eddic poems *Atlakviða, Atlamál,* and *Hamðismál*). Her last request is for a common funeral pyre with Sigurd.

Although *Skamma* numbers an ample seventy-one stanzas, it is elliptical in the early part of the story and detailed only in the elegiac and prophetic speeches from stanza thirty-three on. The motivation for Brynhild's plot against Sigurd is jealousy (the details of her deception are less important and are not specified), and it is possible that the poet knew the version of the story according to which there was a prior betrothal between Sigurd and Brynhild (later told in the lost *Sigurðarkviða in meiri*). Another feature not found in *Sigurðarkviða in forna* is the pressure brought to bear by Brynhild's family in order to make her marry Gunnarr. Brynhild's suicide is not inherited from an earlier version and is likely to be the *Skamma* poet's invention. The monologues and retrospective stance of the poem connect it with the late elegiac poems of the *Edda* (*Guðrúnarkviða* I and *Helreið Brynhildar*). This context suggests that *Skamma* is an attempt to accommodate an old story to a new style. It does not offer a reinterpretation of the story so much as it gives scope for Brynhild's laments. She no longer appears as the decisive heroine of *Forna* but as a bitter and self-destructive victim. The assertiveness of Germanic heroic poetry has given way to the sentimental theme of a woman disappointed in love.

BIBLIOGRAPHY

Edition. Gustav Neckel, ed., *Edda: Die Lieder des Codex Regius nebst verwandten Denkmälern,* rev. by Hans Kuhn (1962), 207–218.

Translation. Henry Adams Bellows, trans., *The Poetic Edda* (1923, repr. 1957, 1969), 421–441; Lee M. Hollander, trans., *The Poetic Edda,* 2nd rev. ed. (1962, repr. 1977), 252–263.

Studies. Theodore M. Andersson, *The Legend of Brynhild* (1980); Finnur Jónsson, "Sagnformen i Sigurðarkviða in skamma," in *Arkiv för nordisk filologi,* **34** (1918); C. Michael Sperberg-McQueen, "The Legendary Form of Sigurðarkviða in skamma," *ibid.,* **100** (1985); Jan de Vries, "Het Korte Sigurdlied," in *Mededeelingen der Koninklijke Nederlandsche Akademie van Wetenschappen,* **2** (1939).

THEODORE M. ANDERSSON

[See also **Atlaviða; Atlamál; Brynhild; Eddic Poetry; Guðrúnarkviða I; Hamðismál; Helreið Brynhildar; Sigurd.**]

SILK provided medieval Europe with its most luxurious textile fabrics. At the dawn of the medieval era, Western Europe imported silk textiles from the Orient; but by the High Middle Ages, Italy had not only established an important sericulture component in her agriculture but become one of the world's major manufacturers of fine silk textiles, with the world's most advanced silk-making technology.

The origins of sericulture lie in ancient northern China and have been attributed to Emperor Huang Ti and Empress Hsi-ling Shih, about 2640 B.C.; but silk cultivation was more likely initiated by peasants of the Huang Ho Valley during the Neolithic era. Over the ensuing millennia, little change occurred in the basic processes of producing silk, the elastic but strong filament of the cocoon spun by the larvae or caterpillars of a variety of moths belonging to the Bombycideae and Saturniidae families of the Lepidoptera order, the most important being the Chinese *Bombyx mori.* According to the ancient Chinese procedure, the eggs of the silk moths (300–500 per moth) are first collected and kept in cold storage until the beginning of the mulberry leaf–producing season, when the eggs are encouraged to hatch by an increase in their air temperature to 25° C (77° F). After hatching and awakening, the caterpillars ("silkworms") feed voraciously for forty-two to forty-five days on chopped mulberry leaves, of which the chief variety are those of the white fruit-bearing *Morus albi.* Toward the end of this feeding period, the silkworms begin secreting, from two parallel glands on their underside, a liquid protein substance called fibroin, which exits through a common orifice at the worm's head, the spinneret, where the two fibroin strands are joined by another glandular secretion, a resinous albuminoid protein mixture called sericin. On contact with the air, the sericin solidifies, cementing the two fibroin strands together. The silkworms continue to produce this filament as one long continuous thread, ranging from 500 to 1,200 meters (about 1,600 to 4,000 feet), in a figure-eight fashion, until completely enveloped by it, that is, by the cocoon so spun. Spinning this cocoon takes between twenty-four and seventy-two hours, with a mean of sixty hours. A kilogram (2.2 pounds) of silkworms can produce about twelve kilograms (26.5 pounds) of silk a year in this fashion.

The protective cocoon allows the silkworm to pupate into the chrysalis stage. After about ten days the chrysalises are ready to break through the cocoon to emerge as moths, at which time, while the cocoon is still fully intact, they are killed by steam or hot-air suffocation—except for those to be retained for breeding.

The subsequent conversion of the cocoon filament into silk yarn for weaving involves essentially two distinct processes known as reeling and throwing. First, suitable cocoons are plunged into boiling water to soften and dissolve some of the sericin (constituting about 25 percent of the fiber); then they are stirred with glass rods, to which the filaments adhere. To provide greater strength and uniformity, three or more filaments are slowly unwound or "reeled" together from their cocoons by a hand crank onto a circular spoke-reel, thus forming a single sericin-united thread. For every ten kilograms (about 22 pounds) of cocoons, this process yields about one kilogram (2.2 pounds) of commercially usable reeled silk, which is marketed as "raw silk" after being rewound (unreeled) into coiled skeins.

To make the silk fully suitable for weaving, however, required the supplementary process known as throwing (from the Old English *thrāwān,* to turn, twist—that is, to add twist to the yarn). For this process, the ancient Chinese (or possibly the Indians) had developed the silk spoke-reel into a hand-powered spool-winder consisting of: (1) a winding-wheel in the form of a rimless spoke-wheel, whose ends were joined together in zigzag fashion by a continuous cord to form a drum-shaped surface; and (2) a horizontally mounted spindle, serving as both bobbin and axle, connected to the spoke-reel's drum by a continuous, oval-shaped driving band. Onto this spindle the throwster (silk-spinner) wound bundles of untwisted filaments from their skeins, which had been soaked in an oil-based emulsion to soften the sericin. Then, using one hand to operate the winding-wheel, the throwster drew the silk filaments from the end of the revolving spindle, whose rapid rotation twisted the silk fibers together as they were drawn off, thus preventing separation, and producing a strong, unified, fully developed yarn that was then wound onto spools. Note that the very nature of the silk filaments permitted the continuous twisting and winding-on of the yarn, in contrast to the treatment of other fibers, for which spinning (drafting and twisting) and winding were separate, intermittent operations, before the fifteenth century. Unreeled silk—that is, silk from a cocoon—and other waste silk fibers, however, were prepared by the same methods used for other textile fibers: originally, by combing and distaff-spinning (on a drop-spindle); subsequently, by carding and by spinning on an Indian or "great" spinning wheel.

Sericulture and silk textile production remained a Chinese imperial monopoly, jealously guarded for well over two thousand years, until about 140 B.C., when, according to legend, some Bombyx eggs and sericulture secrets were smuggled into Khotan (Central Asia, southwest of Sinkiang) and from there into India. By A.D. 300, both sericulture and silk textile manufacturing had spread to Japan and Korea and then, via India, to Sasanian Persia. To the west, the Roman Empire could also boast of having silk-weaving industries, principally in Syria and Egypt, which relied on silk yarns or raw silk imported, from about 50 B.C., by the famed Central Asian "Silk Road." But the Greco-Roman West did not learn the secrets of sericulture itself until the mid sixth century, when, according to Procopius, Emperor Justinian's court historian, two Christian monks succeeded in smuggling Bombyx eggs and mulberry seeds from Central Asia into Constantinople. Silk manufacturing thereafter became a state monopoly, and one of the Byzantine Empire's most important industries. Subsequently, with the Islamic invasions of the eighth century, the Arabs introduced sericulture into Spain, so that, by the early ninth century, silk textile production—of *siklātūn* especially—is recorded at Almería. By the late eleventh or early twelfth century sericulture had also been established in Muslim Sicily; and by the thirteenth century silk textiles were being woven on the Italian mainland itself, principally at Lucca and Bologna.

These two Italian cities were also the site of one of the most important and truly revolutionary technological innovations in the premodern history of textiles: the silk-throwing machine, first recorded at Bologna in 1272, and evidently the creation of a Lucchese exile named Borghesano. Housed in Europe's first true industrial factory, with a central source of water power, this machine permitted two to four operatives to displace several hundred handthrowsters in producing fine, strong silk yarn in a continuous process of drafting, twisting, and winding-on. The machine, about five meters (some sixteen feet) in diameter, consisted of two concentric wooden structures, one revolving and the other stationary. The inner framework rotated about the central vertical shaft (axis), which was driven by an undershot waterwheel. The fixed outer framework supported two rows of twelve horizontal reels or "swifts" each, and below each row a corresponding row of spindles, ten per reel, for a total of 240 spindles. All of these reels and spindles were rotated at their own specific speeds by drum-gears built into the perimeter of the fixed outer framework; the drums, in turn, were rotated by grooved contact with "blades" projecting like spokes from the revolving inner framework. Each spindle contained two essential parts: a rigid bobbin, on which were wound the silk filaments, rotating directly with the spindle itself; and above the bobbin, attached to a pin on top of the spindle, a freely moving conical cap to which was fixed an S-shaped wire "flyer." The silk filaments were fed from the bobbin through the two eyelets of the flyer to the swift-reels above; the differential rotations of the reels, flyers, and spindle-bobbins thus effected a continuous process of upward drafting, twisting, and winding onto the reels, known as "uptwisting." Later models of the fourteenth century, when silk-throwing mills were also established at Florence and Venice, contained four or five rows each of reels and spindles, in varying combinations, with up to 480 spindles.

The silk yarn skeins so spun were then boiled to remove remaining sericin gums, then rinsed, dried, and bleached to a pearly white in hot sulfur fumes, and finally dyed or woven undyed. The weft yarns were generally much more loosely twisted than the warp, such as organzine yarns, consisting of two or more threads doubled and tightly twisted in opposite directions. The very high-twist crepe yarns, on the other hand, with eight to fifteen twists per centimeter (forty to eighty per inch), were used for both warp and weft in weaving.

Silk fabrics, as well as mixed fabrics containing silk yarns, were originally woven in the same manner as were those of other fibers, on variants of the original, vertical loom, whether warp-weighted or fixed with a base beam. Subsequently they were woven on the horizontal box-loom, which first appeared in the West during the eleventh century.

By far the most important development for silk weaving was the introduction, in the thirteenth century, of the Eastern drawloom, whose origins are to be traced not to Han China, as is commonly supposed, but to Sasanian Persia (224–651). The key feature of this loom, whose modern descendant is the jacquard loom (1804), was the "pattern harness" system, which permitted the weaving of intricate and ornate figure designs. Such designs, characteristic of Asian as well as Byzantine and medieval Italian silks, whether damasks, velvets (cut and uncut piles), satins, or brocades, were predominantly of animals and plants, including, from the fifteenth century, the so-called pomegranate figures. Because of their intricacy, these designs required up to a thousand different weave interlacings, an impossibly difficult task on traditional looms, with their limited number of harnesses. The fully developed drawloom, however, greatly facilitated such operations. A perforated board ("comber board") was placed directly over the horizontal warps, in place of the heddle harnesses; through the holes in the board were hung leashes that served as heddle cords, each leash being connected to all the warp ends having the same interlacing. At their lower ends, below the board, the leashes were weighted with lead strips (lingoes) to maintain the proper tension; and, at their upper ends, they were connected to pulley cords. The pulley cords, in turn, were passed through holes in the bottom of a pulley box and over their respective pulleys positioned in the box; then they were carried horizontally to be fastened securely on a side wall. Each pulley cord was connected to a group of leashes that governed all the warps forming a "repeat" in the weave pattern. Usher cites an example of a pattern repeated twenty-eight times in the width of the loom, for which one pulley cord governed twenty-eight leashes and five other cords governed fifty-six each. Each pulley cord was pulled or "drawn" to open its own specific weaving shed, to permit the passage of the weft-bearing shuttle. The very laborious and exacting task of drawing these pulley cords in the assigned order was given to the weaver's assistants, up to four, known as "drawboys," who were stationed high aloft in the loom.

Because of such intricate pattern designs, as well as the very fine, lustrous, resilient, and soft material itself, the best silks were the most aristocratic and most costly of all textiles in the ancient, medieval, and early modern worlds, sometimes rivaled but never surpassed by woolen "scarlets." In medieval Europe, a considerable variety of silks, silk-based fabrics woven with other fibers, and silks interwoven with gold or silver were manufactured: from very light and sheer chiffonlike fabrics to heavy, deep-pile velvets and brocades. For four hundred years, the northern Italian towns maintained virtual supremacy over Europe's silk industry and trades. The major challenge subsequently came from France, whose silk industry was effectively founded at Tours by 1470 (following Louis XI's abortive proposals for one at Lyons, in 1466); growing much more rapidly after the creation of silk-weaving crafts at Lyons in 1536, the French industry succeeded in breaking the Italian hold in the course of the seventeenth century.

BIBLIOGRAPHY

Walter Endrei, *L'évolution des techniques du filage et du tissage du moyen âge à la révolution industrielle* (1968); W. English, "A Study of the Driving Mechanism in the Early Circular Throwing Machines," in *Textile History,* 2 (1971); Robert J. Forbes, *Studies in Ancient Technology,* IV, *Textiles,* 2nd rev. ed. (1964); Agnes Geijer, *A History of Textile Art* (1979); Robert S. Lopez, "Silk Industry in the Byzantine Empire," in *Speculum,* 20 (1945); R. Patterson, "Spinning and Weaving," in Charles Singer *et al.,* eds., *A History of Technology,* II, *The Mediterranean Civilizations and the Middle Ages, c. 700 B.C. to c. 1500 A.D.* (1956); Milton H. Rubin, "Silk," in *Encyclopaedia Britannica,* XX, 14th ed. (1972); Abbott Payson Usher, *A History of Mechanical Inventions,* rev. ed. (1954), 258–303.

JOHN H. MUNRO

[See also **Costume; Scarlet; Technology; Textile Technology; Textiles; Trade;** and frontispiece to this volume.]

SILVERSMITHS. See **Metalsmiths, Gold and Silver.**

SIMÓN DE COLONIA. See **Juan and Simón de Colonia.**

SIMON DE MONTFORT (*ca.* 1165–1218), leader of the Albigensian Crusade. Simon III was the son of Simon II and his second wife, Amicia de Beaumont, sister of Robert, fourth earl of Leicester. On their father's death (1180/1181) Amaury, Simon's older brother, received the county of Évreux and Simon inherited Montfort, Épernon, and Houdan in the Île-de-France. In 1204, on the death of his maternal uncle, Simon became earl of Leicester. King John recognized the title in 1206 only to confiscate the English lands in 1207.

Simon joined the Fourth Crusade in the company of his neighbor Guy, the abbot of Vaux-de-Cernay, but deserted before Zara and shipped to Palestine, from which he returned by 1206. Asked by Odo, duke of Burgundy, to join the Albigensian Crusade in 1208, he agreed after seeking divination in the Psalter. The duke paid well, and it was probably through his influence and that of the abbot of Vaux-de-Cernay that a committee of crusaders in August 1209 chose Simon to be lord of the conquered Trencavel lands. Pedro II of Aragon (Pere I in Catalonia) accepted his homage as viscount in 1211. After defeating Pedro and Raymond VI of Toulouse at Muret, Simon conquered Toulouse and received the count's lands west of the Rhone from the Fourth Lateran Council. Philip Augustus received his homage as count of Toulouse and duke of

Narbonne in 1216. Simon was killed while besieging Toulouse on 25 June 1218 and was buried in the abbey of Hautes-Bruyères near Montfort. He and his wife, Alice, daughter of Bouchard IV of Montmorency, had seven children: Amaury, the eldest, succeeded to his southern lands; and Simon IV became earl of Leicester. The others were Amicia (married Gaucher II de Joigny), Guy (married Perronelle de Bigorre), Robert, Laura (married Gerard II de Piquigny), and Perronelle (nun at St. Antoine-des-Champs).

BIBLIOGRAPHY

Yves Dossat, "Simon de Monfort," in *Cahiers de Fanjeaux,* 4 (1969); Auguste Molinier, "Catalogue des actes de Simon et d'Amauri de Montfort," in *Bibliothèque de l'École des Chartes,* XXXIV (1873); André Rhein, *La seigneurie de Montfort en Iveline* (1910).

FREDERIC L. CHEYETTE

[See also **Albigensians; Aragon, Crown of; Crusades and Crusader States: Fourth; France; Philip II Augustus; Simon de Montfort the Younger; Toulouse.**]

SIMON DE MONTFORT THE YOUNGER (*ca.* 1200–1265), the fourth and youngest son of Simon de Montfort III, leader of the Albigensian Crusade, who became vicomte of Béziers and Carcassonne and eventually possessed most of the county of Toulouse. Simon III, whose mother was an heiress of the Beaumont family in England, claimed and received from King John the earldom of Leicester in 1207 but lost it when he supported Philip II Augustus against John. Little is known about the early years of his son Simon, known as "the younger." In 1230 he went to England, won the favor of Henry III, and a year later obtained the earldom of Leicester.

For some years Montfort was close to Henry III and loyally served him. In 1238 he married Henry's sister Eleanor, widow of the younger William Marshal. The king's brother Richard of Cornwall attempted to block this marriage, but it received papal confirmation in 1239. That same year Montfort quarreled with Henry III over some financial matters, and, leaving with his wife for France, he then went on a crusade. Agreeing upon his return in 1241 to serve Henry III on the disastrous Poitevin expedition of 1242, he thereby regained the royal favor. For the next twelve years he generally adhered to the royal cause, attempting to serve as a moderating influence between the king and the disaffected baronage. He abandoned his hope of accompanying Louis IX of France on his crusade to Egypt in 1248 when Henry III and his council asked him to administer the troubled duchy of Gascony. His firm administration was so disliked by the unruly and factious Gascon lords and the feuding factions of the leading families of the towns, however, that they prevailed upon the indecisive Henry III to permit an investigation. Although acquitted on all charges of maladministration, Montfort departed for France in 1252 because Henry III persisted in accusing him of improper use of royal revenues in Gascony.

When the French nobles offered him the regency of the kingdom made vacant by the death of Louis IX's mother, Blanche of Castile, Montfort, heeding the advice of Bishop Grosseteste of Lincoln, declined and made peace with Henry III in 1253. During the next few years his relations with Henry fluctuated from support to opposition. At Westminster in April 1254, at a great council that included two knights from each shire, Montfort spoke out so effectively against various policies of Henry III that Henry was refused a grant of taxes. Yet Montfort did not break with the royal cause; he even worked with the queen's uncle Peter of Savoy to persuade the pope to relieve Henry from his financial and political commitments concerning the Kingdom of Sicily. When the "Mad Parliament" assembled at Oxford in June 1258, however, Montfort and the earl of Gloucester led the baronial demand for reform. Montfort, who definitely seems to have taken a leading part in drafting the Provisions of Oxford, became a member of the permanent standing executive council of fifteen appointed to supervise Henry III and to govern the realm. In 1261, when the pope released Henry III from his assent to the Provisions of Oxford and to those of Westminster, Montfort, disgusted by this act and by his disagreements with various barons, went to France.

In 1263, convinced that there was no peaceful road to reform, the barons asked Montfort to return and to become the leader of a rebellion to restore the government established by the Provisions of Oxford. Momentarily in a commanding position, Montfort and the barons unwisely agreed to permit Louis IX of France to serve as an arbiter and to abide by his decisions. When in early 1264 Louis IX in the Mise of Amiens rendered his decisions completely supporting Henry III and the powers of kingship inherent in the royal prerogative, war followed, with Montfort leading an opposition composed mostly of younger barons and the towns. Throughout the winter and spring there were inconclusive maneuvers and negotiations. Finally, a royal army marched south to relieve Montfort's siege of Rochester, and in May 1264 the two armies faced each other at Lewes on the downs of southeastern England. On the fourteenth, Montfort's superior leadership prevailed over rashness and panic. Captured were Henry III, his eldest son, Edward, and Richard of Cornwall.

According to the Mise of Lewes then concluded, Edward and his cousin Henry of Almain were to become hostages, the Provisions of Oxford to be reconfirmed, and further reform to be implemented. Montfort reconstituted the baronial executive council, reducing its membership and completely dominating it as well as the realm. Sensing, however, that his government must have a broader base, he began bidding for the support of the knights of the shires and burgesses of the boroughs. For a parliament summoned to meet at London on 22 June 1264 Montfort ordered that four elected knights from each shire should be included. This parliament addressed itself to a reform of the government effective for the rest of Henry III's life. For a second parliament assembled in January 1265 at London, Montfort introduced another innovation: in addition to his baronial supporters he summoned two knights from each shire and two burgesses from each borough to discuss further reform of the realm and necessary taxation. Remaining in session into March, this assembly dealt with implementing the reform agreed to in the Mise of Lewes. To contend that Montfort envisaged the formation of a new representative national assembly would be wrong; he merely intended to enlarge the base of his support and to secure the adherence of the new moneyed and propertied classes. But in moving beyond the old feudal concept of reform and control of the king and in attempting to enlist a broader spectrum of the realm's classes, he unconsciously became an innovator of the representative principle.

The Montfortian political experiment was shortlived. It was too alien to an eight-hundred-year tradition of kingship and depended ultimately upon baronial cooperation, a rapport that seldom existed for long. The chief flaw in Montfort's plan for an executive was the establishment of a kind of triumvirate consisting of the young earl of Gloucester, the bishop of Chichester, and himself. This arrangment quickly failed because the other two members were figureheads and because the barons were suspicious of an executive so narrowly constituted. During the spring of 1265 baronial cooperation deteriorated as Montfort and the earl of Gloucester quarreled over the distribution of certain lands and the control of strategic castles, such as that at Bristol. By May Gloucester had broken with Montfort and had joined other dissident barons in support of Edward, who, having escaped from captivity in Hereford on 28 May, became the leader of the royal cause.

In the hostilities that followed, Montfort was outmaneuvered by Edward. Late in June, Edward captured the town of Gloucester and swiftly advanced upon Kenilworth, where he routed a force led by Montfort's son Simon. He then confronted the Montfortian army at Evesham in Worcestershire and on 4 August reversed the military decision of the previous year. Montfort and his eldest son, Henry, were killed and another son, Guy, was wounded and captured. After Montfort's head was cut off and sent to the wife of Roger Mortimer, his body was buried by the monks of Evesham. Thus ended Montfort and his attempt to restrict royal power. Until the constitutional crisis of 1258–1265 Montfort's career was unremarkable. His fame rests upon his attempt to construct some workable control over the king and royal government and to enlarge his own political support so that it was not solely baronial. Though not the father of representative parliaments, in those assemblies in which he included knights and burgesses Montfort provided Edward I and his successors with a model that proved practical and enduring.

BIBLIOGRAPHY

There are two comprehensive studies on Simon de Montfort: Charles Bémont, *Simon de Montfort,* Ernest F. Jacob, trans. (1930); and Margaret W. Labarge, *Simon de Montfort* (1962). See also C. H. Knowles, *Simon de Montfort, 1265–1965* (1965). There is also much material on Montfort in Ernest F. Jacob, *Studies in the Period of the Baronial Reform and Rebellion, 1258–1267* (1925); Frederick M. Powicke, *King Henry III and the Lord Edward,* 2 vols. (1947); I. J. Sanders, ed., *Documents of the Baronial Movement of Reform and Rebellion, 1258–1267* (1973); Reginald F. Treharne, *The Baronial Plan of Reform, 1258–1263* (1932).

BRYCE LYON

[See also **Barons' War; England: 1216–1485; France: 1223–1328; Henry III; Louis IX; Provisions of Oxford.**]

Resurrection/Ascension and Pentecost. Two panels from a diptych by Simone da Bologna, *ca.* 1360.
THE WALTERS ART GALLERY, BALTIMORE

SIMON USHAKOV. See **Ushakov, Simon.**

SIMONE DA BOLOGNA (**Simone dei Crocefissi**) (*ca.* 1330–*ca.* 1399), Bolognese painter. A pupil and collaborator of Vitale da Bologna (*fl.* 1334–1361), Simone painted numerous crucifix scenes (hence the nickname) and other altarpieces, many of which survive in Bologna. Signed works include a *Crucifix* from S. Giacomo Maggiore (of 1370), a *Coronation of the Virgin* altarpiece from S. Michele in Bosco, and a signed portrait of the Avignon pope Urban V, all in the Museo Nazionale, Bologna. His major fresco cycle is in the Mezzaratta Church, Bologna.

BIBLIOGRAPHY

M. Bernath, "Crocifissi, Simone dei," in Ulrich Thieme and Felix Becker, eds., *Allgemeines Lexikon der bildenden Künstler,* VIII (1913), 141–142; R. Gibbs, "Two Families of Painters at Bologna in the Later Fourteenth Century," in *Burlington Magazine,* **121** (1979); Cesare Gnudi, *Vitale da Bologna and Bolognese Painting in the Fourteenth Century,* Olga Ragusa, trans. (1964); Evelyn Sandberg-Vavalà, "Vitale delle Madonne e Simone dei Crocifissi," in *Rivista d'arte,* **11–12** (1924–1930).

ADELHEID M. GEALT

[See also **Trecento Art; Vitale da Bologna.**]

SIMONE MARTINI (1280's–1344), Sienese painter. Most likely a pupil of Duccio di Buoninsegna (*ca.* 1255/1260–*ca.* 1318), Simone developed a highly personal and decorative style that was of great importance to later Tuscan artists. Simone's first dated work is the 1315 *Maestà* fresco painted for the Palazzo Pubblico in Siena. Based on Duccio's model, Simone's *Maestà* is courtly, mannered, and elegant. What is lost of Duccio's delicacy is gained in Simone's energetic and dazzling style.

In 1319 Simone received a commission for the altarpiece for the Dominican church at the convent of S. Caterina in Pisa (now Pisa, Museo Nazionale), and he probably executed his signed polyptych for the Duomo of Orvieto shortly thereafter. Between 1321 and 1323 documents record Simone's activity for the Palazzo Pubblico of Siena. He restored his 1315 *Maestà* and provided other paintings that have since been lost.

The date 1328 appears on his large equestrian portrait of the condottiere Guidoriccio da Fogliano in the Palazzo Pubblico, a date that may commemorate Guidoriccio's victory over Castruccia Castracane. It is uncertain that the date also reflects the year of the painting's execution.

In 1333 Simone painted one of his most influential works. His *Annunciation,* the first surviving Western altar painting dedicated to this subject, was probably painted for the Siena Duomo (the wings were painted by his brother-in-law Lippo Memmi), and is now in the Uffizi in Florence. (See illustration at "Annunciation.") Copied at least seven times, the *Annunciation* provided a linear, decorative, and psychologically remote alternative to the spatial and psychological realism posited by Giotto two decades before in his fresco (Padua, Arena Chapel). Simone's vision profoundly influ-

The Funeral of S. Martin. Fresco from the S. Martin chapel of S. Francesco at Assisi, *ca.* 1328. ART RESOURCE

enced Sienese and Florentine painters of the mid trecento, notably Barna da Siena, Nardo di Cione, and Orcagna. Simone's panel of St. Louis of Toulouse (Naples, Museo di Capodimonte) shares some stylistic affinities with the *Annunciation,* although its exact date is unknown. An annual grant awarded to Simone by the king of Naples in 1317 has been suggested as the date of the commission.

Simone's major fresco cycle, the S. Martin chapel for the lower church of S. Francesco at Assisi, is undocumented. Generally dated between 1320 and 1330, it is one of the most splendid overall decorations to survive from the trecento. Most likely Simone designed its floor, windows, and vaults, as well as its sumptuously colored, exquisite frescoes. Using works by Duccio and Giotto as sources, Simone transformed them into his own highly refined idiom. His characters move with grace and reserve, while his compositions flow from one frame to another with smooth, easy transitions. The colors, which are delicate and understated, are a marvelous foil to the almost ephemeral creatures inhabiting these frescoes.

In 1340 Simone moved to Avignon. Two ruined frescoes on the portal of the cathedral depicting a *Madonna of Humility* and a *Blessing Christ Surrounded by Angels* are all that survive in Avignon of his activity there.

Some miniatures, notably a frontispiece depicting a Vergilian allegory, have been attributed to him (Milan, Biblioteca Ambrosiana; see illustration at "Petrarch" in volume 9).

BIBLIOGRAPHY

Elizabeth H. Beatson *et al.*, "The St. Victor Altarpiece in Siena Cathedral: A Reconstruction," in *Art Bulletin,* **68** (1986); Ferdinando Bologna, *Gli affreschi di Simone Martini ad Assisi* (1965); Bruce Cole, *Sienese Painting from Its Origins to the Fifteenth Century* (1980); Gianfranco Contini and Maria C. Gozzoli, *L'opera completa di Simone Martini* (1970); Millard Meiss, "The Madonna of Humility," in *Art Bulletin,* **18** (1936); Giovanni Paccagnini, *Simone Martini* (1957), and his article on the painter in *Encyclopedia of World Art,* IX (1964), cols. 502-508; Henk Van Os, *Sienese Altarpieces: 1215–1460: Form, Content, Function,* I (1984); Car Volpe, *Simone Martini e la pittura senese da Duccio ai Lorenzetti* (1965); John White, *Art and Architecture in Italy: 1250–1400* (1966), 233–243.

ADELHEID M. GEALT

[See also **Annunciation** (with illustration); **Assisi; Barna da Siena; Duccio di Buoninsegna; Fresco Painting; Gothic Art; Gothic, International Style; Lippo Memmi; Maestà; Panel Painting; Siena; Trecento Art.**]

SIMONY. In its most general sense, simony is the trafficking in sacred things. In the first three centuries of Christianity, the purchase of church offices and holy orders was not a significant problem. When Christianity became the state religion of the Roman Empire in the fourth century, however, the church was transformed into a wealthy institution whose offices were valuable enough to be bought and sold. In the late Roman Empire, gifts or bribes (*sportulae*) to secular officials were a routine element of doing business, and that outlook began to characterize church officialdom as well. Such venality provoked complaint, and its practitioners were compared to a New Testament villain, Simon the Magician (Magos), a figure of fascination in early Christianity. In the first and second centuries of the Christian era, Simon became the focus of a complex set of historical memories and legends. In particular, Christian heresiologists (beginning with Hegesippus and Irenaeus) regarded Simon as the arch-heretic, the first of those who attempted to corrupt the faith.

As the buying and selling of holy orders and church offices became a serious problem, Simon also became the model of those who bought sacred things. The notion of simony is derived specifically from the account (Acts 8:9–24) of Simon's attempt to buy from the Apostle Peter the power to confer the Holy Spirit by the laying on of hands. Peter rebuked Simon with the words, "May your silver be lost forever, and you with it, for thinking that money could buy what God has given for nothing!" (Acts 8:20).

The terminology of simony evolved slowly. The word derived from Simon's name could refer to all aspects of buying and selling or to buying alone. By the eleventh century the seller in a simoniacal transaction could be designated by a distinct term drawn from the Old Testament. In 2 Kings 5:1–27, the Aramaean general Naaman was cured of leprosy by the prophet Elisha, who refused to take any gift for the cure. Elisha's servant Giezi (Gehazi) went secretly to Naaman and took two talents of silver as a payment for the cure. For the sale of God's free gift, Giezi and his descendants were struck with leprosy. Just as Simon was the type of the buyer, Giezi was the type of the seller in a simoniacal transaction and the expressions *lepra Giezi* and *giezia* designated the crime of selling a holy thing. Gregory I used the expression "simoniacal heresy" (*simoniaca heresis*) to designate the buying and selling of holy things, although it is doubtful that simony was generally regarded as heretical in itself. It was apparently during the bitter quarrel over lay investiture in the eleventh century that the abstract noun *simonia* was coined.

In the fourth and fifth centuries, simony was rather narrowly understood as the giving or taking of money in return for ordination or appointment to church office. The Council of Chalcedon (451) ordered that bishops who ordained or promoted in return for money should be deposed, and those who paid for positions or orders should lose what they bought. Gregory I broadened the notion of what constituted an illicit payment when he remarked in a homily that the simoniacal payment could take one of three forms: the transfer of an object of value (*munus a manu*), the use of flattery or influence to curry favor (*munus a lingua*), or the giving of service with the expectation of a reward (*munus ab obsequio*).

The concept of simony was worked out between the fourth and sixth centuries by prestigious church fathers and was incorporated in theology and canon law. However, the social, economic, and political conditions of early medieval Europe, particularly the pervasive influence of kings and powerful laymen in church appointments, rendered the prohibitions of simony a virtual dead letter. As the patterns of thought and behavior associated with the lay control of church appointments and revenues (*Eigenkirchenwesen*) became entrenched in Germanic Christian kingdoms, the strictures against illicit forms of payment, particularly favor and service, lost their force. Between the ninth and the eleventh centuries, payment of some sort was pervasive in filling church offices, conferring holy orders, and providing the sacraments and other services.

In the vigorous religious movement of the eleventh and twelfth centuries known as the investiture conflict, simony became one of the central issues, along with clerical marriage and lay investiture. The ancient canon law on simony was rediscovered, refined, and expanded. The reformers held suspect any association of payment for a thing that was holy or closely associated with something holy. In different places, times, and circumstances, the accusation of simony was made against stipends for masses or prayers, payments to enter religious life, fees for notaries in ecclesiastical chanceries, fees for the confirmation of ecclesiastical elections, and fees for the burial of the dead. At least one theorist, Cardinal Humbert of Silva Candida (*d.* 1061), challenged the validity of holy orders obtained by simony, although his rigorist views did not prevail.

Beginning in the later eleventh century, the problems involved with defining, detecting, and punishing simony generated a considerable body of casuistry, particularly in the context of the canon law. Just as the investiture conflict ended in compromise, so the more extreme views on simony were tempered by the economic needs of the church in the casuistry of canonists. During this period several important changes occurred. Customary offerings and freewill gifts were legitimated. The *sin* of simony, which lay in the desire to buy or sell a holy thing, was distinguished from the *crime* of simony, which was the carrying out of the wish and had to have an external expression, however subtle or hidden it might be. Canonists came to regard some forms of simony, such as the buying of holy orders, as intrinsically evil, while other forms, such as exchanging one benefice for another, were regarded as evil because the church forbade them, and hence could be dispensed or treated leniently.

Although the theology and canon law surrounding simony were fixed in the aftermath of the investiture conflict during the twelfth and thirteenth centuries, simony in its many forms remained a chronic disciplinary problem in the church until early modern times.

BIBLIOGRAPHY

Émile Amann, "Simon le magicien," and A. Bride, "Simonie," in *Dictionnaire de théologie catholique,* XIV. 2 (1941); John Gilchrist, "*Simoniaca haeresis* and the Problem of Orders from Leo IX to Gratian," in *Proceedings of the Second International Congress of Medieval Canon Law* (Monumenta iuris canonici, ser. C, subs. 1) (1965); Hans-Jürgen Horn, "Giezie und Simonie," in *Jahrbuch für Antike und Christentum,* **8/9** (1965–1966); Jean Leclercq, "Simoniaca heresis," in *Studi Gregoriani,* **1** (1947); Joseph H. Lynch, *Simoniacal Entry into Religious Life: 1000–1260* (1976); Hans Meier-Welcker, "Die Simonie im frühen Mittelalter," in *Zeitschrift für Kirchengeschichte,* **64** (1952/1953); Raymond A. Ryder, *Simony: An Historical Synopsis and Commentary* (1931).

JOSEPH H. LYNCH

[See also **Benefice, Ecclesiastical; Councils (Ecumenical, 325–787); Gregory I the Great, Pope; Investiture and Investiture Conflict.**]

SIMUND DE FREINE (*fl.* 1190–1200), an Anglo-Norman writer, author of the *Roman de Philosophie,* a poem based on Boethius' *De consolatione Philosophiae,* and a *Vie de saint Georges,* which contains some episodes not found in Latin texts devoted to St. George. Simund de Freine was a canon in Hereford and a friend of Gerald of Wales (Giraldus Cambrensis).

BIBLIOGRAPHY

John E. Matzke, *Les oeuvres de Simund de Freine* (1909, rev. ed. 1968).

BRIAN MERRILEES

[See also **Anglo-Norman Literature; Boethius; Gerald of Wales.**]

SĪNĀ, IBN (Abū ʿAlī al-Ḥusayn ibn ʿAbdallāh ibn Sīnā, 980–1037), Islamic philosopher, scientist, and physician, known in the West as Avicenna and in the East sometimes as Bū ʿAlī (the son of ʿAlī) and also as al-Shaykh al-Raʾīs (the foremost among the wise).

Ibn Sīnā was born in the Persian city of Bukhara into an Ismaili family devoted to learning. He exhibited incredible precocity and at an early age mastered the Koran and the religious sciences. By the age of sixteen he was already known as a physician and in that capacity gained access to the royal Samanid library after successfully treating Nūḥ ibn Manṣūr, the Samanid prince. Intense study in this exceptionally wealthy library enabled Ibn Sīnā to master the other sciences, including metaphysics, so that at the end of his life he could mention in his autobiography that he knew no more then than he did at the age of eighteen. He is without doubt the most important self-taught master in Islamic philosophy and medicine, where regular transmission from teacher to student is strongly emphasized.

By the age of twenty-one, Ibn Sīnā had already become a widely known physician and scholar whose services were sought near and far by princes and kings, including Maḥmūd of Ghazna, who captured Bukhara at that time. But Ibn Sīnā had a particular dislike for this famous conqueror, and so departed from his native city to spend the rest of his tumultuous life in various cities of Persia at a time when, as a result of the Turkish migrations, local uprisings, and struggles between local rulers and the central caliphate, Persia and adjacent lands were experiencing a period of continuous disturbance. The physically strong Ibn Sīnā crossed the forbidding desert from Bukhara to the Caspian Sea on foot and survived the arduous journey while his companions perished.

From this exodus onward Ibn Sīnā's life was marked by traveling from one city to another to act as either court physician or, occasionally, government clerk. He traveled for a while in Khorāsān, then went to Rayy to one of the Buyid courts, and from there to nearby Qazwīn. But neither of these cities provided the necessary support to enable him to have the peaceful scholarly life he was seeking. Therefore, he accepted the invitation of another Buyid prince, Shams al-Dawla, to go to Hamadān in western Persia. There he gained the favor of the ruler, becoming the prime court physician and even vizier, as a result of which he had to face political intrigues and was once imprisoned.

In 1022, after the death of Shams al-Dawla and great difficulties that followed for him, Ibn Sīnā left Hamadān and went to Isfahan, where he enjoyed the longest period of tranquillity in his mature life, a period of fourteen years. During this time, in addition to being court physician, he taught regularly at a school that still stands in the old city of Isfahan and composed most of his books. In 1037, while accompanying the ruler ᶜAlāᵓ al-Dawla on a campaign, he fell ill and died shortly thereafter from colic in Hamadān, where his mausoleum, reconstructed in the 1950's, is one of the major historical monuments of Persia to this day.

Because of an incredible power of concentration, which enabled him to dictate even the most difficult works on metaphysics while accompanying a ruler to battle, Ibn Sīnā was able to produce an immense corpus despite the unsettled life he was destined to lead. Up to 276 works have been mentioned as having been written by him, ranging from the monumental *Kitāb al-shifāᵓ* (The book of healing), which is the largest encyclopedia of knowledge composed by one person in the medieval period, to treatises of a few pages. These works cover nearly every branch of knowledge, from metaphysics to medicine, in conformity with the integrating and at the same time encyclopedic genius of Ibn Sīnā.

The *Kitāb al-shifāᵓ* consists of four books devoted to logic, natural philosophy (*ṭabīᶜiyyāt*), mathematics (*riyāḍiyyāt*), and metaphysics (*ilāhiyyāt*). The *Kitāb al-najāt* (The book of deliverance) is a shorter synopsis of the *Shifāᵓ*, while the *Kitāb al-ishārāt wa'l-tanbīhāt* (The book of directives and remarks) represents the last major philosophical work of Ibn Sīnā and the most personal statement of his philosophical views. His other important philosophical treatises include the *Kitāb al-hidāya* (The book of guidance), *ᶜUyūn al-ḥikma* (Fountains of wisdom), *al-Mabdaᵓwa'l-maᶜād* (The book of origin and end), and the *Dānishnāma-i ᶜalāᵓī* (The book of knowledge for ᶜAlāᵓ al-Dawla), which is the first work of Peripatetic philosophy in Persian, and the visionary recitals *Ḥayy ibn Yaqẓān, Risālat al-ṭayr* (Treatise of the bird), and *Salāmān wa Absāl* (Salāmān and Absāl), which comprise a cycle wherein is to be found major elements of his "oriental philosophy." Ibn Sīnā also wrote a number of short treatises on the "hidden sciences" and mystical, theological, and religious subjects, including commentaries on the Koran in which he does not display any specific Ismaili tendencies. It is in fact difficult to judge which interpretation of Islam he followed.

The most important scientific works of Ibn Sīnā are the sections on natural philosophy and mathematics of the *Shifāᵓ* and the *al-Qānūn fi'l-ṭibb* (The canon of medicine), which is perhaps the most famous work in the history of medicine in both East and West. Composed of five books devoted to the principles of medicine, *materia medica,* "head-to-toe" diseases, diseases that are not confined to a specific organ, and compound drugs, this book served as a veritable bible for medicine in the West practically up to modern times, while it continues to be used in India and the Islamic world to this day. Ibn Sīnā also wrote some forty other medical works, including *al-Urjūza fi'l-ṭibb* (Poem on medicine), which was used by medical students to memorize the principles of medicine and pharmacology.

Ibn Sīnā wrote important treatises on language, grammar, and phonetics and devoted many pages of the *Shifāᵓ* to the study of politics and sociology. He was also an accomplished poet, and many of his poems dealing with philosophical and medical subjects in Arabic and Persian have survived.

PHILOSOPHICAL PERSPECTIVE

Ibn Sīnā marks the peak of Islamic Peripatetic (*mashshāᵓī*) philosophy. He brought to completion and perfection the movement begun by al-Kindī, al-Fārābī, al-ᶜĀmirī, and others to harmonize the philosophies of Aristotle and Neoplatonism in the bosom of the unitary teachings of the Koran and in the world of Abrahamic monotheism as it was reasserted through the Islamic revelation. Ibn Sīnā is without doubt the most universal and all-embracing of these Muslim Peripatetics, much more influential in later Islamic history than Ibn Rushd (Averroës), with whom the "Western" interpretation of this school in Spain reached its culmination a century and a half later. Ibn Sīnā placed the seal of his genius upon a grand synthesis that became a permanent intellectual perspective within the Islamic world. Basing himself on the unitary teachings of Islam, he drew from Aristotelian logic and physics, Neoplatonic metaphysics and psychology, and even certain elements of Stoicism and Hermeticism, and constructed a philosophy that marks the beginning of "medieval philosophy" in the Western sense of the term.

Despite being the greatest of the Muslim Peripatetic philosophers, however, Ibn Sīnā was also attracted to a more esoteric and "gnostic" form of wisdom based on inner illumination and the interiorization of the cosmos in the process of the journey of the soul beyond all cosmic manifestation. In his *Manṭiq al-mashriqiyyīn* (Logic of the Orientals), the visionary recitals, and other works, he wrote of that wisdom which was at once illuminative and oriental and which was to receive its full elaboration in the twelfth century by the master of the "school of illumination" (*ishrāq*), Shihāb al-Dīn Suhrawardī.

LOGIC AND LANGUAGE

Along with al-Fārābī and Ibn Rushd, Ibn Sīnā is the greatest of Muslim logicians and the most systematic among them. When he appeared upon the scene, the older school of Baghdad, in which the study of logic was based on the method of writing commentaries upon the *Organon* of Aristotle, had nearly died out, and the new activity of writing independent manuals on logic had not yet begun. Ibn Sīnā stands alone as the link between these two phases. He systematized the earlier work, especially that of al-Fārābī, but Ibn Sīnā's work was not confined to elaboration and systematization. He pondered over the role of logic as at once the tool of philosophy and a branch of it. He provided a detailed theory of hypothetical and disjunctive syllogisms and discussed articulation with respect to both quality and quantity. He elaborated the theory of singular propositions in a manner resembling the Stoics'. He also dealt with the theory of logical definition and classification. These and other features of his logic place him as one of the foremost figures in the development of that discipline in the medieval period.

Ibn Sīnā was also keenly interested in the use of language in relation to logic and to philosophy in general. Not only did he make studies on the origin of language and the relation between a word and its meaning, but he tried to elaborate and elucidate a philosophical vocabulary based on his semantic views. While in Arabic he had to rely on the existing technical vocabulary, which he refined in many instances, in Persian he carried out the much more daring task of seeking to create a whole vocabulary and language to express *mashshāʾī* philosophy for the first time in his other tongue. The *Dānishnāma* is an invaluable document from the point of view of the relation between language and philosophical meaning, and is a most important document for the traditional philosophy of language and semantics.

METAPHYSICS AND COSMOLOGY

Ibn Sīnā has been rightly called the first "philosopher of being," for it was he, rather than the Greek philosophers, who placed the study of being (ontology) at the heart of philosophy. As a result of the influence of the monotheistic revelation, namely Islam, within which he lived and breathed and whose tenets he followed, he considered the study of being to be the heart of that highest science which, since Aristotle, has come to be known as metaphysics. It is true that for Aristotle also the study of being was central, but the meaning of this fundamental concept in the work of the two thinkers is quite different. First of all, the concept of existence does not appear as a definite and clear concept in Greek philosophy as it does in Islamic philosophy, especially with Ibn Sīnā. Secondly, Ibn Sīnā distinguishes between necessity and contingency as a fundamental distinction between Pure Being, which is that of God and is very different from the Aristotelian understanding of being, and the existence of all that is other than Him. God is the Necessary Being (*wājib al-wujūd*), while existents are contingent (*mumkin al-wujūd*) and hence rely in a fundamental way upon the Necessary Being, without which they would be literally nothing. Ibn Sīnā also makes the clear distinction between existence and quiddity, which, along with the distinction between necessity, contingency, and impossibility (*imtināʿ*), form the backbone of his ontology. In all creatures, existence is added to their quiddity or essence. Only in the Necessary Being are they the same. The medieval Scholastic discussions about essence and existence were heavily influenced by Ibn Sīnā and other Islamic philosophers. It is enough to compare the Greek, Arabic, and Latin texts to see that what distinguishes medieval philosophy from Greco-Hellenistic philosophy is rooted in the Avicennian and Farabian discussions of being.

Besides emphasizing the oneness of the Necessary Being in conformity with the unitarian perspective of Islam, Ibn Sīnā also confirms the necessity of the One to give of Itself, to emanate and bring forth manifestation. He bases the creation of the world not only on the Divine Will but also on the Divine Nature. Being both Absolute and Infinite, God cannot but create the world, without which He would not be Creator (*al-khāliq*) as described in the Koran. Hence, there is the first creation or manifestation of the One, which Ibn Sīnā identifies with the Logos or Universal Intellect (*al-ʿaql*). The Intellect contemplates the One as Necessary Being, itself as contingency, and its existence as necessitated by the One. From these three modes of contemplation there issue the Second Intellect, the First Soul, and the First Heaven, the process continuing until the cosmos is generated. Creation is thus related to contemplation, existence to knowledge.

Ibn Sīnā was well aware of both the Aristotelian and Ptolemaic astronomical systems and described both of them in different works. As far as cosmology is concerned, he adopted the scheme of the nine spheres of Islamic astronomy, based on the Babylonian and Greek, and related the emanation of the Intellects, whose idea was connected to Plotinian emanation of the Intellect and the Soul from the One, to the visible heavens. Ibn Sīnā did not, however, fall into any form of so-called pantheism since he always emphasized the contingency of all that exists, from the Universal Intellect to the dust of the earth, before the One Necessary Being. The Second Intellect in this scheme corresponds to the highest heaven above the fixed stars and the Tenth Intellect to the moon, below which begins the world of generation and corruption. In the sublunar world, form and matter are wed together to constitute bodies, and there is constant change, new forms being impinged upon sublunar matter by the Tenth Intellect, which is thus called the "giver of forms" (*wāhib al-ṣuwar;* Latin, *dator formarum*).

The cosmology of Ibn Sīnā also emphasizes the idea of the chain of being whose origin can be seen in Greek philosophy but which in fact was "completed" for the first time only in the *Kitāb al-shifāʾ;* here Ibn Sīnā treated the "three kingdoms" (that is, minerals, plants, and animals) fully, complementing the work of Aristotle in zoology and Theophrastus in botany, and integrating the chain within the natural world into the universal hierarchy of existence reaching to the One, who remains transcendent vis-à-vis the chain. Furthermore, in his "oriental philosophy," Ibn Sīnā developed an esoteric cosmology in which the cosmos was not only described in a scientific manner, but was depicted as a crypt through which man has to journey and which he must ultimately transcend. There are in fact certain Latin apocryphal treatises on the journey of the soul through and beyond the cosmos attributed to Ibn Sīnā.

PSYCHOLOGY

Basing himself on Aristotle's *De anima* and Alexandrian commentators, but also adding elements not to be found in those sources explicitly, Ibn Sīnā developed a faculty psychology based on the relation between the five external and five internal senses. He also classified souls (*nafs*) into the vegetative, animal, and human or rational, each soul possessing certain faculties that are in fact developed fully only in certain species of a particular kingdom. Only in man are all the faculties belonging to all the three souls, which he possesses within himself, fully developed. Ibn Sīnā relates the gradual development of each faculty to the great chain of being, which is based on the fundamental notion of hierarchy and an ever greater degree of perfection as the chain is ascended.

Islamic philosophers such as al-Kindī and al-Fārābī developed the idea of grades and levels of the intellect from the potential to the Active Intellect. This fundamental doctrine, which was known and much debated in the medieval West, received its fullest elaboration in the hands of Ibn Sīnā, for whom the mind receives forms from the Active Intellect and through gradual perfection is able to become united with it.

MATERIAL PHILOSOPHY

The contributions of Ibn Sīnā to the various branches of the natural sciences are too numerous to list in any summary study. His most important work in physics was to develop—within the context of the four Aristotelian causes and the theory of hylomorphism—the criticism of John Philoponos against Aristotle's theory of projectile motion. Ibn Sīnā, like Philoponos, believed that in the case of such motion, a power is imparted to the moving body by the cause that puts the body in motion. Moreover, in contrast to Philoponos, Ibn Sīnā asserted that this power, which he called *mayl qasrī* (Latin, *inclinatio violenta*), would not be dissipated in a vacuum. He also tried to provide a quantitative relation between the velocity and weight of such a body. It was this cardinal idea that, through the writings of Peter Olivi and John Buridan, finally resulted in Galileo's impetus theory. The root of the key concept of momentum can thus be found in Ibn Sīnā's critique of the Aristotelian theory of projectile motion.

In geology Ibn Sīnā displayed some of his acumen in observation and experiment by analyzing meteors and studying the process of sedimentation. But his most important contribution was perhaps in the classification of substances and the systematic study of minerals in a section of the *Shifāʾ* that came to be known in the West as the *De mineralibus* and was attributed to Aristotle until modern times. Ibn Sīnā also made important studies in botany but almost always in relation to the medical properties of herbs.

MEDICINE AND PHARMACOLOGY

Ibn Sīnā is without doubt the most famous of Muslim physicians. In his work the grand synthesis of the Hippocratic, Galenic, and Dioscoridean, as well as the Indian and Iranian, medical traditions reached its most perfect form. The author of the *Qānūn,* which was printed in Latin nearly thirty times before the era of modern medicine and which is still used in the Islamic and Indian worlds, was entitled the "prince of physicians" in Europe, while in the East his fame became so proverbial that he entered into the folk literature of the Persians, Arabs, Turks, and Indian Muslims.

In medicine Ibn Sīnā combined a philosophizing tendency with clinical observation and acumen. He provided a grand framework for medicine by providing a philosophy of medicine based on an inner equilibrium between various temperaments and humors as well as the body and various "souls." He also emphasized the necessity of the ecological balance between the body and the outside environment, which included not only food and diet, whose significance for health he emphasized, but also air and other factors, including even sound. Ibn Sīnā was also a master of psychosomatic medicine and was fully aware of the importance of the health of the mind and the soul for the body.

Ibn Sīnā is credited with the discovery of brain tumors and stomach ulcers. He was the first to diagnose meningitis correctly and realize the contagious character of tuberculosis. He explained cerebral apoplexy and facial paralysis, and was able to distinguish between epileptic seizures and epileptiform hysteria. He studied sterility and sexuality and even proposed surgery for people displaying bisexuality. Besides emphasizing hygiene and preventive medicine, he wrote much on the significance of the correct diet for health, starting with the mother's milk, whose significance for the proper growth of the newly born he underlined. In the use of drugs he emphasized herbs and developed the existing pharmacopeia to an extent that it has served as a foundation for many medical practices to this day in the Islamic world.

INFLUENCE, EAST AND WEST

The philosophy of Ibn Sīnā, although attacked by such Ashᶜarite theologians as al-Ghazālī and Fakhr al-Dīn al-Rāzī, received renewed support in the thirteenth century from Naṣīr al-Dīn al-Ṭūsī and survived in the eastern Islamic world long after the decline of Peripatetic philosophy in Muslim Spain following the death of Ibn Rushd. In fact Avicennian philosophy became a permanent intellectual current in the Islamic world and has had followers to this day. His medical writings, meanwhile, gained universal acceptance throughout the Islamic world and his name became synonymous with Islamic medicine, which is sometimes referred to as *ṭibb-i Bū ᶜAlī* (the medicine of the Ibn Sīnā). In the contemporary revival of Islamic medicine, especially in India and Pakistan, his influence remains substantial. The figure of Ibn Sīnā is a permanent feature of Islamic thought, arts, and sciences whenever and wherever they are cultivated.

In the West, which came to know Ibn Sīnā as Avicenna (through the intermediary of Hebrew sources), the works of the master began to be translated in Toledo under the direction of Dominico Gundisalvo. The most prominent translators were the Jewish Avicennian philosopher Abraham ibn Daud, or Avendeuth, and Gerard of Cremona. In the Sicilian school much attention was paid to Ibn Sīnā, who was translated by Michael Scot. The process of translation of Ibn Sīnā continued throughout the Middle Ages and lasted into the sixteenth century with Andrea Alpego. As a result, much but not all of the *Shifāᵓ*, as well as the *Najāt,* the Autobiography, the *Qānūn,* and smaller works, appeared in Latin, but none of the "oriental philosophy" and such late texts as the *Ishārāt* reached the West.

Although there did not develop a Latin Avicennism in as distinct a manner as Latin Averroism, the influence of Ibn Sīnā is to be seen in nearly all the important later figures of Scholasticism, and he is, after Averroës, without doubt the most influential Islamic philosopher in the West. The direct influence of Ibn Sīnā is to be seen in the Augustinians, beginning with Gundisalvo himself, and in the strand of thought that Gilson has called "Avicennian Augustinianism." His influence is also to be seen in William of Auvergne, Alexander of Hales, Albertus Magnus, Thomas Aquinas, and especially Roger Bacon and Duns Scotus, the last of whom starts his study of metaphysics from a position which is close to that of Ibn Sīnā. But, strangely enough, the latinization of Ibn Sīnā meant also the secularization of the Avicennian universe through the banning of angels, who play such an important role in the Avicennian cosmos, and through a rejection of his theory of the illumination of the mind by the Active Intellect, which he also identified with the angel of revelation. As a result, the Avicenna who came to be so well known to the Latin West gradually parted ways with the Ibn Sīnā whom the Islamic world looked upon even more through the eyes of the Suhrawardian philosophy of illumination.

BIBLIOGRAPHY

Sources. Avicennae de congelatione et conglutinatione lapidum, E. J. Holmyard and D. C. Mandeville, trans. (1927); *Avicenna on Theology,* Arthur J. Arberry, trans. (1951); *Avicenna's Poem on Medicine,* Haven C. Krueger, trans. (1963); *Avicenna's Psychology,* F. Rahman, trans. (1952); *The Life of Ibn Sina,* William E. Gohlman, trans. (1974); *Le livre de science,* Mohammad Achena and Henri Massé, trans., 2 vols. (1955–1958); *Le livre des directives et remarques,* A. M. Goichon, trans. (1951); *The Metaphysica of Avicenna (Ibn Sīnā),* Parviz Morewedge, trans. (1973); *Die Metaphysik Avicennas,* Max Horten, trans. (1907); *La Métaphysique du Shifāᵓ: Livres I à V,* Georges C. Anawati, trans., I (1978); *Psychologie d'Ibn Sīnā,* Ján Bakoš, trans., 2 vols. (1956); *A Treatise on the Canon of Medicine of Avicenna,* O. Cameron Gruner, trans. (1930).

Studies. Soheil Afnan, *Avicenna: His Life and Works* (1958); Georges C. Anawati, *Essai de bibliographie Avicennienne* (1950); Bernard Carra de Vaux, *Avicenne* (1900); Henry Corbin, *Avicenna and the Visionary Recital,* Willard Trask, trans. (1960); Miguel Cruz Hernández, *La metafísica de Avicena* (1949); M. T. D'Alverny, "Avicenna latinus," in *Archives d'histoire doctrinale et littéraire du moyen âge,* **36–45** (1961–1970), **47** (1972); Louis Gardet, *La pensée religieuse d'Avicenne (Ibn Sīnā)* (1951); Étienne Gilson, "Avicenne et le point de départ de Duns Scot," in *Archives d'histoire doctrinale et littéraire du moyen âge,* **2** (1927); Amélie M. Goichon, *The Philosophy of Avicenna and Its Influence on Medieval Europe,* M. S. Khan, trans. (1969); Iran Society (Calcutta), *Avicenna Commemoration Volume,* V. Courtois, ed. (1956); Seyyed H. Nasr, *Three Muslim Sages* (1964) and *An Introduction to Islamic Cosmological Doctrines* (1978); Mazhar H. Shah, *The General Principles of Avicenna's Canon of Medicine* (1966); Roland de Vaux, *Notes et textes sur l'avicennisme latin aux confins des XIIᵉ–XIIIᵉ siècles* (1934); G. M. Wickens, ed., *Avicenna, Scientist and Philosopher: A Millenary Symposium* (1952).

SEYYED HOSSEIN NASR

[See also **Abraham ibn Daud; Alchemy; Alchemy, Islamic; Aristotle in the Middle Ages; Buridan, Jean; Buyids; Contraception, European; Contraception, Islamic; Encyclopedias and Dictionaries, Arabic and Persian; Essence and Existence; Fārābī, al-; Gerard of Cremona; Ghazālī, al-; Ghaznavids; Isfahan; Ismāᶜīlīya; Kindī, al-; Logic, Islamic; Medicine, History of; Michael Scot; Neoplatonism; Pharmacopeia; Philosophy and Theology, Islamic; Rushd, Ibn; Samanids; Scholasticism; Schools, Islamic.**]

ŠINAKAN, the peasant class in Armenian medieval society. The *šinakan* should not be confused with the *ṙamik,* of whom they formed the overwhelming majority but with whom they were not synonymous. The *šinakan* were bound to the soil and subject to taxes, corvées, and mass levies as infantry in wartime, but they were personally free, and some rights were granted to them in ecclesiastical canons.

BIBLIOGRAPHY

R. Khérumian, "Esquisse d'une féodalité oubliée," in *Vostan,* **1** (1948–1949); Hakob Manandyan, *Ditołutᶜyunner hin Hayastani šinakanneri drutᶜyan masin marzpanutᶜyan šržanum* (1925), and *Feodalizma hin Hayastanum* (1934), 160–161, 188–189, 205–210, 304–319; Cyril Toumanoff, *Studies in Christian Caucasian History* (1963), 127.

NINA G. GARSOÏAN

[See also **Armenia, Social Structure.**]

ṢINF (literally, "category" or "class," and used most commonly in its plural form, Arabic: *asnaf;* Turkish: *eṣnāf*) is used in Islamic sources to refer to categories of trade or professional occupations. The assumption that the organization of commerce in medieval Islamic cities is best understood by comparison with developments in European cities that witnessed the emergence of autonomous craft corporations or artisan guilds during the Middle Ages has generated a lively but largely irrelevant debate among Middle Eastern specialists. Publication of an increasing number of firsthand narrative accounts—in particular the *fütüvvetnames*, a genre that gained a special popularity in the period after 1200—now makes it possible to dispense with discussion of the forms that trade organization in the Middle East failed to take and allows us to investigate in greater detail the forms it did take. To avoid confusion with Western guilds, *eṣnāf* will here be translated as "craftsmen associations."

Origins. Islamic traditions of craft organization were strongly influenced by earlier models that originated in Sasanian Iran and that were developed in later centuries in the non-Arab hinterland of the Abbasid empire. These traditions seem to have been introduced to Iraq and Syria together with the Sufi movement, which spread throughout the Middle East during the ninth century, but it is from the late eleventh century that our most detailed information dates. Partly because of the Sufi connection, the rules governing the craftsmen associations had a strong moral and ethical component. The best early source describing the moral requirements for admission to a craftsman association is the *Qabusnama,* written in 1082. As the collapse of centralized political authority accelerated during the era of the "petty kings" (*ṭawāʾif al mulūk*), the caliphs of the late Abbasid empire began to look upon the workmen associations in the cities as potential allies. The caliphs wished to use the workmen associations as a counterbalance against the influence of the military elites, who were capable of holding the caliph virtual hostage in his own realm. Efforts aimed at coordinating the urban youth organizations (*futuwwa*) as a means for consolidating central control and promoting Islamic solidarity in provincial towns cut off from the direct influence of Baghdad reached a head during the period of al-Nāṣir (1180–1225), who was greatly assisted by the movement's philosopher Shihāb al-Dīn ʿUmar Suhrawardī (*d.* 1235). The movement was to have its greatest impact, however, not in consolidating the Abbasid regime (which fell to the Mongols after the sack of Baghdad in 1258), but in preserving traditions of Islamic culture, urban life, and commercial organization in Anatolia and western Iran, both dominated from the mid thirteenth century by an alien, non-Muslim power whose economy relied on the cities but was also shaped by many pastoral concerns.

Under Ilkhanid rule. During the period of Ilkhanid rule, and rule under a variety of successor dynasties (such as the Eretnids of Sivas) who held sway over central and eastern Anatolia after 1335, there was an unstated division of labor in the Islamic missionary movement. Responsibility for propagation of the faith by the sword was delegated to *ghāzīs*, while the task of promoting Islamic civilization and education, especially through encouraging commerce and urbanization, which were held to be indispensable elements of that civilization, fell to exemplary political and spiritual leaders heir to the *futuwwa* traditions called *akhīs*. The responsibilities of the *akhīs* in their civilizing mission were so all-encompassing precisely because Muslim education (*tarbīya*) concerned itself not only with learning and vocational training but also with the formation of sound character and the inculcation of moral values. Apart from their role as directors of craft activity, the *akhīs* performed a number of general functions as community leaders.

What we know of the organization of labor in the Middle East during the thirteenth and fourteenth centuries is learned mostly from the *fütüvvetname* literature written, largely in Persian, during the period of the dominance of the *akhīs*. A strong emphasis on social solidarity is a striking feature of this literature, which was produced during the time of Mongol occupation and disintegration of Muslim political authority. An unusual feature of the codes regulating membership in craftsmen associations was the requirement for apprentices to select, in addition to the master under whom they would pursue their technical training in the craft, two apprentice associates (*yol kardash*) to whom they vowed lifetime devotion. In addition, each member of a craftsman association was entitled, in times of personal, business, or family distress, to borrow funds from the common chest kept under the supervision of officers of the association. These ties helped to promote a strong ethic of mutual help which continued after the apprentice had completed his training and was permitted to open a shop on his own. The nurturing of these lifelong bonds helped to facilitate the circulation of market and business information among merchants who otherwise operated in considerable isolation from one another.

The requirement that a candidate for admission to a craftsman association pass a character test and promise his adherence to a strict moral code may be connected with the concerns of the *akhīs* in their role as community leaders more than as masters of a craft. Careful screening of the membership could prevent granting of rights—equivalent in many ways to rights of citizenship in a town—to elements suspected of harboring strong antiauthoritarian views likely to disrupt the affairs of the community. The attitude of the Sunni establishment to the youth and craftsmen associations in general tended to be strongly condemnatory, and the worldly concerns of the commercial classes dictated a close cooperation with both secular and religious authority. In the absence of any credible or (in the case of the Ilkhanid empire) closely interested higher authority, it was the *akhī*s themselves who determined municipal policy and coordinated commerce. Ankara in the mid fourteenth century is a good example of this kind of administrative setup. The exclusion of certain professions, such as weavers and butchers, from *futuwwa* membership may have had as much to do with the practical need to discourage oversubscription in certain professions as with moral revulsion against the practitioners of such "ignoble" trades.

Under the Ottomans. Futuwwa traditions were further elaborated and the work ethic again redefined by followers of the heroically portrayed and embellished, but probably historical, figure Akhī Ewrān. A work, copied in Konya in the late thirteenth century but probably dating from an earlier period, called the *Laṭāʾif al hikme* (Philisophical anecdotes) and attributed to Akhī Ewrān, expatiates emphatically on the social value that attaches to artisanal skill and development of expertise in the trades in a way strongly reminiscent of the *Qabusnama*. Whether Akhī Ewrān lived in the Seljukid thirteenth century or the Ottoman fifteenth century or is a figure whose historicity should be viewed with skepticism is still unresolved, but his influence on the development of guild traditions in the Ottoman period is undisputed. That *akhī* traditions still flourished in early-fourteenth-century Anatolia is fully documented in Ibn Baṭṭūṭa's travel account. Ibn Baṭṭūṭa notes that part of the broad role *akhī*s played in community affairs was providing hospitality to all Muslim wayfarers, be they merchants, mendicants, or pilgrims, in the *akhī* lodges.

The role played by *akhī*s in organizing the Islamic communities that sprang up along the expanding Ottoman frontier in the Balkans during the fourteenth and early fifteenth centuries is also attested as a typical feature of Ottoman urban growth during that period. As the central state apparatus developed with the transition from frontier state to empire in the mid to late fifteenth century, the overarching powers formerly enjoyed by the *akhī* leaders were gradually eclipsed by officials representing the central state bureaucracy. Within individual craftsmen associations, rituals and traditions associated with their past were preserved, and the patron saint (*pir*) connected with each order remembered and revered. However, these sentimental attachments failed—even within the limited context of commercial affairs—to restore the authority of the headman, called by that time variously *sheikh* or *pir*. By the late fifteenth century this figure's role was confined mostly to ceremony, and the day-to-day administration of the guilds was in the hands of representatives of each profession (*kethüda*) and foremen (*yıghıt bashı*s). These officials were responsible for coordinating guild regulations with central government policy.

It has been generally thought that the Ottoman *eṣnāf* were held in a subservient position by the government and as a consequence rendered powerless to control their own destiny, but acceptance of this conclusion requires more study of the role of the *eṣnāf* in settings outside the major imperial cities. Information emerging from studies of the medium-sized cities and towns of the Ottoman provinces seems to indicate that guilds (apart from those involved in providing the cities with basic necessities, such as foodstuffs, which were more strictly controlled) enjoyed a considerable degree of immunity from unwarranted government intervention.

BIBLIOGRAPHY

For general works on Islamic craftsmen associations see the writings of Gabriel Baer. Especially useful is his "The Organization of Labor," in Bernard Lewis *et al., Wirtschaftsgeschichte des Vorderen Orients in islamischer Zeit,* Teil 1 (1977), 31–52. The standard work for the Islamic city is Ira M. Lapidus, *Muslim Cities in the Later Middle Ages* (1967).

On the origins of the medieval urban tradition, see Kaykavus ibn Iskandar, *A Mirror for Princes: The "Qabus nama,"* Reuben Levy, trans. (1951), esp. chaps. 27, 32, and 43.

On post-Abbasid urban craftsmen associations, see the articles by F. Taeschner and C. Cahen in the *Encyclopaedia of Islam,* 2nd ed. (1960–), cited hereafter as *EI,* 2nd ed., especially "Akhī" and "Futuwwa." *Fütüvvetname* texts have been edited by A. Golpınarlı in his "Islam ve Türk illerinde fütüvvet teşkilatî ve kaynaklarî," Istanbul Üniversitesi, in *Iktisat Fakültesi Mecmuasî,* **11** (1949–1950), 3–354; see in particular the *fatwā* of al-Wardi cited on p. 65 and the list of professions excluded from *futuwwa* membership on pp. 316–318. On Ankara in the fourteenth century see F. Taeschner, "Ankara," *EI,* 2nd ed., I; and A. Tevhid, "Ankarada ahiler hükümeti," in *Tarih-i Encümeni Mecmuasî,* **19** (1329/1913), 1200–1204.

The following works study the role of craftsmen associations in Ottoman urban life. On the *akhi*s and their views on urbanism, see M. F. Köprülü, *Türk edebiyatînda ilk mutasavvîflar* (1918); M. Bayram, "Anadolu Selcuklularî zamanînda ahi teşkilatînîn kuruluşu ve gelişmesi," in Istanbul Esnaf ve sanatkârlar derneği, *Ahilik ve Esnaf* (1986), 175–185; the *Lataʾif al hikme,* a work attributed by Bayram to Akhī Ewrān, Paris, Bibliothèque Nationale, MS Persans A.F. 121. For further discussion on Akhī Ewrān see Köprülü, *op. cit.,* 239ff.; Gölpınarlı, *op. cit.,* 96–97, and F. Taeschner, "Akhī Ewrān," in *EI,* 2nd ed., I. On the role of *akhīs* in the life of provincial towns, see *The Travels of Ibn Baṭṭūṭa, A.D. 1325–1354,* H. A. R. Gibb, trans., II (1959), 416–466; Ö. L. Barkan, "Kolonizatör Türk Dervişleri," in *Vakîflar Dergisi,* 2 (1942), 279–386; and Nikolai Todorov, *The Balkan City, 1400–1900* (1983). On commercial life in the Ottoman urban setting in general, see H. Inalcık, "The Hub of the Ottoman City: The *Bedestan* of Istanbul," in *International Journal of Turkish Studies,* 1 (1979), 1–17.

RHOADS MURPHEY

[See also **Abbasids; Anatolia; Ankara; Baṭṭūṭa, Ibn; Ghāzī; Guilds and Métiers; Ilkhanids; Sasanians; Trade, Islamic.**]

SINFJǪTLI, a legendary hero identified with the tale of the Volsungs. Sinfjǫtli appears in the Old Icelandic sources, the *Poetic Edda* and *Vǫlsunga saga,* as the son and nephew of Sigmundr. He also appears in Old English tradition, in *Beowulf,* as Fitela, the son and nephew of Sigemund. The *Poetic Edda* mentions him in the two poems about Helgi Hundingsbani and in a short prose passage, "Frá dauða Sinfjǫtla," which links the poems of the Helgi cycle to the Sigurd legend. As the half-brother of Helgi, he accompanies him in battle against the sons of Granmarr, performing, before the actual engagement of arms, a ritual verbal duel with Guðmundr. The passage relates the story of his death.

The full story of Sinfjǫtli is told in the *Vǫlsunga saga,* where, as the product of an incestuous union between Signý and her twin brother, Sigmundr, he is the epitome of the Volsung hero. In this account, Signý, to avenge the slaying of her father, Vǫlsungr, by her husband, disguises herself and begets a child with Sigmundr. As the young hero, Sinfjǫtli, approaches manhood, he undergoes a threefold initiation conducted by his parents. In the first trial, he endures unflinchingly as his mother sews his clothes to his skin and then cuts both away. In the second, he successfully bakes bread with flour containing a poisonous snake. And in the third, he joins his father, after the two assume the outward form of a wolf, in slaying a group of men in a forest. At one point during the final trial, Sinfjǫtli kills eleven men single-handedly, and Sigmundr, enraged, bites him on the throat; his wound, however, is quickly healed by a magic leaf. Father and son then return to human form and together exact vengeance on Signý's husband. Finally, the saga relates the circumstances of Sinfjǫtli's death.

In a duel over a woman, Sinfjǫtli kills the brother of Sigmundr's wife, Borghildr. As punishment, Borghildr demands that Sigmundr banish the young hero. Sigmundr refuses, whereupon Borghildr devises a plan. She invites Sinfjǫtli to a banquet and offers him a drink that she has poisoned. Sigmundr, who is impervious to poison, seizes the cup and drains it. Borghildr offers a second cup, and Sigmundr again takes it. The third time, however, Sinfjǫtli himself drinks from it and dies. Grief-stricken, Sigmundr lifts his son's body and carries it on his back to a mysterious ferryman (believed to be Odin, father of all the gods); the ferryman accepts the body and disappears with it in his boat.

The etymology of the name Sinfjǫtli is disputed, but the second element, "fjǫtli," is clearly related to various Germanic words meaning "white-footed" and used as metaphors for "wolf." As a full-blooded Volsung, Sinfjǫtli should be the preeminent member of a family of heroes, whose ancestor and patron is Odin himself. Yet, his role in the extant sources is a comparatively minor one; it is certainly less important than that of Sigmundr or Sigurd. One reason may be found in the social sensitivity regarding the subject of incest. Nevertheless, Sinfjǫtli's story conforms generally to the paradigm of a hero's life proposed by several scholars. It contains, for instance, all the essential elements: divine ancestry, birth as a result of incest, difficult initiation into manhood, and, finally, death by treachery and journey to the land of the dead.

BIBLIOGRAPHY

Henry A. Bellows, ed. and trans., *The Poetic Edda* (1923); R. G. Finch, ed. and trans., *Vǫlsunga saga: The Saga of the Vǫlsungs* (1965); Gustav Neckel and Hans Kuhn, eds., *Edda: Die Lieder des Codex Regius nebst verwandten Denkmälern* (1927, repr. 1962); E. O. G. Turville-Petre, *Myth and Religion of the North: The Religion of Ancient Scandinavia* (1964), 200–201.

KAAREN GRIMSTAD

[See also **Beowulf; Eddic Poetry; Family Sagas, Icelandic; Iceland; Saga; Scandinavian Mythology; Vǫlsunga Saga.**]

SINOPIA, the term for the red ocher wash and brush drawing laid over the arriccio, or first plaster coat, setting out the composition that the fresco painter followed in preparing a wall mural. Most often sketched by the shop master, sinopias defined the overall design of a mural, which provided the best indication of a single master's style, since frescoes were most often the result of a collaborative effort between master and shop assistants. By the fifteenth century, sinopias were gradually replaced by the use of large cartoons.

BIBLIOGRAPHY

Cennino Cennini, *Il Libro dell'arte: The Craftsman's Handbook,* D. V. Thompson, trans. (1933, repr. 1954); Bruce Cole, *The Renaissance Artist at Work* (1983).

ADELHEID M. GEALT

[See also **Arriccio; Fresco Buono; Fresco Painting; Intonaco.**]

ŠIRAK (Shirak) (Greek: Siracene; Georgian: Širaki; Arabic: Sirāj), a district in central Armenia located along the middle and upper course of the Araxes, or Araks, River. Known as Eriahi in Urartian records, Širak perhaps owed its name to an incursion and settlement of the northern Caucasian people called Sirakoi in Greek. Širak was originally a part of the land of Ayrarat (Hebrew: Ararat), the royal domain of the Armenian kings, and its princely dynasty, the House of Kamsarakan, claimed descent from the Kāren-Pahlav branch of the Arsacid imperial house of Parthia. It was thus related to the Arsacid royal house of Armenia, deposed in 428. In addition to Širak, the Kamsarakans also owned the neighboring district of Aršarunik^{c}, from which they were sometimes known as the princes Aršaruni. The Kamsarakans became very important after the loss to Iberia (east Georgia) in 387 of the lands that had formerly lain between Širak and that country. The power of the house was broken by the Arabs, however, after the rebellion of 771/772, when the Kamsarakans sold both of their principalities to the Bagratids and partially migrated to the Byzantine Empire. Thereafter, Širak, now a part of the growing Bagratid holdings, came to form part of the Bagratid kingdom (884–1045), whose capital eventually was settled in Širak at the city of Ani in 961. In 1045 the Bagratid kingdom was annexed by the Byzantines, under whom Širak formed a part of the *Catepanate* (*Katepanikion*) of Iberia with its capital at Ani, but it was lost when Ani fell to the Seljuk Turks in 1064. Širak then passed to the Shaddadids, a Kurdish house (1064–1199), and then to the Georgian Bagratids, who gave it as a fief to the Mχargrdzelids (1201). Overrun by Mongol and Turkoman hordes (thirteenth to fifteenth centuries), Širak became Turkish until occupied by the Russians in 1828.

BIBLIOGRAPHY

Nikolai Adontz, *Armenia in the Period of Justinian,* Nina G. Gersoïan, ed. and trans. (1970); Ghevont M. Alishan, *Širak* (1881); Paolo Cuneo, *L'architettura della scuola regionale di Ani nell'Armenia medievale* (1977); S. T. Eremyan, *Hayastanĕ ĕst "Ašxarhac'oyc'"-i* (1963), 73–74; T. X. Hakobyan, *Hayastani, patmakan, ašxarhagrut^{c}iwn,* 2nd ed. (1968), 138–142; Heinrich Hübschmann, *Die altarmenischen Ortsnamen* (1969); Nikolai I. Marr, *Ani* (1934); V. Minorsky, "Ani," in *Encyclopaedia of Islam,* new ed., I (1960); Cyril Toumanoff, *Studies in Christian Caucasian History* (1963) and *Manuel de généalogie et de chronologie pour l'histoire de la Caucasie chrétienne* (1976, suppl. 1978), 55–56, 96–101.

ROBERT H. HEWSEN

[See also **Ani in Širak; Armenia; Arsacids/Aršakuni; Ayrarat; Bagratids; Kamsarakan; Mongol Empire; Seljuks; Shaddadids; Turkomans.**]

SIRMIUM (modern Mitrovica, Yugoslavia). Situated on the Sava River, Sirmium was a key fortress on the middle Danube. It fell to the Avars in 582 and was later in Bulgar hands. In the early eleventh century it was retaken by the Byzantines, but in 1071 the Pechenegs invaded it, and Sirmium became part of the Hungarian state. Throughout the twelfth century it changed hands a number of times in the wars between Byzantium and the Hungarians. The city was sacked by the Turks in 1396 and again in 1521. In 357 a church council was held at Sirmium at which the Arianism of the Emperor Constantius II was proclaimed as the state religion.

BIBLIOGRAPHY

George Ostrogorsky, *History of the Byzantine State,* Joan Hussey, trans. (1957, rev. ed. 1969).

LINDA C. ROSE

[See also **Arianism.**]

SIR GAWAIN AND THE GREEN KNIGHT. See **Gawain and the Green Knight, Sir.**

SIR ORFEO. The Middle English romance of *Sir Orfeo* has survived in three versions, one from the early fourteenth century and two from the fifteenth century; the earliest version, in the Auchinleck Manuscript (National Library of Scotland, Advocates' MS 19.2.1), is the most authoritative.

Sir Orfeo (this manuscript tells us) was both a king and an expert harpist who lived in "Traciens," as Winchester was once called. One day his wife, Heurodis, to whom he was devoted, fell asleep under a tree in the orchard; in a dream or vision the King of Fairy came to her and told her that the next day she would be carried off to live with him. Orfeo sent an armed company to guard her, but she disappeared from their midst. In his despair at the loss of his beloved wife, Orfeo entrusted his kingdom to his steward and went off to the wilderness, where he lived alone for more than ten years. Sometimes he saw fairy companies in the forest, and one day he recognized his wife among them. He followed them through a hole in a cliff into a beautiful country, where he saw many people who were thought to have died but were still alive; among them was his wife, asleep under a tree identical to the one in his orchard.

In his guise as a poor minstrel Orfeo played to the king of that land. The king, delighted with his performance, offered him any reward he wanted; he chose his wife, and carried her back to earth. When Orfeo came to Winchester and played to the court, his steward recognized the harp and asked him where he had found it; when he said that he had found it beside the body of a man torn to pieces by lions, the steward's grief at the supposed death of Orfeo proved his loyalty. Orfeo and Heurodis lived long and happy lives, and the faithful steward succeeded to the throne.

The prologue to the poem states that it is a Breton lay, and this is probably true; whether it ever existed in a Celtic language, or whether the original was a French imitation of the Breton style, is uncertain, but there is little doubt that the English poem was adapted from a French one. The basic story is plainly the classical story of Orpheus and Eurydice (even the proper names are scarcely altered), in the original Greek version rather than the more familiar Latin version, in which Eurydice is finally lost again; this Greek version is known to have been current in France as early as the eleventh century. The classical story has been much modified under the influence of Celtic legends, particularly of the Celtic concept of the otherworld, *Tír na mBeo,* the land of the living (in contrast with the classical otherworld of the dead).

The English version is told with great charm, and with a skill so sophisticated that it gives the impression of untutored simplicity. The supernatural is treated in such a way that it seems not mere magic, but a glimpse of an alien, awesome, and dangerous world. The love between Orfeo and his wife, and the devotion of the steward, have a human realism and solidity rare in medieval fiction; at the back of everything is a stable society, proof against both the invasion of an alien world and the vicissitudes of human waywardness.

BIBLIOGRAPHY

The standard edition is Alan J. Bliss, *Sir Orfeo* (1954, 2nd ed. 1966). Studies include Dorena Allen, "Orpheus and Orfeo: The Dead and the Taken," in *Medium Aevum,* 33 (1964); Peter J. Lucas, "An Interpretation of *Sir Orfeo,*" in *Leeds Studies in English,* n.s. 6 (1972); J. Burke Severs, "The Antecedents of *Sir Orfeo,*" in MacEdward Leach, ed., *Studies in Medieval Literature in Honor of Albert Croll Baugh* (1961). On the Orpheus legend in general, see John B. Friedman, *Orpheus in the Middle Ages* (1970).

A. J. Bliss

[See also **Middle English Literature; Mythology, Celtic.**]

SIRVENTES. The *sirventes* is an Old Occitan (Old Provençal) lyric genre (called *serventois* in Old French). The Occitan *sirventes* corpus includes about 550 poems, more than 20 percent of the surviving Old Occitan lyrics (by contrast, there are about 1,000 *cansos,* or love lyrics). In the fourteenth century the *Leys d'amors* defined the *sirventes* as borrowing its form and/or melody from a preexisting *canso* or *vers.* According to this same source, the *sirventes* deals with individual or general reproof or blame, to chastise the foolish and the evil; or it can be about some war. It is perhaps because the older elements "serve" the new poem that the form is called *sirventes;* but it has also been held that the song was written by a "servant" (a professional singer?). It is clear that the subject distinguishes the *canso* (which deals with love) from the *sirventes* (which does not).

While a narrower definition of the genre might include only poems that specifically call themselves *sirventes,* the central themes of the poems thus defined can be found in other poems, which may therefore be placed in the same genre. For want of a more detailed nomenclature, there is a tendency to classify as a *sirventes* any poem not fitting any of the other more clearly defined genres.

Subjects widely dealt with in the *sirventes* are mostly personal, moral, political, and religious. In the personal poems, it is possible to discern the professional poet who lives by his ability and performances, and who depends on the generosity of his patrons. Some poems reflect nostalgia. The moral *sirventes* of an early poet like Marcabru (*fl.* 1128–1150) may deal with the mores of a whole class, such as adulterous noblemen who court each other's wives; in the next century, the *sirventes* of Peire Cardenal (1180–*ca.* 1278) bemoan the rising strength of greed (*cobeitatz*) and evil (*malvestatz*) after the Albigensian Crusade.

The troubadours, especially those who were noblemen, often took sides in contemporary political struggles, and some even bore arms in them. Bertran de Born (*ca.* 1140–*ca.* 1215) wrote polemical pieces supporting his patron of the moment, and for this Dante placed him in hell as a sower of discord (*Inferno* 28). The political poems discuss personalities rather than events, often using veiled references that, for modern audiences, render the poems opaque, requiring explanations in footnotes. The religious *sirventes* is generally either a crusading song, which exhorts the hearers to take the cross for the good of their souls, or a complaint of southerners at the abuses they observe in the northern clerics swarming into the Midi in the thirteenth century.

The *serventois* of the trouvères treats many of these subjects; the twelfth-century poets wrote crusading songs, and in the thirteenth century a growing number of nonaristocratic poets introduced personal elements into their lyrics (Colin Muset, Rutebeuf), anticipating the later medieval poetry of Eustache Deschamps and François Villon. The purely political lyric was not much practiced in the north.

BIBLIOGRAPHY

Pierre Bec, *La lyrique française au moyen âge (XIIe–XIIIe siècles),* I (1977), 153, 156–157, and, as ed. and trans., *Nouvelle anthologie de la lyrique occitane du moyen âge* (1970), 122–128; Joseph Bedier and Pierre Aubry, *Les chansons de croisade* (1909); Alfred Jeanroy, *La poésie lyrique des troubadours,* II (1934), 200–212 (repr. in one vol., 1973); Karen Wilk Klein, *The Partisan Voice: A Study of the Political Lyric in France and Germany: 1180–1230* (1971); Robert Lassalle, "Proverbe et paradoxe chez Peire Cardenal, auteur de *sirventés,*" in *Romanistique* (Nice), **14** (1971); Robert Allen Taylor, *La littérature occitane du moyen âge* (1977), a selective and critical bibliography; Suzanne Thiolier-Méjean, *Les poésies satiriques et morales des troubadours du XIIe siècle à la fin du XIIIe siècle* (1978).

F. R. P. AKEHURST

[See also **Bertran de Born; Canso; Colin Muset; Crusade Propaganda; Leys d'Amors; Marcabru; Peire Cardenal; Provençal Literature; Rutebeuf; Vers.**]

SĪS (present-day Kozan), an important city of the Rubenid barony of Cilicia and the capital of the Cilician Kingdom of Armenia (Armenia Minor) from 1198/1199 to 1375. Located in Asia Minor in the valley of the Saros River, the district of Sīs was bounded in the north by Hadjine, in the east by the town and fortress of Kars, in the south by Anazarba, and in the east by the Amanus Mountains. The city and fortress of Sīs were located on an elevated area, the fortress at a height of about 755 feet (230 m), according to the late-nineteenth-century traveler David George Hogarth.

Sīs has been identified with many cities of antiquity, and Ghevond Alishan believed it to have pre-Rubenid origins. It was known to the Byzantines by that name by the beginning of the eighth century. The city was first captured for the Armenians by the Rubenid baron T^c^oros I (1102–1129), but was later taken by the Byzantine emperor John II Komnenos during his campaign in Cilicia in 1137–1138. The Rubenid T^c^oros II (1144–1169) recaptured it in the mid twelfth century.

It was Leo I/II (*d.* 1219), the first king of Cilicia, who constructed the fortress of Sīs and who built the city into the capital of the kingdom. Sīs was not only the seat of the Cilician royal court, but the artistic and intellectual center as well. In 1292, the Armenian *kat^c^ołikosate* moved from Hṙomklay to Sīs, making the latter the religious center of the kingdom as well. It appears to have been the site of the coronation of the later kings of Cilicia, as Tarsus had been that of the earlier kings. Although

Sīs was located along the Venetian and Genoese trade routes to the Far East, it was of secondary commercial importance to the Cilician Kingdom compared with the port of Āyās.

Wilbrand, count of Oldenburg (*d.* 1233), who visited the city with the ambassador of the duke of Austria at the end of 1211, described Sīs as a city of numerous and wealthy inhabitants, including many Greeks, with a well-fortified castle, magnificent gardens, and many orange and lemon trees. There were said to be as many as twenty-three churches in Sīs, foremost among them the cathedral built by Het^cum I (1226–1270) and dedicated to the Holy Wisdom.

Sīs was sacked in 1266 by the Mamluks and was soon further destroyed by an earthquake, after which it never regained its former glory. The Mamluks again invaded in 1275–1276, attempting, but failing, to capture the fortress. A century later, however, in 1375, Sīs fell to the Mamluks, an event that effectively marked the end of the Cilician Kingdom. Remains of the fortress of Sīs still stand today.

BIBLIOGRAPHY

Ghevond Alishan, *Léon le magnifique, premier roi de Sissouan ou de l'Arméno-Cilicie,* G. Bayan, trans., (1888), and *Sissouan; ou, l'Arméno-Cilicie* (1899); Thomas S. R. Boase, ed., *The Cilician Kingdom of Armenia* (1978); Wilhelm von Heyd, *Histoire du commerce du Levant au moyen âge,* 2 vols. (1885–1886, repr. 1959); Wilbrandus de Oldenborg, "Chronicle," in Johann Christian Moritz Laurent, *Peregrinatores medii aevi quatuor* (1864).

ANI P. ATAMIAN

[See also **Anatolia; Armenia; Āyās; Cilician Kingdom; Het^cum I; Hṙomklay; John II Komnenos; Kars; Katholikos; Leo I/II of Armenia; Mamluk Dynasty; Rubenids; Tarsus; Trade, Armenian.**]

SISAKAN. See **Siwnik^c.**

SISEBUT (*r.* 612—620/621), Visigothic king of Spain. A friend of St. Isidore of Seville, the theologian and scholar, Sisebut left several writings of his own that reflect his wide cultural interests, encompassing literature, science, and religion. At the beginning of his reign, he attempted to convert the Jews in Spain to the Christian faith by force, a move that drew the opposition of Isidore. Their friendship, however, survived the resulting strain, and in 612–613 Isidore dedicated to him his *De natura rerum*; he also originally dedicated his mammoth, unfinished encyclopedia, *Etymologiarum sive originum libri XX,* to the king, shortly before the latter's death, around 620.

Sisebut's writings include occasional verse in Latin and eight *Epistolae,* as well as a study of the life and martyrdom of St. Desiderius of Vienne, *Vita vel passio sancti Desiderii episcopi Viennensis.* It is in his letters to Isidore, especially, that Sisebut reveals his versatile mind and extensive reading.

BIBLIOGRAPHY

Franz Brunhölzl, *Geschichte der lateinischen Literatur des Mittelalters,* I (1975), 93–95, 522, with extensive bibliography; Max Manitius, *Geschichte der lateinischen Literatur des Mittelalters,* I (1911), 187–188; *Patrologia latina,* LXXX (1863), 363–384.

EDWARD FRUEH

[See also **Isidore of Seville, St.; Latin Literature; Visigoths.**]

SITULA, a deep, bucket-shaped vessel used in the ancient world for several purposes: utilitarian (to hold water) and religious (to hold the sacred water of the Nile in Egyptian and Roman Isis worship, and to hold the sacrificed bull's blood in Minoan devotion).

Of presumed Egyptian origin, the situla has been found in Etruscan tombs as well as throughout the Roman world into early Christian times. Roman Catholicism has kept the shape of the situla in the aspersory (aspersorium), a simple bucket from which a long-handled sprinkler, called an aspergillum, shakes holy water during liturgical ceremonies.

BIBLIOGRAPHY

G. Lafaye, *Histoire du culte des divinités à Alexandre* (1884); Heinrich Willers, *Die römischen Bronzeeimer von Henmoor, nebst einem Anhange über die römischen Silberbarren aus Dierstorf* (1901).

MARY GRIZZARD

[See also **Early Christian Art.**]

SIWNIK^{c} (Sisakan, Sunitai), the largest principality of Armenia Major and, in the tenth to twelfth centuries, an independent state. Located in the basin of Lake Sevan and in the valleys of the Orotan and the Ałuan (Hageru/Akera) rivers to the south, Siwnik^{c} was a rugged, mountainous, and remote region possessing no cities and few towns. The earliest known seat of its princes was the locality of Siwnik^{c} (now Sisian), but it was later transferred from one fortified site to another. Siwnik^{c} comprised some twelve districts and contained nearly fifty forts (among them; Čahuk, Ernǰak, and Šahaponk^{c}), as well as some 135 monasteries. Many of the latter were important centers of learning in the Middle Ages, especially Glajor, Mak^{c}enoc^{c}, Noravank^{c}, and Tat^{c}ew, the last being the seat of the primate, the metropolitan of Siwnik^{c}. With its rich volcanic soil Siwnik^{c} maintained a prosperous agricultural economy. There were copper mines at Lap^{c}an and a local craft and textile industry.

After the loss of Armenia's easternmost regions to Caucasian Albania in 387, Siwnik^{c} became a borderland of the part of Armenia which had passed under direct Persian suzerainty that same year. After the fall of the Arsacid Armenian monarchy in 428–429, however, the princes of Siwnik^{c} evinced clear separatist tendencies. In the great uprising of 450–451, Prince Vasak of Siwnik^{c} went over to the Persians, and shortly thereafter Siwnik^{c} appears to have been separated from the rest of Persarmenia at its own request and to have been established as the Sasanian Persian province (*šahr*) of Sisakan.

With the fall of Sasanian Iran to the Arabs in the Battle of Qādisīya in 636, Siwnik^{c} was reunited with Armenia under Arab suzerainty. It continued to be ruled by its own dynasty, however, which in the ninth century extended its holdings to the east to include Arc^{c}aχ. At the same time the Siwnids began the custom of placing certain districts under the control of the cadets of the house, who gradually formed semi-independent lines under the suzerainty of the senior prince. Although this practice weakened the house, it did not prevent it from taking advantage of the decline of the Arabs to declare its independence, and about 970 Prince Smbat II (*ca.* 970–*ca.* 998) assumed the title "king of Siwnik^{c}." In its subdivided state, however, the new kingdom was unable to maintain control of its entire territory, and most of northern Siwnik^{c} soon passed to the Bagratid Kingdom of Armenia, probably as a result of the marriage of Catherine (Kotramidē), only child of Vasak VI (*ca.* 998–1019), to Gagik I of Armenia. What was left of Siwnik^{c} remained in the hands of a junior Siwnid line, the princes of Baḷk^{c} or Lap^{c}an.

In 1045 Gagik II of Armenia was forced to cede his kingdom to the Byzantines, but the resistance of the city of Dwin prevented them from reaching Siwnik^{c}; and after the Turks overran Armenia (1064–1071), the Siwnids were able to preserve themselves in Baḷk^{c} as late as around 1170. Thereafter, Siwnik^{c} passed completely under Muslim control, and the Siwnid dynasty survived only in another junior line, the house of Xač^{c}ēn. In 1202 the Georgians conquered Siwnik^{c}, and Queen T^{c}amar the Great (*r.* 1184–1212) gave it to the Hałbakids (Xałbakids) and the Orbelids, two Armenian houses in the Georgian service, the former receiving Vayoc^{c} Jor (northwestern Siwnik^{c}) and the latter obtaining the remainder. After the arrival of the Mongols (1220–1243), these houses, together with the Siwnids of Xač^{c}ēn, managed to retain their lands by accepting Mongol rule and that of whichever Mongol successor state managed to dominate eastern Armenia. Momentarily dispossessed by Tamerlane (from 1387 to 1405), the Siwnids of Xač^{c}ēn regained their lands under the Turkoman Jahān Shāh (1435–1467) and continued to hold them under Iranian suzerainty more or less until the coming of the Russians in the early nineteenth century.

BIBLIOGRAPHY

Nikolai Adontz, *Armenia in the Period of Justinian,* Nina G. Garsoïan, ed. and trans. (1970); Ghevont M. Alishan, *Sisakan* (1893); S. T. Eremyan, *Hayastanĕ ĕst "Ašxarhac^{c}oyc^{c}"-i* (Armenia according to the "Geography") (1963), 80–81, 117; Grigor Mesropi Grigoryan, *Siwnik^{c}i vanakan kalvacatirut'yune IX–XIII darerum* (Monastic lands of Siwnik^{c} in the IX–XIII centuries) (1973); T. X. Hakobyan, *Siwnik^{c}i tagavorut^{c}yunĕ* (The kingdom of Siwnik^{c}) (1966), and *Hayastani patmakan ašxarhagrut^{c}iwn* (Historical geography of Armenia), 2nd ed. (1968), 191–218, 277–279; Robert H. Hewsen, "The Meliks of Eastern Armenia," in *Revue des études arméniennes,* n.s. **9, 10, 11** (1972–1976); Heinrich Hübschmann, *Die altarmenischen Ortsnamen* (1969), 263–266, 347–349; Stepannos Orbēlean, *Patmut^{c}iwn nahangin Sisakan* (History of the land of Sisakan), K. Chahnazarean, ed. (1859); Cyril Toumanoff, *Studies in Christian Caucasian History* (1963), and *Manuel de généalogie et de chronologie pour l'histoire de la Caucasie chrétienne* (1976, suppl. 1978), 71–72, 226–261, 355–360; H. M. Utmazyan, *Siwnik^{c} IX ew X darerum* (Siwnik^{c} in the ninth and tenth centuries) (1958).

ROBERT H. HEWSEN

[See also **Armenia, Geography; Armenia: History of; Bagratids; Gagik I; Gagik II; Georgia; Mongol Empire; Orbēlean, Step^canos; Sasanian History; Turkomans.**]

SIX AGES OF THE WORLD. See **Sex Aetates Mundi.**

SKÁLDATAL, an Icelandic catalog of Norwegian and Icelandic skalds, is preserved in two redactions, one of which takes the list to about 1260, while the other continues to about 1300. The more extensive version is found in Uppsala, De la Gardie 11, the so-called *Uppsala Edda,* from about 1300. The earlier manuscript is *Kringla,* an Icelandic codex from about 1250–1260 containing the text of *Heimskringla* considered nearest to Snorri's own. This manuscript was destroyed in the great Copenhagen fire of 1728, but *Skáldatal* had been transcribed in the late seventeenth century by Árni Magnússon (AM 761 4°). The transmission of *Skáldatal* in association with Snorri's two main works, the *Edda* and *Heimskringla,* suggests that the catalog was produced by the same milieu responsible for preserving Snorri's collections.

Skáldatal lists under each prince the various skalds who composed for him. Haraldr hárfagri (*ca.* 860–931) is given six skalds: Þorbjǫrn hornklofi, Þjóðólfr ór Hvíni, Auðun illskælda, Ǫlvir hnúfa, Úlfr Sebbason, and Guttormr sindri. Nothing of Úlfr's poetry has survived, and only one half-stanza attributed to Auðun and two lines by Ǫlvir have come down to us. Guttormr is said by *Skáldatal* to have also composed for Halfdan svarti and Hákon Aðalsteinsfóstri, but only part of a *Hákonardrápa* survives under his name. *Skáldatal* does not mention the poetess Jórunn skaldmær, to whom are attributed five stanzas addressed to Haraldr hárfagri, nor are the king's own poetic productions mentioned, such as the stanza of a *Snjófríðardrápa* assigned to him in *Flateyjarbók*. *Skáldatal* knows of a Kormákr Ǫgmundarson (*ca.* 930–970), who composed poetry for Haraldr gráfeldr (*r.* in Norway *ca.* 960–970) and Sigurðr hlaðajarl (*d.* 962), only a few fragments of which have survived, but knows nothing of the sixty-four verses (*lausavísur*) attributed to a lovelorn skald in *Kormáks saga*.

The catalog opens with names known from the *fornaldarsögur,* such as Starkaðr the Old, Ragnarr loðbrók, and others who are said to have composed for legendary kings. It ends with fully historical court poets like Snorri's nephews, the brothers Óláfr Þórðarson hvítaskáld and Sturla Þórðarson. The list of skalds is divided into four series: one for Danish, one for Norwegian, and one for Swedish kings, and the fourth naming skalds who composed for lesser dignitaries, such as earls and chieftains. *Skáldatal* contains the names of more than 100 Icelandic skalds whose lives span a period of 350 years, from Egill Skallagrímsson (*ca.* 910–990) to his late descendant Jón murti Egilsson, who, in 1299 recited a praise poem for Norwegian King Eiríkr Magnússon.

Many of the poets listed in *Skáldatal* are now only names. Eleven skalds are said to have composed for King Sverrir of Norway (*r.* 1184–1202), but none of their work has survived. Although most of the extant poetry is addressed to Norwegian rulers and quoted in their sagas, Sverrir seems to have lost out because his saga was written by a contemporary, the Icelandic priest Karl Jónsson, whose direct and personal access to the king eliminated the need for authenticating poetry. Almost no verse on Swedish rulers has been preserved. *Skáldatal* gives Eysteinn Beli, a legendary king of the Swedes, eleven skalds, all but one of whom—Bragi Boddason the Old—are completely unknown to us. If we could only trust *Skáldatal* as to the historical existence of Eysteinn's court poets, most of them a generation older than Bragi, their names would suggest that Bragi's *Ragnarsdrápa* had a skaldic tradition at least thirty years old behind it.

BIBLIOGRAPHY

Skáldatal in *Edda Snorra Sturlusonar* (edition of Den Arnamagnæanske Kommission) (1880–1887), III, 205–752 (text with Latin commentary); Jan de Vries, *Altnordische Literaturgeschichte,* 2nd rev. ed., I (1964), 124–125.

ROBERTA FRANK

[See also **Bragi Boddason the Old; Eddic Poetry; Family Sagas, Icelandic; Fornaldarsögur; Kormáks Saga; Skaldic Poetry.**]

SKALDIC POETRY. In 1153 in the cathedral at Trondheim, a poet recited an encomium on Olaf II Haraldsson, king of Norway (1015/1016–1028) and now her patron saint. Einarr Skúlason's audience included the new archbishop, the three reigning kings of Norway, and their assembled troops. The poem, called *Geisli* (Sunbeam), quickly reviewed Olaf's life down to his fall at Stiklestad and lingered over the battlefield and posthumous miracles that seemed to confirm his worth as Norway's patron. One stanza gave the name of Olaf's sword:

Hneitir frá'k at héti—
hjaldrs—at vápna galdri—
ǫðlings hjǫrr, þess's orra
ilbleikum gaf steikar;
þeim klauf þengill Rauma
þunnvaxin ský gunnar
—rekin bitu stǫ́l—á Stiklar
stǫðum—valbastar rǫðli.

My translation keeps the figurative diction and the order of the clauses, but not the order of the words: "I heard that Hneitir [the Cutter] was called—of battle—at the chant of weapons—the sword of the prince, of the one who gave food to the pale-footed moor-fowl; with that the king of the Raumar clove the thin clouds of battle—the inlaid swords bit—at Stiklestad—sun of the sword-harness." Reduced to essentials, the stanza says, "I heard that the sword of the prince, the one who fed the pale-footed eagle, was called Hneitir. With that sword, the Norwegian ruler clove thin shields at Stiklestad; the inlaid swords bit."

Apparently neither the archbishop nor the kings found it embarrassing to hear praise of the saint's miraculous sword in verse of such colorful secularity, coming from a tradition already some 300 years old and in its origins intimately linked with paganism; what is even more remarkable, they were expected to understand this stanza as it rolled off the poet's tongue. Skaldic verse seems to have been practiced and admired by all the Scandinavian peoples of the Viking age, but we know it chiefly from Norway and Iceland—Icelandic literature preserved the greater part of the corpus.

Old Norse poetry is divided by convention into two types, Eddic and skaldic, although the same poets probably worked in both genres, and a number of early compositions (*Eiríksmál, Hákonarmál,* and *Haraldskvæði,* for example) do not fall neatly into either category. Eddic poetry resembles the rest of early Germanic verse; it tends to be anonymous and uses simple diction and meters to tell a legendary or mythical story. Skaldic verse is the most innovative poetry to develop out of the common Germanic tradition; it is the work of known poets composing in a highly intricate style for known princes and it derives its name from *skald* (poet), the etymology of which—like that of Old English *scop*—is disputed. More than 40,000 lines of skaldic poetry have been preserved, attributed to some 250 poets who lived between 850 and 1400.

THE STRUCTURE OF *DRÓTTKVÆTT*

Einarr's stanza is in *dróttkvætt* (short for *dróttkvæðr háttr*—the meter fit for the *drótt,* the king's band of retainers), the principal verse form of the skalds. The form is characterized by isosyllabism, internal rhyme, relatively free stress in the first half of the line, a caesura, and a cadence with fixed stress at the end of the line, the latter an early verse pattern known from other Indo-European traditions. The eight lines of Einarr's stanza are divided into two "halves" (each called a *helmingr*) by a syntactic break after the fourth line. The poet's basic metrical unit is the couplet, in which each line contains three stresses and six syllables. Each line also has a prescribed ending in a long stressed syllable followed by a short unstressed one. If a line appears to have more than six syllables, the excess is removed either by elision (*frá'k* for *frá ek* in line 1 and *þess's* for *þess es* in line 3) or by "resolution," the practice of allowing two short syllables to stand for one long, heavy one within the first four syllables of the line (*rekin* in line 7 and *stǫðum* in line 8).

The lines of the couplet are linked by alliteration or initial correspondence: two initial sounds in the odd line alliterate with the first syllable of the even line (always stressed). There is also a form of end correspondence or internal rhyme: in each line, the next-to-last syllable—always stressed—chimes with a stressed or semistressed stem in the same line. In even lines, there is *aðalhending* or full rhyme (*galdr-/hjaldrs; steik-/-bleik-*; etc.); in odd lines, *skothending* or half-rhyme, in which different vowels are followed by an identical consonant (*hét-/Hneit-*; *orr-/hjǫrr*; etc.). Of the forty-eight syllables in Einarr's stanza, twenty-four are metrically long and stressed, twelve bear alliteration, eight form half rhyme and eight full rhyme; he had no choice in the placement of eight rhyming and four alliterating syllables.

To make up for these rigid metrical constraints, skalds allowed themselves a good deal of syntactic freedom. Since, for example, the compound place-name Stiklestad did not fit with ease into the skaldic line, Einarr and other poets before him divided the word into grammatically recognizable parts (*Stiklar,* the genitive singular of the river name; *stǫðum,* the dative plural of the Old Norse word for "place"), and then fitted the separate elements—sometimes many words apart—into the half-stanza. In skaldic verse, the sense can be spread over the quatrain in one, two, or three independent clauses, and these clauses may be broken into segments and dispersed throughout the four lines. In both halves of Einarr's stanza, a thought begun in the first couplet is completed only in the second. The last two words of his stanza, for example, are to be construed with the first word of line 5; and the sentence containing this instrumental phrase (with that sword) is itself split by an interposed clause (the inlaid swords bit).

The interlacing of sentence segments in Einarr's first quatrain is even more complex. The opening sentence is intercalated with a relative clause, itself segmented. *Hjaldrs* (of battle) modifies *orra* (bird) in the following line, although it also functions within its own line as a loose modifier of *vápna* (weapons). The periphrasis "at the chant of weapons" can be construed with both the main and relative clauses of the first quatrain, just as the phrase "at Stiklestad" in the second quatrain can be taken with both the main and interposed sentences: "the inlaid swords bit at Stiklestad"; "the king clove shields at Stiklestad." This blended, deliberately unstable syntax is typical of skaldic verse, which frequently seems to be trying to depict concurrent actions concurrently. In this poetry, where meter and patterning form the overriding truth, many things are left in half-darkness; the causal link between phenomena like Einarr's peckish carrion birds and biting swords is usually only suggested. There may have been some system of pointing, something in the poet's delivery perhaps, that helped his audience to hear the connection between words. Each line has a caesura—falling between the rhyming syllables and (in the odd line) also between the alliterating syllables—that often marks syntactic divisions and aids us in ordering clauses. Skaldic syntax, although it remains mysterious, was clearly under the control of traditional laws that are slowly becoming better understood by scholars.

HEITI AND KENNINGS

Many of the nouns in Einarr's stanza (for example, *hjaldr, hjǫrr, þengill, gunnr, valbǫst, rǫðull*) are never found in prose texts or, if they appear, have a different meaning. These nouns are called *heiti* (names) in Old Norse. Lists of *heiti* for the same thing were set down in mnemonic verses known as *þulur*. The difficult word *valbǫst* (which may designate the strap—fastened to a ring on the swordhilt—that was wrapped around the sheath when the weapon was not in use) is found in a *þula* listing names for sword-parts; *hjaldr* is found in a *þula* listing synonyms for battle. Such synonyms probably were never completely interchangeable. The various poetic words for battle (and there are over a score) have different connotations ranging from the terror of war to its noise and intense fury. Of the more than 150 *heiti* for Odin, the god of skalds and warriors, a large number seem to denote different aspects of his nature: the High, the Cherished, Evildoer, Strength, Terrifier, the Flame-eyed, the Walk-weary.

Skaldic verse is a poetry of nouns largely because of the kenning, a distinctive feature that goes hand in hand with rigid metrical requirements and syntactic dismemberment. The kenning divides and multiplies nouns: it is a periphrasis, consisting of two or more substantive members, which takes the place of a single noun. Barely 100 items are expressed by kennings in skaldic verse. These include the warrior, the parts of his body, land, gold, armor, weapons, women, ships, and battles, as well as poetry itself—the trappings of an aristocratic society.

The most characteristic skaldic kenning is a phrase like "ship of the desert." It consists of two terms, one of which is the base word (ship) and the other a noun to which the base word is made to relate (desert). Taken together, the two nouns have a significance (camel) that neither has separately, and this meaning is never that of the base word. Any member of a circumlocution might be expanded by further kennings. Theoretically, the only limit to the length of a kenning is the syllabic capacity of the half-stanza, although by the thirteenth century a kenning of more than five members was considered to be in poor taste.

Many kennings are based on pagan mythological lore. A poet, mourning his drowned son, can call the sea "wounds of the giant's neck," thereby evoking an image of the dying giant Ymir, whose blood as it gushed from his neck created the dark sea. Sometimes we miss the full force of such circumlocutions because the legend or belief to which it alludes is lost, as is perhaps the case with the mysterious kenning for passion—"wind of the giantess"—that occurs in skaldic verse from the tenth to the fourteenth century.

Einarr's stanza contains four simple kennings. The first, "song of weapons," is a characteristic skaldic circumlocution for battle. The second, "bird of battle," is a common skaldic conceit for the raven or eagle: a warrior feeds carrion beasts with the corpses of his slain enemies. The name of any winged creature (except that of the raven or eagle) can serve as the base word in this kenning system. Einarr was free to insert the obligatory definer "of battle" anywhere in his quatrain without having to worry about a loss in comprehension: since bird names almost never occur as base words except to designate the two carrion birds, the name *orri* by itself identifies the appropriate kenning system. Einarr adds the adjective "pale-footed" (really "pale-soled") to specify the eagle, whose pale coloring distinguished him from the dusky raven; normally, however, kennings for raven and eagle are interchangeable. The choice of a particular bird name may have been based on aesthetic considerations (for example, *orri* suggests *orrosta* [battle] and *Orrahríð* a famous battle charge of 1066), or it may have been arbitrary, based solely on metrical needs. Our knowledge of kenning conventions is not yet so secure that we can trace the poet's intentions and subtleties with any confidence.

Einarr's third kenning, designating "shields," has as its base word "clouds," looked upon as protective agents; the definer, *gunnr,* is either the common noun "battle" or the name of a valkyrie. Einarr and his contemporaries seem to have enjoyed incorporating into their kennings mythological names that were also abstract nouns, a kind of poetic euhemerism (for example, *Þróttr* [Odin] but also "strength"). Mythological kennings went out of fashion for at least 100 years after the conversion of the north (especially in the productions of official poets), but the twelfth century ushered in a kind of skaldic renaissance, a renewal of interest in the past and in native traditions. The final kenning of Einarr's stanza designates Olaf's sword, the "sun"—that is, the bright and flashing thing—of the "sword-part."

The second half of Einarr's stanza illustrates a prized feature of skaldic style, the interlacing of two distinct pictures by means of kennings. In this congruent style, the two base words construed with the verb give one meaning: "the sun broke through the clouds"; the two full kennings taken with the same verb, another: "the sword clove shields." If the stanza works, it is because the picture presented on the first level reinforces and enriches the significance of the second. Other levels of meaning are probably present in Einarr's stanza: the sun piercing through the clouds is an image of Olaf himself, the "sunbeam" and "warlike ray" of the poem (*Geisli*), as well as a symbol of his God, the "Sun of Justice and Mercy."

Kennings gave the skald a rich and transforming diction. Some poets preferred to juxtapose unlike kennings in a series of baroque metamorphoses, making a bear turn into a swan that changed into a plank before becoming a tub—all possible base words in ship-kennings. Others used kennings to achieve the greatest possible compression: the skald Þórmóðr Trefilsson fits all three beasts of battle into a single *helmingr* by placing one in a warrior-kenning and one in a carrion-kenning: "the feeder of the raven [here called "swan of blood"] sated the eagle on the food of the wolf."

VARIETIES OF SKALDIC VERSE

Skaldic art tended not to repeat formal patterns such as alliteration, rhyme, or stress schemes in successive strophes of a longer poem. Names for the longer skaldic poem reflect the separateness of its stanzas: *vísur* (verses) is one term for a gathering of stanzas on a single theme; another name is *flokkr*—a "flock" of strophes. The most admired skaldic composition was the *drápa,* a series of at least twenty stanzas broken by one or more refrains at regular intervals. Einarr Skúlason's *Geisli* consists of seventy-one stanzas, broken by one four-line refrain repeated ten times at three-stanza intervals. Numerous single strophes, called *lausavísur* (loose verses), have come down to us. Some were probably composed as independent units; others represent the scattered fragments of lost poems.

Dróttkvætt was the basis of most skaldic meters. Snorri Sturluson's *Háttatal* illustrates some forty-eight possible variations. Most of these have to do with the placement of rhyming syllables: there are measures without rhyme (*háttlausa*), measures with rhymes falling on the first and second stress only (*Fleinsháttr*), measures in which odd lines have no rhyme and even lines have half-rhyme (*munnvǫrp*), measures with all lines having one full rhyme (*rétthent*), or two full rhymes (*alhent*), or end-rhyme (*runhent*). Other variants known to Snorri adjust the number of syllables or the placement of stresses within the line. Þórmóðr Trefilsson achieved his feat of compression in a meter known as *haðarlag* in which the lines consist of only five syllables. A particularly interesting form called *tøglag,* used by some of Cnut the Great's poets, consists of lines of four syllables that obey all the rhyme and alliteration requirements of *dróttkvætt.* An important early skaldic meter without internal rhyme is *kviðuháttr,* in which odd lines have three syllables and even lines four; the oldest poem composed in this measure is Þjóðólfr ór Hvíni's *Ynglingatal,* from around 900. The skaldic innovation most important for the later period is *hrynhent.* The rhymes and alliterations of *dróttkvætt* remained, but the line was extended by two syllables. In the fourteenth century, *hrynhent* took a firm lead over *dróttkvætt* and became the chief meter of the Christian *drápa.*

THE SKALDS

The origins of skaldic verse are obscure. Scholars have sought to demonstrate Celtic influence, yet there seems no reason to assume that this poetry was not a native Norse development. The earliest stanzas to have survived are assigned to Bragi Boddason the Old (*ca.* 835–900). His fragmentary *Ragnarsdrápa* describes the mythological and legendary scenes painted on a ceremonial shield. Another early shield poem is the late-ninth-century *Haustlǫng* by Þjóðólfr ór Hvíni. Skaldic picture poems also included descriptions of wall hangings, horns, and carved wood panels (Úlfr Uggason's *Húsdrápa*); one stanza alludes to a graffito incised on a privy wall by a fuming lover.

The *dróttkvætt* verses of Bragi, Þjóðólfr, and the other early skalds—men like the brilliant Egill Skallagrímsson, Kormakr Ǫgmundarson, and Eyvindr Finnsson Skáldaspillir—have the same basic structure as Einarr's but are less regular: rhymes might be sporadic and not always fall on the penultimate syllable, and a syllable might precede the alliterating sound in the even line. The first skalds were Norwegians (their emergence coincided with a magnification of royal power in late-ninth-century Norway), but soon Icelanders appear to enjoy a virtual monopoly as the court poets of Norway. Skalds included kings, bishops, farmers, outlaws, seven women and, the sagas claim, ghosts and Swedish berserks. The extant sources make no mention of bardic schools, do not tell us whether the skald's manner of composing was rigidly prescribed, whether he wore distinctive garb, or whether his position was hereditary. We know almost nothing about the tenth-century Norwegian court, the institution that presumably dominated the poet's life, providing him with a livelihood and an audience. We do, however, possess a number of treatises from the high medieval period on skaldic poetics: Rǫgnvaldr Kali Kolsson's *Háttalykill,* a twelfth-century *clavis metrica* from the Orkneys; Snorri Sturluson's *Edda* (consisting of *Gylfaginning, Skáldskaparmál,* and *Háttatal*), composed in Iceland around 1220; and the *Third Grammatical Treatise* by Snorri's nephew Óláfr Þórðarson hvítaskáld, a handbook of rhetoric that applies the prescriptions of Latin *artes poeticae* to skaldic verse. These authors—all poets themselves—can be misleading or downright wrong, but modern skaldic scholarship would be severely hampered without them.

The skald composed verse about himself and other skalds, about his art, and about his importance to his patron. Such professional self-consciousness seems to predate by at least a century the eruption of poetic pride audible in Latin verse of the eleventh century and later. The skald usually employed liquid metaphors to refer to his verse: in mythological kennings, poetry is Odin's regurgitated mead, filched from the giants, an offering of nourishment from poet to patron. One tenth-century skald described the act of poetry as a kind of gargle, with Odin's streams—the mead of poetry—resounding like surf against the skerries of the gums (his teeth). The sagas of kings occasionally mention skalds competing with each other for royal favor. Nicknames such as "bad poet," "loud mouth," "serpent's tongue," "praise tongue," "the mouth," and "the plagiarist" suggest that poets at the Norwegian court were not unaware of their colleagues' existence.

The geographic span of the skald's world reached from the New World, Greenland, and the Norse kingdoms of Ireland and England in the west, to Swedish settlements in Russia and Varangian troops in Constantinople in the east. The skald's range of subjects was almost as wide. Whatever was suppressed in the understated, impersonal prose of the sagas—words of defiance, hope, triumph, obscenity, or despair—might surface in its skaldic verses. The poet gloats over a good shield or a good kill, over a boiled sausage or the sacking of a city, laments for a cloak that is too short, for a girl given to another, for his own old age.

The greater part of the skaldic verse composed and preserved between 850 and 1300 involves commemoration and celebration. The skald and his king appear to have had a special relationship in early Scandinavian society: a ruler succeeded to the throne partly through heredity and needed a poet who could recite the royal genealogies to his liking; a prince maintained his power by means of victories, good harvests, and generous gifts, and these, too, were recorded in the eulogies of his skalds, who could confer on him the fame that he and his culture so valued. Such eulogies typically included an initial call to silence, a summary of the prince's outstanding deeds and strengths, and an affirmation that his fame had spread far and wide. Eulogy and lament were joined in the memorial ode, or *erfidrápa,* to which most of the Norse kings between the tenth and twelfth centuries were treated.

The other side of praise is blame. This skaldic genre was known as *níð* (insult, derision). If a prince who provided gifts was hailed, one who did not might be satirized, sometimes—the sagas insist—with devastating results. If eulogy could establish and confirm a man's position, then satire could reduce and destroy it. The early skald seems to have been regarded as a dangerous, uncontrollable man, one in possession of preternatural powers. Twelfth- and thirteenth-century laws still took *níð* very seriously: total outlawry was the punishment for composing a half-stanza containing *níð* or any form of praise that seemed to insult. Poetry in praise of a girl was also punishable by outlawry, apparently because of the spellbinding power such verse was feared to possess.

PRESERVATION OF SKALDIC VERSE

Only a very small part of the total corpus of court poetry is extant. *Skáldatal,* a work from the early thirteenth century, lists over 100 Icelandic skalds who frequented the halls of Scandinavian kings, but many are now only names. Eleven of the poets cited are said to have composed for King Sverre Sigurdsson of Norway (*r.* 1177–1202), but none of their verse has survived. We have only one contemporary record of a *dróttkvætt* stanza from the pagan period: a memorial verse to a Danish chieftain on the Karlevi Stone in Öland. Two difficult skaldic lines in runes also appear on a Swedish copper box, dated to the early eleventh century. Stanzas from the thirteenth and fourteenth centuries, inscribed on rune sticks, have recently been unearthed in Bergen, sole evidence for the late survival of a Norwegian skaldic tradition.

The first extensive skaldic compositions to be recorded on vellum were probably the long Christian poems of the twelfth century, such as *Geisli.* The greater part of the skaldic verse that has come down to us is preserved piecemeal in prose narratives. Almost all of the ninth- and tenth-century extended compositions in our editions have been reassembled from fragments by scholars whose ordering (and sometimes even selection) of the stanzas is often arbitrary. Sometimes a saga author cites a stanza as a historical footnote to corroborate what his prose says; at other times he quotes a stanza as the impromptu utterance of a character in his saga. Many of these verses were undoubtedly once part of longer poems that survived pretty much whole down to the literate period. The prose link accompanying a stanza in a saga occasionally misunderstands the content of the verse altogether. The number of such slips leads to the conclusion that individual stanzas probably acquired their prose commentaries at the time they were first inserted into a saga, after they had been separated from their poetic matrix. The details supplied by the prose regarding the narrative context of any stanza should normally not be taken as reflecting anything more than one medieval author's imaginative reconstruction of how such a poem came to be uttered. Most strophes have come down to us as the works of specific skalds, but at least one is assigned by tradition to three different skalds, and several are assigned to two.

The sagas tell of men and events from the ninth century and later, yet the first saga authors did not compose their texts until the late twelfth and early thirteenth centuries. The authenticity of certain stanzas quoted in these sagas and assigned to skalds who lived two or three centuries earlier is questionable. Skaldic poetry is conservative and preserves archaic forms long vanished from prose: in dating the verse, one can sometimes point to features that are clearly late, but it has proved difficult to isolate early features that could not have been imitated sporadically in later centuries. There is perhaps no reason why early poems—even those composed for occasions more informal than a royal inauguration or funeral—could not have been remembered over three centuries; but there is also no reason why a man telling a saga in the twelfth century or writing one in the thirteenth could not have put a stanza of his own devising (or of someone else's) into the mouth of his tenth-century hero. Some progress has been made in tracing the chronological development of skaldic art; we are now able to recognize certain late innovations in metrical and kenning practice that help us to date a handful of verses. But we still cannot distinguish confidently between "genuine" and "spurious" stanzas.

Twelfth- and thirteenth-century Norse historians do not seem to have worried about the possibility of forgeries in the skaldic corpus. The court poets were recorders of events, men whose profession it was to fix or stabilize memory in a brief statement that would reflect the current political situation or ambition of their patrons. Historical verse of this kind was probably not particularly attractive to twelfth-century forgers, whose "antiquing" had more fertile outlets (for example, love poetry, pagan "odes," first and last utterances of legendary or local heroes, and personal satire) than those afforded by a stanza reporting that one tenth-century earl neatly eliminated the descendants of another earl.

Snorri, in his Prologue to *Heimskringla* (finished about 1235), related that verse by the skalds of Haraldr hárfagri (Harald I Fairhair, *ca.* 850–930) was still remembered by heart, as was that by the court poets of all the succeeding Norwegian kings. Snorri considered the historical content of this court poetry—recited in the presence of the chieftains and their sons—to be entirely trustworthy, if the verses were "sensibly" interpreted. (*Heimskringla* cites verses by over seventy skalds, and Snorri, although far more learned in skaldic poetry and pagan mythology than anyone else we know, appears to misattribute and misunderstand a number of them.) As early as 1180, the Norwegian Theodricus put together a Latin history of his country in which he declared that much of his information came from Icelanders, "among whom memory of past events lives, cultivated in their ancient poems." By 1200, the Danish Saxo Grammaticus had also acknowledged his indebtedness to Icelanders.

Studies of the skalds' historical poetry—if we limit ourselves to stanzas whose contents later poets could have had no conceivable interest in reproducing—may eventually give us a more secure basis on which to date the entire corpus. The meter, diction, and kenning usage of the skalds who composed for the archpagan Hákon inn ríki (Hákon Sigurdsson, ruler of Norway, *ca.* 970–*ca.* 995) differ noticeably from the mannerisms of St. Olaf's poets (1016–1028), whose own stylistic conventions and language contrast in turn with those of the skalds of Haraldr inn harðráði (Harald III Hardråde, *r.* 1046–1066). Analyses of this verse, king by king through the twelfth century, if carried out with extraordinary delicacy, precision, and literary imagination, can provide a chronological framework that may one day make it possible for us to write a convincing history of skaldic art.

Most manuscripts preserving skaldic poetry come from the fourteenth century and later, with some works extant only in seventeenth-century paper copies. Textual corruptions abound in these manuscripts, sometimes leading to partial or complete unintelligibility. Once an error slipped in, confusion was multiplied in subsequent copies by scribes who no longer understood what they were copying or who tried to improve an obviously wrong text. For some stanzas, satisfactory restitution is possible, because the metrical form of the verse provides so much assistance. The elaborate regulation of skaldic art must also have aided in composition and recall. Alliterating and rhyming pairs tend to hang together in the memory, with one member of the pair always ready to produce the other. Most skaldic verse probably was composed orally and privately by professionals and memorized for formal delivery. The best way to experience the pull of this verse—and to grasp how so many stanzas survived intact through the centuries—is to learn one by heart.

Much energy has been expended in this century in a debate over the intelligibility of skaldic verse to its original hearers. No one denies that it is tough poetry, but all court poetry has a certain impulse to difficulty, a desire to outdo all competitors in craftsmanship and knowledge. There can be little doubt that skaldic verse was intended to communicate something to its public, and that this public was trained to prize allusiveness and knottiness in their art.

Finnur Jónsson's monumental edition (1912–1915) of the skaldic corpus is still the standard one. Ernst A. Kock's edition (1946–1949) follows Jónsson's exactly as to content and arrangement of stanzas and relies on Jónsson's two volumes of diplomatic transcripts for manuscript readings (although Kock performs a splendid service in attempting to restore a more natural word order). Much work needs to be done before skaldicists can have confidence in their texts and reference aids. Finnur Jónsson's edition, based on a selection of good manuscripts, was a remarkable achievement, but there are errors of transcription on almost every page, and one can never be sure that the manuscripts not consulted do not have better readings.

Jónsson's admirably thorough revision of the *Lexicon poeticum,* the most complete dictionary of Old Norse poetry, serves as a partial commentary to his own two-volume normalized edition and was the source for Rudolf Meissner's invaluable index of skaldic kennings. The mutual dependence of the standard text edition, standard dictionary, and standard kenning index—combined with the circularity of using Jónsson's chronology and attributions as the basis for our conclusions on linguistic dating—is disquieting. New manuscript readings, a different approach to emendations, or a new understanding of how skaldic poetry works will in some cases dramatically contradict findings based on the standard collections.

Interest in skaldic verse has increased considerably in recent years, and, although a knowledge of the Scandinavian languages and German is still essential for advanced work, there is now a substantial bibliography in English for the nonspecialist. For the historian, the skaldic stanzas of medieval Scandinavia are invaluable primary sources; for the student of religion, the verses transmit a more authentic pagan tradition than anything in the rest of Germanic literature; and for the student of literature, the gemlike brilliance of this compressed, highly polished poetry more than repays the efforts needed to understand it.

BIBLIOGRAPHY

Bibliographies. Carol J. Clover and John Lindow, eds., *Old Norse–Icelandic Literature: A Critical Guide,* in *Islandica,* 45 (1985); Lee M. Hollander, *A Bibliography of Skaldic Studies* (1958); Hans Bekker-Nielsen, *Bibliography of Old Norse–Icelandic Studies* (1963) (see entries *s. v. skaldic* in the index of each volume).

Editions. Finnur Jónsson, *Den norsk-islandske skjaldedigtning,* 4 vols. ([1908], 1912–1915), two volumes of diplomatic texts (IA, IIA) and two of normalized emended texts (IB, IIB), with Old Norse prose renditions translated into Danish; Ernst A. Kock, *Den norsk-isländska skaldediktningen,* 2 vols. (1946–1949), reconstructed texts without translations.

Readers and anthologies. Roberta Frank, *Old Norse Court Poetry: The Dróttkvætt Stanza* (1978); Lee M. Hollander, *The Skalds: A Selection of Their Poems* (1945, repr. 1968); Edward O. G. Turville-Petre, *Scaldic Poetry* (1976).

Standard reference aids. Finnur Jónsson, *Lexicon poeticum antiquae linguae septentrionalis,* 2nd ed. (1931); Rudolf Meissner, *Die Kenningar der Skalden: Ein Beitrag zur skaldischen Poetik,* I (1921).

Literary history. Peter Hallberg, *Den fornisländska poesien* (1962, 2nd ed. 1965), trans. by Paul Schach and Sonja Lindgrenson as *Old Icelandic Poetry: Eddic Lay and Skaldic Verse* (1975); Jan de Vries, *Altnordische Literaturgeschichte,* 2 vols. (1941–1942, 2nd rev. ed. 1964–1967).

Studies. Bo Almqvist, *Norrön niddiktning: Traditionshistoriska studier i versmagi,* I (1965); Theodore M. Andersson, "Skalds and Troubadours," in *Mediaeval Scandinavia,* 2 (1969); Alistair Campbell, *Skaldic Verse and Anglo-Saxon History* (1971); Carol J. Clover, "Skaldic Sensibility," in *Arkiv för nordisk filologi,* 93 (1978); Bjarni Einarsson, *Skáldasögur: Um uppruna og eðli ástaskáldasagnanna fornu* (1961), with English summary; Bjarne Fidjestøl, *Det norrøne fyrstediktet* (1982); Peter G. Foote, "Beginnings and Endings: Some Notes on the Study of Skaldic Poetry," in Régis Boyer, ed., *Les Vikings et leur civilisation* (1976), 179–190, and his essay on Gísli's verses in George Johnston, trans., *The Saga of Gisli* (1963); Gert Kreutzer, *Die Dichtungslehre der Skalden* (1974, 2nd rev. ed. 1977); Hans Kuhn, *Das Dróttkvætt* (1983); Hallvard Lie, *"Natur" og "unatur" i skaldekunsten,* in *Avhandlinger utgitt av Det norske Videnskaps-Akademi i Oslo,* II. Hist.-filos. Klasse, 1 (1957); John Lindow, "Riddles, Kennings, and the Complexity of Skaldic Poetry," in *Scandinavian Studies,* 47 (1975); Klaus von See, *Germanische Verskunst* (1967), 37–52, and "Skaldenstrophe und Sagaprosa," in *Mediaeval Scandinavia,* 10 (1977); John E. Caerwyn Williams, *The Court Poet in Medieval Ireland,* in *Proceedings of the British Academy,* 57 (1971); Alois Wolf, "Zur Rolle der visur in der altnordischen Prosa," in *Festschrift Leonhard C. Franz zum 70. Geburtstag,* Osmund Menghin and Hermann Olberg, eds. (1965); Cecil Wood, "Concerning the Interpretation of Skaldic Verse," in *The Germanic Review,* 33 (1958).

ROBERTA FRANK

[See also **Bjarnar Saga Hítdœlakappa; Bragi Boddason the Old; Drottkvætt; Eddic Poetry; Egill Skallagrímsson; Egils Saga Skallagrímssonar; Eilífr Goðrúnarson; Einarr Helgason Skálaglamm; Einarr Skúlason; Eíriksmál and Hákonarmál; Eyrbyggja Saga; Eyvindr Finnsson Skáldaspillir; Family Sagas, Icelandic; Fóstbrœðra Saga; Gunnlaugs Saga Ormstungu; Hallfreðar Saga; Háttalykill; Háttatal; Kormáks Saga; Norse Flyting; Odin; Saga; Skáldatal; Skáldskaparmál; Snorra Edda; Snorri Sturluson; Þjóðólfr ór Hvíni; Úlfr Uggason.**]

SKÁLDSKAPARMÁL (poetic diction) is the longest section of *Snorra Edda.* It begins with a frame—soon abandoned—in which Bragi, god of poetry, regales a sea king, Ægir, with tales of the gods. Many important myths and heroic legends indeed are recounted, but mostly in explanation of some aspect of poetics. The bulk of *Skáldskaparmál* is an explanation of the metaphoric and metonymic poetic techniques of skaldic verse, primarily kennings and *heiti* (poetic names). The discussion is arranged according to semantic categories common to this poetry, such as men, kings, gold, and weapons, and is quite thorough. Because many of the verses cited are found only here, *Skáldskaparmál* is an invaluable source of the older poetry.

BIBLIOGRAPHY

Much of the literature on skaldic poetry and the *Snorra Edda* is directly or indirectly relevant to *Skáldskaparmál*. See also Arthur G. Brodeur, *The Meaning of Snorri's Categories* (1952).

For an explanation of poetics based largely on Snorri, see E. O. G. Turville-Petre, *Scaldic Poetry* (1976). An English translation of the *Skáldskaparmál* is available in Snorri Sturluson, *The Prose Edda*, Arthur G. Brodeur, trans. (1916, 6th ed. 1967).

JOHN LINDOW

[See also **Eddic Poetry; Gylfaginning; Háttatal; Kenning; Skaldic Poetry; Snorra Edda; Snorri Sturluson.**]

SKANDERBEG (known also as George Castriota and Iskander Bey, 1405–1468), an Albanian who had been sent to the court of Murad II as a hostage and was brought up as a Muslim. After the death of his father, he escaped, reconverted to Christianity, and led the stubborn opposition of the Albanians against the Ottomans in a guerrilla war that lasted from 1443 until his death. In 1444 he organized the League of Lesh, an association of Albanian princes against the Turks, and built a number of fortresses. With help from Venice, Naples, and the pope, he repulsed thirteen Turkish invasions between 1444 and 1466. He is regarded as an Albanian national hero.

BIBLIOGRAPHY

Leften Stavros Stavrianos, *The Balkans Since 1453* (1958).

LINDA C. ROSE

[See also **Albania (Caucasian); Murad II.**]

ŠKAND-GUMĀNĪG WIZĀR (*Shkand-gumānīg Wizār,* Doubt-destroying explanation) is a ninth-century Zoroastrian apologetic text, written originally in Pahlavi, directed against Judaism, Christianity, Islam, and Manichaeism. The author, a layman named Mardānfarrox ī Ohrmazddādān (Martān-Farrux i Ohrmazddātān), explains that he traveled widely and learned of other religions but became convinced of the truth of his own faith. Without the works of other Zoroastrian sages he might have become a Manichaean, he says, and cites their writings in his own argument. The third book of the *Dēnkard* (Acts of the religion), a ninth-century compendium of Zoroastrian teachings, is his principal source; he mentions also Ādurfarnbag ī Farroxzādān (Āturfarnbag i Farruxzātān), the high priest (*hūdēnān pēšōbāy*) of Pārs who debated the apostate Abāliš in the presence of Caliph al-Maʾmūn (*r.* 813–833). The text of the *Škand-gumānīg Wizār* survives in its entirety only in Pāzand (a faulty transcription of Pahlavi into the Avestan alphabet) and in a medieval Sanskrit translation by the Parsi scholar Nēryōsang; the work differs from most of the Pahlavi books in that the argument is pursued in abstract terms, largely without reference to Zoroastrian myth and legend.

The first part of the *Škand-gumānīg Wizār* is devoted to a demonstration of dualism through answers to questions posed by one Mihrayyār ī Mahmadān, presumably a Muslim. Mardānfarrox explains how the good god Ohrmazd could not prevent darkness from attacking light and Ahriman from assaulting the good creation, how the latter is organized defensively to wage battle against evil, and how the grace of Ohrmazd's revelation must presuppose the prior intrusion of an evil alien to this god, the enticements of which man is to resist through the Zoroastrian religion. The author argues also against the Mazdakites and other materialists who deny Ohrmazd's existence.

The second part is a documented polemic against specific faiths: the author's attacks on the Muslims are aimed specifically at the Muʿtazilites, who tended to absolve God of responsibility for evil, attributing it to the devil and to man, and who fought deterministic tendencies in Islam. They were thus closest to the Zoroastrian view; the perceived inconsistencies of their religion were correspondingly most susceptible to argument. In his treatment of Judaism, Mardānfarrox concentrates on contradictions and absurdities in the biblical creation myth and refers both to Scripture and to the Midrashim. In his rebuttal of Christianity (called here *tarsāgīh,* "God Fearing," as in later Persian), he attacks the tenets of the Trinity, the Incarnation, and the Atonement. The argument against the Manichaeans criticizes their perversion of dualist doctrine; it is preserved only in part.

BIBLIOGRAPHY

Texts. Adrien Barthélemy, ed. and trans., *Guzastag Abāliš* (1887), containing Ádurfarnbag's dispute with the apostate, in Pahlavi; Sheriarji D. Bharucha, ed., *Collected Sanskrit Writings of the Parsis,* pt. 4 (1913), Nēryōsang's Sanskrit translation of the text; Jāmāspjī Jamasp-Asana and E[dward] W. West, eds. and trans., *Shikand-gumānīk Vijār* (1887), Pāzand text and Sanskrit translation; Jean P. de Menasce, ed. and trans., *Une apologétique mazdéenne du IXe siècle, "Škand-gumānīk Vičār": La solution décisive des doutes,* n.s., fasc. 30 (1945), Pahlavi text of chaps. 1–5 and Pāzand text of chaps. 6–16, in Roman transcription, with an index of reconstructed Pahlavi forms, a French translation, and a copious commentary, and *Le troisième livre du Dēnkart* (1973), transcribed Pahlavi text with a French translation of the *Dēnkard;* Jacob Neusner, "A Zoroastrian Critique of Judaism (*Škand Gumānīk Vičār,* Chapters 13 and 14: A New Translation and Exposition)," in *Journal of the American Oriental Society,* 83 (1963); E[dward] W. West, ed. and trans., *Sacred Books of the East,* XXIV (1885, repr. 1970), a useful introduction with an out-of-date English translation.

Studies. Mary Boyce, "Middle Persian Literature," in B. Spuler, ed., *Handbuch der Orientalistik,* 1.4.2.1 (1968), 46–47; Jean P. de Menasce, "Zoroastrian Literature After the Muslim Conquest," in *Cambridge History of Iran,* IV (1975), 560–565; Jehangir C. Tavadia, *Die mittelpersische Sprache und Literatur der Zarathustrier* (1956), 92–97.

JAMES R. RUSSELL

[See also **Dēnkard; Mazdakites; Mu^c^tazila, al-; Pahlavi Literature; Zoroastrianism.**]

SKAÐI, in Scandinavian mythology, a mountain-dwelling goddess who hunts on skis with a bow. Snorri in *Gylfaginning* 23 and in *Skáldskaparmál* 1 relates that Skaði was the daughter of the giant Þjazi, whom the Æsir killed. Skaði received as compensation the choice of a husband from among the Æsir, but they allowed her to see only the feet of the candidates. She chose the one with the most beautiful feet, thinking that they must surely belong to Baldr. She had chosen instead the old god Njǫrðr, and their marriage was quarrelsome. Njǫrðr was associated with the sea, whereas Skaði, the *ǫndurdís* (ski goddess), lived in the mountains. They agreed to live alternately nine nights with each other, but Skaði was kept awake by the crying of gulls and Njǫrðr by the howling of wolves. In the *Háleygjatal* it is said that Skaði later married Odin and that they had many sons. Snorri tells that as punishment for the slaying of Baldr, Skaði suspended a poisonous snake over the bound Loki in such a way that the venom dripped into his face.

In the poem *Haustlǫng,* Þjazi is called the father of Mǫrn, which Folke Ström concludes is another name for Skaði. If Ström is correct, then Skaði is revealed as a fertility goddess through Mǫrn's (that is, Skaði's) role in *Vǫlsa þáttr,* which describes a primitive fertility rite involving an equine phallus. Skaði, the ski goddess of the mountains, would thus represent the winter aspect of the annual cycle of fertility, although this same function has also been assigned to Ullr. Another example of the phallic fertility aspect is the story told about Loki, who brought Skaði to laughter after the death of her father by tying one end of a rope to a goat's beard and the other end to his own penis. Loki and the goat both pulled and yelled until Loki fell into Skaði's lap, making her laugh.

The change of dwellings between the sea and the mountains has been viewed as a reflection of the mythological explanation for the alternation of the seasons, the Nordic analogue to the Greek myth of Persephone. If, further, the name Skaði is cognate with the Gothic *skadus* (shadow), then there is a semantic link to the underworld.

The name Skaði is anomalously masculine in its form, while the oldest form of the masculine Njǫrðr was the feminine Nerthus. The figures seem to have switched roles, perhaps as a result of the hermaphroditic nature of fertility deities.

BIBLIOGRAPHY

Hilda R. Ellis Davidson, *Gods and Myths of Northern Europe* (1964), 30, 39–40, 106–107; René L. M. Derolez, *Götter und Mythen der Germanen* (1963), 141–185; Eric Elgqvist, *Ullvi och Ullinshov* (1955), 105–110; *Haleygia-Tal,* in *Corpus poeticum boreale,* I, Gudbrand Vigfusson and F. York Powell, ed. and trans. (1883), 252; Anne Holtsmark, "Skaði," in *Kulturhistorisk leksikon for nordisk middelalder,* XV (1970), 381–382; Folke Ström, *Diser, nornor, valkyrjor* (1954), 25–64; Snorri Sturluson, *The Prose Edda,* Arthur G. Brodeur, trans. (1916, 6th ed. 1967), 36–38, 77, and 91–92; E. O. G. Turville-Petre, *Myth and Religion of the North* (1964), 256–258; Jan de Vries, *Altgermanische Religionsgeschichte,* 2nd ed., II (1957), 259–338.

JAMES E. CATHEY

The Skewṙa Reliquary, depicting St. Gregory the Illuminator and St. Thaddeus. Silver-gilt triptych of 1293. HERMITAGE MUSEUM, LENINGRAD

[See also **Æsir; Baldr; Eyvindr Finnsson Skáldaspillir; Gylfaginning; Loki; Njǫrðr; Odin; Scandinavian Mythology; Skáldskaparmál; Snorri Sturluson; Þjóðólfr ór Hvíni; Ullr.**]

SKEWṘA, an Armenian monastery located near the fortress of Lambron in the Cilician Kingdom of Armenia. Skewṙa was the family monastery of the Het^{c}umid barons and housed a major atelier of the Cilician school of manuscript painting.

Het^{c}um, prince of Lambron, erected the main church at the monastery in 1110. Skewṙa's most remarkable abbot was Archbishop Nersēs of Lambron (Nersēs Lambronac^{c}i, *d.* 1198), a member of the Het^{c}umid family, a distinguished man of letters, a statesman, and an active patron of Armenian miniature painting (Erevan, Matenadaran MS 1568, in 1173; Venice, S. Lazzaro, Biblioteca Armena dei P. P. Mekhitarista, MS 1635, in 1193).

The Skewṙa Reliquary, dated 1293 (Leningrad, Hermitage Museum), an elaborately carved, silver-gilt triptych, is one of the few surviving works of medieval Armenian silversmiths.

BIBLIOGRAPHY

Thomas S. R. Boase, "The History of the Kingdom," in his *The Cilician Kingdom of Armenia* (1978), esp. 15–18, and "Gazetteer," *ibid.,* 182; Sirarpie Der Nersessian, *The Armenians* (1970), 134, *Études byzantines et arméniennes* (1973), 372, 563–579, 705–721, and *Armenian Art,* Sheila Bourne and Angela O'Shea, trans. (1977); Nona Stepanian and Arutyun Tchakmaktchian, *L'art décoratif de l'Arménie médiévale* (1971), 45–46.

LUCY DER MANUELIAN

[See also **Armenia: History of; Armenian Art; Cilician Kingdom; Het^{c}umids; Nerses Lambronac^{c}i.**]

SKÍRNISMÁL (The words of Skírnir) is the title of a twenty-seven-stanza fragment preserved in Codex Arnamagnaean 748, an incomplete, unordered version of the *Poetic Edda.* The poem of Skírnir is found complete in forty-two stanzas in the Codex Regius, entitled *Fǫr Skírnis* (Skírnir's journey). The journey in question takes Skírnir, the servant and friend of the god Freyr, into Giantland to woo Gerðr, a giant's daughter, in the name of his master. Wooing missions and the giant's daughter motif are widely attested in folklore and literature; in Old Norse the closest parallel is *Svipdagsmál,* also an otherworld wooing journey.

Skírnismál thus leads up to but does not depict the union of Freyr and Gerðr. It is, however, this "sacred marriage" of the god of fruitfulness and wealth with a female associated with the earth that probably formed the background of the poem in an agrarian fertility cult—a primitive mythic pattern of worldwide occurrence. Tiny golden plaques apparently portraying the marriage have been found in old cultivated areas in Norway. They are interpreted as votive offerings to ensure Freyr's favor. Gold itself is a special province of Freyr in *Skírnismál* and elsewhere.

Skírnir (the shining one, the ray) may have been an emanation or hypostasis of Freyr in his association with the fructifying sun, but in the poem Skírnir has become an individual unforgettable in his own right.

The story is told entirely through its six dialogues, except for a prose introduction and a few prose transitions. The meter is mostly *ljóðaháttr* (chant meter). It is the dramatic quality (together with the religious background) that makes *Skírnismál* the best evidence in Bertha Phillpotts' case for a cultic drama in Old Norse; however, her argument has not been well received by scholars.

The dramatic skill and humor of the poet are of the highest order. Freyr's lovelorn condition and Skírnir's tentative heroism are brilliantly brought out in the opening dialogues; to portray the dangerous ride through the "flickering flame, dark and knowing," into the Other World, the poet has Skírnir address his horse. Skírnir encounters first a herdsman of Gymir, the father giant; then a servant girl reports the god's arrival to Gerðr, and Skírnir tries to induce Gerðr to marry Freyr by offering her golden apples and the famous ring Draupnir. Next Skírnir threatens and, finally, resorts to a formal curse (stanzas 26–36); Gerðr's resistance vanishes, and a rendezvous in "the windless wood" Barri is agreed on. In the last scene the impatient Freyr demands news of the newly returned messenger and complains comically of the nine-night wait before consummation.

Snorri Sturluson retold this story in his *Prose Edda,* emphasizing the comedy and quoting the last stanza. However, Snorri's version does not contain the curse, and scholars have debated whether the curse belonged to the "original" poem; Ursula Dronke has made a good case that it did.

The poet's light touch has seemed incongruous in an early, deeply heathen poem, and the treatment of love is viewed as late in terms of cultural history. Jan de Vries, therefore, dated the poem to the twelfth century. But Finnur Jónsson has given good reasons for a Norwegian home and a date about 900. Recent consensus, as represented by Einar Ólafur Sveinsson, regards the extant version, a cheerful epithalamium, as somewhere between these extremes but emphasizes the depth of the tradition.

BIBLIOGRAPHY

Editions. Jón Helgason, ed., *Eddadigte,* 3rd ed. (1961); Gustav Neckel, ed., *Edda: Die Lieder des Codex Regius nebst verwandten Denkmälern,* I, 3rd ed. rev. by Hans Kuhn (1962).

English translations. Henry Adams Bellows, trans., *The Poetic Edda* (1923); Lee M. Hollander, trans., *The Poetic Edda,* 2nd rev. ed. (1962); Paul B. Taylor and W. H. Auden, trans., *The Elder Edda: A Selection,* with notes by Peter H. Salus (1969); Patricia Terry, trans., *Poems of the Vikings: The Elder Edda* (1969).

Commentaries. F. Detter and R. Heinzel, *Sæmundar Edda mit einem Anhang,* II (1903), 193–210; Magnus Olsen, *Edda- og Skaldekvad: Forarbeider til kommentar,* VII (1964), 27–46; B. Sijmons and H. Gering, *Die Lieder der Edda,* III, pt. 1 (1927), 217–235.

Standard and general studies. Finnur Jónsson, *Den oldnorske og oldislandske litteraturs historie,* 2nd rev. ed., I (1920), 173–179; Einar Ól. Sveinsson, *Íslenzkar bókmenntir í fornöld* (1962), 276–280; Jan de Vries, *Altnordische Literaturgeschichte,* 2nd rev. ed., II (1967), 104–107.

Articles and special studies. Ursula Dronke, "Art and Tradition in *Skírnismál,*" in Norman Davis and C. L. Wrenn, eds., *English and Medieval Studies Presented to J. R. R. Tolkien on the Occasion of His Seventieth Birthday* (1962); P. Groth, "Sjá hǫlf hýnótt," in *Festskrift til Finnur Jónsson* (1928); A. G. van Hamel, "Gambantein," in *Neophilologus,* **17** (1932); Joseph Harris, "Cursing with the Thistle: *Skírnismál* 31, 6–8 and OE Metrical Charm 9, 16–17," in *Neuphilologische Mitteilungen,* **76** (1975); Vilhelm Kiil, "*Hliðskjalf* og *seiðhjallr,*" in *Arkiv för nordisk filologi,* **75** (1960); Ivar Lindquist, "Kritisk undersökning av sista raden i Skírnismál," in *Studia germanica tillägnade Ernst Albin Kock* (1934); Karl G. Ljunggren, "Anteckningar till Skírnismál och Rígsþula," in *Arkiv för nordisk filologi,* **53** (1937), and **54** (1939); Lars Lönnroth, "*Skírnismál* och den fornisländska äktenskapsnormen," in Bent Chr. Jacobsen, Christian Lisse, Jonna Louis-Jensen, and Eva Rode, eds., *Opuscula Septentrionalia: Festskrift til Ole Widding 10.10.1977* (1977), 154–178; H. Lommel, "Eine Beziehung zwischen Veda und Edda," in *Zeitschrift für deutsches Altertum,* **73** (1936); Fritz Mezger, "A Semantic and Stylistic Study of

Eddic *brek, súsbreki,*" in *The Journal of English and Germanic Philology,* **42** (1943); Felix Niedner, "Skírnis för," in *Zeitschrift für deutsches Alterthum,* **30** (1886); Magnus Olsen, "Fra gammelnorsk myte og kultus," in *Maal og minne* (1909); Bertha S. Phillpotts, *The Elder Edda and Ancient Scandinavian Drama* (1920); Konstantin Reichardt, "Die Liebesbeschwörung in Fǫr Skírnis," in *The Journal of English and German Philology,* **38** (1939); Jöran Sahlgren, *Eddica et scaldica: Fornväst-nordiska studier,* II (1927–1928), 209–303, "Sagan om Frö och Gärd," in *Namn och bygd,* **16** (1928), and "Lunden Barre i *Skírnismál,*" in *Namn och bygd,* **50** (1962); Evert Salberger, "Rístu nú, Skírnir: Ett textställe i Skírnismál 1," in *Arkiv för nordisk filologi,* **72** (1957); F. Otto Schrader, "Beziehung zwischen Veda und Edda," in *Zeitschrift für deutsches Altertum,* **77** (1940); E. O. G. Turville-Petre, "Fertility of Beast and Soil in Old Norse Literature," in Edgar C. Polomé, ed., *Old Norse Literature and Mythology: A Symposium* (1969).

JOSEPH HARRIS

[See also **Eddic Meters; Eddic Poetry; Freyr; Scandinavian Mythology; Svipdagsmál.**]

SKJǪLDUNGA SAGA is an Icelandic saga that is no longer extant. It was the saga of the Skjǫldungar, the oldest royal family in Denmark, telling of more than twenty prehistoric kings from the original ancestor Skjǫldr, son of Odin, to Gorm the Old.

The principal authority for *Skjǫldunga saga* is a treatise on early Danish history written in Latin at the end of the sixteenth century by the Icelander Arngrímur Jónsson the Learned. In this work, Jónsson relied heavily on a now-lost manuscript of *Skjǫldunga saga.* In addition, traces of the saga are to be found, more or less confused in one way or another, in many places in early writings. Snorri Sturluson, for example, used it both in his *Prose Edda* and in *Heimskringla,* where he explicitly refers to it in chapter 29 of *Ynglinga saga.*

Skjǫldunga saga was written about 1200, while a later and longer version of it, which is represented by the so-called *Sǫgubrot* (fragment), was composed in the latter part of the thirteenth century.

The author of *Skjǫldunga saga* had a written genealogy at his disposal. The idea for this genealogy, which may have been written by Sæmundr Sigfússon the Learned (*d.* 1133), probably originated with Sæmundr's family, the Oddaverjar, who claimed descent from the Skjǫldungar. At any rate the genealogy became the backbone of *Skjǫldunga saga* and was later used by the Danish historians Sven Aggesen and Saxo Grammaticus in their historical writings.

The author was, of course, acquainted with various foreign histories, most notably the celebrated *Historia regum Britanniae* of Geoffrey of Monmouth. In all probability he used Frankish dynastic tables (Odin-Skjǫldr) and Frankish works containing the so-called *Urgeschichte,* an account of the migration of Odin and his sons from Asia to the north, where they settled. Yngvi, Skjǫldr's brother, was the ancestor of the Ynglingar, the oldest family of Swedish kings. The date of this immigration can be inferred from a statement that Peace-Fróði, a grandson of Skjǫldr, governed in Denmark at the times of the emperor Augustus and Christ.

If the genealogy is the backbone of the saga, oral sources are its flesh and blood. In oral tradition there were abundant tales about the Skjǫldungar, in poetic form as well as in prose.

Skjǫldunga saga is a heroic story on which killings and acts of revenge between the generations leave their mark. We also find echoes of Viking tales, however. The saga contains few tales of the *Märchen* and folklore type. The author was no uncritical storyteller. He is very much given to explaining the origins and causes of things and events, and even to dating them. He was obviously well versed in the usual etymological and historiographical methods of the Middle Ages. These practices, and his various observations about ancient modes of life, impart to the saga an air of both foreign and native learning.

The author's aim is not only to relate events that directly concern the royal house and the historical and political growth of Denmark, but also to explain the origins of the Nordic peoples and connect their history with world history.

Skjǫldunga saga is a pioneer work in Icelandic literature. It is the first saga of ancient times (that is, it tells of events before the settlement of Iceland). After *Skjǫldunga saga* the Icelanders begin to write histories of nations other than Iceland and Norway (for instance, Denmark, the Orkneys, the Faeroes, Greenland, and Sweden).

Skjǫldunga saga is not an isolated phenomenon but an offshoot of a European literary fashion that has been called "the renaissance of the twelfth century."

There is some circumstantial evidence that Páll Jónsson, bishop of Skálholt from 1195 to 1211, might be the author of the saga.

BIBLIOGRAPHY

Source. For Arngrímur Jónsson's treatise, *Rerum Danicarum fragmenta,* see Jakob Benediktsson, ed., *Arngrimi Jonae opera latine conscripta,* I (1950), and IV (1957). These are volumes IX and XII in the *Bibliotheca Arnamagnaeana;* the former contains the Latin text and the latter a commentary in English. See also Sǫgur Danakonunga, *Islenzk fornrit xxxv,* Bjarni Guðnason, ed. (1982); *Skjoldungernes Saga,* Karsten Friis-Jensen and Claus Lund, trans. with notes in Danish (1984).

Studies. Bjarni Guðnason, *Um Skjöldunga sögu* (1963), and references therein; R. C. Boer, "Studier over Skjoldungedigtningen," in *Årbøger for nordisk Oldkyndighed og Historie* (1922); Andreas Heusler, "Die gelehrte Urgeschichte im altisländischen Schrifttum," in *Abhandlungen der Königlich Preussischen Akademie der Wissenschaften, philosophisch-historische Klasse* (1908), and repr. in his *Kleine Schriften,* II, Stefan Sonderegger, ed. (1969); Niels Lukman, *Skjoldunge und Skilfinge* (1943); Axel Olrik, "Skjoldunga saga i Arngrim Jonssons udtog," in *Aarbøger for nordisk Oldkyndighed og Historie* (1894), and *Danmarks Heltedigtning,* I (1903); Inge Skovgaard-Petersen, "Saxo, Historian of the Patria," in *Mediaeval Scandinavia,* 2 (1969); "Sǫgubrot," in Carl af Petersens and Emil Olson, eds., *Sǫgur Danakonunga* (1919–1925); Einar Ól. Sveinsson, *Sagnaritun Oddaverja* (1937); Elias Wessén, *De nordiska folkstammarna i Beowulf* (1927).

BJARNI GUÐNASON

[See also **Bishops' Sagas; Denmark; Fornaldarsögur; Geoffrey of Monmouth; Iceland; Odin; Orkneyinga Saga; Páls Saga Biskups; Saga; Saxo Grammaticus; Scandinavian Literature; Snorri Sturluson; Sven Aggesen; Vikings.**]

SKRÆLINGS, a term applied by the tenth-century Norse (primarily Icelandic) settlers of Greenland to the natives of that country and the nearby North American coast (Vinland). In Old Icelandic the term *skræling(j)ar* occurs only in this meaning; in Modern Icelandic it can also mean "barbarian," a connotation it evidently had from the beginning. It seems to be derived from a root meaning "dried up, shriveled" (compare the modern Icelandic *skræla* [dry up]). The earliest reference is by Ari Thorgilsson (the Learned), who tells in his *Íslendingabók* (Book of the Icelanders, *ca.* 1130) that when the first Icelanders arrived in Greenland to settle there, they had "found human habitations, fragments of skin boats, and stone implements from which it was evident that the same kind of people had lived there as inhabited Vinland and whom the Greenland settlers called 'Skrælings.'" The reference is to the expedition led by Eric the Red around 986; Ari had it from his uncle, who had been in Greenland and spoken with one of Eric's men.

Modern students have found this and other references that place the Skrælings on the North American mainland puzzling. It is clear that in later years, after the invasion of Greenland by Thule-culture Eskimos (1100–1200), the term was applied only to Eskimos. But even in the Vinland sagas (allowing for the usual white man's arrogance) the descriptions seem to fit Eskimos better than Indians: they were "dark-skinned [literally, 'black'], evil-looking men, with ugly hair on their heads; they were big-eyed and broad-faced" (*Eirik's saga,* chap. 10). Yet it seems that the Norsemen did come into contact with Indians: an arrowhead of indubitable Indian origin has been found on a Greenland farm site, and a Norse coin appeared in an Indian midden in Maine. The dramatic accounts in the sagas may therefore more likely refer to Indians, perhaps Beothuks or Micmacs.

In Ari's time it was still easy to confuse the two, since the Greenlanders had no experience with the Eskimos. The remains they found were probably of the Eskimo Dorset culture, which lasted until about A.D. 100. Contact with the Indians, as pictured in the sagas, was brief and bloody, and ended disastrously for the Norsemen. It was easy for the Norsemen to bracket them all as "barbarians."

In Greenland the Skrælings pushed southward and gradually displaced the Norsemen. For reasons that are unexplained, the latter died out after some five centuries of living in Greenland. Around 1350 it is reported that the Skrælings "possess the whole Western Settlement" (Ívar Bárðarson). When the Eastern Settlement fell silent, there was no one left to record its demise.

BIBLIOGRAPHY

Finn Gad, *The History of Greenland,* Ernst Dupont, trans., I (1970), and "Skrællinger," in *Kulturhistorisk leksikon för nordisk middelalder,* XV (1970), 717–718; Henrik M. Jansen, *A Critical Account of the Written and Archaeological Sources' Evidence Concerning the Norse Settlements in Greenland* (1972), reviewed by Einar Haugen in *Speculum,* **49** (1974); Gwyn Jones, *The Norse Atlantic Saga,* 2nd ed. (1986); Terkel Mathiassen, *Skrælingerne i Grønland* (1935).

EINAR HAUGEN

[See also **Climatology; Exploration by Western Europeans; Missions and Missionaries, Christian; Vinland Sagas.**]

SKYLITZES, JOHN (*ca.* 1040–1100/1110), Byzantine chronicler and high-ranking official at the court of Alexios I Komnenos. His *Synopsis of Histories* comprises the period of 811 to 1057; whether the so-called *Continuation of Skylitzes* until the year 1079 was written by him remains doubtful. For the period down to the mid tenth century, Skylitzes drew on Theophanes Continuatus, and for the second part of the *Synopsis* he used different sources, now lost. The narration is heterogeneous in its manner and contains contradictory social and political tendencies. While in the history of the second half of the tenth century Skylitzes defended the Byzantine church, his attitude toward the ecclesiastical hierarchy after Romanos III became negative. The history of Michael IV is written in an annalistic manner, with abundant dates, while the following section is divided into some chapters arranged topically, without strong chronological sequence, and almost without chronological datings. The principal hero of the last section is the general Katakalon Kekaumenos, whom Skylitzes opposed to the wicked and weak Constantinopolitan rulers and officials.

BIBLIOGRAPHY

Sources. Ioannis Scylitzes Synopsis historiarum, Hans Thurn, ed. (1973); Eudoxus Th. Tsolakēs, *Hē synecheia tēs chronographias tou Iōannou Skylitsē* (1968).

Studies. Herbert Hunger, *Die hochsprachliche profane Literatur der Byzantiner,* 2 vols. (1978), 389–393; A. Kazhdan, "Ioannis Skylitzae Synopsis historiarum," in *Istoriko-filologicheskii zhurnal,* no. 1 (1957), 206–212; Werner Seibt, "Ioannas Skylitzes: Zur Person des Chronisten," in *Jahrbuch der österreichischen Byzantinistik,* **25** (1976); J. Shepard, "Skylitzes on Armenia in the 1040's and the Role of Catacalon Cecaumenus," in *Revue des études arméniennes,* n.s. **11** (1975–1976); M. Sjuzjumov, "Ob istočnikach L'va Djakona i Skilicy," in *Vizantiiskoe obozrienie,* **2** (1916), 106–166.

ALEXANDER P. KAZHDAN

[See also **Byzantine Literature; Theophanes Continuatus.**]

SLAVERY, ISLAMIC WORLD. The average town dweller in the medieval Middle East—Muslim, Christian, or Jew—was bound to have dealings with people who defined their relationships to one another in terms of slavery or clientage—even if he himself was not a slave owner, slave, or former slave. Such relationships were based on the principle that one human being had the right to exercise near-absolute dominion over the life, labor, and person of another human being. Although Islamic jurists consistently maintained that "the original condition [of human beings] is freedom," this principle did not conflict with the basic assumption in the Koran, *ḥadith* literature, and in jurisprudence that the inequality between master and slave, like that between man and woman, was ordained by God.

The great Arabic lexicographer Ibn Manẓūr (*d.* 1311), in his discussion of the word ᶜ*abd* (slave) in his multivolume dictionary, *Lisān al-*ᶜ*Arab* (Language of the Arabs), made the explicit distinction between owner and owned when he cautioned his readers concerning the two plural forms of the word: ᶜ*ibād,* the "worshipers" or "slaves" of God, and ᶜ*abīd,* actual chattel slaves. Every human being, Ibn Manẓūr piously affirmed, was an ᶜ*abd* in the sense of being in a servile state (*marbūb*) in relation to the creator. However, the "Lord of all worshipers as well as of all slaves" had seen fit to designate some people as "slaves for God" and others as "slaves for both God and his creatures." These latter were the ᶜ*abīd mamālīk* (owned ones).

Like Judaism and Christianity, Islam had entered into a world in which, to paraphrase one classical scholar, slavery was "a primordial fact." In the Koran the master-slave hierarchy is taken for granted. The "chattel slave who controls nothing" (16:75) serves both as a metaphor for powerlessness and as an example, in contrast to the prosperous free man, of the omnipotence of God, who "has favored some of you above others in provision" (16:71). The wealthy merchants of Mecca are repeatedly warned that ascribing partners to God is as absurd as if they themselves were to take as partners their own slaves ("those whom your right hand possess"), share their wealth with them, and make them their equals (30:28; compare 16:71,75). Similar language occurs in the discussion of the male-female hierarchy: "men are set over women, for God has favored some of them [that is, men] over others" (4:34). Just as the inequality between master and slave is used as an argument against ascribing partners to God, so the polytheists are ridiculed for assigning daughters to God (Allāt, al-ᶜUzza, and Manāt) when they themselves prefer sons to daughters and practice female infanticide (16: 57–59).

Unlike the inequality between man and woman, that between master and slave is a mutable one. Although there is very little actual legislation regarding slaves in the Koran, masters are repeatedly encouraged to emancipate their slaves as acts of charity (2:177; 90:13) or as expiation for their own wrongdoing (4:92; 5:89). According to the articulation of Islamic slavery by the Muslim jurisprudents, the manumitted slave bears no legal stigma for his slave origin. The male free slave is now "a free man among the free [male] Muslims." The freed female slave, of course, continues to fall within the legally disadvantaged category of women, although her status is definitely improved.

In both the Koran and the *ḥadīth* literature, masters are encouraged to treat both male and female slaves with kindness. Masters should not force their female slaves into prostitution (24:33) and should facilitate the marriages of their slaves of both sexes (24:32). Muslim legal scholars, building on this Koranic basis, argued that whereas masters were not legally constrained to provide adequate physical maintenance (*nafaqāt*) for animals in their possession, they were required to do so for their slaves, who were "among the people with a claim [upon the master]" (*min ahl al-istiḥqāq*), and that claim included proper food and clothing. Similarly, the humanity of slaves was underscored in the recognition of slave marriages. However, the male slave could marry only half the number of wives granted to a free man, and he could not initiate marriage without his master's consent. According to many Muslim jurists, the master possessed the right of *ijbār* (coercion) in marriage over his adult male and female slaves as he did over his minor children. The punishment for adultery in the case of a slave was half that of a free person—an inequality that indicates that the slave marriage was less "sacred" than that of the free person.

Despite the insistence of medieval Muslim jurists that a cruel master should be forced by the local qadi to sell an abused slave, the evidence from chronicles and biographical dictionaries indicates that judicial interference in the master-slave relationship was rare. Social pressure and the informal but powerful mechanism of third-party intercession (*shafāᶜa*) were the most effective and most frequently employed remedies for abuse. The master, however, owned "the physical person" of the slave, and the corporal punishment of slaves (like the corporal punishment of wives and children) was not necessarily perceived as abuse. The slave, as a legally impotent being, was not empowered to sue his master for bodily harm. Among the recognized legal schools, only the Hanafis maintained that a free man could be put to death for killing a slave. More important, perhaps, direct outside interference in the master-slave relationship was seen as a challenge to the social order. Sultan Qānsūḥ al-Ghawrī, himself a freed slave, maintained that he would prefer not to hold a master accountable for the killing of his slave out of respect for the *ḥurma* (sacred honor) of that relationship, just as he would be loath to hold a father accountable for the killing of his son out of respect for the *ḥurma* of fatherhood.

The fact that slavery in the medieval Middle East was primarily an urban phenomenon, deeply embedded in the household system, mitigated against the hardships endured by slaves in societies in which slave labor was a primary relationship of production. Agricultural slavery was rare in the Islamic world. Building projects that required intensive labor were normally carried out by paid workers or by corvée. One of the few attempts to make use of large-scale slave labor occurred in ninth-century Iraq. There, East African slaves were forced to labor in the marshland of lower Iraq under harsh conditions. This venture, which culminated in the famous Zanj revolt, was disastrous.

The absence of agricultural slavery in the medieval Middle East has led some scholars to discount the importance of Islamic slavery. In the absence of reliable data the quantitative history of medieval Islamic slavery remains a matter of conjecture. It is probably true that the actual number of slaves in the Islamic world, if compared with societies based on plantation slavery like that of the pre–Civil War American South, constituted a small percentage of the total free population, both urban and rural. The vital role of slavery in Muslim towns and cities, however, cannot be underestimated. In almost every sector of urban society, the "slaves of the slaves of God"—men, women, and children of diverse origin, background, and training—provided their masters with a broad spectrum of services from cooking, cleaning, and childbearing to managing the finances of great merchant houses and commanding the armies of Islam.

Slaves in the medieval Muslim world bore a common legal status regulated in great detail by Islamic jurisprudence. They did not, however, constitute a monolithic class or group. The "owned ones" shared in the same formal relationship with masters, who might be emirs, merchants, scholars, or craftsmen. Given the high rate of manumission, most slaves would eventually participate in the strong mutual bond of clientage. Each slave's potential for social prestige, economic success, and, in some cases, political power depended on a variety of factors, not the least of which were the circumstances and concerns of the household in which he served. Furthermore, the lot of the individual slave might be determined early on, perhaps in the slave market itself, by certain basic characteristics, such as gender, color, and perceived or ascribed ethnic origin.

Islamic law prohibits the enslavement of any free Muslim or of a Christian or Jew living under Islamic rule in the *Dār al-Islām* (Abode of Islam). There is a great deal of evidence to indicate that second-generation slavery was rare in the medieval Middle East. Most slaves were thus, by definition, outsiders. Indeed, it can be argued that the preferred slave was the child newly acquired from the non-Muslim lands, the *Dār al-Ḥarb* (Abode of War). Muslim jurists describe slavery using the powerful metaphors of illness and death. The enslaved person has lost his or her original condition of freedom and has thus entered into a kind of legal death or, perhaps more accurately, suspended life since he or she can ultimately be "resurrected" through manumission.

The ideology of Islamic slavery could best be described as one that articulated slavery as a social process—a means of converting outsiders into insiders. The helplessness of the newly acquired slave was essential to the working of this process. As in most slave-holding societies, the newly acquired slave was rootless and kinless, a person without a past. His or her original name would be replaced with a distinctive slave name and with the convert patronymic of "son (or daughter) of the slave of God," *ibn* or *bint ᶜabd allāh*. Within this household-centered society, a person's complete name placed him or her within a kinship network, within a religious community, and often within a certain occupational or status group. The name served as a visible sign of a person's social identity, of his circumstances, and of his background. The name of the slave—a name not drawn from the community's common pool of Arabic Muslim names—announced that the slave was a deracinated creature, a person with no network of support who was totally dependent upon his master.

Ideally, the "death" of enslavement would be followed by a period of *tarbīya* (training) of the young slave, in which he or she was socialized into Islam and into the household of the master. The nature of this *tarbīya* varied tremendously from household to household and from slave to slave. The future slave soldier was trained in the use of arms, the future business agent in accounting. Most female slaves were destined for childbearing and/or for household service and were presumably trained accordingly. A small number—who were definitely perceived as investments by their masters—were trained as professional musicians. Most slaves, however, both male and female, appear to have been given a rudimentary Islamic education. There are numerous examples, especially in the biographies of slaves raised in the households of civilian scholars (*ᶜulamāᵓ*), of both male and female slaves who were trained from an early age in the religious sciences and who became recognized scholars in their adult years.

The culmination of the *tarbīya* was, in many cases, manumission in early adulthood. Just as enslavement was described as death, manumission was described as resurrection. The unbeliever who had "died" to his or her former life was now "reborn" as a member of the Muslim community, fully integrated into a social network, the core relationship of which was his bond of loyalty with his manumitter.

The "clientage of manumission" (*walāᵓ al-ᶜitq*) had certain specific legal consequences for both master and slave. The master could inherit from his former slave if the latter died without heirs. The freedman was now part of the master's legally defined agnatic group for purposes of payment of blood money. The most important aspects of the clientage relationship were, however, not articulated in legal terms but expressed in social behavior.

Clientage is repeatedly described in medieval Arabic sources as a kind of artificially created kinship. A commonly quoted *ḥadīth* of the Prophet was "Clientage is flesh like the flesh of kinship; it cannot be sold or given away." The freed slave stood "in place of the paternal cousin" and was known by a *nisba* taken from the name of his manumitter. There is ample evidence both from narrative sources and from surviving documents of waqf (religious endowment) that the clientage relationship was taken quite seriously by both manumitters and freedpeople and often extended for generations.

This model of slavery as a process of socialization—a process articulated in terms of death and resurrection—was an ideal construct that did not necessarily reflect the actual experience of every slave in the medieval Middle East. Some slaves, especially prisoners of war, entered the *Dār al-Islām* as adults. There is strong evidence, however, that adult male slaves, newly acquired and not "formed" by a childhood spent in slavery, were considered to be poor investments. Adult female slaves were not viewed with the same disfavor, probably because the socialization they required for their roles was less intensive than that required for male slaves. Since the female slave produced free, legitimate offspring for her master, her childbearing potential was a crucial determinant of her market value and of her future role.

Some slaves, male and female, lived out their lives in slavery and were never manumitted. The flexibility of Islamic law, which enabled the master to "suspend" the slave's legal disability in regard to contracting and disposing in commercial matters, made the unmanumitted slave a useful and versatile tool for his master. Such a *maᵓdhūn* slave not only engaged in business for his master but could also engage in business for himself and acquire his own capital. One of the many legal vehicles for manumission was the purchase of freedom by the slave himself. It should be emphasized that manumission was not a severance of the master-slave relationship but a transformation of that relationship into what was perceived as an even deeper bond than that of slavery. Manumission appears to have been quite common in the Islamic world, and one could argue that the slavery-to-clientage continuum was one of the most important means of establishing interpersonal networks of loyalty in the urban societies of the medieval Middle East.

The practice of slavery in the Islamic world varied according to the circumstances of time and place. There are certain aspects of Islamic slavery—such as the importance of eunuchs, a small but elite group of slaves who constituted a kind of third gender category—that receive little or no attention in Islamic legal texts. More detailed studies are needed of the daily practice—as opposed to the legal theory—of slavery in specific Muslim societies during particular time periods. The prevalence of slaves and freedpeople in the urban setting, however, makes it clear that within these societies slavery and clientage responded to certain needs that other possible relationships, such as that between employer and employee, failed to meet with the same success.

The emphasis upon the assimilation of the "outsider" slave, the high rate of manumission, the importance of the clientage relationship and the articulation of that relationship in terms of kinship, the diversity in roles and status among people of slave origin, and the complex affiliations between the free, the unfree, and the freed—none of these factors is unique to Islamic society and each can be found in other slaveholding societies. The peculiar combination of these factors, as they were expressed by Muslim jurists and put into practice in daily life, is what makes Islamic slavery unique and makes the study of this institution vital to the social history of the premodern Middle East.

BIBLIOGRAPHY

Ahmed Abd al-Raziq, "Un document concernant le mariage des esclaves au temps du Mamlūks," in *Journal of the Economic and Social History of the Orient,* **13** (1970); Ralph A. Austen, "The Trans-Saharan Slave Trade: A Tentative Census," in Henry Gemercy and Jan S. Hogendorn, eds., *The Uncommon Market: Essays in the Economic History of the Atlantic Slave Trade* (1979); David Ayalon, *Studies on the Mamluks of Egypt (1250–1517)* (1977) and *The Mamluk Military Society* (1979); Robert Brunshvig, "ᶜAbd," in *Encyclopaedia of Islam,* new ed., I (1960); Paul G. Forand, "The Relation of the Slave and the Client to the Master or Patron in Medieval Islam," in *International Journal of Middle East Studies,* **2** (1971); Shelemo Dov Goitein, "Slaves and Slave Girls," in *A Mediterranean Society,* I (1967); Yusuf Fadl Hasan, *The Arabs and the Sudan* (1967); Bernard Lewis, *Race and Color in Islam* (1971); Donald P. Little, "Six Fourteenth-century Purchase Deeds for Slaves from al-Ḥaram al-Sharīf," in *Zeitschrift der deutschen morganländischen Gesellschaft,* **131** (1981), and "Two Fourteenth-century Court Records from Jerusalem Concerning the Disposition of Slaves by Minors," in *Arabica,* **29** (1982); Roy Mottahedeh, *Loyalty and Leadership in an Early Islamic Society* (1980); Hans Müller, "Sklaven," in *Wirtschaftsgeschichte des vorderen Orients in islamischer Zeit,* **6** (1977), and *Die Kunst des Sklavenkaufs* (1980); Rudolf Vesely, "De la situation des esclaves dans l'institution du waḳf," in *Archiv orientální,* **32** (1964); John R. Willis, ed., *Slaves and Slavery in Muslim Africa,* 2 vols. (1985).

SHAUN E. MARMON

[See also **Abode of Islam—Abode of War; Blacks; Concubinage, Islamic; Ḥadīth; Harem; Koran; Law, Islamic; Mamluk Dynasty; Music, Middle Eastern; ᶜUlamaᵓ; Waqf; Zanj.**]

SLAVERY, SLAVE TRADE. Medieval slavery was at first simply a continuation of the slavery of antiquity. Slaves existed almost everywhere in the ancient world, but in order to understand the evolution of this social class in the Middle Ages we need only to consider its position when the Roman state had established its control of the entire Mediterranean world.

In the last years of the Roman Republic, and even more under the empire, the legal position of the slave improved considerably. The power of the master was limited by law. It was forbidden to throw slaves to wild animals, unless this had been ordered by a judicial sentence, and a master who mistreated his slave had to sell him. If the master abandoned a slave who was old or infirm, the slave became free. The courts increasingly supplanted the owner in determining punishment of slaves. The idea that a slave was a person, not just a chattel, although vague at first, became more and more accepted. These changes were a reflection of the Stoic doctrines that had become influential during the first century B.C. At the beginnings of the empire Seneca declared that slavery affected only the body and that the soul remained free. These ideas were rapidly accepted by the jurists, as one can see in a famous text of Florentinus: "Slavery is a convention of the law of nations, whereby a person is subjected, contrary to nature, to the power of another" (*Digest* 1. 5. 4). All rules about slavery were discussed as part of the law of nations. Tryphonius expressed this idea even more clearly: "Freedom is part of natural law, and lordship was introduced by the law of nations" (*Digest* 12. 6. 64). Ulpian gives a fuller definition: "By natural law all men are included in the one name (men), but by the law of nations three terms were introduced, freemen, slaves (their opposites), and third, freedmen" (*Digest* 1. 1. 4). In short, the lawyers recognized the unity of the human race, but accepted the existing social order.

Among the Roman Stoics, Cicero took a position on slavery very close to that of Aristotle, namely that certain peoples were destined by nature to be slaves. Cicero, however, also thought that slavery prevented men of that condition from yielding to their natural tendency to evil. Seneca added another argument—the Fall of Man. During the Golden Age there was no slavery, but when men became corrupt, government, property, and slavery became necessary, and therefore just. This explanation was picked up by Christian writers, and lasted as long as slavery itself.

EARLY CHRISTIAN VIEWS

The Stoic concepts of Roman philosophers and jurists combined with the Old and New Testaments to influence early Christian thought. From the Old Testament came the idea that if master and slave were of the same race and religion, slavery should be barred, but it took centuries for this concept to penetrate the West. Only in the Carolingian age did it appear in the idea of Christian society as one in which no member should be reduced to slavery. However, non-Christian foreigners, even if converted, remained slaves throughout the Middle Ages and even later in the colonies that had slaves. The idea that slavery was a divine punishment for sin can be found in Genesis and was repeated by the church fathers, though it does not occur in the Gospels. According to the Fathers, however, the kingdom of Jesus is not of this world; hence slavery is unimportant if the soul has been freed by turning toward God.

Early Christianity, then, did not fight for an improvement in social conditions, any more than did Gnosticism or Mithraism, which also sought to save the soul rather than to help the body. The church even tried to keep converted slaves from leaving their masters, whether the latter were Christian or pagan. There is no general theory of slavery in the works of the Fathers of the first three centuries, but only allusions to the institution. In their relation to God, slaves are the equals of other men, especially since Christ did not come to save men according to their social condition. The later Fathers went back to Aristotle and once more justified slavery by assuming the intellectual inferiority of the slave. St. Augustine, in the *City of God,* used the argument of inferiority common to slaves, women, and children: "The justice of masters dominating slaves is clear, because those who excel in reason should excel in power."

With Augustine we reach the period of the barbarian kingdoms and the beginning of the Middle Ages. Since the arguments justifying slavery had passed from Rome into Christianity, it is not surprising that the institution itself survived. The slave class had not disappeared, even if new forms of personal dependence had developed and were to persist and grow throughout the early Middle Ages. These new forms of dependence were different from those of late antiquity. The colonus, though he appears in the late empire, was not a slave, and not yet a serf, but the colonate prepared the way, at least in part, for serfdom. Medieval slavery was not

Roman slavery, but it was directly connected with Roman slavery and only gradually developed distinguishing characteristics.

THE BARBARIANS

In Italy the invasion of Alaric and the Visigoths in 410 caused many people to fall into slavery. Other invasions had the same results—those of Attila and the Huns in 452, of the Vandals in 455, of the Heruli under Odoacer in 476. In 493 Odoacer was defeated and killed by Theodoric, king of the Ostrogoths, who ruled from 493 to 526. The edict formerly attributed to the Ostrogoth Theodoric (*Edictum Theodorici*) gives an idea of what had happened to slavery in Italy during this period. Slavery, from this time on, is essentially rural. The subordination of the slave to his master was much harsher than it had been in the late empire. The slave has become a miserable being—he can be killed if he is involved in a lawsuit that concerns his master, burned alive if he has intercourse with a widow (even with her consent) or if he causes a fire. He can have a little money of his own and receive gifts (as in antiquity) but his union with a female slave is not a legal marriage; it is a *contubernium.* She is at best a concubine, not a wife, and the union can be dissolved at will by the master. The harshness of these rules kept the slave in a state of constant terror. He trembled before the overseers, even when they were slaves like himself. Slaves could be freed, but emancipation is mentioned only incidentally in the edict. The slave could be transferred from one estate to another or sent to a town without any regard for his *contubernium* with his unfortunate "wife." He could be assigned to a half-free peasant, who would not treat him better than his master and who might treat him worse, since the peasant was close by and the master far away. The one consolation for a slave was to see that those whose legal position was better than his—the coloni, the half-free peasants who were drifting toward serfdom—were not much better sheltered from the anger of their common master. The society in which the slave had the lowest place was a slave society in which there was little difference between a slave and those who had a slightly superior legal position. Such at least is the inference to be drawn from the penal provisions that comprise the largest part of the Edict of Theodoric.

The emperor Justinian reconquered Italy after the death of Theodoric, but in 568 the Lombard invasions began. Under King Alboin (*ca.* 565–*ca.* 572) they took the place of the Ostrogoths and gained most of northern and central Italy. Since they acquired the lands and slaves of the Romans by violence, and often by murder, they had a larger slave work force than their predecessors. More than a third of the Edict of King Rothari (*Leges Rotharis,* 643) and of the *capitula* of King Liutprand (712–744) deals with the unfree. This shows how numerous they were and how important in the economy. The differences among them, based on differences in their occupations, are clearly shown by the differences in the compensation to be paid for their deaths.

One series of articles in Rothari's Edict puts the *aldii* (unfree Germans) and the *servi ministeriales* on the same level. The latter were slaves (usually of Roman origin) who had special skills and who lived in the master's house. (Such slaves also appear in the *Leges Visigothorum* of Spain, where they are called *idonei* [skilled men].) In general the rural slave has a value half that of a ministerial. The *aldius,* who is at the bottom of the Lombard social scale, is thus worth more than the *rusticanus* (rural slave), who is at the bottom of the Roman scale. Later developments, however, favored the *rusticani,* whose descendants, closer to the land and farther from their masters, became serfs or half-free, while the ministerials continued to be slaves living under the direct control of the master.

Under Liutprand the influence of the church began to be felt with the appearance of the Lombard law of the *manumissio in ecclesia* (freeing a slave in a church), by permitting slaves to enter the clergy with the consent of their master, by the transformation of the *contubernium* into a marriage protected by God, by greater respect for the right of asylum, especially in the case of slaves, and by granting part of the payment for killing a slave belonging to the king to the slave's family (earlier the king would have taken it all). The condition of the slave had perceptibly improved during the century between the Edict of Rothari and the end of Liutprand's reign. Nevertheless, many slaves fled from their masters, even though charters of emancipation were becoming numerous.

NINTH THROUGH TWELFTH CENTURIES

During the period that followed the end of the Lombard kingdom, conquered by the Carolingians in 774, relations of dependence on the lord (an individual or a religious community) were the most important characteristics of the social structure. These relations of dependence involved by far the largest part of the population, but they took many forms, of which the most important were serfdom, which was increasing, and slavery, which was declining. In the period of the barbarian kingdoms—in Italy, Spain, France, Germany, and England—the condition of the servile class is known mainly from the examination of legislative sources; our knowledge of this class in the period from the ninth to the middle of the twelfth century comes from ecclesiastical records, polyptychs, and cartularies. In spite of the fluidity of legal distinctions, the realities of rural economic life made it necessary always to contrast the *homines manuales* (manual laborers) and the *mancipia infra casam*—that is to say, the slaves—with the *homines cum casa et substantia* (men who had a house and goods of their own). The latter, called *rustici, coloni, massarii,* and *manentes,* are always clearly distinguished from the *familia* (the household slaves), who are called *pueri, mancipia, ancillae,* and *servi.* Female slaves were often grouped together in a workshop (*genitium* or *pisele*). At the monastery of Nonantola in Lombardy a large number of female slaves were employed in weaving; they were numerous enough so that a dozen of them could be sent every year to the dependent monastery of S. Michele Arcangelo in Florence to make wool and linen shirts. At Verona, Bishop Rataldus gave the canons a tenth of the clothes made in the workshop. Such an organization had been typical of slavery in the barbarian kingdoms and in the late empire, but it was becoming rare. At S. Giulia of Brescia in the tenth century there were only 741 slaves in a group of 4,700 dependents. Thus, the proportion of slaves to serfs was one to six.

At the same time, however, the slave trade became more important than it had been for many centuries. In southern Italy one finds slaves who came from distant regions; some of them surely had been brought in by slave traders. In 1090 the abbey of Monte Cassino owned, at Tropea in Calabria, a Lombard named Costa. A little later, at Taranto, a gift of slaves included John the Saracen, Theodore the Greek, Demetrios the Greek, Dragius the Bulgar, Costa the Greek, Theodore the Armenian, Simeon the Bulgar, and Maria the Bulgar. In 1057 a marriage contract mentions "a slave girl, Zita, of the Slavic race." To find a Slav in Apulia, so close to the Balkans, is not surprising.

In southern Italy, Amalfi, during the ninth and tenth centuries, was an important center for the export of slaves to the Muslim countries of North Africa. According to the *Life* of Pope Zacharias (741–752), Venice had engaged in this trade in the eighth century. In the *Pactum Lotharii* of 840 between Venice and the Carolingian Empire, Venice promised not to buy Christian slaves in the empire, and not to sell Christians to the Muslims. Thus, non-Christians could still be sold. These slaves, who were, above all, Slavs who were still heathen, had to cross the Alpine passes of Austria in order to reach Venice from central Europe. We are informed about them by a document of 903–906 describing the tolls collected in the region of Raffelstetten near St. Florian on the Danube. This deals with navigation on the Danube from Passau to the Wachau. The boats carried various kinds of merchandise and slaves. There is also mention of Slavic merchants from Bohemia and Russia. Coming from Kiev by way of Przemyśl, Cracow, and Prague, they crossed Bohemia in order to sell slaves, horses, and wax. For each female slave they paid a *tremissa,* and for each male a *saiga,* much less, because more unfree men than women went through the toll station. Further on in the document, Jewish merchants are mentioned; the only stock-in-trade noted for them is slaves. Travel of Jewish merchants in the Alpine region of Austria was common, as the numerous places named *Judendörfer* along the roads indicate.

Jewish merchants played an important role in the slave trade of the ninth and tenth centuries. The most important text on this trade is the *Kitāb al-masālik wa'l-mamālik* (Book of routes and kingdoms) of Ibn Khurdādhbih, written about 847, which describes their itineraries. In this treatise, the merchants are called *radaniya.* They took ship in the south of France, with their cargo of eunuchs, female slaves, young boys, furs, and swords. The Muslim conquest of Spain in 711 made that country an important outlet for merchants selling captive Slavs. In the reign of the caliph al-Ḥakam I (796–822), 5,000 *mamālīk* (singular, *mamlūk*) were settled in Muslim Spain. These were slave-soldiers who did not know Arabic. Soon these *mamālīk* were called *ṣaqāliba* (plural, *ṣiqlābi*), a word derived from the Arabic name for the Slavs. Letters of Agobard, archbishop of Lyons (816–840), acts of the emperor Louis the Pious, and the seventy-fifth canon of the Council of Meaux of 845 allow us to see that caravans of Slavic slaves, often led by Jewish merchants, crossed the Alps to Lyons,

St. Adalbert of Prague interceding with Bolesław I of Poland for the release of three of his subjects from a Jewish slave trader. Bronze relief from the doors of Gniezno Cathedral, 12th century. Now in Muzeum Archeologiczne, Warsaw. FOTO MARBURG / ART RESOURCE

went to the south of France, and embarked there for Muslim Spain. Another route went through the toll station of Walenstadt in eastern Switzerland, from which the Septimer and Splügen passes gave access to Venice. There the slaves embarked for Muslim North Africa. This route is mentioned in 842/843. The use of the Alpine passes and the Austrian valleys for the slave trade directed toward the Muslim world is especially characteristic of the ninth century.

In the tenth century, wars with the Slavs and their subsequent reduction to slavery were above all the work of the German rulers of the Saxon dynasty. As a result, the slave-trade routes were displaced to the north. Jewish merchants and others followed the armies to buy Slavic prisoners. From the banks of the Elbe the caravans of slaves went toward the valley of the Rhine. Rates at the toll-stations of Coblenz, Worms, and Speyer show the payments that the merchants owed for their slaves. From Coblenz, the traders reached Verdun by the valleys of the Moselle and the Meuse. The merchants of Verdun had close relations with Spain, where the number of *ṣaqāliba,* or Slavic slaves, was growing. In the reign of ᶜAbd al-Raḥmān III (912–961), we know that there were at first 3,750, then 6,087, and finally 13,750 *ṣaqāliba* at Córdoba, capital of the Umayyad caliphate. At the end of the reign, there were more than 3,000 *ṣaqāliba* in the palace of Madīnat-az-Zahrāᵓ alone. This palace was in the countryside near the city. Two Arab writers, Ibn Ḥawqal and Ibrahim al-Qarawī, and a passage in the *Antapodosis* of Bishop Liutprand of Cremona show that the Jewish merchants of Verdun were specialists in the castration of *ṣaqāliba* destined for Spain. These eunuchs were so numerous that *ṣiqlābi* lost its original ethnic sense and meant simply eunuch in the entire Muslim world, for from Spain the castrated slaves were exported as far as the Middle East. This long-distance slave trade lasted until the Umayyad caliphate disappeared in the eleventh century.

In the Christian countries traversed by traders with their caravans of slaves (Germany, France), slavery had gradually given way to serfdom. In the north of Spain, little Christian kingdoms were rising and beginning the reconquest of the country from Islam. In these states (León, Castile, Portugal, Aragon, Catalonia—or the county of Barcelona) true slavery no longer existed except for Muslims captured in war. The half-free Christians were by then in a social position whose different ranks were roughly comparable to the serfs of the countries in the west and center of Christian Europe. Even the Muslim slaves who lived on great ecclesiastical estates often became, at the end of several generations, and especially if they were baptized, hereditary serfs of the monasteries. Whether still slaves or already serfs, these Moors were engaged in household or agricultural tasks, when they were not occupied in domestic manufactures. In the towns, above all in Catalonia, some persons had up to ten slaves in their homes. In Portugal there were urban slaves who were blacksmiths and shoemakers. Such slaves could sometimes buy their liberty. Otherwise, the traditional characteristics of the institution persisted: unstable conjugal connections, almost complete absence of legal personal rights, but, nevertheless, the right to have money of their own, which, in turn, made it possible to buy freedom. As long as the Reconquest continued, war was almost the only source of slaves in the Iberian countries. It was only in the last centuries of the Middle Ages that the slave trade brought to Spain, as to other Christian Mediterranean countries, large numbers of slaves from distant regions.

THE PERSISTENCE OF SLAVERY

It was above all the clash between people of different religions that explains the persistence of slavery. In the Mediterranean world Christianity confronted Islam, and the adherents of the two religions reduced each other to slavery whenever they had a chance. Moreover, conversion by itself did not guarantee manumission. In those countries that occupied the lands formerly part of the Roman Empire, medieval slavery, up to the time when the great international slave trade developed, was a continuation of the slavery of antiquity, even though Christianity and Islam had each set their mark on the institution. In central, northern, and eastern Europe this was the case only in certain regions that had bordered the Roman Empire. The result was that beyond these border regions social and economic relations were based on and developed from precedents that were more complex than those of the Mediterranean region. Moreover, northern and central Europe did not become Christian until a somewhat later period. When Christianity did reach this region, it had to confront pagan populations for many years. Conflicts with pagans led to enslavement. Thus, in seventh-century England, Anglo-Saxon paganism was caught between Celtic Northumbria, which had been converted by Irish monks, and Kent, converted by monks sent by the pope. Mercia under King Penda (*ca.* 632–654) was a center of pagan resistance, attacked from the north and the south. On a larger scale, the expansion of the Frankish kingdom into Bavaria and Saxony led to a large number of enslavements before the conversion of these peoples. The first contacts with the Scandinavian world came in the eighth century. These peoples remained pagan for a long time, raided the West, and captured many slaves there. The Slavic countries were also pagan, and this explains why in the ninth and tenth centuries they furnished most of the slaves who were carried through Christian countries to the Islamic area. From the tenth century, however, most of the Slavs became Christian. Vladimir I of Kiev (980–1015) accepted Byzantine Christianity, while Poland, Moravia, Bohemia, and Croatia eventually accepted Roman Christianity. The Serbs and the Bulgars adhered to the Byzantine church. As they became Christian, the Slavic countries ceased to be a source of slaves, but their conversion did not keep them from capturing or buying non-Christian slaves.

The same thing was true of the Byzantine Empire, which was the religious model for most of the Slavic states. Slavery continued to exist until the end of the empire in 1453, at least in theory, since it was never abolished. In fact, by the end of the fourteenth century, slaves were rare in what remained of the Byzantine state. War was no longer a source of slaves, for it was almost always defensive and unsuccessful. Moreover, the Byzantine navy was surpassed by the fleets of Venice and Genoa. Thus, it is not surprising that the slave trade passed through Constantinople without leaving many slaves there; the same thing had happened in Germany and France in the ninth and tenth centuries.

The great international slave trade of the ninth century was based in the Slavic countries. That of the twelfth through fifteenth centuries found its victims, at first, on the shores of the Black Sea, and then in Africa. In the first period, the word *sclavus* appeared in German documents of the tenth and early eleventh centuries with the meaning of slave, just as the word *ṣaqāliba* had the same meaning in Arabic documents. These two terms then faded out, and the reappearance of *sclavus* and its cognates in European languages (French: *esclave;* Italian: *schiavo;* Catalan: *sclau;* German: *sklave*) dates only from the renewal of a large-scale slave trade from the Black Sea at the end of the twelfth century.

This trade was in the hands of the Venetians and especially the Genoese. The word *sclavus* reappears for the first time in a Venetian act of 1192, and then in a Genoese document of 1197. From this time on Genoese and Venetian merchants bought slaves in the Black Sea area—Slavic, if they were Russian or Bulgarian, or called such if they were Caucasian, Tatar, or sold by Tatars. The Italians could trade in the Black Sea only by passing through Constantinople. In Greek, *sklabos* has the meaning of slave only from the end of the twelfth century. This usage could not have become common in Greek unless there had been a spectacular multiplication of the number of slaves who were Slavs, or considered such.

In Egypt the practice of buying Turkish slaves for the army had begun in the ninth century. At the beginning of the eleventh century, however, the great slave trade toward Spain had stopped and Turco-Mongols were imported from the shores of the Black Sea. In the twelfth century this trade increased under the Ayyubid Dynasty (1171–1250). By 1250 the *mamālīk,* or soldier-slaves, were strong enough to seize power and found the Mamluk Dynasty, which governed Egypt until the Turkish conquest of 1517. A decree of the sultan Baybars of 1260 shows that the importation of slaves from the Black Sea was considered essential to preserve Mamluk power in Egypt. In 1281 the Mamluk sultan Qalāʾūn and the Byzantine emperor Michael VIII Palaiologos concluded a treaty giving Muslims of Egypt the right to sail through the Bosphorus to buy slaves in southern Russia. This simply made legal what had been going on before. However, by the end of the thirteenth century, the share of the Italians in this trade had grown to the point of becoming a monopoly. Already in 1289, a Genoese sold in Caffa a slave called "Balaban" from Madjar. *Balaban* is a common Turko-Mongol name meaning soldier-slave, just like the Arabic *mamlūk*. The fact that this slave came from Madjar on the Kuma River shows that slaves were then being sought deep in the Russian backcountry.

During the thirteenth century the role of the Italian traders increased steadily and became dominant by the beginning of the fourteenth century. This is demonstrated by a remonstrance given to Pope Clement V by the ambassadors of the king of Cyprus in 1311 at the Council of Vienne. It was necessary, they said, to clamp down on the Italian ships that were bringing slaves to Egypt and thus increasing the size of the Mamluk army, which was the principal adversary of the Christians trying to reconquer the Holy Land. Sending slaves to Egypt was forbidden by the papacy in 1317, 1323, 1329, 1338, and, finally, 1425. The repetitions show how useless the orders were. The Genoese colony of Kaffa in the Crimea became the great center for exportation of slaves. The treatise of Emmanuel Piloti on his journey to the Holy Land (1420) shows that Genoese ships brought to Alexandria not only Tatars, Circassians, and Russians from the northern shores of the Black Sea, but also Greeks, Albanians, and Serbs, to reinforce the ranks of the Mamluk army. Each year the sultan bought at Caffa at least 2,000 slaves. On the other hand, 2,000 young blacks came from Tunisia and Tripolitania, where the caravan routes across the Sudan ended their journeys. The rest of the trip was made, for the most part, in Genoese ships.

It was the spillover from this trade that reached the Christian Mediterranean world. From Catalonia and Majorca to Sicily, Naples, Genoa, Venice, and the Italian colonies in the eastern Mediterranean, one could find slaves from the Caucacus and the Crimea, Cumans, Circassians, Mingrelians, in addition to Russians, Tatars, Greeks, Bulgars, and Vlachs. There were also blacks coming from Africa, at first through Muslim ports, and later from the Portuguese trading posts of East Africa.

In the Christian countries of the Mediterranean, slaves were much less numerous than in Muslim states, and they did not serve in the army. Nevertheless, in certain Italian towns for which we have quantifiable data, we see that the number of slaves at the end of the Middle Ages was much larger than would be thought if one worked simply from notarized acts of sale or emancipation. If one assumes that in Genoa slaves were about 10 percent of the population in the second half of the twelfth century, the percentage by 1381 would have been about 15 percent. At Palermo in 1480, they were 12.7 percent in what was then the central quarter of the Kalsa. On certain islands from which it was very difficult for slaves to escape, the percentage was much higher. In these islands slaves were used for agricultural work, while in the towns they were chiefly domestic servants. In Venetian Crete, loans were made to finance the importation of large numbers of male slaves to work on the estates of Venetian and Greek landlords. They believed that it was more important to import slaves than horses. At Majorca in 1374, we find property owners who possessed from ten to sixty or more slaves. There were runaway slaves and slave revolts, such as occurred later in the Spanish and Portuguese colonies of America. In 1381 a special police force was created to control rural slaves. Such slaves were chained and locked up for the night in cellars. Most of these slaves came from the Black Sea, as we learn from the accounts of Giacomo Badoer in 1436–1439. This Venetian merchant, established in Constantinople, sent slaves by the hundreds to Majorca. Thus, it is not surprising to find that in 1328 there were some 21,000 slaves in Majorca, or about 36 percent of the total population. In 1428, the population was still about 17.94 percent slave in the rural communities of the island.

Although slavery was an important demographic factor in the Mediterranean world, both Christian and Muslim, it had ceased to be significant in inland France or in western Germany by the tenth or eleventh century. In northern Europe, slavery disappeared when contacts with unorthodox peoples ended. This happened in England before it did in Scandinavia. In Slavic Europe contact with Turko-Mongol nomads created conditions favorable for slavery on both sides, until the time when the nomadic peoples were assimilated. In the Mediterranean countries there were still a large number of slaves, mostly black, during the first half of the sixteenth century. Later, the number of slaves diminished rapidly. The institution vanished in the seventeenth or eighteenth century, depending on the region, generally without a formal act of abolition.

BIBLIOGRAPHY

M. Canard, "Le traité de 1281 entre Michel Paléologue et le sultan Qalā'un," in *Byzantion,* **10** (1935); Reinhart Dozy, *Supplément aux dictionnaires arabes,* 2nd ed., I (1927), 663; Domenico Gioffré, *Il mercato degli schiavi a Genova nel secolo XV* (1971); Anne Hadjinicolaou-Marava, *Recherches sur la vie des esclaves dans le monde byzantin* (1950); A. Haverkamp, "Zur Sklaverei in Genua während des 12. Jahrhunderts," in *Geschichte in der Gesellschaft: Festschrift für Karl Bosl* (1974); Ibn Ḥawqal, *Viae et regna: Descriptio ditionis moslemicae, auctore Abu'l Kasim Ibn Haukal,* in Michael Jan de Goeje, ed., *Bibliotheca geographorum Arabicorum,* II (1873); Johannes Hoffman, "Die östliche Adriaküste als Hauptnachschubbasis für den venezianischen Sklavenhandel bis zum Ausgang des elften Jahrhunderts," in *Vierteljahrschrift für Sozial- und Wirtschaftsgeschichte,* **55** (1968).

Jürgen Jacobi, "Die Rādānīya," in *Der Islam,* **47** (1971); Henry and Renée Kahane, "Notes on the Linguistic History of *Sclavus,*" in *Studi in onore di Ettore Lo Gatto e Giovanni Maver* (1962); Helga Köpstein, *Zur Skaverei im ausgehenden Byzanz* (1966); Ibn Khordadbeh, *Kitab al-masālik wa'l-mamālik,* in Michael Jan de Goeje, ed., *Bibliotheca geographorum Arabicorum,* VI (1889); Gino Luzzatto, *I servi nelle grandi proprietà ecclesiastiche italiane dei secoli IX e X* (1909); al-Maqqarī, *Analectes sur l'histoire et la littérature des Arabes d'Espagne,* Reinhart Dozy *et al.*, eds., I (1855, repr. 1967); Piero Milani, *La schiavitù nel pensiero politico: Dai Greci al basso medio evo* (1972); Hermann Nehlsen, *Sklavenrecht zwischen Antike und Mittelalter: Germanisches und römisches Recht in den germanischen Rechtsaufzeichhungen,* I (1972).

William D. Phillips, Jr., *Slavery from Roman Times to the Early Transatlantic Trade* (1985); Emmanuel Piloti, *Traité d'Emmanuel Piloti sur le passage en Terre Sainte (1420),* Pierre-Herman Dopp, ed. (1958); Dieter Rothenhöfer, *Untersuchungen zur Sklaverei in den ostgermanischen Nachfolgestaaten des Römischen Reiches* (1967); Charles Verlinden, "L'origine de *sclavus* = esclave," in *Bulletin du Cange,* **17** (1943), *L'esclavage dans l'Europe medievale,* 2 vols. (1955–1977), "Une taxation d'esclaves à Majorque en 1428 et la traité italienne," in *Bulletin de l'Institut historique belge de Rome,* **42** (1972), "À propos de la place des Juifs dans l'économie de l'Europe occidentale aux IXe et Xe siècles: Agobard de Lyon et l'historiographie arabe," in *Storiografia e storia: Studi in onore di Eugenio Dupré Theseider* (1974), "Traité des esclaves et cols alpins au haut moyen âge," in *Festschrift für Univ.-Prof. Dr. Herbert Hassinger* (1977), "L'esclavage dans un quartier de Palerme: Aspects quantitatifs," in *Studi in memoria di Federigo Melis,* III (1978), and "Ist mittelalterliche Sklaverei ein bedeutsamer demographischer Faktor gewesen?" in *Vierteljahrschrift für Sozial- und Wirtschaftsgeschichte,* **66** (1979).

CHARLES VERLINDEN

[See also **Agobard; Alaric; Aristotle in the Middle Ages; Ayyubids; Barbarians, Invasions of; Carolingians and the Carolingian Empire; Colonus; Huns; Khurdādhbih, Ibn; Law, German: Early Germanic Codes; Liutprand of Cremona; Lombards, Kingdom of; Mamlūk; Mamluk Dynasty; Ministerials; Odoacer; Ostrogoths; Serf, Serfdom; Theodoric the Ostrogoth; Umayyads of Córdoba; Vandals; Visigoths.**]

SLAVIC LANGUAGES AND LITERATURES

BEGINNINGS OF THE SLAVIC LANGUAGES

Twentieth-century Slavs share a common linguistic heritage. Most scholars believe that there was once a single "proto-Slavic" language known to all Slavs. As late as the ninth and tenth centuries A.D. the ancestors of today's West Slavs (Poles, Czechs, Slovaks), South Slavs (Bulgarians and Yugoslavs, the latter consisting of Serbians, Croatians, Macedonians, and Slovenes), and East Slavs (Ukrainians, Belorussians, and Great Russians) could readily understand one another, despite variations in regional dialects.

Today's Slavs speak twelve or thirteen distinct

languages, if one includes such tongues as West Slavic Kashubian, High and Low Sorbian, South Slavic Macedonian, and Slovenian. While Slavic languages still share similar features, most have evolved to the point of mutual unintelligibility. Much of this linguistic differentiation—together with the development of distinct national literatures—occurred before 1500. The agents of change had been physical separation, wars, invasions, and religious conflicts, with their attendant cultural upheavals. We must also recognize the role of more subtle internal processes by which all languages grow and acquire their own features.

Proto-Slavic. What sort of tongue was proto-Slavic? Roman Jakobson labels it a "Western offshoot of the satem-group of Indo-European languages." Its kinship with other Indo-European languages (Germanic, Iranian, and Baltic in particular) can be observed today: consider the similarities between contemporary Russian and English in words like *kot* (cat), *sestra* (sister), *brat* (brother), *sedlo* (saddle), and *kholod* (cold).

According to a widely held view, the original homeland of proto-Slavic speakers lay within the boundaries of today's Poland, White Russia (Belorussia), and the northwestern Ukraine. Following an evolution of perhaps three thousand years, proto-Slavic broke up into distinct "national" tongues shortly after a written language (Church Slavonic) appeared and the Slavs had begun organizing themselves into separate states (Moravia, Bulgaria, Poland, and Kievan Rus).

Development of a written language. It was among the West Slavs that Slavic literacy got off to a firm start. In 863 two Byzantine missionaries, Constantine (later Cyril, his monastic name) and Methodios, went to Great Moravia (today part of Czechoslovakia) at the invitation of the Moravian prince, Ratislav. Their mission was to provide the prince's subjects with Christian teachings and church services in their own Slavic tongue. Although Greeks, Cyril (Constantine) and Methodios knew the Slavic language spoken in Thessaloniki. Whether it was Macedonian or Old Bulgarian—a point on which scholars have disagreed—that language was then understandable to all Slavs, including the Czech Moravians. Many scholars today believe that Cyril's first step was to devise a Slavic alphabet (Glagolitic), after which both brothers set about translating biblical and liturgical texts into "Slavic."

The Moravians were thus the first Slavs to have a written language. Ironically, it was soon taken from them and passed on, with a new alphabet, to other Slavs in the south and east. German Catholic clergy, who opposed the Slavic Orthodox liturgy, managed to have the co-workers of Cyril and Methodios driven out of Moravia in 885, after Methodios' death (Cyril had died in 869). Methodios' group then went on to recently christianized Bulgaria and Macedonia, bringing with them the translated religious texts and the enduring principle of conducting Slavic services and other cultural activities in the native language. A new alphabet—Cyrillic, so named in honor of Cyril, who himself had devised the Glagolitic alphabet—came into use, steadily replacing the Glagolitic script. Cyrillic, modeled primarily on Greek letters, has survived in modified form to this day as the alphabet of Bulgarians, Ukrainians, Russians, White Russians, and most Yugoslavs. Cyril's original Glagolitic alphabet had largely gone out of use by the twelfth century except in certain areas of Croatia.

Scholars refer to the Slavs' earliest literary language, whether written in Glagolitic or Cyrillic letters, as Old Church Slavonic or Old Slavic. By the eleventh century it was used throughout the Orthodox Slav world, especially for religious subject matter.

Among West Slavs the Latin alphabet prevailed. Certain Slavic sounds, of course, were alien to Latin. To convey such sounds in writing, the fourteenth-century Czechs devised new pairs of Latin letters (the so-called digraphs, such as *cz, sz, rz*). We still find such digraphs in written Polish today, but the Czechs subsequently adopted a system of "diacritic" marks placed over certain letters (for instance, *č, š, ř*). Diacritic marks later came into use among other West and Southwest Slavs (Slovaks, Slovenes, Croatians).

When the "common Slavic" or "proto-Slavic" unity broke down, not only did the grammars and sound systems of the various Slavic tongues undergo change, but their vocabularies evolved independently to such an extent that today one Slavic language's words may resemble only about fifty percent of another's.

Religion—often the religion of a powerful neighbor—played no small part in this process. Moravia and Bohemia provide an example. The first Slavic lands to benefit from Cyril and Methodios' literary activities, Moravia and Bohemia early turned to the Latin alphabet and written language under pressure from the neighboring Roman Catholic Germans.

Latin influence remained strong throughout the Middle Ages; not until the Hussite movement in the fifteenth century did Czech come fully into its own as the national language for prose and poetry alike.

SEPARATION INTO WEST AND EAST SLAVIC

In 1054 occurred the great religious schism that formalized divisions between the Catholic West and the Orthodox East. Latin became dominant among the West Slavs and most Croatians. Old Slavic (in Cyrillic) continued as the liturgical language of Orthodox Slavs, both South and East; it also played a large role in their literature whenever that literature dealt with religious subject matter, even after distinct South and East Slavic languages had emerged. Cyrillic was used for legal documents and secular literature, but such materials tended to be written in the "national" language rather than Old Slavic.

Neighbors could exert linguistic influence without resorting to political or religious pressure: they might simply provide models worthy of emulation. Poland's Christians held religious services in Latin, but by the fourteenth century Czech was becoming the cultivated language of Poland's upper classes in the secular sphere. Later centuries were to see this process reversed, with Czechs eagerly borrowing from Poland. The Bulgarian and Serbian literatures, while written in Church Slavic, were largely based on Byzantine models. Through their translations of Byzantine texts and through their original writings, Bulgarians and Serbs also exerted considerable influence on East Slavs throughout the Middle Ages.

Foreign influences. If some influences (for instance, Byzantine religion and culture in Russia) came about for the most part peacefully, others (Mongol-Tatar in Russia and Turkish in the Balkans) resulted from brutal conquest and domination. Both types are reflected in loanwords. English speakers discover that their Greek-derived words for angel, apostle, bishop, and monastery have close Slavic counterparts (*angel, apostol, episkop,* and *monastyr* in Russian). More down-to-earth Mongol-Turkic words also flooded into Russian (*dengi* [money], *loshad* [horse], *kinzhal* [dagger], *bashmak* [shoe]) and Ukrainian (*bashtan* [vegetable garden], *chaban* [herdsman]), while Turkish words similarly made their way into Serbian and Bulgarian (*budàla* [fool], *čorba* [soup], *kàzan* [kettle], *kòmšija* [neighbor]).

Ukrainian had already begun to emerge as a separate language by the late twelfth century, with the breakup of Kievan Rus. Southwest Rus fell increasingly under Polish domination. After the Mongol invasion (Kiev was destroyed in 1240) and the expansion of the Lithuanian-Polish state, the Ukraine's ties with Northwest Rus (Novgorod) and Northeast Rus (later the Muscovite state) were severely reduced. These developments accelerated the development of Ukrainian as an independent language.

Belorussian did not become a discrete East Slavic tongue (albeit heavily influenced by Polish) until the fifteenth century.

Lexical differences among the Slavic languages resulted not only from foreign borrowings but from more subtle national attitudes and traditions. The Czechs have been more reluctant than the Poles or Russians to adopt words from other languages; the Ukrainian literary language contains more elements of popular vernacular than do Polish or Russian. Each language has its favorite traditional elements (Church Slavic in Russia, archaic words in Czech).

Vocabulary differences. As "cognates," words in Slavic languages frequently resemble each other, yet have acquired different meanings. In Russian *zakhod* means "stopping" (at a place), whereas *záchod* means "toilet" (w.c.) in Czech. *Pozor* means "shame" or "disgrace" in Russian, but "attention" in Czech. The stress in a similar word may vary from language to language: the Russian *úlitsa* (street) becomes *ulíca* in Polish. The languages have grown so far apart that many words with similar meanings have lost all resemblance to each other: "the state" is *gosudarstvo* in Russian, *država* in Serbo-Croatian, *państwo* in Polish.

Phonology, grammar, and syntax differences. Along with lexical differentiation, distinct systems of phonology, grammar, and syntax evolved among the various Slavic languages.

Old Slavic—the written language to which Cyril and Methodios had given an alphabet and literary norms in the ninth century—had by the twelfth century ceased to exist, replaced by several national "recensions," such as Macedonian, Bulgarian, Serbian, and Eastern Slavic or Russian. Subtle evolutionary processes were taking place. While such recensions of Church Slavic were not intended to match the developing spoken languages, they often reflected certain features, such as the loss of "jers" (reduced vowels ъ and ь) in the twelfth century. In final and weak position the jers disappeared altogether; elsewhere they turned into full vowels (*o, e*).

East Slavs had acquired pleophony or *polnoglasie* (for instance, "city" was *grad* in Slavic but *gorod* in Russian), while *g* turned into an *h*-like fricative in Ukrainian. Varying patterns of stress and quantity evolved (accent became fixed on the initial syllable in Czech and the penultimate syllable in Polish). The various Slavic languages also produced dissimilar groups of consonants.

Along with changes in their sound systems, the individual Slavic tongues underwent important modifications in their respective grammars. Whereas proto-Slavic had largely retained the Indo-European system of case declension (nominative, genitive, dative, accusative, instrumental, and locative), the evolving Slavic languages followed different paths of development: Russian retained all six cases, while Bulgarian and Macedonian substituted post-positive particles for earlier case endings. Russian to this day tends to use the genitive for inanimate direct objects of negated verbs; Czech does not. A "personal gender" evolved in several tongues (Bulgarian, Ukrainian, Polish).

The Slavic languages, as a group, retained the basic proto-Slavic and Church Slavic patterns of verbal aspects, voices, and moods, while adopting individual variations too numerous to mention here.

As for syntax, the same basic adherence to proto-Slavic patterns can be discerned in later Slavic word order. Their conjunctions and relative pronouns, however, have displayed "extreme instability" (Jakobson).

The collective effect of all these changes, most of them occurring by the end of the Middle Ages, was to make it difficult and often impossible for Slavs to understand their fellow Slavs from other lands.

WEST SLAVIC LITERATURES

Czech literature. Turning now to the various Slavic literatures that came into being during the Middle Ages, we recall that the Czechs were the first Slavs to have a written literature of their own. Cyril and Methodios translated Greek liturgical, biblical, patristic, and juridical texts into Old Slavic for the Moravians. (Such translations formed an essential part of most Slavic literatures in the beginning.)

Original works now appeared as well, some possibly written by members of the Moravian mission: a vita of Cyril and Methodios, an introductory poem (*proglas*) preceding the translated Gospel, some prayers, an alphabet poem, and others. These pioneering works were of high quality; their authors, after all, included talented and cultured Greeks. Among their poetic devices we find metaphor, antithesis, catalogue, rhetorical questions and exclamations, skillful paraphrase, and the like.

Yet we have seen that the Byzantine legacy to Moravia soon gave way, under German pressure, to Latin models and literary influences. Old Church Slavic (probably written in Glagolitic) did manage to survive a little longer in neighboring Bohemia, where liturgical and patristic texts (vitas of Ludmila and Václav) appeared, and where ecclesiastical works were translated from Latin into Old Church Slavic.

When the Hungarians smashed the Moravian kingdom, the Hungarians (whose King Stephen was knighted by the pope in 1000) blocked further Czech contacts with the East Slavs and Byzantine Greek culture. Czech literature henceforth would be subjected to Western influences: Latin, German, French, Italian, and even English.

Czech literature's short-lived first period, introduced by Cyril and Methodios, was thus followed by a "Romanesque" period lasting until the early fourteenth century (the Premyslid dynasty, ending in 1306). Little survives of Czech literature from this period. Almost untouched by classical Roman or Hellenic Greek culture, Czech Romanesque writings took their Latin models from Italy and Germany. They served liturgical needs, glorified saints, and eulogized Roman Catholicism, which had won out over Byzantine Orthodoxy. Historical writing, always important for the Czechs, now began: a chronicle compiled by the monk Kristián has survived from the end of the tenth century; another, by the diplomat Cosmas, was written in the early twelfth century. Both were in Latin, however. The earliest surviving Czech works were religious songs or hymns in verse, such as *Hospodine, pomiluj ny!* (Lord, have mercy on us!). Probably the finest lyrical work to survive from this era was an anonymous hymn to St. Wenceslas (*Svatý Václave*), the Czechs' martyred patron saint. The hymn consists of three six-line stanzas, each with some rhymed couplets and each ending in "Kyrie eleison!" Other verse from this era includes the Song of Ostrov (*Ostrovská píseň,* twelfth or early thirteenth century) and the Prayer of Lady Kunhuta (*Kunhutina modlitba,* late thirteenth century). Featuring twenty-three four-line stanzas with varying rhyme schemes (*aabb, aaaa, bbbb*) and eight-syllable lines with stressed initial syllable, such verse sometimes produces the effect of syllabo-tonic poetry written in trochaic meter.

The next period, which lasted throughout the fourteenth century, has been characterized as the Czech "Gothic" period. Whereas the preceding "Romanesque" period had borne a heavily religious character, the Gothic century saw a rise of secular culture. King Charles IV (who was also the Holy Roman Emperor Charles I) reigned for three decades (1347–1378), founding Central Europe's first university at Prague in 1348 and ushering in the "golden age of Bohemia." Lay authors (aristocrats, townsmen) joined the clerical, while the clergy itself came under increasing secular influence.

Verse (often eight-syllable lines, rhymed and approximating trochaic in meter) now became the favorite literary form, whatever the genre or subject matter (patristic and allegorical writings, history, epics, and lyric songs). This was a time of increased individuality and national awareness, partly in reaction to pervasive alien influences (French, Italian, and especially German). The so-called Dalimil's Chronicle from about 1314 (the real author is unknown) exhibits such qualities: written in verse, it combines an aristocratic, anti-German bias with Czech sentiments. A similar viewpoint is found in the secular epic *Alexandreis,* adapted from a French model. Another verse epic, the Legend of St. Catherine (*Legenda o svaté Kateřině*), contains elements more typical of later baroque poetry.

The Gothic period also produced satirical poems and secular lyrics, including erotic songs and drinking songs, some penned by students. Czech courtly love songs were probably influenced by German Minnesinger lyrics. In general, Czech songs not only featured rhyme at the line's end but contained extensive internal rhyme (alliteration and other recurrent euphony). The Czechs seem also to have written far more lyric poetry in the Middle Ages than any other Slavs.

The Czechs also enjoyed drama. In the fourteenth century some of the church's Latin Easter plays and Passion plays—such as *Hry tří Marií* (Plays of the three Marys) and *Hry o vzkříšení Páně* (Plays about the Resurrection of our Lord)—were even transformed into popularized works in the Czech vernacular, replete with folk humor and burlesque.

Czech prose now came into its own as well. Numerous translations appeared, including those of the Bible, apocrypha, Marco Polo's travels, and the autobiography of Emperor Charles I.

A major contributor to the development of native Czech prose was Tomáš ze Štítného (*ca.* 1325–1400), who not only translated and adapted, but also produced writings of his own—all dealing with religious themes. Although Tomáš was hardly an original thinker, his works, especially *Řeči besední* (The chats) and *Řeči nedělní a svátečni* (Talks for Sundays and holy days), provided models that set standards for later Czech prose. Well written yet direct and accessible, such prose "brought theology to the people," according to Arne Novák.

A fourth period in Czech literary development was ushered in by the Bohemian reformer Jan Hus, who died at the stake in 1415. Hus attacked the corruption and secularization that he perceived as rampant in the church. He and his followers continued to use Latin in their theological polemics, but turned to the Czech vernacular when drumming up support among the people. In sermons, letters, and other works aimed at the mass audience they combined directness and simplicity with such rhetorical devices as apostrophes and scriptural quotations. Hussite songs, frankly propagandistic, carried this simplicity and directness still further, reserving ornamentation for special effects. Some of Hus's letters read almost like modern Czech, thanks to his simplified spelling, innovative vocabulary, and elimination of archaic grammar. Although the Hussites ultimately lost out, their literary reforms—in orthography, lexicon, and grammar—invigorated the Czech language and provided models of writing that even their opponents came to adopt.

Despite such achievements, the contribution of Hus and his followers to Czech literary development remained otherwise unimpressive. Their brand of fanaticism led them to reject any literature that failed to serve the religious ends for which they themselves were ready to die. German influence later became dominant, and only in the nineteenth century did Czech literature rise to attain new heights.

Polish literature. The other major West Slavic literature was, of course, Polish. But if Czech had already "achieved maturity as an instrument of literary expression" in the Middle Ages (Miłosz), native Polish literature came of age only in the Renaissance, reaching its "golden" era in the sixteenth and seventeenth centuries. Lack of space prevents our discussing this phenomenon in detail. Suffice to say that medieval Polish literature was mostly in Latin. Such was the case for annals and chronicles: the twelfth-century compilation of Gallus Anonymous (a non-Pole, as the name indicates), and the thirteenth-century chronicles of Kadłubek and Baszko, as well as Jan Długosz's fifteenth-century *Annales Poloniae*. Vitas (for instance the Life of St. Adalbert), sermons, and religious songs were also in Latin.

The earliest works to be written in Polish had an exclusively religious content: the fourteenth-century *Kazania świętokrzyskie* (Sermons of the Holy Cross), a religious poem to the Virgin (*Bogurodzica*), and some Christmas carols. Biblical translations (such as the Psalter of Queen Jadwiga, from about 1400) appeared in the late Middle Ages.

The fifteenth century produced such writings as *Rozmowa mistrza ze śmiercią* (A master's conversation with death), Easter songs, a versified legend of St. Alexis, *Żale Matki Boskiej* (The lament of the Mother of God), and two Czech-inspired works: the Lament of a Dying Man and the Song on Wycliffe. More secular and specifically Polish in character was *Pieśń o zabiciu Andrzeja Tęczyńskiego* (The song of Andrzej Tęczyński's murder, 1461).

In the same century a Kraków professor, Jakub Parkoszowić, systematized rules for Polish syllabic verse. Such poetry was theoretically to be written in lines of eight, eleven, or thirteen syllables (in the last two instances with caesura after the fifth or seventh syllables), and feminine rhyme. In practice Polish verse featured "relative syllabification" (Krzyżanowski), with lines of seven or nine syllables appearing in poems whose lines were predominantly eight syllables long; it occasionally violated normal accentuation to accommodate the feminine rhyme.

Polish prose included the apocryphal *Rozmyślanie o zywocie Pana Jezusa* (Meditation on Jesus' life), along with a few surviving letters and legal texts.

SOUTH SLAVIC LITERATURES

Bulgarian literature. Turning now to the South Slavs, we recall that some refugees from Methodios' mission in Moravia made their way to Bulgaria, continued their work there, and prepared the way for a flourishing Old Slavic literature (written in Cyrillic) by the late ninth and early tenth centuries.

Bulgaria not only fell heir to literature produced by the Moravian mission but soon contributed notable translations and original works of its own. Few of these manuscripts have survived, however. In the long run their greatest significance seems to have been as a legacy to Serbs and East Slavs: we know most of the Bulgarian works through copies made in Kievan Rus. They made up that country's bridge to a literary culture.

Some of the translations were religious works. Sermons of John Chrysostom became the *Zlatostrui* (Golden stream); many vitas, some apocryphal works, and collections of stories about monks (*patericons*) became accessible to South Slav (and, later, Russian) readers in Old Slavic translation. The same held true for historical compilations (the chronicles of Malalas and Hamartolos) and "scientific" collections (the Byzantine *Physiologus* became the Slavic *Fiziolog*). Still others included translated belles-lettres (*Stefanit i Ikhnilat*) and encyclopedic collections (notably the Bulgarian model for the Kievan *Izbornik* of 1073).

Authors of Bulgarian or Macedonian works (Clement of Ochrid, Constantin of Preslav, John the Exarch, Kozma the Presbyter) confined themselves largely to religious and philosophical works. In almost every case their sermons, compilations, and polemical writings owed a considerable debt to Byzantine models. But the language was Old Slavic, and here again such compilations as John the Exarch's *Shestodnev* (the Byzantine *Hexaemeron*) passed into the literary legacy of Kievan Rus. A few original legends appeared, of which two (possibly written by Clement of Ochrid) concerned Cyril and Methodios. A certain monk Khrabr left a treatise championing the Slavic language against its detractors.

Serbo-Croatian literature. Others of Methodios' followers had been welcomed in Croatia after their expulsion from Moravia. The Croatian king Tomislav (*r. ca.* 910/914–*ca.* 928) supported them in their work. Whereas the Greek-influenced Cyrillic script had replaced the Glagolitic in Bulgaria, Croatians continued writing in Glagolitic. But Roman Catholicism won out in the area after it became part of the Hungarian empire, and by the fourteenth century the Latin alphabet had replaced Glagolitic almost everywhere. Croatian literature consisted mostly of translated religious texts and a twelfth-century chronicle (*Ljetopis popa Dukljanina*). Under foreign rule, the culturally backward Croatians (like their brothers and sisters in Slovenia and Dalmatia) could produce little literature of their own.

Serbia, on the other hand, maintained close ties with Bulgaria and Byzantium. Like the Bulgarians,

Serbs copied the Slavic texts of Cyril and Methodios and displayed ability in translating (as shown by the twelfth-century Gospel of Prince Miroslav). Serbian monks translated all the Byzantine texts they could get their hands on: chronicles, sermons, sacred verse, and a number of secular works (about Alexander the Great, the Trojan War, *Barlaam and Josaphat, Stefanit and Ikhnilat,* and others).

Biographies of princes and clerical figures enjoyed popularity among the Serbs. Even when dealing with secular heroes, however, such biographies had a strong religious flavor—so much so that they resembled vitas.

The Serbian state reached a high point under Emperor Stefan Dušan (1331–1355). Writing flourished, but because the authors of religious texts adhered to Church Slavic, the gap between the literary language and the evolving vernacular kept widening.

The Turkish victory at Kosovo (1389) brought an end to Serbian independence. Serbian literature did not decline immediately after the Kosovo disaster, of course. The new prince, Stefan Lazarević, wrote lyric poetry, such as *Slovo o ljubve* (A song of love). The tragedy at Kosovo also produced the earliest known Slavic poetess, the nun (former noblewoman) Evfimiya, who around 1399 wrote a moving panegyric to Prince Lazar, who had fallen in the battle.

Bulgars had fought alongside Serbs at Kosovo. After the Turks vanquished Bulgaria in 1393 some Bulgarian monks moved to Serbia, where Turkish rule was relatively lenient at first. Maintaining close ties with Mount Athos and Byzantium, they carried on extensive literary activity in Serbian monasteries. Other Bulgars (and Serbs) migrated to Russia, bringing with them the "second South Slavic influence," whose guiding spirit had probably been Patriarch Evfimii of Trnovo (Bulgaria). Evfimii had introduced reforms to bring Church Slavic closer to fourteenth-century Bulgarian, but had restored archaic Slavic letters and other forms in the process. The Trnovo school also favored a highly ornamental style that came to be known as "word braiding" (*pletenie sloves*)—a way of writing that enjoyed great popularity after reaching Russia.

By the mid fifteenth century the sultan's rule had grown much harsher: in 1459 Serbia became a Turkish province, and the Turks sought to obliterate written evidence of earlier Serbian culture. Elsewhere, South Slavs found themselves under Austrian, Hungarian, or Italian rule. Free literary creativity waned under such conditions.

EAST SLAVIC LITERATURES

Old Russian literature. Some scholars insist that East Slavic literature in the pre-Mongol era was actually "Ukrainian," but most refer to it as "Old Russian," pointing out that the Ukrainian language began emerging only in the late twelfth century (after the decline of Kievan Rus), and that writers in that language gained prominence only after the Middle Ages. "Old Russian" literature was first written in Church Slavic or East Slavic, depending on the subject matter.

A few decades after Kievan Rus had embraced Christianity, Grand Prince Yaroslav the Wise (*d.* 1054) first sponsored literary translation on a large scale. It was now that Bulgarian texts and others began to be copied or translated for Russian readers. Both activities (copying and translating) continued off and on for centuries, under different sponsors and in different locales.

The Russians did not borrow indiscriminately, however. They seem to have taken little from the Orient, for example, and their Greek sources (with or without South Slavic intermediaries) included no works from contemporary Byzantium. Instead, the Russians selected centuries-old sermons of John Chrysostom, Basil the Great, and Gregory of Nazianzus, the chronicles of Hamartolos and Malalas, saints' lives, and novels such as *Barlaam and Josaphat* or *Digenis Akritas.* Various apocrypha likewise enjoyed popularity among Russians.

Soon Russian writers began making their own contributions. Indeed one may speak of a literary "golden age" in Kievan Rus. Most scholars regard Metropolitan Ilarion, Russia's first native son to head the church, as the author of the celebrated *Slovo o zakone i blagodati* (Sermon on law and grace, *ca.* 1050). Written barely a half century after Russia's conversion to Christianity, this work reveals a mastery of Byzantine rhetorical techniques, skillfully adapted to Church Slavic. The Passion and Encomium of Sts. Boris and Gleb the Martyr (*d.* 1015) likewise appeared sometime in the eleventh or early twelfth century. The *Pouchenie* (Precept to my children) was composed by the Kievan grand prince Vladimir Monomakh at about the same time.

Nestor, a cleric in the Kiev Monastery of the Caves (Pecherskaya Lavra), edited a native Russian chronicle—the *Povest vremennykh let* (Tale of bygone years), the compilation of which had begun during the reign of Yaroslav the Wise. Writing in the late eleventh and early twelfth centuries, Nestor also composed a vita of Kiev's St. Theodosius; modeled on Byzantine sources, the vita contained many original features as well. A twelfth-century bishop, Cyril of Turov, wrote eight sermons and twenty-two prayers, which remain models of rhetoric and lyricism (for instance, his Sermon for Easter Eve).

A lay work, *Slovo o polku Igoreve* (Lay of Igor's host, or Igor tale), supposedly written around 1187, is the highly poetic account of a Russian prince's unsuccessful campaign against Kiev's nomadic foes, the Polovtsy. An acknowledged masterpiece, the Tale nevertheless poses problems. Some scholars have claimed, for example, that the Igor Tale is an eighteenth-century hoax, although convincing linguistic and textological arguments can be made against such claims.

The Supplication (or Lament [*Molenie*]) of Daniel the Exile is another secular work dating from the pre-Mongol era. Ostensibly a bid for princely patronage, the Supplication probably belonged to a genre aimed at amusing readers and listeners. The fictitious author, down on his luck, tries to impress the prince with a fawning appeal that combines aphoristic "wit" with blatant flattery. One of the redactions displays an anticlerical spirit rarely encountered in texts from that era; other targets include boyars and women.

The last major work of Old Russian Literature before the Mongol-Tatar conquest was the *Patericon*—a sizeable collection of tales about monks and abbots in Kiev's Monastery of the Caves. Abounding in miracles and ascetic feats, demonology and divine intervention, the tales were read by Russians for hundreds of years; nineteenth-century authors like Gogol acknowledged their influence.

Some scholars have wondered if Kievan Rus knew the genre of secular biography. According to one view, a biography of Prince Alexander Nevsky appeared shortly after his death in 1263 but has been lost; successive efforts by clerical copyists and editors gradually transformed it into the work as we now know it: a princely vita. Others argue that no purely secular biography ever existed: like their Serbian counterparts, Russian biographers (hagiographers) sought to endow their princely subjects with saintly qualities from the outset.

Alexander Nevsky ruled after the Mongol conquest. Manuscripts containing his vita have often included the *Slovo o pogibeli Russkyia zemli* (Discourse on the ruin of the land of Rus), a lyrical work akin to a lament, which may have served as a preface to Nevsky's life.

Very little literature has survived from the first two centuries following the Mongol-Tatar conquest; what remains cannot compare with the best-known works from the earlier period. The chronicles now become "narrower in scope, pale and laconic . . . ; they were artless compilations, mechanically stringing together earlier entries" (Likhachev). Even the *Zadonshchina,* an epic poem celebrating Dmitrii Donskoi's victory over the Tatars in 1380, is no match for the twelfth-century Igor Tale, on which much of it appears to be based.

The second South Slavic influence from Bulgaria and Serbia made itself most felt in hagiography, where the verbose, highly ornamented "word braiding" (*pletenie sloves*) became fashionable and remained the favorite style for religious and official literature well beyond the Middle Ages. Moscow's best-known samples are two vitas written by Epiphanii Premudryi (the Wise): the Life of St. Stefan of Perm and the Life of St. Sergius of Radonezh.

The first Slavic translation of the entire Bible (both testaments) was undertaken by the Novgorod clergy late in the fifteenth century, largely to counter the teachings of the Judaizers, a sect whose reformist ideas in some ways paralleled those of the Czech Hussites.

The fifteenth century also gave us the Journey Beyond Three Seas by the Tver merchant Afanasii Nikitin, a remarkable travel account; earlier samples of this genre (pilgrimage or journey—*khozhdenie*) had been religious. Nestor-Iskander's Tale of the Taking of Constantinople, a military tale, contained many elements of narrative art but also enjoyed popularity for certain passages construed as prophesying Russia's liberation of Constantinople from the Islamic Turks.

Sometime after 1475 a Russian adaptation of the Dracula tale appeared, probably based on Rumanian (Walachian) materials. The work illustrates both the courage and the inhuman cruelty of Vlad Ţepeş (Dracula), onetime governor of Walachia. Some critics see in the Russian tale a pre-Machiavellian model for Moscow's Prince Ivan III: a successful ruler must not hesitate to use deceit and extreme brutality if necessary. Others reject this interpretation, but describe Moscow's Ivan IV (the Terrible) as "the Russian Dracula."

As the medieval era drew to a close, a literature of "Muscovite megalomania" (in the words of Stender-Petersen) emerged, whose dominant themes were Muscovite messianism and glorification of the tsar.

BIBLIOGRAPHY

Antun Barac, *A History of Yugoslav Literature* (1978); Thomas Butler, ed. and trans., *Monumenta serbocroatica* (1980); Dmytro Chyzhevskii, *History of Russian Literature from the Eleventh Century to the End of the Baroque* (1960), *Comparative History of Slavic Literatures,* Richard Porter and Martin Rice, trans. (1971), and *A History of Ukrainian Literature,* George Luckyj, ed., Dolly Ferguson *et al.,* trans. (1975); Francis Dvornik, "Significance of the Missions of Cyril and Methodius" (with replies by H. G. Lunt and I. Ševčenko, and rejoinder), in *Slavic Review,* **23** (1964); Alfred French, ed., *Anthology of Czech Poetry* (1973); Louis J. Herman, *A Dictionary of Slavic Word Families* (1975); Roman Jakobson, *Slavic Languages: A Condensed Survey,* 2nd ed. (1955); Anton Kneževic, *Die Turzismen in der Sprache der Kroaten und Serben* (1962); Julian Krzyżanowski, *A History of Polish Literature,* Doris Ronowicz, trans. (1978); Dmitrii Likhachev, *Poetika drevnerusskoi literatury,* 3rd ed. (1979), and *Razvitie russkoi literatury X–XVII vekov: Epokhi i stili* (1973); Horace G. Lunt, *Old Church Slavonic Grammar* (1955); Czeslaw Miłosz, *The History of Polish Literature* (1969); Arne Novák, *Czech Literature,* P. Kussi, trans., W. Harkins, ed. (1976); Adolf Stender-Petersen, ed. and comp., *Anthology of Old Russian Literature* (1954).

HORACE W. DEWEY

[See also **Alphabets; Bohemia-Moravia; Bulgaria; Cosmas of Prague; Croatia; Cyril and Methodios, Sts.; Indo-European Languages, Development of; Kievan Rus; Muscovy, Rise of; Poland; Primary Chronicle, Russian; Serbia.**]

SLAVS, ORIGINS OF. While the Slavs have constituted the largest ethnic-linguistic group in Eastern Europe since the Middle Ages, there is much controversy regarding their origins and movements in the period prior to the emergence of the first Slavic states during the second half of the first millennium A.D.

One aspect of the controversy concerns the problem of when and where the proto-Slavs separated from the larger Indo-European community. Many scholars maintain that after this separation the proto-Slavs and proto-Balts formed a new community, but its location and dating are the subject of discussion. Perhaps the most heated issue is the location of the proto-Slavic homeland.

Almost every scholar locates the proto-Slavic homeland somewhere between the Volga River in the east, the Oder River in the west, the Baltic Sea in the north, and the Black Sea in the south. Currently, two theories enjoy strong support. One connects the original proto-Slavs with the Lusatian or Lausitz culture, which occupied the area between the Elbe and Vistula rivers from *ca.* 1200 to 500 B.C. The other theory places the Slavic homeland between the Dnieper and Danube rivers and dates it from the third to second millennia B.C. The difficulty with these and similar theories has been to demonstrate a continuity of culture and settlement from the prehistorical period to the time when unquestionable Slavic sites appeared around 500 A.D. Given these problems, some scholars now believe that the original Slavic settlements were scattered over a large area between the Oder and Dnieper rivers and that these proto-Slavic peoples are not necessarily connected with any particular archaeological culture.

The migrations of the Slavs throughout Eastern Europe are usually associated with the movement of the Turkic Avars into the area around the northern Black Sea during the mid-sixth century A.D. and the subsequent expansion of Avar control into the middle Danubian basin. The Slavs inhabiting these regions were either conquered by the Avars or forced to migrate elsewhere. It is believed, for example, that some Slavs fleeing the Avars moved north and east into the southern Ukraine, thus initiating the Slavic settlement of European Russia, which gave birth to the East Slavs, the ancestors of the modern Great Russian, Ukrainian, and Belorussian/White Russian peoples. The Avars launched numerous raids south into the Balkans. The Slavs, either as Avar auxiliaries or on their own, now began to raid and settle throughout the Balkans in large numbers. The Slavic settlement of the Balkans led to the birth of the South Slavs, the ancestors of the modern Bulgarian, Serbian, Croatian, Macedonian, and Slovenian peoples. Finally, Avar domination of the middle Danube apparently opened up this area to Slavic settlement, while a combination of factors brought Slavic migrants as far north as the Baltic coast. These developments led to the emergence of the West Slavs, the ancestors of the modern Czechs, Slovaks, Sorbs, and Poles.

BIBLIOGRAPHY
H. Birnbaum, "The Original Homeland of the Slavs and the Problem of Early Slavic Linguistic Contacts," in *Journal of Indo-European Studies,* 1 (1973); Francis Dvornik, *The Slavs: Their Early History and Civilization* (1956); Marija Gimbutas, *The Slavs* (1971); Witold Hensel, *Die Slawen im frühen Mittelalter,* Waldemar Hein, trans. (1965), and "From Studies on the Ethnogenesis of Slavs," in *Ethnologia Slavica,* 7 (1975); Joachim Herrmann, *Siedlung, Wirtschaft und gesellschaftliche Verhältnisse der slawischen Stämme zwischen Oder/Neisse und Elbe* (1968); Konrad Jażdżewski, *Atlas to the Pre-history of the Slavs* (1948–1949); Karl H. Menges, *An Outline of the Early History and Migrations of the Slavs* (1953); Lubor Niederle, *Slovanské starožitnosti,* 7 vols. (1902–1934), trans. into French as *Manuel de l'antiquité slave,* 2 vols. (1923–1926); Valentin V. Sedov, *Proizkhozhdenie i ranniaya istoriya slavyan* (1979).

THOMAS S. NOONAN

[See also **Avars; Bohemia-Moravia; Bosnia; Bulgaria; Croatia; Kievan Rus; Muscovy, Rise of; Poland; Serbia; Wends.**]

SLUTER, CLAUS (*fl. ca.* 1379–1406), Netherlandish sculptor who ranks with the foremost artists of the later Middle Ages. Probably born in Haarlem, Sluter's name first appears about 1379 in the guild register of the *steenbickeleren* (stone workers) in Brussels. From 1385 until his death in 1406, he worked for Duke Philip the Bold (*r.* 1363–1404) at the Chartreuse de Champmol in Burgundy, first as an assistant to Jean de Marville (*d.* 1389), then, after Marville's death, as master in charge of the duke's sculptural projects. No trace of the master's activity before 1385 survives. The principal remaining sculpture ensembles at the Chartreuse that are documented as his work reveal a sculptor familiar with the most progressive tendencies of the contemporary International Gothic style current in French court centers, particularly Paris, as interpreted by an outstanding artistic genius. In his earliest work, the decoration of the monastery church portal—consisting of the kneeling duke and his wife, Margaret of Flanders (*d.* 1405), being presented by protector saints to a central Madonna (statues completed 1389–1393)—Sluter raises the traditional ex-voto to a new, impressive sense of monumentality; these figures, with their realistically rendered features (the donors' heads are among the finest portraits of the century), and their ample, sculpturally defined drapery, exhibit a self-sufficiency unprecedented in earlier medieval tradition. Located in the center of the cloister and exhibiting an even greater independence from the architectural setting is the sculptor's so-called Well of Moses (*Puits de Moïse*), which originally served to support a monumental group with Christ on the Cross (1395–1403). Six Old Testament figures set against the polygonal base are dramatized as true seers, conscious of the tragic implication of their prophecies relating to Christ's suffering; differentiated in physical type and in psychological attitude, their reactions range from fierce anger to meditative resignation. In his later years Sluter also executed several of the mourning figures for the tomb of Philip the Bold; these, along with the Moses Well statues, represent the artist's culminating achievement. The spatial interest and the astonishing realism that are characteristic of these works point forward to a later generation of Netherlandish artists, notably the painters Master of Flémalle and the Van Eyck brothers, who may be considered Sluter's artistic heirs.

BIBLIOGRAPHY
Henri David, *Claus Sluter* (1951); Robert Didier, "Le monument funéraire de Philippe le Hardi, duc de Bourgogne (1342–1404): Jean de Marville, Claus Sluter, Claus de Werve," in *Die Parler und der schöne Stil 1350–1400: Europäische Kunst unter den Luxemburgern,* V (1980), 20–23; Josef Duverger, *De Brusselsche Steenbickeleren, Beeldhouwers, Bouwmeesters, Metselaars, Enz., der XIVe en XVe eeuw, met een aanhangsel over Klaus Sluter en zijn Brusselsche Medewerkers te Dijon* (1933); Alain Erlande-Brandenburg, "Le portail de Champmol: Nouvelles observations," in *Gazette des Beaux-arts,* 80 (1972); *Les fastes du gothique: Le siècle de Charles V* (exhibition catalog) (1981); *Les pleurants dans l'art du moyen âge en Europe: Musée des beaux-arts, Dijon* (exhibition catalog) (1972); Aenne Liebreich, *Claus Sluter* (1936); Wolfgang Medding, "Herkunft und Jugendwerke des Claus Sluter," in *Zeitschrift für Kunstgeschichte,* 3 (1934); Erwin Panofsky, *Early Netherlandish Painting,* I (1953), 78–81; Georg Troescher, *Claus Sluter* (1932).

J. STEYAERT

[See also **Burgundy; Dijon, Chartreuse de Champmol; Flanders and the Low Countries; Gothic Art: Sculpture; Valois Dynasty; Werve, Claus de;** and illustration overleaf.]

SMARAGDUS OF ST. MIHIEL (*fl.* second and third decades of the ninth century), Carolingian

The Well of Moses. Stone sculpture by Claus Sluter, 1395–1403, at the Chartreuse de Champmol, Dijon. PHOTO: WIM SWAAN

author and abbot. Most probably coming from southern Francia or Spain, he participated in the ecclesiastical and political life of the Carolingian Empire, and, as abbot, teacher, and adviser, produced a varied collection of writings that reflect the wide range of interests and talents of Carolingian scholars. In addition to commentaries on Donatus (*Liber in partibus Donati*) and the Psalms, Smaragdus wrote a commentary on the scriptural passages used in the liturgy, a book of advice for young Louis I the Pious, a collection of readings for monks, poems, and a commentary on the Rule of St. Benedict.

BIBLIOGRAPHY
Franz Brunhölzl, *Geschichte der lateinischen Literatur des Mittelalters*, I (1975), 444–449, 567; Fidel Rädle, *Studien zu Smaragd von Saint-Mihiel* (1974).

JOHN J. CONTRENI

[See also **Benedictine Rule; Carolingians and the Carolingian Empire; Exegesis, Latin.**]

SMBAT I THE MARTYR (*r.* 890–912/914), son of Ašot I and the second Bagratid king of Armenia, who as crown prince held the office of *išxan išxanac*ᶜ (prince of princes). His right to the crown was contested by his paternal uncle Abas, the commander-in-chief (*sparapet*) of the Armenian forces. In 891 Smbat received a diadem from the Abbasid caliph and was officially crowned king of Armenia. He was also recognized by the Byzantine emperor Leo VI as *archōn tōn archontōn* (prince of princes) and "beloved son." During his reign Smbat clashed with Afshīn and Yūsuf (*r.* 901–919), the Sājid emirs of Azerbaijan. In 913 Yūsuf forced Smbat to surrender. He was incarcerated, tortured, and beheaded. Subsequently his body was tied to a beam and displayed in the city of Dwin. Smbat was declared a saint of the Armenian church and annually remembered.

BIBLIOGRAPHY
Katᶜołikos John (Yovhannēs or Hovhannes) Drasxanakertcᶜi, *History of Armenia* (1987); Aram Ter-Ghewondyan, *The Arab Emirates in Bagratid Armenia*, Nina G. Garsoïan, trans. (1976).

KRIKOR H. MAKSOUDIAN

[See also **Armenia; Armenian Saints; Ašot I Mec; Ašot II Erkatᶜ; Azerbaijan; Bagratids; Dwin.**]

SMBAT SPARAPET (1208–1276), otherwise known as Gundstapl (constable), was the commander-in-chief (*sparapet*) of the military forces of the kingdom of Cilician Armenia during the reign of his younger brother, King Hetᶜum I (*r.* 1226–1270). He was the son of Constantine Payl, the regent of the Armenian kingdom, and Dame Alise and related to the Hetᶜumids of Lambron as well as to the royal dynasty of the Rubenids.

Smbat organized the defense of Cilicia against the invading armies of the sultanate of Rum in 1246 and 1259 and the Mamluk sultanate of Egypt in 1276. In 1243 he took part in the embassy that went to Caesarea (Kayseri) to negotiate with the Mongol chief Bayjū. This led to further negotiations that took Smbat in 1248 to Qaraqorum, where he made arrangements for the trip of King Hetᶜum I. He returned to Cilicia in 1250 and in 1254 went back to Mongolia for a second time, accompanying the king to the court of the Great Khan, Möngke. Smbat was instrumental in making an alliance between the Mongols and the Armenian kingdom of Cilicia. He was killed in 1276 in the battle of Sarvandikᶜar, fighting against the Mamluks of Egypt.

Smbat was a member of the Verin or Mec Darpas (supreme court) of the Armenian kingdom, which examined both the domestic and foreign policies of the government. As a jurist he was particularly interested in legal codes. He translated from French the *Assizes of Antioch*, whose original is now lost, and prepared a *Datastanagirk*ᶜ (codex) in Middle Armenian, based on and adapted from the corpus of Mχitᶜar Goš's work.

Smbat is also the author of a historical chronicle, which covers the events of the tenth through eleventh centuries, letters, and poems. His interest in grammar can be detected from notes in his hand in a manuscript. The *Chronicle*, which is considered one of his important contributions, begins with 951/952. The narration of events until 1225 is taken from various older Armenian, Syriac, crusader, and possibly Byzantine sources. The account of events after 1225 is based on his own memories. The work was continued by later chroniclers.

BIBLIOGRAPHY
Sources. "Assizy Antiokhiiskie," A. A. Papovian, trans., in *Banber Matenadarani*, IV (1958); *La chronique attribuée au connétable Smbat*, Gérard Dédéyan, trans. and introduction (1980).
Studies. Sirarpie Der Nersessian, "The Armenian

Chronicle of the Constable Smpad or of the 'Royal Historian,'" in *Byzantine and Armenian Studies,* I (1973), 353–377; Josef Karst, ed., *Sempadscher Kodex,* 2 vols. (1905).

KRIKOR H. MAKSOUDIAN

[See also **Armenia; Armenian Literature; Baybars al-Bunduqdārī; Cavalry, Armenian; Cilician Kingdom; Het^c um I; Het^c umids; Historiography, Armenian; Law, Armenian; Mongol Empire; Mχit^c ar Goš; Qalā^ɔ ūn, al-Manṣūr.**]

SMITHS. See **Metalsmiths, Gold and Silver.**

SNORRA EDDA is the handbook of poetics composed during the 1220's by the Icelandic statesman and man of letters Snorri Sturluson (1178/1179–1241). It contains exhaustive descriptive accounts of metrics, diction, and—to explain aspects of diction—of myth and heroic legend. The meaning of the term *edda,* found in only one manuscript of the text, is not known. Guesses based on etymology associate it with the Old Icelandic nouns *óðr* (poetry) and *edda* (great-grandmother); with the place-name Oddi, the name of the farm where Snorri spent his boyhood as the foster son of the great chieftain Jón Loftsson; and with Latin *edo* in the sense "compose verse." Whatever the meaning of the term, the contents of Snorri's *Edda* are well known. It consists of a prologue followed by three parts: *Gylfaginning, Skáldskaparmál,* and *Háttatal.*

Snorra Edda is preserved in four major manuscripts and several fragments. Of the major manuscripts, the earliest is Codex Upsaliensis (DG 11 4° in the Uppsala University Library, from *ca.* 1300). The other three are the Codex Regius (MS 2367 4° in the Old Collection of the Royal Library in Copenhagen, from *ca.* 1325), Codex Wormianus (MS 242 folio in the Arnamagnaean Collection, Copenhagen, *ca.* 1350), and Codex Trajectinus (MS 1374 in the library at Utrecht, a paper copy of a vellum from the second half of the thirteenth century). The manuscript tradition shows two branches, one represented by Codex Upsaliensis, the other by the remaining three manuscripts. The branches differ primarily in the relative compactness of the texts; Codex Upsaliensis lacks material found in the other manuscripts, and where other manuscripts contain the same text, Codex Upsaliensis tends to be more concise. Which branch is closer to Snorri's original is unknown. Such scholars as K. Müllenhoff, E. Mogk, and Friedrich W. Müller preferred the Uppsala codex, whereas Finnur Jónsson, R. C. Boer, and others have opted for the other branch. Perhaps, as suggested by D. O. Zetterholm, Snorri's original occupied something of a middle ground, and one branch shortened it while the other expanded it. In any case, the most familiar text to modern readers is Codex Regius, for it has formed the basis of most recent editions.

Composition of *Snorra Edda* apparently began in 1222–1223, when Snorri composed a panegyric to King Hákon Hákonarson and Earl Skúli, who had befriended him during a visit to Norway in 1218–1220. The poem contains 102 strophes and is a systematic attempt to exemplify virtually all the metric possibilities of Norse verse; each of the strophes offers an example of a meter, metric variation, or aspect of diction. In its formal virtuosity, the poem alone would qualify as a major achievement in skaldic versecraft, despite its wholly conventional praise of the valor and generosity of Hákon and Skúli. What is truly unique, however, and one of the great monuments of the Icelandic Middle Ages, is the interspersed prose commentary accompanying it. Although seemingly modeled on contemporary Latin scholastics, it is composed in lucid Icelandic and is so clearly presented that it remains fundamental in the study of skaldic poetics. Together the poem and commentary are called *Háttatal* (Enumeration of meters). *Háttatal* now makes up the last part of *Snorra Edda.*

It has been suggested that Snorri was mindful not only of the hospitality he had received in Norway, but also of his failed promise to work for the political assimilation of Iceland under the Norwegian crown. An equally strong impetus, however, must have been a desire to reinvigorate the tradition of skaldic poetry, which was under attack by the church from one side and the new tradition of dance songs from the other. This impetus reveals itself in the section of the *Edda* that Snorri presumably wrote next. Called *Skáldskaparmál* (Poetic diction), it is devoted primarily to the metaphorical and metonymic devices known as kennings and *heiti,* an understanding of which is absolutely essential to composing and understanding skaldic poetry. Kennings, however, are often based on narrative; thus poetry, for example, may be called "Kvasir's blood," because the inspiring mead of poetry was brewed from the blood of Kvasir, the

SNORRA EDDA

wisest man on earth. The narrative on which kennings are based is mythic or heroic, and so Snorri retold much myth and heroic legend in *Skáldskaparmál* in order to clarify certain kennings. Much of *Skáldskaparmál,* however, consists of lists of kennings or *heiti,* arranged according to certain important semantic categories within the poetry.

Skáldskaparmál begins with a frame, soon abandoned, in which a sea-king, Ægir, puts questions to Bragi, god of poetry. Bragi begins by recounting the myth of the near loss of Iðunn and her apples of youth to the giants. Next the origin of the mead of poetry is told, in appropriate detail. Following these two important myths, Snorri turns to poetics, detailing various kennings for gods and poetry, with many examples. The next subject is Thor, whose encounters with Hrungnir and Geirrøðr are recounted. These are followed by discussion of kennings for goddesses, the cosmos, and gold, the latter interrupted by an account of Sif's hair and the gods' acquisition of various treasures. At this point the narratives turn to heroic legend. The Volsung cycle is told at some length, followed by notices of Fróði and Hrólfr kraki. This leads, appropriately, to kennings of gold (again), men, battle, and weapons; after a brief discussion of the eternal battle of the Hjaðningar, the catalog concludes with ships, Christ, and kings. Next come the *heiti:* gods, cosmos, animals, weather, birds, sea, fire, time, kings, and—following an account of Hálfdan the Old—*heiti* for men and numbers, women, parts of the body, language, and wit. *Skáldskaparmál* ends with a theoretical discussion of the device called *ofljóst,* involving the use of homonyms for poetic effect.

As this brief sketch indicates, *Skáldskaparmál* is somewhat amorphous. A certain organizational pattern may be glimpsed, however, in the progressions from Odin to Thor, from gods to heroes, and from kennings to *heiti.* Kennings dealing with more mythic subjects, such as gods, goddesses, and the cosmos, are grouped with the tales of the gods; those dealing with more human subjects, such as warriors, battle, and weapons, are grouped with tales of heroes. The importance of gold is perhaps indicated by its being included in both categories. One can only admire Snorri for this pioneering effort to impose order on a vast system of poetic diction.

After composing *Skáldskaparmál*—by far the longest section of *Snorra Edda*—Snorri apparently felt that a full account of Norse mythology was necessary for understanding of the kenning systems. In undertaking such an account, he returned to a frame device similar to the one abandoned in *Skáldskaparmál.* In this text, however, poetic diction is never mentioned; the myths are recounted as pure narrative in the context of the frame. This section of *Snorra Edda,* which now precedes *Skáldskaparmál,* is the *Gylfaginning* (Deluding of Gylfi).

In some manuscripts *Gylfaginning* begins with an account of how Gefjon plowed up part of the Swedish king Gylfi's land and thus increased the size of Denmark; a skaldic stanza, the only in *Gylfaginning,* is cited. The absence of this material from Codex Upsaliensis has led some observers to regard it as an interpolation. The frame of *Gylfaginning* then begins, as Gylfi sets off, calling himself Gangleri, to test the wisdom of the Æsir (the word means "gods" but here seems to be used euhemeristically). With the Æsir chieftains High, Just-as-High, and Third he wagers his head in a contest of wisdom, putting questions to the three and receiving detailed answers. The questions concern myth and cosmos: the origin and structure of the universe; the identity of the gods; Týr's binding of Fenrir; the identity of the goddesses; Freyr's wooing of Gerðr; Odin's hall, Valhalla; the construction of Asgard; Freyr's ship, Skiðblaðnir; Thor's journey to Útgarða-Loki; his journey to Hymir; the death of Baldr; the punishment of Loki; and Ragnarǫk. Following this tolerably complete account of Norse mythology—of important myths, only those recounted in *Skáldskaparmál* are omitted—the chieftains and their hall vanish. Thus was Gylfi deluded; his interlocutors were wizards, a notion that accords with common medieval conceptions of pagan gods.

The immediate sources for *Gylfaginning* were versions—whether oral or written is unknown—of three Eddic poems: *Vǫluspá, Vafþrúðnismál,* and *Grímnismál.* Snorri cites many stanzas from these poems, and his progression of cosmic history essentially follows that of *Vǫluspá.* Further, the motif of the head wager—though not carried out—is probably derived from *Vafþrúðnismál.* Yet the didactic quality of the question-and-answer format is reminiscent of *Elucidarius* or any catechism, and the result is ironic, perhaps deliberately so. Snorri's lively prose style contributes to this impression.

It seems, however, that pure recounting of pagan myth, even in the format of a dialogue between a

 SNORRA EDDA

putative prehistoric king and three wizards, may not have been wholly acceptable to the church. Apparently for this reason, Snorri composed a short prologue. As it never mentions poetics, it is presumably intended solely as a prologue to *Gylfaginning*. Written from a standard medieval Christian perspective, this prologue sketches a pseudohistorical development of the northern peoples and their religious beliefs. The theoretical basis is a form of euhemerism, in which the Norse gods are derived from kings and heroes who lived long ago. In a learned (and utterly false) etymology, the Æsir are said to have emigrated from Asia. They were led by King Odin, whose foresight informed him that his fortune lay to the north. He settled at Sigtuna, in Sweden, taking land offered to him by King Gylfi, and assigned his sons to other kingdoms in Scandinavia. Because of their great prosperity, and because men had forgotten the true name of God, these "men of Asia" were regarded as gods.

Essentially the same progression is described in the opening chapters of the *Ynglinga saga* in Snorri's *Heimskringla*. It has therefore been suggested that the prologue is a later addition to *Snorra Edda,* and not by Snorri's hand, for it differs greatly in style from *Gylfaginning*. Closer stylistic analysis, however, seems to confirm that the prologue is Snorri's work, and few today would deny it its place in *Snorra Edda*.

It would be difficult to exaggerate the importance of *Snorra Edda*. It is the only complete exposition of Norse mythology stemming from the Middle Ages, and without it interpretation of a great many mythic texts would be difficult, and in some cases impossible. From time to time the degree of Snorri's faithfulness to pagan tradition has been questioned—Eugen Mogk even went so far as to suggest that Snorri founded a "mythological school" that recreated myth from its own imagination—but even today it is not easy to approach Norse mythology without beginning from Snorri's account. Nor is one wise to ignore *Snorra Edda* in the consideration of Norse poetics. Snorri followed the example of the twelfth-century *Háttalykill* and was himself followed by other rhetorico-poetic treatises, but his work represents the zenith. Besides the analysis of poetics, *Snorra Edda* is extremely valuable for its retention of ancient verse, much of it not found elsewhere. Perhaps the most important example is Eilífr Goðrúnarson's *Þórsdrápa*, a tenth-century encomium to Thor found only in *Skáldskaparmál;* but many other examples might be cited, including most of the verse of Bragi the Old, the earliest extant skald (mid ninth century). Here it might also be noted that certain texts are found only in manuscripts of *Snorra Edda*. Codex Wormianus, for example, retains for posterity the so-called First Grammatical Treatise and the Eddic poem *Rígsþula*.

The connection of these works in manuscripts bespeaks the great influence of *Snorra Edda* in medieval Iceland. Skaldic poetry did not die out during the early thirteenth century. Snorri's nephews, Sturla Þórðarson and Óláfr Þórðarson, carried the tradition through the middle of the century, and it continued into the fourteenth century, primarily within the Icelandic church. Certain aspects of the diction were maintained in the *rímur,* a poetic form still in use in recent times (the dance songs that Snorri seems to have disliked never took firm root). Perhaps the greatest influence of *Snorra Edda,* however, lies in the *Poetic Edda*. It is generally considered that the impetus for writing down Eddic poetry came as a direct result of the revival of native poetry stimulated by *Snorra Edda*. If so, we owe the greater part of our knowledge of Norse poetry, skaldic and Eddic, to *Snorra Edda*. To distinguish it from the *Poetic Edda, Snorra Edda* has sometimes been called the *Prose Edda* and (wrongly) the *Younger Edda*.

BIBLIOGRAPHY

Editions. Edda Snorra Sturlusonar, 3 vols. (1848–1887, repr. 1966); Anthony Faulkes, ed., *Prologue and Gylfaginning* (1982); Finnur Jónsson, ed., *Edda Snorra Sturlusonar udgivet efter håndskrifterne* (1931), the standard edition. Other editions are *Edda Snorra Sturlusonar: Codex Wormianus AM 242, fol.* (1924); Willem van Eeden, ed., *De codex Trajectinus van de Snorra Edda* (1913); Anders Grape, Gottfrid Kallstenius, and Olof Thorell, eds., *Snorre Sturlassons Edda: Uppsala-handskriften DG 11,* I.I (1977). The manuscripts may be studied in these facsimile editions: Anders Grape, ed., *Snorre Sturlassons Edda: Uppsala-handskriften DG 11, Facsimileedition i ljustryck* (1962); Sigurður Nordal, ed., *Codex Wormianus (The Younger Edda): MS. No. 242 fol. in the Arnamagnaean Collection in the University Library of Copenhagen* (1931), with a useful introduction; Elias Wessén, ed., *Codex Regius of the Younger Edda: MS No. 2367 4° in the Old Royal Collection in the Royal Library of Copenhagen* (1940), with a useful introduction.

Translations. A complete translation of the *Prologue, Gylfaginning,* and *Skáldskaparmál* is *The Prose Edda,* Arthur Brodeur, trans. (1920); and a translation of the *Prologue, Gylfaginning,* and narrative selections from

Skáldskaparmál may be found in *The Prose Edda: Tales from Norse Mythology,* Jean I. Young, trans. (1964).

Studies. Richard C. Boer, "Studier over Snorra Edda," in *Aarbøger for Nordisk Oldkyndighed og Historie* (1924), and "Studien über die Snorra Edda: Die Geschichte der Tradition bis auf den Archetypus," in *Acta philologica scandinavica,* **1** (1926–1927), 150; Finnur Jónsson, "Edda Snorra Sturlusonar, dens oprindelige form og sammensætning," in *Aarbøger for Nordisk Oldkyndighed og Historie* (1898); Eugen Mogk, "Zur Bewertung des Cod. Upsaliensis der Snorra Edda," in *Beiträge zur Geschichte der deutschen Sprache und Literatur,* **49** (1924–1925), and *Zur Bewertung der Snorra Edda als religionsgeschichtliche und mythologische Quelle des nordgermanischen Heidentums* (1932); Karl Müllenhoff, "UUâra und uuara," in *Zeitschrift für deutsches Altertum,* **16** (1873); Friedrich W. Müller, *Untersuchungen zur Uppsala Edda* (1941); Delmar O. Zetterholm, *Studier i en Snorra-text: Tors färd till Utgård i codices Upsaliensis DG 11 4° och Regius Hafn. 2367 4°* (1949).

Other essential studies are Sigurður Nordal, *Snorri Sturluson* (1920); Walter Baetke, *Die Götterlehre der Snorra Edda* (1950); Anne Holtsmark, *Studier i Snorres mytologi* (1964); and Ernest A. Philippson, *Die Genealogie der Götter in germanischer Religion, Mythologie und Theologie* (1953).

See also Halldór Hermansson, "Bibliography of the Eddas," in *Islandica,* **13** (1920), and Jóhann S. Hannesson, "Bibliography of the Eddas: A Supplement to Bibliography of the Eddas," in *Islandica,* **37** (1955).

JOHN LINDOW

[See also **Æsir; Gylfaginning; Háttatal; Odin; Rímur; Skaldic Poetry; Skáldskaparmál; Snorri Sturluson; Sturla Þórðarson.**]

SNORRI STURLUSON (1178/1179–1241) is Iceland's most renowned and distinguished author. In an age when prose works were mostly anonymous, his name was transmitted to posterity as the author of a mythological and poetical handbook, the *Prose Edda,* and of *Heimskringla,* a history of Norwegian kings. Writers of prose works were infrequently commemorated as authors because their task was thought to be a mere reordering of traditional narratives. For this reason the memory of Snorri as writer was precarious. The names of skaldic poets, however, were often linked to their works. Composed in the intricate and formalized patterns peculiar to the genre, skaldic poems were created for specific purposes. Their intellectual aspect and the memorable circumstances that occasioned composition facilitated remembrance of the poets' names. Ironically, Snorri's prose works have survived, though many of his poems have not. The poems that are extant hardly warrant the fame that his prose works have justly conferred upon him.

Although there are only scraps of information on Snorri's poetic and literary activity, his life as one of Iceland's foremost chieftains is set down in some detail, particularly in the *Íslendinga saga* (part of *Sturlunga saga*), written by his nephew Sturla Þórðarson (1214–1284). The imbalance in the record is the result of two factors. Since political and economic affairs were primary concerns, changes in status were chronicled. Intellectual and poetical aspirations, however, were common among members of the chieftain class. The cultivation of the mind needed, therefore, no special mention.

Snorri was the third legitimate son born from the second marriage of Sturla Þórðarson (Hvamm-Sturla, 1116–1183), a minor chieftain. The family is known as the Sturlungs. The name acknowledges Sturla as the founder of a dynasty that would wield unprecedented power between about 1200 and 1264. Indeed, the period is called "Age of the Sturlungs," an appellation first recorded in the early fifteenth century, but one which seems to have circulated before that time.

Sturla was, by all accounts, a witty, articulate man. His intellectual leanings, a deep and vested interest in law, were intimately linked to his ambition. Knowledge of the law was a prevalent means of self-advancement, which Sturla used, ruthlessly and ingeniously, to increase his power and repute. In the public judicial proceedings the sharpness of his mind found ready recognition. He himself took delight in publicizing his legal entanglements, as he entertained an informed audience with the course of his lawsuits. Snorri did not get to know his father well, but he seemingly inherited a passion for law and a verbal gift for memorable and suspenseful expression.

At the age of two (1181), Snorri was sent to Jón Loftsson (*d.* 1197), Iceland's most powerful chieftain. Acting as arbiter of a notorious lawsuit, Jón offered to foster Snorri. This was an honor Sturla could not refuse. For Snorri this meant an education at Iceland's foremost cultural center, Jón's farmstead Oddi. For several generations Oddi had been renowned for its learning, teaching, splendor, and ties to European ecclesiastical culture. Snorri stayed at Oddi at least until 1199. He thus grew up in a family used to power and one that zealously defended its interests and those of its class.

There are no direct references to formative experiences in Snorri's childhood and youth. The evidence on his intellectual development is, nevertheless, persuasive. At Oddi he seems to have received solid training in law, history, poetry, and saga telling. Oddi was particularly well known as a center for historical learning. Jón himself was proud to be a member of the Norwegian royal house. His mother was recognized, in his presence, as the illegitimate daughter of King Magnus Bareleg (1093–1103). In deliberate imitation of two illustrious Norwegian poetic models, Jón had his ancestry commemorated in a skaldic genealogical poem, "Nóregs konungatal." The commission of the poem testifies to the cultivation of skaldic poetry at Oddi.

The results of Snorri's training were spectacular. Twice he was elected lawspeaker (1215–1218, 1222–1231). The lawspeaker was required to have a prodigious memory. He recited the body of law at the opening of the Althing (judicial assembly) and acted as interpreter in judicial disputes. When Snorri is first mentioned as skald he has already attained honor and repute. The chronicler, his nephew Sturla Þórðarson, notes that Hákon galinn, a powerful Norwegian chieftain, sent to Snorri in return for a poem a magnificent gift: a sword, a shield, armor, and an invitation to visit him at court. By 1230 his reputation as a respected saga writer also seems established. Sturla Þórðarson mentions that his cousin, Sturla Sighvatsson, spent some time at Snorri's farm Reykjaholt to copy the saga books Snorri had composed. Apart from incidental remarks there is only one disparate fact that alludes to Snorri's absorption with saga matter. A trusted household member, Styrmir Kárason (*d.* 1245), had authored a pious saga on Óláfr (Olaf Haraldsson), the Norwegian king and saint (*r.* 1015–1030).

Snorri's quest for power began after Jón's death. The immediate task was to establish himself as chieftain. This required acquisition of wealth (his mother had largely squandered his inheritance) and practice in the prosecution of lawsuits. With his brothers' help he married in 1199 the daughter of and heiress to Bersi the Rich. Bersi's death in 1202 freed him from dependence. He moved to Bersi's farm Borg, the seat of one of his own forebears, the poet and Viking Egill Skallagrímsson, whose saga Snorri may also have authored. In the same period he deeply involved himself in litigation on behalf of Jón's kinsmen, the Oddaverjar, opposing his own brothers and their associates.

Snorri moved swiftly to acquire the influence and sumptuous way of life he desired. In subsequent lawsuits and disputes he would act in his own interest, pitting his strength against the Oddaverjar, assisting his brothers, or vying against the power held by his kinsmen. He became chieftain of several judicial districts or parts thereof. By assiduously tending his livestock he increased the productivity of his farms. By 1206, when he moved to the farmstead Reykjaholt, he was considered affluent. In 1211 he was addressed together with five major chieftains by Archbishop Þórir of Trondheim. The naming of Snorri as a principal testifies to the stature he had achieved within the brief span of twelve years.

Early in the decade Snorri had prepared for a journey to Norway. In Sturla's brief paragraph on the voyage, one senses the urgency with which Snorri had pressed his plan and the disappointment that accompanied the postponement. He had intended to arrive at court as an honored guest. For this purpose he had sent the poem honoring Jarl Hákon galinn and, at Hákon's behest, a poem to Lady Kristín, Hákon's consort. Hákon's unexpected death (1214), however, delayed Snorri's departure for several years.

Snorri finally left for Norway in 1218 and stayed two years. Jarl Skúli (*d.* 1240), regent for Hákon Hákonarson (*r.* 1217–1263), received him with the greatest honor. In 1219 Snorri traveled to Gotland, Sweden, to visit Lady Kristín, now the wife of Lawman Áskell, a powerful functionary. Her parting gift was a historic banner that figured in the 1210 Battle of Gestilsrein between King Eiríkr Knútsson (*d.* 1216) and King Sörkvir Karlsson (*d.* 1210). A year later Snorri was drawn into a bitter feud between the Norwegian crown, acting on behalf of merchants, and the Oddaverjar. Snorri is credited with dissuading Jarl Skúli from invading Iceland, although influential royal advisers had also viewed the enterprise with misgivings. In return Snorri promised to persuade the Icelanders to render homage to the king. In *Heimskringla,* Snorri subsequently depicted the unbridled ambition of strong-willed rulers to subjugate lands close to their grasp.

Snorri left Norway with the highest honors. He had been named *skutilsveinn,* holder of the highest office in the king's retinue, and also, upon his own wish and that of Jarl Skúli, a baron. The parting gifts were lavish, and included the ship that took Snorri home. Yet despite the splendor of his return, the distinction he had received, and the service he had rendered to his country, he was immediately embroiled in the hostilities that had preoccupied him in Norway. There was still deep resentment about the unwarranted slaying of Ormr Jónsson by Norwegian merchants. Ormr's son-in-law Björn Þorvaldsson reproached Snorri for allegedly impeding monetary atonement. Worse still, Snorri's enemies gave a scurrilous twist to a refrain of a poem he had composed for Jarl Skúli. In revenge, Snorri instigated the battle at Breiðabólstaðr in 1221, in which Björn died.

Between 1220 and 1234 Snorri was at the height of his power. This position proved to be more and more hollow. When he married Hallveig, Björn Þorvaldsson's widow, in 1224, he was by far the wealthiest man in Iceland. Yet inability to instill loyalty and to extend respect undermined his authority. The alliances he had fostered by the marriages of his children were short-lived. The avarice he displayed in property settlements, inheritance disputes, and marriage and divorce proceedings aroused discord and rancor. In particular, he proved unable to enlist the support of his sons. Jón died in Norway from a wound inflicted in a brawl. He had set sail because Snorri had at first refused to give him a desirable farmstead as a marriage portion. Órækja proved to be rapacious. Órækja's depredations and Snorri's determination to curb the power of his nephew Sturla Sighvatsson ultimately led to a reversal in fortune.

The year 1235 marked the turning point. Sturla Sighvatsson had returned from a pilgrimage to Rome and from a stay at the Norwegian court. His mercilessness had become more pronounced and his ambition unrestrained. He had long resented Snorri's encroachments upon his power. Despite the imminence of battle, Snorri refused to attack Sturla because of the sanctity of Easter (1236). When Sturla moved against him, he fled. Órækja was given hope for a settlement, but was captured and ordered maimed. The following year, Snorri retreated from a planned attack on Sturla. In the subsequent Battle of Bær, Snorri's ally and kinsman Þorleifr Þórðarson was decisively beaten. That summer Snorri left for Norway (1237).

Snorri's stay in Norway was inauspicious. Hostilities between King Hákon Hákonarson and Jarl Skúli had exacerbated and would end in Jarl Skúli's abortive revolt in 1240. Shortly before Snorri's return in 1239 Jarl Skúli conferred upon him in a secret ceremony the title of jarl. None of the Icelanders present would ever profess knowledge of the entitlement. Nevertheless, in 1240, King Hákon ordered the capture or death of Snorri on a charge of treason and on a lesser charge: Snorri had left for Iceland in deliberate defiance of the king's ban.

In the interim Gizurr Þorvaldsson, Snorri's former son-in-law, had turned into a bitter enemy of Sturla Sighvatsson and covertly also of Snorri. In a savage battle at Örlygstaðir in 1238, in which Snorri's brother Sighvatr and his son Kolbeinn died, Gizurr slew Sturla. King Hákon's command on Snorri's fate was delivered to Gizurr by yet another of Snorri's former sons-in-law, Arni óreiða. With a lack of caution that in Icelandic society traditionally betokens the approach of death, Snorri was unprepared for the nocturnal assault on his life. He ignored all warnings. A fear-ridden priest was forced by Gizurr to divulge the hiding place Snorri had slipped into. No quarter was given. The next morning, by prearrangement, another armed force arrived. One of its leaders was Klængr Björnsson, one of Snorri's disgruntled stepsons.

Snorri had not been given the chance to negotiate with the king, who later professed that he regretted the killing. Nevertheless, the main reason for Snorri's death was that he had tacitly refused to further the king's ambition and interests. For Gizurr, the death of Snorri furthered his quest to rule Iceland. Appointed jarl in 1258, Gizurr was compelled to bring the country, reluctantly, under the king's dominion. The year 1264 saw the surrender of Iceland's political freedom to the crown.

BIBLIOGRAPHY

Sources. Sturla Þórðarson, *Íslendinga saga,* in *Sturlunga saga,* Jón Jóhannesson, Magnús Finnbogason, and Kristján Eldjárn, eds., 2 vols. (1946), and *Hákonar saga Hákonarsonar etter Sth. 8 fol., AM 325 VIII, 4° og AM 304,4°,* Marina Mundt, ed. (1977); Guðni Jónsson, ed., *Byskupa sögur,* 3 vols., 2nd ed. (1953); Gustav Storm, ed., "Oddveria Annall ('Annales breviores'), tildels i udrag, efter AM. 417 4°," in his *Islandske Annaler indtil 1578* (1888), 481.

Translation. Sturlunga saga, Julia H. McGrew with R. G. Thomas, trans., 2 vols. (1970–1974).

Studies. The authoritative work on Snorri Sturluson's life and work is Sigurður Nordal, *Snorri Sturluson* (1920, repr. 1972). See also Gunnar Benediktsson, *Snorri, skáld í Reykholti* (1957); Marlene Ciklamini, *Snorri Sturluson* (1978); Gunnar Karlsson and Helgi Þorláksson, eds., *Snorri: Átta alda minning* (1979); Halvdan Koht,

"Snorre Sturlason," in *Norsk Biografisk Leksikon,* XIV (1962); Sigurður Nordal, "Snorri Sturluson: Nokkurar hugleiðingar á 700. ártíð hans," in *Skírnir,* **115** (1941); Fredrik Paasche, *Snorre Sturlason og Sturlungene,* 2nd ed. (1948); Jacqueline Simpson, "Introduction," in Snorri Sturluson, *Heimskringla, Part One: The Olaf Sagas,* Samuel Laing, trans., rev. ed. (1964). On the political and social background of Hvamm-Sturla's quest for power, see Peter G. Foote, "Sturlusaga and Its Background," in *Viking Society for Northern Research: Saga-Book,* **13,** pt. 4 (1950–1951); W. H. Vogt, "Charakteristiken aus der Sturlungasaga, A. Sturlusaga," in *Zeitschrift für deutsches Altertum,* **54** (1913). On Oddi and the Oddaverja, see Halldór Hermannsson, "Sæmund Sigfússon and the Oddaverjar," in *Islandica* **22** (1932). On the Age of the Sturlungs, see Einar Ól. Sveinsson, *The Age of the Sturlungs: Icelandic Civilization in the Thirteenth Century,* Jóhann S. Hannesson, trans., in *Islandica,* **36** (1953); Jón Jóhannesson, *A History of the Old Icelandic Commonwealth: Íslendinga saga,* Haraldur Bessason, trans. (1974). On the warfare of the period, see Régis Boyer, "La guerre en Islands á l'âge des Sturlungar (XII–XIIIe siècles): Armement, tactique, esprit," in *Inter-Nord,* **11** (1970). For a geographic account of Snorri's journey within Norway, see Finnur Jónsson, "Snorri Sturluson i Norge," in *Historisk tidsskrift* (Oslo), **26** (1924); Halvdan Koht, "Skule Jarl," *ibid.* On Snorri's acquisition of the jarl's title, see Nils Hallan, "Snorri fólgsnarjarl," Björn Teitsson, trans., in *Skírnir,* **146** (1972).

MARLENE CIKLAMINI

[See also **Egill Skallagrímsson; Gylfaginning; Háttatal; Iceland; Norse Kings' Sagas; Óláfs Saga Helga; Skaldic Poetry; Skáldskaparmál; Snorra Edda; Sturla Þórðarson; Sturlunga Saga.**]

SOC. See **Sac and Soc.**

SOCRATES SCHOLASTICUS (*ca.* 380–after 450), a historian who wrote a continuation of Eusebius' *Ecclesiastical History.* He was probably a lawyer and seems to have lived for most of his life in Constantinople, where he was born. He also traveled in the Near East. His history, in seven books, begins with the abdication of Diocletian in 305 and ends in 439. Each book is concerned with the reign of one emperor, and Socrates views political problems as being caused by human sins, so his work concentrates on times of trouble for the church. He makes good use of sources, employing official documents and pointing out the biases of his sources.

BIBLIOGRAPHY

G. Bardy, "Socrate," in *Dictionnaire de théologie catholique* (1905–1950).

LINDA C. ROSE

[See also **Byzantine Literature; Historiography, Byzantine.**]

SOEST, KONRAD VON. See **Konrad von Soest.**

SOFIA. See **Serdica.**

SÓLARLJÓÐ. Most major Christian poems of medieval Iceland are *drápur* in skaldic meters. The most significant exception is the anonymous *Sólarljóð* (Sun song, or, literally, Sun verses) composed in the Eddic meter *ljóðaháttr* and now generally dated to the thirteenth century, usually to its first half, though an argument can be made for a fourteenth-century date. The poem shares with the Christian *drápur* only similar length (82 stanzas), the device of naming the poem in the penultimate stanza, and a concern for christological sun symbolism similar to that in Gamli Kanóki's *Harmsól* and Einarr Skúlason's *Geisli.* Though it alters the genre, *Sólarljóð* is related to continental vision literature involving a soul's journey through hell and heaven; and it also draws—in terms of form, tone, and phrases—on the sapiential *Hávamál* (Sayings of the High One), whose meter it employs, and the apocalyptic *Vǫluspá* (Sybil's prophecy) in such a way as to suggest that the poet is seeking to create a Christian surrogate to these great pagan poems.

The narrative persona of *Sólarljóð* is apparently a dead father who addresses his living son, ostensibly in a dream. The poem begins abruptly with a series of five exempla—accented, as in *Hávamál,* by occasional maxims—illustrating the evil and deceit of the world (stanzas 1–24): a robber whose repentance only causes his death, the uselessness of wealth, a tragic love triangle, pride, deception. The father then offers seven counsels for righteous living (stanzas 25–32), and in stanzas 33–52 his own experience becomes exemplum as he reveals details of his life and death. At the liminal moment between life and death are seven intense stanzas, each beginning with the phrase "Sól ek sá" (I saw the sun). The poem's name is apparently based on these. After experiencing the terror and chill of death, the speaker sat for nine days on the "chair of the Norns"—a detail reminiscent of *Hávamál*'s account of Odin's hanging for nine nights to learn rune magic—before undertaking a journey through the realm of the dead (stanzas 53–74), in which he saw the Sun-Hart (Christ), whose antlers represent his divinity and whose feet symbolize his humanity. As in Dante's *Inferno,* sins and punishments are appropriately matched: the greedy carry burdens of lead to the "castle of avarice," the envious are engraved with bleeding runes. The wayfarer also briefly recounts the joys of the just. Several enigmatic verses follow that evoke the eschatological tone of *Vǫluspá,* and in the two last stanzas (81–82; 83 is a later accretion), the speaker urges the dissemination of the poem's teachings, hopes that he and his son will meet on the "day of joy," and echoes the liturgical "requiem dona eis, domine" in a final prayer.

Sólarljóð is preserved only in late paper manuscripts, the earliest from the seventeenth century. Early scholars, for instance Finnur Jónsson, considered the poem to abound in accretions and suggested dividing it ingeniously into two poems or at least excluding up to forty of its verses. But despite the persistent obscurity of its images and references (the poet invents many names, often symbolic), *Sólarljóð* is, as A. Baumgarten first demonstrated, thematically unified, with the "Sól ek sá" verses at its structural center.

BIBLIOGRAPHY

Editions. Sophus Bugge, ed., *Norrœn fornkvæði* (1867), 357–370; Finnur Jónsson, ed., *Den norsk-islandske skjaldedigtning* ([1908] 1912–1915), A. I, 628–640 (diplomatic), B. I, 635–648 (normalized); Ernst A. Kock, ed., *Den norsk-isländska skaldediktningen* (1946–1949), I, 308–316; Björn M. Ólsen, "Sólarljóð," in *Safn til sögu Íslands,* 5 (1915).

Translations. Lee M. Hollander, trans., *Old Norse Poems* (1936, repr. 1973); Charles Venn Pilcher, trans., *Icelandic Christian Classics* (1950).

Studies. Frederic Amory, "Norse-Christian Syncretism and *Interpretatio christiana* in *Sólarljóð,*" in *Sixth International Saga Conference, Workshop Papers,* I (1985), 1–25; Alexander Baumgarten, "Das altnordische Sonnenlied (*Sólarljóð*)," in *Stimmen der Zeit,* **34** (1888); Detlev Brennecke, "Sólarljóð," in *Kindlers Literatur Lexikon,* VI (1971); Hjalmar Falk, *Sólarljóð,* in Norske Videnskaps Akademi, *Skrifter,* II, Hist.-filos. Klasse, 7 (1914); Bjarne Fidjestøl, *Sólarljóð* (1979); Peter Hallberg, *Old Icelandic Poetry,* Paul Schach and Sonja Lindgrenson, trans. (1975); Jón Helgason, "Norges og Islands digtning," in Sigurður Nordal, *Litteraturhistoria,* II, *Norge og Island, Nordisk kultur,* VIII. B (1953), 99–100; Finnur Jónsson, "Sólarljóð," in *Edda,* 5 (1916), "Et lille gensvar," *ibid.,* and *Den oldnorske og oldislandske litteraturs historie,* 2nd ed., II (1924), 127–131; Njörður P. Njarðvík, "Sólarljóð," in *Kulturhistorisk leksikon for nordisk middelalder,* XVI (1971); Fredrik Paasche, *Kristendom og kvad* (1914), 135–171; George S. Tate, "'Heiðar stjǫrnur'/'Heiðnar stjǫrnur': The Confrontation of Paganism and Christianity in *Sólarljóð,*" in *Sixth International Saga Conference, Workshop Papers,* II (1985); Jan de Vries, *Altnordische Literaturgeschichte,* 2nd ed., II (1967), 71–74.

GEORGE S. TATE

[See also **Eddic Poetry; Einarr Skúlason; Gamli Kánoki; Skaldic Poetry.**]

SOLDIERS' PORTIONS (*stratiōtika ktēmata*), or properties, were hereditary lands registered as belonging to soldiers in return for military service. In order to maintain the army and avoid the need for mercenaries, the law forbade the soldiers from alienating such lands or diminishing their size. Such lands were subject to the demosion tax (basic land tax), but were exempt from other taxes. Imperial legislation first explicitly refers to soldiers' portions in the tenth-century reign of Constantine VII Porphyrogenitos, but their origins are earlier, in the ninth or even eighth or late seventh century.

The origin of soldiers' portions is one of the most controversial issues of Byzantine studies. Soldiers may have acquired vacant lands when dispersed in Asia Minor through purchase, squatting, or seizure in the middle and late seventh century. Gradually the soldiers' obligation to serve may have been shifted to their tax-privileged lands. By the tenth century soldiers' portions had become an important means of financing the Byzantine army. Soldiers' portions were expected to total a value of four pounds of gold, which was increased to twelve pounds in the reign of Nikephoros II Phokas (963–969).

Holders of soldiers' portions were required to provide an armed and equipped soldier if they did not personally serve. In no sense were the holders cultivators of the soil themselves; the term "farmer-soldier" is a misleading modernism. There is no Byzantine Greek compound word indicating that the holder of a soldier's portion was both soldier and cultivator. Other members of soldiers' families may have helped to cultivate the soldiers' lands, however.

No reliable statistics exist concerning the total number of soldiers' portions or of their holders for any given date. It was the military treasury, or *Logothesion tou stratiotikou,* that kept the registers of soldiers' portions. The registration of such lands may have begun early in the tenth century in response to the threat of their disappearance because of the impoverishment of individual holders and because increasingly they were being purchased or otherwise acquired by large landholders and other nonmilitary investors and speculators in land. An undated law of Constantine VII forbade the sale of lands that assured the military service of a soldier; however, it permitted transmission of such lands, the minimum for service being defined as property worth four pounds of gold. In turn, each heir had to make a proportionate contribution to the military service. Not all soldiers' lands were registered, only the amount that was necessary to assure performance of military service. The law of Constantine established a fine for those who held a soldier as a dependent peasant and ordered the restitution of his lands to him. In 962 Romanus II restored soldiers' portions to their correct holders. Emperor Nikephoros II allowed soldiers to regain without compensation lands worth up to four pounds, but raised for the future the minimum wealth to twelve pounds because of changes in armaments.

The soldiers' portions gradually disappeared in the late tenth and early eleventh centuries, because of their absorption by larger private and institutional landholders. This required the government to seek different techniques for financing the upkeep of its land and naval forces, including resort to the hiring of more mercenaries and the eventual creation of the *pronoia.*

BIBLIOGRAPHY

Hélène Glykatzi-Ahrweiler, "Recherches sur l'administration de l'empire byzantin aux IXe–XIe siècles," in *Bulletin de correspondance hellénique,* **84** (1960); John F. Haldon, *Recruitment and Conscription in the Byzantine Army, c. 550–950: A Study on the Origins of the Stratiotika Ktemata* (1979); Michael Hendy, *Studies in the Byzantine Monetary Economy, c. 300–1450* (1985), 634–645; Walter E. Kaegi, "Heraklios and the Arabs," in *Greek Orthodox Theological Review,* **27** (1982); Johannes Karayannopulos, *Die Entstehung der byzantinischen Themenordnung* (1959), 71–88; Paul Lemerle, *The Agrarian History of Byzantium* (1979), 115–156; Ralph-Johannes Lilie, "Die zweihundertjährige Reform: Zu den Anfängen der Themenorganisation im 7. und 8. Jahrhundert, II: Die 'Soldatenbauern,'" in *Byzantinoslavica,* **45** (1984); George Ostrogorsky, *History of the Byzantine State,* Joan M. Hussey, trans., 2nd ed. (1969), esp. 95–98, 133–134, 272–276, 322–323, 329–331; Warren T. Treadgold, "The Military Lands and the Imperial Estates in the Middle Byzantine Empire," in *Harvard Ukrainian Studies,* 7 (1983).

WALTER EMIL KAEGI, JR.

[See also **Byzantine Empire; Cavalry, Byzantine; Law, Byzantine; Logothete; Taxation, Byzantine.**]

SOLEA (schola), in the early Christian church, a walkway fenced with parapets and often slightly elevated. It projected from the chancel barrier into the nave and provided access for the celebrants from the bema to the ambo. It also formed the final axial path for ceremonial entrance processions.

BIBLIOGRAPHY

Thomas F. Mathews, "An Early Roman Chancel Arrangement and Its Liturgical Functions," in *Rivista di archeologia cristiana,* **38** (1962), and *The Early Churches of Constantinople* (1971).

ROBERT OUSTERHOUT

[See also **Ambo; Architecture, Liturgical Aspects (with illustration); Bema.**]

SOLESMES, a Benedictine abbey near Le Mans that has been linked with the restoration of Gregorian chant since the nineteenth century. Founded in 1010 by Geoffroy of Sablé as a priory of Le Mans, the original establishment was destroyed by the English in 1425 and reconstructed some years later. The monastery also suffered setbacks in the wake of the French Revolution.

HISTORICAL BACKGROUND

The main accomplishment at Solesmes rests in the field of liturgical music. Dom Prosper Guéranger (1805–1875), dissatisfied with the truncated, hammered-out plainsong of his day, wished to provide his newly established Benedictine community with choir books in which music was restored to its pristine authenticity as the "perfect expression of the Divine Office." To this end he instructed Dom Paul Jaussions (1834–1870) and Dom Joseph Pothier (1835–1923) to revert to medieval manuscripts in order to reinstate the lost tradition transmitted by neumatic notation. The result of this first exacting inquiry was the publication, in 1864, of the *Directorium chori* (Instructions for the choir) by Dom Jaussions and, in 1883, of the *Liber gradualis* (Chantbook of the Mass) by Dom Pothier, in which the melodies were transcribed in the now familiar thirteenth-century black, square notation on four-line staves and according to the theory of "free oratorical rhythm" already set forth in 1859 by Canon A.-M. Gonthier (1802–1881) of Le Mans.

The appearance of the *Liber gradualis* soon gave rise to a heated controversy, for it was paramount to a scholarly condemnation of the so-called "Neo-Medicean edition" printed by Pustet of Regensburg in 1871. Officially approved—but not imposed—by the Vatican, this very imperfect Neo-Medicean edition was, however, protected by a thirty-year printing privilege. An assistant of Dom Pothier, Dom André Mocquereau (1849–1930), undertook the publication of the monumental *Paléographie musicale* (twenty-one volumes since 1889). This series reproduces in facsimile the most important manuscripts of chant from the different epochs and traditions of its long history. In volumes II and III, for instance, a single piece (the gradual *Justus ut palma*) is reproduced after 219 codices dating from the ninth to the seventeenth century and selected from seven countries, in order to demonstrate the universal agreement of all melodic versions.

In 1904, to end the controversy, Pope Pius X appointed an international commission, presided over by Dom Pothier, with the mandate to bring out a new and faithful edition (*editio typica*) of the chant books. At the outset Solesmes, through Dom Mocquereau, was responsible for the undertaking, but due to irreconcilable differences of opinion on the matter of "ancient" (tenth-century) versus later musical traditions, Mocquereau was excluded from the commission and Pothier carried on the task almost alone, publishing the Gradual for the Mass in 1908 and the Antiphonary for the Office in 1912, without any of the controversial rhythmic signs used in the Solesmes books.

THE METHOD OF SOLESMES

It is impossible to describe in a few words the Solesmes method of performing plainsong without doing injustice to such a complex, nuanced, and artistically beautiful system. Suffice it to indicate that the crux of the problem lies in the determination of rhythm as expressed in the oldest (ninth- and tenth-century) manuscripts in staffless neumes.

According to Dom Pothier, who dealt first with the difficulty of an authentic restoration of plainsong in his *Mélodies grégoriennes d'après la tradition* (1880), the rhythm of the chant derives from the succession, in equal time values, of the tonic (stress) accents of the Latin words: hence the name "free oratorical rhythm," or "accentualist theory."

For Dom Mocquereau, on the contrary, the "free *musical* rhythm" is determined by the melody much more than by the text. Resorting to the additional signs found mainly in the codices of the St. Gall tradition (held by Potheir to be idiosyncratic and therefore discarded from his edition), Mocquereau rejected the principal of accent as irrelevant to the nature of rhythm and described the latter as a movement consisting in a free succession of "rises" (*arsis*) and "falls" (*thesis*) divided into flowing alternations of binary and ternary pulsations unbounded by the "measure." This system was first proposed in volume VII of the *Paléographie musicale* (1901) and fully developed in the two volumes of his magnum opus, the *Nombre musical grégorien* (1908–1927).

This method favored the performance of chant with a nobility of style quite appropriate to the intrinsic mysticism of the Divine Office as sung daily by the monks, although on strictly historical grounds matters may have been very different. Another advantage was to free the concept of rhythm from the tyranny of the bar line imposed by polyphonic music since the thirteenth century, thus bringing out the concealed dynamic and agogic qualities of the musical sentence as a whole.

Solesmes is also opposed to the mensuralists (mostly German, or Jesuit), who, as the name indicates, advocate two or three different time values (longs and shorts) in proportional relation to one another and precisely measured, as in modern music. Although the mensuralists have amassed an impressive amount of historical data to support their views, they have failed so far to produce transcriptions that agree with one another, let alone approach the ethereal beauty of the Solesmes method.

Since 1948, the monks of Solesmes have been involved in the preparation of the first critical edition of the Roman gradual, which will establish the musical text according to a corpus of the earliest notated manuscripts. To replace the *Revue grégorienne* (1911–1964), a journal aimed at furthering in Roman Catholic churches the performance of Gregorian chant, a more scholarly series called *Études grégoriennes* has been published almost annually since 1954.

BIBLIOGRAPHY

Histories of Solesmes include Dom de Mazis, *La charte de fondation du monastère de Solesmes* (1954); and Henri Quentin, *Notice historique sur l'abbaye de Solesmes* (1924).

Studies on Gregorian chant include Willi Apel, *Gregorian Chant* (1958); Eugéne Cardine, *Semiologia gregoriana* (1968); Pierre Combe, *Histoire de la restauration du chant grégorien d'après des documents inédits: Solesmês et l'édition vaticane* (1969); Lucien David, *Dom J. Pothier, abbé de Saint-Wandrille, et la restauration grégorienne* (1943); J. Froger, "Origines, histoire et restitution du chant grégorien," in *Musique et liturgie,* **15–55** (1950–1957); Joseph Gajard, *The Solesmes Method* (1960); André G. Madrignac, *Le chant grégorien: Histoire et pratique* (1984); André Mocquereau, *Le nombre musical grégorien,* 2 vols. (1927), trans. by A. Tone as *A Study of Gregorian Musical Rhythm,* 2 vols. (1932); John Rayburn, *Gregorian Chant: A History of the Controversy Concerning Its Rhythm* (1964); Justine B. Ward, "Gregorian Chant According to the Principles of Dom A. Mocquereau," in *Catholic Education Series: Music,* **4** (1923).

The mensuralist point of view is discussed in Ludwig Bonvin, "The 'Measure' in Gregorian Music," in *Musical Quarterly,* **11** (1929); Eugéne Cardine, "Le chant grégorien est-il mesuré?" in *Études grégoriennes,* **6** (1963); Gregory Murray, *The Authentic Rhythm of Gregorian Chant* (1959) and *Gregorian Chant According to Manuscripts* (1963); J. W. A. Wollaerts, *Rhythmic Proportions in Early Medieval Ecclesiastical Chant* (1956, repr. 1960).

See also Paolo Maria Ferretti, *Estetica gregoriana,* I (1934, repr. 1977); Peter Wagner, *Einführung in die gregorianischen Melodien,* 2 vols. (1895–1905).

YVES CHARTIER

[See also **Antiphonal; Gallican Rite; Gradual; Gregorian Chant; Hymns, Latin; Musical Notation, Western; Plainsong, Sources of.**]

SOLMIZATION, a mnemonic technique used in singing whereby each pitch is assigned a syllable from the series *ut re mi fa sol la* so as to specify the location of that pitch within a scalar arrangement of tones and semitones. The term itself is derived from the coupling of the fifth and third syllables in the set (*sol-mi*-zation). Developed on the basis of Guido of Arezzo's early-eleventh-century teachings, the method was subjected to ongoing elaboration and criticism as it spread throughout Europe. Thorough grounding in the theoretical and practical aspects of so-called Guidonian solmization—the direct antecedent of many present-day sightsinging techniques—became a fundamental component in musical training from the Middle Ages until at least 1600.

In Western civilization, the earliest methodical association of verbal indicators with specific pitches survives in the music theory of ancient Greece. The principal sources, Aristides Quintilianus and the Bellerman Anonymous, make use of the series *ta tē tō te,* with the semitone between the first and second syllables, for tetrachords comprising the two-octave pitch repertory. These tetrachords are related through disjunction (diazeuxis) when separated by a full step (for instance, E F G a to b c d e) or through conjunction (synaphe) when they are linked by a common note (for instance, B C D E to E F G a). The conjunct arrangement demands that the singer omit one of the two names applicable to the pivot, indications being that this common degree was sung as *ta* rather than *te;* as a result, all of the semitones in the system were named identically. Insofar as the controlled suppression of *te* resembles an aspect of the technique later known as "mutation," the Greek method bears comparison with that developed after Guido.

Two concurrent systems for associating more complex verbal cues with complete melodic phrases are found in theoretical and practical sources from the ninth century onward. The first of these, referred to by Aurelian of Réôme about the mid ninth century (*Corpus scriptorum de musica* [*CSM*], vol. 21) and later writers, used a number of apparently meaningless words, such as *noeane* and *noeagis,* to reflect and reinforce the system of modal classification. While the specific mnemonic formulas vary widely from one source to another, links between the *noeane* family as a whole and the Greek tetrachordal syllables have been suggested (Riemann). There are also clear parallels in the intonation formulas, or *echemata,* of Byzantine chant.

Example 1

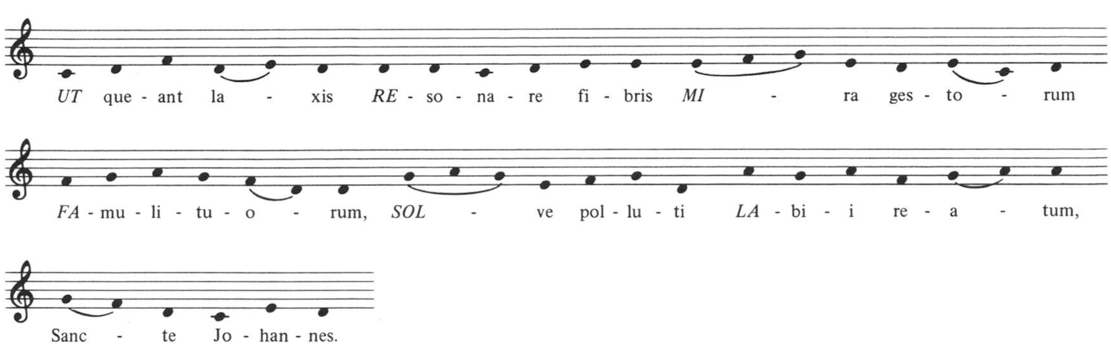

Frequently appearing alongside the *noeane* material is a set of eight Latin texts, each beginning with an ordinal number designating a mode: *Primum quaerite regnum Dei, Secundum autem simile est huic,* and so on. Although not always provided with music, these texts were associated with chant melodies of characteristic modal design. The early-tenth-century tonary of Regino of Prüm (Coussemaker, *Scriptorum de musica mediiaevi* [CS], vol. 2) is among the earliest sources to supply both *noeane* and Latin formulas. The latter gradually came to be cited independently and are copied in theoretical sources long after the *noeane* terms had fallen into disuse. Lambertus' *Tractatus de musica* (*CS*, vol. 1), which dates from about 1270, marks one of last references to the *Primum quaerite* set.

Guido's only direct contribution to solmization appears in his *Epistola de ignoto cantu* (*ca.* 1028; Gerbert, *Scriptores ecclesiastici de musica sacra potissimum* [*GS*], vol. 2). His procedure is based upon the observation that the initial pitches of the first six lines of the hymn *Ut queant laxis* describe a stepwise ascent from C to a, and that if one removes the opening syllable of each of these lines from context, the resultant series of syllables—*ut re mi fa sol la*—will aid in learning unknown chants (Ex. 1).

The assessment of Guido as an innovator is complicated by a number of factors. It is recognized that the text of the hymn is by Paul the Deacon, but the absence of the melody in the form used by Guido from liturgical sources before the thirteenth century suggests that Guido himself adjusted an older version of the melody to suit his pedagogical aims. There is also some possibility that the set of syllables offered by the hymn had been in use in musical instruction prior to Guido's time. In addition, the syllables used by Guido did not enjoy universal acceptance: the series *tri pro de nos te ad* was particularly widespread in theoretical writings, among them five of the earliest manuscripts of the *Epistola.* Finally, Guido did not actually isolate the hexachord as such, nor did he touch in any way in the *Epistola* upon other aspects of solmization as it later developed. Indeed, all that can be confidently claimed is that in positing a fixed relationship between individual pitches and specific mnemonic syllables, Guido's achievement consisted, at the very least, in the synthesis of various elements. Even here, Greek theory provides a precedent, but, apart from the Byzantine scholar Manuel Bryennius (*fl. ca.* 1300), the ancient method of vocalizing seems to have been unknown to medieval musicians.

Guido's second and less direct contribution comes in the seventh and eighth chapters of his *Micrologus* (*ca.* 1026), where he deals with the *affinitas* of pairs of pitches such as A and D, B and E, and C and F. Affinity, contingent upon the separation of the notes in question by the interval of a fourth or fifth, derives from similar configurations of tones and semitones surrounding the paired pitches. Extended to include the coupling of F with B flat, the concept provided an important impetus toward the generation of six-note sets—hexachords—on degrees other than C, and was probably of influence in the development both of hexachordal mutation and of a polyphonic theory reliant upon the vertical combination of notes affiliated through perfect consonances.

Beginning with treatises written as commentaries on Guido's work, the theory of solmization was rapidly disseminated as it became steadily more complex. The hexachordal syllables are explicitly enumerated in the *Commentarium* (1070–1100; Smits van Waesberghe, 1957). The *Liber argumentorum* (1050–1100; *ibid.*) builds hexachords on G's as well as C's, coupling these in a gamut diagram of five overlapping hexachords extending upward to dd. The hexachord on F, requiring a B flat, seems to have been integrated into the system in the late twelfth century, among the earliest sources being the anonymous early-thirteenth-century Louvain treatise (*CS*, vol. 2). Toward the end of the thirteenth century, the gamut of available pitches, shown in the left column of the accompanying table, was extended to include seven complete hexachords, with ee as the uppermost note.

Table 1

ee							la
dd						la	sol
cc						sol	fa
bb						fa	mi
aa					la	mi	re
gg					sol	re	ut
f					fa	ut	
e				la	mi		
d			la	sol	re		
c			sol	fa	ut		
b			fa	mi			
a		la	mi	re			
g		sol	re	ut			
F		fa	ut				
E	la	mi					
D	sol	re					
C	fa	ut					
B	mi						
A	re						
GG	ut						

The use of the hand (usually the left hand) became a mainstay in solmization pedagogy from the eleventh century onward. The hand had long been in use as a calendric device, and had seen musical applications in the area of tetrachordal theory before Guido's time. The first reference to the Guidonian hand as a means of teaching solmization is given by Sigebert of Gembloux at the beginning of the twelfth century, while the drawing of the hand in Monte Cassino, Cloister Archive, manuscript 318, is the earliest known example. The Monte Cassino manuscript, probably copied at the end of the eleventh century from an older French Cluniac source, preserves on the same folio as the hand the notation of the Goliard song "O Roma nobilis" by means of the initial letters of the appropriate solmization syllables. In its developed form, such as that given by Jerome of Moravia, the hand communicated much the same information as the gamut, but enjoyed the advantage of practical utility as a vehicle for demonstration and drill.

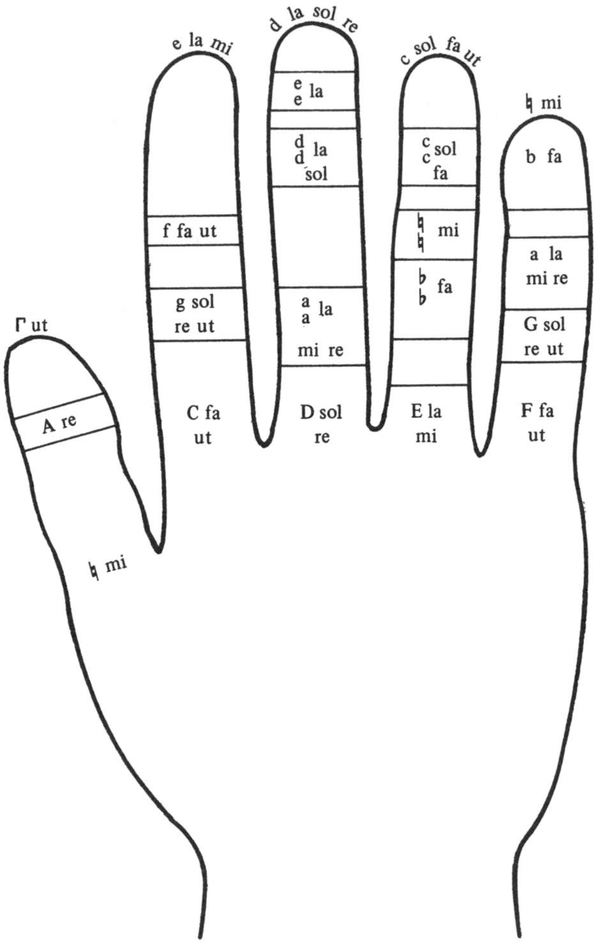

The Guidonian hand

The hexachords on C, G, and F were known as natural, hard, and soft, respectively, the latter two so called because they used either the hard or soft version of the pitch B (that is, B natural as opposed to B flat). Since the ranges of the hexachords overlapped, it became possible, through the technique of mutation, to solmize melodies extending beyond a single six-note set. Mutation involved a shift from one hexachord to another by altering the status of a pivot note. For example, in a stepwise ascent from C to its octave, the a would be converted from *la,* the upper limit of the prevailing natural hexachord, either to *mi,* the third degree of the soft hexachord, or to *re,* the second degree of the hard. The choice of the pivot reflected a desire to delay the mutation as long as possible: the treatises of Amerus (1271; *CSM,* vol. 25), Engelbert of Admont (before 1325; *GS,* vol. 2), and Ugolino of Orvieto (*ca.* 1440; *CSM,* vol. 7) contain diagrams calling for *ut* as the descending and *la* as the ascending syllable before mutation. The opposite technique, wherein the syllables of the new hexachord are introduced at the earliest opportunity, may also have enjoyed some currency.

In addition to a line's range, details of its melodic design exerted a direct influence upon the process of mutation. The presence of the G–c fourth in both hard and soft hexachords meant that the singer's choice between these was based less on a consideration of range than on the need to resolve the intonation of B as *mi* (B natural) or as *fa* (B flat). That all three hexachords could be used in a given melody is clearly implied in the statement, first made in the Louvain treatise and repeated thereafter by most writers on the subject, that a letter with three solmization syllables attached to it could sustain six mutations. Two of these mutations, for example *re* to *ut* and *ut* to *re* on G *sol re ut,* involve the direct transference between soft and hard. The problem of deciding which of these two hexachords was operative at a given time remained problematical until the end of the fifteenth century.

The lack of consensus among theorists is especially evident in the ascending-descending classification of mutations. When undertaken in response to a melody's range, a mutation ending on a syllable from the lower half of the hexachord would be used to ascend, while one ending on *fa, sol,* or *la* would be directed downward. This relationship between the place of each syllable within the hexachord and the subsequent tendency of the line contributed to a division of the syllables into two groups: the *inferiores* (*ut, re,* and *mi*) and the *superiores* (*fa, sol,* and *la*). For mutations involving motion between hard and soft hexachords, however, some writers evidently responded primarily to the fact that the soft hexachord is lower in pitch and that, therefore, any mutation from hard to soft should be considered as descending. Johannes Aegidius of Zamora (1270; *CSM,* vol. 20), Amerus, Marchettus of Padua (1309–1318; Herlinger, 1985), and Jacques de Liège (after 1319; *CSM,* vol. 3) are among those who classify the *ut* to *re* mutation on G *sol re ut* as "descending" for this reason, while other sources, such as Jerome of Moravia, Lambertus, and the *Introductio musice secundum Magistrum de Garlandia* (thirteenth century; *CS,* vol. 1), adhere to the strict distinction underlined by the maxim *Ut, re, mi scandunt; fa, sol, la quoque descendunt.*

The hexachord's internal construction and narrow range made it impossible to deal with melodic leaps of tritones, diminished fifths, minor sixths, and anything wider than a major sixth without an implied mutation. The absence of intervening notes led to anomalous situations, such as the use of *mi–fa* (traditionally associated with the semitone) for both the tritone B to F (Franco of Cologne, thirteenth century; *CS,* vol. 1) and the minor sixth E to c (Louvain treatise). John of Affligem (1100–1121; Babb, 1978) gives *mi–ut* as the solmization for the same leap, while the Louvain treatise continues by using *re–fa* for D to b flat.

Chromatic alteration of pitches in the *musica vera* gamut (GG to ee, with both flat and natural versions of b and bb in the middle and upper octaves) was frequently demanded by cadential voice-leading and by the prohibition of diminished fifths and tritones. Notes governed by added sharps and natural signs were called *mi,* while flattened notes were called *fa* (Marchettus). In general, the transference of solmization syllables to other than their normal locations entailed a shift into *musica falsa,* or *musica ficta,* equated with *falsa mutatio* in the writings of Lambertus, Jacques de Liège, and Philippe de Vitry (*ca.* 1322; *CSM,* vol. 8). Liège cites the conjunction of syllables a third apart, such as *mi* and *sol* on B, as an example of an irregular or false mutation, used here to facilitate an arrival on G sharp below.

The opinions of these theorists notwithstanding, it remains questionable whether semitonal inflections consistently directed the choice of solmization syllables, especially in those frequent instances where the chromaticism was not made explicit through the insertion of accidentals. As dealt with by Lambertus, Elias Salomo (1274; *GS,* vol. 3), and the *Introductio musice secundum Magistrum de Garlandia,* the relationship between *musica falsa* and the act of vocalizing is difficult to determine. Probably referring to the systemic oscillation on B, Bernard of Clairvaux's *Epistola* (*ca.* 1150; *CSM,* vol. 24) calls for the adjustment to be rendered "furtim tamen ac raptim" (covertly and quickly). With respect to solmization, it is probable that many of the adjustments to the musical text were realized *sub rosa.*

In modern terms, the standard range of chromaticism allowed for raised F's, C's, and G's, and lowered E's and A's. To the extent that it was felt necessary to provide a rationale for these notes and their solmization, certain theorists added a number of hexachords to the three in the basic system. Theinred of Dover's use of transposition as a means of deriving hexachords on D and B flat is the earliest known attempt at a systematized approach to the generation of chromatics. The general theory of added hexachords, which were later referred to as *coniunctae,* is echoed and elaborated upon by *Petrus frater dictus Palma ociosa* (*ca.* 1335; Wolf, 1913–1914), the anonymous Berkeley manuscript (*ca.* 1375; Ellsworth, 1984), and numerous writers in the following century, such as Ugolino and John Hothby.

BIBLIOGRAPHY

Three collections contain reprints of many of the medieval treatises cited in the text: Charles Edmond de Coussemaker, *Scriptorum de musica medii aevi* (*CS*) (1864–1876, repr. 1963 in 4 vols.); *Corpus scriptorum de musica* (*CSM*) (1950–); and Martin Gerbert, *Scriptores ecclesiastici de musica sacra potissimum* (*GS*) (1794, repr. 1963 in 3 vols.).

Studies include: Gaston G. Allaire, *The Theory of Hexachords, Solmization, and the Modal System* (1972); Terence Bailey, *The Intonation Formulas of Western Chant* (1974); Jacques Chailley, "*Ut queant laxis* et les origines de la gamme," in *Acta musicologica,* **56** (1984); S[uzanne] C[lercx], "Aux origines de la solmisation," in *Revue belge de musicologie,* **11** (1957); Richard L. Crocker, "Hermann's Major Sixth," in *Journal of the American Musicological Society,* **25** (1972); Oliver B. Ellsworth, trans., *The Berkeley Manuscript: University of California Music Library, MS. 744 (olim Phillipps 4450)* (1984); Jan Herlinger, trans. and ed., *The "Lucidarium" of Marchetto of Padua* (1985); Hans Hickmann, "Ein Beitrag 'zum Problem des Ursprungs der mittelalterlichen Solmisation,'" in *Die Musikforschung,* **10** (1957); Andrew Hughes, *Manuscript Accidentals: Ficta in Focus, 1350–1450* (1972), and "Theinred of Dover," in *The New Grove Dictionary of Music and Musicians,* XVIII (1980); Georg Lange, "Zur Geschichte der Solmisation," in *Sammelbände der internationalen Musikgesellschaft,* **1** (1899–1900); Ina Lohr, *Solmisation und Kirchentonarten,* 2nd ed. (1948); Thomas J. Mathiesen, trans., *Aristides Quintilianus: On Music, in Three Books* (1983); Carl-Allan Moberg, "Die Musik in Guido de Arezzos Solmisationshymne," in *Archiv für Musikwissenschaft,* **16** (1959); Hans Oesch, *Berno und Hermann von Reichenau als Musiktheoretiker* (1961); Hugo Rieman, "Te Ta Tē Tō und No E ANe," in *Zeitschrift der internationalen Musikgesellschaft,* **14** (1912–1913); Franz Ring, "Zur altgriechischen Solmisationslehre," in *Archiv für Musikforschung,* **3** (1938); Charles-Émile Ruelle, "La solmisation chez les anciens Grecs," in *Sammelbände der internationalen Musikgesellschaft,* **9** (1907–1908); Joseph Smits van Waesberghe, *De musicopaedagogico et theoretico Guidone Aretino* (1953), *Expositiones in Micrologum Guidonis Aretini* (1957), and *Musikerziehung: Lehre und Theorie der Musik im Mittelalter* (1969); Walter Wiora, "Zum Problem des Ursprungs der mittelalterlichen Solmisation," in *Die Musikforschung,* **9** (1956).

ARTHUR D. LEVINE

[See also **Aurelian of Réôme; Franco of Cologne; Guido of Arezzo; Jacques de Liège; Noeannoe; Regino of Prüm; Musica Ficta; Musical Notation, Western; Musical Treatises; Vitry, Philippe de.**]

SOLOMON AND MARCOLF are the protagonists in a literary tradition that has roots in Hebrew Scripture and that is still alive today. The tradition was especially productive in the Middle Ages, from which texts survive in more than a half-dozen languages and in nearly as many literary genres. The most influential of these texts is the Latin *Dialogus Salomonis et Marcolfi,* from which are derived not only the majority of the vernacular dialogues, but also dramatic, narrative, and lyric texts in the vernacular.

THE *DIALOGUS SALOMONIS ET MARCOLFI*

The Latin prose *Dialogus* (*D*) consists of two parts. The first is framed by the arrival and departure of Marcolf at the court of King Solomon. Within this narrative frame the two carry on a disputation in which Marcolf opposes each of Solomon's nearly 150 statements with an inconsequent answer. Many of the statements are from Proverbs; others are from other books of the Old and New Testaments, as well as from Cato and elsewhere. Marcolf's responses may take the original with brutal literalness; may mimic the original syntax, filling it with obscene content; or may not establish any connection. The contest is a parody of the scholarly *disputatio,* in which Solomon, representative of the official wisdom of Bible and school, succumbs in the end to the down-to-earth, shameless cleverness of his opponent.

The second part of the *D* comprises a series of anecdotes (many derived from Indo-European tales), in each of which Marcolf gets the better of Solomon. Most of the episodes are organized into one of two series: (1) Marcolf provides proofs for assertions made during a vigil he kept with Solomon; (2) Solomon's famous judgment is followed by his praise of women and, tricked by Marcolf, his denunciation of them. The same cleverness and delight in verbal games that figured in part one are, in part two, developed narratively.

The germ of the contest between Solomon and Marcolf is to be found in Scripture: in the questions put to Solomon by the Queen of Sheba (1 Kings 10:1–3; 2 Chron. 9:1–3), which, along with the king's answers, were recorded in Hebrew legend; and in the exchange of letters between Solomon and Huram (2 Chron. 2:1–16), which, according to a tradition recorded by Josephus, developed into a contest of wisdom, Huram enlisting the aid of Abdemon (or his son). The earliest recorded mention of Marcolf, "contending against the proverbs of Solomon" (Notker Labeo, commentary to Ps. 118:85), indicates that some account of a confrontation between the two (serious like the Hebrew tradition?; irreverent like the *D*?) was known at St. Gall in the tenth century. Indeed, a monastery school is a likely home for the kind of verbal tricks that Marcolf plays on Solomon. Three twelfth-century writers, William of Tyre, Guy de Bazoches (the first and a marginal note to the second explain that Marcolf is the popular name for Abdemon), and Serlo of Wilton, are the first to refer clearly to part two of the *D*. Scholars can no longer determine when the two parts were attached (inconsistencies suggest they were not conceived together), and how their contents changed over the years (the nature of the material and the testimony of the manuscripts suggest there were considerable variations). Although certain gallicisms in the Latin have led some scholars to claim a French or Flemish origin for the *D*, the reference by Notker and the name of Marcolf, as well as the provenience of the extant manuscripts, all make the case for a German genesis much stronger.

The *D* is the most influential of the medieval works in the Solomon and Marcolf tradition. Its popularity is attested by the number of extant manuscripts (nineteen from Germany and two from Poland, all fifteenth-century) and of early printings (twenty-one before 1500 in German, Flemish, Dutch; one from Paris, *ca.* 1500; and one from Venice, 1502), as well as by the number of vernacular works descended from it.

VERNACULAR VERSIONS OF THE *DIALOGUS*

Prose translations of the Latin text were printed in German (over twenty editions, 1482–1670; also two fifteenth-century manuscripts), English (1492), Dutch (1501), Italian (1502), and French (1509). In addition, the *D* was twice translated into German verse. The so-called *Spruchgedicht* incorporates two-thirds of the Latin part one and almost all of part two. In addition, a small amount of new material is introduced in each part, and the story of the abduction of Solomon's wife (related to that in the epic *Salman und Morolf*) is attached to the end. The work is in the four-stress, rhymed couplets of Middle High German courtly epic, a model that may have prompted the introduction of a narrator figure, his professed concern for the "uncourtliness" of the material, and the sporadic appearance of courtly vocabulary. The *Spruchgedicht* seems to have been written in the last quarter of the fourteenth century in the Mosel region. The second German verse translation of the *D* was composed by Gregor Hayden for a Bavarian count between 1459 and 1487. It includes about half the Latin part one and all but the oven episode from part two. Hayden tends to turn the intellectual games of the *D* into moral lessons (Marcolf [!] preaches moderation) and, by turning Marcolf into Solomon's most trusted adviser, reconciles the antagonists in the end (truth, we are told, is helpless without the aid of cunning).

VERNACULAR WORKS DERIVED FROM THE *DIALOGUS*

Material from the *D* tradition figures in a number of works composed in Nuremberg. A *Fastnachtspiel* by Hans Folz (two versions; probably written 1482–1494) is based on selected episodes from part two of the *D*, rearranged but carefully integrated and incorporating (as a dramatic scene) a selection of exchanges from part one. Folz retains both the crudity and the quick intellectuality of the Latin but sets Marcolf (especially in the manuscript version) in a new relation to the larger social order: he has a fixed place in that order (he appears as a peasant and is subject to the moralizing commentary of four peasants) and upsets that order (returning at the end to parody an indulgence seller). Hans Sachs, in three works from 1550, also drew on the *D* tradition—at least on its less crude parts: an episode from part two (Solomon's judgment and its sequel) forming the last two acts of a *comedi;* about forty lines taken nearly verbatim from the *comedi* as well as the genealogies from part one of the *D* figure in a *Fastnachtspiel;* and the first episode of part two, retold in a condensed version as a *Meisterlied.*

At the end of the sixteenth century Giulio Cesare

(della) Croce (*d.* 1609) composed his *Bertoldo.* Besides new material it includes most of the episodes from the *D,* although they have been completely reorganized and King Alboin and Bertoldo have taken the places of Solomon and Marcolf. This work with its two sequels (in the first, Bertoldo's wife, Marcolfa, plays a major role) was translated into German, French, and Spanish. Its great popularity has kept the Solomon and Marcolf tradition alive in Italy, Spain, and Latin America (also in oral tradition, at least in Puerto Rico) until the present day.

DIALOGUES OTHER THAN THE *DIALOGUS*

Two Old English poems of the ninth/tenth centuries known as *Solomon and Saturn* may represent an earlier, more serious tradition of Solomonic dialogues than the *D.* Yet a text of the seventh century, which equates Saturn with Morcholon, suggests that the two traditions are not unrelated. In the first of the Old English poems, Solomon instructs Saturn on the supernatural powers of the Pater Noster; in the second they discuss good and evil, fate and salvation, with Solomon representing the Christian point of view.

Closer to the spirit of the Latin, although they in fact share very little material with it, are two Old French strophic dialogues between Salemons and Marcoul (1160–1240). In the first (edited by Méon), Marcoul answers each of Salemons' statements with parallels from the world of harlots. There are six manuscripts of the work dating from the thirteenth to fifteenth centuries, an undated French printed edition, and one in English from London, around 1527, as well as a bowdlerized translation into Latin. In the second of the Old French dialogues (edited by Crapelet; attributed in the single, thirteenth-century manuscript to a twelfth-century count of Brittany) Marcoul replies to Salemons' remarks (sometimes courtly precepts) from a standpoint less lofty than Salemons' but still completely respectable. There is no narrative in either work, only the rhymed exchanges.

THE MIDDLE HIGH GERMAN EPIC *SALMAN UND MOROLF*

Salman und Morolf, composed in five-line strophes, is generally classified in literary histories under the rubric *Spielmannsepik.* Like other works in this category it falls into two parts, each constructed on the same pattern (the *Brautwerbungsschema*). Here Salman's queen, Salme (originally heathen but captured and baptized by the king), is abducted with her connivance by a heathen king; Morolf discovers their whereabouts and plays tricks on them, then fetches an army (and Salman, part one), defeats the abductor, and returns Salme to Salman. After the second return Morolf kills Salme and Salman marries Affer, the sister of the first abductor. Affer, who had taken Salman's side in part one and later converted to Christianity, represents an alternative to the faithless, heathen Salme, and thus to the essentially negative portrayal of earthly love. The usual contraposition of the protagonists is here transformed; Salman, although structurally the hero, is completely dependent on Morolf, his brother and helper—even the commander of his army. And yet we recognize the traditional Morolf in the repeated tricks and deceptions, some quite crude, that he practices on his enemies and, to a lesser extent, on Salman.

The various stories of the abduction of Salman's wife may have their source in the complications that arise from the biblical Solomon's immoderate love of women (1 Kings 11) and in the talmudic stories of Ashmedai, who, having robbed Solomon of a magical ring, gained power over his lands and wives. An abduction story simpler than but related to the Middle High German epic exists in a sixteenth-century Russian tale; there too, the wife feigns death to aid in her abduction and the king, captured in the attempt to retrieve her, summons his army by blowing three times on a horn. A similar story is told of the Bastard of Bouillon in a fourteenth-century French chanson de geste. The Middle High German epic differs from these tales, however, in the central role played by Salman's brother and helper. Why this role in the abduction story should have come to be filled by Marcolf, Solomon's opponent in the *D* tradition, is not clear. Yet the epic is not the only work to connect the two traditions: both the *Spruchgedicht* and manuscript *S* of the Latin *D* append to their second part, as an additional episode in which Marcolf displays his cleverness to Solomon's discredit, an abduction story clearly related to part one of the epic. And the epic, for its part, incorporates an abbreviated form of an episode from the *D* (Marcolf in the oven). These transpositions, as well as the independent transmission of a single episode of the *Spruchgedicht* (MS *S*), testify to the flexibility shown by all branches of the Solomon and Marcolf tradition.

Although the three extant manuscripts of *Salman*

und Morolf all date from the late fifteenth century (there are also two printed editions: 1499; 1510), the work is generally assumed to have been written in the last third of the twelfth century.

BIBLIOGRAPHY

Sources: The Latin "Dialogus." Walter Benary, ed., *Salomon et Marcolfus* (1914); Piero Camporesi, ed., *Dialogus Salomonis et Marcolphi,* in Giulio Cesare Croce, *Le sottilissime astuzie di Bertoldo: Le piacevoli e ridicolose simplicità di Bertoldino* (1978).

Vernacular versions of the "Dialogus." Edward Gordon Duff, ed., *The Dialogue or Communing Between the Wise King Salomon and Marcolphus* (1892); Friedrich von der Hagen, ed., *Frag' und Antwort König Salomons und Markolfs,* in his *Narrenbuch* (1811); Walter Hartmann, ed., *Salomon und Markolf: Das Spruchgedicht* (1934); Gregor Hayden, *Salomon und Markolf,* in Felix Bobertag, ed., *Narrenbuch* (1885, repr. 1964); Gina Cortese Pagani, ed., *Dialogo di Salomone e Marcolpho,* in *Studi medievali,* **3** (1908–1911); Willem de Vreese and Jan de Vries, eds., *Dat dyalogus of twisprake tusschen den wisen coninck Salomon ende Marcolphus* (1941).

Vernacular works derived from the "Dialogus." Giulio Cesare Croce, *Bertoldo e Bertoldino,* Luigi Emery, ed. (1951); Hans Folz, *Ein spil von könig Salomon und Markolfo,* in Adalbert von Keller, ed., *Fastnachtspiele aus dem fünfzehnten Jahrhundert,* II (1853), "Von dem König Salomon und Markolf und einem Narren," Dietrich Huschenbett, ed., in *Zeitschrift für deutsche Philologie,* **84** (1965), and also in Dieter Wuttke, ed., "Die Druckfassung des Fastnachtspieles von König Salomon und Markolf," in *Zeitschrift für deutsches Altertum und deutsche Literatur,* **94** (1965); Hans Sachs, *Ein comedi, mit acht personen zu recidirn, juditium Salomonis,* in Adalbert von Keller, ed., *Hans Sachs,* VI (1872), and also in Bernhard Arnold, ed., *Hans Sachs' Werke,* II (1884–1885), *Fassnachtspiel, mit 4 personen zu agirn: Von Joseph und Melisso, auch König Salomon,* in Adalbert von Keller and Edmund Goetze, eds., *Hans Sachs,* XIV (1882), and also in Edmund Goetze, ed., *Sämtliche Fastnachtspiele von Hans Sachs,* III, *Elf Fastnachtspiele aus den Jahren 1550 und 1551* (1883), "Marcolfus mit dem kunig Salomo" [*Meisterlied*] in Edmund Goetze and Karl Drescher, eds., *Sämtliche Fabeln und Schwänke von Hans Sachs,* V (1904), 116–117.

Dialogues other than the "Dialogus." Georges A. Crapelet, ed., "Proverbes de Marcoul et de Salemon," in *Porverbes et dictons populaires . . . aux XIIIe et XIVe siècles* (1831), 187–200; Elliot Van Kirk Dobbie, ed., "Solomon and Saturn," in *The Anglo-Saxon Minor Poems* (1942), l–lx, 31–48; John M. Kemble, ed., *The Dialogue of Salomon and Saturnus* (1848), 132–197; Robert J. Menner, ed., *The Poetical Dialogues of Solomon and Saturn* (1941); Dominique M. Méon, ed., "De Marco et de Salemons," in *Nouveau recueil de fabliaux et contes inédits des poetes français . . . ,* I (1823, repr. 1976), 416–436; Thomas Wright, ed., "De Certamine Salomonis et Marcolfi," in *Early Mysteries, and Other Latin Poems of the Twelfth and Thirteenth Centuries* (1838), 131.

The Middle High German epic. Alfred Karnein, ed., *Salman und Morolf* (1979); Friedrich Vogt, ed., *Salman und Morolf* (1880, repr. 1954).

Studies: On the Latin "Dialogus." Giovanni Luigi Biagioni, *Marcolf und Bertoldo und ihre Beziehungen* (1930), 44–100; Maria Corti, "Models and Antimodels in Medieval Culture," in *New Literary History,* **10** (1979); Emmanuel Cosquin, "Le conte du *Chat et de la chandelle* dans l'Europe du moyen âge et en Orient," in *Romania,* **40** (1911), and also in *Études folkloriques* (1922); Michael Curschmann, *"Spielmannsepik": Wege und Ergebnisse der Forschung von 1907–1965* (1968), 19–25; Edward Gordon Duff, ed. *The Dialogue or Communing Between the Wise King Salomon and Marcolphus* (1892), 34–44; Edmond Faral, "Pour l'histoire de 'Berte au grand pied' et de 'Marcoul et Salomon,'" in *Romania,* **40** (1911); Walter Haug, "Theoderichs Ende und ein tibetisches Märchen," in Hugo Kuhn and Kurt Schier, eds., *Märchen, Mythos, Dichtung: Festschrift zum 90. Geburtstag Friedrich von der Leyens* (1963); Wilhelm Kaspars, "Germanische Götternamen," in *Zeitschrift für deutsches Altertum und deutsche Literatur,* **83** (1951/1952); John M. Kemble, ed., *The Dialogue of Salomon and Saturnus* (1848), 1–133, 198–326; Paul Lehmann, *Die Parodie im Mittelalter,* 2nd rev. ed. (1963); Werner Lenk, "Zum Sprichwort-Antithetik im Salomon-Markolf-Dialog," in *Forschungen und Fortschritte,* 39 (1965); Irmgard Meiners, *Schelm und Dümmling in Erzählungen des deutschen Mittelalters* (1967), 134–147, 161–164; H.-Fr. Rosenfeld, "Salman und Morolf," in Karl Langosch, ed., *Die deutsche Literatur des Mittelalters: Verfasserlexikon,* IV (1952) 4–21; Erika Schönbrunn-Kölb, "*Markolf* in den mittelalterlichen Salomondichtungen und in deutscher Wortgeographie," in *Zeitschrift für Mundartforschung,* **25** (1957); Samuel Singer, *Sprichwörter des Mittelalters,* I (1944), 33–57; Friedrich Vogt, ed., *Salman und Morolf* (1880), xli–lxxviii; Willem de Vreese and Jan de Vries, eds., *Dat dyalogus of twisprake tusschen den wisen coninck Salomon ende Marcolphus* (1941), 40–72.

On vernacular versions of the "Dialogus." Giovanni Luigi Biagioni, *Marcolf und Bertoldo und ihre Beziehungen* (1930), 9–26; Ernst Schaubach, *Gregor Hayden's Salomon und Marcolf* (1881).

On vernacular works derived from the "Dialogus." Giovanni Luigi Biagioni, *Marcolf und Bertoldo und ihre Beziehungen* (1930), 26–102; Eckehard Catholy, *Das Fastnachtspiel des Spätmittelalters: Gestalt und Funktion* (1961), 13–138; Dietrich Huschenbett, ed., "Von dem König Salomon und Markolf und einem Narren," in

Zeitschrift für deutsche Philologie, **84** (1965); Gina Cortese Pagani, ed., *Dialogo di Salomone e Marcolpho,* in *Studi medievali,* 3 (1908–1911); Dieter Wuttke, ed., "Die Druckfassung des Fastnachtspieles von König Salomon und Markolf," in *Zeitschrift für deutsches Altertum und deutsche Literatur,* **94** (1965).

On the Middle High German epic. Ingeborg Benath, "Vergleichende Studien zu den Spielmannsepen König Rother, Orendel und Salman und Morolf," in *Beiträge zur Geschichte der deutschen Sprache und Literatur* (Halle), **84** (1962), 312–372, **85** (1963), 374–416; Rolf Bräuer, *Literatursoziologie und epische Struktur der deutschen "Spielmanns"- und Heldendichtung* (1970); Michael Curschmann, *Der Münchener Oswald und die deutsche spielmännische Epik* (1964), 87–100, and *"Spielmannsepik": Wege und Ergebnisse der Forschung von 1907–1965* (1968), 19–25, 81–83; Theodor Frings and Max Braun, *Brautwerbung,* I (*Berichte über die Verhandlungen der Sächischen Akademie der Wissenschaften zu Leipzig, Phil.-hist. Klasse,* 96, 2) (1947); H. W. J. Kroes, "Zum mhd. *Salman und Morolf,*" in *Neophilologus,* **30** (1946); Edyta Połczyńska, *Studien zum "Salman und Morolf"* (1968); H.-Fr. Rosenfeld, "Salman und Morolf," in Karl Langosch, ed., *Die deutsche Literatur des Mittelalters: Verfasserlexikon,* IV (1952), 7–13; Friedrich Vogt, ed., *Salman und Morolf* (1880), i–clx.

JAMES A. SCHULTZ

[See also **Anglo-Saxon Literature; Folz, Hans; Middle High German Literature; Scholasticism, Scholastic Method.**]

SOLOMON BEN ISAAC OF TROYES. See **Rashi [Rabbi Solomon ben Isaac].**

SOLOMON BEN JUDAH IBN GABIROL (Avicebron, Avicebrol) (*ca.* 1020–*ca.* 1058 or 1070), one of Andalusian Jewry's major poets and philosophers. Born in Málaga and raised in Saragossa, Ibn Gabirol transcended poverty and isolation to achieve fame among Jews, mostly for his Hebrew poetry, for which he received patronage in Saragossa and Granada. His poems, some 400 in all, cover all the secular and sacred genres of his day and manifest broad familiarity with both Arabic poetry and Jewish tradition. A number of his poems have been incorporated into the liturgy, the most famous being the long philosophical and yet personal epic *Keter Malkhut* (The kingly crown).

Ibn Gabirol's philosophical prose writing consists of one or two small ethical treatises and a large, extraordinary work of metaphysical speculation. This latter treatise, written in Arabic, has no specific or explicit Jewish references, a fact that contributed, no doubt, to the disappearance of the original version. Although Hebrew selections were rendered by Shem Tov ibn Falaquera in the thirteenth century, it is as the *Fons vitae* (The fountain of life), the twelfth-century Latin translation of Johannes Hispalensus (known too as Aven Dauth and Ibn Daud) and Dominicus Gundissalinus, that the work became well known to the West, where it enjoyed some influence among thirteenth- and fourteenth-century Franciscan thinkers. (Ibn Gabirol, known as Avicebron, was generally thought to be a Muslim.) In Jewish circles the work, in one form or another, affected the thirteenth-century mystics of the Gerona circle as well as diverse Jewish Neoplatonists up to the Renaissance figure of Leone Ebreo (León Hebreo, *d.* 1535).

Fons vitae actually combines at least two major conceptual schemes, Aristotelian hylomorphism and Neoplatonic emanationism. Ibn Gabirol posits the existence of a universal form and matter superimposed upon the Plotinian hypostases of universal intellect, soul, and nature. As universal substances, form and matter are judged to be dual principles of being that offset the single effulgence that "creates" the universal intelligence common to classical Neoplatonism. Universal form and matter in Ibn Gabirol's scheme are understood to actually precede the appearance of this first intelligence; and it too is seen as a hylomorphic entity (*Fons vitae* 1.17; 4.1–6; 5.1, 30, 35).

These teachings find vivid application particularly in the fifth book of this work, where Ibn Gabirol contends that matter is the particular object of divine knowledge, related to God's essence, while form is the expression of divine will (5.30, 42). Form and matter are thus in principle located in the divine being itself. Qua matter, this being is for Ibn Gabirol ever-becoming, potential, the basis for all change and diversity. The divine will builds upon this "material" base. Forms issue forth from God, and the world in its diversity is "created" as a result of the natural affinity of matter for form. Divine unity itself is thus a complex affair, and the universe in its entirety shares with the One the same basic principles of being, which for Ibn Gabirol means that the whole world is infused with God's presence.

SOMNIUM VIRIDARII

BIBLIOGRAPHY
Ibn Gabirol, *Avencebrolis Fons vitae,* Clemens Bäumker, ed. (1895), *La source de vie* in *Mélanges de philosophie juive et arabe,* Salomon Munk, ed. (1859), *La source de vie livre III,* Fernand Brunner, trans. (1950), *The Fountain of Life,* Harry E. Wedeck, trans. (1962), *The Improvement of the Moral Qualities,* Stephen S. Wise, trans. (1902), *Choice of Pearls,* Abraham Cohen, ed. and trans. (1925), *Selected Religious Poems,* Israel Davidson, ed. and Israel Zangwill, trans. (1930), *The Kingly Crown,* Bernard Lewis, trans. (1961), *Salomo Ibn Gabirol: Ostwestliches Dichtertum,* Frederick Bargebuhr, ed. and trans. (1976); Shlomo Pines, "Gabirol, Solomon ben Judah, Ibn," in *Encyclopaedia judaica* (1971), for a full bibliography; Jacques Schlanger, *La philosophie de Salomon ibn Gabirol* (1968).

ALFRED L. IVRY

[See also **Aristotle in the Middle Ages; Hebrew Poetry; Jews in Muslim Spain; Judaism; Neoplatonism; Philosophy and Theology, Jewish: Islamic World.**]

SOMNIUM VIRIDARII (The orchard dream) is one of the most celebrated texts of late medieval Latin literature. The lengthy work was prepared at the command of Charles V of France in the 1370's. In a prologue the narrator addresses the king and explains that, while asleep and dreaming in an orchard, he observed the king and the personifications of temporal and spiritual power together. The two powers summoned a clergyman (*clericus*) and a knight (*miles*) to represent their respective positions in a debate over their differences. An extended dialogue of 552 speeches by the advocates follows, in the course of which all sorts of questions are dealth with, including not only the nature of political power and the proper relationship between lay and clerical authority within Christian society, but also contemporary matters such as the return of the papacy to Rome, the reconquest of Brittany, and the inheritance rights of women. Although anticlerical in tone, the discussion is conducted in orthodox terms. The knightly defender of royal sovereignty and the clerical defender of papal supremacy are equally adept in supporting their cases with materials from the church fathers as well as medieval theologians. This virtual encyclopedia of late medieval political thought concludes with an epilogue in which the narrator awakens and presents his report to the king.

The dream vision was a highly regarded medieval literary form and offered a useful device for the presentation of controversial ideas. Within the formulaic confines of dream literature an author could work secure in the fiction that he was presenting ideas for which he was not personally responsible and confident that his work would be all the more persuasive, in that it assumed the force of a revelation. The *Somnium* appeared in 1376 and was quickly revised, appearing as the *Songe du vergier* in 1378. The differences in the two versions reflect the rapid evolution of political thought at the Valois court in this era of crisis and war. The scholarly *Somnium* is perhaps intended for an audience at court; the shorter (468 speeches), more emphatic *Songe* evidently appeals to a broader audience in its use of the vernacular. Published anonymously, the two editions together bear the marks of hurried committee scholarship producing a tendentious manifesto. The reader is offered an astonishing assembly of unattributed, and sometimes unidentifiable, selections from sources such as the *Disputatio inter clericum et militem* and the *Defensor pacis.* Originality is found less in argumentation than in the editorial judgment that produced this compendium for the defense of autonomous lay authority.

Written at court with royal support, the *Somnium* drew on the intellectual traditions of the University of Paris, as well as the older literature of imperial-papal confrontation, to create a uniquely French text defending the sovereign independence of the kings of France from both papacy and empire. Here emerged the Gallican tradition equivocating between orthodoxy and independence that would climax under the Bourbon monarchs in the works of Pierre Dupuy and Pierre Pithou.

Condemned by Rome and more often exploited as a source than understood as a text, the *Somnium* was nonetheless reproduced and cited regularly from the fifteenth to the eighteenth century. Only since the French Revolution has it won the recognition and scholarly attention it deserves as a monument of late medieval political thought in its own right.

BIBLIOGRAPHY
The earliest surviving manuscripts of the *Somnium* are in Paris, Bibliothèque Nationale, fonds latin, MS 3180C and MS 3459A. The original of the *Songe du vergier* is in London, British Museum, MS Royal 19 C.IV. A modern scholarly edition of the latter work is Marion Schnerb-Lièvre, ed., *La songe du vergier* (1982). A reproduction of the 1668 edition of the *Somnium viridarii*

published by Melchior Goldast is in *Revue du moyen-âge latin,* 22 (1966). A reproduction of the 1731 Brunet edition of the *Songe du vergier* is in *Revue du moyen-âge latin,* 13–14 (1957–1958).

Major modern secondary sources include F. Chatillon, "Notes brèves et premières remarques sur quelques accidents survenus de nos jours dans l'étude du *Somnium Viridarii,*" in *Revue du moyen-âge latin,* 12 (1956), and, with Marion Schnerb-Lièvre, "Avant-propos et les éditions et les manuscrits du *somnium viridarii,*" in *Revue du moyen-âge latin,* 22 (1966); Jeannine Quillet, *La philosophie politique du Songe du vergier (1378): Sources doctrinales* (1977); Jean Pierre Royer, *L'église et le royaume de France au XIVe d'après le "Songe du vergier" et la jurisprudence du Parlement* (1969).

PAUL SOLON

[See also **Charles V of France; Defensor Pacis; Disputatio inter Clericum et Militem; France, 1314–1498; Kingship, Theories of; Political Theory, Western European; Schism, Great; Visions.**]

SONDERGOTIK, a stylistic term (German: *sonder,* "peculiar," and *Gotik,* "Gothic") referring to the supposedly specific German developments in late Gothic architecture of the fourteenth and, especially, fifteenth centuries. The style includes such features as complex geometric ground plans, irregular wall planes, spiral supports, freestanding tracery screens, and intricate vaulting construction and patterns. These features are by no means limited to the Germanic areas of medieval Europe.

Vault of St. Georg, Nordlingen, showing *Sondergotik*-style construction, *ca.* 1450. PHOTO: WIM SWAAN

BIBLIOGRAPHY

Paul Frankl, *Gothic Architecture* (1962), 185–212; Kurt Gerstenberg, *Deutsche Sondergotik,* rev. ed. (1969).

CARL F. BARNES, JR.

[See also **Burghausen, Hanns von; Gothic Architecture; Gothic, Flamboyant; Roriczer, Conrad; Strasbourg Cathedral; Ulrich von Ensingen.**]

SONG OF LEWES (Carmen de bello Lewensi), one of several political poems concerning the period of baronial rule in England (1258–1265). It is a Latin work of 968 lines. The first half celebrates the victory of the army of Simon de Montfort, earl of Leicester, over forces led by King Henry III and his son Prince Edward at Lewes (Sussex) on 14 May 1264. The second half explains the ideal of good governance to which the rebels led by de Montfort aspired. It is an anonymous work, but a strong case has been made that the author was a Franciscan friar who was present at the battle in the entourage of Earl Simon. An equally strong case has been made that the poem was written in the latter half of 1264, that is to say, that it is an almost immediate account of the events at Lewes.

The poem survives in a single manuscript written probably at Reading Abbey. It is not divided into stanzas, but the lines (each usually of thirteen syllables in trochaic meter) are in rhyming couplets, and the syllables at the caesuras in each line are also rhymed in pairs. The style is heavily alliterative.

BIBLIOGRAPHY

A critical edition of the poem is provided by Charles L. Kingsford, ed. and trans., *The Song of Lewes* (1890); and, with revisions of the translation by Sir Maurice Powicke, in *English Historical Documents,* III, 899–912.

WILLIAM CHESTER JORDAN

[See also **Barons' War; Edward I of England; Henry III of England; Simon de Montfort the Younger.**]

SONG OF ROLAND. See **Roland, Song of.**

SORCERY. See **Magic; Witchcraft.**

SÖRLA SAGA STERKA (The story of Sörli the Strong), one of the youngest of the *fornaldarsögur* (stories of ancient times), was probably written in the fifteenth century and survives only in post-medieval manuscripts. There is no indication that the author made use of oral tradition; the central plot is based on chapters 3 and 4 of *Sörla þáttr,* and other materials are borrowed from *Hálfdanar saga Brönufóstra* and elsewhere.

The title hero is a Norwegian prince who, at the age of fifteen, sets out on a Viking expedition with five ships and a band of brave warriors. In the autumn, after winning every battle they fight and adding eight ships to their fleet, Sörli and his men set sail for Norway, but are driven off course to the shores of a strange country, where he kills black people and man-eating ogres, but spares the life of a giantess, who rewards him with her protection and some splendid gifts, including a sword and armor coming from Emperor Maskabert of the Saracens, "which once belonged to the great champion Pantíparus, who ruled Greece after Emperor Agamemnon."

Back in Scandinavia, Sörli is soon put to the test again. One of the kings of Norway has a beautiful daughter, whose hand is sought by a formidable berserk from a faraway country. The rejection of the suitor leads to battle, and the king enlists Sörli's help. The enemy ranks include mighty blacks, a sorcerer who transforms himself into a venom-spewing dragon, and a powerful warrior from Poland riding on an elephant. After winning the battle, Sörli sets out again, this time to Africa and the Red Sea.

Next he fights a naval battle with the legendary Hálfdan Brönufóstri, killing him and taking his dragon-headed longship as war booty. This leads to a series of clashes with Hálfdan's sons, who make one abortive attempt after another to avenge their father. As in *Sörla þáttr,* one of them is killed and the other becomes Sörli's blood brother. The tale ends with a triple wedding: each of the erstwhile enemies marries the other's sister, and one of Hálfdan's warriors marries the princess whose unwelcome suitor Sörli had killed.

Essentially a catalog of battles and other heroic exploits, *Sörla saga sterka* lacks the humor and suspense of earlier Icelandic adventure tales. The author shows little interest in characterization, but more in action. The anticipatory description of the hero tells us that at the age of fifteen he was highly accomplished, handsome in appearance, and exceptionally strong, but it says nothing about his other attributes. Whereas in *Sörla þáttr* it is the hero's greed that makes him attack and kill Hálfdan in order to get the dragon-headed ship, in *Sörla saga sterka* the ship is said to have belonged to Sörli's uncle, whom Hálfdan has killed, so Sörli is fully justified in claiming it. Other writers of adventure tales appear to have grasped the fact that it is inadequate to motivate the hero with nothing beyond a desire to make a name for himself as a fighter and a killer; but the author of *Sörla saga sterka* did not grasp this essential point. The ultimate reward for Sörli's efforts, the hand of his victim's daughter, who is not even given the individuality of a name, seems a clumsy contrivance to reach a conventionally happy ending.

BIBLIOGRAPHY
Guðni Jónsson, ed., *Fornaldarsögur Norðurlanda,* III (1950), 369–410; A. G. van Hamel, "The Saga of Sörli the Strong," in *Acta philologica scandinavica,* 10 (1935/1936).

HERMANN PÁLSSON

[See also **Fornaldarsögur; Hálfdanar Saga Brönufóstra.**]

SOUFFLET (dagger; German: *Blase* or *Fischblase*) was one of the basic motifs used in late Gothic window tracery design. The form, which appears on the Continent in the nave chapels of Amiens Cathedral around 1373, may reflect influence from the Decorated Style of English architecture. Symmetrical and composed of two double-curved bars of tracery, the soufflet became the Flamboyant substitute for the polylobes and oculi of earlier High and Rayonnant Gothic window patterns. This use of sinuous line achieved the complete integration of compositional elements and imparted a sense of organic continuity that is characteristic of late Gothic tracery.

BIBLIOGRAPHY
Lottlisa Behling, *Gestalt und Geschichte des Masswerks* (1944), 28–56; Jean Bony, *The English Decorated Style: Gothic Architecture Transformed, 1250–1350* (1979), 28–29; Wim Swaan, *The Late Middle Ages* (1977), 64, 223.

MICHAEL T. DAVIS

[See also **Gothic Architecture; Gothic, Flamboyant; Gothic, Rayonnant; Mouchette; Tracery.**]

SOZOMEN **(Salamanes Hermeios Sozomenos,** *ca.* 400–*ca.* 450), born in a village near Gaza, was a lawyer trained in the school of rhetoric at Gaza. He later moved to Constantinople, where he wrote his *Ecclesiastical History,* a continuation of Eusebius in nine books. This work, written between 439 and 450, was dedicated to Emperor Theodosius II (408–450) and covers the period from 324 to 439. Sozomen's original intention was to write a history of the church from its origins to his own times, but since others had already written about the earlier period, he summarized it and concentrated on his own times. The period after 421 is treated sketchily, and it is possible that the imperial censor removed some contemporary material. Sozomen used many of the same sources as Socrates Scholasticus as well as other early historians, and was inspired to write his history by the work of Socrates.

BIBLIOGRAPHY
An edition of the Greek text of the *Ecclesiastical History* with Latin translation is in *Patrologia graeca,* LXVII (1859), 843–1,630. A study and short biography is G. Bardy, "Sozomène," in *Dictionnaire de théologie catholique,* XIV, pt. 2 (1941).

LINDA C. ROSE

[See also **Byzantine Literature; Eusebius of Caesarea; Historiography, Byzantine; Socrates Scholasticus.**]

SPĀHBAD (Pahlavi, from Old Iranian **spāda-pati-* "chief of an army"; Armenian loan-word *sparapet,* from the Northwestern Middle Iranian of the Arsacid period), the title of a military commander in Sasanian Iran. Under the Parthians, the noble clan of the Kārēns (from Old Iranian: *kāra-* "army") seem to have possessed the hereditary rank of commanders of the cavalry, and a Parthian family called Spāhbad, of Hyrcania, is mentioned in the third-century trilingual "victory" inscription of Šābuhr I on the Ka^{c}ba of Zoroaster (Ka^{c}ba-yi Zardušt) at Naqsh-i Rustam. Under the early Sasanians, the commander-in-chief was called *spāhbad spāhbadān* (as found in the sixth-century *Letter of Tansar,* the high priest) or *ērān spāhbad,* "commander of Iran": he led the army, exercised diplomatic functions, and administered districts of the country. He commanded regional governors (*marzbān*) in wars; the office of provincial ruler (*pāygōspān*) was subordinate to him.

Xusrō (Khusrau) I (*r.* 531–579) split the office of commander-in-chief among four *spāhbad*s (or *spāhsālār*s, of identical meaning), one for each of the four points of the compass. The army was one of the three estates of ancient Iranian society, and the office of commander was the most prestigious and closest to the Sasanian throne, after the Zoroastrian high priesthood. Xusrō I sought to diminish the potentially dangerous power of the *spāhbad* while seeming to bestow honor on the nobles appointed to the new posts.

BIBLIOGRAPHY
Mary Boyce, trans., *The Letter of Tansar* (1968); Arthur Christensen, *L'Iran sous les Sassanides* (1936, 2nd ed. 1944); Nina G. Garsoïan, "Byzantium and the Sasanians," in *Cambridge History of Iran,* III, pt. 1 (1983), 568–592, esp. 588–589; V. G. Lukonin, "Political, Social, and Administrative Institutions: Taxes and Trade," *ibid.,* pt. 2, 681–746, esp. 689; A. Perikhanian, "Iranian Society and Laws," *ibid.,* 627–680, esp. 642, 645.

JAMES R. RUSSELL

[See also **Ardešīr (Ardashir, Artaxeres) I; Ka^{c}ba of Zoroaster; Naqsh-i Rustam; Šabuhr (Shahpuhr) I; Sasanians; Sparapet; Xusrō I Anōšarwān.**]

SPAIN. See **Aragon; Asturias-León; Castile; Catalonia; Navarre; Valencia.**

SPAIN, CHRISTIAN-MUSLIM RELATIONS

PROBLEMS OF INTERPRETATION

Muslim-Christian interaction was constant and varied from 711 to 1609, and discerning the patterns and meaning within this complexity is an interpretative task of demanding subtlety. The "school" of Américo Castro, which included the Jews in this interaction, saw this dynamic as the basic evolution of Spanish Christian history and character. As textbook stereotypes collapse under advances in the knowledge of Mediterranean and Spanish history, new frameworks for studying the problem become clear. Specific time settings offer altered contexts. Each term of the relationship evolved from decade to decade: The ruralized Iberian Peninsula of 1000, like Western Europe in general, differed from the sophisticated twelfth century, just as Umayyad society differed from the Almoravid; and the thirteenth-century Mudejars differed from those of the fourteenth century. In terrain, few countries were so regionally diverse: The socioeconomic ecologies of the high meseta differed strikingly from the seaward-oriented Mediterranean regions; the Pyrenean from the Andalusian; and northern from southern Valencia. Even within the Aragonese-Catalan realm its two Christian peoples had different languages, moneys, parliaments, calendars, social classes, and economies.

Not only did each pole of the Muslim-Christian interaction regularly change, so that modern historical analysis of the kaleidoscopic relationships had to assume a priori the spatio-temporal isolation of the peninsula in order to limit and organize the data, but also the very fields of cultural interaction and interface constantly changed in their myriad forms: military (wars, crusades, alliances, piracy, armies mutually loaned, weaponry borrowed), commercial (merchant enclaves, commodity interdependence, money linkage), intellectual (metaphysics, medicine, science), artistic (literary themes and genres, linguistic influences, architectural and sculptural influences, musical forms and instruments, and so on), and all the other areas of early medieval acculturation.

Before 1000 the backward Christian Spanish states were under heavy cultural tutelage to their powerful neighbor in Al-Andalus. In the twelfth century, however, formal borrowing by a more self-confident Christian society became a program, transforming Europe profoundly; and in the thirteenth century, Christian Spanish states, already advanced as technological and urban-commercial societies, asserted themselves against a demoralized Al-Andalus while borrowing enthusiastically both across political boundaries and from large enclaves of conquered Muslims.

These interacting and mutually acculturating societies were neither so alien nor so inimical as they appear to modern eyes. Both were forms of a common Hellenistic culture; European subcultures, especially, resonated sympathetically to Byzantine-Iraqi elements under Islamic presidency. Both world religions shared much content and modality; Muslims recognized Christians as a revelational "people of the Book," while to Christians Islam approximated the Arian Christianity professed by the Visigoths during half their rule over Catholic Spain. Peter the Venerable remarked that "they agree with us about many things concerning Christ," more so than the Jews [quoted in James Kritzeck, *Peter the Venerable and Islam* (1964)]. Both societies shared Mediterranean traits, sensibilities, theocratic bias, dress, diet, and rural techniques. The aristocratic and urban classes had similar codes, attitudes, and social structures. (In contrast, the Germanized and parochial northern European societies, with their many pagan borrowings, perceived Islamic elements as scandalously alien.) Yet, a conventional rhetoric of hostility on both sides masked this convergence. Each—Christian and Muslim—remained an exclusivist religious society whose structure subtly altered every common element.

MUDEJARS

Before 1000 informal acculturation was probably the most decisive phase both to and from the Spanish Christian states. During this same period, the Christians' minor border advances were directed into ill-favored, relatively uninhabited buffer zones on the northern and eastern high meseta, whose isolated Islamic populations fled, leaving few Muslims to be absorbed into the backward economies and minimal governments of the Christian states. After 1050 the increasingly prosperous Christians began taking over scattered pieces of the party (*ṭāʾifa*) states, which had emerged from the defunct caliphate. Christians followed the pattern of Islam's *dhimma* in maintaining the conquered communities (Mudejars) as independent enclaves, each with its religious institutions, law, and inner administration intact, but progressively sealed off from the dominant society. The system "tolerated" extensively, but also exiled such communities to humiliatingly inferior status. It followed the logic of both the Christian and the Islamic cosmos: Citizenship and real participation in a religious society required at least nominal membership in that religion, since both the Islamic and the Christian political theories saw society as the earthly expression of religious values and a road to paradise, rather than as a secular autonomy accidentally and adventitiously linked to a religion.

According to Reyna Pastor de Togneri, after the conquest of Toledo in 1085 Alfonso VI borrowed directly and specifically from the Muslims to develop the pattern of Islamic life now called Mudejar. The Mozarabic governor Sisnando Davidiz supposedly instructed him in the "attitudes and norms" proper to this novelty. Similarly, Menéndez Pidal and José Lacarra suggest that Alfonso the Battler of Aragon (*r.* 1104–1134), who served as an adventurous prince with the Cid, borrowed his pattern from the Cid's Valencia. Belief in such mechanical imitations overlooks analogous Latin antecedents, the cumulative impact of informal acculturation between neighbors, and a general Mediterranean cultural substratum.

Restrictions were common but persecution rare; Islamic and Christian authorities alike reserved persecutory energies for their heterodox coreligionists. The elites and classes living under their patronage, including theologians, scientists, and literary figures, tended to emigrate; those ambitious to share in the power structure or in the society as a whole converted. The majority of the Muslim population who remained experienced the social pressures inherent in their subordination and tended to acculturate in many small ways while simultaneously recoiling and hardening in their religious beliefs and social practices. The victorious Christians lived around and among these Muslims, borrowing systematically and often enthusiastically. This "Mudejar fact" eroded progressively as Roman law transformed the tradition, the church, and the presiding sovereignties.

The debated etymology of the term *mudéjar* seems to indicate that its probable source is the Arabic *mudajjan,* a word that combines ideas of permanence and "being left behind." Ramón Martí's thirteenth-century word-list of eastern Spanish Arabic translated the term as *tributarius,* that is, as the *dhimma,* an internal tributary state in mosaic fragments. In their developing Romance tongues, Christians early on began to call Muslims in both Islamic and Christian Spain "Moors," from Classical and early Mozarabic Latin for North Africans; in Latin writing they preferred "Saracens." Derived from the Arabic, the Spanish *aljama* meant both a Mudejar community and its council of sheikhs; the term *morería* meant the Muslim quarter or, by extension, the juridical sum of an area's Mudejars. Like the Christians, most Muslims were farmers and were prized for their agricultural skills. The extent to which a normal contingent of merchants, craftsmen, jurists, and professionals remained at a given conquered locality needs much study. Mudejars, like Jews, came directly under the king's protection and theoretical jurisdiction; in practice either the king or a lord (ecclesiastical or lay) had immediate jurisdiction and collected rents. To the scandal of northern European lords, Mudejar militia performed army service for their Christian rulers.

In Portugal and on Spain's meseta from the 1030's, tribute paid to the newly aggressive Christians prepared the way for pacts with the Mudejars. The fall of Toledo (1085) supplied an early example of these agreements; Mudejars retained their residence, religion and main mosque, property, security, tax obligations, and rights to emigrate or to return. Similarly in 1094 the Cid offered Valencia the traditional guarantees, including its own administrative, fiscal, and religious personnel, former tax obligations, and retention of farms under the new landlords. Twenty years later Alfonso I the Battler conquered the eastern meseta so rapidly that 70 percent of his subjects in Aragon were Muslims. Terms for the surrender of the Saragossa district in 1118 allowed Mudejars to keep Islamic religious, legal, fiscal, and administrative systems; he guaranteed all property except that specifically vacated by treaty (for example, he ordered them to vacate the capital for the suburbs).

Similar treaties or constitutions marked the Christian advance down the Ebro Valley. By laws of war a quick and total victory could not forestall or control a massacre, while a delayed victory won the conquered only a safe-conduct exile. Thus each side found it advantageous not to allow a siege to develop beyond the point of the traditional negotiated peace. Christian lords preferred an undamaged and prosperous tax-paying community, especially since Christian immigrants were relatively scarce and any king would feel proud to be an imperial "ruler of three religions" on the Byzantine and Islamic model. Tudela in northeast Aragon supplies our earliest intact charter, interlinear Arabic-Latin in the lost original (1119), spelling out the usual guarantees: no Christian could enter a Moor's house or farm uninvited, nor could labor service be required of Moors, nor could their arms be confiscated. Tortosa at the Ebro's mouth surrendered by a similar pact (1148), as did Lérida and Fraga near the Aragonese-Catalan border (1149). Though few exemplars of such pacts survive, James I the Conqueror of Aragon (Joume I in Catalonia) persuaded Muslims to surrender by pointing to general past custom: "I have many Saracens in my country; my dynasty kept them formerly in Aragon and Catalonia"; all preserved their religio-social structure "just as well as if they were in the country of the Saracens."

The surges of the "Reconquest" in the eleventh and twelfth centuries gave each small state a portion of the Mudejar population and transformed the dynamics of their societies. The Berber invasions, first Almoravid and then Almohad, halted these two Christian advances, each time stabilizing and allowing mutual consolidation. Then, in the confusion attending Almohad collapse for a half century after the Battle of Las Navas de Tolosa in 1212, both Castile-León and Aragon-Catalonia swept relentlessly over the heartlands of Al-Andalus, leaving only a tributary rump sultanate behind Granada's mountains. The new Mudejar communities contrasted with those of the previous two military surges, because they were larger, more cohesive, and more capable of serious revolts. Castile settled Christians in the larger conquered cities, organizing rural Muslims into extensive estates under lay or ecclesiastical lords. The Valencian or Mediterranean littoral scattered its Christian colonial minority widely, both in populations atolls and in some regions mixed with the Muslims in the characteristic small-farm pattern. Yet these generalizations obscure not only the distinct dynamic followed by various regions (Murcia, the Balearics, Valencia, and Andalusia) but the separate patterns within a region (for example, northern, southern, and central Valencia experienced different levels of Christian immigration and different patterns of political and agricultural organization).

Revolts at Murcia in 1266 and in the Valencian kingdom in each decade from 1240 to 1280, and those connected with Abū Yūsuf's invasion of 1275, afforded the Christian kings excuses for expelling Mudejar leaders, confiscating choice lands and towns, and thinning out the feared Muslim masses, which in turn increasingly ruralized Mudejar populations. Interchange in the form of technological and linguistic borrowings, popular fashions and entertainment, and commerce nevertheless continued. From the Black Death of the mid fourteenth century, the Mudejar constitutions for either renegotiations or agreements for settling new lands grew harsher in their economic and legal impositions. Restrictive laws by church and state, not too serious an irritant in the thirteenth century, increased in virulence and effectiveness during the fourteenth.

REGIONAL EVOLUTION

Manuscript materials for the Mudejars abound from the thirteenth century on, particularly for Mediterranean Spain; but whether royal, municipal, ecclesiastical, or private, they remain largely unstudied. Histories have relied until recently on legal, chronicle, literary, and artistic evidence, plus a very narrow range of charters. Thus, we know much about Mudejar liberties, the repressive laws that eroded them, the elementary workings of their administrative-judicial-religious structure, and their contributions to architecture. More serious research since the 1930's has accelerated dramatically, a phenomenon celebrated by the First International Symposium on Mudejarism, at Teruel in 1975.

In the upland kingdom of Aragon, large communities of Muslims lived around Tudela and the lower Aragon and Albarracín regions, and along the Ebro and Jalón rivers, where for many years Muslims outnumbered Christians. Only the area of Saragossa suffered a population drain, causing Alfonso the Battler to forbid Muslim emigration from there. Except for the forced removal, by treaty, of Muslims to the suburbs, their daily lives continued on preconquest levels on personally owned farms subject to "share" taxes (*exaricos*). French, Castilian, Catalan, and Aragonese settlers joined the mixture of Muslims, Jews, and Mozarabs. Moors under seigniors paid higher taxes than royal Moors and enjoyed less power as communities; but their freedom to sell and move elsewhere inhibited seignorial harshness. Late censuses (from 1495) show Muslims as 11 percent or perhaps 15 percent of the total population (Joan Reglá argues for 20 percent). Although a minority in the cities, Muslims preponderated in many towns and over the most productive farmlands. Sixteen percent were royal, the rest seignorial. The kingdom's economy depended heavily upon these valued tenants, and the impact of their craftsmen in construction was widespread.

In the twelfth and thirteenth centuries, as economic crises diminished seignorial income, Mudejar liberties were limited. By 1300 exploitation, erosion of privileges, and religious intolerance had worsened the condition of the Mudejars. There was a decline in social status of Aragonese Mudejars, especially in rural areas, due to ecclesiastical pressures. Except in large towns or where Christians grossly predominated, Muslims lived and mingled with Christians. Their council of family heads met weekly in the mosque and occasionally with Christians for joint projects. Each *aljama* (Mudejar district or community) had an *alamín* executive with *adelantados* as consultors and a qadi (*alcadí*, "judge" or "magistrate"). A lifetime *alcadí general* conducted an appeals court. An *alfaquí* cared for each mosque, taught school, and presided at worship.

After the Battle of Las Navas de Tolosa (16 July 1212), in which Alfonso VIII, king of Castile (*d.* 1214), defeated the Muslims, the whole of central Iberia, "the most prosperous region of medieval Spain," lay open for conquest. Ferdinand III of Castile-León (*r.* 1217–1252) swept through the region, taking for Castile such cities as Córdoba (1236), Murcia (1243), and Seville (1248). He garrisoned his conquered territory, moved the Moorish communities outside the large cities, buffered the Granadan frontier with the estates of great families and military orders, parceled the countryside into seignories, and mounted an intensive Christian immigration.

Castilian Mudejars soon became a very small minority within the predominant Christian population. They became rather irrelevant despite their disproportionate artistic contributions. Having flourished from the eleventh to the mid thirteenth century, Mudejars began leaving Castile for the attractions of Granada. This hemorrhage of the Mudejar population is particularly evident in the later fourteenth century as a result of the Black Death and its attendant economic dislocations, loss of privileges, and demographic catastrophes, which affected peasant societies everywhere in Europe. Those Mudejars remaining outside Granada settled around the larger urban areas. Long after the devastation of the Black Death in the mid fourteenth century, a fifteenth-century tax list for 120 *aljamas* showed 22 percent of their total around Toledo-Cuenca, 22 percent around Ávila-Burgos-Palencia-Segovia, 17 percent around Cartagena, 11 percent around Cádiz-Córdoba-Seville, and 5 percent around Badajoz-Coria. Recent immigration had concentrated the important urban-artisan Mudejar group at Burgos. Military orders possessed large numbers of Mudejars. Thirty *aljamas* numbered less than twenty households, thirty had twenty to fifty, thirteen had fifty to one hundred, and seven had over one hundred (two of them over 200). Restrictive legislation increased, beginning around 1250, and contributed to a ghettoizing trend from 1268 on, reinforced by church legislation from 1335. These restrictive laws were established as principle in 1412 but were always poorly enforced. Laws restricted the medical (1332) and nursemaid (1252) professions, many crafts (1400's), contact at weddings, employment as servants, and even the use of Romance first names. The actual success of such legal campaigns still lies hidden in the unexplored archival data, but in all probability this social stigmatization progressively diminished intercultural exchange.

After Castile's definitive conquest of the territory of Murcia in 1266, its Mudejars emigrated massively over the next fifty years, the remnant falling under the control of the large estates. Murcia's Granadan frontier experienced both Muslim-Christian warfare and cooperation (the latter in such areas of common concern as livestock grazing and bandit control). Ferdinand IV reported in 1305 that "because of wars and other ills the greater part of the Moors are dead and others fled." Henry IV (*r.* 1454–1474), ignoring restrictive laws by Sancho IV and Alfonso XI, protected remaining communities, appointing an *alcalde mayor*. City Mudejars held lowly jobs but monopolized some crafts, such as ceramics and iron- and stonework. All seem "a minority, very diminished, of extreme poverty," on a frontier inviting banditry; but only archival research can clarify these impressions.

The Balearics, a Christian-Islamic crossroads before and after their conquest beginning in 1229, outshone Barcelona in North African trade by the early fourteenth century. Juridically recognized Muslim communities did not form. Last-ditch defense had led to the mass expulsion of Moors (1230–1231). Fortunately, emigration to Africa by sea was cheap and attractive. King James claimed that 2,000 Moors "remained in the mountains." According to some authors, Mudejars were assimilated into the large body of Christian settlers, but Elena Lourie has demonstrated from archival sources that free Muslims remained on all three islands, and, on Majorca, in considerable number as both farmers and artisans. Their juridical blackout conceals a semi-Mudejar persistence, since Muslim merchants operated from the Balearics freely.

Having evacuated areas conquered in the late-eleventh- and early-twelfth-century Christian advance, Muslims concentrated by the mid twelfth century in Lérida and Fraga.

In the mid fourteenth century in the mainland territories belonging to Aragon, there were Muslims living in and outside the *aljama,* supplying the crown with a professional cavalry and playing a prominent role in the medical profession. By far the most fascinating Mudejar society was in the kingdom of Valencia, a conquest and component of the realm of Aragon. The region is the most varied in Spain, still legendary among Muslims as a "paradise," intensely cultivated, possessed of one of the most famous irrigation systems of history, and integrally connected through its commercial cities with North Africa. The Christian conquest, accomplished by isolating and bypassing fortifications, and by negotiating with the Muslims to surrender their forts and towns on good terms, had precluded the expulsion of Moors except at Burriana and the capital. Later rebellions led to local expulsions. After thirty years, James the Conqueror estimated the Muslim-Christian proportion at 100,000 to 30,000. Despite the usual loss in elites, Muslims remained in force, amounting to nearly half of all Moriscos at the time of the seventeenth-century expulsion. Their mosque schools were magnets for northern Mudejars, their militia valued in the royal armies, their common Arabic language and their identity intact as a "nation" (the Morisco claim). As with other Mudejars, their history divides into a series of stages: reasonable autonomy in the thirteenth century; growing harassment in the fourteenth, with increasing hostility especially after the Black Death; and deep troubles in the fifteenth, including the sack of the capital city's *morería* in 1455 and their identification as supporters of the oppressive nobility in the later revolt of the Germanies. At each stage their relationship both with their colonial overlords and with their farmer neighbors varied in context and quality.

A thirteenth-century stratum of Muslim lords formed part of Valencia's Christian feudal order. Despite rental taxes, Muslims owned their farms and could sell, will, divide, or subrent them. A small-farm way of life characterized both Muslims and Christians and at first brought about an integration of the two peoples, but later Christian immigration eventually displaced the Muslims, forcing them into predominantly Islamic rural hinterlands. Interior immigration in the fourteenth century favored royal jurisdictions; by the late fifteenth century the balance reversed, most Muslims becoming seignorial.

Mudejar influence on Valencian life, especially in language and medicine, was pervasive. Campaigns of conversion by the mendicant orders, particularly by the celebrated Dominican "language" schools for theologico-metaphysical dialogue in Valencia (and in Murcia and Tunis), had limited success. (In anti-Moor rioting in 1276, converts suffered as cultural kin.) Mudejar ceramic (Manises, Paterna) and paper (Játiva) industries were internationally famous. Transforming the royal chancery, Játiva's paper allowed extensive details to be recorded for this most symbiotic of Muslim-Christian societies. Mixing and recoil were simultaneous, acculturation mutual, but ethnic division perduring.

FORMAL CULTURAL BORROWING

The opinion that the conquered Muslims were naturally bilingual is a consensus rapidly losing support; many or most of the progressive Muslims acquired the local Romance tongue or lost their Arabic altogether, especially in the Castilian realms. ᶜĪsā ben Jābir in 1462 summarized the *sunna* in the Castilian vernacular. A literature also developed in Romance using Arabic characters, called *aljamiado* (foreign). Arabic intellectual culture flowed into Europe by a process of selective translation from 1000 on, helped by continual absorption of Mudejar communities, by the growing wealth of the conquering Christian states, and especially by the intellectual developments in a newly urbanized and commercially affluent Europe. A diffused tradition of translations, at points so diverse as ninth-century Ripoll, eleventh-century Tarragona, and twelfth-century Pamplona, saw its most celebrated center rise at mid-twelfth-century Toledo around Archbishop Raimundo and Gerard of Cremona (*d.* 1187). The more organized mid-thirteenth-century renaissance at the court of Alfonso X the Learned had more Castilian than European impact, favored Romance over universal Latin, and showed a wide range of interest from chess treatises to Islamic literature. The focus of the selective translation of Arabic writings (itself an index of cultural distancing) was the metaphysical works of Ibn Sīnā (Avicenna) and Ibn Rushd (Averroës), which greatly influenced European thought. Translations were also made of works on medicine, mathematics, and geography. The Koran was translated into Latin in 1143 by Robert of Ketton for Peter the Venerable, and then into Castilian and Catalan. The polymath Ramon Lull (*d.* 1316) went directly to Arabic sources, as did the physician

Arnau de Vilanova (*d.* 1311); but the Arabist Juan de Segovia (*d.* 1458), who delved far more deeply than most scholars into the Islamic culture, was a lonely figure in an age still basically unsympathetic to that culture, except on a superficial level. Yet, converts to Islam, like the Joachimite Franciscan Anselm Turmeda (*d. ca.* 1425), were not rare.

The great medieval jurist, the Dominican Raymond of Peñafort (*d.* 1275), devoted his last decades to theological dialogue through the schools of Arabic he had helped found in the conquered regions; he probably persuaded Thomas Aquinas to begin writing his *Summa contra gentiles* to aid that Spanish enterprise. Al-Andalus music and poetry influenced European troubadours in an intricate Romance-Arabic mutual interchange. Castile's systematic diffusion of Islamic literary and creative elements stamped its late-blooming culture profoundly, a culture that later carried these elements to the New World. Most of the more obviously Arabic-derived words in the Castilian vernacular flooded in during the thirteenth century.

The influence of Mudejar art is basically in the sphere of architecture; Mudejar craftsmen, traveling throughout Spain, mixed Islamic and Christian architectural elements in a wide variety of proportions. Seen today especially at Seville, Tarazona, Teruel, Toledo, and Saragossa, this architecture can be divided into a courtly and a popular style. One brilliant example, Seville's Alcázar, is largely the work of Toledan Mudejars with Granadan help. Featuring geometric and arabesque motifs, colored tiles, clever brickwork and carpentry, elaborate ceilings, the horseshoe arch, and stucco, the style appeares in churches, palaces, town gates, fortifications, and humble dwellings. By 1300 it rivaled the Gothic style on the meseta, then combined with the Gothic for a century of maximum occidentalization; in the late fifteenth and sixteenth centuries it turned into the Plateresque style, its influence apparent in decorative rather than structural elements.

CONCLUSION

The conquest of Granada brought about the final, brief appearance of the Mudejar way of life. The loose union of the Aragonese-Catalan realms with those of Castile in 1475 pitted a rising world power against an emirate torn by civil war (1482–1492). The piecemeal preliminary conquests and the city of Granada itself received traditional constitutions of surrender, followed by the usual emigration of elites, removal of Moors from the main cities to suburban *morerías,* isolated revolts, and the arrival of 40,000 Christian immigrants (mostly to the royal cities, while Mudejars dominated elsewhere). For a decade Ferdinand and Isabel backed Mudejar liberties, while the pro-Arabic archbishop Hernando de Talavera of Granada won Mudejar affections. When Portugal expelled its Mudejars in 1496/1497, the monarchs opened Spain to them. But these were the decades of the Spanish Inquisition, wholesale Jewish expulsion, and the full development of a centralizing monarchy. Suddenly, heavy taxes and the virtual replacement of Talavera by the cruel archbishop Ximénez de Cisneros of Toledo, with his inquisitorial "reconciliation" of those ex-Christian Muslims protected by treaty, led to a revolt in 1500 and to the end of the Mudejar status. Muslims had the savage choice of conversion or exile (with their children left behind). This "choice" was then extended over the entire Castilian realm. The Aragonese-Catalan realms elicited Ferdinand's oath against further extension, later broken by his grandson the emperor Charles V, in 1525. Reasons for this extension—from hypocritical expedience to greed, popular pressure, or reasons of state—are still being debated. Jocelyn Hillgarth lays the responsibility squarely on Isabel and her instrument Cisneros, with her ideology of religio-social unity and determination to force the pace of conversion; Andrew Hess locates her action within a wider Mediterranean and Castilian dynamic.

The Mudejars ceased to exist, replaced by Moriscos, or nominal Christians. There had been little effort at a general conversion before the twelfth century; indeed the preoccupation with conversion, from 1085 through the thirteenth century, aimed rather at the Moorish rulers and influential men. Serious general efforts began with the thirteenth-century mendicants and continued with such sporadic pressures (resented and resisted by Christian lords) as the fanatic proselytizing associated with Vincent Ferrer (*d.* 1419). From 1500 on the Christians imposed mass baptisms, Christian names, and the burning of Arabic books. An underground of pretended converts arose, as did a fifth column in contact with the Ottoman Turks. As often with seemingly unassimilable minorities, expulsion followed in 1568–1570 at Granada, and universally in 1609. However, this Morisco tragedy belongs to modern rather than medieval Spanish history.

BIBLIOGRAPHY

John Boswell, *The Royal Treasure: Muslim Communities in the Crown of Aragon in the Fourteenth Century* (1977); Robert I. Burns, *The Crusader Kingdom of Valencia,* 2 vols. (1967), "Christian-Islamic Confrontation in the West," in *American Historical Review,* **76** (1971), "Renegades, Adventurers, and Sharp Businessmen: The Thirteenth-century Spaniard in the Cause of Islam," in *Catholic Historical Review,* **58** (1972), *Islam Under the Crusaders: Colonial Survival in the Thirteenth-century Kingdom of Valencia* (1973), *Medieval Colonialism: Postcrusade Exploitation of Islamic Valencia* (1975), "Mudejar History Today: New Directions," and "Piracy as an Islamic-Christian Interface in the Thirteenth Century," in *Viator,* **8** (1977) and **11** (1980), respectively, *Moors and Crusaders in Mediterranean Spain* (1978), "Muslim-Christian Conflict and Contact in Medieval Spain: Context and Methodology," in *Thought,* **54** (1979), and "Societies in Symbiosis: The Mudejar-Crusader Experiment in Thirteenth-century Mediterranean Spain," in *Fifteenth International Congress of Historical Sciences,* I (1980); Isidro de las Cagigas, *Los mudéjares,* 2 vols. (1948–1949); Louis Cardaillac, *Morisques et chrétiens: Un affrontement polémique, 1492–1640* (1977); José María Casciaro, *El diálogo teológico de Santo Tomás con musulmanes y judíos* (1969); José María Font Rius, "La carta de seguridad de Ramón Berenguer IV a las morerías de Ascó y ribera del Ebro (siglo XII)," in *Homenaje a Don José María Lacarra de Miguel,* I (1977); Luis García Ballester, *Historia social de la medicina en la España de los siglos XIII al XVI* (1976); Thomas F. Glick, *Islamic and Christian Spain in the Early Middle Ages* (1979); Pierre Guichard, "Un seigneur musulman dans l'Espagne chrétienne: Le 'raʾīs' de Crevillente (1243–1318)," in *Mélanges de la casa de Velázquez,* **9** (1973).

Jocelyn Hillgarth, *The Spanish Kingdoms, 1250–1516,* 2 vols. (1976–1978); John E. Keller, *Alfonso X, El Sabio* (1967); James Kritzeck, *Peter the Venerable and Islam* (1964); José María Lacarra, "La conquista de Zaragoza por Alfonso I," in *Al-Andalus,* **12** (1947); Miguel A. Ladero Quesada, *Los mudéjares de Castilla en tiempo de Isabel I* (1969); Henri Lapeyre, *Géographie de l'Espagne morisque* (1959); Richard Lemay, "Les traductions de l'arabe au latin," in *Annales: E.S.C.,* **18** (1963); Guy Liauzu, "La condition des musulmans dans l'Aragon chrétien aux XIe et XIIe siècles," in *Hespéris Tamuda,* **9** (1968); Elena Lourie, "Free Moslems in the Balearics Under Christian Rule in the Thirteenth Century," in *Speculum,* **45** (1970); Angus MacKay, *Spain in the Middle Ages: From Frontier to Empire, 1000–1500* (1977); George Makdisi, "The Scholastic Method in Medieval Education," in *Speculum,* **49** (1974); Ramón Martí, *Vocabulista in Arábico,* Celestino Schiaparelli, ed. (1871); Eero Neuvonen, *Los arabismos del español en el siglo XIII* (1941); Joseph O'Callaghan, *A History of Medieval Spain* (1975); *Simposio internacional de mudejarismo* (1975); Donald Thaler, "Mudejars of Aragon During the Twelfth Century and the Thirteenth Century" (diss., Princeton, 1973); Klaus Wagner, *Regesto de documentos del archivo de protocolos de Sevilla referentes a judíos y moros* (1978).

ROBERT I. BURNS, S.J.

[See also **Almogaváres; Almohads; Almoravids; Aragon, Crown of; Castile; Catalonia; Cid, History and Legend of; Granada; Hispano-Mauresque Art; Lull, Ramon; Mozarabic Art; Mudéjar Art; Navarre; Portugal; Raymond of Peñafort, St.; Reconquest; Valencia; Vincent Ferrer, St.**]

SPAIN, MUSLIM KINGDOMS OF. Al-Andalus ("Vandal land"?) is both myth and history. Romantic image projects a brilliant countercaliphate monolithically flourishing throughout seven centuries. Professional history is presented as either narratives of rulers, administrations, institutions, and civil wars, or transcendent analyses of poetry, intellectual fields, and creative arts. Particularly fascinating subjects are Spanish Islam's contributions to Western culture and, conversely, the Romance elements found in Islamic poetry and art. A grand tradition of narrative history (surveyed by Monroe, Manzanares), in contrast to primarily literary-cultural studies (surveys by Chejne, Vernet, Watt-Cachia), culminated in the publication of a magisterial synthesis, covering the period until 1031, by Évariste Lévi-Provençal. Meanwhile, an older controversy, on the continuity or discontinuity of culture after the Arabic conquest, reached a critical new stage in the works of Claudio Sánchez Albornoz and Américo Castro. Recent decades have seen the expansion of narrative data and a widening of contextual horizons, as well as the emergence of revolutionary interpretations. This discussion shall (1) trace a traditional chronological-political survey, with ethnoreligious and cultural notes, and (2) introduce current structural reinterpretations and narrative additions.

NARRATIVE

According to later accounts that are at least partly legendary, the Islamic conquest of Byzantine North Africa (by 701; Tangier, 708) encouraged a probe into Spain by Ṭāriq ibn Ziyād (711). Implausibly, by some accounts, the probe was invited by the losers in the Visigothic civil war or helped by the

MUSLIM SPAIN (711–1031)
(AL-ANDALUS)

disaffected Jews; it may have been undertaken (improbably) in cooperation with Byzantine Ceuta's exarch Count Julian, whose daughter had been seduced by the usurper king Roderick. After Ṭāriq's Arab officers and 12,000 Berbers dispersed Roderick's army, Mūsā ibn Nuṣayr, the Maghrib's governor, and his 18,000 men occupied Seville, Saragossa, and most of Spain (712–714). The caliph in Damascus, however, recalled both leaders. Because of the distance between Damascus and Spain, as well as the conquerors' benign neglect, twenty governors followed in bloody, chaotic succession (714–756); six of these were imposed by soldiers during 725–730 alone. Meanwhile, Syrian (northern) Arabs imported their feud against Yemenite (southern) Arabs into Spain, and other elements rallied around each in clientage. Military probes seized Barcelona, Carcassonne, and Nîmes until the overextended Muslims were finally repulsed by Eudes of Aquitaine and Charles Martel near Poitiers in 732. In Spain's northwest, Pelayo, king of Asturias, rallied followers to victory at Covadonga in a semilegendary episode that inaugurated the "Reconquest" (718). Each former Roman province survived as a *kūra* under a *wālī* (governor). The "Reconquest" eventually straightened the Coimbra-Toledo-Saragossa frontier to a line connecting Badajoz-Toledo-Saragossa, each a march (*thagr*) enfolding heartland Al-Andalus in Spain's south and east. The bleaker center and north became a no-man's-land, requiring long-distance raids by both Muslims and Christians as a tactical pattern and simultaneously attracting Christian settlers.

The last Umayyad to escape his dynasty's destruction by the new Abbasid caliphate established Islam's first autonomous emirate as ᶜAbd al-Raḥmān I of Al-Andalus (756–788). Poet, builder, and organizer, he ruthlessly suppressed a dozen revolts, introduced more Syrian supporters, encouraged the growing power of the conservative-pragmatic Malikite jurists, and coped with both expanding Asturias and Charlemagne's invasion (to help the Abbasid governor and faction at Saragossa in 778). Succeeding emirates (Hishām, 788–796; al-Ḥakam, 796–822) shone splendidly despite repressive massacres, Christian raids, and the loss of Barcelona to Carolingian Franks (801). Since Islam had made the Mediterranean a vast market stretching from Spain to inner Asia, the innovator ᶜAbd al-Raḥmān II (822–852) found himself ruling an urbanized, commercially affluent complex. He centralized the fisc, introduced Abbasid-model bureaucracies and officials, strengthened a fleet against Viking raids, suppressed local Hispano-Muslim (*muwallad*) revolts such as the Ebro Valley's Banū Qasī rebellion, and dealt with the "voluntary martyr" movement of his Christian subjects (850–859).

A half-century of troubles plagued the next three emirs: over two dozen *muwallad* revolts (especially by Ibn Ḥafṣūn), the virtual independence of the Saragossa frontier, Viking attacks (855, 859)—all a prelude to the brilliant recovery and golden age of ᶜAbd al-Raḥmān III (912–961) and his son al-Ḥakam II (961–976). ᶜAbd al-Raḥmān III made Al-Andalus a Mediterranean sea power; seizing Ceuta in 931 and harrying the North African coast, he influenced the Fatimid withdrawal of their capital from Ifrīqiya to Egypt; his corsair fleets plundered the Rhône Valley and penetrated Alpine valleys. Against heterodox Fatimid pretensions, he boldly assumed the title of caliph (929), and with his mercenary armies reinforced by masses of imported slaves (*ṣaqāliba*), he neutralized León-Navarre. He undertook ambitious hydraulic and building programs (especially the palace city Al-Zahrāʾ and the finishing elements of Córdoba's Great Mosque); began the first regular mintage of gold coins, with serious impact on the economy; presided over a capital rivaling Constantinople and Baghdad in splendor and culture; and received embassies from Emperor Otto I the Great, Hugh of Arles ("king of Italy"), Marquis Guido of Tuscany, and the Spanish Christian kingdoms.

Technically the caliphate survived until 1008 or even 1031, a half-dozen nonentities continuing the dynasty, with Hammudid interludes. In fact, however, Spanish unity had fragmented disastrously by about 1000. The rise of the Amirid vizier al-Manṣūr to de facto power (981–1002; "king" in 996) masked the decay. This Napoleonic general managed two decades of domestic peace and fifty victorious campaigns—burning Barcelona and Santiago, devastating Coimbra and León, and subduing Morocco. Political control then dissolved into coups, revolts, anarchy, and eventually a generalized bloodbath that invited intrusion by Christian Spanish armies as allies.

Postcaliphal Spain saw city-principalities emerge. Their shifting borders, checkerboard alliances, dynasty changes, and ephemeral members impede exact enumeration. Twenty or thirty appeared, but five regions were prominent: three extensive frontier marches—Badajoz (under the Aftasids), Toledo (under the Dhū 'l-Nunids), and Saragossa (under the Hudids)—plus Seville (under the Abbadids) and Granada (under the Zirids). Collectively they were "party" (*ṭaʾifa*) rulers because each dynasty represented a contending ethnic faction: Berbers (Albarracín, Badajoz, Granada, Toledo); the vizier's Amirid dynasty and slave allies, particularly unstable (Almería-Murcia, Valencia, Tortosa, Denia-Balearics); and especially Hispano-Arabs, the largest (and native) bloc (Alpuente, Seville-Córdoba, Saragossa). Incessant strife invited Christian help, resulting in tributary status for many (especially Badajoz, Granada, Seville, Toledo), and led to Castilian and Italian naval invasions. Wealthy and cultivated, but without hegemony or dynastic legitimacy, each principality decorated its claims with an elaborate and hedonistic court, cultural patronage, sovereign coinage, and building programs. Their tribute gold (*parias*) flowed north, strengthening Christian kingdoms but being recycled through purchases of Islamic technology and arts.

After Alfonso VI of Castile conquered the Toledo march in 1085 and the Cid took the Valencian coast, a delegation from the Abbadid ruler of Seville, the Aftasid of Badajoz, and the Zirid of Granada, representing the endangered petty states, invited the severely reformist Almoravids from North Africa. After founding Marrakech (*ca.* 1070), these Ṣanhāja Berbers and allies had expanded from the Senegal basin to western Algeria, professing Abbasid loyalties and a Malikite mysticism; the *ribāṭ,* the border monastery-fortress, is the root of their name. After defeating Castile at Zallaga (modern Sagrajas) in 1086 (and again at Uclés in 1108), the Almoravids turned on the party "kings," taking Seville, Granada, and Badajoz in 1094; Valencia in 1102; and Saragossa in 1110, "africanizing" Islamic Spain as an imperial province. Perhaps these purists eventually assimilated Spanish luxury or antagonized the local aristocracy. They were challenged, in turn, by an exclusivist religio-social movement, the Almohads (Arabic: *al-Muwaḥḥidūn,* those who proclaim the Oneness of God). Centering on the Maṣmūda tribe of Atlas mountaineers and their mahdi, Muḥammad ibn Tūmart, they swallowed Morocco and (from 1145) Spain. They made Seville the capital of their territory, which stretched from the Atlantic to Tripoli; negotiated with Saladin against crusader Palestine; and declared their own countercaliphate. Their hundred-year rise and fall gave them only brief control of Spain. After the 1195 Battle of Alarcos, one of Islam's greatest victories over Christendom, the empire suffered a terrible defeat at Las Navas de Tolosa (1212) by Spain's Christian states.

While the Almohads were convulsed in civil wars, Muḥammad ibn Hūd nearly established a new Al-Andalus in eastern Spain, but his assassination in 1238 renewed the Spanish chaos. With Almohad control effectively gone by 1223 (though the rival Marinids did not decisively supplant them in Africa until 1269), James the Conqueror of Aragon-Catalonia raided the Valencian border in 1225, seized the island of Majorca in 1229 and the Valencian lands in 1232–1245, and tightened control during subsequent campaigns. Meanwhile, Castile-León, under Ferdinand III and his son Alfonso X the Learned, took Córdoba (1236), Jaén (1246), Seville (1248), Murcia (1243–1244 provisionally, 1266 definitively), and Cádiz (1262). While James intruded into Algerian-Tunisian affairs, Alfonso raided Moroccan Salā, inaugurating the African penetration the Cid had envisioned.

From this wreckage Muḥammad ibn Naṣr (Ibn al-Aḥmar) built a principality at Jaén from 1232 (recentering it at Granada 1237–1246) that extended from Gibraltar to Almería and some sixty miles inland. Concealed by sheltering mountains, it played Christian states against Marinids to maintain independence. Sometimes a tributary or ally of Castile, sometimes a channel for a Moroccan threat, and sometimes a buffer, Granada experienced its greatest brilliance from 1344 to 1396, particularly during the reign of Muḥammad V (1354–1391). It lost Gibraltar to Castile in 1462, and in 1492, after a decade of war (Ronda was lost in 1485, Málaga in 1487, and Almería in 1489), surrendered as a Mudéjar province to Ferdinand and Isabella's confederated states. Surviving longer than the emirate, caliphate, *ṭāʾifa,* or Berber dynasties, the highly arabized and homogeneous Granada alternated in war and peace with Christian Spanish states, influencing their architecture and culture, particularly in Castile.

Al-Andalus comprised competing ethnic groups, especially before 1100: (1) the "Arab" elite, with Syrian and Yemenite factions, expanding by clientage, intermarriage, and immigration; (2) the far larger Berber waves from different sections of North Africa, feuding tribes with a common language that were inclined to pastoral-rural roles; (3) the slave class, especially those imported for the bureaucracy and the army, progressively freed as new converts; and (4) the overwhelming majority, native Spaniards who were born Muslims (*muwalladūn*) or were recent converts (*musālima*). Each Muslim group was further diversified by social strata and ranged from aristocrats, castellans, and urban notables to farmers, craftsmen, and the lower classes. Certain functions (merchant, chivalrous horseman, savant) cut across social and ethnic diversity, especially the religious jurist (*faqih*) and the powerful qadi (judge).

Jews and Mozarabs were harmoniously tolerated under Koranic *dhimma* precepts, as contract tributaries. They were excluded and restricted in some ways, but they mingled with the Muslims in others. Each enjoyed an internally autonomous community under its own leaders and laws. Jews contributed splendidly to Al-Andalus culture, and their thoroughly arabized educated classes supplied statesmen, physicians, and merchants. Immigration, particularly during the caliphate, swelled the already large Visigothic Jewish population. Almohad persecution sent many north, intensifying the Jewish role in Christian-Arab cultural interaction. Mozarabs (Arabic: *mustaʿrib,* "arabized") included both arabized and Romance (various dialects) Christians, who at first made up the bulk of the population. By extension the term Mozarab applies to their Hispano-Visigothic liturgy, music, script, architecture, and art (especially the various Beatus codices). At Córdoba, Saragossa, and their most important later center, Toledo, the Mozarab *dhimmi* lived intermixed with Muslims; cities such as Valencia built extra- or intramural *mozarabías.* An aristocratic Christian count, with judge and tax collector, administered each community; parishes, dioceses (three metropolitanates), and many monasteries (fifteen around Córdoba alone) framed a religious life, which was in regular communication with Latin Christendom but troubled by syncretic and Eastern heterodoxies. Mozarabs allied with *muwallad* rebellions were associated as supporters by the caliphate and al-Manṣūr and fled Almoravid-Almohad persecution. Actively linked to the north, Mozarabs' merchant role and regular emigration as monks and settlers in León-Castile-Aragon had a disproportionately high impact on language, society, and art. They contributed little to Al-Andalus learned and literary culture and were sometimes collaborationists in the Reconquest.

Évariste Lévi-Provençal surveyed the elegant caliphal society, with its administrative and institutional officials, irrigation marvels, city plans, art, industry, and trade. Andrew Watson has explicated the "green revolution" of new crops (700 to 1100, then diminishing). C. E. Dubler and S. M. Imamuddin outlined the industrial, economic, and social data over the course of Al-Andalus history. Even a cursory glance at the intellectual and creative glories, however, would demand a small volume: the sciences (especially astronomy, in particular during the eleventh century), geography, metaphysics, agricultural and botanical research, music, mysticism, travel, law, theology, history, medicine, and poetry (especially before 1100 and including the celebrated *kharja*—the envoi or final lines, often in Romance, in the Spanish-Arabic poems called *muwashshaḥ*). The pace and program of Eastern influence attract current interest. Europe's "twelfth-century renaissance"—troubadours, hospitals, and Scholasticism—fed on this. A roll call of the world greats must include the following: in philosophy, Ibn Bājja (*d.* 1138), Ibn Rushd (*d.* 1198), and Maimonides (*d.* 1204); in medicine, al-Rāzī (*d.* between 923 and 932) and the surgeon Abū Khasim (*d.* 1009); in poetry, Ibn Quzmān (*d.* 1160) and the great polymath Ibn Ḥazm (*d.* 1064); in travel, Ibn Jubayr (*d.* 1217) and Ibn Baṭṭūṭa (*d.* either 1368/1369 or 1377); in geography, Aḥmad al-Rāzī (*d.* 936), al-Bakrī (*d.* 1094), and, despite his work in distant Sicily, al-Idrīsī (*d.* 1165); in history, Ibn al-Khaṭīb (*d.* 1374); and in mysticism, Ibn ᶜArabī of Murcia (*d.* 1240). Despite North African provenance, both Ibn Khaldūn (*d.* 1406) and al-Maqqarī (*d.* 1631) provide mines of information on Al-Andalus. Al-Andalus controlled access to the Sudanese gold routes from 850 to 1250, sometimes through Berber sultans; this access fueled its economy, agricultural advance, and marvelous architecture such as the Great Mosque of Córdoba, Seville's Giralda, and the profusion of baths, palaces, mosques, country estates, and castles that served as the backdrop to gracious living.

INTERPRETATIONS

Cultural and literary specialties aside, recent research has moved in two significant directions: toward filling the gap in information on the party, Berber, and Granada states, and toward reinterpreting and even dismantling much of the previous consensus on structural evolution. Ambrosio Huici amassed the details on political development of the Almohad empire and, more impressively, of the Valencian regions from conquest to Reconquest. Monographs now illuminate *ṭāᵓifa* Granada (Handler), Albarracín (Bosch Vilá), Alpuente (Mateu y Llopis), Badajoz and Carmona (H. R. Idris), Denia (Rubiera), Toledo (Dunlop, Pastor de Togneri), and Saragossa (Turk). Local historians have clarified the Islamic centuries at Almería (Tapia Garrido), Lérida (Pita Mercé), and Orihuela (Vilar). Epalza has revolutionized the historiography of the eastern regions. Muᵓnis and Bell studied the Almoravids. Nasrid Granada has occupied a school of historians, from Juan Carriazo and M. A. Ladero Quesada to Cristóbal Torres Delgago, Aḥmad Mujṭār al-ᶜAbbādī, Wilhelm Hoenerbach, Julio Caro Baroja, and especially Rachel Arié. Thus Granada's intricate tapestry has been minutely examined, including its "resolutely opportunist" foreign policy, literature of virtuosity rather than of creativity, complex social-ethnic strata, advanced medicine, feeble merchant marine dependent on the Genoese and the Catalans, magnificent military and palace architecture, romantic but crippling frontier warfare, and fervent religion both Sufi and Malikite.

Interpretative problems begin with the Arab conquest. Are its narratives folkloric conceits, at best loosely related to the invasion reality (Dozy, Glick), or a fantasy concealing a wholly peaceful penetration via Muslim merchant-missionaries (Olagüe, challenged by Guichard)? Did cruel Visigoths persecute the Jews so relentlessly that they invited complicity with invasion (Katz), or is this overstated (Bachrach)? Were Christians so disaffected toward an exploitative establishment church that they soon drifted toward Islam (Watt-Cachia, Ashtor), or did they resist mass conversion until the caliphate (Glick)? Was the voluntary martyr movement of the 850's a last explosion of minority zealotry (Chejne) or an echo of Carolingian neoimperial ideology, harbinger of the Reconquest (Waltz), and has the movement suffered from careless analyses by otherwise eminent historians (Colbert, Wolf)? Were the Visigoths swiftly arabized but, though nominally converted, only tardily islamized under the Berbers (Watt), or was religiocultural progress a single phenomenon? Were educated Christians participants in Arabic culture and a bridge to Christendom (Menéndez Pidal, Pastor de Togneri, Chejne), or did they generally resist all but marginal arabization, coining the word "Mozarab" very late to mock a stratum of cultural renegades, and thus both freeze their church in an irrelevant past and communicate to Asturias-León its stubborn Visigothic ideology (Contarino)? A traditionalist historiography, from Francisco Simonet and Julián Ribera to Sánchez-Albornoz and Henri Terrasse, finds Al-Andalus a "European Islam"; an Eastern religion presides over European structures and society, with Córdoba nearer in essence to Paris than to Baghdad. Castro's school counters with a fully Islamic society that later joined Christians and Jews and formed a *convivencia,* yielding un-European Spanish Christians. This continuity-discontinuity polemic recurs in many areas, from poetry and philology to Visigothic and Mozarabic studies.

Were Hispano-Muslims naturally Malikite zealots, therefore backing the Berber dynasties against the self-indulgent upper classes (Watt-Cachia), or were they hostile to that conservative, narrow orthodoxy of the "Arabs," overthrowing it for the "liberal puritanism" of spirit over letter under Berber-slave allegiance (Monroe)? Or did the central Sunnite government at Córdoba spread and intensify Malikitism deliberately to forestall the fanatically expanding Shiite Fatimids of North Africa (Epalza)? Must we stop speaking of an Al-Andalus form of feudalism (Chalmeta) and resist Karl Wittfogel's classification of Spain as an agromanagerial hydraulic community (Glick)? Was tribalism a negligible factor under the Umayyads

(Lévi-Provençal) or central and pervasive (Guichard)? Were Spanish Muslims commonly bilingual, using Romance and Arabic down to the late Reconquest (Lévi-Provençal and most commentators), or did they lose Romance before that time (Bramon, Burns, Sanchis Guarner)? Was the position of women unique, a touchstone of aberrant arabization (Chejne and many others), or did it reflect standard Islamic behavioral patterns (Guichard)? Was Granada a "city of the Jews" and founded by them (as many argue), or does this view rest on misread sources (Spivakovsky)?

Did the Spanish Christian states, and eventually Europe, borrow the idea of crusades from the holy war of Al-Andalus (Castro)? Was crusade a purely Christian experience that first appeared in Spain (Goñi Gaztambide)? Were Spain's Christian-Muslim wars not crusades (H. E. Mayer)? Were the wars prior to 1000 secular (Menéndez Pidal) or religious (Lomax)? Did the Cluniacs in the Christian north and the Berber dynasties in the Islamic south simultaneously introduce or aggravate the religious component (Chejne), or did the papacy transform the religious element (Bishko, Goñi Gaztambide)?

Did the caliphate "fall," imperial grandeur disintegrating into anarchy (the consensus), or did the Bulliet-curve of religious conversions tardily islamize Al-Andalus, rendering unnecessary and irrelevant the central controlling autocracy of the "Arabs," as now-matured regional states and economies emerged to supplant it (Glick)? Was the control of the caliphate largely illusory beyond the central Baetic portion, and was the Berber role less pastoral and subordinate than has been represented (Guichard)? If the caliphate fell, was it because Islamic politics outran religious ideology, so that a materialistic upper class exploited religion to maintain an ever more unwieldy amalgam of Persian and elitist structures, while the swelling urbanized masses had no middle class to mediate the resultant selfish particularisms (Watt-Cachia); or, conversely, did a burdened and alienated middle class plunge into economic crisis as population outran technology, government poured tax revenues into armies and display, and the nomad invasions along the southern Mediterranean coast shattered the commerce network (Pastor de Togneri)?

Has a mistaken belief that Castile was the heartland of Christian Spain distorted historians' perception of pre-Almohad Al-Andalus, emphasizing its frontiers in the north rather than its position on the Mediterranean sea-lanes, thus slighting it as a naval, commercial world power (Burns)? The wider Mediterranean context, including Spain obliquely, is helping to dispel narcissistic preoccupation with peninsular neighbors (Goitein, Lewis, Lombard). Reinterpretations of the Islamic city (I. M. Lapidus) and of western Mediterranean trade patterns (Dufourcq) supply further context.

Representative structural reinterpretations include the models by James Monroe, Pierre Guichard, Míkel de Epalza, and Thomas Glick. Monroe argues that the agrarian, landed "Arab" establishment lost out to the disdained mercantile, urban, egalitarian, neo-Muslim middle class; thus ᶜAbd al-Raḥmān III represents an ideological break with the past, a refounding and shifting of base for the central power, and a replacement of tribal by national solidarity. The underlying class, rather than ethnic, tensions had previously issued in patriotic risings during government weaknesses and had been anti-Malikite and liberal. The new *muwallad* triumph related to the emerging commercial revolution of tenth-century Europe, to patronage of learning, and consequently to a cultural upcurve. Monroe's reversal of the caliphate's role—not an autumnal culmination before anarchic collapse, but a novel sociostructural and cultural advance—throws light on the neglected *ṭāᵓifa* states. Thus maritime Denia's annexation of the Balearics, invasion of Sardinia, "restoration" of the caliphate, and florescence under a former Christian Italianate sultan belong at center stage.

Guichard concentrates on the significant themes of tribalism and women. Rejecting current assumptions, he finds the Berber element more numerous and influential than the Arabic and both of them decidedly tribal in structure and mentality. According to Guichard, tribalism spread through clientage and persisted until urbanization and the military reforms of al-Manṣūr finally reduced its impact. This explains much of Umayyad Spain's "fragility." Despite pre-Islamic elements, social structure was characteristically Islamic, clearly so in regard to the status and behavior of women. Very early in its history, the more highly developed Islamic culture assimilated, dominated, and replaced the barbarized native model.

Glick has synthesized various current interpretations, especially of technological, economic, and sociological trends, with his own insights. Following Richard Bulliet's logarithmic curve of conversions, Glick argues that by 900 barely a quarter of Visigoths had converted and that Islamic society comprised a colonial minority dominating the cities. Explosive mass conversion then "coincided closely" with the reign of ᶜAbd al-Raḥmān III, and by 1100 a full 80 percent of the natives had converted. Along with a great influx of Berbers, these conversions forever changed the social composition, swamped the establishment caliphate, and set off an evolution toward a less tribal, more homogeneous, and revitalized culture. This drastic change expressed the peaking urbanism, regional economies, and the conversion demography. The density of the Muslim population now demanded educational expansion and by 950 had created a high culture proper to Al-Andalus. Consequently the xenophobic Almoravid-Almohad dynasties could confront the Reconquest with a wholly Muslim state and force out much of the Mozarabic and Jewish remnants. Cultural heterogeneity and revolts before 900 were merely normal: tribal society mandated feuding to test power distribution, while tribal infrastructure guaranteed stability at socio-institutional levels. The thirty or so rebellions during the reign of ᶜAbd Allāh (888–912) were the last tribal maneuvers before the conversion curve outmoded that dynamic; but the nontribal slave party states proved less stable than the coalitions of the ethnic states. Meanwhile, the Islamic Mediterranean imperium had formed a massive common market (though European Christians entered it mostly after their own urban rise in the 900's). This re-urbanized Al-Andalus and opened it to Iraqi culture. From data on mosque capacity, Córdoba apparently numbered 25,000 in the late 700's, 75,000 in the 800's, and 90,000 in 950. Seville went "from 52,000 in the tenth century to 83,000 in the eleventh; Toledo from 28,000 to 37,000, Granada from 20,000 to 26,000, Zaragoza from 12,000 to 17,000, Valencia from 11,000 to 15,000, and Málaga from 10,000 to 20,000" (Glick). Cities followed both a communications axis running from Fés to Toledo, centered on Córdoba-Seville, and another from Saragossa to Tortosa and then to the Balearics and Valencia. Each city interacted intimately with its surrounding countryside. Leopoldo Torres Balbás has made a life's study of the evolution, detailed physical elements, and peculiarities of Al-Andalus cities.

As the course of Al-Andalus has been reinterpreted from Arab conquest through the Almoravids, and as historians have reworked the themes of Granada, the Almohad society has been relatively neglected. Ambrosio Huici Mi[illegible]nda has traced the narrative political detail, and literary, intellectual, and artistic aspects do not lack their scholars. But the social and institutional elements lie embedded largely in charters of the conquering Christians, neglected by Arabists and Hispanists alike. Robert I. Burns has exploited Aragonese-Catalan records to suggest the Valencian Almohad structures, which the Christian conquest distorted and transmogrified in that first generation. Families of city notables, traditional crops and taxes, men of learning, taverns and baths, land-tenure arrangements, mosques and boundaries, courts and customs, castle dynasties, and anthroponymic-toponymic data all appear together in archaeological detail. This vision of an incipient Mudéjar society mirrors in a diffract and tortured way the twilight synthesis of the Almohads; similar recoveries from the abundant Christian records can offer a token return to Islam for the cultural riches it dispensed to Christendom here over so many centuries.

BIBLIOGRAPHY

James T. Monroe surveys major authors, themes, and controversies in his *Islam and the Arabs in Spanish Scholarship* (1970), to be supplemented with Manuela Manzanares de Cirre, *Arabistas españoles del siglo XIX* (1972). Besides general Islamic finding aids like J. D. Pearson, *Index Islamicus: 1906–55* (1958), with supplements, especially useful are the abstracts under "Musulmanes" in each issue of *Índice histórico español* (1953–). Anwar G. Chejne, *Muslim Spain* (1974), supplies a bibliography of over 400 Arabic manuscripts, catalogs, and published Arabic works both primary and secondary, with translations indicated. The *Encyclopaedia of Islam,* new ed. (1960–), is a mine of essays and specific data. Brief surveys are Ángel González Palencia, *Historia de la España musulmana* (1925, rev. ed. 1945); Juan Vernet Ginés, *Los musulmanes españoles* (1961); and William Montgomery Watt and Pierre Cachia, *A History of Islamic Spain* (1967).

Texts and studies. Aḥmad Mujṭār al-ᶜAbbādī, *El reino de Granada en la época de Muḥammad V* (1973); ᶜAbd Allāh (ibn Zirīd), *El siglo XI en la Iª persona: Las "Memorias" de ᶜAbd Allāh, último rey Zīrī de Granada,* Évariste Lévi-Provençal and Emilio García Gómez, trans. (1980); Rachel Arié, *L'Espagne musulmane au temps des Naṣrides (1232–1492)* (1973), and *España musulmana (siglos VIII–XV)* (1982); Eliyahu Ashtor, *The Jews of Moslem Spain,* Aaron Klein and Jenny M. Klein, trans., 3 vols. (1973–1984); Bernard S. Bachrach, "A Reassessment of Visigothic Jewish Policy, 589–711," in *American Historical Review,* 78 (1973); Morales Belda, *La marina de al-Andalus* (1970); A. Bell, *Les almoravides et les almohades* (1970); Julian Bishko, "The Spanish and

Portuguese Reconquest (1095–1492)," in Kenneth M. Setton, ed., *A History of the Crusades,* III (1975); Lucie Bolens, *Les méthodes culturales au moyen-âge d'après les traités d'agronomie andalous* (1974); Jacinto Bosch Vilá, *Albarracín musulman* (1959); Dolors Bramon, *Contra moros i jueus* (1981); Robert I. Burns, *Islam Under the Crusaders: Colonial Survival in the Thirteenth-century Kingdom of Valencia* (1973), "Socioeconomic Structure and Continuity: Medieval Spanish Islam," in A. L. Udovitch, ed., *Land, Population, and Society: Studies in the Economic History of the Middle East* (1979), and *Muslims, Christians, and Jews in the Crusader Kingdom of Valencia* (1984).

Isidro de las Cagigas, *Los mozárabes,* 2 vols. (1947–1948); Juan Caro Baroja, *Los moriscos de Granada* (1957); Juan Carriazo, *En la frontera de Granada* (1971); Américo Castro, *The Spaniards,* W. F. King and Selma Margaretten, trans. (1971); Enrico Cerulli, *Nuovo ricerche sul Libro della scala e la conoscenza dell'Islam in Occidents* (1972); Pedro Chalmeta Gendrón, "Le problème de la féodalité hors de l'Europe chrétienne: Le cas de l'Espagne musulmane," in *Actas del II Coloquio hispano-tunecino de estudios históricos* (1973), and *El "señor de zoco" en España: Edades media y moderna, contribución al estudio de la historia del mercado* (1973); Edward P. Colbert, *The Martyrs of Cordoba (850–859)* (1962); Vicente Contarino, *Entre monjes y musulmanes: El conflicto que fué España* (1978); Federico Corriente, *A Grammatical Sketch of the Spanish Arabic Dialect Bundle* (1977); Reinhart Dozy, *Histoire des musulmans d'Espagne jusqu'à la conquête de l'Andalousie par les almoravides (711–1110),* 4 vols. (1861), 2nd ed. by Évariste Lévi-Provençal, 3 vols. (1932), trans. of 1861 ed. by F. G. Stokes, *Spanish Islam* (1913, repr. 1972); Charles E. Dufourcq, *L'Espagne catalane et le Maghrib aux XIIIe et XIVe siècles . . .* (1966); César E. Dubler, *Über das Wirtschaftsleben auf der iberischen Halbinsel vom XI. zum XIII. Jahrhundert: Beitrag zu den islamisch-christlichen Beziehungen* (1943); D. M. Dunlop, "The Dhunnids of Toledo," in *Journal of the Royal Asiatic Society* (1942), "Notes on the Dhunnids of Toledo," *ibid.* (1943), and *Arabic Science in the West* (1958).

Mikel de Epalza, *Moros y moriscos en el Levante peninsular: Introducción bibliográfica* (1983); Emilio García Gómez, *Poemas arábigo andaluces,* 5th ed. (1971); Thomas F. Glick, *Irrigation and Society in Medieval Valencia* (1970) and *Islamic and Christian Spain in the Early Middle Ages* (1979); Solomon D. Goitein, *A Mediterranean Society: The Jewish Communities of the Arab World . . .,* 4 vols. (1967–1983); José Goñi Gaztambide, *Historia de la bula de la cruzada en España* (1958); Pierre Guichard, *Structures sociales "orientales" et "occidentales" dans l'Espagne musulmane* (1977); Andrew Handler, *The Zirids of Granada* (1974); Ibn ʿAbd al-Munʿim al-Ḥimyarī, *La péninsule ibérique au moyen âge d'après le Kitāb al-rawḍ al-miʿtār . . .,* Évariste Lévi-Provençal, ed. and trans. (1938); *Historia mozárabe: Ponencias y comunicaciones presentadas al I Congreso internacional de estudios mozárabes* (1978); Wilhelm Hoenerbach, *Spanisch-islamische Urkunden aus der Zeit der Naṣriden und Moriscos* (1965); Ambrosio Huici Miranda, *Colección de crónicas árabes de la Reconquista,* 4 vols. (1952–1955), *Las grandes batallas de la Reconquista* (1956), *Historia política del imperio almohade* (1957), and *Historia musulmana de Valencia,* 3 vols. (1970).

H. R. Idris, "Les Birzālides de Carmona," in *al-Andalus,* 30 (1965), and "Les Afṭasides de Badajoz," *ibid.;* S. M. Immamuddin, *A Political History of Muslim Spain* (1961, 2nd ed., rev. and enl., 1968), and *Socio-Economic and Cultural History of Muslim Spain, 711–1492 A.D.* (1965); Solomon Katz, *The Jews in the Visigothic and Frankish Kingdoms of Spain and Gaul* (1937); Ibn Khaldūn, *Histoire des berbères et des dynasties musulmanes de l'Afrique septentrionale,* William McGuckin, baron de Slane, trans., 4 vols., new ed. by Paul Casanova (1925–1956), and *The Muqaddimah: An Introduction to History,* Franz Rosenthal, trans., 3 vols. (1958, 2nd ed. 1967); Miguel A. Ladero Quesada, *Granada: Historia de un país islámico (1273–1571)* (1969); Roger Le Tourneau, *The Almohad Movement in North Africa in the Twelfth and Thirteenth Centuries* (1969); Giorgio Levi della Vida, "I mozarabi tra Occidente e Islam," in *L'Occidente e l'Islam nell'alto medioevo,* II (1965); Évariste Lévi-Provençal, *L'Espagne musulmane du Xème siècle: Institutions et vie sociale* (1932), and *Histoire de l'Espagne musulmane,* 3 vols. (1950–1953, 2nd ed. 1967), both rev. and trans. by Emilio García Gómez as *España musulmana hasta la caída del califato de Córdoba (711–1031 de J. C.),* in Ramón Menéndez Pidal *et al.,* eds., *Historia de España,* IV (2nd ed. 1957) and V (2nd ed. 1965); Archibald R. Lewis, *Naval Power and Trade in the Mediterranean, A.D. 500–1100* (1951); Derek W. Lomax, *The Reconquest of Spain* (1978); Maurice Lombard, *L'Islam dans sa première grandeur* (1971), trans. by Joan Spencer as *The Golden Age of Islam* (1975); Consuelo López-Morillas, "Aljamiado Studies Since 1970," in *La corónica,* 4 (1975).

Maḥmūd ʿAlī Makkī, *Ensayo sobre las aportaciones orientales en la España musulmana y su influencia en la formación de la cultura hispano-árabe* (1968); Aḥmad ibn Muḥammad al-Maqqari, *The History of the Mohammedan Dynasties in Spain,* abridged trans. by Pascual de Gayangos, 2 vols. (1840–1843, repr. 1964); Felipe Mateu y Llopis, *Alpuente, reino musulman* (1944); Ramón Menéndez Pidal, *La España del Cid,* 2 vols. (1929, 7th ed. 1969), abridged trans. of 1st ed. by Harold Sunderland, *The Cid and His Spain* (1934); J. M. Millás-Vallicrosa, *Nuevos estudios sobre historia de la ciencia española* (1960); James Monroe, *The Shuʿūbiyya in Al-Andalus: The Risāla of Ibn García and Five Refutations* (1970);

Ḥusayn Muʾnis (Mones), "La división político-administrativa de la España musulmana," in *Revista del Instituto egipcio de estudios islámicos* (Madrid), **5** (1957), and "Le rôle des hommes de religion dans l'histoire de l'Espagne musulmane jusqu'à la fin du califat," in *Studia islamica,* **20** (1964); ʿAlī ibn Mūsā ibn Saʿīd, *Moorish Poetry: A Translation of the Pennants, an Anthology Compiled in 1243,* Arthur J. Arberry, trans. (1953); Ignacio Olagüe, *Les arabes n'ont jamais envahis l'Espagne* (1969), abridged as *La revolución islámica en Occidente* (1974).

Reyna Pastor de Togneri, *Del Islam al cristianismo, en las fronteras de dos formaciones económico-sociales: Toledo, siglos XI–XII* (1975); *idem* and Marta Bonaudo, "Problèmes d'assimilation d'une minorité: Les mozarabes de Tolède (de 1085 à la fin du XIIIe siècle)," in *Annales: E.S.C.,* **25** (1970); Basilio Pavón Maldonado, *Arte toledano: Islámico y mudéjar* (1973); Henri Pérès, *La poésie andalouse en arabe classique au XIe siècle* (1937, 2nd ed. 1953), and "Les éléments ethniques de l'Espagne musulmane et de la langue arabe au Ve–XIe siècle," in *Études d'orientalisme dediées à la mémoire de Lévi-Provençal,* II (1962); Rodrigo Pita Mercé, *Lérida árabe* (1974); Julián Ribera Tarragó, *Disertaciones y opúsculos,* 2 vols. (1928); M. J. Rubiera Mata, *La taifa de Denia* (1985); Claudio Sánchez Albornoz, *La España musulmana según los autores islámicos y cristianos medievales,* 2 vols. (1946, 4th ed. 1974), and *España, un enigma histórico,* 6th ed., 2 vols. (1976), trans. by Colette J. Dee and David S. Reher as *Spain: A Historical Enigma,* 2 vols. (1975), esp. I, chaps. 3–4; Manuel Sanchis Guarner, "Época musulmana," in Miguel Tarradell *et al.,* eds., *Historia del país valencià,* I (1965); Francisco J. Simonet, *Historia de los mozárabes de España* (1897–1903, repr. 1967); Erika Spivakovsky, "The Jewish Presence in Granada," in *Journal of Medieval History,* **2** (1976).

José A. Tapia Garrido, *Almería musulmana,* 2 vols. (1976–1978); Henri Terrasse, *L'art hispano-mauresque dès origines au XIIIe siècle* (1932), and *Islam d'Espagne: Une rencontre de l'Orient et de l'Occident* (1958); Cristóbal Torres Delgado, *El antiguo reino nazarí de Granada (1232–1340)* (1974); Leopoldo Torres Balbás, *Ciudades hispanomusulmanas,* Henry Terrasse, ed., 2 vols. (1970); ʿAfīf Turk, *El reino de Zaragoza en el siglo XI de Cristo (V de la hégira)* (1978); Dominique Urvoy, *Le monde des ulémas andalous du V/XIe siècle: Étude sociologique* (1978); Juan Bautista Vilar, *Orihuela musulmana* (1976); Juan Vernet Ginés, *La cultura hispanoárabe en Oriente y Occidente* (1978); J. Waltz, "The Significance of the Voluntary Martyrs of Ninth-century Córdoba," in *Muslim World,* **40** (1970); David Wasserstein, *The Rise and Fall of the Party-Kings* (1985); Andrew M. Watson, "The Arab Agricultural Revolution and Its Diffusion, 700–1100," in *Journal of Economic History,* **34** (1974).

ROBERT I. BURNS, S.J.

[See also **Abbasids; Agriculture and Nutrition; Alfonso X of Castile; Almohads; Almoravids; Andalusia; Aragon, Crown of; Astrology/Astronomy; Asturias-León; Barcelona; Baṭṭūṭa, Ibn; Berbers; Caliphate; Castile; Charles Martel; Córdoba; Crusade, Concept of; Geography and Cartography, Islamic; Ghazālī, al-; Granada; Ḥazm, Ibn; Idrīsī, al-; Islam, Conquests of; Jews in Muslim Spain; Jihad; Khaldūn, Ibn; Kharja; Maimonides, Moses; Manṣūr, al-; Minorities; Mozarabic Art; Mozarabic Kharjas; Mozarabic Rite; Poitiers, Battle of; Qadi; Rāzī, Abū Bakr; Rushd, Ibn; Seville; Toledo; Trade; Urbanism; Valencia; Vikings; Visigoths; Zirids.**]

SPANDREL. (1) The triangular surface between an arch and the horizontal and vertical sides of a rectangle enclosing it, or the wall surface between two arches in an arcade; often ornamented. (2) The surface of a vault between two adjacent ribs, also called a vault field.

GREGORY WHITTINGTON

[See also **Arch; Rib; Vault.**]

SPANISH ERA, a chronological system based on the epoch of 38 B.C., believed to commemorate the Roman pacification of Spain and the imposition of a tribute by Augustus. The Spanish era first appeared in sepulchral inscriptions in the northwest of the Iberian Peninsula at the end of the third century. Bishop Idatius (*d.* 470) employed it in dating his *Chronicle,* and the Visigothic King Athanagild (*r.* 554–567) gave it official status. The era is thirty-eight years in advance of the standard dating of the Christian era. It was never widely used in Aragon, Catalonia, or Valencia, where dating according to the year of the Incarnation was common. King John I of Castile abolished this dating in 1383, as did the Portuguese in 1422.

BIBLIOGRAPHY

Luis Sánchez Belda, "Era Hispánica," in *Diccionario de Historia de España,* I (1952), 999; Luis García de Valdeavellano, *Historia de España,* 2d ed., I, pt. 1 (1955), 264.

JOSEPH F. O'CALLAGHAN

[See also **Calendars and the Reckoning of Time.**]

SPANISH LANGUAGE

DELIMITATION

Under the label "Old Spanish" it is customary to subsume a number of closely related dialects of Romance stock spoken in the central section of the Iberian Peninsula, approximately between 1100 and 1500. Not included in this alliance of dialects are, to the west of the center, Old Galician–Portuguese; and, to the east, Old Catalan, which, in turn, falls into various subdialects, such as Old Valencian and Old Balearic. One must further subtract, across the Pyrenees, Old Gascon, despite the common descent and strong mutual affinity among all the languages and dialects so far mentioned. Totally unrelated to Old Spanish, despite a not inconsiderable number of loan words and, possibly, "loan meanings," "loan constructions," and the like, were: (1) Basque, in the north, on the southwestern slopes of the Pyrenees, and (2) Hispano-Arabic, in the south (a variety closely akin to Moroccan or Maghrebi Arabic). Hebrew was not used as a spoken tongue among Spanish Jews (Sephardim), although Biblical and post-Biblical Hebrew were widely cultivated by them, as a matter of both theological and aesthetic concern. To this extent, Hebrew must be placed, within the context of Old Spanish culture, on virtually the same level as Latin. Greek remained unknown to Christian inhabitants of the peninsula during the four centuries at issue. Also, Visigothic, once the language of an elite, appears to have been thoroughly forgotten by the eighth century.

Old Spanish was by no means a homogeneous language, least of all at the start. First, it fell into a variety of rather sharply delimited dialects, and these dialectally colored forms served as vehicles for literature (or, at least, for written texts, such as contracts and municipal laws). Then again, one observes major variations across time: After an extended period of uninhibited experimentation (before 1250) one recognizes a century and a half of relative consolidation or standardization, with the royal court serving as the source of all tacitly issued norms. With the advent of a new hierarchy of cultural prestige, around 1400, a novel trend set in which led, once more, to fragmentation and diversification, especially on the level of style.

Aside from regional variation and temporal shifts, there no doubt existed social dialects. Fortunately, a few specimens of the speech of medieval rustics have been preserved, for instance in Juan Ruiz' mid-fourteenth-century masterpiece, *Libro de buen amor,* and in certain short pastoral plays toward the very end of the fifteenth century, where low-class speech and the use of Sayagués (a subdialect of rural Salamancan, to the west of Castile) have been almost inextricably blended.

Finally, it is worth remembering that Old Spanish was a language shared by Christians, Muslims, and Jews, all of whom, in characteristically medieval fashion, insisted on using each group's separate alphabet for essentially the same language. Nevertheless, both the power of religious traditions and the fact that religious communities were enmeshed in the social stratification of the day undoubtedly contributed toward endowing Old Judeo-Spanish and the Spanish of the kingdom of Granada with certain noteworthy peculiarities.

Since Spanish was not exported to the New World before the discoveries of Columbus, medievalists are not directly concerned with New World Spanish. Also, because the Jews unwilling to be converted to Catholicism were forced to leave Spain that same year, the "post-exilic" phases of Judeo-Spanish (Ottoman Empire, North Africa, Holland) will here be excluded from further consideration, as will also be the Spanish exported to the Canary Islands.

RECORD OF RESEARCH

Early studies (to 1800). Curiosity about Old Spanish started at an early date. In the didactic writings composed by teams of clerics and translators at the court of Alfonso X the Learned, in the third quarter of the thirteenth century, numerous key words were etymologized. In the year 1492, crucial in so many respects, the humanistic philologist Antonio de Nebrixa issued his *Gramática de la lengua castellana,* which, in addition to describing the language at the threshold of the Golden Age of Spanish literature, also related some of its significant features to Latin and, at least by implication, to earlier forms of medieval Spanish. With the Renaissance spirit in full bloom, antiquarian curiosity developed vigorously; in the sixteenth century Argote de Molina, busying himself with a "classic" mid-fourteenth-century text (Don Juan Manuel's *El conde Lucanor*), compiled a rudimentary glossary of antiquated, that is, Old Spanish, terms. A few decades earlier, Juan de Valdés, a resident of Naples, in his Platonic *Diálogo de la lengua* (written *ca.* 1535, but not published until 1737), commented on various changes undergone by Spanish as it emerged from the Middle Ages. In the early seventeenth century, two etymological dictionaries shot through with references to Old Spanish were prepared; the one that was published, by Sebastián de Covarrubias, abounded in often long-winded discussions of obsolete (that is, Old Spanish) terms. (The unpublished one was by Francisco del Rosal.) The erudite compilers of the original dictionary of the Royal Spanish Academy (1726–1739) put to good use the works of these pioneers; thereafter, Francisco de Berganza extracted many antiquated words from a wide spread of documents, while toward the very end of the eighteenth century Tomás Antonio Sánchez appended glossaries of words no longer readily understandable to the layman to each of his four consecutive volumes of Old Spanish poetic texts. These glossaries were eventually amalgamated into a single book.

Nineteenth-century studies. While interest, from 1500 to 1800, thus centered almost exclusively about the Old Spanish lexicon (plus a scattering of proverbial sayings), the pendulum began to swing in the opposite direction with the advent to prestige and influence of the historico-comparative method in the Napoleonic era. Grammar then gradually took precedence over etymology, and Old Spanish was intensely studied as an intermediate link between Vulgar Latin (the assumed fountainhead of Romance languages) and Golden Age (or Classical) as well as modern Spanish. The center of research moved overnight from Spain to Germany (and adjoining countries). The few Spaniards still interested in the medieval prototype of their own tongue (for instance, Pedro Felipe Monlau) adopted the new German perspective, as established, chiefly, by Friedrich Diez, in the successive editions of his comparatively and diachronically slanted Romance grammar and—hierarchically and chronologically subordinated to it—his similarly tilted etymological dictionary. The sprinkling of Frenchmen, Italians, Portuguese, Englishmen, and Americans (chiefly Longfellow and Ticknor) who were at all interested in the exploration of Old Spanish responded to the lure of the historical method, rallying around its German spokesmen. The historicist movement reached its peak in the grammatical and, later, also etymological writings of Swiss-born Wilhelm Meyer-Lübke.

Twentieth-century studies. While Spain gradually lost its earlier initiative and leadership, except on the humblest level of data-gathering, several Spanish-American countries asserted themselves impressively. Starting in the 1860's and toiling indefatigably—first in Bogotá and later in Paris—until his death in 1911, the Colombian Rufino José Cuervo reconstructed Old Spanish pronunciation and studied the spelling, the lexicon, and the syntax of medieval Spanish texts with the dedication and precision of a mystic turned scientist. Of the two talented German linguist-philologists who, while still young and flexible, settled in Santiago de Chile, Rodolfo (Rudolf) Lenz and Federico (Friedrich) Hanssen, it was the latter who (until his death in 1919), in fifty or so exemplary monographs, studied fine details of Old Spanish grammar (with emphasis on morphology) and metrics, introducing the dialectological dimension. Toward the end of his life, Hanssen synthesized his vast knowledge in a magnificent historical grammar, of which there exists an earlier German and a later and more elaborate Spanish version.

It was the great Ramón Menéndez Pidal (1869–1968)—the Spanish counterpart of Germany's Jakob Grimm—who, singlehandedly, reversed the trend, moving back to Madrid the center of Old Spanish studies for a period of a half-century. The two basic goals—which he reached—of Menéndez Pidal qua student of Old Spanish were, first, to intertwine the investigations into medieval texts and modern dialects (such as Asturo-Leonese) and, second, to advance, through minute, scrupulous inspection of selected nonliterary texts (for instance, charters and glosses), our knowledge of preliterary, or archaic, Old Spanish (tenth and eleventh centuries). Menéndez Pidal's *Cid* grammar and lexicon and, above all, his unsurpassed masterpiece, the *Orígenes del español,* in which he adopted the cartographic projection of linguistic facts from dialect geographers, represent the all-time peak of research in Old Spanish. Such foreign scholars as evinced special interest in Old Spanish flocked to Menéndez Pidal's headquarters in Madrid (Centro de Estudios Históricos) or, at least, coordinated, in one way or another, their own inquiries into Old Spanish with those of the recognized leader in that field. This applies to such figures as Erik Staaff (in Sweden), Arnald Steiger (in Switzerland), Giambattista Pellegrini (in Italy), Fritz Krüger and Max Leopold Wagner (in Germany), and C. Carroll Marden and J. D. M. Ford (in the United States).

In the post–World War II period one no longer can point to any country, or even continent, as monopolizing leadership in Old Spanish studies.

The share of North American involvement has been steadily increasing, both in size and in quality, along the axes of precision and of imagination.

SOURCES OF INFORMATION

Difficulties of research. To reach the best sources of information (and the right tools of research) on Old Spanish as a whole—or on any narrower problem relating to Old Spanish—happens to be an excruciatingly difficult task. This regrettable state of affairs is due to two apparently unrelated reasons. For one thing, there is no dearth of competently crafted research tools (bibliographies, annual reports and digests, indexes, announcements of studies in progress, and the like), but the bits of information are almost hopelessly scattered. One runs into all sorts of gratuitous overlaps and counterproductive delays and procrastinations in publication dates; and certain reference books show a disappointingly low level of typographic tidiness, all of which threatens to slow down the briskness of advance by a painfully wide margin.

Another, equally vexing, major difficulty stems from the fact that, counter to expectation, the most stimulating and authoritative treatments of Old Spanish—again, either globally or with respect to individual problems—are not readily identifiable if one is guided, in the search, chiefly by the label "Old Spanish." This point deserves to be stressed heavily, because in this respect Old Spanish clashes sharply with a variety of other medieval occidental languages, notably Old and Middle English, Old and Middle High German, and Old French. While for all those languages (or characteristic phases of languages) there exists a profusion of often excellent and entirely up-to-date research tools, above all, separate dictionaries and either descriptive or historical grammars exclusively so oriented, pitifully few explicit and specific sources of information of comparable prestige can be cited for Old Spanish. Also, as if to make things worse, such sources, once they have been identified, as a rule turn out to be antiquated or otherwise defective. Two examples may suffice: If a researcher insists on working with a dictionary of Old Spanish complete in itself, he or she runs the risk of being eventually guided to Julio Cejador y Frauca's posthumous *Vocabulario medieval castellano* (1928), which is notoriously undependable, starting with the pervasive inaccuracy of the loci of quoted illustrations. Let the researcher voice a desire to be assigned a special, self-contained grammar of Old Spanish, and he or she will before long be holding either the original (1908) or the revised (1921) handbook of Adolf Zauner, *Altspanisches Elementarbuch*—which, to mention solely its most venial shortcoming, is thoroughly obsolete. All in all, less than 5 percent of valuable writings on Old Spanish are, one ventures to guess, immediately identifiable by the use of this helpful explicit tag.

The deeper reasons for such a confusing situation cannot be investigated here in any detail; briefly, many writers on this subject and the overwhelming majority of their readers, past, present, and prospective, especially those educated in the Spanish-speaking countries, have tended to see in Old Spanish not a separate entity, inviting sharply delimited and highly specialized study, but simply an early stage or phase of Spanish, a sort of prelude to the great Classical Age—the two "Golden Centuries" (*Siglo* or *Siglos de Oro,* roughly from 1500 to 1700), and beyond. Underlying this emotional attitude of the modern reader's far-reaching self-identification with the distant past is the objectively verifiable fact that an average educated native speaker of Spanish—or a foreigner of comparable background who has acquired a respectable knowledge of modern Spanish—is in a position to understand rather well, except perhaps for a few obsolete words or "tricky" constructions, any medieval Spanish passage; far better, as a matter of fact, than a college-trained Anglophone can ever hope to grasp Chaucer, let alone assimilate *Beowulf.* This peculiar situation, to which the untrained modern Italian's ability to cut a path through the writings of Dante, Boccaccio, and Petrarch offers the closest parallel, conceivably offers both a clue to, and a lame excuse for, the scarcity of scholarly literature overtly dedicated to Old Spanish.

Aids to research. How, then, does the uninitiated reader stand a chance to recognize the most promising leads when working with, let us say, a library catalog? Only a few hints can here be supplied. Again and again one discovers that the terms "Old Spanish" or "Medieval Spanish" have been replaced by implications or paraphrases. Thus, in lieu of adding an appropriate qualifier to "Spanish" (or, alternatively, "Castilian" in its wider and looser use), specialists have deferred to the taste of their anticipated lay readers by leaving the key word "Spanish" itself unqualified, while defining their books as "historical" dictionaries or grammars; one is reminded, in this context, of the Madrid Academy's two successive attempts (first, in 1933;

then, after the Civil War, in 1960) to launch a *Diccionario histórico de la lengua española.* Also, on the side of grammatical sketches, one thinks of two masterpieces, Hanssen's *Gramática histórica de la lengua castellana* and Menéndez Pidal's *Manual de gramática histórica española.* In all three ventures, Old Spanish is very prominently, though of course not exclusively, represented—as a matter of fact, the authors involved, regardless of their private tastes, simply could not help placing Old Spanish in the center of events once they had opted for the diachronic perspective. There may also be a reference to the presumed starting point of the development; witness Menéndez Pidal's *Orígenes del español* (which, it will be recalled, is basically an account of medieval Spanish in its embryonic form, immediately antecedent to the flowering of vernacular literature—not of the provincial Latinity that ultimately gave rise to Spanish). On a distinctly more rudimentary level, words and phrases suggestive of evolution, as in the title of Robert K. Spaulding's moderately sophisticated *How Spanish Grew,* virtually guarantee a generous share of attention to Old Spanish.

In addition to these almost apologetic allusions and circumlocutions, used in recoil from the alleged pedantry of such a straightforward label as "Old Spanish," one must be prepared to ferret out valuable shreds of information from books and journals devoted to the Romance language family as a whole, or to one of its branches or subbranches (assuming the validity of this slightly controversial imagery), for instance, Western Romance, or Ibero-Romance, or Hispano-Romance, or Hispanic. This approach and its terminological apparatus have, traditionally, been far more popular in Central Europe—the headquarters of comparatism ever since 1800—than in the Spanish- or English-speaking countries; whatever the constellation of circumstances, this trend of thinking must be taken into account. Moreover, with the current blossoming of linguistics in its many guises all over North America, younger scholars in this country have been gradually falling into step with standard European usage. Rather characteristically, where F. González Ollé would speak of *Los sufijos diminutivos en castellano medieval* (1962), the preferences of his American contemporaries would be split: J. E. Algeo is satisfied with viewing function and development of the concessive conjunction "in Medieval Spanish," whereas C. Blaylock, depending on his choice of the most rewarding angle, may confine the discussion of a problem to Spanish, with an implied stress on its early stage, or expand the perspective to Hispano-Romance (beside Ibero-Romance) or even to Romance as a whole. But whatever the projection favored in each instance, studies so titled are apt to deal in searching detail with Old Spanish.

For those coming to Old Spanish from linguistics rather than medieval literature it is worth bearing in mind that in the first decades of the twentieth century some of the finest studies in Old Spanish were undertaken by philologists and could thus be found in elaborate, annotated editions of chosen Old Spanish texts. A first-class edition of a challenging text was in those days equipped with a carefully thought-out grammatical sketch, aimed at distinguishing, so far as that goal was attainable, between the language of the author (not infrequently anonymous) or of the translator, on the one hand; and, on the other, that of the scribe or copyist. Special issues of major relevance to the literary scholar, for instance the approximate date of composition as well as the regional provenience of the chosen text or manuscript, invited painstaking linguistic analysis. Some of these older inquiries have remained unsurpassed and must still be appealed to at every step. Menéndez Pidal's magisterial "critical" editions of *Elena y María* (Old Leonese) and the *Poema de Yúçuf* (or *de José*) (Aljamiado) are treasure troves of information for the student of Old Spanish; the same scholar's standard-setting edition, in three volumes, of the *Cantar de mío Cid* exceeded his own strictly grammatical writings, inasmuch as the grammar, for once, included a big chunk of syntax, while the glossary poured out heavily substantiated etymological information. Moreover, in support of genetic conjectures and semantic definitions, the author cited, or even quoted at length, near-parallel passages culled from other texts, some of them unpublished, hence difficult of access. In later decades of the twentieth century, such almost ostentatious exuberance would hardly have been encouraged. A somewhat leaner and probably better-balanced grammatical, lexical, and metric commentary was offered in C. Carroll Marden's masterly edition of the *Libro de Apolonio.* Almost completely unindexed, hence difficult of consultation, is Karl Pietsch's grammatical volume accompanying his meticulous edition of *[Old] Spanish Grail Fragments.* To this day there exists, for the unhurried reader, no more rewarding source on selected problems of Old Spanish syntax than this companion volume; if one bothers to combine it with certain articles from Pietsch's pen—particularly those channeled through *Modern Philology*—the aggregate of lexical information thus conveyed will likewise turn out to be astonishingly rich. In the 1970's the lengthy Introduction to Dana A. Nelson's edition of the *Libro de Alexandre,* for all the controversiality of its central thesis, and the long string of articles surrounding that venture, yielded important side dividends for the study of straight grammatical issues in Old Spanish (for instance, the temporal and regional distribution of *-er* and *-ir* verbs). Even a short text of hotly debated provenience, such as the *Auto de los reyes magos,* titillated grammatical curiosity (witness J. M. Solá-Solé's paper).

Important research tools. Having made clear these crucially important points and having, accordingly, included in the appended bibliography numerous items whose relevance to Old Spanish is not at once revealed by their titles, I may now revert to a brief critical survey of available sources of information on progress of inquiries into Old Spanish and on the whereabouts of inventoried knowledge.

One can set off the following categories of reports, straight bibliographies, indexes, and similar genres of critical and informational literature:

(1) Critical distillations of recent scholarship. Old Spanish figures in the decennial guide—which spans the difficult, in part chaotic, World War II years—by Alvin Kuhn, *Die romanischen Sprachen,* and is prominently represented in Kurt Baldinger's almost overdocumented monograph, *La formación de los dominios lingüísticos en la Península Ibérica,* a book whose hybrid and slightly elusive character can be best inferred from the descriptive subtitle of the much slimmer German original, *Querschnitt durch die neueste Forschung und Versuch einer Synthese* (Overview of the newest research and a tentative synthesis). That is, the author, apropos his circumstantial account of the crystallization of a medieval Spain's linguistic areas, examines in a critical vein literally hundreds of contributions by linguistic analysts, mainly to Old Spanish. The third major study so tilted is Diego Catalán's substantial book-length venture *Lingüística iberorománica: Crítica retrospectiva.* A special place must be reserved for the two volumes of Madrid's *Enciclopedia lingüística*—a string of middle-sized reports, many of them relevant to Old Spanish, by seasoned specialists (a few of them foreigners) framed by two major pieces by R. Menéndez Pidal and D. Alonso.

(2) Critical annual distillations of current scholarship. The best time-tested enterprise of this type is Great Britain's series *Year's Work in Modern Language Study.* The relevant section, "Spanish, I: Language," rose to considerable prominence under the unforgotten stewardship of Ignacio González-Llubera, a scholar endowed with great finesse, throughout the 1950's. The better fruits in each year's harvest are listed, and the best are, moreover, summarized and assessed, with some attention given, for good measure, to earlier critical appraisals, whenever available.

(3) Bibliographies of Spanish linguistics, in which Old Spanish, traditionally, receives the lion's share of attention. The currently most copious and least antiquated work of this kind is Homero Serís' *Bibliografía de la lingüística española* (1964). The compiler was a professional bibliographer, but hardly an expert linguist in his own right. The inevitable result of this imbalance was that, if as a "sleuth," Serís unearthed numerous half-forgotten items, his classificatory arrangements, conversely, sometimes lacked forcefulness. An earlier, more modest experiment along the same line was Hensley C. Woodbridge and Paul R. Olson's *Tentative Bibliography of Hispanic Linguistics,* assembled around the gradually unfolding oeuvre of a single scholar whose productivity the compilers apparently admired. On the positive side of the ledger, the authors paid heightened attention to such critical reactions to the books caught in their dragnet as had captured their attention.

Discernibly less impressive, as regards comprehensiveness, neatness, and classificatory cogency, is Pauline Cook Hall's *Bibliography of Spanish Linguistics: Articles in Serial Publications.* As a consequence of the programmatic exclusion of books, it qualifies only as an occasional supplement to the better-balanced reference works.

(4) Annual and related bibliographies. Far and away the most sweeping and, at the same time, the tidiest series meeting this description is, unquestionably, the *Linguistic Bibliography* subsidized by UNESCO, edited by J. J. Beylsmit, and sponsored by the Dutch-Flemish publishing house Spectrum. By combing through the pages reserved for General Romance, Hispanic, and Spanish proper, one is apt to isolate quickly and efficiently such items as—judging from their titles—have a bearing on Old Spanish. There are numerous cross-references; the

typographic standard is consistently high; and, with rare exceptions, all pertinent book reviews have been raked in.

There exist alternative and supplementary sources of information, less neatly geared to the annual format. Easily the oldest and most prestigious is the chain of skillfully indexed and subdivided *Supplement bände* (as distinct from the string of *Beihefte*) to the *Zeitschrift für romanische Philologie,* Germany's leading quarterly in this domain. Note also the periodic bibliographic listings, verging on exhaustiveness, in the back of various journals (some of them extinct by the 1980's), such as Madrid's *Revista de filología española,* Buenos Aires' *Revista de filología hispánica,* and Mexico City's *Nueva revista de filología hispánica.* The Modern Language Association's Annual Bibliography reserves one volume for linguistics (and this is the volume to watch for those in search of information on Old Spanish qua language). Incidentally, the MLA has for years been collecting information not only on studies actually published, but also on research projects anounced.

(5) More specialized bibliographies. Of great potential value to those concerned with all aspects and facets of Old Spanish has been, since 1951, Harry F. Williams' *Index of Medieval Studies Published in Festschriften, 1865–1946, with Special Reference to Romanic Material.*

(6) Of limited use to the lexicologist and etymologist, but of none at all to the grammarian among students of Old Spanish, are sundry volumes aiming to serve as master indexes to such Spanish words (many of them distinctly medieval) as have come up for discussion in certain categories of scholarly writings. Thus, Carmen Fontecha's *Glosario de voces comentadas en ediciones de textos clásicos* is, actually, little more than an alphabetical guide to footnotes in over one hundred annotated editions of older texts (including a sprinkling of those assignable to the late Middle Ages). Miguel Romera-Navarro's *Registro de lexicografía hispánica* is deceptive, coming as it does from a noted expert in Baroque literature. The book is very poorly organized and has not been checked for accuracy, consistency, and the like; it is a bewildering hodgepodge of diverse lexical indexes and lists, including inventories of dialect words which, strictly, do not qualify as specimens of Spanish.

Among the unpublished, but classified, collections of Old Spanish material, generally accessible to qualified researchers, let me single out the Old Spanish Dictionary produced by, and housed in, the University of Wisconsin's Medieval Seminary of Hispanic Studies (Madison), a project originally launched by Antonio García Solalinde (*d.* 1937) and later very energetically pursued by Lloyd A. Kasten. The kernel of that collection is the lexicographic inventory of Alfonsine writings (didactic prose of the late thirteenth century). Another exceptionally rich repository of words extracted from texts of all periods, starting with the literature of the Middle Ages, has been prepared by a team of workers trained by such directors of research as Julio Casares and, after his death, Rafael Lapesa and S. Fernández Ramírez at the Seminario Lexicográfico attached to Madrid's Real Academia Española upon the conclusion of the Civil War.

Some excellent work on Old Spanish is entombed in unpublished doctoral dissertations; to cite but one example, the single best-organized Old Spanish glossary, at least in my experience, has been Marion A. Zeitlin's almost exhaustive vocabulary, a Berkeley dissertation, to the two extant versions (MSS *E* and *M*) of Chancellor Pero López de Ayala's long-winded didactic poem *Rimado de palacio* (*ca.* 1390). The *Dissertation Abstracts* project has been in operation since 1938 and has provided guidance to relevant doctoral theses available in microfilm and/or amenable to xerographic reproduction. A bird's-eye view of such material, plus its assessment by a seasoned expert, remains a desideratum.

THE PATTERN OF PERIODIZATION

To simplify matters, this article has so far deemphasized the temporal and regional varieties of Old Spanish. However, the language that prevailed around the year 1100 undeniably differed in several important respects from the one more clearly amenable to observation four centuries later, at the threshold of the modern age. To come to grips with this problem of variation, one is well advised to separate, for the sake of neatness, the axis of time from the axes of space, even though such separation is doomed to be somewhat artificial and not always attainable, inasmuch as in certain backward territories older modes and fashions of communication are easily apt to entrench themselves and thus to suffer from a lag, all of which makes a consolidated spatio-temporal, or an even more ambitious socio-spatio-temporal, approach almost mandatory as the ultimate goal. Also, one is occasionally tempted to discriminate between a philologist's and a linguist's perspectives.

The testimony of texts (that is, philological evidence) allows us to segment Old Spanish into three rather neatly circumscribed periods.

Early Old Spanish. Preserved in several poetic texts (involving both vernacular and learned genres of composition) and a few fairly short texts in prose, all of them still worded in an experimental key, early Old Spanish extended approximately from 1100 to 1250. The texts (for instance *Auto de los reyes magos, Disputa del alma y el cuerpo*) show strong dialectal coloring; though stirrings of certain traditions begin to develop, writers and copyists can afford to remain staunchly individualistic.

Standardized or classical Old Spanish. Represented by a few excellent poetic texts (including the two consecutive versions of Juan Ruiz' *Libro de buen amor, ca.* 1330, 1343) and the many, in part lengthy, specimens of didactic prose (legal, historiographic, narrative, moralizing, "scientific," recreational), standardized Old Spanish was pushed, first, by King Alfonso the Learned and, later, by his talented, unruly nephew Don Juan Manuel. Within this stream of events the language, between the two extreme points, from about 1250 to about 1400, appears almost completely stabilized, although the immobilization of its growth was doubtless artificial, enforced from above, rather than corresponding to actual grass-root preferences (which, one gathers from circumstantial evidence, continued to change ceaselessly at the usual rate of attrition).

Late Old Spanish. The Galician-Portuguese musico-literary infiltration, a fresh influx of Gallicisms (including an admixture of Provençalisms and Catalanisms), plus the first wave of Italianisms, whipped up by the winds of Humanism and the Renaissance, greatly modified Spanish in the fifteenth century. Along with this erratic foreign influence came the less spectacular, but steady, erosion of the medieval syntax, which was to last until the opening decades of the following century (for this period of transition see the commendably tidy, statistically underpinned array of facts in H. Keniston's *Syntax of Castillian Prose*).

Vocabulary and grammatical forms. Characteristic of Early Old Spanish were certain words that later fell into desuetude, such as *¡ya!* (oh!) and *goír* (to enjoy); or, more interestingly, others that during the subsequent period were temporarily banished from the literary language, but eventually reappeared, presumably after having gone "underground" for a while, surviving in folk speech alone, to the strict exclusion of the polished literary language. Thus, for "nobody" one finds in the earliest texts *nadi* beside the fuller variant *omne nado* (man born [anywhere], that is, anyone), or, alternatively, *ne(n)guno, ninguno* (not even one). After 1250 *nadi* was banished from the approved set of pronouns, but, with the gradual relaxation of the Alfonsine canon, after 1400 emerged from oblivion as *nadie.*

Further typical of the experimental early period was the protracted rivalry of vernacular and learned (or partially learned) forms, for instance, *egreja* beside *eglesia* (church), *trist-eza* beside *trist-icia* (sadness). The so-called "semilearned" forms often exhibit an erudite shape of the suffix, arrived at through purposeful imitation of (Church) Latin models, and a vigorously modified, at times badly distorted shape of the root (or radical), for instance, *gan-ancia* (earning, gain), from non-Latin (Visigothic) *gan-* plus exquisitely refined *-ancia* (comparable to English *-ancy*), in unexpected preference to truly vernacular *-ança;* or *femencia, fimencia* (fervor, passionate belief), which, in its first half, involves an almost violent distortion of the underlying model word *vehementia,* under the impact of *fe(e)* (faith), while its second half preserves, with flawless accuracy, the derivational suffix *-encia;* or else *premencia, primencia* (pressure [of heavy taxes]), which blends as many as three elements: (1) the *prim-* ingredient of *prim-icia(s)* (first fruits, conceived of as an exactable tax); (2) the learned suffix *-encia,* perhaps erroneously substituted for *-icia(s);* plus (3) the radical *prem-, prim-,* extracted from a rapidly aging verb *prem-er, -ir* (to press). Of this motley material *ganancia* has been kept to this day; *femencia* was preserved long enough to reach the next evolutionary stages, *(h)emencia,* and was then discarded, lacking as it did the continued support of *fe; premencia* was rapidly eliminated; *tristeza* dislodged *tristicia,* while *e-, i-glesia* ousted *(e)greja* except in a few place-names.

Subject as it was to constant gropings and vacillation, this initial period could not be homogeneous. One major change occurred toward the end of this period: In many instances, the vowels *-e* and even *-o,* temporarily dropped, began to be restored. Thus, *noch* (night), from Latin *nocte,* reverted to the fuller form *noche; lueñ* (far), from Latin *longē*, either regained the status of a two-syllable word (*lueñe*) or yielded ground to a competitor (*lexos,* today *lejos*). Similarly, *dueñ* (master), from Latin *dominu,* became, once more, *dueño,* except for fossilized *dueñ de (casa)* > *duende* (hobgoblin). Rafael Lapesa has associated this many-faceted change with the rejection, by speakers of Spanish, of a clipped style too closely reminiscent of French and Provençal models to please the staunchly independent Spaniards.

At the peak of the Old Spanish period the lexicon still abounded in words at present no longer readily understood (for instance, *cedo* [early], *alfayate* [tailor], *deçir* [to descend], *troçir* [to pass, cross over]), but the profusion of variants was gradually brought under control. Thus, for "sweet" the Latinized form *dulce* was favored more and more, while the numerous vernacular counterparts (*duz, doz, duce, doce*), which lacked similar authority, vanished by and by from the literary language, if not from variegated dialect speech. The forms of address were *tú* and *vós,* as in French, and the corresponding possessives were *to* and *vuestro.* Falling diphthongs, such as *au, eu,* and *ei,* for a while almost barred (except in a few such words as *peine* [comb]), gained a foothold anew, through the introduction of Latinisms or semi-Latinisms (*actu*> *auto* [act, action]); through internal development (*debdo*>*deudo* [kindred], *debda*>*deuda* [debt]); or through the continued infiltration of Provençalisms, such as *afeitar* (to embellish with affectation, put make-up [of women]; later, to shave [of men]). A much sharper line than before was drawn between the conjugation classes in *-er* and *-ir.*

While some of these processes continued unabated in Late Old Spanish, a succession of new cultural fashions reshaped the lexicon. Certain native words all of a sudden soared to new prominence, among them *lindo* (beautiful), still used chiefly as a qualifier of royal princesses (from Latin *lēgitimu* [well-mannered, well-dressed, like a legitimate princess, and unlike a monarch's daughter born out of wedlock]). Portuguese poetry and music became a great attraction, and Spanish poets began to compose in Portuguese, though medievalists disagree on the intended purity of that medium, with the late Henry R. Lang and R. Lapesa occupying unreconcilable positions on this score. Several lexical borrowings occurred: For native *fallar* (or, later, *hallar*) *menos* (to miss) it became fashionable in tone-setting circles to substitute the Old Portuguese cognate *achar menos,* which was ultimately confused with native Spanish *echar* (to throw), genetically unrelated; hence *echar menos* and, in the end, the totally opaque *echar de menos.*

During the Late Old Spanish period the development of rising diphthongs (*ie, ue*) reached its point of saturation, and examples of secondary monophthongization became more frequent: *dixieron* (they said) gave way to *dixeron* (hence modern *dijeron*); *aviespa* (wasp) and *ariesta* (fish-bone) contracted to *avispa* and *arista,* respectively; *fruente* (forehead) shrank to *frente.*

To this more or less neatly articulated tripartite edifice of Old Spanish one may add, by way of prelude, a few glimpses that highly specialized observers stand a chance to catch of Archaic Spanish, that is, an incipient evolutionary stage known from a fragmentary corpus of texts, strictly nonliterary in the north, but poetic in the south. The retrieval of this priceless material and its subsequent analysis started toward the very end of the nineteenth century, when J. Priebsch published a few hundred tenth-century glosses from a manuscript traceable to the monastery of Silos; that is, interlinear and marginal translations, into a nascent form of the Spanish vernacular, made by an apprentice cleric assigned certain readings in Church Latin. Thirty years later Menéndez Pidal, in his sensationally impressive *Orígenes del español,* added to this already known series of "Glosas silenses" a comparable series of even cruder and possibly a bit older glosses from a similar "crib" traceable to the monastery of San Millán ("Glosas emilianenses"), interpreting the entire material thus gathered in a remarkably ingenious and forceful fashion.

In addition to glosses, today's analyst also has at his or her disposal charters, that is, all sorts of accurately dated and localized contracts; the oldest among these documents clearly predate, by a sizable margin, the earliest literary texts, such as the *Auto de los reyes magos,* the Cid epic, and the short but pungent *Disputa del alma y el cuerpo.* Thirdly, since the 1950's a major success has been scored, through combined efforts of Hispanists and Orientalists, in the decipherment of eleventh-century refrains (*muwashshaḥat*) couched in part in spontaneous Old Andalusian and attached to highly artistic poems composed in Classical Arabic or in Medieval Hebrew. From this bric-a-brac of specimens of exceedingly early uninhibited Romance speech one can distill a—not necessarily unified—Archaic Spanish, unmistakably different from Early Old Spanish. To cite just a few among its most striking features, the title *doña* (Mrs., prefixed to the first name) and the corresponding noun *dueña* (lady, mistress) were not yet completely separated in the eleventh century; the gamut of variants, *domina, dompna, duanna,* often preceding the title *donna* (that is, *doña*) in sequences such as *illa dompna donna Sancia,* shows the tenuous connection. Also, in lieu of the early literary forms of the definite article *el, ell* (before vowel), *lo, la* . . . , reminiscent of their modern descendants, one finds in archaic texts the fuller variants *el[l]o, el[l]a* . . . (later preserved only as stressed, or disjunct, personal pronouns), a cogent proof of the common descent of articles and pronouns from essentially the same Latin series: *ille, illu, illa* . . . , subject to different stress patterns. Finally, within the paradigm of the verb "to be," one detects, in the present indicative, forms totally at variance with what one tends to expect, coming as one often does from direct contact with older and, a fortiori, later literature: *yes* ([thou] art), *yet* ([he, she, it] is).

There is no philological access to any still earlier phase of Spanish, which one is at liberty to tag "Proto-Spanish" and which would fill the half-millennium lacuna (fifth to tenth century) between late provincial Latin and the earliest samples of Archaic Spanish. Linguistic reconstruction empowers us to formulate conjectures and hypotheses, sometimes arrived at through appeal to the comparative method. It is customary to mark such undocumented, but very often cogently argued, forms by an asterisk to set them off from the inventory of verifiable forms. But the advocacy and practice of that method, and the championship of the concrete results it yields with respect to "Proto" languages, are no longer under the jurisdiction of studies in Old Spanish.

The entire procedure of periodization, which is obviously geared to dependable dating of texts as prima facie evidence, is immensely complicated by the fact that a major gap in time is likely to separate the actual composition of a given literary work (the didactic genres included) from the preparation of, perhaps, the one manuscript preserved—conceivably the copy of a copy. These remote descendants suffer, as far as evidence for a language state is concerned, from the medieval copyist's uninhibited readiness to adjust grammar, meter, and wording to the taste of his own generation (*remozamiento* [rejuvenation]). Thus, even if younger Hispanists no longer accept as an article of faith Menéndez Pidal's stubbornly upheld dating of the *Cid* epic's lost original (namely *ca.* 1140), everyone continues to agree that a long interval, far in excess of one century, separates that event from the actual copying carried out by Per Abbat in, precisely, 1307. This major discrepancy forces scholars to ponder, in examining every feature of the *Poema,* whether it is best ascribed to the author or should instead be credited to the copyist, who in all likelihood also acted as a self-appointed reviser. While it is relatively easy, in such detective work, to "crack" the naive reviser's "deceits," the more sophisticated medieval modernizers practiced almost impenetrable "cover-ups."

Because private documents (deeds, contracts, licenses) were copied less zestfully, if at all, by posterity and because their phrasing often reflects local (municipal) speech preferences rather than mirroring the arbitrary decisions of a royal chancellery (or *scriptorium*), students of Old Spanish have made a point of issuing, with paleographic meticulosity, regional collections of such charters. We owe the three standard collections of this sort to the scrupulous scholarship of Erik Staaff (for the kingdom of León), Menéndez Pidal (for the kingdom of Castile), and Tomás Navarro (for the kingdom of Aragon). Staaff's florilegium of texts is preceded by a penetrating study, which elicited a thorough, finely nuanced review by Menéndez Pidal. The latter's book (*Documentos lingüísticos de España: Reino de Castilla*) is a bare collection of magisterially edited texts; the analysis flowing from this material was offered one lustrum later, in the aforementioned *Orígenes del español.* In closing the circle Tomás Navarro has supplied the chosen texts shorn of any attempt at analytical interpretation (admittedly the editor's juvenilia included research in Aragonese conjugation). Closely akin to this selection of material and slant of study has been research concerned with the language of medieval city ordinances, carried on in Spain proper (A. Castro, F. de Onís); later, on a grandiose scale, in Sweden (G. Tilander); more modestly in France; and very modestly in the United States (A. C. Jennings). Finally, V. R. B. Oelschläger—a student of Solalinde's and Castro's at Madison—single-handedly prepared a vocabulary of dated appearances of Old Spanish words (until *ca.* 1230), as transmitted by documents and the oldest literary texts (chiefly those authored by Gonzalo de Berceo).

THE DIALECTS OF OLD SPANISH

From the start—indeed, especially at the outset—Old Spanish appears very strongly, though not rigidly, dialectalized. The dialect zones are not, to any major extent, outgrowths of the old provincial boundaries bequeathed by the Roman Empire at the time of its disintegration (fourth and fifth centuries); neither do the divisions constitute, *grosso modo,* late repercussions of the old frontiers between the tribal domains of pre-Roman times. They came into existence and began to harden during the Reconquest, as the Christians, at first pushed back to the extreme north by the steamroller of the Moorish invasion and conquest (eight and ninth centuries), began to fight back and gradually reconquered the entire peninsula, reaching the old Visigothic capital of Toledo in the eleventh century, the fertile valley of the Guadalquivir in the thirteenth, and the last Moorish strongholds (Granada, Málaga) in mountainous Andalusia toward the end of the fifteenth century.

It is customary to slice the territory of the old Christian north into three major dialect zones—Asturo-Leonese, Castilian, and Navarro-Aragonese—each marked by lexical, phonic, and grammatical peculiarities and corresponding for a while to separate political entities: kingdom of León; county, later kingdom of Castile; kingdoms of Navarre and Aragon.

The Asturo-Leonese territory. The Asturo-Leonese dialect, and bundle of sub-dialects (which Menéndez Pidal, as late as 1906, called Leonese for short), stretched to the north and the west of Old Castile. Its northern half, adjoining the sea (Bay of Biscay), is a kind of eastward prong of Atlantic, that is, Galician-Portuguese, language and underlying material civilization as well—what F. Krüger used to call *nordwestiberische Volkskultur* (northwestern Iberian folk culture)—a label acceptable only if one associates Iberian with the square-shaped peninsula as a whole rather than with the ancient Iberians (who happened to settle in the east rather than the west). In Leonese proper (the speech of the territory surrounding the old town of León, once a stronghold of Roman legions) these "Atlantic" features are less sharply pronounced. There exist relatively few and not very important texts couched in Old Asturian; in contrast, Old Leonese was a major vernacular vehicle for the written word. Thus, most manuscripts of the lawbook *Fuero Juzgo* and a crucially important version (MS O) of the medieval *Alexander* epic exhibit sharply silhouetted Leonese idiosyncrasies. One recognizes Old Leonese texts by some of the following recurrent features: the syllable-initial clusters *pr-, br-, cr-,* and so on, are favored over *pl-, bl-, cl-;* the rising diphthongs *ue* (beside *ua*) and *ie* seem to alternate haphazardly with the corresponding monophthongs *o* and *e,* and, moreover, are not necessarily tied to word stress, as was the case in Old Castilian; palatal *l* /ʎ/ makes its appearance where Old Castilian displays /ž/ between vowels, that is, in words like *ojo* (eye), *muger* (woman, wife, modern *mujer*), from Latin *oculu* and *muliere,* respectively; the word-medial *-bd-* consonant cluster, highly characteristic of Old Castilian, is represented by *-ld-* in Old Leonese, in local counterparts of *cabdiello* (chieftain), *cobdo* (elbow), *cobdicia* (greed).

Old Castilian territory. In similar fashion, one can set aside certain features once peculiar to Old Castilian proper, that is, to the medieval dialect of Burgos and the adjoining area, which was to become later known as the province of Old Castile (as against New Castile, the territory to the south surrounding the city of Toledo and also encompassing Madrid, a place not yet prominent in the Middle Ages). To the superficial beholder, these idiosyncrasies turn out not to be exactly conspicuous, inasmuch as they for the most part coincide with the familiar characteristics of standard Spanish—the obvious result of the eventual elevation of Castilian to a higher rank than that of just another dialect. Not so in the Middle Ages, where, if one can at all invoke a hierarchy of dialects, Castilian, in its slow rise, for a while was not even *primus inter pares,* the first among its peers.

Typical of medieval Old Castilian so defined were, above all, certain traits of consonant structures, for example, a strong predilection for palatal *l* spelled *ll: llegar* (to arrive), *calle* (street, lit. mountain path), *cuello* (neck); in these cases adjacent dialects might use *pl-,* or *pr-,* or *-l-,* instead. Further characteristic of this centrally located dialect par excellence was the emergence of an affricate consonant, spelled *ch* and pronounced, from the start, /č/, where rival dialects, more conservatively from the historian's vantage, make do with *-it* after the vowel. Thus, Old Castilian *mucho* beside *muy(t)* (much, very) clashes with *muito,* usually spelled *muyto,* just as Old Castilian *lech(e)* (milk) corresponds to *leite* in circumjacent territories.

Almost self-contradictory, not to say grotesque, in the evolutionary perspective are the two facts that, first, in a very deep lexical layer, Castilian allowed the /^{d}ž/ sound to disappear, word-initially, where the consensus of cognate languages was for its retention (*enero* [January], as against Portuguese *janeiro,* French *janvier,* Italian *gennaio,* from *Iā-* or

Iē-nuāriu), but, second, at a later date introduced /ž/ into a niche of its sound system that had been kept for palatal *l* /ʎ/ in closely related languages, as when *ojo* /ožo/ (eye) (at present /oχo/) opposes Portuguese *olho* /oʎu/ and French *œil,* originally /oʎ/. To round out the picture, let me cite a negative characteristic: Old Castilian, in ever-widening circles drawn around a diminutive nuclear area, shed its *f,* both in word-initial and in word-medial intervocalic positions, allowing it to become, first, *h* and later, in actual pronunciation if not in official spelling, zero: Hence *fierro*>*(h)ierro* (iron) *filo*> *(h)ilo* (thread), *fazer*>*(h)azer* (to do, make; modern *hacer*), *rafez*>*rahez* (cheap). These four traits of the sound system were very striking, as was indeed the staccato rhythm, and, they all, at the outset, made Castilian sound to the ears of "spoiled" speakers of soft-sounding neighboring dialects as a distinctly rude and rustic parlance.

Not one whit less noteworthy than these internal characteristics was the external circumstance that the early speakers of Castilian carried with them, in real life, a marked aptitude for vigorous territorial expansion, through military prowess and peaceful settlement alike. On their northeastern flank the "tough" Castilians consistently pushed back the Basques into the West Pyrenean valleys—or out into the sea. Their southward drive was ostensibly aimed at wresting New Castile from the Moors; but they somehow contrived to conduct the Reconquest in fanlike fashion, elbowing their way into areas that the less dynamic Leonese and Aragonese might with equal if not greater justification have claimed for their own expansion. Through this aggressive attitude the speakers of Old Castilian tended to impose their dialect not only on the conquered Moors but also on fellow Christians, and in the end succeeded in equating their private brand of Castilian with prestigious standard Spanish.

Navarro-Aragonese territory. The easternmost dialect of medieval Christian Spain—Navarro-Aragonese—ceased to be a vehicle of an important literature long before the formal unification of the crowns of Castile and Aragon under the Catholic Monarchs. (One can observe that by that time the center of gravity in the domain controlled by the Crown of Aragon had shifted to Catalonia, and that Old Catalan could not, by any stretch of imagination, be subsumed under Old Spanish.) In the late twelfth and early thirteenth centuries, however, Navarro-Aragonese was still in full bloom. The differences between Old Navarrese and Old Aragonese, few and very slight, were correctly diagnosed and formulated by Mark G. Littlefield. Conceivably the single most striking phonic feature of the dialect was the preservation (or successful restoration?) of the initial clusters *cl-, fl-, pl-,* so that Old Navarro-Aragonese *clave* matches Old Castilian *llave* (key), *flama* corresponds to *llama* (flame), and *plorar* (cry) packs as much weight as does *llorar.* (In classical and modern Spanish, true enough, *clave, flama,* and *plorar* also eke out a marginal existence, but, for the most part, boast only figurative meanings.) Navarro-Aragonese also displayed certain morphological identification tags, as when it staunchly favored the *-ir* over the *-er* conjugation, pitting *cullir* (compare French *cueillir*) against western *colher* and central *coger* (to pick). Also, it showed a measure of independence in matters of spelling.

There is no dearth of legal texts (*Fueros de Aragon, de la Novenera, de Navarra*), poetic writings (*María Egipcíaca, Libro de Apolonio, Alexandre*), and didactic treatises (*Vidal mayor*) traceable to the culture of the Ebro Valley and the southern slopes of the Pyrenees—which was closely integrated with Old Gascon (or Béarnais), stretching beyond the mountain ridge toward the Garonne Valley. Equally important, the region of La Rioja, which produced the peninsula's major early-thirteenth-century poet known by name, Gonzalo de Berceo, was a western prong of Navarre in the late Middle Ages, before becoming, on a lower rung of the ladder, an eastern sector of Old Castile. Still awaiting a plausible explanation is the culturally piquant fact that several Aljamiado texts written by unconverted Muslims (such as the *Poema de Yúçuf* or *de José,* narrating with Koranic orchestration the plight of the biblical patriarch), as well as a sprinkling of Old Judeo-Spanish compositions, show throughout an Old Aragonese, rather than an Old Castilian, hue.

The Old Andalusian (Mozarabic) dialect, which survived in Christian communities for four long centuries after southern Spain had been overrun and firmly seized by the Moors, has been pieced together very slowly, since the pertinent material must be painstakingly distilled in its entirety from Arabic sources, so that its handling requires the expertise of a trained Orientalist. Shortly before the end of the nineteenth century there became available a rather sizable dictionary, compiled by F. J. Simonet, containing solely pickings of Hispano-

Romance words which, for the sake of authentic "local color," Moorish travelers, geographers, and historians would allow to percolate into their writings and reports. By the middle of the twentieth century, two additional repositories of long-buried Mozarabic speech were tapped: the refrains (*muwashshaḥat*), partly in the vernacular, that tied together stanzas composed in impeccable Arabic (or Hebrew), and a collection of vernacular phytonyms, that is, plant names, which an unidentified Arabic botanist—a splendid observer not only of flora but also of folk usage—had obligingly recorded for posterity in Arabic transliteration. This treasure trove of frequently obscure Romance words was made available by that fine Madrid Arabist Miguel Asín Palacios almost immediately after the Civil War and has since been put to use systematically by Menéndez Pidal, chiefly in the bold 1950 revision and expansion of his *Orígenes,* and by J. Corominas in his imaginatively conceived, if a shade capriciously executed (and both quaintly and pretentiously titled), four-volume etymological dictionary, the *Diccionario crítico-etimológico de la lengua castellana.* Mozarabic preserved several extraordinarily archaic features, maintaining as it did the falling diphthongs /aj/ and /aw/ just the way they had been used in colloquial Late Latin. On the other hand, Mozarabic overtook Castilian in their common drift toward apocope, as when the widespread diminutive-hypocoristic suffix *-iello* (from Latin *-ellu*) was allowed to shrink to *-iel*; witness such familiar place-names as *Maciel* and *Montiel* (the latter corresponding to Spanish *montecillo*). Finally, in certain environments the southerners, through permutation of affricates, would use /č/ where the northerners welcomed /ts/, hence the later competition between such words as *aguaza* and *aguacha* (stagnant water).

Bilingualism and bidialectalism. The Old Andalusian refrains involved a moving tribute to bilingualism, but they were not isolated in transmitting this message of split loyalty, except for the special dosage of exoticism for once added to the formula. Actually, one finds all over the peninsula abundant traces both of full-scale bilingualism and of its paler "sidekick"—mere bidialectalism. Along the pilgrim route strung out across northern Spain, all the way from travelers' shelters in the Pyrenees to the shrine of Santiago de Compostela in far-off Galicia, small contingents of speakers of Old French and/or Old Provençal settled down in a Hispanophone environment, a situation that prompted R. Lapesa to reinterpret one of the oldest collections of municipal ordinances, the *Fuero de Avilés* (1155), famous for its recalcitrance to smooth analysis, as a hybrid text composed of Old Asturian and Old Provençal nuggets. A small residue of the aforementioned tenth-century glosses translated difficult-to-retain Latin words not into Old Navarro-Aragonese, but also into Basque, conjuring up the background image of a Basque-Navarrese speech community. And a male Jew living in tenth-century Muslim Spain may be credited with having acquired fluency in Maghrebi Arabic, with having readily understood Mozarabic (that is, the local form of Romance), and presumably also with having known how to make himself understood in it, to say nothing of the command of Hebrew and Aramaic required by his religion—quite a virtuoso performance turned in on a daily basis.

Bidialectalism also asserted itself, as Castilian, in the course of its precipitate southward advance, as a result of its aforementioned "jostling" movement began to shade off into Asturo-Leonese and Navarro-Aragonese. The many castilianized versions of, say, Leonese and Riojan originals are simply the other side of the same coin. Witness the mid-fourteenth-century epic *Poema de Alfonso XI,* which, judging from Yo ten Cate's and D. Catalán's separate investigations, represents a crudely castilianized version of a (lost) Leonese prototype. As the last surviving islets of Mozarabic speech were, one by one, wrested from the Moors and absorbed into Christian Spain, another, short-lived, variety of bidialectalism inevitably developed. Immediately after the close of the Middle Ages the "push" of Spaniards in various directions increased this motley character of speech, vividly portrayed by the contemporary playwright Bartolomé de Torres Naharro and analyzed by the best connoisseur of the early Renaissance theater, Joseph E. Gillet.

After the spadework successfully carried out by several pioneers (Hanssen and Staaff, among others), it was, once more, Menéndez Pidal who, in 1926, proposed a model or paradigm for the total dialectal configuration of medieval Spain, short of the Atlantic and the Mediterranean coasts. According to that view, the Asturo-Leonese, the Navarro-Aragonese, and the Mozarabic (or Old Andalusian) clusters of subdialects were, at the outset, closely related to one another; the lone atypical dialect was Old Castilian, whose surge in an area adjacent to the Basque domain and subsequent rapid advance, in the direction of the Rock of Gibraltar, cleft the peninsula, as it were. While the advocate of this hypothesis adduced several valid-sounding arguments (such as the preservation of *f-* in local descendants of *fīliu* [son] or of palatal *l* [ʎ] in those of *oculu* [eye] both in the west and in the east, over against Old Castilian [h]>[zero] and [ž], respectively, in the very same slots), one can with equal cogency defend a rival scheme, where different sound-correspondences, neglected by the Madrid scholar, were involved. Thus, Latin *d* between vowels disappeared rapidly in the west (compare Portuguese *nĩu,* later *ninho* [nest], *pés* [feet], *vau* [ford], from ancestral *nīdu, pedēs, vadu*); the central dialects displayed all sorts of inconsistencies (Old Spanish *nío* beside *nido,* but only *pies* and only *vado*); while in Old Riojan, used to the east of Old Castile, *piedes* (feet) was the variant originally favored, for instance by Berceo. One recognizes a gradient, with west and east representing extremes rather than tending to coincide in their preferences. The regional distribution of *-d-* apparently preceded by centuries the phenomena that were to capture Menéndez Pidal's attention.

PRONUNCIATION AND SPELLING

Except for details of prosody and morphophonemics (for instance, the stress pattern of *sinífica* [signifies] once tolerated, as against modern *significa,* and the closer dependence of the rising diphthongs on the main stress), the vowels of Old Spanish were the very same as those found in today's language. Conversely, within the ranks of consonants the resemblance of the medieval to the present-day pronunciation was discernibly less close: medieval Spanish lacked today's celebrated *jota* /χ/, as in *general, joven, mujer,* but—as if by compensation—boasted one voiced and one voiceless prepalatal, [ž] and [š], spelled *g* (also *j,* even *i*) and *x,* respectively, quite apart from also having a [č], spelled *ch* and preserved to this day virtually intact. Late Old Spanish, for a short while, also had an evanescent /h/, which represented ancestral /f/ on its way to zero. In addition, Old Spanish placed at the disposal of its speakers a pair of dental affricates, /^{t}s/ and /^{d}z/, spelled *ç* and *z,* which in the end were deaffricated. Word-medially, it pitted /s/ against /z/, spelled *-ss-* and *-s-* respectively, as in *viesso* (verse) beside *casa* (house). *V* and *b* remained contrastable phonemes (as they have done to this day in, say, French and Italian); but there was a clear-cut tendency for *b-* to replace *v-* in individual words, witness *bivir* (to live), *bermejo* (red), *bellido* (handsome), as against more conservative Portuguese *viver, vermelho,* and *velido.* The lisped dental, /θ/, characteristic of today's Peninsular—rather than New World—pronunciation, was absent from Old Spanish. Before 1500, there was a clear distinction between /r/ and /R/, but the range of these phonemes was not necessarily the same as at present: certain manuscripts would tend to use *crr-* and *grr-,* etc., apparently involving /R/ rather than, as at present, /r/. On the transmutation of Old Spanish into Golden Age and modern pronunciation, the classical treatise goes back to Cuervo; for a more venturesome interpretation, appealing to peculiarities of Basque as a possible source of interference, see André Martinet's controversial 1952 paper, compared to which A. Alonso's studies—a posthumous magnum opus surrounded by numerous satellite articles—may be described as almost hugging the ground of philological overdocumentation. In the aggregate, these studies constitute a sequel to H. Gavel's strictly medievalistic inquiry.

For innovative Romance sounds, that is, those alien to the old Roman inventory of phonemes, different spellings were tried out in the old dialects. For palatal *n* /ɲ/, Galician-Portuguese adopted the graphy of Old Provençal troubadours, namely *nh,* while Castilian used *nn* (later *ñ*) and Navarro-Aragonese *ny.* The distribution is entirely symmetric with respect to the renditions of palatal *l* /ʎ/: *lh* (again an echo of Provençal usage), *ll,* and *ly.* Note that the sharp distinction between *ç* and *z,* and even *j* and *ch,* was not enforced before the Alfonsine era (*ca.* 1270), when the scope of *y* was also widened. Far and away the most authoritative treatment of Old Spanish graphemics will be found in a chapter of Menéndez Pidal's often-praised *Orígenes.* To mark transliteration from Arabic or Hebrew scripts, scholars make use of boldface.

BIBLIOGRAPHY

Delimitation. William D. Elcock, *The Romance Languages* (1960, rev. ed. 1975); William J. Entwistle, *The Spanish Language, Together with Portuguese, Catalan, and Basque* (1936, repr. 1962); Ramón Menéndez Pidal, *El idioma español en sus primeros tiempos* (1927); Rebecca R. Posner, *The Romance Languages: A Linguistic Introduction* (1966); Robert K. Spaulding, *How Spanish Grew* (1943); John B. Trend, *The Language and History of Spain* (1953).

Record of research. Gonzalo Argote de Molina, "Vida de don Juan Manuel: Discurso de la poesía antigua castellana. Index de la lengua antigua castellana," in Don

Juan Manuel, *El conde Lucanor* (1575, repr. 1642), and *Nobleza de Andaluzía* (1588, repr. 1961, 1975); Francisco de Berganza, *Antiguedades de España, propugnadas . . .* , 2 vols. (1719–1721); Ramón Cabrera, *Diccionario de etimologías de la lengua castellana,* Juan M. Ayegui, ed., 2 vols. (1837); Américo Castro, *Glosarios latino-españoles de la edad media* (1936); Sebastián de Covarrubias Horozco, *Tesoro de la lengua castellana, o española,* Martín de Riquer, ed. (1943); Rufino J. Cuervo, *Diccionario de construcción y régimen de la lengua castellana* (A–D), 2 vols. (1886–1893, repr. 1953–1954), of vol. 3 (E) several fascicles, ed. by Fernando Antonio Martínez *et al.,* appeared during 1959–1987, and *Obras,* Fernando A. Martínez and R. Torres Quintero, eds., 2 vols. (1954).

Friedrich Diez, *Grammatik der romanischen Sprachen,* 3 vols. (1836–1844, rev. ed. 1870–1872, 5th ed. 1882), and *Etymologisches Wörterbuch der romanischen Sprachen* (1853, rev. 3rd ed. in 2 vols. 1869–1870, 5th ed. 1887); Jeremiah D. M. Ford, "The Old Spanish Sibilants," in *Harvard Studies and Notes in Philology and Literature,* 7 (1900), and *Old Spanish Readings, Selected on the Basis of Critically Edited Texts . . .* (1906, rev. 2nd ed. 1911, repr. 1934, 1939, 1966); Friedrich Hanssen, *Spanische Grammatik auf historischer Grundlage* (1910), later version, *Gramática histórica de la lengua castellana* (1913, repr. 1945), and *Estudios: Métrica, gramática, historia literaria,* 3 vols. (1958), with bibliography of Hanssen's writings; Fritz Krüger, *Studien zur Lautgeschichte westspanischer Mundarten* (1914); Rudolf Lenz, *La oración y sus partes: Estudios de gramática general y castellana* (1920, rev. 3rd ed. 1935).

Yakov Malkiel, "Old and New Trends in Spanish Linguistics," in *Studies in Philology,* **49** (1952), "Era omme esencial . . ." (bio-bibliographic essay on R. Menéndez Pidal, 1869–1968), in *Romance Philology,* **23** (1969–1970), "Comparative Romance Linguistics," in Thomas A. Sebeok, ed., *Current Trends in Linguistics,* IX, *Linguistics in Western Europe* (1972); Gregorio Mayáns i Siscar, ed., *Orígenes de la lengua española, compuestos por varios autores,* 2 vols. (1737, repr. 1873); Ramón Menéndez Pidal, "Notas para el léxico románico," in *Revista de filología española,* 7 (1920), *Orígenes del español: Estado lingüístico de la Península Ibérica hasta el siglo XI* (1926, rev. 3rd ed. 1950), and *Toponimia prerrománica hispana* (1952); Wilhelm Meyer-Lübke, *Grammatik der romanischen Sprachen,* 4 vols. (1890–1902), trans. by E. Rabiet, A. Doutrepont, G. Doutrepont, and A. Counson as *Grammaire des langues romanes,* 4 vols. (1890–1906), *Einführung in das Studium der romanischen Sprachwissenschaft* (1901, rev. 3rd ed. 1920), trans. and rev. by Américo Castro as *Introducción a la lingüística románica* (1926), and *Romanisches etymologisches Wörterbuch* (1911, rev. 3rd ed. 1930–1935); Pedro F. Monlau, *Diccionario etimológico de la lengua castellana . . .* (1856, 2nd ed. 1881, repr. 1941), and *Discursos leídos ante la R. Academia Española . . . Del origen y la formación del romance castellano* (1859).

Antonio de Nebrixa, *Gramática de la lengua castellana, Muestra de la istoria de las antigüedades de España, Reglas de orthographia en la lengua castellana,* Ignacio González-Llubera, ed. (1926), and *Vocabulario de romance en latín* (1495?, rev. ed. by the author 1516), ed. by Gerald J. MacDonald (1973); Eero K. Neuvonen, *Los arabismos del español en el siglo XIII* (1941); Hans-Josef Niederehe, *Die Sprachauffassung Alfons des Weisen: Studien zur Sprach- und Wissenschaftsgeschichte* (1975); Giovanni Battista Pellegrini, *Grammatica storica spagnola* (1950); Francisco del Rosal, "Origen y etymología de todos los vocablos originales de la lengua castellana" (unpubl.; lost original dated 1601; single eighteenth-century copy in Biblioteca Nacional, Madrid; for lemmata beginning with A–D, see Samuel Gili y Gaya, *Tesoro lexicográfico (1492–1726),* fasc. 1–4 (1947–).

Tomás Antonio Sánchez, ed., *Colección de poesías castellanas anteriores al siglo XV,* 4 vols. (1779–1790), amalgamated into a single book as *Vocabulario de voces anticuadas . . .* (1842); Erik Staaff, *Étude sur les pronoms abrégés en ancien espagnol* (1906); Arnald Steiger, "Contribución al estudio del vocabulario del *Corbacho,*" in *Boletín de la Real Academia Española,* **9** (1922), and *Contribución a la fonética del hispano-árabe y de los arabismos en el ibero-románico y el siciliano* (1932); F. Courtney Tarr, "A Bibliography of the Publications of C. Carroll Marden," in *Modern Language Notes,* **47** (1932); Oiva Johannes Tallgren (Tuulio), "La Z y Ç del antiguo castellano iniciales de sílaba, estudiadas en la inédita *Gaya* de Segovia," in *idem,* ed., *La Gaya, o Consonantes de . . . , manuscrito inédito del siglo XV* (1907); María L. Vázquez de Parga, "Bibliografía de don Ramón Menéndez Pidal," in *Revista de filología española,* **47** (1964); Max L. Wagner, *Caracteres generales del judeo-español de Oriente* (1930), and "Etymologische Randbemerkungen zu neueren iberoromanischen Dialektarbeiten und Wörterbüchern," in *Zeitschrift für romanische Philologie,* **69** (1953).

Sources of information. Academia Española, *Diccionario histórico de la lengua española* (A–E), 2 vols. (1933–1936), and *Diccionario histórico de la lengua española,* Rafael Lapesa Melgar *et al.,* eds. (1960–); James E. Algeo, "The Concessive Conjunction in Medieval Spanish and Portuguese: Its Function and Development," in *Romance Philology,* **26** (1972–1973); Kurt Baldinger, *Die Herausbildung der Sprachräume auf der Pyrenäenhalbinsel: Querschnitt durch die neueste Forschung und Versuch einer Synthese* (1958), rev. as *La formación de los dominios lingüísticos en la Península Ibérica,* Emilio Lledó and Montserrat Macau, trans. (1963, 1970); Curtis Blaylock, "Substratum Theory Applied to Hispano-Romance," in *Romance Philology,* **13** (1959–1960), "The Monophthongization of Latin AE in

Spanish" and "Hispanic Metaphony," *ibid.,* **18** (1964–1965), "Assimilation of Stops to Preceding Resonants in Ibero-Romance," *ibid.,* **19** (1965–1966), and "The Romance Development of the Latin Verbal Augment -SK-," *ibid.,* **28** (1974–1975); Ralph S. Boggs *et al., Tentative Dictionary of Medieval Spanish,* 2 vols. (1946); Eugenio de Bustos Tovar, *Estudios sobre asimilación y disimilación en el ibero-románico* (1960).

Diego Catalán, *La escuela lingüística española y su concepción del lenguaje* (1955), and *Lingüística iberorománica* (1974); Julio Cejador y Frauca, *Vocabulario medieval castellano* (1929); *Enciclopedia lingüística hispánica,* Manuel Alvar *et al.,* eds., 2 vols. (1960–1967); Carmen Fontecha, *Glosario de voces comentadas en ediciones de textos clásicos* (1941); Pauline Cook Hall, *A Bibliography of Spanish Linguistics: Articles in Serial Publications* (1957), first publ. as a supplement to *Language,* **27** (1956); Alwin Kuhn, *Romanische Philologie,* I, *Die romanischen Sprachen* (1951); *Linguistic Bibliography for the Year . . .* (1949–); Charles Carroll Marden, ed., *Libro de Apolonio, an old Spanish Poem,* 2 vols. (1917–1922); Ramón Menéndez Pidal, *Poema de Yúçuf: Materiales para su estudio* (1952), *idem,* ed., *Cantar de mio Cid: Texto, gramática y vocabulario,* 3 vols. (1908–1911, rev. 2nd ed. 1944–1946), "*Elena y Maria* (disputa del clérigo y el caballero): Poesía leonesa inédita del siglo XIII," in *Revista de filología española,* **1** (1914), and *Crestomatía del español medieval,* rev. by Rafael Lapesa and María Soledad de Andrés, 2 vols. (1965–1966).

Dana A. Nelson, "Generic vs. Individual Style: The Presence of Berceo in the *Alexandre,*" in *Romance Philology,* **29** (1975–1976), and *idem,* ed., *El libro de Alixandre: Reconstrucción crítica* (1979); Karl Pietsch, "On the Language of the Old Spanish *Grail Fragments,*" in *Modern Philology,* **13** (1915–1916) (the promised concluding segment never appeared), and *idem,* ed., *Spanish Grail Fragments* [George T. Northup, trans.], 2 vols. (1924–1925); Miguel Romera-Navarro, *Registro de lexicografía hispánica* (1951); Homero Serís, *Bibliografía de la lingüística española* (1964); José M. Solá-Solé, "El *Auto de los Reyes Magos:* ¿Impacto gascón o mozárabe?" in *Romance Philology,* **29** (1975–1976); Harry F. Williams, *An Index of Medieval Studies Published in Festschriften, 1865–1946, with Special Reference to Romanic Material* (1951); Hensley C. Woodbridge and Paul R. Olson, *A Tentative Bibliography of Hispanic Linguistics* (1952); Adolf Zauner, *Altspanisches Elementarbuch* (1908, rev. ed. 1921); Marion A. Zeitlin, "A Vocabulary to the *Rimado de palacio*" (diss., Univ. of California at Berkeley, 1931).

The pattern of periodization. Américo Castro and Federico de Onís, eds., *Fueros leoneses de Zamora, Salamanca, Ledesma y Alba de Tormes* (1916); Joan Corominas, "Problemas por resolver: *Lindo,*" in *Anales del Instituto de Lingüística de Cuyo,* **1** (1941–1942); Ramón J. Cuervo, "*Lindo,*" in *Revue hispanique,* **9** (1902); Charles B. Faulhaber, "Neo-traditionalism, Formulism, Individualism, and Recent Studies on the Spanish Epic," in *Romance Philology,* **30** (1976–1977); Emilio García Gómez, ed., *Las jarchas romances de la serie árabe en su marco* (1965, 2nd ed. 1975); Max Gorosch, ed., *El fuero de Teruel* (1950), reviewed by Malkiel in *Language,* **31** (1955); Augustus C. Jennings, "A Linguistic Study of the Cartulario de San Vicente de Oviedo" (diss., Columbia Univ., 1941); Hayward Keniston, *The Syntax of Castilian Prose,* I, *The Sixteenth Century* (1937); Henry R. Lang, ed., *Cancionero gallego-castelhano: The Extant Galician Poems of the Gallego-Castilian Lyric School (1350–1450)* (1902); Rafael Lapesa, "La apócope de la vocal en castellano antiguo: Intento de explicación histórica," in *Estudios dedicados a Menéndez Pidal,* II (1951). Yakov Malkiel, "Antiguo español y gallegoportugués *trocir* 'passar,'" in *Nueva revista de filología hispánica,* **10** (1956), "Le nivellement morphologique comme point de départ d'une 'loi phonétique': La monophtongaison occasionelle de *ie* et *ue* en ancien espagnol," in *Mélanges . . . offerts à Jean Frappier* (1970), "En torno al cultismo medieval: Los desciendentes hispánicos de DULCIS," in *Nueva revista de filología hispánica,* **24** (1975), and "Multi-conditioned Sound Change and the Impact of Morphology on Phonology," in *Language,* **52** (1976); Ramón Menéndez Pidal, ed., *Documentos lingüísticos de España,* I, *Reino de Castilla* (1919); Ian Michael, ed., *Poema de mío Cid* (1976, rev. ed. 1978); Thomas Montgomery, "Complementarity of Stem-Vowels in the Spanish Second and Third Conjugations," in *Romance Philology,* **29** (1975–1976); Tomás Navarro Tomás, ed., *Documentos lingüísticos del Alto Aragón* (1957); Dana A. Nelson, "The Domains of Old Spanish *-er* and *-ir* Verbs: A Clue to the Provenience of the *Alexandre,*" in *Romance Philology,* **26** (1972–1973); Victor R. B. Oelschläger, *A Medieval Spanish Word-List: A Preliminary Dated Vocabulary of First Appearances up to Berceo* (1940); J. Priebsch, ed., "Altspanische Glossen," in *Zeitschrift für romanische Philologie,* **19** (1895); Jean M. V. Roudil, ed., *Les fueros l'Alcáraz et d'Alarcón* (1968); Juan Ruiz, Arcipreste de Hita, *Libro de buen amor,* Raymond S. Willis, ed. (1972), Anthony N. Zahareas, ed. (1978), and other editions.

Colin Smith, ed., *Poema de mío Cid* (1972); José M. Solá-Solé, ed., *Corpus de poesía mozárabe: Las harǧa-s andalusies* (1973); Erik Staaff, *Étude sur l'ancien dialecte léonais d'après des chartes du XIIIe siècle* (1907), reviewed by Menéndez Pidal in *Revue de dialectologie romane,* **2** (1910); Samuel M. Stern, ed., *Les chansons mozarabes: Les vers finaux (kharjas) en espagnol dans les muwashshahs arabes et hébreux* (1953, repr. 1964); Gunnar Tilander, ed., *Los fueros de Aragón, según el manuscrito 458 de la Biblioteca Nacional de Madrid* (1937), *Los fueros de la Novenera* (1951), *Vidal mayor: Traducción aragonesa de la obra In excelsis Dei thesauris* *de Vidal de Canellas,* 3 vols. (1956), reviewed by Malkiel in *Language,* **35** (1959), and *Fueros aragoneses desconocidos promulgados a consecuencia de la gran peste de 1348* (1959); Knud Togeby, "L'apophonie des verbes espagnols et portugais en *-ir,*" in *Romance Philology,* **26** (1972–1973).

The dialects of Old Spanish. Manuel Alvar, *El fuero de Salamanca: Lingüística e historia* (1968), and *idem,* ed., *Vida de Santa María Egipcíaca,* 2 vols. (1970–1972); Miguel Asín Palacios, ed., *Glosario de voces romances registradas por un botánico anónimo hispano-musulman (siglos XI–XII)* (1943); Yo ten Cate, ed., *Poema de Alfonso XI,* 2 vols. (1942–1956); Joan Corominas, *Diccionario crítico etimológico de la lengua castellana,* 4 vols. (1954–1957), and *Breve diccionario etimológico de la lengua castellana* (1961, rev. 3rd. ed. 1973); Steven N. Dworkin, "Therapeutic Reactions to Excessive Phonetic Erosion: The Descendants of RIGIDU in Hispano- and Luso-Romance," in *Romance Philology,* **28** (1974–1975); Víctor Fernández Llela, *Gramática y vocabulario del Fuero Juzgo* (1929); Joseph E. Gillet, ed., *Propalladia and Other Works of Bartolomé de Torres Naharro,* III, *Notes* (1951); Fritz Krüger, "Die nordwestiberische Volkskultur," in *Wörter und Sachen,* **10** (1927), and *El léxico rural del noroeste ibérico,* Emilio Lorenzo y Criado, trans. (1947).

Rafael Lapesa, *Historia de la lengua española* (1942, rev. 6th ed. 1965), and *Asturiano y provenzal en el Fuero de Avilés* (1948); *El libro de Alexandre,* Raymond S. Willis, ed. (1934); Mark G. Littlefield, "The Riojan Provenience of Escorial Biblical Manuscript I.j.8," in *Romance Philology,* **31** (1977–1978); Consuelo López-Morillas, "Aljamiado *akošegir* and Its Old Provençal Counterparts: Studies in the Romance Transmission of Latin CŌN-S-," *ibid.,* **28** (1974–1975); Yakov Malkiel, "Paradigmatic Resistance to Sound Change: The Old Spanish Preterite Forms *vide, vido* Against the Background of the Recession of Primary *-d-,*" in *Language,* **36** (1960); Ramón Menéndez Pidal, *El dialecto leonés,* Carmen Bobes, ed. (1962); Gergard Rohlfs, *Le gascon: Études de philologie pyrénéenne* (1935, rev. 2nd ed. 1970); Francisco J. Simonet, *Glosario de voces ibéricas y latinas usadas entre los Mozárabes* . . . (1888, repr. 1967); Theodoricus Catalanus, *El libro de los caballos: Tratado de albeitería del siglo XIII,* Georg Sachs, ed. (1936); José María Yanguas y Miranda, *Diccionarios de los fueros del reino de Navarra* . . . , 2 vols. (1828–1829, repr. 1964).

Pronunciation and spelling. Amado Alonso, "Las correspondencias arábigo-españolas en los sistemas de sibilantes," in *Revista de filología hispánica,* **8** (1946), *De la pronunciación medieval a la moderna en español,* Rafael Lapesa [and María Josefa Canellada], eds., 2 vols. (1955–1969, rev. 2nd ed. of vol. 1, 1967), and a bibliography of Alonso's works in *Nueva revista de filología hispánica,* 7 (1953); Rufino J. Cuervo, "Disquisiciones sobre antigua ortografía y pronunciación castellanas" (1895), rev. version in his *Obras inéditas,* Félix Restrepo and P. U. González de la Calle, eds. (1944); H. Gavel, *Essai sur l'évolution de la prononciation du Castillan depuis le XIVe siècle* . . . (1920).

Yakov Malkiel, "Derivational Transparency as an Occasional Co-determinant of Sound-Change: A New Causal Ingredient in the Distribution of *-ç-* and *-z-* in Ancient Hispano-Romance," in *Romance Philology,* **25** (1971–1972), "Old Spanish *bivo, bevir, visque, vido:* A Preliminary Analysis," in *Studies in Honor of Lloyd A. Kasten* (1975), and "In Search of 'Penultimate' Causes of Language Change: Studies in the Avoidance of /ž/ in Proto-Spanish," in *Current Studies in Romance Linguistics,* Marta Luján and Fritz Hensey, eds. (1976); André Martinet, "The Unvoicing [Devoicing] of Old Spanish Sibilants," in *Romance Philology,* **5** (1951–1952), rev. and trans. in his *Économie des changements phonétiques: Traité de phonologie diachronique* (1955), 297–325.

YAKOV MALKIEL

[See also **Alexandre, Libro de; Aljamiado Literature; Apolonio, Libro de; Aragon; Asturias-León; Auto de los Reyes Magos; Berceo, Gonzalo de; Cantar de Mío Cid; Castile; Castilian Literature; Judeo-Spanish; Kharja; López de Ayala, Pero; Mozarabic Literature; Navarre, Kingdom of.**]

SPANISH LATIN LITERATURE. Latin Literature composed by inhabitants of the Iberian Peninsula during the Middle Ages (variously called Hispano-Latin or Spanish Latin Literature) rested on the solid foundation of Christian Latin writings from the third, fourth, and early fifth centuries, best exemplified by the Christian epic of Juvencus (*fl.* 330's) and the hymns of Prudentius (348–*ca.* 410).

With the Germanic invasion (409), the fifth century was a period of upheaval in Spain; but at the beginning of the century a last representative of Hispano-Roman culture, Paulus Orosius, following St. Augustine, wrote his *Historia adversus paganos* (418) to prove that Christianity was not the cause of the evils suffered by the Roman Empire. After Orosius there is little of literary value until the works of St. Martin of Braga (*ca.* 515–579). His *Formula vitae honestae* (after 570) is a moralizing work that presents the four cardinal virtues for a lay audience; the doctrines and probably much of the language were based on the writings of the Spanish philosopher Seneca (*d.* A.D. 39).

Under the Visigoths, the great age of Latin letters was the seventh century; the major figure was St.

Isidore of Seville (*ca.* 560–636), schoolmaster to the Middle Ages. His *Etymologiae* contain in twenty books an encyclopedic résumé of the learning of antiquity. Other works include theological treatises and histories. The style of his *Differentiae* and *Synonyma*—short periods, rhymed prose, antitheses, anaphora, asyndeton, and heavy use of synonyms—was imitated by St. Ildefonsus of Toledo (*ca.* 607–667) in his *De virginitate sanctae Mariae contra tres infideles,* the first of many Spanish works devoted to Mary. Other figures of note in Visigothic Spain are the historian John of Biclaro (*ca.* 540–621); Braulio, bishop of Saragossa (*ca.* 585–651), whose letters paint a vivid picture of contemporary life; and Eugenius II, bishop of Toledo (*d.* 657), the best poet of his age.

This active literary life ended with the Muslim invasion (711), in large part because the general level of the Latin educational system—in both the Christian north and Islamic south—declined precipitously. Latin letters continued to be cultivated under the Muslims, but their last important manifestation occurred in mid-ninth-century Córdoba when St. Eulogius (*d.* 859) and Paul Albar (Paulus Alvarus, *ca.* 800–*ca.* 861) wrote in defense of contemporary martyrs. Alvarus' impassioned *Indiculus luminosus* (854) is remembered today chiefly for its lament that young Christians had turned to Arabic and no longer cultivated or could even read Latin. In the north the Christian states that emerged in the course of the eighth century were absorbed in the struggle against Islam; there was little leisure for cultural activities. During the first several hundred years one can mention Beatus of Liébana's commentary on the Apocalypse (*In apocalypsin, ca.* 786) and the *Chronica* (*ca.* 883) of Alfonso III, king of Asturias, which initiated a series of official histories that continued until the end of the Middle Ages and beyond. For poetry during this period we must turn to the Mozarabic hymnary, the ancient liturgy of the Visigothic church.

The suppression of this Mozarabic liturgy at the end of the eleventh century is symptomatic of what happened in other spheres of Spanish intellectual and cultural life as well. The heritage of Isidore gave way increasingly to extrapeninsular trends, from Latin Europe and the Islamic Orient. European influence is seen clearly in the *Tractatus Garsiae Toletani Canonici de Albino et Rufino* by an anonymous canon of Toledo, perhaps the most successful work of the period. An antipapal satire, the first (1099) of many similar pieces from all over Europe, it recounts the visit of Archbishop Grimoardus (a pseudonym) of Toledo to Rome in order to obtain an appointment from Pope Urban II; he brings with him the relics of Saints Rufinus (gold) and Albinus (silver). This attack on simony parodies to devastating effect the homilies and sermons on the relics of martyrs. Although written in prose, the piece's parodic spirit resembles that of contemporary goliardic poetry, a genre to which Spain contributed very little, with the exception of the *Carmina Rivipullensia,* twenty love poems found in a late-twelfth-century manuscript from the monastery of S. María de Ripoll (Catalonia). Although possibly of French origin and certainly of French inspiration—not surprising, given the close ties of the Spanish March with France—they were probably composed in Ripoll itself, the home of a poetic tradition going back at least to the eleventh century. The Ripoll songs resemble those of the *Carmina Burana,* with their commonplaces of springtime love, stylized descriptions of the lover and the act of love, dream sequences, and Ovidian reminiscences.

The flood of scientific and philosophical texts, both ancient Greek and medieval Arabic, which entered Latin Europe via the various schools of translators (particularly Toledo) had an immense effect on the nascent scholasticism of the twelfth century. Equally influential for literature was the *Disciplina clericalis* (after 1106) of a converted Jew, Petrus Alfonsi of Huesca. Organized around a simple frame story of a father giving advice to his son, this collection of stories, proverbs, and sententiae from the East became one of the basic sources for later tellers of tales, from the *Gesta Romanorum* to Boccaccio and even Cervantes.

An innovation in twelfth-century histories was an interest in the exploits of individuals. The *Chronica Adefonsi imperatoris* (*ca.* 1147) is still the official history in that it narrates the actions of Alfonso VII, king of Castile and León; but the *Historia Roderici* (*ca.* 1110) is dedicated for the first time to the deeds of a nonroyal personage, the legendary Cid *campeador,* Rodrigo Díaz de Vivar. Hispano-Latin historiography culminates in the thirteenth century with Lucas, bishop of Túy (*d.* 1249), and Rodrigo Jiménez de Rada (1170/1180–1247), archbishop of Toledo. The former's *Chronicon mundi* (1236) continues the genre of universal history, while the latter's series of historical works—such as the *Historia Gothica* (1243)—tells the story of each of the successive ethnic groups that invaded the Iberian Peninsula.

In Spain, as in the rest of Europe from the thirteenth century on, Latin increasingly gave up its literary functions to the vernacular languages, although it remained the language of schoolroom and church. Literally hundreds of Spanish figures from the thirteenth to the fifteenth centuries contributed to the learned disciplines. For example, the canonist Raymond of Peñafort (*d.* 1275) organized the collection of papal decretals of Pope Gregory IX (1234). The *Summulae logicales* of Peter of Spain (*d.* 1277), later Pope John XXI, served as a beginning textbook on logic for centuries all over Europe. Another enormously popular handbook was the *Manipulus curatorum* (1333), a manual for parish priests, by Guido of Monte Roterio, from Teruel. Ramon Lull, Mallorcan mystic and evangelist (*ca.* 1233–1316), left a career in the royal service in order to undertake the conversion of the Muslim world to Christianity through the use of his *Ars,* a system by which he could prove by necessary and strictly logical reasons all the doctrines of the Christian faith.

In the fifteenth century one may cite Alfonso Fernández de Madrigal (El Tostado, *d.* 1455), theologian at Salamanca; Raymond Sabunde of Barcelona (*d.* 1436), rector of the University of Toulouse, whose *Theologia naturalis* (1433) inspired Montaigne; and Fernando of Córdoba (*d.* 1486), who astonished Europe with the breadth of his learning. Counter to this traditional scholastic current ran another, that of Italian humanism, which begins to appear in Spain—first in Catalonia, via the papal court at Avignon—toward the end of the fourteenth century. Beginning as an interest in translations of the classics, by the second half of the fifteenth century humanism had begun to affect above all historical writing, a trend reflected in the *Paralipomenon Hispaniae* of Cardinal Joan Margarit i Pau (1421–1484) and the *Gesta Hispaniensia* of Alfonso de Palencia (1423–1490). The reform of the teaching of Latin, however, the basis for a true understanding of the classics and a renovation of Latin letters, began only in the last quarter of the century through the efforts of Antonio de Nebrija (Antonio Martínez de Cala y Jarava, 1444–1522), whose *Introductiones Latinae* (1481) continued in use as a textbook well into the nineteenth century. Although best known for this work, for his grammar of Spanish—the first printed grammar of any of the vernacular languages (1492)—and for his Spanish-Latin dictionaries, Nebrija was also an occasional poet in impeccable hexameters. The impressive flowering of neo-Latin literature in sixteenth-century Spain can be attributed in large part to his educational efforts.

BIBLIOGRAPHY

Tomás y Joaquín Carreras y Artau, *Historia de la filosofía española: Filosofía cristiana de los siglos XIII al XV,* 2 vols. (1939–1943); Ottavio Di Camillo, *El humanismo castellano del siglo XV,* Manuel Lloris, trans. (1976); Manuel C. Díaz y Díaz, *Index scriptorum Latinorum medii aevi Hispanorum,* 2 vols. (1958–1959), and *De Isidoro al siglo XI: Ocho estudios sobre la vida literaria peninsular* (1976); Ursicino Domínguez del Val, "Herencia literaria de padres y escritores españoles de Osio de Córdoba a Julián de Toledo," in *Repertorio de historia de las ciencias eclesiásticas en España,* **1** (1970); Charles B. Faulhaber, "Las retóricas hispanolatinas medievales (s. XIII–XV)," *ibid.,* **7** (1979); *Iberian Fathers,* Claude W. Barlow, trans., 2 vols. (1969); Edward James, ed., *Visigothic Spain: New Approaches* (1980); Therese Latzke, "Die Carmina erotica der Ripollsammlung," in *Mittellateinisches Jahrbuch,* **10** (1975); Klaus Reinhardt and Horacio Santiago Otero, *Biblioteca biblica ibérica medieval* (1986); Francisco Rico, "Las letras latinas del siglo XII en Galicia, León y Castilla," in *Ábaco,* **2** (1969), and *Nebrija frente a los bárbaros* (1978); José Riesco Terrero, "La metafísica en España (siglos XII al XV)," in *Repertorio de historia de las ciencias eclesiásticas en España,* **4** (1972); Isaías Rodríguez, "Autores espirituales españoles en la edad media," *ibid.,* **1** (1970); Isidoro Rodríguez, "Literatura latina hispana del 711 hasta Trento," *ibid.,* **2** (1971).

CHARLES B. FAULHABER

[See also **Beatus Manuscripts; Braulio of Saragossa, St.; Cantar de Mío Cid; Cid, History and Legend of; Disciplina Clericalis; Encyclopedias and Dictionaries, Western European; Eulogius of Córdoba; Eugenius II of Toledo; Hisperic Latin; Ildefonsus, St.; Isidore of Seville, St.; Latin Literature; Lull, Ramon; Orosius; Peter of Spain; Prudentius; Raymond of Peñafort, St.**]

SPANISH LITERATURE. Literature in Spanish is treated below in the following twenty articles:

Spanish Literature (survey)
- **Ballads**
- **Bible Translations**
- **Biography**
- **Chronicles**
- **Dawn and Spring Songs**
- **Drama**
- **Epic Poetry**
- **Hagiography**

Instructional Works
Lost Works
Lyric Poetry
Popular Poetry
Romances
Satire
Sentimental Romances
Sermons
Translations
Troy Story
Versification and Prosody

Additional articles on related topics are cited in cross-references at the end of each essay.

SPANISH LITERATURE

THE BEGINNINGS

Traditional lyric. The history of Spanish vernacular literature begins about the year 900. Its prehistory, though undeniably present, is shadowy and eludes definition. Arabic literary historians of the twelfth century tell us that the characteristically Hispano-Arabic verse form known as the *muwashshaḥ* was invented, circa 900, by Muqaddam, or Muḥammad, of Cabra, who took verses in the language of the people and built his poems round them. The language of the people, as we see in texts from a later period, could mean either Mozarabic (the variety of Hispano-Romance spoken in Muslim Spain) or Vulgar Arabic. Muslim Spain, at that time the greater part of the peninsula, was largely bilingual, with a racially mixed population and a thriving Jewish community. Thus it was natural that cultured Arabic poets should draw on traditional song in Romance as well as in their own tongue, and that Hebrew poets should imitate them.

The earliest datable *muwashshaḥ* with a Romance *kharja* is a Hebrew poem by Yosef al-Katīb ("the Scribe"), composed not later than 1042. Allowing time for the *kharja* to circulate before Yosef heard it and used it for his own work, about 1000 seems a reasonable date for this first surviving lyric in a Romance language. Extant *muwashshaḥs* in Arabic or Hebrew contain over sixty *kharja*s that are largely or partly in Spanish (linguistic mixture is a feature of the *kharja*s, as of the society that produced them). The manuscripts, especially those in Arabic script, are hard to read, and even the language of some *kharja*s is in dispute. Some, however, belong unmistakably to a tradition of women's love song that is found elsewhere in the peninsula, in other parts of the former Roman Empire, and even further afield. The *kharja*s exhibit notable coincidences of theme and vocabulary with the *villancicos* of later medieval Castile and the *cantigas de amigo* of Galicia and Portugal; in addition, their verse form resembles that of the *villancicos*. The much earlier appearance in writing of the *kharja*s seems to be a historical accident; cultured poets alone could give written form to these songs—individually ephemeral yet collectively of astonishing persistence—and Muslim Spain had cultured poets before the Christian north.

It is probable that from a very early stage the whole peninsula had a flourishing tradition of women's love song, and that this was part of an even wider tradition. Recent investigation shows that *kharja*s, *cantigas de amigo,* and *villancicos* share a formulaic system that is found also in the early popular lyrics of northern France, and that presumably goes back to Vulgar Latin oral lyrics of the empire, lost except for occasional ambiguous references. In all probability, the tradition is even more widespread and ancient. Similarities have been noted with the love songs of classical Greece, and some coincidences with Slavic lyric suggest that the Hispanic songs may be one branch of a popular poetic tradition rooted in the early Indo-European period. Thus the *kharja*s, which seen from one angle exemplify the uniqueness of Spain's culture, resulting from the coexistence of Christians, Moors, and Jews, on closer inspection provide important evidence of the European roots of Spanish literature.

The earliest epics. The earliest Spanish epic is probably *Siete infantes de Lara* (or *de Salas*), the story of a family feud leading to treacherous murder and bloody revenge; it bears a striking resemblance to the *Nibelungenlied. Siete infantes,* like other Spanish epics of the earliest period, was probably composed orally, using a system of formulas (later, extant, epic texts that were clearly composed in writing make such substantial use of formulaic language that they must have inherited it from an oral past). None of the earliest epic poems survives, but their incorporation into later chronicles makes it possible to reconstruct the plots, often in great detail, and even to extract lines of verse (550 lines in the case of *Siete infantes*) from the chroniclers' prose. Some scholars believe in a Spanish epic tradition before *Siete infantes,* a tradition dealing with the fall of Spain to the Moors and the beginnings of the Reconquest, and descending in an unbroken line from the Germanic epic of the Visigoths, but the evidence for this is very weak. Other scholars have sought to connect the Spanish poems with an Arabic epic tradition, but here also there are difficulties that have not been overcome.

Siete infantes takes for granted a historical situation, of coexistence punctuated by border raids, which by the late tenth century no longer existed. For this reason, it can hardly have been composed much later than 1000. It was followed by further epics dealing with events—real and fictitious—under the first counts of Castile. The later poems of the counts cycle, which have not been preserved but can be more or less clearly traced in chronicles and other texts—*La condesa traidora, Romanz del infant García, Cantar de Fernán González*—have important features in common, perhaps because *Siete infantes* set the pattern. Their plots of treachery and vengeance do not sufficiently distinguish them from other epic cycles, but the prominent role of women is a more unusual feature. Indeed, female characters dominate the action in most of the counts cycle. It is also noteworthy that all of these epics are connected with tomb cults in the monasteries and churches of Old Castile and León, though the evidence is insufficient to determine whether cults gave rise to epics or vice versa. Ecclesiastical connections are not restricted to the counts cycle, but are found in most medieval Spanish epics. So is a basis of historical fact: although the historical accuracy of these poems is much slighter than was once supposed, it is nevertheless a good deal more substantial than in the medieval epics of most other countries. Another continuing feature of Spanish epic, from *Siete infantes* to the late *Mocedades de Rodrigo,* is that although the Moors are enemies in battle, they are not the treacherous villains presented in the *Chanson de Roland*. The real villains are other Christians, often members of the hero's own family, and a generous and honorable Moorish character may be used to point a contrast (in *Siete infantes,* the avenging hero Mudarra is half Moorish). An even more striking feature is the prominence of sexuality from the earliest poems onward. This, together with the dominant women of the counts cycle, shows that Spanish epic cannot have been an exclusively male concern.

The poetic quality of *Siete infantes* is clear from the lines of verse that have been reconstructed, and from the story preserved in the chronicles. This lost epic seems, indeed, to have been one of the masterpieces of medieval Spanish literature. It left its mark not only on chronicles but on ballads, and through them on the drama of Spain's Golden Age. Spanish epic has displayed an astonishing ability to survive across the centuries and in various genres.

Latin literature. In the eleventh century, then, vernacular literature consists of oral poetry, both lyric and epic. Written literature in Spain, apart from the transmission of few *kharja*s, is in Latin, Arabic, or Hebrew. Spaniards (more accurately, natives of the Iberian Peninsula) had been writing in Latin for over a thousand yeras; Seneca, Lucan, Quintilian, and Martial are the great names from the classical period, with Prudentius and Orosius from the last days of the Roman Empire. These, however, show no awareness of themselves as Spanish authors (although this is how they are now often regarded in Spain). They are Latin writers who happen to come from the peninsula, and there is a very slow transition to those later medieval Spanish writers who happen to express themselves in Latin. The transition perhaps begins in Visigothic Spain, now politically separated from the Roman Empire; the leading Hispano-Latin author of this period is St. Isidore of Seville (*ca.* 540–636). The present article, devoted to vernacular literature, cannot go beyond a token acknowledgment of the great mass of writing in Latin, some of it of great importance; but one must always remember that almost all written prose and poetry in medieval Spain depends to some extent on the Latin tradition, whether from within or from beyond the peninsula. For further discussion, see "Spanish Latin Literature" in this volume.

THE TWELFTH CENTURY

Late in the eleventh century, or in the first half of the twelfth, the assassination of King Sancho II of Castile (1072) was commemorated in two epics, the vernacular *Cantar de Sancho II,* for oral delivery to a popular audience, and the Latin literary epic *Carmen de morte Sanctii regis*. Both are lost, but may be traced in chronicles. The relation between them is uncertain, as is the mode of composition of the *Cantar*. It seems likely, however, that the poet of the *Cantar* saw his work as a continuation of the counts of Castile cycle. Other heroic verse in Latin was written at this time: the *Carmen Campidoctoris,* a panegyric to Rodrigo Díaz de Vivar, el Cid, and the *Poema de Almería,* which celebrates the capture of Almería from the Moors by Alfonso VII.

The Cid was praised in prose as well as verse; the *Historia Roderici,* probably composed about the middle of the century, sees the hero's career through the eyes of his supporters, and it is dangerous to use it as an impartial historical source. The *Poema* (or *Cantar*) *de mío Cid,* the greatest of vernacular Spanish epics, is often said to have been composed in the first half of the twelfth century, but is very probably a work of the early thirteenth.

Literature in the learned tongues of the peninsula—Latin, Arabic, and Hebrew—flourished at this time. Just before the century began, García, canon of Toledo, composed a notable satirical poem, the *Garsuinis,* and a twelfth-century manuscript from the Catalan monastery of Ripoll preserves what may the first consciously fashioned cycle of love poems in medieval Europe (*Carmina Rivipullensia*). Another innovation is *Disciplina clericalis,* by the converted Jew Petrus Alfonsi (*b. ca.* 1062, baptized 1106). This is a collection of exempla, chiefly from Oriental sources, which acclimatizes in Europe a narrative genre that had long enjoyed a vogue in Arabic and before that in Sanskrit.

A development with even more far-reaching consequences was the growth of several centers of translation and, in the second half of the twelfth century, the establishment in Toledo of a highly organized and prolific school grouped round Gerard of Cremona. Arabic works had been translated into Latin before, notably in tenth-century Ripoll, but the twelfth-century centers, and especially the Toledo school, were on a much bigger scale. Scholars from all over Europe came to these hubs of intellectual activity, and from them emerged scientific and philosophical treatises that gave to the Latin West not only the finest products of Arabic thought, but also a number of important Greek works with their Arabic commentaries. Spain, a cultural bridge between the Arabic and Latin worlds, thus played a vital part in the twelfth-century renaissance. From Muslim Spain came two of the leading philosophers of the century: Averroës (Ibn Rushd, 1126–1198) and Maimonides (1135–1204), who wrote in both Hebrew and Arabic.

In the second half of the century, we find the first clear cases of vernacular literature composed in (rather than merely reduced to) writing. The most important of these is a play. Latin liturgical drama, which flourished in Catalonia, has left relatively little trace in Castile, but the vernacular *Auto de los reyes magos* is, despite its brevity, a work of remarkable quality. Composed for Epiphany presentation at Toledo Cathedral, it dramatizes the clash between the old and new dispensations, and in the final scene of a dispute between Herod's rabbis it provides the dramatic equivalent of two Christian iconographic traditions: the blindness of Synagoga and her incipient reconciliation with Ecclesia. The *Auto* has no successors. There are occasional and ambiguous references to dramatic performances, but not until the fifteenth century do we find further plays in Castilian, or even clear references to lost works. The other vernacular works of this period are significant not for their literary quality but because they are the first specimens of historical writing in Spanish: brief annals in Navarrese, the earliest of which may have been composed in 1186. The real achievements of twelfth-century peninsular historiography are in Latin (for instance, the *Historia silense, ca.* 1116) and in Arabic, but in the misnamed *Corónicas navarras* (they do not have the length or structure of chronicles) and in the slightly later Aragonese *Liber regum* (between 1196 and 1209) we see the first faint glimmers of what will, some seventy years later, become a vigorous tradition of vernacular historiography.

THE THIRTEENTH CENTURY

The epic. The longest, and by far the best, of the extant Spanish epic texts is the *Poema de mío Cid,* probably composed in the Burgos region circa 1207. Its author is anonymous (the Per Abbat who is named in the explicit seems to be the scribe). Study of the text, however, reveals much; the poet was thoroughly familiar with legal procedure, and his cast of mind was that of a lawyer or administrator. He made use of written sources (though probably not as intensively as some recent criticism suggests), but he also drew on oral poetic techniques, especially a formulaic style. The proportion of formulaic language is much too high to be the result of chance, but is far lower than in any poem whose oral composition is proven. The conclusion that this is a cultured poet's adaptation of the oral style is supported by recent analysis, which shows a close resemblance in the use of repetitions by *Mío Cid* and by nineteenth-century Yugoslav poems composed in writing but in the traditional style. This modification is not confined to style; the *Mío Cid* poet uses the familiar epic theme of vengeance, but in place of the slaughter that forms the climax of *Odyssey, Chanson de Roland,* or *Nibelungenlied,* or the savagery of execution in *Siete infantes* or

Infant García, we find a civil action in court that vindicates the hero and humiliates the villains. In the duels that follow, blood is shed but no lives are lost.

The moderation in the poet's presentation of the hero's vengeance occurs equally in the stylistic details. In the battle descriptions, the numbers of warriors are realistically small, and though there are great feats of valor they remain within the bounds of credibility. The poet very seldom makes explicit judgments; with a self-effacing restraint unusual in an epic poet, he prefers to imply judgment of the characters through the action, through use of imagery, or in what other characters say about them. This quality of prudent restraint, of *mesura,* is shared by the poet and his hero; the Cid, like Beowulf but unlike Roland, Siegfried, or Gonzalo González of *Siete infantes,* blends *fortitudo* with *sapientia.* This does not save him from a tragic dilemma when the king, to whom he is passionately loyal and who has just restored him to favor after an exile caused by the intrigues of his enemies at court, proposes that the Cid's beloved daughters should marry the Infantes de Carrión (Leonese members of the effete higher nobility). The marriages end disastrously, when the Infantes beat and abandon their young wives in the oak forest of Corpes, but the Cid's courage and *mesura,* aided by the hard-won support of the king, wipe out the dishonor, and the hero's daughters are happily remarried to royalty. This is that rarity among epics, a story with a happy ending. The story, moreover, is convincingly told, with theme, style, and structure supporting each other and combining to produce the desired result.

Other epics of the thirteenth century are reworkings of much older poems of the counts of Castile cycle. The *Poema de Fernán González,* of about 1250(?), combines the lost *Cantar de Fernán González* with literary, folkloric, and hagiographic material to serve the interests of the monastery of S. Pedro de Arlanza as well as those of Castilian patriotism. The connection between *Mío Cid* and another monastery, S. Pedro de Cardeña, is evident (Cardeña plays a prominent part early in the poem, and the monks developed a thriving tomb cult of the Cid), but it is not easy to establish a causal relationship. In the case of the *Poema de Fernán González,* there is no problem; the poet is clearly an Arlanza monk who aims to inspire devotion, and stimulate gifts, to the monastery by stressing its connection with the first count of independent Castile. Alone among Spanish epics, this poem uses not the traditional epic meter (assonating lines arranged in laisses of varying length), but the learned verse form known as *cuaderna vía.* The poem is seriously incomplete, and is thus hard to compare with the almost complete *Mío Cid,* but, despite *Fernán González*'s obvious merits, it seems to fall well short of *Mío Cid* in both stylistic and structural qualities. Other reworkings are a second *Siete infantes de Lara* (*ca.* 1300?), which improves the structural balance of the original, and a second *Cantar de Sancho II.* The effect of the latter reworking is to detach the story of Sancho's murder from the fringes of the counts cycle, where the original poem seems to have placed it, and to make it a forerunner of *Mío Cid.* The young Cid's part in the story is enhanced, and the dominant role of Princess Urraca is reduced. The Cid cycle is completed by the *Gesta de las mocedades de Rodrigo,* showing the beginnings of the hero's career.

The last-named poem, like the reworked *Sancho II* and *Siete infantes,* is lost, but like them it can be reconstructed in outline. The use of chronicle texts to reconstruct epics raises a serious problem: since almost every chronicle, and in some cases almost every manuscript, has a slightly different version of the epic stories it incorporates, how much of the variation should be attributed to the differing tastes of chroniclers, and how much to the use of different poetic sources? In the cases mentioned above, the differences are so great that poems have fairly clearly been reworked, and as more chronicle manuscripts are examined the number of such reworkings grows. Given the loss of most epic texts, chronicles and ballads become an indispensable source for our knowledge of the Spanish epic tradition.

One thirteenth-century epic remains to be mentioned: the hundred-line fragment of *Roncesvalles,* a derivative of the *Chanson de Roland.* The surviving lines present Charlemagne's lament for the dead heroes, in a vigorous style that seems to owe something to *Siete infantes.* The circulation of Carolingian epic in Spain was bound to raise some nationalistic resentment, and the lost *Bernardo del Carpio* embodied this in another story of treachery and vengeance.

The clerecía poets. The most notable non-epic poems are concentrated in the first half of the century, though precise dating is difficult or impossible. The majority are in the new *cuaderna vía,* an adaptation of a verse form from across the Pyrenees. It has long been known that the *cuaderna vía* poems (also referred to as *mester de clerecía*) are associated with the monasteries and universities of Old Castile and the Leonese border. The latest research suggests that this poetic movement (in which the poets have a common literary program, and are aware of each other's writings) may have begun at Palencia, the first Spanish university, in the 1220's. Many of the teachers at Palencia were French or had studied in France, and they may well have brought with them the alexandrine lines and the monorhymed quatrains that were given Spanish form in *cuaderna vía*. It may also be significant that the earliest and longest poem in the new meter, the *Libro de Alexandre* (late 1220's), has as its principal sources works by French poets: the *Roman d'Alexandre,* and the Latin *Alexandreis* by Gautier de Châtillon. The most likely hypothesis is, then, that a French-trained Palencia poet launched a new school of poetry with the *Libro de Alexandre.* Moreover, the launching was a conscious act: the first stanzas of the poem contain a veritable literary manifesto.

Such a development would come most easily in the vigor and ambition of a new university, and the university atmosphere is clearly perceptible in the poem. Thus the twelfth-century renaissance in France, which, as we have seen, depended on Spain for much of its intellectual sustenance, seems to have repaid the debt by stimulating the first literary movement in Spanish. At almost the same time, cultured lyric poets in Galicia and Portugal were adapting the genres and verse forms of Provençal in the courtly love poetry of the *cantigas de amor* and in the satirical and often scurrilous *cantigas d'escarnho e de mal dizer.* This movement (which led the cultured poets to take an interest in the traditional oral lyric of their region, and to produce the written texts of *cantigas de amigo*) seems to have been due not to the twelfth-century renaissance but rather to the *camino francés,* the pilgrim route from southern France to the Galician shrine of Santiago de Compostela.

The *Libro de Alexandre,* reflecting the duality of its principal sources, is of mixed genre; fundamentally a romance, it also has elements of the literary epic. This poem's carefully woven structure, its use of figural technique to point its moral, and its vivid descriptive passages effectively transmit the grandeur of its central theme: the hero of supreme ability and dazzling achievement who conquers the world but, through an increasingly apparent flaw, brings about his own downfall. Obviously an exemplum for rulers, less obviously a moral lesson for all its readers, this is one of the best of the many medieval works on Alexander the Great.

Alexandre has been attributed to Gonzalo de Berceo, a priest attached to the monastery of S. Millán de la Cogolla, who was born at the end of the twelfth century and died before 1264. The attribution, which is made in one of the manuscripts, has recently been supported on grounds of similarities of language between *Alexandre* and the known works of Berceo, but these are probably due to direct influence and to a common formulaic system in the thirteenth-century *clerecía* poems. The poetic persona that emerges from *Alexandre* is markedly different from that presented in Berceo's works.

Berceo's first poem is the *Vida de San Millán de la Cogolla* (early 1230's?), in which the new poetic form is applied to a purpose at once devout and economic. The monastery had fallen on hard times, and a monk had forged a document entitling it to tribute from a wide area. Berceo's adaptation of a Latin prose life of the saint may be largely a pretext for a rendering of the forged *privilegium,* which forms the poem's climax. The poem is good: well structured, convincing in its narrative, and made livelier by its borrowing of epic material and of stylistic devices of the minstrels. What is more, Berceo's plan seems to have succeeded, for the monastery's economic position improved. If the chronology suggested is correct, the *clerecía* school thus begins with a poetically ambitious re-creation of classical antiquity and with the use of poetry for urgently practical ends. The dichotomy is, of course, not total; *Alexandre* has a moral point to make, and Berceo, even in the *Vida de San Millán,* seems to enjoy exercising his poetic gifts. Yet the two tendencies are there, and they continue in later *clerecía* works, with the practical aims being more often dominant. Those aims are, however, generally pious rather than economic. Only the *Poema de Fernán González,* which, as an epic, is set apart from other *clerecía* poems, clearly follows the example of Berceo's first work by serving the economic interest of a particular monastery.

Berceo's other poems, narrative or expository, with some lyrical elements, fall into three categories: hagiographic, Marian, and doctrinal. The first category, chiefly concerned with local saints, spans his entire literary career, from the *Vida de Santo Domingo de Silos* (probably the immediate successor to the *Vida de San Millán*) to the *Vida de Santa Oria* of his old age; the *Martirio de San Lorenzo* is incomplete. The most famous of the Marian poems—indeed, of all Berceo's works—is the *Milagros de Nuestra Señora,* twenty-five miracle stories with an allegorical introduction to the book. The Virgin is presented in varying moods: tender, fierce in defense of her devotees, in one story furiously jealous; but the overall message is the same—she will protect those who revere her. Lyrical elements are stronger in the *Duelo de la Virgen* and the *Loores de Nuestra Señora.* The former contains a watchman's song that blends popular and liturgical elements. The Marian and hagiographic poems, aimed at encouraging devotion, are addressed to a wide public. It is for this reason that Berceo borrows from the *juglares* (minstrels); he is competing with them for an audience. (The role of the minstrels in medieval Spanish literature is hotly disputed. It is clear that they were the transmitters of much poetry, and they presumably composed the early oral epic, but some scholars believe that they played a much larger part, composing epics and other poems over several centuries.) Berceo's doctrinal works, *Signos del Juicio Final* and *Sacrificio de la misa,* are designed for a more restricted audience. *Sacrificio* in particular, although carefully expository, is pitched at a fairly high intellectual level. These two poems may still be addressed to the laity, but to a laity in some measure already educated. They may reflect in one way, and the Marian and hagiographic poems in another, the improvement of religious education among the laity, one of the most important concerns of the Fourth Lateran Council.

One other major *clerecía* poem was composed at this time: the *Libro de Apolonio* (1240's?), like *Alexandre,* is a romance with a classical subject, though of a different kind. This version of the story of Apollonius of Tyre, still redolent of the primitive folkloric associations of the original, its plot filled with violence, natural calamities, and sexual sin, reaches the standard happy ending of Greek romance in a way that points a Christian moral. Later poems in *cuaderna vía,* of uncertain dating, are on the fringes of the *clerecía* school. They are works of moral philosophy (*Castigos y exemplos de Catón, Proverbios de Salamón,* and *Libro de miseria de omne*), hagiography (*Vida de Sant Alifonsso,* and lost works on Mary Magdalene and the founder of the Dominicans), and Marian devotion (*Gozos de la Virgen*). These have been variously dated from the mid thirteenth to the late fourteenth century; recent research points to the earlier part of this period. None seems to reach the literary level of Berceo, *Alexandre,* or *Apolonio.*

Other poems. Another important class of thirteenth-century poems is composed in rhymed couplets with an octosyllabic basis but considerable irregularity of meter and of rhyme. This verse form, like *cuaderna vía,* seems to be an adaptation of a form favored by twelfth-century French poets (Chrétien de Troyes wrote in octosyllabic couplets). Generically and thematically, also, they adapt trans-Pyrenean fashions. Most of them seem to be roughly contemporary with the *clerecía* poems, but attempts to date them more precisely are usually arbitrary. They do not form a school, but have occasional links with *clerecía* poetry. Three are debate poems. The *Disputa del alma y cuerpo* (only the first part survives) may be the earliest extant nondramatic poem written in Castilian; it changes the emphasis of the criticism in its French original. *Elena y María* uses the tradition of the knight-clerk debate to give a scathingly satirical picture of society; both knight and priest are shown, in this abusive debate between their mistresses, to betray their essential social function. A third European debate tradition, that of water and wine, forms the second part of Lope de Moros' *Razón de amor,* the first part being a love narrative with strong lyric elements. This subtle, beautiful, and enigmatic poem, which blends Provençal and popular Hispanic influences, is much discussed by scholars.

Hagiography is represented—very differently from the extant *cuaderna vía* saints' lives—by the *Vida de Santa María Egipciaca.* Like the body-soul debate, this is a frequent subject in medieval Spanish verse and prose. Not only does the thirteenth-century *Vida* offer vivid pictures of Mary of Egypt's life as a harlot and of her years of penitence in the desert; it improves on its French original by borrowing lyric motifs and techniques from the Hispanic tradition. The *Libre dels tres reys d'Orient* (the misleading title given in the manuscript) or *Libro de la infancia y muerte de Jesús* reshapes material from an apocryphal gospel to provide a tightly structured illustration of the working of grace through baptism. Metrically distinct from the other poems in couplets (it has longer lines, grouped in stanzas with a refrain) is *¡Ay Iherusalem!* (late 1240's), a lament for the fall of the city to the Saracens in 1244. Like its contemporaries, this is a Spanish representative of a European genre—but, in this case, rather surprisingly so. Spanish concentration on the Reconquest, to the almost total exclusion of the crusades in the Holy Land, makes a Spanish crusading poem something of an oddity. The very existence of *¡Ay Iherusalem!*—a splendid poem in its own right—illustrates the extent to which thirteenth-century Spanish poetry is rooted in a European tradition.

The rise of vernacular prose. Poetry, as we have seen, dominates vernacular literature in the first half of the thirteenth century, and its center is the monasteries and universities of the north. The most important prose works are in Latin: the histories by Lucas, bishop of Túy, and Rodrigo Ximénez de Rada, archbishop of Toledo. The Toledo school of translators continued to produce Latin versions of Arabic works. Yet vernacular prose begins to develop from its fitful late-twelfth-century origins. About 1220, a second, Castilian, version of *Liber regum* was composed, and a geographical treatise, *Semejança del mundo,* combines and where necessary modifies two Latin sources. This more sophisticated approach looks forward to the achievements of Alfonso el Sabio's reign. *Fazienda de Ultra Mar,* a combination of pilgrim's guide to the Holy Land with biblical material, once thought to be the earliest vernacular prose work, is probably a thirteenth-century translation of a Latin book. A few decades later, an excellent work of local history is written, the *Crónica de la población de Ávila.*

Ferdinand III (St. Ferdinand), who ruled Castile from 1217 to 1252, is famous for the reconquest of much of Andalusia and for the final union of León with Castile (1230), but politico-military triumphs did not absorb all his energies. He began the long series of vernacular legal works by having the Visigothic legal code translated (*Fuero juzgo*), and the *Libro de los doce sabios* may have been written for him. This is probably the first Spanish work of wisdom literature (a collection of classical and Oriental sententiae, within a perfunctory narrative framework). Like most such works, it has an Arabic original, as do the earliest vernacular exemplum collections, produced at the end of Fernando's reign and the beginning of the next. In 1251 the then Prince Alfonso (*b.* 1221) commissioned *Calila e Dimna,* a Spanish version of the Indian collection of tales, *Panchatantra,* which had reached Arabic via Persian. Two years later, his brother Fadrique had another collection, the *Book of Sindibad,* translated as *Libro de los assayamientos de las mugeres* (generally known as *Libro de los engaños*). *Calila,* and still more *Engaños,* have strong narrative frames, which in the latter case contributes to the overall moral of the tales. *Engaños* is the first of several Spanish *Sindibad* (or *Seven Sages*) versions. The production of these two works of fiction, at the dawn of the Alfonsine era of utilitarian translations, may be explained by the increasing vogue of the popular sermon: the mendicant friars and other popular preachers needed a large stock of exempla to illustrate their points and to hold the attention of their audiences.

Alfonso X el Sabio (*r.* 1252–1284) was a political failure, but the success that eluded him in one sphere was gained in another. Even though some of his intellectual enterprises suffered from the unrealistic ambition that marked him as king, he succeeded in establishing Castilian as a normal vehicle for learned prose, in equipping the language with a wider vocabulary and more flexible syntax, and in creating a large and varied body of legal, historical, and scientific works. Building on the well-established Toledo school, he formed an international team of scholars, translators, and artists.

Intellectuals who in Ferdinand's reign would have made their career in the monastery or the university were increasingly attracted to the service of his successor. The center of literary life shifted from northern Castile to the Toledo region, and the emphasis moved from verse to prose. The change was not total, but it was clear and substantial. Some of the manuscripts from Alfonso's scriptorium survive, and give a clear impression of the care with which the work was executed. The intellectual preparation was equally careful. The prologue to his *Libro de la ochava esfera* tells us that he suppressed any passages that were redundant or in bad Spanish, replacing them with something more appropriate, and that he corrected the language of the text.

Alfonso's first legal works are the *Fuero real* (1255), a unified municipal legal code for the whole kingdom, which was the only one to be promulgated in his lifetime, and the *Espéculo,* a first draft of his longest legal work, the *Siete partidas.* This vast encyclopedic compilation (1256–1265, twice revised after 1272) is based on a diversity of Spanish and foreign sources. It was too ambitious and controversial to be acceptable during his reign (part of it was involved in the quarrel with his son Sancho over the law of succession). It was finally promulgated a century later, and its influence was both profound and long-lasting. Last came the *Setenario* (early 1280's?), an encyclopedic manual of ecclesiastical law, which like the *Siete partidas* has a sevenfold structure.

Both of the king's historical works were left unfinished, one because it was conceived on too vast a scale, the other because the collapse of his imperial ambitions made its planned climax irrelevant. The *Estoria de España* (*Primera crónica general*) was begun fairly soon after Alfonso succeeded to the throne. As well as the history of Spain, it gives great attention to that of the Roman (and the Holy Roman) Empire. It seems that this double treatment was inspired by Alfonso's ambition to wear a double crown, and that the *Estoria* was to find the culmination of both its aspects in Alfonso, king of Castile and Holy Roman emperor. When the dream became unrealizable (1273), Alfonso abandoned the *Estoria de España* and concentrated his collaborators' efforts on a history of the world, the *General estoria.* It is as if he planned to encompass intellectually a world that he could no longer hope to dominate politically, but that ambition too was beyond him. The *General estoria,* which dovetails secular and biblical history in great detail, breaks off as it approaches the birth of the Virgin Mary. Even the resources available to Alfonso could not bring so huge a task near to completion. Among the material incorporated we find the first prose romances in Spanish: stories of Thebes, Troy, and Alexander are as much a historical source for Alfonso's team as are the epics prosified in the *Estoria de España.* Although the *General estoria* still found readers in the fifteenth century, it was the *Estoria de España* that had the greatest success, setting the pattern of Spanish historiography for three centuries.

While Alfonso's legal and historical works, like thirteenth-century poetry, look toward Europe, his scientific works look southward. They make Arabic science (chiefly astronomical) available in Castilian, and they too are voluminous. One, the *Tablas alfonsíes,* was still used in Renaissance Europe. Religious literature was also included in the Alfonsine program, and was not confined to Castilian: Bernardo de Brihuega wrote saints' lives in Latin, and Alfonso (probably with collaborators) composed in Galician-Portuguese the *Cantigas de Santa María* (miracle stories and songs of praise). The king's choice of this language for these and other poems shows the extent to which it was the accepted medium for courtly poets in Castile. Translation of the Bible, however, was into Castilian, as much in the separate vernacular texts as in the *General estoria.*

The reigns of Alfonso's successors Sancho IV (1284–1295) and Ferdinand IV (1295–1312) did not keep up the intellectual momentum, but some interesting works were written (exact dating is seldom possible). Several wisdom books are probably of this period, notably *Libro de los cien capítulos, Bocados de oro,* and *Poridat de las poridades,* all from Arabic. In exemplum literature there are *Castigos e documentos del rey don Sancho* and, on the fringes of the group, *Libro de la vida de Barlaam e del rey Josapha de India,* a christianized life of Buddha with interpolated tales. Other traditions are represented by the encyclopedic *Lucidario,* from a Latin original, and the *Historia de la donzella Teodor,* which in successive reworkings transmits knowledge by question and answer, and which is based on a tale from *The Thousand and One Nights.* Two important prose romances from Ferdinand's reign will be mentioned in the next section. The literary production of these reigns shows the extent to which Alfonso succeeded in establishing Castilian as a natural vehicle for prose writing, and the nature of the works reflects the continuing concern for the education of the laity.

THE FOURTEENTH CENTURY

The reign of Alfonso XI. As in the thirteenth century, so in the fourteenth, a great king ruled for most of the first half of the century. Alfonso XI (*r.* 1312–1350) succeeded to the throne in infancy, assumed full power in early adolescence, and pressed forward the Reconquest vigorously. He probably commissioned a hunting treatise, the *Libro de la montería,* and a prose version of the *Roman de Troie;* and a short lyric is attributed to him. His reign is notable for the vigor and the diversity of its literary development, especially in prose. The major figures of Juan Ruiz in poetry and Juan Manuel in prose are surrounded by many interesting, often anonymous, writers.

The prose romance, which became the dominant form of Spanish fiction in the fifteenth and sixteenth centuries and deeply influenced the tastes of Renaissance Europe, first established itself as a genre in the early fourteenth. The *General estoria,* as we have seen, incorporated several romances, but the first prose romance to be written as a separate work is the *Libro del cavallero Zifar* (*ca.* 1301), probably by Ferrán Martínez, (*d.* 1309), a canon of Toledo. *Zifar* is more overtly didactic than most

King Alfonso X el Sabio with his musicians, scribes, and chancery officials. Miniature from the *Cantigas de Santa María, ca.* 1265. REAL BIBLIOTECA DE SAN LORENZO DEL ESCORIAL, MADRID, COD. T.I.1

romances, conveying its Christian message partly by a figural technique based on biblical echoes, and owing something to sermon structure; it incorporates a substantial section of wisdom literature. No single source had been found for this tale of a knight who by virtue and God's favor restores the fortunes of his family and becomes a king, but it may owe something to an oriental tradition. The romance is carefully and rather elaborately structured. A few years later the *Gran conquista de Ultramar,* an adaptation of French crusade poems, incorporates a substantial romance, the *Caballero del Cisne,* and blends historical events with romance narrative technique. This blend is found in a number of fourteenth-century chronicles.

Zifar and *Gran conquista* were written in Ferdinand IV's reign, but the composition of romances did not become frequent until Alfronso XI was, at least nominally, on the throne. In 1313 or 1314 Juan (or João) Vivas produced a Hispanic version of the *Roman du Graal,* the post-Vulgate cycle of Arthurian romances. The language of this version is disputed, and it survives partially in both Castilian and Portuguese texts. Later in the century, the prose *Tristan* was adapted into Castilian and Aragonese. The best Hispanic descendant of the Arthurian tradition is *Amadís de Gaula,* not a version of a French romance but an original development. *Amadís* was composed in the early fourteenth century, and seems (only a fragment of this original version survives) to have ended the story of love-inspired knightly valor with a tragic conflict between father and son. Garci Rodríguez de Montalvo's late-fifteenth-century reworking, which began the Amadís vogue in the Renaissance, dilutes the tragedy of the original. Several romances on the Trojan War derive from Benoît de Sainte-Maure's *Roman de Troie* or Guido delle Colonne's *Historia destructionis Troiae,* sometimes with a blend of other sources. All but one are in prose. The exception, now known as *Historia troyana polimétrica,* mixes prose and verse. The best of the Spanish Troy books, it gives additional emphasis to courtly love; its date has been put as early as *ca.* 1270 and as late as *ca.* 1350. Other romances, almost certainly from Alfonso's reign, are preserved in a manuscript that also contains saints' lives. They derive from French sources, and stress the role of virtuous women (*Otas de Roma, Una santa enperatriz, Un cavallero Plácidas, El rey Guillelme, El enperador Carlos Maynes de Roma*). The strong link between hagiography and romance in these texts is found less obviously in some later romances.

Overtly didactic writing is found in prose hagiography (for instance, in two versions of the Mary of Egypt story); in two attempts to replace Oriental-based wisdom literature by collections of Western sententiae (*Dichos de los santos padres,* by Pedro López de Baeza, and *Libro del consejo e de los consejeros,* attributed to Pedro Gómez Barroso, *ca.* 1270–*ca.* 1349); in sermons (all that survives is a homily composed about 1327–1338 by López de Baeza); in the *Montstrador de la justicia* and *Libro de las tres gracias* of the converted Jew Alfonso de Valladolid (1270–1349); and in the works of Juan Manuel (1282–1348).

Juan Manuel, a nephew of Alfonso el Sabio, was an active and devious politician whose ambition was inflamed by the conviction that his branch of the family had been wrongly excluded from power. This conviction can be seen most clearly in the partly autobiographical *Libro de las tres cazones* (sometimes called *Libro de las armas, ca.* 1337–1342), which memorably depicts the young Juan Manuel's meeting with the dying King Sancho IV. His best-known work is the *Libro del conde Lucanor et de Patronio* (completed 1335), which seems to have been planned as a "Libro de los exemplos" (fifty-one exempla, comprising part I of the present work) plus a "Libro de los proverbios" (wisdom literature, parts II–IV), with a final and more theoretical part V. The fundamental theme of the exempla, which are arranged in a master-and-pupil frame story, is the need to save one's soul while living successfully in this world. It has been well said that Juan Manuel uses this fiction to impose his own view of a society in which he felt ill-used and betrayed. Similar concerns shape his other major work, the *Libro de los estados* (*ca.* 1327–1332). The starting-point for *Estados* is the legend of Barlaam and Josaphat, and the emphasis is not on the theoretical structure of society but on how, within that structure, a man may save his soul. Book I deals with the laity (in practice, the nobility), and book II with the clergy. Five other works by Juan Manuel are extant: a chronicle of Spain (*Crónica abreviada,* early 1320's), a hunting treatise (*Libro de la caza, ca.* 1325), two works of moral and philosophical advice (*Libro del cavallero et del escudero, ca.* 1326, and *Libro infinido, ca.* 1336–1342), and a Marian book (*Tratado de la Asunción,* after 1342). A number of other works, including a volume of poems, are lost. Juan Manuel was aware of himself as a writer—much more so than most of his contemporaries—and was as concerned for his literary as for his political reputation. This is made explicit in both versions of his prologue to his collected works (*ca.* 1335, *ca.* 1342).

Juan Manuel's contemporary Juan Ruiz, who describes himself as archpriest of Hita, also felt the need to collect his works, but went further, gathering the poems of many years into a single book under the title *Libro de buen amor* (1330). Some of the text was no doubt written to provide an overall structure of fictional autobiography for previously independent poems; even so, the structure is at times uncomfortably loose. Two of the extant manuscripts represent the original *Libro,* while a third contains an expanded version (1343; but some scholars deny the existence of two versions). The 1343 *Libro* has a prose prologue in the form of a sermon, explaining the work's didactic and literary aims. The didactic statement, here as throughout the *Libro,* is rendered ambiguous by parody. The *buen amor* of the title has various meanings: the love of God, courtly love, an old procuress. Diversity characterizes the book at every level: in verse form (*cuaderna vía* alternates with a great variety of lyric stanzas), in content (narratives of love affairs, exempla, encounters with wild mountain women, a mock battle, didactic exposition, religious lyric, a lament), and in tone (serious, parodic, devout, ambivalent). Part of the diversity is attributable to composition over a long period, but part must come from Juan Ruiz's temperament. Sources and analogues for almost all sections have been found in the Western European literary tradition, but some critics have seen Arabic or Hebrew influence also. The wealth of lyrics in the *Libro* (and still more are mentioned but not included in the extant text) bears out the author's claim in the prologue that he would set an example of poetic composition. Galician-Portuguese was still the standard language for cultured lyric, and by writing his in Castilian Juan Ruiz may have hoped to achieve, single-handedly, a poetic revolution. He may even have succeeded.

One of the most important and persistent of Spanish poetic genres, the ballad, is first traceable in the reign of Alfonso XI. Traditional ballads (as opposed to poems in ballad meter by cultured poets) are of three main kinds: those from literary sources (including epics), adventure or novelesque ballads that are part of an international stock, and ballads arising directly from a historical event. Only the historical ballads can be dated with any precision, and the earliest event from which a ballad sprang (the prior of San Juan's defiance of the king) occurred in 1328. We cannot know what preceded this; perhaps the first Spanish ballads arose from epics (the meter is similar), but it is equally possible that the genre was born under the pressure of history, and that epic and other literary ballads followed, with adventure ballads last of all. The origin of traditional Spanish balladry is thus mysterious, and its death has not yet come, though it may be near. The social conditions that favored the tradition have largely passed away, even among the dispersed Spanish Jews, who have preserved many old ballads.

At the end of Alfonso's reign comes Rodrigo Yáñez's *Poema de Alfonso XI* (1348), a new kind of popular epic in octosyllables, composed in writing but using a formulaic system. Its subject matter is largely historical, and its relation to the prose *Crónica de Alfonso XI* remains uncertain. The poet borrows techniques from *clerecía* poetry, traditional epic, and (in his treatment of the king's adulterous relationship with Leonor de Guzmán) the literature of courtly love. Political prophecy is used as a structural device, and social criticism is prominent. The manuscript breaks off in the year 1344.

Civil war and Trastámaran rule. The confident achievements of Alfonso's reign ended in the outbreak of the Black Death (1348), the king's premature demise, and the troubled rule of his son Pedro I (1350–1369), known variously as the Cruel and the Just. From this shaken and newly pessimistic society comes one great poem, the *Proverbios morales* of Rabbi Shem Tov ibn Arduṭiel ben Isaac (Santob de Carrión), a carefully structured and melancholy work of wisdom literature, with touches of personal lyricism. Shem Tov is the only medieval writer to be a significant figure in both Castilian and Hebrew literature. (Other poems by Jewish authors of this period are minor.) *Aljamiado* literature, by Muslim writers living under Christian rule, is ascribed by some scholars to this period, but it is very hard to date, and may be largely post-medieval. As the discontents of Pedro's reign, and his quarrel with his bastard half-brother Henry (Enrique) de Trastámara (Henry II, 1369–1379), moved toward civil war, propaganda ballads were composed on both sides. Pedro lost the war; he was murdered by Henry, and though loyalist resistance lingered on, it eventually collapsed. Consequently it is mostly the ballads by the Trastámaran supporters that survive. At this time also begin the frontier ballads, inspired by skirmishes with the Moors. The earliest event referred to is the siege of Baeza (1368). Their beginning coincides with the decline of the traditional form of the epic, though epics continued to circulate for some time (the new octosyllabic epic remained vigorous until the early sixteenth century). The last epic in traditional meter that we possess is *Mocedades de Rodrigo* (*ca.* 1360–1370), a reworking of the thirteenth-century *Gesta de las mocedades*. The poet is a cleric from Palencia, and his aim is to help his diocese at a critical time by linking its fortunes to the youthful (and sensationally fictionalized) deeds of the Cid.

Aragonese writers were relatively untouched by the troubles of Castile. The most important is Juan Fernández de Heredia (*ca.* 1310–1396), grand master of Rhodes in the Order of Knights Hospitalers. He was a bibliophile and, like Alfonso el Sabio, both an author and a patron of authors. He was responsible for translations of Thucydides, Plutarch, and Marco Polo; for wisdom literature (*Secreto secretorum, Libro de actoridades, Rams de flores*), for the *Grant crónica de Espanya* (based partly on the Alfonsine *General estoria*), and for chronicles of the Catalan conquest of the Morea. As with Alfonso, it is difficult to know how much of this is the work of the patron himself. Another Aragonese, Pedro de Luna (the schismatic Pope Benedict XIII, 1394–1423), composed, probably in the late fourteenth century, the *Libro de las consolaciones de la vida humana,* which contains a number of exempla. In Castile, Pedro Fernández Pecha (*d. ca.* 1400), founder of the Hieronymite Order, wrote his *Soliloquios,* religious meditations with deep emotion and elaborate style.

The last major writer of the century is Pero López de Ayala (1332–1407), chancellor of Castile, who was deeply involved in the Trastámaran wars. He defected from Pedro's side, and seems never to have come to terms with this action. His chronicles of the reigns of Pedro and the first four Trastámaran monarchs follow an earlier fourteenth-century tradition of single-reign chronicles by Fernán Sánchez de Valladolid, who was also chancellor of Castile (reworkings of the Alfonsine *Estoria de España* also continue throughout this century and the next). There is, however, a significant modification: López de Ayala seeks not so much to inform as, with great narrative skill, to convince readers (and himself?) that his desertion of Pedro was justified. He was a prolific author: apart from the chronicles, he wrote a hunting treatise (*Libro de la caça de las aves*), translated Livy, Boccaccio, St. Gregory, the Book of Job, and possibly a Troy romance, and composed much poetry. Most of his poetry is collected in his *Rimado de palacio,* a long and pessimistic meditation that moves from Ayala's own sins to human nature and the state of society, ending with an adaptation of Gregory's commentary on Job. The *Rimado* incorporates a number of religious lyrics, but is mostly in *cuaderna vía.* It is the last important poem in that meter, and Ayala is a conservative poet who is rejected by a new generation, the first group of courtly poets to write their lyrics in Castilian. The chief figure of the group is Alfonso Álvarez de Villasandino (*d. ca.*

1424), who began to write in Galician around 1370 but, ever attuned to changes in fashion, turned increasingly to Castilian when it became apparent that the Galician-Portuguese courtly tradition was dying. Villasandino and his contemporaries begin the extraordinary flowering of late medieval courtly verse in Castilian, which has been justly termed the troubadour revival.

THE REIGN OF JOHN (JUAN) II

Courtly poetry and fiction. Once the practice of using Castilian for the cultured lyric was established, it spread to an astonishing extent. The work of some 700 Castilian fifteenth-century poets survives, and we know of many other poets whose work is lost. This poetry is a development of the Galician-Portuguese courtly tradition, and thus—at one remove—of Provençal. Yet it is no mere imitation. It makes increasing and creative use of elements from Petrarch and Dante, from the French and Catalan poets, and from a native popular tradition. It was collected in *cancioneros* (songbooks), and though these do not contain musical notation before the late fifteenth century, the lyric *canciones,* in octosyllabic meter, were at first designed for singing (later *canciones* were written to be read, and the *cancioneros musicales* are filled with other verse forms, such as *villancicos*). The *cancioneros* also contain *decires,* longer narrative or didactic poems; these use either octosyllables or the dodecasyllabic *arte mayor,* which replaced *cuaderna vía.*

The earliest collections are the *Cancionero de Baena* (first version *ca.* 1430, completed 1445) and *de Palacio (ca.* 1438–1444). The former, compiled by the *converso* (Christian of Jewish origin) Juan Alfonso de Baena, was made for John II (*r.* 1406–1454), himself a minor poet. Baena contributes poems and a theoretical preface. The anthology contains the work of several generations. The oldest poets represented (beginning *ca.* 1370) often write in Galician: the leading figures are Pero Ferrús, Garci Fernández de Jerena, and Macías, chiefly remembered as a tragic lover. Then comes Villasandino, soon followed by a new and innovating generation led by Francisco Imperial (of Genoese origin, *d. ca.* 1409). Imperial introduced the Italian hendecasyllable and Dantesque allegory. Some of his contemporaries were concerned with moral and theological questions (Fernán Pérez de Guzmán and the *conversos* Ferrán Manuel de Lando and Ferrán Sánchez Calavera) or social criticism (Diego de Valencia, Ruy Páez de Ribera). The youngest generation of *Baena* poets includes Álvaro de Luna (*ca.* 1390–1453), constable of Castile and author of a courtly treatise, *Libro de las virtuosas e claras mugeres* (1446).

The two greatest poets of John II's reign were too young for representation in the *Cancionero de Baena.* Íñigo López de Mendoza, marqués de Santillana (1398–1458), is a poet of extraordinary range: courtly *canciones* and *decires,* sonnets, *serranillas* (adaptations of the pastourelle), allegorical poems on politics (*Comedieta de Ponza*), on other writers (*Coronación de Mossén Jordi de Sant Jordi, Defunssión de don Enrique de Villena*), and on love (*Triunfete de Amor, El sueño, Infierno de los enamorados*), philosophical poetry, political satire. He devoted most attention to his sonnets, trying to naturalize the Italian form in Castilian, but the allegories and the *serranillas* are the most highly regarded by posterity. Santillana also wrote, in a letter (*carta*) to Dom Pedro de Portugal, an outline critical history of European poetry (*ca.* 1449)—a remarkable achievement at a time when literary criticism as we know it scarcely existed. Juan de Mena (1411–1456), Latin secretary to the king, wrote love lyrics, an elaborate panegyric to Santillana (*La coronación,* 1438), some prose works that included commentaries to his own poems, and, at the end of his life, the grimly didactic *Coplas contra los pecados del mundo.* His masterpiece is *Laberinto de Fortuna* (1444), a political allegory with brilliant descriptive passages that tries to raise Spanish as a poetic language to the level of Latin.

Not all the literature of love at this time is in verse. Juan Rodríguez del Padrón, a *Baena* poet, wrote *Triunfo de las donas,* defending women against their detractors, translated Ovid's *Heroides* (*Bursario*), and founded a genre: *Siervo libre de amor,* a partly allegorical account of his unfortunate love affair, includes a tale of two tragic lovers that is the prototype of the sentimental romance. Another kind of fiction is Pedro del Corral's *Crónica sarracina* (*ca.* 1430), a historical romance masquerading as history. Its subject is the fall of Spain to the Moors, and it gives prominence to love.

Didactic literature. Some didactic work is contained in *Baena* and in the poetry of Santillana and Mena, but much is in prose. A good deal of fifteenth-century didactic writing continues earlier medieval traditions, as in two exemplum collections. One, the *Libro de los exenplos por a.b.c.* by Clemente Sánchez de Vercial (*d. ca.* 1434), is an alphabetically arranged reference book, the longest collection of exempla in Spanish. The other, *Libro de los gatos* (perhaps late fourteenth century), a version of Odo of Cheriton's *Fabulae,* is notable for the pungency of its social criticism. Other exempla are contained in the most famous didactic work of this period, the *Arcipreste de Talavera* (1438, sometimes called *Corbacho*) by Alfonso Martínez de Toledo (1397/1398–1468). Martínez, archpriest of Talavera and canon of Toledo, wrote this book as a warning against lust. The book's structure and persuasive techniques owe much to the sermon, especially the popular sermon; as well as exempla there are lively satirical descriptions and imitations of popular speech. Women are the chief target of the satire; the extent of the author's misogyny is disputed. Martínez also wrote saints' lives and a historical compendium that draws chiefly on the Alfonsine chronicle tradition.

The influence of sermons is pervasive in late medieval didactic literature, but sermon texts in the vernacular are rare before the fifteenth century (it seems that of the countless sermons preached, few were written down). Two survive from the fourteenth century (one by Pedro López de Baeza, the other by Pedro de Luna) and in the early fifteenth century we find the first extant group of texts; though attributed to Pedro Marín, they are the Castilian sermons of the famous Valencian preacher St. Vincent Ferrer.

A didactic poem that draws on the pulpit tradition is the *Dança general de la Muerte.* The dragging of all ranks of society into Death's dance exemplifies the words of the preacher that open the poem. This work is based on the French *Danse macabre,* but has a stricter organization, and makes skillful use of image patterns. The tenor of the poem is deeply pessimistic; almost all the characters are destined for Hell. A similar pessimism in found in most of the fifteenth-century body-soul debates (one in prose, several in verse) that revive an earlier tradition, but in one of these poems, *Revelación de un hermitaño,* an angel rescues the soul at the last minute.

Conversos played an important part in the didactic writing of this period, as priests and as members of the growing class of *letrados* (graduates in law) who served the crown. This may partly account for the suspicion and even hostility with which humanistic learning was generally viewed. One family was especially prominent: the Santa Marías or Cartagenas, whose head was Pablo de Santa María (*ca.* 1352–1435), successively chief rabbi and bishop of Burgos. He wrote in both Spanish and Latin, drawing on his rabbinical knowledge for commentary on the Scriptures; some minor Hebrew works, written before his conversion, are also extant. His son Alfonso de Cartagena (1384–1456), also bishop of Burgos, wrote a variety of didactic works, Latin and vernacular, and as chief Castilian delegate to the Council of Basel made a famous speech asserting his country's precedence over England (1434). The nun Teresa de Cartagena, granddaughter of Pablo de Santa María, wrote a treatise on the spiritual benefits of illness (*Arboleda de los enfermos,* 1450's?), and, when criticized for this, defended the right of women to authorship in her *Admiración operum Dey* (in vernacular, despite the title). This is the first piece of feminist writing in Spanish.

Even greater suspicion than that felt for *conversos* was directed at the Old Christian nobleman and polymath Enrique de Villena (1384–1434). Villena, translator of Vergil and Dante, wrote on the moral application of Greek mythology (*Doze trabajos de Hércules,* before 1417), medicine (*Tratado de la lepra, ca.* 1421–1422), cookery (*Arte cisoria,* 1423), a *Tratado de la consolación* (1423), the evil eye (*Tratado del aojamiento,* mid 1420's), the language of poetry (*Arte de trovar,* 1433), and other subjects. His voracious intellectual curiosity, thought unsuitable for an aristocrat, led to suspicions of black magic, and much of his library was burned after his death by Bishop Lope de Barrientos, supposedly on the orders of John II. (Barrientos, *b.* 1382, was himself an author: *Tractado de caso y fortuna, Contra algunos cizañadores de la nación de los convertidos del pueblo de Israel,* and several other works.)

In this area of literature as in others, the number of works composed in the fifteenth century is so much greater than in earlier periods that one has to be more selective. Among the most interesting are *De cómo al ome es necesario amar,* by Alfonso de Madrigal (1400?–1455), known as el Tostado, bishop of Ávila and a prolific writer in Latin as well as Spanish (his commentary on the *Chronici canones* of Eusebius is important for fifteenth-century intellectual history); and the *Visión deleitable* (*ca.* 1438) of Alfonso de la Torre. The *Visión,* a compendium of medieval knowledge within an allegorical framework, draws heavily on St. Isidore, Alain de Lille, Aquinas, and Maimonides.

From chronicle to biography. Reworkings of the

Alfonsine *Estoria de España* continued as vigorously as ever in the fifteenth century, and the old tradition of universal history is represented—this time in verse—by Pablo de Santa María's *Edades del mundo* (1418). Chronicles of individual reigns also continue, and make increasing use of narrative techniques borrowed from the romances. There are several versions of a *Crónica de Juan II.* The growing interest in individual description and analysis of character (already perceptible in López de Ayala's chronicles) reaches a peak in the *Generaciones y semblanzas* of Fernán Pérez de Guzmán (*ca.* 1378–1460?), incisive sketches of the great men of the recent past, in which the author makes a real, though not always successful, effort to avoid bias.

Full-length biographies, hitherto reserved for royalty and saints (the twelfth-century Latin biography of the Cid is a rare exception), are developed with great success by fifteenth-century writers. An outstanding example is *El victorial* or *Crónica de don Pero Niño* (1448) by Gutierre Díez de Games (*b.* 1378?), at once biography, military history, and travel book (Pero Niño's raids on the English coast are described in vivid detail). The assumptions of the book are those of the chivalresque romances, and this is probably how Pero Niño saw his own career. Real-life knights-errant abound in fifteenth-century Spanish documents, and one long account of a real incident (the *Libro del Passo Honroso,* 1434, by the notary Pero Rodríguez de Lena) reads like an implausible romance: the knight Suero de Quiñones seizes a bridge and holds it for a month against all comers in honor of his mistress.

As Spanish envoys and explorers extended their range, indigenous rivals to Marco Polo's book were composed. In 1403–1406, Ruy González de Clavijo led an embassy from Henry III to Tamerlane the Great (his wife, Nayor Arias, wrote a moving poem on his departure). A careful account, *Embajada a Tamorlán,* was composed by him and several collaborators in the few years that followed his return (he died in 1412); it contains lively descriptions of scenes and customs. Pero de Tafur's *Andanças e viajes* (written or reworked after 1453) describes his travels in Europe and the Mediterranean in 1436–1439. He shares Clavijo's taste for local color but, partly because of the longer gap between travel and writing, he is less reliable factually. These books are, of course, partly autobiographical, but the chief emphasis is on things seen by the authors. In the brief *Memorias* of Leonor López de Córdoba (1362/1363–*ca.* 1412), dictated to a notary at the end of her life, all the interest is concentrated on the author and her reactions to her experiences. This memoir by a survivor from the losing side in the Trastámaran wars is the first extant book in Spanish by a woman author.

Literature and politics: The end of John II's reign. The last decade of the reign was darkened by growing violence against the *conversos,* and by the overthrow of the king's chief minister, Álvaro de Luna. Luna had long been the real power in the kingdom, strengthening the government with the aid of the *letrados,* curbing the ambitions of the nobles, protecting the *conversos.* A *converso*'s reaction to the gathering troubles is given in the pessimistic meditation of *Libro de la consolación de España* (late 1430's or 1440's). In 1449 anti-*converso* rebels seized Toledo and launched a systematic persecution. Their manifesto, the *Memorial contra los conversos* of Marcos García de Mora, a *letrado* of peasant origin, and the countermanifesto, Fernán Díaz's *Instrucción del Relator,* give us an unusually clear picture of the ideological bases of the conflict and of how the immediate participants felt. A more philosophical defense of the *conversos* is made in Alfonso de Cartagena's *Defensorium unitatis christianae.*

Luna's defeat of his enemies at the Battle of Olmedo (1445) is satirically commemorated in the *Coplas de ¡Ay panadera!,* which heaps ridicule on the combatants. The propaganda of his enemies took many forms, from palace gossip to major poetry. Santillana's *Bías contra Fortuna* (1448) is a philosophical reaction to the imprisonment of his cousin, for which Luna was partly responsible, but in the later *Favor de Hércules contra Fortuna* philosophy gives way to invective. Mena's *Laberinto,* as we have seen, is a political poem; it seeks to persuade John II to throw his full weight behind Luna's policies. It succeeds as poetry, but fails politically; the king gave way to pressure, and Luna was arrested and executed without trial (1453). Santillana's *Doctrinal de privados* rejoices in his fall, and puts into the mouth of the dead man a confession of guilt. The views of Luna's supporters survive in the *Crónica de don Álvaro de Luna,* probably by his servant Gonzalo Chacón.

THE END OF THE MIDDLE AGES

Literature and politics: Henry (Enrique) IV and civil war. John II outlived Luna by only a year. His son Henry IV (1454–1474) was a weak king without a strong minister. His liking for Moorish styles at court was one of the pretexts for the nobles' intrigues against him, and for an attempt to depose him. The case against him is put with skill and venom in a Latin chronicle, the *Décadas* of his Latin secretary Alfonso de Palencia (1423–1492), and he is defended by his official historian, Diego Enríquez del Castillo, in the *Crónica de Enrique IV*. Palencia's *Batalla campal de los perros contra los lobos* seems to be a covert attack on the aristocratic feuds in the closing years of John II's reign and the beginning of Henry's; both sides in the feuds are condemned, probably from the viewpoint of a nascent civic humanism on the Italian model. A blistering picture of Henry's rule is given in two poems: the populist *Coplas de Mingo Revulgo,* perhaps by Fray Íñigo de Mendoza, and the conservative *Coplas del Provincial* (*ca.* 1474), filled with accusations of sexual vice. *Mingo Revulgo,* the best of the satirical *Coplas,* was printed with a commentary by the historian Hernando del Pulgar (*ca.* 1425–after 1490). One other poem of Henry's reign directs its satire at more localized social conditions: a reworked and expanded *Dança de la Muerte* reflects life in Seville in the 1460's.

Chronicles and didactic writing under the Catholic Monarchs. Henry died in 1474 and was succeeded by his half-sister Isabella. When her husband Ferdinand succeeded to the throne of Aragon in 1479, the two kingdoms were effectively united. The Catholic Monarchs pressed forward the long-neglected Reconquest, and Granada surrendered in 1492. They countered popular unrest against the *conversos* by setting up the Spanish Inquisition. This, and monarchic absolutism, moved Spain increasingly in the direction of a closed society, especially after the expulsion of the unconverted Jews in 1492. The literature of the period reflects the beneficial aspects of the Catholic Monarchs' rule, not only because it was imprudent to do otherwise, but also because they brought stability and favored literature and learning.

An early reaction to changed conditions is the *bachiller* Palma's *Divina retribución sobre la caída de España* (1478?), which celebrates the defeat of a Portuguese invasion as a reversal of the disastrous Battle of Aljubarrota a century earlier. Both Hernando del Pulgar and Alfonso de Palencia chronicled the successful campaign against Granada, and wrote general accounts of the reign, while Pulgar adapted the biographical technique of Pérez de Guzmán in his *Claros varones de Castilla.* The portraits are shrewd, even though tact often replaces Pérez de Guzmán's candor. Full-length biography is well represented by the *Hechos del condestable Miguel Lucas de Iranzo* (perhaps written by Pedro de Escavias, *ca.* 1420–late 1490's). This narrates its subject's part in the events of Henry's reign in Andalusia. The *Libro del infante don Pedro de Portugal* gives a fanciful account of a voyage in the 1420's, and *Mandeville's Travels* was translated.

Didactic literature is as varied as it is plentiful. There is political theory, in the *Suma de la política* and the *Vergel de príncipes* by Rodrigo Sánchez de Arévalo (1404–1470, also a chronicler). The Augustinian Martín de Córdoba (*d.* 1476) wrote Latin scriptural commentaries (now lost), treatises on Fortune, on predestination, and on women (*Compendio de la Fortuna, Tratado de la predestinación, Jardín de nobles donzellas*), and an *Ars praedicandi.* Juan de Lucena, probably a *converso,* wrote the *Libro de vita beata* (1463), an imaginary dialogue on true happiness between Santillana, Mena, and Alfonso de Cartagena, and a warning (now lost) to the Catholic Monarchs about the procedures of the Inquisition in its early days. The works of Diego de Valera (1412–1488?), besides chronicles of Henry IV and the Catholic Monarchs, and poetry, include *Tratado de Providencia contra Fortuna, Defensa de virtuosas mugeres,* and *Doctrinal de príncipes.* Hernando de Talavera (1428–1507), first archbishop of Granada, composed treatises on various questions of practical morality (for instance, *De cómo se ha de ordenar el tiempo para que sea bien expendido*) and pastoral care (*Breve forma de confesar*). He was famous for his sermons, and at least one survives, as does his answer to a group of Seville *conversos* who criticized his preaching (*Católica impugnación,* 1481). Several collections of sermons by other preachers of this period are extant, including one by the Franciscan Ambrosio Montesino (*d.* 1513), who also wrote religious lyrics (*Coplas sobre diversas devociones y misterios*) and translated Ludolph of Saxony's *Vita Christi.* The other leading religious poets of this time are Íñigo de Mendoza (*ca.* 1425–*ca.* 1507), another Franciscan, whose *Coplas de Vita Christi* (1467–1468, 1482) have great dramatic power; Diego de San Pedro, whose *Pasión trobada* (1470's) goes even further, verging on rudimentary drama; the *comendador* Román (*Trovas de la gloriosa Pasión* and *Coplas de la Pasión con la Resurrección,* 1480's); and the Carthusian Juan de Padilla (1467?–1520), author of *Retablo de la vida de*

Cristo and *Los doce triunfos de los doce apóstoles,* long poems with elaborate numerical structures.

Fiction: Romances and the birth of the novel. The adaptation into Spanish of French romances continued in the second half of the fifteenth century; the best are probably *Flores y Blancaflor, El conde Partinuplés,* and *Historia de la linda Melosina.* This was the great period of the sentimental romance, a native Spanish genre that was soon to acquire European popularity. Rodríguez del Padrón's example was followed by Dom Pedro de Portugal (1429–1466), all of whose extant works are in Castilian. *Sátira de la infelice e felice vida* (early 1450's?—there may have been a Portuguese original some years earlier) is, like *Siervo libre de amor,* an allegorical presentation of an unfortunate love affair; it verges on the sentimental romance without fully becoming one. (Pedro left two other works: a long poem on the evils of the world, and a lament for his sister.)

A closer approach to the sentimental romance is the anonymous *Triste deleytaçión* (1460's?), written in Castilian by a Catalan, but the classic works of the genre are by Diego de San Pedro and Juan de Flores. Little is known of the life of San Pedro, but Flores—previously a biographical enigma—is now known to have been a royal chronicler (probable author of *Crónica incompleta de los Reyes Católicos,* late 1470's) and perhaps rector of the University of Salamanca. San Pedro (also a courtly and religious poet) wrote two romances, *Arnalte y Lucenda* and *Cárcel de Amor,* as well as a pseudo-sermon on courtly love, though at the end of his literary career he disowns these works in his poem *Desprecio de la Fortuna. Arnalte* (*ca.* 1481) is the story of a man whose love is unrequited, who kills his successful rival in a duel, and who ends his days in a symbolic desert of frustration. In *Cárcel de Amor* (1492), the narrator, who in the earlier work had merely listened to Arnalte's story, becomes directly and emotionally involved in the action, precipitating by his misjudgment the tragic ending that he had hoped to avert. The question of whether Laureola really reciprocated Leriano's love is never resolved; her final rejection of him causes a suicide with strong religious overtones. This is the masterpiece of the genre: psychologically penetrating; tightly structured, with allegory, discourse, and action integrated; emotionally powerful. Nicolás Núñez wrote a brief sequel.

Flores' two romances, *Grisel y Mirabella* and *Grimalte y Gradissa,* are probably influenced by San Pedro. Requited and consummated love in one, unrequited love and betrayal in the other, lead to the inevitable disasters: suicide, the desert of frustration. A third work by Flores, *Triunpho de Amor,* is a mythological treatment of love rather than a sentimental romance. *Triunpho* was long lost, and rediscovered only in 1976, along with the anonymous *Coronación de la señora Gracisla* (a historical roman à clef), which is probably also by Flores. The standard opening situation of a sentimental romance is the starting point for Luis de Lucena's attack on women, *Repetición de amores.* The sentimental romances blend elements from Italian fiction such as Boccaccio's *Fiammetta,* the chivalresque romances, Ovid's *Heroides,* and courtly poetry. In most of them, there is also a disconcerting element of savagery, which contrasts with their courtly setting. This has been variously interpreted.

Garci Rodríguez de Montalvo's extensive reworking of *Amadís de Gaula,* though not printed until 1508, seems to have been completed by the early 1490's. It inspired a long series of sequels and translations. Soon afterward, there was a radical innovation in late medieval fiction: the first European novel. The *Comedia* (later *Tragicomedia*) *de Calisto y Melibea,* soon renamed *Celestina* by its public, began as an attempt by an unknown author to write in Spanish a humanistic comedy on the model of the Latin works then flourishing in Italy. Fernando de Rojas (*d.* 1541), a *converso* lawyer who had studied at Salamanca, took over this story of a seduction aided by an old go-between, with its low-life scenes of servants and prostitutes, and steered it to a tragic ending which owes much to the plot of the sentimental romance. The lover Calisto is shown, under his cover of courtly phrases, as a self-indulgent egotist. He, his servants, and the go-between, Celestina, meet violent deaths; his mistress, Melibea, kills herself; and her aged father, Pleberio, is left to lament in bitterly pessimistic tones.

Rojas tells us that his aim is to warn against illicit love, bad servants, and go-betweens. This cannot be wholly accurate, since the aristocratic Calisto is presented in a worse light than his servants, but a grimly moralistic view seems to be implied in this picture of the destructive power of the passions. The role of witchcraft in the work (Celestina is witch as well as procuress) is much debated, as is the connection between Rojas' attitudes and his *converso* status. The first version, in sixteen acts, was printed in 1499, a year or two after Rojas wrote acts II–XVI (we cannot date the anonymous act I). He soon, though, he says, reluctantly, expanded it to twenty-one acts. Although it is entirely in dialogue, it was not designed for stage performance, and its length, complexity, structure, and depth of characterization are those of the novel rather than the drama (though, of course, Rojas cannot have realized that he was writing in a genre that was new to Europe). Having written an innovatory masterpiece while still young, he seems to have abandoned literature—certainly, no other work of his is known.

Cancionero poetry. The flowering of late medieval lyric in Spanish was not confined to the peninsula. Spanish poets wrote at the Neapolitan court of Alfonso V the Magnanimous of Aragon. Their work was collected in a *cancionero* from about 1460, and from this descend three extant *cancioneros: Stúñiga, Roma,* and *Marciana.* The striking feature of this group of poets, whose leading members are Carvajal, Juan de Dueñas, Juan de Andújar, Pedro de Santa Fe, Juan de Tapia, and perhaps Lope de Estúñiga, is that despite long residence in Italy they continued to write in the standard Spanish fashion, quite unaffected by Italian poetic developments. The *Cancionero de Herberay des Essarts* reflects the taste of the Navarrese court in the third quarter of the century and shows greater interest in the popular tradition than any other *cancionero* of this period.

The largest of all is the *Cancionero general,* compiled by Hernando del Castillo (begun *ca.* 1490, published 1511). Castillo's aim was to include all the poetry he could find from Mena's time onward, with any earlier work that had retained its popularity. He must have come fairly close to success, since the 1511 edition contains over a thousand poems (others were added in later editions). The poetic production of the reigns of Henry IV and the Catholic Monarchs, collected in this *cancionero,* is remarkable for the number of poets represented (some 200), for the progressive restriction of the metrical and lexical range of the *canciones,* and for the final section of obscene poems (*Obras de burlas provocantes a risa,* the heirs of the Galican-Portugues *cantigas d'escarnho e de mal dizer*). This obscene poetry is often by writers whose courtly and even religious verse appears elsewhere, and it has been plausibly suggested that some of the abstract vocabulary of the *canciones* ("gloria," "muerte") is a system of sexual euphemism. The large number of poets, especially among the nobility, in the latter part of the century corresponds to an increase in the creation of hereditary titles. It seems to be part of a devotion to the externals of aristocratic life as the old institutions and values lose their power.

Some *Cancionero general* poets, and others of this period, are represented in the *Cancionero musical de Palacio,* one of the few that include the music of these songs. Among the earliest generation of *Cancionero general* poets the best is Gómez Manrique (*ca.* 1412–*ca.* 1490), exceptionally skillful in versification, and the author of love poems, satires, and an outstanding elegy (*Coplas para el señor Diego Arias de Ávila*). Other leading poets of this generation are Pero Guillén de Segovia, author of a dictionary of rhymes (*Gaya ciencia*), and the *converso* satirist Antón de Montoro.

The most prominent poets of the Catholic Monarchs' reign are the *converso* Juan Álvarez Gato, author of amatory, moral, and religious verse (the last category being deeply influenced by Hernando de Talavera); Rodrigo Cota, another *converso* and author of the *Diálogo entre el Amor y un viejo,* in which an old man who yields to love is humiliated; Diego López de Haro, an accomplished love poet; and Gómez Manrique's nephew Jorge. Jorge Manrique (*ca.* 1440–1479) wrote good love poems and satires, but he is famous for the *Coplas que fizo por la muerte de su padre* (1479), the greatest elegy in Spanish. This gives emotional power to the Christian commonplaces on death and the soul by a pattern of emotive images arranged in a careful structure that leads from general reflections to individual consolation. Among the other poets of this reign are those famous in other genres, such as Diego de San Pedro and the dramatist and musician Juan del Encina (author of an *Arte de poesía castellana*); Quirós (his other name is uncertain), whose *canciones* are closest to the metrical norm; and Florencia Pinar, the only woman poet of whom we have more than a few lines, who uses animal imagery to great effect in her love poems. The poets of the *Cancionero general,* unlike those of *Baena,* have begun to incorporate in their courtly verse two main types of Castilian traditional poetry, the ballad and the *villancico;* these remain part of the repertoire of cultured poets throughout the sixteenth century.

Drama. After the *Auto de los reyes magos,* there is a gap of over two centuries without any reliable evidence of drama in Castile. In the fifteenth century, a dramatic tradition grows up, first at Toledo

Cathedral and then at the University of Salamanca. Records have been discovered at Toledo of dramatic productions for Corpus Christi going back to the early part of the century, and the titles are known of twenty-five plays performed in the 1490's. One of these Toledo plays has survived: the *Auto de la Pasión* of Alonso del Campo (*d.* 1499), which draws heavily on San Pedro's *Pasión trobada* and, like its anonymous contemporary the *Auto de la huida a Egipto,* gives an immediate and vivid picture of the biblical events. An earlier play is Gómez Manrique's *Representación del Nacimiento de Nuestro Señor,* which uses a variety of techniques (broad comedy, mumming, a shepherds' scene, a lyric) to make its doctrinal point, that Nativity and Crucifixion are indissolubly linked.

In the 1490's two important religious and secular dramatists and musicians were rivals at the University of Salamanca: Juan del Encina (1468–1529/1530) and Lucas Fernández (1474–1542). Encina wrote between thirteen and fifteen plays; Fernández, who was influenced by Encina, wrote seven. From their time onward, Spain has a continuous tradition of secular as well as religious drama.

Humanism and the growth of postmedieval forms. The Catholic Monarchs encouraged humanistic learning for the first time in Castile, even bringing Italian humanists such as Pietro Martire d'Anghiera and Lucio Marineo Siculo into their service (the latter wrote *De laude Hispaniae,* 1499). Juan de Lucena's *Epístola exhortatoria a las letras* is a gesture of support for the monarchs' policy. The two most important Spanish humanists of this period are Alfonso de Palencia and Antonio de Nebrija (1444?–1522). Palencia, as we have seen, wrote chronicles and political allegory; he was also a geographer, a lexicographer (*Universal vocabulario en latín y romance,* 1490), a translator of the classics, and an exponent of a civic humanism on the Italian model. Nebrija wrote Latin verse and a large number of Latin prose works; his best-known work is *Gramática de la lengua castellana* (1492).

The end of an exclusively medieval literature in Spanish comes at different times for different genres. The lyric is still securely medieval in 1511, when Castillo publishes the *Cancionero general,* but by the early 1530's Garcilaso de la Vega is writing unmistakably Renaissance poetry. In the drama, a turning point comes when Encina spends some time in Rome and writes Italianate plays (one is staged in 1513). In prose fiction, a perceptible change is much longer delayed. The first picaresque novel and the first pastoral romance do not appear until the 1550's, and until then the sentimental romances, *Amadís, Celestina,* and their descendants reign unchallenged. In learned prose, on the other hand, a change is noticeable even before 1500; Nebrija is hardly medieval except in his date of birth.

Yet even when Renaissance forms are established, the medieval ones do not die. A few examples must suffice. The *Cancionero general* was still being expanded until 1557, and reprinted until 1573. When Florián de Ocampo wanted to publish a history of Spain in 1541, he adapted a descendant (*ca.* 1400) of the thirteenth-century *Estoria de España,* and Ocampo's book was reprinted as late as 1604. Alfonso de la Torre's *Visión deleitable,* based on sources at least three centuries old, was reprinted until the 1550's, then translated into Italian, and then retranslated into Spanish and published in 1663. *Flores y Blancaflor* (fifteenth century) and *La donzella Teodor* (*ca.* 1300) were sold in cheap popular editions in the nineteenth century. Ballads of medieval origin are still sung today in some areas. In Spanish, medieval literature is still, though tenuously, with us.

BIBLIOGRAPHY

General bibliographies and reference works. José Amador de los Ríos, *Historia crítica de la literatura española* (1861–1865); David J. Billick and Steven N. Dworkin, *Lexical Studies of Medieval Spanish Texts: A Bibliography of Concordances, Glossaries, Vocabularies and Selected Word Studies* (1987); James F. Burke, "Spanish Literature," in Thomas D. Cooke, ed., *The Present State of Scholarship in Fourteenth-century Literature* (1982); *La Corónica: Spanish Medieval Language and Literature Newsletter* (1972–) [contains bibliographies and surveys]; Alan Deyermond, *A Literary History of Spain: The Middle Ages* (1971; amplified Spanish translation, 1973, 1988) [includes extensive bibliographical references], and *La edad media,* in Francisco Rico, ed., *Historia y crítica de la literatura española,* I (1980, *Suplemento 1,* 1988) [surveys of scholarship 1945–1978, with bibliographies]; José María Díez Borque, ed., *Historia de las literaturas hispánicas no castellanas* (1980) [major sections on Hispano-Latin, Hispano-Arabic, and Hispano-Hebraic literatures, plus extensive treatment of medieval literature in Catalan, Galician, Navarrese, and Aragonese]; Charles B. Faulhaber, *Libros y bibliotecas en la España medieval: Una bibliografía de fuentes impresas* (1987) [a fundamental guide to the contents of medieval Spanish libraries], and *idem et al., Bibliography of Old Spanish Texts,* 3rd ed. (1984) [detailed listing of literary MSS and incunabula]; Francisco López Estrada, *In-*

troducción a la literatura medieval española, 5th ed. (1983) [contains discussions of genres, themes, and methods]; Walter Mettmann, ed., *La littérature dans la péninsule ibérique aux XIVe et XVe siècles,* in *Grundriss der romanischen Literaturen des Mittelalters,* IX (1983–); Klaus Reinhardt and Horacio Santiago-Otero, *Biblioteca bíblica ibérica medieval* (1986) [a bio-bibliographical guide to some 150 authors, Latin and vernacular, who deal with biblical material]; *Repertorio de historia de las ciencias eclesiásticas en España* (1967–) [includes surveys of important aspects of medieval literature]; Julio Rodríguez-Puértolas, ed., *Historia social de la literatura española (en lengua castellana),* I (1979) [a Marxist account of medieval and Renaissance literature, especially useful for bibliographical coverage of this approach to literature]; P. E. Russell, ed., *Spain: A Companion to Spanish Studies* (1973) [contains linguistic, historical, artistic, and musical surveys, as well as treatment of literature, with brief bibliographies]; Homero Serís, *Manual de bibliografía de la literatura española* (1948–1954) [only the first two parts were published; they are valuable for their thematic arrangement of the material] and *Guía de nuevos temas de literatura española,* D. W. McPheeters, ed. (1973) [suggestions for research topics compiled from Serís' notes after his death, therefore outdated in parts, but contains information and ideas not readily available elsewhere]; José Simón Díaz, *Bibliografía de la literatura hispánica,* II (3rd ed. 1984) and III.ii (2nd ed. 1965) [uneven in coverage and in quality, but by far the fullest bibliography; supplements appear regularly in *Revista de literatura*].

Genres, forms, movements. Carlos Alvar, *La poesía trovadoresca en España y Portugal* (1977), *idem,* ed., *Textos trovadorescos sobre España y Portugal* (1978), and *idem* and Ángel Gómez Moreno, *La poesía lírica medieval* (1987); Ana María Álvarez Pellitero, "Aportaciones al estudio del teatro medieval en España," in *Anuario de filología española,* **2** (1985); Samuel G. Armistead, "A Critical Bibliography of the Hispanic Ballad in Oral Tradition (1971–1979)," in *El romancero hoy: Historia, comparatismo, bibliografía crítica* (1979); Egla Morales Blouin, *El ciervo y la fuente: Mito y folklore del agua en la lírica tradicional* (1981); Roger Boase, *The Troubadour Revival: A Study of Social Change and Traditionalism in Late Medieval Spain* (1978); Diego Catalán, *De Alfonso X al conde de Barcelos: Cuatro estudios sobre el nacimiento de la historiografía romance en Castilla y Portugal* (1962), *Siete siglos de romancero (historia y poesía)* (1969), and *idem et al., Teoría general y metodología del romancero pan-hispánico: Catálogo general descriptivo* (1984); Pedro M. Cátedra, *Dos estudios sobre el sermón en la España medieval* (1982); Jane E. Connolly, *Translation and Poetization in the "Quaderna vía": Study and Edition of the "Libro de miseria d'omne"* (1987); Jerry R. Craddock, *The Legislative Works of Alfonso X, el Sabio: A Critical Bibliography* (1986); Alan Deyermond, "The Lost Genre of Medieval Spanish Literature," in *Hispanic Review,* **43** (1975), and *El "Cantar de Mio Cid" y la épica medieval española* (1987); Ottavio Di Camillo, *El humanismo castellano del siglo XV,* Manuel Lloris, trans. (1976); Richard B. Donovan, *The Liturgical Drama in Medieval Spain* (1958); Brian Dutton *et al., Catálogo-índice de la poesía cancioneril del siglo XV* (1982); José Manuel Fradejas Rueda, *Ensayo de una bibliografía de los libros españoles de cetrería y montería (s. XIII–XVII)* (1985); Margit Frenk, *Las jarchas mozárabes y los comienzos de la lírica románica* (1975), and *Estudios sobre lírica antigua* (1978); Álvaro Galmés de Fuentes, "Influencias sintácticas y estilísticas del árabe en la prosa medieval castellana," in *Boletín de la Real Academia Española,* **35** (1955) and **36** (1956); Michel Garcia, "L'historiographie et les groupes dominants en Castille: Le genre chronistique d'Alphonse X au Chancelier Ayala," in Augustin Redondo, ed., *Les groupes dominants et leur(s) discours* (1984); Albert Gier and John Esten Keller, *Les formes narratives brèves en Espagne et Portugal,* in *Grundriss der romanischen Literaturen des Mittelalters,* V (1985) [in German]; Fernando Gómez Redondo, "Fórmulas juglarescas en la historiografía romance de los siglos XIII y XIV," in *La Corónica,* **15** (1986–1987); María Jesús Lacarra, *Cuentística medieval en España: Los orígenes* (1979); J. N. H. Lawrance, "The Spread of Lay Literacy in Late Medieval Castile," in *Bulletin of Hispanic Studies,* **62** (1985); Pierre Le Gentil, *La poésie lyrique espagnole et portugaise à la fin du moyen âge,* 2 vols. (1949–1953); Humberto López Morales, *Tradición y creación en los orígenes del teatro castellano* (1968), and "Sobre el teatro medieval castellano: *Status quaestionis,*" in *Boletín de la Academia Puertorriqueña de la Lengua Española,* **14** (1986); José Antonio Maravall, *Estudios de historia del pensamiento español, I, Edad media,* 2nd ed. (1973); Francisco Rico, *Predicación y literatura en la España medieval* (1977), and "La clerecía del mester," in *Hispanic Review,* **53** (1985); Nicholas G. Round, "Renaissance Culture and Its Opponents in Fifteenth-century Castile," in *Modern Language Review,* **57** (1962); Joaquín Rubio Tovar, ed., *Libros españoles de viajes medievales (selección)* (1986); Justina Ruiz de Conde, *El amor y el matrimonio secreto en los libros de caballerías* (1948); Nicasio Salvador Miguel, "'Mester de clerecía,' marbete caracterizador de un género literario," in *Revista de literatura,* **41** (1979); Benito Sánchez Alonso, *Historia de la historiografía española,* I, 2nd ed. (1947); Harvey L. Sharrer, *A Critical Bibliography of Hispanic Arthurian Material,* I, *Texts: The Prose Romance Cycles* (1977); N. D. Shergold, *A History of the Spanish Stage: From Medieval Times Until the End of the Seventeenth Century* (1967); Ronald E. Surtz, ed., *Teatro medieval castellano* (1983); Robert B. Tate, *Ensayos sobre la historiografía peninsular del siglo XV* (1970); Barry Taylor, "Old Spanish Wisdom Texts: Some Relationships," in *La Corónica,* **14** (1985–1986); Isabel Uría Maqua, "Sobre la unidad del mester de clerecía del siglo XIII: Hacia un replantamiento de la cuestión," in *Actas de las III Jornadas de Estudios Berceanos* (1981); John K. Walsh, "Juan Ruiz and the *Mester de clerezía:* Lost Context and Lost Parody in the *Libro de Buen Amor,*" in *Romance Philology,* **33** (1979–1980); Jane Whetnall, "'Lírica femenina' in the Early Manuscript *Cancioneros,*" in *What's Past Is Prologue: A Collection of Essays Presented to L. J. Woodward* (1984); Keith Whinnom, *La poesía amatoria de la época de los Reyes Católicos* (1981), and *The Spanish Sentimental Romance 1440– 1550: Critical Bibliography* (1983).

Themes and influences. Ricardo Arias y Arias, *El concepto del destino en la literatura medieval española* (1970); Américo Castro, *España en su historia: Cristianos, moros y judíos* (1948), reworked as *La realidad histórica de España* (1954), trans. by Edmund L. King as *The Structure of Spanish History* (1954); Alan Deyermond, "The Interaction of Courtly and Popular Elements in Medieval Spanish Literature," in *Court and Poet: Selected Proceedings of the Third Congress of the International Courtly Literature Society* (1981); Harriet Goldberg, "Two Parallel Medieval Commonplaces: Antifeminism and Antisemitism in the Hispanic Literary Tradition," in Paul E. Szarmach, ed., *Aspects of Jewish Culture in the Middle Ages* (1979), and "Riddles and Enigmas in Medieval Castilian Literature," in *Romance Philology,* 36 (1982–1983); Otis H. Green, *Spain and the Western Tradition: The Castilian Mind in Literature from El Cid to Calderón,* 4 vols. (1963–1966); John Esten Keller and Richard P. Kinkade, *Iconography in Medieval Spanish Literature* (1984); María Rosa Lida de Malkiel, *La idea de la fama en la Edad Media castellana* (1952), "La visión de trasmundo en las literaturas hispánicas," in Howard R. Patch, *El otro mundo en la literatura medieval* (1956), and *La tradición clásica en España* (1975); Derek W. Lomax, "The Lateran Reforms and Spanish Literature," in *Iberoromania,* **1** (1969); Francisco López Estrada, "Las mujeres escritoras en la Edad Media castellana," in Yves-René Fonquerne and Alfonso Esteban, eds., *La condición de la mujer en la Edad Media* (1986); Juan de Dios Mendoza Negrillo, *Fortuna y Providencia en la literatura castellana del siglo XV* (1973); Ramón Menéndez Pidal, *Poesía juglaresca y juglares* (1924), reworked as *Poesía juglaresca y orígenes de las literaturas románicas: Problemas de historia literaria y cultural* (1957); María Rosa Menocal, *The Arabic Role in Medieval Literary History: A Forgotten Heritage* (1987); Colbert I. Nepaulsingh, *Towards a History of Literary Composition in Medieval Spain* (1987); Alexander A. Parker, *The Philosophy of Love in Spanish Literature 1480–1680,* Terence O'Reilly, ed. (1985); Malcolm K. Read, *The Birth and Death of Language: Spanish Literature and Linguistics, 1300–1700* (1983); Francisco Rico, *El pequeño mundo del hombre: Varia fortuna de una idea en las letras españolas,* 2nd ed. (1986); Elias L. Rivers, *Quixotic Scriptures: Essays on the Textuality of Hispanic Literature* (1983); Nicholas G. Round, "The Shadow of a Philosopher: Medieval Castilian Images of Plato," in *Journal of Hispanic Philology,* 3 (1978–1979); Luciana de Stefano, *La sociedad estamental de la baja Edad Media española a la luz de la literatura de la época* (1966); John K. Walsh and B. Bussell Thompson, *The Myth of the Magdalen in Early Spanish Literature* (1986); Keith Whinnom, *Spanish Literary Historiography: Three Forms of Distortion* (1968).

ALAN DEYERMOND

[See also **Aljamiado Literature; Arthurian Literature, Spanish and Portuguese; Asturias-León; Cantigas de Amor, Amiga, and Escarnio; Castile; Cid, History and Legend of; Converso; Cuaderna Vía; Galician-Portuguese Poetry; Kharja; Mester de Clerecía; Mester de Juglaría; Mozarabic Literature; Villancicos;** and individual authors and works.]

SPANISH LITERATURE: BALLADS. The Spanish ballad or *romance* is usually defined as an epico-lyric narrative poem in sixteen-syllable lines, each line being divided into two eight-syllable hemistichs, with a single assonant rhyme used throughout. In point of fact, a number of ballads contain more than one assonant series, and certain narrative poems in nonballad meters (hexasyllabic or octosyllabic parallelistic couplets, for instance) are often included in the Hispanic ballad canon or *romancero.*

VARIETIES OF BALLADS

In its thematic content, the early ballad corpus (*romancero viejo*) is usually divided into various different subtypes: for example, epic, Carolingian, historical, classical, Arthurian, and novelesque ballads. The epic ballads include many of the themes known to the medieval Spanish epic: *Fernán González, Infantes de Lara, Mocedades de Rodrigo, Cerco de Zamora, Cantar de mío Cid.* A certain number of early ballads are probably based directly on the epics, having originated as fragments detached from the longer poems and subjected to varying degrees of subsequent adaptation. Many *romances épicos,* however, are not of direct tradition but follow intermediate chronistic narratives.

Carolingian ballads are based on medieval Spanish translations (or adaptations) of Old French chansons de geste. Among the poems represented are the

Chanson de Roland, Maynet, Chanson des Saisnes, Aymeri de Narbonne, Aïol, Floovent, Ogier le Danois, and *Beuve de Hantone.* Other narratives, originally extrinsic to the French epic, have been absorbed into the Carolingian milieu, such as the pseudo-Carolingian ballads *Conde Dirlos* and *Gaiferos.*

Historical ballads include numerous propagandistic poems, concerning Pedro I "the Cruel" of Castile (*r.* 1350–1369) and a rich assortment of narratives on the frontier wars with the Muslims (late 1300's to 1492). There are few authentically medieval ballads on classical themes; they include the *Judgment of Paris* and an *Abduction of Helen of Troy,* based on some medieval interpretation of the Homeric story, a *Death of Alexander,* which follows a narrative different from *El libro de Alexandre,* and a ballad derived from a medieval legend concerning Vergil. Arthurian *romances,* including poems on Tristan and Lancelot, are extremely rare.

The novelesque category must be viewed as a catch-all in which narratives of quite diverse origin have been brought together. Here various different genres and individual works have inspired Spanish ballad narratives: *pastourelles, romans d'aventure,* sentimental novels, romances of chivalry, and, most important of all, the European traditional ballad (especially, but not exclusively, that of France) have all made their contributions. In the above-mentioned categories, there are, of course, also independent original compositions that depend on no earlier source. It is possible to identify various features of style that distinguish certain ballad subtypes: Among the historical ballads, those concerning the frontier wars with the Muslims of Granada (*romances fronterizos*) are more given to detailed description than are other types of ballads, while Carolingian *romances* use certain formulaic verses not found in other subtypes.

In style the ballads are characterized by their terseness, simplicity of language, and general absence of extensive description; they are highly dramatic, often in dialogue, and little given to the marvelous and supernatural. Formulaic diction is often used. The ballad's style, like that of the epic and the early lyric, has been defined as intuitive: it suggests more than is actually stated, thus leading the reader (or hearer) to supply on his own the narrative's background details. Some of the masterpieces of Spanish balladry are "fragmentistic," breaking off at a critical point and leaving us to imagine the denouement's multiple possibilities. Fragmentism as a stylistic device, with its abrupt beginnings and endings, is ultimately relatable to the genre's origins in "fragments" separated from longer epic narratives. The ballad's perspective is usually universal (rather than nationalist or regional); it is often antiregal and anticlerical; there is little attention to explicit religiosity or moralization; and, far from being puritanical, it often evinces a strong sexuality.

Some ballads undoubtedly originated as fragments of epic poems. Ramón Menéndez Pidal has hypothesized that minstrels, having been asked for an "encore," might have repeated an epic's most dramatic episodes, thus providing their audiences—especially an essentially illiterate public, more adept at memorizing than are literate moderns—with sufficient exposure to the text so that they could easily have learned the crucial scenes. Most authentic *romances épicos* concern, in fact, the epic narratives' peak points, and many contain allusions and obscure details that take on full significance only when seen in the context of the entire epic story from which they derive.

Along with a certain number of ballad narratives, the early *romancero* probably borrowed its formulistic diction and its octosyllabic meter from the epic's anisosyllabic assonant verses, broken, like the *romance* line, into two hemstichs. In the *Cantar de mío Cid,* seven-syllable verses are more frequent than eight-syllable verses, which occupy second place in order of frequency, followed by verses of six, five, nine, ten, and four syllables, respectively. The late (*ca.* 1365) and poorly copied *Mocedades de Rodrigo* is undoubtedly more octosyllabic than were earlier epics. The *romances* may well represent a continuation of this drift toward octosyllabism, and indeed the earliest ballad texts still evince a certain syllabic irregularity not unlike that of the epics. All the same, the octosyllable was also common in the early lyric, long before the first documentation of *romances,* and it seems likely that the lyric may also have played a role in the ballad's origins.

EARLY HISTORY OF THE MEDIEVAL BALLAD

Rather than deriving from the epic alone, it is probable that the ballad's origins were characterized by the same generic and thematic complexity attested at later stages. At very least, the epic, the lyric, and the trans-Pyrenean strophic ballad must all have contributed early on to its formation. It is impossible, however, to study the early Spanish ballad without taking into account its later manifestations. A vast majority of the poems, though medieval in origin, cannot be documented until the sixteenth century, and the modern oral tradition, in its turn, attests to a number of medieval narratives that were never printed during the early period. The ballad tradition, from its medieval genesis to the latest modern versions, forms a single continuum, whose individual segments are essentially inseparable from the whole.

The first known *romance* text dates from 1421, when Jaume de Olesa, a Mallorcan law student in Florence, copied *La dama y el pastor.* It is obvious that this Castilian ballad, transcribed in a mixture of Castilian and Catalan, must already have circulated in oral tradition over an extended period in order to have reached Mallorca, on the outer fringe of the Hispanic linguistic domain. Clearly, *romances* were being sung long before the date of this first known text. Diego Catalán has shown that *El prior de San Juan* must have been composed shortly after the narrative's events (1328); the ballads of Pedro the Cruel are likewise contemporary. Manuscript copies and allusions to the genre as a whole are scarce during the fifteenth century: Juan Rodríguez del Padrón copied (or adapted) three traditional texts around 1450 in the *Cancionero del British Museum* (British Library, Add. 10431). A number of versions quite different from or unknown to the later printings are recorded in the late-fifteenth-to-early-sixteenth-century manuscript *Cancionero musical de Palacio.*

During the reign of Ferdinand and Isabella (1474–1504), the ballad attained a vigorous, universal popularity in all strata of Spanish society, a popularity it would maintain for more than a century. The earliest printed texts are the broadside of *El conde Dirlos* published in Saragossa (about 1510) and several traditional texts absorbed by Hernando del Castillo's *Cancionero general* (1511). The first half of the sixteenth century was the dominant period of the *pliegos sueltos* (loose sheets, corresponding, approximately, to English broadsides or, more exactly, to chapbooks). Ballads were printed, with multiple re-editions, on sheets of cheap paper folded to form booklets of eight or more pages and priced at a pittance. The *pliegos sueltos* were ephemeral literature par excellence. Innumerable issues were lost in their entirety, and many more have survived only in single copies. The principal collections are those of Madrid, Biblioteca Nacional: Marquis of Morbecq; Paris, Bibliothèque Nationale; London, British Library; Prague, University Library; and Cracow, Biblijoteka Jagiellónska. *Pliegos* continued to be printed into the nineteenth century, but with a few exceptions (*Gerineldo, Conde Alarcos, Marqués de Mantua*), they do not concern early ballads.

The first book-length publication devoted exclusively to *romances* was printed by Carles Amorós in Barcelona (about 1525): *Libro en el qual se contienen cincuenta romances.* Only the first four sheets of a second edition have been preserved. The book was, however, an exception, for it is not until more than two decades later, around 1548, when the Flemish printer Martin Nutius (Nucio) published in Antwerp his *Cancionero de romances* (known as the *Cancionero de romances, impreso en Amberes sin año*), that other book-length collections begin to appear. The success of Nucio's venture soon led to the printing of additional collections: an amplified *Cancionero de romances* (1550) and Esteban G. de Nájera's *Silva de romances* (1550–1551). *Romances viejos* monopolized Spanish ballad anthologies for the next thirty years. Nucio's collection saw multiple re-editions, and the three parts of Nájera's *Silva* were repeatedly anthologized in the shorter *Silvas recopiladas.* Other important collections were Juan Timoneda's *Rosas de romances* (1573) and the much-reprinted *Flor de enamorados* (1562).

Abundant reprintings, in which a single ballad variant may be successively reproduced without essential change, suggest a deceptive unity and sameness in the *romances viejos* that contrast completely with its later development in oral tradition. The early *romances,* just like those in modern tradition, must have existed in multiple, protean, constantly changing texts, only one of which, by chance, may have had the good fortune to be printed. And once consecrated in print, that single version was usually reprinted over and over again by subsequent editors, who never bothered to refer back to the oral tradition. Rare indeed are ballads such as *El prisionero* or *Domingo era de Ramos* and *Ya comienzan los franceses,* which early printings have preserved in two significantly different forms. Yet, as soon as we go beyond the restricted purview of the early printings and their re-editions, the diversity and variability of the *romancero viejo* become immediately clear. The sixteenth-century Portuguese *Cancioneiro musical e poético da Biblioteca Públia Hortênsia,* independent of the activities of Spanish editors, gives us Castilian texts that are as different in relation to those of the *cancionero* canon as might be any two parallel samplings from the modern tradition.

Pliegos sueltos and *cancioneros* are not our only sources for the reconstruction of the early tradition. The Golden Age theater, *vihuelista* manuals, *ensaladas,* literary allusions, proverbial expressions, pen trials, and early Judeo-Spanish hymn incipits all help to confirm the rich diversity of the *romancero viejo.* Spanish dramatists often used ballads in their *comedias,* not only as a major source for plot material but also in innumerable citations (including some essentially complete texts). The sources used are not infrequently independent of contemporary printing and attest to the typical variablity of oral texts.

Another major source of early ballad variants are the instruction manuals of *vihuela* (guitar) masters. The texts—usually abbreviated—that accompany their adaptations of traditional ballad tunes are often different from those of contemporary printers. *Ensaladas* (miscellany poems composed of single verses taken from previous compositions) are a rich and still largely unexplored source that sometimes documents otherwise unknown texts. The innumerable allusions to *romances* in sixteenth- and seventeenth-century literature remain uncataloged for Spain; the Portuguese corpus has been admirably systematized by Carolina Michaëlis de Vasconcelos. So popular was the *romance* that some key verses became proverbial and were an important component in Hispanic folk speech. Though not all variations go back to the ballads themselves, some apparently do. The possible documentation of Spanish ballads in pen trials, which obviously call upon memory rather than any written source, has yet to be explored.

Another important documentary source are the first lines of Spanish ballads used as tune indicators in collections of Hebrew hymns sung in the eastern Mediterranean and Moroccan communities of Sephardic Jews expelled from Spain in 1492. Evidence of ballad incipits (some sixty different narrative types are represented) dates from as early as 1525 and continues throughout the sixteenth century, as well as in seventeenth-, eighteenth-, and nineteenth-century piyutim collections.

LATER SCHOLARSHIP

During the seventeenth and eighteenth centuries and much of the nineteenth, the *romancero viejo* went "underground"; or, according to Menéndez Pidal, it was in a "latent state" (*estado latente*), largely unnoticed by the learned strata of society, but very much alive in the oral traditions of the illiterate and of rural peasantry. Only rarely was this almost total documentary silence broken on the peninsula by some sporadic, isolated written testimony. The eighteenth-century Sephardic tradition, on the other hand, offers a rich assortment of manuscripts dating from 1702 onward and providing documentation for thirty-four different ballad themes, many of medieval provenience.

Agustín Durán's massive *Romancero general,* first published in five volumes (1828–1832), under the influence of Romanticism's concern with popular poetry—and even today a fundamental research instrument—did not, however, contain a single oral testimony. Only in the second edition (2 vols., 1849–1851) are a few isolated modern Andalusian and Asturian texts incorporated. In Portugal the earliest substantial collections of modern ballads was João Baptista de Almeida Garrett's *Romanceiro* (1843–1851). The first major collection in Castilian did not appear until more than three decades later, when Juan Menéndez Pidal published his *Poesía popular: Colección de los viejos romances que se cantan por los asturianos* (1885). The first major Sephardic collection, by Abraham Danon, appeared in 1896 (*Revue des études juives,* 32–33). Castile itself did not emerge from its latent state until 1900, with the early fieldwork of Ramón Menéndez Pidal and María Goyri, which produced, among other treasures, a previously unknown medieval ballad, *La muerte del príncipe Don Juan* (1497). Spanish America yielded no extensive collection until Julio Vicuña Cifuentes' Chilean *Romances populares y vulgares* (1912). The Canary Islands were not satisfactorily documented until 1969, and numerous unknown areas and scattered outposts still remain to be explored.

Today, however, in confirmation of Menéndez Pidal's theory of the pan-Hispanic distribution of the *romancero,* we have ballad evidence even from the most exotic and isolated corners of the Hispanic world (Alghero, Goa, Guam, the Philippines, Louisiana, Tunisian *moriscos*), and massive collections have been formed from every major tradition. The most important are, for the Castilian-speaking areas of Spain, the vast, still largely unedited archive of Menéndez Pidal and the Santander collection of José María de Cossío and Tomás Maza Solano; for Portugal, Theófilo Braga, José Leite de

Vasconcellos, and Manuel da Costa Fontes. Gisela Beutler's *Estudios sobre el romancero español en Colombia* (1977) offers the most extensive Spanish American collection and is an indispensable starting point for the complex bibliography of that tradition. Diego Catalán's *La flor de la marañuela* (2 vols., 1969) is central to our knowledge of the Canarian tradition. The most important Judeo-Spanish collections are those of Menéndez Pidal and of S. G. Armistead, J. H. Silverman, and Israel J. Katz, both still in great part unedited, and the printed *romanceros* of Moshe Attias, Paul Bénichou, Arcadio de Larrea Palacín, Zarita Nahón, Rina Benmayor, and Oro A. Librowicz, among others.

Every branch of the modern tradition has, in some way, elucidated our knowledge of the *romancero viejo,* and as fieldwork goes forward new and dramatic discoveries can still be expected. Scholarly work on the *romancero,* largely historicist until quite recently, has now turned to other and equally important concerns. Paul Bénichou's *Creación poética en el romancero tradicional* (1968) heralded a new interest in ballad poetics and in the oral tradition as a creative process. Even more recently, scholarship is addressing ballad semiotics, computerized poetic analysis, and the *romancero*'s sociological implications.

BIBLIOGRAPHY

As starting points for all Hispanic ballad studies, see Ramón Menéndez Pidal, *Romancero hispánico,* 2 vols. (1953), and *Estudios sobre el Romancero* (1973). Ferdinand J. Wolf and Conrad Hofmann, *Primavera y flor de romances,* 2 vols. (1856), is still the best scholarly collection, re-edited and supplemented by Marcelino Menéndez y Pelayo, *Edición nacional de las obras completas,* XXIV and XXV (1945). Antonio Rodríguez-Moñino's monumental *Diccionario bibliográfico de pliegos sueltos poéticos: Siglo XVI* (1970), and *Manual bibliográfico de cancioneros y romanceros,* 4 vols. (1973–1978), plus innumerable ancillary editions and critical works, are indispensable. Excellent modern anthologies, among others, are Juan Alcina Franch, *Romancero antiguo,* 2 vols. (1969–1971); Michelle Débax, *Romancero* (1982); Mercedes Díaz Roig, *El romancero viejo* (1976); Giuseppe Di Stefano, *El romancero* (1973); Sylvanus Griswold Morley, *Spanish Ballads* (1911, numerous reprs.); Germán Orduna, *Selección de romances viejos de España y América* (1975); and C. Colin Smith, *Spanish Ballads* (1964, repr. 1969).

Menéndez Pidal's *Flor nueva de romances viejos,* 3rd ed. (1938, numerous reprs.), offers beautiful synthetic texts based on both the sixteenth-century and modern traditions. A good, though brief, selection in English translation is William S. Merwin, *Spanish Ballads* (1961). The entire Hispanic ballad corpus is being brought together in the massive *Romancero tradicional de lenguas hispánicas* (collected by María Goyri and Ramón Menéndez Pidal), Diego Catalán *et al.,* eds. (1957–).

Concerning the use of traditional formulas, see Ruth House Webber, *Formulistic Diction in the Spanish Ballad* (1951). On ballad style, values, and perspectives: C. Colin Smith, "On the Ethos of the *romancero viejo,*" in N. D. Shergold, ed., *Studies of the Spanish and Portuguese Ballad* (1973). On the genetic connection with the medieval epic: Menéndez Pidal, *La epopeya castellana a través de la literatura española,* 2nd ed. (1959), 137–140; Samuel G. Armistead, "Epic and Ballad: A Traditionalist Perspective," in *Olifant,* 8 (1981); and *idem,* Joseph H. Silverman, and Israel J. Katz, *Judeo-Spanish Ballads from Oral Tradition,* I: *Epic Ballads* (1986). On the earliest evidence of ballads: Diego Catalán, *Siete siglos de romancero* (1969), 15–56. On the oral character and variability of the early tradition: Armistead, "Neo-individualism and the *Romancero,*" in *Romance Philology,* 33 (1979–1980). On early ballads in Portugal: Carolina Michaëlis de Vasconcelos, *Romances Velhos em Portugal,* 2nd ed. (1934). On early ballad music: Miguel Querol Gavaldá, "Importance historique et nationale du *romance,*" in *Musique et poésie au XVIe siècle* (1954). On ballad lines as tune indicators: Armistead and Silverman, "El antiguo romancero sefardí: Citas de romances en himnarios hebreos (siglos XVI–XIX)," in *Nueva revista de filología hispánica,* 30 (1981). On the modern tradition and its crucially important connections with the early *romancero:* Armistead *et al., El romancero judeo-español en el Archivo Menéndez Pidal: Catálogo-índice de romances y canciones,* 3 vols. (1978); Diego Catalán, *Por campos del romancero: Estudios sobre la tradición oral moderna* (1970), "El romancero medieval," in *El comentario a textos,* IV, *La poesía medieval* (1983), and *idem et al., Catálogo general del romancero,* 3 vols. (1982–1984); Antonio Sánchez Romeralo *et al., Bibliografía del romancero oral* (1980); on creativity in oral tradition: Paul Bénichou, *Creación poética en el romancero tradicional* (1968). The edited proceedings of two international colloquia provide additional perspectives on all aspects of Hispanic balladry: Coloquio Internacional Sobre el Romancero, 1st, Madrid, 1973, *El romancero en la tradición oral moderna* (1973), and Coloquio Internacional, 2nd, *El romancero hoy,* 3 vols. (1979).

S. G. Armistead

[See also **Alexander Romances; Arthurian Literature; Assonance; Cancionero General; Cantar de Mío Cid; Chansons de Geste; Matter of Britain, France, Rome; Troy Story; Vergil in the Middle Ages.**]

SPANISH LITERATURE: BIBLE TRANSLATIONS. Some fifteen biblical manuscripts have come down to us from the Old Spanish period (roughly 1200–1500). Two date from the thirteenth century, the rest from the late fourteenth and fifteenth centuries. They form several manuscript families whose precise interrelation has not been determined. A few are written in Catalan and show strong French textual influence. The others are in Castilian, some with dialectal overlays. Nearly all the manuscripts are incomplete or fragmentary.

Of particular significance in the cultural history of Spain is the coexistence of Christian Bibles based on the Vulgate with versions of Hebrew origin. Each tradition influenced the other, despite the great differences between them.

The two earliest biblical texts are representative in this sense. The older one, from the Hebrew with a possible intermediary version in Latin or dialectal French, has been published under the title *Fazienda de Ultra Mar.* Not strictly a Bible, it contains selections and summaries of material on the most memorable Old Testament heroes and prophets, presented within the framework of an itinerary of the Holy Land. Apparently it was conceived as a repository of ancient Jewish popular lore. The peculiar format may have been intended to avoid censure by authorities, a presumption supported by the presence of a spurious introductory letter in which Archbishop Raimundo of Toledo, who in fact died in 1151, perhaps a century before the writing of the text, purportedly requests its composition from one Almeric, archdeacon of Antioch, whose identity has not been verified. The version is simply written and invaluable as a cultural and linguistic document. Though based on the Hebrew, it draws upon the Vulgate and makes reference to the New Testament.

The other thirteenth-century text was originally a two-volume Bible; only the second part is extant as *Biblia Escurialense* 6 (Biblioteca de El Escorial, San Lorenzo de El Escorial). It dates from around the 1260's and was known to the group of historians who compiled the *General estoria* under the direction of King Alfonso X (*r.* 1252–1284). Some of the books carry prologues of St. Jerome, and to some are added glosses taken from the *Collectanea* of Peter Lombard, indicating a French textual background. The language is direct and often eloquent in its simplicity; from the choice of everyday words and expressions it is plain that this Bible was meant to be read by (or more accurately, read to) people with little knowledge of Latin.

Limited diffusion of these early Bibles, and their lack of intellectual or linguistic pretensions, must explain why they contributed little to the vocabulary of Spanish literature. When, after a lapse of over a century, new versions began to appear, they were written for nobles rather than for common people. Among a number of valuable manuscripts, the Bible of Alba (1422–1433) deserves particular mention. Prepared by Rabbi Mosse Arragel of Guadalajara at the order of a Christian nobleman and under his supervision, it tries to reconcile the Hebrew and Latin traditions, sometimes offering two alternative readings. Its beautiful miniatures also combine rabbinical and Christian elements.

In the Middle Ages, vernacular Bibles were frequently regarded with official suspicion in Spain, as elsewhere. Interchange among Christians and Jews enriched the translations but increased their vulnerability to censure. How many manuscripts were destroyed cannot be guessed, but the few remaining bear witness to an impressive scholarly output.

BIBLIOGRAPHY

Editions. Oliver H. Hauptmann, ed., *Escorial Bible I-j-4: I: The Pentateuch* (1953), a Hebrew-based text; Moshé Lazar, ed., *La Fazienda de Ultra Mar* (1965); Thomas Montgomery, ed., *El Evangelio de San Mateo según el manuscrito Escurialense I-I-6* (1962); *idem* and Spurgeon W. Baldwin, eds., *El Nuevo Testamento según el manuscrito Escurialense I-I-6* (1970).

Studies. Margherita Morreale, "Apuntes bibliográficos para la iniciación al estudio de las Biblias medievales en castellano," in *Sefarad,* **20** (1960), and "Vernacular Scriptures in Spain," in *The Cambridge History of the Bible,* II (1969), 465–491, and bibliography 533–535; Carl Otto Nordström, *The Duke of Alba's Castilian Bible: A Study of the Rabbinical Features of the Miniatures* (1967).

THOMAS MONTGOMERY

[See also **Bible; Exegesis, Jewish; Spanish Language; Spanish Literature.**]

SPANISH LITERATURE: BIOGRAPHY. The tradition of biographical literature in the peninsula stems, as elsewhere in Western Europe, from the twin streams of classical and patristic culture. The hagiographical genre was explored by many Hispano-Latin writers from St. Isidore, St. Ildefonsus, and Braulius onward, leading eventually in the thirteenth century to the versified romance narratives of Gonzalo de Berceo on Riojan saints (derived from Latin sources) and anonymous works like the *Vida de Santa María Egipciaca.* Hagiographies continued to be written through the fourteenth and fifteenth centuries, with the often recurring theme of the *Vida de San Ildefonso*: from the earliest example by the so-called "beneficiado de Ubeda" to the *Vida de San Isidoro* and *San Ildefonso* copied by Alfonso Martínez de Toledo, archpriest of Talavera, completed about 1444. The Suetonian tradition, through intermediaries, inspired the thirteenth-century *Liber illustrium personarum* of Juan Gil de Zamora and certain passages of the *Crónica de España* of Alfonso X. A more powerful secular thrust came from the epic, the prose romance, and the chivalresque ethic, which, combined with the evolving romance chronicles and popular treatises on the moral virtues, produced the richest vein of biographical works in the fifteenth century.

There are five extant examples of varying worth, and all deal with idealized noble protagonists drawn from contemporary history. The first, *El Victorial* or *Crónica de Don Pero Niño* (*fl.* 1379–*ca.* 1458), attributed to Gutierre Díez de Games, states its aims clearly: "La causa material en aquesta obra es oficio e arte de caballería: la causa eficiente es quien la fizo: la causa formal es loar los fechos de un buen cavallero: la causa final es provecho" (In this work the material cause is the office and the art of chivalry; the efficient cause lies in the one who created this work; the formal cause is the praise of the deeds of a good knight; the final cause is the benefit of all). It deals with the upbringing, career, and amours of a true knight in Spain, France, England, and the Mediterranean up to 1446. In contrast with this blend of fantasy, legend, and chronicle is the *Crónica de don Miguel Lucas de Iranzo* (constable of Castile during the disturbed reign of Enrique IV of Castile, and alcaide of Jaén from the 1460's to 1471), stopping short of Lucas' assassination in 1473. As distinct from the larger landscape of the previous work, this concentrates on the patterns of life, customs, ceremonies, and frontier warfare of a provincial noble recorded by someone who knew his subject intimately, variously named as Luis de Castillo, Gonzalo Mexía, and Pedro de Escavias, with the balance of favor leaning toward the last, alcaide of neighboring Andújar, a known poet and chronicler. The most famous, most compelling, and most erudite biography, *La crónica de don Álvaro de Luna,* attributed to Gonzalo Chacón, *comendador* of Montiel and a figure of some substance in the court of Ferdinand and Isabella, also deals with a constable of Castile. There are no digressions as in the *Victorial* and few details of intimate life as in *Lucas de Iranzo.* It was probably written sometime after the execution of Don Álvaro in 1453 and retouched near the end of the century by a politically minded courtier with strong literary pretensions who wished to demonstrate, through highly emotional apostrophe, harangue, dialogue, and sententious meditation, the dedicated concern for the common weal of his protagonist, who in the final scenes assumes the attributes of a Christ-like figure.

Two other biographies of minor aristocrats that have not yet been properly assessed are Alonso de Maldonado's *Hechos de don Alonso de Monroy, clavero y maestre de la orden de Alcántara* and the anonymous *Historia de don Rodrigo Ponce de Léon, marqués de Cadiz.* Both are incomplete, probably written in the first years of the sixteenth century. The former is preserved as a prologue to a lost translation of Appian's *Civil Wars* and records the personal exploits of Don Alonso in Extremadura up to 1475 against a background of siege, robbery, assault, and famine, interlaced with fragments of contemporary song. The latter restricts its narrative to the role of Don Rodrigo as a crusader against the Moors and a dedicated supporter of Ferdinand and Isabella in their campaign against Granada. It breaks off in 1488. Of the autobiographical tradition there is only one surviving example, the remarkable and emotional memoirs of Leonor López de Córdoba, daughter of a supporter of Pedro I of Castile, dictated in the early fifteenth century.

Of a different but allied tradition are two collections of biographies or *semblanzas,* one by the noble Fernán Pérez de Guzmán (*ca.* 1378–*ca.* 1460), and the other by the *converso* royal secretary and historian Hernando del Pulgar (*d. ca.* 1493), who chose the former as his model. Guzmán's *Generaciones y semblanzas* is a collection of thirty-four brief portraits (three kings, a queen, twenty-two nobles, seven prelates, and a clerk) sketched near the end of his life as a worldly-wise, disabused minor noble, from his rural retreat in Batres. Traces of the Suetonian and Sallustian approach to history are close to the surface, and the vices and virtues of a self-regarding nobility are dispassionately analyzed in laconic prose. It is difficult to argue positively for any humanistic impact here, but a Senecan stoicism is certainly present in his judgments, in the value of adversity, and the praise of generosity. Guzmán is also the author of a large body of poetry in traditional forms in which the note of moral sententiousness is uppermost. His most ambitious projects were the *Setecientas* and the *Loores de los claros varones.* He also made a vernacular adaptation of the *Mare historiarum* of the Dominican Giovanni della Colonna and instigated translations of Seneca's *Moral Epistles* and Sallust's *Jugurthan War* and *Conspiracy of Catiline.* These latter may have contributed to the presentation of the *Generaciones.*

The classical heritage is much more evident in the *Claros varones de Castilla* of Pulgar (after 1483), but the historical context in which it is set is significantly distinct. Included are one king, Enrique (Henry) IV, fifteen nobles, eight prelates, and two intercalated addresses to Queen Isabella, which allow a slightly more elaborate treatment of the *semblanza.* For Pulgar, the anguish and confusion of the days of Pérez de Guzmán were yielding to a new era in Castile in which individual achievements could match and even outstrip those of Roman history. Whereas Guzmán was reserved and laconic, often dismissive, Pulgar is expansive and dynamic, ironic and allusive, setting his subjects more explicitly against the backdrop of contemporary history and dramatizing their attitudes in narrative, dialogue, and declamatory address. Pulgar, as a royal dependent and official historian, is at pains to emphasize those qualities that lead to strength rather than attack those that lead to weakness. In creating for Castile her own present-day set of heroes, he reflects the desire of Ferdinand and Isabella to act with tact and moderation toward the nobility in the aftermath of a civil war so as to bring a single-minded concentration to bear on the campaign against Granada, which had not been completed before he finished the *Claros varones.* His official history, the *Crónica de los reyes católicos,* has inevitably a larger brief; its aim was to trace the dramatic change in the political fortunes of Castile from the marriage of Ferdinand and Isabella to the last phase of the Granadine campaign in which events follow in an ineluctable succession under the guidance of Providence. This and other works in a similar mold are contrived to present a triumphal conclusion to decades of feud and dissension, a theme reinforced by works in Latin in the humanist vein by native Spaniards or Italians such as Lucius Marineus Siculus.

BIBLIOGRAPHY

Editions. Gonzalo Berceo, *La vida de San Millán de la Cogolla,* Brian Dutton, ed. (1967), *El martirio de San Lorenzo,* Pompillo Tesauro, ed. (1971), *El poema de Santa Oria,* Isabel Uría Maqua, ed. (1976), and *La vida de Santo Domingo de Silos,* B. Dutton, ed. (1978); *Crónica de don Álvaro de Luna,* Juan de Mata Carriazo, ed. (1940); *De operibus historicis Johannis Aegidii Zamorensis* (1913), Georges Cirot, ed.; Gutierre Díez de Gámez, *El Victorial: Crónica de don Pero Niño,* Juan de Mata Carriazo, ed. (1940); *Estoria de Santa María Egipciaca,* Roger M. Walker, ed. (1972); *Hechos del Condestable Don Miguel Lúcas de Iranzo,* Juan de Mata Carriazo, ed. (1940); *Historia de los hechos del marqués de Cadiz,* in *Colección de documentos inéditos para la historia de España,* CVI (1893), 143–317; Alonso de Maldonado, *Hechos del maestre de Alcántara Don Alonso de Monroy,* Antonio Rodríguez-Moñino, ed. (1935); Alfonso Martínez de Toledo, Arcipreste de Talavera, *Vidas de San Ildefonso y San Isidoro,* José Madoz, ed. (1952); Fernán Pérez de Guzmán, *Generaciones y semblanzas,* Robert B. Tate, ed. (1965); Hernando de Pulgar, *Claros varones de Castilla,* Robert B. Tate, ed. (1971), reviewed by Alberto Várvaro in *Romance Philology,* **27** (1973–1974); *Repertorio de príncipes de España y obra poética del alcalde Pedro de Escavias,* Michel García, ed. (1972); *Vida de Santa María Egipciaca,* Manuel Alvar, ed., 2 vols. (1970–1972); *Vida de San Ildefonso,* in *Biblioteca de autores españoles,* **57** (1898).

Studies. Juan B. Avalle Arce, *El cronista Pedro de Escavias: Una vida del siglo XIV* (1972); Reinaldo Ayerbe-Chaux, "Las memorias de doña Leonor López de Córdoba," in *Journal of Hispanic Philology,* **2** (1977); Alan D. Deyermond, *La edad media,* in *Historia de la literature española,* I (1973); Michel García, "À propos de la chronique du connétable Miguel Lucas de Iranzo," in *Bulletin hispanique,* **75** (1973); E. Michael Gerli, *Alfonso Martínez de Toledo* (1976); Antonio Giménez, "El problema del género en la *Crónica de don Álvaro de Luna,*" in *Boletín de la Real Academia Española,* **55** (1975); Harriet Goldberg, "Moslem and Spanish Christian Literary Portraiture," in *Hispanic Review,* **45** (1977); Ralph de Gorog and Lisa de Gorog, "La atribución de las 'Vidas de San Ildefonso y San Isidro' al Arcipreste de Talavera," in *Boletín de la Real Academia Española,* **58** (1978); Theodore L. Kassier, "The Thetorical Devices of the *Vida de Santa María Egipciaca,*" in *Anuario de estudios medievales,* **8** (1972–1973); Warren F. Manning, "An Old Spanish Life of St. Dominic: Sources and Date," in *Mediaeval Studies in Honor of Jeremiah D. M. Ford* (1948); Juan A. Marichal, "G. Díez de Games y su Victorial," in *Imago Mundi,* **1** (1954); Franco Meregalli, *Cronisti e viaggiatori castigliani del*

Quattrocento (1957); Madeleine Pardo, "Un épisode du *Victorial:* Biographie et élaboration artistique," in *Romania,* **85** (1964); B. Sánchez Alonso, *Historia de la historiografía española,* I (1941); Robert B. Tate, *Ensayos sobre la historiografía peninsular del siglo XV* (1970).

ROBERT B. TATE

[See also **Alfonso X of Castile; Berceo, Gonzalo de; Biography, Secular; Castile.**]

SPANISH LITERATURE: CHRONICLES. In the Middle Ages many believed in the Gothic personality of Christian Spain. Her kings, in this view, were literally of the same line as the Goths Recared and Receswinth; Pelayo, first king of the Reconquest, was accounted also a Goth and successor to the tragic Roderick, who "lost" Spain. One can see what this implies. Muslim rule becomes a mere episode, Christian Spain a continuous entity, and the Reconquest a genuine restoration. This set of beliefs is the organizing principle for a large body of chronicles and histories. It is first expressed in the important *Chronicle of Alfonso III* (ninth–tenth centuries) and appears in the elegant *Chronicle of Silos* (twelfth century), an abortive biography of Alfonso VI of León. *Silos* is in turn partly incorporated in the *Chronicle of Nájera* (twelfth century) and in the influential compilation *Chronicon mundi* of Lucas of Túy (thirteenth century). The contemporary *De rebus Hispaniae* of Archbishop Rodrigo Jiménez de Rada of Toledo also preserves the Gothic myth. Finally, that great vernacular compilation, the *Estoria de España,* also known as the *Primera crónica general,* composed under the direction of Alfonso X of Castile, translates most of Rodrigo and parts of Lucas and so puts the theme of the Gothic succession at the center of its large stage.

These works are all what one could call general chronicles. They begin with events remote in time from their authors, the Creation for Lucas and Alfonso, the reign of Hercules for Rodrigo, the accession of Vitiza for the author of *Silos.* The *Chronicle* of Pelayo of Oviedo (twelfth century), that of Nájera, and the *Chronicon* of Lucas all incorporate or presuppose the world chronicle and the Gothic history of Isidore of Seville and certain other texts, and they continue down to the time of the reigning monarch. Recent history for all of these works is that of western Spain, León and Castile. Of the lot, Rodrigo, Nájera, and Alfonso favor Castile. Nájera and Alfonso make extensive use of Castilian epic literature to add bulk to their histories of Castile, scanty in Leonese chronicles. The eastern half of Christian Spain gets its due in a brief general history of its own, the very influential *Chronicle of San Juan de la Peña* (fourteenth century). This work is also a compilation; its account begins with matter from Rodrigo on Hercules and on the Goths and ends with an original section on the united monarchy of Aragon-Barcelona.

Alfonso's two great torsos, the *Estoria de España* and his universal history, the *Grande e general estoria,* full of Josephus and Comestor, are vast mosaics of ancient and medieval texts, quite in the manner of a Vincent of Beauvais or of an Otto of Freising. But the Alfonsine compositions are the masterpieces of the genre, articulated more elaborately than their predecessors, and more systematically and deliberately thematic and didactic. The first of these works enjoyed a spectacular fortune in the peninsula; it was read and copied down to the Renaissance, both in its original form and in a series of important variants and partial texts, a development much studied. Alfonso's achievement was duplicated in the mid fourteenth century in Aragon. Juan Fernández de Heredia and his circle produced, among other works, Aragonese versions of Thucydides and Plutarch and, interesting for us, a lengthy *Grant crónica de Espanya,* heavily dependent on Alfonso.

Spanish histories on more limited subjects are of different sorts. There are many sets of annals covering events as late as the fourteenth century. The most modern of these works are regional and limited in their information, but not all; a few are generally Spanish in scope. In a different mode the *Historia compostelana* is a lively narrative of the rule of Gelmírez, the powerful first archbishop of Santiago. A contemporary Latin memoir of the Cid survives, the *Historia Roderici.* A broader panorama is presented in the splendid quasi-epic *Chronica Adefonsi imperatoris,* an account of the pan-Spanish rule of Alfonso VII. The work tells the remarkable story of the monarch's consolidation of power and of a series of his campaigns against the Muslims. Catalan historiography comes into its own in a group of superb chronicles, those of James I, Bernat Desclot, and Ramón Muntaner, witnesses to the growing power of Aragon and Barcelona in the thirteenth and fourteenth centuries. In Castile royal chronicles exist for every king from Alfonso X on.

The ones for the reigns of Pedro I the Cruel and the first Trastámaras are by no less a writer than the chancellor Pero López de Ayala. The chronicle of Pedro the Cruel is in every sense brilliant historiography; its account of the gradual collapse of Pedro's rule is subtle, exact, and complete.

Historical literature in fifteenth-century Castile is extensive. The reigns of Henry IV and of the Catholic Monarchs were honored by chronicles by writers as distinguished as Alfonso de Palencia, Diego de Valera, and Hernando del Pulgar. The histories of the humanist Palencia, Tacitan in style and conception, are the masterpieces of the lot and the sources of several of the others on the period. But perhaps the liveliest commentaries on the times are found not in histories nor chronicles but in biographies, Pérez de Guzmán's brilliant *Generaciones y semblanzas,* Hernando del Pulgar's companion *Claros varones de Castilla,* a life of the royal favorite Álvaro de Luna, and others.

BIBLIOGRAPHY

Texts. Alfonso X of Castile, *General estoria,* I, Antonio García Solalinde, ed. (1930), *General estoria,* II, A. G. Solalinde, Lloyd A. Kasten, and Victor R. B. Oelschläger, eds., 2 vols. (1957–1961), and *Primera crónica general,* 2nd ed., Ramón Menéndez Pidal, ed., 2 vols. (1955); *Crónica de Alfonso III,* Agustín Ubieto Arteta, ed. (1971); *Crónica de don Álvaro de Luna,* Juan de Mata Carriazo, ed. (1940); *Crónica de San Juan de la Peña,* A. Ubieto Arteta, ed. (1961); Bernat Desclot, *Crónica,* M. Coll i Alentorn, ed., 5 vols. (1949–1951), trans. by F. L. Critchlow as *Chronicle of the Reign of King Pedro III of Aragon* (1928); Juan Fernández de Heredia, *La grant crónica de Espanya, libros I y II,* Regina af Geijerstam, ed. (1964); *Historia compostelana,* in *Patrologia latina,* CLXX (1853); *Historia silense,* Justo Pérez de Urbel and Atilano González Ruiz-Zorilla, eds. (1959); Jaime [James] I of Aragon, *Chronica i comentaris del . . . Rei En Jacme Primer,* Marian Aguiló i Fúster, ed. (1873), completed by Ángel Aguilo (1905), trans. by John Forster as *Chronicle of James I, King of Aragon* (1885).

Pero López de Ayala, *Crónicas de . . . don Pedro, don Enrique II, don Juan I, y don Enrique III,* in Cayetano Rosell y López, ed., *Crónicas de los reyes de Castilla,* I, II (1875, 1877, repr. 1953); Lucas of Túy (Lucas Tudensis), *Chronicon mundi,* in Andreas Schottus, ed., *Hispaniae illustratae,* IV (1608); Ramón Muntaner, *Crónica,* E. B., ed., 9 vols., 2nd ed. (1927–1952), trans. by Lady Goodenough as *The Chronicle of Muntaner,* 2 vols. (1920–1921); Alfonso de Palencia, *Alphonsi Palentini gesta hispaniensia . . .* (1834), incomplete, trans. by A. Paz y Mélia as *Crónica de Enrique IV,* 5 vols. (1904–1909), repr. in 3 vols. (1973–1975); Fernán Pérez de Guzmán, *Generaciones y semblanzas,* Robert B. Tate, ed. (1965); Hernando de Pulgar, *Claros varones de Castilla,* Robert B. Tate, ed. (1971); Ximénez de Rada, Archbishop Rodrigo of Toledo (Rodrigo Toledano), *De rebus Hispaniae,* in *Opera,* III (1793, repr. 1968).

See also B. Sánchez Alonso, *Historia de la historiografía española,* I (1941).

CHARLES F. FRAKER

[See also **Alfonso X; Chronicles; Cid, The, History and Legend of; Isidore of Seville, St.; López de Ayala, Pero; Otto of Freising; Vincent of Beauvais.**]

SPANISH LITERATURE: DAWN AND SPRING SONGS. The coming of dawn and the celebration of spring are characteristic themes of the old Spanish lyric. Dawn usually has an erotic connotation; it can be the time chosen to serenade the loved one ("Recordad, mis ojuelos verdes / ca la mañana dormiredes") or the melancholy hour of separation ("Ya cantan los gallos, buen amor, y vete / Cata que amanece"). Spring songs belong to a very ancient tradition, which Gaston Paris related to the origins of medieval lyric poetry ("Entra mayo y sale abril / ¡Tan garridico le vi venir!").

BIBLIOGRAPHY

Dionisia Empaytaz, *Antología de albas, alboradas, y poemas afines en la Península Ibérica hasta 1625* (1976); Edward M. Wilson, "Iberian," in Arthur T. Hatto, ed., *Eos: An Enquiry into the Theme of Lovers' Meetings and Partings at Dawn in Poetry* (1965).

ANTONIO SÁNCHEZ ROMERALO

[See also **Villancicos.**]

SPANISH LITERATURE: DRAMA. In Spain, as elsewhere in Europe, the earliest documented testimony of the existence of a liturgical drama is associated with the Easter liturgy. The oldest *Quem quaeritis* in Spain is found in an eleventh-century breviary from the Benedictine monastery of Silos, written in Mozarabic script. Along the pilgrimage routes at Huesca to the east and Santiago de Compostela to the west, several more examples of the *Quem quaeritis* dialogue from the eleventh and twelfth centuries have been found. The heaviest concentration of extant texts is located in the

Catalonian region. The twelfth-century *Visitatio sepulchri* from the Benedictine monastery of Ripoll has been called the "earliest complex Latin Resurrection play" in Europe. The merchant scene appears here almost a hundred years before it does in any other documented text, having possibly originated in the region within a vernacular dramatic context. Easter plays are also presented at Vich and Santa María del Estany and numerous other locations in nothern Catalonia.

Gerona was particularly active in the Christmas season. Numerous references to the performance of Christmas plays are recorded in its fourteenth-century *consueta* (ceremonial breviary). The popular custom of electing an *episcopellus* (a "boy bishop") on 28 December was also practiced here, and a very realistic performance of the martyrdom of St. Stephen took place on 26 December. It is also significant that Gerona and Majorca in the Balearic Islands offer the earliest examples of dramatization within the Mass; in Majorca plays were presented in the vernacular during the celebration of the Divine Office.

Although no liturgical dramatic texts in Latin have been found in Toledo, it was in this city's cathedral library that one of the earliest dramas in the vernacular in Europe was found. The *Auto de los reyes magos* is a 147-verse Epiphany play from the twelfth century. Its polymetric versification and alternating rhyme schemes add depth and subtlety to the characterization of the Three Kings, Herod, and his advisers, and contribute to shape agile and rapid-moving dialogues.

Despite the frequent references to religious dramatic performances in the vernacular in and around Toledo, no other texts from this period have been found. The possible existence of a nonreligious secular drama is supported by secondary documentation. The councils of Valladolid (1228), Lérida (1229), Tarragona (1317), and Aranda (1473) include admonitions to the clergy not to participate in theatrical activities other than religious plays. Alfonso X in his legal encyclopedia, *Las siete partidas* (1256–1263), mentions, besides the traditional Easter and Christmas plays, the *juegos de escarnio,* widely thought to refer to secular commercial theatrical entertainment.

Religious devotion and dramatic entertainment are joined in the feast of Corpus Christi. The pageantry of the feast generated at an early date its own type of drama. The Valencian mystery plays combine local popular allusions to places and figures familiar to the audience with the traditional religious theme.

One type of performance peculiar to Spanish soil is the dramatization of the monologue of the Sibyl. Although the ceremony is documented as early as the tenth century at Ripoll (perhaps even earlier at Córdoba, in the ninth century, within the Mozarabic liturgy), its origins are obscure, and the first attempt at impersonation is not recorded until 1440 at Gerona.

BIBLIOGRAPHY

James P. Wickersham Crawford, *Spanish Drama Before Lope de Vega,* rev. ed. (1937, repr. 1967); Richard B. Donovan, *The Liturgical Drama in Medieval Spain* (1958); O. B. Hardison, Jr., *Christian Rite and Christian Drama in the Middle Ages* (1965); Karl Young, *The Drama of the Medieval Church,* 2 vols. (1933, repr. 1967).

José M. Regueiro

[See also **Alfonso X; Auto de los Reyes Magos; Drama, Liturgical; Drama, Western European; Mozarabic Rite; Siete Partidas; Visitatio Sepulchri.**]

SPANISH LITERATURE: EPIC POETRY. The development of Spanish epic poetry probably began with oral traditions. To these would belong the short, semihistorical *cantos noticieros,* of which a few appear to have been incorporated in the later, partially extant, long epic poems. They are, however, not to be confused with the presumably much later, concise, strictly episodical *romances* (ballads) of the period after 1350, some of which are regarded as modernizations of particularly impressive *tiradas* (stanzas) of the epic, whose irregular versification they tend to normalize (fourteen-to-sixteen-syllable lines). Apart from these antecedents, which were recited or sung in the Castilian language, there were several preserved or reconstructible Latin forerunners. These include the brief, incomplete *Carmen Campidoctoris* (a song praising the Cid *campeador,* "expert of the battlefield," written perhaps as early as in the 1090's, during the lifetime of the protagonist) as well as fragments of the *planctus Carmen de morte Sanctii Regis,* and the *Poema de Almería.* The first two were followed by the extensive *Cantar* (or *Poema*) *de mío Cid* (composed and rewritten between the beginning of the twelfth and that of the thirteenth century) and the partly reconstructed *Cantar del*

Sancho II y del cerco de Zamora, respectively. A primitive stage in the formation of the French and Spanish epic legends of Roland is represented by the Latin summary contained in the *Nota Emilianense* (late eleventh or early twelfth century), and another more recent one in the Spanish *Roncesvalles* fragment (thirteenth century).

Several epics have survived only in the form of prose reductions found in the text of the medieval Castilian chronicles that preserved whole hemistichs and countless assonances. They therefore lent themselves to reconstructions, such as those of portions of *Sancho II* and *Infantes de Lara* (or *Salas*) and smaller, yet significant, sections of *Cid.* Ironically, the best-preserved works, the *Fernán González* and the *Alfonso XI,* are those of the later period (after 1250), written in meters different from those of the more genuine, early products of the Castilian epic. In the already "decadent" *Mocedades de Rodrigo* (or *del Cid*), which recounts the youthful exploits of the hero, the original minstrel versification (*mester de juglaría*) is retained. The latter poem helped to initiate a further stage in the epic development that led to the "historical" drama of the Spanish Golden Age and eventually to Pierre Corneille's *Le Cid* of the French classical stage. Other epic cycles are preserved in late medieval *romances,* notably that of *Rodrigo el último godo,* the last Visigothic king, responsible for the loss of Spain to the Arabs, and that of *Bernardo del Carpio,* a fictitious Spanish leader who opposed the imperialistic Carolingian Franks and was believed by the Spaniards to have caused the death of Roland in the Pyrenees. Literary critics have pointed out the reciprocal influences of Spanish and French epic poetry, citing as examples the two *Gestas de los infantes de Lara* and the *Cid* cycle.

There has been much justifiable speculation about a lost Spanish original of the *Cantar de mío Cid,* of which the extant version would constitute an amplified re-elaboration. In spite of its duality—structural, thematical, and stylistical (as has at length been explained by the supporters of that theory)—due to its double authorship, this first product of the preserved epic written in the Castilian language surpasses in quality all subsequent works of the genre. It consists mainly of the successful portrayal of a shrewd and determined, yet reputedly restrained (*mesurado*), hero who successively loses and regains both his personal honor on the chivalric plane and his family honor on the feudal plane—a characterization that compares not unfavorably with those of Roland and Charlemagne in the contemporary French epic.

BIBLIOGRAPHY

Bulletin bibliographique de la Société Rencesvals, I (1958–); Miguel Garci-Gómez, ed., *Cantar de mío Cid* (1977); Miguel Magnotta, *Historia y bibliografía de la crítica sobre el "Poema de mío Cid"* (1976); Ramón Menéndez Pidal, ed., *Poema de mío Cid* (1911 and later eds.), *Reliquias de la poesía épica española* (1951), and *Cantar de mío Cid: Texto, gramática, y vocabulario,* 3rd ed., 3 vols. (1954–1956); Ian Michael, ed., *The Poem of the Cid,* Rita Hamilton and Janet Perry, trans. (1975), *Olifant,* **1–8** (1973–1981); Colin Smith, ed., *Poema de mío Cid* (1972).

ERICH VON RICHTHOFEN

[See also **Cantar de Mío Cid; Cid, The, History and Legend of; French Literature; Mester de Juglaría; Mocedades de Rodrigo.**]

SPANISH LITERATURE: HAGIOGRAPHY. In the early vernacular literature of Castile, no theme is more richly represented than that of the lives of the saints. The presence of these hagiographic legends is so prominent in the medieval psyche and in the cycle of festivals that ordered life in the Middle Ages that Américo Castro has spoken of a "hagiographic" mythology. Moreover, these sanctoral tales often provide the designs and motifs for other genres in this era: the romance, the epic, the apologue, the ballad.

In addition to the numerous compilations of the lives of the saints in Old Spanish (especially translations of Jacopo da Voragine's *Legenda aurea* [1258]) and to the extensive incidental applications of the lives of the saints in early literature and folklore, there are numerous early texts that give literary form to the life of a saint or to the miracles connected with the legend of a saint.

HAGIOGRAPHIC POEMS

Several long poems, either in popular narrative forms or in *cuaderna vía,* recount the legends of saints. Both these types are indebted to French originals or models. Two thirteenth-century poems of the lyric or *juglar* (minstrel) type survive: *La vida de Santa María Egipciaca,* derived from the Old French *La vie de sainte Marie l'Egyptienne,* with several shifts of narrative focus, and *Libro de la infancia y muerte de Jesús,* also called *Libre dels tres reys d'orient*. The *Libro de la infancia* recounts the flight of the Holy Family into Egypt, and incorporates the legend of the good thief St. Dismas. Both poems are undoubtedly records of recited or sung poems (probably performed with musical accompaniment).

The principal writings of Gonzalo de Berceo (*ca.* 1196–*ca.* 1264), the first Spanish poet whose name is recorded, were hagiographies in *cuaderna vía*. Berceo's production (which should be studied in the editions of Brian Dutton) emphasizes the life and miracles of saints connected with the great Benedictine monasteries of San Millán de la Cogolla and Santo Domingo de Silos. Two of his longer poems are devoted to the abbots: *Vida de San Millán de la Cogolla* (from the Latin original by St. Braulio, bishop of Saragossa) and *Vida de Santo Domingo de Silos* (from the Latin original by Grimaldus). Another local saint—a virgin-recluse of the convent associated with the monastery of San Millán—is the subject of Berceo's *Vida de Santa Oria*. Berceo also wrote a *Martirio de San Lorenzo,* though the last part is missing. In all four hagiographies there is some proselytizing: mention is made of the sights and cults at the monasteries or affiliate convents or sanctuaries, and reminders are made of financial promises to the church.

Other poets of the *mester de clerecía* also wrote lives of saints, following the general form and the precise hemistich-length formulas of Berceo in their elaboration. The *Vida de Sant Alifonsso por metros* in 276 quatrains was composed by a poet known as the "Beneficiado de Úbeda," probably at the start of the fourteenth century. Another poem in *cuaderna vía*—no doubt parallel in length and structure to Berceo's hagiographies—is the *Vida de Santo Domingo de Guzmán,* of which only the opening stanzas have been preserved.

Although there are no lengthy hagiographic poems after the fourteenth century, legends of the saints are a constant theme in poetry (for example, the tale of St. Nicholas and the poor man in Pero López de Ayala's *Rimado de palacio*; capsule biographies in the *Libro de miseria de omne*; and "loores de santos" among the poems of Fernán Pérez de Guzmán). The marqués de Santillana turned toward religious poetry late in his life: legends of saints are included in the *Sonetos fechos al itálico modo*; his longer work, the *Canoniçaçión* of Vincent Ferrer and Pedro de Villacrezes, is a blending of hagiography and stylized allegorical settings.

HAGIOGRAPHY IN PROSE

Apart from the multiple translations and reworkings (principally unedited) of the *Legenda aurea* and short biographies in the great sanctoral compilations and the collections of exempla, there are numerous separate longer biographies. Most are translations of Latin sources (sometimes, through Old French); only some have been edited. Several distinct translations of *Barlaam y Josaphat* are available. Two different prose renditions of the legend of S. María Egipciaca circulated widely in the fourteenth and fifteenth centuries. Other extensive prose lives in Old Spanish include those of Catherine of Alexandria, Dominic of Guzmán, Dominic of Silos, Ildefonsus, Isidore of Seville, Martha, Mary Magdalen, and Thomas Aquinas. Other inedited prose texts include the *Miragros de Santiago* (reworked from the Codex Calixtinus), the *Tratado de San Francisco,* and the *Vida de San Ginés de la Xara* (apparently, an original work in Old Spanish, with a debt to the French epic tradition). The life of St. Eustace has the texture of early romance (it was copied in the same manuscript with secular romances), and the motifs of his legend are conspicuous in medieval Hispanic texts.

Among the saints whose lives have been edited (as given in the Old Spanish translations of the *Legenda aurea* and related compilations) are Barlaam and Josaphat, Blaise, Justina and Cyprian, Dominic, Lucy, Macarius the Egyptian (the Elder), Mary of Egypt, and Patrick. But these texts are a minuscule sampling beside the vast corpus of unedited prose hagiographies. To date, no significant study has been made of the affiliations among more than a dozen extensive Old Spanish *sanctorales*—all using the *Legenda aurea* as frame text, but with numerous interpolated biographies, including those of Spanish saints and those in the Franciscan movement.

A number of otherworld or visionary legends tied to the cults of the saints exist (or are known to have existed) in Old Spanish prose form. The *Purgatorio de San Patricio* is conserved in a lengthy text and in several distinct translations of the *Legenda aurea.* The *Revelación de San Pablo* (based upon the *Visio Pauli*) was printed in Seville in 1494. The most important text of an otherworld romance is the *Visión de Túngalo,* a fourteenth-century manuscript from Toledo (derived from the eleventh-century *Visio Tnugdali*) that was rediscovered in 1978. Technically, the work is not a saint's life or adventure, but its conception and narrative segments are closely allied to the legends of Sts. Patrick, Paul, and Amarus.

One of the more original and interesting of the peninsular otherworld texts is the *Vida de San Amaro*. It is, to use the Arabic term, an *imram*—the description of a (sea) voyage ending with a vision of the earthly paradise. The surviving medieval manuscript is fragmentary, but the text of the full tale was printed several times in the sixteenth century. The work is an amalgam of the descriptive elements in the *Voyage of St. Brendhan* and other visionary tracts.

Several prominent writers of the fifteenth century also contributed prose texts on the lives or miracles of the saints. Alfonso Martínez de Toledo wrote or at least supervised the composition of a long prose version of the life of Ildefonsus (closely related to the rhymed *Vida de San Alifonsso*) and another of Isidore of Seville. Álvaro de Luna's *Libro de las virtuosas e claras mujeres* is derived principally from Boccaccio's *De claris mulieribus* but includes an extensive supplement with biographies of twenty-one female saints—almost all taken from translations of the *Legenda aurea*. Diego Rodríguez de Almela, chaplain and chronicler of Queen Isabella, wrote a *Conpilación de los miraglos de Santiago*. Finally, the anonymous reworking called *Estoria de los quatro dotores de la santa eglesia* gives ample biographies of Sts. Ambrose, Augustine, Gregory the Great, and Jerome.

BIBLIOGRAPHY

Poetry. Dominic of Guzmán: W. F. Manning, "Una antigua *Vida de Santo Domingo* en verso: ¿Ha existido en algún tiempo?" in *Analecta Sacra Tarraconensia,* **40** (1967). *Dominic of Silos:* Gonzalo de Berceo, *Vida de Santo Domingo de Silos,* Brian Dutton, ed. (1978). *Emilianus:* Berceo, *Vida de San Millán de la Cogolla,* Dutton, ed. (1967). *Ildefonsus:* Manuel Alvar Ezquerra, ed., *Vida de San Ildefonso* (1975). *Lawrence:* Berceo, *El Martirio de San Lorenzo,* Dutton, ed. (1981). *Mary Egyptian: La vida de Santa María Egipciaca,* María Soledad de Andrés Castellanos, ed. (1964), and *The Life of Saint Mary of Egypt,* Michele Schiavone de Cruz-Sáenz, ed. (1979). *Oria,* also *Aurea, Auria:* Berceo, *Vida de Santa Oria,* Dutton, ed. (1981).

Prose texts. Amarus: O. Klob, "A vida de Sancto Amaro: Texte portugais du XIVe siècle," in *Romania,* **30** (1901). *Barlaam and Josaphat:* John E. Keller and Robert W. Linker, eds., *Barlaam y Josaphat* (1979). *Blaise:* Mario L. Schiff, ed., "Vida de Sant Blas, mártir" (Bibl. Nac. Madrid, MS 10252), in *La bibliothèque du Marquis de Santillane* (1905). *Catherine of Alexandria:* Hermann Knust, ed., "Vida de Santa Catalina," in *Geschichte der Legenden der h. Katarina von Alexandrien und der h. Maria Aegyptiaca* (1890). *Dominic of Guzmán:* R. Menéndez Pidal, ed., "Vida de Santo Domingo de Guzmán," in his *Crestomatía del español medieval,* II (1966). *Dominic of Silos:* Berceo, *Vida de Santo Domingo de Silos,* Dutton, ed. (1978). *Eustace:* Hermann Knust, ed., "De un cavallero Plácidas que fue después cristiano e ovo nonbre Eustacio," in his *Dos obras didácticas y dos leyendas* (1878). *Francis of Assisi:* G. Gasca Queirazza, S. J., "Una *vita* di San Francesco d'Assisi in antico Castigliano," in *Studi di lingua e letteratura spagnola,* **31** (1965). *Genesius Sciarensis:* John K. Walsh, "French Epic Legends in Spanish Hagiography: The *Vida de San Gines de la Xara* and the *Chanson de Roland,*" in *Hispanic Review,* **50** (1982). *Ildefonsus:* Walsh, ed., "Vida de San Ildefonso" (Bibl. Nac. Madrid, MS 12688), in *Vida de Sant Alifonsso por metros* (1988), and Alfonso Martínez de Toledo, "Vida de San Ildefonso," in his *Vidas de San Ildefonso y San Isidoro,* José Madoz, ed. (1962). *Isidore of Seville:* Martínez de Toledo, "Vida de San Isidoro," ibid.; *James the Greater:* Randall Sipes, ed., "A Critical Edition of the *Cõpilación . . . ,*" (diss., Univ. of North Carolina, Chapel Hill, 1972). *Joseph of Arimathea*: Karl Pietsch, ed., "El Libro de Josep Abarimatia," in his *Spanish Grail Fragments,* I (1924); *Justina and Cyprian:* Antonio Sánchez Moguel, ed., *Memoria acerca de el mágico prodigioso de Calderón* (1881). *Lucy:* Á. González Palencia, "La doncella que se sacó los ojos: Para la leyenda de Santa Lucía," in his *Historias y leyendas* (1942). *Macarius the Egyptian:* Dwayne C. Carpenter, "An Egyptian Saint in Medieval Spanish Literature: St. Macarius the Elder," in *La corónica,* **8** (1980). *Martha and Mary Magdalen:* E. Michel, ed., "Vidas de Santa María Magdelena y Santa Marta: An Edition of the Old Spanish Text" (diss., Univ. of Chicago, 1930). *Mary Egyptian:* B. Bussell Thompson and John K. Walsh, eds., *La vida de Santa María Egipçiaca* (1977). *Patrick:* Galo Francisco González, "Una versión inédita de la *Vida de S. Patricio,*" in *La corónica,* **10** (1982). *Paul the Apostle:* F. Secret, "La Revelación de Sant Pablo," in *Sefarad,* **28** (1968). *Thomas Aquinas:* Luis G. Alonso Getino, ed., *Leyenda de Santo Tomás de Aquino, siglo XIV* (1924).

Visionary texts. B. Bussell Thompson and John K. Walsh, eds., *Historia del virtuoso cavellero don Túngano* (1985).

JOHN K. WALSH
B. BUSSELL THOMPSON

[See also **Berceo, Gonzalo de; Cuaderna Vía; Hagiography, Western European; Mester de Clerecía.**]

SPANISH LITERATURE: INSTRUCTIONAL WORKS. Instruction was offered by monastic and cathedral schools, tutors, and the university. Memorization of rudiments formed the basis; oral explication of whole or epitomized texts was the principal method. Although vernacular glosses and word lists appeared early, and eventually vernacular works provided a considerable part of instructional and theoretical matter, Latin was used throughout the Middle Ages—for instance, Isidore of Seville's *Etymologiae,* a source of basic knowledge from its appearance (*ca.* 620) until well into the Renaissance. Typical later texts were Juan Gil de Zamora's *Ars musica* (*ca.* 1300) and *Dictaminis epithalamium* (before 1282), Alfonso de Benavente's *Ars et doctrina studendi et docendi* (1453) for law students, and Ruy Sánchez de Arévalo's *Speculum vitae humanae* (1467–1468) on career choice.

Another factor was Moorish coexistence with Christians (711–1492). When Arabic civilization flowered, the substantial Jewish population in turn brought Hebrew literature and learning to their highest point since the biblical period. The resulting contact between cultures provided access to a rich body of knowledge, disseminated by various paths. After his conversion from Judaism, Pedro Alfonso, for example, utilized his linguistic proficiency to compile an important collection of tales, the *Disciplina clericalis* (after 1106), destined for Christian readers. Al-Fārābī's *Iḥṣaʾ al-ʿulūm* (Catalog of the sciences), which drew substantially from Plato and Aristotle, illustrates one link in the transmission of Greek thought to Toledo and then to Europe. In the twelfth century, the archdeacons Juan Hispano and Domingo Gundisalvo collaborated in translating, the former rendering the Arabic into Spanish, the latter turning the vernacular into Latin. Moses Maimonides' *Moreh Nevukhim* (Guide for the perplexed, 1190) was twice translated into Hebrew (from the original Judeo-Arabic); from the Hebrew a Latin version was derived in the thirteenth century and a Castilian version in the fifteenth century by Pedro de Toledo.

From the early thirteenth century on, vernacular works grew steadily more numerous. They include translations from the Arabic, such as *Poridat de poridades* (a "mirror of princes") and *Libro de los buenos proverbios,* and more original but still derivative works such as *Semejança del mundo* (after 1222), *Doze sabios* (1237), and *Flores de derecho* of Jacobo de las Leyes. These works, which appeared during the youth of Alfonso X, heralded the expansion of scholarly productions during his reign.

That growth slowed in the following century. Guides of conduct, however, flourished: Juan Manuel's *Libro del cavallero et del escudero* (1326–1327), *Libro infinido* (1336–1337), and *Libro de los estados* (1330); and the *Regimiento de príncipes* (*ca.* 1345), Juan García de Castro-Jeriz' glossed version of Egidius Colonna's *De regimine principium.* Also noteworthy are *Libro de los caballos* (thirteenth century), Juan Manuel's *Libro de la caza* (*ca.* 1325), Alfonso XI's *Libro de la montería* (before 1350), and Pero López de Ayala's *El libro de las aves de caça.*

During the early fifteenth century, interest in "new science" (*nueva ciencia*) increased the tempo of book production. After a midcentury lull, production was quickened by the spread of printing. To translations of medical works such as Arnald of Villanova's *Recetario de diversas enfermedades* and Lanfranc of Milan's *Cirugía menor* were added Alfonso Chirino's *Menor daño de medicina,* Diego de Cobas' *Cirugia rimada* (1412), and Francisco Lopez de Villalobos' *Sumario de medicina* (1490–1500). Enrique de Villena wrote a manual of carving, *Arte cisoria, o Tratado del arte de cortar del cuchillo* (early fifteenth century), and alchemy was presented in *Imagen de la vida.* Alfonso de la Torre used allegorical narration to elucidate the liberal arts and ethics in *Visión delectable de la filosofía y artes liberales* (*ca.* 1440). Poetics was treated by Villena in *Arte de trovar* (1433); in Pero Guillén de Segovia's rhyming dictionary, *La gaya ciencia* (1475); and in Juan del Encina's *Arte de poesía castellana* (1496). Antonio de Nebrija translated his *Introductiones latinae* (1481) into Spanish and then wrote *Gramática sobre la lengua castellana* (1492). His *Vocabularium* superseded Alfonso de Palencia's *Universal vocabulario en latín y en romance* (1490). Access to Arabic was offered by Fray Pedro de Alcalá in the *Arte para ligeramente saber la lengua aráuiga,* together with the *Vocabulista aráuiga en letra castellana* (1501).

BIBLIOGRAPHY

Anthony Cárdenas *et al.*, *Bibliography of Old Spanish Texts* (2nd ed. 1977, 3rd ed. 1984); Charles Faulhaber, *Latin Rhetorical Theory in Thirteenth and Fourteenth Century Castile* (1972); Ángel González Palencia, *El arzobispo don Raimundo de Toledo* (1942); Mario Schiff, *La bibliothèque du marquis de Santillane* (1905); Israel Zinberg, *A History of Jewish Literature,* Bernard Martin, ed. and trans., I (1972).

EDWIN J. WEBBER

[See also **Dictamen; Disciplina Clericalis; Elucidarium and Spanish Lucidario; Encyclopedias and Dictionaries, Western European; Exemplum; Isidore of Seville; Manuel, Don Juan; Mirror of Princes.**]

SPANISH LITERATURE: LOST WORKS. No separate full-length study on the lost works of medieval Spanish literature has yet appeared. Excerpts from a tentative catalog were published by A. D. Deyermond in 1977, and an article by C. C. Smith appeared in 1984. Early assessments tend to put the losses as high, but the quality of evidence is inevitably uneven and criteria can vary enormously. A proper survey will serve to correct impressions of the relative proportions of what has survived, since the agents of conservation in earlier periods will tend to favor some categories against others. In the peninsula many important libraries have been destroyed or dispersed. For example, the Escorial library lost 4,000 manuscripts in a fire in 1671 and it was heavily pilfered in the 1820's; in 1734 the old royal palace was destroyed by fire. Monastic collections sustained their heaviest losses in the nineteenth century. The Civil War of 1936–1939 did not respect university libraries or the collections of bibliographers. To the present day adequate catalogs are not available even for some main deposits of manuscripts, so works deemed lost are continually emerging. The present survey, therefore, must be considered conjectural and selective.

It has always been accepted that the early secular lyric has had a low survival rate and that the few extant and incomplete texts of heroic narrative poetry represent a small fraction of the whole, whereas religious and devotional works stood a greater chance of being preserved. No independent Castilian lyric texts have survived prior to the mid fourteenth century. But we have evidence that songs in the vernacular appeared by around 1100. Fragments of lyric transcribed in Arabic or Hebrew characters were identified in 1948 as part of a Hispano-Semitic verse form, the *muwashshaḥ,* and a case has been made that this whole form may be derived from a lost Romance tradition. Such a hypothesis has been questioned primarily on the grounds that the evidence available is not strong enough. In early poetic narratives there are traces of lyric conventions of dawn songs and spring songs but without evidence as to which peninsular vernacular was used; one fragment of a Castilian parallelistic lyric, *Çorraquin Sancho,* has survived with an epic subject datable to the mid twelfth century. There is much less evidence for the existence of a learned Castilian lyric until the *Libro de buen amor* of Juan Ruiz appears in the mid fourteenth century.

The existence of lost epic narratives is more easily attested, if only because we have the direct evidence of some 5,000 lines of extant texts, none complete. Supporters of the neotraditionalist theory argue for the existence of a chain of epics composed by secular *juglares* from Visigothic times to the appearance of surviving texts. Much of the support derives from the supposed presence in medieval chronicles of material deriving from nonhistorical sources, stretching from ninth-century Latin histories to the thirteenth-century Castilian *Estoria de España,* in which acknowledgment is made to "cantares" and "fablas de gesta." Such references do not carry equal weight, and if one demands explicit evidence of the presence of compositions in narrative verse form and not legend or folktale or prose accounts in Latin or the vernacular, then the case for most of the supposed works listed by Menéndez Pidal in his *Reliquias de la poesía épica española* is decidedly weak. It may be that the *Condesa traidora* or the *Romanz del infant García* derive from or are associated with foundation legends or tomb cults as well as the supposed lost epic ancestor of the extant *cuaderna vía* poem on the Castilian count Fernán González.

The issue is by no means closed, and the hypothesis that a cycle of epics on the early counts of Castile once existed is not without substance. The strongest case for lost epics in this cycle is that of the *Siete infantes de Lara,* for which some scholars advocate a date of around 1000 and a length of about 1,500 lines. To the thirteenth century can be attributed another vengeance poem, the *Cantar de Bernardo del Carpio.* As for the cycle related to the Cid, support has weakened for Menéndez Pidal's "two poets" theory involving prior versions of the extant *Cantar de mío Cid* and there is an equal reluctance to posit subsequent reworkings. The supposed *Cantar del rey Don Sancho y del cerco de Zamora* has been the subject of excessive editorial reconstruction. It could well derive from a prose version of a lost Latin poem of monastic origin, but the matter is still under discussion. Another episode of the Cid's youth, the *Jura de Santa Gadea,* probably never had independent status but might have served as a link between the two aforementioned narratives. There is firmer evidence for the existence in the thirteenth or fourteenth century of a lost predecessor to the surviving incomplete *Mocedades de Rodrigo.*

In the post-epic period there are few reasons for supposing a vanished tradition of learned lyric in Castilian in the thirteenth and early fourteenth centuries. Nor is there evidence for the disappearance of much pious, devotional, hagiographical, or gnomic poetic narrative. Brian Dutton has argued for the attribution to Berceo of lost works on the translation of the remains of Riojan saints; only the prologue survives of an anonymous commentary to Shem Tov's *Proverbios morales.* As for popular verse, there are clear signs of ballad literature emerging before the mid fourteenth century, and certainly it must have flourished during the period of the Trastámaran civil wars, but such poetry as was political and satirical would tend to disappear with the special conditions that gave rise to it. More substantial are the losses in early prose texts, originals or translations, attributable to the "Alfonsine school" as well as other historical or pseudo-historical works, treatises on lapidaries, games, or the chase: for example, the Dominican Fray Jaeme de Solís, *Tratado del juego de Axedrez.* From the evidence of the general prologue to Don Juan Manuel's works, several of these have not survived, and a number of later fourteenth-century chronicles have gone astray, by authors such as Jofre de Loaisa, Fernández de Heredia, Juan de Alfaro, and Pérez de Correa.

In the fifteenth century, losses in this genre are particularly marked, covering known authors like Enríquez del Castillo, Alfonso de Toledo, Pero Fernández Niño, Juan de Mena, Santillana, Rodríguez del Padrón, Gonzalo García de Santa María, Alfonso de Palencia, Pedro de Torres, Martín García, Pedro de Argüello, Tristán de Silva, and Diego Fernández de Mendoza. As for moral and devotional literature of the fourteenth and fifteenth centuries, one could mention *Voz del grillo* (Pedro Gómez Barroso?); Antonio de Carrión, *Batalla de la riquesa et pobreza;* Alfonso de Valladolid, *De las batallas del señor;* Lope Fernández de Minaya, *Libro de confesión;* and an anonymous work entitled *Arttminia* once possessed by Gallardo. Library catalogs of the counts of Haro, Santillana, Peter of Portugal, and Queen Isabella now become a useful source for lost items, particularly in the genre of vernacular translation; Martín de Lucena's gospel translations, Gómez de Zamora's translation of Orosius, and also classical translations by or for López de Ayala, Enrique de Villena, Pero Díaz de Toledo, Alonso de Maldonado, Diego de Belmonte, and others.

A great deal more in the area of narrative prose romance, particularly Arthurian, may not have survived. Only fragments of the Grail story have come down, and early versions of the Lancelot and Tristan romances could well have existed. Evidence for this is present in the *Cavallero Zifar,* the *Amadís* fragment, the *Demanda del Sancto Grial,* and García de Salazar's *Bienandanzas.* It is also more than likely that there are lost versions of early Castilian Troy romances, Alexander material, and narratives of exotic voyages. Because these genres have been neglected by scholars, it may be that many items like *Oriflama* by Rodríguez del Padrón lie undiscovered in libraries; witness the recent discovery of a Castilian version of *Persefores.*

It is impossible here to deal in any detail with the substantial losses of poetic texts in the late fourteenth and fifteenth centuries. Prosodic treatises have disappeared (Juan Manuel, Enrique de Villena, Juan de Mena). Works attributed to Santillana (*Los votos del pavón*), the two writers named Diego de San Pedro, Juan de Padilla, and Guillén de Ávila, for instance, are not extant. Recent interest in *cancionero* poetry has served to identify supposedly lost collections, mainly due to the labors of Aubrun, B. Dutton, A. Rodríguez Moñino, and J. Steunou and L. Kapp. The *cancionero* parent to *Stúñiga,* which covers poetry written in the Neapolitan court of Alfonso V, is missing, as is the original of Guillén de Segovia. References exist to about nine others still unlocated, while another known half-dozen or more are incomplete. As for single poems, items so far recorded may well take the total well beyond 200, but this is no more than a beginning, as bibliographical research has only just begun. Authors include Rodrigo de Borja, Juan and Pedro Buyl, Ramón Carroz, Diego de Castilla, Luis de Espindola, Juan de Gayoso, Juan de Hinestrosa, Manuel de León, Iñigo Manrique, Rodrigo Puerto Carrero, Alonso Rebolledo, Martín de Tavara, Sancho de Velasco, and Miguel de Vilanova.

In drama, scholars have noted in the past the remarkable paucity in Castile of Latin and vernacular dramatic entertainments of all types, especially when compared with Catalonia or Valencia. No convincing explanation has yet been offered. A tradition of early vernacular drama associated with court and church may have existed, but it is doubtful that it produecd more than a few works, and it is not until the mid fifteenth century that vernacular texts appear associated with gospel accounts. Account books recently discovered in Toledo Cathedral, however, indicate that there may be more texts of actual plays than was hitherto suspected.

It cannot be said, as it has been of English literature, that if all the lost works prior to the known *Amadís,* Garcilaso, and the *Celestina* were to be found, then the whole of medieval Spanish literature would appear in a different light. Distortions are present, it is true, but other distortions of an opposite type have certainly been caused by overenthusiastic attention to hypothetical losses in certain fields like the epic and the ballad as compared with sermon literature, prose hagiography, and narrative fiction or romance. The topic of lost literature in Castile is in its infancy, and no definitive statement can as yet be made.

BIBLIOGRAPHY

Samuel G. Armistead, "The 'Mocedades de Rodrigo' and the Neo-individualist Theory," in *Hispanic Review,* **46** (1978); Juan B. Avalle Arce, "El Poema de Fernán González: Clerecía y juglaría," in *Philological Quarterly,* **51** (1972); Louis Chalon, *L'histoire et l'epopée castillane du moyen âge: Le cycle de Cid, le cycle des comtes de Castille* (1976), and "La historicidad de la leyenda de la Condesa Traidora," in *Journal of Hispanic Philology,* **2** (1978); Alan D. Deyermond, *Edad media,* in *Historia de la literatura española,* I (1973), "The Lost Genre of Medieval Spanish Literature," in *Hispanic Review,* **43** (1975), "Lyric Traditions in Nonlyrical Genres," in *Studies in Honor of Lloyd A. Kasten* (1975), "Medieval Spanish Epic Cycles: Observations on Their Formation and Development," in *Kentucky Romance Quarterly,* **23** (1976), "The Lost Literature of Medieval Spain: Excerpts from a Tentative Catalogue," in *La corónica,* **5** (1977), *idem,* ed., *Mío Cid Studies* (1977), 13–47, 113–128, "The *Mocedades* as a Test Case: Problems of Methodology," in *La corónica,* **6** (1978), and "The Problems of Lost Epica: Evidence and Criteria," in *Hispanic Review* (in press); Ursicino Domínguez del Val, "Obras desaparecidas de padres y escritores españoles," in *Repertorio de historia de las ciencias eclesiásticas en España,* **2** (1971); Brian Dutton, ed., *La vida de San Millan de la Cogolla de Gonzalo de Berceo* (1967), 60–61, 165.

Enciclopedia universal ilustrada, VIII, 665–668; Charles B. Faulhaber, "Neo-traditionalism, Formulism, Individualism, and Recent Studies on the Spanish Epic," in *Romance Philology,* **30** (1970); John E. Keller, "An Unknown Castilian Lyric Poem: The Alfonsine Translation of 'Cantiga X' of the 'Cantigas de Santa María,'" in *Hispanic Review,* **43** (1975); J. N. H. Lawrance, *Un tratado de Alonso de Cartagena sobre la educación y los estudios literarios* (1979), 54; D. W. Lomax, "Algunos autores religiosos, 1295–1350," in *Journal of Hispanic Philology,* **2** (1978); Alonso de Maldonado, *Hechos del maestre de Alcántara Don Alonso de Monroy,* Antonio Rodríguez-Moñino, ed. (1935), prologue; Warren F. Manning, "An Old Spanish Life of St. Dominic: Sources and Date," in *Mediaeval Studies in Honor of Jeremiah D. M. Ford* (1948); Nancy F. Marino, "Una parte del cancionero perdido de Martínez de Burgos: El debate entre Alfonso Álvarez de Villasandino y el abad del Arzobispo," in *Revista de archivos, bibliotecas y museos,* **79** (1976); H. Salvador Martínez, *El "Poema de Almería" y la épica románica* (1975), 384–388; Ramón Menéndez Pidal, *Reliquias de la poesía épica española* (1951), xvi, and *La leyenda de los infantes de Lara,* 3rd ed. (1971), reviewed by Deyermond in *Hispanic Review,* **42** (1974); I. Michael, "The Spanish *Perceforest:* A Recent Discovery," in *Studies in Medieval Literature and Languages: In Memory of Frederick Whitehead* (1973); Agustín Millares Carlo, *Introducción a la historia del libro y de las bibliotecas* (1971); José María Millás Vallicrosa, *Las traducciones orientales en los manuscritos de la Biblioteca Catedral de Toledo* (1942), 158–159, 285–312.

Frederick J. Norton, "Lost Spanish Books in Fernando de Colón's Library Catalogue," in *Studies in Spanish Literature of the Golden Age, Presented to Edward M. Wilson* (1973), and *A Descriptive Catalogue of Printing in Spain and Portugal, 1501–1520* (1978), see p. 5 for Guillen de Avila's *Egloga interlocutoria . . .* ; Fernán Pérez de Guzmán, *Generaciones y semblanzas,* Robert B. Tate, ed. (1965), 15, 101; Erich von Richthofen, *Tradicionalismo épico-novelesco,* Ana Ma Aznar *et al.,* trans. (1972), 55–65; Francisco Rico, "Corraquín Sancho, Roldán y Oliveros: Un cantar paralelístico castellano del siglo XII," in *Homenaje a la memoria de Don Antonio Rodríguez-Moñino* (1975); Juan Rodríguez de la Cámara [ó del Padrón], *Obras,* Antonio Paz y Mélia, ed. (1884), xxviii; Antonio Rodríguez-Moñino, *La colección de manuscritos del Marqués de Montealegre (1677)* (1951), and *Historia de una infamia bibliográfica, la de San Antonio de 1823: Realidad y leyenda de lo sucedido con los libros y papeles de Don Bartolomé José Gallardo* (1965); P. E. Russell and A. R. D. Pagden, "Nueva luz sobre una versión española cuatrocentista de la *Ética a Nicomaco:* Bodleian Library MS SPAN D1," in *Homenaje a Guillermo Guastavino* (1974).

C. Colin Smith, "The Cid as Charlemagne in the *Leyenda de Cardeña,*" in *Romania,* **97** (1976), "The Diffusion of the Cid Cult: A Survey and a Little-Known Document," in *Journal of Medieval History,* **6** (1980), and "On the 'Lost Literature' of Medieval Spain," in *Guillaume d'Orange and the Chansons de Geste: Essays Presented to Duncan McMillan* (1984); Jacqueline Steunou and Lothar Kapp, *Bibliografía de los cancioneros castellanos del siglo xv y repertorio de sus géneros* *poéticos,* I (1975); Carmen Torroja Menéndez y María Rivas Palá, *Teatro en Toledo en el siglo xv: "Auto de la Pasión" de Alonso de Campo* (1977).

ROBERT B. TATE

[See also **Amadís de Gaula; Arthurian Literature, Spanish and Portuguese; Berceo, Gonzalo de; Cantar de Mío Cid; Castile; Catalonia; Cavallero Zifar, Libro del; Cid, The, History and Legend of; Cuaderna Vía; Fernán González, Poema de; Grail, Legend of; Latin Literature; López de Ayala, Pero; Manuel, Don Juan; Mena, Juan de; Mocedades de Rodrigo; Rodríquez del Padrón, Juan; Ruiz, Juan; San Pedro, Diego de; Santillana, Marqués de; Shem Tov; Valencia; Villena, Enrique de.**]

SPANISH LITERATURE: LYRIC POETRY. The word Spanish in the title of this article refers not to all the languages used in Spain, but to the Galician-Portuguese, Castilian, Leonese, Navarro-Aragonese, and Mozarabic dialects. The word lyric is used in the sense that Wolfgang Kayser applies it in *Das sprachliche Kunstwerk,* where he interprets genre (citing Emil Staiger, Ernst Cassirer, and Heinrich Junker) as a concept rooted in the three persons of all known languages; so that, basically, the lyric is the genre in which an ego expresses itself emotionally. By comparison, in the dramatic genre, the ego becomes a second person ("you"), and engages another "you" in intentional intersubjective dialogue, while in the epic genre the ego becomes a third person ("he," "she," or "it") that narrates objectively. In addition to these three genres Kayser identifies three attitudes common to each of them; so that in the case of the lyric genre, for example, one finds three distinct attitudes: a purely lyric attitude, which Kayser identifies with the language of song; a dramatic attitude, which he terms apostrophe; and finally an epic attitude, which he calls enunciation.

Thus Kayser's classification of genres and attitudes is helpful in clarifying one of the major confusions of literary categories: if one is discussing a song, for example, which includes dramatic dialogue, one can, according to Kayser, speak of a work written in the lyric genre and, where the dialogue is concerned, in a dramatic attitude. Likewise, a novel interspersed with lyric poetry, can be classified as written in the epic genre and lyric attitude. These distinctions are crucial to any discussion of medieval Spanish lyric poetry because in medieval Spain, as elsewhere, the dominant literary attitude for all genres was lyric; so that one finds many epic and dramatic works in medieval Spain (the *Cid,* the *Libro de buen amor,* the *Milagros,* the *Auto de los reyes magos*) written in a lyric attitude.

It is safe to assume that everywhere people have always sung lyrics, many of which have not survived. In a magnificent attempt to capture some of the elements of this universal genre, Cecil M. Bowra collected songs among hunting-and-gathering societies where lyrics have been transmitted in unwritten form. In Bowra's book, entitled *Primitive Song* (1962), there is the following convincing description of the genesis of lyric as told to the explorer Knud Rasmussen by an Eskimo named Orpingalik:

> Songs are thoughts sung out with the breath when people are moved by great forces and ordinary speech no longer suffices. Man is moved just like the ice-floe sailing here and there out in the current. His thoughts are driven by a flowing force when he feels joy, when he feels fear, when he feels sorrow. Thoughts can wash over him like a flood, making his breath come in gasps and his heart throb. Something like an abatement in the weather will keep him thawed up. And then it will happen that we, who always think we are small, will feel still smaller. And we will fear to use words. But it will happen that the words we need will come of themselves. When the words we want to use shoot up of themselves—we get a new song.

By substituting for Orpingalik's Eskimo setting (ice floes, and so on) a more appropriate Spanish one (stag hunting, for example) we can arrive at a reasonably accurate conception of the nature of those ancient lyrics of Spain that have not reached us in their pristine form. It is feasible to imagine that these lost songs covered a wide range of human emotion and activity: there must have been work songs, love songs, battle songs, laments, lullabies, ritual songs, songs meant simply to entertain, and many others.

It is certain that songs like these existed because, although they have been lost, evidence has survived that they were suppressed in Spain. In 589, sixty-two bishops of the church met at Toledo and decided that "the irreligious custom practiced by the people on saints' days, whereby those who ought to be performing holy offices indulge themselves in lewd songs and dances, ought to be entirely eradicated." In 591, the bishop of Cartagena, Licinianus, expressed his disapproval of the lustful songs used in certain dances. In his *Rules for Monks* (chap. 5), Isidore of Seville advised against shameful love songs such as those sung by secular workers while they worked, and he recommended instead other songs and stories appropriate to the service of Christ. St. Valery of Bierzo (León, seventh century) made it quite clear that, if he had his way, a man called Justo who was well known for entertaining people with his secular songs and music would never have been ordained as presbyter. As late as the thirteenth century, a document instructing priests how to conduct confession urges them to ask confessants if they sang lustful songs on fast days, and it notes that sinners dislike listening to Mass, but take delight in listening to burlesque songs (*cantares de las caçurias*).

In the fifteenth century, the Marqués de Santillana, in his famous letter to the commander in chief of the Portuguese army, divided poetry into three hierarchical categories: sublime, mediocre, and inferior (*ínfimo*). By sublime he understands poems written in Greek and Latin; by mediocre he means works written in Romance languages by learned poets like Guido Guinizzelli and Arnaut Daniel; by inferior he refers to "those who compose, without any order, rule or count, ballads and songs in which people of low and servile station take delight." It is obvious from these documents, dated between the sixth and the fifteenth century, that there was a deliberate attempt in medieval Christian Spain to suppress lyrics that either were not religious, or stemmed from the lower class, or both. As a direct result of this suppression, it would appear that much of medieval Spanish lyric poetry has survived mainly as a reaction to the idiom of the common people; members of the ecclesiastical and noble classes reproduced only those lyrics which could be made to serve the moral and social aims of the church and the court. Some examples of this reaction to popular idiom are provided by the *muwashshaḥ*s, the *Razon de amor,* the *Libro de Buen Amor,* and *La Celestina,* where lyrics are embedded in a setting presumed to be morally or culturally superior to them.

*MUWASHSHAḤ*S AND *KHARJAS*

In the tenth century, in Muslim Spain, a new form of Arabic poetry was invented called the *muwashshaḥ,* that is, a poem that resembles a *wishaḥ*—either a leather belt inlaid with precious stones or a double-stringed necklace of pearls or other gems. The *muwashshaḥ* consists normally, in its complete form (*tāmm*), of eleven stanzas, six of which are of equal length, linked by a common rhyme and separated by five monorhymed stanzas of equal length, but each with different rhymes. The six stanzas linked by rhyme are called returns (*qufl*s), and the five with different rhymes are called strophes (*bayts*); so that one variation of a complete *muwashshaḥ* is as follows: *AA* (*qufl,* also called *maṭlaᶜ*) *bbb* (*bayt*) *AA, cccAA, dddAA, eeeAA, fffAA.* Sometimes, *bayt* and *qufl* are counted as one stanza, in which case there are obviously five stanzas instead of eleven. When the first *qufl* is omitted the *muwashshaḥ* is said to be bald (*aqra*). The last *qufl,* on the other hand, cannot normally be omitted from a *muwashshaḥ,* and, more importantly, it is given a special name (*kharja,* or exit). In fact, although the *kharja* comes at the end of the *muwashshaḥ,* it is not only the most important part of the poem but also the poet's point of departure. As translated by Samuel M. Stern, in *Hispano-Arabic Strophic Poetry* (1974), Ibn Sanāᵓ al-Mulk, a twelfth-century Egyptian literary historian, explains that

> the kharja is the spice of the *muwashshaḥ,* its salt and sugar, its musk and amber. It is the close of the muwashshah; it must, therefore, be beautiful; it is its seal; nay, it is the beginning, although it is at the end. What I mean by saying it is the beginning is that the composition of the poem must begin with it. The composer must start with it before committing himself to a particular metre or rhyme . . . and build the muwashshah on it, having found the basis, holding the tail fast and putting the head on it. (p. 34)

Another important rule for the *kharja* concerns the language in which it is written: although the rest of the *muwashshaḥ* is written in classical Arabic or in Hebrew, the *kharja* should preferably be frivolous and racy, or, according to Ibn Sanāᵓ al-Mulk, "hot and burning, close to the language of the common people and the phraseology of thieves. If it employs the classical form of the language, in the same way as the rest of the strophes and *qufl*s that precede it, the *muwashshaḥ* is not a *muwashshaḥ* anymore in the true sense of the word." Classical language is permitted in the *kharja* only under certain exceptional circumstances. On the other hand, a foreign language (*ajamīya*) is deemed suitable for the *kharja,* including, of course, the Romance dialect (Mozarabic) spoken by the Christians who lived in Muslim Spain; the racy quality deemed desirable in vernacular Arabic *kharja*s is also required of *kharja*s in a foreign language.

Although *kharja*s in a Romance language were

known to exist, they were not rediscovered until 1948, when Samuel M. Stern found some twenty of them in Hebrew *muwashshaḥ*s composed by Jewish poets of Spain. Stern's discovery has altered what was known about the history of Spanish and Romance lyrics, and scholars are still engaged in formulating new and instructive questions and answers as a consequence of the romance *kharja*s first published by Stern in 1953. What, for example, did the *muwashshaḥ* poets borrow from the common people? Did they merely use the racy vernacular words of the common people, or did they also borrow their songs? These questions are prompted, but not satisfactorily answered, by Ibn Sanā᾽ al-Mulk's statement that "some of the later poets are unable to compose a *kharja* and, therefore, employ the *kharja* of another poet." Satisfactory answers cannot be forthcoming until a definitive text of the *kharja*s is available. Since Stern's discovery, some seventy *kharja*s have been published which seem to contain a significant number of Romance words, but only a handful of these *kharja*s (less than a dozen) can be said to have been definitively deciphered. The difficulty, sometimes insoluble, lies mainly in the vowelless nature of the unpointed Semitic script in which the *kharja*s (forty-five in Arabic, twenty-six in Hebrew script) have been transmitted. Some of the words now believed to be Romance might conceivably be Arabic, Hebrew, Persian, or some macaronic mixture of these languages.

In spite of the enormous difficulties of the texts, some conclusions can be attempted about the *kharja*s. First of all, it seems clear from what is known at present that the earliest poetry to have survived in written form in any Romance language is the *kharja* that was composed before 1042, which reads, "Tanto amare tanto amare habib tanto amare / enfermeron olios nidios e dolen tan male" (So much loving, so much loving, darling, so much loving / brilliant eyes fell ill and now hurt so badly). This is one of the few *kharja*s that seem to have been deciphered to the satisfaction of most critics. It is found at the end of a Hebrew *muwashshaḥ* composed by Joseph the Scribe (Yusuf al-Ramādī) as a panegyric to the famous vizir Samuel ibn Nagrella and his brother Isaac. Since all the words in this *kharja,* except one (*habib*), are Romance, Ibn Sanā᾽ al-Mulk's claim that *kharja*s were sometimes composed in Romance has been documented; so that, even if it turns out that all the remaining seventy *kharja*s are not in Romance (which is unlikely) it cannot mean that Romance *kharja*s never existed but simply that they have not been found or have not been deciphered.

Secondly, the evidence now available also indicates that the *muwashshaḥ* was invented in Spain by a poet who composed in Arabic, and that Jewish poets played a major role in spreading the popularity of the *muwashshaḥ* to Christian Spain and to the rest of the Muslim world, especially Egypt. It has been argued with a great deal of feasibility that one of the candidates for invention of the *muwashshaḥ,* Muqaddam ibn Muᶜafā, may have been a Christian recently converted to Islam, whose mother tongue was Romance. Whatever the merits of this argument, it remains indisputable that Muqaddam wrote Arabic poetry, and that Arabic and Hebrew poets in Spain were the first to pay serious attention to the cultivation of popular lyrics in Romance. Until further evidence to the contrary, it seems wise to conclude that the influence of the *muwashshaḥ* and its *kharja* emanated from Muslim to Christian Spain and not vice versa. It is well known that one composer of Hebrew *muwashshaḥ*s, Todros Abulafia, was a member of the Christian courts of the Spanish kings Alfonso X and Sancho IV.

Finally, it can be stated confidently that even if the *kharja*s were not originally popular lyrics borrowed by the *muwashshaḥ* poets, they soon became very popular among the common people. From some of the writings of Maimonides we learn that *muwashshaḥ*s, in Hebrew and Arabic, were greatly in vogue among the Jews of Egypt and that they were sung at drinking parties as well as at marriage celebrations. Maimonides strongly disapproved of this practice. Thus we can assume that some Jewish religious authorities in Spain opposed the songs of the common people with a virulence equal to that of the Christian bishops referred to above. But the religious authorities must have been forced to concede to the popularity of the *muwashshaḥ,* because we know from Ibn Sanā᾽ al-Mulk that *muwashshaḥ*s were adapted as *contrafacta* for religious purposes with their vulgar *kharja*s intact:

> A *muwashshaḥ* that has for its subject the contempt of the world is called by a special name: *mukaffir.* It has as its special feature that its meter and its rhymes follow the pattern of a well-known *muwashshaḥ,* and that it ends with the *kharja* of the latter. All this is done in order to show that it has been composed for the purpose of doing penance for the original *muwashshaḥ,* and of entreating God's forgiveness for its author. (Stern, p. 81)

SECULAR LYRICS OF CHRISTIAN SPAIN

It cannot be proved that Christian poets in Spain borrowed from the Jews and Arabs the idea of embedding a popular song in a work that pretends to be morally superior to the song; the idea is simple enough to be susceptible of polygenesis. Yet it is true that, after the invention and popularity of the *muwashshaḥ*, the embedding of lyrics became a constant practice in medieval Spanish literature. In the first half of the thirteenth century an anonymous Spanish poet composed a narrative in verse that seeks to warn clerics about the dangers of succumbing to lustful desires. The work, entitled *Razón de amor,* tells how the author, a cleric well versed in poetry as well as in the art of courtly love, meets for the first time with his lover, whom he has never before seen. They enjoy themselves physically at this first meeting until the woman announces abruptly that she must leave. Her departure leaves the cleric disconsolate and, in his words, as if near death. What seems to save the author's life is the timely appearance of a dove which, by its action as the symbolic representative of the wisdom of the Holy Spirit, instructs the author that only the wine of Holy Communion, not the water of carnal lust, will satisfy his thirst for love. When the woman first appeared to the cleric she was singing a song, and the author takes care to copy the complete lyrics of this song as an intergral part of his work.

As in the case of the *kharja*s, it cannot be decided whether the author borrowed this song from the common people and then composed his work around it, or composed the song specifically for his work. In any event, the song is clearly secular, and like the secular *kharja*s in religious *muwashshaḥ*s, its intent is to serve as an example for the morality of the religious context that surrounds it. It matters little whether or not the author's intent is sincere; the overriding point is that, even if he is merely seeking an avenue to transmit lustful songs, the suppressive environment in which the author is composing prefers that the setting in which he places lustful material be patently religious and morally defensible.

The same moral intent, sincere or ambiguous, can be attributed to the famous song about the bakerwoman (*Cruz cruzada, panadera*), which the Archpriest of Hita, Juan Ruiz, inserts into his fourteenth-century *Book of Good Love* (*Libro de buen amor*). *The Book of Good Love* is a long narrative in verse that tells, as its principal story, how an archpriest who has had little success in love affairs becomes a disciple of the God of Love. After the archpriest has received specific instructions from the God of Love, Don Amor, and from his wife, Doña Venus, he has a series of amorous adventures with women, the majority of which are failures. The song about Cruz, the bakerwoman, is one that the archpriest says he composed (before he became a disciple of Love) after the man he chose to carry his messages to Cruz, Ferrand García, stole her away from him. The Archpriest of Hita calls his poem about Cruz a "burlesque song" (*troba caçurra*), which is the same kind of song (*cantares de las caçurias*) that people preferred listening to, rather than listening to Mass, according to the complaint in the document on confession cited earlier. It is perhaps because burlesque songs like these were suppressed by church authorities that the archpriest takes care to mention (sincerely or not) that his poem about Cruz is meant as an example against such stupidity: "Out of my great grief I wrote this burlesque song; if any lady hears it, let her not disdain me because of it, for I should call myself stupid and more than an ass if I did not compose a mocking song from such a big joke on me."

It might be significant that the Archpriest of Hita composed his song about Cruz in the form of a *zajal,* a form of poetry closely related to the *muwashshaḥ*. The *zajal* differs from the *muwashshaḥ* in that it is written in vernacular as opposed to classical Arabic, in that only half of the initial *qufl* is repeated as a return, and in that it has no *kharja;* so that a typical pattern for a *zajal* would be *AA, bbbA, cccA, dddA, eeeA, fffA,* which is precisely the form of the poem about Cruz. It might also be significant that the Archpriest's *zajal*-like song about Cruz is written, not unlike religious *muwashshaḥ*s, in such a way that, if necessary, it could be interpreted in a religious manner: the poem's references to seeing the light, losing the Cross, taking a narrow path, eating the sweetest bread, a deceitful traitor, are all easily understood in a religious Christian context.

In addition to the poem about Cruz, the Archpriest of Hita inserted into his *Book of Good Love* nine songs about the Virgin Mary, four pastoral songs (*serranillas*) about encounters with mountain women, two songs about the Passion of Jesus Christ, four begging songs, and one song of prayer to the goddess Fortune; eight of these songs are also in zajalesque form. The Archpriest of Hita writes in several parts of his book that he composed other songs, but the lyrics of these, unlike the ones referred to above, were not copied in the texts that have been transmitted to us. Critics can only conjecture whether these omissions were expurgated, or whether the Archpriest himself failed to include them. In any event, we can be sure that the songs which have been lost were varied and popular (even among Jews and Moors) because the Archpriest writes:

> After this I composed many dance-songs and quicksteps for Jewesses and Moorish girls and for ladies in love, and for instruments of the usual kind: if you don't know the music for one of these songs, pick it up by ear from a singing girl. I composed a few songs of the kind that blindmen sing, and some for scholars who gad about at night, and for many others who go from door to door: scurrilous songs and mocking songs, there would not be room for them on ten folios.

One hundred years after the archpriest composed his book it was still common for courtly ladies, like the one in the *Razón de amor* and the ones to whom the archpriest frequently addressed himself, to sing popular songs; the note of caution and, sometimes, condemnation that existed in the earlier songs is still present in the fifteenth-century ones. For example, in a fifteenth-century composition attributed both to the Marqués de Santillana and to Suero de Ribera, a poet tells in well-measured, polished lines of his encounter with three women who are singing songs. Two lines of each song are copied at the end of each stanza, and these lines are of uneven length and in a language less refined and more vernacular than the language of the other lines, somewhat reminiscent, that is, of the *muwashshaḥ* and its *kharja,* with respect to language. The lines of the popular songs the women are singing do not tell of the joys of love, but rather they emphasize what women must suffer on account of love: "They are spying on me / I have never seen such spies," "The girl who is in love / How will she sleep alone?" and so on. These brief lines are, most probably, *villancicos,* the name that is given in the fifteenth century to that part of a zajalesque poem that resembles the return (*qufl*) of the *muwashshaḥ* and the *zajal.* Later, these *villancicos* and their glosses, like the *muwashshaḥ,* were adapted for religious purposes, and by the seventeenth century the *villancico* came to be almost synonymous with Christmas and Easter carols.

The final medieval example of popular lyrics embedded in a work that pretends to moral or cultural superiority is found in *La Celestina,* a work that claims to have been written "in reprehension of crazy lovers who . . . call their loved ones their God." In Act 19 of this work, Melibea (the loved one whom Calisto calls his God) and her servant Lucrecia sing songs while they await Calisto's arrival in the garden of Melibea's home. The song Melibea sings alone ends with what seems to be a *villancico:* "Midnight is past and he is not here / Tell me if someone else is detaining him." Melibea's song also uses in its first stanza the word *alborada,* which is the name for the type of popular dawn song that tells of lovers who are reunited at dawn, as distinguished from the *alba,* in which lovers who have spent the night together part at dawn. This meeting in the garden leads to the death of Calisto as he scales the garden wall and to Melibea's suicide on account of Calisto's death.

ECCLESIASTICAL AND COURTLY LYRICS

For the purposes of this discussion, the medieval Spanish lyric is divided into three convenient classes: the secular lyric popular among the common people, the ecclesiastical lyric preferred and sanctioned by the church, and the courtly lyric practiced by the nobility and by those who, by association, appended themselves to the noble class. The evidence indicates that the most vibrant of these three types in medieval Spain was the popular lyric, which attracted the attention first of the Arabic nobility and, much later, of their Christian counterparts. This popular poetry was so resilient that ecclesiastical authorities, who tried continually to suppress it, were forced instead to adopt it for their own use. Mere fragments only of this powerful popular lyric have survived, mainly as precious gems embedded in ecclesiastical and courtly works.

About the ecclesiastical lyric, little more needs to be said. The vernacular lyric on ecclesiastical themes did not thrive as well as it might have partly because Latin remained the official language of the church, so that, besides the religious songs of Juan Ruiz mentioned above, only a few ecclesiastical lyrics have been transmitted. During the first half of the thirteenth century, Gonzalo de Berceo rendered three Latin hymns on the Virgin Mary in Castilian verse, and he composed another work ("Eya Velar") that seems to combine liturgical elements of the Passion of Jesus with the popular tone and rhythm of the type of popular work song sung by night watchmen and jailers. Several works contain variations of set prayers in the vernacular, as, for example, Doña Ximena's prayer for her exiled husband in the *Cantar de mío Cid;* the prayer of the Archpriest of Hita (for release from prison, symbolic or real) at the beginning of the *Book of Good Love;* the prayer of the Christians (after the Moorish invasion of Spain in 711) in the *Poema de Fernán González;* and Tarsiana's prayer as her life is threatened by Teófilo in the *Libro de Apolonio.* At the end of the fourteenth and beginning of the fifteenth century, Pero López de Ayala inserted some twelve religious songs, nine of them in the form of the *zajal,* into his *Rhymed Book of the Palace* (*Libro rimado del palacio*). Eleven of these songs are prayers either to God or to the Virgin Mary, and one of them is a lament for the author's imprisonment, set in the religious context of putting aside all worldly cares. Later in the fifteenth century, the Marqués de Santillana wrote two songs to the Virgin Mary and one short prayer.

Most of what is known about the courtly lyric in medieval Spain is due mainly to the intense interest, from the middle of the fifteenth century onward, in collecting anthologies of poetry (*cancioneros*). Individual poets presented their poems to patrons in notebooks (*cuadernos*), which were stored in the libraries of the patrons and later copied and amalgamated to form *cancioneros* (*cancioneiros* in Portuguese). Three of the most important *cancioneros* (the *Cancioneiro da Ajuda, Cancioneiro da Biblioteca Nacional,* and *Cancioneiro da Vaticana*) contain over 1,700 poems written in Galician-Portuguese by at least 150 poets between the years 1198 and 1354. Three kings are known to have been the principal supporters of these courtly poets: Ferdinand III of Castile, Dinis of Portugal, and Alfonso X of Castile: Dinis and Alfonso were also prodigious poets in their own right. The lyrics cultivated in these three courtly collections are of three basic types: *cantigas de amigo, cantigas de amor,* and *cantigas de escarnio e de maldizer.* The first two are love songs that are distinguished one from the other in that the *cantiga de amigo* pretends to represent the point of view of women in love, and in them, the woman's words are heard first; the *cantiga de amor,* on the other hand, purports to represent the man's perspective, and in them, the man's words are heard first. The *cantigas de escarnio e de maldizer* can be about any subject, including love, but their aim is to vilify or ridicule. The difference between *escarnio* and *maldizer* is that the former uses double entendre, whereas the latter says plainly what it means. All three types of cantigas may use a refrain, but the refrain and different forms of structural parallelism are more typical of the *cantigas de amigo.* The *cantigas de amor* and *cantigas de escarnio e de maldizer,* on the other hand, do not normally use parallelistic stanzas (although they may use parallelism of thought), and they frequently omit the refrain, in which case they are called not *cantigas de refran* but *cantigas de meestría* (or *maestriá*). Both the *cantigas de refran* and the *cantigas de meestría* should preferably end with one or more climactic stanzas of one to four lines linked by rhyme either to the last stanza of the *cantiga de meestría* or to the refrain of the *cantiga de refran.* For obvious reasons, therefore, scholars have compared the Galician-Portuguese lyrics of these three *cancioneiros* with the form and content of the lyrics of the Provençal troubadours; apart from the themes of courtly love, the lyrics of both languages also share forms such as the political satire of the sirventes, the lament (*planto*), the debate (tenson), the descort, and the form that resembles the *serranilla,* the pastourelle. The *cantigas de amigo* have also been compared with the *kharjas*, but what has been written in this regard will be of little value until the *kharjas* are properly edited.

Some forty-two of the Galician-Portuguese lyrics have been attributed to Alfonso X, king of Castile and León (*r.* 1252–1284). The vast majority of these (thirty-nine) are *cantigas de escarnio e de maldizer,* several of which are blatantly pornographic; the remaining three are *cantigas de amor.* If King Alfonso X wrote any *cantigas de amigo,* none has as yet been found; he was certainly capable of composing *cantigas de amigo,* because he borrows their parallelistic structure for several of his other cantigas; but, on the other hand, he might have composed only *cantigas de amor,* since only these have survived among the love lyrics. In any event, King Alfonso apparently vowed to stop composing love lyrics to ordinary women, and to write lyrics to the Virgin Mary alone: "And what I would like is to sing praise / to the Virgin, Mother of Our Lord / . . . and therefore I / want to be from now on her troubadour/ . . . and also / I should like to stop composing from now on / for any other women." The quotation is from the song that serves as a prologue to Alfonso's famous collection of 427 songs in praise of the Virgin Mary, the *Cantigas de Santa María.* The majority of these songs do not concern us directly in this article because they are really narratives written in the lyric attitude, this is, brief stories that tell, in verse, the miracles attributed to the Virgin Mary. Forty-two of these songs, however, are strictly lyrical in that they are hymns of praise to the Virgin; Alfonso interspersed these hymns at regular intervals of ten, in imitation, most likely, of the pattern of rosary beads of his time. These forty-two hymns are written for the most part in the form of the *zajal.*

According to the marqués de Santillana, Galician-Portuguese was, up to the end of the fourteenth century, the favorite language of medieval Spanish courtly lyric poets, even of those like King Alfonso X, whose native dialect was Castilian. From the middle of the fourteenth century, the favored language of courtly lyric began to shift from Galician-Portuguese to the dialects of Castile, Aragon, and Navarre; the principal courts that patronized these lyrics were those of John II of Castile (*r.* 1406–1454), Charles III of Navarre (*r.* 1389–1425), Alfonso V of Aragon (*r.* 1416–1458), and John II of Aragon (*r.* 1458–1479). It has been calculated, conservatively, that in these fifteenth-century Spanish courts over 900 poets are known to have composed works that have been collected in over 140 *cancionero* manuscript sources and several other printed volumes. Many of these compositions are not strictly lyrical: the anthologists themselves differentiated between lyrics, which they normally called *cantigas,* and other narrative poems in a lyrical attitude, which they called *decires.* The *decires* covered a wide variety of themes, including pieces composed for special occasions (like births, deaths, coronations), philosophical debates, Dantesque allegories, and religious topics. The main subject of the *cantigas* is love, but even here, many of the songs are stilted and perfunctory and seem to lack a convincing lyrical quality. Clearly, for these courtiers, poetry had become less a vehicle for lyrical expression than a public display of skill and manners, a courtly joust with words. These opinions can be confirmed by a quick perusal of any of the five principal *cancioneros:* the *cancioneros de Baena, de Estúñiga, musical de palacio, de Herberay,* and the *Cancionero general.* With the lyrics of most of these fifteenth-century courtly poets we are far removed from the songs that the Eskimo Orpingalik described as "thoughts sung out with the breath when poeple are moved by great forces and ordinary speech no longer suffices"; we are much closer, in fact, to "ordinary speech."

If one were forced to single out, for reasons of space, one of these 900 poets, a most convenient choice would be the marqués de Santillana (1398–1458). Santillana was one of the most powerful courtiers and men-at-arms of his time, while at the same time he was both a poet in his own right and a patron of poetry. He would perhaps expect to be remembered for his narrative *decires,* which are, for the most part, Dantesque allegories; but in fact his contributions to lyric poetry as a historian, critic, and poet are of greater value to literature than his pretentious nonlyrical *decires.* As a historian and critic, Santillana wrote a long letter to the chief of the Portuguese army, who had asked him for a collection of his poems; in this letter Santillana transmits the first known critique of Castilian poetry, and he demonstrates clearly that he is fully aware of the lyrical tradition to which he contributes. As a lyric poet Santillana is best known for transforming the *serranilla* and its Provençal counterpart, the pastourelle, into a refined courtly form; the hideous mountain women of the archpriest of Hita become, in Santillana's *serranillas,* beautiful ladies whose high-born sentiments and courtly manners force the poet to swear that he would never have known that they were mountain lasses. Santillana was also the first Castilian poet to have attempted the Italian sonnet. His *sonetos, fechos al italico modo* (sonnets made in the Italian mode) are, understandably, not perfect, but they mark in the history of Spanish lyric poetry a distinct period of transition from medieval to Renaissance, and they point the way to the inimitably beautiful sonnets of his great-nephew, the Renaissance poet Garcilaso de la Vega (1501–1536).

BIBLIOGRAPHY

Editions. Alfonso X, *Cantigas de Santa María,* Walter Mettmann, ed., 4 vols. (1959–1972); Elza P. Machado and José P. Machado, eds., *Cancioneiro da Biblioteca Nacional antigo Colocci-Brancuti,* 8 vols. (1949–1964); Carolina Michaëlis de Vasconcellos, ed., *Cancioneiro da Ajuda,* 2 vols. (1904); José J. Nunes, ed., *Cantigas d'amigo dos trovadores galego-portugueses,* 3 vols. (1926–1928, repr. 1971); Juan Ruiz, *Libro de buen amor,* Raymond S. Willis, ed. and trans. (1972); Marqués de Santillana, *Poesías completas,* Manuel Durán, ed., II (1980).

Studies and bibliographies. Cecil M. Bowra, *Primitive Song* (1962); Richard Hitchcock, *The "Kharjas": A Critical Bibliography* (1977); Wolfgang J. Kayser, *Das sprachliche Kunstwerk* (1948), trans. by María D. Mouton and V. García Yebra as *Interpretación y análisis de la obra literaria* (1961); Rafael Lapesa, *La obra literaria del marqués de Santillana* (1957); Alfred Morel-Fatio,

"Textes castillans inédits du XIIIe siècle," in *Romania,* **16** (1887); Colbert I. Nepaulsingh," "'The Song of Songs' and the Unity of the 'Razón de amor,'" in his *Towards a History of Literary Composition in Medieval Spain* (1987); Manuel Rodrigues Lapa, *Cantigas d'escarnho e de maldizer dos cancioneiros medievais galego-portugueses* (1965, 2nd ed. 1970); José M. Solá-Solé, *Corpus de poesía mozárabe* (1973); Samuel M. Stern, *Hispano-Arabic Strophic Poetry* (1974); Jacqueline Steunou and Lothar Knapp, *Bibliografía de los cancioneros castellanos del siglo XV y repertorio de sus géneros poéticos,* 3 vols. (1975); José Vives, ed., *Concilios visigóticos e hispano-romanos* (1963), 133.

COLBERT I. NEPAULSINGH

[See also **Alfonso X; Cancionero General; Cantiga; Cantigas de Amor, Amigo, and Escarnio; Celestina, La; Courtly Love; Decir; Fernán González, Poema de; Galician-Portuguese Poetry; Kharja; López de Ayala, Pero; Mozarabic Literature; Razón de Amor; Ruiz, Juan; Santillana, Marqués de; Villancicos.**]

SPANISH LITERATURE: POPULAR POETRY. Popular culture is sometimes the result of cultural diffusion from centers of more sophisticated learning. There were three areas in the Iberian Peninsula of such importance in the Middle Ages: the south, at Córdoba, which was one of the great European centers of culture (eighth to eleventh centuries); the northeast, with the French-influenced county of Catalonia (ninth century onwards); and the northwest, with its concentration of towns along the route to Santiago de Compostela (ninth century onward).

Medieval Spanish culture is hard to define. In a land where fighting and raiding was the norm along the Moslem-Christian borders, it was only natural that the safety of townships was often preferable to the ill-defended country areas. The devastating raids and campaigns caused by the confrontation of Muslims and Christians lasted on and off for over 750 years (711–1492). In the three above-mentioned areas, however, glimpses may be caught of music and dance, folk custom and drama, and folk narrative in ballad form.

The presence of cave paintings and prehistoric remains in parts of northern Spain suggests that from paleolithic times there have been inhabitants with an advanced culture completely capable of fostering music in the form of work songs, ritual dance, and lyric. The survival of Basque traditions—indeed of their language and physical traits as well—implies that their culture might well reach back to paleolithic man. Therefore it would be no surprise to find that in Spain, particularly in the mountains and valleys around the confines of the central meseta (northern Spain, the Ebro Valley, eastern Spain, the Guadalquivir Valley, and others), a flourishing popular culture has existed since earliest times.

In the field of medieval popular poetry, there were four clear-cut verse styles, all of them possibly stemming from one original tradition. These were the *kharja* from the Muslim south, a refrain occurring at the end of the poetic form known as the *muwashshaḥ;* the *villancico,* a poem generally on a love theme, also with a recurring refrain, coming mainly from Castile; the *cantiga de amigo,* from Galicia, which has a structure usually built up on a parallelistic principle—that is, with one line nearly repeating in its words the line preceding it. Another Muslim-inspired verse form was the *zajal,* which also possessed a refrain. All four forms were very likely closely connected with dances and in particular—as Alan Deyermond suggests—with the double-ring dance or the dance circle with a central figure in the middle. Boat songs, pilgrim songs, and dance songs (*barcarolas, cantigas de romería, bailadas*) all had their origins in the work song and were often chanted by women (as also in the case of the *kharja*). Shepherd songs such as the *pastorela* were also popular. In the field of ritual dance, the *jota* was very likely connected with fertility rituals.

Many of the themes of such songs and dances treated of love, friendship, or praise, but there are also mocking songs that were probably connected with the ritual wishing of good fortune, or that took the form of satires: such were the *cantigas de escarnho e de mal dizer* (Galicia) or *cantigas de escarnio* (Castile). Some of these would seem to have taken on a dramatic form rather akin to the dance-dramas of the Quiché today in Guatemala or the Quechua in Bolivia and Peru. There is, moreover, evidence that pre-Christian (and particularly Roman) customs still survived well into the Middle Ages in Spain, for example, the Roman Saturnalia and the Lupercalia: these found expression in the Christian tradition of the boy bishop, or the ritual beating for fertility purposes of women by men. There also existed vernacular religious drama, imported perhaps from France, which flourished in works like the *Auto de los reyes magos,* a twelfth-century manuscript fragment.

Finally, another branch of popular culture stems from the north-south confrontation of Christian and Muslim or from the internecine struggles between emerging Christian states. Epic and heroic tales were composed celebrating border raids, battles, and family dramas (*Siete infantes de Lara*), Castilian efforts to free themselves from León (*Fernán González*), squabbles between members of the royal family (*Siege of Zamora*), or cult figures like Rodrigo Díaz, the Cid. These in the main were not written down until incorporated in thirteenth- and fourteenth-century compilations, the best-known of which is the *Primera crónica general.* The composition of the *Cantar de mío Cid* is dated, however, about 1200. The themes treated in these legends also found their way into ballad form, and the *romanceros,* collections of these short poems, began to be written down in the fifteenth century.

BIBLIOGRAPHY

Alan D. Deyermond, *A Literary History of Spain: The Middle Ages* (1971); Douglas Gifford, "European Folk-Tradition and the 'Afrenta de Corpes,'" in Alan D. Deyermond, ed., *"Mío Cid" Studies* (1977); Richard Hitchcock, "The Fate of the Kharjas: A Survey of Recent Publications, in *Bulletin of the British Society for Middle Eastern Studies,* 12 (1985); Angus Mackay, *Spain in the Middle Ages* (1977); Ian Michael, "Spanish Literature and Learning to 1474," in Peter E. Russell, ed., *Spain: A Companion to Spanish Studies* (1973); Samuel M. Stern, *Les chansons mozarabes* (1953, repr. 1964), but for later opinions see Richard Hitchcock, *The "Kharjas": A Critical Bibliography* (1977), 60–61; Robert Stevenson, "Spanish Music," in P. Russell, ed., *op. cit.,* 543–567.

DOUGLAS GIFFORD

[See also **Auto de los Reyes Magos; Cantigas de Amor, Amigo, and Escarnio; Cantar de Mío Cid; Fernán González; Kharja; Mozarabic Literature; Villancicos.**]

SPANISH LITERATURE: ROMANCES. The traditional use of the term "novel" in criticism written in Spanish, as in the title "novel of chivalry," is not particularly appropriate; there is little about these works that resembles the modern novel. The word "romance" describes the genre better. In addition, the term "chivalry," is proper only if used in its broadest sense, as chivalrous actions and behavior are only part of what is portrayed in these works. Basically, they are adventure stories, sometimes with hagiographic or moral overtones, which involve a somewhat mythicized hero in a series of quests, loves, dangerous encounters, and the like. We possess only a few medieval examples of this genre, whose flowering came principally in the sixteenth century and whose influence on Cervantes and other authors of the period was notable.

The origins of the genre harken back to the Byzantine novel, the popular Alexandrine legends, and Semitic sources. Another important influence is the French Arthurian material, principally the *Roman du Graal,* which appears to have been translated into one of the Romance dialects of the Iberian Peninsula in the first quarter of the fourteenth century. Unfortunately this translation is now lost.

Three other examples of the genre make their appearance toward the end of the thirteenth century and at the beginning of the fourteenth. The *Libro del cavallero Zifar* is artistically the most important of them. It is somewhat atypical in that, although there are obvious Arthurian influences, the Semitic tradition has also intervened, and it is likely that the book's author bore in mind the methods of figural construction, a technique used by medieval writers based upon the activities of exegetes of the Bible who attempted to show how real events in the Old Testament prefigured or foreshadowed real happenings in the New Testament. *El cavallero del Cisne,* a recapitulation in Spanish of the swan-knight legend, appears in the *Gran conquista de Ultramar,* a long composition having to do with the crusades. The *Historia troyana polimétrica* acclimatizes the Trojan material to the peninsula, combining verse and prose in a manner somewhat reminiscent of the Menippean satire.

The most primitive version of the *Amadís de Gaula,* of which only a fragment survives, also dates from the fourteenth century. The rendition that we possess (printed 1508) is drawn from the reworking executed by Garcí Rodríguez de Montalvo about 1492.

BIBLIOGRAPHY

Alan Deyermond, "Libros de caballerías y 'novela' sentimental," in his *Edad media,* vol. I of Francisco Rico, ed., *Historia y crítica de la literatura española* (1980).

JAMES F. BURKE

[See also **Alexander Romances; Amadís de Gaula; Arthurian Literature, Spanish and Portuguese; Cavallero Zifar, Libro del; Spanish Literature: Troy Story.**]

SPANISH LITERATURE: SATIRE. Medieval "Spanish" satire, that is, satire written in one of the Romance languages of the Iberian Peninsula, dates from as early as the twelfth century in the eastern part of the peninsula. Since this area was closely related politically and culturally to the south of France, the earliest troubadours wrote in Provençal and their attacks dealt mainly with political affairs of the region. Those poets born in Catalonia and Aragon shifted gradually to writing in Catalan, but the northern influence remained strong. The most popular themes were the vileness or cowardice of political enemies, sexual aberrations of a rival, and the defects of rich and powerful barons and rulers. Misogyny, anticlericalism, and social criticism were also popular themes, increasingly so in the fourteenth and fifteenth centuries.

From the twelfth century on, the northwestern part of the Iberian Peninsula produced, in addition to a rich body of love lyrics, a large number of *cantigas de escarnio y maldezir* (songs of ridicule and slander). Although all of the poets wrote in Galician-Portuguese, many were attached to the thirteenth-century Castilian courts of Ferdinand III and Alfonso X (the latter an accomplished poet himself who composed some powerful satires) or accompanied armies in the wars against the Moors. Their satire was aimed at other poets, courtesans, avaricious or poverty-stricken nobles, both male and female religious, doctors, cowardly soldiers, and homosexuals. Personal vanities, belief in auguries, and unequal marriages were also ridiculed.

Since the courtly poetry, even in the central area of the peninsula, was written in Galician (and it was this poetry that was preserved), Castilian verse satire is relatively late. The earliest manifestation is probably the *Elena y María* or *Disputa del clérigo y el caballero* (*ca.* 1280). Within the European tradition of "disputes" on the relative merits of clerics and knights, the Castilian poem accentuates the satirical aspect, especially against the cleric. Two great fourteenth-century poets include satire in their masterpieces: Juan Ruiz' subtle *Libro de buen amor* humorously censures worldly and enamored clerics, as well as other classes; the more austere satire of Pero López de Ayala's *Rimado de palacio,* although directed primarily against the low state of morality and the simony of ecclesiastics, also includes the royal court, lawyers, judges, and merchants.

The instability of the government, the rise and fall of royal favorites and power struggles of the nobility, gave rise to considerable political satire in the fifteenth century, including works by the Marqués de Santillana, Gómez Manrique, and Juan Álvarez Gato. Anonymous sociopolitical satires flourished, as did expressions of personal and regional rivalries. Drinking and eating habits and excesses in dress were criticized. The presence of many *conversos* (converted Jews or their descendants) is an important factor in the literature of the fifteenth century. They were objects of attacks both by "old Christians" and by some of their fellow converts, but they themselves also produced much of the satirical writing of the period, in which one can perceive the black humor of a group alienated from and persecuted by the main body of society. Although satire in medieval Spain did not produce a masterpiece (Juan Ruiz' work is a masterpiece, but it is not primarily or uniquely a satire), it was a literary mode much cultivated in the three major Romance languages that developed in the peninsula.

BIBLIOGRAPHY

Kenneth R. Scholberg, *Sátira e invectiva en la España medieval* (1971).

KENNETH R. SCHOLBERG

[See also **Cantigas de Amor, Amigo, and Escarnio; Converso; López de Ayala, Pero; Ruiz, Juan; Santillana, Marqués de.**]

SPANISH LITERATURE: SENTIMENTAL ROMANCES. The Spanish sentimental romances are a type of prose fiction that flourished during the second half of the fifteenth century and beginning of the sixteenth. The major examples are: Juan Rodríguez del Padrón, *El siervo libre de Amor* (1440?) Diego de San Pedro, *Cárcel de amor* (1492), and Juan de Flores, *Grisel y Mirabella* and *Grimalte y Gradissa* (1495). Some would also include Juan de Segura's *Proceso de cartas de amores* (1548) in spite of its late date. These romances, which total fourteen at the most, span a period of more than a century and exhibit radical differences. Some critics separate what they refer to as the bourgeois erotic romances from the aristocratic "purely sentimental" ones. San Pedro, for example, is vastly different from Flores: while the former writes about unconsummated love, in the latter consummation is taken for granted. This disparity has been studied in terms of sources, Flores being considered closer to a possible Italian model, Boccaccio's *Elegia di Madonna Fiammetta,* while San Pedro's writings show evidence of the influence of the *cancionero.*

Menéndez Pelayo was the first to define, delimit, and discuss in detail the sentimental romances. Since his study, critics have added new works or subtracted titles from the original list of novels; redefined the genre; debated as to whether it is a novel, a romance, or a transitional form; and have even questioned the very existence of this type of prose fiction. It is difficult, however, to quarrel with Menéndez Pelayo's original assessment: the fifteenth century witnessed the appearance of a genre distinct from the usual types of medieval fiction. If this group of works parallels the chivalric romances in the combination of heroic and amorous exploits, it is distinct in its conciseness and in the stress on sentiment rather than on bellicose practices. The chivalric romances overwhelm with action and stress the superhuman qualities and triumphs of the hero, while the sentimental romances are practically static and underline more human qualities. Psychology, whether masculine or feminine, is a central concern in the latter form: the man pursues and laments while the woman, a veritable "belle dame sans merci," resists passion and rejects pleas for mercy, adducing reasons of honor.

These short romances share a number of characteristics. Among them are the tendency to allegorize, a propensity toward the epistolary form, and an autobiographical flavor conveyed through an inflated rhetorical style. Characterization is important but always assumes certain courtly modes: the submission and service of the lover, who must preserve humility and secrecy, and the initial and often continued indifference of the lady. She is frequently associated with the virtuous ideal, although this view is somewhat ambiguous due to her lack of "charity"—a duality based on the opposition of the code of love to the code of honor. Although many have seen in this idealization a kind of feminism, others reject this notion because the lover often must separate his spiritual adventure from the earthly quest since the woman proves unworthy. Sentimental romances usually end tragically: the convent at times proves to be the ultimate obstacle for the lovers, although more often death, even in the form of suicide, provides the irrevocable separation. Since the lover's ideal is unrealizable in this world, he resorts to death or to a kind of imprisonment that yearns for oblivion.

BIBLIOGRAPHY

Frederick A. de Armas, "Algunas observaciones sobre *La cárcel de amor,*" in *Revista de estudios hispánicos* (Alabama), **8** (1974); Dinko Cvitanovic, *La novela sentimental española* (1973); Peter N. Dunn, "Narrator as Character in the *Cárcel de amor,* in *Modern Language Notes,* **94** (1979); Armando Durán, *Estructura y técnicas de la novela sentimental y caballeresca* (1973); Barbara Matulka, *The Novels of Juan de Flores and Their European Diffusion* (1931); Martín de Riquer, "*Triste deleytaçión:* Novela castellana del siglo XV," in *Revista de filología española,* **40** (1956); J. Scudieri Ruggieri, "Un romanzo sentimentale: Il 'Tratado notable de amor' di Juan de Cardona," *ibid.,* **46** (1963); Carmelo Samona, "Per una interpretazione del *Siervo libre de amor,*" in *Studi ispanici,* **1** (1962); José Luis Varela, "Revisión de la novela sentimental," in *Revista de filología española,* **48** (1965); Pamela Waley, "Love and Honor in the *novelas sentimentales* of Diego de San Pedro and Juan de Flores," in *Bulletin of Hispanic Studies,* **43** (1966); Bruce Wardropper, "El mundo sentimental de la *Cárcel de amor,*" in *Revista de filología española,* 37 (1953); Keith Whinnom, *Diego de San Pedro* (1974).

FREDERICK A. DE ARMAS

[See also **Boccaccio, Giovanni.**]

SPANISH LITERATURE: SERMONS. Medieval Spanish preaching has never been studied, few sermons have been cataloged, and hardly any have been published. Sermons were certainly delivered in medieval Spain in all the major languages spoken there (Latin, Arabic, Spanish, Portuguese, Catalan, and, perhaps, Hebrew, Basque, and Berber), but most of the surviving texts are in Latin. Many probably represent what was actually said to monastic or other congregations capable of understanding Latin, from the sixth-century *Homilia de monachis perfectis* and the homilies of St. Leander and St. Isidore, through the fifty-four surviving sermons of St. Martín of León (*d.* 1203) and down to the Renaissance. Other Latin texts, however, are mere outlines, written before or after the actual delivery of sermons preached in the vernacular, sometimes to clerics, but perhaps more frequently to lay congregations. Examples of these are the hundreds of surviving sermon outlines in Latin of Juan de Aragón, archbishop of Toledo (1319–1328), and of St. Vincent Ferrer (1350–1419).

Very few texts, in contrast, appear to have survived in Castilian, although this may be simply because no systematic search has yet been made for them. The earliest is *Qué sinifica el hábito de los frailes de Santiago* (*ca.* 1329) by Pedro López de Baeza, a friar of the military Order of Santiago; this work explains the allegorical meaning of the friars' accoutrement and exhorts them to fulfil their military duties against the Muslims. By 1400 it was becoming more common to write a sermon down in the vernacular, as can be seen from the *Libro de las consolaciones de la vida humana* of Pope Benedict XIII (*r.* 1394–1423). The first big collection of sermons to survive in Castilian is that of the secular priest Pedro Marín, which he dedicated in 1425 to a Castilian noble and which deals with the virtues, beatitudes, and works of mercy; its publication is planned by Pedro Cátedra. A later collection is the *Libro de los evangelios desde adviento hasta la dominica de Pasión* of the Dominican Juan López de Salamanca (*d.* 1479); and other preachers such as Archbishop Hernando de Talavera (1428–1507) and the Hieronymite Gonzalo de Frías are known to have left collections of their sermons, but these have not yet been found. In general, much less is known for certain about vernacular sermons in Castilian than about those in Catalan.

Nevertheless, the surviving texts do not suggest that Castilian preaching varied greatly from the Western European norm. The same structures are found, with *divisio intra* (learned sermons) and *extra* (popular sermons), and groupings according to the liturgical year, saints' days, and special occasions such as funerals and political crises. The sources are also similar: the Bible, the church fathers, the classics, exempla, and the observance of daily life. The usual auxiliaries are also found: *artes praedicandi* (guides to preaching, such as those by Martín de Córdoba and others by non-Castilians such as Francesc Eiximenis and Ramon Lull); and collections of exempla, which are especially rich since Spain was the home of translations from the Arabic (for example, the *Disciplina clericalis* of Petrus Alfonsi and the *Libro de los exenplos por a.b.c.* of Clemente Sánchez de Vercial). Finally, there are the literary derivatives: devotional works (such as *Vencimiento del mundo*) and parodies (*Libro de buen amor, Sermón de amor*).

BIBLIOGRAPHY

Derek W. Lomax, "The Lateran Reforms and Spanish Literature," in *Iberoromania,* **1** (1969), and "Pedro López de Baeza, 'Dichos de los Santos Padres' (siglo XIV)," in *Miscelánea de textos medievales,* **1** (1972); Francisco Rico, *Predicación y literatura en la España medieval* (1977); Isafas Rodríguez, "Autores espirituales en la edad media," in *Repertorio de historia de las ciencias eclesiásticas en España,* **1** (1967).

DEREK W. LOMAX

[See also **Ars Praedicandi; Disciplina Clericalis; Eiximenis, Francesc; Exemplum; Lull, Ramon; Preaching and Sermon Literature, Western European; Ruiz, Juan; Vincent Ferrer, St.**]

SPANISH LITERATURE: TRANSLATIONS. The written records of Spanish begin with translations: interlinear glosses in twelfth-century Latin documents. Literary translation comes much later, and at first it cannot easily be distinguished from original composition. Some of the most important works of the thirteenth century are free adaptations from French (*Disputa del alma y el cuerpo, Vida de Santa María Egipciaca*) or from Latin (*Libro de Apolonio,* Gonzalo de Berceo's *Milagros de Nuestra Señora* and his saints' lives). In the fifteenth century there were more clearly defined frontiers between original work and translation, or between *translatio* (the process of [cultural] transference) and strict translation. Translation, in our modern sense, was part of the Latin literature of Spain before it was a vernacular activity, and scientific and philosophical works were translated earlier than purely literary ones. Latin versions of Arabic works were made at the monastery of Ripoll in the tenth century, and there were several major centers of translation in the twelfth, with Toledo attaining predominance later in the century. In at least some cases a Castilian draft was the intermediary between the Arabic original and the Latin end product, but none of these drafts have survived.

King Alfonso X (*r.* 1252–1284) built on the work of the Toledo school, directing the major effort into the production of Castilian texts (though translation into Latin continued into the fifteenth century). Thus Castilian became the main channel by which Arabic culture (itself a transmitter of Indian, Persian, and Greek material) reached Western Europe. Scientific work was carefully and closely translated by the Alfonsine team, while contemporary versions of Oriental story collections, such as *Calila e Dimna* and *Libro de los assayamientos de las mujeres* (*de los engaños*), were made with greater freedom. Between these extremes are translations incorporated into the Alfonsine historical works, which are in general fairly close, but are sometimes medievalized (a reference to bullfighting is added to a passage of Orosius). There are also occasional pseudo-translations: legends of the Cid passed off by a monk of San Pedro de Cardeña as a translation of an Arabic chronicle by Ibn al-Faraj were accepted at face value by the Alfonsine team.

In the second half of the fourteenth century, Juan Fernández de Heredia directed a major program comparable to, though smaller than, the Alfonsine achievement: the making of Aragonese versions of moral and historical works in Latin, French, and Greek. The translation from Greek (for example, of Thucydides) may have been direct, rather than from a Latin or Arabic version. A couple of generations later, the Marqués de Santillana was a leading patron of translators: many versions of classical and medieval works (including the first Spanish translation of Plato) were made for him. The activity of Italian humanists began to affect Spanish translators in Santillana's time, and Alfonso de Cartagena felt confident enough to challenge Leonardo Bruni in the 1430's on his method of translating Aristotle's *Ethics*. At this time we also find several cases of authors translating their own works: Enrique de Villena's *Doze trabajos de Hércules* was composed in Catalan, Pedro de Portugal's *Sátira de la infelice e felice vida* in Portuguese, and both authors turned their work into Castilian. In the second half of the fifteenth century Alfonso de Palencia translated some of his Latin writings into Castilian and some of his Castilian into Latin.

The range of foreign authors translated into medieval Spanish is wide: Classical Latin (Cicero, Livy, Ovid, Sallust, Seneca and Pseudo-Seneca, Vergil), Medieval and Renaissance Latin (Gregory the Great, Aeneas Sylvius, Boccaccio, Petrarch); French (Brunetto Latini, Marco Polo, Honoré Bonet); Italian (Boccaccio, Dante); Provençal (Matfre Ermengaud); Catalan (Lull); Portuguese (Pedro de Barcelos); Greek (perhaps Plutarch), Arabic (Koran, Abenragel), as well as Hebrew (Old Testament). Others were translated at second hand: Greek authors from Latin and Arabic versions (Aristotle, Homer), Sanskrit and Persian from Arabic. One English work, Gower's *Confessio Amantis*, was translated into Portuguese by an Englishman and thence into Castilian. Translation, however, can operate in two directions. Spanish books were translated into Latin, French, Portuguese, and Catalan during the Middle Ages; in the sixteenth century major works of medieval Spanish literature appeared in English, French, and Italian. Spain received, but she also gave.

BIBLIOGRAPHY

Georg Bossong, *Probleme der Übersetzung wissenschaftlicher Werke aus dem Arabischen in das Altspanische zur Zeit Alfons des Weisen* (1979); Manuel Díaz y Díaz, *Las primeras glosas hispánicas* (1978); Hans Ulrich Gumbrecht, "Literary Translation and Its Social Conditioning in the Middle Ages: Four Spanish Romance Texts of the 13th Century," in *Yale French Studies,* **51:** *Approaches to Medieval Romance* (1974); María Rosa Lida de Malkiel, "La tradición clásica en España," in *Nueva revista de filología hispánica,* 5 (1951), repr. in her *La tradición clásica en España* (1975); Anthony Luttrell, "Greek Histories Translated and Compiled for Juan Fernández de Heredia, Master of Rhodes, 1377–1396," in *Speculum,* 35 (1960); Gonzalo Menéndez Pidal, "Cómo trabajaron las escuelas alfonsíes," in *Nueva revista de filología hispánica,* 5 (1951); José María Millás Vallicrosa, *Las traducciones orientales en los manuscritos de la Biblioteca Catedral de Toledo* (1942); Margherita Morreale, "Apuntes para la historia de la traducción en la edad media," in *Revista de literatura,* 15 (1959); Evelyn S. Procter, *Alfonso X of Castile, Patron of Literature and Learning* (1951), 6–23, 113–139; Peter Russell, *Traducciones y traductores en la Península Ibérica (1400–1550)* (1985).

ALAN DEYERMOND

[See also **Alfonso X; Bible; Santillana, Marqués de; Translation and Translators, Western European.**]

SPANISH LITERATURE: TROY STORY. In the Iberian Peninsula the Troy romance was popular from the thirteenth century onward. Benoît de Sainte-Maure and Guido delle Colonne are the main sources for these Spanish versions, although the Troy material in the Castilian Alexander romance, the *Libro de Alexandre* (early thirteenth century), uses the *Ilias latina,* and the section of Alfonso X the Learned's *Grande e general estoria* (begun in 1272) devoted to Troy uses Dares as well as Benoît. In the fourteenth century Alfonso XI commissioned a Castilian prose translation of Benoît (1350), which was twice translated into Galician Portuguese (one of these Galician manuscripts is bilingual with Castilian and contains material from the *Grande e general estoria*). A second prose version of the prosified Benoît, the *Historia troyana polimétrica* (probably fourteenth century), has original inserted poems in Castilian that are generally considered to be the best of the peninsular Troy material. The poems concentrate particularly on the Troilus story, which is presented in terms of courtly love. A wide variety of metrical forms are employed in the poems.

A fourteenth-century Castilian rendering of Guido delle Colonne and other sources (including the *Grande e general estoria*) is the *Sumas* of Leomarte. Other fourteenth-century prose versions of Guido delle Colonne exist in Aragonese (Juan Fernández de Heredia) and Catalan (Jaume Conesa, *ca.* 1370), and there is an anonymous Castilian translation in the early fifteenth century. Guido delle Colonne remained popular in Castile in the fifteenth century and was translated by Pedro de Chinchilla in 1443. Finally, the printed *Crónica troyana* (1490), sometimes attributed to Pero López de Ayala (*d.* 1407), depends mainly on Guido delle Colonne. The fifteenth century also saw a renewed interest in the Homeric original and its derivatives: the poet Juan de Mena (*d.* 1456) translated the *Ilias latina,* and Pedro González de Mendoza translated Piero Candido Decembrio's Latin version of the *Iliad.*

BIBLIOGRAPHY

Sources. Alfonso X, *General estoria: Segunda parte,* Antonio G. Solalinde, Lloyd A. Kasten, and Victor R. B. Oelschläger, eds., II (1961), 87–169; *Cronica troyana: Códice gallego del siglo XIV de la Biblioteca Nacional de Madrid,* Manuel Rodríguez and Andrés Martínez Salazar, eds. (1900); *Crónica troyana: Manuscrito gallego del siglo XIV no. 10.233, Biblioteca Nacional Madrid,* Kelvin M. Parker, ed. (1978); Guido delle Colonne, *La corónica troyana,* Frank P. Norris, ed. (1970); *Historia troyana,* Kelvin M. Parker, ed. (1975); *Historia troyana en prosa y verso,* R. Menéndez Pidal and E. Varón Vallejo, eds. (1934), abridged in Menéndez Pidal, *Tres poetas primitivos* (1958); Leomarte, *Sumas de historia troyana,* Agapito Rey, ed. (1932); *El libro de Alexandre,* Raymond S. Willis, ed. (1934); Juan de Mena, *La 'Yliada en Romance' según la impresión de Arnao Guillén de Brocar (Valladolid, 1519),* Martín de Riquer, ed. (1949); *La versión de Alfonso XI del "Roman de Troie,"* Kelvin M. Parker, ed. (1977).

Studies. Marina Scordilis Brownlee, "Towards a Reappraisal of the *Historia troyana polimétrica,*" in *La corónica,* 7 (1978); *Les histories troyanes de Guíu de Columpnes tradujdes al catalá en el XIV^en^ segle per En Jacme Conesa,* R. Miquel y Planas, ed. (1916); Agapito Rey and Antonio García Solalinde, *Ensayo de una bibliografía de las leyendas troyanas en la literatura española* (1942); Solalinde, "Las versiones españolas del *Roman de Troie,*" in *Revista de filología española,* 3 (1916).

DOROTHY SHERMAN SEVERIN

[See also **Alexander Romances; Alexandre, Libro de; Alfonso X; Benoît de Sainte-Maure; Catalan Literature; Mena, Juan de; López de Ayala, Pero; Troy Story.**]

SPANISH LITERATURE: VERSIFICATION AND PROSODY. Medieval Spanish versification and prosody evolved mainly from medieval Latin verse systems designed for popular appeal. The earliest known Spanish line and stanza patterns are varied, with none, apparently, predominating before the thirteenth century. Line measure was based on either predetermined beat distribution or syllable count involving special rules. Single-unit lines (*verso de arte menor*) ranged up to nine syllables in length, longer lines normally being divided in the middle by a caesura. Early stanzas, some patterned in both long and short verse, contained from two lines to several. Full rhyme was generally preferred to assonance, in both end rhyme and interior rhyme. Purpose dictated form, so that a popular refrain was variously structured, as in the *refrán* or the *kharja*; song stanzas were monostrophic, as in the *¡Eya velar!* of Gonzalo de Berceo (*ca.* 1196–*ca.* 1264); a short narrative might be composed in loosely measured form, as in *Razón de amor*; dramatic verse in a given piece could be polymorphous, fitting speech to circumstance, as in the *Auto de los reyes magos* (second half of the twelfth century), modeled metrically on the Latin *sequentia* (Spanish: *secuencia* or *prosa*); epic verse might be arranged in a *tirada* or *serie* in monorhymed assonance, as in the *Cantar* (*Poema*) *de mío Cid.* All were based on the principle of rhythmic harmony.

In the thirteenth century, when the vernacular was clearly becoming an acceptable medium for "learned" poetry, and the *cuaderna vía* the favored metric form for works on serious topics, the essential rules for the Spanish syllable-count system that has since prevailed were being established. This system, based on the principle of metrical equivalency rather than on that of simple enumeration of syllables actually present, allowed for modifications that reduced the monotony of strict count. Contraction, apocope, aphaeresis, diaeresis, synizesis, and syncope, each permitted under certain conditions, afforded some relief from the rule of obligatory hiatus between contiguous vowels of separate words, as did the system of hemistich-end and line-end count, in which both oxytones and proparoxytones are measured as if they were paroxytones. Long poems were generally composed in long lines, with mid caesura creating balanced hemistichs.

In the *Cantar de mío Cid,* for instance, syllables per hemistich range around seven—from four to ten—but the work permits a reading in which each hemistich contains two regularly timed stress beats producing a grave *one*-TWO//one-*TWO* cadence. *Cuaderna vía*'s *alejandrino* verse, on the other hand, minces along at the even rate of 1, 2, 3, 4, 5, 6́, (7)// 1, 2, 3, 4, 5, 6́, (7) syllables, the sameness relieved mainly by a fluctuating secondary stress on one or two of the first four syllables of each hemistich. Short poems of the time were best served by single-unit verse, as in the anonymous *Razón de amor* (early thirteenth century), with its lines hovering around the enneasyllabic, or in the near-trochaic syllable-numbered lines of the "Profecía de Casandra," from the *Historia troyana polimétrica* (*ca.* 1270), which contains poems in other single-unit meters.

In his *Libro de buen amor* (early fourteenth century), Juan Ruiz interspersed more than a score of variously designed pieces among his *cuaderna vía,* purposely to illustrate the versification craft of his day. No doubt reflecting current usage, about two-thirds of these poems are in octosyllables, some with regularly placed half-lines or otherwise fractioned lines (this device was known as *pie quebrado*). The rest are in six- or seven-syllable verse, or in modified adonics—(o)óooóo—or, once, in a patterned distribution of five- and seven-syllable lines. His stanzas, from four to ten lines each, range in form from the basic *zéjel* quatrain (*aaab*/*cccb*/ *dddb*/ . . .) to a ten-line *copla de pie quebrado* with a complex rhyme scheme. His *coplas de arte menor* are of both seven and eight lines, identical stanza end rhymes gracing one poem. Significant are his selections in double octosyllabic (8 + 8) *cuaderna vía.*

A favored fourteenth-century stanza is the quatrain rhyming *abab,* as in Shem Tov's heptasyllabic (Spanish count) *Proverbios morales,* or in the *Poema de Alfonso XI* (1348), in which the verse hovers around the octosyllable in length, and some rhymes have consonants with acoustic equivalence in lieu of identical sound.

By the late fourteenth century, overuse of anacrusis in the hemistichs, as in Pero López de Ayala's *Rimado de palacio,* threatened to merge the *alejandrino* with the double octosyllable *romance* meter. As the *alejandrino* thus declined, it was replaced by the relatively fixed-beat *verso de arte mayor,* evolved from the medieval Latin double adonic and deemed the most elegant of fifteenth-century meters. The *cuaderna vía* likewise yielded to the *copla de arte mayor,* the stanza so brilliantly polished by Juan de Mena in his epic *Laberinto de fortuna* (1444). The *verso de arte mayor,* by century's end stiff and monotonous from overregularization, was soon to give way to the supple Italianate hendecasyllable. Accentual verse derived from the single adonic, as in Santillana's *Moçà tan fermosa,* finally merged with the simple hexasyllable. Common fifteenth-century stanzas in single-unit verse are the *copla de arte menor,* the *copla de pie quebrado,* the *seguidilla,* and the *zéjel* and its variations. The *villancico* (carol) form remained loose. Preference for astrophic over stanzaic structure in the *romance* was marked. Attempts to introduce the Italian sonnet failed, despite Santillana's notable effort.

Juan del Encina's poetry illustrates, and his *Arte de poesía castellana* (1496) and Antonio de Nebrija's treatise *La prosodia i silaba* (1492) well summarize, the medieval poets' achievements and the period-end state of the art, when beat-measure and divided verse were about to be discarded in favor of the single-unit, syllable-count line shaped according to rules that arrested the creep of amorphism and, with the aid of the fifteenth-century adaptation to Spanish of the Italian glide device of synaloepha, countered the rigidity and halting effect of obligatory hiatus and provided a smooth flow to all verse.

Medieval poets' most lasting contribution to Spanish prosody was, perhaps, the modernization of syllable-count verse, most notably of the octosyllable, which, by the end of the fifteenth century, had been given the graceful form it bears today.

BIBLIOGRAPHY

Charles V. Aubrun, "La métrique du 'Mio Cid' est régulière," in *Bulletin hispanique,* **49** (1947); Alfredo Carballo Picazo, *Métrica española* (1956), a bibliography; Dorothy Clotelle Clarke, *Morphology of Fifteenth-century Castilian Verse* (1964); Juan del Encina, "Arte de poesía castellana," in *Cancionero de Juan del Encina* (1496, facs. ed. 1928); Pierre le Gentil, *La poésie lyrique espagnole et portugaise à la fin du moyen âge,* II, *Les formes* (1952); Sylvanus Griswold Morley, "Recent Theories About the Meter of the *Poema de mio Cid,*" *PMLA,* **48** (1933); Tomás Navarro, *Métrica española: Reseña histórica y descriptiva* (1965, 4th ed. 1974); Antonio de Nebrija, *Grámatica castellana,* Pascual Galindo Romeo and Luis Ortiz Muñoz, eds., 2 vols. (1946), I, "Libro segundo"; Julio Saavedra Molina, *El verso de arte mayor* (1946), and "El verso de clerecía," in *Boletín de filología* (Santiago de Chile), **6** (1950–1951); Antonio Sánchez Romeralo, *El villancico* (1969); Colin Smith, "La métrica del *Poema de mio Cid:* Nuevas posibilidades," in *Nueva revista de filología hispánica,* **28** (1979).

DOROTHY CLOTELLE CLARKE

[See also **Alfonso XI, Poema de; Assonance; Auto de los Reyes Magos; Berceo, Gonzalo de; Cantar de Mío Cid; Copla; Cuaderna Vía; Kharja; Laisse; López de Ayala, Pero; Mena, Juan de; Mester de Clerecía; Razón de Amor; Ruiz, Juan; Shem Tov.**]

SPARAPET, an Armenian term meaning "commander-in-chief of the army," etymologically derived from the Parthian *spadapat* (*spad* [army], *pat* [leader], which in turn derives from Old Persian: *spadapaitis*). Because of the destruction of Iranian sources at the time of the seventh-century Arab invasions of Iran, more is known about the Armenian *sparapet* than about his Iranian counterpart (*Eran-spahbad*), even though both the term and the institution probably were borrowed from Iran.

According to Arthur Christensen, the *Eran-spahbad* was head of the Iranian army until the time of Xusrō I (531–579). As a result of Xusrō's reforms, the single *Eran-spahbad* was replaced by four *spahbad*s, one in charge of each of the major Iranian frontiers. The survival of Armenian historical sources treating fourth-through-seventh-century events permits a closer look at this official. However, the Armenian *sparapet* and the Iranian *spahbad* may have had different duties and prerogatives.

The office of *sparapet* was the hereditary charge of the lordly Mamikonean family. Precisely when this office was instituted or abolished is unclear, although the sources record Mamikoneans occupying the position by the early fourth century, and the removal of this office from the Mamikoneans probably coincided with their emigration to Byzantium in the eighth to tenth centuries. The martial prowess of the Mamikoneans, plus the fact that their office (as with most others in Arsacid Armenia) was held hereditarily by right and not by appointment, made this family frequent rivals of Armenia's kings for dominance in the country's affairs. As such, the Armenian *sparapet* differed from his Iberian (Georgian) counterpart (*spaspet*), who apparently held a noninheritable office that included civil as well as military functions. The relevant, authentic fourth- and fifth-century Armenian sources that speak of Mamikonean *sparapet*s are the histories of P^{c}awstos Buzand, Koriwn, Agat^{c}angełos, and Łazar P^{c}arpec^{c}i. These sources permit the construction of a list of Mamikonean *sparapet*s from 303 until 506.

BIBLIOGRAPHY

Sources. P^{c}awstos Buzandac^{c}i, *History of the Armenians,* Robert Bedrosian, trans. (1985); Łazar P^{c}arpec^{c}i (Ghazar P^{c}arpec^{c}i), *History of the Armenians,* Robert Bedrosian, trans. (1985); Sebēos, *History,* Robert Bedrosian, trans. (1985).

Studies. Nicholas Adontz, *Armenia in the Period of Justinian,* Nina G. Garsoïan, ed. and trans. (1970); Robert Bedrosian, "The *Sparapetut^{c}iwn* in Armenia in the Fourth and Fifth Centuries," in *Armenian Review,* **36** (1983); Arthur Christensen, *L'Iran sous les Sassanides,* 2nd ed. (1944); Nina G. Garsoïan, "Prolegomena to a Study of the Iranian Aspects in Arsacid Armenia," in *Hantes Amsoria,* **90** (1978); Cyril Toumanoff, *Studies in Christian Caucasian History* (1963); Geo Widengren, "Recherches sur le féodalisme iranien," in *Orientalia suecana,* **5** (1956).

ROBERT BEDROSIAN

[See also **Armenia, Social Structure; Arsacids; Historiography, Armenian; Koriwn; Łazar P^{c}arpec^{c}i; Mamikonean; P^{c}awstos Buzand; Sasanian History; Xusrō I Anōšarwān.**]

SPEAR. See **Lance.**

SPERBER, DER. This *Märe* of about 370 lines is preserved in eleven manuscripts, making it the second most frequently transmitted of the genre. The manuscript tradition and dialectal features suggest that *Der Sperber* was composed in the Alemannic region of Germany in the later thirteenth century. It contains verbal echoes of the works of Hartmann von Aue and apparently was familiar to authors of later *Mären.*

Der Sperber recounts the tale of a young woman who has grown up in a cloister, knowing nothing of the outside world. One day from the cloister wall she sees a knight riding past with a sparrow hawk (*Sperber*) perched on his wrist. When she expresses her admiration for the bird, he tells her it is for sale; when she complains that she has no money, he offers it to her in exchange for her love. The young woman has no idea what "love" is, but is sure she does not have any. The knight assures her he will be able to find it on her person if she will let him search. She agrees and accompanies him to an orchard, where he "searches" her three times, gives her the hawk, and departs. The girl hurries to the prioress and boasts of her purchase, but the prioress, outraged at her folly, thrashes her.

Hoping to regain the prioress' favor, the girl accosts the knight as he rides past the next day and demands that he take back the hawk and return her love. He agrees, "returns her love" twice, then a third time when she insists on full restitution, and leaves. She returns elated to the prioress, who realizes her own responsibility for this latest misfortune and accepts it philosophically.

Der Sperber is gracefully written and carefully composed. The heroine is characterized through direct speech (nearly half the text), which brings out especially her ingenuous pleasure in sexual intercourse. Her comments on the bird are innocently amusing: "If only its beak weren't crooked, it would be perfect. I'm sure it sings beautifully." The sparrow hawk is a symbol of chivalric status but also suggests erotic relations, being frequently associated with women in medieval German literature. *Dulceflorie* and *Das Häslein* are *Mären* similar in plot.

BIBLIOGRAPHY

The text can be found in Friedrich Heinrich von der Hagen, ed., *Gesammtabenteuer,* II (1850, repr. 1961), 23–35, and in Heinrich Niewöhner (see below, 15–44). Studies include David Dalby, *Lexicon of the Mediaeval German Hunt* (1965), 210–213; Hanns Fischer, *Studien zur deutschen Märendichtung* (1968, 2nd ed. 1983), 403–404 and *passim;* Heinrich Niewöhner, *Der Sperber und verwandte mhd. Novellen* (1913, repr. 1970); Joachim Suchomski, *"Delectatio" und "Utilitas": Ein Beitrag zum Verständnis mittelaltlicher komischer Literatur* (1975), 194–195.

STEPHEN L. WAILES

[See also **Hartmann von Aue; Häslein, Das; Mären; Middle High German Literature; Walther von der Vogelweide.**]

SPERVOGEL AND HERGER, German poets of the twelfth century whose lively and vigorous epigrammatic commentary on human nature preceded Walther von der Vogelweide's *Spruchdichtung.* The primary sources for Spervogel and Herger are manuscripts *A, C,* and *J.* Ambiguity in the manuscripts regarding attribution of individual stanzas, however, has given rise to critical speculation, sometimes ingenious, that complicates the problem of identifying the two poets. Spervogel is generally considered to be a fictitious name, possibly derived from the word for sparrow. In manuscript *C,* for example, the poet is depicted with a spear from which several birds hang; the name appears also in his poetry (*Des Minnesangs Frühling,* 20.18). Some critics have suggested that the phrase *mîn geselle Spervogel* ("my companion Spervogel") refers to another poet. However, there is now general agreement that the poet meant himself and not another singer. While Spervogel may not have been his baptismal name, it seems to have been fairly common, probably as a nickname. Various associations may have made it especially attractive to traveling singers, among them the tradition of the sparrow as a bird of wisdom, an attribute that the poet may ascribe to himself, as in stanza 20.9.

The major disagreements over identification have centered on the second poet, since three names appear in his stanzas: Herger, Kerlinc, and Gebehart. The manuscripts, however, also include his work under Spervogel and Young Spervogel. Because of his rhymes and syntax, as well as his mention of the death of Walther von Hausen (25.21), which occurred about 1170, there is general agreement that Herger is the older of the two poets. At this point, however, complications begin. Some earlier critics suggested that Gebehart or Kerlinc was really the author. Others proposed Spervogel Anonymous, Spervogel II, or the Older Spervogel.

Manuscript *A,* the oldest of the major minnesong collections, contains twenty-six stanzas attributed to Spervogel and twenty-seven to Young Spervogel. Of the twenty-six under Spervogel's name, eleven are credited to him in *Des Minnesangs Frühling;* the remaining fifteen belong to Herger, as do thirteen of those listed in *A* under Young Spervogel. Herger is complete in *A.* Manuscript *C* contains all the stanzas that scholars believe are Spervogel's; and *J,* from the mid fourteenth century, has thirteen of Spervogel's stanzas. The most recent editors of

 SPERVOGEL AND HERGER

Des Minnesangs Frühling wisely decided toprint both manuscript transmissions of Spervogel, since C and J show different tendencies: J is explanatory and offers words and phrases intended to make more explicit and concrete those passages that in C seem to strive for a more poetic effect.

Herger was probably from the Rhine region, where he seems to have been active between 1150 and 1180; he may have been twenty to thirty years older than Spervogel. Although his work has been called the bourgeois lyric of the twelfth century, such a summation does not convey its variety. His poetry contains the first extant examples in German literature of the animal story, as well as other types of *Sprüche* that appear for the first time in German: the demand for support and the lament on personal poverty. He also offers religious lyrics as well as observations on life gleaned from his own seemingly difficult existence.

The scope of his poetry reflects Herger's apparently broad education. He knew the Germanic tales, as shown in his reference to Fruot, the Danish king legendary for his generosity (25.19–20). His religious poetry reveals knowledge of church teachings. The wolf fable could suggest familiarity with monastery animal fables.

Herger's poetry is arranged in five groups of five stanzas each (pentads) plus a triad and a single stanza; the manuscript arrangement probably reflects his original intent. Recent work has shown that the relationships among these stanzas are often closer and more subtle than earlier critics had believed; the failure to see these internal relationships may have been in part due to the controversies surrounding the characteristics of a *Spruch*. Unlike later writers in this genre, Herger was concerned not with the problems and politics of life at court but with the cares of daily life. He complains about the lot of the homeless poet who has neglected to provide himself with a home for the time when he might no longer be in favor with his patron (pentad II). In pentad IV he compares the lot of the redeemed Christian with that of the damned sinner. The first three stanzas of pentad III relate dealings with the notorious wolf, telling first of the foolish man who lets the wolf into his sheep pen and then of the wolf that goes to a monastery to repent its sins and thinks itself reformed until it is sent to guard the sheep.

In spite of the relatively small amount of Herger's poetry that has survived, his range is quite remarkable. The various song types display sure use of language on several levels of style—from the earthy and robust description of quarreling dogs (III.5) to the exalted language reminiscent of the Psalmist (VI.3).

In contrast with Herger, Spervogel wrote for a courtly audience that enjoyed poems about bravery in battle (20.25) and courtly ladies (24.1), as well as vigorous and pithy comments on human behavior couched in proverblike statements about animals (20.9, 21.5, 23.21), and general, ironic comments on the human condition (20.1, 21.21, 22.25). The absence of religious poetry also could point to Spervogel's preoccupation with court life. Just when he was active is unclear, but Walther's quotation of him, as well as his use of the older term *helde* instead of *ritter* for a noble warrior, probably would date him about 1180–1190, a decade or so before Walther became well known. His social standing may have been roughly that of his audience, since he seems to speak to them as equals (24.25), but he probably was not as well off as they were. Stanza 22.9 sharply bemoans the adverse effects of poverty on the poet's creative powers as well as on his social standing, and indicates a passing familiarity with impecuniousness. Recent critical work has confirmed this tentative conclusion. Otto Ludwig's analysis of Spervogel's use of the priamel, a form that unites various statements under a general observation, has shown that stanzas previously considered only didactic—such as 21.29, 21.13, and 21.5—contain a veiled request for support from his patron.

One of the services that Spervogel rendered and which he tactfully emphasized was that of counselor. A number of his stanzas stress the value of good counsel to a lord, noting that a wise adviser can save noble families from degeneration (24.25) and can ensure an honorable reputation to him who follows it (20.17). Spervogel often gives rather pointed advice to his courtly audience with images and comparisons drawn from daily life, as in stanza 23.21: A prudent man should not fill his ship too full; if a husband buys his wife too many luxurious and beautiful clothes, he may find there is an illegitimate child to be baptized. In 21.11 he states that a light in a strange man's hand is of little use to the blind man, and in 23.33–34 that when the straw with its wheat has filled the granary and the chest of the rich man, it becomes dung. Spervogel's wide range of themes and his pithily elegant use of language mark him as a worthy predecessor of Walther von der Vogelweide.

BIBLIOGRAPHY

Source. Hugo Moser and Helmut Tervooren, eds., *Des Minnesangs Frühling,* 2 vols. (1977).

Studies. Salomon Anholt, *Die sogenannten Spervogel sprüche und ihre Stellung in der älteren Spruchdichtung* (1937); Walter Blank, *Die kleine Heidelberger Liederhandschrift* (1972); Carl von Kraus, *Des Minnesangs Frühling: Untersuchungen* (1939); Martin Liechtenhan, *Die Strophengruppen Hergers im Urteil der Forschung* (1980); Otto Ludwig, "Die Priameln Spervogels," in *Beiträge zur Geschichte der deutschen Sprache und Literature,* **85** (1963), repr. in Hugo Moser, ed., *Mittelhochdeutsche Spruchdichtung* (1972); Hugo Moser, "Die Sprüche Hergers: Artzugehörigkeit und Gruppenbildung," in W. Foerster and K. H. Borck, eds., *Festschrift für Jost Trier zum 70. Geburtstag* (1964); Helmut Tervooren, "Doppelfassung bei Spervogel," in *Zeitschrift für deutsches Altertum und deutsche Literatur,* **99** (1970); Joachim Teschner, "Das bîspel in der mittelhochdeutschen Spruchdichtung des 12. und 13. Jahrhunderts" (Ph.D. diss., Bonn, 1970).

VICKIE ZIEGLER

[See also **Biblical Poetry, German; Chivalry; Courtly Love; Fables; German Literature: Lyric; Middle High German Literature; Minnesingers; Walther von der Vogelweide.**]

SPIERINC, CLAEYS (also Spirinc, Spierinck, or Clay Nicholas Spierinc) (*fl.* late fifteenth century), Flemish illustrator, illuminator, and calligrapher. He worked in Brussels, Ghent, and Amsterdam, as well as at the court of Duke Charles the Bold of Burgundy. The oldest extant example of his work (London, British Museum, Harley MS 2943) is a book of hours dated 1486. The book of hours at the Fitzwilliam Museum in Cambridge (MS James 136) is most characteristic of his style. Spierinc was foremost a calligrapher, as is evident in the stylistic treatment of his figures. His work is characterized by bold, incisive lines rendered at the expense of convincing pictorial space. It also demonstrates an interest in lavish decorative motifs and is exceptional in its attention to organic forms and to creating harmony between miniatures and border designs when compared with other works produced in the last years of the fifteenth century.

Jesus discoursing on the Law. Miniature by Claeys Spierinc from a book of hours dated 1486. London, British Museum, Harley MS 2943, fol. 127v. COURTESY OF THE TRUSTEES OF THE BRITISH LIBRARY

BIBLIOGRAPHY

Alexander Willem Byvanck, *La miniature dans les Pays-Bas septentrionaux* (1937), 105–108; Reginald Howard Wilenski, *Flemish Painters, 1430–1830,* 2 vols. (1960), I, 36–39.

JENNIFER E. JONES

[See also **Book of Hours; Manuscript Illumination, European.**]

SPINELLO ARETINO (**Spinello di Luca di Spinelli**) (*b. ca.* 1346–1410), painter, active in Florence from about 1373, and father of Parri Spinelli. Called a pupil of Agnolo Gaddi, Spinello in his art demonstrates affinities with Sienese painting, notably the works of Bartolo di Fredi and Barna da Siena. Numerous paintings and fresco cycles testify

Pope Alexander III entering Rome. Scene from the fresco cycle (1408–1410) of Spinello Aretino in the Palazzo Pubblico, Siena. BROGI 15071 / ART RESOURCE

to a long, active career, which included collaborations with Niccolò di Pietro Gerini and Lorenzo di Niccolò. Important surviving works include the restored fresco cycle, S. Miniato al Monte, Florence (*ca.* 1386–1387); the frescoes of the Camposanto in Pisa (*ca.* 1391–1392); the chapel of St. Catherine in Antella (*ca.* 1387–1388); and a cycle, the *Life of Alexander III,* in the Palazzo Pubblico, Siena (1408–1410), with the assistance of Parri.

Spinello's animated, vigorous style, which explores volume and pictorial depth while maintaining a decorative unity, forms an important transition between late Trecento and early Renaissance Florentine painting.

BIBLIOGRAPHY

Richard Fremantle, *Florentine Gothic Painters* (1975).

ADELHEID M. GEALT

[See also **Bartolo di Fredi; Barna da Siena; Fresco Painting; Gaddi, Agnolo; Lorenzo di Niccolò di Martino; Niccolò di Pietro Gerini.**]

SPIRITUAL LADDER. See **John Klimakos.**

SPOLIA (Latin, "spoils"; singular, *spolium*). The term refers to architectural remains, particularly Roman columns, capitals, and entablatures, incorporated in medieval buildings, and, by extension, to the reuse of materials in other mediums. Such reuse of ancient building parts was a common practice in the Middle Ages, especially in Italy.

GREGORY WHITTINGTON

[See also **Construction: Building Materials; Early Christian and Byzantine Architecture; Romanesque Architecture.**]

SPRUCHDICHTUNG. See **German Literature: Lyric.**

SQUARCIONE, FRANCESCO (1394/1397—*ca.* 1468), a Paduan painter whose place in Renaissance art in northern Italy has not been securely established. Squarcione's role as head of a workshop and his relationships with his notable pupils (Andrea Mantegna, *ca.* 1431–1506, among them) are of great interest for the history of art. Evidence suggests that he was well regarded as a master, although his hard-edged, eclectic style now appears uninspired.

A polyptych for Leon de Lazzara with the Penitent Jerome and other saints (1449–1452; Padua, Museo Civico) and a signed half-length *Madonna and Child* (Berlin-Dahlem, Staatliches Museen, Gemäldegalerie) form the core works of his oeuvre.

BIBLIOGRAPHY
Miklòs Boskovits, "Una ricerca su Francesco Squarcione," in *Paragone,* **28,** no. 325 (1977); Deborah Lipton, "Francesco Squarcione" (diss., New York Univ., 1974); Michelangelo Muraro, "Francesco Squarcione, pittore 'umanista,'" in *Da Giotto al Mantegna,* Lucio Grossato, ed. (1974), 68–74, cat. no. 80.

CAROL TALBERT PETERS

SQUINCH, a corbeling, usually a small arch or series of projecting arches or a half-conical niche, thrown diagonally across a corner of a square or rectangular space to support a round or polygonal superstructure. The squinch is common in the Byzantine and Islamic worlds, as well as in the West; it is used to carry domes, lanterns, crossing towers, and the like.

GREGORY WHITTINGTON

[See also **Dome (with illustration); Vault.**]

SQUIRE, ESQUIRE. In the twelfth century (the first that provides us with much evidence) the various words that we would translate as "squire" (Latin *armiger* or *scutifer*, Old French *escuier*, Occitan *escudier*) almost always meant a knight's personal servant. The squire's duties were manifold: literature of the period reveals squires serving their masters at table, carrying their messages, and running their errands. On campaign, squires stood watch, set up camp, and foraged for the host; but they do not seem to have fought on the battlefield. In war and peace alike, however, the squire's most important function was caring for his master's arms, his armor, and especially his horses. On the march, the squire rode one of his master's horses (the rouncy) and led the warhorse (*destrier*), which was too valuable to serve as the knight's usual mount.

Historians have traditionally depicted the squire as a youth of knightly birth whose service constituted a form of military apprenticeship that culminated in his own knighting. Late-twentieth-century scholarship has shown that this picture overestimates the squire's status, at least in the twelfth century. Most squires appearing in the literature of that era were professional servants performing their duties for pay; they had no claims to knighthood and need not have been young. In northern Italy, the gap in status between knights and their squires left its mark on the tenurial system. There a peasant of the highest rank might hold a squire's fief (*feudum scutiferi*) in return for maintenance of a horse and service to his master in the host. This arrangement clearly presupposes a permanent, indeed inheritable, distinction between knight and squire. Though young men aspiring to knighthood did serve a kind of apprenticeship, those undergoing it were seldom called squires until the thirteenth century. Evidence from southern France suggests a preference in the 1100's for the term *damoiseau* (Occitan: *donzel*; Latin: *domicellus*) as the word for a young nobleman, before and after knighting; it also reveals that the responsibilities of such a youth, though similar to those of a professional squire, emphasized personal attendance on the knight, and downplayed the less honorable and more onerous tasks of caring for horses and gear. Eventually, resistance to the use of the word "squire" to describe the gently born waned, and by 1300 the term's base connotation seems to have disappeared.

Meanwhile, the gradual restriction of knighthood to a smaller circle among the upper classes created new meanings for the term "squire" during the thirteenth century. As sons of knightly families came to postpone and even forgo their own dubbings, they required a title to distinguish themselves from their social inferiors. Perhaps because it emphasized their connection to the chivalric title they no longer consistently claimed, squire became one of the words used to denote a man of gentle birth who was not knighted. In the fourteenth century such squires gained the right to coats of arms, and by 1400, in England, they constituted a distinct grade of the lesser nobility below the knights but above mere gentlemen. Similarly, as the title of knight came to refer not to all armored cavalry, but only to an elite of the best-equipped, squire came into use in military documents as one term for the nonknightly heavy horseman.

BIBLIOGRAPHY
Relevant sources include Matthew Bennett, "The Status of the Squire: The Northern Evidence," and Linda M. Paterson, "The Occitan Squire in the Twelfth and Thirteenth Centuries," both in Christopher Harper-Bill and

Ruth Harvey, eds., *The Ideals and Practice of Medieval Knighthood: Papers from the First and Second Strawberry Hill Conferences* (1986); François Menant, "Les écuyers ("scutiferi"), vassaux paysans d'Italie du nord au XIIe siècle," in *Structures féodales et féodalisme dans l'Occident méditerranéen (X^e^–XIIIe siècles)* (1980); Nigel Saul, *Knights and Esquires: The Gloucestershire Gentry in the Fourteenth Century* (1981); S. T. H. Scoones, "Écuyer," in *AUMLA: Journal of the Australasian Languages and Literature Association,* **41** (1974).

DONALD F. FLEMING

[See also **Arms and Armor; Cavalry, European; Chivalry; Class Structure, Western; Knights and Knight Service; Nobility and Nobles.**]

ST. See **Saint.**

STAFF (**stave**), a line or lines used to notate musical pitch. The earliest methods of staff notation appeared in pedagogical manuals; but they were not adopted in practical compilations. Certain plainchant sources after about 1000 used heightening to indicate relative pitch. In the following century, Aquitanian manuscripts attempted greater prescriptiveness through their use of a drypoint line. Guido of Arezzo's influential *Aliae regulae* (*ca.* 1030) is the earliest treatise to advocate the use of lines (some of them colored) for alternate pitches. Although Guido did not specify the number of lines to be used, the four-line staff has been the standard for plainchant since the twelfth century.

Because of the wider range of multipart music, French polyphonic sources from the thirteenth century on adopted a five-line staff. With few exceptions, this became the standard in the Middle Ages and has remained so.

BIBLIOGRAPHY

David Hiley, "Staff," in *The New Grove Dictionary of Music and Musicians,* XVIII (1980), 54–55.

ARTHUR D. LEVINE

[See also **Guido of Arezzo; Music, Western European; Musical Notation, Western; Musical Treatises; Neume.**]

STAGECRAFT. See **Drama.**

STALACTITE VAULT. See **Vault.**

STANTIPES. See **Dance.**

STAR VAULT. See **Vault.**

STARKAÐR is an exceptional warrior and poet of Danish legend. Both his impressive martial feats and his poetry are recorded in two somewhat different versions in the thirteenth-century Danish chronicle *Gesta Danorum* by Saxo Grammaticus, who translates the poetry into Latin prose, and in *Gautreks saga,* an Old Icelandic *fornaldarsaga,* whose oldest manuscript dates from the fifteenth century.

Saxo portrays Starkaðr as the model traditional warrior, the defender of conservative standards of heroic behavior. His prodigious strength assures a career as a professional soldier; he fights loyally and bravely in the armies of many princes and in single combat against a number of the most formidable legendary warriors. Among Starkaðr's many professional attachments, Saxo stresses his relationship to the Danish king Fróði; he is made a retainer and serves Fróði and his son for many years. Later he becomes attached to King Olo, or Áli the Bold, and is bribed to murder him in his bath by the noblemen of the realm. Grieved by this deed and almost too aged to walk, Starkaðr longs for death. However, because he remains fearfully strong, he must finally pay someone to slay him with his own sword. In a final act of defiance, his severed head bites the ground as it falls.

The basic portrait drawn of Starkaðr by Saxo is confirmed by the account in *Gautreks saga,* although the saga focuses more on the hero's early years and specifically on his service with the Norwegian king Víkarr. This service ends tragically when Starkaðr is requested to sacrifice Víkarr to Odin (Óðinn). We learn of Starkaðr's special relationship to Odin and of the curious meeting between the warrior and the gods, in which Odin blesses him with long life, money and weapons, victory in every battle, and the art of poetry, while Thor (Þórr) counters with corresponding curses: that he shall commit three atrocious acts; that he shall never own property; that he shall be grievously wounded in every battle; and that he shall never remember a line of poetry he composes.

Of particular interest to scholars is Starkaðr's relationship to the giants and to the gods Odin and Thor. According to *Gautreks saga,* Starkaðr's grandfather, also named Starkaðr, was a giant who was killed by Thor. Saxo mentions tales about Starkaðr's giant ancestry but remains skeptical about their veracity. Because of his great strength and his role as the invincible protector of his friends against their opponents, Starkaðr has been seen by some as the sole example in the heroic legends of a Thor-hero. On the other hand, there are cogent arguments for linking him to Odin; chief among these are his exceptional talent as a poet and his physical appearance, which also seems to confirm his giant origins. Even in his youth he looked old and ugly. It is Odin who takes Starkaðr's side against Thor in *Gautreks saga.* Although Saxo alludes to the rumor that Starkaðr was born with an extraordinary number of arms and that Thor tore off four of these, giving him a more human contour, this tale may simply be another version of the story of Thor's battle with the giant Starkaðr as related in *Gautreks saga* and also by the tenth-century skald Vertliði Sumarliðason in his poem celebrating the deeds of Thor. If Starkaðr was a giant in the earliest tradition, it is clear that both Saxo and the author of *Gautreks saga* have humanized him. As a humanized giant known to legend as a great warrior and skillful poet, he could have served as the ideal literary model for certain giant-like human warriors and poets of the sagas, such as Egill Skallagrímsson and Grettir Ásmundarson.

BIBLIOGRAPHY

Marlene Ciklamini, "The Problem of Starkaðr," in *Scandinavian Studies,* 43 (1971); Georges Dumézil, *The Destiny of the Warrior,* Alf Hiltebeitel, trans. (1970), 82–95; Kaaren Grimstad, "The Giant as a Heroic Model: The Case of Egill and Starkaðr," in *Scandinavian Studies,* **48** (1976); Axel Olrik, *Danmarks Heltedigtning,* II (1910); Hermann Pálsson and Paul Edwards, trans., *Gautreks Saga and Other Medieval Tales* (1968); E. O. G. Turville-Petre, *Myth and Religion of the North* (1964), 205–211; Saxo Grammaticus, *History of the Danes,* Peter Fischer, trans., and Hilda E. Davidson, ed., I (1979), bks. 6–8.

KAAREN GRIMSTAD

[See also **Chronicles; Fornaldarsögur; Gautreks Saga Konungs; Odin; Saxo Grammaticus; Scandinavian Literature; Scandinavian Mythology; Thor.**]

STATIONS OF THE CROSS (also known as the Way of the Cross) is an exercise in Christian piety in which the participant centers his devotion on representations of specific scenes of Christ's Passion, from his being condemned to death to his entombment and even resurrection. Pious visits and pilgrimages to the actual or supposed sites of these events in Jerusalem began in patristic antiquity, the most celebrated account of which is by the fifth-century Spanish nun Egeria (*Itinerarium Egeriae*). These visits continued throughout the Middle Ages, although at times they were inhibited by the presence of the Muslims in Jerusalem. From the fourteenth century the Franciscans instituted the Holy Circulus, or devotional processions from site to site, and in the fifteenth century the stops along the route were described by the English pilgrim William Wey (1458/1462) as stations.

Devotion to Christ's passion began to spread from the twelfth century; together with the crusades this contributed heavily to the spiritual desire for the Stations of the Cross. Pictorial representation of the last events in Christ's life on earth were commonplace from the eleventh century on; and on the floors of such Gothic churches as those at Rheims, Amiens, and Chartres labyrinthine depictions served as a sort of ersatz for the pilgrim journey to Jerusalem.

By the fifteenth century, especially in the Low Countries, booklets, often illustrated, were made to assist the user in contemplating and participating privately in the Passion of Christ. Although the practice of building shrines or churches in which the events of Christ's life were remembered goes back at least to the fourth century in Jerusalem, it was not until the fifteenth century in the West that a series of shrines erected to commemorate the Passion specifically became commonplace and were used, together with the devotional booklets, to assist the participant in the Way of the Cross.

Freestanding Stations of the Cross go back at least to the early fifteenth century, such as those of the Dominican Álvarez, who set up in the monastery of Scala Coeli near Córdoba a series of seven chapels and oratories, each decorated with a painting representing a scene from the Passion. Other notable early examples are those of the Franciscan Philip of Aquila (1456), the so-called "Jerusalemberg" of Lübeck (1468), the famous relief stations of the "Seven Falls of Christ" by Adam Krafft in Nuremberg (1490/1505), and the Calvary of Varallo (1486–1491).

In the late Middle Ages the number and the specific scenes from the life of Christ varied greatly, from seven in German-speaking lands to as many as forty-three elsewhere. The process of standardizing these scenes to the fourteen known today began in the late sixteenth century.

BIBLIOGRAPHY
Ubald d'Alençon, *Le chemin de croix dans la religion, dans l'histoire et dans l'art* (1923); Karl A. Kneller, *Geschichte der Kreuzwegandacht von den Anfängen bis zur völligen Ausbildung* (1908); Albert Storme, *The Way of the Cross: A Historical Sketch,* Kiernan Dunlop, trans. (1976); Herbert Thurston, *The Stations of the Cross* (1906, repr. 1914).

ROGER E. REYNOLDS

[See also **Holy Week; Itinerarium Egeriae; Krafft, Adam; Passion Cycle.**]

STATUTE. Since the early sixteenth century the term "statute" has been used in England to describe a legislative act of the crown in parliament. Legislation—that is, the conscious and deliberate changing of legal rule by competent authority—obviously has a history that antedates written records. In England, however, "statute" is first applied to legislation made in the name of the king during the thirteenth century.

The earliest series of royal proclamations called a statute by the nineteenth-century editors of *The Statutes of the Realm* were those issued by a great council held at Merton in 1236. It is unclear why these "provisions," the term used in the document, came to qualify as the earliest statute, while like measures, before and after 1236, did not. In all probability the early-nineteenth-century editors of the official version of the statutes merely followed established tradition in this matter. What is clear is that there were many forms of legislation in thirteenth-century England—charter, writ, and ordinance, to name only three others—and that by the end of the thirteenth century "statute" is often used to describe pieces of this increasingly frequent legislation.

The acts designated by contemporaries as statutes were of the greatest variety, in terms of both form and content. The Statute of Gloucester (1278) was, its preface states, established and ordained by the king. The Statute of Mortmain (1279) was a royal writ addressed to the justices of common pleas. The Statute of Acton Burnell (1283) avows that the king and his council ordained and established this legislation. According to the Statute of Westminster II (1285), "The Lord King in his Parliament at Westminster . . . caused to be recited the many oppressions and defects of the laws, with a view to supplementing the statute made at Gloucester, and published these statutes following." In this last case, association of the king with the emerging institution of parliament in the enactmant of statutes foreshadows the future. Yet long after the end of the reign of Edward I (1307) it remained uncertain either that the term "statute" would come to signify the highest and most solemn form of legislation or that such legislation would be invariably linked to parliament.

The medieval style preferred three words when one would suffice, and thus any given enactment was likely to be said to contain statutes, ordinances, and provisions. Modern scholars have especially tried to distinguish "statute" from "ordinance" in medieval usage, but the terms seem to have been used interchangeably throughout the fourteenth century.

Whatever the name, these legislative acts reflected a struggle between king and parliament for control of legislative power. As early as the Statute of York (1322) it was being urged that common consent in parliament was essential in certain instances. Yet even by the end of the fourteenth century the notion that statutes needed parliamentary sanction had not been firmly established. However, the confirmation of nonparliamentary legislation by subsequent act of parliament, as in the 1388 enactment of the Statute of Laborers (1351), seems to indicate the growth of some such idea.

Even after 1400, two difficulties had to be surmounted before "statute" could become a technical term. First, it had to be reserved exclusively for enactments by the king and parliament. This seems a relatively simple matter, though synonyms long continued to be used together with "statute." Second, the content of legislation continued to escape the control of parliament because the final text of a statute was drafted by the crown, which frequently employed language that subverted the wishes of the assembly. Parliament, and the Commons in particular, remedied this by establishing control over both the initiation and the final wording of statutes during the first half of the fifteenth century.

Finally, there is the question of parliament's formal role in statute-making. The first half of the fifteenth century also saw the earliest use of the phrase "by authority of parliament" in the preamble to a statute. This recognized parliament as something more than a body that requests statutes: parliament as a body lends its authority to the statute. The fifteenth century also saw the Commons gain equal stature with the Lords. No longer are the Commons mere petitioners for statutes; they, like the Lords, advise and assent in respect to the statutes. Throughout all these changes the agreement of the king remained essential. Without royal assent nothing was possible.

The formula used by the first Tudor monarch in the enactment of statutes nicely sums up the complex constitutional development of the previous two centuries.

> The king our sovereign Lord Henry VII at his Parliament holden at Westminster . . . by the assent of the Lords spiritual and temporal and the commons in the said parliament assembled and by the authority of the same parliament hath done to be made certain statutes and ordinances in manner and form following.

BIBLIOGRAPHY

Sources. A. Luders *et al.*, eds., *The Statutes of the Realm,* I (1810). Many of the statutes are also available in David C. Douglas, ed., *English Historical Documents,* III–IV (1969).

Studies. Stanley B. Chrimes, *English Constitutional Ideas in the Fifteenth Century* (1936); W. S. Holdsworth, *Sources and Literature of English Law* (1925); Charles H. McIlwain, *The High Court of Parliament and Its Supremacy* (1910), and *Constitutionalism and the Changing World* (1939); F. W. Maitland, *The Constitutional History of England* (1908); Theodore F. T. Plucknett, *Statutes and Their Interpretation in the First Half of the Fourteenth Century* (1922), and *Legislation of Edward I* (1949); H. G. Richardson and G. O. Sayles, "The Early Statutes," in *Law Quarterly Review,* 50 (1934), and *The English Parliament in the Middle Ages* (1981).

T. A. SANDQUIST

[See also **Assize; Charter; Edward I of England; Law, English Common; Magna Carta; Mortmain; Ordinance; Parliament; Westminster, Statutes of.**]

STAVE. See **Staff.**

STAVE CHURCH. See **Church, Types of.**

STEELMAKING. Steel is an alloy of iron with carbon, and the quality of the steel is determined in large measure by the amount of carbon present. The near absence of carbon yields a soft, malleable, or "wrought" iron; the presence of more than about 2 percent carbon produces the very hard, but also very brittle, "cast" iron. Cast iron, furthermore, becomes fluid if heated sufficiently, and it can therefore be cast in a mold; wrought iron, however, can be shaped easily, but never becomes really fluid. Steel is intermediate in the carbon-iron spectrum between these two extremes. It normally has from 0.15 to 1.5 percent carbon.

However, the qualities that distinguish steel from both wrought and cast iron—its tensile strength, its resistance to blows, and its ability to take and to retain a sharp cutting edge—are not due only to the proportion of carbon present. They also depend on the processes of tempering and annealing, by which the crystalline structure of the metal is given a particular form. The very sophisticated art of steelmaking consists of imparting to a mass of iron these chemical and physical properties.

The actual nature of the changes involved in steelmaking became known only in the nineteenth century, as a result of metallurgical research. As late as 1722, when Réaumur published his treatise on *L'art de convertir le fer forgé en acier* (The art of converting forged iron into steel), knowledge of the changes brought about in the metal was scanty, and his explanations, though recommending themselves to his contemporaries, ceased a generation or two later to be tenable.

In the absence of scientific knowledge, methods of steelmaking were discovered empirically. Essential processes were not readily distinguished from the incidental and irrelevant, and metallurgy as a whole had the air more of magic than of science. Steelmaking was a kind of alchemy, and the smith himself was enveloped in a kind of mystique.

Iron was in ancient and medieval times smelted from its ore on a hearth or in a low furnace. It came out as a spongy mass or "bloom," containing scoriae as well as carbon and chemical impurities. Its qualities would depend in part on the ore used, in part on the temperature at which it had been smelted. A high temperature permitted the metal to absorb more carbon, though it is improbable that

Blacksmith shop with smelting furnace. Drawing from a 14th-century Franco-Flemish treatise (MS Sloane 3983, fol. 5r) on astronomy. COURTESY OF THE TRUSTEES OF THE BRITISH LIBRARY

an iron of the quality of true cast iron could have been made in a hearth or low furnace. (There is, nevertheless, a passage in Pausanias which suggests that cast iron was occasionally produced in classical times.) The bloom of metal from the hearth would more likely be low in carbon, and repeated heating on the hearth under a jet of air would tend to oxidize and remove much of the carbon that had been absorbed from the fuel.

The other factor controlling the quality of the metal was the nature of the ore itself. Some ores—notably those of Styria in the eastern Alps and of the area around Siegen in western Germany—contained small amounts of manganese. The manganese not only served to "cleanse" the metal of deleterious matter such as sulfur, but also, alloyed with the iron, improved its quality as a steelmaking material. It was the quality of the ore as much as the empirical skills of the ironworkers that endowed certain steels with such high qualities during the Middle Ages. Armor that dented and swords that bent had probably been made from a steel too low in carbon, while the weapon that shattered on impact had certainly too high a carbon content.

The methods of adjusting the carbon content of iron and of tempering tools and weapons must have been discovered at an early date. The soft iron taken from the hearth showed little improvement over bronze as a material for tools or weapons. Only steel could have been a serviceable material for armor plate and cutting tools, though a softer iron would have been used for the wire from which chain mail was made. It was steel, not iron, that displaced bronze in the last centuries before Christ.

Broadly speaking, two methods of making steel were in use during the Middle Ages. The first, and probably the older, was the so-called "natural" process. It consisted in so adjusting the bellows on the smelting hearth that a metal with the requisite carbon content was produced. Only the best ores could be made to yield a "natural" steel in this way, but among them were those of Eisenerz, in Styria.

The other process consisted in producing a low-carbon or soft iron and then recarburizing it to the desired extent. This became by far the most important method of making steel during the Middle Ages. At its simplest it was a "cementation" or case-hardening process. Theophilus thus described it in the twelfth century in his account of the making of a steel file:

> Burn the horn of an ox in the fire and scrape it. Mix with it a third part of salt and grind it vigorously. Then put the file into the fire and, when it is red hot, sprinkle this composition over it on every side. When the coals are strongly blazing, open them up and hastily blow all around so that the hardening does not

diminish. Immediately take out the file and quench it evenly in water. (Hawthorne, trans.)

The horn of an ox was merely part of the magic; charcoal would have served as well. The metal absorbed enough carbon at the surface (case-hardening) to give it the hard quality expected of a file. The inside of the file, however, would have consisted of a much softer metal, and the ability of the file to resist a blow would not have been great. For weapons, cutting tools, and armor, a metal of more even quality and texture was needed, and this could be obtained only by repeated forging.

A third method obtained steel from high-carbon, or "pig," iron, by oxidizing and removing much of its carbon. This method was used in the Weald of England in the sixteenth century, but it is unlikely to have been important very much earlier, because the blast furnace, which yields a high-carbon iron, had not yet been invented.

At a later date it was the practice to produce steel of even quality by melting it down in sealed crucibles. There is little direct evidence that this technically very demanding process was used in medieval Europe. Crucible steel was, however, produced in India at a very early date, and, as wootz steel, was exported to Persia and the Middle East. There it was used in the manufacture of the swords marketed in Damascus. These owed their very high reputation not only to the quality of the metal used in their manufacture, but also to the process of welding together thin strips of crucible steel. This produced a streaked, "watered," or "damascened" appearance. A similar welding process was used by the Moors in Spain and was probably derived from the Middle East. This Spanish steel was well known in the weapons of Toledo.

The quality of medieval steel owed much to the tempering and annealing to which it had been subjected. As iron is heated, its crystalline structure changes. If the hot metal is then plunged into cold water, it retains this new crystalline structure, which becomes "frozen." This process of heating and then "quenching" in cold water is known as tempering. The character of the steel depends in part on the temperature at which it has been tempered. Such a steel is hard, but sometimes also brittle. The brittleness can be remedied by annealing—that is, by reheating the metal and allowing it to cool slowly.

Both tempering and annealing were used by medieval steelmakers. The causes of the physical changes that take place in the metal are now known through microscopic examination; these causes were unknown in the Middle Ages. One can only guess at the amount of trial-and-error experimentation that led to the development of the steelmaking processes. It is easy to see how a process could have been "lost" and then rediscovered. It must be noted, furthermore, that a process developed for an iron made from one particular ore might be quite ineffective for an iron derived from another.

Evidence from crystallographic examination of surviving Roman tools and weapons shows that recarburization and tempering and annealing processes were practiced, in classical times, though not always with complete success. These techniques continued to be used during the early Middle Ages. The Vikings, for example, appear to have mastered them, and they were widely used in Merovingian and Carolingian France. By the twelfth century, iron was being made in many parts of Europe, and, since soft iron had only a limited usefulness, it follows that a considerable part of this iron must have been used to make steel by a recarburization process. One can only estimate the amount of iron and steel produced. A hearth is unlikely to have made more than two or three tons of metal a year. There were hundreds of hearths, but their aggregate production remained small. Styria, one of the most noted of all European steelmaking areas, probably made no more than 2,000 tons a year during the early fourteenth century, its period of greatest prosperity. Great Britain probably produced less than 1,000 tons a year, only part of which would have been converted to steel. Other areas that produced an iron regarded as suitable for "steeling" were the Bilbao region of northern Spain, the lower Rhineland (especially the district around Siegen), central Sweden, and the Alps of northern Italy. Osmund iron from Sweden was imported into England by the merchants of the Hanseatic League, and much of it was probably converted into steel after import. However, the Steelyard, the London headquarters of the League, derived its name not from the commodity which it certainly handled, but rather from the steel balance used for weighing goods.

Steel seems generally to have been made in rural areas, owing to the large quantities of charcoal used, but it was fabricated into armor, weapons, and tools largely in the cities, where the armorers and swordsmiths sometimes formed important and powerful guilds.

Steel was transported either in small ingots (*Stahl-*

kuchen, or steel cake) or in bundles (or garbs) of forged strips. (There is evidence in furnace accounts of the sixteenth century of the use of barrels and "firkins" for packing and transporting these small strips of steel.) Rhineland steel was shipped by merchants of Cologne and Soest and other towns of the region to consuming centers, of which London and Paris must have been among the more important, and Styrian steel helped to supply the armorers of northern Italy.

Steel was an expensive commodity, and a "steel cake" fetched more than ten pence in the early fourteenth century. In consequence it was used sparingly. A technique was even developed of welding a steel edge on to an iron tool or weapon, so that its sharpness could be maintained.

Steel of poorer quality was used for arrow tips, horseshoes, plowshares and coulters, and the tires of wooden wheels, and for the fittings of crossbows and of other war machines. Such steel was produced very widely. In England it was made in the Weald to the south of London and in the Forest of Dean, where the king controlled an iron-smelting and steelmaking industry, from which his castles were supplied with arrows and other weaponry.

BIBLIOGRAPHY

General. A useful, but not exhaustive, guide to the literature is Peter M. Molloy, *The History of Metal Mining and Metallurgy: An Annotated Bibliography* (1986).

Sources. The medieval treatise by Theophilus on metallurgy and other practical arts is of great interest. There are two modern English translations: C. R. Dodwell, trans., *Theophilus* (1961); John G. Hawthorne and Cyril S. Smith, trans., *Theophilus on Divers Arts,* 2nd ed. (1979).

Treatises from the early modern period are also useful. For a selection of English translations, see Cyril S. Smith, ed., *Sources for the History of the Science of Steel, 1532–1786* (1968); see also Georgius Agricola, *De re metallica,* Herbert C. and Lou H. Hoover, trans. (1912); Martin Lister, "The Manner of Making Steel, and Its Temper," in *Philosophical Transactions,* **17** (1693), 865–870; Anneliese G. Sisco and Cyril S. Smith, ed. and trans., *Réaumur's Memoirs on Steel and Iron* (1956); Cyril S. Smith and Martha T. Gnudi, trans., *The Pirotechnia of Vannoccio Biringuccio* (1942); Hermann W. Williams, Jr., trans., "A Sixteenth-century German Treatise, *Von Stahel und Eysen,*" in *Technical Studies in the Field of the Fine Arts,* **4** (1935).

The financial accounts of an early modern metallurgical enterprise are available in D. W. Crossley, ed., *Sidney Ironworks Accounts, 1541–1573* (1975).

Studies. Leslie Aitchison, *A History of Metals,* 2 vols. (1960); Kenneth C. Barraclough, *Steelmaking Before Bessemer,* 2 vols. (1984); Ludwig Beck, *Die Geschichte des Eisens,* 5 vols. (1884–1903); R. J. Forbes, *Studies in Ancient Technology,* 2nd ed., VIII (1971) and IX (1972), and "Extracting, Smelting, and Alloying," in Charles Singer *et al.,* eds., *A History of Technology,* I (1954), and "Metallurgy," *ibid.,* II (1956); Rhys Jenkins, "Notes on the Early History of Steel Making in England," in *Transactions of the Newcomen Society,* **3** (1924); John U. Nef, "Mining and Metallurgy in Medieval Civilization," in M. Postan and E. E. Rich, eds., *The Cambridge Economic History of Europe,* II (1952); H. R. Schubert, *History of the British Iron and Steel Industry* (1957).

Archaeology. There is a growing archaeological literature. See, for instance, David Crossley, *The Bewl Valley Ironworks, Kent, c. 1300–1730* (1975); Jaap Ypey, "Au sujet des armes avec damas soudé en Europe," in *Archéologie médiévale,* **11** (1981).

NORMAN J. G. POUNDS

[See also **Arms and Armor; Bells; Bronze and Brass; Cannon; Charcoal; Clocks and Reckoning of Time; Coal, Mining and Use of; Hanseatic League; Metallurgy; Metalworkers; Mining; Swords and Daggers; Technology, Western; Theophilus; Tools, Agricultural.**]

STEFAN LAZAREVIĆ (*r.* 1389–1427), ruler of Serbia, inherited the Serbian throne as a minor (his mother, Milica, was regent) after his father, Prince Lazar, was killed at Kosovo (1389). Opposed by Hungary, the Ottomans, and possibly Vuk Branković (a prominent Serbian noble), Milica accepted Ottoman suzerainty. Stefan maintained this policy, developing close relations with Sultan Bāyazīd I (1389–1402), which enabled him to gain greater control over the Serbian nobility. He led Serbian troops in support of Bāyazīd I at the battles of Rovine (1395), Nicopolis (1396), and Ankara (1402). After Timur (Tamerlane) defeated and captured Bāyazīd at Ankara, Stefan shed Ottoman vassalage. In Constantinople, en route home, the Byzantine emperor granted him the title "despot."

Opposed by his nephew George Branković and having tense relations with Bāyazīd's son Suleyman, who then controlled Ottoman Europe in the Ottoman civil war following the Ankara defeat among the brothers Suleyman, Musa, and Mehmed, Stefan became a vassal of Hungary's King Sigismund, who awarded Stefan the Mačva banate and Beograd for life. With Sigismund's aid he concluded satisfactory truces with his two opponents. In

1409–1410, he briefly lost some southern lands to his brother Vuk, whom Suleyman supported; however, when Musa killed Vuk, Stefan regained these lands. Sigismund awarded Stefan in 1411 the rich Bosnian mining town of Srebrnica. Stefan enjoyed good relations with Sultan Mehmed I after he emerged the victor from the Ottoman civil war in 1413. Mehmed awarded Stefan considerable territory between Niš and Sofia.

In 1421 Balša Balšić of Zeta died without sons; he left his lands to Stefan. Owing to Venetian action, Stefan was able to obtain only part of Zeta, including Bar and Budva; Serbia again reached the Adriatic. In 1426 a council at Srebrnica declared, since Stefan had no sons, his nephew George Branković heir. At Tati this decision and Serbia's vassalage to Hungary was confirmed by Sigismund. The Tati meeting disturbed Sultan Murad II, who attacked Serbia; Stefan made peace with him. He then defended Srebrnica from a Bosnian attack. He died in July 1427.

Stefan built several monasteries, including Manasija. A literary figure, he executed translations from the Greek as well as original compositions. Konstantin Filozof wrote his biography.

JOHN V. A. FINE, JR.

[See also **Bāyazīd I; Lazar Hrebeljanović; Ottomans; Serbia.**]

STEFAN NEMANJA (*r. ca.* 1168–1196), Grand *župan* of Raška (Serbia). Four brothers, led by Grand *Župan* Tihomir, the eldest, assumed leadership of the Serbian lands, probably through Byzantine machinations, between 1166 and 1168. Tihomir was soon overthrown and eventually killed in battle by his younger brother Stefan Nemanja. The three remaining brothers (Nemanja, Miroslav, and Stracimir) divided their territory; Nemanja held Raška and the Grand *Župan*'s title. A Byzantine attack forced Nemanja into submission in 1172. He remained a loyal Byzantine vassal until Emperor Manuel I's death in 1180. In the 1180's Nemanja acquired Zeta (Duklja), assigning it to his eldest son, Vukan. He also expanded to the southeast. In 1190 the Byzantines defeated him, but recognized Serbia's independence and allowed Nemanja to retain his acquisitions of Leskovac, Vranje, the Kosovo, Zeta, and part of northern Albania. He abdicated in 1196. His second son, Stefan, succeeded.

Becoming a monk, taking the name Simeon, Nemanja first resided at Studenica, the great monastery he had built. He then moved to Mt. Athos, where the Byzantine emperor, Alexios III, granted him for the Serbs the dilapidated monastery of Hilandar (Khilendar). Nemanja and his son Sava made Hilandar into a major monastery, which throughout the Middle Ages remained a leading Serbian cultural center. Soon after his death, Nemanja was canonized. His sons Sava and Stefan wrote biographies of him. The dynasty he founded ruled Serbia until 1371.

JOHN V. A. FINE, JR.

[See also **Sava, St.; Serbia; Stefan Prvovenčani.**]

STEFAN PRVOVENČANI (the First-crowned, *r.* 1196–1227). Stefan became ruler of Serbia (Raška) when his father, Stefan Nemanja, abdicated in 1196. He was soon attacked by his elder brother, Vukan, holder of Zeta (Duklja). In 1202 or 1203 Vukan drove Stefan from his lands. Within a year, possibly with Bulgarian aid, Stefan regained his throne. Fighting continued until their brother Sava mediated peace in 1208. However, war soon resumed, continuing sporadically under Vukan's son and successor, George, until Stefan annexed Zeta in about 1216.

In 1214 Stefan repelled a joint Bulgarian-Latin invasion of Serbia and also an attack by Michael I of Epiros into Zeta. This permanently stopped Epirote expansion at Serbia's expense. In 1217 he was crowned Serbia's first king by a papal legate. The flirtation with Rome was unpopular with many of his subjects and with the church organization; it was to be short-lasting. In 1219 his brother Sava won Nicaea's recognition for an independent Serbian church. Stefan built the monastery Žiča, the first seat of the autocephalous Serbian archbishop. At Žiča, a church council was held in 1221 which proclaimed a translation of the Byzantine Nomocanon the law of the Serbian church. Stefan wrote a biography of his father, Nemanja (St. Simeon). He died in 1227, to be succeeded by his son, Radoslav (1227–1234). Two other sons followed on the throne: Vladislav (1234–1243) and Uroš I (1243–1276).

JOHN V. A. FINE, JR.

[See also **Sava, St.; Serbia.**]

STEFAN TOMAŠ (*r.* 1443–1461), king of Bosnia. A son of King Ostoja (*r.* 1398–1404, 1409–1418), Stefan Tomaš became king of Bosnia in 1443 after Tvrtko II died. Stefan Vukčić of what is now Hercegovina refused to recognize him. War broke out between them, lasting from 1443 to 1446, when Stefan Tomaš after a divorce married Stefan Vukčić's daughter, Katarina. The pope, having already recognized him as king, announced in 1446 that Stefan Tomaš had abandoned the Bosnian church for Catholicism. Under Stefan Tomaš Catholicism made considerable progress. He built Catholic churches and many Bosnians accepted the Catholic faith.

Bosnia in this period suffered periodic Ottoman raids and lost much of its eastern territory, including Vrhbosna (Sarajevo) in 1451. Ottoman raids became particularly grave after 1456. Stefan Tomaš fought with Serbia (1448–1450) over Srebrnica, a rich mining town. In 1458, right after Despot Lazar Branković of Serbia died, Bosnia seized eleven towns along the Drina. To make peace Stefan Tomaš' son Stefan Tomašević married the late despot's daughter, receiving Smederevo as her dowry. In 1459 the Turks conquered Smederevo. Faced with the Turkish threat, Stefan Tomaš, hoping for Western aid, yielded to papal pressure and in 1459–1460 gave Bosnian church clerics the choice of converting to Catholicism or exile. Most agreed to convert. The king seized much Bosnian church land. Stefan Tomaš died in July 1461.

JOHN V. A. FINE, JR.

[See also **Bosnia; Bosnian Church; Serbia.**]

STEFAN TOMAŠEVIĆ (*r.* 1461–1463), king of Bosnia. Stefan Tomašević married Jelena (who took the name Maria), daughter of Despot Lazar Branković of Serbia. He received Smederevo in 1459 as her dowry and probably the title of despot. However, he failed to adequately defend Smederevo and the Turks conquered it that same year. When his father, King Stefan Tomaš, died in July 1461, he became king of Bosnia. A papal legate crowned him in November 1461. His close ties with the papacy were a contributing cause of the Ottoman invasion of 1463, which conquered Bosnia. Stefan Tomašević—Bosnia's last king—was captured by the Turks at Ključ and beheaded at Jajce.

JOHN V. A. FINE, JR.

[See also **Bosnia; Serbia.**]

STEFAN UROŠ II MILUTIN (*r.* 1282–1321), ruler of Serbia. Milutin, the second son of King Uroš I (1243–1276), acquired the Serbian (Raškan) throne at an assembly of nobles at Deževo in 1282, which deposed (allegedly for reasons of health but more likely for political reasons) his elder brother Dragutin (1276–1282). Dragutin retained an appanage centered in the mining town Rudnik; Dragutin's son Vladislav was proclaimed heir to the throne. In 1284 Dragutin's father-in-law, the Hungarian king, granted him a principality to the north of Raška along the Sava and Danube rivers. Milutin, as part of Charles of Anjou's coalition against Byzantium, in 1282 took Skopje, which became his main residence.

During the next seventeen years Milutin warred on two fronts: (1) In the north, he supported Dragutin against the Bulgarian state of Vidin, leading to gains for Dragutin. This caused difficulties with the Nogaj Tatars (Vidin's suzerains), with whom Milutin was forced in the mid 1290's to conclude a treaty by which his eldest son, Stefan Dečanski, had to become a Tatar hostage. Troubles with the Nogajs ended after the Golden Horde destroyed them in 1299. (2) In the south against Byzantium, Milutin carried out a series of campaigns that conquered northern Macedonia. His gains were recognized in a 1299 Byzantine-Serbian treaty by which Milutin married Simonida, the daughter of Andronikos II. It was his fourth marriage. The frontier with Byzantium was established: Ohrid (Ochrid), Prilep, Štip, and Strumica became the Byzantine border fortresses.

In 1299, after the Nogajs' fall, Dečanski escaped home, receiving Zeta as an appanage. Dragutin probably believed this threatened Vladislav's succession. Many nobles, probably opposed to Milutin's peace with Byzantium, supported Dragutin. War followed between the two brothers, beginning in 1301 or 1302 and lasting, presumably sporadically, until a treaty in 1312 restored prewar conditions. In 1314, probably incited by nobles in Zeta, Dečanski revolted. He was defeated by Milutin, allegedly blinded, and exiled until 1320 to

STEFAN UROŠ IV DUŠAN

Constantinople. When Dragutin died in 1316, Milutin absorbed Dragutin's Serbian lands and arrested Vladislav. His state still was not tranquil. Various nobles in his northern Albanian lands revolted in 1318. Disorders continued until his death in October 1321, when civil war erupted among his sons Constantine and Dečanski and his nephew Vladislav.

Milutin supported mining, which provided cash for mercenaries to balance the independent-minded nobility. He was the first Serbian ruler to coin money. He had close ties with the church, which actively supported him in his war against Dragutin. Simonida's presence led to increased byzantinization (charter forms, titles, and so on) at the Serbian court. Milutin also initiated *pronoia*s—the Byzantine land-for-service system—in Serbia.

JOHN V. A. FINE, JR.

[See also **Bulgaria; Serbia.**]

STEFAN UROŠ IV DUŠAN (*r.* 1331–1355), ruler of Serbia. Stefan Dušan, the eldest son of Stefan Dečanski (1321–1331), received the title "young king" in 1322; through most of his father's reign he administered Zeta. In 1331, according to biased sources, Dečanski's advisers convinced him to deprive Dušan of succession. Dušan was persuaded to revolt by the Zeta nobles. In the ensuing battles Dečanski was captured and imprisoned. Dušan was crowned king in September 1331. The nobles, alienated by Dečanski's failure to follow up the Velbužd victory (1330) and attack Byzantium to acquire new lands to the south, willingly supported Dušan. They also seem to have dominated him early in his reign. He was powerless to prevent his father's murder in November 1331.

In late 1331 he made peace with the new Bulgarian regime, which had ousted his aunt, Anna, from power, and sealed it by marrying Tsar John Alexander's sister, Jelena. Good relations with Bulgaria continued throughout his reign. In 1332 he suppressed a separatist revolt in Zeta. In 1334, by supporting a Byzantine rebel, he acquired Ohrid (Ochrid), Prilep, and Strumica. A treaty with Byzantium (1335), recognizing these gains, freed his troops to successfully repel a Hungarian invasion. Civil war erupted in Byzantium in 1341 between John Kantakuzenos and a regency. Dušan took advantage of it, first by supporting Kantakuzenos and later the regency, to gain: the remainder of Macedonia and Albania (1344), Serres, Drama, and the Chalcidic Peninsula, including Mt. Athos (1345), and Epiros and Thessaly (1347–1348). He assigned the newly conquered regions to relatives or commanders to administer. Thus he doubled his state's size. However, his strength should not be exaggerated. He acquired these lands during a Byzantine civil war when few troops could defend them and he did it all through sieges without a single open-field battle.

In 1346 a great council at Skopje (attended by leaders from Mt. Athos, the Bulgarian [Trnovo] patriarch and the archbishop of Ohrid) raised the Serbian archbishop to patriarch. The new patriarch then crowned Dušan emperor (tsar) of the Serbs and Greeks. (The patriarch of Constantinople responded by excommunicating Dušan and the Serbian patriarch in 1351.) At his coronation, his son Uroš was crowned king and nominally given the Serb lands to rule. Dušan the emperor—who in fact ruled the whole state—had particular responsibility for "Romania," the Greek lands. He allowed them to retain Greek as their official language and most of their existing laws and institutions. He even left many Greeks as local officials and holders of *pronoia*s (fiefs). The Serbian lands received Serbia's first public law code, which Dušan promulgated at an assembly in 1349. Further articles were issued at a second council (1353/1354). With success, Dušan became ambitious to capture Constantinople and become *the* emperor. Action was delayed to repel another Hungarian invasion (1354). Then, while still dreaming of his attack, Dušan died of a stroke, aged forty-seven, in December 1355.

Though Dušan rose from a semi-puppet of the aristocrats to become their master, he never changed the structure of his state. He eventually obtained obedience from the nobles through their interest in booty from his campaigns plus reliance upon foreign (especially German) mercenaries. His failure to establish centralized institutions and his permitting the nobles to retain great authority in their counties meant the basis for separatism remained; his empire disintegrated piecemeal during the reign of his son and successor, Uroš V (1356–1371).

JOHN V. A. FINE, JR.

[See also **Bulgaria; Byzantine Empire: History; Serbia.**]

STEFAN VUKČIĆ KOSAČA (1435–1466), Bosnian noble. Stefan Vukčić in 1435 inherited from his uncle, Sandalj Hranić, a semi-independent principality within the Bosnian kingdom. It extended from the Neretva mouth north to Konjic and east to the Drina and Lim rivers. Soon Stefan extended his authority south to Nikšić and acquired most of the present-day Montenegrin coast. He warred against Radoslav Pavlović, 1435–1439, and against Bosnia's king, Stefan Tomaš, 1443–1446. The king married Stefan's daughter, Katarina, in 1446 to end that war. Stefan supported Serbia against Bosnia in their 1448–1450 war. During it (in 1448) he declared his independence from Bosnia by dropping his title *vojvoda* of Bosnia and assuming that of *herceg* of Hum and the Coast. In 1449 he changed this to *herceg* of St. Sava after the famous Serbian saint whose relics rested in his monastery, Mileševo. From this title his principality became known as Hercegovina, a name surviving to the present.

Needing money for Ottoman tribute and obtaining insufficient revenue from customs and tolls, Stefan sought to make Novi (Hercegnovi) a major port. He imported weavers and by marketing salt he challenged Dubrovnik's salt monopoly. In protest Dubrovnik banned its merchants from Hercegovina. This quarrel turned into war (1451–1454). Various Bosnians (including the king) and the *herceg*'s son Vladislav supported Dubrovnik; Venice supported Stefan. Peace, restoring matters to their prewar state, was concluded with Vladislav in 1453 and Dubrovnik in 1454.

In 1463 the Ottomans invaded, conquering Bosnia and occupying most of Hercegovina. When this campaign was over, the *herceg*, who had withdrawn with his army to the coast, returned, ousting the Ottoman garrisons left behind. For assisting them to recover western Bosnia, the Hungarians granted him the counties of Krajina and Završje. Venice, feeling unable to defend from the Turks its possessions at the Neretva mouth, granted these to Stefan. During the next two years the Turks regained most of Hercegovina, but Stefan still retained a small coastal holding at his death in 1466. Stefan belonged to the Bosnian church, but tolerated the Catholic and Orthodox faiths.

BIBLIOGRAPHY

S. Ćirković, *Stefan Vukčić-Kosača i njegovo doba* (1964).

JOHN V. A. FINE, JR.

[See also **Bosnia; Dubrovnik.**]

STEINMAR. The author of the fourteen songs found under the name Her Steinmar in the Manesse Manuscript is usually identified with a Berthold Steinmar, who appears between 1251 and 1294 in documents drawn up at or near Klingnau in northern Switzerland. However, the evidence that connects the poet to Berthold is flimsy, and the poems may well belong to someone else. In any event, echoes of Ulrich von Liechtenstein and Tannhäuser in his verse, and traces of one of his songs in several works by Johannes Hadlaub, indicate that the Steinmar of the manuscript composed during the second half of the thirteenth century.

Although he uses the timeworn framework and motifs of the traditional minnesong, Steinmar revitalizes them with fresh, often realistic language. His lady is like a rose in the morning dew; she raises his spirits like the falcon's wings that drive it skyward; she fills him with the joy of a soul leaving purgatory. Some of the similes are so noncourtly and exaggerated that they have the effect of parody, although this was not Steinmar's chief aim. The singer's heart leaps about like a pig in a sack and struggles like a dragon to break out of his breast and go to his lady; to escape the pangs of love, he dives like a swimming duck that is attacked by falcons; his lament could awaken the compassion of an anvil. Most of the songs have nature introductions, one of which is unmatched for vivid expression: the singer wishes to become green with the grain of the field, bloom with the flowers, sing with the birds, send forth leaves with the trees, and condense into drops with the dew.

In four of the works, a peasant girl is the subject instead of a highborn lady, with results that are humorous without being grotesque or absurd. The dawn song (*tageliet*) that describes the awakening of the peasant lovers by the herdsman's call is a charming composition that does not need the parody to sustain it. And in two other songs, the simple heroine who goes barefoot in the cold evokes sympathy as well as a smile when she refuses to admit a lover to her bed unless he can give her a pair of shoes. She is quite different from Neidhart von Reuental's coarse villagers. One noncourtly work is a harvest song (*Herbstlied*), believed to be the first of its kind in German. It tells the story of a singer whose lady does not reward him, and so he decides to leave her and sing the praises of Harvest. He then recounts the gargantuan feats of eating and drinking that he will perform in honor of his new patron. This song was apparently the model for later harvest songs and may have inspired many of the drinking and glutton songs of the late Middle Ages.

Other significant features of Steinmar's verse include refrains (which sometimes vary from stanza to stanza), appeals to his listeners, and, in one poem, highly complex metrical and rhyme patterns. In an age of virtuosity, Steinmar was not exceptional as a craftsman, but none of his contemporaries had his talent for making characters and situations both lifelike and interesting.

BIBLIOGRAPHY

The texts of Steinmar's verse and a survey of the early secondary literature appear in Karl Bartsch, ed., *Die Schweizer Minnesänger* (1886, repr. 1964), CVI–CXXI, 170–188. Recent studies include Karl Stackmann, "Herr Steinmar, Berthold," in Karl Langosch, ed., *Die deutsche Literatur des Mittelalters: Verfasserlexikon,* IV (1953), 267–271; Helmut de Boor, *Die deutsche Literatur im späten Mittelalter: Zerfall und Neubeginn, 1250–1350* (1962), 338–340, 345; Diether Krywalski, "Untersuchungen zu Leben und literaturgeschichtlicher Stellung des Minnesängers Steinmar" (Ph.D. diss., Munich, 1966); Eckehard Simon, "Literary Affinities of Steinmar's *Herbstlied* and the Songs of Colin Muset," in *Modern Language Notes,* **84** (1969).

J. WESLEY THOMAS

[See also **German Literature: Lyric; Johannes Hadlaub; Middle High German Literature; Minnesingers; Neidhart von Reuental; Tannhäuser; Ulrich von Liechtenstein.**]

STEPʿANOS ASOŁIK TARŌNECʿI (Stephen of Tarōn) (*fl.* late tenth–early eleventh centuries), Armenian historian, the author of a *Universal History,* which he was commissioned to write at the order of the Armenian katʿołikos Sargis (992–1019). The *History* is composed of three books: the first covers the period from the time of the first man to that of the conversion of the Armenians to Christianity; the second book contains the history of Christian Armenia until the establishment of the Bagratid kingdom in 884; the third book, which is the history of Bagratid Armenia, ends with the year 1004. For the period from 930 to 1004 (book III, chaps. 8–48), Asołik is exceptionally valuable, since he is a primary and often an only source. His *History* is a matter-of-fact description of the events. Asołik is the first Armenian historian to have made a systematic use of chronology in his account.

BIBLIOGRAPHY

Sources. Stepʿanos Asołik Tarōnecʿi, *Histoire universelle,* I, Édouard Dulaurier, trans. (1883) and II, Frédéric Macler, trans. (1917), *Patmutʿiwn tiezerakan* (1885), *Des Stephanos von Taron armenische Geschichte,* Heinrich Gelzer and August Burckhardt, trans. (1907), and *Vseobshchaia istoriya Taronskogo Asokh'ika po prozvaniiu,* M. Emin, ed. (1864).

Studies. Manuk Abełean, *Hayocʿ hin grakanutʿean patmutʿiwn,* III (1968); A. Ter Łewondean, "Tʿuakanutʿeamb žamanakagrutʿiwnē hay patmagrutʿean mēǰ," in *Patmabanasirakan Handēs,* **1** (1979).

KRIKOR H. MAKSOUDIAN

[See also **Armenia, History of; Armenian Literature; Bagratids, Armenian; Historiography, Armenian.**]

STEPHEN I OF HUNGARY, ST. (*ca.* 975–1038), last grand prince (997–1000) and, as Stephen I, first Christian king (1000/1001–1038) of Hungary. Born Vajk in Esztergom (Gran), he was the only known son of Grand Prince Géza (970/972–997) and his wife, Sarolt (also called Beleknegini [white lady]), daughter of Gyula, the lord of Transylvania. In 995 Stephen (Vajk) married Gisela, daughter of Duke Henry of Bavaria and sister of Emperor Henry II. They had one son who reached adulthood, Imre (Emericus or Henry), and several daughters.

Stephen is justifiably regarded as the founder of the medieval kingdom of Hungary even though the bases for his work had been laid by his predecessors. The enserfment of the free semi-nomads and the settlement of servile villages on princely domains had begun generations earlier. Following the 955 defeat at Lechfeld (near Augsburg), Stephen's grandfather Taksony encouraged peaceful contacts with the West, and after the end of the incursions into Byzantium (*ca.* 970), the prince's armed retinue was gradually settled on the land. In 973 Géza asked Emperor Otto I to send missionaries, and the ruling family, together with many nobles, were baptized in the Latin rite. Still, the definitive turn to a church-supported monarchy and the concomitant social changes were the achievements of Stephen, who, educated in a baptized, though hardly Christian, household under the influence of St. Adalbert of Prague, was aware of the need to model his realm on the example of the feudal West. When Stephen succeeded his father, most of the Carpathian basin was already united under the rule of his family. He had, however, to contend with the oldest member of the ruling clan, the pagan Koppány, who in the tradition of *senioratus* (inheritance by the oldest living male of the family) claimed the throne and, in the tradition of the levirate, the bed of Sarolt. Having been girded with a sword in a knightly manner by his Western retainers, Stephen defeated Koppány with the help of his superior heavy cavalry and auxiliary troops supplied by the related tribes, such as the Kabars. Koppány was cruelly quartered, perhaps on the insistence of the reportedly fierce Sarolt, and his extensive properties were distributed to churches and retainers.

Stephen's next major move, the request for papal and imperial sanction to organize the Hungarian church and be crowned as Christian king, cannot be reconstructed exactly from the contradicting reports of the different legends. The best sources (Thietmar von Merseburg, Hildesheim Annals) agree that Stephen received an apostolic blessing and probably also a crown and a lance from Pope Sylvester II, as well as the concurrence of Otto III in his elevation. This step, often distorted in nationalist and politically motivated interpretations, has to be seen in the context of both the general "pacification" of Europe around 1000 and Otto's and Sylvester's idea of *renovatio* of a Christian empire that was to include the newly converted Hungary without formal (feudal) ties to either Rome or the imperium. (Neither pope nor emperor is mentioned in the formulas of Stephen's few authentic charters, although they were written by a former imperial notary.) The papal authorization for the foundation of a metropolitan see in Esztergom (which gave rise to later claims to legatine status, and in modern times to the "apostolic" title of the kings of Hungary) was probably delivered by a pupil of St. Adalbert, Asherik/Anastasius, who remained a counselor and collaborator of Stephen and a representative of the new Hungarian church abroad, having been its third archbishop. Crowned either on Christmas Day 1000 or on 1 January 1001, most probably in a ceremony following the Mainz Sacramentary (Mainz Ordo), Stephen became the first Christian king east of the Ottonian Empire.

The elevation in rank and the simultaneous "incorporation" of Hungary into Latin Christendom stabilized the foundations of the medieval kingdom. Its significance cannot be overestimated; even though Stephen kept close contacts with the Eastern church and the *basileus* (Byzantine emperor) and Hungary remained open to Byzantine influence well into the twelfth century, his final decision for the Latin West defined the country's fate for a millennium. The new king was immediately challenged in the east of the country. The Greek Orthodox lord of Transylvania, Stephen's uncle Gyula, resisted the king's unifying attempts and had to be subjugated by force (1003). A short while later, Ajtony, chief of the "black Magyars" (Kabars?), attempted to consolidate an autonomous territory along the lower Tisza and to intercept the important royal salt shipments from Transylvania; he also may have been in alliance with the Greeks. Stephen's campaign, in which Ajtony, and with him the last opponent of the monarchy, fell, can be dated 1003–1008 on the basis of Bruno of Querfurt's missionary journey into those parts in 1004.

Strengthened by the international acceptance of his royal authority and victorious over his rivals, Stephen could now turn to the organization of the kingdom and the church. He completed the confiscation, begun by his predecessors, of two-thirds of all tribal land for the crown, leaving one-third as allodial property to the chiefly families or—in the case of rebelling chiefs—granting it to his new retainers, Magyars and foreign "guests" (*hospites*) alike. The backbone of Stephen's government was the royal county (*megye,* civitas). Some forty-eight of these were founded by him—not all at the same time—of which twenty-four were marches (frontier districts). As a rule, the settlement and pasturage area of a clan were transformed into such a unit with an existing or newly built castle as its center and a count (*comes*) appointed by the king at its head. The count led the settled warriors, descendants of the ruler's retinue (*jobagiones castri*), in the royal host and supervised the villages of specialized royal servants (plowmen, craftsmen, hunters, fishers, guards) as well as the dependent peasants and slaves on the royal domain. He was also judge and administrator of all free men in his district. This system, in many respects parallel to contemporary Polish and Czech developments, most resembled the Lombard *civitates* of the eighth through tenth centuries.

While most counties had definite boundaries coinciding with archdeaconries, the border counties extended from an inland core to the frontier wasteland and were in charge of guarding the "gates" leading into the country, such as passages through marshland and mountain passes. The duty of guarding the border was often assigned to tribes

STEPHEN I OF HUNGARY, ST.

related to the Magyars, such as the Székely, Pecheneg, and Kaliz, who came with them into the Carpathian basin and retained their free military status for many centuries. Toponymic and later documentary evidence suggests that some thirty-five to forty powerful families (many of whom gave their names to the counties of which they were the first *comites*) and more than 100 minor ones constituted Stephen's new ruling stratum, several of them having been the king's knights from western lands. The royal household, which had been itinerant in Stephen's younger years and later became increasingly sedentary, was governed by a count of the palace (count palatine; Latin: *comes palatii*) and consisted of the typical medieval royal office-holders (marshal, treasurer, steward, and so forth). A small chapel served also as a chancery. Whether the queen, who was in charge of extensive properties mainly in western Hungary, had a separate household, as later became the rule, is uncertain. The tradition of the preceding century, to delineate a "ducal" territory for the heir, seems to have been retained for Stephen's son, Imre.

The commander of the royal bodyguard, now mostly of Varangian (Kievan Norman) origin, received a special area, or "shoreline," along the Danube for pasture and two (winter and summer) residences. Parallel to the administrative and military structure, Stephen established the Hungarian church. The creation of the archbishopric of Esztergom was followed by that of ten bishoprics (some of which were not completely established in Stephen's lifetime), mostly at the centers of royal family domains, endowed with rich landed property, and placed under the protection of the *comes*. A church was to be built and a priest supported by every ten villages, and the whole population had to pay tithe. Stephen's monastic foundations, besides generous grants and exemptions for the Benedictine abbey of Pannonhalma/Martinsberg (which received much of the spoils of the Koppány campaign), include Pécsvárad in the south, Zalavár (at the site of Mosaburg, residence of a former Slavic prince), the hermitage of Bakonybél, and a second nunnery in the north.

Considering its close connection with the royal domain, Stephen's ecclesiastical system can be best described as a "state church" rather than as a Germanic-type "proprietary church," although there were family monasteries founded by great landowners as burial and memorial centers of the clans. The greatest number clergy were called by Stephen from abroad—Italy, Bohemia, Lorraine—and the fewest from Germany, in order to forestall the traditional claims of ecclesiastical overlordship (some based on the forgeries of Bishop Pilgrim of Passau) of the Bavarian metropolitans on Hungary. Bishop Gerard of Csanád was born near Venice, the hermit saint Svorad-Andreas was an Istrian, and Asherik/Anastasius was probably Lotharingian. Slavic loanwords for ecclesiastic terms suggest that South-Slav (Slovene) priests played a role in the conversion of Hungary. In Stephen's monastic policies the influence of the Lotharingian (Gorze, Hirsau) reform is more conspicuous than the Cluniac, although the king corresponded with Abbot Odilo of Cluny.

A major arrangement of Stephen's later years was the reopening of the old pilgrimage route overland to Jerusalem across western Hungary to the Byzantine frontier that now coincided with the country's southern borders, due to the defeat of the Bulgarian Empire. Stephen founded hostels and way stations on the route, and additional ones in Ravenna, Rome, Constantinople, and Jerusalem. The royal residence was transferred close to the route, to Székesfehérvár (*Alba Regia*), where Stephen founded a royal church, inspired by the palace chapel at Aachen. Stephen's court already had been host to such men as Duke Bruno, brother of Henry II; the Czech Anastasius, who escaped the bloodbath of Libice and became archbishop of Esztergom; and the exiled sons of the Anglo-Saxon king Edmund Ironside, who came there via Kiev (Edward's daughter, St. Margaret of Scotland, was born in Hungary). With the new pilgrimage route many Western travelers passed through the country. Some, such as Bishop Gerard, stayed, while others, such as the hermit Gunther, returned repeatedly.

Two books (*libri*) of laws, containing some fifty paragraphs, are traditionally regarded as having been issued by Stephen. One of them has survived in a twelfth-century manuscript, the other in later copies only. Their measures were based largely on older Western laws and synodal decrees, codifying religious duties (observance of the Sabbath, payment of tithes, burial in holy ground, punishment for pagan practices) and protecting the new institutions of royal and private property. Wergilt—assessed in cattle—was different for each of the three classes: lords (*comites*), warriors (*milites*), and commoners (*vulgares*). Some violent offenses, however, were punished according to the traditional nomadic "eye for an eye" principle. Although

STEPHEN I OF HUNGARY, ST.

Stephen regulated the fairs (ordering that they be held on Sundays), his coins, minted on the pattern of Regensburg *denarii,* were hardly for internal trade. They were, more in concert with early medieval fashion, symbols of sovereignty and means of royal munificence. An important document on Stephen's policies is the *Libellus de institutione morum,* written by an unknown author (Asherik?) in the king's name as a "mirror of princes" addressed to his son. Besides the conventional emphasis on piety and righteousness, it stresses the importance of the royal council (*senatus*), of the leading men and warriors, and especially of the foreigners (*hospites*) who came to strengthen the country.

The last decade of Stephen's life was overshadowed by warfare and the problem of succession. Animosity between Bolestav Chrobry, duke of Poland, and Stephen led to several wars; pagan Pechenegs attacked Transylvania; and in 1030 Emperor Conrad II led an army into western Hungary. In 1031 Prince Imre, son and heir of Stephen, fell victim to a hunting accident. Stephen decided to pass over his immediate relatives, whom he may not have trusted to continue his Christian-feudal state building, and named his nephew, Peter Orseolo (son of the doge of Venice), as his successor. The choice did not prove to be a happy one: Peter's rule led to uprisings and German interventions, and it was finally under the sons of Stephen's cousin Vazul (Basil), whom the old king had blinded in order to exclude him from power, that his work was restored and continued. The evidence on these matters and on the one or more attempts on Stephen's life became greatly distorted in later chronicles and cannot be entirely disentangled; the authors, writing under kings who, like all kings of Hungary until 1301, were Vazul's and not Stephen's descendants, attempted to preserve both the saintly image of the kingdom's founder and the honor of the ruling dynasty's actual ancestor—for example, blaming Queen Gisela for the cruel punishment of Vazul. Stephen, plagued for many years by illness and grief over his son's death, died on 15 August 1038, a contemplative and pious old man.

Characteristically, probably also due to clerical preference, it was this image and not that of a militant, active statesman that for centuries defined the memory and iconography of Stephen. He was buried (in Byzantine fashion) in a redecorated Roman sarcophagus in the nave of his new royal basilica. In 1083 Stephen, together with his son and Bishop Gerard, was canonized with papal permission. A head reliquary of Stephen that was in Székesfehérvár for many centuries is now lost; a hand relic (the "holy right hand") survived many adventures and is now in the treasury of St. Stephen's Basilica in Budapest. In Hungary, 20 August, the day of the transfer of his relics, was celebrated as the saint's day; it was the date for the annual royal court during the Middle Ages and remained a popular feast day well into the twentieth century. (In 1948 it was renamed the Day of the Constitution.) The Roman calendar lists him now under the saints of 16 August.

BIBLIOGRAPHY

Sources. The best information can still be gained from the eleventh- and twelfth-century legends. *Vita maior* and *Vita minor,* D. W. Wattenbach, ed., in *Monumenta Germaniae historica: Scriptores,* XI (1854), 222–242; Bishop Hartwik's *Vita S. Stephani regis,* in *Acta sanctorum, September,* I (1746), 562–575; critical edition by Emma Bartoniek in Imre Szentpétery, ed., *Scriptores rerum Hungaricarum tempore ducum regumque stirpis Arpadianae gestarum,* II (1938), 365–440; a German translation by Thomas von Bogyay in Thomas von Bogyay, János Bak, and Gabriel Silagi, eds., *Die heiligen Könige* (1976). For passages in the Hungarian Chronicle surviving in later redactions, see the edition by A. Domanovszky in Szentpétery, ed., *Scriptores rerum Hungaricarum,* I (1937), 311–323, which may go back to near-contemporary sources but which were later distorted. References to Stephen in foreign sources were collected in Ferenc Albin Gombos, *Catalogus fontium historiae hungaricae,* I (1937), nos. 2001–2056.

Studies. Archivum Europae centro-orientalis, **4** (1938); János M. Bak, "Sankt Stefans Armreliquie im Ornat König Wenzels von Ungarn," in *Festschrift Percy Ernst Schramm,* I (1964); Thomas von Bogyay, "Über den Stuhlweissenburger Sarkophag des hl. Stephan," in *Ungarn-Jahrbuch,* **4** (1972), *Stephanus rex: Versuch einer Biographie* (1975), and "Adalbert von Prag und die Ungarn: Ein Problem der Quellen-Interpretation," in *Ungarn-Jahrbuch,* **7** (1976); Josef Deér, "Der Anspruch der Herrscher des 12. Jahrhunderts auf die apostolische Legation," in *Archivum historiae pontificiae,* **2** (1964), and "Aachen und die Herrschersitze der Arpaden," in *Mitteilungen des Instituts für österreichische Geschichtsforschung,* **79** (1971), both reprinted in *Byzanz und das abendländische Herrschertum,* Peter Classen, ed. (1977).

Dezsö Dercsényi, "Hungarian Art in the Age of St. Stephen," in *New Hungarian Quarterly,* **11** (1970); Georges Duby, *L'an mil* (1967); Hansgerd Göckenjan, *Hilfsvölker und Grenzwächter im mittelalterlichen Ungarn* (1972); György Györffy, "Zu den Anfängen der ungarischen Kirchenorganisation auf Grund neuer quellenkritischer Ergebnisse," in *Archivum historiae pontifi-*

ciae, **7** (1969), "Der Aufstand von Koppány," in *Studia turcica,* Lajos Ligeti, ed. (1971), *Autour de l'état des semi-nomades: Le cas de la Hongrie* (1975), "Die Entstehung der ungarischen Burgverfassung," in *Acta Archaeologica Academiae scientiarum Hungaricae,* **28** (1976), "Zur Frage der Herkunft der ungarländischen Deinstleute," in *Studia slavica,* **22** (1976), and *István király és müve* (1977), pt. II of which is translated in *Wirtschaft und Gesellschaft der Ungarn um die Jahrtausendwende* (1983).

Gyula Moravcsik, "The Role of the Byzantine Church in Medieval Hungary," in *American Slavic and East European Review,* **6** (1947); Jean-Pierre Ripoche, "La Hongrie entre Byzance et Rome: Probleme du choix religieux," in *Ungarn-Jahrbuch,* **6** (1974/1975); Percy E. Schramm, *Kaiser, Rom und Renovatio* (1929); Jenö Szücs, "König Stephan in der Sicht der modernen ungarischen Geschichtsforschung," in *Südost-Forschungen,* **31** (1972); Peter von Váczy, *Die erste Epoche des ungarischen Königtums* (1935).

JÁNOS M. BAK

[See also **Benedictines; Bruno of Querfurt, St.; Cluny, Order of; Gerard of Csanád, St.; Germany: 843–1137; Gorze; Hirsau; Hungary; Magyars; Mirror of Princes; Odilo of Cluny, St.; Otto I the Great, Emperor; Poland; Stephen, Crown of St.; Sylvester II, Pope; Székesfehérvár; Thietmar von Merseburg; Wergild.**]

STEPHEN II, POPE (*ca.* 710–757), was born in Rome and reared in the Lateran Palace. Hence, from the time of his accession to his pontificate in 752 he represented Roman pride in the face of Lombard and Byzantine threats to papal independence. In the winter of 753/754 Stephen traveled to France to gain the support of Pepin III, who then twice intervened in Italy in military campaigns against the Lombards on the pope's behalf (755 and 756). Pepin's "donation" to Stephen in 756 of lands formerly held by the Lombards and Byzantines, extending from Ravenna on the Adriatic to Narni in the central Italian interior, is often regarded as a landmark in the formation of the papal states.

BIBLIOGRAPHY

Erich Caspar, *Pippin und die römische Kirche* (1914); Léon Levillain, "L'avènement de la dynastie carolingienne et les origines de l'état pontifical, 749–757," in *Bibliothèque de l'École des Chartes,* **94** (1933); Peter Partner, *The Lands of St. Peter* (1972).

ROBERT E. LERNER

[See also **Papal States; Pepin III and the Donation of Pepin.**]

STEPHEN HARDING. See **Harding, Stephen.**

STEPHEN OF ORLÉANS. See **Stephen of Tournai.**

STEPHEN OF TARON. See **Step^{c}anos Asołik Taronec^{c}i.**

STEPHEN OF TOURNAI (also known as Stephen of Orléans, 1128–1203), prominent canonist and church administrator, was born at Orléans. He studied at Bologna and Chartres, served as abbot of Euverte from 1167, and in 1176 was named abbot of the important monastery of Ste. Geneviève in Paris. The culmination of his career came in 1192, when he was appointed bishop of Tournai, where he remained until his death. In addition to playing a very influential role in the ecclesiastical and political life of France, Stephen left a significant collection of documents and letters relating to his activities. He is the author of an important *Summa* on the *Decretum* of Gratian, as well as of several poems, liturgical compositions, and sermons.

BIBLIOGRAPHY

Sources. Jules Desilve, ed., *Lettres d'Étienne de Tournai* (1893); Michael McCormick, *Index scriptorum operumque latino-belgicorum medii aevi: Nouveau répertoire des oeuvres médiolatines belges,* pt. III, vol. II (1979), 278–285, and, with P. Fransen, *ibid.,* pt. III, vol. I (1977), 74–75, 107–108.

Studies. Johann Friedrich von Schulte, *Die Summa des Stephanus Tornacensis über das Decretum Gratiani* (1891); Joseph Warichez, *Étienne de Tournai et son temps, 1128–1203* (1937).

MICHAEL MCCORMICK

[See also **Decretists.**]

 STEPHEN, CROWN OF ST.

The crown of St. Stephen. Gold bands decorated with enamel plates depicting Emperor Michael VII Doukas (center) and the co-emperors Constantine Porphyrogenitos and Géza I. BILDARCHIV FOTO MARBURG/ART RESOURCE

STEPHEN, CROWN OF ST., the traditional name for the royal crown of Hungary at least since the late thirteenth century, attributing it to the first Christian king of the country. The existing diadem is an arched crown (*Bügelkrone*), consisting of a gold band 24.5 inches (62 centimeters) in circumference, decorated with gems, enamel plates, translucent arch- and gable-form enamels, and pendant chains, and surmounted by a cruciform band with enamel plates and a simple gold cross on top. The crown received its present form sometime in the thirteenth century. The crown that Stephen I may have received from Pope Sylvester II, probably a band with gems and lilies as depicted in the king's portrait on the coronation mantle, was lost during the decades following his death. It may have been sent to Rome as booty of war by Emperor Henry III when the king of Hungary, Peter Orseolo (1038–1041, 1044–1046), became his vassal, and it may have been there as late as the seventeenth century. The identification of the surviving crown with that of St. Stephen remained unchallenged until the nineteenth century, along with a forged "bull of Sylvester" on its donation.

Although doubts about its date and origin were raised as early as 1880, Hungarian and foreign experts were hampered in their investigations by the special status accorded the crown jewels, and until 1945 their judgments were also impeded by political considerations. Scholarly studies under less constrained conditions since the late 1940's have resulted in a number of serious hypotheses on the origin and history of the crown. The gold band is Byzantine (*corona graeca*) and can be dated on the basis of the iconography and inscriptions of its enamels. The two main protruding plates depict Christ Pantokrator (front) and Emperor Michael VII Doukas (rear), the eight smaller plates the archangels Michael and Gabriel; the saints George, Demetrius, Cosmas, and Damian; and two rulers, co-emperors Constantine Porphyrogenitos and Géza, "pious king of Turkia"—that is, Géza I of Hungary (1074–1077).

This program, and the size and the form of the diadem, suggest that the crown was originally made for Géza's Greek queen, the daughter of Theodulus Synadenus. The bluish-green, fishscale-decorated, translucent enamel *pinnae* are of the highest Byzantine craftsmanship; hence it is more than likely that they, too, belonged to the queen's crown sent from Constantinople. The pendants (*cataseistae*), nine gold chains ending in trefoils, are also characteristic of Greek crowns; hence they may have belonged to the original *corona graeca*.

The cruciform arch with enamel plates in late Romanesque style, depicting Christ and eight apostles, and bearing Latin inscriptions (*corona latina*), was added later, having been removed from an unknown object. This is suggested by the fact that four apostles are missing and that the arms had to be bent to fit the Greek band. The style and technique of the enamels and of the two decorative lines of pearls suggest a date in the third quarter of the twelfth century. As to its original use, it may have been an *asteriskos,* a frame of the domelike cover for a liturgical paten used in the Eastern church. The top plate with the image of Christ, very similar to the Pantokrator plate of the Greek enamels, was drilled through to permit the fastening of the gold cross. This barbaric procedure suggests that the *corona latina* had no special significance previously (thus rendering false the assumption that it was a reliquary crown of St. Stephen's) but, rather, that the cross was a spiritually valuable object, perhaps a pectoral cross of the "holy king"; this relic-like quality may explain the early references to the *sacra corona.* (The original medieval cross was replaced by the present one in the sixteenth century.)

The most likely sponsor of such a composite crown—Byzantine and Latin, "imperial" in form and perhaps also connected to St. Stephen—is Hungarian king Béla III (1172–1196), who grew up in Constantinople and who (as despot Alexios) had been for years heir presumptive to Manuel I Komnenos but, after his return to Hungary, accepted its traditional Latin orientation and enhanced the country's power and independence from both empires. No exact date for the crown can be established. The appellation "St. Stephen's Crown," first known to have been used in 1292, emerged in the troubled years following the civil war between King Béla IV (1235–1270) and his son Stephen V (1270–1272), during which time "a crown" was carried off to Bohemia. The immediate reasons for this attribution are unknown. In the mid 1960's, Josef Deér assumed that the crown might have been placed in the position of an "authentic" insignia of old when it had to replace a lost crown thought to have been St. Stephen's; it is also possible that King Andrew III (1290–1301) sought a symbolic association with the "holy king" because his legitimacy was challenged. From the late thirteenth century on, the crown and a number of other insignia were regarded as having been those of St. Stephen, just as elsewhere banners, thrones, and crowns were attributed to Charlemagne, Edward the Confessor, and St. Wenceslas.

At the same time, the specific crown acquired a particular significance in the inauguration of Hungarian kings. As there were no descendants in the male line of the founding dynasty after 1301, coronation with the crown was seen as crucial for establishing legitimacy. Thus, the Angevin king of Hungary, Charles I Robert (1308–1342), had to be crowned three times: once as a claimant to the throne, once with a "replacement" crown anointed by the papal legate, and finally with "St. Stephen's" crown, which had to be recovered from a baron opposing his succession because the nation did not recognize his rule without the "holy" insignia. This growing veneration was also expressed in reports on miraculous events surrounding the crown; it had been lost by King Otto at night, but found intact the next day "as if it had been invisible." It explains why the widow of King Albert had the crown stolen in 1440 in order to have her newborn son (Ladislas V Posthumous) crowned with it; he was eventually accepted by the Hungarians, but only after the coronation of another king with a crown "declared valid" by the estates. King Matthias I (1458–1490) was ready to pay some 80,000 florins to redeem the crown from Emperor Frederick III. From this time on, the crown, which had earlier been kept in the treasury of Székesfehérvár or in a royal castle, was entrusted to specially elected officers of the realm (the estates). The unique status of the crown as a "holy" and "authentic" insignia of rulership also influenced the metaphorical expressions relating to the crown in Hungarian chancery practice and law.

During the twelfth through fourteenth centuries the term *corona* occurs in formulations similar to those of other (mostly earlier) European charters signifying royal power, kingship, or "crown" property, but from the late fourteenth century on, the expression *corona regni* acquired a more "constitutional" meaning as an abstract subject of authority. During interregnums or disputed successions, sovereignty was imputed to the *sacra corona regni Hungariae,* which was seen as a kind of corporation comprising king and nobility. In this sense, using the language of the "organic" state (John of Salisbury), István Werböczy (1458–1541), author of a highly influential collection of Hungarian customary law, *Tripartitum opus iuris consuetudinarii Hungariae* (1514), used the concept of the "body of the holy crown" and its members to signify the privileged noble *natio.* This notion, introduced to support the claim to equal liberty of all landowning nobles (*una et eadem nobilitas,* one and the same nobility), remained an integral part of the estates' rhetoric well into modern times.

After 1526 the crown was taken to Transylvania and then to Vienna, was later returned to Buda, and later still was buried after the defeat of the 1848–1849 revolution. It was used for the coronation of almost all kings of Hungary until 1916. During World War II the Hungarian Nazi (Arrow-Cross) government took the crown jewels when retreating to Germany, where the insignia later fell into the hands of the U.S. Army. They were returned to Budapest in January 1978 and have been kept since in a special exhibit at the National Museum.

Other traditional insignia of the kings of Hungary include a scepter (a tenth-century Fatimid carved crystal ball, perhaps part of an older scepter, embedded in a twelfth-century gold-filigree head and a decorated gilt-silver staff), a gilded orb surmounted by a Byzantine-style double cross (fourteenth century, replacing a lost one), a coronation mantle (the only piece genuinely contemporary with Stephen I, having been an ecclesiastical garment donated by him and his queen to the basilica of Székesfehérvár and recut for secular use), and a sword. Medieval sources refer to "St. Stephen's" tunic, shoes, and so forth. The lance that Stephen holds in his portrait on the mantle may have been sent to Rome by Emperor Henry III. A tenth-century "royal" sword, attributed to St. Stephen, came in the fourteenth century to Prague, where it remains.

BIBLIOGRAPHY

János M. Bak, *Königtum und Stände in Ungarn im 14.–16. Jahrhundert* (1973); Magda Bárány-Oberschall, *Die Sankt Stephans-Krone und die Insignien des Königreiches Ungarn,* 2nd ed. (1974); Thomas von Bogyay, "L'iconographie de la 'porta speciosa' d'Esztergom et ses sources d'inspiration," in *Revue des études byzantines,* 8 (1950), and "Ungarns heilige Krone," in *Ungarn-Jahrbuch,* 9 (1978); Josef Deér, *Die heilige Krone Ungarns* (1966); Dezső Dercsényi, "The Hungarian Crown," in *New Hungarian Quarterly,* **19** (1978); Eric Fügedi, "Coronation in Medieval Hungary," in *Studies in Medieval and Renaissance History,* n.s. **3** (1980); Manfred Hellmann, ed., *Corona regni* (1961); Patrick J. Kelleher, *The Holy Crown of Hungary* (1951); Éva Kovács and Zsuzsa Lovag, *The Hungarian Crown and Other Regalia,* Peter Balabán, trans., rev. by Mary and András Boros-Kazai (1980); Gyula Moravcsik, *Byzantium and the Magyars,* Samuel R. Rosenbaum, trans. (1970); Gerhard Seewann, "Die Sankt-Stephans-Krone, die heilige Krone Ungarns," in *Südost-Forschungen,* 37 (1978).

JÁNOS M. BAK

[See also **Enamel; Hungary; Stephen I of Hungary, St.; Székesfehérvár.**]

STETHAIMER, HANNS. See **Burghausen, Hanns von.**

STIACCIATO (**schiacciato;** literally, "flattened out") is a term applied to the lowest or finest form of relief, in which the projection of the sculpted form is kept to a minimum. One of the most noted examples (considered by scholars to be the first) of *relievo stiacciato* is Donatello's *St. George and the Dragon* predella, carved for the Or San Michele, Florence, about 1417.

BIBLIOGRAPHY

Bruce Cole, *The Renaissance Artist at Work* (1983), 122; Horst W. Janson, *The Sculpture of Donatello* (1963), 30–32, in which *stiacciato* is discussed in detail; Leonard R. Rogers, *Relief Sculpture* (1974).

ADELHEID M. GEALT

[See also **Donatello.**]

STICHERON (plural, stichera; from Greek *stichos,* "verse"), a common hymnographic accretion associated with the psalm verses (*stichoi*) in the Byzantine Orthodox Office (vespers and matins). These verses, some of them going back to the sixth or seventh centuries and possibly earlier, are monostrophic and vary considerably in length. They appear with a simple syllabic notation in an anthology, the *Sticherarion,* beginning in the tenth century.

BIBLIOGRAPHY

Enrica Follieri and Oliver Strunk, eds., *Triodium Athoum,* in *Monumenta Musica Byzantinae* (MMB), IX (1975); Carsten Höeg, Henry J. W. Tillyard, and Egon Wellesz, eds., *Sticherarium, ibid.,* I (1935); Roman Jakobson, ed., *Fragmenta chiliandarica palaeoslavica, Sticherarium, ibid.,* V/A (1957); Jørgen Raasted, "Some Observations on the Structure of the Stichera in Byzantine Rite," in *Byzantion,* **28** (1958), 529–541; Oliver Strunk, "The Chants of the Byzantine-Greek Liturgy," in his *Essays on Music in the Byzantine World* (1977), 297–335; Henry J. W. Tillyard, *The Hymns of the Sticherarium for November,* in MMB, Transcripta II (1938), *The Hymns of the Octoechus, ibid.,* Transcripta III, V (1940 and 1949), and *Hymns of the Pentekostarium, ibid.,* Transcripta VII (1960); Egon Wellesz, *A History of Byzantine Music and Hymnography* (1949, 3rd ed. 1963).

NICOLAS SCHIDLOVSKY

[See also **Heirmos; Hymns, Byzantine; Music, Byzantine; Troparion.**]

STICHOMETRY (Greek: *stichos,* "verse" or "line"). Presumably in connection with the cost of their labor, Greek and Latin scribes of antiquity

St. George and the Dragon. Marble *stiacciato* relief by Donatello, *ca.* 1417, from the St. George Tabernacle, Or San Michele, Florence. ALINARI/ART RESOURCE

sometimes tallied the number of lines they had copied when they reached the end of a page or a work. Medieval copyists occasionally transcribed these stichometries along with the texts of their ancient exemplars. These relics of the classical book trade can thereby illuminate the text and physical form of the distant ancestors to surviving medieval copies.

BIBLIOGRAPHY

Robert Clavaud, "Remarques sur la stichométrie dans les manuscrits médiévaux," in *Revue d'histoire des textes,* 5 (1975); Eric G. Turner, *Greek Manuscripts of the Ancient World* (1971), 19.

MICHAEL MCCORMICK

[See also **Codicology, Western European; Manuscript Books, Production of; Scriptorium.**]

STIKARION (sticharion), the basic long, straight-sleeved undertunic worn by Orthodox clergy, often of rich material to distinguish it from civilian wear. Items indicating clerical rank or status, such as the omophorion of bishops, were worn over the stikarion. It is comparable with the Western alb.

BIBLIOGRAPHY

Nicole Thierry, "Le costume épiscopal byzantin du IXe au XIIIe siècle d'après les peintures datées," in *Revue des études byzantines,* **24** (1966), esp. 310.

LESLIE BRUBAKER

[See also **Costume, Byzantine; Omophorion; Paludamentum (with illustration); Vestments.**]

STJEPAN KOTROMANIĆ (*r.* 1318–1353), ban (ruler) of Bosnia, was the son of Stjepan Kotroman, who held lands in the north of greater Bosnia. After a period of exile in Dubrovnik, Kotromanić obtained the Bosnian banovina in central Bosnia under obscure circumstances in about 1318. At first he was in a subordinate position to the Šubići of Bribir. By 1322, after a Šubić civil war had weakened that family, Kotromanić asserted his own independence. He was soon allied with the king of Hungary, Charles I (Charles Robert, *r.* 1308–

1342), his nominal overlord; Charles's support throughout his reign enabled Kotromanić to greatly expand his state. In 1324 he acquired Sol (Tuzla) and Usora as well as the western Bosnian regions of Završje and the Krajina, including the towns of Livno, Duvno, Glamoč, Imota, and the port of Makarska.

Between 1322 and 1325 Kotromanić established his suzerainty over the Hrvatinići, lords of the Donji Kraji. In 1326 he took advantage of disorders among the Serbs to acquire a sizable portion of Hum. He managed a decentralized state, in which the aristocrats enjoyed considerable autonomy in their counties. He also presided with great tolerance over three faiths (each strong in particular regions): Catholicism, Orthodoxy, and the Bosnian church. He established friendly relations with the Franciscans and in 1339–1340 allowed them to establish a mission in Bosnia. The Franciscans have remained in Bosnia without a break to the present. Shortly after the mission's establishment, Kotromanić himself converted (probably from Orthodoxy) to Roman Catholicism.

Under Stjepan Kotromanić's rule Bosnia began to develop its rich mineral resources, and several mines (silver and lead) were opened, greatly increasing Bosnia's wealth and its commercial contacts abroad (particularly with Dubrovnik). Kotromanić built a strong army that not only successfully subdued neighboring noblemen but also repelled an attack from Dušan's Serbia in 1351. Kotromanić died in 1353 and was buried in the Franciscan monastery at Visoko, his main residence. His young nephew Tvrtko I (1353–1391) succeeded.

BIBLIOGRAPHY

John V. A. Fine, Jr., *Late Medieval Balkans* (1987).

JOHN V. A. FINE, JR.

[See also **Banat; Banus; Bosnia; Bosnian Church; Hungary; Serbia; Tvrtko I.**]

STOCKTON, THOMAS (*fl.* 1509–1525), English sculptor, the king's chief joiner in the Tower of London from 1510 to 1525. From 1509 to 1515 he was also master carver at King's College Chapel, Cambridge, and designed—though he did not necessarily personally carve—the outstanding stone sculpture in the antechapel. He was master joiner at Archbishop Thomas Wolsey's York Place, Westminster, from 1515. His functions encompassed the carving of wooden fittings and embellishment rather than just structural carpentry.

An antechapel of King's College Chapel, Cambridge, with stone carvings designed by Thomas Stockton, 1509–1515. PHOTO: WIM SWAAN

BIBLIOGRAPHY

Howard M. Colvin, ed., *The History of the King's Works*, III, *1485–1660*, pt. 1 (1975), 32–33, 192; John H. Harvey, *English Medieval Architects: A Biographical Dictionary Down to 1550* (1954), 252–253; Lawrence Stone, *Sculpture in Britain: The Middle Ages* (1955, 2nd ed. 1972), 228–229.

BARRIE SINGLETON

[See also **Cambridge, University of; London.**]

STONE, a weight for dry products in the British Isles, generally of 14 pounds (6.350 kg). Variations, however, ranging from 5 to 32 pounds (2.268 to 14.515 kg), were used for certain items such as the following: almonds, 8 pounds; alum, generally 8 pounds but occasionally 13.5 pounds; beef, London, 8 pounds, but Herefordshire, 12 pounds; cumin, 8 pounds; flax, generally 14 pounds but occasionally 16 pounds; glass, 5 pounds; hemp, generally 16 pounds but sometimes 20 and 32 pounds; lead, generally 12 pounds but occasionally 15 pounds; pepper, sugar, and wax, 8 pounds; and wool, generally 14 pounds but Herefordshire, 12 pounds, Gloucestershire, 15 pounds, and Wales, 17 pounds. The stone was frequently referred to as a half-quartern. In medieval manuscripts variant spellings of the stone include stan, stæn, stane, stayne, steane, sten, ston, stoone, and stonne.

RONALD EDWARD ZUPKO

[See also **Weights and Measures, Western European.**]

STOSS, VEIT (*fl.* 1477–1533), celebrated Franconian sculptor active in Kraków and Nuremberg. His most massive and powerful early works are in Kraków, especially the St. Mary Altarpiece (1477–1489) and the red marble tomb of King Casimir IV, dated 1492. In Nuremberg after 1496 he specialized in carved and painted limewood. Stoss's work is noted for its swirling drapery, deep carving, and active figures: St. Sebald Church (St. Sebalduskirche) *Crucifixion* with the two mourning figures of Mary and John, dated about 1506/1507 and 1520; St. Lawrence Church (St. Lorenzkirche) *Rosary Annunciation,* executed 1517–1518; and the Bamberg Altarpiece of 1520–1523.

The *Rosary Annunciation*, a wood carving by Veit Stoss, 1517–1518. PHOTO: WIM SWAAN

BIBLIOGRAPHY

Michael Baxandall, *The Limewood Sculptors of Renaissance Germany* (1980), 191–202, 266–274; Rainer Kahsnitz, ed., *Veit Stoss in Nürnberg* (1983); Zdzisław Kępinski, *Veit Stoss* (1981); Eberhard Lutze, *Viet Stoss,* 4th ed. (1968); Theodor Müller, *Sculpture in the Netherlands, Germany, France, and Spain, 1400 to 1500* (1966), 125–128, 180–183.

LARRY SILVER

STOWELL, JOHN (*fl.* second half of the fifteenth century), was a freemason of Wells regularly employed at the cathedral from 1457/1458. By 1470

Remains of a reredos to the Virgin by John Stowell, based on a Jesse Tree (reclining figure) in St. Cuthbert's Church, Wells, 1470. COURTAULD INSTITUTE, LONDON

he was important enough to contract with the city corporation to provide a large reredos to the Virgin based on a Jesse Tree in the south transept of St. Cuthbert's Church. The remains of this work were discovered in 1848 and still survive.

BIBLIOGRAPHY

John H. Harvey, *English Medieval Architects: A Biographical Dictionary Down to 1550* (1954), 254; Thomas Serel, *Historical Notes on the Church of St. Cuthbert's in Wells* (1875), 19–23; Lawrence Stone, *Sculpture in Britain: The Middle Ages* (1955, 2nd ed. 1972), 227.

BARRIE SINGLETON

[See also: **Tree of Jesse.**]

STRASBOURG CATHEDRAL, dedicated to the Virgin and celebrated for its sculptural and stained glass programs and for its varied architecture. The choir and part of the transept date from between 1176–1179 to about 1225 and are late German Romanesque in style. The nave, built between 1236/1237 and 1274, is French Court Style Gothic. The west facade was built by Master Erwin (von Steinbach?), beginning in 1277. The single octagon tower was built by Ulrich von Ensingen between 1399 and 1419, and its 466-foot (142-meter) spire, completed in 1439, was built by Johannes Hültz von Köln.

BIBLIOGRAPHY

Louis Grodecki, "Les arcs-boutants de la cathédrale de Strasbourg et leur origin," in *Gesta,* **15,** (1976), 43–51; Hans Reinhardt, *La cathédrale de Strasbourg* (1972), see esp. 259–262 for a bibliography; Wim Swaan, "Strasbourg," in his *The Gothic Cathedral* (1969), 163–170, for a general summary.

CARL F. BARNES, JR.

[See also **Erwin, Master; Gothic Architecture; Gothic Art: Sculpture; Ulrich von Ensingen.**]

Original drawing for the west facade of Strasbourg Cathedral, showing design with figures of the Virgin and Apostles. Ink drawing on parchment by Michael Parler, *ca.* 1385. PHOTO: WIM SWAAN

STRASBOURG OATHS. On 14 February 842, Louis the German and Charles the Bald met at Strasbourg and swore oaths of alliance against their brother, the emperor Lothar. Each swore in the language of the others' followers, Louis in French and Charles in German; their followers swore in their own languages. The oaths are recorded by Charlemagne's grandson Nithard in his *Historiarum libri IV.* The German oaths, apparently imperfectly understood by the scribe, are in a form of the Rhenish or Middle Franconian dialect. Linguistically far more significant are the French oaths, being the first document in the French language, which had by now emerged from Latin as a distinct Romance idiom.

BIBLIOGRAPHY

Sources. The oaths are in book 3, chap. 5, of Nithard's *Histories.* See Ernestus Müller, ed., *Nithardi historiarum libri IIII* (3rd ed. 1907, new ed. 1956); Nithard, *Histoire des fils de Louis le Pieux,* Ph. Lauer, ed. and trans. (1926) (Latin text and French translation). For an English translation, see Bernhard W. Scholz and Barbara Rogers, trans., *Carolingian Chronicles: Royal Frankish Annals and Nithard's Histories* (1970). The oaths are also available in W. Foerster and E. Koschwitz, *Altfranzösisches Übungsbuch,* 5th ed. (1915).

Studies. Siegfried Becker, *Untersuchungen zur Redaktion der Strassburger Eide* (1972); J. K. Bostock, *A Handbook on Old High German Literature,* 2nd ed. (1976), 187–189; A. Tabachovitz, *Étude sur la langue de la version française des serments de Strasbourg* (1932).

D. R. McLINTOCK

[See also **Carolingians and the Carolingian Empire; French Language; German Language; Nithard.**]

STRATEGOS (Greek; plural, *strategoi*), Byzantine general and, in the middle Byzantine period (seventh through eleventh centuries), the usual title of the commander of a theme or of a thematic army and its military district. Appointed by, and removable at the will of, the emperor, he was responsible for military affairs within his theme. He mustered and commanded the soldiers of the theme in defensive and offensive operations, but his power was subject to the control or check of the theme's *protonotarios* or *chartoularios,* who controlled respectively the theme's finances and supplies.

The *strategos* periodically received a salary in gold from the emperor. He was forbidden to acquire land in, or to marry a woman from, the theme while exercising authority over it.

Toward the end of the tenth century, *katepano* or *dux* frequently became the official designation of the local military commander, rather than *strategos,* although the last term continued to be used for some commands. By the middle of the eleventh century, *dux* or *doux* had become the common designation for the local military commander, while the *krites* or judge emerged to head the separate sphere of civilian affairs. The old thematic organization had thus lost its coherence. Historians and other writers, however, continued to use *strategos* informally to refer to a general.

BIBLIOGRAPHY

John B. Bury, *The Imperial Administrative System in the Ninth Century* (1911, repr. 1958); Hélène Glykatzi-Ahrweiler, "Recherches sur l'administration de l'empire byzantin aux IXe–XIe siècles," in *Bulletin de correspondance hellénique,* **84** (1960), esp. 36–52; Nicolas Oikonomides, *Les listes de préséance byzantines des IXe et Xe siècles* (1972).

WALTER EMIL KAEGI, JR.

[See also **Byzantine Empire: Bureaucracy; Byzantine Empire: History; Dux; Katepano; Logothete; Themes.**]

STRATHCLYDE, KINGDOM OF. The kingdom of Strathclyde, or Cumbria, existed from the fifth to the early eleventh century and was centered originally in the Clyde Valley in southwest Scotland. Its main stronghold was at Dumbarton. The history of Cumbria is largely unknown. None of the annals or lore of the Cumbrians has survived, and their history is based on occasional mentions of them in the records of their neighbors and on an incomplete list of their kings.

The Cumbrians were a Celtic people who spoke Brythonic, a *P*-Celtic language akin to Welsh and Breton. Their kingdom emerged out of the Damnonii, an Iron Age tribe. Scholars have theorized that the Romans organized the kingdom as a federate state to help defend Hadrian's Wall, but this is doubtful. Although the Cumbrians may have been federate allies (*foederati*), tribes along the Roman frontier commonly evolved more sophisticated political arrangements. Moreover, once the Romans withdrew in the late fourth century, a series of similar kingdoms emerged south of Strathclyde.

The first actual mention of Cumbria is from the mid fifth century, when St. Patrick reproved Coroticus, king of Dumbarton, for slave raiding in Ireland. Aside from this, nothing is known about Strathclyde or the other British kingdoms in the north during the fifth and most of the sixth century. In the 580's and early 590's, however, it raided the new kingdom of Bernicia, and Riderch of Strathclyde took part in one of these expeditions. These raids may have been intended to stop German settlement in the north, but if this was the hope, they failed. Although the actual chronology of the Northumbrians' expansion is debatable, during the early seventh century they conquered all the British kingdoms in the north except Strathclyde. By about 640 Strathclyde was confined to the Clyde Valley and Ayrshire. Northumbria bordered it to the south and east, Pictland to the northeast, and the Irish kingdom of Dál Riata to the north. This constellation of kingdoms was stable until the ninth century.

From archaeology and the poetry of the northern Britons one can form a general picture of conditions in the kingdom. After the departure of the Romans, the natives probably reoccupied their old hill forts. They lacked a money economy and practiced mixed farming in which herding was dominant. In material culture the Roman interlude had made little difference; in religion this was not the case. The Cumbrians were converted to Christianity, probably by their British neighbors to the south, and had a bishopric in the sixth century. Government also had changed. It was in the hands of a warrior-king who maintained a war band. His warriors protected the king and raided his neighbors, and they were rewarded with loot and a constant flow of mead and wine.

Although the names of some of the early kings are known, their exploits were imperfectly recorded. Presumably they centered on cattle raids, and in these Strathclyde probably had the advantage over the Northumbrians and Picts. It was poorer than the eastern kingdoms, and its warriors could easily raid the east through the wild and thinly populated hills. The best way to control such raids was for the eastern kings to make the kings of Strathclyde their dependents; and for some years before 685, Cumbria was in fact under the lordship of the Northumbrians. Later, the Picts and Northumbrians, at first separately and then in alliance, unsuccessfully tried to become the overlords of the Cumbrians in the 740's and 750's.

This uneasy relationship between Strathclyde and the Northumbrians and Picts became completely unbalanced in the ninth century, when Vikings entered the Irish Sea. These Vikings were Norwegians who had settled in the Hebrides and established bases along the Irish coast. They raided all the kingdoms around the Irish Sea and may have destroyed Dál Riata, Strathclyde's northern neighbor. Mentions of Cumbria disappear from the annals, and it is clear that beginning in the 840's the Vikings freely crossed its territory to raid the new kingdom of Scotia in the east. These forays recurred throughout the rest of the century and into the next. In 870 the Vikings took Dumbarton and enslaved its inhabitants. The impact of these depredations is obscure, especially because the kings of Strathclyde somehow expanded their kingdom as it was being destroyed. They may have retreated into the hills and capitalized on the weakness of Northumbria, or they may have simply allied with the Vikings. In any case, they became lords of the hill country east of the Clyde and of all the land around the Solway Firth.

At its height, Strathclyde may have stretched as far south as the Mersey, and it was in effect a Cumbrian-Viking condominium. From around 900 the Vikings raided Yorkshire and the Midlands through Cumbria, and there was extensive Viking settlement in the southern part of the kingdom. During this period the Cumbrians probably lost the records of their past and began to abandon Brythonic in favor of Gaelic, which was introduced into the southwest by the hated *Gall-ghàidhil* (Celts who had become Vikings). Strathclyde was, in fact, in the process of becoming Galloway, the land of the *Gall-ghàidhil,* and the only reason anything is known of its history after 870 is that the Anglo-Saxon and Scottish kings repeatedly tried to pacify it. They obtained the submission (alliance) of the Cumbrian kings five times in the tenth century and invaded and wasted Cumbria three times (945, 972, and 1000). Neither of these expedients ended raids from the west. The Cumbrian kings were too weak to control the movement of Vikings through their kingdom, and their people were too poor to be vulnerable to raids. A line of native kings was able to stay in power throughout the century, and the situation improved only as the power of the Vikings slowly waned. The kingdom lasted until after around 1018, when Owen the Bald, the last known king, died, and Malcolm II, king of Scots, seized power in Strathclyde in unchronicled circumstances. Cumbria thus became part of Scotland, but it was many years before the new kings made their power real outside Clydesdale or the Galwegians stopped their slave raids into England.

BIBLIOGRAPHY

Sources. The main sources for the history of Strathclyde are the Annals of Ulster and the Annals of Tigernach. These and most other mentions of the Cumbrians can be most easily consulted in *Early Sources of Scottish History, A.D. 500 to 1286,* Alan O. Anderson, ed. and trans., I (1922). For the pedigree of the kings of Strathclyde, see A. W. Wade-Evans, *Nennius's History of the Britons* (1938), 101–114. This meager material is sometimes supplemented with John of Fordun, a fourteenth-century historian, but most of his statements concerning Cumbria lack any known basis.

Studies. The most important discussions of Strathclyde are Hector Munro Chadwick, *Early Scotland* (1949), 136–158; Kenneth Jackson, "The Britons in Southern Scotland," in *Antiquity,* **29** (1955); D. P. Kirby, "Strathclyde and Cumbria: A Survey of Historical Development to 1092," in *Transactions of the Cumberland and Westmorland Antiquarian and Archaeological Society,* n.s. **62** (1962). The last of these cannot be trusted after about 900 and should be studied only in conjunction with P. A. Wilson, "On the Use of the Terms 'Strathclyde' and 'Cumbria,'" *ibid.*, n.s. **66** (1966). For Northumbrian-Cumbrian relations after 900, see William E. Kapelle, *The Norman Conquest of the North* (1979), esp. 33–39, 138–141. Archibald A. M. Duncan provides the most judicious treatment of Strathclyde in his *Scotland: The Making of the Kingdom* (1975). The best general introduction to the post-Roman period is Leslie Alcock, *Arthur's Britain* (1971).

Progress in reconstructing the history of Cumbria can come only from specialist studies in a number of disciplines. Annual bibliographies of this material appear in *Scottish Historical Review* and *Scottish Studies.* The following is a selection of such work. Kenneth Jackson provides an introduction to the warrior ethos of the early northern Britons in *The Gododdin* (1969). There is a summary of the archaeology of these kingdoms in Lloyd Laing, *The Archaeology of Late Celtic Britain and Ireland* (1975), 20–45. On the question of the reliability of the British genealogies, consult M. Miller, "Historicity and the Pedigrees of the Northcountrymen," in *Bulletin of the Board of Celtic Studies,* **26** (1975); and D. P. Kirby's criticism of her views, *ibid.,* **27** (1976). W. F. H. Nicolaisen and J. MacQueen have discussed the place-name evidence in a series of articles in *Scottish Studies,* esp. **4** (1960), **8** (1964), and **17** (1973). Finally, the conversion of the northern Britons to Christianity is currently being reassessed. See A. C. Thomas, "The Evidence from North Britain," in M. W. Barley and R. P. C. Hanson, eds., *Christianity in Britain, 300–700* (1968).

WILLIAM E. KAPELLE

[See also **Celtic Languages; Dál Riata; England, Anglo-Saxon; Malcolm II of Scotland; Picts; Scotland: History; Vikings.**]

STRATIOTAI (singular, *stratiōtēs*), the ordinary Greek word for Byzantine soldiers in all periods, including soldiers who were recruited from both Greek and foreign ethnic groups, and referring to both foot and mounted troops. The soldier's arms included a sword and a lance, but the bow was especially important between the sixth and the tenth century. His terms of recruitment varied, but there was probably no general conscription. Limited chain mail or plate and a metal helmet normally protected him. He supported himself by diverse means, including rations in kind (*siteresia, annonae*), a periodic cash salary and donatives on special occasions, and revenues from his landed properties that were supplemented by special tax exemptions. Substantial numbers of soldiers enjoyed revenues from "soldiers' portions" or properties (*stratiōtika ktemata*) in the ninth and tenth centuries, and from state grants of *pronoia* (fiefs) in the twelfth and thirteenth centuries.

BIBLIOGRAPHY

Hélène Ahrweiler, "Recherches sur l'administration de l'empire byzantin aux IX–XI siècles," in *Bulletin de correspondance hellénique,* **84** (1960), esp. 5–24; Gilbert Dagron and Haralambie Mihaescu, *Le traité sur la guérilla de l'empereur Nicéphore Phocas* (1986), 224–250, 266–269; Paul Lemerle, *The Agrarian History of Byzantium* (1979), 115–156.

WALTER EMIL KAEGI, JR.

[See also **Pronoia; Soldiers' Portions; Strategos; Themes; Warfare, Byzantine.**]

STRATIOTIKA KTEMATA. See **Soldiers' Portions.**

STRENGLEIKAR. In the southwest of Norway around 1270 a vellum manuscript was produced containing, among other things, translations into Old Norse of twenty-one Old French lais. Keyser and Unger gave these works the title *Strengleikar* (literally, string games or stringed instruments), since that is one of the words used in the text to translate the Old French term lais. The main part of the *Strengleikar* manuscript is now in the library of the University of Uppsala under the designation codex De la Gardie 4–7; four mutilated leaves of the same manuscript are in the Arnamagnæan Institute in Copenhagen (AM 666b, 4°). There are no other manuscript copies of this text except for a recently identified *Gvímars saga,* a sister manuscript to the first lai in the *Strengleikar* collection: *Guiamar* (Old French *Guigemar*).

The *Strengleikar* are in prose and thus take their place among other Old Norse prose renderings of Old French poetry made during the reign of King Hákon Hákonarson (*r.* 1217–1263). Some of the other works translated were *Erec et Enide* (*Erex saga* in Old Norse), *Yvain* (*Ívens saga* in Old Norse), the *Perceval* of Chrétien de Troyes (*Parcevals saga*), and the *Tristan* of Thomas (*Tristrams saga*).

The twenty-one lais in the *Strengleikar* collection can be grouped as follows: (1) eleven correspond to lais in the Harley collection (London,

British Library, MS Harley 978), traditionally attributed to Marie de France—only *Éliduc,* the longest of the Harley lais, is missing in *Strengleikar;* (2) six others also have extant French originals, but not in the Harley collection—*Desiré Tydorel, Doon, Lecheor, Nabaret, Graelent;* (3) four exist today only in *Strengleikar,* their Old French sources having been lost.

If the Old French manuscript from which the *Strengleikar* were translated still survived, then the *Strengleikar* would have little importance beyond that of a skillful example of Old Norse translation style. Since that Old French manuscript is not extant, the *Strengleikar* have a wider, and twofold, value: for textual criticism and for literary history.

Where the Old French originals exist, the *Strengleikar* are often useful in determining the correct reading of the Old French text; as the sole representative of an important early French manuscript, the *Strengleikar* manuscript is one of the three main repositories of lais (along with the Harley MS and Paris, Bibliothèque Nationale, nouv. acq. fr. 1104), and its readings have to be considered as part of the textual tradition of the lais.

By preserving four lais that would not otherwise have come down to us, the *Strengleikar* perform a valuable service for literary history. The first of these four, *Gurun,* tells about the successful wooing of a maiden who has a well-meaning but strict dwarf as her guardian. The *Lai of the Beach* (*Strandar strengleikr*) tells how William the Conqueror ordered a lai (in this case a musical composition) to celebrate a happy period he spent at Barfleur, waiting for a good wind to take him across the Channel. *Richard the Old* (*Ricar hinn gamli*) tells how the daughter of the king of Brittany (Richard) got around her strict father by getting her guards drunk and then going off to meet her lover. The fourth of these *strengleikar* apparently has the same name as one of the lais in the Harley collection, the *Lai of Two Lovers* (*Tveggia elskanda strengleikr*). Its setting, though not its theme, is untypical for a Breton lai: the son of the Roman emperor and the daughter of the duke of Piacenza flee from their warring fathers, hide in a cave that is sealed off by a snowstorm, and die in each other's arms.

BIBLIOGRAPHY

Carol J. Clover, "*Vǫlsunga saga* and the Missing Lai of Marie de France," in *Sagnaskemmtun: Studies in Honour of Hermann Pálsson on His 65th Birthday,* Rudolph Simek, Jónas Kristjánsson, and Hans Bekker-Nielsen, eds. (1986); Robert Cook and Mattias Tveitane, eds., *Strengleikar: An Old Norse Translation of Twenty-one Old French Lais* (1979); Marianne E. Kalinke, "Gvímars saga," in *Opuscula* (Bibliotheca Arnamagnæana, XXXIV), 7 (1979), 106–139, and with P. M. Mitchell, *Bibliography of Old Norse-Icelandic Romances* (1985), 105–114; Rudolf Keyser and Carl Richard Unger, eds., *Strengleikar eða Lioðabok* (1850); Jean Rychner, ed., *Les lais de Marie de France* (1966); Prudence Mary O'Hara Tobin, ed., *Les lais anonymes des XIIe et XIIIe siècles* (1976).

ROBERT COOK

[See also **Elis Saga ok Rosamundu; French Literature: To 1200; Hákonar Saga Hákonarsonar; Lai, Lay; Marie de France; Scandinavian Literature.**]

STRICKER, DER ("the knitter," perhaps of words into verse), pseudonym of a thirteenth-century German poet. Little is known with certainty about Der Stricker. Nonetheless, some assumptions can be made from his writings. For example, dialectal traits suggest that he came from Franconia, but topical allusions and the manuscript tradition itself indicate that he spent a good part of his literary career in Austria. His earliest work is dated from about 1220; he is thought to have been active until at least 1250. His pen name, the form and themes of his writings, and a brief self-characterization (in *Die Frauenehre* [Honor of ladies], lines 137–145) lead one to conclude that he was an itinerant professional poet. But who his patrons were and which communities he lived in are matters of conjecture.

Considered the first professional narrative writer in the history of German medieval literature, Der Stricker composed all his work in rhymed, octosyllabic couplets. His invariability of form is counterbalanced by a great variety of genres: two epics in the courtly manner, totaling more than 20,000 lines; a comic biography of the priest Amis, a panegyric on women in general as well as an attack on ill-natured women, and a poem on the Mass, ranging from 900 to 2,500 lines in length; beast fables, prayers, and comic as well as moralistic *Mären;* and more than 100 didactic poems on social, moral, and theological subjects. (He wrote no lyric poetry.) In all, Der Stricker's style is simple, unadorned, and impersonal. Because such a style lends itself to imitation, scholars cannot be certain that all works in the canon are the poet's own.

Der Stricker is believed to have begun his career with *Karl der Grosse,* a revision of the twelfth-century *Rolandslied* (Song of Roland), a version of the *Chanson de Roland.* This was long thought to be merely a technical polishing of the verse and a smoothing of the narrative, but recent scholars (von der Burg, Schnell) have found evidence of political tendencies in his additions to, and slight modifications of, the story. Der Stricker may have revised the epic to flatter partisans of the reigning Hohenstaufen dynasty, whose members claimed descent from Charlemagne. His original Arthurian romance, *Daniel von dem Blühenden Tal,* was probably composed after *Karl der Grosse,* but not later than 1230. Opinion regarding its merits varies. While most consider it a clumsy imitation of Hartmann von Aue's *Iwein,* interesting only for its replacement of courtly spirit with a kind of ethical pragmatism, some scholars (Henderson, Brall) contend that it is a structurally sophisticated work with a coherent political message. Modern readers generally have placed both *Daniel* and *Karl der Grosse* low in the ranks of German narrative from this period. On the other hand, contemporaries of Der Stricker apparently admired his work. Rudolf von Ems (*ca.* 1240), for example, mentions him twice as a notable epic poet, and *Karl der Grosse,* which has come down to us in more than forty manuscripts, was very popular in the Middle Ages.

Attempts have been made to establish the relative chronology of the shorter works, but these have rested on suspect assumptions (for example, that Der Stricker wrote his amusing stories in his youth and his religious poems later). Since Der Stricker wrote on commission, or in the hope of reward from a particular individual or group, his choice of subject and manner of treatment depended to some degree on the tastes of others. Granting his role in determining the general character of his work—that he wrote no legends, for instance, surely can be taken to indicate a personal distaste for this aspect of popular religion rather than lack of interest in it by the public—we nonetheless must imagine Der Stricker responding to perceived opportunities. He may well have written, within the very same year, his group of prayers for a religious community and a group of comic tales for a bourgeois audience.

Of Der Stricker's works, those best known to modern readers are the sixteen *Mären* (stories). These are the earliest known examples of the genre, so that Der Stricker may be regarded either as its creator or—assuming that the genre already existed as popular, recited poetry—as the first writer to bring the *Märe* to a level of sophistication warranting its preservation on parchment. Most of Der Stricker's *Mären* represent the comic aspect of the genre, depicting everyday conflicts between the wise and the foolish. Two stories, however—*Der arme und der reiche König* (The poor and the rich king) and *Der junge Ratgeber* (The young counselor)—lack ludicrous elements and thus are moralistic *Mären.* Several tales, such as *Die eingemauerte Frau* (The immured lady) and *Die drei Wünsche* (The three wishes), contain ethical or religious doctrines in the guise of farcical happenings, while others, such as *Ehescheidungspräch* (Talk of divorce) and *Der unbelehrbare Zecher* (The incorrigible toper), are subtle explorations of common psychological states. In their form and choice of subjects (misunderstandings, deceptions, marital conflicts), Der Stricker's stories are typical of the *Mären* of the period; they are untypical in their role as vehicles of a strong philosophical intelligence.

Comparatively little attention has been given to Der Stricker's didactic and theological poems, which, until the editions of Schwab and of Moelleken *et al.,* were usually published in rare and obscure sources. A major inspiration for these poems, we may reasonably assume, was the Fourth Lateran Council, which convened in 1215, at the start of the poet's career. It has been established, for example, that Der Stricker was familiar with certain of the canons enunciated by that body; indeed, penitential theology and practice, one of its most important concerns, appears as the dominant theme in his numerous shorter poems. Arguing from a traditional viewpoint, that of the central Scholastics of the twelfth century, Der Stricker urges his fellow men to admit their profound sinfulness and turn to God in the hope of forgiveness. Reflecting the renewed importance of sacramental penance in the church after Lateran IV, he repeatedly stresses the necessity of contrition, confession, and satisfaction. In one group of poems, he espouses for all Christians an ascetic form of existence that recalls the penitential life of the Franciscans, but the likelihood that he was affiliated with this order seems small when one considers that his poems contain no reference to it or to St. Francis (who was canonized in 1228). Taking up the traditional plea of wandering poets that the nobility be generous with its wealth, Der Stricker goes a step further and, citing Jesus' parables of stewardship, argues that all excess property belongs to the poor.

Although Der Stricker's art lacks breadth, it holds penetrating formulations in central areas of the moral life. While Der Stricker had no gift for sustained narrative, he was nonetheless a masterful innovator within short forms. Coming at the end of the florescence of chivalric literature in Germany, he is among the most interesting of secondary poets.

BIBLIOGRAPHY

Sources. Karl Bartsch, ed., *Karl der Grosse von dem Stricker* (1857, repr. 1965); Hanns Fischer, ed., *Der Stricker: Verserzählungen,* I (4th ed. 1979), II (3rd ed. 1984); Klaus Hofmann, *Strickers "Frauenehre"* (1976); Wolfgang Wilfried Moelleken, Gayle Agler-Beck, and Robert E. Lewis, eds., *Die Kleindichtung des Strickers,* 5 vols. (1973–); Michael Resler, ed., *Daniel von dem Blühenden Tal* (1983); Gustav Rosenhagen, ed., *Daniel von dem Blühenden Tal* (1894, repr. 1976); Ute Schwab, *Die bisher unveröffentlichen geistlichen Bispelreden des Strickers* (1959) and, as editor, *Der Stricker: Tierbispel* (1960).

Studies. Helmut de Boor, *Die deutsche Literatur im späten Mittelalter: Zerfall und Neubeginn,* pt. 1 (1962), 231–247; Helmut Brall, "Strickers *Daniel von dem Blühenden Tal,*" in *Euphorion,* **70** (1976); Joachim Bumke, "Strickers 'Gäuhühner,'" in *Zeitschrift für deutsches Altertum und deutsche Literatur,* **105** (1976); Udo von der Burg, *Strickers "Karl der Grosse" als Bearbeitung des "Rolandsliedes"* (1974); Hanns Fischer, *Studien zur deutschen Märendichtung,* 2nd ed. (1983), 145–148, 405–417, 521–528; Ingeborg Henderson, *Strickers Daniel von dem Blühenden Tal: Werkstruktur und Interpretation . . .* (1976); John Margetts, "Non-feudal Attitudes in Der Stricker's Short Narrative Works," in *Neuphilologische Mitteilungen,* **73** (1972); Hedda Ragotzky, *Gattungserneuerung und Laienunterweisung in Texten des Strickers* (1981); Rüdiger Schnell, "Strickers 'Karl der Grosse': Literarische Tradition und politische Wirklichkeit," in *Zeitschrift für deutsche Philologie,* **93** (1974), spec. iss.; Stephen L. Wailes, "Stricker and the Virtue *Prudentia:* A Critical Review," in *Seminar,* **13** (1977), and *Studien zur Kleindichtung des Stricker* (1981).

STEPHEN L. WAILES

[See also **Chivalry; Courtly Love; Exemplum; Fables; Hartmann von Aue; Mären; Middle High German Literature; Minnesingers; Rolandslied; Scholasticism, Scholastic Method.**]

STRINGCOURSE, a continuous molding, platband, or projecting masonry course running horizontally across the face of a building. Stringcourses are often placed at floor level, to mark the division into stories. When continuous with a row of window sills or lintels, a stringcourse is also called a sill course or a lintel course.

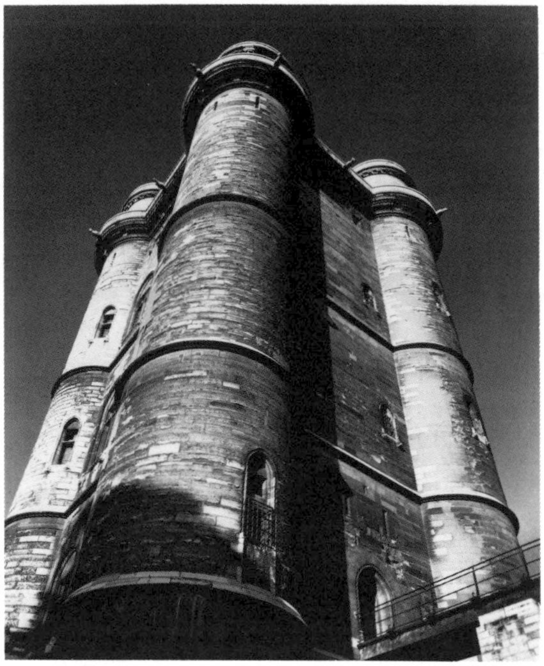

Stringcourses on the keep of the Château de Vincennes, Paris, 13th-century French Gothic. PHOTO: WIM SWAAN

GREGORY WHITTINGTON

[See also **Molding.**]

STUDIOS MONASTERY, a Byzantine monastic residence located in the southwest corner of Constantinople. Although dedicated to St. John the Baptist, the monastery was commonly known by the name of its original benefactor, the patrician Studios, who established it in 463 to house a community of *akoimetoi* ("sleepless ones," so called because they maintained a perpetual recitation of the Divine Office). The monastery had a varied history. Depopulated by the iconoclast emperor Constantine V (*r.* 741–775), it experienced a dramatic revival after the energetic Theodore became abbot in 799; within a few years the number of monks increased to more than 700.

Unlike prior Byzantine monasteries—which had tended to be loosely organized, with abbots often practicing a life of ascetic seclusion—Studios under Theodore adopted a strict, cenobitic order, in accordance with the monastic rules of St. Pachomius, St. Basil the Great of Caesarea, and Dorotheus of Gaza. Individual asceticism was subordinated to community life as monks worked and worshiped together under the constant paternal supervision of the abbot. In time, the monastery became a center for iconography and hymnography. It also maintained an important scriptorium that is credited with introducing into Byzantium the minuscule style of writing.

The monastery's rigorous insistence on doctrinal orthodoxy and moral purity often set the Studites at odds with the civil and ecclesiastical establishment. They were dispersed after the recrudescence of iconoclasm in 814 but quickly regained their former eminence and sense of independence after the restoration of orthodoxy in 843. The rule and liturgical order of Studios exerted a strong influence on other monastic establishments during the Middle Ages, particularly on Mt. Athos and in Russia.

The monastery was virtually destroyed during the Latin occupation of Constantinople (1204–1261); it was rebuilt in 1290. After the fall of the city to the Turks in 1453, the monastery's church was converted into a mosque; severely damaged by fire in 1782, it stands today as a roofless ruin.

BIBLIOGRAPHY

Hans-Georg Beck, *Kirche und theologische Literatur im byzantinischen Reich* (1959), 213 and *passim;* H. Delehaye, "Stoudion-Stoudios," in *Analecta Bollanda,* 52 (1934); J. Leroy, "La vie quotidienne du moine Studite," in *Irénikon,* 27 (1954).

JOHN H. ERICKSON

[See also **Athos, Mount; Basil the Great of Caesarea, St.; Byzantine Church; Constantine V; Divine Office; Iconoclasm, Christian; Monasticism, Byzantine; Pachomius, St.; Theodore of Studios.**]

STUDIUM GENERALE. See **Universities.**

STURLA ÞÓRÐARSON (1214–1284), Icelandic poet and historian, was a nephew of the celebrated historian Snorri Sturluson. He grew up in western Iceland and stayed at various times in Snorri's house, becoming influenced by his uncle's historical studies and political efforts to maintain Iceland's independence from Norway. After Snorri's death in 1241, Sturla assumed an important role among Icelanders opposed to King Hákon's plans to dominate their country, offering at every opportunity resistance to the king's agents, notably Gizurr Þorvaldsson. Sturla was lawspeaker in 1251. At length, however, in 1262 Iceland was forced to submit to Norway's will. In his *Íslendinga saga,* preserved in the collection known as *Sturlunga saga,* Sturla records the history of the age of the Sturlungs, describing the bloody feuds, the ideas that animated the various sides, and the moral corruption that finally brought about the loss of Iceland's independence. In the process he offers valuable glimpses into Icelandic social life.

In 1263, Sturla journeyed to Norway, arriving just after Hákon Hákonarson had left on what was to prove a fatal military expedition to Scotland. He met Hákon's son, Magnús, who had been crowned king. Magnús' attitude, however, made it clear that the former resister was not welcome at court. Nevertheless, when Magnús and his wife, Ingiborg, embarked on a boat trip to the south of Bergen, Sturla was invited to go along. One evening the poet narrated to the crew a story (probably a *fornaldarsaga,* now lost) about the giantess Huld. He told the story "better and more fully than anyone there had ever heard it told before." The queen noticed the merry gathering around Sturla, and the next day the royal couple summoned him to repeat the story to them. Henceforth they were friends.

The following spring, when news of Hákon's death reached Norway, Magnús asked Sturla to write his father's biography. *Hákonar saga Hákonarsonar,* the last of the great Old Norse kings' sagas preserved entire, was completed, or nearly completed, in 1265, according to a remark in the saga itself. Some fifteen years later (most likely 1278–1280), Sturla wrote the very last of the royal sagas, *Magnúss saga lagabœtis* (Saga of Magnús the law amender), which is based, according to *Sturlunga saga,* on letters and on the king's own instructions. Of this saga only two sheets of parchment are preserved.

Sturla remained in Norway until 1271, when he was sent home with a new code of laws, the *Járnsíða,* for the Icelanders. Under the code, which took effect in 1272, Sturla assumed the newly created office of *lögmaðr* (lawman), responsible directly to the Norwegian king. Some years later, when the office was divided, Sturla became *lögmaðr* for the northwestern part of the country, likely until 1283. In 1277–1278 he spent a year in the Faeroe Islands and in Norway. Thereafter, it is generally assumed, he concentrated on his literary activities.

It is difficult to say which of his other works Sturla wrote during his later years and which of them he had written earlier. Apart from those mentioned above, we know that he wrote one version of *Landnámabók* (*Sturlubók, ca.* 1275–1280), elaborating a text from the early thirteenth century, and several poems in skaldic verse, most of them quoted in his *Hákonar saga.* Moreover, three anonymous works have been attributed to him: *Kristni saga,* perhaps Sturla's version of an older, somewhat shorter text; *Laxdœla saga;* and *Grettis saga,* the preserved text of which is believed to be based on an original and shorter work, now lost, by Sturla.

BIBLIOGRAPHY

Gunnar Benediktsson, *Sagnameistarinn Sturla* (1961); Rolf Heller, "*Laxdœla* und *Sturlunga saga,*" in *Arkiv for nordisk filologi,* **76** (1961); William Paton Ker, "Sturla the Historian," in his *Collected Essays,* Charles Whibley, ed., II (1925, repr. 1967); Marina Mundt, *Sturla Þórðarson und die "Laxdœla saga"* (1969); Sigurður Jóhannesson Nordal, "Sturla Þórðarson og *Grettis saga,*" in *Studia Islandica,* **4** (1938); Pétur Sigurðsson, "Um *Íslendinga sögu* Sturlu Þórðarsonar," in *Safn til sögu Islands,* **6**, nos. 2–4 (1933–1935).

MARINA MUNDT

[See also **Family Sagas, Icelandic; Fornaldarsögur; Grettis Saga Ásmundarsonar; Hákonar Saga Hákonarsonar; Iceland; Laxdœla Saga; Norse Kings' Sagas; Snorri Sturluson; Sturlunga Saga.**]

STURLAUGS SAGA STARFSAMA (The story of Sturlaugr the Industrious), one of several "adventure tales" among the *fornaldarsögur* (stories of ancient times) that are without any historical basis. It was written in Iceland, probably about 1300. It appears to be older than *Göngu-Hrólfs saga,* which refers to it and whose title hero is said to be the son of Sturlaugr.

After introducing the protagonist, a chieftain's son in Norway, the narrative begins with his first quest. Sturlaugr sets out to ask for the hand of Ása, an earl's daughter in another province, but she rejects him, not wishing to marry someone staying at home and doing nothing except help his mother with the housework. Another suitor, King Haraldr, forces Ása's father to promise the girl to him. Then a berserk seeks her hand and challenges the king to a duel. The king is too old to fight, and Sturlaugr agrees to take care of the berserk on condition that Ása become his wife. The king has no option, so Sturlaugr and Ása go ahead and celebrate their wedding. With advice and guidance from Ása's wise foster mother, Véfreyja, Sturlaugr succeeds in killing the berserk, whose brother, Franmar, then tries to take revenge, but Sturlaugr wins that second duel as well, and the two become blood brothers and friends for life.

None too pleased with losing his fiancée, King Haraldr takes revenge by sending Sturlaugr on a dangerous mission to find a certain aurochs horn and bring it to him. Following a clue provided by Véfreyja, Sturlaugr discovers that her sister, Queen Snælaug of Hundingjaland, is the only person who knows its whereabouts, and she tells him that it is kept in a Permian temple, dedicated to Thor, Odin, Frigg, and Freyja, and also that no one but Sturlaugr can fetch the horn. When Sturlaugr and his blood brothers finally reach the temple, they find Thor sitting there in all his glory, surrounded by sixty priestesses, one of whom is wielding a mighty sword. Sturlaugr succeeds in getting the aurochs horn, but one of his blood brothers is killed in the attempt. He brings the horn to the king and then sets out on an expedition to Permia and Hundingjaland, killing the kings of both countries.

Back in Sweden, where Sturlaugr is now the king, he and his blood brother make solemn vows for the future: Sturlaugr to find out the origin of the aurochs horn, and Franmar to get into bed with Princess Ingigerðr of Russia. On Véfreyja's advice, Sturlaugr sends one of his men to abduct a Lappish princess, who then marries that man in the belief that he is Sturlaugr. On their wedding night, the bridegroom asks her about the horn, and she tells the whole story. Sturlaugr overhears by eavesdropping, and then sets fire to the house, killing the bridal couple. Franmar's efforts to get into bed with the Russian princess are at first thwarted by her hostile attitude, but with Sturlaugr's help and after a battle in which her father is killed, Franmar's vow is ultimately fulfilled.

The description of the *Hundingjar* (the cynocephali), who bark like dogs, is based on an Icelandic translation of Isidore of Seville or some other medieval authority. But the opening paragraph of the tale, stating that Scandinavia was settled by people from Asia, under the leadership of Odin, is borrowed from Snorri Sturluson's *Edda.*

BIBLIOGRAPHY

Sophie A. Krijn, "Sturlaugssagaen og Sturlaugsrimur," in *Arkiv för nordisk filologi,* **41** (1925); Otto J. Zitzelsberger, ed. and trans., *The Two Versions of Sturlaugs saga Starfsama* (1969).

HERMANN PÁLSSON

[See also **Berserks; Fornaldarsögur; Frigg; Gǫngu-Hrólfs Saga; Isidore of Seville, St.; Odin; Snorri Sturluson; Thor.**]

STURLUNGA SAGA (The saga of the sons of Sturla) is a compilation of fourteen sagas, if we count *Arons saga* (The saga of Aron) among them and if we consider *Ættartölur* (The genealogies) a saga; the compilation dates from about 1300. Like the other great compilations of medieval Icelandic writings (*Hauksbók, Flateyjarbók,* and *Möðruvallabók*), it includes narratives which differ in form as in content but which are all demonstrably sagas. Distinctively, the narratives compiled in *Sturlunga saga* are almost entirely contemporary histories written by men who themselves took part in many of the events they recorded. The earlier title of the collection was *Íslendinga saga hin mikla* (The great saga of the Icelanders), and reflects the central importance both thematically and structurally of the longest saga in the compilation—*Íslendinga saga* (The saga of the Icelanders). The title given later by Árni Magnússon (*d.* 1730) and still in use, *Sturlunga saga,* reflects the conviction already developed by Árni's time that one family, the Sturlungs, epitomized thirteenth-century Icelandic culture both in its savage feuds and violent enmities and also in its literary and intellectual vigor.

The *Sturlunga* offers both history and fiction; it contains the first substantial vernacular histories, not chronicles, after Ári's *Íslendingabók* and the *Landnámabók.* It also contains fictionally treated stories and single events which lead at once to the major issues and problems in the development of medieval Icelandic literary traditions.

Often in the *Sturlunga,* the authors, like all Icelandic writers passionately convinced that in historical fact lies the fundamental motivation for an individual's or a family's actions, inform their fictions by the narrative sequences, the references to common beliefs and practices, and the sense for chronology that encompass historical narrative (for example, see the interweaving of public and private scenes in the story of Þorgils skarði at the Norwegian court in *Þorgils saga skarða* [The saga of Þorgils skarði]).

Medieval hagiography enjoyed a vigorous development in Iceland, and it, too, variously and dramatically influenced secular biography in style and attitudes (for example, *Hrafns saga Sveinbjarnarsonar* [The saga of Hrafn Sveinbjörn's son] and *Prestssaga Guðmundar góða* [The saga of the priest Guðmundr the Good]).

Most remarkably, however, *Sturlunga*'s historians reflect the uniquely Icelandic influence of fictional writing on historical writing, an influence that led historians to adapt and even imitate the fictional techniques of pace, structure, and characterization already brilliantly developed in the great family sagas which were written before and during the lifetime of Sturla Þórðarson, the author of *Íslendinga saga.*

The *Sturlunga* compilation presents the history of Iceland from 1119 to 1284; its compiler, Þórðr Narfason, was a friend of Sturla Þórðarson and a lawman who lived at Skarð, near the central sites of many events in *Íslendinga saga.* He died in 1308, twenty-four years after Sturla's own death.

Þórðr understood Sturla's intention to write the history of his country during the twelfth and thirteenth centuries so as to give a panoramic yet immediately vivid story as his famous uncle, Snorri Sturluson, had given in his *Heimskringla* (History of the kings of Norway). Þórðr understood also, apparently, that Sturla hoped by the sequence of his separate sagas about leading Icelanders to heighten the contrasts in moral and social integrity between the late twelfth century and the mid thirteenth century, when Iceland tragically destroyed its own independence and became subject to the Norwegian church and state.

But Þórðr was a compiler, not a writer, and he failed to comprehend what Vigfusson rightly calls the "poetry" in Sturla's conception of Iceland's history. In an effort to explain Sturla's work and its significance, Þórðr wrote a short preface, known as Sturla's *Formáli* (Preface), in which he tried to distinguish between those sagas written before Sturla's work, sagas which concerned events in Iceland before the death of Brandr Sæmundarson (1201), and sagas which concerned events after Brandr's death but which were "little written" before Sturla composed his saga. As a preface to Sturla's history, Þórðr's comment does little to clarify the relationship of *Íslendinga saga* to the whole of the *Sturlunga* but much to clarify the compiler's principle that the chronology of the events should determine the narrative sequence.

Þórðr, probably at Sturla's request, selected several sagas about individual Icelanders' lives and gathered them together with *Íslendinga saga* in order to expand the history to the years before Sturla began his story. Þórðr further added the *Ættartölur,* and patched up some contradictions between sagas in two or three instances. Sturla's narrative covers events between 1183 and 1264, by which date Iceland was no longer independent, economically or ecclesiastically. Sturla himself died in 1284. (For the most eloquent accounts of Sturla's gifts as a historian, see Vigfusson's prolegomena to his edition of *Sturlunga;* for the fullest account of the relationship of *Íslendinga saga* to the whole of the *Sturlunga* compilation, see R. G. Thomas' introduction to the English translation of *Sturlunga.*)

The compilation comes down to us in two vellum manuscripts: Króksfjarðarbók (AM 122 A fol.) and Reykjarfjarðarbók (AM 122 B fol.). Both were known to be in the western fjords of Iceland in the seventeenth century. Reykjarfjarðarbók was probably written during the late fourteenth century; it was copied in the seventeenth century but after that suffered great damage—folios were removed to make covers for new books, or to be used as dress patterns, and so forth—so that when Árni Magnússon assembled it in the eighteenth century only about thirty folios, many of them in fragments, remained of an estimated 180 folios. Króksfjarðarbók was also written during the fourteenth century, perhaps mid century, and was also copied during the seventeenth century. Of its estimated original tally of 139 folios, we have 110, but many are in fragmentary condition. There are approximately forty extant paper manuscripts, as well as one eighteenth-century Latin translation. Although five major printed editions since 1816 have greatly increased our knowledge of the texts of *Sturlunga,* exact knowledge of the relationships of Reykjarfjarðarbók and Króksfjarðarbók to their sources is limited by compiler Þórðr Narfason's own detailed knowledge of Iceland's history as well as of Sturla's selective methods as a historian who did not intend to repeat other sagas' narratives. Had Þórðr altered less, and bequeathed a less amorphous manuscript to us, the more "incoherent" compilation might have given us a more direct vision of authorial character and craftsmanship.

The fine contemporary edition of the *Sturlunga,* by Jón Jóhannesson, Magnús Finnbogason, and Kristján Eldjárn, prints the sagas in the following order: Vol. I—*Geirmundar þáttr heljarskinns, Þorgils saga ok Hafliða, Ættartölur, Haukdœla þáttr, Sturlu saga, Formáli, Prestssaga Guðmundar góða, Guðmundar saga dýra, Hrafns saga Sveinbjarnarsonar, Íslendinga saga;* Vol. II—*Þórðar saga Kakala, Svínfellinga saga, Þorgils saga Skarða, Sturlu þáttr, Arons saga.*

Geirmundar þáttr heljarskinns is a *þáttr,* that is, a short narrative (literally, "a single strand of rope"), and gives, genealogically, the tale of the origin of Geirmundr's name, *heljarskinn* (black-skinned).

Þorgils saga ok Hafliða is a full saga about two chieftains, Þorgils and Hafliði, equally dignified, politically astute, and socially powerful. Their feud is bitter but their actions are not savage; the denouement contrasts reconciliation with the anticipated possibilities of vengeance, and is achieved by recourse to Christian principles of forgiveness and generosity. In the introduction to her edition of this saga, Ursula Brown gives a forceful and sensitive analysis of the dramatic and rhetorical structure of the saga, suggesting how much less "objective" it is in style and tone than later sagas in the *Sturlunga;* in so doing, she finely demonstrates its "moral, ironic, and personal" theme.

Haukdœla þáttr is again a very short piece, one of Þórðr's compiler's threads, which ties in the genealogy of the men of Haukadal with the preceding *Ættartölur.*

Sturlu saga is the saga of the first Sturla, Sturla of Hvammr, whose feuds and disputes during the years 1148 to 1183 illustrate the litigious road to power in his time and place yet also reflect the author's dispassionate appreciation of a shrewd man's use of the legal system without abusing all care for justice.

Formáli, as mentioned above, is Sturla's preface.

Prestssaga Guðmundar góða is the biography of Guðmundr the Good, a militant preacher, an intransigent defender of ecclesiastical power, and a man of remarkable intellectual and emotional fervor. The life of Guðmundr Arason, bishop at Hólar from 1203 to 1237, is told in several versions in different sagas, but the two fullest and most coherent are in *Sturlunga* and the separate Bishop's Saga, edited and printed under title *Byskupa sögur.* The

STURLUNGA SAGA

style of this life of Guðmundr Arason is somewhat clumsily hagiographic, and combines romantic admiration for a legendary hero with deep trust in the miraculous healing powers of the priest. It is not entirely clear how much of this saga was composed before, and how much especially for, the *Sturlunga,* but it is clear that the compiler of *The Life of Guðmundr Arason* knew Guðmundr in Iceland, even "was with him in Iceland in his circuits when priest, but . . . did not go abroad with him" (Vigfusson, "Prolegomena," cxxiii).

Guðmundar saga dýra tells briefly, in narrow focus, the central events, from about 1184/1185 to 1212, in the career of Guðmundr the Noble, as his intense dispute with Önundr led to Guðmundr's burning of Önundr in 1197. Guðmundr then enters a cloister, and the saga concludes anticlimactically, without either Christian or heathen principles elicited. The saga was probably composed shortly after 1212, the date of Guðmundr's death.

Hrafns saga Sveinbjarnarsonar is again a secular biography with echoes of hagiographic tones, and tells of the remarkable Hrafn, the son of Sveinbjörn, a surgeon, musician, woodcarver, and generally talented and generous man who was hated and envied by Þorvaldr of Vatnsfjörðr, and eventually brought down by him. There is a full life of Hrafn elsewhere, but only the latter half of his story is included in the *Sturlunga.* This part aptly reflects the decay of order and trust in the Icelandic Commonwealth as it destroyed individual men's moral security.

Íslendinga saga, the heart of the *Sturlunga,* contains 200 chapters of differing lengths, so that there is a rise and fall in the narrative rhythm, providing a controlled sense of the continuing but increasingly tragic crises in the history. At the beginning, Sturla picks up the echoes of Hvamm-Sturla's disputatious life; recounts the youth of Sturla's three sons by his second wife—Þórðr, Sighvatr, and Snorri—and suggests their different interests; brings back the impact of Bishop Guðmundr when dating his return to Iceland; and concentrates this first section on the murderous death of Hrafn Sveinbjarnarson. Sighvatr, Sturla's son, moves to the north, and from here onward the forces from the north are largely his supporters; those in the south and west, Snorri Sturluson's. Snorri Sturluson's political career now embroils him more and more against Bishop Guðmundr and often against his own brothers. Sturla, the son of Þórðr Sturluson, gives a fuller portrait of his cousin, Sturla, Sighvatr's son, than of Snorri Sturluson, and it is clear that the reckless and dashing young Sighvatsson is the romantic but self-destroying hero of this part of the saga.

The fullest detail and the deepest comprehension of the interwoven events of Icelandic history comprise chapters 45 through 195, and cover the years from 1222 to 1260: the Sauðafellraid (chap. 74); the violent marauding of their fellow men by Snorri's illegitimate son, Órækja, and his band; the criminal activities of Kolbeinn the Young; the Apavatnraid (chap. 129) in 1238; the battle at Ørlygsstaðir (chap. 138); the burning at Flugumýrr. All of these events mark the gradual loss by Snorri Sturluson of power and independence, and anticipate the growing might of the Sturlungs' enemy, Gizurr Þorvaldsson, who ultimately receives the title of *jarl* (earl) from King Hákon of Norway, and rules over Iceland in the name of Norway's monarchs.

Sturla's gifts as a historian are less apparent in the balanced use of detail throughout each section of his story than they are in the vivid portraits of single characters—the rash, courageous, proudly defiant Sturla Sighvatsson; the taciturn, ironic, magnanimous Sighvatr Sturluson; and Snorri Sturluson himself, here seen not as the great historian and poet but as the ambitious and grasping politician, not as the scholar of history and literature but as a vacillating and suggestible victim of Norwegian power politics. Sturla's judgments on the leading men of his lifetime are implied, as in the traditional style of the family sagas, by their laconic remarks and by their actions. He says no more about himself, either when he is captured at Ørlygsstaðir or when he is treacherously taken by Gizurr.

Sturla has two major problems as a historian of these events: that he himself was so close to them (as Snorri was not to the events in his histories of Norwegian kings), and that he was primarily a storyteller, not a political analyst. His saga is, therefore, a moving story of the failures, ambitions, noble dreams, and ignoble failures of single men during the decline of the Icelandic Commonwealth; it is not primarily a historian's social and political commentary on the causes of that decline.

Sturla's language is rich and his syntax flexible, moving easily from colloquial to formal; he uses dreams and dream strophes to heighten the sense of impending doom or to underline one man's taunting comment on another's dishonorable action or motive. When we remember that Sturla also wrote the *Grettis saga* as we have it, and that he wrote the more conventional history *Hákonar saga Hákonarsonar* (The saga of Hákon, son of Hákon), we can see the more clearly that in his *Íslendinga saga* he consciously attempted to use the fictional sagas' techniques of characterization and dramatic dialogue to strengthen the sense of human truth in his historical saga.

Þórðar saga Kakala takes us forward in the life of the Sturlungs' avengers. Þórðr, the son of Sighvatr, and thus Sturla's cousin, was humorously nicknamed the cackler, chatterer, bubbling little pot, but he was a man of more serious discipline and integrity than his nickname suggests. Much of his life was spent in Norway after he outwitted his enemy Kolbeinn's plots against him and survived the bloody sea-battle at Flói. He constantly tried to win the Norwegian kings' and leading men's sympathy for Icelandic independence, especially in ecclesiastical matters, but the Norwegian king distrusted Þórðr's trustworthiness and kept him almost as a prisoner until his death in Norway (1256). In this saga the sharply visualized scenes and vividly realized personalities remind us of *Íslendinga saga,* but the tone is very different; a disillusioned eye for the internecine slaughter focuses our feeling on Þórðr's triumph over his enemies, bought at the cost of a noble adversary's death. The lament for Brandr Kolbeinsson exceeds even Sturla's sense of pathos; it is fully tragic (chap. 39).

Svínfellinga saga is the story of the men of Svínafell during the years from 1248 to 1252 and is the only saga in the compilation which records events in the southeastern corner of Iceland, where Ormr Jónsson was the most notable chieftain. The central feud concerns Ormr's sons, who, after his death in 1241, are first favored and then envied by Ögmundr, Ormr's brother-in-law. After his wife's death, Ögmundr seems to have fallen into hitherto unsuspected savagery and distrust; he finally ambushed and killed two of his nephews. Conventional repentance and the imposition of penalties followed, whereby the murderous loss of life was presumably compensated.

Þorgils saga Skarða returns to the Sturlung family, for it recounts the career of Böðvar's son Þorgils the Harelip, the chivalric and daring Icelander who, at the court of the Norwegian king, won the king's trust and favor, and in 1252 was sent back to Iceland as precisely that sort of commissioner Snorri Sturluson had tried to become. Þorgils was the son of Sturla's half-brother, and a young man whom Sturla always loved and admired. For many years Þorgils succeeded in balancing the claims of his own family, which was not sympathetic to his Norwegian allegiance, with his responsibility to the Norwegian king. The saga portrays this success as the result of Þorgils' understanding of peace and capacity for just administration, not as the sign of a selfish or unreliable commissioner. But Þorgils' death by treachery echoes the murder of Snorri Sturluson in 1241; here again, in 1258, the anarchy bred of envy, ruthless ambition, and immoral use of the heroic vengeance code wiped out the older moral ethos of Iceland.

Sturlu þáttr is the brief account of some of the final occurrences in Sturla Þórðarson's life, primarily his meeting with King Magnús in Norway and his success as a storyteller to the king and his queen. It also contains the specific statement that Þórðr Narfason spent the winter of 1271 with Sturla, and concludes with the dates of Sturla's life; he died in 1284, "when he was seventy years old," and thus had been born in 1214.

Arons saga tells of Hjörleifr's son Aron, a thirteenth-century hero whose career is later than that of the *Sturlunga* but whose saga has often been included with the *Sturlunga.* (The English translation of the *Sturlunga* does not include this story of a familiarly fearless, even rather old-fashioned, outlaw-hero.)

Although Sturla Þórðarson's *Íslendinga saga* is the heart of the *Sturlunga* compilation, the shorter sagas also have their historical and literary identities; they embody shifts in tone from Sturla's, sometimes romantic, sometimes caustic and satiric. They include, in the story of Þorgils skarði, a return to the earlier sense of honor as we read of it in the great family sagas such as *Njála* and *Gísla.* They dramatize, as in the story of Þorgils and Hafliði, the possibilities of mediation and reconciliation in contrast to the certain anarchism and destruction of vengeance. Most of all, the shorter sagas brought together by the compiler, Þórðr, surround Sturla's *Íslendinga saga* with a vast, ever-changing countryside of individuals whose world was fundamentally altered by the murder of Snorri Sturluson in 1241 (chap. 151 in *Íslendinga saga*).

BIBLIOGRAPHY

Sources. Ursula Brown, ed., *Þorgils saga ok Hafliða* (1952); Halldór Hermannsson, ed., *The Saga of Thorgils and Haflidi* (1945); *The Life of Gudmund the Good, Bishop of Hólar,* G. Turville-Petre and E. S. Ólszewska, trans. (1942); Jón Jóhannesson, Magnús Finnbogason, and Kristján Eldjárn, eds., *Sturlunga saga,* 2 vols. (1946); Kristian Kaalund, ed., *Sturlunga saga,* 2 vols. (1906–1911); *Sturlunga saga,* Julia McGrew, trans., I (1970), and Julia McGrew and R. George Thomas, trans., II (1974); Gudbrand Vigfusson, ed., *Sturlunga saga, Including the Íslendinga Saga of Lawman Sturla Thordsson and Other Works,* 2 vols. (1878).

Studies. Gunnar Benediktsson, *Ísland hefur jarl* (1954), and *Sagnameistarinn Sturla* (1961); Úlfar Bragason, "On the Poetics of *Sturlunga*" (diss., Univ. of California at Berkeley, 1986); Ólafia Einarsdóttir, *Studier i kronologisk metode i tidlig islandsk historieskrivning* (1964); R. J. Glendinning, "Saints, Sinners, and the Age of the Sturlungs: Two Dreams from the *Íslendinga Saga,*" in *Scandinavian Studies,* 38 (1966); Sigurður Nordal, *Sturla Þórdarson og Grettis saga* (1938), and "Sagalitteraturen," in *Nordisk kultur,* VIII, pt. B (1953), 180–273; Björn M. Ólsen, *Um Sturlungu* (1897); Pétur Sigurðsson, *Um Íslendinga sögu Sturlu Þórðarsonar* (1933–1935); Einar Ól. Sveinsson, *The Age of the Sturlungs,* Jóhann S. Hannesson, trans. (1953); R. George Thomas, "The Sturlung Age as an Age of Saga Writing," in *Germanic Review,* 25 (1950); Stephen Norman Tranter, *Sturlunga Saga: The Rôle of the Creative Compiler* (1987).

JULIA H. MCGREW

[See also **Family Sagas, Icelandic; Gísla Saga Súrssonar; Grettis Saga Ásmundarsonar; Iceland; Njáls Saga; Norway; Snorri Sturluson; Sturla Þórðarson; Þættir.**]

STYLUS (Latin: *stilus,* long, pointed instrument), an ancient and medieval instrument made of metal, wood, ivory, or the like, which served chiefly for writing on wax tablets. In the early Middle Ages, the stylus was also widely used for ruling and for making nearly invisible drypoint annotations (glosses in the vernacular, liturgical notes, and so forth) on parchment books. Typically, one end of the stylus was sharp, for writing, while the other was rounded or flat and used to erase.

BIBLIOGRAPHY

Bernhard Bischoff, *Mittelalterliche Studien: Ausgewählte Aufsätze zur Schriftkunde und Literaturgeschichte* , I (1966), 88–92.

MICHAEL MCCORMICK

[See also **Ruling; Wax Tablets; Writing Materials.**]

SUDA, perhaps meaning "palisade" or "bulwark," a large tenth-century Byzantine dictionary and encyclopedia. The Byzantines inherited the Hellenistic passion for epitomizing and organizing ancient learning, history, and literature. The disruptions of the seventh and eighth centuries stifled such activity, but during the relative peace of the Macedonian period Byzantines once again looked to classical antiquity and collected remnants of a heritage they found all the more precious because it was now perilously reduced. Within this flourishing genre, the *Suda* justly claims preeminence.

At least from the time of Eustathios (twelfth century) until about 1930, readers assumed that an editor named "Suidas" had created the lexicon. After Ada Adler demonstrated that *Suda* was the collection's title, for another thirty years scholars debated the elusive meaning of that word. Nikolaus Walker has summarized the various arguments in an article published in 1962.

The work contains about 30,000 lemmata in a variation of alphabetical order, with vowels and diphthongs ordered by sound. So αι follows not α, but δ; after ζ come ει, η, ι, all of which the Byzantines pronounced ē (as do Greeks today); ω follows ο. Scholars used to assume that the *Suda* drew this material directly from ancient texts. The immediate sources, however, have almost invariably been proven to be other collections, including the extensive *Excerpts* of Constantine VII Porphyrogenitos (905–959), the chronicle of George the Monk (*fl.* mid ninth century), Diogenes Laertius (*fl.* early third century), and the biographical dictionary of Hesychios of Miletos (*ca.* 500). Occasionally the compilers added extracts culled at random from a complete *corpus,* that of Callimachus, for example, and of the emperor Julian. The collectors seem to have consulted the *Palatine Anthology* (*Anthologia Palatina, ca.* 980, a revision of an *Anthology* by Constantinus Cephalas dating from the late ninth century), as well as texts and scholia for Homer, Sophocles, and Aristophanes.

The *Suda* simply presents this hodge-podge, blissfully neglecting uniformity and demonstrating little historical sense or critical discrimination. Careless errors, conflicting multiple glosses for a single lemma, and peculiar distortions betray the hasty composition and want of governing intelligence. For scholars who exercise appropriate caution, however, the *Suda* offers a treasury of ancient and late antique learning that is otherwise lost. While showing the respectful admiration that linked Constantinople to Athens, the *Suda* also repeatedly illustrates the chasm between the two, for instance, by treating literary masterpieces as philological curiosities, proposing allegorical interpretations of classical statues or demythologizing antique tales, deflating pagan gods through euhemerism and allegory or even attacking paganism head on. Such entries make the *Suda* a provocative and revealing monument of Byzantium.

BIBLIOGRAPHY

Ada Adler, *Suidae lexicon,* 5 vols. (1928–1938, repr. 1967–1971), and "Suidas," in Pauly-Wissowa, ed., *Realencyclopädie des klassischen Altertumswissenschaft,* ser. 2, IV (1931), 675–717; Emily Albu Hanawalt, "The *Suda* on the Pagan Gods," in *East European Quarterly,* **13,** no. 4 (1979); Romilly J. H. Jenkins, "The Hellenistic Origins of Byzantine Literature," in *Dumbarton Oaks Papers,* **17** (1963); Karl Krumbacher, *Geschichte der byzantinischen Litteratur* (1897, repr. 1970); Nikolaus Walter, "*Suda*: Ein Literaturbericht zum Titel des sogenannten Suidas-Lexicons," in *Das Altertum,* **8** (1962).

EMILY ALBU HANAWALT

[See also **Classical Literary Studies; Constantine VII Porphyrogenitos; Encyclopedias and Dictionaries, Byzantine; George the Monk.**]

SUDAN. See **Nubia.**

ṢUFFA, an Arabic word meaning "raised floor" or "bench" (hence the English "sofa"). The word is most often found in the Arabic sources in connection with the *ahl al-ṣuffa,* those who, either from poverty or from lack of a dwelling in Medina, encamped within the *ṣuffa* of Muḥammad's house. In that context *ṣuffa* is thought to refer to the roofed portico of palm trees at one end of the courtyard. In later Iranian sources it is most frequently used to designate the raised platform on which tombstones were placed. Another common usage is in the sense of *īwān* (*eyvān*), since the *ṣuffa* was usually raised above the level of the courtyard.

BIBLIOGRAPHY

K. A. C. Creswell, *Early Muslim Architecture,* 2nd ed. (1969); W. Montgomery Watt, "Ahl al-Ṣuffa," in *Encyclopaedia of Islam,* 2nd ed., I (1960).

BERNARD O'KANE

[See also **Eyvān; Islamic Art and Architecture.**]

SUFISM. See **Mysticism, Islamic.**

SUGER OF ST. DENIS (1081–1151). Abbot of St. Denis from 1122 to his death, Suger was the successful head of a leading royal abbey north of Paris, a valued counselor to two kings, a great architectural innovator, and a perceptive historian of his times. He was born probably in Argenteuil, near Paris, or in St. Denis. Suger and his biographer, the monk Guillaume, repeatedly acknowledge that his family was of "humble" origin, which almost certainly means that they belonged to the lesser nobility of the Île-de-France. His father, Hélinand, appears in the necrology of St. Denis, and two brothers, Pierre and Raoul, are also known. Descendants of the line at the end of the twelfth century were knights and bore the surname "de St. Denis."

Suger was given as an oblate to the monastery of St. Denis at the age of nine or ten. The first decade he spent in study at the priory of St. Denis de l'Estrée, where he must have come to the attention of Abbot Adam, who, toward the close of 1103, sent him to a monastery near Fontevrault in Normandy to continue his education. By 1106 he had returned to St. Denis, in time to represent the abbot at the Council of Poitiers. The following year Adam appointed him *prévôt* of the largely devastated priory of Berneval in Normandy. Suger spent two strenuous years reclaiming lost rights and restoring lands to cultivation. Encouraged by this success, Adam transferred him, in 1109, to Toury-en-Beauce, which is not far from Chartres. This was one of the abbey's most important domains and, like Berneval, subject to repeated attacks from neighboring lords. Once again, Suger tells us, he succeeded in transforming the domain "from sterility to fecundity."

While still a student at St. Denis de l'Estrée, Suger had formed a lasting friendship with a fellow student, the young Prince Louis, later Louis VI. As early as 1108 Suger was sufficiently intimate at court to be present at confidential talks between the reigning king, Philip I, and the crown prince. He accompanied Louis VI on most of his military expeditions against the rebellious vassals of the Île-de-France and was commissioned by Louis to negotiate with one of the most troublous, Hugues du Puiset, in 1122. Throughout this period, Suger appears to have been particularly concerned with affairs of the church. Louis employed him as am-

The reconstructed choir of the abbey church of St. Denis, dedicated by Suger in 1144. FOTO MARBURG/ART RESOURCE

bassador to represent Capetian policies at the papal court in a series of missions to Pope Paschal II in 1112, to Gelasius II in 1118, and to Calixtus II in 1122. It was while returning from this last voyage that Suger learned of the death of Abbot Adam and his own election as abbot of St. Denis.

Under Suger's direction, St. Denis prospered as never before. By his own account, he more than tripled the domainal revenues of the abbey. No administrative detail was too insignificant to escape his concern, from the regulation of liturgical practice to the provisioning of wheat and the cutting down of trees. He established new towns at Carrières-St.-Denis (shortly before 1137) and Vaucresson (1146). (Historians are doubly favored by his decision to record for posterity his varied labors on behalf of the church in his *Liber de rebus in administratione sua gestis* [On the things done in his administration].) At the same time, he scoured the abbey's archives to discover forgotten claims to lands and rights, which he prosecuted with zeal, notably in the case of the priory of Argenteuil, then occupied by nuns under the direction of Heloise, the former mistress of Abelard. In 1129, on the basis of a charter that he himself forged, Suger successfully established the abbey's rights to Argenteuil, ejected the nuns, and recovered the monastery for St. Denis.

In 1127, Suger undertook a much-needed reform of the abbey, which had become lax under the governance of Abbot Adam and the target of a scathing attack by St. Bernard. His reform abolished the worst abuses of the brothers and returned them to a strict observance of the monastic rule.

Suger's accomplishments as abbot of St. Denis were most strikingly displayed in his reconstruction of the abbey church, which was to serve the rest of Europe as a model of a new architectural style, the Gothic. The building campaign was conducted in three stages, beginning with the west facade, which Suger completed in 1140 (except for the west towers). He then turned east and rebuilt the choir, which he dedicated in 1144, commemorating the ceremony in a *Libellus alter de consecratione ecclesiae Sancti Dionysii* (On the consecration of the church of St. Denis). Finally, he began work on the nave, which, however, remained incomplete during his lifetime.

In the choir, walls were pierced by tall windows of stained glass that reduced wall surfaces to frames and let in a flood of light, embodying the Gothic ideal of luminosity, intended to instruct the worshiper that there was a reality beyond that perceived by the senses, the "true light," as Suger wrote, "to which Christ is the door." This striking innovation in architectural design was the result of Suger's personal metaphysic, derived from a reading of Pseudo-Dionysius the Areopagite, a fifth-century Neoplatonic writer whom legend identified with St. Denis, apostle to France and patron of the abbey. On the basis of the Dionysian theory of emanations, Suger saw art as a means to lift the mind from the contemplation of the material world to an understanding of the power and majesty of God. His church was meant to be an image of God; its construction, to serve the "edification" of the faithful.

Despite Suger's many responsibilities as abbot, he was in constant attendance at the royal court. The *Chronicle of Morigny* singled him out as "the most famous and best advocate at the court of the king," and from 1127 to 1137 his name appears as witness to numerous royal charters. Although temporarily in eclipse at the beginning of Louis VII's reign (1138–1143), Suger thereafter re-emerged as a principal counselor of the king. When Louis took the cross in 1146, Suger was named regent of France. From 1147 to 1149 he governed the realm in the king's absence, successfully quelling the revolt led by Louis' brother, Robert of Dreux, in the spring of 1149.

Suger made himself the chronicler of the events in which he played such a vital part. His life of Louis VI, the *Vita Ludovici Grossi,* composed between 1138 and 1144, and the beginning of his life of Louis VII (*Historia gloriosi regis Ludovici septimi*), which death prevented him from completing, are among the most important works of royal history in the first half of the twelfth century. They initiate a long series of regnal histories written at St. Denis to record, and in recording to celebrate, the deeds of France's ruling monarchs.

Suger's final year was spent in preparation for a new crusade, but death cut short his plans. According to his biographer, his many achievements won him the respect of his contemporaries, who bestowed upon him the affectionate title of *pater patriae,* father of his country. He died 13 January 1151, at the age of seventy, and was buried at St. Denis.

BIBLIOGRAPHY

Sources. The standard edition of Suger's works remains *Oeuvres complètes de Suger,* A. Lecoy de la Marche, ed. (1867), which also contains the life of Suger by Guillaume of St. Denis. Suger's fragment on Louis VII, along with an edition of his life of Louis VI, is in Auguste Molinier, ed., *Vie de Louis le Gros par Suger suivie de l'Histoire du roi Louis VII* (1887). A French translation of the life of Louis VI, with a Latin text, is available in Henri Waquet, ed. and trans., *Vie de Louis VI le Gros* (1929, repr. 1964).

Erwin Panofsky has provided English translations, with Latin texts, from several of Suger's writings that bear on the construction of the church of St. Denis. See Erwin Panofsky, ed. and trans., *Abbot Suger on the Abbey Church of St.-Denis and Its Art Treasures* (1946). A second edition of this volume was issued in 1979, with revised bibliography by Gerda Panofsky-Soergel.

See also *Suger: Comment fut construit Saint-Denis,* Jean Leclercq, trans. (1945), a French translation of Suger's *De consecratione*; Jules Lair, "Fragment inédit de la Vie de Louis VII préparée par Suger," in *Bibliothèque de l'École des Chartes,* **34** (1873).

Studies. Marcel Aubert, *Suger* (1950); Éric Bournazel, *Le gouvernement capétien au XIIe siècle* (1975); Otto Cartellieri, *Abt Suger von Saint-Denis, 1081–1151* (1898); Sumner McKnight Crosby, *L'abbaye royal de Saint-Denis* (1953), *The Royal Abbey of Saint-Denis in the Time of Abbot Suger (1122–1151)* (1981), and *The Royal Abbey of Saint-Denis from Its Beginnings to the Death of Suger, 465–1151,* Pamela Z. Blum, ed. (1987); Paula Lieber Gerson, ed., *Abbot Suger and Saint-Denis* (1986); Achille Luchaire, *Louis VI le Gros* (1890, repr. 1964); Otto von Simson, *The Gothic Cathedral* (2nd ed. 1962); Gabrielle M. Spiegel, *The Chronicle Tradition of Saint-Denis: A Survey* (1978), 44–52, and "History as Enlightenment: Suger and the *Mos Anagogicus,*" in Paula Gerson, ed., *Abbot Suger and Saint-Denis* (1986); Thomas G. Waldman, "Abbot Suger and the Nuns of Argenteuil," in *Traditio,* **41** (1985); Walter Wulf, *Die Kapitellplastik des Sugerbaus von Saint-Denis* (1979).

GABRIELLE M. SPIEGEL

[See also **Abelard, Peter; Antiquarianism and Archaeology; Bernard of Clairvaux, St.; Gothic Architecture; Grandes Chroniques de France; Louis VI of France; Paschal II, Pope; Provost; Pseudo-Dionysius the Areopagite; St. Denis, Abbey Church.**]

SULTAN, a title denoting the holder of political authority. In Arabic, *sulṭan* (a loanword from Aramaic *sholṭānā*), originally signified (political) power, might, authority. It was applied to individuals by the tenth century, if not earlier, and was used by some Fatimids (907–1171) and Maḥmūd of Ghazna (977–1032), as well as others. The Seljuk era introduced a greater specificity in its usage. Toghrıl-Beg was given this title by the caliphate in 1051 as a sign of the supreme political authority he wielded in the Islamic world. In an age in which the Abbasids no longer possessed spiritual authority, it was a means by which a secular authority could be legitimized. The title was passed on to the Ayyubids, Mamluks, and Ottomans, among others.

BIBLIOGRAPHY

Ibn al-Athīr, *Al-Kāmil fī't-Ta'rīkh,* C. J. Tornberg, ed. (1851–1876), IX, 92; Aṭ-Ṭabarī, *Ta'rīkh aṭ-Ṭabarī,* M. Ibrāhīm, ed., 10 vols. (1962–1967), IX, 518; Vasilii V. Barthold, *Turkestan Down to the Mongol Invasion,* V. Minorsky, trans. (1977); Clifford E. Bosworth, *The Ghaznavids* (1963); P. M. Holt, "The Position and Power of the Mamluk Sultan," in *Bulletin of the School of Oriental and African Studies,* 37 (1975); Johannes Hendrik Kramers, "Sultan," in *Encyclopaedia of Islam,* 1st ed., IV (1934), 543–545; A. K. S. Lambton, "The Internal Structure of the Seljuq Empire," in *The Cambridge History of Iran,* V (1968).

PETER B. GOLDEN

[See also **Ayyubids; Caliphate; Islamic Administration; Mamluk Dynasty; Seljuks.**]

SUMER IS ICUMEN IN, a mid-thirteenth-century musical composition for six voices, set in a four-part unison canon over a two-part round. Probably originating at Reading Abbey, England (hence its variant name: Reading Rota), the Summer Canon figures among the best-known works of the Middle Ages.

Two voices singing a "rondellus" provide the harmonic substructure. Their music, labeled "pes" (the ground bass) in the unique source (British Museum, Harley MS 978, fol. 11v), consists of a pair of short phrases constructed as counterpoints to each other (Ex. 1).

Above the pes appears a lengthier melodic line that, according to the verbal instructions or "canon" in the manuscript, is performable as a "rota" (round or unison canon) by two to four singers.

The basses' constant alternation of the first and second notes of the mode generates a bell-like sense of motion between two "chords." The scale employed produces a "major" cast, further enhanced through clear triadic sonorities. For the most part, the upper voices proceed in the lilting long-short pattern of the first rhythmic mode, with phrases (4 + 4 + 2 + 4 + 4 + 6) somewhat independent of the foursquare pes.

Above the reiterated "Sing cuccu nu, sing cuccu," the upper voices perform either of two texts. The first, a Middle English poem in praise of "sumer" (that is, "spring" or "warm weather") has given the work its popular title; beneath this appears a Latin poem for Easter, *Perspice christicola.*

In several respects, including date of composition and provenance, the Summer Canon was for some time the subject of scholarly debate. Although these matters are now generally agreed upon, discussions of three general issues continue: the earliest recoverable version, the order of composition, and the relationship of the work to oral and written traditions.

In its present state, the manuscript reveals erasures and notational emendations. Whereas the majority of the deleted pitches are recoverable, the revisions remain problematical. The earlier version utilized a combination of squares, later converted through the addition of stems, and rhomboid lozenges, some of which were changed into squares. Restoration of the original notation bears upon discussions of rhythm and the compositional process.

The priority of the texts and the notation has also been queried. Whereas current opinion inclines toward the addition of the Latin as the last step, paleographical and textual analysis has led at least one author on the subject to place the Latin poem before either the English or the music. It has also

Example 1

been suggested that both texts and music were the work of a single individual.

The combination of rota and rondellus places the Summer Canon on a high level of craftsmanship and sophistication. Moreover, if the likeness between the pes and an Easter antiphon is more than coincidental, the resultant affinity with procedures in the contemporaneous motet supports an assessment of the work as clearly indebted to written tradition.

On the other hand, links to oral and improvisatory traditions have been defended, principally on the basis of the simple round used in the pes. The notion that the upper parts might reflect a technique for extemporizing short phrases over a static foundation was put forward in 1983, although the melody's phraseology argues against too ready an acceptance of such a view.

Sumer Is Icumen In offers an outstanding instance of synthesis on two levels: compositional technique and written versus oral traditions. Its importance to the history of music is further heightened by its position as the sole piece of six-voice polyphony before the fifteenth century, and by its relationship with stylistic developments occurring in English and continental music of the period.

BIBLIOGRAPHY

Source. Ernest H. Sanders, ed., *English Music of the Thirteenth and Early Fourteenth Centuries* (Polyphonic Music of the Fourteenth Century, XIV) (1979), 5 (nos. 4a, 4b).

Studies. Manfred F. Bukofzer, *"Sumer is icumen in": A Revision* (1944); Shai Burstyn, "Gerald of Wales and the *Sumer* Canon," in *The Journal of Musicology,* 2 (1983); E. J. Dobson and Frank Ll. Harrison, *Medieval English Songs* (1979); Jacques Handschin, "The Summer Canon and Its Background," in *Musica disciplina,* 3 (1949), 5 (1951); Frank Ll. Harrison, "Rota and Rondellus in English Medieval Music," in *Proceedings of the Royal Musical Association,* **86** (1959–1960), and *Music in Medieval Britain,* 4th ed. (1980), 141–144; Wolfgang Obst, "'Sumer Is Icumen In'—A Contrafactum?" in *Music and Letters,* **64** (1983); Nino Pirrotta, "On the Problem of 'Sumer Is Icumen In,'" in *Musica disciplina,* 2 (1948); Edmund Reiss, *The Art of the Middle English Lyric* (1972); Ernest H. Sanders, "Duple Rhythm and Alternate Third Mode in the 13th Century," in *Journal of the American Musicological Society,* **15** (1962), "Tonal Aspects of 13th-century English Polyphony," in *Acta musicologica,* **37** (1965), and "Sumer Is Icumen In," in *New Grove Dictionary of Music and Musicians,* XVIII (1980), 366–368; B. Schofield, "The Provenance and Date of 'Sumer Is Icumen In,'" in *Music Review,* **9** (1948); James Travis, "A Possible Celtic Origin for the Reading Rota," in *Miscellanea musica celtica* (Institute of Medieval Music: Musicological Studies, XIV) (1968).

ARTHUR D. LEVINE

[See also **Middle English Literature: Lyric; Polyphony; Rota.**]

SUMMA. See **Scholasticism.**

SUMMA DE LEGIBUS NORMANNIE. See **Custumals of Normandy.**

SUMPTUARY LAWS, EUROPEAN. In the southern French town of Alais in 1253 the municipal authorities decreed that young couples could no longer celebrate their marriages with torchlight parades through the streets. There was at the time insufficient timber in the district to permit this traditional extravagance, and wood was needed for many other economic necessities. In 1340, in Portugal, all peons, "those who [did] not have enough wealth to possess horses" and who were residing in towns, were forbidden to wear furs and jewelry because it did not become their station. The ordinances containing these proscriptions were repeated in 1391 and around 1441. In 1637 the city fathers of Protestant Basel severely restricted the sorts and amounts of gifts that sponsors could give their godchildren at christenings. Extravagance was unseemly and an abomination to pure religion.

These three examples give some indication of the three major explanations for the remarkable persistence of sumptuary laws (laws limiting consumption) in human history: (1) the necessity to respond to economic realities, (2) the perceived need to emphasize the hierarchies of social status, and (3) the belief that superfluous consumption was irreligious. Oftentimes a combination of these factors resulted in sumptuary legislation.

Although the whole of the Middle Ages was touched by sumptuary laws, the period of the most feverish legislative activity was the late Middle Ages. Of course, more evidence has survived from the later period in general, but the impression of increasing concern about consumption in the fourteenth and fifteenth centuries seems justified by several considerations. In the first place, by the early fourteenth century the expansion of population had put enormous pressure on the productive resources of Europe. To this extent the spate of "national" sumptuary laws (England from the time of Edward III; Portugal from 1340; the German principalities in the fourteenth century) is related to the increasing concern over bread prices and other social problems, and is similar to the explosion of sumptuary legislation associated with the economic crisis of late antiquity.

Although the economic issue was perhaps uppermost, the social dislocations following the great wars of the fourteenth and fifteenth centuries and the plagues of the same period led to sumptuary legislation with a rather different aim. As social categories became more fluid (entrance into the nobility, for example, increased as noble families died out through war and pestilence; fiefs entered the hands of bourgeois by purchase), there was an atavistic attempt to maintain the rigid distinctions nostalgically associated with an earlier period, and to do so especially by means of laws on dress. To be sure, laws respecting appropriate dress for differing classes can be found in the thirteenth century, but it was only in the fourteenth century and later that the full panoply of regulations came into prominence; and this coincided with a revolution in noble dress that took it to Olympian heights of ostentation. In this sense it was not conspicuous consumption itself that was reprehensible—that was expected of and appropriate to the nobility—but conspicuous consumption by bourgeois and parvenu non-nobles that seemed to threaten the social order.

The other motivation, besides economic necessity and class tensions, that stimulated sumptuary laws was religious sensibilities. Again, religion was closely related to questions of economic well-being and appropriate social styles. In a world of much want, gluttony was a particularly horrible sin. Late medieval meditations on the passion of Jesus expend enormous numbers of words on his phrase "I thirst," using it to discourse at length on the evils of not sharing and of indulging one's appetite. Nearly sixty-three printed pages of one set of meditations are devoted to this single point.

It was inevitable, too, that the clergy would be the object of sumptuary legislation. Widely criticized for their indulgence, they were caught between professing the ideal of Christian poverty and maintaining a style of life appropriate for a highly privileged and wealthy caste in Europe. Large parts of the great Spanish law code, the *Siete partidas,* deal in detail with the sorts of dress that are permitted and not permitted for clergymen. The Reformation gave a new and sharper edge to such legislation wherever Protestantism gained the upper hand.

It was one thing to issue laws concerning consumption; it was quite another to enforce them. The prevailing opinion seems to be that enforcement, except in the first flush of enthusiasm after passage, was lax. Punishments, when there was enforcement, were usually limited to fines of varying severity and, if dress was at issue, forfeiture of the apparel that had been inappropriately worn. The purchase of licenses to wear prohibited articles is occasionally documented in the fifteenth century and may have occurred earlier.

BIBLIOGRAPHY

The classic study of consumption is Henri Baudrillart's *Histoire de luxe,* 4 vols. (1878–1880). The bibliography on sumptuary laws is immense. A few of the many works are Frances E. Baldwin, *Sumptuary Legislation and Personal Regulation in England* (1926); Veronika Baur, *Kleiderordnungen in Bayern* (1975); Liselotte C. Eisenbart, *Kleiderordnungen der deutschen Städte* (1962); Étienne Giraudias, *Étude historique sur les lois somptuaires* (1910); Kent R. Greenfield, *Sumptuary Law in Nürnberg* (1918); A. H. de Oliveira Marques, *Daily Life in Portugal in the Late Middle Ages,* S. S. Wyatt, trans. (1971); John M. Vincent, *Costume and Conduct in the Laws of Basel, Bern, and Zurich* (1935).

WILLIAM CHESTER JORDAN

[See also **Class Structure, Western; Costume, Western European; Siete Partidas.**]

SUMPTUARY LAWS, ISLAMIC. Sumptuary laws in Islam fall into two categories: those relating to Muslims and those relating to non-Muslims.

Sumptuary regulations for Muslims go back to the early Muslim community (*umma*) in Medina. Several suras of the Koran promise the righteous silk clothes in paradise (for instance, 44:53). However, the Koranic condemnation of the nonchalance of the wealthy toward religion, and the general feeling that Judgment Day was nigh, made Muḥammad decide that luxurious clothes, jewelry, and household utensils were inappropriate in this world. Most of the canonical *ḥadīth* collections relate that Muḥammad received a silk robe (*farrūj*) as a gift. He put it on and began to pray in it, then suddenly pulled it off as if it were loathsome, declaring that such a garment was unseemly for the God-fearing. According to tradition, he eventually forbade seven things: silver vessels, gold rings, silk garments, brocade, a striped silken fabric from Egypt called *qassī,* satin, and tanned hides. Many other proscribed luxury fabrics are mentioned in the *ḥadīth* literature. Exceptions were made for individuals suffering from lice and pruritus. Women apparently were exempted from the prohibition on gold jewelry and silken garments. The *ḥadīth* collections are almost unanimous in condemning the practice of ostentatiously trailing one's garments along the ground. Wearing one's garments too long was considered to be a sign of libertinism. Furthermore, certain styles of draping one's mantle are strictly censured in the *ḥadīth,* apparently because they caused the pudenda to be exposed.

Certain dress restrictions for Muslims were promulgated in early Umayyad times. Arab troops serving in the Persian territories were forbidden to wear Iranian-style clothing. The initial reason was probably for security, but later it was to stem the tide of assimilation. Arab soldiers were reportedly punished for wearing the Persian cuirass (*khaftān*) and leggings (*rān*).

Most of the sumptuary laws for Muslims soon fell into desuetude with the rise of a large leisured class in the new empire. The nouveaux riches invented a considerable body of countertraditions in which the Prophet is quoted as permitting silks, brocades, and other luxury fabrics. Only occasionally were sumptuary laws imposed upon Muslims in later times. These usually were enacted under zealous, puritanical reformers and were short-lived. For example, the Fatimid caliph al-Ḥākim in 1014/1015 forbade shoemakers to make outdoor footwear for women. The founder of the Almohad religious movement, the Mahdi Muḥammad ibn Tūmart, forbade the wearing of sandals with gilded laces and turbans that were not in the Muslim fashion. He also did not permit men to wear certain styles of robes that he considered effeminate. However, these restrictions did not continue under al-Ḥākim's or the Mahdi's successors.

The principal sumptuary laws for non-Muslims originated in the period of the Arab conquests and became more detailed with the passage of time. These laws were known as *ghiyār* (differentiation). Their main purpose was to mark clearly the distinction between believer and nonbeliever. These laws first appeared in the Pact of ᶜUmar and were originally inspired by security considerations. Non-Muslims were forbidden to wear Arab-style headgear (specifically, the turban and the *qalansuwa*), military dress, or certain robes. They were not to wear their hair or beards like Arabs. Christians—though apparently not Jews or at first Zoroastrians—had to wear a distinguishing outer belt, the *mintag* or, more commonly, the *zunnar* (plural, *zanānīr;* compare Greek *zonarion*). Non-Muslims could not ride horses, use ordinary saddles—but only packsaddles—on their mounts, or carry arms. They could not wear rings engraved with Arabic signets.

Many of the specific prohibitions developed during the first two Islamic centuries, although the general ban on imitating Muslim fashion goes back to the conquests of the seventh century. The restrictions against non-Muslims building their homes higher than those of Muslims are, on the other hand, clearly from a later time, when the two groups lived side by side. This last prohibition was rarely enforced, although during the intolerant Mamluk period there were instances of vigilante mobs tearing down the upper stories of houses and shops belonging to non-Muslims—as happened, for example, in Cairo in 1301.

With the passage of time the main raison d'être for the Islamic sumptuary laws for non-Muslims seems to have been to fulfill the Koranic injunction to humble unbelievers (9:29). The Abbasid caliph al-Mutawakkil in 849/850 commanded that non-Muslim men wear honey-colored *ṭayālisa* and *zunnārat.* The men were to attach two buttons to their *qalansuwa*s and to wear a patch on the breast and the back of their outer clothing that was four fingers in diameter and of a different color than the garment.

Laws governing dress went in and out of force until Mamluk times. From the mid thirteenth century on, they were more strictly applied. The famous decree of Sultan al-Malik al-Ṣāliḥ, issued in 1354, not only reiterated the restrictions of the Pact of ᶜUmar but also added new ones. Non-Muslims were henceforth limited in the size of their turbans: No more than ten ells of winding cloth could be used. This was reduced to seven ells in 1419 by order of Sultan al-Malik al-Mu'ayyad, who further decreed that the sleeves of non-Muslims' robes should be narrow in cut (wide sleeves were a mark of respectability). Even riding upon donkeys was now forbidden to non-Muslims within city limits. The various sumptuary regulations for non-Muslims in the Islamic world went in and out of effect throughout the later Middle Ages and into modern times. They were continuously applied with great rigor in late medieval Persia, Yemen, and Morocco.

The implementation and oversight of the sumptuary laws for both Muslims and non-Muslims was usually the responsibility of the *muḥtasib,* an official who was both a censor of public morals and an inspector of markets.

BIBLIOGRAPHY

Stanley Lane-Poole, *A History of Egypt in the Middle Ages,* 4th ed. (1925, repr. 1968), 126; Reuben Levy, *The Social Structure of Islam* (1962), 334–338; Norman A. Stillman, *The Jews of Arab Lands* (1979), 26, 68–71, 83, 92, 158–159, 167–168, 269–274; Yedida K. Stillman, "Libās," in *Encyclopaedia of Islam,* new ed., V (1986); Yedida K. Stillman and Norman A. Stillman, "Libās: Iran," *ibid.;* Bertold Spuler, *Iran in früh-islamischer Zeit* (1952), 515; A. S. Tritton, *The Caliphs and Their Non-Muslim Subjects* (1970), 115–126; Ibn al-Ukhūwa, *Ma^c^ālim al-qurba,* Reuben Levy, ed. (1938, repr. 1968), 5, 10–16, 25, 51–53 (English section); Arent J. Wensinck, *A Handbook of Early Muhammadan Tradition* (1927, repr. 1971), *s.v.* "Clothes."

YEDIDA K. STILLMAN

[See also **Costume, Islamic; Costume, Jewish; Ḥadīth; Islam, Religion; Muḥammad; Muḥtasib; Textiles, Islamic.**]

SUNDIALS. The ancient world had several instruments telling the hour of the day from the position of the sun as defined by the shadow of a pin (gnomon or style) falling on a surface engraved with hour lines showing "seasonal" hours, dividing the time from sunrise to sunset into twelve equal parts (and thus of varying lengths through the year). The theory of the sundial is found in Ptolemy's *Analemma* and Vitruvius' *De architectura,* book IX.

The mathematical science of gnomonics (or dialing) was lost in the Dark Ages. The first medieval sundials appeared about 800 (some scholars date this appearance as early as 670); these were very crude and imprecise scratch dials on the south walls of churches. More precise forms emerged with the growing knowledge of geometry and spherical astronomy. The altitude dials, showing the hour from the altitude of the sun above the horizon, include

Angel with sundial, south tower of Chartres Cathedral, 12th century. FOTO MARBURG/ART RESOURCE

the portable quadrant, the *horologium viatorum,* or traveler's sundial, with a horizontal style casting its shadow on the outer surface of a cylinder, and the ring dial, in which a hole in a cylindrical ring admitted a ray of the sun to fall on hour lines drawn on the inner surface. Other types show the hour from the direction of the sun as defined by either its azimuth or its hour angle. Azimuth dials usually have a vertical gnomon on a horizontal surface. Hour-angle dials have a gnomon or style parallel to the axis of the Earth and can be easily adapted to show the equal, or astronomical, hours commonly used today.

All sundials have to be correctly placed with respect to the meridian. In the portable dials of the late Middle Ages this was often achieved by a built-in magnetic compass. Such dials were produced in great numbers in Augsburg and Nuremberg, and spread rapidly in the wake of the mechanical clock, which required frequent adjustment to solar time. This development also explains the enormous increase of books on gnonomics from the sixteenth to the eighteenth century.

BIBLIOGRAPHY

Maximilian Bobinger, *Alt-Augsburger Kompassmacher* (1966); Joseph Drecker, *Theorie der Sonnenuhren* (1925); Kathleen Higgins, "The Classification of Sundials," in *Annals of Science,* 9 (1953); R. R. J. Rohr, *Die Sonnenuhr—Geschichte, Theorie, Funktion* (1982); Ernst Zinner, *Alte Sonnenuhren an europäischen Gebäuden* (1964).

OLAF PEDERSEN

[See also **Calendars and Reckoning of Time; Clocks and Reckoning of Time; Nuremberg; Scientific Instruments.**]

SUNNA is an Arabian concept, traceable to the pre-Islamic era, the *Jāhilīya,* that in early Islam evolved into a concept comparable with orthodoxy. In a juridical sense it came to mean recommended (normative) behavior, specifically of the prophet Muḥammad. The semantic development of the term is complex and can be divided into various stages.

In the *Jāhilīya* the term *sunna* generally denoted "way," "course," "manner of acting," but not necessarily "normative behavior." *Sunnas* from the pre-Islamic era were integrated into Islam.

In the Koran the term *sunna* occurs sixteen times, mostly with regard to the "way" in which God dealt with the people to whom He had sent prophets, and who disobeyed and rebelled against the heavenly messages conveyed to them (for instance, 8:38; 17:77; 33:38, 62; 35:43).

Especially during the first century of the Muslim community's existence, politics and religion were inextricably intertwined. In early Islam no political event or sociological trend can be assessed properly unless religious undertones are fully taken into consideration. And every development in religious thinking is interlaced with the sociopolitical tendencies of the day. It should, therefore, not come as a surprise that *sunna* emerges among the political concepts of the period.

Where the "way" or *sunna* of the Muslims of the first generation is gradually adopted by the nascent Islamic community as normative, that generation's success in holding the community together and protecting it from disuniting forces soon becomes idealized in the thinking of later generations.

During the time of the four "rightly guided" caliphs (Abū Bakr, 632–634; ᶜUmar ibn al-Khaṭṭāb, 634–644; ᶜUthmān ibn ᶜAffān, 644–656; ᶜAlī, 656–660/661), the concept of *sunna* was often made applicable to their "rule" and "custom," creating precedents. There are explicit references to the "*sunna* of Abū Bakr" and the "*sunna* of ᶜUmar," as well as the "*sunna* of the two ᶜUmars" (ᶜUmar ibn al-Khaṭṭāb and the Umayyad caliph ᶜUmar ibn ᶜAbd al-ᶜAzīz, 717–720). In a reference to the gang of murderers of the third caliph, ᶜUthmān, the term is used in the pejorative context "*sunna* of wrongdoing." *Sunna* is used in a positive as well as a pejorative sense to indicate the "manners" or "rulings" of various Umayyad caliphs.

The concept *sunna* played a central role in the deliberations resulting from the controversy between ᶜAlī and Muᶜāwiya, the founder of the Umayyad dynasty—for instance, the expression "the *sunna* that is righteous, binding the people together rather than leading them into disunity." *Sunna* is here virtually synonymous with "Islam" or "the new order" but commanding political rather than religious loyalty.

Parallel to the development in a political sense, the term evolved with a religious or, to be more precise, juridico-theological connotation. In texts dealing with the first century of Islam (622–720), there are occasional references to the *sunna* of the Prophet beside that of the first caliphs, but it is perhaps not unwise to interpret all these references only after scrutinizing their provenance, authorship, and/or chronology. It is often wrong to identify *sunna* preceded by the definite article (*as-sunna*) automatically as that of the Prophet (*sunnat al-nabī*) in contexts describing the situation in the Islamic world during its first century. Only in the course of the second century (720–816) did the concept *sunna* of the Prophet gradually eclipse the concept *as-sunna,* denoting the *sunna* of the early Islamic community comprising that of the Prophet and his immediate successors and/or closest associates. The first to emphasize the *sunna* of the Prophet alongside the *sunna* of the community at large was, according to ancient Muslim sources, ᶜUmar ibn ᶜAbd al-ᶜAzīz, and the first to grant the *sunna* of the Prophet the official status of second root of Muslim law—after the Koran and complementary to it—was Muḥammad ibn Idrīs al-Shāfiᶜī (*d.* 820). From the latter's lifetime on, *as-sunna* came to mean almost exclusively the *sunna* of the Prophet and no longer the *sunna* of the Prophet as well as that of his closest associates. However, in a letter attributed to the Abbasid caliph al-Mahdī, dated to 776, *sunna* of the Prophet and *sunna* in both a positive and a pejorative general sense were still used in one and the same context.

The vehicle by means of which the *sunna* was transmitted during the first two centuries of Islam to find its way ultimately to Islamic law was the *ḥadīth* (plural, *aḥadith*), the recorded sayings and deeds of early Muslims. Initially the *ḥadīth* included the rulings, precepts, and prohibitions of the Prophet, but also those of his companions and those of the next generation, the so-called successors. But as a result of the emphasis on *sunna* of the Prophet, initiated by Shāfiᶜī, *ḥadīth* became almost exclusively devoted to the *sunna* of the Prophet. For this reason the oldest preserved *ḥadīth* collections contain, next to prophetic *aḥadīth,* a number of *aḥadīth* ascribed to companions or successors, a division that gradually disappears with time. Collections compiled after, say, 850 may contain only by way of exception an utterance attributed to someone other than Muḥammad; the bulk are ascribed to the Prophet himself. *Ḥadīth* and *sunna* have sometimes erroneously been taken to be virtually synonymous, but *ḥadith* is really the concrete record of a *sunna,* which is an abstract.

With the narrowing down of the broad concept *as-sunna* to *sunna* of the Prophet exclusively, there emerged sayings attributed to the Prophet that, in the oldest redactions preserved, were ascribed to other authorities. In the absence of Koranic occurrences of *sunna* in the connotation "*sunna* of the Prophet," later Koran exegesis tries to trace the concept *sunna* in that particularly restricted sense in other Koranic concepts. The best-known example of such a concept is *ḥikma* (wisdom). Closer inspection reveals that among the earliest (available) Koran commentators, the identification of *ḥikma* with "*sunna* of the Prophet" is unknown or at least left unmentioned. In the commentaries of Mujāhid ibn Jabr (*d.* 722), Muqātil ibn Sulaymān (*d.* 767), and Sufyān al-Thawrī (*d.* 778), most of the time *ḥikma* is not elucidated at all. In the commentary of al-Ṭabarī (*d.* 923) only the early authority Qatāda ibn Diᶜāma (*d.* 735) is quoted as having glossed *ḥikma* as *as-sunna,* but in a broad sense: at 2:129, Qatāda explains *ḥikma* as *as-sunna,* but at 3:48, *ḥikma* as *as-sunna* is applied to that *ḥikma* in which God instructs Jesus, not Muḥammad. It is Shāfiᶜī who bracketed the Koranic *ḥikma* with *sunna* of the Prophet. Furthermore, the famous Koran verse "You had in God's Messenger an excellent example" (33:21), inevitably adduced by medieval exegetes in support of the Koran's alleged emphasis on the prophetic *sunna,* is not even commented upon in that sense by al-Ṭabarī, let alone by his predecessors. The *ḥadīth* collection of Aḥmad ibn Ḥanbal (*d.* 855), *Musnad*, contains the earliest identification of the "excellent example" from 33:21 with the *sunna* of the Prophet.

Shortly after Shāfiᶜī the term *sunna,* definitively narrowed down to that of the Prophet, became the hallmark of those who opposed the Abbasid-backed Muᶜtazilite inquisition (833–848). The "people of the *sunna* and the community," a phrase that may have been current for more than a century, denoted in general those Muslims who were not characterized by "pernicious innovations" or turmoil-abetting political ideologies. Whereas *sunna* of the Prophet had been wielded as a weapon by virtually everybody—including the early Abbasid caliphs, their supporters, and their politico-dogmatic opponents—after the successful demobilization of the Muᶜtazilite inquisitors and their adherents, the *sunna* of the Prophet became the sole property of those who are still generally felt to have had the right on their side, who became identified in short with what we term orthodoxy. An orthodox Muslim, a Sunnite (in Arabic: *sunnī*), emerged from some two centuries of tumultuous dispute that had given way to bloody civil war and to dogmatic hairsplitting and intellectual intolerance.

From the beginning of the ninth century, Muslim orthodoxy has had various creeds at its disposal. Apart from those (probably erroneously) attributed to Abū Ḥanīfa (*d.* 767), such as *Al-fiqh al-akbar, Al-fiqh al-absaṭ*, and *Maᶜrifat al-madhāhib,* the first available creeds are those of Ḥumaydī (*d.* 834), Muḥammad ibn ᶜUkāsha (*fl.* 840), Aḥmad ibn Ḥanbal, his son ᶜAbd Allāh (*d.* 903), Yaᶜqūb ibn Sufyān al-Fasawī (*d.* 890), and al-Ḥasan ibn ᶜAlī ibn Khalaf al-Barbahārī (*d.* 941). Most material in these creeds is ascribed to late-eighth-century *ḥadīth* scholars such as ᶜAbd Allāh ibn al-Murbārak (*d.* 797), Sufyān ibn ᶜUyayna (*d.* 814), and Wakīᶜ ibn al-Jarrāḥ (*d.* 812). What *sunna* in these creeds amounts to may be summarized as follows.

The Sunnite is to believe unconditionally in the doctrine of predestination: only God determines whether a believer will attain paradise or burn in hell. Belief is expressed in words as well as deeds, both of which require the proper intention (*nīya*). One's religiosity is subject to fluctuation: it can increase as well as decrease. The Sunnite is not to indulge in dogmatic dispute. Fighting in the holy war is a duty even under the leadership of an ungodly overlord. Any ritual prayer (*ṣalāt*) behind any prayer leader (*imām*) is valid, unless the imam is known to uphold heretical (for instance, Jahmite) ideas. No one of the prophet's companions may be cursed, the most excellent of them being Abū Bakr, ᶜUmar, ᶜUthmān as well as ᶜAlī (here the Muslim creed for the first time distances itself officially from the political upheaval stemming from the succession of the Prophet). The Koran is to be considered the uncreated word of God. God's attributes (*ṣifāt*) should not be made the subject of discussion except by means of those terms he uses to describe himself in the Koran. The believer is not to ask "why" or "how" with regard to God. The believer may be subjected in his grave to a (painful) interrogation at the hands of the angels of death, Munkar and Nakīr. The believer will see God after death with his own eyes, and also other features of the life hereafter, such as the Basin (*ḥawḍ*), the Bridge (*ṣirāṭ*), and the Scales (*mīzān*). The Prophet may mediate before God for those believers who deserve it.

Finally, the creed of Barbahārī contains the crucial statement attributed to the pious Bishr ibn al-Ḥārith (*d.* 842): *sunna* and Islam are in essence identical.

Whereas during the inquisition the Muᶜtazilites demanded the flogging of those who refused to embrace their views, the Sunnites stipulated the beheading of their opponents. After allegedly having been a minority, the Sunnites gained the upper hand, expecially as a result of the polemics of a renegade Muᶜtazilite, ᶜAlī ibn Ismāᶜīl al-Ashᶜarī (*d.* 935), directed against his former associates. The Sunnites' former fanaticism was toned down, making room for a steadily increasing tolerance. This was, for example, expressed in Ashᶜarī's use of the appellatives "the people of the ritual prayer [*ṣalāt*]" "the people of the [common] direction for prayer [*qibla*]," or "the people of Islam" as comprising various groups of innovators, including the Muᶜtazilites. However, in the creed of Fasawī, adhering to any innovative doctrine definitively invalidates the performing of Islam's major religious rites, such as the *ṣalāt* and the pilgrimage. In Ashᶜarī's writings, and also in those of al-Māturīdī (*d.* 944), Islam found a solid basis for its orthodoxy. Phrases such as "people of the *sunna* and the community" were substituted for "people of the *sunna* and righteousness."

Hence the term *sunna* developed a particular connotation in Islamic law. Among the five value judgments assessing the (de)merits of a human action, *sunna* came to mean "recommended," the equivalent of *mandūb* and *mustaḥabb* (desirable); a *sunna muᵓakkada* became the qualification of an action, the neglect of which was deemed reprehensible, whereas a *sunna nāfila* became a term for any pious, strictly voluntary activity. None of these technical terms is found in the *Risāla* of Shāfiᶜī.

BIBLIOGRAPHY

Sources. Barbahārī's creed in Ibn Abī Yaᶜlā, *Ṭabaqāt al-Ḥanābila,* M. H. al-Fiqī, ed. (Cairo, 1952), II, 18–44; Yaᶜqūb ibn Sufyān al-Fasawī's creed in his *K. al-maᶜrifa wa 't-taᵓrīkh,* A. D. al-ᶜUmarī, ed. (Baghdad, 1974–1976), III 385–403; Aḥmad ibn Ḥanbal, *K. as-sunna,* edited with his *Ar-radd ᶜalā 'l-Jahmīya wa 'z-zanādiqa* (1968); Ḥumaydī's creed in his *Musnad,* Aᶜẓamī, ed. (Beirut, n.d.), II, 546ff; Muḥammad ibn ᶜUkāsha's creed in Ibn ᶜAsakīr, *At-taᵓrīkh al-kabīr (Tahdhīb),* Badrān, ed. (Damascus, 1951–1973), III, 131ff.

Studies. Western studies include Zafar I. Ansari, "Islamic Juristic Terminology Before Sāfiᶜī: A Semantic Analysis with Special Reference to Kūfa," in *Arabica,* **19** (1972); M. M. Bravmann, "Sunnah and Related Concepts," in his *The Spiritual Background of Early Islam* (1972); P. Crone and M. Hinds, *God's Caliph: Religious Authority in the First Centuries of Islam* (1986); Louis Gardet and M. M. Anawati, *Introduction à la théologie musulmane* (1948, 2nd ed. 1970); M. Hinds, "The Ṣiffīn Arbitration Agreement," in *Journal of Semitic Studies,* **17** (1972); G. H. A. Juynboll, *Muslim Tradition* (1983), 30–39; Theodoor W. Juynboll, *Handbuch des islamischen Gesetzes* (1910), 59ff.; Henri Laoust, *Les schismes dans l'Islam* (1965) and, as ed. and trans., *La profession de foi d'Ibn Baṭṭa* (1958); Richard J. McCarthy, *The Theology of al-Ashᶜarī* (1953); Tilman Nagel, "Das Problem der Orthodoxie im frühen Islam," in *Studien zum Minderheitenproblem in Islam,* I (1973), and *Rechtleitung und Kalifat* (1975); Joseph Schacht, *The Origins of Muhammadan Jurisprudence* (1950, rev. and enl. 1967) and "Sur l'expression 'Sunna du Prophète,'" in *Mélanges d'orientalisme offerts à Henri Massé* (1963); Laura Veccia Vaglieri, "Sulla origine della denominazione 'sunniti,'" in *Studi orientalistici in onore di Giorgio Levi della Vida,* II (1956); Arent J. Wensinck, *The Muslim Creed* (1932, repr. 1965).

G. H. A. Juynboll

SUNNITES

[See also **Abū Bakr; Abū Ḥanīfa; ʿAlī; Ashʿarī, ʿAlī ibn Ismaʿīl al-; Caliphate; Ḥadith; Ḥanbal, Aḥmad ibn Muḥammad ibn; Imam; Islam, Religion; Jihad; Koran; Muʿāwiya; Muḥammad; Qibla; Sects, Islamic; Shāfiʿī, al-; Ṣiffīn; ʿUmar I; ʿUmar II.**]

SUNNITES (from Arabic *sunnī,* "of the *sunna*"). Sunnite is the appellative of those Muslims who have become identified with Islamic orthodoxy. Sunnites as a religious group emerged toward the end of the seventh century; they were usually referred to as *ahl as-sunna* (people of the *sunna,* or the religious party), mostly in contrast to the *ahl al-bidaʿ*, the people following innovative doctrines. Perhaps the earliest juxtaposition of these two appellatives is found in a saying attributed to Muḥammad ibn Sīrīn (*d.* 728), who may be presumed to have made the statement about 700. We do find an earlier appellative: *ahl as-sunna wa 'l-jamāʿa* (the people of the *sunna* and the community), but in this expression the connotations of the term *sunna* are still predominantly political rather than religious.

To distinguish those Muslims who most faithfully followed the concept of Islam established during Muḥammad's last years in Medina (622–632) from those who fell away from that original concept was, during the first fifty years after the Prophet's death, a matter of distinguishing between political rather than religious factions. The party of Muḥammad's son-in-law ʿAlī, the Shīʿa, upheld ʿAlī's claim to the caliphate against Muḥammad's first three successors: Abū Bakr (632–634), ʿUmar (634–644), and ʿUthmān (644–656). After ʿUthmān's murder, when ʿAlī became caliph (656–660/661), allegiance was refused to ʿAlī by the Prophet's companions Ṭalḥa and al-Zubayr, supported by the Prophet's widow ʿĀʾisha—all three defeated in the Battle of the Camel (656)—and Muʿāwiya, governor of Syria, who claimed vengeance for his kinsman ʿUthmān's assassination. Muʿāwiya and ʿAlī faced each other on the battlefield at Ṣiffīn (657–658), a conflict settled by an arbitration committee. The decision prompted a large part of ʿAlī's followers to desert him and form the Kharijites.

The Muslims who had not joined any of those dissenting parties may be considered the precursors of the *ahl as-sunna.* Among older appellatives for these Muslims are such expressions as "the people of the *salāt*" (prayer ritual) and "the people of the *qibla*" (direction of prayer).

A member of the *ahl as-sunna* is called a *sunna.* The first people known by that name are contemporary with Ibn Sīrīn. An older category of early Muslims, which might conceivably be entitled to the label "religious party," is that of the *qurrāʾ* (what this name means is still a matter of dispute), found everywhere in the Islamic empire, even among Shiites and Kharijites. They cease to be mentioned in early Islamic historical sources after the putting down in 703 of the rebellion led by Ibn al-Ashʿath, in which they participated; their disappearance neatly coincided with the emergence of the *ahl as-sunna.* Sunnites became increasingly numerous in the course of the eighth century but were still a minority compared with the followers of the mainly politico-doctrinal factions referred to above.

Sunnites are identified with the transmission of *ḥadīth* (pl., *aḥadith*), but this should not be taken to mean that any Sunnite's *ḥadīth* transmission automatically indicates expertise in this matter. Quite the opposite, in fact, appears to be the case with early Sunnites. This seems to be reflected also in the distinctly derogatory name *ḥashwīya* (literally "stuffers"; figuratively "rabble"), used by friend and foe alike in connection with the *ahl al-ḥadīth wa 's-sunna* to describe *ḥadīth* transmitters whose traditions betray both naïveté, on the one hand, and a fair amount of fabrication, on the other. But it is striking that Islam's most articulate early Sunnites, such as ʿAbd Allāh ibn al-Mubārak (*d.* 797), Wakīʿ ibn al-Jarrāḥ (*d.* 812), and Sufyān ibn ʿUyayna (*d.* 814), are nowhere identified with *ḥadith* fabrication, even if their pivotal role in the faith (*imān*) seems to point in that direction.

After the Muʿtazilite inquisition (*miḥna*) instituted by the Abbasid Maʾmūn in 833 and abolished under Mutawakkil in 848, Sunnites propagated and became identified with a form of Islam based upon personal piety and observation of ritual laid down in *aḥadith* that, in an increasingly elaborate manner, claim to preserve the prophetic example (*sunnat al-nabī*). The most important Sunnite spokesman during and after this period was Aḥmad ibn Ḥanbal (*d.* 855). The Sunnites gradually came to be considered the representatives of the only true form of Islam that would guarantee eternal salvation in paradise.

During the first century and a half after the Prophet's death, only the reigns of Abū Bakr and ᶜUmar, and the first half of ᶜUthmān's, were considered to constitute a model society upon which later Muslims should pattern themselves; but from the beginning of the ninth century, that period plus the final half of ᶜUthmān's reign, as well as ᶜAlī's, was for the first time regarded as the most ideal period in Islamic history, whose example was to be followed.

Today most Muslims are Sunnites. Shiites form the majority only in Iran and North Yemen, and minorities of various numbers in Lebanon, Syria, Iraq, Afghanistan, and Pakistan. An offshoot of the Shiites, the Ismailis, is scattered in India and East Africa. Kharijites are found in small numbers in southern Algeria and Oman. Major Sunnite religious centers are the Al-Azhar mosque in Cairo and the Zaytūnīya in Tunis.

BIBLIOGRAPHY

For a representative cross section of the earliest Sunnites up to the middle of the ninth century, see G. H. A. Juynboll, "Some New Ideas on the Development of *Sunna* as Technical Term in Early Islam," in *Jerusalem Studies in Arabic and Islam,* 6 (forthcoming). See also Wilferd Madelung, *Religious Schools and Sects in Medieval Islam* (1985), chap. 1: "Early Sunnī Doctrine Concerning Faith as Reflected in the Kitāb al-Īmān of Abū ᶜUbayd al-Qāsim ibn Sallām (D. 224/839)," repr. from *Studia islamica,* 32 (1970); Ibn Tahir al-Baghdadi, *Moslem Schisms and Sects,* Abraham S. Halkin, trans. (1978). Further sources and studies can be found in the bibliography for *Sunna* in this volume of the Dictionary.

G. H. A. Juynboll

[See also **Abū Bakr; ᶜĀᵓisha; ᶜAlī; Caliphate; Ḥadīth; Islam, Religion; Muᶜāwiya; Muḥammad; Sects, Islamic; Ṣiffīn; Sunna; ᶜUmar I.**]

SŪQ, an Arabic word meaning shopping area or market in an urban setting. Its Iranian equivalent is the *bāzār* (bazaar), and it is the word *bāzār* that took precedence in the Turkish world.

As it appeared in its most classical form, as in Aleppo, the *sūq* was a network of streets, usually but not necessarily covered, almost entirely devoted to retail trade and to artisanship. Each street or group of streets was usually restricted to a single commodity or activity, for example, bookselling, leatherwork, and so on. The aristocracy of the *sūq* was usually the cloth merchants. Every city had a *sūq*. Large cities could have more than one, but, as a rule, one *sūq* dominated, and merchandise or materials were brought to it from all over. The origin of the *sūq* is still unclear, although it clearly relates to the great mercantile ensembles of the classical Roman city, especially in its Near Eastern variants. The best-preserved *sūq*s are in Aleppo, Cairo, and Fēs.

Persian bazaar or *sūq,* a European engraving from *ca.* 1867. THE BETTMANN ARCHIVE

Oleg Grabar

[See also **Aleppo; Cairo; Damascus; Fairs; Fēs; Trade, Islamic; Urbanism, Islamic World.**]

SURTR (Surt), the black fire giant (or demon) in Scandinavian mythology. At Ragnarǫk, the end of the world, the fire giant Surtr will lead the attack against the gods. His host will ride down the Rainbow Bridge, Bifrǫst, breaking it and, therewith, the path constructed by the gods between the heavens and earth. Strophe 52 of *Vǫluspá* says, "Surtr journeys from the south with fire; the sun of the gods of the slain shines from his sword." The heavens are rent, mountains tumble, trolls are loosed, and men tread the Hel path. The forces of Surtr meet the gods on the plain Vígríðr (*Vafþrúðnismál,* 18) or the island Óskópnir (*Fáfnismál,* 14). The god Freyr lacks his sword, which he had given to Skírnir in order to get the giantess Gerð, and is felled by the sword wielded by Surtr—perhaps Freyr's own. Snorri quotes *Vǫluspá* 52, in *Gylfaginning,* 4, and concludes from *Vǫluspá* 51, that the first world was Múspell (or Múspellr) to the south, where intense heat prevails. Surtr guards the boundary of the land of Múspell with a flaming sword. The "sons of Múspell" (*Gylfaginning,* 13) vanquish the gods, and at the end of the battle the earth is swept by fire, then rises rejuvenated from the waters in a new beginning.

The name Surtr has to do with the adjective *svartr* (black), and thus with the notion of being blackened by fire. If the mythologem of the black fire giant originated in continental Scandinavia, it must have been reinforced by the geology of Iceland, where frequent and dramatic volcanic activity actualized the vision of the world ending in flames.

BIBLIOGRAPHY
Hilda R. Ellis Davidson, *Gods and Myths of Northern Europe* (1964), 37; Anne Holtsmark, "Surtr," in *Kulturhistoriskt Lexikon för nordisk medeltid,* XVII (1972), 439–442; Sigurður Nordal, ed., *Vǫluspá,* B. S. Benedikz and John McKinnell, trans. (1978), 102–103, 104; Snorri Sturluson, *The Poetic Edda,* Henry Adams Bellows, trans., 2 vols. in 1 (1969), esp. 20–22, 73, 110, 376, and *The Prose Edda,* Arthur Gilchrist Brodeur, trans. (1916), 16–17, 24–25; Edward O. G. Turville-Petre, *Myth and Religion of the North* (1964), 275–285, esp. 281–284; Jan de Vries, *Altgermanische Religionsgeschichte,* I (1935, repr. 1956), 250, and II (1937, repr. 1957), 413.

JAMES E. CATHEY

[See also **Eddic Poetry; Freyr; Gylfaginning; Muspilli; Ragnarǫk; Scandinavian Mythology; Snorri Sturluson; Vǫluspá.**]

SURVEYING. The Romans had a highly developed, if rigid, system of land surveying based on a pair of sticks that were crossed at right angles. This instrument, called a *groma,* allowed the Romans to lay out their towns and fields very precisely, but all angles had to be 90 degrees. Several manuals were written on the Roman technique, and the *Corpus agrimensorum romanorum* was copied through the Middle Ages, as were other technological writings, such as Vitruvius on architecture (*De architectura*), Frontinus on the aqueducts of Rome (*De aquis urbis Romae*), and Hyginus Gromaticus on the layout of a Roman military camp (*De munitionibus castrorum*).

None of this material had much practical influence in the Middle Ages, and there are very few sources that give an idea of how surveying was done in the medieval period. One piece of evidence is a survey map of Wildmore Fen in England, dating from around 1300. More generally, there are indications that medieval surveyors could accurately measure distance but not angles.

Medieval architects were quite good at measuring angles, of course, but even in the cathedrals the larger dimensions display angular irregularities that are not seen in the smaller dimensions, where the mason could work directly with ruler, compass, and template.

On the even smaller scale of the plan, there can be charming irregularities, as in the twelfth-century plan for the water supply system of Canterbury Cathedral, or very careful drafting, as in the ninth-century plan for the monastery at St. Gall, which shows a clear influence of the Roman system of 90 degrees. Precise angular measurement in a plan, however, does not mean that the architect had the ability to build a building that accurately reflected the plan.

Modern land surveying is based on triangulation and developed in the sixteenth century. However, since the first surveyor's transit was most probably inspired by the astrolabe, it seems fair to say that modern surveying is firmly based in medieval astronomy.

BIBLIOGRAPHY
Oswald A. W. Dilke, *The Roman Land Surveyors* (1971); Walter Horn and Ernest Born, *The Plan of St. Gall,* 3 vols. (1979); Allie Wilson Richeson, *English Land Measuring to 1800* (1966); Lon R. Shelby, "The Geometrical Knowledge of Mediaeval Master Masons," in *Speculum,* **47** (1972); Robert Willis, "The Architectural History of the Conventual Buildings of the Monastery of Christ Church in Canterbury," in *Archaeologia Cantiana,* 7 (1868).

WILLIAM K. WEST

[See also **Astrolabe; Astronomy; Construction: Engineering; Geography and Cartography; Gothic Architecture; Mathematics; Navigation; Portolan Chart; St. Gall, Monastery and Plan of.**]

SUSO, HEINRICH (*ca.* 1295–1366), also known as Seuse and under the cognomen Amandus, was a German Dominican friar, famous for his mystical writings, who was often referred to as "the minnesinger of mysticism." Suso was born in Constance or Überlingen in southern Germany. His father, a knight, was interested above all in hunting, hawking, and jousting, while his mother, whose family had landholdings near the small town of Süs (or Seuse) on Lake Constance, was a tender-hearted, very religious woman. It is clear that Heinrich took after her. After her death he showed his great devotion to her by assuming her name.

Suso joined the Dominican convent in Constance when he was thirteen or fourteen and led the routine life of a novice until eighteen, when he underwent a sudden change, a conversion that caused him to practice an asceticism of unparalleled severity. For ten years he lived in complete seclusion, wearing a hairshirt and various nail-studded devices, and voluntarily suffered the tortures of hunger and thirst. After these years of self-mortification, another change took place in Suso: in 1324 he entered the world again as a student at the Dominican *studium generale* in Cologne, where, in all likelihood, he met his idol, the great Meister Eckhart.

Like his contemporary Johannes Tauler, Suso was not chosen for advanced theological studies in Paris. Rather, he was sent to his old convent in Constance to teach the novices and to do pastoral work in neighboring cloisters and monasteries. Because of the papal interdict against Emperor Ludwig of Bavaria, the Dominicans who remained loyal to Rome had to leave their convents; and Suso spent roughly eight years in exile in the Scots monastery in Constance (1339–1347). In 1348 he was involved in a private scandal and, as a victim of vicious slander by a woman who accused him of fathering her child, was forced to abdicate the office of prior, to which he was elected in 1344; he also had to move to Ulm, where he apparently spent some peaceful years until his death on 25 January 1366.

Suso's written legacy bears evidence of a very productive life. He was not as powerful a preacher as Tauler or even Eckhart, and there are only a few extant sermons that can be attributed to him; his books, however, were among the most popular readings in the late Middle Ages not only in Germany but also in France, Italy, the Netherlands, and England.

His first work, the *Büchlein der Wahrheit* (*Little Book of Truth*), written around 1327, is an introduction to the mystical way which emphasizes that one should strive to lead a pious life, but also that the *unio* with God can only come about through God's grace. Some of the ideas developed along this line seem written in defense of Meister Eckhart, who at that time was coming under attack for some of his mystical teachings. Possibly because of his loyalty to his teacher, Suso was temporarily removed from his office as lector. The *Book of Truth* is significant for its content but also because in it Suso makes systematic use of the dialogue (between "Disciple" and "Truth"), a literary form which until then was only scarcely used in German.

Suso's second book, the *Büchlein der Ewigen Weisheit* (*Little Book of Eternal Wisdom, ca.* 1327–1334), has been called by H. S. Denifle "the finest fruit of German mysticism" and, though far removed from the intellectual heights of Eckhart's theological speculation, is a masterpiece of devotional literature. Written for nuns, it develops (again in the form of a dialogue) the idea that man can get to know God only through the humanity of Christ. Suso's language, with its admixture of knightly imagery and religious symbolism, is truly poetic and in its lyrical quality rivals that of the great minnesinger Heinrich von Morungen.

The same poetic spirit effuses from two works of which Suso is the spiritual author and redactor but which were written down by a nun, Elsbeth Stagel. These are the *Grosses Briefbuch* (*Great Book of Letters, ca.* 1360; an abridged version of this book was circulated as *Briefbüchlein,* or *Little Book of Letters*) and the *Vita,* or *Life* (*ca.* 1362). Both these books allow unusual psychological insights into Suso's highly complex artistic mind and are, therefore, of special interest to the modern student of the Middle Ages.

Suso's only extant Latin work is an expanded translation of the *Book of Eternal Wisdom* with the title *Horologium sapientiae* (*Clock of Wisdom, ca.* 1327–1334), which enjoyed incredible diffusion and became one of the most popular medieval works of literature. Some scholars claim that Suso planned to write a *Book of Examples,* the so-called *Exemplar,* in which he wanted to present in scholarly form his theological system. There is a "Prologue" to such a work but its authorship cannot be ascertained.

As a mystic, Suso marks a point of transition, a development away from the intellectual mysticism of Eckhart to a more emotional mysticism in which intellectual speculation has no part. Though Suso's works contain the vocabulary and some of the key concepts developed by Eckhart, the spirit permeating his mysticism is clearly not that of Eckhart but that of Bernard of Clairvaux and the Song of Songs. Emphasis is never on the intellect but always on emotion, that is, love, and the *via contemplativa* always seems inferior to the *via illuminativa.* In contrast to Eckhart, Suso also stresses the role of the historical Christ. Because of the greater tangibility of his teachings, Suso was more popular throughout the Middle Ages than Eckhart and even Tauler. Modern philosophers, on the other hand, have not been as attracted by him as they are by Eckhart, who offers them a more cohesive philosophical system.

BIBLIOGRAPHY

Editions and translations. Heinrich Seuse, *Deutsche Schriften,* Karl Bihlmeyer, ed. (1907, repr. 1961); *Horologium sapientiae,* Pius Kunzle, ed. (1977), a revision of *Horologium sapientiae,* Joseph Strange, ed. (1861); Henry Suso, *The Life of the Servant,* James M. Clark, trans. (1952); *Little Book of Eternal Wisdom* and *Little Book of Truth,* James M. Clark, ed. and trans. (1953).

Studies. J. A. Bizet, *Suso et le minnesang* (1945, 1947), and *Henri Suso et le déclin de la scholastique* (1946); James M. Clark, *The Great German Mystics* (1949); Ray C. Petry, "Henry Suso," in his *Late Medieval Mysticism* (1957), 245–258; Friedrich-Wilhelm Wentzlaff-Eggebert, *Deutsche Mystik zwischen Mittelalter und Neuzeit,* 3rd ed. (1969).

ERNST H. SOUDEK

[See also **Eckhart, Meister; Mysticism, Christian: German; Tauler, Johannes.**]

SUTRI, SYNOD OF. This synod of German, Burgundian, and Italian bishops was called by Emperor Henry III in 1046 with the intention to reform the papacy and to end a period of moral and political crisis. The synod formally deposed an antipope, Sylvester III, who had opposed Pope Benedict IX for a seven-to-eight-week period in 1045. It also deposed the reigning pope, Gregory VI, who was accused of simony for having secured Benedict's resignation through a payment of £1,000 to £2,000. At the Synod of Rome (1046), Benedict IX was formally deposed and Henry's candidate, Suidger of Bamberg, was elected as Pope Clement II. Henry's actions inaugurated a series of non-Roman popes who lifted the papacy out of the sphere of local family politics and took the lead in the religious reforms of the mid eleventh century.

The events leading to the synod, the motives of Henry, and the actions taken by the synod remain a part of the debate over the nature and impact of the investiture conflict. Before Sutri, the papacy had played no role in the movement for religious reform. Rather, it had been a prize claimed by various Roman families. From 1012 to 1045 the see of St. Peter was firmly in the hands of the Tuscolani family. Although the Tuscolan pope Benedict IX (1032–1045), "blessed in name but not in actions," was politically astute, he was noted for his dissolute life. Late in 1044 a faction led by a branch of the Crescenzi family temporarily drove Benedict from the city and installed their own pope, Sylvester III. In March 1045 Benedict regained the city and his throne, only to abdicate shortly thereafter in favor of Gregory VI. The reasons for his abdication still are not clear. Some contemporaries claimed that he resigned in order to marry; others said he resigned in contrition for his misdeeds; and it is probable that he recognized the weakness of his political position in central Italy.

Although Gregory VI was recognized by all, including the emperor, it was at this time that Henry chose to intervene. He seems to have acted out of a combination of political and moral concerns. He wished to reduce the pretensions of native Italian families, including the Tuscolani, to which both Benedict and Gregory may have been related. Imperial policy was based on the support of churchmen, but it was never intended to include direct political or legal domination of the papacy. Henry certainly felt that as emperor he had an obligation to cleanse the papacy of simony. While Gregory VI was known for his participation in the reform of local churches in Rome, it was widely acknowledged that he had approved, if not directly made, the payments to his predecessor, Benedict IX. Thus he was a simoniac.

Contemporaries nearly unanimously applauded imperial actions at Sutri and Rome. Several sources report that Gregory resigned, but it is more likely that he was deposed by the council and taken to Germany by the emperor. He was accompanied by Hildebrand, the future Gregory VII, who never forgot or accepted the imperial role at the synods of Sutri and Rome. Gregory VI died in exile in late 1047 or early 1048.

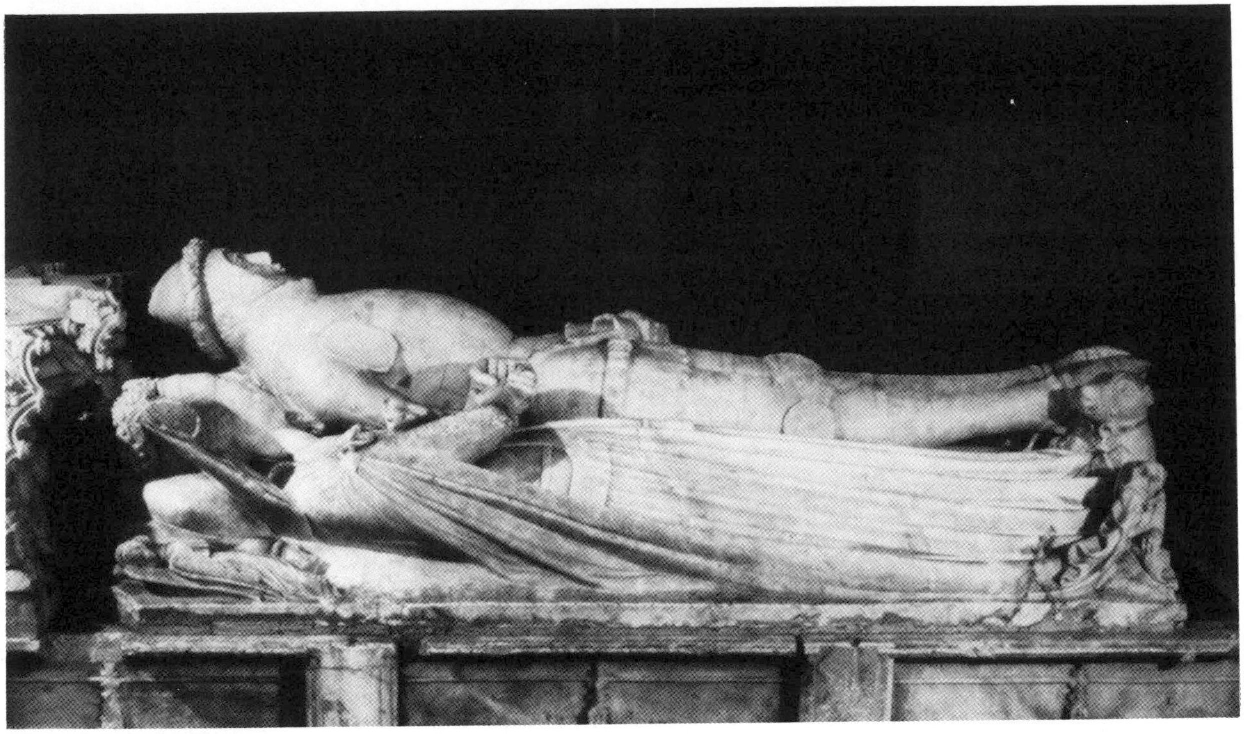

Tomb of Ralph and Katharine Greene. Alabaster sculpture by Robert Sutton, 1418, in Lowick, Northamptonshire. RONALD SHERIDAN

BIBLIOGRAPHY

The most important sources for the synod are Beno the Cardinal Presbyter, "Gesta Romanae ecclesiae contra Hildebrandum," Bonizo of Sutri, "Liber ad amicum," and "De ordinando pontifice auctor Gallicus," all of which are edited in *Monumenta Germaniae historica: Libelli de lite,* I (1891) and II (1892). The most thorough discussion of all the sources is Giovanni Battista Borino, "L'elezione e la deposizione di Gregorio VI," in *Archivio della R. Società romana di storia patria,* 39 (1916). More balanced conclusions are in Gerd Tellenbach, *Church, State, and Christian Society at the Time of the Investiture Contest,* R. F. Bennett, trans. (1940), 169–177; Ovidio Capitani, "Benedetto IX," in *Dizionario biografico degli italiani,* VIII (1960); Klaus Jürgen Herrmann, *Das Tuskulanerpapsttum (1012–1046): Benedikt VIII, Johannes XIX, Benedikt IX* (1973), 153–163. See also Reginald Lane Poole, *Studies in Chronology and History* (1934), 185–222. On Henry's Italian policy, see Cinzio Violante, *Studi sulla cristianità medioevale,* 2nd ed. (1975), 249–290. See also Giovanni Battista Borino, "Invitus ultra montes cum domno papa Gregorio abii," in *Studi Gregoriani,* 1 (1947); Augustin Fliche, *La réforme grégorienne,* I (1924), esp. 92–113; Charles Joseph Hefele and Henri Leclercq, *Histoire des conciles,* IV (1973), pt. 2, 981–994.

DUANE J. OSHEIM

[See also **Antipope; Church, Latin: to 1054; Henry III of Germany; Investiture and Investiture Conflict; Papacy; Simony.**]

SUTTON, ROBERT (*fl. ca.* 1415), a carver of Chellaston, Derbyshire. He contracted in 1418 with the slightly better known Thomas Prentys to build the tomb of Ralph Greene and his wife, Katharine, which survives at Lowick, Northamptonshire. The somewhat anonymous features of the effigies and of the contract specifications are probably typical of the sculptural trade that operated around the alabaster quarries in the Midlands.

BIBLIOGRAPHY

Arthur Gardner, *Alabaster Tombs of the Pre-Reformation Period in England* (1940), 5–7; Lawrence Stone, *Sculpture in Britain: The Middle Ages,* 2nd ed. (1972), 179–180, 198.

BARRIE SINGLETON

[See also **Prentys, Thomas.**]

SUTTON HOO is a site near the town of Woodbridge, Suffolk, England, on the Deben River estuary about seventy miles northeast of London, where a ship burial of the seventh century was discovered and excavated in 1939. The word "hoo" means "spur of a hill." The ship, in the largest of at least fifteen barrows found there, had almost completely disappeared, although its size and construction could be determined from the impression it left in the mound. The contents of the grave other than the ship constitute the most significant treasure hoard of the early Middle Ages in Europe.

The ship was about 89 feet (27 m) long and 14 feet (4.2 m) wide amidships. It had been placed in the mound with the bow facing away from the river, and a burial chamber had been erected in its center. Many of the grave goods were in the west end of the chamber. No trace of the deceased was found at the time of the excavation, but the most recent analyses of the mound's contents indicate a body had been present.

The most unusual objects were found at the western edge of the burial chamber. An iron stand, 5.5 feet (172 cm) high, may have been an emblem or standard borne in processions, but its exact purpose is not known. A stone bar or whetstone, 2 feet (61 cm) long, is carved at each end with four heads directed to the points of the compass. A recent reconstruction has one end of the whetstone surmounted by a bronze stag on an iron ring, although this was formerly thought to be part of the iron standard. A parallel exists, albeit in a much smaller example, in a bronze pin surmounted by an animal figure with four human faces directed to the points of the compass, which was found at Hagested in Denmark. The whetstone is believed to have been a royal scepter.

The weaponry in the grave is similar to that in finds in Sweden, at Vendel and Valsgärde in the Uppland district near Stockholm. The Sutton Hoo "warrior" was supplied with a helmet, always rare in Germanic archaeology, which is ornamented with designs known in Swedish (Germanic) art of the sixth century. His shield, now almost entirely decayed, was round and of wood, with an iron central boss and decorative gilt-bronze plaques akin to others found at Vendel (an inhumation cemetery of the sixth to eighth centuries). The rusted remains of an iron sword about 34 inches (85 cm) long are supplied with a gold and garnet pommel and gold guard plate; the pommel is also paralleled in Swedish finds. However, it should be pointed out that the Swedish inhumation boat graves at Vendel and Valsgärde contain little gold and do not appear to have been royal burials. Kings' graves at Old Uppsala, the legendary seat of Sweden's pagan rulers, are sixth-century barrows containing cremations.

Helmet from Sutton Hoo, 7th century. Iron, bronze, silver, and gilt fragments on a restored base. MICHAEL HOLFORD

Among other notable finds in the Sutton Hoo grave were a set of ten silver bowls (eight well preserved) that fit into one another (see illustration at "Celtic Arts"); a pair of nielloed silver baptismal spoons inscribed with the names Saul and Paul in Greek; a large bronze hanging bowl adorned with enamel and millefiori; a large silver dish marked with the control stamps of the Byzantine emperor Anastasius (491–518); a lyre of maplewood (in a beaverskin bag of which traces remain); and a pair of drinking horns of aurochs decorated with silver-gilt foil.

The most beautiful of the objects found at Sutton Hoo are a great buckle of gold, 5.2 inches (13.2 cm) long, weighing 14.6 ounces (414.62 g), ornamented in a style known from Vendel; a purse lid framed in gold with plaques executed in garnets and millefiori glass (see illustration at "Enamel, Millefiori"); and gold, garnet, and millefiori shoulder clasps. The purse, presumably of leather or some textile that has completely disappeared, contained thirty-seven "Merovingian" gold coins (weighing between 1.06 and 1.38 grams), three unstruck blanks, and two small gold bars or ingots. The forty smaller pieces may be symbolic payment to the forty oarsmen the Sutton Hoo ship is calculated to have had. The two ingots, together weighing about eight times as much as the average coin, may have been the wages of the helmsman. The only positively datable coin is of the Frankish king Theodebert II (595–612).

Nearly a generation of scholars have proposed various names for the occupant of the Sutton Hoo grave. Their arguments were based on two assumptions: (1) the coins seemed to indicate a burial about 650 or 660, and (2) the absence of a body was a sign that the deceased was a new Christian, in an England undergoing conversion, who was buried as a Christian elsewhere but given a pagan rite at Sutton Hoo by those who might not have embraced the new faith. The presence of baptismal spoons was taken as evidence of a recent conversion.

The latest proposal discards both assumptions. The coin hoard is now believed to have been assembled about 625, and chemical analysis of the soil in the mound indicates a body once was present but has completely decayed. Raedwald, an East Anglian king who had been converted to Christianity but lapsed into paganism, and who died about 625, is the likely occupant of the Sutton Hoo grave.

BIBLIOGRAPHY

Rupert Bruce-Mitford, *Aspects of Anglo-Saxon Archaeology: Sutton Hoo and Other Discoveries* (1974), and *The Sutton Hoo Ship Burial: A Handbook,* 3rd ed. (1979); Angela C. Evans, *The Sutton Hoo Ship Burial* (1986); Charles Green, *Sutton Hoo* (1963); Robert Howard Hodgkin, *A History of the Anglo-Saxons,* 2 vols., 3rd ed. (1952).

SIDNEY L. COHEN

[See also **Celtic Art; Migration Period Art; Scandinavia: Before 800.**]

SUYŪṬĪ, AL- (Abū 'l-Faḍl ᶜAbd al-Raḥmān ibn Abī Bakr Jalāl al-Dīn) (1445–1505), one of the most prolific scholars of medieval Islamic times. He came from a prominent family of the Egyptian town of Asyūṭ. His father died when the boy was only five, and the family was long in financial difficulty. But academic and governmental connections ensured that al-Suyūṭī could begin his studies, and within a short time he showed himself to be a talented and diligent student. He first studied the Koran, jurisprudence, and grammar, then pursued a long and grueling program for further advanced work. His particular strengths, in his opinion, were grammar and jurisprudence, followed by rhetoric, elegant literary prose (*inshāᵓ*), and *ḥadīth*. He also took up, at various times in his career, Koranic exegesis, belles lettres, history, logic, dogmatics, mathematics, and medicine. But as his views became more rigidly orthodox he gave up logic, considering it a sacrilege. He also refused to study scholastic theology (*kalām*) and prided himself on his ignorance of philosophy. He had Sufi contacts and was interested in mysticism but gave the subject serious attention only late in his life.

At the age of only seventeen, al-Suyūṭī received his licenses to teach and to pronounce formal legal opinions (*fatāwā*). He then spent time traveling through Egypt in search of further learning and twice went on pilgrimage to Mecca. By 1466 he was back in Cairo and teaching regularly. His energy and dedication quickly gained him a reputation as one of the most eminent scholars of Egypt. He held numerous important academic posts in Cairo and also devoted himself to a phenomenal writing career: He composed more than 500 works, many of which were acclaimed throughout the Islamic world.

At the same time, however, al-Suyūṭī was highly controversial. He had enormous self-confidence, was unbearably arrogant, and believed himself to be the *mujaddid,* the religious reviver expected at the turn of each century—in this case, the Muslim year 900 (1494)—to restore Islam to its true path. He repeatedly plunged into bitter disputes with his colleagues (often over trifles), vilifying them as imbeciles and charlatans. Not surprisingly, he always had enemies and detractors and was repeatedly the object of intense criticism; he was even in personal danger. In 1498, the members of the Baybarsīya Sufi convent at which he was *shaykh* (master) carried him off and threw him into a fountain. When this quarrel expanded in 1501 to include the sultan al-ᶜĀdil Ṭūmān Bāy among his enemies, al-Suyūṭī had to go into hiding. With this, his career came to an ignominious end. He retired a disappointed and bitter man and refused to return to public life when his old position at the

SVARFDÆLA SAGA

Baybarsīya was offered to him again three years later. He chose to remain in seclusion until his death. He was widely mourned and has ever since been regarded as one of the greatest scholars of Mamluk Egypt.

Much of al-Suyūṭī's fame derives from his vast number of works. Many of these were pamphlets pertaining to his numerous disputes; others were unfinished works. Those he did see through to completion were generally derivative in nature; seldom original, he was repeatedly accused of pirating the work of others. Indeed, he was fond of selecting a topic, compiling relevant information from a wide variety of sources, and then recasting, annotating, and reworking the material into his own new book. Nevertheless, his compilations were, and today remain, extremely useful to scholars. He greatly facilitated access to an enormous range of source material and preserved from destruction much that would otherwise have been lost to modern researchers.

BIBLIOGRAPHY

Sources. Al-Suyūṭī, *History of the Caliphs,* H. S. Jarrett, trans. (1881), and *Islamic Cosmology,* Anton M. Heinen, ed. and trans. (1982).

Studies. Carl Brockelmann, *Geschichte der arabischen Litteratur,* II, and *Supplement,* II, 2nd ed. (1937–1949), 180–204 and 178–198, respectively; E. M. Sartain, *Jalāl al-Dīn al-Suyūṭī* (1975).

LAWRENCE I. CONRAD

[See also **Ḥadīth; Koran; Law, Islamic; Mamluk Dynasty; Mysticism, Islamic; Philosophy and Theology, Islamic.**]

SVARFDÆLA SAGA (Saga of the people of the Svarfaðar Valley) is preserved in a paper transcript (*ca.* 1650) of a lost fifteenth-century vellum and in some forty copies of the transcript; the text contains several minor lacunae and one crucial one, several chapters in length, near the middle of the story. In its present form, the work, written around 1350, is partly a reconstruction of a lost *Svarfdæla saga* from around 1250. Sturla Þórðarson (1214–1284) knew the original work, but the relationship of the extant one to *Landnámabók* and earlier sagas is complex and obscure. The story consists of three parts, which differ markedly from each other in content and style.

In the first part, which is based largely on motifs from *Örvar-Odds saga* and other *fornaldarsögur* (stories of ancient times), a young Norwegian named Þorstein slays two formidable Vikings, thereby winning fame, fortune, an earl's daughter in marriage, and the cognomen *svörfuðr* (tumult), from which the district Svarfaðardalr in Iceland is said to derive its name. Grief at his wife's death and disagreement with the national policies of King Harald Fairhair impel Þorstein to leave Norway and settle in Iceland.

The second part, which seems to be based largely on local traditions, treats of the many feuds between Þorstein's descendants, led by his son Karl the Red, and their adversaries, the kinsmen and followers of the chieftain Ljótólfr. Much of the violence is caused by a kinsman of Karl named Klaufi, who is a berserker while alive and, following his death, a revenant who goes about wielding his severed head as a weapon. A reconciliation between the feuding parties is frustrated by the stubborn pride of Yngvildr Faircheek, who is successively the concubine of Ljótólfr and the wife of Klaufi (whose death she has treacherously brought about) and of a man named Skíði. As a result, Karl the Red is slain.

The final section consists of a combination and elaboration of the taming-of-the-shrew theme and of motifs from an early *Amlóða saga* (Story of Hamlet). Karl Karlsson, born after the death of his father, Karl the Red, masquerades as a speechless fool until age twelve, when he takes fearful vengeance for his father's slaying. After banishing Skíði and striking off the heads of Yngvild's children before her eyes, he twice sells her into slavery abroad. Only after she has learned to sympathize with the suffering of others is she returned to Iceland, but neither Ljótólfr nor Skíði will have anything to do with the woman they regard as the cause of their greatest difficulties. The story ends with a tenuous reconciliation among the adversaries in the "valley of tumult."

BIBLIOGRAPHY

Svarfdæla saga, in Guðni Jónsson, ed., *Íslendinga sögur,* VIII (1947), 119–215; *Svarfdæla saga,* in Jónas Kristjánsson, ed., *Íslenzk fornrit,* IX (1956), lxvi–xcii, 129–208.

PAUL SCHACH

[See also **Berserks; Fornaldarsögur; Landnámabók; Norway; Örvar-Odds Saga; Sturla Þórðarson.**]

SVEN AGGESEN (*b. ca.* 1130). A member of one of the noble families of Jutland, Sven refers in his work to his grandfather Christiern Svensen and to his father, Agge, who participated on the side of Erik Emune in the civil wars unleashed by the murder of Cnut (Canute, Knud) Lavard (1131). Sven may have belonged to the royal retinue or *hirð,* and was present at the destruction of Jomsborg (Julin) by Cnut IV Valdemarsen in 1185. It has been suggested that Sven studied at the school of Chartres, but this is a conjecture based primarily on his use of Bernard of Chartres's famous dictum on "being as dwarves sitting on the shoulders of giants" (*esse quasi nanos gigantium humeris insidentes*), a commonplace phrase.

Two brief works by Sven are preserved: the *Lex castrensis,* an account of the *Witherlogh* (law of compensation), which is a code of behavior and legislation for the king's guard, and the *Brevis historia regum Dacie,* a brief history of Denmark that encompasses both legendary and historical episodes.

The *Lex castrensis* appears to have been written first; chapter 11 refers to the history as a future project. Based on a short vernacular account of the laws, the *Lex* consists of a foreword and fourteen chapters. The introduction explains why it is necessary that the laws should be written down. The first four chapters describe the origin of the *Witherlogh* in the days of Cnut the Great: how the king's fame drew to him a multitude of warriors of very different backgrounds and temperaments, among whom the occasions for hostility and strife were numerous; and how Cnut decided to institute a law for these men who made up his *hirð,* so that they could all be judged by a common standard of conduct. Subsequent chapters deal with the minor services that the men owe each other (such as taking each other's horses to water), the king's obligations toward his warriors, termination of service to one's lord, the *huskarlestefne* or council of the king's men and its authority on issues of slander and verbal offense, the procedure for property claims, how Cnut the Great was the first to break the new law by killing one of his men, compensation for a wound inflicted on a fellow warrior, compensation for a blow given with the hand or with a weapon, offenses committed against fellow warriors who have not been recognized as such, and penalties for high treason against king and country.

In *Gesta Danorum* X.xvii, Saxo Grammaticus gives a rather free account of the *Witherlogh.* There is a third version extant in Danish, which is likely to be secondary and based on Sven's and Saxo's descriptions.

The *Brevis historia regum Dacie* covers in very short compass the same scope as Saxo's vast *Gesta*: legendary history (Danish *oldhistorie*) and the Danish kings from Harald I Bluetooth to Cnut IV Valdemarsen. The legendary section is minimal, consisting of a list of kings' names interrupted by rather full accounts of the story of Wermund and Uffo, including the latter's fight against the Saxon champions at the Eider, and of the story of Thyra, "Denmark's ornament," and her financing of the Danevirke, a fortification at the Danish border with Germany. The properly historical section of Sven's work keeps more even proportions in the space allotted to the various kings, and emphasizes Danish enmity toward and independence from the German empire, a theme already sounded in the legendary chapters.

Sven undoubtedly used oral sources in his history, and in the later chapters much information must derive from family traditions. His written sources are limited, among them Ælnoth's *Vita et passio* of St. Cnut, the liturgical office of Cnut Lavard, perhaps the Roskilde Chronicle. His rather pedestrian Latin contains many echoes of Vergil, Lucan, Statius, Sallust, and Martianus Capella, as well as numerous references to classical mythology and to the Vulgate, all of which make the hypothesis of an education at Chartres rather more likely.

Sven's work was first edited by Stephan Hansen Stephanius in 1642, from a manuscript at the Copenhagen University Library that was later destroyed in a fire. The present standard text was established by M. C. Gertz on the basis of a copy of another manuscript made by Klaus Kristoffersen Lyskander around 1570 and preserved in the Arnamagnaean collection (AM 33 4°). In spite of numerous omissions and misunderstandings, Lyskander's copy provides a more complete and trustworthy text, and clearly reflects a better manuscript than was available to Stephanius.

BIBLIOGRAPHY

Sources. En ny text af Sven Aggesøns værker (1916); *Sven Aggesøns historiske skrifter, oversatte efter den paa grundlag af Codex Arnamagnaeanus 33, 4°, restituerede nye text,* Martin C. Gertz, trans. (1967).

Study. Ellen Jørgensen, *Historieforskning og historieskrivning i Danmark indtil aar 1800* (1931).

JOAQUÍN MARTÍNEZ-PIZARRO

[See also **Bernard of Chartres; Cnut the Great; Denmark; Knud Lavard; Martianus Capella; Roskilde Chronicle; Saxo Grammaticus; Vergil in the Middle Ages.**]

SVERRIS SAGA, the saga of the Norwegian king Sverre Sigurdsson (*r.* 1184–1202), is preserved in four medieval manuscripts and in vellum fragments. AM 327 4° (*ca.* 1300) is considered to have the best text, whereas *Eirspennill* (*ca.* 1300) is somewhat abridged.

Sverre, a self-proclaimed illegitimate son of King Sigurðr munnr, was raised in the Faeroe Islands and educated as a priest. He traveled to Norway in 1176 and became leader of the *Birkibeinar* party the following year, but his claim to kingship was opposed by King Magnús (the son of *Jarl* Erlingr skakki and the first Norwegian monarch to be crowned by the church, in 1163/1164). Sverre's victory over Magnús (who died in 1184) brought short-lived peace, but new pretenders staged uprisings from 1185 until 1195. In 1196 a new power group supported by the church, the *Baglar* party, began to back claimants to the throne. The controversy between the two parties continued almost unbroken for fifteen years after Sverre's death in 1202.

According to the saga's prologue, Karl Jónsson (*d.* 1212/1213), abbot of the Icelandic monastery Þingeyrar, wrote the first section of the saga under Sverre's personal direction (1185–1188/1189). That part is known as *Grýla* (bogeyman; so named because of Sverre's ever-increasing power), but it does not cover much material. The later part of the saga is said to be based on eyewitness accounts, some of which were written down soon after the events. One manuscript, *Flateyjarbók,* contains an expanded version of the prologue.

Grýla probably extended only to chapter 31 (1178), but the transition to the following section is gradual. The entire saga was most likely completed by 1210. The account is thus almost contemporary with the events, and its overall historicity, even in details, is generally accepted.

An unevenness in composition is due at least in part to different sources. The four compositional sections correspond to phases of Sverre's career: (1) chapters 1–31 (*Grýla*), (2) chapters 32–100 (1178–1184/1185), (3) chapters 101–128 (1185–1195), and (4) chapters 129–182 (1196–1202). *Grýla* contains motifs from saints' lives, fairy tales, and legendary sagas, and portrays Sverre, especially through his dreams, as God's and St. Óláfr's chosen one. The second section reveals the best literary composition in its interweaving of narrative strands and employment of oratory. The third section is brief and lacks cohesion, but the last section is again artistic and fuller.

A slight change at chapter 100 in the general uniformity of style and composition may be the result of composition at different times by the same author. Characteristic figurative expressions in the narrative text and in direct discourse bind the saga together. Since these expressions are found in *Grýla,* Karl Jónsson may have completed the entire work himself.

Oratory, which may preserve authentic material, is employed extensively and consistently in the literary composition. Sverre in particular is masterfully portrayed through his occasional orations. His speeches are original and are distinguished by irony, humor, metaphors, proverbs, and quotations.

BIBLIOGRAPHY

Sources. Sverris-saga: The Saga of King Sverri of Norway, J. Sephton, trans. (1899); *Sverris saga etter Cod. AM 327 4°,* Gustav Indrebø, ed. (1920, repr. 1981).

Studies. Lárus H. Blöndal, *Um uppruna Sverrissögu* (1982); Geoffrey M. Gathorne-Hardy, *A Royal Impostor: King Sverre of Norway* (1956); Ludvig Holm-Olsen, *Studier i Sverres saga* (1953).

JAMES E. KNIRK

[See also **Norse Kings' Sagas; Norway; Saga.**]

SVETI CXOVELI, the largest surviving Georgian religious building and burial place of the Georgian kings. The cathedral Sveti Cχoveli (life-spending pillar) is the seat of the *kat^{c}ołikos* (head of the Georgian church) in the ancient capital of Georgia, Mc^{c}χet^{c}a. According to the donors' inscription on the east facade, it was built between 1010 and 1029 under Kat^{c}ołikos Melχisedek (*r.* 1010–1033) by the architect Arsukisdze. The cathedral replaced the dilapidated fifth-century basilica of King Waχtang I Gurgaslani, which in turn had been erected on the site of a fourth-century wooden church. The remains of Waχtang's basilica were excavated from 1970 to 1971. The protective wall and fortifications surrounding the largest part of the cathedral derive from the eighteenth century, but the beautiful gate of the *mandra* (gatehouse) is contemporary with the cathedral. The exterior walls of the cathedral, enlivened by polychromatic effects (green and red sandstones) and enhanced by articulated, rhythmically arranged blind arcades encompassing figural and decorative patterns, evoke a sense of grandness and logic.

BIBLIOGRAPHY
Adriano Alpago-Novello, *Art and Architecture in Medieval Georgia* (1980); Rusudan Mepisashvili and Vakhtang Tsintsadze, *Arts of Ancient Georgia* (1977, repr. 1979); L. Muskhelishvili, "Mtsḩetis sveti cḩovelis tadsris idsvelesi tsartserebi da mati damonid-ebuleba Mexhisedek Katolikosis anderdstan," in *Ars georgica,* 1 (1942), with French summary, "Les plus anciennes inscriptions de la cathédrale de Mtzkhétha et leurs rapports au testament du catholicos Melchisédech"; N. P. Severov and G. Tshubinashvili, *Mtskheta* (1946); G. Tshubinashvili, "K voprosu o pervonačalnykh formakh Mtskhetskogo Kafedrala," in *Ars georgica,* 5 (1959), with German summary.

WACHTANG DJOBADZE

[See also **Georgia: Political History; Georgian Art and Architecture; Georgian Church and Saints; Georgians (Iberians); Mc^{c}χet^{c}a; Waχtang I Gurgaslani.**]

SVIPDAGSMÁL. The poem *Svipdagsmál,* as we know it today, is an amalgamation of two poems, *Grógaldr* and *Fjǫlsvinnsmál,* found only in manuscripts of the *Poetic Edda* that date from the end of the seventeenth century or later. It was Sophus Bugge who, as a result of his investigations of the Danish and Swedish ballad cycle about Sveidal, suggested joining the two poems and calling the product *Svipdagsmál.* Scholars agree that the poem is relatively recent, probably from the thirteenth century.

Grógaldr is a poem of sixteen stanzas in the verse style called *ljóðaháttr.* A young man comes to his mother's (Gróa's) grave and awakens her from the dead. He has been cursed by his stepmother to wander until he finds the maiden Menglǫð, and he asks for his mother's protection on the dangerous journey. She responds with nine charms to guard him against water, cold, the attacks of enemies, fetters, the perils of the sea, dead Christian women, and the superior wit of threatening giants. Then she sinks back into the grave.

The young man's journey is not related, and the poem *Fjǫlsvinnsmál,* of fifty stanzas, also composed in *ljóðaháttr,* begins with his arrival at the dwelling of Menglǫð. Fjǫlsviðr (Very Wise) is a giant guarding the dwelling whom the young man, first calling himself Vindkaldr (Wind-Cold), engages in a standard wisdom dialogue. Vindkaldr questions Fjǫlsviðr about the nature of the stronghold, its guardians and special features. He learns that it is quite impossible for anyone to enter save Svipdagr, for whom the impossible will be possible. He then reveals himself as Svipdagr and is united with Menglǫð.

The tale told in the poem has features in common both with the Welsh story of Culhwch and Olwen found in the *Mabinogi* and with the Grail legend. *Svipdagsmál* also contains a number of similarities to other Eddic poems. Its basic theme immediately recalls the events of both *Skírnismál* and the legend of Sigurd and Brynhild. While its etymology is disputed, the name Svipdagr obviously has some connection with "day" and occurs in the prologue to Snorri's *Edda* and in Saxo Grammaticus as the name of a king, as well as the name of a warrior in Snorri's "Skálds kaparmál" and *Heimskringla.* In addition, the hero gives his father's name as Sólbjartr (Sun-Bright). Freyr's name means "lord" and that of Freyr's servant Skírnir, "shining." As in both *Skírnismál* and the Sigurd legend, the maiden to be wooed lives in an enclosure, surrounded by fire, that opens only to the chosen suitor. In *Grógaldr* the waking of the dead woman for aid is analogous to scenes in *Baldrs draumar, Vǫluspá,* or Hervör's waking of her father, Angantýr, in *Hervarör saga.* The chanting of charms is reminiscent of the "Ljóðatal" passage in *Hávamál.*

On the question of the nature of the poem's source there are two prevailing opinions. For example, as the main proponent of the first opinion, Jan de Vries considers the basic fairy tale as presented in the ballad cycle and also in the Celtic material to be primary and the poem as an attempt to adapt that fairy-tale plot to an older mythical form. However, the actual journey with all its dangers prophesied by the dead woman Gróa—in fact the heart of the fairy tale— is missing from the texts. The principal advocate of the second opinion, Lotte Motz, has suggested that the poem has its roots in ancient initiation ritual. Svipdagr has no identity until he has successfully endured the tortures of his initiation, represented by the charms, and gained the wisdom needed for his new role,

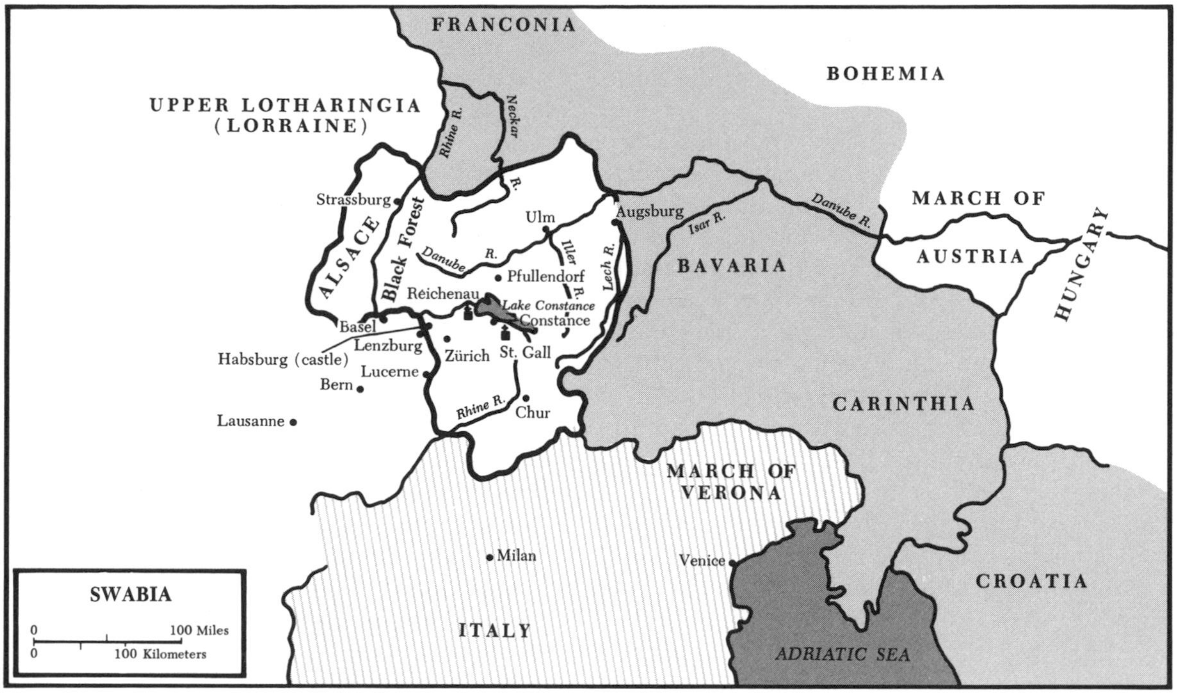

symbolized by the encounter with Fjǫlsviðr. At the end he is revealed in his new identity as Svipdagr, the royal consort of Menglǫð, who can variously be linked to the earth goddess, Freyja, or even his mother, Gróa.

BIBLIOGRAPHY

Henry A. Bellows, trans., *The Poetic Edda* (1923, repr. 1957); Sophus Bugge, ed., *Norrœn Fornkvæði* (1867); Lotte Motz, "The King and the Goddess: An Interpretation of the Svipdagsmál," in *Arkiv för nordisk filologi,* **90** (1975); Franz R. Schröder, "Svipdagsmál," in *Germanisch-romanische Monatsschrift,* **47** (n.s. **16**) (1966); Jan de Vries, "Om Eddaens Visdomsdigtning," in *Arkiv för nordisk filologi,* **50** (1934), and *Altnordische Literaturgeschichte,* II (1942, repr. 1967), 524–527.

KAAREN GRIMSTAD

[See also **Baldrs Draumar; Brynhild; Eddic Poetry; Grail, Legend of; Hávamál; Hervarar Saga Ok Heiðreks Konungs; Mabinogi; Sigurd; Skírnismál; Vǫluspá.**]

SWABIA (Alamannia) can refer to the territory in which the Alamanni settled (roughly the federal state of Baden-Württemberg, western Bavaria, Alsace, German Switzerland, and Vorarlberg); to the Alaholfingian duchy, the newer stem duchy that existed between 911 and 1268; and more narrowly, to the territory between the Black Forest and the Lech River, north of the Rhine River. The changes in Swabia's borders and the modern division of the region among Germany, France, Switzerland, and Austria can be attributed largely to the Alamanni's failure to achieve any lasting political unity.

The Alamanni were a confederation of several tribes. During the Carolingian period the name of the most important tribe, the Suebi or Suevi, who originally lived along the Elbe, was applied to the entire group and its territory, Swabia.

The Alamanni appeared on the Main River in 213. In 259/260 they crossed the *limes,* the defensive line the Romans had built between the Rhine and upper Danube, and occupied the Decuman Fields, the Roman military zone between the *limes* and the Rhine. The Alamanni made repeated incursions into Gaul and Italy but were driven back, most notably by Julian the Apostate at the Battle of Strassburg in 357.

In the fifth century they conquered Alsace, north-central Switzerland, and the area between the Iller and Lech rivers. Eastern Switzerland and Vorarlberg were germanized very slowly. The arrival of the Bavarians on the Danube at the beginning of the sixth century prevented the expansion of the Alamanni beyond the Lech, while the Burgundians blocked the Alamanni's advance west of the Aare River.

The Franks were the Alamanni's most formidable rivals. Clovis defeated the Alamanni decisively at the Battle of Zülpich (Tolbiac) in 496 and occupied Alsace and northern Alamannia, that is, the area between the Main and the mid Neckar Valley, which became part of Franconia. Ten years later, Clovis suppressed an uprising of Alamanni. The remaining Alamanni accepted the protection of King Theodoric of the Ostrogoths in 506/507; but in 536, after the Byzantine invasion of Italy, all of the Alamanni submitted to the overlordship of the Franks.

The various Alamannic tribes originally retained their own kings—fifteen are mentioned in connection with the Battle of Strassburg—but in the fifth century they were united under a single ruler. The Franks abolished the Alamannic monarchy and replaced the kings with dukes, who belonged to the old royal house but were selected by the Frankish kings. The first known dukes were two brothers, Leutharis and Bucelin, who invaded Italy and whose army was annihilated by the Byzantines in 554. Like the Merovingians, the Alaholfingians divided the duchy among themselves. One branch of the ducal house, the Ettichone, governed Alsace until the middle of the eighth century. The center of the main Alamannic duchy was located west of Lake Constance.

The most important consequence of the Alamanni's incorporation into the Frankish realm was their conversion to Christianity. They had conquered the Decuman Fields before Constantine's conversion, but in the late Roman Empire there were bishoprics in Strassburg, Augst, Windisch, Chur, and Augsburg that survived the Alamannic invasion (the episcopal sees of Augst and Windisch were subsequently transferred to Basel and Lausanne, respectively). The tribal leaders had accepted the new faith by the end of the sixth century, but most of the Alamanni converted during the seventh century. This was the result of Frankish pressure, contact with the surviving Roman Christians, and the activity and example of wandering monks, most notably St. Columbanus, who arrived at Lake Constance in 610, and his disciple, Gallus. The latter founded a cell that around 720 became the monastery of St. Gall. The origins of the main Swabian bishopric, Constance, which was first mentioned in 613, are shrouded in darkness; but its location at the center of the duchy suggests that the duke played the leading role in its foundation. It was the largest German diocese but had a small endowment.

The pace of Christianization is evident in the two extant law codes. The *Pactus legis Alamannorum,* which was compiled about 613, referred to the church in only two places, whereas the *Lex Alamannorum,* which appeared about 718, devoted one of its three sections (chaps. I–XXII) to the church.

The decline of the Merovingians made the Alamannic dukes virtually independent, but the Carolingian mayors of the palace restored Frankish authority. Pepin II waged several campaigns against Dukes Gottfried and Willehari between 709 and 712. Charles Martel conducted several expeditions against Gottfried's son, Duke Lantfrid (712–730); promoted the monastery of Reichenau, which St. Pirmin had founded in 724, as a center of Frankish influence; and abolished the duchy in 730. After Charles's death in 741, the Alamanni, led by Lantfrid's brother Theudebald, rebelled; but Pepin the Short and Carloman crushed the revolt and executed the rebellious magnates in the so-called Bloodbath of Cannstadt (746). It is noteworthy that the *Lex Alamannorum,* which was probably revised under Charlemagne, unlike the earlier *Pactus,* did not recognize the existence of a separate estate of nobles. The mayors reorganized Alamannia into counties and appointed Franks as counts. Reichenau and St. Gall became major centers of the Carolingian renaissance.

Nevertheless, the magnitude of the changes ought not to be exaggerated. The native nobility survived and intermarried with the Frankish imperial aristocracy to form the Swabian nobility of later centuries. Charlemagne's wife, Hildegard, was a scion of the old Alamannic ducal house. More important, the *Lex Alamannorum,* the bishopric of Constance, which included most of Swabia, and the Carolingians' grant of Alamannia to their sons as a subkingdom—to Charles II the Bald in 829 and to Charles III the Fat in 876—helped to preserve the Swabians' stem identity.

This proved to be of crucial importance in the revival of the stem duchy in the crisis precipitated at the beginning of the tenth century by the extinction of the Carolingian dynasty and the Magyar invasions. Two lineages of the imperial aristocracy vied for power. Margrave Burchard of Raetia was executed in 911 for trying to make himself duke. The count palatine, Erchanger, who had led the resistance to the Magyars, was elected duke at a tribal assembly in 915 but was executed by his brother-in-law, King Conrad I, in 917. He was succeeded by Burchard's son, Burchard II (917–926), who submitted to King Henry I in 919 but retained the duchy. Henry asserted his authority in 926 by appointing a non-Swabian, Hermann I (926–949), a cousin of Conrad I, as duke and by taking control of the Swabian church.

During the Saxon and early Salian periods, the dukes were the king's representatives in Swabia, enfeoffed with royal and church lands and responsible for maintaining the peace and leading the Swabian contingent into battle. They were, however, comparatively weak figures. The kings preferred to select non-Swabians, often minors, who had no independent source of power in Swabia, as dukes. The office was not hereditary, but hereditary claims were not ignored. For example, Burchard II's widow married Hermann I and their daughter married Otto the Great's son, Liutolf, who was duke from 949 to 953; Liutolf was succeeded by Burchard III (954–973), the son of Burchard II. Conflicts with the crown involved dynastic rather than Swabian issues: Liutolf's revolt against his father in 953, Hermann II's candidacy for the crown in 1002, and the rebellion of Ernst II (1015–1030) against his stepfather, Emperor Conrad II.

This changed in the eleventh century. In the process of developing their own territorial lordships, the Swabian nobles became conscious of their membership in patrilineal dynasties and associated with the castles they built to secure their holdings. The names of some of these Swabian dynasties resounded in subsequent European history: Hohenstaufen, Welf, Habsburg, and Hohenzollern. This sense of family identity was further strengthened by the foundation of dynastic monasteries, such as the Habsburg abbey of Muri. While these reformed houses usually were conveyed to the papacy, the lineages retained the hereditary advocacies. This established a link between the nobles and Rome, which endangered the monarchy during the investiture conflict.

The papal party elected the duke of Swabia, Rudolf of Rheinfelden (1057–1079; *d.* 1080), as antiking in 1077, and Rudolf's son Berthold (1079–1090) succeeded him as duke. King Henry IV responded by enfeoffing the first Hohenstaufen duke, Frederick I (1079–1105), who married Henry's daughter, with the duchy in 1079. Frederick's opponents included not only the Rheinfelder but also two other lineages of ducal rank: the Zähringer, whose holdings were concentrated west of the Black Forest, and the Welfs, whose Swabian lands were situated northeast of Lake Constance. Frederick's own domains were confined to northeastern Swabia and Alsace.

After Berthold's death in 1090, the Rheinfelden inheritance passed to his brother-in-law, Berthold of Zähringen, who was elected as the antiduke in 1092. Berthold's brother, Bishop Gebhard of Constance (1084–1110), and his mentor, Abbot William of Hirsau (1069–1091), were the clerical leaders of the Gregorian party. Henry IV was reconciled with the Welfs in 1096, and in 1098 Berthold of Zähringen renounced his claims to the duchy and received the advocacy of Zurich as compensation. The Welf and Zähringen territories obtained de facto independence from the duchy. The Zähringer's attention was increasingly focused thereafter on western Switzerland, particularly after King Lothair enfeoffed them with the rectorate of Burgundy in 1127.

Swabia was a secundogeniture of the Hohenstaufen after they mounted the German throne in 1138. The Hohenstaufen's dynastic lands in Swabia had been comparatively small; Frederick I Barbarossa (1152–1190), who served as regent for his young cousin and sons, the nominal dukes, remedied this. He obtained the advocacies of various churches, such as Augsburg and Reichenau; forced them to enfeoff the Hohenstaufen cadets with church lands; and above all acquired, especially after 1167, the holdings of Swabian dynasties who had died without heir, such as the counts of Lenzburg and Pfullendorf. His biggest acquisition was the purchase of the domains of his childless maternal uncle, Welf VI. Frederick promoted the development of such cities as Gmünd and Ulm. By the end of the twelfth century, Swabia increasingly meant this Hohenstaufen territory.

After Frederick's youngest son, Philip, became king in 1198, Swabia was linked with the crown in a personal union and lost its separate identity. This association of Swabia with Germany is reflected in the French word for Germany, *Allemagne*; the name of the Alamanni, who had settled next to the Franks, was thus applied in France to all of Germany. Emperor Frederick II did not neglect Swabia. When Berthold V of Zähringen died without heir in 1218, the Zähringer's imperial fiefs, including the advocacies of Zurich and Schaffhausen and the cities of Bern and Solothurn, reverted to the *Reich*. Their alods were divided between Berthold's brothers-in-law, the counts of Kyburg and Urach (most were eventually acquired by the Habsburgs). Frederick's own urban foundations included Esslingen, Nördlingen, and Rottweil.

The identification of Swabia with the Hohenstaufen spelled its doom. In spite of later efforts by the Habsburgs, most notably by the first Habsburg king, Rudolf (1273–1291), to revive the duchy, it ended with the execution of the last male Hohenstaufen, Conradin, in 1268.

The fall of the Hohenstaufen left Swabia politically fragmented. The approximately forty cities in the Hohenstaufen duchy became imperial cities. Various nobles, who had been ducal vassals, and imperial ministerials formed the *Reichsritterschaft*, the imperial knighthood directly subject to the crown. There were approximately fifty ecclesiastical lordships, among them Constance, Ellwangen, and Kempten. The lesser noble dynasties, like the counts of Zollern and Fürstenberg, created dwarf states. The Habsburgs, who since 1135 had been the landgraves of Alsace and who had extensive holdings in Switzerland, which they lost to the Swiss Confederation in the fourteenth and fifteenth centuries, assembled sizable domains on both sides of the Black Forest and around Lake Constance, but failed to shape them into a principality. The holdings of the margraves of Baden, a cadet line of the Zähringer, in the Upper Rhine Valley remained divided among several branches of the lineage until the eighteenth century. The most successful dynasty was that of the counts of Württemberg, the chief rivals of the Habsburgs, who created in the Neckar Valley the most united state in Swabia, the duchy of Württemberg (1495). Swabia was the most politically fragmented area of the old *Reich*, but that fragmentation nourished a rich cultural life.

BIBLIOGRAPHY

Karl Siegfried Bader, *Der deutsche Südwesten in seiner territorialstaatlichen Entwicklung* (1950, repr. 1978); Heinrich Büttner, *Staufer und Zähringer im politischen Kräftespiel zwischen Bodensee und Genfersee während des 12. Jahrhunderts* (1961) and "Staufische Territorialpolitik im 12. Jahrhundert," in *Württembergisch Franken*, 47 (1963); *Laws of the Alamans and Bavarians*, Theodore John Rivers, trans. (1977); Helmut Maurer, *Der Herzog von Schwaben: Grundlagen, Wirkungen und Wesen seiner Herrschaft in ottonischer, salischer und staufischer Zeit* (1978); Theodor Mayer, "The State of the Dukes of Zähringen," in Geoffrey Barraclough, ed. and trans., *Mediaeval Germany, 911–1250: Essays by German Historians*, II (1938); Wolfgang Müller, ed., *Zur Geschichte der Alemannen* (1975); Karl Schmid, "Adel und Reform in Schwaben," in Josef Fleckenstein, ed., *Investiturstreit und Reichsverfassung* (1973); Hermann Tüchle, *Kirchengeschichte Schwabens*, 2 vols. (1950–1954); Karl Weller, "Die staufische Städtegrundung in Schwaben," in *Württembergische Vierteljahrshefte für Landesgeschichte*, n.s. **36** (1930), and *Geschichte des schwäbischen Stammes bis zum Untergang der Staufer* (1944), the only general history, but marred by pro-Nazi overtones; *Die Zeit der Staufer: Geschichte, Kunst, Kultur. Katalog der Ausstellung [Stuttgart, 1977]*, 5 vols. (1977–1979).

JOHN B. FREED

[See also **Alamanni; Barbarians, Invasions of; Bavaria; Carolingians and the Carolingian Empire; Charlemagne; Charles Martel; Clovis; Columbanus, St.; Frederick I Barbarossa; Gall, St.; Germany; Habsburg Dynasty; Henry IV of Germany; Hohenstaufen Dynasty; Investiture and Investiture Conflict; Julian the Apostate; Law, German; Mayor of the Palace; Merovingians; Ostrogoths; Pepin II; Pepin III and the Donation of Pepin; Pirmin, St.; Theodoric the Ostrogoth.**]

SWEDEN. In the early Middle Ages Sweden was undiscovered as far as the rest of Europe was concerned. In the sixth century the Gothic historian Jordanes and the Byzantine Procopius provided a few glimpses, probably drawn from itineraries of Roman traders, sailors' stories, and testimonies of Scandinavian and Erulian officers in the armies of Gothic Italy and Byzantium. According to these authors, the west coast of present-day Sweden was inhabited by small tribes of local importance, but inland and on the Baltic coast we hear of at least three major tribes: the Gauts (Goths) south of Lake Vänern, the Austrogauts (Ostrogoths) east of Lake Vättern, and, most important, the Swedes around Lake Mälar, at that time a bay of the Baltic cutting deep into the country. Between the regions of these tribes were vast forests, and the country was generally very sparsely populated.

We know from place-names that Germanic tribes inhabited present-day Sweden at least from the beginning of the Middle Ages, living in small villages and engaging in primitive agriculture, cattle breeding, hunting, and fishing. The small tribes on the west coast were early incorporated into the

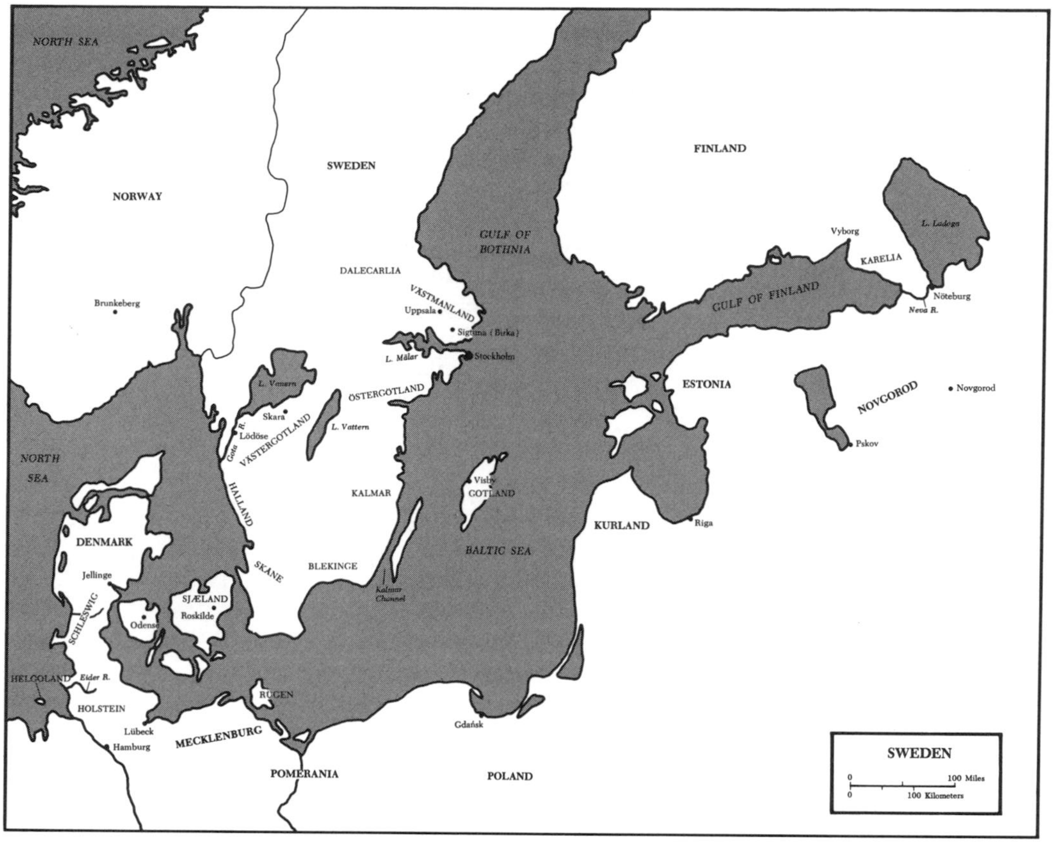

kingdom of the Danes, which was the most densely populated and most powerful Scandinavian realm until the end of the Middle Ages. The Swedes and the Ostrogoths were oriented toward the Baltic, while the Goths were an inland tribe on the Göta River, an outlet to the North Sea. We know from archaeological research that the peoples of Sweden traded with the Romans and the Greeks, and later with the Irish, the Anglo-Saxons, and the Franks; but we have no traces of towns until the Viking Age. There existed a trading center at Helgö on Lake Mälar from the fourth century, with international connections east and west and with a highly specialized handicraft (production of needles and fibulae). Whether it had a permanent concentration of people large enough for it to be called a town is not known.

How and when the main tribes were united into the kingdom of Sweden is a matter of speculation. We know that such a kingdom existed in the middle of the ninth century as a Baltic dominion, containing not only the coastal regions to and beyond the Kalmar Channel in the south but also with a foothold in Kurland and probably some influence over the islands in the Baltic. It is not known whether the Goths were incorporated at that time, but at the beginning of the eleventh century they were subjects of the Swedish king. In the twelfth century, however, they had for some time a king of their own, and at the beginning of the thirteenth century Sweden was still a rather loose federation comprising the three main tribes; the Swedes had the right to choose and depose the common king, and the other tribes had the right to accept or reject the Swedish candidate. During the thirteenth century Sweden developed into a society of privileged estates of clerics, nobles, and burghers, with an administration and a capital, the new port and fortress town of Stockholm.

NINTH TO ELEVENTH CENTURY

In the Viking Age long-distance trade with the Arab countries in the east profited the seafaring people of the Mälar provinces and of the island of Gotland, especially their chieftains. Sweden also benefited from a good climate for agriculture and the expansion of cultivated land. A new town, Birka, on an island in Lake Mälar, rapidly became a center of international trade and a temporary residence of the king of Sweden. According to the *Life of St. Ansgar* (*ca.* 865) and the ecclesiastical chronicler Adam of Bremen (1070's), the king of Sweden had very little power except in time of war, when he commanded the armed forces of the kingdom. The local leaders of the peasant society held real control of daily life and were the kingmakers. There was also a spiritual power in Sweden: the pagan cult site of Uppsala. In midwinter a great sacrifice was held here at which the king was expected to officiate, and an important market took place in connection with this rite.

The Viking Age kingdom of Sweden was very unstable. Like the emerging kingdoms of Denmark and Norway, it was a maritime kingdom; the waterways linked the different parts of the realm and even the regional units. In the sparsely populated countryside no administrative authority kept the highways open and fit for use through the vast and uninhabited forests, and harsh weather made all roads impassable for long periods. But the many lakes and rivers offered good transportation in the warm season and travel by sleigh over ice in winter. The Scandinavians had developed a marvelous type of ship: light and swift, with a shallow draft but seaworthy even in stormy seas. The ships made it possible to keep together the separate parts of the Swedish kingdom and to penetrate the rivers of Eastern Europe for trading purposes. In periods when the navies of other powers dominated the Baltic, the Swedish kingdom suffered the risk of falling apart; at other times the Swedish kings and warriors invaded neighboring areas and played a dominant role in the area.

We know the names of some mid-ninth-century Swedish kings, who with some reluctance gave Christian missionaries permission to work in the country, but after that there is a long period about which we know little. At the end of the tenth century there seem to have been several invasions into the heart of Sweden, threatening the sanctuary of Uppsala, that were beaten back. A warrior king, Erik the Victorious, is said to have achieved this success, and also to have conquered Denmark temporarily with the help of King Bolesław of Poland. After Erik's death the king of Denmark, Sweyn Forkbeard, rapidly regained supremacy in the Scandinavian waters, and conquered England and Norway. Under Erik's son Olof, Sweden became a satellite of the Danish North Sea empire.

In the tenth century three new port towns came into existence: Sigtuna, replacing nearby Birka, which had been destroyed; Visby, on Gotland; and Lödöse, on the Göta River, the port of Västergötland, the country of the Goths. This country was christianized at that time, probably by English missionaries, and its Christianity was stabilized in the middle of the eleventh century when a diocese was organized from the archbishopric of Bremen with its center in the new city of Skara. The kings of Sweden were Christians beginning with Olof Eriksson, according to Scandinavian royal custom in the late Viking Age. They were, however, expelled from Sweden proper by the pagan opposition: first Olof Eriksson and then, about 1080, Inge and Halsten. In both cases they had to take up residence in Christian Västergötland.

TWELFTH TO THIRTEENTH CENTURY

The stubborn paganism in the Mälar region had its roots in the Uppsala cult site and in the supremacy of the local chieftains, who held sacral functions and were naturally conservative. During the eleventh century, however, there emerged a new social class of traders and Viking soldiers who gained wealth in foreign countries. They were Christians like their trading partners and former comrades-in-arms in Western Europe and Russia, and they must in the long run have helped the kings to undermine the pagan authorities. About 1100 a revolutionary change took place in the central parts of Sweden: ecclesiastical and royal administrations were organized, with dioceses and uniform military districts. From then on, the kings held the governing power, though their rule was often disputed. Out of eight kings in the twelfth century, five were killed by their enemies. This meant the slow and often violent conquest of the country by the king and his retainers, with help of the church, against the resistance of the freeholders, led by the provincial great families. In Sweden, as in Denmark and Norway, the kings had to ally themselves with an aristocratic group in order to hold power. In the middle of the thirteenth century, however, the dynasty of St. Erik (*d.* 1160) was united with the family of the *jarls* (earls) of Sweden, and in 1250 Valdemar, the son of the powerful regent, Earl Birger, was made king by his father, who had previously crushed the freeholders' army in battle, imposed permanent taxes on them, and beheaded their leaders, members of the former royal family.

During the long period of civil wars the territory of the Swedish kingdom had expanded to the east. Western and central Finland (that is, the south of present-day Finland) were incorporated. Northern Finland, however, was still wilderness, with the exception of some lake districts and the coast of the Gulf of Bothnia. How this conquest was accomplished is for the most part unknown; ecclesiastical sources mention crusades, and some fighting may have taken place, but the tribe in this part of Finland, the Tavasts (Häme), were regarded by the Russians as allies of the Swedes, and there is no indication that strong military measures were needed to keep the country under the dominion of the king of Sweden. There were Swedish settlements along the coast of both sides of the Gulf of Finland, which indicates some form of coexistence. But relations with the Estonians south of the gulf were hostile, with frequent raids across the Baltic, until the Danes conquered Estonia in 1219. The Karelians in eastern Finland were allies and dependents of the Russian principality of Novgorod, and it was in their area that the expansionist interests of the Swedes were concentrated. From the Viking Age on, they were interested in trade with Russia, and here the missionary interests of the Catholic church were united with traditional Swedish economic interests. In the twelfth century the merchant farmers of the island of Gotland and the burghers of Visby had become the leading mercantile power in the Baltic and aimed at dominance of the Russian trade, especially with rapidly growing Novgorod. The Gotlanders formed a nearly independent merchants' republic that paid tribute to the kingdom of Sweden and belonged ecclesiastically to a Swedish diocese; they led the way in expansion eastward. In 1240, with Russian principalities falling to the invading Mongols, the earl of Sweden tried to conquer Novgorod but was defeated by Alexander Nevsky. In 1288 King Magnus I Ladulås of Sweden capitalized on the civil war on Gotland to have his supremacy of the island recognized, and a few years later the marshal and regent of Sweden, Torgils Knutsson, made a serious attempt to establish Swedish dominion in Karelia and on the Neva River to control the waterways into Russia, especially to Novgorod. A war of several decades over sea power in the east was thus launched.

Within Sweden canon law was accepted in 1248, celibacy was imposed on the clergy, and donations of real estate by testament gradually became respected. Ecclesiastical exemptions from taxes and military duty were contested but eventually recognized. Still, in the decades around 1300, the provincial aristocrats resented the independent position and growing power of the papal church. In the last half of the thirteenth century a new aristocracy was created by enfeoffing the king's men; new families were rapidly amalgamated with the old ones, especially since granting of royal castles and their fiefs was dependent on feudal oaths of fidelity. The king's council was recruited from both old and new aristocracy and from the ecclesiastical hierarchy. It is important, however, to note that feudalism in the continental sense was never introduced into Sweden. The fiefs never became hereditary, and the soil belonged to its private owners, for the most part peasants and their families.

The change in Swedish society in the thirteenth century was connected with a change in the transportation system. By ecclesiastical initiative, highways were cleared through the forests, and the royal officials took control of them from the peasant communities. This meant a unification of the provinces, but it also meant that small, well-equipped cavalry forces, based at castles, could maintain order in the communities. Professional warriors now took over the fighting, and the bishops and high nobility dominated society. The geography of the country still imposed restrictions on their power, however. A greedy landowner who pressed his tenants too much or an unreasonably demanding bailiff always risked the possibility that a farmer would take his portable buildings and his cattle, and disappear into the forest. A peasantry in revolt could always retreat into the forests, where it was easy to organize death traps for pursuing cavalry. Even the burning of farms and villages was no lasting catastrophe for the inhabitants, since there was plenty of wood for constructing new buildings. But these possible actions by the common people were a threat only on the local level. Peasants did not constitute a significant political force until they were able to mobilize and organize large fighting units.

FOURTEENTH CENTURY

In the late 1290's the forces of Sweden were concentrated in the "crusade" against Karelia and Novgorod. It was initially successful: the greater part of Karelia was taken permanently, and controlled by the port and fortress of Vyborg; a stronghold was also erected on the Neva and Swedish cavalry raided the surrounding area. But at the beginning of the fourteenth century civil war broke out in Sweden; King Birger Magnusson was opposed by his younger brothers, the dukes Erik and Valdemar. Most of the nobility sided with the dukes, while the church was loyal to the king. The civil war, fought in several rounds, absorbed the energies of the kingdom until it ended in a catastrophe for the royal family: in 1317 King Birger treacherously captured and murdered the dukes and the following year he was driven out of the country by a general uprising. In this dynastic vacuum only one possible candidate for the throne survived: the three-year-old son of Duke Erik, Magnus Eriksson. He was given oaths of allegiance by the aristocracy on the traditional stone at Mora Meadow and at the same time inherited the kingdom of Norway from his maternal grandfather. In the name of the child a confederation of bishops and nobility, for the first time united into an aristocratic upper class, governed Sweden.

In the meantime the crusade into Russia failed: the stronghold on the Neva was lost and the Swedes lost control of the Russian trade, which was rapidly taken over by the Hanseatic League. After the civil war the Swedish armed forces in the east secured Vyborg and southern Karelia, and in 1323 concluded the Peace of Nöteburg with Novgorod, which for the first time defined an eastern border between Swedish Finland and Russian Karelia (from the Karelian Isthmus across present-day Finland to the Gulf of Bothnia). This made swift colonization of the very sparsely populated northern part of Sweden essential to the governing powers, and they tried to promote it by various means.

The period after the bitter dynastic war was one of chivalry. The regency was determined to secure a constitution reflecting aristocratic control of the kingdom. In the 1320's a detailed law code was drawn up covering future elections of kings; it stipulated a representative assembly from the main provinces to gather at Mora Meadow, and oaths to be exchanged between the king and the electing body that restricted the king's powers of taxation and forced him to entrust castles and fiefs to the native aristocracy. But as an adult King Magnus was a resolute and ambitious man with autocratic tendencies. He had resources in Norway; in Skåne, a Danish province that elected him king in a moment of political division; and in his brothers-in-law, the counts of Namur. He also had supporters in the aristocracy, and for many years he managed to balance the aristocratic opposition.

The Swedish state suffered from economic weakness due to the primitive agricultural structure of the society. The art of war in fourteenth-century Europe required professional soldiers trained in the use of specialized equipment, and this demanded in turn large amounts of capital. When an armed conflict arose, even if it was an internal conflict, both parties had to engage allies with better resources than the domestic nobility. In addition, the Black Death struck parts of Sweden in 1349/1350 and accentuated a decline in agriculture, diminishing the income of both king and aristocracy. When the tension between King Magnus and his council hardened into civil war in the 1350's and 1360's, Magnus asked King Waldemar Atterdag of Denmark for help; the aristocracy turned to the duke of Mecklenburg, who had married the king's sister. The result was that the Danes reconquered Skåne and took Gotland by armed invasion, while the Mecklenburgers conquered most parts of Sweden and made a son of the duke, Albrecht of Mecklenburg, king of Sweden. In 1374 King Magnus drowned in a shipwreck off the Norwegian coast. His surviving son, King Håkon of Norway, maintained his hold on the Vänern provinces and his claim to all of Sweden.

In Sweden, King Albrecht was soon confronted by the same aristocratic opposition as his predecessor, and the situation was complicated by the immigration of Mecklenburg nobility who claimed Swedish castles and fiefs as payment for their military services. The aristocracy, which soon absorbed most of the immigrant knights, gained control at an early stage, but in the late 1380's King Albrecht forced an open conflict, relying on help from Mecklenburg, with its superior cavalry. In 1388 the council of Sweden had to turn for help to the queen-regent of Denmark, Margaret, widow of Håkon Magnusson and mother of his son Olof, who died just as the conflict in Sweden broke out. Margaret was recognized as sovereign in all three Scandinavian kingdoms, and in 1389 her army defeated the Mecklenburgers in battle, taking Albrecht and his son prisoners. This ended the civil wars in Sweden for nearly half a century.

FIFTEENTH TO SIXTEENTH CENTURY

Margaret, one of the most remarkable political personalities in Scandinavian history, gained control over the aristocracy in all her kingdoms. She kept firm control of castles and income, and in Sweden she introduced a crushing taxation and took back all estates that the church and the nobility had appropriated in the Mecklenburg period. In her foreign policy she had to confront the Mecklenburgers and, periodically, the great power of the Baltic, the Teutonic Order. She also had to deal with the claims of privileges from the Hanseatic League, and she tried to negotiate the return of the duchy of Schleswig from the counts of Holstein under the crown of Denmark. Her death in 1412 was an irreparable loss for the royalty of the three united kingdoms. Margaret had chosen her great-nephew Erik of Pomerania and had him crowned king of Denmark, Norway, and Sweden in the Swedish town Kalmar in 1397. According to her plan he should have been recognized unconditionally, but some of the most prominent members of the aristocracy of Sweden presented their conditions (their claims, however, remained unanswered). King Erik, when he took over the government in 1412, proved to be no cautious diplomat but rather a militant autocrat. In 1426 he fought a war over Schleswig against the powerful counts of Holstein, who were later joined by the Hanseatic League. King Erik pressed his subjects, including the privileged estates, for support, but the tax burden drove them into opposition.

In Sweden land rents decreased steadily in the first decades of the fifteenth century as a result of the general agricultural depression. The educated groups in Swedish society were remarkably aware of constitutional theory and practice from the conflicts over the position of the royalty in the fourteenth century, and when King Erik tried to break canon law by appointing a new archbishop of Uppsala in 1432, the ecclesiastical hierarchy refused to obey. The conflict spread in the following two years to the aristocracy, and in 1434 a great rebellion broke out among the peasants and miners of Västmanland and Dalecarlia (Dalarna), headed by Engelbrekt Engelbrektsson, a mine owner. After some weeks the church and the nobility joined forces with the peasantry and recognized Engelbrekt as head of the rebel army. King Erik, who had been involved in peace negotiations with the Hanseatic League, tried to restore his authority with Danish help, but in 1436 the Danes joined the opposition. The peasants' leaders, Engelbrekt and Erik Puke, were murdered; the aristocracy, represented by the council of the kingdom, now took over the government and occupied castles and fiefs. Erik of Pomerania was formally deposed in 1439 and after two years was succeeded by his nephew Christopher of Bavaria, who had to accept harsh restrictions on his power. During his reign Sweden was in reality governed by regents belonging to the nobility.

In 1448 Christopher died without heir, and the marshal and regent of Sweden, Karl Knutsson Bonde, obtained support for his own election as King Charles VIII of Sweden. The Danes elected a German count, Christian of Oldenburg, and a bitter fight broke out over who would rule the united kingdoms of Scandinavia. Karl Knutsson, by far the weaker combatant, never gave up, although he had to flee the country twice. After his death in 1470, his nephew Sten Sture was made regent by the partisans of King Karl, and he dealt King Christian a crushing defeat at Brunkeberg, near Stockholm. After that the council governed Sweden as an aristocratic republic, nominally recognizing the king of Denmark and Norway as a sovereign. Sten Sture, in the meantime, was able to raise sufficient funds to pay armed forces loyal to him. Out of the civil wars the Swedish parliament of estates was organized in the mid fifteenth century as a political instrument of the national, anti-Danish forces. Its backbone was the miners of Dalecarlia and the merchants of Stockholm, capitalist groups able to equip mail-clad troops of their own. The regency became a standing institution and the kings were kept out of the country by force.

In 1520, however, King Christian II made a grand effort with an international army of professional German soldiers, French artillerymen, and Danish noblemen, equipped with the help of his brother-in-law, Emperor Charles V. The invasion came in the winter, and the regent at that time, a namesake but not a relative of Sten Sture, was mortally wounded by a cannonball in the first encounter. After that the defense broke down, in spite of stubborn local fighting, and in the fall Stockholm surrendered. Christian II was proclaimed king of Sweden without constitutional restrictions. In a terrible act of vengeance, the famous Bloodbath of Stockholm, many supporters of the Swedish regent were summarily executed.

This was a rather foolish show of strength, since King Christian could not afford to keep his grand army in Sweden. A rebellion started in Dalecarlia, led by a young nobleman, Gustav Vasa, an unusually strong-willed and intelligent man who proclaimed himself regent in 1521. After two years of fighting, Sweden was freed of Christian's followers, and Christian himself was deposed by an aristocratic rebellion. Gustav Vasa was proclaimed king of Sweden and thus became the founder of a new dynasty.

BIBLIOGRAPHY

Hans Andersson, *Urbanisierte Ortschaften und lateinische Terminologie: Studien zur Geschichte des nordeuropäischen Städtewesens vor 1350* (1971); Ingvar Andersson, *Källstudier till Sveriges historia, 1230–1436* (1928) and *A History of Sweden,* Carolyn Hannay, trans. (1956); Sture Bolin, "Om Nordens äldsta historieforskning," in *Lunds Universitets Årsskrift,* **27** (1931), "Mohammed, Charlemagne, and Ruric," in *Scandinavian Economic History Review,* **1** (1953), and "The Agrarian Life of the Middle Ages: Scandinavia," in *Cambridge Economic History of Europe,* II.1 (1966); Johannes Brøndsted, *The Vikings,* Kalle Skov, trans. (1965); Svend Gissel, Eino Jutikkala, Eva Österberg, Jørn Sandnes, and Björn Teitsson, *Desertion and Land Colonization in the Nordic Countries, c. 1300–1600* (1981).

Erik Lönnroth, *Sverige och Kalmarunionen, 1397–1457* (1934, repr. 1969), *Statsmakt och statsfinans i det medeltida Sverige* (State power and state finance in medieval Sweden, with a summary in German) (1940, repr. 1984), "The Representative Assemblies in Mediaeval Sweden," in International Congress of Historical Sciences, 10th, Rome, 1955, *Relazioni,* VII (1955), "The Baltic Countries," in *Cambridge Economic History of Europe,* III.4 (1963), "Government in Medieval Scandinavia," in *Recueils de la Société Jean Bodin pour l'histoire comparative des institutions,* **24** (1966), "Communications, vie économique et modèles politiques des Vikings en Scandinavie," in Centro italiano di studi sull'alto medioevo, *I Normanni e la loro espansione in Europa nell'alto medioevo, Settimane di studio,* **16** (1969), "Die Goten in der modernen kritischen Geschichtsauffassung," in *Studia gotica* (1972), *Gotland, Osteuropa und die Union von Kalmar,* Acta Visbyensia, 4 (1973), "Genesis of the Scandinavian Kingdoms," in his *Scandinavians* (1977).

Beata Losman, *Norden och reformkoncilierna, 1408–1449,* with summary in German (1970); Lucien Musset, *Les peuples scandinaves au moyen âge* (1951); Sven Ulric Palme, "Les impôts, le statut d'Alsnö et la formation des ordres en Suède (1250–1350)," in Roland Mousnier, ed., *Problèmes de stratification sociale* (1968); Michael Roberts, *The Early Vasas: A History of Sweden, 1523–1611* (1968); Jerker Rosén, *Svensk historia I* (History of Sweden I) (1962); Peter Sawyer, *The Age of the Vikings,* 2nd ed. (1971); Henrik Schück, "Riksdagens framväxt, tiden intill 1611," in *Riksdagen genom tiderna* (1985), English version in press; Inge Skovgaard-Petersen, "The Coming of Urban Culture to Northern Europe," in *Scandinavian Journal of History,* **3** (1976); The Museum of National Antiquities (Statens historiska museum), *Vendel Period Studies,* **2** (1983); Lauritz Ulrik Absalon Weibull, *Nordisk Historia* (Scandinavian history), 3 vols. (1948–1949).

Erik Lönnroth

[See also **Adam of Bremen; Birka; Black Death; Denmark; Erikskrönikan; Gotland; Hanseatic League; Jordanes; Law, Swedish; Nevsky, Alexander; Norway; Novgorod; Procopius; Scandinavia; Ships and Shipbuilding, Northern Europe; Vikings; Warfare, Western European.**]

SWINESHEAD (Suicet, Suincet, Suisseth, Swyneshed, and other various forms). There may well have been three men of this name associated with Oxford University in the mid fourteenth century. Alfred B. Emden lists a John de Swyneshed who was a Merton College fellow in 1340 and 1346 to 1347, became a bachelor of civil and canon law, and died in October 1372 with no surviving writings. Second, there was a Richard de Swyneshed, also a Merton College fellow in 1344 and 1355, author of the *Liber calculationum* (Book of calculations) and of other short works on motion. Third, Emden lists a Roger de Swyneshed, who was a doctor of theology, Benedictine monk at Glastonbury, and author of a two-part treatise on logic, *De obligationibus* and *De insolubilibus* (On obligations and on insolubles), and a work on physics, *De motibus naturalibus* (On natural motions), both before 1338.

The existence of a distinct person named John Swineshead with degrees in law seems fairly certain. Whether there were two different Swinesheads associated with Oxford in the middle third of the fourteenth century, both writing about physical and logical topics, is open to greater doubt. In the manuscripts of the works at issue there is much confusion concerning first names. For instance, *De obligationibus* and *De insolubilibus* are variously ascribed to "Rogeri Suincet," "mag. Jo. Swinished de anglia doctoris in sacra theologia," and "Ricchardi Suisset doctoris anglici," among others.

The works all belong to the same intellectual context at Oxford. Both the *De motibus naturalibus* and the *Liber calculationum* make use of Thomas Bradwardine's *De proportionibus velocitatum in motibus* (On the ratios of velocities in motions) of 1328, and both have characteristics associated with the so-called Oxford Calculators, slightly junior associates of Bradwardine (*d.* 1349) at Oxford. In his *Regulae solvendi sophismata* (Rules for solving sophismata) of 1335, William Heytesbury (*ca.* 1313–1372), one of these Oxford Calculators, cites the opinion on insolubles to be found in the Swineshead treatise *De insolubilibus*. The *De motibus naturalibus* in turn seems to betray familiarity with Heytesbury's *Regulae*. The short works on motion ascribed to Richard Swineshead cite the work of John of Dumbleton (*d. ca.* 1349), another Oxford Calculator.

But even though all of the works ascribed to any of the Swinesheads belong to the same context, there was no apparent medieval effort to distinguish two different Swinesheads. Despite the multiplicity of first names, opinions were often ascribed simply to Swineshead with no first name given. This seems to be evidence against distinguishing Roger from Richard. Perhaps the Swineshead who was a fellow of Merton also wrote the *De obligationibus* and *De insolubilibus* and *De motibus naturalibus* and went on to become the monk of Glastonbury, possibly changing his name when he entered monastic life. It would not be surprising if the Merton College fellow obtained a theological degree, although, since one would not expect to find a Benedictine monk at Merton, the time at Merton would have had to precede entrance into the order. If the identification of Roger and Richard were accepted, however, one would need to consider whether the *De motibus naturalibus* and *Liber calculationum* could conceivably have been written by the same person, something that at first perusal seems rather unlikely; the *De motibus naturalibus,* for instance, rejects Bradwardine's view of the relations of forces, resistances, and velocities whereas the *Liber calculationum* accepts it. In sum, without more evidence, the distinction between Roger and Richard must be considered tentative.

The two-part work *De obligationibus* and *De insolubilibus* was written before 1335, since it is cited in Heytesbury's *Regulae*. Treatises on obligations concerned a special sort of logical "combat" popular in medieval universities. In an obligation, one participant, the respondent, obligated himself to concede some original proposition (often something factually false) stipulated by the second participant, called the opponent, plus anything that followed logically from it and anything that was both true in fact and logically irrelevant (*impertinens*) to what had already been conceded. By proposing propositions to be conceded or denied, the opponent tried to lead the respondent into contradicting himself. Swineshead's position on obligations was called the "new response" by Robert Fland in the mid fourteenth century and was adopted by some later logicians.

The treatise on insolubles concerns seemingly well-formed but self-contradicting propositions, such as "I am telling a lie." Assuming that such a proposition falsifies itself, Swineshead concluded that a false proposition may signify principally what is the case, that in a good inference something false can follow formally from what is true, and that mutually contradictory propositions can both be false at the same time—conclusions often debated in the later literature.

The *De motibus naturalibus* covers definitions of motion and time, generation, alteration, augmentation, local motion, causes of motion, and maxima and minima. Each type of motion is treated first from a physical point of view and second from a logico-mathematical point of view. Swineshead rejects Bradwardine's view about the correct relation of forces and resistances to the resulting velocities and argues that where there are resistances, the velocities are proportional to the difference between force and resistance. He has an idiosyncratic view according to which if two bodies are altered and one gains a single uniform degree more than the other, there will be no ratio between their alterations.

The *Liber calculationum* is divided into sixteen treatises covering measures of intension and remission, rarity and density, augmentation, powers, difficulty of action, maxima and minima, the special problems of reaction, and whether an elemental body falling in a tunnel through the center of the earth would come to rest at the center. It does not discuss the physics of these various categories and motions but limits itself to alternative views of how things should be measured. Emphasis is placed on complicated and counter-intuitive imaginary cases, with relatively great mathematical ingenuity in deriving results of the various positions. While later mathematicians, including Leibniz, were inclined to admire the *Liber calculationum,* it epitomized to Italian humanists the scholastic technicality and quibbling detail to which they were so much opposed. As author of this work, Swineshead was known as "the Calculator."

BIBLIOGRAPHY

For a detailed discussion of Swineshead, emphasizing the scientific works, see John E. Murdoch and Edith D.

Sylla, "Swineshead, Richard," in *Dictionary of Scientific Biography,* XIII (1976), 184–213. For biographical details and the reasons for distinguishing Roger from Richard, see Alfred B. Emden, *A Biographical Register of the University of Oxford to A.D. 1500,* III (1959), 1,835–1,837, and James A. Weisheipl, O.P., "Roger Swyneshed, O.S.B., Logician, Natural Philosopher, and Theologian," in *Oxford Studies Presented to Daniel Callus* (1964).

For a discussion of some of the ideas of the *De motibus naturalibus,* see Edith Sylla, "Medieval Concepts of the Latitude of Forms: The Oxford Calculators," in *Archives d'histoire doctrinale et littéraire du moyen âge,* 40 (1973). Treatise 11 of the *Liber calculationum* concerning the motion of a body through the center of the earth is edited in Michael Hoskin and A. G. Molland, "Swineshead on Falling Bodies: An Example of Fourteenth-century Physics," in *British Journal for the History of Science,* 3 (1966). For an attempt to place the *Liber calculationum* in the context of logical disputations at Oxford see Edith Sylla, "The Oxford Calculators," in Norman Kretzmann *et al.,* eds., *The Cambridge History of Later Medieval Philosophy* (1982).

EDITH DUDLEY SYLLA

[See also **Aristotle in the Middle Ages; Bradwardine, Thomas; Buridan, Jean; Burley, Walter; Oxford University; Physics.**]

SWITZERLAND (Schwyz), originally the name of a mountainous territory of approximately 350 square miles (900 square km), rich mainly in forests and pastures, separating the two lakes of Zurich and Lucerne. Despite its weak economic and demographic importance, this region gave its name to a confederate state formed at the end of the Middle Ages at the expense of the Holy Roman Empire. To speak of "Switzerland" before the fifteenth century would be anachronistic; in fact, the Swiss Confederation, a unicum in the medieval world, was the result of the convergence of interests between a small federation of mountainous territories jealous of their independence and a few cities, mainly Bern and Zurich, anxious to maintain their status of free imperial cities and to enlarge their rural territories. The sense of belonging to one independent state emerged much later.

EARLY HISTORY: 600–1100

The present-day Swiss Confederation constitutes neither a geographic, ethnic, nor linguistic unit. The main part consists of the northern Alpine massif, of which the major bulwark is the St. Gotthard, at the junction of the high valleys of the Rhône, Ticino, Rhine, and Reuss. Passages from one valley to another have always existed; however, until the beginning of the thirteenth century, this massif presented a natural obstacle to international traffic. It was circumvented by going up the Rhine to Chur and from there toward Como and Milan by passes, or by following the roads on the plain. The Swiss plateau, or Mittelland, extends from Lake Geneva to Lake Constance and is almost 185 miles (300 km) long and from 12 to 43 miles (20 to 70 km) wide. It is in this small and rather differentiated zone that the majority of the population has been concentrated and urban life developed. The plateau is connected to the Alpine foreland by navigable lakes with complicated contours (Constance, Zurich, Lucerne, Zug). In the north it fans out on the basin of the Aare, a tributary of the Rhine. In the west the lakes of Neufchâtel and Biel separate the plateau from the Jura buttress. The ancient land of the Helvetii, strongly romanized in its western part (plateau, Jura, and Upper Rhône Valley), much more superficially in the Alpine zone, had been colonized in the fifth century by two rather different Germanic peoples, who are at the origin of the linguistic division that has lasted until the present.

In 443 the Burgundian people, weakened by a crushing defeat seven years earlier at the hands of the Huns on the Rhine, obtained from the Roman general Aëtius the authorization to settle in Sapaudia, a territory that must have corresponded to the south of Lake Geneva (Savoy), the land of Vaud, the Upper Rhône Valley (Valais), and a part of Burgundy. The kingdom of the Burgundians, with Lyon and Geneva as capitals, had a rather brief life. In 515 King Sigismund founded the abbey of St. Maurice at Augaune in Valais; but by 534 his kingdom was destroyed by the Franks and he himself was killed. The Burgundian kingdom disappeared, at least as a national state, even if the successive partitions of the Frankish kingdom, allotted to one or the other members of the Frankish dynasty under the Merovingians, gave at times the appearance of a "kingdom of Burgundy." The Burgundian people, small in number, seem to have been rapidly absorbed by the pre-existing Gallo-Roman population. This western portion of the future Switzerland retained Roman dialects (Franco-Provençal).

Things went differently in the eastern territories,

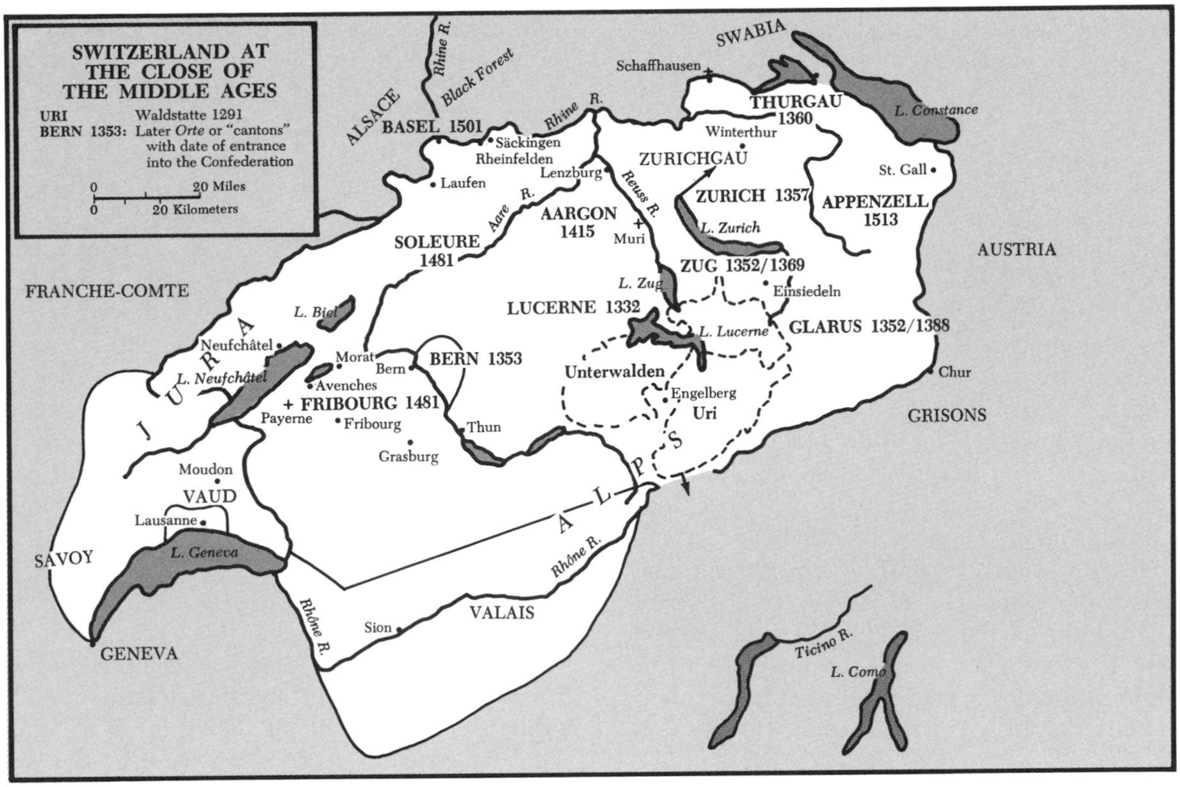

particularly on the banks of the Rhine and the upper Alpine valleys, where the Alamanni, based in southern Germany and Alsace, settled themselves progressively in great numbers. Written testimony about this people in the fifth and sixth centuries is scarce. We know of their progress mainly through archaeological findings and toponymics, both imprecise. The Alamanni overran the local population of the Aare Valley. Their advance forced the bishopric of Windisch (in present-day Aargau) to be moved toward Avenches, in romanized country, and from there toward Lausanne. In the Alps they penetrated deeply into the northern St. Gotthard valleys. The Chur region and the Upper Rhine Valley were not germanized, even though they later belonged to Alamannic territory. It is only in the middle of the thirteenth century that German-speaking peoples settled in the Upper Rhine Valley (Graubünden) and in Upper Valais.

The Alamanni were conquered by the Franks around 496 after a difficult war. From then on their territory, while maintaining a rather large autonomy, became part of the Merovingian kingdom. An episcopal see had existed in Basel since the Roman era and was reorganized in the seventh century. A new see was founded in Constance around 600. Monasteries were founded at Reichenau, on Lake Constance, and at St. Gall. Around 730 the mayor of the palace Charles Martel began the subjection of the Alamanni, which was successfully accomplished by his son Carloman in 746. Important domains were then incorporated into the royal treasury and Frankish counts eliminated a large portion of the aboriginal aristocracy; however, the territorial organization left important traces. The organization into gaus (regions) probably dates from the Alamannic period and lasted subsequently on the left bank of the Rhine (Zurichgau, Aargau, Thurgau).

The division of the Carolingian empire in the ninth century brought about the formation of new territoral entities. In 888 the count of Auxerre, Rudolph, was proclaimed king at St. Maurice in Valais by the powerful noblemen; he tried immediately to restore Lotharingia as it had been established by the Verdun treaty. Thwarted in this plan by the Carolingian Arnulf, he had to limit his ambitions to the region he had governed before his accession to the throne, mainly present-day French-speaking Switzerland. His successors extended their power to the Rhône Valley and Provence, and also to a part of Alamannic territory. Around 914 Rudolph II took advantage of the troubles stirred up by the succession in Swabia to extend his possessions to Thurgau. However, he clashed with the new duke of Swabia, Burckhardt, who defeated him at Winterthur (919). A reconciliation followed, marked by the marriage of Rudolph to Burckhardt's daughter, Bertha, then by a joint expedition to Italy, during which the duke was killed trying to save his son-in-law, who had to abandon Italy.

Queen Bertha, founder of the monastery at Payerne, left a vivid impression in Swiss historical chronicles. However, the Burgundian kings in Alamannic territory left few diplomatic traces, except in Basel, where the "Rudolphians" held on to their possession of a concession from the German king Henry I. Taken as a whole, the ancient Alamannic country, or duchy, of Swabia formed one of the basic units of the new Holy Roman Empire. Equally attracted by imperial subinfeudation, the kingdom of Burgundy was annexed at the death of the last "Rudolphian" by the emperor Conrad II in 1032.

For many centuries thereafter these territories of future Switzerland found themselves incorporated into a far greater entity. The linguistic boundary between *terra romana* and *terra theodica* did not correspond to a precise political division. Practically, the framework of the large territorial principalities was more or less weakened, while new land groupings, sometimes very far apart, were benefiting the great feudal families. Around the episcopal cities principalities were established, to the benefit of the see, and endowed most often with rights pertaining to count or king; such was the case with Lausanne, Sion, and probably Geneva, by virtue of the concessions of the Burgundian king to Emperor Otto I. Around 1040 the bishop of Basel, due to his countship, received important concessions of lands and mines from Emperor Henry III.

The development of lay seignories is more difficult to grasp because of deficient source material from the early Middle Ages. One can note, however, the rise in the middle of the eleventh century of the counts of Lenzburg, who established themselves between Lake Zurich and the Reuss River; more important were the counts of Rheinfelden, whose castle stood in Aargau. Their possessions extended from the Upper Rhine Valley to the region of Vaud, and around 1041 they also obtained fiefs of the bishopric of Basel. In 1057 Rudolph of Rheinfelden married Agnes, sister of Emperor Henry IV, and received the duchy of Swabia. However, instead of concentrating his efforts on the development of a territorial principality, he agreed during the conflict between Henry IV and the papacy to lead the side opposed to his brother-in-law and then was elected king in 1077 by some of the German princes. After several battles of varying success, Rudolph was killed 15 October 1080. A part of his domains, in particular those in Vaud, were given to the bishops who had remained faithful to the emperor. On the other hand the Rhine Valley possessions were recovered by the united Zähringen family. As for the duchy of Swabia, the emperor had given it in 1079 to one of his most faithful partisans, Frederick of Büren, founder of the Hohenstaufen line.

An accord concluded in 1098 between the Hohenstaufens and the Zähringens confirmed the partition of Swabia between the two houses. The Hohenstaufens kept the actual duchy, along with important domains in southern Germany. Their influence to the south of the Rhine was limited. They were mainly represented there by the vassal family of Lenzburg. The Zähringens, renouncing the duchy of Swabia, kept the ducal title attached to their own house as well as important domains and fiefs from the Black Forest to the Alps. The accord of 1098 allotted them Zurich, "nobilisium Sueviae oppidum" (the most noble town of the Swiss), according to the chronicler Otto of Freising.

THE ZÄHRINGEN DYNASTY

The Zähringens were the first dynasty whose field of action corresponded in large part to the territory of present-day Switzerland. Their original castle stood in Breisgau (today in southern Germany), but they had many possessions in the Aare Valley and in other regions of present-day Switzerland. Their recovery of Rheinfelden and Zurich made them the most powerful local dynasty. In 1127 Emperor Lothair, who wanted to restore imperial authority over the kingdom of Burgundy, delegated his powers to Duke Conrad of Zähringen by investing him with the rectorship of Burgundy. By this title, Conrad of Zähringen intervened in the regions of Vaud and the Jura, where he clashed victoriously with the counts of Burgundy and Geneva. He does not seem to have been active in the southern part of the kingdom. In 1156 his son Berchtold renounced the rectorship in favor of the new emperor, Frederick Barbarossa, who had just married Beatrice of Burgundy and was inaugurating an active policy in the kingdom of Burgundy. To compensate for his renunciation, Berchtold of Zähringen received the seignorial protection of the three romanized bishoprics of Geneva, Lausanne, and Sion, which theoretically extended his sphere of influence beyond present-day French-speaking Switzerland. Practically, he could hold on to neither Geneva nor Sion, and he retroceded his rights to the counts of Geneva and Savoy, who themselves faced the opposition of the local bishops.

In Lausanne Duke Berchtold entered into conflict around 1186 with the bishop; the boundary of respective zones of influence was a permanent source of difficulties. The power of the Zähringens remained limited by the power of the Hohenstaufens. The networks of influence crisscrossed on both sides of the Rhine. The accession of Conrad III as king in 1138 and of Frederick Barbarossa in 1152 did not eliminate the rivalry of the two great Swabian families, who, however, avoided open conflict. Frederick Barbarossa was particularly interested in the romanized lands near his own Burgundy countship, granting diplomas to the abbeys of Payerne, Romainmôtiers, and Val de Travers. In the east he was mainly interested in controlling the road leading from Lake Constance to Lake Como in Italy, by acquiring in the name of the duchy of Swabia the seignorial protection of the bishopric of Chur.

The Zähringens were most successful in their original domain and in the frontier zone between the Germanic and French-speaking regions. The urban landscape was greatly modified by their founding of new cities. This had begun in 1120 with the founding of Freiburg in Breisgau. Around 1157 Fribourg was created, and, in 1191, Bern and Thun.

The extinction of the Lenzburg line in 1173 led to a territorial readjustment; the Zähringens saw a rival house, closely linked to that of Swabia, disappear. In these circumstances they were able to consolidate their position in Zurich, where the Lenzburgs had until then kept certain rights, and in the Uri Valley. In 1191 the new duke, Berchtold V of Zähringen, suppressed an uprising of the nobility in the French-speaking region. His house was at the zenith of its territorial power. In 1197 Berchtold refused the imperial crown, which had been offered to him by the archbishop of Cologne. Berchtold died without heir in 1218, and that led to the breakup of the duchy of Zähringen. Emperor Frederick II seems to have recovered the imperial functions connected with the duchy, namely the seignorial protection of Zurichgau. The principal cities—Zurich as well as the newly founded cities of Bern and Fribourg—more or less openly demanded incorporation into the empire. As to the division of the patrimonial possessions, those on the right bank of the Rhine fell to the lords of Urach, those on the left to the Kyburgs.

The extinction of the Zähringens brought about a new dispersal of feudal power. This had already begun during the lifetime of Berchtold V, when Count Thomas of Savoy, master of some of the Alpine passes, had taken hold of Moudon in the Vaud region, by a concession of King Philip II Augustus in 1207, which had launched the first conflict with the old duke of Zähringen. A son of Thomas, Peter of Savoy, built himself a vast domain in the French-speaking region and extended his influence as far as Bern. The city of Bern, fearing for its independence, put itself under his protection.

The real successors of the Zähringens were the Kyburgs. This family, whose castle was near Zurich, had recovered in 1172–1173 an important portion of the Lenzburg heritage. Around 1180 Count Hartmann of Kyburg founded the city of Winterthur. The Kyburgs owned rich lands in the present-day cantons of Zurich and Aargau; they were also landgraves of Thurgau. Ulric of Kyburg, son-in-law of Berchtold of Zähringen, inherited in 1218 the portion of his father-in-law's domains situated south of the Rhine, namely Fribourg and Thun.

The Kyburg dynasty did not, however, attain the position enjoyed by the Zähringens. Weakened by a partition in 1250, they died out with the deaths of Counts Hartmann V in 1263 and Hartmann IV in 1264, heads of both branches of the family, thus opening the way for the Habsburgs.

The Habsburgs took their name from a castle situated in Aargau, which was built around 1020. They also had rich possessions in Alsace. Through the ages they significantly enlarged the small territory, delineated by the Aare and the Ruess, which has kept the name of Eigen ("own"), where they had founded the abbey of Muri. Werner of Habsburg was in 1135 landgrave of Upper Alsace and protector of the Alsatian abbey of Murbach, itself belonging to Lucerne. In 1173 his family recovered more of the Lenzburg possessions: the seignorial protectorate of the abbey of Säkingen on the Rhine, the domain of Willisau and of Sempach, and the protectorate of the territories of Schwyz and Unterwalden. They also acquired countship rights to Aargau and Zurichgau. The end of the Zähringen line in 1218, while not directly enriching them, gave the Habsburgs free rein in an area where the spheres of influence were still badly defined. A family partition in 1232 weakened their situation by creating a Habsburg-Laufenburg line. However, the most dynamic and better-endowed branch had at its head from 1239 on a particularly enterprising and active figure, Rudolph. He at first attached his fortunes to that of the last emperor of the Hohenstaufen house, Frederick II, who was at the time engaged in his last conflict with the papacy. At home, on the contrary, the Kyburgs and the Habsburg-Laufenburgs were on the pope's side. The death of Frederick II in 1250 did not compromise greatly the position of Count Rudolph, who tried, year after year, to strengthen his patrimony by using the seignorial protectorates of the big monasteries and by claiming his rights to the countships of Turgau, Aargau, and Zurichgau. At the same time he was busy buying back most of his fiefdoms from the Laufenburg branch. The extinction of the Kyburgs offered Rudolph an opportunity to rebuild the old Zähringen domain. In 1263 the count of Habsburg recovered Fribourg, Laufen, and Grasburg, the next year the other possessions. From then on he entered into rivalry with the count of Savoy, whose sister was the widow of the last Kyburg, Marguere. In 1266–1267 a war set the partisans and adversaries of Peter of Savoy and his allies—in particular the cities of Bern and Morat—against the Habsburg count. An agreement was reached between the two adversaries: the Kyburg inheritance remained in Rudolph's hands and constituted a dowry for Marguerite of Savoy. Peter of Savoy kept all his French-speaking positions as well as his protectorate over Bern and Morat.

In 1268 the death of Peter of Savoy freed Rudolph of his major rival. He spent the next five years consolidating his position in the Aare and Rhine valleys. With the acquisition of the seignorial protectorate of St. Gall, he succeeded in creating a contiguous territory. Faced with the bishop of Basel's opposition, he attacked that city; it was there in September 1273 that he received the news of his own election as emperor (king of Germany). Rudolph's accession to the throne did not fundamentally modify his territorial policy; rather it reinforced this policy by allowing him to combine his prerogatives of sovereign and landowner. In 1282 Rudolph marched against the Savoyard possessions, attacked Payerne, and detached Bern from the Savoyard lands.

Rudolph's reign marks a turning point in Habsburg history: From 1282–1283 the conquest of vast territories from Ottokar II of Bohemia opened up a new field of action to the dynasty; Albert, son of the emperor, received as fiefs Austria and Styria, thus distancing the Habsburgs from their original territory; and, finally, in certain cases, where the Habsburg domination had apparently not penetrated deeply, resistance appeared right after Rudolph's death.

THE WALDSTÄTTE

The original core of the Swiss Confederation was formed in a limited, mountainous, and, for a long time, isolated territory called, from the thirteenth century on, the *Waldstätte* (forest districts). It included the plateau of Schwyz, Uri in the Upper Reuss Valley, and Unterwalden to the south of Lake Lucerne. Unterwalden itself was divided between Niwalden, the part nearest the lake, and Obwalden, which formed a little valley. Until the twelfth century these territories seem to have lived without any particular common links, practicing subsistence-level mixed farming, poorly adapted to the natural conditions. There has been much discussion on the original "freedom" of the inhabitants. In fact they had not escaped feudal obligations; the monasteries of Engelberg, Zurich, and Einsiedeln were strongly entrenched and collected rents, and different lay or ecclesiastical lords maintained their agents there.

Quite rapidly breeding became a major endeavor in these territories, attested to in the documents of the abbey of Engelberg (1190) and in the *Urbar* of Einsiedeln (1217). This economy, which required the common use of pastures, the gathering of cattle at fixed dates, and the foreign marketing of products, led to an early consciousness of common interests, to the formation of associations (*Markgenossenschaften*), and to the common administration of a territory. Thirteenth-century documents show that a syndic (*Ammann*) was at the head of each valley and a *Landammann* was responsible for each territory. These figures, chosen locally and endowed with jurisdictional powers, were the intermediaries between seignorial power and the community residents.

The opening to traffic of the St. Gotthard Pass, which most recent historians (Bergier, for example) place around 1220, certainly provided a stimulant to the local economy by allowing exportation of products. It also bestowed wealth and power, in particular on the inhabitants of the Uri Valley, right at the foot of the St. Gotthard, who are sometimes given the credit for building the stone bridge in the rugged Schollenen Pass. This attribution corresponds well to the idea of the dynamism and pugnacity of this mountain people.

The manner in which the Habsburgs became masters of the valleys is not completely clarified; apparently Schwyz and Unterwalden had belonged to the Lenzburgs, who had exercised ancient seignorial rights there before 1173. Uri depended for the most part on the Fraumünster Abbey in Zurich, whose protectorate might have been passed from the Zähringens to the Habsburgs in 1218. In 1217 the count of Habsburg, Rudolph the Elder, appears in a charter "as solicitor and protector by legitimate heredity of the people of Schwyz." Generally the Habsburgs sought to convert into patrimonial rights their local prerogatives, whether they had an actual seignorial character or whether they derived from the exercise of countship or solicitor's rights. However, the interference of these powerful dynasties in a region that had heretofore benefited from relative neglect seems to have been badly received. The first breach in Habsburg power was caused by the newly acquired people of Uri, doubtlessly emboldened by the new perspectives offered by the opening of the St. Gotthard Pass. In 1231 they petitioned Henry, son of the emperor Frederick II. Henry bought back the protectorate of Uri from the count of Habsburg and united it with the empire by establishing a charter in which he agreed never to alienate them.

The example of Uri was followed in 1240 by the inhabitants of Schwyz and Unterwalden, who petitioned Emperor Frederick II at his Faenze camp and obtained in turn a charter of mediatization. The acts of 1231 and 1240, however, did not have immediate effect, because the emperor, who was in Italy, had other worries than to uphold the mountaineers against their lords. But mediatization within the framework of the empire became the main aspiration of the *Waldstätte,* an aspiration that was obstinately opposed by the Habsburgs. In 1247 Count Rudolph of Habsburg had Schwyz and Obwalden returned to his authority. Ten years later, his nephew of the same name imposed his arbitration on the internal quarrels of the inhabitants of Uri. He also reinforced his position by buying back the Kyburg and Habsburg-Laufenburg rights and by assuming for himself the actual control of the St. Gotthard Pass. His election as king of Germany (emperor) allowed him to unite, without appeal, his imperial and seignorial prerogatives. He recognized the imperial mediatization of the inhabitants of Uri in 1274, but not that of the other communities. Furthermore, he seems to have respected local customs for the most part, while the mountain people adjusted to his authority. A Schwyz contingent even distinguished itself in the imperial army during an expedition in Burgundy in 1289.

The death of Emperor Rudolph on 15 July 1291 liberated the centrifugal forces that his strong personality had kept in check in the empire and gave birth to an insecure climate. As soon as the news arrived the representatives of Uri, Schwyz, and Niwalden, fearing trouble or excessive claims, got together to conclude a defensive pact of a perpetual nature, which the inhabitants of Obwalden joined shortly thereafter. Although the act of 1291 had been preceded by similar ones and although it contains only rather cautious clauses (mutual assistance in case of outside aggression, refusal to accept judges from other countries, a rough outline of a method for settling disputes between allies by arbitration), the pact has been considered retroactively as the act of foundation of the Swiss Confederation. This is historically, but not judicially, correct. The pact was followed by an alliance between Schwyz and Uri with the city of Zurich. It was a very temporary alliance, but one that foreshadowed the extension of the emerging Confederation. The alliance helped Zurich at least to resist an attack by Albert of Austria, son of Rudolph of Habsburg, who was unable to take the city and did not risk attacking the inhabitants of Schwyz in their mountains.

In November 1297 the new king of Germany, Adolf of Nassau, who was hostile to the Habsburgs, confirmed the mediatization of Schwyz and Uri. But he lost his life the following year in a battle against the Habsburgs; Count Albert then became emperor.

As in the days of Rudolph, the accession of a Habsburg as emperor meant that the liberties won by the forest cantons would not be acknowledged. That there were numerous tensions between the Confederation and lords and cities faithful to the Habsburgs, as well as with officials of the sovereign, we know from local sources as well as from the legends created later on to explain the emancipation of the *Waldstätte,* such as the story of William Tell and the bailiff Gessler, figures often evoked but not historically authenticated. At the unexpected death of Albert in 1308, the Habsburgs found themselves separated from the imperial crown for over a century, but with their territorial power reinforced. The new emperor, Henry VII of Luxembourg, solemnly confirmed the mediatization of the cantons, extending it to the whole of Unterwalden, but he also subjected them to an imperial judge (1309). The requirements of his Italian policy, however, led him to consider the protestations of Dukes Frederick and Leopold of Habsburg. After having encouraged the different protagonists in their claims, he died suddenly in 1313, opening up a new battle for succession in Germany. While Duke Frederick was contending for the imperial crown with Louis of Bavaria, his brother Leopold was busy reinforcing the cohesion of the hereditary domains of the house of Habsburg. On their side, the *Waldstätte* felt war was coming. Complementing the natural defense offered by their mountains, they obstructed the valleys with palings and barriers. Apparently sure of their forces, the people of Uri invaded the abbey of Engelberg in 1309. And in January 1314 the people of Schwyz invaded the abbey of Einsiedeln, pillaged it, and imprisoned the monks. At once King Frederick banished the culprits from the empire and his brother Leopold attacked with his large army. In the autumn of 1315 the duke personally was leading about 2,000 knights and attendants to Schwyz, when he was surprised on 15 November at the Morgarten Pass between a wall of rock and a marsh. Incapable of deploying in battle formation, the Austrian knights were massacred by the mountaineers, lying in ambush. The duke was able to flee, but the battle assured for a long time the independence of the *Waldstätte,* which immediately renewed the alliance of 1291. The new act of 1315 reinforced the existing bond by prohibiting each of the participants from accepting a foreign seigniory without the consent of the two others. King Louis of Bavaria, happy to annoy his Habsburg adversaries, encouraged the brave mountaineers, but he did not send them any material assistance. He hurriedly confirmed their freedoms. Later on he sometimes succumbed to the temptation of dealing with the Habsburgs at their expense. The Habsburgs accepted in 1318 a truce, which was periodically renewed. Basically, however, they had renounced none of their claims.

THE CITIES

In the Mittelland intense commercial and manufacturing activity developed during the twelfth and thirteenth centuries, in which many cities and market towns of recent seignorial foundation participated. However, no urban center experienced growth comparable to that of other regions in Europe. It seems that no city had more than 5,000 inhabitants, with the exception of the cathedral cities of Basel and Geneva. Basel entered into the Confederation at the end of the Middle Ages (1501), Geneva much later.

Lucerne occupied the most central position, at the western shore of its lake. An early monastic center, it had passed into Habsburg seignorial protection in the thirteenth century and as such had frequently been drawn into the wars against the *Waldstätte.* However, Lucerne's economic interests were closely linked to those of its riparian neighbors, since it acted as a relay on the waterway leading to the St. Gotthard route. Thus in 1332 Lucerne formed a perpetual alliance with the *Waldstätte,* while still preserving, at least formally, the Habsburg rights.

Zurich's situation was rather different; it was an ancient city which gave its name to a gau. The presence of two royal abbeys, endowed with important domains, had favored the development of a large clergy and noble class, while the town, endowed already in the year 1000 with commercial privileges, developed its activities at the crossroads of the main thoroughfare joining the Rhine Valley to northern Italy, as well as those leading to the French-speaking region and southern France. Otto of Freising noted it as the largest city in Swabia. With the extinction of the Zähringens in 1218, Zurich gained the status of free imperial city. In 1245 the burghers sided with the emperor against the pope. On this occasion part of the clergy was chased from the city, which soon acquired a strong city council and claimed for itself toll, coinage, and market rights formerly held by the clergy.

The local nobility, at first dominant in the council, had to make more and more room for the new urban patricians rising from the merchant class; but new tensions became evident at the beginning of the fourteenth century between the city council and the guilds, which had been excluded from municipal functions. In 1336 the knight Rudolph Brun succeeded in uniting the forces of the nobility and the craft guilds and imposed a new constitution. Until his death in 1360, Brun was to exercise much influence in Zurich. The constitution and Zurich's economic interests induced the city to treat the Habsburgs with consideration because they challenged routes of access. The 1291 alliance with the *Waldstätte,* which had led Zurich into open warfare with Albert of Habsburg, seems parenthetical. (Indeed Zurich had sent reinforcements to Duke Leopold after his defeat at Morgarten.) The Habsburgs maintained solid support among the local nobility, whose members voluntarily served in their domains. The quarrel between Zurich and the Habsburgs occurred following incidents between the new rulers and members of the local nobility, the Rapperswils, who supported members of the old city council. In 1350 Brun and his friends narrowly escaped a coup at the hands of the Rapperswils.

Bern was a new city, founded in 1191 by the duke of Zähringen for military rather than economic purposes, as a point of support against the French-speaking regions. In 1218 the city obtained from the emperor confirmation of its liberties and, it seems, the status of free imperial city. Threatened by the counts of Kyburg, Bern found support in 1240 in Peter, son of the count of Savoy, who was then building a seigniory in the Vaud region. King Rudolph forced Savoy to renounce its trusteeship over Bern in 1282 and forcibly subdued the city, which had refused his constitution, in 1289. However, its status was modified neither by Rudolph nor by his successors. Unlike Zurich, Bern was not a big commercial center and the importance of its craftsmen (mostly weavers) was not comparable to that of Zurich's or Fribourg's. The local nobility had always maintained an important place in the city government. The nobility and the burghers, and the city itself, pursued a policy of acquiring property by using all appropriate means, especially by buying and mortgaging. At the beginning of the fourteenth century Bern had become the center of an important domain but had alienated all its neighbors. It had to face a seignorial coalition including Fribourg and the bishop of Basel. Allied with Solothurn, it succeeded in defeating its adversaries at the Battle of Laupen (1339). Although it had maintained connections with the Habsburgs, Bern drew closer to the *Waldstätte,* mainly to discourage uprisings of its own rural subjects in the Oberland, who were not indifferent to the Confederates.

Other cities played a more passive role in the development of the Confederation. The abbatial cities of St. Gall and Schaffhausen were commercial cities of cloth merchants. Basel and Constance, cathedral towns, kept up equal relations with both sides of the Rhine. Lausanne and Geneva, two other cathedral towns, in the French-speaking region, were encircled by Savoyard territory. Fribourg, which remained in Habsburg territory at the beginning of the fourteenth century, maintained precarious relations with its neighbor, Bern.

THE DEVELOPMENT OF THE CONFEDERATION

If the entry of Lucerne into the alliance in 1332 brought an urban element to the *Waldstätte,* one can say that the Confederation was profoundly changed by the almost simultaneous entry of Zurich (1351) and Bern (1353). From then on the urban element was predominant; the alliance was strengthened but had to take into account thereafter the differences of interest between its constituents. The internal tensions of its members influenced the policy of the whole. Toward outsiders, particularly the Habsburg house (which remained master of a Helvetic territory vaster than the Confederation itself), the policy of the more dynamic Confederates often tended to prevail; the others followed whether they liked it or not. Leadership was thus assumed in turn by Zurich, Lucerne, Schwyz, and Bern, and always most aggressively.

The alliance system was both flexible and complex, in no way resembling a constitution of a federal state. Lucerne had allied itself to the *Waldstätte,* while maintaining formally the Habsburg's rights, which still allowed the nomination of the local *Schultheiss* (mayor). Zurich allied itself with the *Waldstätte* and Lucerne, Bern only with the *Waldstätte.* Bern had its own network of alliances, especially with Soleure. Bern felt only indirectly bound to Lucerne and Zurich and showed it during the war of 1386 by not declaring hostilities immediately. In the absence of an organization, the allies had perfected a procedure of consultation; common affairs gave rise to meetings of all, or at least some, allies. Until the middle of the fifteenth century they succeeded in reconciling, as well as possible, the respective positions and in avoiding confrontation among themselves. They also made common resolutions like the *Pfaffenbrief* (priest's charter) of 1370, by which the Confederates assumed their own jurisdiction by forbidding recourse to ecclesiastical courts. The alliance had been extended in 1352 to include the rural regions of Glarus and

Zug. But that had to be annulled under Austrian pressure.

Indeed, the Habsburgs did not remain inactive. In 1354 they obtained the help of Emperor Charles IV, who laid siege to Zurich, but soon lifted it. Shortly after, the Habsburgs obtained the countship of Rapperswil. The tension grew in 1379, when the dukes of Habsburg proceeded to divide their lands. Duke Leopold acquired the possessions in Germany, Alsace, and Tyrol, providing new ardor to revive the rights of his house. This time the cities were chiefly responsible for initiating the new hostilities. Zurich and Lucerne had multiplied the recruitment of *Pfahlburger,* that is, burghers who were Austrian subjects. Zurich destroyed the Austrian stronghold of Rapperswil in 1385 and received the abbot of Einsiedeln as a burgher. The same year Lucerne seized the Austrian stronghold of Rothenburg and concluded a pact of *combourgeoisie* (reciprocal rights) with the cities of Sempach and Wolhusen. Duke Leopold decided to attack the rebellious cities. The battle took place at Sempach on 9 July 1386; the duke was defeated and killed.

The Confederate victory was completed with the uprising of the inhabitants of Glarus against Austrian domination. Supported by reinforcements from Schwyz, the Glaronese defeated a counteroffensive at Näfels in 1388. With Zug, which entered the alliance in 1364, Glarus became the eighth canton (*Ort*) of the Confederation. The Bernese in turn entered the war, threatening Fribourg, which had remained faithful to the Habsburgs. Then the intervention of the Swabian towns led to a new truce in 1389.

The success of the war had not exhausted the Confederates' vitality, but the absence of immediate peril led to a certain slackening of existing bonds. While each confederated city increased its rural territory, the mountainous cantons were taking daring initiatives. Schwyz supported the peasant populations of Appenzell and of the St. Gall region against their lord-abbot. And the village subjects of the cities of Lucerne and Zug requested arbitration by the other confederates. The people of Uri crossed the St. Gotthard, annexing Valle Leventina; they pushed momentarily into Italy to Domodossola, but had to turn back when confronted by the dukes of Milan and Savoy.

In 1415, thanks to a new conflict between the Habsburgs and Emperor Sigismund, the Bernese, encouraged by the emperor, drew the allies into the conquest of Austrian Aargau, dividing the territory among themselves. Part was allotted to Bern; the rest remained a subject territory administered in common by the Confederates. Such "common domain" (*Gemeinen Herrschaften*) territories were to increase in the second half of the fifteenth century and necessitate the appointment of bailiffs designated by all the Confederates. The conquest of Aargau and those that followed are thus at the origin of a permanent communal organization.

However, the Confederation was still to undergo a long and serious internal crisis. From 1439 to 1450 a war set Zurich against the other Confederates and challenged the very foundations of the alliance. The cause was a territorial conflict between Zurich and Schwyz, both of which coveted the inheritance of the last count of Tottenburg. At first the armed conflict remained limited to Zurich and some rural cantons. But the head of the house of Habsburg, Frederick, who had just been made king, wanted to capitalize on the bitterness of the inhabitants of Zurich and recover the hereditary lands of his own house. On 17 June 1442 he concluded a treaty of alliance with Zurich, which quickly provoked all the other Confederates to rise against him. The war took a very violent turn, marked by dramatic incidents such as the Confederates' execution of Zurich prisoners. Siege was laid to Zurich itself in June 1444. However, the unexpected arrival of an army of French mercenaries (Armagnacs) at the behest of King Frederick forced the Confederates to lift the siege after a bloody battle at St. Jakob an der Birs. It was only in 1450 that peace was re-established. The war had made apparent Austria's powerlessness to re-establish its position on the left bank of the Rhine. Drawing a lesson from these events, the cities of Fribourg, St. Gall, and Schaffhausen, the abbeys of St. Gall and Reichenau, and the region of Appenzell exchanged Austrian trusteeship for an alliance with the Confederates. With the occupation of Thurgau by the Confederates in 1460 and the purchase of Winterthur by Zurich in 1467, Austrian domination over the left bank of the Rhine was terminated.

THE PEACE OF BASEL (1499)

The war with Burgundy marked the entrance of the Confederates (or "Swiss") into European history. The origin of the conflict was the fate of southern Alsace (Sundgau) and of the last Habsburg possessions on the Rhine, which Duke Sigismund of Habsburg had pledged to the powerful duke of

Burgundy, Charles the Bold. The alliance of the Habsburgs with the house of Burgundy represented a serious danger for the Confederation.

Charles the Bold imposed his tutelage on the duchess of Savoy, on whom depended the major part of French-speaking Switzerland. Anxiety then spread mainly to the western cities, Fribourg, Soleure, and especially Bern, which had established special relations with Basel and the cities of Alsace. At this point, the Bernese diplomat Diesbach negotiated with the king of France, Louis XI, an old adversary of the Burgundians, the grant of large subsidies to feed the armed resistance.

The brutality of the Burgundians reconciled Duke Sigismund with the Confederates. Prompted by Bern, they took part in the reconquest of Alsace in the spring of 1475; they also invaded the Savoyard territory of Vaud. There Duke Charles took to the field with a large army, but he suffered two crushing defeats at the hands of the Confederates' army, one at Grandson on 2 March 1476, the other at Morat the following June. This victory over the most powerful prince of Europe established the military reputation of the Confederates' army.

The spoils recovered in the Burgundian camp were fabulous, but these successes were poorly exploited. After having invaded and ransomed the Vaud region and Franche-Comté, the Confederates abandoned their conquests, with the exception of a few forts shared with Bern and Fribourg. The majority of the Confederates, mainly among the *Waldstätte,* thus expressed their distrust of Bernese initiatives. The differences among Confederates, particularly between town and country, remained alive at the end of the fifteenth century. Following very laborious negotiations, civil war was averted by the Compromise of Stans (1481), by which Fribourg and Soleure were admitted as de jure members, but which left intact the independence of the different cantons. But, as the Confederate soldiers were more and more in demand as mercenaries by the greater powers, the concept of a common foreign policy became questionable.

Nevertheless, the consciousness of unity, if not national, at least confederal, was dawning just as the military power of Switzerland began arousing growing hostility in the neighboring states. The attempt of Emperor Maximilian I, a Habsburg, to impose in 1495 upon the Confederation a system of regular taxation created new tensions. Differences also arose following judgments rendered by the imperial court against St. Gall, Appenzell, and Schaffhausen. In 1499 a series of local incidents unleashed a violent war between the Germans and the Austrians on one side and the Swiss and the inhabitants of the Grisons (formerly Raetia) on the other. The military superiority of the Confederates forced the emperor to negotiate a peace treaty on 22 September 1499 in Basel. While the treaty did not recognize explicitly the Confederates' sovereignty, the peace of Basel is considered to be the de facto recognition of the separation of Switzerland from the empire.

At that time, the Confederation (increased in 1501 by the admission of Basel) had approximately attained its present boundaries with Germany. Still to be captured in the south were the Grisons and Valais, small republics, with interests closely linked to those of the Confederates. Ticino belonged to the Milanese. In the west the French-speaking territories remained in great part under Savoyard sovereignty. The cathedral cities of Lausanne and Geneva, broadly autonomous, remained outside the Confederation, despite the existence of special accords with Fribourg, for example.

BIBLIOGRAPHY

Die Alpen in der europäischen Geschichte des Mittelalters (1965); *Atlas historique de las Suisse/Historischer Atlas der Schweiz,* Hektor Amman and Karl Schib, eds. (1958); *Atlas historique français: Savoie . . . Genève,* Jean-Yves Mariotte and André Perret, eds. (1979); Marcel Beck, R. Moosbrugger-Leu, and Stefan Sonderegger, "Volks- und Sprachgrenzen in der Schweiz im Frühmittelalter: Mit besonderer Berücksichtigung der burgundisch-alemannischen Grenze," in *Schweizerische Zeitschrift für Geschichte,* 13 (1963); Heinrich Büttner, *Schwaben und Schweiz im frühen und hohen Mittelalter* (1972); Paul Guichonnet, ed., *Histoire et civilisations des Alpes* (1980); Albert Hauser, *Schweizerische Wirtschafts- und Sozialgeschichte* (1961); Jean-Yves Mariotte, "Le royaume de Bourgogne et les souverains allemands du haut moyen âge," in *Mémoires de la Société pour l'Histoire du Droit et des institutions des anciens pays bourguignons, comtois et romands,* 23 (1962); Bruno Meyer, "Die Entstehung der Eidgenossenschaft: Der Stand der heutigen Anschauungen," in *Schweizerische Zeitschrift für Geschichte,* 2 (1952); Hans Nabholz *et al., Geschichte der Schweiz,* I (1932); Daniel Reichel, ed., *Grandson 1476: Essai d'approche pluridisciplinaire d'une action militaire du XVe siècle* (1976); Fritz Wernli, *Die Entstehung der schweizerischen Eidgenossenschaft: Verfassungsgeschichte und politische Geschichte in Wechselwirkung* (1972); Hermann Wiesflecker, *Kaiser*

Maximilian I, II, *Reichsreform und Kaiserpolitik, 1493–1500* (1975).

J. Y. MARIOTTE

[See also **Alamanni; Barbarians, Invasions of; Burgundians; Carolingians and the Carolingian Empire; Charles Martel; Dante Alighieri; Germany; Habsburg Dynasty; Hohenstaufen Dynasty; Holy Roman Empire; Maximilian I, Emperor; Mayor of the Palace; Swabia.**]

SWORDS AND DAGGERS. The sword (Danish: *svaerd;* Dutch: *zwaard;* German: *Schwert;* French: *épée;* Italian: *spada;* Spanish: *espada,* from Late Roman *spatha*) was the only weapon in early man's arsenal designed solely for the killing of other persons and not developed from hunting equipment (spear, bow and arrow) or tools (knife, axe, pruning hook). For this rather sinister reason the sword is universally regarded as the most noble of weapons. Medieval epics celebrate the sword, for instance, Roland's Durendal or King Arthur's Excalibur, because of the awe and even magic surrounding this weapon par excellence.

Technically a sword is a straight cutting-and-thrusting weapon, usually with a double-edged blade more than two feet (61 cm) in length; daggers are for thrust only and average between ten and eighteen inches (25–45 cm) in total length. The main components of both are the blade and the hilt; the basic elements of the hilt are the guard, the grip, and the pommel. Accessories for sword and dagger are scabbard and belt.

ANCIENT SWORDS AND SWORDSMITHING

In classical antiquity the Roman legionnaire's sword (*gladius*) had a blade approximately two feet long, with parallel edges, a sharp triangular point, and a central ridge running all the way to the point for reinforcement; it was designed for the thrust from the cover of the large shield (*scutum*). The hilt of the *gladius* consisted of four elements: the semicircular guard, the tubular grip, the globular pommel, and the button. These elements were threaded onto the long tang of the blade, with the tip of the tang peened over and riveted into the button. The Roman cavalry sword (*spatha*) was of the same shape, but had a blade three feet in length. It was designed for slashing rather than stabbing, though it was also suitable for the thrust. The *gladius* was carried on a shoulder baldric on the legionaire's right side; the spatha hung on the cavalryman's left.

Outside the Roman world the Celtic warriors used three-foot-long slashing swords; their hilts of wood, horn, or bronze were made in a single piece of a peculiar X-shape, sometimes with anthropoid features. Medieval swords adopted the Roman hilt construction but followed Gaulish prototypes for their long blades.

The requirements for a good sword blade are obvious: it should hold a keen edge, and it should not break or bend out of shape under a heavy blow. Unfortunately, the material properties of iron and steel are such that these desirable qualities are mutually exclusive. The more steel is hardened, the more brittle it will become; soft iron is tough and hard to break, but it is easily deformed and loses its edge.

As a way out of this dilemma, the ancient bladesmiths laboriously hammer-welded together thin strips of steel and iron of varying hardnesses to form the core of the blade and added, separately, edges of very hard steel. For extra cohesiveness the core strips were braided or twisted like ropes; when polished, the finished blade showed patterns of light and dark hues that looked like spotted snakeskin (German: *wurmbunt*) and were poetically described as writhing or fighting dragons and serpents. This technique was used by Celtic smiths of the late La Tène period (*ca.* 250 B.C.). To produce these high-quality blades with the celebrated "dragonskin pattern," it was essential that a strict temperature control of the steel under the hammer be observed. This could be achieved only by closely watching the changing colors of the heated metal from dark red to white-hot, which was best done in the dark of the night. This seemingly secretive working at night added to the superstitious awe that surrounded the smith, who fashioned instruments that could take life, and elevated the value of his works into the realm of magic.

These pattern-welded swords were the weapons of the warriors of the early Middle Ages who became the heroes of medieval epics (Beowulf, King Arthur, Siegfried, Dietrich von Bern). Good swords were rare, and therefore expensive, which put them out of reach of the common warrior. As late as Charlemagne's reign, a sword was not among the weapons required for a fighting man on foot, though it was for a horseman.

Steel for sword blades has to have qualities different from those required for armor plates. With

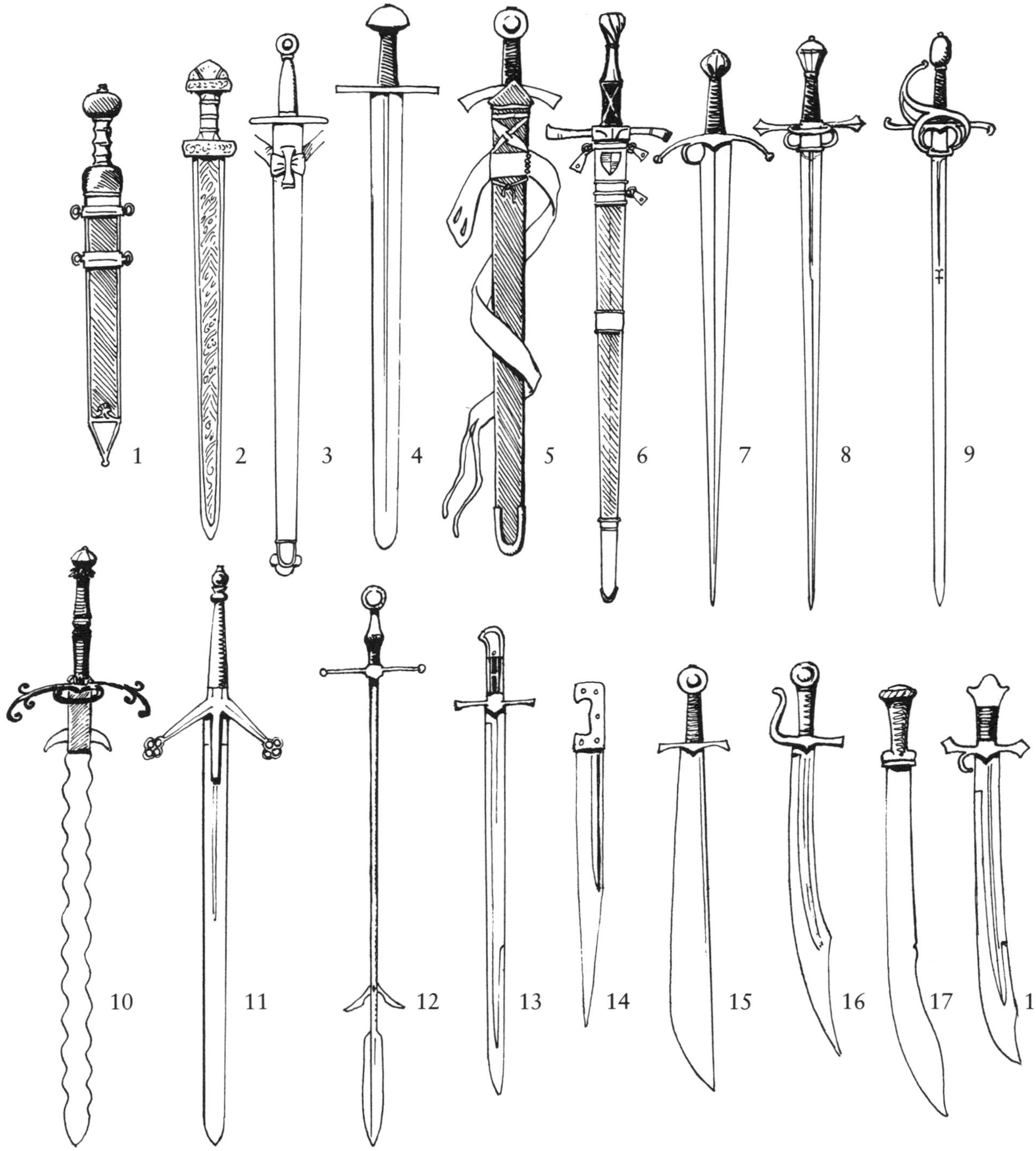

Types of medieval swords: (1) Roman *gladius,* 1st–3rd c.; *(2)* Viking sword with pattern-welded blade, hilt type VII, *ca.* 900; *(3)* Sasanian sword in scabbard, early disk pommel, *ca.* 700; *(4)* Sword with "Brazil nut" pommel, type XI, pommel type A, 12th–13th c.; *(5)* Sword with curved quillons, wheel pommel, scabbard, and belt, type XII, pommel type K, 13th c.; *(6)* Sword with "half-and-a-half" grip and scabbard, type XVIII, pommel type T, 15th c.; *(7)* Sword with fingerguard loop, type XV, pommel type T, *ca.* 1400; *(8)* Early rapier with side rings and double "arms of the hilt," 16th c.; *(9)* Fully developed rapier with "swept" hilt, knuckle bow, guard branches, side rings, and "arms of the hilt," 16th–17th c.; *(10) Bidenhander*; *(11)* Scottish claymore; *(12) Schweinschwert*; *(13)* Hunting sword; *(14) Seax*; *(15) Falchion*; *(16) Storta*; *(17) Malchus*; *(18) Dusägge.* ALL DRAWINGS BY AUTHOR

the limited technology of the early Middle Ages, and in ignorance of trace elements, smiths knew only from experience that ore from a certain mine was more suitable than that from another. For this reason industrial centers of blade smithing were usually in different locations than armor-producing centers. The three most renowned centers for sword manufacture—all going back at least to Roman times—were Toledo, Passau on the Danube (at the border between Austria and Bavaria), and Solingen (in the Rhineland, near Cologne). Toledo blades were highly prized, but Passau blades enjoyed a special reputation. Their distinctive mark was the image of a wolf engraved and inlaid in brass on the blade; skillfully launched rumors convinced prospective customers that these "wolf blades" possessed magical qualities and brought good luck. By the fifteenth century the wolf mark was imitated by Solingen and even Toledo smiths in order to enhance their wares.

The best-known type of swords with pattern-welded blades are the so-called Viking swords, which have blades that seem to have been made mostly in the Rhineland for export and were furnished with hilts made by local Scandinavian craftsmen. These Viking hilts as a rule have a massive oblong guard, only about one inch (2.5 cm) wider than the blade, and a pommel made in two parts. Its lower element, the pommel bar, parallels the guard in shape and decoration; it is surmounted by a semicircular or triangular cap covering the spot where the tang is riveted into the pommel bar. Among the sword blades of the Viking period are specimens with inscriptions inlaid with bold letters in different colors of steel: ULFBERH+T, INGELRIÍ, GICELIN. Evidently these are the names of the smiths; Gizelin is the name of a local saint in the Rhineland, and Ulfberht could be an early form of the name of the Solingen swordsmiths' clan, Wolffertz.

The Viking sword is generally considered to be the prototype of the medieval knightly sword. Indeed, among swords from the high days of chivalry down to the late thirteenth century there are various pommel types outwardly resembling the Viking pommel forms, named "Brazil nut," "tea cozy," and "cocked hat" shapes by modern antiquarians. However, there is a structural difference insofar as these medieval pommels are of one solid piece, instead of two separate elements, as their supposed prototypes were. Also, the guards of these knightly swords are much more slender, with quillons of up to four inches long on either side of the blade. Finally, a new type of pommel, disk-shaped, with a central boss like the hub of a wheel, appeared with increasing frequency. These long swords with long quillons and disk pommels are found as early as Sasanian representations of the fifth to sixth centuries and in Byzantine art of the ninth and tenth. For this reason it is more likely that this type of hilt was a fashion imported directly from Byzantium, though "Brazil nut" and "cocked hat" pommels were influenced by "Viking" styles.

TYPES AND STYLES OF SWORDS

The sword is a weapon that has to be carefully tuned to the person of its wielder, and therefore no two of them are exactly alike, though there are clear-cut trends and fashions, both local and international, recognizable among their representations in art and among the surviving swords themselves.

Viking hilts were classified as types I–VII by Mortimer Wheeler; to this system types VIII and IX were added by Ewart Oakeshott. This was done in order to allow for a smooth transition to the medieval knightly sword, which was subdivided by Oakeshott into ten groups, X–XX, mainly on the basis of the shape and length of the blade and the presence of one or more grooves or ridges. Oakeshott also established a classification system for pommel types, A–Z.

The two basic types of sword blades are, first, one with more or less parallel edges and one or more grooves (their purpose is to lighten the blade and at the same time stiffen it, in the manner of an I-beam), designed for slashing blows (Oakeshott X, XI, XII, XIII, XIV, XX), and second, a blade for the thrust, with straight edges tapering to a sharp point, with a central ridge running all the way to the point as its reinforcement (Oakeshott XV and XVIII). There are also three intermediary types, one (Oakeshott XVII) having flat, tapering blades and two others (XVI and XVIIIa) with grooves halfway down the blade and reinforcing ridges from there to the point.

During the eleventh through fourteenth centuries the blades of the first group dominated, while those of the second group are found from after 1350 to the middle of the sixteenth century. Aside from these chronological distinctions, it also has to be kept in mind that there is a preference for the slashing blow in countries north of the Alps and for the thrust in Italy, Spain, France, and Portugal.

SWORDS AND DAGGERS

From the late tenth century on, the guard with long quillons had been of a cross shape that acquired religious significance during the crusades and in regions, such as Spain and the Baltic, where century-long struggles of Christians against "infidels" or "pagans" took place. In the cathedral of Seville, for instance, a sword thought to be King Ferdinand III's is kept as a relic, mounted upright like a cross; and cruciform swords were the badges of the military-religious orders of Santiago in Spain and the Brethren of the Sword in Livonia.

From the thirteenth century on, there was a marked tendency to give the quillons a slight downward curve to allow more freedom for the hand in swordplay, but the symbolic value of the cross shape ensured that the straight quillons never disappeared entirely. In fencing, sword strokes were blocked with the shield, but when the shield became obsolete through improvements in body armor during the fourteenth century, parries had to be executed with the sword itself. For a firm and precise thrust, the index finger was often locked over the foreward quillon; now this finger came in grave danger of being sliced off in a parry. For its protection a semicircular loop was added to the foreward quillon; its first example is in a Sienese painting of the Crucifixion by the Master of the Codex of St. George (1340/1350), now at The Cloisters in New York. By the middle of the fifteenth century this single loop had been doubled, probably as much for practical reasons—in order to give the swordsman a chance to use both edges—as for aesthetic ones, to make the guard symmetrical with these "arms of the hilt." After 1400 it became increasingly frequent for quillons to be recurved, either the foreward quillon turned slightly upward and the rear quillon down, or the foreward quillon bent inward and the rear one outward.

The grip of the sword hilt was usually of wood, covered with leather to prevent splitting; for extra reinforcement it could be wrapped with cords or wire. Up to the fourteenth century grips were quite short, just wide enough for the grasp of the hand. The massive pommel kept the center of gravity close to the fist and balanced the blade. When armor was made increasingly of plates (mid fourteenth century), slashing blows became less effective; instead precise thrusts had to be directed at the "chinks in armor." For a better balance for the thrust, the grip was gradually elongated; shortly before 1400 it received a characteristic bottle-shaped form. Because it was now almost two palms' width long, this grip is called "hand-and-a-half" or, less elegantly, "bastard sword grip."

The scabbard, necessary to carry a sword safely, consisted of two shaped slats of wood, covered with leather or fabric, and fitted with metal mountings securing potentially vulnerable parts. Chapes for the scabbard tip were always present, and occasionally there were also ferrules for the scabbard mouth. These ferrules were usually fitted with rings for the carrying straps of the belt, a method going back to the construction of the *gladius* scabbard. Most scabbards of the twelfth to fourteenth centuries had the soft leather of the scabbard mouth cut to a blunt point to fit tightly over the guard of the sheathed sword, in order to keep dust and rain out. The belt, of soft white leather, was attached to the scabbard by splicing with strips cut from the belt itself. In Western Europe the belt had elaborate buckles, but in countries under German influence, east of the Rhine, one end of the belt was split and the opposite end had a pair of small slits through which the straps of the split end were passed and then tied with a slipknot. After the middle of the fourteenth century, a heavy metal-studded belt, the *dupsing,* was worn to hold the newly developed fitted body armor of plates in position, and the sword was hung from it. The newly introduced breastplates also gave support to a chain that could be attached to the sword hilt to keep it within reach when the sword was knocked out of the knight's fist. Though there are many representations of these scabbards with spliced-on belts, only two originals have survived: that of the sword of King Sancho IV el Bravo of Castile (*d.* 1295), from his tomb in the cathedral of Toledo, and that of the sword of Fernando de la Cerda (*d.* 1270), in the monastery of Las Huelgas at Burgos.

Highly specialized sword types were the tuck (Middle French: *estoc*), with a very long blade of triangular or rhomboid cross section for extra stiffness, designed for the mail-piercing thrust in the fifteenth century, and the oversize swords for use with both hands. Their main representatives were the German *Bidenhander* (both-hander), with total length of up to 77 inches (196 cm), and the Scottish claymore (*claidheamh mör,* great sword). *Bidenhander* swords are characterized by two parrying hooks about a handspan in front of the guard; those with wavy blades are called *flamberges.* Claymores have small wheel pommels and unusual guards with straight extensions along the blade and tapering quillons pointing downward at an angle of about

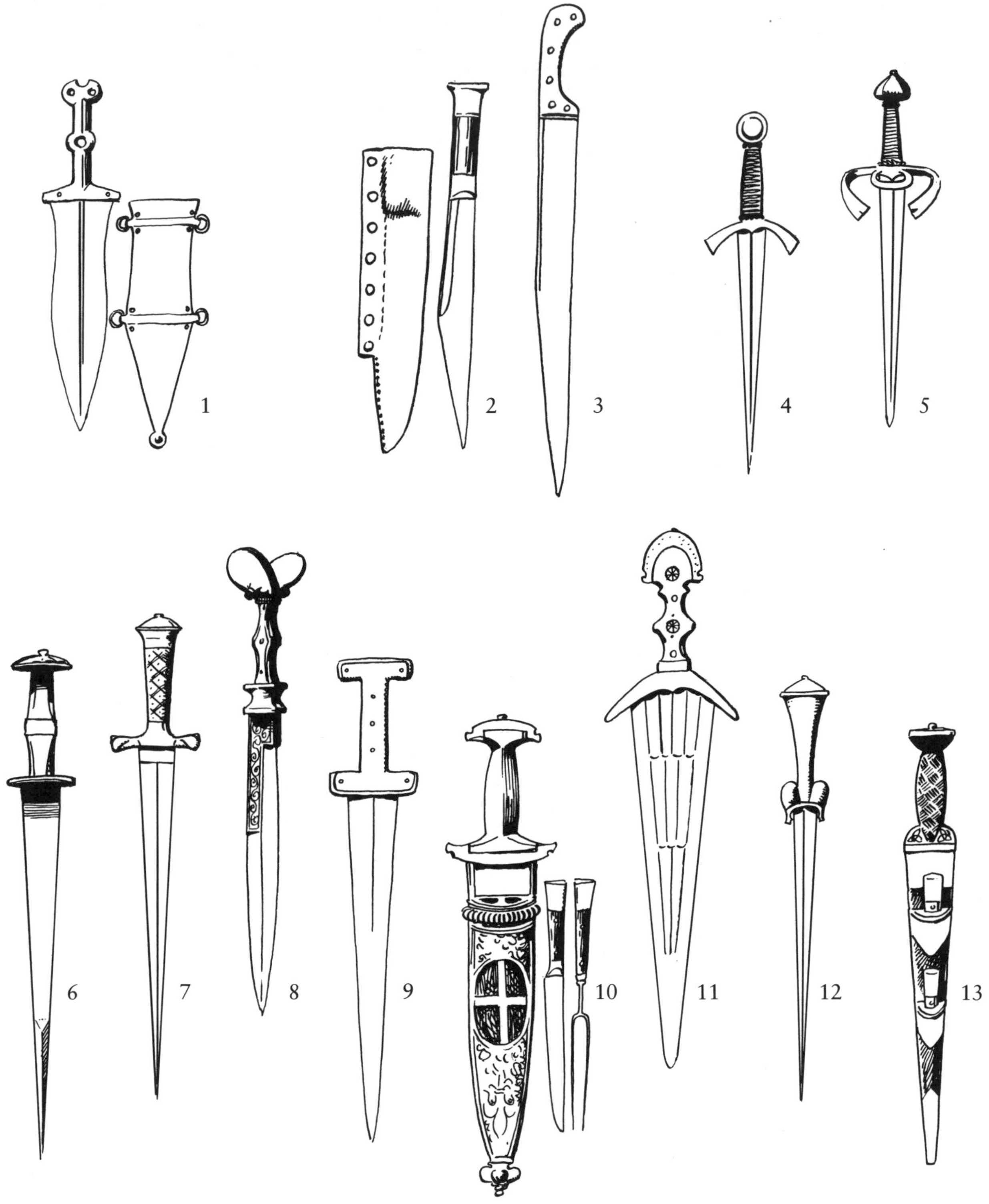

Types of medieval daggers: (1) Roman *pugio*; *(2)* and *(3) Scramasaxes*; *(4)* Poniard, quillon dagger; *(5)* Parrying dagger for left hand; *(6)* Rondel dagger; *(7) Kruismes*; *(8)* Eared dagger; *(9) Baselard*; *(10)* Swiss dagger; *(11)* Italian *cinquedea*; *(12)* Kidney dagger or ballock knife; *(13)* Scottish dirk. ALL DRAWINGS BY AUTHOR

SWORDS AND DAGGERS

45 degrees. Though they are not fighting weapons, in connection with two-handed swords mention should be made of executioners' swords. Their very wide blades have parallel edges and squared-off tips, often decorated with the symbols of capital punishment, such as gallows and wheel, inlaid in brass.

Specialized weapons that are not swords in the strict sense are the German *Schweinschwert,* with a cross-guard hilt, a rodlike blade with a lanceolate tip, and a toggle like a boar spear, for hunting wild boar from horseback; and the "hunting sword." The latter is actually an oversize hunting knife, single-edged and with a grip built up from two plaques riveted to either side of the tang. It was developed from the old Germanic *seax,* a machete-like tool or weapon of the migration period that gave the Saxons their name.

Single-edged swords with curved blades are sabers (from the Hungarian *szab,* to cut). The medieval European forms are the *falchion,* the *storta* (in Italy), and the *Malchus* and *Dusägge* (in Germany). *Falchion* and *storta* often have the foreward quillon bent upward at a right angle to form a knuckle guard; all of them owe much of their shape, especially the clipped point of the blade, to Eastern influences.

DAGGERS

The dagger was once an everyday accessory of a man's costume. Most common was the "kidney dagger" (a Victorian euphemism for the original ballock knife) worn upright in front of the body, together with a belt pouch (like its descendant, the Scottish dirk) and the sporran. With its single-edged, sharply pointed blade it was a household tool as well as a handy weapon in an emergency. Its scabbard usually had an extra compartment for a small byknife. Another weapon was the rondel dagger, with a disk-shaped guard and sometimes a matching pommel plate capping the grip. Because of its strong blade capable of piercing mail, it is also romantically named *misericordia* or *Gnadgott,* suggestive of the coup de grace. The most exotic dagger type was the eared dagger of fifteenth-century Italy and Spain, in the sixteenth century also found in France and England. Its peculiar shape, with two flaring "ears" topping its grip, has been found in Near Eastern bronze daggers of the second millennium B.C. It was evidently derived from a prototype carved from the upper joint of a shinbone.

Local dagger types were the Italian *cinquedea,* with a wide ("five fingers") tapering blade, its surface compartmented by shallow grooves arranged in decorative groups, a horseshoe-shaped guard, and a flat grip of horn and bone attached to the tang by large tubular rivets filled with delicate brass rosettes; and the Swiss dagger (*Schweizerdolch*). The Swiss dagger had a characteristic I-shaped grip and a scabbard mounted in gilded brass, decorated with biblical, allegorical (Dance of Death), or patriotic (William Tell's shot at the apple) scenes in relief. The scabbard also contained two smaller compartments for a byknife and a two-pronged fork—presumably for an early form of fondue at the campfire. Ironically, this strictly national Swiss dagger type was chosen as the model for the honor dagger of the Nazi SA storm troopers, though without the knife and fork.

Of *cinquedeas* there exist sword-size specimens; the *Schweizerdegen,* the sword-length version of the Swiss dagger, was the national sidearm of the Swiss citizen-soldiers of the fifteenth century. Often daggers were shaped like miniature editions of swords, with quillons and wheel- or pear-shaped pommels, clearly meant to be part of a garniture of matching sword and dagger. This ensemble became almost de rigueur for the fashion-conscious gentleman of the sixteenth and seventeenth centuries, after the fencing style with rapier and left-hand dagger (*main-gauche*) had been firmly established.

BIBLIOGRAPHY

Elis Behmer, *Das zweischneidige Schwert der germanischen Völkerwanderungszeit* (1939); Howard L. Blackmore, *Hunting Weapons* (1971); Claude Blair, *European and American Arms, ca. 1100–1850* (1962); Wendelin Boeheim, *Handbuch der Waffenkunde* (1890, repr. 1966); Ada Bruhn-Hoffmeyer, *Middelalderens tveaeggede svaerd,* 2 vols. (1954); Hilda R. E. Davidson, *The Sword in Anglo-Saxon England* (1962); Bashford Dean, *Handbook of Arms and Armor* (1930); Guy Francis Laking, *A Record of European Armor and Arms Through Seven Centuries,* 5 vols. (1920–1922); James G. Mann, *An Outline of Arms and Armour in England from the Middle Ages to the Civil War* (1969); Paul Martin, *Arms and Armour,* René North, trans. (1967); Helmut Nickel, *Ullstein-Waffenkunde* (1974); A. Vesey Norman, *Arms and Armour* (1964) and *The Rapier and the Small Sword, 1460–1820* (1980); R. Ewart Oakeshott, *The Sword in the Age of Chivalry* (1964); Jan Petersen, *De Norske Vikingsverd* (1919); Harold L. Peterson, *Daggers and Fighting Knives of the Western World* (1968); William Reid, *Arms Through the Ages* (1976); Hugo Schneider, *Schwerter und Degen* (1957); Heribert Seitz,

High altar of St. Kilian's Church, Heilbronn. Wood sculpture by Hans Syfer, 1498. WÜRTTEMBERGISCHE LANDESBILDSTELLE

Blankwaffen, 2 vols. (1965–1968); Eduard Wagner, *Cut and Thrust Weapons* (1967); Frederick J. Wilkinson, *Swords and Daggers* (1967) and *Edged Weapons* (1971).

HELMUT NICKEL

[See also **Arms and Armor; Knights, Knight Service; Metalworkers; Steelmaking; Warfare, Western European.**]

SYFER, HANS (*d.* 1509). An early-sixteenth-century Middle Rhenish sculptor active from the 1480's to 1509, Syfer continued the physiognomic detail and animated individualism of Nikolaus Gerhaerts and Nicholas Hagenauer (or von Hagenau) in stone works. His principal carvings were *Mount of Olives,* commissioned in 1505 (fragments, Speyer Cathedral), *Crucifixion,* commissioned in 1501 (Stuttgart, St. Leonhard's), and the high altar of St. Kilian, dated 1498 (Heilbronn, including a self-portrait).

BIBLIOGRAPHY

Michael Baxandall, *The Limewood Sculptors of Renaissance Germany, 1475–1525* (1980), 284; Werner Fleischhauer, "Zu Hans Syfer," in Hans Wentzel, ed., *Form und Inhalt: Kunstgeschichtliche Studien* (1950), 203–210; M. L. Hauck, "Der Bildhauer Conrad Sifer von Sinsheim und sein Kreis in der oberrheinischen Spätgotik," in *Annales universitatis saraviensis,* 9 (1960), 197: R. Schnellbach, *Spätgotische Plastik im unteren Neckargebiet* (1931), 9, 147; E. Zimmermann, "Plastik," in *Spätgotik am Oberrhein, 1450–1530* (1970), 165.

LARRY SILVER

[See also **Gerhaert, Nikolaus; Hagenauer, Nicholas.**]

SYLVESTER II, POPE (**Gerbert d'Aurillac,** *ca.* 945–1003), monk, mathematician, teacher, bishop, and pope (998–1003). Born in the Auvergne region of France, Gerbert studied at the Benedictine monastery of St. Géraud in Aurillac, leaving it in 967 to accompany Borel, count of Barcelona, to Catalonia, where he continued his studies under Bishop Atto of Vich. In 970 he went with Borel and Atto to Rome, where he came to the favorable attention of Pope John XIII. He also made the acquaintance of Otto I, Holy Roman emperor.

Gerbert was assigned to Adalbero, archbishop of Rheims, and successfully reorganized the cathedral school. He was particularly influential in the teaching of mathematics. His best-known pupil was Fulbert (*ca.* 960–1028), who went on to establish a school at Chartres and in 1006 became bishop there. Other distinguished pupils taught by Gerbert were Robert, son of Hugh Capet, who later became King Robert II of France; Richer of St. Remi, who was to become Gerbert's biographer; and Adalbold, later bishop of Utrecht.

Gerbert is known to have constructed armillary spheres for the teaching of astronomy and to have used polar sighting tubes. He used a special form of the abacus for teaching calculation. It consisted of a board having twenty-seven columns combined in groupings of three, headed (from left to right) by *C* (*centum*), *D* (*decem*), and *S* or *M* (*singularis* or *monad*). Higher decimal units were accommodated in other columns with appropriate designations. The counters were inscribed with the symbols equivalent to each of the ten digits. With this device it was possible to perform addition, subtraction, multiplication, and division.

In 983 Gerbert was appointed abbot of Bobbie,

but he returned to Rheims the following year and became involved in political activity that led to the election and coronation of Hugh Capet as king of France (987), in which Gerbert assisted. He was appointed archbishop of Rheims in 991, but despite his appeal to the new pope, Gregory V, he did not obtain approval of this title. He left the position six years later, amid considerable controversy, to follow the court of Emperor Otto III through Germany and Italy.

During his stay at Madgeburg between 994 and 995, Gerbert is known to have made an *horologium* for the purpose of taking the altitude of the polestar. No description of the instrument has survived, and it has been speculated that it was either an astrolabe or some form of sundial. It was probably in this period that he used sighting tubes for observing the polestar.

In 998 Gerbert was appointed archbishop of Ravenna. With the unexpected death of Pope Gregory V in 999, Otto III appointed Gerbert to succeed him. He was the first Frenchman to ascend the papal throne, taking the name Sylvester II.

During his short reign Sylvester was an authoritarian reformist, denouncing nepotism and simony among the clergy and demanding celibacy. He directed attention to the needs of the Holy Land and the expansion of the church in Eastern Europe. It may have been Sylvester who sent the holy crown, symbol of the admission of Hungary to the Christian community, to King Vajk, who was baptized as Stephen and later canonized.

Many writings attest to his work and influence in theology and science, but there is considerable uncertainty about the authenticity of surviving manuscripts attributed to him.

BIBLIOGRAPHY

Sources. Oeuvres de Gerbert, Alexandre Olleris, ed. (1867); *Lettres de Gerbert (983–997),* Julien Havet, ed. (1889).

Studies. Oscar G. Darlington, "Gerbert the Teacher," in *American Historical Review,* **52** (1947); José María Millas y Vallicrosa, *Nuevos estudios sobre historia de la ciencia española* (1960); François Picavet, *Gerbert, un pape philosophe* (1897); Paul Tannery, ed., *Mémoires scientifiques,* V (1922), arts. 5, 6, 10.

SILVIO A. BEDINI

[See also **Adalbero of Laon; Adalbold of Utrecht; Astronomy; France: 987–1223; Mathematics; Otto III, Emperor; Radolph of Liège; Richer of St. Remi; Scientific Instruments.**]

SYMEON THE NEW THEOLOGIAN, ST. (949–1022), one of the greatest mystics of Eastern Christianity, and author of catechetical homilies, theological and ethical "chapters" (short rules), and *Hymns.* Having first lived as a novice in the great cenobitic community of Studios in Constantinople under the spiritual direction of the elder Symeon the Pious, he received his tonsure in the neighboring monastery of St. Mamas. Around 980 he became abbot of St. Mamas and was ordained a priest.

Following the tradition of early monasticism and, particularly, the fourth-century writings of Pseudo-Macarius, Symeon, in his preaching and his writings, insistently affirmed that *personal experience* represents the true reality of the Christian faith. "I beg you," he addresses his monks, "let us try, in this life, to see and contemplate [Christ]. For if we are deemed worthy to see Him *sensibly,* we shall not see death; death will have no dominion over us (Rom. 6:9)" (*Catechetical Homilies*; see Krivocheine, p. 240). This insistence on the experiential *event* as the content of Christianity led Symeon to be exigent with his monks, critical of the ecclesiastical hierarchy, and daring in some of his innovations. For example, he initiated spontaneously in his monastery a liturgical veneration of his spiritual father, Symeon the Pious, and defended the practice of private confession to lay monastic elders. Some modern historians have associated his thought with the charismatic, anti-institutional sect of the Messalians. However, the accusation of Messalianism was never leveled against him during his life (although he spent some time in exile after a conflict with ecclesiastical superiors) and, in contrast with Messalianism, he was always a fervent promoter of extreme eucharistic realism. In fact, by recognizing him as a saint, Byzantine Christianity admitted the legitimacy of a tension in the church between formal institutions and conscious spiritual experience. Of this tension Symeon was the living example.

BIBLIOGRAPHY

Nicetas Stethatos, *Un grand mystique byzantin: Vie de Syméon le Nouveau Théologien (949–1022),* Irénée Hausherr, ed. (1928); his writings (with French translation) are in the collection *Sources chrétiennes,* LI–CLXXXXVI, *passim* (1957–1973). The most comprehensive general study is Basil Krivocheine, *In the Light of Christ: St. Symeon the New Theologian—Life, Spirituality, Doctrine* (1986).

JOHN MEYENDORFF

[See also **Byzantine Church; Liturgy, Byzantine Church; Studios Monastery.**]

SYMEON METAPHRASTES, a Byzantine writer of the end of the tenth century. According to Yahya of Antioch and the eleventh-century Georgian writer and scholar Ep^{c}temi Mc^{c}ire (Ephrem the Less), he was a contemporary of Emperor Basil II (*r.* 976–1025) and Patriarch Nicholas Chrysoberges (979–991); he became a famous writer in the sixth year of Basil's reign, about 982. Though both Yahya and Ep^{c}temi call Symeon a logothete, his identification with Symeon the Logothete, historian and author of an epitaph for Stephen, the son of Romanos I Lekapenos (*r.* 920–944), is questionable, since the Logothete's literary activity reached its peak in the middle of the tenth century. Metaphrastes was a typical exponent of tenth-century encyclopedism, the hallmark of which was the tendency toward collecting and compiling. His chief goal was to gather and unify hagiographic legends; he collected lives of saints, disposed them in accordance with the ecclesiastical calender (from September to August), and stylistically edited them. Michael Psellos described his purpose: old acts of martyrs and saints' lives became obsolete as Byzantine scholarship grew, and Symeon tried to update them to meet the needs of his time. His editorial techniques, however, were inconsistent. At least twelve old texts were included unchanged; some texts written by Symeon's contemporaries did not undergo any alterations; and some were actual *metaphraseis* (paraphrases), embellished according to the taste of the tenth century, sometimes enlarged and sometimes shortened. Ep^{c}temi adds that Symeon eliminated heretical distortions from saints' lives. Symeon's collection, the Menologion, contains 148 texts. Most pieces in the Menologion are saints' lives, but other items, such as Constantine VII's speech on the translation of Christ's image from Edessa, are included. The texts are especially abundant for the winter months, whereas the texts from March on are scanty. Symeon's Menologion became an official tool for church services; about 700 manuscripts containing its parts are preserved.

It is difficult to determine which other works belong to Symeon's legacy. There is some poetry ascribed to him, as well as excerpts from the church fathers. Other works would seem rather to have been done by other persons, such as Symeon the Logothete or Symeon Hieromonachos *tu Scholariu.*

BIBLIOGRAPHY

A. Ehrhard, *Überlieferung und Bestand der hagiographischen und homiletischen Literatur der griechischen Kirche* (1937).

ALEXANDER P. KAZHDAN

[See also **Byzantine Literature; Hagiography, Byzantine; Historiography, Byzantine; Symeon the Logothete; Yahya of Antioch.**]

SYMEON OF BULGARIA (*r.* 893–927), ruler of Bulgaria. Destined for a church career by his father, Boris I (852–889), Symeon was sent in about 878 to Constantinople to study. He acquired a fine education and a good enough knowledge of Greek for Byzantine sources to call him "the Half-Greek." He returned to Bulgaria around 888, becoming a monk at the Ticha monastery near Preslav, where he was active translating Byzantine works into Slavonic. After his father abdicated, his eldest brother Vladimir (889–893) succeeded. Vladimir tried to restore paganism. Boris left the monastery he had entered and overthrew Vladimir. He convened a council at Preslav (893) which, releasing Symeon from his vows, declared him prince of Bulgaria.

Preslav became the capital and Symeon spent lavishly on it, making it a splendid city. He also maintained literary interests, sponsoring many translations of Byzantine legal, religious, and historical works. Under him the first original Bulgarian works appeared (those of John the Exarch and of the monk Hrabr'). Slavonic also became the official language of Bulgaria's church and state. The Cyrillic alphabet for Slavonic triumphed over Glagolitic during his reign. Symeon supported commerce. When in 894 the Byzantines transferred the Bulgarian market from Constantinople to Thessaloniki, causing disadvantages for Bulgarian merchants, Symeon declared war. The Byzantines persuaded the Hungarians to invade Bulgaria. They caused much destruction before Symeon got the Pechenegs to attack the Hungarians' homeland. The Hungarians were driven from the steppes; they settled in present-day Hungary. Symeon then won a major victory over the Byzantines at Bulgarophygon, leading to a treaty (897) restoring the

Bulgarian market to Constantinople and Byzantine tribute to Bulgaria.

Peace lasted until 904. Then, after an Arab raid damaged the fortifications of Thessaloniki, Symeon was tempted to attack it. The Byzantines bought him off with a new treaty, recognizing Bulgarian rule of Macedonia—long held without Byzantine recognition—and granting Symeon more Thracian territory. Peace lasted until 913, when the Byzantine emperor, Alexander, refused Bulgaria tribute. Alexander then died. The unstable situation existing in Constantinople stirred Symeon's ambitions to conquer Constantinople and become emperor. He marched on Constantinople, where he was received by the regent and patriarch, Nikolaos I Mystikos, who agreed that Symeon's daughter should marry the child emperor, Constantine Porphyrogenitos. Nikolaos also crowned Symeon, probably "emperor of the Bulgarians." Constantine's mother then staged a coup and renounced this agreement. Symeon went to war again. The war continued until shortly after his death in 927. In the course of it he won a major victory over the Byzantine army at Anchialo (917); frequently raided Byzantine Thrace, on occasion plundering Constantinople's suburbs; and once led a major raid through Greece.

In 919 Symeon held a council in Bulgaria which raised his archbishop's rank to patriarch. The patriarch then crowned Symeon, probably "emperor of the Romans," the imperial title he was seeking. After a series of intrigues in Serbia by which Bulgaria and Byzantium alternately placed their clients on that throne, Symeon invaded Serbia and annexed it in 924. When the deposed Serbian ruler fled to Croatia, a Byzantine ally, Symeon in 926 sent troops to invade Croatia. The Bulgarians were soundly defeated. In 927 Symeon led his armies once again toward Constantinople, but he died en route. His son Peter succeeded.

John V. A. Fine, Jr.

[See also **Boris; Bulgaria; Peter of Bulgaria.**]

SYMEON THE LOGOTHETE (Symeon Magister) (before 912–after 987), Byzantine chronicler. Symeon held the office of logothete of the drome and was probably identical with Symeon Metaphrastes. His chronicle, beginning with the Creation, ending in 948 and composed soon thereafter, is mostly a copy of earlier sources with few literary pretensions. Popular among both Byzantines and Slavs, it was freely interpolated, continued, plagiarized, and translated into Slavonic. Now that many of its sources are lost, it is the best narrative source for most of the period from 813 to 948. Unfortunately, thus far only plagiarizations and translations of the text have been edited. The published text ascribed to "Symeon Magister" is an interpolated version of Symeon's chronicle (with fabricated dates) which scholars now term the "Pseudo-Symeon."

BIBLIOGRAPHY

Sources. Leo Grammaticus, *Chronographia,* Immanuel Bekker, ed. (1842), Greek text with Latin translation, is a close plagiarization of Symeon's chronicle. Symeon Magister, *Chronographia,* Immanuel Bekker, ed. (1838), is the Pseudo-Symeon.

Studies. Herbert Hunger, *Die Hochsprachliche profane Literatur der Byzantiner,* I (1978), 349–351 and 354–357, provides a bibliography of the secondary literature. Gyula Moravcsik, "Sagen und Legenden über Kaiser Basileios I," in *Dumbarton Oaks Papers,* **15** (1961), contains a complete list of the manuscripts of the chronicle and a comprehensive edition of a sample of the text. Warren T. Treadgold, "The Chronological Accuracy of the *Chronicle* of Symeon the Logothete for the Years 813–845," in *Dumbarton Oaks Papers,* **33** (1979), is a study of the chronicle's sources and accuracy for the early ninth century.

Warren T. Treadgold

[See also **Byzantine Literature; George the Monk; Hagiography, Byzantine; Historiography, Byzantine; Logothete; Magistros; Slavic Literature.** See **Symeon Metaphrastes** for the view that the two were different men.]

SYNAGOGUE, the central institution of Judaism for the last 2,000 years. *Synagōgē* is a Greek word meaning assembly or gathering; its Hebrew equivalent is *bēt keneset.* The origins of the synagogue are not documented, but there are many theories as to its beginnings. Some scholars argue that the synagogue originated in the seventh century B.C. during the "Deuteronomic reformation" of King Josiah, when local shrines (*bamoth*) were destroyed and all worship was centered in Jerusalem. Since not all people could make the long journey to the central sanctuary at Jerusalem, it is assumed that substitute local places of worship, protosynagogues, arose. Other scholars believe in a third-century B.C. beginning of the synagogue in Helle-

Interior of a Gothic synagogue in Spain, showing Torah reading from the *bimah, ca.* 1350. BY PERMISSION OF THE BRITISH LIBRARY, LONDON, MS OR. 2884, fol. 17v

nistic Egypt because the literature of the period describes *proseuchai* (prayer houses), which are equated with synagogues. The most widely held theory is that the synagogue originated in the sixth century B.C. It is argued that the destruction of the holy temple in Jerusalem demanded a substitute place of worship in Babylonia, and the synagogue filled the void in exile. All hypotheses are based on arguments of silence—arguments with no archaeological or textual evidence, biblical or nonbiblical, to support them. The earliest written evidence of the existence of the synagogue is found in such first-century sources as the writings of the Jewish historian Flavius Josephus (37–95) and the New Testament.

It is most likely that the synagogue originated following the Hasmonean revolt in Judea (second century B.C.), which ushered in new Jewish classes and institutions. The Pharisees, a new democratic scholar class, came to power and radically restructured the existing Pentateuchal religion. They used the Hebrew Bible as a proof text to forge a novel twofold legal system known as the Written Law and the Oral Law. The goal of the earlier cultic religion had been to ensure the fertility of the land through animal sacrifices offered by priests at the temple in Jerusalem. The cultic religion was grounded in the Pentateuch and had flourished in Palestine for 1,000 years. By contrast, the goal of the new Pharisaic religion was to assure the individual of salvation after death and of bodily resurrection in the messianic age. It was believed that salvation and resurrection could be attained by each individual (without temple, sacrifices, or priests) through the observance of laws (*halakhoth*) systematically set down in the divinely revealed twofold law. The synagogue, one of the unique Pharisaic institutions, became an important meeting place where, through prayer and ceremonies, each individual Jew could affirm loyalty to the twofold Pharisaic law.

Although the synagogue was originally designated by its Greek name, *synagōgē,* it has been known as *bēt keneset* (Hebrew), *be kanishta* (Aramaic), *scola* (Latin), *scuòla* (Italian), *Schule* (German), and *Shul* (Yiddish). *Mikdash me*ᶜ*at* (small sanctuary) is another common term for synagogue. From the nineteenth century on, the synagogue was called a temple by Reform Jews.

The architecture of the synagogue closely followed contemporary non-Jewish structural and stylistic forms. In the Byzantine period, the classical basilica frequently served as a model for the synagogue. In Europe, Romanesque and Gothic buildings were adapted for synagogal use. These adaptations were, of course, modified to conform to the requirements of Jewish worship and the restraints imposed by the society in which the Jewish minority lived. While early synagogues, such as the third-century Dura Europos synagogue in Syria, had biblical scenes painted on their walls, and later Palestinian synagogues were decorated with figural mosaic floors, most medieval and later synagogues have sparse artistic decoration.

The most important object in the synagogue is the Pentateuchal scroll (Torah) handwritten on parchment. The Torah is likened to both a princess and a bride, and as such is regally adorned. Often it is clothed with embroidered textiles and silver objects. The silver adornments may be a crown (*atarah* or *keter*), finials (*rimmonim*), a case (*tik*), a pointer (*yad*), and a "breastplate" or shield (*tas*). The textiles are a Torah binder (*mappah*) and a mantle (*me*ᶜ*il*). Torah scrolls are housed in special arks (variously called *tevah, aron kodesh,* and *heikhal*). In the early period of the synagogue's existence, the Torah scrolls were kept in a portable ark, stored in an adjoining room and brought into the synagogue for services only. Gradually the ark became stationary. Generally it was positioned to face toward Jerusalem (in many cases east), for Jerusalem was to be the site of the ultimate messianic fulfillment, with the rebuilding of Solomon's temple and the resurrection of the dead. In front of many Torah arks there hangs an embroidered curtain (*parokhet*), often with a valance (*kapporet*). An eternal light (*ner tamid*) is suspended in front of and above the ark curtain. In many synagogues a nine-branched lampstand is found to the right of the ark. This lampstand (*menorah*) was intended for the celebration of the Hanukkah holiday, when the kindling of eight lights recalled the Hasmonean victory over the Syrians in 165 B.C. and the associated miracle of the lights that occurred when the temple was cleansed.

Next to the Torah ark the most important synagogue furnishing is the pulpit (called *bimah, tevah,* or *almemar*), from which the Torah is read. The Torah ark and the *bimah* varied in the degree of emphasis placed on each of them. In medieval Ashkenazi (German) synagogues the *almemar* predominated, often standing in the center of the synagogue. In Italian synagogues the Torah ark and the *bimah* were given equal prominence. From the nineteenth century on, the Torah ark has been the most significant feature of many synagogues.

The role of women in the synagogue is problematic. In the early and medieval synagogues there does not seem to have been a separate place where women had to sit. In the late Middle Ages a so-called *Weiber Schule* (an adjoining building for women) was added. Later separate galleries or balconies for women were introduced. Today, liberal synagogues seat men and women together. The reciting of prayers and the reading of the Torah are the most important elements of the synagogue.

BIBLIOGRAPHY

Joseph Gutmann, *The Dura-Europos Synagogue* (1973), *idem*, ed., *The Synagogue: Studies in Origins, Archaeology, and Architecture* (1975), *Ancient Synagogues: The State of Research* (1981), and *The Jewish Sanctuary* (1983); Rachel Wischnitzer, *The Architecture of the European Synagogue* (1964).

JOSEPH GUTMANN

[See also **Dura Europos; Jewish Art; Judaism; Liturgy, Jewish.**]

SYNAXARY (Synaxarion), a collection of short accounts of the saint or feast of the day appointed to be read in the Eastern churches in the course of matins (orthros). The synaxary may either take the form of an independent book (the "Great Synaxary") or be incorporated into the Menaion, the series of books containing propers for the liturgical year. The term comes to be used virtually interchangeably with "menologion" to designate a collection of longer saints' lives arranged according to the liturgical year but intended for private devotional reading. Even less appropriately, the term is also used to designate a simple listing of the calendar feasts along with references to their proper scriptural readings (the "Little Synaxary"). The synaxary in the proper sense of the word is found in a variety of forms in the Eastern rites, of which the Byzantine enjoys the widest diffusion.

Although earlier manuscripts with extensive hagiographic pictorial cycles for individual saints exist, the oldest illustrated synaxary is the so-called Menologion of Basil II (*r.* 976–1025), of which only the first volume—illustrating the months of September through February with 430 miniatures—remains (Vatican Library, MS gr. 1613, dated *ca.* 985). Here, as in the more frequently illustrated Metaphrastian Menologion (apparently developed from synaxaria in the second half of the tenth century), the life of each saint is introduced and/or followed by an illustration, usually a portrait, an image of martyrdom, or an essential episode from his or her life.

BIBLIOGRAPHY

G. Bayan, "Le synaxaire arménien der Ter Israël," in *Patrologia orientalis,* **5–6, 15–16, 18–19, 21** (1910–1926); Hans-Georg Beck, *Kirche und theologische Literatur im Byzantinischen Reich,* XII, 2.1 (1959), 251–252; H. Engberding, "Synaxarion," in *Lexikon für Theologie und Kirche,* **9** (1964); Sirarpie Der Nersessian, "The Illustrations of the Metaphrastian Menologium," in Kurt Weitzmann, ed., *Late Classical and Medieval Studies in Honor of Albert Mathias Friend, Jr.* (1955); Ivor Ševčenko, "The Illuminators of the Menologion of Basil II," in *Dumbarton Oaks Papers,* **16** (1962).

LESLIE BRUBAKER
JOHN H. ERICKSON

[See also **Armenian Saints; Byzantine Art: 843–1453; Byzantine Church; Liturgy, Byzantine Church; Menologion; Symeon Metaphrastes.**]

SYNDIC (Latin: *syndicus*), a legal agent of urban governments in cases before the emperor (Theodosian *Code,* 16.2.42; Justinian's *Digest,* 50.4.18.13).

In the mid thirteenth century, with the reception of Roman civil law and its terminology, the term was used to describe several distinct offices. In Italy a *sindaco* could be the legal agent of a commune, especially in international relations, though the term was also used of the *gonfaloniere.* In Spain and France a *syndicus* could be an assessor of a local court or a local overseer.

In Germanic central Europe the *syndicus* was the legal counsel of a commune before high courts or in diplomatic matters, as well as an adviser on internal matters. The *syndicus* was a distinct official in very large communes or those involved in chronic litigation, but in middling towns the office was often compounded with that of the municipal clerk (*Stadtschreiber*), who by the fifteenth century usually had some legal training. Into the fourteenth century, the *syndicus* was usually a cleric, but by the middle of the fifteenth century he was usually a layman with an academic degree. In the Netherlands from the fifteenth century on, the *syndicus* or *pensionaris* was the chief professional administrator answerable to a provincial estate assembly. In canon law, the *syndicus* was the legal agent of religious houses, collectivities, and even entire orders.

BIBLIOGRAPHY

Charles Du Fresne Du Cange, *Glossarium mediae et infimae latinitatis,* VII (1886), 690–691; Jacob and Wilhelm Grimm, *Deutsches Wörterbuch,* X.4 (1942), 1,421–1,423; Eugen Haberkern and Joseph Friedrich Wallach, eds., *Hilfswörterbuch für Historiker* (1964), 577, 607; Theodor Mommsen and Paul Krueger, eds., *The Digest of Justinian,* Alan Watson, trans., 4 vols. (1985); Clyde Pharr *et al.,* eds. and trans., *The Theodosian Code and Novels* (1952, repr. 1969); Walther von Wartburg, *Französisches etymologisches Wörterbuch,* XII (1966), 495–497.

STEVEN ROWAN

[See also **Codex Theodosianus; Corpus Iuris Civilis; Law** (various articles).]

SYNEKDEMOS. See **Hierokles.**

SYNKELLOS, title of a high official of the patriarchate of Constantinople. Ecclesiastics designated by the title *synkellos* (person sharing one's quarters, or confidant) appear in sources of the fourth century. Generally monastics with priestly or diaconal rank (for instance, an archdeacon, *synkellos* of Archbishop Cyril of Alexandria in the early fifth century), they played a leading role as advisers and administrative assistants of leading bishops and patriarchs.

By the seventh century in Constantinople the patriarchal *synkellos* could be simultaneously in charge of several administrative functions at the patriarchate and was often regarded as successor-designate to the patriarch. His importance grew to the point that protocol granted him precedence over a metropolitan. Eventually the appointment of the *synkellos* was reserved to the emperor, so that he became the sovereign's delegate at the patriarchate. He was frequently invested with diplomatic missions involving both the state and the church.

By the tenth century the title of *synkellos* began to be attributed to bishops. It was often granted to several ranking metropolitans simultaneously. They would then be members of both the patriarchal synod and the senate. The inflation of titles, characteristic of the late Byzantine period, led to the appearance of *protosynkelloi,* who were headed by a "great *protosynkellos*" (*megas protosynkellos*). It appears that during the Palaiologan period (1261–1453) the title became purely honorific, and was bestowed upon bishops and other ecclesiastics without involving concrete administrative duties.

BIBLIOGRAPHY

Hans-Georg Beck, *Kirche und theologische Literatur im byzantinische Reich* (1959), esp. 68–69, 102–103, 118–119; V. Grumel, "Titulaire de métropolites byzantins, I: Les métropolites syncelles," in *Revue des études byzantines,* 3 (1945).

JOHN MEYENDORFF

[See also **Clergy, Byzantine; Metropolitan; Patriarch.**]

SYNODIKON OF ORTHODOXY, solemn proclamation drawn up in 843 to mark the "triumph of orthodoxy" over the iconoclastic heresy and read annually since then in the Orthodox church on the first Sunday of Lent. It was revised several times in the course of the Middle Ages, chiefly to laud more recent patriarchs of blessed memory and to anathematize new heretics and their teachings. The most important of these revisions were made in the Komnenan period (eleventh century), when the Neoplatonism of John Italos (*ca.* 1025–after 1082) and a number of christological errors were condemned, and in the fourteenth century, when the theology of Gregory Palamas (1296–1359) concerning the divine "energies" was given formal approbation.

BIBLIOGRAPHY

Jean Gouillard, "Le synodikon de l'Orthodoxie: Edition et commentaire," Centre de Recherches d'Histoire et Civilisation Byzantines, *Travaux et mémoires,* **2** (1967).

JOHN H. ERICKSON

[See also **Christology; Councils, Byzantine; Gregory Palamas; Heresies, Byzantine; Iconoclasm, Christian; John Italos; Neoplatonism; Philosophy and Theology, Byzantine; Plato in the Middle Ages.**]

SYNTHRONON. In the Early Christian and Byzantine church, the synthronon was a bench or series of benches for use by the clergy, normally set within the curvature of the apse. Frequently in the eastern Mediterranean the benches were stepped in arrangement, resembling the cavea of a Roman theater, with a special, central throne for the bishop. Benches could also be provided in straight rows on either side of the bema.

BIBLIOGRAPHY

Richard Krautheimer, *Early Christian and Byzantine Architecture* (1975).

ROBERT OUSTERHOUT

[See also **Architecture, Liturgical Aspects (with illustration); Early Christian and Byzantine Architecture.**]

SYRIA. Medieval Syria included the territories of the modern states of Syria, Lebanon, Israel, and Jordan, and a small part of modern Turkey. Of ancient settlement, the area was the birthplace of Christianity, the center of the Umayyad dynasty in Damascus, and the primary locus of the conflict between Christians and Muslims that is known as the crusades.

At the end of the classical period, Syria remained one of the plums of the Roman Empire. The general demographic and economic decline of the empire was less severe in Syria than elsewhere. For example, Syria still possessed a dense network of cities, the number of which increased from 145 to 197 during the sixth century A.D. Similarly, east of Antioch new olive groves came into being in the fifth and sixth centuries. Syrians were the leading merchants trading wine, olive oil, silk, glass, and Indian spices with the western Mediterranean region. Syria (including Upper Mesopotamia) at the end of the sixth century had some 7 million inhabitants, about as many as Egypt or Asia Minor each—a figure that remained unsurpassed during the Middle Ages.

The large majority of the inhabitants of Syria were Jacobite Christians speaking a variety of Semitic dialects or languages (Aramaic, Arabic). As Monophysites (believing in a single, human-divine nature of Christ) they watched with growing disaffection Byzantine concessions made to the Dyophysite popes in Rome (who believed in Christ's double nature) during the sixth and early seventh centuries in order to secure the possession of the western exarchates, Ravenna and Sicily. No Christian unity existed in Syria.

Religious disunity was followed by political instability. During the tumultuous reign of the Byzantine usurper Phokas (602–610), the Persians invaded Syria. Heraklios (610–641) succeeded in driving the Persians out again, but destruction was considerable, particularly in Jerusalem and Palestine. The emperor was still in Syria supervising Byzantine reconstruction efforts when in 629 the first Muslim Arab expeditionary corps of about 3,000 troops appeared near the Dead Sea. Under orders from the prophet Muḥammad in Medina, the Muslims sought an alliance with local Jacobite Arab *foederati* tribes, on whom the Byzantine defense of the desert border rested. But these tribes preferred Byzantine subsidies over uncertain promises from the Muslim upstarts and repelled them.

Four years later, in 633, the Muslims reappeared. After Muḥammad had rallied Mecca, a search for allies in the north became unnecessary and a policy of unification with the Arab tribes in Syria was adopted. In several encounters between 634 and 638 the Muslim Arabs defeated the Christian Arab and Greek armies. A counteroffensive by Heraklios with Arab and Egyptian recruits collapsed in 639. The Aramaic-speaking Jacobites watched the collapse without coming to the rescue

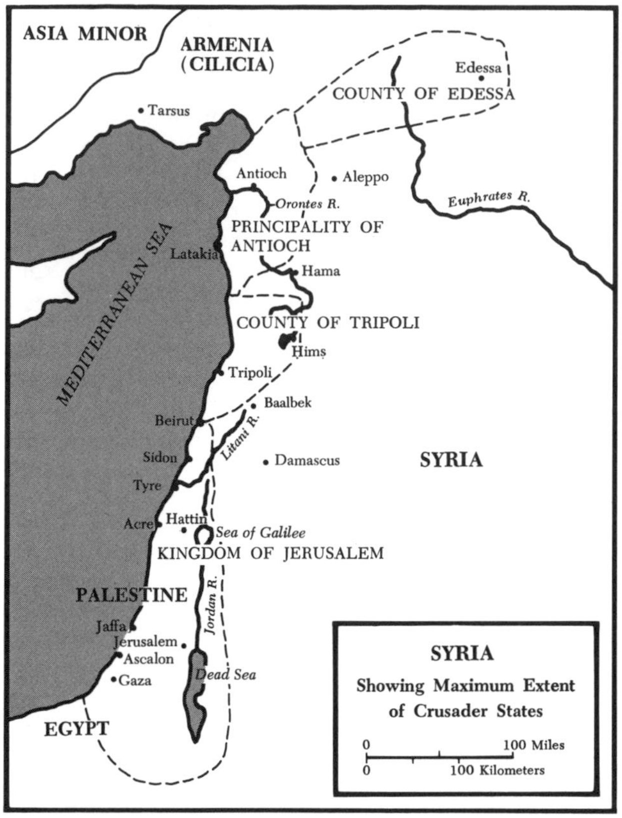

SYRIA
Showing Maximum Extent
of Crusader States

of their orthodox emperor, and almost all of Syria came under Muslim rule.

During the Muslim Arab conquest the second caliph, ᶜUmar ibn al-Khaṭṭāb, visited Syria personally (638), in a move that might have had millennial overtones: Jerusalem was the holy center of the world, and he entered it with the claim of being the Redeemer (*al-fārūq*).

Contrary to ᶜUmar's wishes, the governor of Syria, Muᶜāwiya ibn Abī Sufyān (who later became caliph), did not garrison his troops in encampments separate from the indigenous population, as was done in Iraq and Egypt. Instead, he distributed them among the four (after 680, five) military districts (*junds*) into which Syria was divided. There, both the 30,000 Muslim Arab immigrants and the much larger mass of Christian Arab Syrians either received, or had confirmed, possession of the pastures, orchards, and fields of the interior, in return for constant military preparedness against the Byzantines along the new frontier on the upper Euphrates. The Christian Arabs, former Byzantine *foederati,* quickly converted to Islam and merged with the immigrants to form an Arab ruling class which was considerably larger than that of Iraq or Egypt.

Under the caliphal dynasty of the Umayyads (661–750), Syria, or *al-Shaᵓm* (the north) in Arabic nomenclature, became the center of a vast empire which at its zenith in 711 stretched as far west as Spain and as far east as India, and traded with China. Taxes collected from the Christians in Syria and one-fifth of all booty acquired on the frontiers flowed into the capital at Damascus, providing the caliphs with a princely income. In addition, the caliphs were extraordinary agricultural entrepreneurs, building castles in the steppes, complete with irrigated orchards, vineyards, and fields. Christian craftsmen adorned these castles with mosaics, frescoes, and statues in the Byzantine style. The cosmopolitan court was little disturbed by the censure of representative art that religious scholars began to proclaim in the early 700's as the foundations of Islamic law and theology were being laid.

The most important caliph of the Umayyad dynasty was ᶜAbd al-Malik (685–705), who built the mosaic-covered Dome of the Rock in Jerusalem and created an efficient central administration in Damascus. He enlarged the earlier office of the "seal" into a chancery, Arabic became the official language of correspondence, and an imperial gold and silver currency was minted. However, since the Umayyads wavered between the policies of Arab supremacy and Islamic universalism, the results of centralization remained modest. In Syria, with its considerable indigenous Arab population, the first policy was reasonable, whereas in the provinces the vastly outnumbered Arabs had no choice but to seek collaborators from among the non-Arabs, who could be rallied only through a policy of universalism. During the Abbasid revolution, whose supporters in Iran espoused the cause of universalism, the Umayyads were overthrown (750).

Syria was now relegated to the periphery of a new empire centered further east, in Baghdad. It functioned as an appanage for Abbasid family members until Caliph al-Muᶜtaṣim (833–842) decided to phase out unruly Arabs from the standing army and replace them with more pliable Turkish cavalry forces. The horsemen were recruited as young slaves (*ghilmān*) in Central Asia, and after military training and conversion to Islam they entered regular army service as freedmen. Turkish generals in Baghdad dispatched junior officers with troop support to serve as governors in Syria, with the obligation to forward the tax surplus or pay tribute to Baghdad. Arabs in the Syrian *jund*s (or *ajnād*) were pruned from the military payroll and dropped from the ruling class.

These expensive Turks—each Turk had to be purchased, trained, salaried, and equipped with bow, arrow, lance, saber, mail, and horse—were not numerous and therefore had to concede a certain degree of autonomy to the urban population, particularly in the largest cities, Damascus and Aleppo. Politically ambitious associations of young men (*aḥdāth*) arose in these cities. One source mentions them for the first time in 895–896, when the Tulunid emir Jaysh contemplated a replacement of his unruly Turkish cavalry with Damascene *aḥdāth* infantry. For the next seventy-five years *aḥdāth* provided troops used by urban notable leaders (*ruʾasāʾ*) from commercial and landowning families, often of Umayyad descent, to defend the cities against the Turks.

A similar condominium prevailed after North African Berbers replaced the Turks in the garrisons in 969. They served under the Shiite caliphate of the Fatimids in Cairo, which disputed Sunni Abbasid leadership for about 250 years, on grounds (among others) of a more direct relationship to the Prophet Muḥammad, by way of his daughter Fāṭima. Although eliminated from the ruling class, urban Arabs in Syria preserved a degree of self-determination under both the Turkish and the Berber governors.

The Turks returned to Syria in 1057, this time as free tribal immigrants, championing Sunni Islam in the name of the Abbasids and driving the Fatimids from northern Syria. These Turks, under the leadership of the Seljuk dynasty of sultans, were more numerous than their *ghilmān* predecessors and therefore succeeded in reducing and eventually suppressing Syrian urban autonomy. They established a large sultanate that stretched from Iran and Iraq to Syria and Asia Minor but broke apart into smaller realms in 1092, seven fateful years too short to prevent one of the most extraordinary movements of the Middle Ages—the First Crusade of Western Christianity—from reaching its goal, the liberation of the church of the Holy Sepulcher from Muslim "infidel desecration." As a result, in Syria the Seljuk successor states were thrown back to the interior, while the crusaders established their kingdom along the coast.

The preaching of the First Crusade by Pope Urban II (1088–1099) had succeeded in mobilizing the astounding number of some 60,000 European peasants and knights, many with their families. Under the leadership of a half-dozen prominent French, English, German, and Sicilian knights, most marched the entire distance on foot, enduring hunger, disease, winter, battle, and siege. A majority died or melted away, but the remnant of about 15,000 was enough to storm Fatimid-held Jerusalem during the night of 14–15 July 1099. After large-scale massacres of Muslims and Jews, many crusaders settled down. Their numbers increased by the mid twelfth century to about 250,000 immigrants.

The crusader kings of Jerusalem parceled out some 700 villages—almost as many as under the Byzantines—in the form of assignments (*iqṭāʿāt*) to about 600 landed knights who represented the military backbone of the realm. The *iqṭāʿ* was the prevalent form of landholding in the Middle East during the High Middle Ages; it was essentially a tax district without demesne or boon services. The peasants were still largely Christian, although increasingly they became members of the Maronite church. (This church arose in the mid eighth century, espousing a compromise between Monophysitism and Dyophysitism; it recognized the jurisdiction of the pope in 1181.) Cereal farming was about twice as productive as in Europe, and the villages excelled in growing sugarcane and fruits or vegetables (cherries, peaches, artichokes, asparagus) novel to the Europeans. Commerce flourished, and the value of the manufactured goods and spices traded (such as silk, glass, pepper, cinnamon, and cloves) exceeded that of the merchandise exchanged in Muslim Alexandria. The Western Christian immigrants profited handsomely from agricultural and commercial opportunities.

In the long term, however, the Kingdom of Jerusalem had no chance of survival. Once the Muslims had recovered from the shock of the initial massacres, their numerical superiority proved overwhelming. Under the banner of a Muslim version of the crusades, also directed toward the liberation of Jerusalem from the "infidel," Turkish cavalry and Arab infantry retook the Holy City on 2 October 1187. Emir Saladin (Ṣalāḥ al-Dīn, 1174–1193), the inspiring, Kurdish-descended leader of the Muslims and founder of the Ayyubid dynasty (1174–1250), nevertheless made one crucial mistake: had he taken the strategically more important but less glamorous port city of Tyre first, it is probable that Jerusalem would have fallen just as easily as it did but the crusaders would not have hung on along the coast for another century.

Saladin's descendants never regained the initiative. It was only through the more unified Mamluk sultanate, centered in Egypt, that the crusaders eventually lost their kingdom. Unlike the Seljuks, the Mamluks held on to the older freedman tradition discussed above and replenished their ranks through the purchase of Turkish slaves. The Mamluks could assemble as many as 12,000 cavalry, ten times what the crusaders were able to recruit from the ranks of the lords and the military orders. They settled tens of thousands of Turkish, Kurdish, and Mongolian auxiliaries in the steppes of Syria's interior and embarked on a systematic destruction of crusader castles, ports, and villages, so as to deprive the enemy of strategic facilities. To the sound of trumpets, cymbals, and drums Sultan al-Ashraf (1290–1293) stormed Acre on 18 May 1291. The remaining crusader stronghold surrendered by 14 August and only the island of Ruwad held out until 1303.

The destruction wrought on the province during the later crusades was profound and substantially reduced the agricultural base. Scores of villages disappeared in Palestine. Cities were somewhat better off since they now participated in an international spice trade channeled exclusively through Mamluk territories. Nevertheless, the overall population shrank and remained relatively reduced throughout the period of the Black Death (1347–1349) and its twelve aftercycles, lasting until about 1500.

While the Mamluks were searching for a successful policy of recovery from economic decline, the Ottomans in Asia Minor expanded. Their empire dated from the period immediately after the Black Death, and their more innovative sultans, less dependent than their Egyptian colleagues on cavalry, had prudently equipped themselves early on with the newly developed firearms. When the Ottomans invaded Syria in 1516 their army defeated the Mamluks; the next year the Ottomans were in Egypt, and the Mamluk dynasty was no more.

During the Middle Ages, Syria was the crown jewel of the first Arab empire and the spearhead of an expanding Europe. But it was, in addition, sacred land for Jewish, Christian, and Muslim pilgrims, all of whom yearned to see their Holy City—Jerusalem.

BIBLIOGRAPHY

Fred M. Donner, *The Early Islamic Conquests* (1981); Andrew S. Ehrenkreutz, *Saladin* (1972); Nikita Elisséeff, *Nūr ad-Dīn: Un grand prince musulman de Syrie au temps des Croisades,* 3 vols. (1967); Claus-Peter Haase, "Untersuchungen zur Landschaftsgeschichte Nordsyriens in der Umayyadenzeit" (diss., Kiel, 1975); Axel Havemann, *Riʾāsa und qaḍāʾ: Institutionen als Ausdruck wechselnder Kräfteverhältnisse in syrischen Städten vom 10. bis zum 12. Jahrhundert* (1975); Peter M. Holt, *The Age of the Crusades: The Near East from the Eleventh Century to 1517* (1986); R. Stephen Humphreys, *From Saladin to the Mongols: The Ayyubids of Damascus, 1193–1260* (1977); Robert Irwin, *The Middle East in the Middle Ages: The Early Mamluk Sultanate, 1250–1382* (1986); Ira M. Lapidus, *Muslim Cities in the Later Middle Ages* (1967, new ed. 1984); Huda Lutfi, *Al-Quds al-Mamlūkiyya: A History of Mamlūk Jerusalem Based on the Ḥaram Documents* (1985); ᶜAbd al-Munᶜim Mājid, *Ẓuhūr khilāfat al-Fāṭimīyīn wa-suqūṭuhā fī Miṣr* (1968); Matti Moosa, *The Maronites in History* (1986); Joshua Prawer, *The Crusaders' Kingdom: European Colonialism in the Middle Ages* (1972); Kamal S. Salibi, *Syria Under Islam: Empire on Trial, 634–1097* (1977); Muhsin D. Yusuf, *Economic Survey of Syria During the Tenth and Eleventh Centuries* (1985); Suhayl Zakkār, *The Emirate of Aleppo, 1004–1094* (1971).

PETER VON SIVERS

[See also **Abbasids; Aleppo; Antioch; Ayyubids; Byzantine Empire: History; Caliphate; Crusades and Crusader States; Damascus; Dome of the Rock; Fatimids; Heraklios; Islam, Conquests of; Jerusalem; Lebanon; Mamluk Dynasty; Maronite Church; Marwān, ᶜAbd al-Malik ibn; Monophysitism; Muᶜtaṣim, al-; Muᶜāwiya; Ottomans; Palestine; Phokas; Roman Empire, Late; Saladin; Sasanian History; Seljuks; Tulunids; ᶜUmar I ibn al-Khaṭṭāb; Umayyads.**]

SYRIAN CHRISTIANITY refers to those oriental churches whose liturgical language is Syriac; "Syrian" does not imply any necessary connection with Syria, either as a geographical or as a political entity. By about the third century Syriac had become the main literary language of non-Greek-speaking Christians in the eastern provinces of the Roman Empire and in the Sasanian Empire further east. Beginning as the local Aramaic dialect of Edessa (whose king, Abgar V the Black, had, according to a legend already known to Eusebius, corresponded with Jesus), Syriac rapidly spread eastward via missionaries, and by 635 had reached west China (recorded in a Chinese-Syriac bilingual inscription dated 781). Classical Syriac survives to the present day as a liturgical language, and modern dialects are still spoken in parts of southeast Turkey, Syria, Iraq, and western Iran.

THE FOUR SYRIAC CHURCHES

The fifth-century christological controversies divided Syrian Christianity into four ecclesiastical bodies: the church of the East (so-called Nestorians); the Syrian Orthodox church (so-called Monophysites, or Jacobites, after Jacob Baradaios, *d.* 578); the Melchite church (from Syriac *malkā,* emperor, since they followed the imperial position on Christology defined at the Council of Chalcedon in 451); and the Maronite church (after the monastery of St. Maron, in southern Syria).

Church of the East. The church of the East rejected the Council of Ephesus (431), and, ever since a series of synods held between 484 and 497, it followed the Antiochene tradition of Christology, as exemplified above all by Theodore of Mopsuestia (*d.* 428), many of whose works survive only in Syriac translation (Nestorius features in East Syrian synods first in the seventh century). The chief theologian of this church was Babai the Great (*d.* 628).

Prior to the Arab invasions, adherents of the church of the East were nearly all found within the Sasanian Empire, where, by about 600, Christians formed a sizable minority of the population. The seat of their patriarch, or katholikos, was at Seleucia-Ctesiphon, the winter residence of the Sasanids. During the fourth and fifth centuries, hostilities with the Roman Empire had at times resulted in persecution, most extensively under Šābuhr II in the 340's; by the sixth century, however, aristocratic converts from Zoroastrianism were most likely to suffer martyrdom.

After the collapse of Sasanian rule before the Arab invaders in the 640's the relationship between the church of the East and the new state remained largely unchanged (indeed the roots of the Ottoman *millet* system stretch back to the late Sasanian period). As "people of the book," the Christian population had dhimmi status, which involved certain rights subject to the payment of the jizya, or poll tax. Although medieval sources, both Muslim and Christian, speak of the "Covenant of ᶜUmar" (ᶜUmar ibn al-Khaṭṭāb, 634–644) as setting out the relationship between the Muslim rulers and their subject Christian minorities, it is clear that these arrangements evolved only gradually over the course of a century or more. Conversions to Islam on a large scale took place only in areas such as Qatar and Oman and were due to economic rather than religious pressures. Many Christians continued to hold high administrative office, though in due course this increasingly gave rise to outbreaks of Muslim resentment.

The ninth century, with its intellectual ferment centered on the "House of Wisdom" at the Abbasid capital, Baghdad, witnessed remarkable cooperation among Muslim, Jewish, and Christian scholars. The letters of the patriarch Timothy I (*d.* 823) indicate the existence then of nineteen metropolitan sees, considerably more than are attested in seventh-century sources; most of the new sees were in Central Asia and India, and this represents the apogee of the church of the East's missionary expansion eastward.

In the thirteenth century the Mongol conquerors at first favored the Christian populace over the Muslims, and Hulagu, who effected the final collapse of the Abbasid caliphate in the sack of Baghdad (1258), had a Christian wife, while Argun (1284–1291) employed an East Syrian monk from Peking as his emissary to the Christian powers of Europe (Rabban Ṣauma's account of his journey survives). Shortly after Argun's death the Mongols turned against Christianity and officially adopted Islam. The fourteenth century, culminating in the ravages of Tamerlane, was a period of rapid decline.

Syrian Orthodox church. The Syrian Orthodox church rejected the doctrinal formulation of the Council of Chalcedon stating that the incarnate Christ is one "in two natures" (the draft, which had "out of two natures," would have been acceptable). Their theological position, based on Cyril of Alexandria's, was elaborated above all by Severus, patriarch of Antioch (deposed 518, *d.* 538), who wrote in Greek, and by Philoxenus of Mabbug (*d.* 523), and was the same as that of the Armenian, Coptic, and Ethiopian Orthodox churches. The Syrian Orthodox were mainly to be found in what is now southeast Turkey, Syria, and (from the late sixth century onward) Iraq. Their patriarch had the title "of Antioch," but after 518 his seat was not fixed. Second to the patriarch was the "maphrian of the East," whose seat was at Tagrit (Takrit/Tikrit) on the Tigris from 629 to 1156 (and subsequently variable).

Since the Syrian Orthodox had been harshly treated by Heraklios, the change from Byzantine to Arab rule was seen as a change from one unsympathetic ruler to another. It was not until the late eighth century that Syriac sources mention any mass conversions to Islam in Syria or northern Mesopotamia. In the ninth century Syrian Orthodox scholars contributed to the intellectual activity of the time, writing in both Syriac and Arabic. The late tenth century, with the Byzantine reconquest of northern Syria, brought renewed contact with the Byzantine world, and in the ensuing centuries this was strengthened thanks to the removal of the patriarchal seat to a monastery near Melitene (Malatya).

The crusades proved perhaps more disastrous for the Syrian Orthodox church than for any other oriental Christian community. Regarded as heretics by the Latins and as collaborators by the local Muslim populace, the Syrian Orthodox never saw their initial hopes fulfilled, and in the long run Christian support first for the crusaders and then for the Mongol invaders constituted one of the main causes for the almost total eclipse of Christianity in the Middle East over the course of the fourteenth and fifteenth centuries.

Melchite and Maronite churches. The Melchites and Maronites formed the Christian population of Syria that adhered to the Council of Chalcedon. Their emergence, in the course of the seventh and eighth centuries, as two separate ecclesiastical bodies, each with its own patriarch of Antioch, is shrouded in obscurity, though connected with the repercussions of the Monothelite controversy. For the Melchites Syriac was but one of four different liturgical languages in use, the others being Greek, Christian Palestinian Aramaic, and (from the eighth/ninth century) Arabic. Syriac survived vestigially until the late Middle Ages, when it was replaced entirely by Arabic. The Maronite church, on the other hand, has retained Syriac as a liturgical language to modern times. As a literary language, however, Arabic replaced Syriac from about the ninth century in both communities; thus they play a very minor role in the history of Syriac literature.

The crusades brought the Maronites more than the other oriental Christian communities into contact with Europe. They offered considerable help to the crusaders and their allegiance to the See of Rome dates, according to William of Tyre, from 1182. Their patriarch Jeremiah attended the Lateran Council (1215) in person (the Maronites of Cyprus, however, submitted to Rome only in 1445).

SCHOOLS AND MONASTERIES

In the fifth century a number of theological schools are known to have existed in Edessa, most famous of which was the "School of the Persians," closed in 489 at the orders of Zeno as a hotbed of Nestorianism. Most of the teaching staff crossed into the Persian empire and reestablished the school in Nisibis. The School of Nisibis, whose statutes of 496 survive, served as the main channel by which the Antiochene Christology of Theodore of Mopsuestia reached the Persian church. By the mid sixth century the school's reputation was known to Cassiodorus (by way of Junilius Africanus, whose *Instituta regularia divinae legis* had in part been inspired by Paul of Nisibis).

The church of the East had several other schools in Sasanian Persia, some of which continued into the Arab period; that at Gundisapur, in particular, was famed for its medical tradition.

In the third and fourth centuries northern Mesopotamia had developed distinctive forms of ascetic life, which could be described as "protomonastic." But from the late fourth century onward this indigenous tradition was incorporated into the Egyptian model, and such was the prestige of Egyptian monasticism that later Syriac legend attributed the introduction of monasticism into northern Mesopotamia to an Egyptian, Mar (St.) Awgen/Augen (Eugenios) of Clysma and his disciples (reputedly in the fourth century).

Throughout the history of the Syriac churches, monasteries have served as one of the main transmitters of Syriac culture. The names of several hundred of these are known from the sixth century, and some of them became famous centers of learning.

The early sixth century witnessed a monastic revival, led by Abraham of Kashkar, in the church of the East. From the monastery he founded on Mt. Izla (northeast of Nisibis) many further monastic foundations were made in the late sixth and the seventh centuries, mostly in northern Iraq. These are described in two ninth-century works, Ishoᶜdnaḥ's *Book of Chastity* and Thomas of Margā's *Book of Superiors (Governors)*. Best known of these monasteries was Beth ᶜAbe, renowned for its liturgical and musical traditions. Another monastery particularly influential in liturgical matters was the "upper monastery" in Mosul, which flourished in the ninth and tenth centuries. During the ninth century the monks of Dair Qunni (about ninety kilometers [sixty miles] southeast of Baghdad) played a significant role in creating the atmosphere of cooperation between Christian and Muslim scholars, characteristic of that century. Many of these monasteries survived until the Mongol invasions; a few even remain to the present day.

During the sixth and seventh centuries monks of certain Syrian Orthodox monasteries gained a reputation for their work of translations from Greek (notably those of Mar Zakkai, near Kallinikos, and Qenneshre, both on the Euphrates). In the early seventh century the monastery of the Ennaton (ninth milestone), outside Alexandria, saw the production of two monuments of biblical scholarship, the Syro-Hexapla (Paul of Tella's translation of Origen's revised Septuagint text) and the Harklean New Testament, translated by Thomas of Harkel; both are meticulous renderings of the Greek. In northern Iraq the most important scriptorium, from the eighth century onward, was the monastery of Mar Mattai, perched on mountains southeast of Mosul.

Throughout late antiquity and the Middle Ages a region where monasticism always flourished was the mountainous area north of Nisibis, known as Ṭūr ᶜAbdīn (a few of these monasteries still function today). From the tenth to the thirteenth century the monastery of Barsaumas, near Melitene, served as an important center of Syriac culture and for part of the time was the residence of the patriarch.

Of utmost importance for its preservation of a large number of old Syriac manuscripts (now the basis of the Vatican and British Library Syriac collections) was the Syrian monastery in Wadi'n Natrun, between Cairo and Alexandria. Many of these had been collected by a remarkable abbot, Moses of Nisibis, in the early tenth century.

Two Melchite and Maronite monastic centers may be singled out. In the tenth to eleventh centuries Melchite monasteries in the region of Antioch undertook many translations into Syriac of Greek liturgical texts when their rite was byzantinized. Perhaps in the ninth century the Maronite center of gravity shifted from southern Syria to what is today Lebanon, and there the "Holy Valley" (southeast of Tripoli) became the home of several monasteries, including the Qannūbīn (*kenobion*), from 1440 the patriarchal residence.

SYRIAC LITERATURE

Syrian Christianity gave birth to an extensive literature in Syriac, but to no other distinctive artistic tradition (architecture and illumination, for example, generally follow the local idiom).

The golden age of Syriac literature lasted until the seventh century. The earliest major writers, Aphrahat and Ephraem (both fourth century) exhibited a largely unhellenized form of Christianity, while all subsequent writers increasingly came under the influence of Greek thought and rhetoric. Ephraem's outstanding poetry may have contributed to the emergence of early Byzantine hymnography, and he was well known to Greek and Latin writers in translation (though many of the texts attributed to him in Greek, Slavonic, and Latin are not genuine). Subsequent to the fifth-century schisms the main literary figures among the Syrian Orthodox were Philoxenus (whose writings present a remarkable synthesis of native Syriac and Greek theological traditions) and the poet Jacob of Serugh (*d.* 521), author of a large corpus of verse homilies, mainly on biblical topics. In the church of the East, Narsai (*d. ca.* 502), head of the School of Nisibis, another poet-exegete, and the theological writers Cyrus of Edessa (sixth century) and Babai (*d.* 628) were prominent.

From the seventh to the thirteenth century creative writing gave way to encyclopedic learning. The main Syrian Orthodox writers, almost all polymaths, were Severus Sebokht (*d.* 666/667), author of a work on the astrolabe; Jacob of Edessa (*d.* 708); George (*d.* 724), bishop of the Arab tribes; Moshe bar Kēphā (*d.* 903); Dionysius bar Ṣalibi (*d.* 1171); Jacob bar Shakkō (*d.* 1241); and Bar Hebraeus (*d.* 1286), one of the most learned men of his time. The twelfth century witnessed something of a literary renaissance.

In the church of the East the most important writings of the seventh to eighth centuries are on the monastic life, while the ninth century was a period of great literary activity during which Syriac scholars (of all the churches) played an important role in the transmission of Greek learning to the Arab world. From this time come several massive biblical commentaries, such as that by Īshō ᶜdād of Merv. This exegetical tradition was subsequently transmitted to the Christian Arab world by Ibn aṭ-Ṭaiyib (*d.* 1043). Later East Syrian writers include Elias bar Shināyā of Nisibis (*d.* 1046) and ᶜAbdishoᶜ bar Berīkha (*d.* 1318), author of a famous catalog of Syriac writers.

The third period, from the fourteenth century onward, was one of decline for all the Syriac churches, and the literature of this period is of minor importance.

SYRIAN CHRISTIANITY

Historical writing. Several important Syriac chronicles survive, culminating in three vast world histories produced in the twelfth to thirteenth centuries by Syrian Orthodox writers: the patriarch Michael (*d.* 1199), an anonymous writer of the "chronicle to the year 1234," and Bar Hebraeus. All three are of considerable value, especially for the crusader period. The main earlier chronicles to survive are by John of Ephesus and Pseudo-Zacharias Rhetor of Mytilene (both sixth century), Pseudo-Dionysius of Tel-Mahré (eighth century), and Elias bar Shināyā of Nisibis (mainly tables). Several shorter chronicles contain useful materials for sixth- to ninth-century history.

Monastic literature. This includes local monastic histories, lives of notable abbots, monastic rules, and treatises on the spiritual life. On this last subject Syriac writers produced some works of enduring interest. Important authors include John of Apamea, or "the Solitary," (early fifth century); Philoxenus; Stephen bar Ṣūdhaili (early sixth century), probable author of *The Book of the Holy Hierotheos,* a remarkable work of pantheist character; Martyrius, or Sāhdōna, and Isaac of Nineveh (both seventh century); Joseph the Seer and John Saba or the Elder (both eighth century).

Four main strands within Syriac spirituality can be discerned: (1) the native tradition of Ephraem, the fourth-century *Book of Steps* and John the Solitary; (2) the Pseudo-Macarian homilies; (3) the works of Evagrius; and (4) the Pseudo-Dionysian corpus. (The Macarian homilies and writings of Evagrius were translated into Syriac in the fifth century, the Pseudo-Dionysian corpus translated in the early sixth and revised in the late seventh.) All writers from the sixth century onward exhibit varying admixtures of all four traditions.

Translation activity. Between the fourth and ninth centuries a vast number of Greek texts, mainly religious, were translated into Syriac, and by the early seventh century highly sophisticated techniques of "mirror" translation had been developed. Among these translations are several works whose Greek original has been lost (for example, by Theodore of Mopsuestia, Evagrius, and Severus, who had all fallen out of favor with the Greek ecclesiastical authorities).

Of particular importance was the intermediary role of Syriac translators in the transmission of Greek learning to the Arab world, especially in the fields of philosophy and medicine, thus giving them a place in the chain that linked one strand of medieval Western Aristotelianism with its Greek origins. In philosophy, Syriac scholars focused their attention on Aristotle's logical works (the *Organon*), and here the main translators/commentators were Probus of Antioch (probably early sixth century, though often dated to the fifth); Sergius of Reshaina (*d.* 536), who also translated the Pseudo-Dionysian corpus and Pseudo-Aristotle's *De mundo*; Athanasius II (683/684–687), Syrian Orthodox patriarch; Jacob of Edessa; and George, bishop of the Arab tribes. In the flurry of translation activity in ninth-century Baghdad the most famous figure was Ḥunayn ibn Isḥāq al-ᶜIbādī. Ḥunayn's procedure was often to translate from Greek into Syriac (since a long tradition of technical translation was available) and then into Arabic. Commentaries on the *Organon* continued to be written later, but after the ninth century Muslim Aristotelian scholarship parted company with its Christian roots.

The other area of Greek philosophy that attracted Syriac translators was that of popular ethics (including some works whose Greek original is lost). Among medical writings translated into Syriac, works by Galen were paramount.

In the sixth and seventh centuries translations were also made into Syriac from Middle Persian. These include Pseudo-Callisthenes' Alexander romance and the Indian tales known as *Kalīla wa-Dimna.*

Translations from Syriac into Greek were comparatively rare. Most significant in this category are various works by Ephraem; some hagiography (notably the oldest form of the legend of Alexis); some monastic writings (notably those of Isaac of Nineveh, made in Palestine in the ninth century); and the Apocalypse of Pseudo-Methodios, whose Syriac original perhaps dates to about 692. From the various Greek versions derive the many Slavonic and Latin reworkings.

BIBLIOGRAPHY

General. Julius Assfalg and Paul Krüger, *Kleines Wörterbuch des christlichen Orients* (1975); Sebastian P. Brock, "An Introduction to Syriac Studies," in J. H. Eaton, ed., *Horizons in Semitic Studies* (1980).

Literature. Anton Baumstark, *Geschichte der syrischen Literatur* (1922); Rubens Duval, *La littérature syriaque,* 3rd ed. (1907); Rudolph Macuch, *Geschichte der spät und neusyrischen Literatur* (1976); Ignacio Ortiz de Urbina, *Patrologia syriaca,* 2nd ed. (1965); William Wright, *A Short History of Syriac Literature* (1894).

Sources. Albert Abouna, trans., and Jean M. Fiey,

intro., *Anonymi auctoris chronicon ad annum Christi 1234 pertinens,* II (1974); Ernest A. W. Budge, trans., *The Book of the Governors by Thomas of Marga* (1893), *The Discourses of Philoxenus* (1894), *The Monks of Kûblâi Khân* (1928), and *The Chronography of Gregory Abu'l Faraj (Bar Hebraeus)* (1932); Jean-Baptiste Chabot, trans., *Chronique de Denys de Tell-Mahré, IVe partie* (1895), and *Chronique de Michel le Syrien* (1899–1924, repr. 1963); Frederick J. Hamilton and Ernest W. Brooks, trans., *The Syriac Chronicle Known as That of Zachariah of Mitylene* (1899); Frederick S. Marsh, ed. and trans., *The Book of the Holy Hierotheos* (1927); Alphonse Mingana, ed. and trans., *Early Christian Mystics* (1934); James A. Montgomery, trans., *The History of Yaballaha III, Nestorian Patriarch, and of His Vicar, Bar Sauma* (1927); Robert Payne Smith, trans., *The Third Part of the Ecclesiastical History of John, Bishop of Ephesus* (1860); Arent J. Wensinck, *Mystic Treatises by Isaac of Nineveh* (1923).

Studies. Aziz S. Atiya, *A History of Eastern Christianity,* 2nd ed. (1980); Sebastian P. Brock, *Syriac Perspectives on Late Antiquity* (1984), chaps. 5, 6, 7, and "Syriac Spirituality," in Cheslyn Jones *et al.*, eds., *The Study of Spirituality* (1986); Brian Colless, "The Place of Syrian Mysticism in Religious History," in *Journal of Religious History,* 5 (1968); Pierre Dib, *History of the Maronite Church,* S. Beggiani, trans. (1971); Jean M. Fiey, *Assyrie chrétienne,* 3 vols. (1965–1968), *Chrétiens syriaques sous les Mongols* (1975), and *Chrétiens syriaques sous les Abbasides* (1980); J. Gribomont, "Documents sur les origines de l'église maronite," in *Parole de l'orient,* 5 (1974); Wolfgang Hage, *Die syrisch-jakobitische Kirche in frühislamischer Zeit* (1966); Ernst Honigmann, *Le couvent de Barsauma et le patriarcat jacobite d'Antioche* (1954); Peter Kawerau, *Die jakobitische Kirche im Zeitalter der syrischen Renaissance,* 2nd ed. (1960); Judah B. Segal, *Edessa: The Blessed City* (1970); Arthur Vööbus, *History of Asceticism in the Christian Orient,* 2 vols. (1958–1960), and *History of the School of Nisibis* (1965); William A. Wigram, *The Assyrians and Their Neighbours* (1929); William G. Young, *Patriarch, Shah, and Caliph* (1974).

Bibliographies. Sebastian P. Brock, "Syriac Studies 1960–1970" and "Syriac Studies 1971–1980," in *Parole de l'orient,* 4 (1973) and 10 (1981/1982); Cyril Moss, *Catalogue of Syriac Printed Books in the British Museum* (1962).

SEBASTIAN P. BROCK

[See also **Bar Hebraeus; Byzantine Church; Councils (Ecumenical); Christology; Church, Early; Cyril of Alexandria, St.; Dionysius of Tel-Mahré; Edessa; Eutychios the Melchite; Maronite Church; Melchites; Michael the Syrian; Monophysitism; Monothelitism; Nestorianism; Nestorius; Nisibis; Sasanian History; Zacharias of Mytilene.**]

SYRIAN RITES. Syrian-rite liturgies are usually divided into two major branches: the East Syrian, or Assyro-Chaldean, and the West Syrian, or Syro-Antiochene. Three principal liturgical centers—Jerusalem, Antioch, and Edessa—had a major influence on the origins of these rites. Of these, only Edessa was a true center of Syriac culture and literature, the other two being Greek-speaking cities with Syriac-speaking minorities.

The East Syrian rite was that of Mesopotamia in the Persian Empire; its roots can probably be traced back to Edessa. The center of the rite was the katholikosate of Seleucia-Ctesiphon, on the Tigris River south of Baghdad in present-day Iraq. In 410 the Synod of Seleucia attempted to unify and fix liturgical customs for the whole region. Before that time the rite had developed under the influence of such figures as St. Ephrem of Edessa (*d.* 373), who is said to have borrowed the rhythms and tunes of the unorthodox hymns earlier made popular by Bardesanes of Edessa (*d.* 222); Ephrem's contemporary Jacob, bishop of Nisibis (*d.* 338); Simeon, katholikos of Seleucia-Ctesiphon (*d. ca.* 341/344), who is credited with arranging the daily office into "choirs" or "weeks"; and Marutha of Martyropolis (*d.* before 420).

Other important contributors were Narsai of Nisibis (*d.* 502), Babai the Great of Kakhar (*d.* 628), and especially Katholikos Išʿyahb II of the Upper Monastery of Mar Gabriel on the Tigris at Mosul, who is said to have put in order the *Hudra* (the book of the Divine Office for Sundays, feasts of the Lord, and the period called "Fast of Ninevah"), and to have reformed the services of baptism and ordination. It seems that at least from the seventh century there were used in the Eucharist the old Anaphora of the Twelve Apostles and two others, imported from Antioch but remodeled according to East Syrian traditions, that were attributed to Theodore of Mopsuestia and Nestorius.

A number of new liturgical compositions, especially Psalter collects, were composed or taken from older collections by Patriarch Elias III (*d.* 1190), alias Abū Ḥalim, including a liturgical book that still bears his name. Shortly after that Katholikos Yabhalaha II (1190–1222) gave final form to the *Gazza,* the collection of hymns, antiphons, prayers, and homilies for all the feasts of the year. Later this was augmented in the *Warda,* or *Rose,* named after George Warda (*d.* before 1300), who with his contemporary Šlemon was a prolific writer of antiphons (*'onyata*).

The East Syrian liturgical commentators Gabriel Qatraya bar Lipah (*ca.* 615), Abraham bar Lipah (seventh century), and especially the anonymous ninth-century compiler of the *Expositio officiorum* attributed to George of Arbela all give a good picture of the early liturgical practices in the East Syrian rite.

The West Syrian rite is a synthesis of native Syrian elements with material translated from Greek liturgical texts of Antiochene and hagiopolite provenance. This synthesis came largely from Syriac, non-Chalcedonian monastic communities in the Syriac-speaking hinterlands of Syria, Palestine, and Mesopotamia. With the rupture of the Monophysites and the church of Constantinople, these Syriac-speaking Christians were organized into an independent church under Jacob Baradaios (*d.* 578) and thus were called Jacobites.

During the seventh and eighth centuries, under the great Jacobite doctors and patriarchs, the West Syrian liturgy grew with the addition of new hymns and a number of eucharistic anaphoras, and with the development of the rites of baptism and penance. Definitive codification came in the second half of the twelfth century with the work of Dionysius bar Ṣalibi (*d.* 1171) and a contemporary, Michael the Great (Michael the Syrian, *d.* 1199), to whom the Antiochene pontifical is attributed. Throughout the Middle Ages the Jacobite church continued to be influenced by Byzantine customs, whether by direct contact after Syria was reconquered by the empire in 968 or through Jerusalem, whose liturgy was closely connected with that of Constantinople.

Part of the Syro-Antiochene tradition is the rite of the Maronites, who take their name from the saintly anchorite Maron (*d. ca.* 410), in whose honor a monastery was founded at Apamea, at the head of the Orontes, in the fifth century. The Maronite rite seems to be a synthesis that probably goes back to Syriac-speaking Chalcedonian communities in Syria, which maintained their independence from the Greek-speaking centers of the coast. Later they were byzantinized, but the ancient Syrian rites and traditions were preserved and developed by monks who went into the mountains of Lebanon at the beginning of the eighth century. With the crusades the Maronite church came into contact with the West, resulting in progressive Latin influence.

BIBLIOGRAPHY

Donald Attwater, *The Christian Churches of the East,* 2 vols. (rev. ed. 1961); Michel Breydy, *L'office divin dans l'église syro-maronite* (1960); Frank E. Brightman, *Liturgies Eastern and Western,* I (1896, repr. 1965); Humphrey W. Codrington, *Studies of the Syrian Liturgies* (1952); Irenée H. Dalmais, *Eastern Liturgies,* Donald Attwater, trans. (1960); H. Husmann, "Eine altorientalische christliche Liturgie: Altsyrisch-melkitisch," in *Orientalia Christiana periodica,* **42** (1976); S. H. Jammo, "L'office du soir chaldéen au temps de Gabriel Qatraya," in *L'orient syrien,* **12** (1967); Archdale A. King, *The Rites of Eastern Christendom,* I (1947, repr. 1972); William F. Macomber, "A Theory on the Origins of the Syrian, Maronite, and Chaldean Rites," in *Orientalia christiana periodica,* **39** (1973); J. Mateos, "Les matines chaldéennes, maronites, et syriennes," *ibid.,* **26** (1960); Roger E. Reynolds, *The Ordinals of Christ from Their Origins to the Twelfth Century* (1978); Sévérien Salaville, *An Introduction to the Study of Eastern Liturgies,* adapted from the French by Msgr. John M. T. Barton (1938); Robert F. Taft, "On the Use of the Bema in the East-Syrian Liturgy," in *Eastern Churches Review,* **3** (1970), and *The Liturgy of the Hours in East and West* (1986); G. Winkler, "Das Offizium am Ende des 4. Jahrhunderts und das heutige chaldäische Offizium, ihre strukturellen Zusammenhänge," in *Ostkirchliche Studien,* **19** (1970).

ROGER E. REYNOLDS

[See also **Antiochene Rite; Christian Church in Persia; Church, Early; Maronite Church; Monophysitism; Nestorianism; Syrian Christianity.**]

SZÉKESFEHÉRVÁR (Latin: Alba Regia; German: Stuhlweissenburg), after Esztergom (Strigoniae, Gran), is the oldest royal center in medieval Hungary. Its basilica was founded by Stephen I of Hungary about 1018 along the "pilgrims' route" near the burial monastery of the princely family. Annual royal courts were held, most kings crowned, and many buried here until 1526. The Crown of St. Stephen and other insignia were entrusted to the *custos* of the basilica at least until the fourteenth century. The tax exemptions and other liberties of the "Latin" settlers (granted about 1130) served as examples for several early city charters.

BIBLIOGRAPHY

J. Deér, "Aachen und die Herrschersitze der Arpaden," in *Mitteilungen des Instituts für österreichische Geschichtsforschung,* **79** (1971); Errik Fügedi, "Der Stadtplan von Stuhlweissenburg und die Anfänge des Bürgertums in Ungarn," in *Acta historica Academiae Scientiarum Hungaricae,* 15 (1969), repr. in Fügedi, *Kings, Bishops, Nobles, and Burghers in Medieval Hungary,* János M. Bak, ed. (1986); Hansgerd Göckenjan, "Stuhlweissenburg—eine ungarische Königsresidenz vom 11–13. Jahrhundert: Forschungsbericht," in Klaus Zernack, ed., *Beiträge zur Stadt- und Regionalgeschichte Ostund Nordeuropas* (1971), 135–152; György Székely, "Wallons et Italiens en Europe centrale aux XIe–XVIe siècles," in *Annales Universitatis Scientiarum Budapestinensis de Rolando Eötvös nominatae: Sectio historica,* 6 (1964).

JÁNOS M. BAK

[See also **Hungary; Stephen I of Hungary, St.; Stephen, Crown of St.**]

ṬABARĪ, AL- (al-Ṭabarī Abū Jaʿfar Muḥammad ibn Jarīr ibn Yazīd ibn Kathīr, 839–923), noted Islamic scholar who was born in Āmul (Amol), in northern Iran. After displaying unusual intellectual gifts as a child, he was sent off, as was the custom, to study with various scholars in the leading centers of Islamic learning. His travels took him initially to al-Rayy and later to Baghdad, Basra, al-Kufa, Syria, and Egypt (876–877). He ultimately returned to Baghdad, where he died.

Al-Ṭabarī, acknowledged as a scholar of vast erudition and wide interests, was considered by some as the most learned of all his contemporaries. As an exegete, he was the outstanding authority of his time in all aspects of Koranic studies. He was among the greatest historians and also a leading scholar in *ḥadīth* (Koranic tradition), Islamic law, and Arabic grammar. He took an interest as well in ethics, mathematics, and medicine. His output was prodigious even by medieval standards of productivity. One tradition has it that he wrote forty pages a day, day in, day out, for forty years; another that his total output came to 30,000 pages for his commentary on the Koran and a similar number for his monumental history.

In matters of law, he followed initially the "school" (*madhhab*) of the Shāfiʿites, but later established a *madhhab* of his own in Egypt, called after him the Jarirīyah. His approach to law did not take root, however, and his school was not considered among the leading *madhhab*s. On matters concerning *ḥadīth,* he initially followed the school of Aḥmad ibn Ḥanbal, but he later broke with them at some risk to himself. He reportedly wrote a number of works, but his enduring reputation is based largely on his vast Koranic commentary of thirty volumes, *Jāmiʿ al-bayān fī tafsīr al-Qurʾān,* and his quintessential chronicle, *Taʾrīkh al-rusul wa'l-mulūk* (The chronicle of prophets and kings).

The chronicle begins with a prolegomenon on the relationship between history and time and then proceeds to record events from creation to the year A.H. 302 (July 915); the printed editions include various closing remarks and addenda by other scholars. The history is thus divided into pre-Islamic and Islamic times. The former segment deals with the ancient Iranians, Israelites, and the Hellenistic world as well as the pre-Islamic Arabs. Here Ṭabarī relies on various ancient traditions that percolated into the world of Islam, probably via converts to the new faith. The traditions dealing with the ancient Israelites (which for Muslims includes materials on Christians) are often found in the Koranic commentary as well.

The arrangement of the pre-Islamic material is not entirely systematic. Ṭabarī often interrupts his discussion of a particular civilization only to come back to it at some later point in the work. On the whole he presents loose time sequences organized according to the dynastic arrangement. With the beginning of the Muslim calendar, reckoned from the prophet Muḥammad's emigration (hegira) from Mecca to Medina (16 July 622), events are described in connection with a particular year. Ṭabarī was not the first Muslim historian to utilize the annalistic arrangement (the earliest extant text is that of Ibn Khayyāṭ al-ʿUsfuri, *d.* 854). However, no known work, regardless of arrangement, matched the magisterial scope of the *Taʾrīkh.*

Al-Ṭabarī's detailed reporting usually consists of a series of short, detached statements, more often than not preceded by an *isnād* or chain of authority, according to a practice followed in the religious sciences. The same event is often reported from the perspective of the different authorities on whom Ṭabarī relied. At times, the various accounts contradict one another as regards certain particulars, but the author rarely expresses his own judgments as to the veracity of the individual accounts. Indeed, many earlier historical traditions are known only through the *Taʾrīkh,* which had a tendency to displace from currency earlier and presumably thinner sources, hence its indispensable value to modern historians.

At the conclusion of each year there are usually brief notices, consisting of terse statements dealing with government appointments as well as with other incidental information. However terse, these notices are extremely valuable for tracing larger patterns of provincial government and add to the importance of the *Taʾrīkh* as the single most important source for the study of early Islamic history.

The great commentary on the Koran shows a similar care for detail and attention to earlier sources. As with the history, the author brings together the views of a wide variety of scholars going back to the earliest commentators. Taken as a whole, the *Tafsīr* represents a major advance in koranic exegesis, not only as regards the amount of material presented (the author allegedly dictated this work to one of his students, a venture that was said to have lasted seven years), but also because of the systematic way he treated the individual verses.

Where appropriate, the author made full use of his great knowledge of Arabic grammar and philology, as well as *ḥadīth* literature. The exegesis also shows great concern for theological and legal matters suggested by the Koran. Some of the material is common to the history, particularly where the sacred text discusses the affairs of the ancient Israelites. It would appear that the author was well aware of the far-ranging literature dealing with that subject and cites it extensively. The views of earlier exegetes are given, most often with a full chain of authorities. Where a consensus has developed among various exegetes, it is duly noted by Ṭabarī; the same is done for differing views. Given the wide range of sources listed, one is able to reconstruct a great deal of an earlier exegesis that is no longer extant.

Al-Ṭabarī's indefatigable energy has already been noted. Having memorized the Koran by the age of seven, he began a productive career that extended almost until his death. His work ethic and writing set a standard for medieval Muslim scholarship that was never surpassed.

BIBLIOGRAPHY

A brief listing of all the major secondary sources dealing with Ṭabarī, as well as the various editions and manuscripts of his work, and references to him in the medieval Arabic biographical literature can be found in Fuat Sezgin, *Geschichte des arabischen Schrifttums,* I (1967), 323–328.

JACOB LASSNER

[See also **Encyclopedias and Dictionaries, Arabic and Persian; Historiography, Islamic; Koran.**]

TABLION, a richly decorative woven square of material, often of silk or gold thread studded with gems, applied to the front of a cloak or mantle (chlamys). It identifies the wearer as an office-holder and is most commonly seen on warrior saints such as George and Demetrios, particularly in Early Christian and Byzantine art. An example is the embroidered tablion on the chlamys worn by St. Demetrios (standing between donors), depicted in a seventh-century mosaic at Hagios Demetrios, Salonika. Imperial examples include the richly embroidered tablion worn by the emperor Justinian I on his paludamentum and those worn by two state officials standing to his right in the mosaic panel at S. Vitale, Ravenna.

BIBLIOGRAPHY

John Beckwith, *Early Christian and Byzantine Art* (1970, repr. 1979), 114, 375; Mary G. Houston, *Ancient Greek, Roman, and Byzantine Costume and Decoration,* 2nd ed. (1947, repr. 1963), 136.

BARBARA OEHLSCHLAEGER-GARVEY

[See also **Byzantine Empire: Bureaucracy; Costume, Byzantine; Early Christian Art; Paludamentum** (with illustration).]

TABRĪZ. The principal city of Azerbaijan province in northwest Iran, Tabriz is situated in the fertile valley of the Aji Chai (Talkheh) River within the foothills of Mount Sahand. Its location makes it a natural entrepôt for trade between the Iranian plateau and countries to the north and west. It is also a principal market for the agricultural products of this rich province and a prime location for manufacture.

As Tauris, Tabriz was the capital of Armenia under Trdat III (IV) (fourth century), but at the time of the Arab conquest of Iran (642), it was little more than a village. So it remained until the caliphate of al-Mutawakkil (*d.* 861), when a certain Ibn al-Rawād built his palace there and subsequently enclosed the community that grew up around it with a wall.

By the following century Tabriz had become a large town with a Friday mosque and extensive, well-watered orchards. During these early centuries it was obliterated three times by earthquakes (791, 858, and 1042), with great loss of life, but it was completely rebuilt after each disaster.

During the period of Seljuk supremacy in Iran (eleventh and twelfth centuries), Tabriz grew to be the principal city of Azerbaijan, with a widespread reputation for its tabby (*ᶜattābī*) silks, velvets, and woven stuffs.

The city was spared destruction by the Mongols in 1221 when the ruling atabeg, Muzaffar al-Din, was able to buy the attackers off. The Ilkhanid period (1256–1353) was the great period in Tabriz's history. It was the dynasty's capital for the last four decades of the thirteenth century, and the final Ilkhanid to rule from Tabriz, Maḥmūd Ghāzān (*r.* 1295–1304), in particular did much to expand and beautify the city, ordering the construction of mosques, schools, hospitals and asylums, libraries, baths, caravansaries, and an observatory.

Tabriz was subsequently the capital of three dynasties in succession: that of the Qara Qoyunlu during the reign of Mīrzā Jāhān-Shāh (*d.* 1466); that of the Aq Qoyunlu ruler Uzun Ḥasan (*d.* 1478), who defeated Abū Saᶜīd and seized Tabriz in 1469; and, more than a century later, of the Safawid dynasty, when Shah Ismāᶜīl I defeated the last Aq Qoyunlu, Murād (*d.* 1501).

The proximity of Tabriz to the border of Ottoman Turkey, with which the Safawids were almost continously at war, made it a risky choice as capital. The Safawids soon moved their court, first to Qazvin and then to Isfahan. Tabriz was held several times by the Ottomans, including the period from 1585 to 1603 and from 1724 to 1730.

During the Qajar period (1779–1925) the continuing struggle between Iran and Russia gave Tabriz a strategic importance. It was made the governorate of the heir apparent, and the site of the modernization of Iran's army and the manufacture of modern armaments.

In the early twentieth century, the people of Tabriz played a leading role in the constitutionalist movement that led to the overthrow of the Qajar dynasty and, ultimately, to the establishment of the Pahlavis.

BIBLIOGRAPHY

Cambridge History of Iran, IV (1975); Guy Le Strange, *The Lands of the Eastern Caliphate* (1966); Ghulam H. Muṣaḥib, ed., *Dāᵓirat al-maᶜārif-i Fārsī* (1966).

JEROME W. CLINTON

[See also **Aq Qoyunlu; Azerbaijan; Ghāzān, Maḥmūd; Ilkhanids; Iran, History: After 650; Isfahan; Ottomans; Qara Qoyunlu; Trdat III (IV) the Great, St.**]

The *tabula ansata* of Orestes, an ivory diptych, 530. VICTORIA AND ALBERT MUSUEM, LONDON

TABULA ANSATA (ansate tablet), a rectangular frame or tablet with handlelike projections, usually trapezoidal, used to contain an inscription. The motif appeared on sarcophagi of the third and fourth centuries, such as that of Adelphia (*ca.* 340, now in the National Museum at Syracuse), in manuscripts such as the Calendar of 354, and on ivory panels from the fourth through the sixth century, such as the Symmachi-Nicomachi diptych of 388–401 (now in London, Victoria and Albert Museum, and Paris, Musée de Cluny) and numerous consular diptychs, such as those of Areobindus (506, Constantinople; now in Paris, Musée de Cluny) and Orestes (530, Rome; now in London, Victoria and Albert Museum).

BIBLIOGRAPHY

Henri Stern, *Le calendrier de 354: Étude sur son texte et sur ses illustrations* (1953), 120–121; Wolfgang F. Volbach, *Elfenbeinarbeiten der Spätantike und des frühen Mittelalters* (3rd ed. 1976), nos. 8–11, 14–18, 21, 24, 31, 55, 62.

LESLIE BRUBAKER

[See also **Ivory Carving.**]

The Farewell of the Apostles, 1408, from Taddeo di Bartolo's fresco cycle depicting the life of the Virgin, in the Chapel of the Virgin, Palazzo Pubblico, Siena. ALINARI / ART RESOURCE

TABULA PEUTINGERIANA. The Tabula Peutingeriana, which is named after its discoverer, Konrad Peutinger (1465–1547), German antiquarian, diplomat, and economist, is the only extant example of the *itineraria picta* (road map) that was intended as a portable map of the military roads of the Roman Empire. It probably dates from the fourth century, although its various parts may be earlier or later; the existing copy dates from the thirteenth century. The Tabula is attributed to Castorius and is composed of a long, narrow strip in twelve sections, the dimensions of which (21 feet [6.4 m] by 1 foot [0.3 m]) distort the shape of the countries depicted. It is in six colors and contains not only the distances between major points of the empire but also a variety of natural features, such as mountains and rivers. Small towns are marked by houses, larger ones by walls and towers, and watering places by bathhouses. The map extends from Britain to the mouth of the Ganges—essentially the world known to the Romans of that time—but most of Britain and Spain and the western part of North Africa are missing. The Tabula is now in Vienna, Österreichische Nationalbibliothek.

BIBLIOGRAPHY

Konrad Miller, *Itineraria romana: Römische reiswege an der Hand der Tabula peutingeriana* (1916, repr. 1964), and *Die Peutingersche Tafel* (1916, 2nd ed. 1929, repr. 1962); Henry F. Tozer, *A History of Ancient Geography* (2nd ed. 1935).

LINDA C. ROSE

[See also **Geography and Cartography.**]

TABULAE CERATAE. See **Wax Tablets.**

TADDEO DI BARTOLO (*ca.* 1362–1422), Sienese painter. Probably a pupil of Bartolo di Fredi, Taddeo di Bartolo is still insufficiently appreciated for his originality and advanced pictorial thinking. Important works include a large altarpiece dated 1389 in the church of S. Paolo in Collegarli; a *Crucifixion* dated 1395 (now in the Museo Nazionale e Civico di S. Matteo); and a polyptych with the *Assumption of the Virgin* dated 1401 in the duomo of Montepulciano. His greatest surviving achievement is his fresco cycle depicting the life of the Virgin (*ca.* 1407–1414) in the Palazzo Pubblico in Siena. His interest in natural observation produced remarkable experiments in foreshortening without ever giving over his image entirely to rational space, because his painting, true to Sienese tradition, was geared to an emotional experience on the part of the viewer.

BIBLIOGRAPHY
Bruce Cole, *Sienese Painting in the Age of the Renaissance* (1984); Sibilla Symeonides, *Taddeo di Bartolo* (1965).

ADELHEID M. GEALT

[See also **Bartolo di Fredi; Fresco Painting; Siena.**]

TAFUR, PERO DE (*ca.* 1416–*ca.* 1484), a Spaniard born in Córdoba, traveled in the East and left an account of his travels which provides a great deal of firsthand information on that region in the fifteenth century. He went to the Holy Land, where he disguised himself as a Muslim and so was able to enter the mosque of ᶜUmar; he witnessed the election of the grand master of the Hospitalers on Rhodes, and saw Constantinople, which was already in terminal decline. Since Pero was a trader, his account contains a great deal of information on fifteenth-century commerce.

BIBLIOGRAPHY
Pero Tafur, *Travels and Adventures, 1435–1439,* Malcolm H. I. Letts, ed. and trans. (1926); Rafael Ramírez de Arellano, "Pero Tafur," in *Boletín de la Real Academia de la Historia,* **41** (1902).

LINDA C. ROSE

[See also **Travel and Transport.**]

TAGMATA (singular, tagma), general Byzantine Greek word for military units. In its restricted meaning it refers to the elite professional Byzantine mobile guards and expeditionary forces that were attached to the emperor and were normally stationed at or near Constantinople. There were four (later five) imperial tagmata: the *scholae, arithmos* or Watch (*vigla*), *numera, excubitors,* and the *hikanati.* The *numera* and the regiment of the walls also guarded imperial prisons and part of the palace walls. The tagma of *foederati* was exceptional. Originally composed of foreigners, it was stationed in the Anatolik theme in central Asia Minor and was commanded by a turmarch. Except for the drungarios of the *arithmos,* the other tagmatic commanders held the rank of domestics. The second in command in each tagma was a *topoteretes* or lieutenant, followed by a *chartularius.* The exact sizes of the tagmata are impossible to determine. Some scholars accept Arab geographers' figures of 4,000 troops or more per tagma, but others believe that the total tagmatic forces did not exceed 4,000.

The names of some tagmata were very old but it may be that the four imperial tagmata as efficient mobile corps date back to a reorganization in the reign of Constantine V (741–775), after his downgrading of the Opsikian theme. Nikephoros I (802–811) created the *hikanati.* The tagmatic units were not merely ceremonial palace guards but elite and well-equipped shock troops that constituted some of the best imperial formations. Individual soldiers were selected with care for their loyalty to the person and policies of the reigning emperor and probably were recruited from diverse domestic and foreign sources, but there is no conclusive proof. The tagmata were at the height of their prestige and efficiency between the late eighth and middle of the eleventh centuries. Emperor John I Tzimiskes (969–976) created the short-lived tagma of the Immortals (*athanatoi*).

The tagmatic armies were distinct from the thematic armies, yet the decline of the thematic armies accompanied the creation of additional tagmata, each under a *dux* or *katepano.* The financing and provisioning of the tagmatic armies are obscure. Normally the domestic of the schools took precedence over other tagmatic commanders, even commmanding entire joint tagmatic and thematic armies.

BIBLIOGRAPHY
John B. Bury, *The Imperial Administrative System in the Ninth Century* (1911, repr. 1958); Hélène Glykatzi-Ahrweiler, "Recherches sur l'Administration de l'Empire byzantin aux IXᵉ–XIᵉ siècles," in *Bulletin de correspondance hellénique,* **84** (1960), esp. 24–33; John F. Haldon, *Byzantine Praetorians: An Administrative, Institutional, and Social Survey of the Opsikion and Tagmata, c. 580–900* (1984); Nicolas Oikonomides, *Les listes de préséance byzantin des IXᵉ et Xᵉ siècles* (1972), esp. 329–333; Warren T. Treadgold, "Notes on the Numbers and Organization of the Ninth-century Byzantine Army," in *Greek, Roman, and Byzantine Studies,* **21** (1980).

WALTER EMIL KAEGI, JR.

[See also **Anatolikon, Theme of; Constantine V; Domestic; Dux; John I Tzimiskes; Katepano; Nikephoros I; Opsikion, Theme of; Stratiotai; Warfare, Byzantine.**]

ṬĀHIR IBN AL-ḤUSAYN (*d.* 822), known as Dhu'l-Yamīnain, "the man with two right hands" or "the ambidextrous" (either because of his prowess in battle or his liberality), was the founder of a line of governors who succeeded each other hereditarily in Khorāsān during the period of the Abbasid caliphate.

Although Ṭāhir's family later claimed Arab lineage and membership of the tribe of Khuzāᶜa, they in fact came from eastern Iran and were clients (*mawālī*) of the incoming Arab warriors. The family's fortunes were made by their support of the winning side, that of the Abbasids, in the Umayyad-Abbasid civil warfare of 746–750, and members of the family were rewarded by provincial governorships at Pūshang and Harāt in what is now western Afghanistan. They were effective in suppressing the religious and social discontent that affected much of the Iranian countryside at this time.

Ṭāhir became the confidant of the caliph Hārūn al-Rashīd, and in the civil strife (consequent upon the latter's death in 809) between his two sons al-Amīn and al-Ma'mūn, al-Ma'mun's adviser al-Fadl ibn Sahl made Ṭāhir commander of the army sent from Ray to confront al-Amīn's forces at Hamadān (811). Ṭāhir defeated al-Amīn's forces and advanced on the caliph al-Amīn, now beleaguered in Baghdad.

Baghdad was taken by al-Maᵓmūn's troops in 813, and Ṭāhir's Persian soldiers killed al-Amīn. Some sources state that al-Ma'mūn later held Ṭāhir personally responsible for his brother's death. His star was nevertheless very much in the ascendant. Appointed governor of Al-Jazīra (northern Iraq and northeastern Syria), with his base at Raqqa on the Euphrates, he acquired further lucrative offices in Iraq and Baghdad that members of his family were to hold for more than a century to come. Ṭāhir's palace in Baghdad, the Harīm Ṭāhir, was particularly opulently appointed.

In 821 Ṭāhir was made governor of all the lands east of Iraq—that is, of the whole Iranian world. According to the sources, he deliberately sought the office in order to remove himself from the center of the caliphate, fearing a change of attitude on the part of al-Maᵓmūn. Once established in the east at his capital, Merv (now Mary, in the Soviet Union), Ṭāhir began to omit the caliph's name from the Friday sermon (*khutba*) and from the coinage. Both of these acts were considered to be virtual declarations of independence; however, at this point he died.

Whatever Ṭāhir may have intended, al-Ma'mūn and later caliphs did not hesitate to appoint his sons and descendants to high offices in both Khorāsān and Iraq. It is possible that the significance of Ṭāhir's independent act was not so great as it appears. The subsequent Tahirids were all faithful vassals of the caliphs, punctilious in the fulfillment of their gubernatorial obligations.

Although of Persian origin, Ṭāhir is said to have been highly literate in Arabic, and appreciative of its literature; he was the patron of several of the leading poets and prose stylists of the age, and to him is attributed an epistle, addressed to his son ᶜAbd Allāh, on statecraft and wise behavior, which anticipates the later flowering of the "mirror for princes" genre in Islamic literature.

BIBLIOGRAPHY

W. Barthold, *Turkestan Down to the Mongol Invasion,* V. Minorsky, trans., 4th ed. (1977), esp. 207–209; C. E. Bosworth, "The Tahirids and Arabic Culture," in *Journal of Semitic Studies,* **14** (1969), "An Early Arabic Mirror for Princes: Ṭāhir Dhū'l-Yamīnain's Epistle to His Son ᶜAbdallāh (206/821)," in *Journal of Near Eastern Studies,* **29** (1970), and "The Ṭāhirids and Ṣaffārids," in *Cambridge History of Iran,* IV (1975); Mongi Kaabi, *Les Ṭāhirides au Ḫurāsān et en Iraq* (Tunis, 1983), 69–219; P. Thillet and D. Sourdel, "Documents et notules," pt. 2, "Les circonstances de la mort de Ṭāhir Ier au Hurāsān en 207/822," in *Arabica,* **5** (1958), 66–69.

C. E. BOSWORTH

[See also **Abbasids; Hārūn al-Rashīd; Iran; Maᵓmūn, al-; Mirror of Princes; Tahirids.**]

TAHIRIDS, a family of arabized Persians. They played a prominent role in the early Abbasid caliphate as holders of several important administrative and police offices in Iraq and western Persia. And they were governors of Khorāsān or eastern Persia, where they formed a short-lived line that spanned four generations, from 821 to 873.

The prehistory of the family is rooted in service to the early Arab governors in Sīstān (in southeastern Persia). They then participated alongside of the Abbasid insurgents in the revolution of 746–750 (one of whose epicenters was Khorāsān), which toppled the Umayyad caliphs of Damascus and replaced them with the Abbasids of Iraq and Baghdad. As a reward for their services, various members of the family were given provincial gov-

TAHIRIDS

ernorships in their native eastern Persia. Thus, they started out as clients of Arab governors and gradually themselves assumed an Arab identity—their ninth-century poets and propagandists praised them as affiliates of the Arab tribe of Khuzāᶜa.

Ṭāhir ibn al-Ḥusayn (called Dhu'l-Yamīnain, "the ambidextrous") fought for the victorious al-Maᵓmūn in the latter's civil war with al-Amīn over their father Hārūn al-Rashīd's inheritance of the caliphate. He thereby gained lucrative offices in Iraq and the governorship of Khorāsān just before he died in 822. The sources relate that Ṭāhir made moves toward asserting his independence in Khorāsān, but these cannot have amounted to much, since the caliph maintained his son Ṭalḥa there. Possibly al-Maᵓmūn judged it prudent to leave that distant province in indigenous hands. Certainly, the family retained all its other positions in Iraq, and none of the subsequent Tahirid governors showed any signs of desiring any degree of de jure independence.

Ṭalḥa is a somewhat vague figure, but his brother ᶜAbd Allāh (governor 828 or 829–844) left a deep impression on contemporary history and Arabic culture. He spent much of his career suppressing unrest in Egypt, Syria, and Iraq that resulted from the fratricidal warfare. Then in Khorāsān he quelled Alid risings after 828, establishing control over the imperfectly islamized Caspian coastlands and supporting the Samanid vassal governors in Transoxiana against threats from the steppe Turks. These last formed a vital source of slave-soldier manpower in the caliphate. Much of the Tahirids' indispensability in the east and also much of their personal wealth came from control of this traffic. ᶜAbd Allāh at the same time governed other parts of Persia, such as Kirmān and Ray, and was administrator of central Iraq and commander of the guard in Baghdad. The total income from his territories amounted to 48 million dirhams a year. His court at Nishapur was a splendid center for Arabic literature to which several of the greatest poets of the time resorted for patronage, and he and his son ᶜUbayd Allāh are themselves mentioned as composing melodies. Like other subsequent Tahirids, he maintained a respectful attitude toward his Abbasid master, forwarding regular tribute and dutifully acknowledging caliphal supremacy on his coinage. He remained in his own territory and never visited the caliphal court.

On his death, the caliph al-Wāthiq eventually confirmed ᶜAbd Allāh's son Ṭāhir II as governor. Little is recorded of him, though we know that the Persian countryside continued to be disturbed by political, social, and religious movements expressing resentment at outside domination. Meanwhile, ᶜAdb Allāh's other son, Muḥammad, controlled the family interests in the west until his death in 867. When Ṭāhir II died, Muḥammad ibn ᶜAbd Allāh refused to leave Iraq, so the caliph had to appoint Ṭāhir's young son Muḥammad to Khorāsān. It was the latter's misfortune that his rule coincided with a powerful and enduring revolutionary Shiite movement in the Caspian provinces. The period also witnessed the rise in Sīstān of the aggressive Saffarid brothers, Yaᶜqūb and ᶜAmr, who built up their own powerful empire, which at one time nearly overwhelmed the caliphate itself. Muḥammad ibn Ṭāhir was unable to withstand them, and in 873 he lost Nishapur and Khorāsān to Yaᶜqūb; he then retired to Iraq. There thus ended fifty years of Tahirid dominance in Khorāsān, which had probably been thus maintained hereditarily by the caliphs because it provided continuity at a time when the caliphate in the west was falling into increased instability. The Tahirids did, however, retain offices in Iraq well into the tenth century.

The Tahirids are regarded very favorably in Islamic sources as upholders of the aristocratic, orthodox Sunni tradition against religious dissidence, heresy, and social unrest in the province. By contrast, the Saffarids are regarded as baseborn adventurers. The Tahirids certainly supported the Arab-Persian landowning classes, but they also did much to ensure stability and agricultural prosperity in Khorāsān. Equitable rulers, they protected the peasantry from undue exploitation and watched over the conduct of local officials. A book on irrigation and water rights commissioned by ᶜAbd Allāh ibn Ṭāhir from leading experts in Iraq and Persia is said to have remained authoritative in Khorāsān for two centuries. The Tahirids encouraged cultivation and sought to open the caravan routes (from Iraq across northern Persia to Transoxiana, the Central Asian steppes, and the Far East) that brought many luxury articles into the Islamic world. We may therefore characterize the period of the Tahirids in Persia as one of enlightened absolutism. They upheld the existing social order and the caliph's ultimate authority. Only with the eruption of the Saffarids from Sīstān was the pattern of caliphal control in the east irrevocably shattered.

BIBLIOGRAPHY

Sources. Ibn al-Athīr, *Chronicon* (1851–1876); Gardīzī, *Zayn al-akhbār* (Tehran, 1347/1968); Miskawayh, *Tajārib al-umam,* V–VI (1907–1917); Ṭabarī, *Annales,* 3rd ser., II–IV (1879–1901).

Studies. In addition to the bibliography under Tāhir, see C. E. Bosworth, *The Islamic Dynasties: A Chronological and Genealogical Handbook* (1967) and "The Ṭāhirids and Persian Literature," in *Iran,* 7 (1969); Edward G. Browne, *A Literary History of Persia,* I (1902).

C. E. BOSWORTH

[See also **Abbasids; Alids; Caliphate; Hārūn al-Rashīd; Iran; Iraq; Mamluk Dynasty; Ma$^{\supset}$mūn, al-; Nishapur; Saffarids; Samanids; Transoxiana; Umayyads; Ya^{c}qūb ibn Layth.**]

TAILLE, TALLAGE. The French word *taille* and the English word "tallage" correspond to the Latin *tallia,* which in the documents of the eleventh and twelfth centuries is best translated as "exaction." That is to say, it meant an appropriation of property that fell between "taxation" and "extortion": payment by a weaker person to a stronger one for purposes that were neither completely "public" nor completely "private," under circumstances in which the element of compulsion was much in evidence.

At the same time, these documents used other words (like *tolta*) that also meant exaction. This typically medieval inclusion of several apparently synonymous terms in the same document (frequently a charter granting exemption) arises from the fact that the words were only roughly synonymous. For instance, *tallia* denoted not only an exaction, but also a method of exaction related to the practice of using notched sticks ("tallies") to keep accounts.

The underlying meaning of *tailler* (to cut) was also preserved in documents of the fourteenth century relating to the French currency. The *taille* of a particular coinage was the number of coins "cut" from a mark of silver.

Thus the word tallage has the ambiguities characteristic of medieval terminology relating to fiscal institutions. In one context it meant an exaction that was detested because it implied inferior status. In another context it gradually came to describe a method of assessing taxes—by apportionment (*répartition*). At times, both connotations are present, and it is not always clear when a *taille* was mainly an exaction and when it was primarily a tax assessed in a particular way. These considerations make it difficult to generalize about tallages in a short article, and it should be stressed that the ensuing remarks attempt to describe, somewhat superficially, the different kinds of tallage encountered in medieval history.

There have been two main ways of classifying medieval tallages: (1) the personal *taille* vs. the territorial *taille* and (2) the seigneurial *taille* vs. the municipal *taille* vs. the royal *taille.* Neither method deals very satisfactorily with chronological or regional differences, but the second is preferable. The seigneurial *taille* was an exaction levied by lords on people under their control. The municipal *taille* referred to taxes levied by urban governments on their inhabitants. The royal *taille* is best described in the restricted sense of a tax levied by the French crown during the last four centuries before the revolution of 1789. This royal *taille* was peculiarly French, and its assessment was subject to geographical variations in which the personal vs. territorial factor is relevant.

THE SEIGNEURIAL *TAILLE*

Medieval historians have always devoted a great deal of effort, often fruitlessly, to seeking the origins of various early modern institutions. The word *taille* first appears in the eleventh century in its seigneurial form, as an exaction levied by powerful lords on powerless peasants. Whether its roots were Roman, Germanic, or Carolingian is really immaterial. The truism that the powerful have always been able to appropriate the property of the weak does not contribute much to our understanding of the *taille.* What is clear is that the word *tallia* was used by the eleventh century (along with other words) to describe such exactions. During the next three centuries, tallages more closely resembled taxes in the modern sense than did other seigneurial dues.

The scarcity of documents in the tenth century makes one cautious about attributing new developments to the eleventh, but we do find increased mobility on the part of peasants, some of whom left their ancestral villages and moved to other communities as *hospites.* These migrations gave rise to disputes when the former lord and the new lord each claimed tallage. These jurisdictional disputes and the records they have left were, by their nature, exceptional cases, but they have persuaded some historians that the first lord was entitled to personal tallage and the second (usually an ecclesiastical body) was able to exact it as a territorial levy.

Another development associated with the eleventh century was the rise of the castle-holding seigneur, who wielded vast powers of questionable legality that were derived from the ban—the police power of the state, as we should now call it. These castellans are first attested in France, where they escaped the authority of the counts in many regions and began to exercise formerly public powers as hereditary private rights. The lay and ecclesiastical lords who controlled castles forced the peasants and lesser fighting men into a deeper subjection than had been known by free men previously. Many seigneurial powers over peasants appear for the first time after this period, and the old distinction between free and unfree peasants lost much of its meaning. After conquering England in 1066 the Normans imposed a somewhat similar regime on the population there, and the same sort of lordship began to spread in Germany as the investiture struggle undermined public authority.

From the eleventh century on, the tallage was perhaps the most onerous personal burden imposed on peasants by lords. It was an arbitrary exaction, usually of money, the lord being able to take what he thought the peasant could pay. Some modern scholars have seen it as the basic identifying feature of servitude, and it was certainly regarded as such in some regions. The seigneurial tallage, however, began to change as the mobility of peasants accelerated. The clearing of forests and the founding of new communities created a demand for labor. To attract peasants, lords offered "liberties," and to keep their own peasants from leaving, other lords found it expedient to ameliorate their condition. They often did so for a price, however.

The granting of franchises or liberties usually included references to tallage, a fact that underscores its unpopularity as a degrading burden. In some cases, tallage was simply abolished; more often it was converted to a fixed annual payment. As prices gradually rose through the twelfth and thirteenth centuries, the fixed *taille* became less burdensome to the peasants and less valuable to the lords, but its great virtue in the eyes of the peasant was that it was fixed. Heavy exactions might be hard to bear, but to the medieval mentality arbitrary ones were far worse. In the fourteenth century, the expression "tallageable-at-will" described people who still were subject to arbitrary tallage and were, on that account, considered to be servile. Payment of a fixed *taille,* even a heavy one, did not have the same degrading connotation.

The fixed tallage in the twelfth and thirteenth centuries was by no means always derived from formerly arbitrary exactions on rural manors. It could be established by lords as a means of commuting to cash payments one or more other seigneurial dues that formerly had been rendered in kind or had been irregular in nature. At the outset, before these dues were affected by inflation, the lord might find it to his own advantage to replace them with such a regular and more predictable payment in cash. We also find the fixed tallage used to obtain a guarantee of stable currency from a lord who operated a mint. The fixed tallage thus proved to be a flexible instrument for commuting various forms of seigneurial revenue into a more convenient form. Sometimes such a tallage remained a personal levy; more often it was owed by a community and subject to apportionment among the members, a mode of assessment that became a characteristic feature of tallages.

THE MUNICIPAL *TAILLE*

When we speak of commutation or enfranchisement, we are led to the second aspect of tallage—the so-called municipal *taille.* Enfranchisements of groups were far more common than enfranchisements of individuals, and the communities most likely to receive liberties were those completely controlled (or founded) by a single lord. Large cities with several lords often had to fight for their liberties. Lords granted charters more freely to market towns, villages, and other communities that were not subject to multiple jurisdiction. When such charters established a fixed payment to the lord, it generally was a lump sum imposed on the community, rather than individual payments by those who had formerly been tallageable-at-will. It is at this point that we can observe the *taille* becoming territorial rather than personal and being assessed by the characteristic method of *répartition.*

In effect, when the inhabitants of a town were released from the old seigneurial tallage (arbitrary and personal in nature) and allowed to substitute a fixed lump sum, the government of that town was being empowered to raise the money from the inhabitants. All who lived in the community for a year and a day were normally deemed eligible to enjoy its liberties, and the municipal tax levied to raise the lump sum applied to those who resided in the territory where the liberties (and jurisdiction) of

TAILLE, TALLAGE

the municipality were in force. Such municipal taxes themselves came to be known as *tailles*. In fourteenth-century France, the word *taille* appears far more frequently as a municipal tax than as a seigneurial exaction. The word had come to apply to municipal taxation in general, not only the taxes levied to pay a lump sum to the lord or the king but also those to repair fortifications or finance other municipal needs.

These municipal *tailles* took many different forms. Often they were assessed on the sale of foodstuffs and merchandise, but they could be based on property or income. The form of tax was often determined by the economic interests of those who controlled the town government. Wealthy oligarchies came under bitter attack for adopting regressive forms of municipal taxation, and political opposition frequently forced urban governments to assess taxes by *répartition*—apportionment based in principle upon ability to pay.

THE ROYAL *TAILLE*

As the term became less associated with a degrading personal exaction by a seigneur, and more associated with assessment by *répartition,* we begin to encounter the first signs of the royal *taille*. These first signs appear toward the beginning of the fourteenth century. Under the name of *taille* it would be peculiar to France, but some of its roots would be found elsewhere as well. When a government in the thirteenth or fourteenth century levied an extraordinary subsidy for some purpose (such as a war, a crusade, or the ransom of a monarch), it frequently negotiated with towns for lump sums, and these, like the earlier substitutes for seigneurial *tailles,* were raised by municipal taxes on the inhabitants.

Taxation by means of lump-sum payments by communities became quite common in Mediterranean Europe. In fourteenth-century Languedoc, for instance, first individual towns, then entire seneschalsies, and then the whole region paid royal taxes based on apportioned lump sums. The word for such a tax was generally not *tallia* but *focagium,* meaning "hearth tax" (the French *fouage*). The lump sums were apportioned among communities on the basis of their taxable households (hearths), and the communities could then raise the money by whatever means they chose. Increasingly the method of *répartition* came to be used, because of widespread suspicion that a wealthy clique was manipulating municipal finances to the disadvantage of the majority.

After the mid fourteenth century, the *focagium* in southern France began to diverge in an important way from its counterpart in the north. Not only did the enumeration of hearths become an administrative fiction unrelated to actual households, but the hearths referred to a particular form of property—generally urban and described as being *roturier* in nature (that is, having been held originally by someone who was neither noble nor cleric). This development arose from the fact that nobility in Mediterranean Europe was not restricted to a rural military aristocracy but included city dwellers who held certain offices or practiced certain professions. When the apportioned *fouage* finally began to be called a *taille* in southern France (by the fifteenth century), lawyers began to characterize it as the *taille réel* because it was based on a certain category of real property rather than on actual households.

In northern France, some royal taxes had been based on lump sums paid by towns, but by the 1340's these had largely disappeared in favor of indirect taxes on consumer goods. At a more local level, however, the tradition of municipal *tailles* made itself felt in regional assemblies that met to deal with problems of peace-keeping in the 1350's and 1360's. These often levied special apportioned hearth taxes to meet the needs of local defense. Late in 1363, an assembly representing a large part of the Languedoil "nationalized" this principle by granting the king a *fouage* to finance military measures against brigandage. It was to produce an average of three francs per taxable household, but was graded from one to nine francs according to ability to pay. The hearth in this sense referred to a household unit whose wealth exceeded a certain minimum. The mode of apportionment resembled the *répartition* associated with the *taille,* but the tax was levied directly, without the intermediary of lump sums imposed on communities.

This *fouage,* however, proved to be the immediate ancestor of the royal *taille* in the northern two-thirds of France, in that it was an apportioned direct tax bearing on rural as well as urban inhabitants. With minor changes and interruptions, it ran until 1380, when Charles V canceled it. Within a few years, however, the French government found that it could no longer manage without direct taxation. It finally adopted the idea of occasional special taxes, called *tailles*. At first these were lump sums calculated as a percentage of the anticipated

TAILLE, TALLAGE

revenues from the *aides* (royal indirect taxes) in a given region, but assessed according to the sort of apportionment used for the earlier *fouage.* A number of these "great tallages" were imposed by the royal government—in 1384, 1386, 1387, 1388, 1396, and 1406—always ostensibly for some specific purpose like a military campaign or the marriage of the king's daughter.

These taxes were more popular with the bourgeois than the *aides,* for the latter bore mainly on the towns and increased the price of goods sold, while the royal *tailles* affected the large rural population as well. The nobles of the Languedoil, most of whom lived in the country, disliked the *tailles* for the same reason. It is true that the government, in imposing the *taille* of 1388, had declared that nobles who met certain requirements would be exempt, but it would be many years before noble status would be any guarantee of exemption from royal *tailles,* and the lords of this period were not eager to see their peasants heavily burdened by royal exactions.

We find many references to royal *tailles* in France between 1420 and 1440, when the kingdom was politically divided and in deep financial distress. Charles VII controlled the part of the realm south of the Loire, which included regions with at least two different fiscal traditions. The monarch summoned frequent assemblies of the Estates General, and these granted *tailles* or *aides* on most occasions. Except in 1428 and 1436, however, the *aides* were replaced by *tailles* in most regions when provincial Estates met to ratify the grants of the central assemblies. One infers that the nobles, who preferred *aides* to *tailles,* had less political influence in the provincial assemblies than in the Estates General.

In 1439 the need to deal with brigandage was as great as it had been in 1363, when the Estates had first authorized the royal *fouage.* Once again the Estates resorted to direct taxation. The *taille* granted in 1439 resembled others levied in the recent past, but it was to be collected in addition to the *aides,* which had been back in force on a regular basis since 1436. The *taille* granted in 1439, moreover, did not expire after its stated length of time, one year. Because a revolt in 1440 prevented any new assembly from meeting to cancel or renew the *taille,* the king continued to collect it, although the Estates were not convened again for nearly thirty years.

Historians have attributed great importance to the *taille* of 1439, not because it was at all novel by that date, but because it became permanent thereafter. For the next three and a half centuries it was the most important source of royal revenue in France. In 1460, it produced about 1.2 million pounds, and thereby constituted about two-thirds of the crown's income. Up to this point its relative importance had not increased greatly over the *fouage* levied from 1363 to 1380, but in the reign of Louis XI (1461–1483) the receipts from the *taille* soared to an annual rate of 3.9 million pounds. Such an increase would not have been possible without a great improvement in the economic state of the kingdom, but it naturally gave rise to considerable resentment. Those who governed in the name of his young successor reduced the *taille* to 1.5 million pounds, and its next great increase did not occur until the sixteenth century. Even in 1484, however, the *taille* remained the most crucial source of revenue for the French government, and there was little effective opposition to the crown's practice of determining each year the amount it needed and assessing it without reference to any central assembly.

In its matured form, the French royal *taille* was a lump sum determined by the king's financial officers and apportioned among the provinces of France. The criteria used in this apportionment included economic factors, national and regional custom, and current political circumstances. Inevitably, the more heavily taxed regions came to regard this apportionment as excessively arbitrary and unfair. The further apportionment of each region's quota was carried out under the supervision of provincial estates or royal officers, depending on local traditions. Exemptions from the royal *taille* appeared almost as early as the tax itself. Most nobles, clergy, and universities and selected types of officials had secured exemptions by the end of the Middle Ages, but these had not yet become permanently enshrined in law.

Although the *taille* experienced a lengthy evolution, in a sense it came full circle in France. Under the *ancien régime* many people considered the royal *taille* as arbitrary and degrading as its remote seigneurial ancestor of the eleventh century.

BIBLIOGRAPHY

Thomas N. Bisson, ed., *Fiscal Accounts of Catalonia Under the Early Count-Kings (1151–1213),* 2 vols. (1984); Georges Duby, *La société aux XIe et XIIe siècles dans la région mâconnaise* (1953); Theodore Evergates,

Feudal Society in the Bailliage of Troyes Under the Counts of Champagne, 1152–1284 (1975); John Bell Henneman, *Royal Taxation in Fourteenth-century France: The Captivity and Ransom of John II, 1356–1370* (1976); Maurice Rey, *Le domaine du roi et les finances extraordinaires sous Charles VI, 1388–1413* (1965); Richard W. Southern, *The Making of the Middle Ages* (1953); Carl Stephenson, "The Origin and Nature of the *Taille,*" in his *Mediaeval Institutions: Selected Essays,* Bryce D. Lyon, ed. (1954), 41–103.

JOHN BELL HENNEMAN

[See also **Accounting; Ban, Banalité; Banking, European; Castellan; Charles V of France; Charles VII of France; Commune; Corvée; Feudalism; Gabelle; Knights and Knight Service; Maltolte; Reclamation of Land; Taxation, French; Urbanism, Western European; Villages: Community.**]

TÁIN BÓ CÚAILNGE (The cattle raid of Cooley), the most important early Irish saga, is the closest approximation in medieval Irish tradition to a heroic narrative of epic dimensions. Although it is associated with ancient Ulster, its influence on other Irish literary texts spreads far beyond its original scope as a saga of the northern half of Ireland and affects every aspect of the tradition. It continued to be copied down to the nineteenth century, even though Fenian heroic lore had usurped it in popular oral tradition. As a result of the numerous translations made into English in the late nineteenth century, it has become a basic ingredient of the political, educational, and cultural consciousness of the modern Irish nation-state.

The textual history of the *Táin* is complex. Most scholars assume that the text had a long oral prehistory that preserved intact many elements of La Tène Celtic heroic culture such as headhunting, fighting from war chariots (a practice that was obsolete in the Gaul of Caesar's day but survived in Britain), and taboo and totemic preoccupations. An initial formulation for these stories in the fourth century has been suggested with the first written treatments beginning in the seventh century. The earliest extant text of the elaborated saga containing all the essential elements of the tale occurs in an eleventh-century manuscript, *Lebor na hUidre* (Book of the dun cow). Called Recension I (with the text completed from fifteenth-century manuscripts), this text can be dated on linguistic grounds to the ninth century. Recension II, complete in a manuscript from the second half of the twelfth century known as the Book of Leinster, is a fresh retelling of the saga in contemporary linguistic and stylistic guise and is usually considered as the work of a single revising author. There is also a later third version which combines elements of the earlier versions.

The complex textual history of the *Táin bó Cúailnge* is reflected in the great variety of literary styles present in its various forms, ranging from archaic verse to prose sequences of elaborate rhetorical complexity. While continual oral retellings must have been present through the medieval period and while the later recensions are of great interest, the version of the story in Recension I, nevertheless, remains the principal focus of scholarly interest.

The essential elements of this version are as follows: The armies of Queen Medb of Connaught in the west and of her consort Ailill, with allies drawn from all over Ireland, attack the province of Ulster in order to win a prized black bull (Donn Cúailnge) belonging to an Ulsterman. The warriors of Ulster and their king, Conchobor mac Nessa, are afflicted by a mysterious illness, the result of a curse by the goddess who gave her name to the royal residence of Emain Macha. A young warrior, Cú Chulainn, is left to defend the province alone; with the help of his divine father, Lug, he succeeds in warding off the invading forces by fighting a series of single combats until the men of Ulster recover from their torpor. The saga ends with a great pitched battle, a fight to the death between the two champion bulls from each side, and an ensuing peace that lasts for seven years.

In its long history the tale has been elaborated in several ways and bears many of the marks of oral compositional techniques and transmission. The result is a narrative of varying coherence. The unifying factor in the saga is the clear focus on Cú Chulainn. From the point of view of Indo-European epic, he has been seen as an archaic Herculean figure displaying features such as elaborate battle-frenzy techniques, trickster qualities, and magical powers, and there is one long flashback section relating the boyhood exploits of Cú Chulainn that shows him apparently undergoing the ordeals of warrior-band initiation rites. More restrained and conventional epic themes are the contrast between ineffective king and resourceful warrior, the roles of malign goddess and helper of god, and a fight to the death between two foster brothers.

The constant glorification of warriors and war is

countered somewhat by the often farcical and comic treatment of heroic assumptions and by a larger framework of reference that, especially in the introductory scene-setting tales, includes the peaceful values of the court, artisans, farmers, and women. Memorable and fully rounded characters are created, often from the debris of an older mythicopolitical system, as in the case of Queen Medb, originally a sovereignty goddess of the central province, who appears in the *Táin* as an anarchic, amoral figure of masterful feminine intrigue.

If the tale can be characterized on a basic level as an archaic example of the archetypal Indo-European cattle raid, its long history and paramount place in Irish literary tradition ensure for the *Táin bó Cúailnge* consideration as a text of true epic status.

BIBLIOGRAPHY

Sources. Ernst Windisch, *Die altirische Heldensage Táin bó Cúalnge nach dem Buch von Leinster* (1905); Cecile O'Rahilly, ed., *Táin bó Cúalnge, from the Book of Leinster* (1967), and *Táin bó Cúailnge: Recension I* (1976).

Studies. James Carney, "Early Irish Literature: The State of Research," in *Proceedings of the Sixth International Congress of Celtic Studies* (1983), 113–130; Myles Dillon, ed., *Irish Sagas* (1959, repr. 1968); Kenneth H. Jackson, *The Oldest Irish Tradition: A Window on the Iron Age* (1964); Rudolf Thurneysen, *Die irische Helden- und Königsage bis zum siebzehnten Jahrhundert* (1921).

Ann Dooley

[See also **Irish Literature; Irish Literature: Saga.**]

TALENTI, FRANCESCO (*fl.* 1351–1369), architect, first documented in Orvieto, 1325, later active in Florence, where he is mentioned from 1351 to 1369 as *capomaestro* (foreman) of the building works of the cathedral. The extent of his contribution there (whether the implementation of old designs or the innovation of bold new ones) is disputed by modern scholars. The upper three stories of "Giotto's" bell tower are generally considered his work.

The campanile of the cathedral of Florence, 1334–1359, with upper three stories designed by Francesco Talenti. ALINARI/ART RESOURCE

BIBLIOGRAPHY

Cesare Guasti, *Santa Maria del Fiore: La costruzione della chiesa e del campanile secondo i documenti tratti dall'Archivio dell'opera secolare e da quello di Stato* (1887); Gert Kreytenberg, *Der Dom zu Florenz: Untersuchungen zur Baugeschichte im 14. Jahrhundert* (1974), reviewed by Marvin Trachtenberg in *Art Bulletin,* **61** (1979), and a reply by Kreytenberg, *ibid.,* **62** (1980); Marvin Trachtenberg, *The Campanile of Florence Cathedral: "Giotto's Tower"* (1971).

Dale Kinney

[See also **Brunelleschi, Filippo (with illustration); Trecento Art.**]

TALIESIN. Taliesin is the name of one of the five poets mentioned by Nennius in his *Historia Brittonum* as being renowned for their poetry among the British (that is, the Celtic peoples of Britain) in the second half of the sixth century; the others are Talhaearn, called "the Father of Poetic Inspiration," Aneirin, Blwchfardd, and Cian, whose epithet is often translated "Wheat of Song." Of these poets, only Aneirin's name remains attached to any extant poetry.

Despite the traditional early date for his floruit, poetry attributed to Taliesin survives chiefly in a manuscript of the late thirteenth century known as *The Book of Taliesin.* The sixty or so poems contained therein include poems to historical persons, religious and scriptural poems, prophecies, and poems of an arcane nature, which some scholars have seen as belonging to a separate tradition. The historical poems attributed to Taliesin match well the chronology provided by Nennius, and it seems clear that Taliesin must have been court poet to Urien, king of Rheged (southwest Scotland, broadly speaking), who flourished in the last quarter of the sixth century, and to his son Owain.

This is the poet whom scholars believe was an actual historical figure, as opposed to the legendary figure of Taliesin, subject of a tale known as *Hanes Taliesin* (Tale [or Story] of Taliesin). The *Hanes Taliesin* exists in manuscripts no earlier than the sixteenth century and tells of a youth named Gwion Bach, who either inadvertently or by design gained access to the three drops of magical knowledge and poetic inspiration destined for the ugly son of the witch Ceridwen. After a chase characterized by much shapeshifting, the witch swallowed the lad, then gave birth to him in due course. He was then set adrift and eventually discovered by Elphin, son of a wealthy squire in North Wales, during the time of the historical King Maelgwn of Gwynedd. He was named Taliesin, and when he was thirteen years of age he set out for the court of Maelgwn, where he confounded the royal poets and established himself as the chief poet of the Western world. Many of the arcane poems in *The Book of Taliesin* treat themes that reflect the career of this legendary poet. In some of those and in the poems that belong to the *Hanes* itself, the poet appears as a personification of wisdom, an archetypal being who has existed through all time and space, in many forms, and who knows all things. This lore echoes material found elsewhere in Celtic cultures involving the notion of an archetypal poet and the acquisition of supernatural or divinely inspired knowledge.

BIBLIOGRAPHY

Patrick K. Ford, *The Mabinogi and Other Medieval Welsh Tales* (1977); A. O. H. Jarman, "Taliesin," in *idem* and Gwilym Rees Hughes, eds., *A Guide to Welsh Literature,* I (1976), 51–67; Ifor Williams, *Chwedl Taliesin* (1957) and *The Poems of Taliesin,* J. E. Caerwyn Williams, trans. (1968).

PATRICK K. FORD

[See also **Aneirin; Mabinogi; Mythology, Celtic; Nennius; Welsh Literature.**]

T^{c}ALIN, an Armenian town, once the capital of the Kamsarakan princes, is notable for its large cathedral, the small church of St. Astuacacin (both seventh century), and numerous fifth- or sixth-century stelae carved with figured compositions.

The cathedral, probably erected by a Kamsarakan prince in the second half of the century, is a longitudinal domed structure, one of the most imposing Armenian churches in size and height. Its plan is a synthesis of the older basilical domed churches of Armenia (Gayianē, Mren) and the cruciform or trefoil type. Three of its apses, semicircular on the interior and polygonal on the exterior, project outward from the walls of the church. Four freestanding central piers, linked by arches, supported the dome (now collapsed) with pendentives to make the transition from the square bay to the circular drum. The exterior of the drum and apses have blind arcades with geometric and floral motifs. The structure has been severely damaged by earthquakes.

There are remnants of wall paintings on the interior confirming testimony by the monk Vrt^{c}anēs K^{c}ert^{c}oł (sixth/seventh century) that Gospel cycles were painted in early Armenian churches. Scenes include a theophanic vision in the apse (as at Mren and Lmbat), Christ's entry into Jerusalem, saints, and apostles.

The church of St. Astuacacin, according to an inscription, was erected by Nerses Kamsarakan probably in the 630's. A small, domed, central-plan church with three semicircular apses, it is a freestanding cruciform on the exterior with rectangular arms (similar to churches at Alaman and Lmbat). Squinches are used to ease the transition from the square central bay to the semicircular drum on which the dome rests.

The stelae at T^{c}alin were originally from a ruined basilical church nearby. Some are carved on all four sides with figured images and include scenes with the Virgin and Child enthroned, the baptism of Christ, angels, and representations of King Trdat (Tiridates) III the Great (*r. ca.* 259–314) with a boar's head, in accordance with the legend surrounding the conversion of Armenia to Christianity in 314.

BIBLIOGRAPHY

Architettura medievale Armena: Roma, Palazzo Venezia, 10–30 giugno 1968 (1968); Sirarpie Der Nersessian, *The Armenians* (1969) and *Armenian Art,* Sheila Bourne and Angela O'Shea, trans. (1978); Varaztad

Harouthiounian and Morous Hasrathian, *Monuments of Armenia* (1975); Harry F. B. Lynch, *Armenia: Travels and Studies*, I (1901, repr. 1965); Josef Strzygowski, *Die Baukunst der Armenier und Europa*, I (1918); N. M. Tokarskii, *Architektura Armenii IV–XIV vv* (1961).

LUCY DER MANUELIAN

[See also **Armenia: History of; Armenian Art; Gayianē, Church of; Kamsarakan; Mren, Church of; Trdat III (IV) the Great, St.**]

TALLIES. See **Taille, Tallage.**

TALMUD, EXEGESIS AND STUDY OF. There are two Talmuds, the Jerusalem (also called the Palestinian) and the Babylonian. Both are essentially expansive comments on and interpretations and analyses of the Mishnah, which was edited and redacted by Rabbi Judah the Prince about the beginning of the third century. The sages of the period beginning with the death of Judah and ending with the editing and redaction of the two Talmuds are known collectively as interpreters, or amoraim (sing., amora). It is their words that make up the vast majority of attributed remarks in both Talmuds. Both Talmuds also contain many unattributed comments, which are called the comments of the anonymous (*setam*). The quantity of the *setam* is far greater in the Babylonian Talmud, where it weaves intricate arguments and discussions into the attributed comments of the amoraim. The Mishnah and Talmud are divided into large units, called orders; these, in turn, are divided into smaller units, called tractates.

The Jerusalem Talmud was edited in two locations. The majority of it was edited in Tiberias near the end of the fourth century; the order *Nezikin* had been edited in Caesarea about fifty years earlier. These dates are accepted by virtually all modern scholars.

The Jerusalem Talmud does not refer to its own editing, whereas the Babylonian Talmud does comment on its own editing. Traditionally, the editing of the Babylonian Talmud has been attributed to Ravina and Rav Ashi, on the basis of an ambiguous comment in the tractate *Bava Mezia* 86a that Ravina and Rav Ashi mark the end of teaching (*horaʾah*). It is not clear whether *horaʾah* refers to a final ordering or a final editing, although this is how Rashi understands the passage. It is also not clear whether the Ravina referred to is Ravina I (*d.* 422) or Ravina II (*d.* 499 or 501). Modern scholars differ, as well, on the dating of the *setam* portions of the Babylonian Talmud. Most date them from before Rav Ashi (*d. ca.* 427); others date them from the period between Rav Ashi and Ravina II, and refer to these anonymous sages as the *setamaim*. All agree that Rav Ashi played a significant role in the editing of the Babylonian Talmud and that it was virtually completed by the end of the fifth century.

THE SAVORAIM

The Babylonian scholars after the period of the amoraim are known as savoraim (sing., savora). The period of the savoraim is still shrouded in considerable mystery. Primary information about them comes from *Iggeret Sherira Gaon* (987) and from *Sefer ha-Kabbalah* of Abraham Ibn Daud (1160). Sherira dates the period from 499 to 540, and Ibn Daud dates it from 502 to 689.

Sherira defines the activity of the savoraim as rendering decisions similar to *horaʾah* and giving explanations of the things that had been left unsettled in the Babylonian Talmud. The extent of their involvement in further editing of the Babylonian Talmud is unclear, though there are sections of the Talmud that are attributed to them by virtual universal agreement. In addition, some of the technical terminology in the Babylonian Talmud is attributed to them.

With the end of the period of the savoraim, a turning point is reached. The Talmud is completed, and the efforts of the sages turn toward explaining and interpreting it, rather than continuing a process of editing it or adding to it.

THE GEONIM

The next period is referred to as the gaonic period. Gaon (pl., geonim) is the title given to the heads of the academies, who were appointed by the exilarch, at the cities of Sura and Pumbedita. The period begins at the end of the sixth century and continues until the middle of the eleventh century. The names of only a few of the geonim are well known, including Yehudai, Amram, Saadiah, Sherira, Samuel ben Ḥofnī, and Hay. The academies exerted great influence on the entire world Jewish community, serving as supreme courts and as the authoritative interpreters of Jewish law. It is during this period that the Babylonian Talmud became the dominant one, and the term "Talmud" came to mean the Babylonian Talmud alone. Indeed, it is only in modern times that there has been a resurgence of interest in and study of the Jerusalem Talmud.

From this period on, the primary focus of Jewish study became the Talmud, which was studied for its own sake and as the basic source of Jewish law. Thousands used to come to the academies for a month-long public forum (*kallah*). These *kallot,* devoted to the study of the Talmud, took place twice a year, in fall and spring, under the direction of the gaon. A different tractate of the Talmud was reviewed at each one.

The basic genres of talmudically based literature that evolved during this period continued to be utilized throughout the Middle Ages and, indeed, into modern times. The first genre is commentary. Gaonic commentaries tend to be of two types: either very short and concise explanations of difficult words or phrases or very long, exhaustive analyses of entire talmudic sections. Very few of the gaonic commentaries have survived in anything approaching complete form. Most are known primarily through quotations from them by later talmudic exegetes, in whose writings references to them abound.

A subcategory of the commentary genre is composed of the works that were intended to be introductory treatises to the Talmud (*sifrei mevo*ᵓ*ot*). Since the Talmud served as the primary source for Jewish law, one of the major functions of this group was to provide guidance concerning appropriate decision-making, particularly where the Talmud records disagreements among amoraim. These treatises also include historical material. Two very important examples of this genre have survived (most have not). *Seder Tannaim ve-Amoraim* (884), of unknown authorship but probably Suran, has both historical and methodological sections. *Iggeret Sherira Gaon* (987), extant in two versions, is primarily historical. It continues to be the primary historical source for the talmudic and gaonic periods.

The second genre of this period is the codes of talmudic law (*sifrei halakhot*). The earliest codes were mainly systematic compilations of the legal sources relevant to a given topic, almost always accompanied by a decision on those issues that were a matter of disagreement in the Talmud. (The Talmud itself, although the basis of law, is not systematically organized: it can deal with the same subject matter in many different places.) Among the best known of the gaonic period are: *Halakhot Pesukot* (Halakhic decisions) of Yehudai Gaon (second half of the eighth century); *Halakhot Gedolot* (Large Halakhah) of Simon Kayyara (eighth or ninth century), which, in part, is organized according to the order of the Talmud; the thematic legal treatises of Saadiah (*d.* 942), only one of which has survived intact; and similar works of Samuel ben Ḥofnī (*d.* 1013) and Hay (*d.* 1038). In addition, the *She*ᵓ*iltot* of Aḥa of Shabḥa (first half of the eighth century) should be included in this category, although it is unique insofar as it is organized according to the order of the sections of the Torah rather than thematically or following the order of the Talmud, and it contains a significant mixture of legal and nonlegal material.

The third genre of literature to flower during the gaonic period is that of the responsa, or questions and answers (*she*ᵓ*elot u-teshuvot*). Though antecedents exist in the Talmud itself, it is only during this period that it becomes a literary form and an independent genre.

At the beginning of the period, the questions addressed to the geonim and their academies came mainly from the Babylonian community itself and were often answered orally. From the middle of the eighth century, however, written queries were addressed to them from all over the Jewish world, with a significantly larger number coming from Spain and North Africa. The questions included requests for interpretation of difficult passages in the Talmud, questions of history, theology, and belief, and, most often, queries requesting legal guidance in matters that had arisen in the community.

Questions were answered primarily during the *kallah* months. The gaon listened to a discussion of the issue in the academy and then dictated his answer, which was transcribed by the scribe of the academy and set off to the questioner. The answers could vary in length from a few brief words to an entire treatise. *Iggeret Sherira Gaon,* for example, is a response to a query addressed to Sherira by the North African community of Al-Qayrawān (Kairouan). Responsa of a legal nature were answered in the name of the entire academy and were considered to be definitive and authoritative, not merely the expression of an opinion.

Of the tens of thousands of responsa written during this period only several thousand have survived. The most prolific segment of the period in terms of responsa output was the final segment, with nearly half of the surviving gaonic responsa attributable to Sherira and his son Hay.

The responsa were almost entirely based on the Talmud, and they furthered the entrenchment of the Talmud as the central focus of Jewish study. Virtually every responsum entails study of the Talmud and its exegesis.

THE RISHONIM

The same three basic categories—commentary, codes, and responsa—remain the primary modes of literary expression in the period following the gaonic period, although significant modifications are introduced in each.

The gaonic period came to an end with the decline of the academies in Babylonia (Iraq) and the founding of academies of Jewish learning in other countries. The period that followed is referred to as the period of the early scholars, or "first ones" (*rishonim,* sing., *rishon*). Beginning, therefore, in the mid eleventh century, it continued until late in the sixteenth century, ending with the publication of the *Shulḥan Arukh* by Joseph Caro in 1565 and the composition of glosses to it by Moses Isserles (*d.* 1572). The three genres of literary activity in the period of the *rishonim* will be treated separately, but it must be stressed that there is a significant—and inevitable—degree of overlap among them because the Talmud stands at the core of each of them.

The commentary literature of this period can be divided into two major components. The first, explanation (*perush;* pl., *perushim*), tries to explain the text of the Talmud in order to make it more comprehensible. During the early part of the period of the *rishonim* there were two distinctly different approaches to talmudic explanation. The Sephardic Spanish and North African schools tended to summarize the contents of the passage in a clear and holistic fashion, with little concern for line-by-line analysis and discussion of detail, except when necessary. The Ashkenazic Franco-German schools, on the other hand, reflected great concern with virtually every detail of the passage, usually at the expense of a systematic and methodological analysis of the passage as a whole. An example of the Sephardic approach is the commentary of Ḥananel ben Ḥushiʾel, a sage of the first half of the eleventh century, from Al-Qayrawān. An example of the Ashkenazic approach is the commentary of Gershom ben Judah, a well-known Germanic scholar of the end of the tenth and beginning of the eleventh centuries.

Few of the *perushim* of Gershom have survived, except in the writings of his students and their students. One such person is Solomon ben Isaac, known by the acronym Rashi (1040–1105), who was the student of Jacob ben Yakar and Isaac ben Judah, students of Gershom. Rashi's talmudic commentary is the *perush* par excellence. Written in a clear and concise manner, interweaving his own comments into the very words of the Talmud, Rashi, more than any other, has made the Talmud accessible to nonscholars. The brilliance of his commentary lies in the fact that it speaks to both the beginner and the great scholar, each of whom finds Rashi an indispensable tool to understanding the Talmud.

Novellae (*ḥiddushim*) comprise the second component of the commentary genre. Novellae involve depth analysis of the principles and bases of talmudic discussions with an eye toward expanding upon it, reconciling contradictions between talmudic passages, comparing and analyzing parallel sources, establishing the correct version of the text, deducing law, and establishing matters of history, chronology, and talmudic methodology.

Among the Ashkenazic communities, this literature is embodied primarily in additions (*tosafot*). The exegesis of the tosafists originated as comments, analyses, and expansions on the commentary of Rashi. But shortly after the death of Rashi, the genre grew into an independent method of study not restricted to "additions" to Rashi. After Rashi's death, the teachings of Ḥananel and Isaac Alfasi (1013–1103) found their way to the Franco-German communities and were incorporated into the discussions of the tosafists. The early giants of the tosafists were Rashi's grandsons Isaac, Samuel, and Jacob, sons of Meir, husband of Rashi's daughter Jochebed. Among these the greatest was Jacob, known as Rabbenu Tam (*d.* 1171). He and his nephew Isaac ben Samuel of Dampierre (*d. ca.* 1198) were the prime formulators of the tosafistic method and pattern.

Among the early Sephardic *ḥiddushim* are those of Joseph ibn Migash (1077–1141) and Abraham ben David of Posquières (*ca.* 1125–1198). Their *ḥiddushim,* written in a style close to that of the Sephardic commentators, were not analyses of Rashi's commentary. The earliest Sephardic commentator to refer to the *tosafot* in his *ḥiddushim* is Meir ha-Levi Abulafia (*ca.* 1170–1244). After that, the writings and method of the tosafists made real inroads into the Sephardic communities through the work of Moses ben Naḥman, also known as Naḥmanides (*ca.* 1194–1270), and became firmly established during the days of his successors, Solomon ben Abraham Adret (*ca.* 1232–1310) and Yom Tov ben Abraham Ishbili (*ca.* 1250–1330). Asher ben Jehiel (*ca.* 1250–1327), who came to Spain from Germany, was the first to participate actively in both communities and to combine the methods of both. From the days of these sages, the study and method of the tosafists became as much a part of the Sephardic tradition as of the Ashkenazic tradition.

Literature codifying the law in the period of the *rishonim* takes two forms, one of which is much less directly connected with talmudic exegesis than the other.

Three exceptionally important codes demonstrate the general evolution of the literature. The earliest, *Sefer ha-Halakhot* of Isaac Alfasi (known as the Rif), written in the mid eleventh century, basically follows the pattern of the *Halakhot Gedolot* of the gaonic period. It is arranged according to the order of the Talmud, and the legal decision is prefaced by a summary of the talmudic discussion. In the Rif's work, these prefaces are generally much longer than in similar gaonic halakhic works.

The second important code of the era is the *Mishneh Torah* (also known as *Yad ha-Ḥazakah*) of Maimonides (1135–1204). Written between 1177 and 1187, this work broke new ground in codification by its daring. Maimonides composed a systematic and thematically organized code that omitted all references to the talmudic sources or disagreements, and that included only a single, briefly stated conclusion. This style of code is referred to as a book of decisions (*sefer pesakim*) rather than as a book of laws (*sefer halakhot*).

In reaction to the Maimonidean code, the commentators on the *Mishneh Torah* focused primarily on identifying the sources for Maimonides' decisions and, in the process, often spelled out disagreements reflected in those sources. Thus, Maimonides' attempt to write a decisive and unambiguous code spawned a literature that restored the very items that he had intended to delete.

The final codifier of the period is Joseph Caro (1488–1575), whose code is in two parts. One, the *Bet Yosef,* written as a type of commentary to *Sefer ha-Turim,* by Jacob ben Asher (*ca.* 1269–*ca.* 1340), is, in fact, an extensive *sefer halakhot.* It quotes, discusses, and analyzes the halakhic material until Caro's time on each subject and ends with a conclusion. The second, the *Shulḥan Arukh,* completed in 1563, presents a definitively worded statement of Caro's conclusion in the *Bet Yosef.* The *Shulḥan Arukh* is the *sefer pesakim* that complements the *sefer halakhot* in the *Bet Yosef.* In these two works together, Caro accomplished the dual goal of providing a definitive and unambiguous legal decision without severing the decision itself from the exegesis of the sources that led to it.

Of the three basic genres during the period of the *rishonim*, the responsum literature is by far the most voluminous. Though a precise number of responsa is impossible to give, it is probably somewhere between 250,000 and 300,000. They provide a virtual treasure trove of material covering not only matters of practical law (their primary function) but also of biblical interpretation, philosophy, theology, and history.

From the eleventh century on, we find responsa authored by the leading sages of Germany, France, Spain, North Africa, Italy, Egypt, Israel, and Turkey. They do not come in equal numbers from each country in each century, however. Most of the sages who wrote *perushim, ḥiddushim, sifrei halakhot,* and *sifrei pesakim* also wrote responsa, and many other sages did, as well.

Throughout the period, the talmudic exegesis remained the backbone of the responsa, for the Talmud remained the primary focus of Jewish learning and law. There are, however, some differences between responsa of the *rishonim* and those of the geonim. None of the postgaonic academies enjoyed the same degree of authority as the gaonic academies of Babylonia. The responsa of the *rishonim,* therefore, were not usually written in the definitive style of those of the geonim. They were more the recommendations of the individual respondents than the authoritative conclusions of an entire academy. Expressions like "Thus it seems to me" or "In my opinion" become common. In addition, as the period of the *rishonim* progresses, the responsa tend to become more lengthy and expansive, with the author feeling some compulsion to be as detailed as possible, quoting not only the Talmud but the geonim and earlier *rishonim* as well, in order to buttress the validity and authoritativeness of his response. Finally, toward the end of the period, the subject matter of the responsa tends to be restricted to the primary goal of legal decision-making.

From the completion of the Talmud until modern days, the Talmud has been the primary focus of traditional Jewish study. Its interpretation, exegesis, and implications are examined and recorded in three genres of literature which continue to be written even now: commentary, codes, and responsa.

BIBLIOGRAPHY

Chanoch Albeck, *Introduction to the Talmud: Babli and Yerushalmi* (in Hebrew) (1969); Simḥah Assaf, *Tekufat ha-Geonim ve-Sifrutah* (1955); Menachem Elon, *Jewish Law: History, Sources, and Principles* (in Hebrew) (1973), with an extensive bibliography, 1,373–1,393; David Halivni, *Sources and Traditions: A Source* [of] *Critical Commentary on the Talmud* (in Hebrew), II (1975), 1–12, and III (1982), 5–27.

JOEL ROTH

[See also **Abraham ben David of Posquières; Abraham ibn Daud; Exegesis, Jewish; Gaonic Period; Gershom ben Judah; Jacob ben Meir; Law, Jewish; Naḥmanides, Moses; Rashi (Rabbi Solomon ben Isaac); Responsum Literature, Jewish.**]

TAMAR (Tᶜamar, Tamara, *r.* 1184–1212), the daughter of Giorgi III and co-ruler of Georgia with him from 1156 to 1184. Queen Tamar faced strong opposition to her full exercise of power on her ascension to the throne. Forced to make the katholikos Mikel Mirianisdze her chief adviser and executive (*chkondideli-mtsignobartukhotsesi*) and to demote her commander-in-chief (*amirspasalar*) Qubasar, Tamar attempted, and at first failed, to reduce the power of the oppositional nobility. The noble council (*darbazi*) required her to marry a Russian prince, Yurii, son of Andrei Bogoliubskii of Rostov-Suzdal (1185), but after the death of Mikel the queen began to assert her own authority.

Quickly divorced, Tamar chose the Ossetian prince David Soslan as her husband and consort. Together they were able to put down a rebellion of Georgian nobles (1191) that aimed at restoring Yurii. Tamar found loyal support in the Mχargrdzeli (Zakarid) family and in the second decade of her reign used their military and diplomatic skills to expand her kingdom. At Shamkhor in 1195 the Georgians defeated a Muslim coalition under Abū Bakr, the atabeg of Azerbaijan. In 1199 Tamar's army retook Ani and gave it to the Mχargrdzelis. At Basian in 1203/1204 Georgians defeated Rukn al-Dīn, sultan of Rum. Dwin, Shamkhor, and Ganjak were annexed to Georgia, and the queen commanded an empire which extended into Azerbaijan and Armenia. In 1204 Tamar aided her relatives, the Komnenoi, to establish the empire of Trebizond. Independent of Byzantium and dominant in Caucasia, Georgia under Tamar reached the zenith of its power and prestige in the Middle Ages.

Although the noble council continued to function and the queen never achieved autocratic powers, the "feudal" system in Georgia operated in the twelfth century to keep the more powerful dynastic princes from fragmenting the kingdom. With great commercial centers now within Georgia's frontiers, industry and commerce brought new wealth to the country and court. Tribute and booty added to the royal treasury, and with wealth came an outburst of literary and artistic culture. The flourishing feudal society with its Eastern variant of the chivalric ideals was depicted in the verse of Shotᶜa Rustaveli's epic (*The Man in the Panther's Skin*). Tamar's reign marked the height of the "Golden Age" of Georgian history and culture.

BIBLIOGRAPHY

N. A. Berdzenishvili, *et al., Istoriya Gruzii, I: S drevneishikh vremen do 60-kh godov XIX veka* (1962); Mariam D. Lordkipanidze, *Peodaluri sakartvelis politikuri gaertianeba* (1963), and *Istoriya Gruzii, XI–nachalo XIII veka* (1974); I. Mantskhava, "The Golden Age of Georgia," in *Asiatic Review,* **37** (1941), 366–376, 798–809; J. M. Rogers, "The Mχargrdzelis Between East and West," in *Atti del primo simposio internazionale sull'aste Georgiana, Bergamo, 28–30 guigno 1974* (1977), 257–272; Cyril Toumanoff, "On the Relationship Between the Founder of the Empire of Trebizond and the Georgian Queen Thamar," in *Speculum,* **15** (1940), and "Armenia and Georgia," in *Cambridge Medieval History,* IV.1 (1966).

RONALD GRIGOR SUNY

[See also **Amirspasalar; Atabeg; Bogoliubskii, Andrei; Dwin; Ganjak; Georgia: Political History; Giorgi III; Komnenoi; Shotᶜa Rustaᶜveli; Trebizond; Zakarids.**]

TAMERLANE (**Timur Leng**) (1336–1405), the conqueror of central Eurasia and much of the Near and Middle East. Descended from the (Turkic) Barulas clan, his lack of Genghisid blood precluded the proclamation of his own khanate. A leg wound led to his name "Timur the Lame" (Turkish: Aqsaq Timür; Persian: Timur Leng). His father was Taraghai, a relatively important emir. In his early career, Tamerlane—a master opportunist and political manipulator—maneuvered between the various factions contending for power in Transoxiana. In 1361 he became the emir of Tughluq Timür (*d.* 1367), a leading Chaghatayid figure. He quickly turned on him and, using Du'a, another Chaghatayid prince, as a figurehead, he gathered up power in this anarchic region in the name of Genghisid unity. Although claims were made of a kinship tie with the Genghisids, Tamerlane never pressed it, scrupulously maintaining that he was only an emir for the lawful rulers (from 1388 he also used the title sultan but always as the subordinate of whatever Genghisid he had placed on the throne). The closest Genghisid affiliation that he officially proclaimed was that of *Kürgen* (Mongolian, "son-in-law") by virtue of his marriage to the daughter of Chaghatayid Qazan Khan.

Through a combination of military ability and guile, Tamerlane became master of Transoxiana by 1370. His program was to reconstitute the entire Genghisid empire. Over the next decade he established his control over the Chaghatayid khanate. By 1384 Khorāsān was in his possession, and in 1386–1388 he campaigned in western Persia, Transcaucasia, and eastern Anatolia. He was then diverted by his one-time protégé Toqtamish, who, having become ruler of the Golden Horde, had turned on him. Following successful campaigns against the Golden Horde (1388–1391), Tamerlane again moved on western Persia, Transcaucasia, Mesopotamia, and eastern Anatolia (1392–1397, briefly interrupted by another victory over the Golden Horde in 1395). His eastern Anatolian ventures aroused the Ottoman sultan. But, before further complications could ensue, Tamerlane had turned toward India, where he campaigned (1398–1399) amidst even greater carnage than normally attended his triumphs. He returned to the Near East, campaigning against the Mamluks in Syria. Damascus was invested in 1400–1401. Once taken, the city was pillaged mercilessly for three days and many of its inhabitants massacred, apparently without the approval of Tamerlane. His presence was a provocation to the Ottoman sultan Bāyazīd I, and the inevitable contest between the two took place in 1402 at Ankara, where Bāyazīd was defeated and captured. Tamerlane went on to plunder as far as İzmir (Smyrna). He died in 1405 while preparing for a massive assault on China.

Tamerlane's empire was made in and governed from the saddle. Little was done to establish a government in the conquered areas. They were simply despoiled and left, usually to be conquered again. Despite the intention of reestablishing the Genghisid realm and Tamerlane's relatively sophisticated, strict Sunni Islamic faith, he was unable to rise above the level of a steppe marauder. Tamerlane, like other steppe figures before him, needed a continual series of victories to maintain his tribal union and satisfy his followers' desire for booty. His empire, hastily thrown together to the accompaniment of great slaughter, did not long survive him.

BIBLIOGRAPHY

Sources. Ibn Arabshāh, *Tamerlane,* J. H. Sanders, trans. (1936, repr. 1976); Ruy González de Clavijo, *Embassy to Tamerlane, 1403–1406,* Guy Le Strange, trans. (1928); Mirza Muḥammad Haider Dughlat, *Ta'rīkh-i Rashīdī: A History of the Moghuls of Central Asia,* N. Elias, ed., E. D. Ross, trans. (1895); Niẓām al-Dīn Shāmī, *Histoire des conquêtes de Tamerlan, intitulée Ẓafarnāma, par Niẓāmuddīn Šāmī, avec les additions empruntées au Zubdatu-t-Tawārīh-i Bāysunġurī de Ḥāfiẓ-i Abrū,* Felix Tauer, ed. (1937); Sharaf al-Dīn ᶜAlī Yazdī, *Zafarnāma,* M. ᶜAbbāsī, ed., 2 vols. (1957); Thomas of Medzoph, *Exposé des querres de Tamerlan et de Schah-Rokh dans l'Asie occidentale, d'après la chronique arménienne inedite de Thomas de Medzoph,* Felix Neve, trans. (1860).

Studies. B. Akhmedov, "Iz politicheskoi istorii Khorezma v XV v," in *Izvestiya Akademii Nauk Uzbek, SSR* (1960); V. V. Barthold, *Four Studies on the History of Central Asia,* II, *Ulugh-beg,* V. Minorsky and T. Minorsky, trans. (1958); Lucien Bouvat, *L'empire mongol (2ᵉ phase)* (1927); Boris D. Grekov and A. Yu. Yakubovskii, *La horde d'or et la Russie,* François Thuret, trans. (1961); Hilda Hookham, *Tamburlaine, the Conqueror* (1962); Ibragim M. Muminov, *Rol i mesto Amira Timura v istorii Srednei Azii v svete pismennykh istochnikov* (1968); Hans R. Roemer, "Neuere Veröffentlichungen zur Geschichte Timurs und seiner Nachfolger," in *Central Asiatic Journal,* 2 (1956); L. V. Stroeva, "Vozniknovenie gosudarstva Timura," in *Uchenye zapiski Leningradskogo Gosudarstvennogo Universiteta* (1952), and "Borba kochevoi i osedloi znati v Chagataiskom gosudarstve v pervoi polovine XIV v," in *Pamyati Akademika Ignatiya Yulianovicha Krachkovskogo: Sbornik statei* (1958), 206–220; A. Yu. Yakubovskii, "Timur," in *Voprosy istorii,* 8–9 (1946).

PETER B. GOLDEN

[See also **Anatolia; Ankara; Bāyazīd I, Yildirim; Damascus; Genghis Khan; Golden Horde; Iran, History: After 650; Khan; Mamluk Dynasty; Mongol Empire; Muscovy, Rise of; Samarkand; Transoxiana.**]

TANCRED (canonist, *ca.* 1185–*ca.* 1236) was a leading canonist of the Bolognese school. He rose to prominence between 1210 and 1215, during which period he composed apparatuses of glosses on *Compilationes prima* and *secunda,* which became the *glossae ordinariae* on their respective collections. Tancred revised these works after 1220, when he also produced the *glossa ordinaria* to the *Compilatio tertia.* One of the most important features of Tancred's apparatuses was his scrupulous attribution of his predecessors' glosses, so that much of what we know of their activities derives from Tancred's work. Some scholars have attributed the *Compilatio quinta* to Tancred, since Honorius III addressed the bull of publication (1226) to him. In addition to his work on the decretals, Tancred composed the most influential *Ordo iudiciarius* of his time and a *Summa de sponsalibus et matrimonio.*

BIBLIOGRAPHY

Stephan G. Kuttner, *Repertorium der Kanonistik (1140–1234)* (1937); Charles Lefebvre, "Formation du droit classique," in *L'âge classique (Histoire du droit et des institutions de l'église en Occident,* 7 [1965]).

STANLEY CHODOROW

[See also **Law, Canon: After Gratian.**]

TANCRED (crusader, 1075/1076–1112). The early life of Tancred is poorly recorded. His father was Odo the Good Marquis; his mother was Emma, the daughter of Robert Guiscard. His uncle Bohemond persuaded him to take the cross in September 1096. He spent the remaining years of his life in the Near East, attempting to gain territory at the expense of the Greeks, the Provençals, the Turks, and even his uncle.

Tancred played an important role in the success of the First Crusade. His first encounter with the Turkish allies of the Byzantines at Vardar and his refusal to take an oath of allegiance to Byzantine emperor Alexios I Komnenos marked him as a daring fighter and an ambitious young man. Following the fall of Nicaea in 1097, Tancred led a diversionary force into Cilicia and gained Tarsus. Baldwin, brother of Godfrey of Bouillon and count of Edessa, forced him to abandon Cilicia, however, and return to the main army.

Tancred participated in the siege of Antioch in 1098. Ruthless at times, he decapitated some Turkish prisoners and sent their heads to Adhémar, bishop of Le Puy, as a tithe. Following the fall of Antioch, Tancred became involved in the rout of Kerbogha, the Turkish governor of Mosul, and the slaughter of the fleeing Turks.

Following the resumption of the march to Jerusalem, Tancred allied with Raymond of St. Gilles for a short time but soon switched his loyalty to Godfrey of Bouillon. He revealed his territorial ambitions by seizing Bethlehem while en route to Jerusalem. When the defense of Jerusalem broke down, Tancred plundered the temple and gained great wealth. Arnulf, chaplain of Robert of Normandy, attacked his seizure of the temple treasures, but Tancred managed to keep most of the booty, and in turn gave some money to the church.

Tancred assisted Godfrey in defeating al-Afḍal at Ascalon, and for a few months thereafter he attempted to take Haifa, Tiberias, and Jaffa. The death of Godfrey in 1100 brought Tancred's enemy Baldwin to Jerusalem to claim the kingship. Tancred continued his conquests in Galilee but failed to win the friendship of Baldwin, despite the fact that they settled their differences at Haifa in March 1101. That same year Tancred was asked to become regent of Antioch during the captivity of his uncle Bohemond. His activities in Galilee had strengthened the kingdom of Jerusalem, and his departure left Baldwin with a free hand in Palestine. During his regency of Antioch, Tancred devoted most of his time to regaining Cilicia and capturing Laodicea. Bohemond's return in 1103 again left Tancred with few lands and the ill will of his uncle: Bohemond, angered by his nephew's failure to help gain his release, had forced Tancred to return all territory taken when he was regent. Tancred retained two small castles, however. As fate would have it, Bohemond, caught between the Greeks, the Provençals, and the Turks, abandoned Antioch and again left the regency to his nephew in 1104; then he returned to the West to gain support for his fight against Alexios.

Tancred defeated the Greeks and Turks during the ensuing years of his regency and formed an alliance with William Jordan, count of Cerdagne, who hoped to gain control of the county of Tripoli.

After spending years helping in the conquests of Syria and Palestine and as prince of Galilee and regent of Antioch, Tancred died 12 December 1112. His legacy was an expanded Christian influence in the Near East, which ensured the success of later crusaders for decades.

BIBLIOGRAPHY

John Hugh Hill and Laurita Lyttleton Hill, *Raymond IV, Count of Toulouse* (1980); Robert Lawrence Nicholson, *Tancred* (1940); Ralph of Caen (Radulphus Cadomensis), *Gesta Tancredi in expeditione Hierosolymitana,* in *Recueil des historiens des croisades: Historiens occidentaux,* III (1866); Ralph Bailey Yewdale, *Bohemond I, Prince of Antioch* (1924, repr. 1980).

JOHN HUGH HILL

[See also **Alexios I Komnenos; Baldwin I of Jerusalem; Bohemond I, Prince of Antioch; Crusades and Crusader States; Robert Guiscard.**]

TANNHÄUSER. The poet who called himself *tanhusere* in four of his songs appears in no official document and is mentioned by no contemporary except the anonymous author of a ballad of which he is the hero. It is possible that the name is simply a humorous pseudonym with the meaning "backwoodsman." References in his works to historical events and people and to his own experiences indicate that he composed from about 1245 to about 1265, spent some time in Nuremberg, and lived for a while in Vienna as a protégé of Duke Friedrich II of Austria; his account of a journey to the Middle East is probably fictional. The compositions generally ascribed to the poet include seven *Leiche* (metrically virtuosic songs akin to the lai), six minnesongs, four *Spruch* cycles (a *Spruch* is a single-strophe, often didactic song), and two melodies—a rather large number of extant works for a minnesinger of his time.

Tannhäuser is known primarily for his *Leiche.* Five are dance *Leiche*—probably the earliest extant in German literature—and have a lighthearted, joking manner appropriate to their function. The versicles fall into groups that form more or less distinct segments according to content and sometimes according to rhythm. Relatively few different *Töne* are used, which gives several *Leiche* the appearance of *Lieder* and suggests that the poet was not very inventive with regard to musical composition. The minnesongs consist of summer songs, winter songs, and *minne* parodies. The summer and winter songs were probably sung for dancing (the parodies may have been used for the same purpose); unlike the dance songs of Neidhart von Reuental, they have no narrative. Tannhäuser's minnesongs reveal a skillful use of form to emphasize content and avoid monotony. The *Spruch* cycles develop specific themes and are more realistic than the other verse. Moreover, the scale of moods is greater, ranging from genuine sorrow at the death of Duke Friedrich to the broad humor of complaints about hard biscuits and salty meat. Structurally they are less complex than the minnesongs, with simpler rhyme schemes and more regular metrical patterns. Frequent touches of irony and occasional parody characterize the *Sprüche,* except for four that are openly didactic. The two melodies consist largely of similar variations on a brief central theme, but they are pleasant and show considerable technical ingenuity. One of them is to a *Spruch* cycle, the other is the only extant music to a dance *Leich.*

Tannhäuser was the most original minnesinger of his day, an innovator in both style and subject matter. He composed the first direct travesties in lyric verse of the idea of service of ladies, wrote the earliest songs with a courtly milieu—except the dawn songs—to give a frank account of love's fulfillment, and initiated the use of repetition and catalogs as a deliberate stylistic device of lyric poetry. The most noteworthy characteristic of his verse is its irony, the chief objects of which are the standard conventions of courtly lyric and epic literature. Humor is drawn from conceits and stereotypes by distorting them with incongruent or incompatible material or by exaggerating them as parody.

BIBLIOGRAPHY

Texts and extensive bibliographies of works on Tannhäuser and the Tannhäuser ballad appear in Helmut Lomnitzer and Ulrich Müller, eds., *Tannhäuser: Die lyrischen Gedichte der Handschriften C und J* (1973); and J. Wesley Thomas, *Tannhäuser: Poet and Legend* (1974).

See also Dietz-Rüdiger Moser, *Die Tannhäuser-Legende: Eine Studie über Intentionalität und Rezeption katechetischer Volkserzählungen zum Buss-Sakrament* (1977).

J. WESLEY THOMAS

[See also **German Literature; Middle High German Literature; Minnesingers; Neidhart "von Reuental."**]

TANSAR, LETTER OF. See **Letter of Tansar.**

TANUTĒR, an Armenian title derived from *tun* (house) and *tēr* (lord). It seems to have been used interchangeably with *nahapet* and to have been the equivalent of the Georgian *mamasaχlisi.* The *tanutēr* was the head or senior member of a medieval Armenian noble house. He led the clan in all secular undertakings, assumed its hereditary office, supervised its domains, and commanded its military contingents in wartime. Despite the great authority and power of the *tanutēr,* he originally administered all the affairs of his family with the help and advice of his *sepuh*s (cadets), and did not personally own the joint hereditary lands of his house until the transformations of the later Middle Ages.

BIBLIOGRAPHY

Émile Benveniste, *Le vocabulaire des institutions indo-européennes,* I (1969), 296, 305; Cyril Toumanoff, *Studies in Christian Caucasian History* (1963).

NINA G. GARSOÏAN

[See also **Armenia, Social Structure.**]

TAO. See **Tayk^{c}.**

TAPESTRY, ART OF. Narrowly used, the word "tapestry" refers to a specific weaving technique or, more broadly, to hangings or coverings produced by this or other methods. Ancient forms of the word—*tapēs* (Greek), *tapeta* (Latin), *tapis, tapiz* (Old French)—all designate a covering for walls, floors, or couches. In this sense the famous twelfth-century embroidery of Bayeux is properly called a tapestry, for it was intended to hang on a wall. The typical tapestry of medieval Europe, however, was woven, rather than embroidered, in a weft-faced weaving technique. The extraordinary number made in this difficult and expensive medium shows how well tapestries met contemporary architectural and social needs. Tapestry's development as an art and an industry was dependent on a steady supply of excellent wool (preferably English) delivered by an efficient mercantile system; a pre-existing cloth industry from which skilled weavers and dyers could be drawn; and a stratified society with sufficient wealth at the top to support an industry of grand luxe.

ARCHITECTURAL AND SOCIAL USES

Tapestry's first purpose was to provide splendid decoration that confirmed the wealth and rank of the owner and transformed bare stone walls into sumptuous backdrops for castle life and church ceremonial. Even in the cold, drafty halls of northern Europe, tapestries were valued less as insulators than as exponents of the princely way of life. Majestic in scale and brilliantly colored, they were designed in series to illustrate saints' lives or the exploits of secular heroes, ancient and contemporary. Occasionally they were based on plays or romances, or depicted scenes of daily life: noble sport and peasant labor. Tapestries of monumental size lined public rooms, while sets of medium-sized panels curtained off "chambers" within the great halls, creating more intimate and comfortable spaces. The repetition of their chosen themes on pillows, bed hangings, and accessories provided a total textile environment.

The ease with which tapestries could be transported recommended them to the landed nobles, who took them from castle to castle and even onto the battlefield. They suited a multi-residence mode of life as rugs suit the nomads of Central Asia. The tops of many tapestries show damage or repair, the result of having been torn by nails at each installation. Their transportability encouraged their use as a means of transferring wealth. They passed as gifts between the rich and powerful and served at least once as a prince's ransom. Tapestries have a prominent place in inventories drawn up at the death of princes and lesser persons of substance.

Tapestries answered the social need for entertainment and instruction during house-bound winter months of boredom and inactivity. They appealed to audiences on every level, from the illiterate many to the highly educated few. The simplest viewer had no trouble "reading" these sermons and romances in wool. Miracles and violent combat were the preferred subject matter, drawn from the Old Testament, the *Golden Legend* of Jacobus de Voragine, the popular *Biblia pauperum,* and, more rarely, the New Testament. The narrative unfolded in episodes leading from wall to wall; or several scenes, representing progressive action, might appear together in one panel.

The oldest surviving French tapestry, the *Apocalypse* (1375–1380, now at Angers, Musée des Tapisseries), shows the cataclysmic events surrounding the end of the world, as revealed to St. John on the island of Patmos. Jean Bondol (Jan

Rabbit-Hunting with Ferrets. Franco-Flemish tapestry, 1460–1470, probably from Tournai. THE FINE ARTS MUSEUM OF SAN FRANCISCO, GIFT OF THE M. H. DE YOUNG ENDOWMENT FUND, 39.4.1

Boudolf, Jean de Bruges, *fl.* 1368–1381), the designer, followed manuscripts illustrating the book of Revelation. Other designers, inspired by the *Biblia pauperum,* bracketed New Testament scenes with the Old Testament stories believed to prefigure them. The *Golden Legend,* which fleshed out the lives of the saints with lively incident and homely detail, proved an inexhaustible source for tapestry designers, as it did for contemporary playwrights.

A fifteenth-century document records preparations made for a tapestry intended for the church of the Madeleine at Troyes. First, an ecclesiastic wrote the story. Then an artist painted a small model on paper to give the words a visual form. Then another specialist, the cartoon designer, enlarged the small model, or *petit patron,* to a full-scale pattern for the weavers to follow. His role was critical, requiring an intimate understanding of the weaver's craft to transpose the artist's image into the less flexible medium of weaving. The bare outlines were painted on cloth in grisaille (in the documented case on bed linen sewn together for the purpose), with only brief notes on colors. The cartoon's summary nature left the weaver with ample opportunity to exercise artistic judgment.

Fifteenth-century tapestries are generally borderless, although an architectural frame or arcade, perhaps a classical legacy, sometimes separated figures or incidents. The idea of a window through which one looked into deep space had not yet evolved. Little interest was shown in representing depth, more remote figures simply being higher on the field. The horizons were extremely high, producing combined elevation and aerial views. Turned to show the most expressive silhouette, figures appeared flattened. Borders became conventional about 1500 as the three-dimensional goals of Italian painting began to alter the nature of tapestry design.

Egypt has yielded the earliest examples of tapestry weaving (1406–1398 B.C., from the tomb of Thutmose IV, now at the Cairo Museum), but the

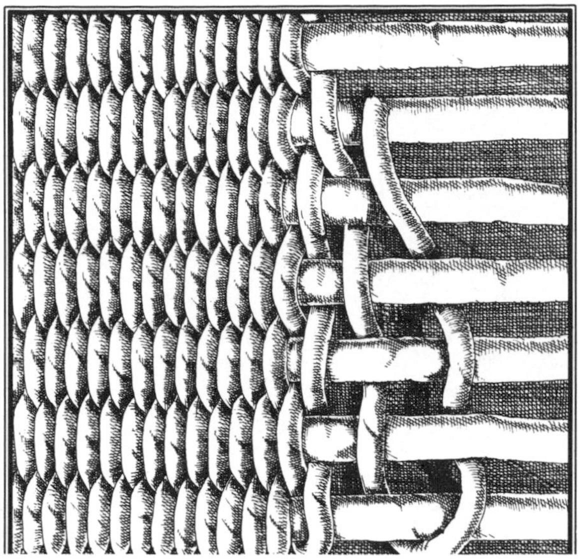

Tapestry weaving in progress, showing weft and heavier warp threads. AUTHOR'S COLLECTION

Weaving on a high-warp loom. 10th-century engraving depicting strings (*lisses*) attached to a section of warp and the passing of the weft-loaded bobbin. REPRODUCED FROM *L'ENCYCLOPEDIE OU DICTIONNAIRE RAISONNÉ DES SCIENCES, DES ARTS, ET DES MÉTIERS*, 1763

art was probably not indigenous, for no further examples appear in graves for nearly a thousand years. Syria may well have been the ultimate source. Tapestry in the form of bands, squares, and roundels decorated Egyptian tunics from the third to tenth centuries of the Christian era. They appear as bobbin darning, the dyed woolen weft interlaced on the warp in a simple over-under technique, then tightly packed to cover the warps completely. How the technique was transmitted to Europe is not known. The oldest European pieces date from the eleventh to thirteenth centuries. The *Cloth of St. Gereon* (originally at Cologne, now in various museums), the *Baldishol* in Oslo, and the pieces at Halberstadt Cathedral in Germany are small in scale. Medium-sized tapestries, representing an intermediate stage of development, have not survived from that early period. Large-scale tapestries appeared suddenly in the fourteenth century, examples of an art already fully mature.

TECHNIQUES

The warp threads that provided the tapestry's skeletal strength were usually coarse, undyed wool, held under tension on a wooden loom. The weft threads interlacing the warps at right angles were brilliantly colored with vegetable dyes. The design was built up entirely by the weft in the course of the weaving. The loom needed to be only as wide as the height of the tapestry if the design was woven sideways. The long warp threads were wound around the end beams and paid out as needed. When the tapestry was completed and taken from the loom, it was given a quarter turn before hanging to bring the design into proper axis. The benefits of weaving the design sideways were tapestries of greater horizontal length, less distortion, and finer lines.

A firm grid was formed by passing the fine weft threads alternately over and under the heavier warp threads. A comblike tool was used to pack the weft so that the warp was completely covered and visible only as ridges beneath the surface. When the tapestry was hung, these ridges would run in a horizontal direction and serve to unify the design.

Two kinds of looms were used for tapestry weaving: the high-warp (*haute lisse*) loom, set up like a vertical screen, and the low-warp (*basse lisse*) loom, resembling a long, narrow table. Both high-warp and low-warp weavers worked from the back of the tapestry, sitting on low stools. In both cases, strings (*lisses*) attached to the warp threads enabled the weaver to move them in groups, creating a shed through which to pass the weft-loaded bobbin. The high-warp weaver had to draw forward a section of warp with one hand while passing the bobbin through with the other.

The low-warp weaver changed the shed with his feet by stepping on pedals that raised and lowered the harnesses with attached groups of odd and even

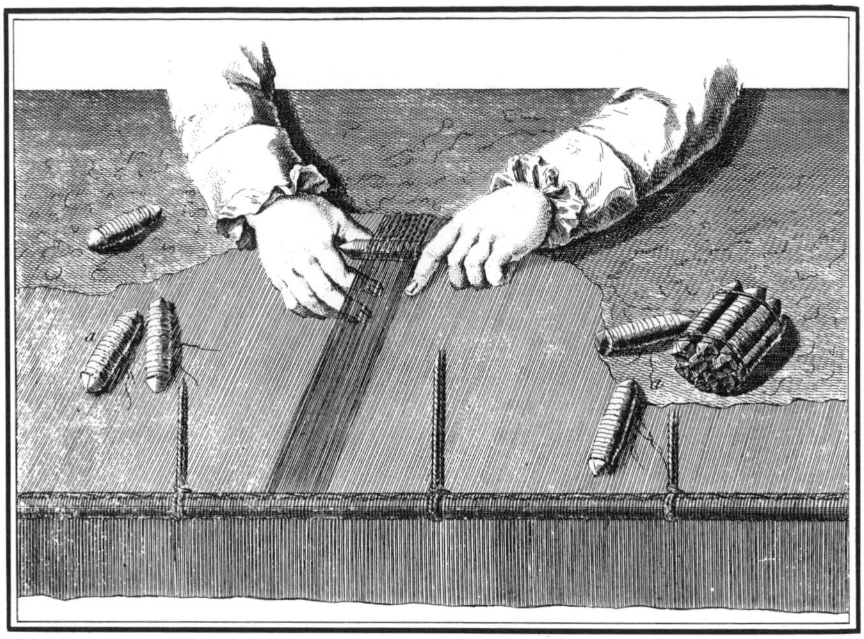

Weaving on a low-warp loom. REPRODUCED FROM *L'ENCYCLOPEDIE OU DICTIONNAIRE RAISONNÉ DES SCIENCES, DES ARTS, ET DES MÉTIERS*, 1763

warps. The advantage lay in having both hands free for weaving.

High-warp weavers needed greater skill and were more highly paid. Their weavings were considered less mechanical. They marked the outlines of the design to be followed on the warps themselves and frequently consulted the full-scale cartoon posted behind them. They could see the finished face of the tapestry by walking around to the front of the loom.

The cartoon prepared for the low-warp weaver had to be reversed, since the low-warp process produces a mirror image. The cartoon was cut into strips and the strips were laid, one at a time, beneath the warp threads. The weaver looked down through the threads to follow the cartoon pressed closely beneath them. The work went faster, with the aid of the pedals, but there was the disadvantage of being able to see only small sections of the finished work by slipping a mirror between the warp and the cartoon. The low-warp weaver saw the tapestry as a whole only after it had been cut from the loom. Several weavers worked together on a large tapestry, each controlling about twenty inches (50.8 cm). The smooth joinings were evidence of their great skill.

Tapestry weaving is distinguished by its discontinuous weft. In ordinary weaving, the shuttle carrying the weft is thrown from selvage to selvage. In tapestry weaving, the weaving does not progress evenly in this way. The weaver works with one color at a time, carrying the bobbin to the edge of the color area as indicated by the cartoon, then changing shed and reversing the direction of the bobbin. This interruption of the warp grille results in the formation of slits between color areas. In most medieval tapestries, these slits were left until the weaving was finished and then sewed shut with needle and thread. There were other ways of dealing with slits, and, in the most skillfully made examples, the choice seems to have been made on aesthetic grounds. Sometimes minor slits were purposely left unsewed. The resulting small shadows were exploited to add expressiveness to features or to suggest rough, textured surfaces. Where the closest joining was desired, the threads were interlocked by wrapping weft threads, singly or doubly, around each other between the warps. Another method, called dovetailing, created a strong but ragged line—weft threads from adjoining color areas were passed alternately, singly or doubly, around the same warp thread.

MATERIALS AND DYES

Wool, undyed for the warp and dyed in bright colors for the weft, was the sole material of the *Apocalypse* (1375–1380). By 1466 weavers were

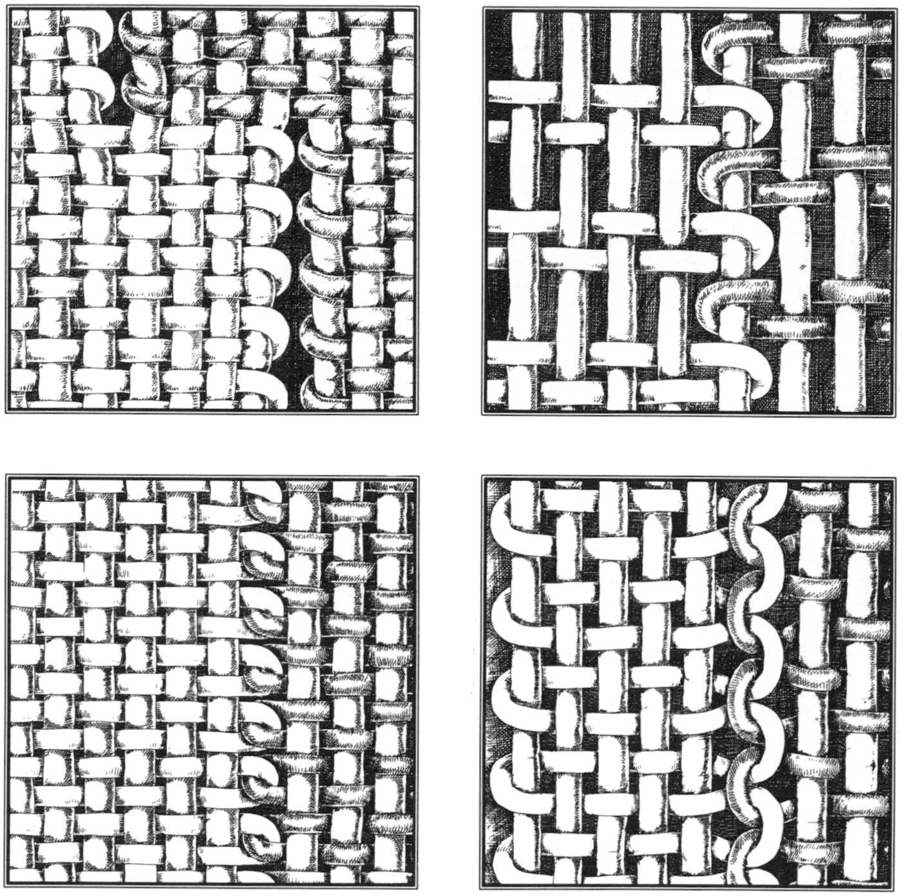

Discontinuous weft of tapestry weaving. Clockwise from upper left: formation of slits; dovetailed wefts; double interlocking; single interlocking. AUTHOR'S COLLECTION

using wool, silk, silver, and gold, as in the *Tapestry with Arms of Burgundy* (Bern, Historisches Museum). English wool was preferred for its strength and durability. It was produced in small quantities, pooled at fairs, shipped to collection points, and exported to such continental weaving centers as Ghent and Bruges, to be woven into fabric for clothing or used for tapestries.

Large-scale cloth production and tapestry weaving were both guild controlled and subject to rules that protected both the product and the weavers. Dyestuffs, especially, were carefully monitored. Only those that had proved resistant to light were approved. Woad (*Isatis tinctoria*), also called pastel, supplied the blue color that was later furnished by indigo (*Indigofera tinctoria*) when the opening of the sea route to India made it the cheaper source. The former source's leaves produced dye by fermentation; then a reduction agent, such as stale urine, was used to release the dye into solution. Weld (*Reseda luteola*), "the dyer's mignonette," usually provided the yellow. To accept the dye, fibers had to be prepared by using a mordant. Madder plants (*Rubia tinctorum*), the source of a warm red, also required a mordant (often alum) in the dyeing process. In later tapestries, reds were supplied by the insect bodies of kermes (*Coccus ilicus*) and cochineal (*Coccus cacti*).

The strict limitation of dyestuffs to sources of proven stability resulted in the remarkable survival of color in older tapestries. Available shades were limited to about two dozen, thus precluding realistic effects, had they been desired. Weavers did seek a way to avoid stained glass effects, however, by using hachures to blend colors. These interpenetrating, comblike extensions of adjacent color areas at first seemed aimed at softening color transitions, and later at suggesting three-dimensional form. When guild regulations relaxed and the number of available colors multiplied, gradations of color,

TAPESTRY, ART OF

King Arthur with three cardinals from the *Nine Heroes* series. Paris, 14th century. NEW YORK, THE METROPOLITAN MUSEUM OF ART, THE CLOISTERS COLLECTION, MENSEY FUND, 1932 (32.130.3a)

without hachures, were used to achieve three-dimensional and pictorial effects.

LEADING WEAVING CENTERS

The commissions and protection of wealthy patrons encouraged the concentration of the most skillful weavers in recognized centers. The downfall of these princely patrons often resulted in the decline of centers and the rise of their rivals. The first focus seems to have been Paris. Nicolas Bataille (late fourteenth century), master weaver and entrepreneur, was established there, and the *Apocalypse* series was woven there under his direction. The superiority of Paris was challenged by Arras toward the end of the century, perhaps because of its access to better material. English occupation of Paris in 1420 brought the industry there to an end.

The reputation of Arras continued to grow until the name of the town became attached to the product: arras (English), *arazzi* (Italian), and *paños de ras* (Spanish). The mighty dukes of Burgundy kept looms busy until mid century with important commissions. The supremacy of Arras began to falter as Tournai, to the north, came forward. The capture of Arras by Louis XI in 1477 left Tournai without a serious competitor.

Tapestries were being woven in Bruges, Audenarde (Oudenaarde), and Brussels in the second half of the fifteenth century, but Tournai had ducal patronage. The typically crowded and tumultuous scenes associated with tapestries attributed to Tournai may reflect Burgundian taste. Sieges, plagues, and declining patronage hurt Tournai in the third quarter of the century. Old cartoons were reused at Tournai, while Brussels was developing a new style emphasizing luxurious fabrics. By 1500 Brussels had taken the lead. Superior designers, organization, and perfected technique allowed it to dominate the market, both domestic and foreign. Low-warp looms speeded up production and guild rules, dating from mid century, assured quality. The painters' insistence on a major role in designing the cartoon paved the way for the Raphael commission (1515–1516) that changed the course of tapestry production for four centuries.

Although Raphael was commissioned by Pope Leo X to design the series the *Acts of the Apostles* for the Sistine Chapel, the choice of Pieter van Aelst of Brussels to execute the weaving established Brussels as the leading center. Raphael's pictorial style imposed new goals and new problems for the weaver. Its deepening perspective, low viewpoint, and central focus made tapestries in the Late Gothic style instantly outmoded.

The *Apocalypse* is the most famous surviving fourteenth-century tapestry. The King Arthur piece from the *Nine Heroes* (New York, The Cloisters) dates from the same period. Among the celebrated series from the fifteenth century are the *Devonshire Hunting Tapestries* (London, Victoria and Albert Museum), the *Lady with the Unicorn* (Paris, Musée de Cluny), and the *Hunt of the Unicorn* (New York, The Cloisters).

BIBLIOGRAPHY

Anna G. Bennett, *Five Centuries of Tapestry* (1976); Adolph S. Cavallo, *Tapestries of Europe and of Colonial Peru in the Museum of Fine Arts, Boston,* 2 vols. (1967); Julien Coffinet and Maurice Pianzola, *Tapestry* (1974);

Margaret B. Freeman, *The Unicorn Tapestries* (1974); Roger A. d'Hulst, *Flemish Tapestries from the Fifteenth to the Eighteenth Century* (1967); Madeleine Jarry, *World Tapestry from Its Origins to the Present* (1969); Joseph Jobé, ed., *Great Tapestries,* Peggy Oberson, trans. (1965), 9–76, 226–264; W. S. Sevensma, *Tapestries,* Alexis Brown, trans. (1965); Geneviève Souchal, *Masterpieces of Tapestry from the 14th to the 16th Century* (1974); William G. Thomson, *A History of Tapestry from the Earliest Times to the Present Day* (3rd ed., rev. 1973); Mercedes Viale Ferrero, *Tapestries,* Hamish St. Clair-Erskine and Anthony Rhodes, trans. (1969); George Wingfield Digby and Wendy Hefford, *The Devonshire Hunting Tapestries* (1971) and *The Tapestry Collection: Medieval and Renaissance* (1980).

ANNA G. BENNETT

[See also **Bataille, Nicholas; Biblia Pauperum; Bondol, Jean; Golden Legend; Rugs and Carpets; Textile Technology; Textile Workers; Wool.**]

TAPESTRY, MILLEFLEURS. The French *millefleurs* ("a thousand flowers") describes tapestries distinguished by a profusion of plant forms, arranged in an overall background pattern or "planted" naturalistically in the foreground. The flowers are often botanically precise. Their symbolic import, however, is conjectural. The origin of the type is uncertain, originally attributed to the Loire Valley and more recently assigned to Brussels.

BIBLIOGRAPHY

Margaret B. Freeman, *The Unicorn Tapestries* (1976), 213ff., 239.

ANNA G. BENNETT

TAQ-I BOSTAN, a rock-cut grotto of the Sasanian period located near Kermānshāh in northwestern Iran. Carved at a spring near the base of a mountain, it consists essentially of two adjacent *eyvāns* of unequal size. The smaller bears in its rear wall a sculpted group of Šābuhr III (*r.* 383–388) and his father. The large *eyvān* is generally attributed to Xusrō II Abarwēz (591–628), who presumably is represented in the investiture scene with the deities Anāhitā and Ahura Mazda on the rear wall. An equestrian figure below, clad in chain mail and bearing a lance and shield, may also represent Xusrō, although an allegorical interpretation is

Detail from a *millefleurs* tapestry, the *Tapestry with Arms of Burgundy,* French, 1466. BERNE, MUSÉE HISTORIQUE. PHOTO: S. REBSAMEN

possible. Large reliefs on the side walls show the king hunting wild boar and stag in the company of courtiers and musicians. These panels, rendered with a wealth of detail, provide unique source material for the study of Sasanian textiles and jewelry.

The proximity of Taq-i Bostan to the important road that linked Baghdad with Central Asia must have enhanced its popularity with medieval geographers and poets who attempted to explain the main figures in the reliefs. The knight was seen as Xusrō himself, mounted on his horse Shabdīz. The king's love for this fabulous animal was taken by some to be the monument's raison d'être. The figures of Anāhitā and Ahura Mazda were thought to be Xusrō's Christian wife, Shīrīn, and the *Mōbadān mōbad,* high priest of Sasanian Zoroastrianism. This latter figure was later identified with Farhād, Xusrō's general and overseer of work at Taq-i Bostan, whom the twelfth/thirteenth-century poet Niẓāmī of Ganja credited with having carved the grotto as an ecstatic gesture of his love for Shīrīn.

The true significance of Taq-i Bostan, at least in its final phase, is probably reflected in the decoration of the facade. Winged females of Byzantine inspiration occupying the spandrels beneath a crenellated cornice may allude to Xusrō's victory in 591, shortly after his coronation, over the usurper Bahrām VI Čōbēn. The reliefs portraying the king as a mighty hunter are appropriate to a hunting preserve, to which the grotto probably belonged.

BIBLIOGRAPHY

The basic study of the monument is Ernst Herzfeld, *Am Tor von Asian* (1920), 57–103. Excellent photographs of the reliefs are in Shinji Fukai and K. Horiuchi, *Taq-i-Bustan,* 2 vols. (1969–1972). For representations of costume and textiles at Taq-i Bostan, see Elsie Holmes Peck, "The Representation of Costumes in the Reliefs of Taq-i Bustan," in *Artibus Asiae,* **31** (1969); Carol M. Bier, "Textiles," in Prudence Oliver Harper *et al., The Royal Hunter: Art of the Sasanian Empire* (1978), an exhibition catalog. For Taq-i Bostan in Islamic literary tradition, see Priscilla P. Soucek, "Farhād and Ṭāq-i Būstān: The Growth of a Legend," in Peter J. Chelkowski, ed., *Studies in Art and Literature of the Near East: In Honor of Richard Ettinghausen* (1974).

LIONEL BIER

[See also **Bahrām VI Čōbēn; Eyvān; Mōbadān Mōbad; Sasanian Art and Architecture; Sasanian History; Xusrō II Abarwēz.**]

TARA. The hill of Tara (Gaelic: Temair Breg) in County Meath, Ireland, is an ancient site, 501 feet (153 m) high, containing earthworks and a passage grave. Tara is celebrated in medieval Irish literature as the seat of kings, and in the literature the kingship of Tara is often equated with the sovereignty of Ireland. This equation is a fiction, since Ireland did not enjoy a centralized monarchy, but it is true that in the early Middle Ages the Uí Néill king of Tara would normally be the most powerful king in Ireland. In the eleventh century an elaborate doctrine was developed of an immemorial high kingship of Ireland centered at Tara, and this doctrine enjoyed some currency until very recent times.

BIBLIOGRAPHY

D. A. Binchy, "The Fair of Tailtiu and the Feast of Tara," in *Ériu,* **18** (1958); Francis J. Byrne, *Irish Kings and High-Kings* (1973); D. L. Swan, "The Hill of Tara, County Meath: The Evidence of Aerial Photography," in *Journal of the Royal Society of Antiquaries of Ireland,* **108** (1978).

TOMÁS Ó CATHASAIGH

[See also **Ireland, Early History; Uí Néill.**]

TARASIOS (*ca.* 730–806), a layman with theological training, was secretary to Empress Irene, who had him made patriarch of Constantinople, an office he held from 784 to 806. In agreement with her policy, he supported the restoration of icons at the Second Council of Nicaea in 787. Subsequently, he came into conflict with the zealots, who severed communion with him because he supported Emperor Constantine VI when the latter divorced his wife and married his mistress in 795. A nearly contemporary *Life of Tarasios* by the deacon Ignatios survives.

BIBLIOGRAPHY

Tarasios' writings are in *Patrologia graeca,* XCVIII (1860), 1,423–1,500. His *Vita* was edited by I. A. Heikel in *Acta societatis scientiarum Fennicae,* **17** (1891). See also Hans Georg Beck, *Kirche und theologische Literatur im bzyantinischen Reich* (1969), 489; V. Grumel, ed., *Les regestes des actes due patriarcat de Constantinople,* I, fasc. II (1972), nos. 350–373; Giovanni D. Mansi, ed., *Sacrorum conciliorum nova et amplissima collectio,* XII (1936), 1,119–1,128, and XIII (1947), 208–356, 399–472; George Ostrogorsky, *History of the Byzantine Empire,* Joan Hussey, trans. (1957, rev. ed. 1969), 177–181.

LINDA C. ROSE

[See also **Byzantine Church; Byzantine Empire: History (330–1025); Councils (Ecumenical, 325–787); Iconoclasm, Christian; Irene, Empress.**]

TARŌN (Tarawn, Taraun; Arabic: Ṭarūn; Greek: Taronitis), a district of southwestern Armenia, west of Lake Van, comprising the broad Plain of Muš and watered by the rivers Aracani (Greek: Arsanias; Turkish: Murad-su) and Meḷ (Turkish: Karaçay). The name Tarōn was used for three distinct entities:

First, Lesser Tarōn (1,486 sq mi/3,800 sq km),

divided into (1) West Tarōn, once a temple state centered at the shrine of Vahagn at Aštišat, which belonged to the house of Vahevuni (Vah[n]uni), hereditary high priests of Armenia, but which passed to the Gregorids, hereditary patriarchs of Armenia, after the conversion of Armenia to Christianity (*ca.* 314), and then to the Mamikonids through marriage (before 438); (2) East Tarōn, centered at the castle of Oḷakan (Strabo: Olanē; Tacitus: Castellum Volandum), belonging to the princes of Sḷkuni, who were dispossessed by the Mamikonids in the fourth century and are last heard of in the mid fifth century; and (3) Aspakunik^c or Aspakuneac^c Jor (Valley of Aspakunik^c), which had no known princes and could have belonged to either East or West Tarōn.

Second, Greater Tarōn (2,970 sq mi/7,700 sq km), consisting of the three entities above together with the districts of (1) Aršamunik^c, which (from its name) may have once belonged to the descendants of Arsam, Orontid king of Sophene, but which in historical times was held by the house of Mandakuni until the latter disappeared (*ca.* 500) and, like East and West Tarōn, passed to the Mamikonids; (2) Palunik^c, in the valley of the tiny river Menaskut (Turkish: Boghan), whose princes migrated to the region of Lake Van in the fourth or fifth century and whose territory, with the town of Ciwnkert (or Porpēs; Turkish: Borbas), passed to the Mamikonids as well; and (3) Xut^c (or Xoyt^c), a tribal territory in the Taurus Mountains that became Mamikonid at about the same time.

Third, Tarōn or Koḷmn Tarōnoc^c (region of Tarōn), a name occasionally applied by the Armenians to Tawruberan or Turuberan (9,650 sq mi/25,000 sq km), the Armenian name for the Byzantine province of Inner Armenia (established in 591). This province included all of the above six districts and thirteen others until the Arab invasions of the seventh century. Ecclesiastically, Mamikonid Tarōn formed a separate episcopate that was the see of the bishop of the Mamikoneans par excellence, one of the three attached to the Mamikonid house. In the eighth century the Mamikonid lands passed to the Bagratids, under whom Tarōn formed a separate principality.

The Mamikonids had taken refuge from the Bagratids in the empire, and when the Byzantines annexed Tarōn in 966/967, the Mamikonids appear to have resettled there. In 1058 Tornik Mamikonean drove the Turkish invaders from Tarōn, and after the Byzantine defeat at Manazkert (1071) he founded the line of the Tornikids at Muš, who held Greater Tarōn with Ašmušat, Hašteank^c, and Sanasunk^c (Sasun) until dispossessed by the Muslim shahs of Armenia (Shāh-Arman) in 1189/1190. Thereafter, Tarōn ceased to have a separate existence, passing successively to the Mongols, the Turkomans, and, finally, under Sultan Selim (*r.* 1512–1520), to the Ottoman Turks. Tarōn was one of the most fertile and densely populated districts of Armenia, and Armenian sources cite some 150 towns, villages, forts, and monasteries there. The main roads from central Armenia to Mesopotamia passed through the plain, as did the southern road from central Armenia to Anatolia.

BIBLIOGRAPHY

Nikolai Adontz, *Armenia in the Period of Justinian,* Nina G. Garsoïan, ed. and trans. (1970); Sowren T. Eremyan, *Hayastanĕ ĕst "Ašχarhac^{c}oyc^c"-i* (Armenia according to the "Geography") (1963), 85, 116; T. X. Hakobyan, *Hayastani patmakan ašχarhagrut^{c}iwn* (Historical geography of Armenia), 2nd ed. (1968), 165–168, 280–282; Heinrich Hübschmann, *Die altarmenischen Ortsnamen* (1904, repr. 1969), 325–327; Cyril Toumanoff, *Studies in Christian Caucasian History* (1963) and *Manuel de généalogie et de chronologie pour l'histoire de la Caucasie chrétienne* (1976, suppl. 1978).

Robert H. Hewsen

[See also **Armenia: Geography; Armenia, History; Armenian Arab Emirates; Bagratids (Bagratuni), Armenian; Gregorids; Mamikonean; Manazkert.**]

TARSUS. Located near the mouth of the Cydnus River in Asia Minor, Tarsus had been an important city as the capital of the Roman province of Cilicia, and later became a major center of early Christianity as the birthplace of St. Paul. Tarsus was occupied by the Arabs in 831, captured by the Byzantine emperor Nikephoros II Phokas in 965, and taken by the Seljuks before the First Crusade.

After the First Crusade, the city was in dispute among Cilician Armenia, Byzantium, and the principality of Antioch. The Armenians gained control of the city by 1173, and Bohemond III of Antioch formally ceded it to Ruben III of Cilicia in 1183. Although one of the principal cities of the Cilician kingdom, Tarsus was, by this time, fast losing its importance as a trading center to Ayas through the silting of the Cydnus River.

There was an Armenian bishop in Tarsus from

the end of the tenth century, and it was later an important archdiocese. The cathedral of Tarsus became the site of the anointment and coronation of many of the early kings of Cilicia, including Leo I/II, Het^cum I, Leo II/III, and Ošin. Under Ošin (*r.* 1308–1320), there was considerable building activity in Tarsus, including a castle and a new cathedral dedicated to the Virgin.

Tarsus was raided by the Mamluks in 1275 and again in 1318. During the reign of King Constantine III/V (1344–1363), Tarsus, along with Adana, was ceded to the Mamluks.

BIBLIOGRAPHY

Ghevont M. Alishan, *Sissouan; ou, L'Arméno-Cilicie* (1899); Thomas S. R. Boase, ed., *The Cilician Kingdom of Armenia* (1978); Wilhelm Heyd, *Histoire du commerce du Levant au moyen âge,* 2 vols. (1885–1886, repr. 1959).

ANI P. ATAMIAN

[See also **Anatolia; Armenia, Geography; Armenia: History of; Antioch; Cilician Kingdom; Crusades and Crusader States; Het^cum II; Het^cumids; Leo I/II of Armenia; Rubenids.**]

TAT^cEW. The monastery of Tat^cew in the province of Siwnik^c, now in the Soviet Union, was one of the most important religious and cultural centers of Armenia from the ninth century on. Theologians, philosophers, scholars, doctors, scribes, and manuscript painters, as well as important secular figures, were associated with this large, wealthy, and powerful monastic complex. Tat^cew was also the repository of numerous manuscripts, documents, and archives. Bishop Step^canos Orbelean, a thirteenth-century Armenian historian, drew on them for his *History of the Family and the Province of Siwnik^c*, which includes a history of the monastery, its structures, its university, and its scholarly and artistic activity.

Perched on an almost impregnable mountain plateau and protected by towered walls, the complex includes three churches, several *gawit^c*s (large vestibules for assemblies), a refectory, a library, storerooms, workshops of various kinds, baths, domestic structures, and a fifteen-meter-high, free-standing column-stele, constructed for the most part between the ninth and the late thirteenth century. These structures are in various states of repair due mainly to an earthquake in 1931.

After the monastery was generously endowed with lands and properties in 844 by the princes of Siwnik^c, the church of S. Grigor Lusaworič was constructed in 848, later rebuilt in 1295 by Bishop Orbelean. The main church, dedicated to Sts. Paul and Peter, was erected between 895 and 906. Other medieval structures include a *gavit^c*, now destroyed, built in 1043; the church of St. Astuacacin in 1087; and the "swaying stele" dedicated to the Holy Trinity, probably constructed in 895. The inscriptions at Tat^cew are a rich source of historical information.

The monastery is also noted for its school of manuscript painting (for example, Gregory of Tat^cew, *The Gospel of 1297,* Erevan Matenadaran MS 7482), the wall paintings commissioned in 930 (probably executed by Frankish painters), and interesting relief sculpture.

Tat^cew was the scene of a popular uprising in the early tenth century.

BIBLIOGRAPHY

Architettura medieval armena: Roma, Palazzo Venezia, 10–30 Giugno 1968 (1968), 125; Marie Felicité Brosset, trans, *Histoire de la Siounie par Stéphannos Orbélian,* 2 vols. (1864–1866); Sirarpie Der Nersessian, *The Armenians* (1969), and *Armenian Art,* Sheila Bourne and Angela O'Shea, trans. (1977, 1978); Lidiya A. Durnovo, *Armenian Miniatures,* Irene J. Underwood, trans. (1961), 138–139; Varaztad Harouthiounian and Morous S. Hasratian, *Monuments of Armenia* (1975), 90–94.

LUCY DER MANUELIAN

[See also **Armenian Art; Gawit^c; Siwnik^c.**]

TATIAN MANUSCRIPTS. In the sixth century Bishop Victor of Capua discovered a Gospel harmony (a composite of the four Gospels) that he tentatively—and correctly—attributed to Tatian, a Syrian who compiled such a work, the Diatessaron, about 170. Victor had the work copied (or perhaps translated) between 541 and 546, and provided with chapter and verse from the Gospels. The resulting Latin text eventually found its way to the abbey of Fulda (whence it is known as *F*), probably deposited there by Boniface, the abbey's founder. Between 832 and 842 a German translation of the harmony was entered, side by side with a Latin version not identical with *F,* in a manuscript now at St. Gall and known as *G.* The German translation apparently was based neither on *F* nor on the accompanying Latin, but on a version containing Old Latin readings not found in either. There is evidence that several manuscripts of the German translation once existed, but *G* is the only complete text now extant. A closely related text, generally thought to be a copy of *G*, was copied by Junius; his copy is now in the Bodleian Library, Oxford.

It was formerly thought that the German translation was made from the Latin of *F* or *G*, and divergences from the supposed original were seen as evidence of the translator's freedom and of the state of ninth-century German. It is now clear that deviant renderings are more likely to be due to the original from which the translator was working. For example, in both *F* and *G*, Matthew 4:8 (Tatian 15:5) reads "et ostendit ei omnia regna mundi." The translation reads "inti araugta imo allu thisu erdrichu," in which the last two words render an Old Latin reading "regna huius mundi" or "regna mundi huius." And in *F* and *G*, Luke 2:9 (Tatian 6:1) reads "et ecce angelus domini stetit iuxta illos"; the German rendering "quam thara gotes engil inti gistuont nah in" seems strikingly free until one learns that the Old Tuscan translation of the Diatessaron, which can have had no direct connection with the German, reads "e l'angelo di dio venne e stette allato a lloro."

It was formerly thought that *F* was the ancestor of all Western versions of the Diatessaron and that the German translation was made at Fulda under Hrabanus Maurus. Although the authority of *F* is now questioned, Fulda may still be the home of the German translation; no other place has a better claim. The translation was clearly the work of a team, though it is impossible to say how many members it had. Some parts of the translation are slavish; others show evidence of thoughtful rendering. The work of copying is easier to describe. One scribe wrote only Latin. Six wrote both Latin and German, each copying both the Latin text and the corresponding German. The sixth scribe, whom some have imagined to be Hrabanus himself, corrected the whole. All except one, whose language has Alamannic features, share a largely uniform phonology that is commonly called East Frankish and is taken to be that of the Fulda scriptorium. The accidence is less uniform. The vocabulary has some remarkable affinities with Old English, but these are demonstrably due not to borrowing under Anglo-Saxon influence (as was once asserted), but to a common lexical heritage different from that of more southerly German. The language of the text is relatively archaic and has stronger links with the dialects of the north (and with Old English) than are found in other Old High German documents.

BIBLIOGRAPHY

J. Knight Bostock, *A Handbook on Old High German Literature,* 2nd ed. (1976), 157–168; Helmut de Boor, *Die deutsche Literatur von Karl dem Grossen bis zum Beginn der höfischen Dichtung,* 3rd ed. (1957), 44–46; Curt Peters, *Das Diatessaron Tatians* (1939); J. Rathofer, "Ms. Junius 13 und die verschollene Tatian-Hs. B. Präliminarien zur Überlieferungsgeschichte des ahd. Tatian," in *Beiträge zur Geschichte der deutschen Sprache und Literatur* (Tübingen), 95 (1973); *Tatien: Lateinisch und altdeutsch mit ausführlichen Glossar,* Edward Sievers, ed. (1872, rev. and enl. ed. 1892); H. Vogels, *Beiträge zur Geschichte des Diatessarons in Abendland* (1919).

D. R. McLintock

[See also **Bible, Armenian; Fulda; Hrabanus Maurus.**]

TATWINE OF CANTERBURY (*d.* 734), born in Mercia in the late seventh century, was appointed presbyter in the monastery of Bredon in Worcester. In 731, he was consecrated archbishop of Canterbury. He was the author of two works: the *Ars Tatvini,* a grammatical work on the eight parts of speech, influenced by Priscian and especially Donatus; and the *Aenigmata,* written sometime between 722–731, comprised of forty metrical riddles based on Eusebius.

BIBLIOGRAPHY

Corpus christianorum: Series latina, CXXXIII–CXXXIIIA (1968); Max Manitius, *Geschichte der lateinischen Literatur des Mittelalters,* I (1911), 203–207.

Nathalie Hanlet

[See also **England: Anglo-Saxon; Grammar; Priscian; Riddles.**]

TAULER, JOHANNES (*ca.* 1300–1361), famous German preacher who combined a mystical inclination with theological learning and a genuine missionary zeal. Tauler was born in Strasbourg, a hub of religious activity during the Middle Ages, as

TAULER, JOHANNES

the son of a wealthy burgher. He joined the Dominicans at their Strasbourg convent in 1314/1315 and is documented at the *studium generale* of his order in Cologne in 1324, when Meister Eckhart, the great master of speculative mysticism, was teaching there.

Tauler's penchant for preaching soon surfaced and the administrators of his order, Eckhart perhaps one of them, sent him among the people rather than to Paris for further theological study. Some scholars wrongly concluded that Tauler was a doctor of theology, which would have implied study at St. Jacques in Paris, but it has been proven that this was not the case. Instead, Tauler spent all of his life in or around Strasbourg, Cologne, and Basel.

Tauler's education and learning were typical for a *frater docti,* a teaching friar: he was most heavily influenced by the Bible, Peter Lombard's *Sentences,* and St. Thomas' *Summa theologiae.* There are, however, also traces of Neoplatonism in his works, which may have come about through reading of Plotinus, St. Augustine, Pseudo-Dionysius the Aeropagite, John Scottus Eriugena, Avicebron, and Maimonides, or more indirectly through the influence of Meister Eckhart.

To date, there are seventy-nine sermons that are definitely attributable to Tauler. These, and a letter to a nun, constitute only part of the works on which Tauler's fame is based because there is a vast canon of devotional literature falsely attributed to Tauler that distorted the picture of the real man. It is, therefore, advisable to keep in mind whether a certain scholar speaks of the true Tauler or of "Pseudo-Tauler." The problem of authenticity of the works was not clarified until 1910, the date of publication of Ferdinand Vetter's edition of Tauler's sermons, and all secondary literature antedating that event should be read with caution.

Tauler belongs to a triad of great German mystics of whom Meister Eckhart is the most intellectual and Heinrich Suso the most emotional and lyrical. Tauler lies in between the other two: he is less intellectually inclined than Eckhart, but more so than Suso; more emotional than Eckhart, but less so than Suso. His major ideas and his working vocabulary are essentially Eckhartian. In Tauler's sermons we find all the key concepts of speculative mysticism, such as Ground of the Soul, Spark of the Soul, and Birth of God as Word in the Soul. Unlike Eckhart, however, Tauler presents these concepts in a more easily digestible, almost down-to-earth manner. He is not so much concerned with the theoretical aspects of the *unio mystica* as with the practical way of attaining it. His chief concern throughout all of his sermons is with the method by which the soul can be readied for the entry of God into the "Ground" (the *Seelengrund*), and he always clearly distinguishes between God and the created world to which the soul belongs. Because of this scholastic orthodoxy, and perhaps also because he was all too aware of what had happened to Eckhart, Tauler never ran into trouble with the papal authorities and none of his writings were ever banned or suppressed.

All of Tauler's works are in German and it is unlikely that he wrote anything in Latin. His task was to preach to nuns and laymen who had scanty or no knowledge of Latin. He did this with unrivalled mastery and it is safe to say that in his lifetime his reputation as a preacher was exceeded by nobody. His sermons are powerful in content and tone; they are, according to Evelyn Underhill, "trumpet calls to heroic action upon spiritual levels." His prose is rich in images and metaphors but almost void of the abstractions and paradoxes that confounded Eckhart's audiences. Tauler also shied away from Eckhart's tendency to retreat into an intellectual monologue; rather, he preferred the rhetorical form of the dialogue to explain or clarify a complex theological point.

Tauler's works were widely circulated throughout the Middle Ages and his fame for a long time eclipsed that of the more brilliant but also more abstruse Eckhart. The works falsely attributed to Tauler also heightened his popular appeal, and Luther's recommendation, albeit based on a work Taulerian in spirit but authored by somebody else, caused many a Protestant during and after the Reformation to see in Tauler a kindred spirit.

BIBLIOGRAPHY

Editions and translations. Ferdinand Vetter, ed., *Die Predigten Taulers,* Deutsche Texte des Mittelalters, XI (1910); Adolphe L. Corin, *Sermons de J. Tauler et autres écrits mystiques,* 2 vols. (1924–1929); Elizabeth Strakosch, *Signposts to Perfection* (1958), the only reliable translation of some of Tauler's sermons.

Studies. James M. Clark, *The Great German Mystics* (1949); Dick Helander, *Johann Tauler als Prediger* (1923); Friedrich Wilhelm Wentzlaff-Eggebert, *Deutsche Mystik zwischen Mittelalter und Neuzeit,* 3rd ed. (1969).

ERNST H. SOUDEK

[See also **Eckhardt, Meister; Mysticism, Christian: German; Suso, Heinrich.**]

TAVERNIER, JEAN LE. See **Jean le Tavernier.**

TAXATION, BYZANTINE. Byzantine taxation is the direct continuation of the later Roman one; its evolution was conditioned by the changes in the administrative system (such as the creation of the themes) as well as by the profound modification of the general economic situation that prevailed after the seventh century.

DIRECT TAXATION

Direct taxation mainly concerned agricultural production, which undoubtedly constituted the basis of the Byzantine economy. The basic taxable unit was the village (*chorion*), the inhabitants of which were solidary in their fiscal obligations. In other words, if one villager died or disappeared, his pairs (other villagers), who might cultivate his land, had also to pay his part of the state taxes, at least until a revision of the cadastre was made and a partial fiscal exoneration (*sympatheia*) was granted to the village. A piece of land that remained abandoned for thirty years was declared to be a *klasma,* became state property, and could be sold to an individual either at a very low price, or with the obligation to pay one-twelfth of its regular taxes. Moreover, "fiscal villages" possessed communal properties (such as pastures), for which taxes were paid by the community as a whole. The fiscal obligations of each individual were thus reassessed at the local level, through the complicated procedure of *epibolé,* every time the cadastre was revised; but by the eleventh century the tendency to establish a unified rate of *epibolé* for the whole empire appeared.

Big landowners constituted separate taxable units. In the fiscal vocabulary they were called "persons" (*prosopa*), as opposed to villages. Their domains, called *proasteia,* were cultivated by tenants, by dependent tenants (*paroikoi*), or by slaves. They were supposed to assume the same fiscal obligations as the villages.

A geographical region containing several basic taxable units was called an *enoria*; several *enoriai* formed a *dioikesis,* the largest provincial fiscal unit, which sometimes corresponded to a whole theme, sometimes to a part of it.

Although the *strategos* wielded full powers inside his theme, at least until the tenth century, taxation was in the hands of special officials who, although administratively subordinate to him, reported directly to the central financial administration at Constantinople. The revision of the cadastre and the establishment of the amount of the taxes was the work of subordinates of the logothete of the genikon (*anagrapheis, epoptai, exisotai, dioiketai*). The census of the military lands was done by the *chartularioi,* subordinates of the logothete of the stratiotikon. All fiscal obligations concerning the postal service and the maintenance of the roads were controlled by the logothete of the drome. The protonotarios of the theme, a subordinate of the imperial sakelle, appears to have been the head of the financial services of the province.

The main taxable good was land, classified, for fiscal purposes, into three categories according to its productivity. The basic tax on it (*demosios kanon, demosion*) was established at 4.17 percent of its value per year. For example, one nomisma per year was due for twenty-four *modioi* (about 24,000 square meters) of land of first quality, for forty-eight *modioi* of second quality, and for seventy-two *modioi* of third quality. This principle survived until the end of the empire, with one difference: in the fourteenth century, as tax collectors had to deal almost exclusively with large domains, they applied a flat rate of one nomisma for fifty *modioi* of land of all qualities.

From the eighth century on, this basic tax gradually increased with the addition of special and "temporary" taxes, such as the *dikeraton* (one-twelfth nomisma), and the *hexaphollon* (one-forty-eighth nomisma), introduced by Leo III for the repairs of the walls of Constantinople, and the *synetheia* and the *elatikon,* which were supposed to pay for the expenses of tax collectors and of their armed escorts. But these taxes ended by being incorporated into the basic one. This basic tax had to be paid in gold nomismata (*charagma*), which were not readily available in the countryside.

The land tax was paid by the landowner. Several other taxes were paid by the individuals who cultivated the land, whether they owned it or not. The *kapnikon* (hearth tax), similar to the *capitatio,* was paid by each farmer's household. To this basic personal tax was added a second one, proportionate to the farmer's productivity; it was evaluated according to the number of oxen he possessed and, consequently, to the quantity of land he could cultivate efficiently. This tax was called *synone* (the ancient *coemptio,* with the difference that it was paid in specie). It and the *kapnikon* were calculated according to the principle of 4.17 percent of the value. For instance, a *paroikos* with one pair of oxen paid one nomisma, while another with just one ox paid half a nomisma, and so on.

Special tithes (*dekate*) were paid for the use of pastures by the owners (individuals or village collectivities) of all kinds of domestic animals producing revenue, especially sheep, swine, and bees.

There was also a long list of extraordinary corvées (*aggareia*) and taxes that could be exacted whenever the need appeared: for cultivating state land; for building or repairing roads (*odostrosia*), bridges (*gephyroktisia*), fortresses (*kastroktisia*), and warships (*katergoktisia*); for providing fortresses or army detachments with victuals at low prices. Particularly unpopular was the obligation to provide quarters to state officials or military that were passing through (*aplekton*) and, even worse, to provide winter quarters to an army contingent (*metaton*). Equally unpopular was the participation in extraordinary levies of lightly armed soldiers (archers, lancers, sailors). In the eleventh century the list of these extraordinary exactions (*epereiai*) became extremely long and undoubtedly contributed to the general dissatisfaction of farmers with their central government.

Not all farmers were subject to the abovementioned exactions. Those who were inscribed as regular soldiers or sailors were exempted from all these *epereiai.* Their land, branded as "military land" (*stratiotike ge*), had a special, hereditary obligation called the *strateia*; the owner should have the necessary equipment and serve, whenever asked, in the armed forces of his theme. If, for some reason, he was unable personally to perform his military duties, he had to pay a tax, also called *strateia,* amounting to the sum that was necessary for hiring a mercenary to replace him for one campaign (four to six nomismata in the tenth and eleventh centuries). The obligations were proportionate to the means of each individual (in the tenth century one could serve as a heavily armed horseman, as a lightly armed horseman, as an infantry soldier, or as a sailor). When soldiers were too poor to assume the whole obligation by themselves, it could be shared by groups of two or more persons. A similar system existed for groups of people who were in charge of the postal service and of the care and feeding of the horses that were needed for it (*exkoussatoi ton dromou*).

Tax exemptions were granted by the emperors to big landowners, state officials, and ecclesiastical institutions, especially monasteries. It has to be stressed, however, that such exemptions mainly concerned the secondary taxes or corvées, and very seldom the basic property tax of the land.

A constant tendency of the Byzantine fiscal system was to transform the various obligations of physical service into fiscal obligations paid in specie that could be levied even when there was not an apparent need for them, thus increasing the burden on the contributors. Such practices favored the development of farming out the taxes of whole provinces to individuals, who could thus make considerable profits at the expense of taxpayers, especially when the monetary system was destabilized in the eleventh century. Tax farming became frequent in the eleventh century and was generalized in the subsequent ones.

The emperors of the tenth century, in a deliberate effort to protect small landowners, issued a series of measures, the most important of which was the *allelengyon* established by Basil II in 1004, obliging the big landowners to make full payment of their poor neighbors' taxes. This measure was repealed by Romanos III (1028–1034). In the meantime, the social composition of the countryside had rapidly changed: the domains of the state and of wealthy individuals constantly increased while the cultivators of the land were increasingly reduced to the status of *paroikoi.* From the twelfth century on, the fiscal system, without being modified in its basic principles, was adjusted to the new reality—a reality that became all the more evident with the development of the *pronoia* as the main means for financing the army and the imperial administration.

The survey, carried out by an *apographeis,* became an essential part of the calculation, collection, and, mainly, redistribution to *pronoia* holders (*pronoiarioi*) of the fiscal revenues. Land was taxed at a flat rate of one nomisma per fifty *modioi.* Each *paroikos* was taxed proportionately to his possessions and to his potential productivity (*oikoumenon*), and was still liable to corvées (usually the equivalent of twelve to twenty-four workdays per year). These taxes went either to the state or to his lord, who might be a *pronoiarios* or a tax-exempt landowner. In the last two cases, the state was deprived of all its fiscal revenues except for fines or "rights" (*aer*) that the villagers had to pay in case of murder or of rape, or if they discovered a hidden treasure.

INDIRECT TAXATION

The basic indirect tax was the *kommerkion,* which replaced the Roman *octava* and was calculated at 10 percent of the value of the merchandise. The rate remained unchanged until 1348, when John VI Kantakouzenos reduced it to 2 percent, in the hope that by this measure Byzantine merchants could compete with their Venetian and Genoese counterparts.

It is not clear whether the *kommerkion* was a customs duty or a sales tax. Most probably it was a combination of both. Special officials called the *kommerkiarioi* levied it at the ports or trade centers of the empire. These offices were eventually farmed out to individuals.

Beyond the basic *kommerkion* there were several secondary taxes, for example, the tithe on wine (*dekateia oinarion,* obviously a customs duty), the *pratikion* (obviously a sales tax), and various local duties paid for crossing a bridge, for using a port, and for weighing merchandise. Trade in slaves was also subject to a special tax, at least in the tenth century.

This system of indirect taxes varied through the centuries. Tax exemptions were granted to individuals and certain institutions treated as "moral persons"—especially monasteries—usually on a very limited scale. Foreign merchants obtained much more important exemptions, especially the Venetians (privileges in the tenth century; complete immunity from 1082), the Genoese (privileges in the twelfth century, complete immunity from 1261), the Pisans, the Catalans, and the French. This fiscal policy that favored foreigners was partly responsible for the decline of Byzantine trade from the twelfth century on.

BIBLIOGRAPHY

Hélène Antoniadis-Bibicou, *Recherches sur les douanes à Byzance* (1963); G. I. Bratianu, *Privilèges et franchises municipales dans l'empire byzantin* (1936); Franz Dölger, *Beiträge zur byzantinischen Finanzverwaltung besonders des 10. und 11. Jahrhunderts* (1927, repr. 1960); K. V. Hvostova, *Osobennosti agrarnopravovyh otnošenii v pozdnej Vizantii XIV–XV vv.* (1968); Jacques Lefort, "Fiscalité médiévale et informatique: Recherche sur les barèmes pour l'imposition des paysans byzantins au XIVe siècle," in *Revue historique,* **252** (1974); Nicolas Oikonomides, "Das Verfalland im 10.–11. Jahrhundert: Verkauf und Besteuerung," in *Fontes Minores,* **7** (1986); George Ostrogorsky, "Die ländliche Steuergemeinde des byzantinischen Reiches im 10. Jahrhundert," in *Vierteljahrschrift für Sozial- und Wirtschaftsgeschichte,* **20** (1928), and "Pour l'histoire de l'immunité à Byzance," in *Byzantion,* **28** (1958); H. F. Schmid, "Byzantinisches Zehntwesen," in *Jahrbuch der Österreichischen byzantinischen Gesellschaft,* **6** (1957); Nicolas G. Svoronos, "Recherches sur le cadastre byzantin et la fiscalité aux XIe et XIIe siècles: Le cadastre de Thebes," in *Bulletin de correspondance hellénique,* **83** (1959); Diogenes A. Xanalatos, *Beiträge zur Wirtschafts- und Sozialgeschichte Makedoniens im Mittelalter, hauptsächlich auf Grund der Briefe des Erzbischofs Theophylaktos von Achrida* (1937).

NICOLAS OIKONOMIDES

[See also **Agriculture and Nutrition, Byzantine; Allelengyon; Byzantine Empire: Bureaucracy, Economic and Social Structure; Epibolé; Farmers' Law; Mints and Money, Byzantine; Nomisma; Paroikoi; Postal and Intelligence Services, Byzantine; Pronoia; Stratiotai; Tithes.**]

TAXATION, CHURCH. The taxes paid by the clergy fall under two headings: those levied by the pope and those imposed by national sovereigns. The two systems of taxation overlapped, however, because taxes approved by the pope could be assigned to kings. The secular rulers were supposed to use the revenue for a pious purpose, normally the mounting of a crusade, and sometimes they actually did so.

Papal revenues in the Middle Ages were extraordinarily varied. The establishment of the papal states in Italy in the eighth century naturally led to the popes being supplied with revenues similar to those received by temporal rulers—such as tolls, fines, fees, compositions, and tallages. With the growing prestige of the papacy and its increasing commitments, the popes tried to increase their revenues by demanding payments and dues of diverse kinds. It became common, for instance, for monasteries to secure independence from the temporal jurisdiction of the diocesan bishop by the payment of annual dues (the *census*) to the pope, into whose ownership the monastic house technically had passed. The sums involved in such payments were never large.

In return for papal protection and favor, kings and princes sometimes paid tribute to the Holy See. Probably the earliest instance was that of a duke of Poland at the close of the tenth century; by the early thirteenth century the kings of Castile, Aragon, Portugal, and England paid tribute on occasions;

but though the sums were often large, the payments were irregular and often in arrears.

The best known of such national tributes was Peter's pence, originating in England, perhaps in a payment first made by the Mercian king Offa at the end of the eighth century. The sums involved were comparatively insignificant, the English annual tax being fixed at £199 6s. 8d., the supposed equivalent of a penny a household. The money was collected by the parish priest and delivered by him to the rural dean; from the dean it passed to the archdeacon and usually to the bishop, who handed it to the papal collector, all the recipients except the last retaining some part of what was received. Peter's pence was paid irregularly and was often in arrears. In 1205, Pope Innocent III tried to extract the full amount but failed.

After the mid thirteenth century the papacy developed the concept of taxes on ecclesiastical benefices. These taxes, the annates and the various forms of *servitia,* were important sources of revenue for the late medieval popes, especially the Avignon papacy. They were founded on the belief that the pope had an ultimate right as universal ordinary to dispose of all ecclesiastical benefices and dignities.

The payments known as *servitia* (services) were made by the higher clergy—patriarchs, archbishops, bishops, and abbots—on the occasion of their appointment or confirmation by the pope in his consistory (the regular meeting of pope, cardinals, and lesser officials). The payments consisted of common services (*servitia communia*), which were shared between the camera of the pope and the camera of the college of cardinals, and petty services (*servitia minuta*), which were divided among the officers and servants of the pope and the college.

Such dues developed into fixed payments in the third quarter of the thirteenth century—the *servitia minuta* were first mentioned in 1263—and became fixed as one-third of the annual income in the benefices. The Avignon popes extended the right to include all ecclesiastical dignities; during the pontificate of John XXII (1316–1334) the two cameras received 1,123,003 florins from the *servitia communia.* These dues were delivered at the camera by the debtors or their agents; local collectors were commissioned only to collect the sums due if the debtors failed to pay.

Annates were a similar development. They were fees for appointments to prebends and other benefices that were subject to papal reservation, had a revenue of more than six marks a year, and were confirmed by the pope outside the consistory, on condition that the benefice did not pay *servitia.* A portion of the first year's revenue of a benefice, originally a third of the annual income, annates were first appropriated to papal use by Clement V in 1306. In 1316 John XXII reserved the annates of a large number of benefices that were to fall vacant within the next three years; the number of vacancies was increased by the constitution *Ex secrabilis* in 1317. Ten years later the pope reserved for a year the annates of all benefices falling vacant at the apostolic see, a device adopted by his successors. In the fifteenth century the term "annates" was also used to describe the *servitia* paid by bishops and abbots.

The subsidies (*subventus*) and income taxes demanded by the popes were more universal in their application and aroused increasing criticism from the clergy, upon whom, for the most part, the burden of payment fell. Subsidies may be compared with feudal aids, in that money was to be used for a particular purpose. An example is the request of Pope Urban II in 1093 that the prelates of Aquitaine, Gascony, and Lower Burgundy provide him with money to assist in the recovery of the apostolic see from the antipope Clement III. In 1166 a similar request was made to the archbishop of Rheims by Pope Alexander III. In 1184, Pope Lucius asked for an aid from the English king and clergy, but the clergy opposed the demand. The large subvention of 10,000 marks that Pope Innocent IV requested from the English clergy in 1244 was much criticized, but the English bishops agreed at the Council of Lyons in 1245 to collect an aid of 6,000 marks.

Papal income taxes grew out of the need to finance crusades. In 1166 and 1188 the English and French kings levied a tax on the income and chattels of their lay and clerical subjects for this purpose. The first direct papal taxes were levied by Innocent III in 1199, when he ordered all clergymen to pay one-fortieth of their ecclesiastical income for one year in aid of the Holy Land. In the thirteenth century his successors made increasing use of the right to levy a general tax upon the clergy. Such payments could be enforced by ecclesiastical censures.

At first such taxes actually paid for crusades. Increasingly, however, the money was granted to princes who had glibly promised to mount a crusade but never got around to carrying out the promise. In such cases, the papal collector was empowered to hand over the money to papal merchants for transfer to the papal camera, but much was often retained by the king. A papal income tax might be imposed for a period as short as one year or as long as six years. The tax might be imposed on the clergy of the universal church or on the clergy of a single country or group of provinces. The first two income taxes, that of 1199 and the triennial twentieth imposed by the Fourth Lateran Council in 1215, had been levied on income that the payers themselves assessed; later valuations were computed by collectors empowered to oblige the clergy under oath to reveal its ecclesiastical revenues and receipts. Pope Innocent IV instituted special papal collectors.

ENGLAND

Regular papal taxation fell heavily on the English clergy in the reign of Henry III and was often stoutly resisted. In 1225 Pope Honorius III, wishing to procure a fixed endowment for the Roman curia, requested the bishops to convert a prebendal stall in every cathedral to the use of the apostolic see, and to secure a fixed income to be assessed according to their wealth from bishops, monasteries, and collegiate churches. Henry III's advisers told the bishops that consent to this proposal would be tantamount to a breach of their service to the crown as barons. The clergy, meeting in London in May 1226, opposed the proposed grant, alleging that it would infringe the rights of local churches, and that in any case the annual tribute of 1,000 marks paid in accordance with the terms of King John's submission to Innocent III should exempt England. In 1239, to assist Pope Gregory IX against the emperor, Henry III allowed bishoprics beneficed in England to be deprived of a tithe of their annual revenues, so long as clerks in his own service were exempt, and he allowed the papal legate, Cardinal Otho, to make arrangements for a general subsidy. The clergy strenuously resisted the levy; and while its collection continued after the legate's departure in January 1241, much of the money was never paid.

In 1252, on the pretext of going on a crusade, Henry III obtained from Innocent IV a grant of a tenth for three years, promising that he would set out for the Holy Land in 1256. In 1254 the pope extended the period of the grant to five years, thus enabling the king to pay for the furtherance of his son Edmund's claims to the Sicilian throne.

This grant was to be based not on the ancient assessment of the churches but on a new and more stringent valuation. In England taxes on the clergy were assessed differently from the lay taxes on movables, being calculated on the rental value of estates rather than on actual revenues. Walter Suffield, the bishop of Norwich, who, with the bishop of Chichester and the abbot of Westminster, had been appointed a papal collector, was entrusted with the task of drawing up the new valuation. He wrote to every rural dean, requiring each of them, and three or four rectors, to take an oath to assess the benefices according to a just estimation; for each cathedral, responsibility for the assessment was placed on the dean and three or four canons; for each religious house, the abbot or prior and three or four monks. The bishop's assessment was thought by the king's advisers to be insufficiently severe, and in 1255 a papal nuncio, Rostand, came to England under a papal mandate to supersede the three collectors and to supervise a new assessment incorporating both temporalities and spiritualities. The revised assessment was criticized by the English clergy, so much so that the new valuation was dropped.

In 1266, Pope Clement IV authorized the payment of a tenth for three years "according to the true value [*verus valor*] and not according to the ancient estimation." In practice the assessment made under the supervision of the bishop of Norwich was still employed, on the understanding that the clergy would pay the difference if the "true value" proved to be higher. In 1267, King Henry III sent his clerks to all English bishops to make a new assessment of temporalities on the valuation of the common people (*plebs*), who were summoned to give evidence. This led in 1269 to a strong protest by the convocation of Canterbury against making grants to laymen and being committed to such grants by the bishops. The protesting clergymen alleged that churches assessed at ten marks in the previous valuation were now assessed at thirty-six, and they refused to pay.

In 1274, at the Second Council of Lyons, Pope Gregory requested a universal tenth for six years for the Holy Land. Raymond de Nogaret, a papal nuncio, and John of Darlington, a Dominican, were appointed papal collectors for England. They had great difficulty collecting the tax, the clergy representing that the new assessment was too high. The monks were so reluctant to pay that the abbot and chapter of the abbey of St. Albans were excommunicated for failing to pay.

To advance his plans for a crusade, Gregory X had offered any king who took up the cross the yield of a tenth within his kingdom. Edward I secured the grant of a tenth for his dominions on these grounds; but other affairs prevented him from going on a crusade, and confronted by a financial crisis caused by the Welsh war in 1277, he requested the pope in 1278 to grant to him the money gathered by the collectors. Nicholas III refused, but he offered 25,000 marks to cover the cost of preparations if the king took the cross and promised to return the money if he did not fulfill his vow. Edward I did not, however, accept the offer.

In 1283 Edward seized the papal tenths collected, though later he agreed to return the money. He eventually persuaded Martin IV, and later his successors Honorius IV and Nicholas IV, that he had every intention of setting out on a crusade, and he actually took the cross in 1287. In 1289, Nicholas IV agreed that the proceeds of a tenth collected in England should be paid to the king, and a new tenth was to be authorized for six years.

On 18 March 1291, Oliver Sutton, bishop of Lincoln, and John of Pontoise, bishop of Winchester, were empowered to act as papal collectors. They instructed the bishops to supervise a new valuation. In practice the clergy had refused to accept the previous valuation, made in 1276, and once more paid according to the valuation made by the bishop of Norwich in 1254. The clergy complained that the assessors of 1291 had doubled, trebled, or even quadrupled the verdicts of juries. In 1254 the income of the English clergy had been assessed at £101,000, in 1276 at £213,980, and in 1291 at £210,660. Although there was some revision of the assessment in 1293 and again in 1318, the valuation of 1291 remained, in England, the basis of taxation of the clergy until 1535.

The election of the Gascon Bertrand de Got as Pope Clement V in 1305 was advantageous to Edward I, for he ordered the English clergy to pay the king an annual tenth for the next seven years, avowedly with the object of recovering the Holy Land. During the last five years of his reign, Edward I obtained some £70,000 from the clergy by means of the tenths levied by but not paid to the papacy. Later English kings enjoyed a higher proportion of the income tax imposed on the clergy than did the papal camera. Similar developments occurred in other countries. Alfonso III of Aragon (Alfons II in Catalonia, 1285–1291) planned a crusade against Granada and was indignant that the pope should grant only a tenth of clerical incomes for two years, whereas the French king had received a similar grant for six years.

By the early fourteenth century European princes held that they were entitled to tax their clergy, whether or not they had papal permission. This had been an issue as early as the twelfth century. At the Third Lateran Council in 1179, Pope Alexander III, concerned with the situation in the Italian city-states, condemned lay rulers who imposed taxes on the clergy, asserting that only voluntary gifts conceded by the bishops on grounds of need were allowable. In 1207 an English great council, including bishops as well as lay magnates, consented to the levy of a thirteenth, but the clergy opposed the levy. The bishops, "to be quit of the aid," agreed to pay substantial sums voluntarily, but Archbishop Geoffrey of York refused to pay, appealing to the pope on the principle of the "real immunity of the clergy" from lay taxation and threatening to excommunicate any of his clergy or tenants who paid the tax. The archbishop went into exile and was supported by the pope. Canon 46 of the Fourth Lateran Council (1215) forbade the clergy to pay any tax or even to make a voluntary gift to the secular power without papal permission. In October 1269 the English clergy refused to pay a subsidy to the king because the pope had not been previously consulted.

The issue of lay taxation of the clergy became increasingly serious as time passed. Edward I tried to impose taxes on the clergy in 1275, but the clergy refused, noting that it was already paying a tenth to the papacy. In 1279 the convocation of Canterbury agreed to a request for a fifteenth to meet the expenses of the king's Welsh wars, and in 1280 the convocation of York agreed to a tenth for two years. In 1283, however, the convocation of Canterbury refused a grant toward the costs of the Welsh wars because no representatives of the lower clergy were present at the assembly. Eventually the convocation of Canterbury granted the king a triennial twentieth. The last tax to be based on the assessment of 1254 was the clerical tenth of 1291, a grant made in return for the expulsion of the Jews from England.

In 1294, Edward I made an unprecedented demand of a half based on the new and harsher assessment of 1291; but the clergy voted only two-tenths. Edward threatened reprisals that obliged the clergy to yield; however, collection of the tax proved difficult. By Michaelmas 1295 only some £66,000 out of an estimated total of £101,000 had been received.

In November 1295 the king demanded a new aid; he accepted the offer of a tenth, based on the assessment of 1291, but the collection proved difficult, only £11,243 of the full amount (£20,000) having been received by September 1296. Boniface VIII's bull, *Clericis laicos,* issued in 1296, prohibiting the payment of taxes to the secular power, though not specifically aimed at Edward I, strengthened Archbishop Thomas Winchelsea's resistance to the king's demands. When the king demanded a further clerical aid, Winchelsea ordered the clergy to refuse to pay. Edward did manage, however, to obtain £22,810 from the clergy by placing it outside his protection and then permitting it to regain his favor by accepting a fine for the restoration of his protection, which enabled him to take money without having to offer defiance to the pope.

In 1297 the clergy proved more willing to grant taxes, the convocation of Canterbury granting a tenth and the convocation of York a fifth, to assist the king in his war against the Scots. Archbishop Winchelsea, however, insisted that the money collected should be paid directly to the New Temple, and that there should be no secular interference by royal officials. Edward I did not receive any further subsidies directly from the English clergy after 1297, but all in all he received some £300,000 from ecclesiastical taxes (in comparison he received about £500,000 from the laity).

There continued to be many occasions when the clergy refused to make grants: in 1319 the clergy refused to make a grant because it lacked papal permission; in 1329 because it believed that the subsidy contributed by the laity was adequate for the king's requirements, and in any case the clergy could barely support the pope's burdens. Members of the clergy sought repeatedly to make their grants conditional on the redress of grievances. Thus, in the winter of 1377 the convocation of Canterbury granted the king two-tenths on condition that the temporal lords and commons made a grant of a fifteenth and a tenth; the convocation also stipulated that such money as it granted should be expended only in defense of the realm of England and on the king's wars. In December 1383 the convocation of Canterbury made two grants of half-tenths, the first without condition, the second only on condition that no truce with France be signed. In 1384 the laity agreed to give two-fifteenths to the king if the clergy would give two-tenths. This evoked a strong remonstrance from Archbishop Courteney, who insisted that the English church was free and should not be taxed by the laity. But, as a rule, the taxation of the clergy worked well, and generally, if occasionally grudgingly, it conceded what the king requested.

THE CONTINENT

The experience of other nations was not dissimilar to that of England. Rulers took some proportion of the taxes authorized by the pope and levied taxes on the clergy. In 1285, Pedro III of Aragon (Pere II in Catalonia) obliged the Catalan clergy to help him defend Catalonia against the French "crusade," which was accompanied by a papal legate. In 1294, Sancho IV of Castile told his officials to compel his bishops and abbots to contribute money toward the war against the Muslims.

In France, Philip IV demanded a contribution from the clergy and churches to help him in his war against Edward I of England. Taxation of the property of the churches in France was novel. In practice, however, despite a refusal by Nicholas IV in 1292, the popes allowed the French king to levy the tenths he requested, usually justifying the tax on the grounds that the royal purposes were in the church's interest. Unlike his predecessors, Louis IX and Philip III, Philip IV levied tenths (and annates) without papal consent and for the defense of his realm. No other group of the king's subjects was taxed so harshly or, except for war subsidies, contributed such revenue.

In 1294 a series of provincial synods of the French clergy granted Philip IV a tenth for two successive years, though they sought to attach conditions to their grants while reciting their grievances. When in 1296 the king demanded and obtained another tenth, Pope Boniface VIII issued the aforementioned bull *Clericis laicos,* prohibiting the levying of any imposition upon the clergy by any lay power without previous permission of the Holy See. Eventually, however, in the face of stern reprisals by which the king forbade the export of gold and silver and expelled the papal tax collectors, the pope was obliged to retreat. A full council of the French church was held at Paris in March 1297. It granted a double tenth. On 31 July 1297 the pope, by the bull *Etsi de statu,* authorized the French king to ask for an aid whenever, in his judgment, the realm was in peril. From this the government appears to have believed that tenths were now conceded as regular payments, in spite of protests from the clergy.

When the quarrel between Boniface VIII and Philip IV was renewed in 1301, the pope forbade the clergy to pay any money to the king. In 1303 the king called a council of clergy to Paris to request a grant; the clergy agreed, at the same time making demands for the reform of the administration in return for the twentieth it had voted. The government, realizing the constitutional implications of such demands, eventually, and reluctantly, yielded in part. Similar negotiations occurred in 1303–1304, producing further concessions, though there were still protests from the clergies of Rouen, Sens, and Tours, whose archbishops refused to pay the double tenth requested. This represented the high peak of clerical resistance to lay taxation.

In 1305 the election of a friendly pope, Clement V, led to agreement between king and pope. All tenths after 1305 were granted by agreement with the pope. Clement V granted a tenth in 1310 and 1312, and a tenth for six years in 1313, nominally for a crusade. The French clergy was no longer able to win concessions from the French crown and could not impose permanent restrictions on the royal power of taxation.

The situation in other countires was similar. Papal taxation was bitterly resented in Castile, but in 1247 Innocent IV granted the *tercias,* a third part of the ecclesiastical tithe, the original purpose of which was the upkeep of the church's fabric, to Ferdinand III to fight against the Muslims. Ferdinand's successor, Alfonso X, levied the *tercias* for purely political purposes, and they were treated henceforth as a source of regular income for the Castilian crown in spite of occasional protests, such as that made by Boniface VIII in 1301. The financial contribution made by the clergies of Castile and León to the crown's budgets was very substantial.

THE LATE MIDDLE AGES

During the Great Schism (1378–1449) there was some decline in the payments the clergy made to the papal camera as *servitia* and annates; resistance to such taxes was encouraged by the attempt of the Council of Basel (1431–1449) to abolish them. In France there was a sharp decline in the amount of such payments in the fifteenth century; but elsewhere, as in Germany and Poland, assessments were actually increased.

In view of the encroachment of secular rulers on papal taxes, the papacy had to devise new forms of taxation to compensate for its losses—for instance, increased payments for the issuance of bulls, chancery taxes, "compositions," (sums collected through the apostolic penitentiary for the compounding of penances), fees for visitations to Rome, and issues of such papal graces as indulgences and dispensations. Such taxes were levied by papal collectors, officials of the papal camera who held diplomatic status in the regions to which they were accredited.

By the closing years of the Middle Ages, lay powers not only taxed their clergy, practically at will, but also shared in the profits of papal taxation. A king could demand payments to allow the export of money as well as take a share in the profits. For instance, in respect to indulgences, a third generally went to the fabric of the church to which the indulgence had been granted, a third to the papal camera (in some cases as much as a half and, in the case of plenary indulgences, as much as two-thirds), and a third to the sovereign.

BIBLIOGRAPHY

H. S. Deighton, "Clerical Taxation by Consent, 1279–1301," in *English Historical Review,* **68** (1953); Jean Favier, "Temporels ecclésiastiques et taxation fiscale: Le poids de la fiscalité pontificale au XIVe siècle," in *Journal des savants* (1964), and *Les finances pontificales à l'époque du grand schisme d'Occident, 1378–1409* (1966); Rose Graham, "The Taxation of Pope Nicholas IV," in her *English Ecclesiastical Studies* (1929); Gabriel Le Bras, *L'immunité réele* (1920); Peter Linehan, *The Spanish Church and the Papacy in the Thirteenth Century* (1971); William E. Lunt, *The Valuation of Norwich* (1926), "Clerical Tenths Levied in England by Papal Authority During the Reign of Edward II," in *Anniversary Essays in Mediaeval History by Students of Charles Homer Haskins* (1929, repr. 1967), "The Consent of the English Lower Clergy to Taxation During the Reign of Henry III," in *Persecution and Liberty: Essays in Honor of George Lincoln Burr* (1931, repr. 1968), *Papal Revenues in the Middle Ages,* 2 vols. (1934), *Financial Relations of the Papacy with England,* 2 vols. (1939–1962), and *Accounts Rendered by Papal Collectors in England, 1317–78,* Edgar B. Graves, ed., *Memoirs of the American Philosophical Society,* **70** (1968); Peter D. Partner, "*Camera papae*: Problems of Papal Finance in the Later Middle Ages," in *Journal of Ecclesiastical History,* **4** (1953), and "The 'Budget' of the Roman Church in the Renaissance Period," in E. F. Jacob, ed., *Italian Renaissance Studies* (1960, repr. 1966); C. Samaran and G. Mollat, *La fiscalité pontificale en France au XIVe siècle*

(1905); C. J. Nederman, "Royal Taxation and the English Church: The Origins of William of Ockham's 'An princeps,'" in *Journal of Ecclesiastical History,* 37 (1987); Jane E. Sayers, *Papal Government and England During the Pontificate of Honorius III (1216–27)* (1984); Joseph R. Strayer, *The Reign of Philip the Fair* (1980); *idem* and Charles H. Taylor, *Studies in Early French Taxation* (1939); Dorothy B. Weske, *Convocation of the Clergy* (1937).

VIVIAN H. H. GREEN

[See also **Annate; Aragon, Crown of (1137–1479); Benefice, Ecclesiastical; Boniface VIII, Pope; Bull, Papal; Cardinals, College of; Church, Latin: Organization; Clement V, Pope; Clericis Laicos; Consistorium; Convocations of Canterbury and York; Councils, Western; Crusades and Crusader States; Curia, Papal; Dispensation; Indulgences; Innocent III, Pope; John XXII, Pope; Nuncio, Papal; Papacy, Origins and Development of; Papal States; Peter's Pence; Philip IV the Fair; Schism, Great; Simony; Tithes.**]

TAXATION, ENGLISH. Roman Britain experienced the gamut of imperial taxation, including taxes in money, in kind, and in services. Most of these taxes presumably disappeared with Rome's legions, and the rest with the disorganization caused by the German invasions. When the German warriors came to Britain, they disdained to pay taxes, which were impositions, in their view, to be expected only from the unfree. They fought for their chieftains but only as an honor. The chieftains may have had a larger share of conquered lands and booty, but this was hardly taxation.

The food renders, or feorms, payable to the king as king appear to be the earliest taxes for the support of the monarchy. They may just possibly have been vestiges of taxes taken by the Romano-British chieftains. Also early were certain service taxes such as cartage, building royal halls and villages, and hospitality for the king and his servants. Military service or fyrd, fortress building, and bridge building were required of all freemen before the end of the eighth century.

These early taxes were assessed by the hide, originally the holding of one family, but for taxation purposes apparently a subdivision of the hundred. Villages were rated at *x* number of hides, and the villagers divided the taxes according to the size of their holdings. Feorm was presumably paid thus, and the borough garrisons of King Alfred (849–899) were certainly recruited at the rate of one man per hide. It was probably Alfred who also established the obligation of every 300 hides to furnish a ship; and in 1008 every ten hides was responsible for a boat and every eight for a helm and breastplate.

Royal authorities levying tolls. Drawing from the *Canterbury Psalter.* Trinity College, Cambridge, MS R.17.1, fol. 230r, *ca.* 1148–1149. BY PERMISSION OF THE MASTER AND FELLOWS OF TRINITY COLLEGE, CAMBRIDGE

A monetary tax collected by the hide was devised in 991 by the government of Ethelred the Unready to bribe Danish invaders to go home. After several of these extraordinary gelds, in 1012 a tax began to be collected annually to support the king's Danish allies and later his professional troops, and it became known as "heregeld." The gelds were collected by the king's reeves along with his other revenues. The ealdormen, after 1016 the earls, were ultimately responsible for the tax collections and may have shared in them. Even if much was lost in the the collection, the yields were phenomenal: in the year 991, £10,000 was collected; in 1018, £82,000. Thus England had the most advanced system of direct taxation in Western Europe at the end of the Old English period.

Indirect taxes were known in England from at least the eighth century. But their ubiquity is exceeded only by their obscurity. Tolls were taken on goods offered for sale in markets, others for passage through ports or boroughs. These tolls were apparently levied by royal authority, but payment in one market or port did not relieve the merchant from paying in another. On the other hand, many churches, some cities, and some foreign lands had exemptions for all their men to trade without tolls in one, some, or all English markets. The tolls, moreover, were often merged with other dues, some of which were commutations of service taxes and feorms, others rents and profits of justice, all being paid under the name of "customs." The king's reeves were the collectors of all these customs except when the borough was farmed to the burgesses or some other persons or granted to a thegn like any other estate. Not a few of these farmers or grantees would seem to have added to the royal tolls or created new ones on their own authority. Rates and yields are unknown, but Offa (757–796), Ethelred the Unready (978–1016), and Cnut the Great (1016–1035) all showed their interest in foreign trade, and they may have been influenced by the financial returns of tolls. Although other reasons were given when Edward the Confessor remitted the tax on hides in 1051, increased revenues from indirect taxation must have made it possible.

AFTER THE NORMAN CONQUEST

The Norman Conquest brought to England the Norman and Angevin kings, who introduced continental institutions and at the same time maintained those of the English. They kept the fyrd (the duty to bear arms), the hidage (or land tax), and the tolls; they introduced scutage and feudal aids, tallage, new taxes on trade, and taxes on the Jewish moneylenders they brought into England.

The obligation of every freeman to bear arms was never lost sight of, and in 1181 Henry II issued his Assize of Arms, which established the kinds of arms men were required to have according to three levels of wealth assessed by juries. Henry III (1216–1272) elaborated on this system, requiring service from all between the ages of fifteen and sixty according to five levels of wealth, defined by equating a certain value of chattels with landed incomes. The system was given a definitive statement in Edward I's Statute of Winchester in 1285.

Hidage and carucage. The Norman kings were quick to revive the tax on hides, which they called the danegeld. By the end of his reign, in 1135, Henry I seems to have made hidage an annual tax but also increased the number of hides that were exempt, and the yield from a normal hidage dropped to about £2,500. Stephen (1135–1154) promised to abolish the tax, and Henry II only took it twice, allowing it to lapse after 1162. A land tax was revived in 1194, but it was assessed not on hides but on plowlands and eventually on plows. This plow tax, or carucage (from the Latin *carruca,* or plow), was based on a new assessment each time it was levied, and thus the inflexibility of the hidage should have been obviated except for an element of artificiality found in local assessments. But carucage still did not tap the real wealth of the king's subjects; its rate varied only between two and five shillings; and its yield was correspondingly disappointing, about £5,500 being collected in 1220. A carucage in 1224 on the lands of the clergy only was the last to be taken.

Tolls. Tolls continued to be collected under the Norman and Angevin kings. They also had the right of purveyance—that is, the right to requisition goods they needed or wanted at special prices and have them delivered to wherever they wanted them. The tax in purveyance arose from the price differential, the free cartage service, and often a long delay in payment. Related to purveyance was the right of prisage, by which the king took wine from each shipment into England for his own use; in time the rule was one tun from a ship carrying between ten and nineteen tuns, two from ships with twenty or more tuns. In the twelfth century, and possibly earlier, the kings imposed a tax on exports called lastage and a tax on imports called scavage to be paid in addition to the older local customs. The Angevin kings sometimes imposed a maltolte (an unaccustomed toll, especially one taken at a high rate). The best documented of these maltoltes was the fifteenth King John levied from at least 1201 to 1206 on all goods imported or exported. Collections reached about £5,000 in two and a half years. John promised in Magna Carta to lay no more maltoltes except in time of war, and his son is not known to have taken any.

Jews. The Norman kings introduced into England a certain number of Jews, who settled in the larger towns of the kingdom and engaged in crafts, in trade, and above all in moneylending. As the king's Jews they were always subject to his special taxation. When the Saladin Tithe was collected in 1187, Christians in England were said to have contributed £70,000, the Jews £60,000. John taxed the Jews in 1210, according to one chronicler, in the amount of £44,000. In 1241, Henry III took 20,000 marks. Ultimately, the goose that laid the golden eggs was stifled by this overtaxation, and Edward I expelled the poverty-stricken remnant of the Jews in 1291.

Tallage. The Norman and Angevin kings laid other kinds of wealth under contribution by asking for *dona* or *auxilia,* gifts or aids, from the churches and the royal demesnes, especially the towns. After 1177 the term tallage (from the Old French *taillies,* to cut) was used with increasing frequency for the taxes on the royal demesnes. London resisted tallage and gave aids until 1255, but then the great city was finally tallaged. This "cut" of personal wealth was regarded as a lord's right, but it was subject to negotiation as to amount. Typically, the king's officers gave a manor or borough the opportunity to compound in a lump sum for the tax and then allocate it among themselves as they wished; but if a satisfactory composition was not made, then the king's tallagers assessed it per capita "according to property." If the town government assessed the tax on the inhabitants, it might not be as fair as the king's men: a poll tax taken in London to pay the city's part of King Richard's ransom produced a revolt, the poor people demanding that the tax be collected in proportion to wealth. Under Henry II a tallage of the whole royal demesne amounted to about £4,000 or £5,000; in 1210 John took a very heavy one of more than £8,000; the fourteen tallages of Henry III ranged from about £6,000 down to £1,500 when London was not taxed. Edward I and Edward II took only one tallage each, in 1304 and 1312, and Edward III revoked a tallage he ordered in 1332. He did not, however, renounce the right to tallage, but tallages were superseded by higher-yielding subsidies.

Scutage. When the Normans introduced feudalism into England, it was to provide them with a cavalry army. By 1100, however, the Norman kings permitted their vassals to pay a monetary composition instead of serving in person. This composition came to be called "shield-money," or scutage (from the Latin *scutum,* or shield), and was levied on the knight's fee. Those barons who did not bring their due service to a properly summoned feudal host were obliged to pay from ten shillings to three marks on a knight's fee. They could recoup this payment by collecting scutage from their own tenants, and therefore the effective incidence of scutage fell upon the lowest level of feudal tenants. If, as sometimes happened, the lords had enfeoffed more knights than they owed the king, they might make money on a scutage. Henry II tried to maximize the yield of scutage by requiring his barons to pay on all their fees, but the effort was successfully resisted. Richard then took from his barons fines that were larger than the scutage should have amounted to. John collected scutages nearly every year, some by false pretenses, and thus he precipitated the barons' demand in 1215 for the right to consent to scutages. Since Henry III was obliged to accept from his barons new quotas of service that were only fractions of the old ones, he levied no scutages after 1258, and efforts of his successors to revive scutage as a significant tax failed.

Feudal aids. Feudal service included aids payable by vassals for their lord's necessities. The uncertainty of occasions for aids in the twelfth century led to their being limited in the Magna Carta to ransom, marriage of the lord's eldest daughter, and knighting of his eldest son. On other occasions a lord might collect gracious aids if his men consented to them. In 1110 Henry I took an aid of three shillings on a hide for his daughter's marriage, but in 1168 Henry II for his daughter's marriage levied an aid of one mark per knight's fee, on the model of the scutage. Henceforth, these feudal aids were collected on the basis of the knights' fees and were usually charged at the same customary rate of about two marks to a fee until 1275, when it was fixed by statute at twenty shillings.

TAXES ON MOVABLES

Under the Angevins, then, English royal taxation included the tax on hides or carucates paid by all landowners, the tallage paid by the men of the royal demesnes, especially the towns, and feudal scutages and aids, paid by those who held land in fee. When the king needed extraordinary revenue, he could levy all three of these taxes at once in order to lay all kinds of taxpayers under contribution. Thus, after Richard the Lionhearted was captured in Austria in 1192 and held for a ransom of £100,000, his subjects were taxed to the utmost to provide this enormous amount. In England a hidage was assessed at the rate of two shillings; a tallage of ten shillings or more was made on the royal demesne; the Jews were taxed heavily; a feudal aid was taken at twenty shillings a knight's fee; the whole wool crop of the Cistercians and Gilbertines was taken; the plate of all the churches was confiscated; and some clergymen paid a tenth and a twentieth. But above all, a tax of a fourth of movable wealth or revenue was taken from every person in the realm. This was the kind of tax the kings needed in a time of inflation, when the taxes at inelastic rates on fixed assessments like hidage and scutage were losing much of their value. It was also a tax that tapped new kinds of wealth in a society with increasing mercantile and industrial components.

The origin of the tax on movables lay in the financing of the crusades. In 1166 the pope asked for aid to the Holy Land, and the kings of France and England responded by laying a tax upon their subjects, which amounted in England to a fortieth of movables spread over five years. This idea was picked up in the Holy Land itself in 1183 and again in France and England in 1185 at the rate of a hundredth. Then in 1187 the Saladin Tithe was called for by the papacy. Imposed on the clergy of Europe by ecclesiastical sanctions, it was established in France and England by the joint action of Kings Philip II Augustus and Henry II. All the subjects of the two kings who did not themselves take the cross were required to pay a tenth of their incomes and movables, omitting only the necessities of their professions. In France the outcry led Philip to promise that neither he nor his descendants would ever take such a tax again, and it was a century before Philip IV did. In England there were complaints, but the English were more accustomed to royal taxation than the French. The moneys collected reached gratifyingly large proportions, and when Richard's ransom required a similar amount of money, the Saladin Tithe offered an obvious precedent.

In his wars with Philip Augustus, King John found the tax on movables irresistible. In 1203, besides a scutage and a tallage, he took a seventh of the movables on the demesnes of his English tenants-in-chief, and in 1207 a thirteenth of revenues and movables was collected with the consent of the magnates. The yield of the thirteenth amounted to more than £60,000. But not even John dared take such a burdensome tax often, and indeed the next tax on movables came in the minority of his son. In 1225 the great council assented to the levy of a fifteenth for the defense of Aquitaine, provided a new Charter of Liberties was issued. Setting the pattern for all future taxes on movables, the fifteenth was not levied on taxpayers without goods from which at least one penny of tax was due. Even so, collections amounted to no less than £38,000, nearly twice as much as the normal annual revenue at that time.

Henry III was granted a fortieth in 1232 and a thirtieth in 1237, but with increasing opposition. When he asked for more taxes on movables, his barons demanded the right to supervise his expenditures. Since he would not submit to this, they refused him further extraordinary taxes. But his son Edward I was able to take the taxes on movables relatively frequently, levying nine of them in the thirty-five years of his reign. Yields varied, of course, according to the rate, but comparisons of the tax bases show that the most productive tax by far was that of 1290, which was granted in return for the expulsion of the Jews, while the least productive was that of 1297, which was the fourth in four years. This succession of taxes in 1294–1297 showed a progressive diminution of tax bases, partly due no doubt to tax evasion but also probably to real reductions in taxable wealth, since the taxes were taken on capital goods. But the administration of the taxes gained in efficiency throughout, and by the end of the reign the taxes on movables had become a fixture in the extraordinary revenue of the English kings.

TAXING THE CLERGY

Parallel with the evolution of the taxes on movables went that of the taxes on clerical incomes. The Saladin Tithe had been collected from the clergy by papal order, and in the thirteenth century the popes enlarged upon that foundation. Innocent III ordered a fortieth in 1199 for the Fourth Crusade and in 1215 a twentieth for three years to support the Fifth Crusade. In the reign of Henry III the English clergy were taxed by the pope twelve times in twenty-four years. With all these taxes a great deal of experience was gained in assessing and collecting clerical income taxes. Several valuations were made, the most famous being that of the bishop of Norwich in 1254, which included the temporalities as well as the spiritualities of the clergy. The result was a considerable increase in the tax base and yield of clerical taxes, much to the gratification of the pope and also the king, to whom the pope often granted the revenues generated.

Edward I sought to maximize his tax income by taxing the clergy directly. On his demands the two convocations of Canterbury and York separately granted several taxes on their income ranging from tenths to thirtieths, each usually for a period of three years. For example, on the expulsion of the Jews the clergy granted Edward a tenth. A new valuation of clerical incomes was made in 1291 that approximately doubled the assessment of the Valuation of Norwich; attended by loud complaints at its establishment, it became the definitive one for the rest of the Middle Ages. Aside from Edward's direct taxes of the clergy, he obtained a number of papal grants of tenths levied on the English clergy. Over his whole reign Edward has been estimated to have received about £300,000 from ecclesiastical taxes, which may be compared to the £500,000 collected from the taxes on movables.

IMPORT AND EXPORT TAXES

New mercantile wealth attracted new taxes in Edward's reign. In 1266 Henry III gave to his son and heir control of the foreign merchants in England, including the right to give or withhold licenses to trade in England and to take customs on their imports and exports. Edward did indeed levy a tax and farm it to Italian merchants for 6,000 marks a year. The "new aid" was much resented, and in 1275 Edward replaced it with a custom levied in parliament on wool, woolfells, and hides. From 1294 to 1297 a maltolte was adopted by agreement of an assembly of merchants to pay six times the amount of the customs on a sack of wool; this lowered the price of wool in England and led to much resentment on the part of producers. In 1297 all the wool and fells and leather were ordered seized to be sold by the king, helping to produce the constitutional crisis of that year, the effect of which was the king's abandonment both of the seizure of wool and of the maltolte. The king continued, however, to collect the "old custom" of 1275. Only in 1303 was a "new custom" of half the rate of the old custom added as a surcharge on exports of wool, fells, and leather by foreign merchants, along with new dues on wine, cloth, and wax, and an *ad valorem* tax of three pence on the pound (called the poundage) for other exports and imports. In return the alien merchants received a charter of liberties that gave them virtually the same rights to trade in England that English merchants had. Partially suspended in 1309 for a year and then abolished in 1311, this new custom was restored in 1322 to last till modern times. The yield of both old and new customs averaged about £18,000 each during the last four years of the reign of Edward I and clearly was an important addition to royal revenue.

THE LATE MIDDLE AGES

The fourteenth century began, then, with royal taxation firmly based on the three taxes on movables, on clerical incomes, and on exports and imports. All these taxes required consent, and parliament's assumption of leadership in this role gives the period much of its constitutional interest. Royal attempts to supplement parliamentary taxation by the revival of obsolete taxes like tallage and scutage either yielded little money or produced great opposition. Occasional until the beginning of the Hundred Years War, the taxes then became nearly continuous, national rather than merely royal. The taxes themselves did not remain unchanged, as parliament and the king negotiated their passage each time.

The customs on foreign merchants continued essentially the same, but English merchants were pressed by the king to grant him similar or more extensive rates as emergency measures. As early as 1308 a number of English merchants had commuted royal prisage by a payment of two shillings per tun of wine, and eventually parliament granted the king such a tax, called tunnage. In 1347 the council imposed a tax on other merchandise at the rate of six pence on the pound, and under the name of "poundage" parliament later confirmed this tax as well. Each grant of tunnage and poundage was made for a fixed term of years until 1398, when Richard II was given the subsidy on wool, wool fells, and leather for life. On the average, export-import taxes produced about £12,000 a year.

The subsidy. Corruption and evasion led the taxes on movables to be changed into taxes on land by a decision in 1334 not to reassess the property of the taxpayers but to fix a quota for each vill that the taxpayers could then divide among themselves. The yield of a fifteenth on the country and a tenth on the boroughs and ancient demesne amounted to just over £38,000, and this came to be called a subsidy, parliament meeting the king's needs for money by granting one or more subsidies to be paid over varying periods. The Black Death made the unchanging assessment very inequitable, and it was necessary for parliament to give relief to decayed vills, which reduced the value of a subsidy to about £30,000 by 1485. When parliament granted lay subsidies, the clergy met in their two convocations and separately granted tenths of their incomes. The clerical tenths continued to be paid on the Valuation of 1291, though the exemption of livings worth less than ten marks reduced the yield somewhat below the nominal £20,000 a tenth should have brought.

Parliamentary experiments. Parliament also experimented with new taxes in the late fourteenth and early fifteenth centuries. In 1371 it was determined to raise £50,000 by assessing each parish according to its wealth, "the parishes of greater value to be aiding and contributing to the parishes of lesser value." This was clearly an attempt to get away from the inequity and inflexibility of the fifteenths and tenths, which were a great annoyance to the politically important landed classes who had to pay them. So also were the poll taxes of 1377, 1379, and 1380, each person being subject to the tax but "the strong aiding the weak," so that no one payed less than a groat, no one more than sixty groats. The fact that the last of these taxes provoked the Peasants' Revolt meant that it was not levied again. Instead, parliament experimented with income taxes in the first half of the fifteenth century. The rates of these taxes were so low as to yield very little, but they are interesting attempts to supplement the subsidies, which remained the principal tax on the landed interest. A further innovation was a short-lived tax on aliens, apparently in reprisal for taxes Englishmen had to pay abroad and not very productive of revenue.

Benevolences. Altogether the Lancastrian kings had a well-developed tax system to support their policies, including the renewal of the French war by Henry V. In 1415 parliament granted him the customs on wool as well as tunnage and poundage for life, and all his successors in the century had similar grants. But the other taxes required consent of parliament or convocation. When Edward IV became king in 1461, he determined to rule as much as possible without parliament, and after 1473 instead of parliamentary subsidies he relied upon irregular taxes called "benevolences," so-called since men were asked to make payments to the king for his goodwill. Those who might be tempted not to make these payments were threatened with the king's ill will, and few were willing to risk the consequences. The medieval legacy of royal taxes was complete.

NONROYAL TAXATION

England was a highly centralized state for a medieval kingdom, and royal taxation was, by far, the most highly developed in the land. But the king was not the only beneficiary of English taxation. The church, for one, levied heavy taxes on all Englishmen from an early day. Soul scot originated as a voluntary offering to a priest at the graveside for the salvation of the soul of a dead person, but a tenth-century doom made it obligatory, and it probably survived the Middle Ages in the form of the mortuary of second-best chattel due the parish priest. Also found in the same dooms, though probably centuries old by then, were plow alms, which were paid to the parish priest in the amount of a penny for every plow team. Churchscot was already levied as an annual tax by Ine's laws of about 694; under a twelvefold penalty for nonpayment, all free households had to pay the minster an amount of grain in proportion to the holding and occasionally a hen.

The tithe gradually emerged as the principal tax for the support of the church: every Christian was required to pay a tenth of his or her agricultural income, chiefly in the form of grain or livestock. In 786 a legatine council required the payment of tithe by everyone; but it was not until the tenth century that Edgar imposed an eightfold penalty for nonpayment of tithes. Two-thirds of the tithes were supposed to go to the minsters and one-third to the parish church, but many lords seem to have paid their tithes where they wished. Also by the beginning of the tenth century Romescot or Peter's Pence was being collected at the rate of a penny on every hearth and sent to the pope as a gift of the English people. While neither this nor plow alms was a heavy burden, churchscot, soul scot, and especially the tithe were.

Attempts were made from the thirteenth century to extend the things tithed to personalty, but these were not successful. A clerical constitution of 1343 to include underwood raised great opposition in parliament, and in general tithe was paid by ancient prescription. Peter's Pence became a fixed payment to the pope in the amount of £199. 6s. 8d. a year, though far more was collected to enrich the English prelates. The clergy, in turn, continued to be taxed by the pope as well as by the king, though papal tenths and subsidies were taken with decreasing frequency. But increasing amounts of English money were collected for the papacy as "annates," the incomes of vacant benefices and their assessed value for one year after they were filled. Visitation taxes and service taxes were other, lesser burdens the English clergy paid to papal collectors, who lived and worked in England continuously from 1304 until the separation of the English church from Rome by Henry VIII.

Taxation by lords. All lords, including the churches having lordship, tallaged their men on their demesnes as the king tallaged his men. Those lords who held lands that were formerly royal demesne were often limited in their right of tallage to times when the king tallaged his men. But the great majority of lords were free to tallage their men as often as they could, and typically they took annual taxes.

This institution of tallage was at first taken as

aids or gifts, but gradually came to be a mark of villeinage. While tallage was only one of many manorial dues, it was often very lucrative. Other dues were frequently services, either in person or commuted into money payments. Many of these were probably economic to start with, but some, such as hundred penny and tithing penny, were political in origin.

Free men gave their lords aids, by right limited to the three cases named in the Magna Carta, otherwise by grace. The king sometimes wrote letters to the men of a lord asking them to give the lord aid. But essentially aids were granted by the lords' men as the king's men granted him aids. The basis for assessment of seigneurial aids would seem to be knight's fees in at least some but not all cases. Altogether, seigneurial taxes may have been as heavy as ecclesiastical.

Borough taxes. Boroughs, like manors, could be tallaged by their lords, and at those times the boroughs would tax their inhabitants to pay the tallage. But boroughs might also have need of money for their own corporate purposes "for protection and common benefit," as it was put in a charter of 1305 for King's Lynn. Then they might obtain the right from their lords to take tallages or other aids by the assent of the community. London developed a tax on rents in the thirteenth century, but a tax on movables was the usual practice then. Before the end of that century local taxation had become "frequent, even regular." There was much complaint of fraud and especially of the exemption of the patricians from taxation. Other boroughs were not so sophisticated in their taxation as the capital city. But the Cinque Ports had by the fourteenth century evolved "compositions," divided among three groups of ports, to pay their common expenses.

CONCLUSION

In sum, England was a well-taxed land in the Middle Ages, though one can only guess at the burden. Ecclesiastical and seigneurial taxes may have been the heaviest because they were taken most frequently. Direct royal taxes were only taken as frequently in the fourteenth and fifteenth centuries, and only in the reign of Edward I were the assessments probably near the true valuation. Indirect royal taxes (the customs, subsidies, tunnage, and poundage) appear to have borne heavily on the grazing interest at times, but otherwise occasioned remarkably little reaction beyond grumbling.

The principal complaint, climaxing in the Peasants' Revolt of 1381, came on the issue of fairness. In general, the English taxes were proportional to property, and this principle appears to have been strongly entrenched in the English political system. There was also a progressive principle, too, in the exemption of the poor from the taxes on movables. The complaints of Londoners about the twelfth-century poll tax were widened with the nationwide poll taxes of the late fourteenth century. Although these taxes were graduated, they reached down to tax even the poorest; the near-poor were taxed at rates greater than they were accustomed to pay; and the richest were taxed no more than sixty times the poorest even if their incomes might be a thousand times as much. The exemption of the rich from taxes was another source of complaint, and the Yorkist institution of benevolences, extracted primarily from the rich, should have been popular with the typical taxpayers.

Generally speaking, in the country neither the cotters nor the lords paid taxes on their main sources of income, respectively wages and rents; and in the towns neither the wage laborers paid on their wages nor the merchants on their profits. The principal taxpayers appear to have been the villeins and freeholders in the country and the craftsmen of the towns, who were the primary producers of the wealth that was taxed, both directly in movables, tithes, and seigneurial tallages, and also indirectly in export and import duties. Aside from questions of equity, differential taxation of this sort may have hindered capital formation. But the revenue produced made possible the remarkably aggressive foreign policy of the medieval English kings as well as the power and glory of the aristocracy, both temporal and spiritual.

BIBLIOGRAPHY

A basic list of references on English taxation will be found in Edgar B. Graves, ed., *A Bibliography of English History to 1485* (1975), esp. 483–491, 495–499. Full bibliographies on clerical taxation are given in the works of William E. Lunt: *Accounts Rendered by Papal Collectors in England, 1317–1378,* Edgar B. Graves, ed. (1968), *Financial Relations of the Papacy with England,* 2 vols. (1939–1962), and *The Valuation of Norwich* (1926).

For general background, the pertinent volumes of the Oxford History of England have not yet been replaced: Frank M. Stenton, *Anglo-Saxon England,* 2nd ed. (1947); Austin Lane Poole, *From Domesday Book to Magna Carta, 1087–1216,* 2nd ed. (1955); Frederick M. Powicke, *The Thirteenth Century, 1216–1307,* 2nd ed. (1962);

May McKisack, *The Fourteenth Century, 1307–1399* (1959). William Stubbs, *The Constitutional History of England,* 3 vols. (1880), is still indispensable for its listing of medieval taxes. For economic history see Edward Miller, "The Economic Policies of Governments: France and England," in M. M. Postan *et al.*, eds., *The Cambridge Economic History of Europe,* III (1963), 290–340.

Monographs that proved particularly useful for this study were: J. Goronwy Edwards, *The Second Century of the English Parliament,* J. S. Roskell, ed. (1979); Robin E. Glasscock, ed., *The Lay Subsidy of 1334* (1975); Norman S. B. Gras, *The Early English Customs System* (1918); G. L. Harriss, *King, Parliament, and Public Finance in Medieval England to 1369* (1975); Ada E. Levett, *Studies in Manorial History,* H. M. Cam *et al.*, eds. (1938); Thomas Madox, *Firma burgi* (1726) and *The History and Antiquities of the Exchequer of the Kings of England,* 2nd ed., 2 vols. (1769); Sydney K. Mitchell, *Studies in Taxation Under John and Henry III* (1914) and *Taxation in Medieval England,* Sidney Painter, ed. (1951); William A. Morris and Joseph R. Strayer, eds., *The English Government at Work, 1327–1336,* II; *Fiscal Administration* (1947); Katharine M. E. Murray, *The Constitutional History of the Cinque Ports* (1935); Sidney Painter, *The Reign of King John* (1949); Michael Prestwich, *War, Politics, and Finance Under Edward I* (1972); James F. Willard, *Parliamentary Taxes on Personal Property, 1290 to 1334* (1934); Gwyn A. Williams, *Medieval London: From Commune to Capital* (1963).

Articles include Fred A. Cazel, Jr., "The Tax of 1185 in Aid of the Holy Land," in *Speculum,* **30** (1955), "The Fifteenth of 1225," in *Bulletin of the Institute of Historical Research,* **34** (1961), and "Royal Taxation in Thirteenth-century England," in *L'impôt dans le cadre de la ville et de l'état* (1966), 99–120; Helena M. Chew, "Scutage Under Edward I," in *English Historical Review,* **37** (1922), and "Scutage in the Fourteenth Century," *ibid.,* **38** (1923); Eric John, "The Imposition of the Common Burdens on the Lands of the English Church," in *Bulletin of the Institute of Historical Research,* **31** (1958); J. H. Round, "The Great Carucage of 1198," in *The English Historical Review,* **3** (1888); Carl Stephenson, "The Origin and Nature of the *Taille,*" in his *Mediaeval Institutions: Selected Essays,* Bryce D. Lyon, ed. (1954), 41–103, and "The Seignorial Tallage in England," in H. van der Linden *et al.*, eds., *Mélanges d'histoire offerts à Henri Pirenne,* II (1926), 465–474; A. Tomkinson, "The Carucage of 1220 in an Oxfordshire Hundred," in *Bulletin of the Institute of Historical Research,* **41** (1968).

FRED A. CAZEL, JR.

[See also **Borough (England-Wales); Cnut the Great; Danegeld; England; Exchequer; Feudalism; Hide; Magna Carta; Maltolte; Peasants' Rebellion; Pipe Rolls; Reeve; Saladin; Scutage; Taille, Tallage; Thegn; Tithes; Trade, European; Wine; Wool.**]

TAXATION, FRENCH. Taxation is a process by which wealth in private hands is conveyed into public hands, that is, to the state. The meaning was clear enough in the Roman *res publica,* as it is in a modern state, but in most of Europe, for most of the Middle Ages, the distinction between public and private was so blurred that the term "taxation" is anachronistic.

When we apply to medieval France what we now mean by "taxation," we find that it had three aspects: (1) that which ordinary people had to pay to their political rulers, (2) the revenues which the crown of France collected, and (3) those royal revenues which most resembled taxes in the modern sense of the term. The last of these achieved significance by the fifteenth century, when France acquired the character of a modern state; but for centuries "taxation" existed only in its first two aspects. The history of medieval French finance was an evolutionary process, in the course of which taxation as we understand it gradually developed.

The burdensome land taxes of the later Roman Empire had largely perished by the seventh century. Landowners resented them, and most Germanic peoples perceived direct taxation as a sort of tribute incompatible with free status: the seizure of a weaker person's property by a stronger person, not a contribution to the common welfare as represented by the state. Tolls on commerce survived, but the limited volume of trade in the centuries of Frankish rule restricted the receipts from tolls.

Aside from the profits of their landed estates, the Frankish kings obtained several sorts of revenue: (1) booty (in land or movables) acquired through conquest or confiscations from rebels, (2) "gifts," which were concealed direct taxes collectible only by strong kings, (3) proceeds of justice, a portion of the fines levied in both civil and criminal cases by the ruler in whose court they were decided, and (4) mint profits, insofar as the king operated mints and collected more than was needed to pay the cost of their operation.

The revenues of important magnates paralleled those of the kings. Custom and the realities of power compelled the kings to share their booty with their warrior chieftains. Magnates exacted payments from their men, or "gifts" if the latter were of free status. Judicial and monetary profits, supposedly reserved to the king, could often be appropriated by the magnates when the kings were weak, as could the revenues from tolls on commerce.

At every level, landlords exacted payments from

the masses of their subject peasants, free and unfree. Many of these were payments in kind—agricultural produce and labor services. The marketing of agricultural surpluses gave the landlords revenue. It is abundantly clear that from the seventh through tenth centuries the possession of land was what determined wealth and power. The strong kings were those with vast landholdings; so also were the strongest magnates. Grants of land were a major means of rewarding followers or "paying salaries" to troops and officials. Revenues from agriculture were an important component in the "budget" of anybody exercising political authority.

It thus would appear that during the Merovingian and Carolingian periods (*ca.* 480–*ca.* 980) the distinction between what was public and what was private had become progressively more blurred. The confusion of the two sectors became even more pronounced as a result of developments that occurred in the succeeding century.

Around 980, royal authority was weak and restricted in territorial extent, but regalian powers were still being exercised by the counts in many parts of France. These former provincial officials had become autonomous, hereditary rulers in their regions, in defiance of both the king and those marcher lords who were trying to set up territorial principalities. Inside their counties they preserved most of the public functions with which their forebears had been entrusted by the Carolingian kings, exercising military, fiscal, and judicial authority over all free men except those residing in ecclesiastical immunities. In the eleventh century, however, many counties began to disintegrate in favor of a smaller unit based on the castle. In many regions, counts found themselves reduced to the position of being merely one of perhaps a dozen castle-holding lords in the old *pagus*.

During the eleventh century, the castellans became the effective rulers of much of rural France, especially north and east of the Loire. These lords subjugated the free peasants and lesser landlords, and took into their own hands most judicial, military, and fiscal functions. Even in regions with a strong territorial ruler, such as Anjou or Normandy, the castellans had become the embodiment of government for the masses of rural people, nearly all of whom were subject to such seigneurs.

The fragmentation of once-public functions into what we would call private hands created the state of affairs out of which the fiscal history of Capetian France developed. Above the peasants were knights, or fighting men. Those who possessed lands were lesser seigneurs who found themselves gradually drawn into the orbit of some castellan, holding their land in fief from him and serving him as vassals. This so-called feudal relationship eventually came to determine the relations of many castellans with each other and with the king or territorial prince if such a person exercised power in their region.

Conditions were far from static between the eleventh and fourteenth centuries, but we can summarize what passed for "taxation" in those centuries. Ordinary folk owed their lord traditional rents and labor services, which began to look more like taxes when they were commuted to payments in money. Now they also had to pay him an assortment of fees arising from his control over the court they attended, his authority over the bulk of the uncleared forest, his responsibility for the maintenance of roads and bridges, and his exclusive operation of important facilities like mills, ovens, and winepresses. These fees went by such names as *corvées* and *banalités*. Peasants also often had to pay for the privilege of marrying outside the lordship, and most of them were also subject to tallages and poll taxes, which the lord could exact merely because of his power over them. From the point of view of the peasant, these many payments were what constituted taxation between the eleventh century and the late fourteenth.

These same payments formed the bulk of the lords' seigneurial revenues. A really important lord had additional ones, arising from mineral rights or treasure trove, the protection of an important market or fair, or lordship over a town that might yield lucrative rents and tolls. A lord of this importance would have many vassals who attended his court, owed him a sum when they inherited a fief, and had to contribute "aid" when the lord knighted his eldest son, required a dowry for his daughter, or needed to be ransomed from a captor. Wars, and especially crusades, also were occasions for such aids. Fiefs in the hands of a minor or unmarried woman fell under the lord's wardship, while a fief left vacant reverted to the lord, who might grant it to another vassal for a price. All these sums obtained from vassals constituted the lord's feudal, as opposed to his seigneurial, revenues.

A special case is afforded by the mints, which lost their public character later than the other symbols of royal power but became largely proprietary during the eleventh and twelfth centuries. Most lords in this period did not alter their currency purely to make large profits, but different currencies changed at different times, creating problems with exchange rates and the settlement of debts. Territorial lords came under pressure to maintain stable coinage. In some places they did so in return for a regular tax on hearths. Elsewhere the tax was more like a fixed seigneurial tallage. In the southwest, large occasional payments were exacted. Thus although the coinage was treated by lords as another source of seigneurial revenue, it led directly to some taxes in the modern sense and remained a matter of great concern to the economically active classes.

The king of France was a great seigneur and feudal lord. Little more than an important castellan around 1000 (except for especial authority over churches), the king had become a powerful territorial prince by the reign of Louis VII (1137–1180), and the huge additions to the royal domain between 1204 and 1229 turned the French monarch into a major European ruler. Yet throughout this evolution, and for nearly another century thereafter, the king drew his revenue almost entirely from the seigneurial and feudal sources just described. It was, by the thirteenth century, much greater in magnitude than that of other lords, but was very similar in type. The royal income thus came from a multitude of sources, usually in small amounts, and efficient "estate management" had a good deal to do with the royal financial position. These revenues, few of which we should associate with taxation, long continued to be called the "ordinary revenues" of the crown. They still constituted nearly half the royal income in the 1320's, but probably amounted to less than a tenth of it by the end of the fourteenth century.

The French monarchy had become a major power by the mid thirteenth century, thanks to the great expansion of the royal domain in the preceding generation. It was not yet a strong state in the institutional sense, and the next two centuries witnessed an often painful evolution from feudal monarchy to national state. In the relatively peaceful and prosperous thirteenth century, the need to supplement ordinary revenues was not yet urgent, but some extraordinary endeavors did strain royal resources. The crusades of Louis IX required substantial sums from the French towns, and they were asked for more in 1250 to ransom the captured royal army. Philip III's campaigns in Languedoc and Aragon required special aids; and soon after Philip IV became king in 1285 he sought to collect a tax for his own knighting.

What was happening in France was the beginning of a process whereby some traditional ordinary revenues were being expanded to the point of becoming extraordinary. Vassals, as we have seen, owed their lord certain feudal aids, but now the crown was trying to extend to a far greater number of subjects the obligation to pay a special tax for a royal crusade or ransom or knighting. These efforts to generalize limited traditional "taxes" came at a time when the experts in Roman and canon law were asserting doctrines of necessity and the common welfare to justify extraordinary royal taxes. Finally, the recurrent crusades and the "imperial papacy" of the thirteenth century had increased the diversion of church revenues to the crown. What was not yet clear was whether the clergy made their contributions as royal subjects or as representatives of the international church. It was under these circumstances that the outbreak of Anglo-French war in 1294 inaugurated the "age of the war subsidy."

THE AGE OF THE WAR SUBSIDY

The war subsidy was a special tax, of whatever form, that was levied to pay the extraordinary expenses associated with a war. For about a century, the crown had occasionally levied *aides de l'ost* based, essentially, on the commutation of military service, but the increasing warfare after 1294 made subsidies recurrent to the point where they finally became almost annual in nature. Lasting until 1356, when the capture of a French king led to the establishment of regular taxation, the age of the war subsidy was a critical period of transition from the age of dependence on revenues of seigneurial or feudal origin to a time of true taxation based ultimately on the needs of a sovereign state.

From the point of view of the legists, the king exercised sovereign powers as "emperor in his own kingdom." He could demand subsidies in cases of "evident necessity" for the defense of the realm. Philip IV invoked this principle several times in the 1290's, trying unpopular excises and also levying several general taxes based on income. Repeated levies, even at very low rates, began to cause uneasiness on the part of those who distrusted the king's proclamation that a state of necessity existed. In the less sophisticated eyes of the non-lawyer, the king's power was based on the feudal-seigneurial tradition: he was the supreme suzerain of the realm. In this context, he could require his men to aid him in military emergencies, but the assistance could take the form of personal service, not simply a financial payment. Earlier *aides de l'ost* or war subsidies had generally taken the form of financial composition (*finances*) in lieu of personal service, and beginning in 1302 Philip IV adopted this basis for levying taxes. It was slower and more cumbersome but more acceptable politically, and it tied taxation more closely to a genuine state of war. This system required that the king issue a general call to arms before trying to collect money. Depending on one's viewpoint, this requirement was its greatest strength or its greatest weakness.

Except for a large subsidy in 1304, the first third of the fourteenth century was notable for low tax receipts that the government tried to supplement by unpopular expedients based on the generalizing or stretching of traditional revenues. The age of the war subsidy was marked not only by such expedients but also by two other characteristics: (1) the stubborn refusal of most Frenchmen to pay subsidies in times other than outright war, and (2) a tendency in practice to invert the teachings of the legal theorists on the right to tax. Romano-canonical legal principles gave the king the right to determine the existence of an emergency justifying taxation, but required him to obtain in some procedural way the consent of those whose rights were affected. The French taxpayers, by contrast, were not much concerned about the question of consent, as long as the "necessity" was indeed "evident." If, however, they doubted the king's claim of necessity (and they often did so because they defined it in much more local terms than did the king), they resisted taxation strongly. What they wanted was to give counsel on the need for a tax when the matter was in doubt, not the right (or duty) to consent to taxes that were obviously justified. Representative assemblies, particularly central assemblies of the estates, had been rare in France, and the revival of such meetings in the first quarter of the century was mainly a royal effort to get favorable endorsement ("good counsel") for potentially controversial policies. There seems to have been little interest in making such assemblies act as consenting bodies, and it was the crown, not the three estates, that would have benefited from doing so in this period.

The clergy did not render military service, and they were part of an international church as well as being royal subjects. The ambiguity of their position came to a head in 1296 when Boniface VIII forbade the clergy to contribute to the Anglo-French war. The swift and hostile royal response induced the pope to amend his position, permitting the clergy to contribute to defense. The French prelates, who included some able canonists, tended to support Philip IV in his quarrels with Boniface, but they were the one segment of French society that did insist on the right to consent to taxation. Philip IV and his successors obtained a "clerical tenth" with great regularity, but they found that the French clergy could drive a hard bargain. They soon found it preferable to obtain consent from the friendly French-speaking popes who reigned after 1305. The tenths were supposedly to support crusades.

In the generally peaceful years between 1305 and 1313, Philip IV found that ordinary revenues no longer were sufficient. To supplement them he squeezed money from Jews, Italian moneylenders, and the hapless Templars, and he aroused a storm of litigation by trying to generalize feudal aids. The next war subsidy, in 1313, he canceled and returned when the conflict was averted. When he failed to follow this embarrassing precedent under similar circumstances a year later, widespread rebellion broke out against continued collections.

At this point (late 1314), Philip IV died, and the short reigns of his three sons were politically troubled. Louis X and Philip V first used representative assemblies to persuade the public that taxes were needed. This tactic facilitated slightly the collection of war subsidies but utterly failed in 1321 to produce a tax in peacetime. Assemblies for fiscal purposes went into eclipse. The crown in these years turned the customs service into an important fiscal institution, levying a tax called *haute passage,* which took the form of licenses to export wool and cloth, and imposing the *droit de rève,* which was basically an ad valorem duty of four deniers per livre on exports.

Charles IV obtained subsidies for wars with England and Flanders (1323–1326), but leaned heavily on loans, extortions from Jews and Italians, and mint profits obtained by weakening the currency. Philip VI had to abandon manipulation of the currency, but he and Charles both used commissioners of inquiry (*enquêteurs*) to identify and fine those individuals and communities that were guilty of infringing on royal rights or jurisdiction. Philip again tried the unpopular generalization of customary feudal aids.

Prolonged warfare with England resumed in 1337, but the indecisive skirmishing of the early years made it difficult to persuade people to pay subsidies. Philip VI had to resume weakening the coinage and extorting funds from moneylenders. The lack of regular taxes left France militarily unprepared at the end of each truce, while the public insistence that subsidies be tied closely to a state of outright conflict led the king to adopt the expedients that people found oppressive and tyrannical. In the 1340's taxation did gradually become more uniform and regular. The northern two-thirds of France (Languedoil) paid subsidies in the form of modest indirect (merchandise) taxes. In the 1350's these rose to 2.5 percent and tended to be granted annually by local or regional assemblies of estates. Affecting mainly the urban population with lower incomes, these taxes did help break down the close connection between subsidies and outright fighting. In southern France (Languedoc) subsidies remained closely tied to a state of war. They increasingly took the form of a lump sum apportioned among the communities of a district and raised by the urban governments through municipal taxes of their choice.

These signs of greater uniformity developed only slowly, and as a truce neared its expiration date in 1345 the royal government faced its usual lack of resources for military preparations. In an attempt to overcome this chronic problem, the crown now proposed that each region raise a tax to pay a certain number of men-at-arms (the quotas evidently being based on figures for hearths or households). The form of tax and the method of collection would be left entirely to local people. This plan was not approved, and the English went on to win great victories. Finally, in 1347, the estates found the royal plan attractive and endorsed it. Collection of a large subsidy based on this principle was under way when the Black Death reached France. The plague proved particularly important for French taxation because it ruined not only a large subsidy but also one in which the Estates General had finally played a major role.

As the kingdom gradually recovered from the effects of the plague, it fell increasingly into the pattern of annual indirect taxes granted by local estates in Languedoil and smaller but more frequent hearth taxes (*fouages*) granted in Languedoc by assemblies of the entire region. These last were apportioned lump sums based on pre-plague hearth figures. The subsidies of the 1350's remained low and did not suffice for military needs once the English resumed their war effort. After 1354, moreover, collections were inhibited in wealthy Normandy by the hostility of many nobles led by the Évreux branch of the royal family. John II suffered increasing financial distress and had to resume the immensely unpopular manipulations of the coinage for profit. Still inadequately financed, the French suffered new defeats in 1355 and 1356, like those of a decade earlier but with two crucial differences: first, the king was captured; and second, the Estates General could not unite to remedy the financial situation.

Just as they had done eight years before following English triumphs, the estates met in Paris in December 1355 and authorized a tax based on the salaries of so many troops. This assembly, however, went further and took control of the form and collection of the taxes instead of leaving these matters to regional assemblies that were sensitive to local particularism. The attempt to ordain and collect a uniform set of taxes for all of Languedoil ran into immediate opposition and seems to have been a tactical error. As heavy and regressive indirect taxes, they were resented in the towns, and subsequent meetings of the estates in 1356 had to replace them with a levy that would increase the obligation of wealthier people (especially nobles). None of these assemblies, however, made concessions to local autonomy, and the estates were unable to produce the money they had promised. They had lost considerable credibility by the time John II was captured at Poitiers in September.

THE GROWTH OF REGULAR TAXATION

The king's capture was the most decisive single event in the history of medieval French taxation. On the one hand, it created a political situation in which the Estates General became completely discredited as a part of the tax-raising process. On the other hand, it led directly to the establishment of permanent and regular taxation, first because the king had to be ransomed, and second because the kingdom had to finance measures against the unruly soldiers left unemployed by the ensuing truce and treaty.

Having already raised doubts about their ability to produce the taxes they promised, the estates from October 1356 to February 1358 declined to deal with the problem of securing the king's release. Instead, they advanced a mixture of constructive reforms and selfish personal vendettas. They granted high taxes for prosecuting the war, steadily increasing the burden on the nobility. Wealthy bourgeois, although taxed more heavily than in the past, were assessed more lightly than their noble counterparts. In the absence of financial records, we must doubt that much money was actually collected. Nobles began to boycott the recurrent assemblies, which fell increasingly under bourgeois domination and tended to pursue class interests. Both the royal government (represented by the dauphin, who would reign as Charles V) and the nobility lost all confidence in such assemblies. They began to bury their own differences and draw together politically, embracing some of the more popular reform proposals. By the end of 1358, it was evident that taxation and reform would be accomplished outside the arena of central assemblies of estates.

The treaty for John II's release that was ratified in 1360 required a large ransom that could be paid only by means of heavy annual taxes, the first in French history to be levied in peacetime over the entire realm. One of these was the *gabelle,* a special tax on salt that had been tried before, but the two major taxes were a levy on wine (initially about 8 percent and later raised to 25 percent on retail sales) and what we should call a "value-added tax" of 5 percent on other commodities. These were known as the *aides,* an appropriate term for payments to ransom one's lord. They were actually levied for all but two of the next fifty-seven years, and the term *aide* gradually became synonymous with a general indirect tax. These taxes all bore mainly on the urban population, and their enactment was accompanied by a stabilization of the coinage. The entire package must have been quite acceptable to the rural rich—the seigneurs—but it was not popular in Languedoc, where the apportionment of taxes among the towns on the basis of hearths had become a deeply engrained tradition. By 1362, the southern towns arranged to replace the *aides* with an equivalent tax in the form of lump-sum payments that accorded with Occitanian custom. This action had the effect of creating a customs barrier between northern and southern France. To prevent evasion of the *aides,* it had proved necessary to impose a new duty of 5 percent, called the *imposition foraine,* on all goods exported outside the parts of France where the *aides* were in force. Despite some subsequent interruptions, this group of taxes arising from the royal ransom remained a basic part of the French fiscal structure for four centuries.

If war subsidies had been justified by evident necessity, so also had the new regular taxes, in the sense that the making of peace was a matter of necessity. Peace, however, soon became a dubious blessing because of the violence of unemployed soldiers. Many local districts had to levy additional taxes to buy off these marauders or hire some troops to fight the others. By the end of 1363, in Languedoil, these local initiatives were incorporated into a royal policy by the adoption of a hearth tax (*fouage*) averaging three francs but scaled according to wealth. It was earmarked for the payment of troops to control brigandage. Several years later, Languedoc took a similar step on a more provisional basis, and the resultant revenues financed what would be called in later times a standing army.

This new direct tax lasted through the reign of Charles V (1364–1380) and contributed greatly to the military victories that have given this monarch a favorable reputation. It was the ancestor of the *taille,* which was to have an even greater future than the taxes levied for the royal ransom. The French did not, however, abandon their view that taxes were really "extraordinary" revenues. When the victories gave way to military stalemate, taxes began to encounter violent resistance (1379–1384). Charles V canceled the *fouage* on his deathbed, and the succeeding regime had to cancel the other taxes as well and go through lengthy negotiations with various assemblies to get new taxes in 1381. The setback, however, proved to be temporary. The *aides* and *gabelle* were back in force in 1382 and remained so for another thirty-five years, after rebellions against them were suppressed. The *fouage,* which affected the nobles and the ravaged countryside, was not restored, but by the mid 1380's the crown was imposing periodic *tailles,* which began as surtaxes on the *aides* but soon became apportioned direct taxes like the former *fouage.* The *tailles* long remained occasional taxes, geared to some special need like the old war subsidies. To reduce opposition, the crown granted exemption (1388) to hereditary nobles who pursued military careers.

The fiscal system of the 1360's survived the reaction of 1380, but the insanity of Charles VI (1392) and the ensuing princely rivalries finally ruined it. English conquests after 1415 accelerated the decline, and in 1417 the competing French factions canceled the *aides* in hopes of winning popularity. The most immediate result was a resumption of the monetary mutations abandoned in 1360.

Charles VII (1422–1461) was in serious financial and military straits in the first decade of his reign, and he made a great effort to revive the Estates General as a possible institution for raising taxes. Frequent assemblies granted taxes (usually *tailles*), but their delays and insistence on local ratification disappointed the crown and cost these assemblies a final opportunity to play a major role in the fiscal process.

The crisis of the early fifteenth century was of such magnitude that it is not surprising that the fiscal regime of the 1360's collapsed. What is noteworthy is that so much of it survived for so long and that its revival came about so quickly once the conditions were favorable. In 1435 a treaty with Burgundy ended the French civil conflict and permitted offensive measures against the English. The estates subsequently authorized reimposition of the *aides* and *gabelle,* and the government again stabilized the coinage. The treaty of 1435 and a truce with England in 1444 led to a serious revival of brigandage by disbanded troops, and in 1439 the estates granted a *taille.* The government levied it henceforth without further consultation and used the money, as it had with the *fouage* of 1363, to support a standing force of paid men-at-arms. This force, fully organized by the ordinances of 1445, was able to suppress internal disorder and complete the expulsion of the English from the country.

Henceforth, the French crown relied primarily on taxes that had first appeared in the 1360's as a consequence of John II's capture in battle: the *aides* (replaced in Languedoc by the *équivalent*), the *gabelle* on salt, and the *taille* or apportioned hearth tax, which closely resembled, and was the successor to, the *fouage* of the 1360's and 1370's. In addition, there remained the customs duties, of which the *imposition foraine* was most important. The old clerical tenth, which had been an almost annual tax through the fourteenth century (generally granted by the pope), had begun to lose this regularity after 1380, but in practice the crown in the fifteenth century obtained steady revenues from the church as a result of grants by the French clergy. The coinage, which had been so frequently manipulated for royal profit in the age of the war subsidy and again between 1417 and 1438, did not play this role thereafter. Modest mutations dictated by economic conditions aroused no hostility.

During the age of the war subsidy, the crown had developed two financial institutions: the Treasury, which handled receipts and disbursements of royal funds and operated much like a bank, and the Chamber of Accounts, which acted as an auditing and adjudicating body. After the crown first proposed subsidies in the form of salaries for troops (1345), with locally appointed collectors, the idea was taken up by the estates, and the collectors (*élus*) were named by the central assemblies in the later 1350's. When the *aides* were imposed at the end of 1360, these *élus* became royal officers. At first, the *élu* supervised collections in a diocese of the church, but as the districts were subdivided they lost connection with other administrative units and became known as *élections.* In some regions appointment of *élus* remained in the hands of provincial estates. The supervisory auditors of the *élus,* first established by the Estates General of 1355, bore various titles in which the word *généraux* always appeared. Under Charles V they became the "councillors-general," and toward 1390 they began to act also in a judicial capacity as the "Court of the Aids." One of their main tasks was to rule on claims of tax exemption, which had been granted to certain kinds of nobles in 1388 (for the *taille*) and 1393 (for the *aides*). Henceforth the Court of the Aids dealt with extraordinary revenues, while the Chamber of Accounts was most involved with the older ordinary revenues, although it had a broader competence.

By 1460, taxation had come of age. The *taille* was reckoned to produce about 1 million pounds, the *aides* and *gabelle* about 550,000, and the ordinary revenues only 50,000. Under Louis XI the *taille* was adjusted to meet royal needs and more than tripled in amount. A popular reaction compelled its reduction to around 1.5 million pounds in 1484, but the *taille* still provided two-thirds of the royal revenue.

BIBLIOGRAPHY

Elizabeth A. R. Brown, "Subsidy and Reform in 1321: The Accounts of Najac and the Policies of Philip V," in *Traditio,* **27** (1971), "*Cessante causa* and the Taxes of the Last Capetians: The Political Applications of a Philosophical Maxim," in *Studia Gratiana,* **15** (1972), and "Taxation and Morality in the Thirteenth and Fourteenth Centuries: Conscience and Political Power and the Kings of France," in *French Historical Studies,* **8** (1973); Georges Duby, *La société aux XIe et XIIe siècles dans la région mâconnaise* (1971); Theodore Evergates, *Feudal Society in the Bailliage of Troyes Under the Counts of Champagne, 1152–1284* (1975); John Bell Henneman, *Royal Taxation in Fourteenth-century France: The Development of War Financing, 1322–1356* (1971), and *Royal Taxation in Fourteenth-century France: The Captivity and Ransom of John II, 1356–1370* (1976); Maurice Rey, *Le domaine du roi et les finances extraordinaires sous Charles VI, 1388–1413* (1965); Joseph R. Strayer and Charles H. Taylor, *Studies in Early French Taxation* (1939); Charles H. Taylor, "The Composition of Baronial Assemblies in France, 1315–1320," in *Speculum*, **29** (1954), and "French Assemblies and Subsidy in 1321," *ibid.*, **43** (1968); Adolphe Vuitry, *Études sur le régime financier de la France avant la Révolution de 1789*, 3 vols. (1878–1883); Martin Wolfe, *The Fiscal System of Renaissance France* (1972).

JOHN BELL HENNEMAN

[See also **Accounting; Ban, Banalité; Banking, European; Black Death; Boniface VIII, Pope; Carolingians and the Carolingian Empire; Castellan; Charles V of France; Chivalry, Orders of; Clericis Laicos; Corvée; Estate Management; Fairs; Feudalism; France; Gabelle; Hundred Years War; Kingship, Theories of; Knights and Knight Service; Languedoc; Law, French; Lombards; Markets, European; Mints and Money, Western European; Normans and Normandy; Philip IV the Fair; Salt Trade; Taille, Tallage.**]

TAXATION, ISLAMIC. The image of the Middle East as the archetypal commercial entrepôt reflects Western interest in and awareness of the Islamic world. In fact, the basis and bulk of the Islamic world's wealth and prosperity, throughout the Middle Ages, was its agriculture. The agricultural poverty of the area is a modern phenomenon totally foreign to its earlier history. The commerce of the Middle East was supported by the Islamic world's productive agriculture.

Long-distance, high-value trade was conducted by merchants who tended to evade taxation. Trade was, in fact, frequently carried out by individuals who were also high government officials and hence in a position to evade taxation (Abbasids), by the rulers of the state (Fatimids), or by the state itself as a monopoly (Mamluks). Therefore, agricultural taxation will be the focus of this article.

Eastern sources detail elements of the abstract theoretical nature of taxation and provide anecdotal information on assessment and collection. Egyptian sources, on the other hand, include documents that provide a wealth of information on the actual assessment and collection of taxes. Documentary sources include tax receipts, fragments of tax registers, and administrative correspondence dating from just after the Arab conquest through the Middle Ages. Egyptian narrative sources also include largely intact administrative "how-to" tax manuals, as well as encyclopedias of administrative procedures written by government officials involved in the actual administration of taxation.

Several factors, which fluctuated widely with successive dynasties, had a major impact on the revenues remitted to the central government from agricultural taxation. These factors were land tenure, the frequency with which the land was surveyed and crops were assessed, who assessed and collected taxes, and rates.

LAND TENURE AND TAXATION

The article on Islamic land tenure in this *Dictionary* sets out the jurists' classical explanation of Islamic land tax, especially with regard to the distinction between *kharāj* and ᶜ*ushr* land. *Kharāj* land was defined as state land conquered by Arab Muslims from unbelievers. ᶜ*Ushr* designated land owned by Muslims and, therefore, subject to the ᶜ*ushr* (tithe), half the rate of taxation of *kharāj* land.

The work of Albrecht Noth has uncovered contradictory substrata of evidence with regard to the status of land tenure established by the Arabs at the time of the original Arab conquests (634–640). Between the end of the seventh century and the beginning of the eighth, the Umayyad rulers introduced changes in the original status. Jurists later rationalized those changes by introducing new traditions imputing what was, in fact, a new status, retroactive to the time of the original Arab conquests.

The purpose of the Umayyad changes was to redefine the ᶜ*ushr* land of the Sawād (southern Iraq) as *kharāj* land and so displace private Muslim owners, thereby enhancing the fisc. In Egypt, where few Arabs had settled, ᶜ*ushr* land was redefined as *kharāj* land to displace the Coptic church, which had been allowed to retain possession of its land and which constituted the primary landholder in Egypt.

The change in status of the greater part of land in Egypt to *kharāj* gave the state the right to tax at a higher rate and was accompanied by the introduction of direct taxation of individuals. Under the previous designation the fisc had collected taxes indirectly and, to a large extent, through the Coptic church. At the local level a native Egyptian notable apportioned his district's assessment among individuals. This same local notable collected the taxes he had assessed and then remitted them to the fisc.

The Arab administration was entirely dependent on a subordinate level of administrators who were native Egyptians. This situation resulted in frequent and large-scale tax evasion by the native Egyptian administrators.

Papyrological evidence from Egypt, a totally independent source, corroborates Noth's findings, based on narrative sources, that later jurists had rewritten the traditions to justify Umayyad changes in land tenure. By the jurists' explication of tax status, all of Egypt was *kharāj* land. Yet the term *kharāj* is not attested in any published Arab document until the Abbasid period (773). And even then, the jurists' definition of *kharāj* as "state land" is never apparent in Egyptian documents. Instead, *kharāj* is used interchangeably to refer to "tax levied on agricultural land" and to "rent."

ASSESSMENT AND COLLECTION

From the Greek, Coptic, and Arabic papyruses we know that following the Arab conquest Egypt was administered largely through the Coptic church. This was of necessity, as no Arabs, other than a few high-level personnel, settled in Egypt until nearly a century later. Intrusion of the central government at the local level was first felt as a result of the concerted efforts on the part of the central administration to replace Coptic administrative personnel with Muslims beginning about 717, a very slow process, according to the testimony of the documents, which indicate that Coptic officials continued in place well into the eighth century.

Egyptian narrative sources indicate a periodic survey by the central government by the end of the seventh century/beginning of the eighth. Introduction of an annual survey conducted by representatives of the central government is attested in the documents as early as 798. The annual survey entailed revised, and possibly increased, biannual tax assessments and may be related to the coterminus outbreak of first Coptic, then both Coptic and Arab, revolts in Egypt, all associated in the sources with tax assessment (for instance, "shortening the measuring rod").

In Egypt, agricultural taxes were initially assessed in the fall on the basis of the preceding spring's survey figures. That initial assessment could be subject to revision when the next spring survey was conducted. The biannual assessment procedures were necessary in Egypt because the annual inundation of the Nile washed away and laid down land. A similar procedure would have been necessary in the Sawād.

By the mid ninth century the central administration had furthered its control of taxation by separating the assessment and collection procedures. This was accomplished by assigning separate personnel to these responsibilities. This step, documented in the Arab papyruses, was probably more effective than had been replacing Copts with Muslims, which seems to have suffered from a lack of available personnel. By assigning separate responsibility and liability, the central administration could exercise a far greater degree of control over each function and hence maximize returns to the central fisc. Tax officials, who both assessed and collected taxes, had been in a position to overassess—while underreporting—taxes assessed and actually collected, pocketing the difference.

The annual survey, subject to reassessment and conducted by officials of the central government, continued until perhaps the early Fatimid period (*ca.* 1036). It was reinstituted in 1121, only to be rendered ineffective sometime after 1179 with the advent of the Ayyubid regime, which introduced the system of military estates (*iqṭā*ᶜ). The effect of military estates on the assessment procedures was to reunify, as had been the case in the first two centuries of Arab rule in Egypt, the assessment and collection procedures in the hands of interested parties (now the holders of military estates).

There were several more attempts by the state to regain control of taxation by putting its own officials in charge of assessment on military estates, thereby again separating assessment and collection personnel on the majority of arable land in Egypt. The last effort at central control, however, failed; the 1315 assessment figures were still being used in 1468.

ASSESSMENT AND TAX RATES

Irrigation. Methods of assessment depended first on irrigation. Passively irrigated land was seasonally watered by the annual flood and basin irrigation in Egypt and the Sawād, and by rainfall elsewhere. Actively irrigated land was watered year-round by waterwheels, wells, or *qanāt*s (underground canals).

Passively irrigated land was assessed on the basis of a survey, annual in the more prosperous historical periods, at a rate per *faddān* (6.368 sq m) of a particular land category. Land categories (of which thirteen, including pasture, are enumerated for Egypt) indicated crop rotation, fallowing, and irrigation—and hence which crop or crops could be successfully cultivated in a given agricultural season.

Actively irrigated land was assessed in a triennial survey that noted the area, number of seedlings and trees, their age, and age-specific tax rates. It was used for commercial crops—orchards, indigo, sugarcane, and vines—that required a high initial investment and a long period of maturation before a return on investment could be realized. Rates of taxation on actively irrigated land were assigned for each specific *faddān,* taking into account the actual number and productive capacity of trees, bushes, and vines, and then calculated at the local level. These taxes were not subject to revision but were established for a three-year period, at the end of which a new survey would be conducted and a new assessment established.

Tax rates. Egyptian narrative sources indicate three methods of assigning tax rates tied to particular crops or groups of crops. First was taxation by *faddān,* the method of assessment liable to revision on the basis of the spring survey. Second was taxation by negotiation; the land, though surveyed in spring, would not be subject to reassessment of the initial fall areal assessment figures. Finally, there was an assigned rate of taxation applicable to actively irrigated land. All three methods are continually detailed in narrative Egyptian sources through the fifteenth century.

No systematic evidence that would allow comparative levels of taxation is available. However, a late-twelfth-century Egyptian administrative source lists variable rates depending on yield. Onions and garlic yielded a crop valued at 10 to 20 dinars per *faddān,* on which the tax was 2 dinars, a rate of from 10 percent to 20 percent. A *faddān* of sugarcane produced processed sugar valued at between 20 and 100 dinars, depending on the area, on which the tax is listed as 7.5 dinars, a rate of from 7.5 percent to 37.5 percent. Indigo yielded a crop valued at 26 dinars per *faddān,* taxed at 3 dinars, a rate of 11.5 percent. Orchards and vineyards, crops subject to the triennial survey, were taxed at one-quarter of a dinar per *faddān* in the first year and 3 dinars in the fourth year.

Tax payments in kind and in money. Payments in money and in kind are both documented from early Islamic Egypt through the fifteenth century. A fifteenth-century narrative sources states that in Upper Egypt most tax was collected in kind, while in Lower Egypt taxes were collected in cash. A thirteenth/fourteenth-century source notes that in Syria taxes were collected in kind "on the threshing floor." Such collection is also documented in Egypt.

Tax farms. Under the Umayyads (661–750), the central government at Damascus appointed resident governors to the provinces. Their responsibilities included remitting tax revenues to the fisc. This proved unsatisfactory, and with the Abbasids (750–1258) administrative and financial responsibilities were separated. A resident financial official was responsible for an indeterminate portion of the provincial taxes. The remainder of the provincial taxes were raised through tax farms. In this system, Baghdadi notables gave bonds for the revenue of large parts of a province, whole villages, and/or districts, and then were liable for the taxes of that territory. The precise terms of tax farming have not been worked out. However, in the Abbasid period the fisc apparently retained the right to assess taxes on tax farms, with the tax farmer being then a contractor, not an autonomous fiscal agent.

Tax farming was practiced earliest and to the widest extent in the eastern provinces. It was introduced much later and less extensively practiced in Egypt. The introduction of the *iqta*ᶜ system, starting in the East in the tenth century and in Egypt only in the late twelfth, began systematic military tax farming in which the fisc surrendered its rights to assess and collect taxes on military estates.

OTHER TAXES

Maks (plural: *mukūs*), documented as the *ᶜushr* in seventh-century Egypt, subsumed customs and excise taxes as well as all manner of noncanonical taxes by the Fatimid period. Information on import and export taxes in Egypt is considerable but sporadic and incomplete. Juridically, rates were tied to the religion of the individual paying the tax, but in practice they were tied to value and preferential trading status.

BIBLIOGRAPHY

Walther Björkman, "Maks," in *Encyclopaedia of Islam,* 2nd ed., VI (1987); Clifford E. Bosworth, "Abū ᶜAbdallāh al-Khwarāzmī on the Technical Terms of the Secretary's Art," in *Journal of the Economic and Social History of the Orient,* 12 (1969); Claude Cahen, "Contribution à l'étude des impôts dans l'Égypte médiévale," *ibid.,* 5 (1962), and the following articles in *Encyclopaedia of Islam,* 2nd ed.: "Ḍarība" and "Djizya," II (1965), and "Kharādj," IV (1978); Richard S. Cooper, "Ibn Mammātī's Rules for the Ministries: Translation with

Commentary of the *Qawānīn al-Dawāwīn*" (diss., Univ. of California, 1973); Gladys Frantz-Murphy, "Agricultural Tax Assessment and Liability in Early Islamic Egypt," in *Atti del XVII Congresso internazionale di papirologia,* III (1984), "Land Tenure and Social Transformation in Early Islamic Egypt," in Tarif Khalidi, ed., *Land Tenure and Social Transformation in the Middle East* (1984), and *The Agrarian Administration of Egypt from the Arabs to the Ottomans* (1986); Ibn Mammāṭī, *Kitāb qawānīn al-dawāwīn,* A. S. ^cAṭīya, ed. (1943); al-Makhzūmī, *Kitāb al-minhāj fī ^cilm kharāj miṣr,* Claude Cahen and Yūsuf Rāgib, eds. (1986); Albrecht Noth, "Zum Verhältnis von Kalifer Zentralgewalt und Provinzen in Umayyadischer Zeit," in *Die Welt des Islams,* n.s. **14** (1973), and "Some Remarks on the 'Nationalization' of Conquered Lands at the Time of the Umayyads," in Tarif Khalidi, ed., *Land Tenure and Social Transformation in the Near East* (1986); al-Nuwayrī, *Nihāyat al-arab fī funūn al-adab,* VIII (1931); al-Qalqashandī, *Ṣubḥ al-a ^oshā,* III (1919–1922); Hassanein Rabie, *The Financial System of Egypt A.H. 564–741/A.D. 1169–1341* (1972).

GLADYS FRANTZ-MURPHY

[See also **Abbasids; Agriculture and Nutrition: Islamic World; Ayyubids; Caliphate; Fatimids; Irrigation; Islam, Conquests of; Islamic Administration; Tenure of Land, Islamic; Trade, Islamic; Umayyads.**]

TAXT-I SULEIMAN, a term meaning "throne of Solomon," was first applied in the Ilkhānid period (1256–1353) to a hill 87 miles (140 km) southeast of Lake Urmia in Iranian Azerbaijan and to the architectural remains on its flat summit. European travelers in the nineteenth century enthusiastically noted the site's salient features, which include a small lake within an oval fortification wall with gates and towers. Two decades of German excavation on the site in the 1960's and 1970's exposed a complex dating essentially from the late Sasanian period. Clay sealings discovered in the debris have confirmed a long-held theory that the ruins are those of the sanctuary of the Atur Gushnasp (*ātur-i gušnasp*), one of the three great fires of Sasanian Zoroastrianism.

Recent attempts to interpret the remains by analogy with modern Parsi cult practice have resulted in conflicting explanations as to how the sanctuary was used. While the function of most of the vaulted chambers and columned halls remains speculative, it is probable that the eternal flame was housed in one of two originally domed chambers at the center of the complex (the *atashgah*) and carried periodically to the adjacent chamber (*char taq*) to be used by the priests before the eyes of the faithful.

The first Sasanian king to foster connections between this "fire of warriors" and the Persian monarchy seems to have been Bahrām V Gōr (420–438), who visited the sanctuary following a successful campaign against the Chionites and who dedicated there the crown of his vanquished enemy. Later kings, following Bahrām's example, made pilgrimages to the place, lavishly endowing the temple with gifts. Traces of a large *eyvān* (*iwan*) hall that opened on the lake from the west may have belonged to a Sasanian pavilion connected with the shrine.

In the late twelfth century the poet Niẓāmī of Gandja (*d.* 1209), who was apparently familiar with the site (then called Shiz), fancifully reconstructed the ruins as an impressive palace in his epic romance of Alexander. Taχt-i Suleiman flourished again briefly under the Ilkhanids when a palace was built over the Sasanian remains.

BIBLIOGRAPHY

Of the excavation reports for Taχt-i Suleiman, the following are the most useful: Hans H. von der Osten and Rudolf Naumann, eds., *Takht-i Suleiman: Vorläufiger Bericht über die Ausgrabungen von 1959* (Teheraner Forschungen, I) (1961), for the topography of the site and a description of the enclosure wall; Naumann *et al.,* "Takht-i Suleiman und Zendan-i Suleiman," in *Archäologischer Anzeiger* (1965), 619–799; Naumann and Dietrich Huff, "Takht-i Suleiman: Bericht über die Ausgrabungen 1965–1973," *ibid.* (1975), 109–204; and Dietrich Huff, "Takht-i Suleiman," in *Archäologische Mitteilungen aus Iran,* n.f. **10** (1977), 211–230. For a concise review of the problems surrounding the site's identification and function, see Klaus Schippmann, *Die iranischen Feuerheiligtümer* (1971), 309–357. See also G. Gropp, "Neupersische Überlieferungen vom Heiligtum auf dem Taχt-i Soleiman," in *Archäologische Mitteilungen aus Iran,* n.f. 10 (1977), 243–291, for references to Taχt-i Suleiman in medieval Persian epic poetry.

LIONEL BIER

[See also **Azerbaijan; Bahrām V Gōr; Eyvān; Ilkhanids; Iranian Literature; Sasanian Art and Architecture; Sasanian History; Zoroastrianism.**]

TAYK^c (Georgian: Tao), an Armenian-Georgian principality located in the lower valley of the Čoroχ (present-day Çoruh) River and in the valleys of its tributaries, in what is now northeastern Turkey. Tayk^{c} is an ethnic name and corresponds to that of the people called Daiaeni by the Assyrians (eleventh century B.C.). Diauehi by the Urartians (eighth century B.C.), and Taochoi (Taochi, in Xenophon) by the Greeks (fourth–fifth centuries B.C.). Tayk^{c} appears to have been acquired by the East Georgian kingdom of Iberia (fourth–third centuries B.C.), then by Artaxiad Armenia (second century B.C.), forming a part of Armenia until A.D. 772, that is, for nearly a millennium. During this period Tayk^{c} was ruled by the Armenian-Georgian house of Mamikonean and consisted of four districts lying west of the principality of Koł (Georgian: Kola) in a semicircle around the three districts that formed the Dimak^{c}sid principality of Bołχa.

At the Byzantine-Persian partition of Armenia in 387, Tayk^{c} became Persian, and its western border formed a part of the boundary between the two empires. In 591, however, the Persian frontier was pushed much further east, and Tayk^{c} passed to the Byzantines, who apparently added to it Koł and Bołχa to form the province of Armenia Interior (*Armenia profunda*). This, with its eight districts, corresponds to the greater Tayk^{c} of medieval Armenian sources. After 772 Georgian sources refer to Upper or Thither Tao (southwest Tayk^{c}) and Lower or Hither Tao (northwest Tayk^{c}), the former of which had recently passed into Bagratid hands, while the latter was held by the Iberian Guaramids. By 813, however, both Taos were Bagratid and thereafter remained in the Iberian rather than the Armenian sphere of influence. By the tenth century Bagratid Tao/Tayk^{c} and a part of neighboring Klarǰet^{c}i formed a vassal state of the Byzantine Empire, whose Georgian Bagratid ruler Dawit^{c} (David) the Great of Tao (*d.* 1000) was styled *curopalate;* but, by 1008, Tayk^{c} was an integral part of the united Bagratid Kingdom of Georgia.

A rugged, mountainous region, early Tayk^{c} had no cities, the residence of its princes being first at Eraxani, then at the fortress of Tayoc^{c} K^{c}ar, and then at the village of Išχan. The population of Tayk^{c} was of mixed Armenian and Georgian origin, toponyms in both languages being found there as well as a number of Georgian, that is, Greek Orthodox, monasteries (for example, Oski and Bana), along with those of the Armenian church (for example, Išχan and Vac^{c}ejor). Other forts in Tayk^{c} included Bołχa, Ok^{c}ałe, Tortum, Azord, and Berdagrak. In the golden age of Georgia, from the eleventh to the thirteenth century, Tayk^{c} became very prosperous. Trade routes developed to the Black Sea, and commercial towns, such as Artvin, Ardahan, and especially Ardanuš, arose. Greater Tayk^{c}, later called Mosχika (Meschia), has been Turkish since the sixteenth century, but the local population is still largely composed of Georgian Muslims.

BIBLIOGRAPHY

Nikolai Adontz, *Armeniya v epokhu Iustiniana* (1908), and the English edition, *Armenia in the Period of Justinian,* Nina G. Garsoïan, ed. and trans. (1970); Sowren T. Eremyan, *Hayastanĕ ĕst "Ašxarhac^{c}oyc^{c}"-i* (Armenia according to the "Geography") (1963), 84, 118; T. X. Hakobyan, *Hayastani patmakan ašxarhagrut^{c}iwn* (Historical geography of Armenia), 2nd ed. (1968), 260–262; Heinrich Hübschmann, *Die altarmenischen Ortsnamen* (1904, repr. 1969), 276–278, 357–361; T. Marut^{c}yan, *Xoraguyn Hayk'* (Deep Armenia) (1978); H. Y. Tašean, "Tayk' drac'ik' ew Xotorjur patmakan-tełegrakan usumnasirut'iwn," in *Handes amsorya,* **84,** 4–6, **87,** 1–3 (1970–1973); Cyril Toumanoff, *Studies in Christian Caucasian History* (1963), and *Manuel de généalogie et de chronologie pour l'histoire de la Caucasie chrétienne* (1976, suppl. 1978), 96–101, 116–118, 331–339, 424–428.

ROBERT H. HEWSEN

[See also **Armenia, Geography; Armenia: History of; Bagratids, Armenian; Bagratids, Georgian; Curopalates; David of Tao; Georgia: Geography and Ethnology; Georgia: Political History; Trade, Armenian.**]

ṬAYLASĀN, a large, dark shawl or mantle worn by men in the Muslim world over the turban and down on the back and shoulders. It either was left flowing or was gathered in front to create a cowl or hoodlike effect. Sometimes, it was merely worn on the shoulders.

The *ṭaylasān* was originally a Persian winter garment (although the traditionalist al-Bukhārī mentions a headcovering by this name worn by the Jews of Khaybar in Muḥammad's time). It was considered so typically Iranian that a common insult for Persians was *ya 'bn al-ṭaylasān* (O son of the *ṭaylasān*).

During the Abbasid caliphate, the *ṭaylasān* was adopted by Arabs and was worn from Spain to the borders of India. However, the question was raised from time to time by jurists of the Hanbalite and Malikite schools whether or not wearing it was to be considered an act of *bid^{c}a* (heretical innovation). The great Egyptian Shafi^{c}ite scholar

Seated figure (far right) wearing a *ṭaylasān* or *ṭarḥa* over his turban. Miniature from al-Ḥarīrī's *Maqāmāt, ca.* 1300. British Museum, MS Add. 22.114, fol. 15. BY PERMISSION OF THE BRITISH LIBRARY

al-Suyūṭī (*d.* 1505) wrote several treatises dealing with the *ṭaylasān,* including a collection of traditions justifying the wearing of it.

From the High Middle Ages until recent times, the *ṭaylasān,* and a similar shawl called the *ṭarḥa,* became a distinctive badge of judges and legal scholars, who were referred to as *arbāb al-ṭayālisa* and *aṣḥāb al-ṭayālis* (*ṭaylasān* wearers). Shawls of this kind were also among the robes of office of oriental Christian and Jewish religious leaders. It has even been suggested that the *ṭaylasān* may be the forerunner of the Western academic hood.

The *ṭaylasān* appears in the Genizah documents as both a man's and a woman's garment. The woman's *ṭaylasān* was made of luxurious fabrics such as the iridescent *qalamūnī.*

The *ṭaylasān* is shown in illustrated manuscripts of al-Ḥarīrī's *Maqāmāt,* usually in depictions of qadis.

BIBLIOGRAPHY

Albert Arazi, "Noms de vêtements et vêtements d'après al-Aḥādīt al-Ḥisān fī Faḍl al-Ṭaylasān d'al-Suyūṭī," in *Arabica,* 23 (1976); Reinhart P. A. Dozy, *Dictionnaire détaillé des noms des vêtements chez les Arabes* (1845), 254–262, 278–280; Richard Ettinghausen, *Arab Painting* (1962), 106 (the captions on pages 106 and 107 should be reversed); Edward W. Lane, *Arabic-English Lexicon,* V (1874), 1, 866c–1,867a; Reuben Levy, "Notes on Costume from Arabic Sources," in *Journal of the Royal Asiatic Society,* n.v. (1935), esp. 334–335; Norman A. Stillman, *The Jews of Arab Lands: A History and Source Book* (1979), 167, 181–182; Yedida K. Stillman, *Female Attire of Medieval Egypt* (1972) and "Libās," in *Encyclopaedia of Islam,* new ed., V (1986).

YEDIDA K. STILLMAN

[See also **Costume, Islamic; Costume, Jewish.**]

TAYMĪYA, IBN (al-Shaykh Taqī al-Dīn Aḥmad ibn Taymīya) (1263–1328), Muslim scholar and teacher. In terms both of the effect that he had on his contemporaries and of the influence that his writings exerted on succeeding generations of Muslims, Ibn Taymīya was one of the most dynamic intellectuals of the Islamic Middle Ages. Like Aḥmad ibn Ḥanbal (*d.* 855), the founder of the school of jurisprudence to which he adhered, Ibn Taymīya was a thinker dedicated to the fundamental principles of Islam, adamant in opposition to accretions to the faith and practice, and defiant of the political pressures that were exerted on him by the state. As a result of his strong, uncompromising stand he gained great fame during his lifetime, even though substantial portions of it were spent in prison.

Ibn Taymīya's life was divided between Damascus and Cairo, the two principal cities of the Mamluk Empire, which held back the Mongol invasions and provided a refuge for Muslims who fled in their path. Ibn Taymīya was one of those refugees; as a boy of six, he left his birthplace in northern Mesopotamia and with other members of his family settled in Damascus in 1269. There he received a traditional religious education and at the age of twenty-one, in 1284, succeeded his father as teacher of *ḥadith* at a college in the city. Little is known of his life thereafter, until almost ten years later, when he first became involved in public incidents that gained him notoriety and led to his periodic incarceration by the rulers of the Mamluk state. These incidents reached a climax in 1305–1306, as a result of imprudent attacks that Ibn Taymīya launched against the teachings of Ibn ʿArabī (*d.* 1240), the great exponent of pantheistic mysticism in Islam. He was subjected to a series of inquisitions on his religious beliefs—first in Damascus, then in Cairo—to which he was summoned as a result of the intervention of one of Ibn ᶜArabī's influential disciples with a high-ranking Mamluk official.

For the next four years Ibn Taymīya was in and out of prisons in Cairo and Alexandria on a variety of pretexts, including his views on the divine attributes and the power of intercession of the prophet Muḥammad and saints. Inevitably he became a political issue in the struggle among various Mamluk candidates for the sultanate and their clerical supporters; however, there is little if any evidence for the claim that Ibn Taymīya harbored political ambitions for himself.

In 1313 Ibn Taymīya returned to Damascus as spiritual exhorter to an army that had set out from Egypt to fight the Mongols. In Damascus he resumed teaching and at the same time produced many of his more important works relating to Islamic law, including *fatāwā* (singular, *fatwā*; authoritative opinions on points on Islamic religious law). It was these latter opinions, particularly on divorce, that again earned the displeasure of the authorities; in 1318 a former supporter, the great sultan al-Nāṣir Muḥammad, commanded him to be silent on this issue. Defiance of this order landed Ibn Taymīya in prison for five months, and again in 1326, when he inveighed against the popular practice of visiting the tombs of saints. When he continued to circulate his views from prison, he was denied pen and paper. A few months later he died. His funeral was the occasion for a great public demonstration of mourning. Ironically, his tomb in Damascus became the object of pilgrimage.

The great popularity that Ibn Taymīya enjoyed during his lifetime and the respect that he continues to command can best be explained in terms of his single-minded devotion to the pristine Islam of the Muslim forefathers and his willingness to pit his convictions against the might of the political and religious establishment. The motives that led the Mamluk authorities to squelch Ibn Taymīya lay not so much in the nature of his beliefs as in his popularity and his unfailing ability to arouse public controversy and disorder. His writings still have currency in some areas of the Muslim world, particularly in Saudi Arabia.

BIBLIOGRAPHY

The standard Western source for the life and writings of Ibn Taymīya is still Henri Laoust, *Essai sur les doctrines sociales et politiques de Takî-d-Dîn Aḥmad b. Taimîya* (1939). Two more recent articles help to broaden our understanding of him: Donald P. Little, "Did Ibn Taymiyya Have a Screw Loose?" in *Studia islamica,* **41** (1975), 93–111; George Makdisi, "Ibn Taymīya: A Ṣūfī of the Qādirīya Order," in *American Journal of Arabic Studies,* **1** (1973), 118–129.

DONALD P. LITTLE

[See also **Caliphate; Fatwā; Ḥanbal, Ahmad ibn Muḥammad ibn; Mamluk Dynasty; Mysticism, Islamic; Philosophy and Theology, Islamic; Sufism.**]

TBILISI (Georgian; Armenian: Tpᶜłis; Persian/Arabic: Tiflīs; Russian: Tiflis) (41° 40′ N, 44° 45′ E), the principal city of South Caucasia, capital first of East Georgia (Iberia) and then of the united Georgian kingdom (twelfth to fifteenth century). Tbilisi was founded in 455/458 by King Waχtang I Gurgaslani (447–522) in the district of Paruar at the source of several warm springs (Georgian: *tbili,* "warm"). Excavations, however, reveal continuous settlement since 3000 B.C., and the fort called Suris Cᶜiχē seems to have been located here before the city's foundation. The original Tbilisi consisted of a citadel on a hill with a walled town (Kala) extending down to the banks of the river Kura. Later in the eighth/ninth century, a new section, Isani, developed on the north; the inhabitants built a double wall and added a ditch to the defenses. A typical oriental town of narrow, winding streets and small squares, Tbilisi had no formal plan until after its occupation by the Russians in 1801.

After the Georgian king David II (IV) the Builder recaptured the city from the Seljuk Turks in 1122, Tbilisi became the capital of a pan-Caucasian Georgian empire and the center of the Georgian golden age (1122–1225/1226). Here were schools teaching philosophy, theology, history, and law; the works of Firdawsī and Nizami were translated; and Georgian intellectuals, such as Šaχruχadze, Mose Xoneli, Ioane Šavteli, and Šotᶜa Rustᶜaveli, gathered to work. Tbilisi was also a great commercial center at this time, with caravansaries and several large bazaars that attracted merchants from Persia, Syria, the Byzantine Empire, and all Caucasia. The resident merchants, largely Armenians, played a great role in the life of the city. Chief among the monuments of Tbilisi were Seon (Sion) Cathedral (sixth century, rebuilt 1710), the Ančᶜisχati Church (sixth century to 1675), the Lurǰi (Lurdzh, "blue")

Monastery founded by Queen Tamar the Great (1187–1212), the Bethany Monastery and Didubia Church (twelfth century), the Meteχi Church (thirteenth century), and the Džvaris Mama Church (fifteenth/eighteenth centuries). The original royal palace had been located in Kala, but after 1122 a new one and several others were erected in Isani.

Taken by force some forty times in its history, Tbilisi was destroyed by the Khwārizmshāh Jalāl al-Din in 1231, captured by the Mongols in 1234, and stormed eight times by Tamerlane (1386–1403). Thereafter, the city declined in prosperity until the nineteenth century.

BIBLIOGRAPHY

William E. D. Allen, *A History of the Georgian People* (1932, 2nd ed. 1971); Károly Gink and Erzsebet Csemegi-Tompos, *Georgia Treasures, Towers, and Temples* (1975), 39–40, 86, 89–90; S. N. Kakabadze, *K istorii nazvaniya goroda Tiflisa* (1928), 60–67; David Marshall Lang, *The Last Years of the Georgian Monarchy: 1658–1832* (1957), and *The Georgians* (1966); Mindia Lashauri, "The Fifteen-hundredth Anniversary of Tbilisi," in *Caucasian Review,* 7 (1958); Rusudan Mepisashvili and Vakhtang Tsintsadze, *The Arts of Ancient Georgia* (1979); Jules Mourier, *Guide au Caucase,* 2 vols. in 1 (1894).

ROBERT H. HEWSEN

[See also **Albania (Caucasian); Bagratids, Georgian; Caucasia; David II (IV) the Builder; Georgia: Geography and Ethnology; Georgia: Political History; Georgian Art and Architecture; Georgian Literature; Kura River; Mongol Empire; Seljuks; Shotᶜa Rustᶜaveli; Tamar; Tamerlane; Waχtang I Gurgaslani.**]

TE DEUM, a Latin hymn in prose sung after the last responsory at matins on Sundays and feast days, at the end of liturgical dramas, in processions, and for thanksgiving on festive occasions. The text is a *psalmus idioticus*—that is, a text written in imitation of the psalms, composed probably by 350. In medieval liturgical books, it is found with the canticles for the Divine Office at the end of the psalter.

The melody exhibits the characteristics of the fourth ecclesiastical mode: E final, A reciting note, encompassed by a range of an octave C–C. After the opening intonation, the verses to "quos pretioso sanguine redemisti" are set to two archaic psalmodic formulas that are closely related to formulas in the Yemenite cantillations of the Torah. Each sets a continuous portion of the text and is varied according to the number of syllables in each verse. The first portion is punctuated by the threefold exclamation of "sanctus," set to a distinctive motive that is used later to begin the verses "patrem immensae maiestatis" and "sanctum quoque paraclitum spiritum." Following the second portion, the verse "aeterna fac cum sanctis tuis" is set to a melody that appears to be an antiphon; the hymn may, then, have ended here at an earlier stage in its history. Versions of this melody are used for the next two verses, and then the next five verses are set to the second reciting formula. Finally, another version of the antiphon melody concludes the hymn on the verse "in te domine speravi."

The verse "tu patris sempiternus es filius" appears as an example of organum in the *Musica enchiriadis* (*ca.* 900), and the final verse was set in English discant around 1300. Other festive performances, which used instruments, are documented and may have been set in improvised polyphony.

BIBLIOGRAPHY

The most detailed account of the hymn and its melody is the article by Ruth Steiner and John Caldwell, "Te Deum," in *The New Grove Dictionary of Music and Musicians,* XVIII (1980). The discussions in Peter Wagner, *Die Einführung in die gregorianischen Melodien,* III (1921, repr. 1962), 224–228, and in Willi Apel, *Gregorian Chant* (1958), 409 and 509, although based on the modern version of the chant, are useful.

JAMES GRIER

[See also **Divine Office; Gregorian Chant; Hymns, Latin; Mass; Poetry, Liturgical.**]

TEACHING CENTERS. See **Schools; Universities.**

TECHNOLOGY, BYZANTINE. For the Byzantine literati, preoccupied as they were with questions of theology and philosophy, the subject of technology held little interest. They were disdainful of the marketplace, as well as of the mechanical and industrial arts necessary for its efficient operation: hauling, lifting, tinting, alloying, and soldering. Thus, the corpus of literature on the subject that has come down to us from Byzantine authors, whether in the form of commentaries on ancient treatises or original essays, is quite small. Indeed, in examining the question of Byzantine technology and in assessing strides made by the Byzantines in this area, we are dependent not only upon written texts but also upon the culture's material remains. The competence of the Byzantines in engineering, for example, is evident from various structures in the capital, such as the aqueduct of Valens, the city's massive land walls, and the splendid church of Hagia Sophia.

Counterpoises. Through the survival of hundreds of glass weights we are aware of a major Byzantine innovation in weighing. Prior to 500, the empire had employed bronze counterpoises for the weighing of coin and commodities, but early in the sixth century, due perhaps to an increase in population in the capital and an accompanying acceleration in commercial activity, the chief administrative official of Constantinople began to issue glass counterpoises. Unlike bronze weights, which had to be filed to secure the required weight and then engraved with a mark of value, glass counterpoises could be "mass-produced" in molds using a measured amount of glass in a ladle and then stamped with a value mark and/or an inscription indicating the authority behind the weight's issue. As often happened, this innovation was adopted by the Arabs and further refined, while the Byzantines, struggling to preserve the integrity of their frontiers, abandoned their own creation in the later decades of the seventh century. Also typical is the fact that the party, or parties, responsible for this important, but mundane, development in weighing are anonymous.

Mechanics. Byzantium played a significant part in the progress of medieval technology, but a portion of this significance derives from its role as a "swing culture," that is, a civilization that preserved the ancient past and passed on this knowledge to its neighbors, the Latin West and the Arab East. Among the more important authors whose work was transmitted were the Hellenistic mechanicians Philo of Byzantium and Hero of Alexandria and the later Greek mathematician Pappus of Alexandria. Philo (early second century B.C.) wrote a manual on applied mechanics in nine books; most of this work is lost, but there survives in Greek the fourth book (on catapults) and in Arabic a discussion of pneumatics and pneumatic machines. Of the *Mechanics* of Hero (dates uncertain) only excerpts survive in Greek (Vaticanus graec. 218), but the

Blacksmiths pounding an anvil. Italian engraving of a Hellenistic water-driven theatrical machine devised by Hero of Alexandria, 1647. DIBNER LIBRARY, SMITHSONIAN INSTITUTION, WASHINGTON, D.C.

text in its entirety was translated into Arabic in the ninth century by Qusṭā ibn Lūqā of Baalbek at the command of the Abbasid caliph al-Musta^{c}īn (*r.* 862–866).

The excerpts in Greek are known through the writings of Pappus of Alexandria (*fl.* early fourth century), a gifted mathematician who produced an extensive *Mathematical Collection* (*Synagoge*) in eight books. The *Collection* includes commentaries on higher geometry and treatises on theoretical and applied mechanics by Archimedes, Philo of Byzantium, and, as noted, Hero. In Book VIII, Pappus, basing himself on Hero, discusses five simple machines, including the wheel and axle, lever, pulley, wedge, and screw. Book VIII (preserved in Vaticanus graec. 218) lacks its final section, but the whole of the book survives in a ninth-century Arabic translation. The passage of this book, first into the Islamic world and later into the West, had an important impact on technological developments among Byzantium's neighbors and foes. The Latins eventually surpassed Byzantium in the uses of gears, pulleys, and wind-driven machines.

As regards the application of technology, perhaps the best-known examples are Greek fire and the marvelous automata of the imperial throne room of the Triclinium of the Magnaura palace. The term "Greek fire" refers to a crude oil substance that was used with a projection device to set

Greek fire used in a naval battle. Miniature from the Skylitzes Codex, Madrid, Biblioteca Nacional, *ca.* 1300. FOTO MAS

enemy ships on fire. The oil was projected by means of a bronze pump (*siphon*); the direction of the flow was controlled by a bronze-bound swivel tube. Greek fire played a key role in saving the capital from capture by siege in 674 and 717, and later in 941. We might note, however, that in the design of catapults and ballistae the Byzantines seem not to have progressed beyond Pappus and his predecessors. From historical notices (the *Book of Ceremonies* 2.15) and the account of the traveler Liutprand of Cremona (Book VI, chapter 2) we know that one of the most spectacular sights at the capital was the automata. These mechanical singing birds, roaring lions, and moving beasts delighted visitors to the imperial throne room of the Magnaura. Such mechanisms may well have derived from a knowledge and use of Hero's works on pneumatic and mechanical devices.

Scientific instruments and farming. In addition to "toys," however, the Byzantines also had an interest in scientific instruments. The sixth-century author John Philoponus, whose commentary on the *Physics* of Aristotle was particularly influential, wrote a treatise on the astrolabe. The subject also fascinated the fourteenth-century historian Nikephoros Gregoras, who wrote two treatises on the astrolabe, based on Ptolemy and Philoponus. In the first treatise, of which there are at least twenty-six extant manuscripts, he discusses how an astrolabe should be constructed, revealing an extraordinary curiosity about this device.

Although Byzantine authors in general exhibit a distinct indifference toward ordinary instruments and tools, it is noteworthy that they had a certain interest in farm tools and equipment, as witnessed by a number of illustrated manuscripts of Hesiod's *Works and Days* (of 260 manuscripts, 14 have illustrations), as well as by illustrated texts of Gregory Nazianzus' *Homilies.* These illustrations depict a wide range of farm implements, including carts and yokes, plow beams, yoke beams, and plowshares, mattocks, threshing sledges and draghoes, winnowing forks and vinedresser's knives, handsaws, hatchets, an auger, and a chisel. In the autograph of Demetrios Triklinios (Marcianus graec. 464, dated 1316) we find superb illustrations of metal instruments that constitute "the impressive, informative, and 'realistic' evidence for Byzantine ironmongery we have."

The interest of the Byzantines in farming is further attested by the tenth-century *Geoponica,* a manual on farming techniques and procedures for storing agricultural products. The *Geoponica* also contains recipes for the veterinary care of bees, pigs, and horses. The health of horses was of direct concern to the state, particularly in light of the use of heavily armed cavalry units (*cataphracti*) in the campaigns of Nikephoros II Phokas and John I Tzimiskes. It is not surprising that the tenth century should witness the production of a deluxe edition of the *Hippiatrika* (Berlin, Staatsbibliothek, Phillips 1538), a manual on the care and treatment of horses. If Byzantine landowners had applied technology in a massive way to farming, the empire would have reaped handsome dividends in the form of increased population and revenues. For the arable to expand, for seed yields to increase, and for the introduction of new crops, such as cotton and rice—summer crops with high water requirements—flooding along riverbanks had to be controlled and irrigation systems set in place. But clearing, irrigation, and planting are expensive operations that require massive infusions of venture capital. The main sources of such capital resided in the hands of the church and the magnates, but the church needed its wealth to pay its clergy, maintain its religious foundations, and assist the poor; and the magnates were for the most part content to add land to their holdings simply by swallowing up the arable of the weaker and less fortunate.

Alchemy. The literati paid little attention to the production of articles of everyday life, but there exists within the context of alchemy an interesting body of "popular" literature concerning the industrial and fine arts. Of the many texts dealing with alchemy is the third-century Leyden Papyrus X, which contains many prescriptions for the treatment of metals, the manufacture of alloys, and the imitation of precious metals. We might recall that alchemy was concerned with the transmutation of base metals into silver or gold. Although there are four elements in nature, alchemists believed that there was a fifth entity, which, if it could be identified and controlled, could be used to accomplish such transmutations.

Alchemy and the industrial and fine arts were linked by the fact that, in a certain sense, artisans regularly performed such transmutations in their workshops. Casting rings, belt buckles, and brooches of iron, bronze, or lead, they then proceeded to coat these objects of base metal with silver in order to enhance their appeal and create an illusion of luxury. For the same reasons artisans applied gilt to objects of base metal or added glass paste, in place of semiprecious stones, to open-work jewelry. Then again, dyers, catering to clients with small pocketbooks, used inexpensive dyes to imitate the colors of the murex shell. Merchants, for their part, had an interest in tests for the purity of silver or gold and the care of silver and gold objects, such as the removal of oxides.

The flavor of the various recipes is found in alchemical texts, as in the following passages in Leyden Papyrus X (quoted in Cohen and Drabkin, *A Source Book in Greek Science,* pp. 364, 365):

> How silver is purified and made brilliant. Take a part of silver and an equal weight of lead; place in a furnace and keep up the melting until the lead has just been consumed; repeat the operation several times until it becomes brilliant.
>
> If you wish to test the purity of gold, remelt it and heat it; if it is pure it will keep its color after heating and remain like a piece of money. If it becomes white, it contains silver; if it becomes rougher and harder some copper and tin; if it blackens and softens, lead.
>
> A procedure for writing in letters of gold. To write in letters of gold, take some mercury, pour into a clean vessel, and add to it some gold in leaves; when the gold appears dissolved in the mercury, agitate sharply; add a little gum, 1 grain for example, and after letting stand, write in the letters of gold.

The practicality of some recipes is well illustrated by the last prescription. By combining gold and mercury a gold amalgam is produced in a form that will remain sufficiently liquid for the time necessary to apply the letters; after drying, the gum provides a coating that protects the letters against wear.

Alchemical writings cover the whole range of the industrial and fine arts. We find instructions for the manufacture and tinting of glass, as well as for the coloring of paints. A summation of coloring techniques came to be codified in the *Painter's Handbook*. Alchemical literature continued to be produced to the end of the empire, with many manuscripts dating from the fourteenth century. The flow of such literature can be gauged by noting that the listing of such manuscripts in the *Catalogue des manuscrits alchimiques grecs* published by the International Union of Academies (1924–1932) required eight volumes.

It is generally accepted that technological innovation at Byzantium ceased with the tenth century. With the Latin conquest of 1204, Byzantium seems even to have lost what it knew regarding the higher sciences. Nevertheless, the shimmering majesty of its mosaic icons illustrates the adept touch that Byzantium had in the fine arts, a touch that it had at the beginning and retained right to the end.

BIBLIOGRAPHY

Gerard Brett, "The Automata in the Byzantine 'Throne of Solomon,'" in *Speculum,* **29** (1954); Anthony H. M. Bryer, "Byzantine Agricultural Implements: The Evidence of Medieval Illustrations of Hesiod's *Works and Days,*" in *The Annual of the British School of Archaeology,* **81** (1986); Marshall Clagett, *Greek Science in Antiquity* (1955), 168–181; Morris R. Cohen and I. E. Drabkin, *A Source Book in Greek Science* (1958), 183–256, 360–366; A. M. Doyen-Higuet, "The *Hippiatrica* and Byzantine Veterinary Medicine," in *Dumbarton Oaks Papers,* **38** (1984); J. Haldon and M. Byrne, "A Possible Solution to the Problem of Greek Fire," in *Byzantinische Zeitschrift,* **70** (1977); O. Neugebauer, "The Early History of the Astrolabe," in *Isis,* **40** (1949); George Sarton, *Introduction to the History of Science,* I (1927), 195, 208–211, 337; K. Vogel, "Byzantine Science," in *Cambridge Medieval History,* IV.2 (1967).

JOHN W. NESBITT

[See also **Agriculture and Nutrition: Byzantium; Alchemy; Gems and Jewelry; Geoponica; Greek Fire; Metalsmiths, Gold and Silver; Mints and Money, Byzantine; Translation and Translators, Byzantine; Warfare, Byzantine; Weights and Measures, Byzantine.**]

TECHNOLOGY, ISLAMIC. Islamic technology is a major link in the general history of technology. Because insufficient attention has been given to this subject it does not occupy the place it deserves in Western literature. Charles Singer, in an epilogue to volume two of *A History of Technology,* remarks that from the ninth century until the fourteenth, "Islam was technologically far superior to Western Europe." He adds that during this period and in nearly all branches of technology "the best products available to the West were those of the Near East." He concludes that "technologically, the West had little to bring to the East. The technological movement was in the other direction."

The factors behind the rise of Islamic civilization and its technological achievements are numerous. Economic factors include the agricultural revolution, the rise of the large cities, the inherited skills in trades and crafts, and the flourishing of international trade. The cultural factors include the ideology of Islam and the unity of the Islamic world, and the role of Arabic as a language of science, culture, and daily life.

Technological subjects were considered an integral part of the philosophical sciences. The engineer (*al-muhandis*) enjoyed a high status in society, and

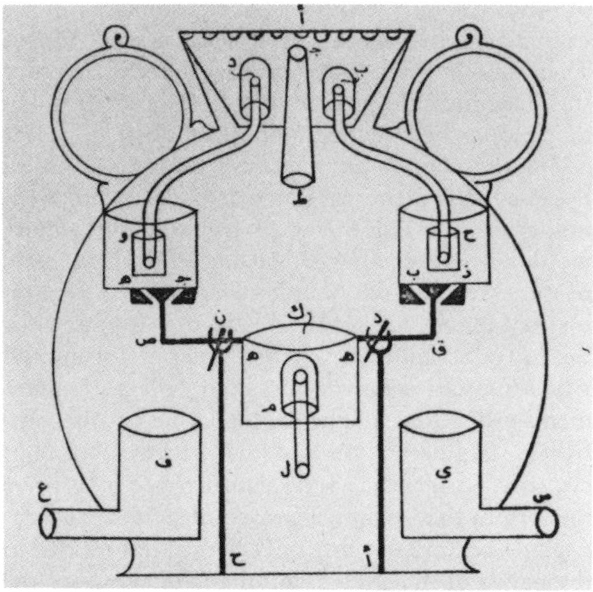

Automata vessel from the *Book of Ingenious Devices* of the Banū Mūsā, 9th century. © 1979 D. R. HILL, REIDEL, DORDRECHT

the artisan felt pride in being a member of a guild, where perfection in the craft was considered a form of worship.

MECHANICAL TECHNOLOGY

Literature. Several sources in Islamic mechanical technology have been published. *The Book of Ingenious Devices* (*Kitāb al-ḥiyal*) of the Banū Mūsā (three brothers: Muḥammad, Aḥmad, and al-Ḥasan, "sons of Mūsā"; ninth century) was published in its original Arabic text and in English. This is the most important book on automata, and it shows notable advances upon the works of the Hellenistic authors. There are 103 models in the existing manuscripts.

The book of al-Jazarī^c (*fl. ca.* 1181–*ca.* 1206), *Kitāb fī ma^crifat al-ḥiyal al-handasīya* (Book of knowledge of ingenious mechanical devices), is the most important document on machines, from any cultural area, from ancient times until the Renaissance. The complete Arabic text has been published, and also the English translation. The book deals with water clocks, trick vessels, fountains, perpetual flutes, water-raising machines, and miscellaneous other devices, including a piston pump driven by a paddle wheel, a remarkable machine for three reasons: the application of the double-acting principle; the conversion of a rotary to a recipro-

Bloodletting device. Miniature from a copy of al-Jazarī^{c} illuminated between 1250 and 1300. COURTESY OF THE FREER GALLERY OF ART, SMITHSONIAN INSTITUTION, WASHINGTON, D.C.

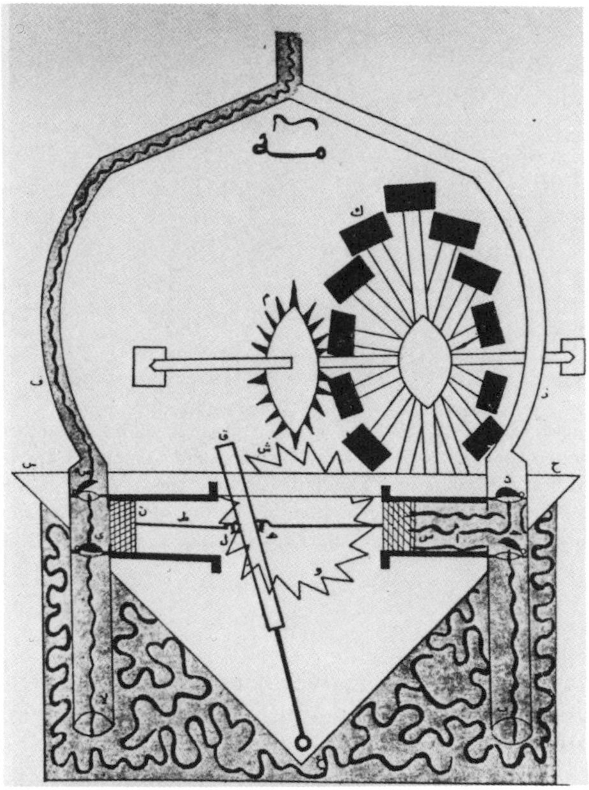

Water-driven two-cylinder pump with paddle wheel. Drawing from a copy of al-Jazarī^{c}, *ca.* 1315. Reproduced from the edition of A. Y. al-Hassan © 1979 I.H.A.S., ALEPPO

cating motion; and the earliest known use of true suction pipes. It therefore has an important place in the development of the steam engine and of modern reciprocating pumps.

Islamic engineers never described common, familiar, or everyday machinery. They interested themselves in recording only ingenious and unfamiliar inventions.

Waterpower. Waterpower was exploited extensively; for example, tidal mills were in use at Basra, in present-day southern Iraq, before the tenth century. The needs of such large Islamic cities as Baghdad made large-scale milling of cereals essential, and large ship mills were moored to the banks of the Tigris and Euphrates. Al-Bīrunī (*d. ca.* 1050) mentions that waterpower was used in driving trip hammers for paper mills in Samarkand and in crushing gold ores. Water mills were used for processing sugarcane, sawing timber, and raising water.

Wind power. Joseph Needham writes that "the history of windmills really begins with Islamic culture and in Iran." From an early date in Islamic history windmills were used extensively in Sistan. They were horizontal in type. According to R. J. Forbes, "the invention spread throughout the Moslem world and beyond it to the Far East." Forbes says that "as crushing mills, they were a feature of the Egyptian sugar cane industry and thence travelled to the West Indies when Arabic experts from Egypt were lured to help and establish the first sugar plantations." Needham is of the opinion that by the sixteenth century the Islamic horizontal windmills had become well known in Europe. He thinks that "this must surely have been a Westward transmission from Iberian culture originally derived from Muslim Spain."

The supply of water for irrigation and other purposes has always been a vital consideration in Islamic lands. The *shādūf* (counterpoised sweep for raising irrigation water), the *sāqiya* (a waterwheel with buckets), and the *nā^{c}ūra* or noria (waterwheel)

Light cannon (*midfa*ᶜ) on a carrying stick (right) and other gunpowder weapons. A drawing after the Leningrad Arabic Military Manuscript (İstanbul, Topkapi Seray, 7416), 13th century. From J. R. Partington, *A History of Greek Fire and Gunpowder.* © 1960 W. HOFFER & SONS, LTD., CAMBRIDGE

were very common, whether animal- or water-driven. Al-Jazarīᶜ and Taqī al-Dīn describe several other types of pumps.

Arabic mechanical treatises abound with the technical details of pumps, water and mechanical clocks, automata, fountains, mechanical toys, instruments, and perpetual-motion machines.

OTHER BRANCHES OF ISLAMIC TECHNOLOGY

We can mention only very briefly the other main branches of Islamic technology.

Civil engineering. Islamic civil engineering includes architectural technology, roads and bridges, irrigation, dams, and surveying. High offices in the government were occupied by engineers and architects who were in charge of these public enterprises. The superintendent of irrigation of Marw, for example, had under him 10,000 workers, each with a specified job. Al-Muqaddasī (*d. ca.* 1000) describes a massive hydraulic project in tenth-century Iran: "ᶜAḍud al-Dawla closed the river between Shīrāz and Iṣṭakhr by a great wall. . . . The water formed a lake and rose. Upon it on the two sides were ten norias, . . . and beneath each noria was a mill, and it is today one of the wonders of Fārs. There he built a city, the water flowed through canals and irrigated 300 villages."

Military technology. Rich material is available on Islamic military technology. During the twelfth and thirteenth centuries a considerable number of military treatises were composed. They deal with horsemanship, archery, tactics, military organization, and weapons. They are also rich sources on mechanical and chemical technology and the metallurgy of iron and steel.

Gunpowder is the main subject of several treatises. Ḥasan al-Rammāḥ (*d.* 1294–1295) gave the first account of the purification and crystallization of saltpeter. There are more than seventy recipes for gunpowder in al-Rammāḥ's book alone. This is a compilation of material that had been established for a long time. An earlier chemical work dating back to the tenth or eleventh century gives seven recipes for gunpowder.

Rockets and torpedos carrying fire and grenades are also described in treatises. Specifications give the weight of the rocket's paper, the weight of the gunpowder, and the carrying load. The *qidr* (pot) was a main siege weapon and was thrown by trebuchets.

Cannon were first used in the thirteenth century. Although some modern historians express doubts about the use of cannon in siege as early as the thirteenth century, the first illustrations of a portable cannon and the formula for its gunpowder occur in an Arabic treatise during this period. In addition, the historian Ibn Khaldūn (*d.* 1406) described the use of cannon in the year 1274 in al-Maghrib. Military treatises mention that a light cannon (*midfa*ᶜ) was used by the Mamluk armies to confuse and frighten the Tatars in the battles of 1260 and 1303. Cannon were used in the siege of Huesca in Spain in 1324. According to al-ᶜUmarī, by 1340 out of the six main siege engines belonging to Islamic armies, three used gunpowder, and cannon was one of these.

Shipbuilding. Shipbuilding was a major industry for the construction of both merchant vessels and warships. There were many naval dockyards in the Muslim world. The word "arsenal" comes from *dār al-ṣināᶜa,* the Arabic word for a dockyard. The summit of Islamic achievement in navigation is represented in the writings of Ibn Mājid (fifteenth century). But as early as the tenth century sailors in the Gulf ports had maps, books, and files that they relied upon for nagivating to India and beyond. The introduction of the maritime compass to Islam, about the beginning of the thirteenth century, marked a significant step in the progress of navigation.

Chemistry. Rich Arabic sources are available on

chemical technology. Equipment and unit processes are described in detail. Distillation was utilized on a large scale. The properties of alcohol were noted by Jābir ibn Ḥayyān (eighth century). Al-Kindī (ninth century), al-Fārābī (tenth century), al-Zahrāwī (Abulcasis; *d.* 1013), and Ibn Bādīs (*d.* 1061) all mention the distillation of alcoholic beverages. The distillation industries included rosewater and perfumes, oils and fats, and petroleum. Descriptions of the preparation of mineral acids appear in the writings of Jābir, al-Rāzī (*d. ca.* 935), and later writers. These include nitric acid, aqua regia, and sulfuric and hydrochloric acids. Some organic acids were prepared. Alkalies were in great demand for making glass, glazes, and soap. Natron was found in its natural state in Egypt. *Al-qalī* was the fused ashes of a Syrian shrub. Al-Rāzī gave a recipe for caustic soda.

Soap was another product of the chemical industry. Hard soap was first produced in Islamic lands. Glass was an ancient Near Eastern industry that flourished and developed in Islam. Syria was a major manufacturing center, and a treaty for technology transfer was concluded in 1277 with Venice, by which that Italian city-state acquired the secrets of Syrian glassmaking. Islamic ceramics also reached a high level of craftsmanship, and important innovations in this art were introduced. Inks, pigments, and paints were given special attention as writing materials. Several manuscripts deal with their preparation. Dyes were important products for the textile industry.

Textile and paper manufacturing. Textiles constituted the leading industry in the Islamic world. Such English words as "damask" and "muslin" reflect the effect of Islamic textiles in the West, where Islamic silk was greatly valued. The state factories were organized in production lines. The spinning wheel was in use at an early date. Multispindle machines of silk threads were in use in the tenth century. Looms with foot treadles were developed, and the drawloom became widely used.

The introduction of the paper industry to Islamic lands was a milestone in history. It started with Chinese war prisoners in Samarkand in the eighth century. Soon paper factories were established in Baghdad and Syria. They spread westward until they reached Muslim Spain and Sicily. According to Dard Hunter, the major innovations in the technology of paper were Islamic. They advanced papermaking into a real industry.

The techniques of manufacturing leather were well established. The manufacture of the Islamic cordovan leather in Córdoba became famous over Europe. Bookbinding also attracted the attention of authors, who wrote numerous treatises on it.

Agricultural technology. The Islamic agricultural revolution affected most aspects of agricultural and food technology. To feed the populations of large cities, flour milling became a major industry. Water-driven hammers were used in rice mills for husking the rice. Sugar was a basic Islamic industry. It necessitated a high technological competence. The technology of sugar refining was transferred to Europe, China, and the West Indies. Edible vegetable oils, especially olive and sesame oils, were basic commodities, and oil presses were abundant. Cooked foods and drinks were sold in the cities, and authors wrote books on cooking. Treatises on agriculture give information on the storage of agricultural products. Other sources discuss food preservation. Quality control and the prevention of the adulteration of foods were discussed in the manuals on the *ḥisba* (a government department in charge of inspecting weights and measures and the quality of goods at markets to prevent cheating) and in other sources.

Mining technology. Mining played an important role in the Islamic world. Information on Islamic mines occurs in various Arabic works, especially those dealing with geography, alchemy, and mineralogy. Underground and open-cut mining methods were used. There is information about the tools of the miners, the windlasses, illumination, ventilation, and drainage of the mines. Waterwheels were installed in stages to drain the mines. In dressing the ores, water-driven trip hammers were used. The exploitation of corals and pearls was a thriving industry as well. Innovative designs of diving equipment and of dredging machines are described in Arabic technical literature.

Much information on metallurgy is available. This includes the nonferrous metallurgy of gold, silver, copper and its alloys, and other metals. Wrought iron, cast iron, and steel were made. Iron was produced from local iron ores. Steel was produced in crucibles in the molten state. Patterned swords with the *firind* or *jawhar* (both words refer to wavy marks, streaks, and grain of the sword) were made from Damascus steel. Works by al-Bīrūnī (*d. ca.* 1050), al-Kindī, and several other authors contain rich information on the making of steel and its heat treatment.

BIBLIOGRAPHY

Sources. Ibn Bādīs, *ʿUmdat al-kuttāb wa ʿuddat dhawī al-albāb* (MSS in Cairo, Gotha, and Chicago), English ed., Martin Levey, trans., in *Transactions of the American Philosophical Society,* n.s. 52, pt. 4 (1962); Banū Mūsā, *The Book of Ingenious Devices,* Donald R. Hill, ed. and trans. (1979), and *Kitāb al-ḥiyal* (Arabic text), A. Y. al-Hassan, ed. (1981); ʿAbu al-Rayhān al-Bīrūni, *Kitāb al-jamāhir fī maʿrifat al-jawāhir,* F. Krenkow, ed. (1936); Ibn al-Rizzaz al-Jazarī, *The Book of Knowledge of Ingenious Mechanical Devices,* Donald R. Hill, trans. (1974), and *Al-jāmi ʿbayn al-ʿilm wa al-ʿamal al-nāfiʿ fī ṣināʿat al-ḥiyal* (A compendium on the theory and practice of the mechanical arts), A. Y. al-Hassan, ed. (1979); Ibn Khaldūn, *Kitāb al-ʿibar,* VII (1971); Ibn Mājid, *Kitāb al-fawāʾ id fī uṣūl ʿilm al-baḥr wa al-qawāʿid* (1921–1923); *Al-makhzūn jāmiʿ al-funūn* (MSS in Leningrad, İstanbul [Topkapi Seray, 7416], and Paris [Bibliothèque Nationale, 2826]); Abu ʿAbd Allah Shams al-Din al-Muqaddasī, *Aḥsan al-taqāsīm fī maʿrifat al-aqālīm,* M. J. de Goeje, ed. (1906); Najm al-Din al-Ḥasan al-Rammāḥ, *Al-furūsiyyah wa al-manāṣib al-harbiyyah* (Paris, Bibliothèque Nationale, MS 2825); al-ʿUmarī ibn Faḍl Allah, *Al-taʿrif bi al-muṣṭalah al-sharīf* (Cairo, 1312H).

Studies. Pierre Eugène M. Berthelot, *La chimie au môyen age,* II (1893); Robert James Forbes, *Studies in Ancient Technology,* 9 vols. (1955–1964), II; Ahmad Y. al-Hassan, "Iron and Steel Technology in Medieval Arabic Sources," in *Journal for the History of Arabic Science,* 2 (1978), *Taqī al-Dīn and Arabic Mechanical Engineering* (in Arabic) (1976), and, with Donald R. Hill, *Innovation in Islamic Technology* (1981) and *Islamic Technology: An Illustrated History* (1986); Joseph Needham, *Science and Civilisation in China,* 5 vols. (1954–1965), II, 560–566; Charles J. Singer, E. J. Holmyard, and A. R. Hall, *A History of Technology,* 5 vols. (1954–1958), II (1956), 754–767.

AHMAD Y. AL-HASSAN

[See also **Agriculture and Nutrition, II: The Mediterranean Region; Alchemy, Islamic; Arabic Numerals; Archimedes in the Middle Ages; Basra; Bīrūnī, Muḥammad ibn Aḥmad Abū 'l-Rayḥān al-; Ceramics, Islamic; Compass, Magnetic; Distilled Liquors; Glass, Islamic; Irrigation; Khaldūn, Ibn; Leather and Leatherworking; Manuscript Books, Binding of, Islamic; Muqaddasī, al-; Navies, Islamic; Paper, Introduction of; Silk; Textiles, Islamic.**]

TECHNOLOGY, TREATISES ON. The written record documenting the history of medieval technology is sparse and incomplete. Despite a surge of technological growth, few conventional sources record this activity, and those which have come down to us were often produced not by artisans but by observers lacking a familiarity with technical processes. Since medieval craftsmen were illiterate or only marginally literate, information about techniques was transmitted from master to apprentice orally. There was little need to put craft secrets into writing. This only makes the documents that do survive all the more precious, for when artisans took pen in hand, it was in response to far-reaching social and psychological changes. The technological treatises are the lenses through which these changes can be viewed.

ANCIENT TREATISES

Unlike conventional scientific and philosophical treatises, European technological writings owed very little to ancient sources. Greek and Roman works on engineering and the practical arts were few in number, and while their influence was felt in Islam, they did not become an integral part of the Western European tradition until the Renaissance. These treatises reflected an intensely aristocratic society in which manual labor was condemned as being suitable only for slaves. Greek treatises on mechanics were highly theoretical, openly avoiding any discussion of the application of techniques to practical purposes. An anonymous work of the school of Aristotle, entitled *Quaestiones mechanicae* (third century B.C., possibly by Strato), for example, discusses thirty-five problems relating principally to the lever and balance (for instance, "why a wedge exerts great force and splits great bodies"), but only incidentally gives information about practical applications of mechanical principles to tools and techniques.

Although the study of mechanics flourished at Alexandria in late antiquity, there was little interest in the actual construction of machines, except perhaps for the building of automata, puppets, and mechanical playthings. Ctesibius (*fl.* 270 B.C.) is credited with inventing the water organ, water clock, and double-piston force pump (known as the *Ctesibica machina,* or "Ctesibian device"). His work on pneumatics (described by Vitruvius) is lost. Philo of Byzantium, who lived a generation after Ctesibius, wrote a textbook on mechanics that included sections on the lever, the catapult, pneumatics, automata, warfare, and the construction of seaports, but only fragments of the work are extant. Philo's pneumatic inventions, including a variety of ingenious toys and trick vessels, were probably devised for entertainment or experimentation, although he is also credited with designs for new forms of weaponry. The most famous works in the Alexandrian tradition were by Hero of Alexandria (first century); Hero's *Pneumatica* and his *Automata* had a strong influence in medieval Islam and in the West during the Renaissance. These works contain detailed descriptions of trick fountains, "magical" apparatuses, automatic door openers, and aeolipiles. Whether these machines were ever built by Hero or his contemporaries is still an open question. Nevertheless, the designs illustrate the work of inventors of the first order.

Ancient treatises on the art of war also contained technological information. Among these works are Hero's *Belopoeica,* on artillery; a handbook by Bito (*ca.* 240 B.C.) on catapults; the artillery manual of Philo of Byzantium (*Belopoeica*); and *De rebus bellicis* (*ca.* 370), the work of an anonymous Roman reformer. The latter treatise offers a number of imaginative, if impractical, proposals for new military inventions, including scythed chariots, siege machines, artillery, and portable pontoon bridges. It was the only ancient work on military technology known in the West before the fifteenth century. Finally, the tenth book of Vitruvius' *De architectura* describes artillery, military engines, and lifting devices used in the construction of buildings.

ISLAMIC TREATISES

The ancient technological tradition flourished in Islam. Part of Hero's *Mechanica* was translated into Arabic by Qusṭā ibn Lūqā about 864, and Philo's *Pneumatica* appeared in Arabic in the fourteenth century. These works undoubtedly stimulated the interest of Arab engineers and contributed substantially to their writings. Arabic treatises on technology, like those of the Alexandrian school, displayed little interest in practical applications. Written mainly by engineers employed in the courts of the great Muslim caliphs, these lavishly illustrated treatises were devoted almost exclusively to the construction of ingenious mechanical devices (*ḥiyal*) and automata designed to provoke wonder and aesthetic pleasure.

Our knowledge of Arab mechanical engineering comes from four main treatises. A book on the making of water clocks attributed to Archimedes is a very early Muslim work, possibly written toward the end of the eighth century. It is certainly not an authentic work of Archimedes, but the fact that the unknown author who wrote the work so attributed it suggests that this ancient Greek mathematician and supposed instrument maker was greatly revered in Islam.

About 850, Ahmad ibn Mūsā, one of three famous sons of a certain Mūsā ibn Shakir, who are known collectively as the Banū (sons of) Mūsā, composed an influential work on trick vessels, fountains, self-trimming lamps, and musical automata. The Banū Mūsā, who had been brought up in the court of the caliph al-Maʾmūn, were celebrated for their knowledge of the sciences and mathematics. Ahmad's work, *Kitāb al-ḥiyal* (Book of ingenious devices), was written very much in the spirit of Hero and Philo, and hence is important in showing the transmission of the Alexandrian mechanical tradition in Islam. The designs of the Banū Mūsā, however, were much more sophisticated than anything that had appeared earlier. In particular, a preoccupation with automatic controls and the use of self-operating valves, timing devices, and delay systems distinguishes the mechanical ingenuity of the Banū Mūsā from the relatively simple mechanical concepts of Hero and Philo.

The third Arab engineering treatise was by Riḍwān ibn Muḥammad al-Saʿātī, who in 1203 wrote a lengthy work dealing with the repair of a monumental water clock over the Jayrūn Gate in Damascus. Riḍwān's work exists in only one manuscript, from the sixteenth century; a complete edition of the work has not been published.

The most important Arabic treatise on technology is the *Kitāb fī maʿrifat al-ḥiyal al-handasīya* (Book of knowledge of ingenious mechanical devices) of Ibn al-Razzāz al-Jazarīʿ (*fl. ca.* 1181–*ca.* 1206), a court engineer in the service of the Artuqid rulers of Diyarbakir in southeastern Turkey. Al-Jazarīʿ had spent twenty-five years under the patronage of this family, having entered its service about 1180/1181; the work on *ḥiyal* was thus completed about 1205 or 1206. This treatise is altogether superior to earlier Arabic writings on technology. Unlike the Banū Mūsā, whose talents were devoted mainly to the design of imaginative and curious devices, al-Jazarīʿ's interests were more those of an engineer. He described a much wider range of machines and displayed a greater interest than his predecessors in designing machines for practical use. In the fifth book of the treatise, for example, al-Jazarīʿ describes several interesting designs for pumps and water-lifting devices. While earlier writers had been vague about the construction of their machines, al-Jazarīʿ carefully de-

Water-lifting device described by al-Jazarī^c. Miniature from a 13th-century copy of his works. MUSEUM OF FINE ARTS, BOSTON. THE GALOUBEW COLLECTION

scribes each phase of construction, specifying measurements, procedures, and the materials to be used. Mechanically, this treatise is the most sophisticated work in the entire Arabic corpus, since al-Jazarīᶜ incorporated all of the components used by his predecessors and introduced many of his own. Al-Jazarīᶜ's monumental water clocks provided spectacular visual effects: circles representing the zodiac rotated at constant speed; birds discharged pellets from their beaks to sound the hours; and doors opened at regular intervals to reveal musicians performing on their instruments. These effects were achieved by ingenious application of conical valves, tipping buckets, and segmented gears, which did not enter the general vocabulary of European machine design until the sixteenth century.

Clearly, very few of the ingenious devices encountered in Arabic technological treatises were intended to relieve the burdens of human labor. They were meant only to amuse the aristocratic audiences for whom they were built. Frivolous though this aim may seem to the modern Western observer, the designers of *ḥiyal* may actually have made significant contributions to the development of modern science and technology. Historians have observed that the preoccupation with automata in Greece, in Islam, and later in Europe was one of the factors that led to the development of rationalistic, mechanistic explanations of natural phenomena. Indeed, the mechanically sophisticated astronomical clocks of the fourteenth, fifteenth, and sixteenth centuries may well have stimulated natural philosophers into imagining the entire cosmos as a gigantic clockwork, an attitude that was immensely fruitful in the development of modern science. In addition, the makers of *ḥiyal* made important contributions to the development of machine design, the outcomes of which, among other things, are vending machines, mechanical calculators, and the modern computer.

Although al-Jazarīᶜ's treatise was extremely popular in Islam (fourteen Arabic copies exist), its influence on practice is unfortunately not known. Nor is it possible, in the present state of our knowledge, to determine the extent to which the Islamic treatises in general influenced European technology. One possible avenue for the transmission of Arabic technology into Europe was the court of Alfonso X the Wise at Seville. Alfonso commissioned the translation of a number of Arabic scientific treatises, including works on the design of astronomical instruments, which are contained in the *Libros del saber de astronomía* and the *Dos libros de las armellas.* A treatise on machines entitled *Kitāb al-asrar fī nataᵓij al-afkār* (Book of secrets of the results of thoughts), by one Ibn Khalaf al-Murādī (eleventh century), was copied at Alfonso's court around 1266. This work is similar in scope to al-Jazarīᶜ's treatise, in that it includes models of water clocks and automata, but is distinguished from other Arabic treatises by the inclusion of large machines with powerful prime movers. In this respect at least, the treatise seems to resemble more closely the European treatises than other Arabic works on *ḥiyal.*

EUROPEAN TREATISES

Medieval European treatises on technology were entirely different from those produced in ancient Greece, Byzantium, and Islam. In the first place, few dealt with the construction of automata; nor were they, like Hero's *Mechanica,* theoretical treatises devoted to solving problems in mechanics. Almost completely divorced from the Alexandrian school, the West produced treatises that were in general devoted more to the application of engineering concepts to practical purposes, such as construction or warfare. Second, these writings usually took the form not of systematic treatises but of compilations of recipes and workshop notes, or of drawings of machines accompanied by meager textual annotations.

These characteristics were in part the result of changes in the social status of artisans and of new attitudes toward work that emerged in the Latin West. As early as the sixth century, when Benedict of Nursia laid the foundations of Western monasticism, manual labor was accorded an exalted status that was unknown in the classical world. According to the Benedictine monastic rule, "Laborare est orare": Work is worship. Historians have seen in the Benedictine rule the basis of a new ethos sanctifying the active life and man's dominion over the earth. These attitudes surfaced in the eleventh century, as cathedral builders left indelible traces all over Europe of the capacity of humans to control and harness the forces of nature.

Simultaneously, as commercial activity quickened in the West, craftsmen began to enjoy new freedom, wealth, and enhanced social status. By the twelfth century, intellectuals were beginning to adjust theory in accordance with established practice. Hugh of St. Victor, writing in the 1120's, divided knowledge into theoretical arts, practical arts (ethics), the arts of discourse, and the mechanical arts, thereby elevating technology to the same plane as the sciences. Thus, in both attitude and social fact, manual labor was released from its former servile status and given new dignity.

Latin treatises. The earliest Latin treatises reflecting these developments were, not surprisingly, products of monastic workshops and scriptoria, where craftsmanship and learning mingled according to the precepts set down by St. Benedict. As monks sifted through the sparse literary remains of antiquity, they found and copied many technical recipes relating to the decorative arts: painting, gilding, metalwork, dyeing, and glassmaking. Many of these recipes can be traced back to Alexandrian alchemical treatises, such as the early-fourth-century Leyden and Stockholm papyri.

The earliest Latin treatise comes to light around the year 800 in the form of two manuscripts. Codex 490 of the Biblioteca Capitolare in Lucca, Italy, contains a collection of Latin technical recipes known as *Compositiones variae.* It is a compilation based mainly on Italian practice but is greatly influenced by Greco-Byzantine learning, and also contains traces of Arab and Spanish influences. The manuscript was undoubtedly preserved for its recipes for making pigments, preparing parchment, and writing in gold, as such knowledge would have been of great interest to monks engaged in illuminating manuscripts.

Contemporary with the Lucca manuscript was the *Mappae clavicula,* a compilation of similar scope. Although only two extended copies of the *Mappae clavicula* survive (tenth and twelfth centuries), the work is known to have existed in the ninth century in the library of the Benedictine monastery at Reichenau, an important center of both artistic activity and the revival of learning stimulated by the Carolingian court.

Mappae clavicula and *Compositiones variae* are part of a very large family of technical recipe books that were scattered widely throughout European monasteries. Scores, if not hundreds, exist in European libraries today. These handbooks probably served as introductions to novice craftsmen or as workshop reminders to experienced artisans. They are certainly not step-by-step instructional treatises, nor do they always reflect the most advanced practices of the day. The *Mappae clavicula,* for example, was badly garbled by centuries of transmission through monastic scriptoria, and many of its recipes make no technical sense whatsoever. This does not mean that such texts serve no useful purpose; it only means that the modern historian must approach them carefully, always bearing in mind that the medieval craftsman "spoke" with his hands and not his pen. Consequently, evaluations of these treatises must be supplemented by detailed laboratory examination of medieval paintings, textiles, ceramics, and metalwork.

One outstanding exception proves this rule. It is *De diversis artibus,* a treatise written in the 1120's by one Theophilus, who has been plausibly identified as Roger of Helmarshausen, a Benedictine monk and noted metalworker. Whether or not this identification is correct, the author of this work was undoubtedly an experienced craftsman who was completely up-to-date in his knowledge of techniques. Equally apparent is the strong religious motivation underlying the work; writing against the Cistercians' puritanical denunciations of ornamentation in the churches, Theophilus defends "the embellishment of the material house of God." Indeed, the work as a whole is an account of all the skills required for decorating a church, from the making of chalices and censers to the construction of organs and the casting of bells for the tower.

Theophilus describes techniques for preparing the pigments for painting shrines and manuscripts; he explains how to make glass in the form of windows, vessels, mosaic tesserae, and glazes; and in the third book he gives detailed instructions for a wide range of metalwork. This section of the work is exceptional for its detail and clarity. Theophilus begins by telling how to set up the workshop and furnish it with tools. He then gives precise directions for making a chalice and a censer, and for applying enamel, niello, and jewels. Toward the end of book III, Theophilus gives a vivid description of a process for casting large bells that was not improved on until the sixteenth century.

De diversis artibus is a unique document. No other medieval technical treatise matches it for clarity, detail, or range of subjects treated. Unlike most writings on the arts, which were merely random compilations of earlier recipes, *De diversis artibus* is a balanced, systematic, and unified instruction manual designed for the express purpose of teaching younger artisans. The extent of its influence on practice is impossible to ascertain, although we do know that the work was frequently copied: it exists in at least twenty manuscripts dating from the twelfth to the fifteenth centuries. But even if *De diversis artibus* did not train generations of craftsmen, who no doubt learned their skills in traditional ways, it had an enduring influence on attitudes toward technology.

Few new treatises on technology appeared in the Latin West before the fourteenth century. Around 1235, the architect Villard de Honnecourt produced a sketchbook based on observations made in France, Lausanne, and Hungary. Although it is not primarily a technological treatise, it does contain a few drawings of machines and carpenter's tools, including a water-driven sawmill that uses a sapling spring to return the saw blade, a screw jack, a saw for leveling wooden piles, a trebuchet, and a mechanical bird. The sketchbook also reveals Villard's curiosity about perpetual motion, and confirms that such an interest was shared by many of his contemporaries. Villard's *perpetua mobilia* were wheels of pivoted hammers and pivoted tubes of mercury. Peter Perigrinus of Maricourt, in his *Epistola de magnete* of 1269, depicted a *perpetuum mobilium* based on the magnet. Fanciful though such notions were, they suggest that even in the thirteenth century, writers on technology were coming to think of the universe as a vast reservoir of forces to be tapped at will.

The design of complex instruments, such as clocks and astrolabes, took pride of place in the technological treatises of the fourteenth century. The Arab tradition reappeared in the West in the form of translations from Arabic works on astronomical instruments, such as the *Libros del saber de astronomía* of Alfonso X of Castile. In 1271, Robertus Anglicus left the first description of the design of mechanical clocks. Thereafter, a continuous line of such works appeared, including Richard of Wallingford's *Tractatus horologii astronomici* (*ca.* 1330), giving the first description of a weight-driven clock, and Giovanni de' Dondi's *Tractatus astrarii,* a treatise on the construction of a very complex astronomical clock that Dondi, a physician, built between 1348 and 1364. Dondi's clock became one of the marvels of his age. Although it disappeared in the sixteenth century, the treatise he left describing it is so detailed that two modern reconstructions of the clock have been made (one can be seen at the Smithsonian Institution in Washington, D.C.).

Dondi was neither the first nor the last physician to be concerned with instrument making. Indeed, practically every important technological treatise of the fourteenth and fifteenth centuries came from the pen of a medical doctor. One explanation for this, which has been suggested by Lynn White, jr., lay in the revival in the West of medical astrology, a complex and exact discipline demanding careful celestial observations and elaborate computations. These professional requirements, according to White, led medical astrologers to make improvements on astronomical instruments and clocks, and the skills gained in these endeavors spilled over into other areas of mechanical, civil, and military engineering.

The fourteenth century also gave us the first of a long series of illustrated treatises on military technology. In 1335, Guido da Vigevano, a physician in the court of King Philip VI of France, presented his monarch with a treatise on new and improved means for reconquering the Holy Land. The treatise, entitled *Texauris regis Franciae acquisitionis terre sancte de ultra mare* (Paris, Bibliothèque Nationale, fonds Latin 11015, fols. 32–55), was in two parts. The first contained medical advice for protecting one's health in the field, and the other was devoted to siege engines. Some of Guido's proposals were quite novel: machines made of portable, prefabricated elements; the use of interchangeable parts; paddle-wheel boats propelled by crankshafts; and a war wagon propelled by a windmill mounted on its top. These designs seem to be completely original; there is nothing like them in the works of the ancient writers on artillery, which in any case would not have been known by Guido. Though he was not a practicing engineer, Guido was a good observer, for his designs, though impractical, were firmly rooted in a knowledge of the crafts.

After 1400, the number of technological treatises produced in Europe increased dramatically. Whereas there are few surviving written records detailing technological activities in the early Middle Ages, in the fifteenth century there was a sudden deluge of such documents. The range of subjects treated also expanded. Although the earlier recipe collections continued to be copied throughout the medieval period, the fifteenth-century treatises introduced a dynamic, exploratory attitude toward machine design and the application of mechanical power to all sorts of military and industrial uses. Clearly, the appearance of these treatises reflected a growing consciousness in late medieval Europe of power technology. Indeed, as Lynn White, jr., has suggested, the late medieval engineers were "power conscious to the point of fantasy."

This new consciousness alone, however, does not explain why, in the fifteenth century, craftsmen and engineers suddenly began to write down what earlier generations had been content to transmit by word of mouth. Other factors must be taken into account. First, the level of literacy in Europe rose substantially. Even craftsmen outside of monastic orders began learning to read and write; indeed, many guilds required literacy for entrance into apprenticeship. In addition, social changes affected the status of people engaged in technology. Foremost among these changes was the rise of the professional engineer, who found employment in the courts of political rulers.

As warfare became more complex tactically and technologically, men who could design and build siege engines and fortifications became valued public servants. In peacetime, the engineer assisted in various construction projects, such as designing bridges, canals, roads, and public fountains; or, like the Arab engineers, he designed clocks and automata to embellish the royal court. Leonardo da Vinci, in a famous letter to Lucovico Sforza (Il Moro), offered these and many other services in his attempt to gain employment. Although the letter is usually taken as an indication of Leonardo's manifold genius, it may also be a sign that he knew what was expected of a Renaissance engineer.

Engineering treatises. The increasing complexity of technology, the enhanced status of the engineer, and rising literacy rates combined to produce a new awareness of the value of preserving and transmitting technical knowledge in writing. On the simplest level, this new attitude manifested itself in a profusion of handbooks and collections of recipes representing almost every traditional craft activity. As new technologies came into being, they too brought forth technical manuals. With the introduction of cannon into warfare, for example, a series of master gunners' handbooks appeared. Characteristic of these texts is the *Feuerwerkbuch* (*ca.* 1420), a didactic treatise composed largely of recipes for making gunpowder and other incendiary compositions, plus a few simple rules governing the art of ballistics.

In addition to recipe books, the fifteenth century saw the appearance of a large group of illustrated treatises on mechanical and military engineering. The illustrations in these works were not simply ornaments; they served an important didactical purpose as well. While ordinary language is sufficient to give instructions for mixing ingredients (as in a recipe), none of the languages of medieval Europe, whether Latin or the vernaculars, could adequately express the complex spatial relationships treated in machine design. To convey such information, medieval engineers made drawings, and used words simply to label the parts of a machine or to explain its function. As Bert Hall has pointed out, crude though these drawings often were, their introduction constitutes an important shift in the medium through which technological information was communicated.

The engineering treatises of the fifteenth century fall into two main traditions: German and Italian. The German school begins with Konrad Kyeser's *Bellifortis* (*ca.* 1405; Göttingen, Universitäts-bibliothek, Cod. phil. 63). As the title of this work (Strong war) suggests, Kyeser's interests were chiefly in military technology. Although some of the devices he describes might also have been used for non-military purposes (for instance, an Archimedes' screw, the first since antiquity), the bulk of *Bellifortis* deals with siege engines, artillery, firearms, and chariots of war. Several types of cannon are illustrated, including a multiple-barreled rotating cannon, and one long section contains recipes for making explosives copied from the treatise of

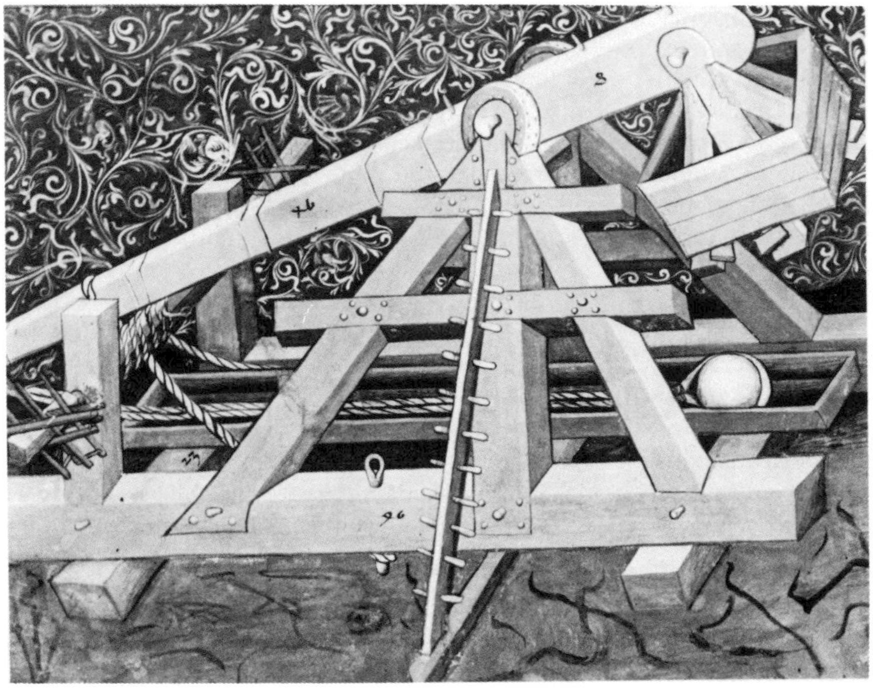

The trebuchet from Konrad Kyeser's *Bellifortis, ca.* 1045. Göttingen, Universitätsbibliothek, Cod. phil. 63. Reproduced from the edition of G. Quarg. © 1967 VERLAG DES VEREINS DEUTSCHER INGENIEURE, DUSSELDORF

Marcus Graecus known as the *Liber ignium* (Book of fires). A stunning picture of a great trebuchet includes exact specifications for its construction. At the same time, the *Bellifortis* is filled with magical themes, astrological symbols, and references to marvelous devices. Legends of Alexander the Great permeate the work. The chariots and battering rams carry figures of demons or fantastic, terrifying animals. One section of the *Bellifortis* includes magical recipes extracted from the ever-popular "book of marvels" attributed to Albertus Magnus. Eccentric though these interests seem to modern minds, they were typical of the engineers of the fifteenth century. Magic, which aims at controlling the forces of nature, provided a natural intellectual framework for technology; and, at the same time, it elevated the aspirations and dreams of engineers to fantastic heights.

Another important treatise in the German tradition is a Munich manuscript (Bayerische Staatsbibliothek, Cod. Lat. Monacensis 197, pt. I) known as the "Manuscript of the Hussite Wars' Engineer," so called because it was formerly thought to have been composed by an engineer active in the Hussite campaigns. The editor of the manuscript, however, has shown that it is actually the work of two authors, the first part dating from about 1472–1475, and the second from about 1486–1492. The manuscript consists of a series of drawings of machines, primarily military, such as crossbows, siege engines, and windlasses designed for lifting heavy cannon. In addition, there are drawings of machinery for less strictly military purposes, such as cranes, grain mills powered by wind and water, a stone-polishing machine, and devices for hollowing out wooden pipes. The drawings in this text are in general quite crude, and display no sense of proper artistic perspective. They are, nevertheless, of considerable interest in documenting the history of machine design, since they are among the earliest illustrations to show mechanical details. One incomplete drawing, for example, illustrates a method for pulling mine wagons to the surface on wooden rails. Another shows a grain mill driven from two power sources. Another depicts the "double-acting crane of Nuremberg," which was in use in the fifteenth century. The text also illustrates several uses of what was undoubtedly the most important innovation of the fifteenth century: the rod-and-crank system. Several of these designs employ flywheels as governors to eliminate "dead spots" in the system. This idea was later explored with great sophistication in Francesco di Giorgio's sketchbook.

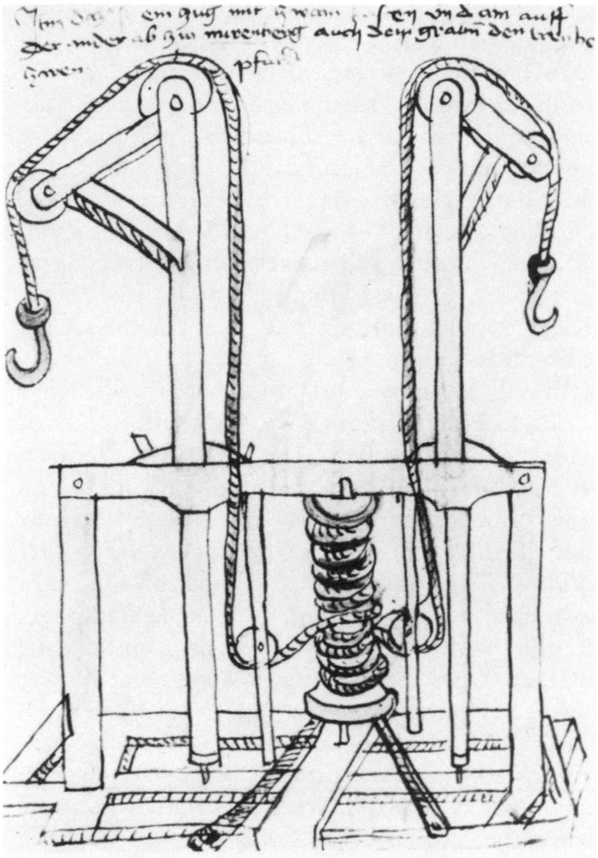

The double-acting crane of Nuremberg. Munich, Bayerische Staatsbibliothek, Cod. Lat. Monacensis 197, *ca.* 1472–1475. Reproduced from Bert S. Hall, ed., *The Technological Illustrations of the So-called "Anonymous of the Hussite Wars."* © 1979 DR. LUDWIG REICHERT VERLAG, WIESBADEN

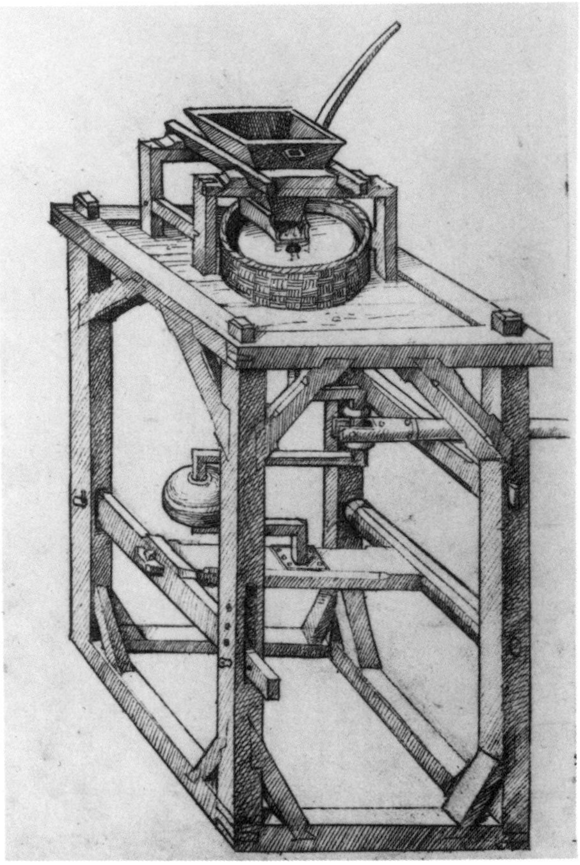

Reconstruction of a grain mill of *ca.* 1480. Reproduced from Willy F. Storck, *Das Mittelalterliche Hausbuch.* © 1912 E. A. SEEMANN, LEIPZIG

The last decades of the fifteenth century saw the appearance of technical treatises that were influenced by new artistic styles developed by Italian and Flemish artists. The best example of this is the *Mittelalterliche Hausbuch* (*ca.* 1480) of the anonymous Master of the Amsterdam Cabinet. In addition to garden and workshop scenes, this beautiful manuscript contains many drawings of machinery for military and industrial uses. Although the text is not novel (being composed mainly of alchemical, medical, and pyrotechnical recipes), the drawings are outstanding in both aesthetic quality and mechanical detail.

The Italian tradition opens with a treatise on machines by Giovanni da Fontana (*ca.* 1420; Munich, Bayerische Staatsbibliothek, Cod. icon. 242). In spite of the title later attached to this manuscript, *Bellicorum instrumentorum liber,* military instruments dominate only in the first part; the remainder is a potpourri of mechanical subjects, including designs for hoists, fountains, aqueducts, automata, a combination lock, and a mechanical car. Although Fontana's treatise seems closely related to the German school, some of his drawings, particularly those of automata, indicate that he was familiar with the Alexandrian mechanical tradition.

The fifteenth-century Italian treatises on technology reflect dramatically the rise of the artist-engineer, a type completely different from those who wrote about technology earlier. Classical education and extensive practical experience combined to produce an approach to engineering problems that was at once more rational and more experimental than that found in the German school. One source of the machine designs of the quattrocento architects was Filippo Brunelleschi, who designed a number of revolutionary techniques for the construction of the dome of the cathedral of S. Maria

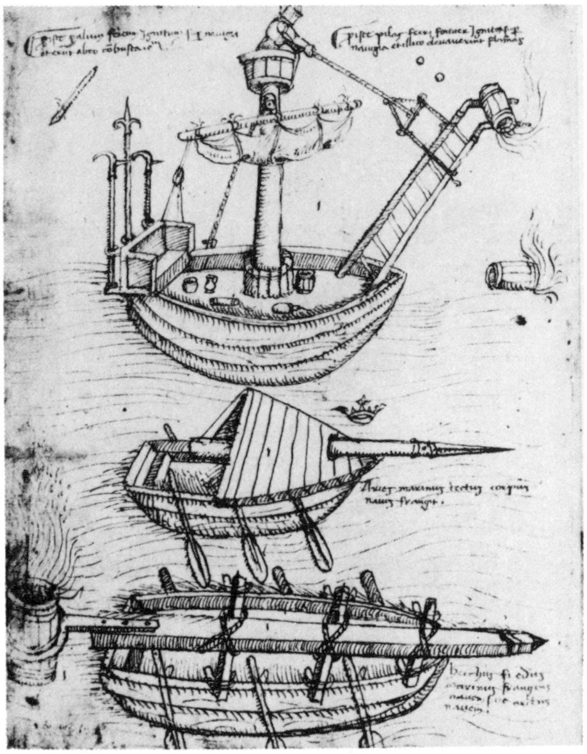

Battleships depicted in the *De machinis* of Taccola, 1449. Reproduced from the edition of Gustina Scaglia. © 1971 DR. LUDWIG REICHERT VERLAG, WIESBADEN

del Fiore in Florence. Although he wrote nothing about these machines, his ideas influenced many architects and builders. The *Zibaldone* of Buonaccorso Ghiberti, for example, contains a number of drawings of Brunelleschian machines, including cranes, hoists, and load positioners.

Brunelleschi's influence is also apparent in the notebooks of Mariano di Jacopo, il Taccola, an artist and engineer known in his day as the "Archimedes of Siena." Taccola, who knew Brunelleschi personally, wrote two illustrated treatises on machines. *De ingeneis,* completed in 1433 and dedicated to Emperor Sigismund, is devoted mainly to civilian technology but contains numerous designs for military machines as well. The work pictures cranes, aqueducts and pumps, mills (including floating mills), assault ladders, towers, battering rams, and trebuchets.

Taccola's other treatise, entitled *De machinis,* was completed in 1449. It is similar in scope to the earlier work, although its drawings are somewhat more realistic and display greater attention to mechanical detail. It is possible that *De machinis* was stimulated in part by Kyeser's *Bellifortis,* which Taccola probably knew, for the work is devoted mainly to military technology, and some of Taccola's compositions are similar to those found in Kyeser manuscripts. Significantly, *De machinis* was one of the first engineering treatises to be organized according to classes of machines. It is divided into ten books devoted, respectively, to ladders, battering engines, bridges, bombards and guns, lifting devices, pumps, mill systems, tunnels, horsemen, and marine warfare.

Among the many artists influenced by Taccola's work was Francesco di Giorgio Martini, the great Sienese painter, sculptor, and architect. Between 1482 and 1501, Francesco recorded his ideas in a series of manuscript works that are collectively titled *Trattati de archittetura, ingegneria e arte militare.* This treatise reveals one of the most innovative technological minds of the age. Its pages are filled with experimental designs of mills using different types of gearing systems and power sources; of pumps and aqueducts; of lifting machines, "automobiles," and dredges. Francesco experimented with water turbines and exploited compound cranks and connecting rods for a wide range of applications. As an architect, he also designed construction machines, such as cranes, jacks, pile drivers, and load positioners. Clearly, Francesco wanted to explore every possible combination of mechanisms known to him, and to apply these to every conceivable purpose. While this attitude sometimes seems naive, its innocence produced novel and interesting results. The value of Francesco's treatise was recognized immediately, and it influenced generations of engineers. Francesco was repeatedly plagiarized, even in his own lifetime; Leonardo owned and annotated one of the manuscripts of his work, and the drawings were later copied in many of the "theaters of machines" of the sixteenth century.

With Leonardo da Vinci we reach the climax of quattrocento developments in mechanical technology. Indeed, Leonardo's explorations into mechanics transport us at once from the Middle Ages to the threshold of the scientific revolution. Unfortunately, Leonardo wrote for himself and not for others. His notebooks, written in mirror writing, were unread by technologists of his and subsequent generations, and his ideas made virtually no impact whatsoever on the development of European technology. Nevertheless, the notebooks give us a glimpse of Leonardo the inventor at work, and are for this reason priceless documents for understanding his creative genius.

Like all Renaissance engineers, Leonardo advised political rulers on military matters; consequently, his notebooks contain many drawings of engines of war. He produced several designs for multiple-barreled cannons, and he investigated problems relating to the trajectory of a cannonball. He was particularly fascinated, however, with automation, and this concern is apparent in both his military and his civil technology. One of his most elegant designs is of an automatic file cutter. He also designed automatic screw-cutting machines, a device for automatically stamping gold foil, and numerous machines for the textile industry. There are, indeed, ingenious gadgets for almost every conceivable purpose in Leonardo's notebooks.

Madrid Codex I reveals another side of Leonardo's technological activity. This manuscript appears to be a working draft of a formal treatise on abstract and applied mechanics. Leonardo intended to write a work not just on machines but also on mechanisms, analyzing the conditions that lead to the rational assembly of useful machines. Thus he was particularly concerned with the problem of friction arising in gear wheel trains and bearings. He experimented with a surprising array of roller and ball bearings to reduce friction, and examined many different drive systems. Moreover, Leonardo's drawings are not merely static representations of conventional concepts; they are attempts to solve problems through pictures, and reveal vividly the process by which he developed his mechanical concepts.

With Leonardo, the medieval phase of technological literature closes. A new epoch opens with the appearance of printed books on technology, the earliest of which was Roberto Valturio's *De re militari* (1472). This work was typically humanistic in its use of classical writings on military subjects but thoroughly medieval in its illustrations, which were borrowed directly from standard works like Kyeser's *Bellifortis* and the manuscripts of Taccola. In the 1480's a series of German works on Gothic design appeared. After 1529, when the *Feuerwerkbuch* was printed by Christian Eginolph at Strassburg, technological writings literally streamed from the presses. A series of technical handbooks known as the *Kunstbüchlein* was printed in many editions beginning in 1531–1532, and these eventually made their way into the numerous "books of secrets" of the sixteenth and seventeenth centuries.

All of these works are directly related to the medieval treatises on the decorative arts. Also drawing extensively from medieval technological writings was a series of richly illustrated sixteenth- and seventeenth-century "theaters of machines," whose influence is evident as late as the French *Encyclopédie*. Hence, a continuous line of manuscripts and printed books links the medieval technological tradition to the Industrial Revolution.

BIBLIOGRAPHY

Only a few of the treatises have been published; for unpublished manuscripts, see Gille (below). Modern editions include Helmuth Bossert and Willy F. Storck, ed., *Das Mittelalterliche Hausbuch* (1912); Theodore Bowie, ed., *The Sketchbook of Villard de Honnecort,* 2nd ed. (1962); A. Rupert Hall, "Guido's *Texaurus,* 1335," in Bert S. Hall and Delno C. West, eds., *On Pre-Modern Technology and Science* (1976), 11–52; Bert S. Hall, *The Technological Illustrations of the So-called "Anonymous of the Hussite Wars"* (1979); Donald Routledge Hill, trans., *The Book of Knowledge of Ingenious Mechanical Devices by Ibn al Razzāz al Jazarī* (1974), and *The Book of Ingenious Devices . . . by the . . . Banū Mūsā* (1979); Leonardo da Vinci, *The Madrid Codices,* Ladislao Reti, ed., 5 vols. (1974); Lon R. Shelby, ed., *Gothic Design Techniques* (1977); Cyril Stanley Smith and John G. Hawthorne, eds., "*Mappae clavicula,*" in *Transactions of the American Philosophical Society,* **64**, pt. 4 (1974); John R. Spencer, trans., *Filarete's Treatise on Architecture,* 2 vols. (1965); Mariano di Jacopo Taccola, *Liber tertius de ingeneis ac edifitiis non usitatis,* James H. Beck, ed. (1969), and *De machinis: The Engineering Treatise of 1449,* Gustina Scaglia, ed., 2 vols. (1971).

Studies of the treatises and their social and intellectual contexts include Silvio A. Bedini and Francis R. Maddison, "Mechanical Universe: The Astrarium of Giovanni de' Dondi," in *Transactions of the American Philosophical Society,* **56**, pt. 5 (1966); Marshall Clagett, "The Life and Works of Giovanni Fontana," in *Annali dell' Istituto e museo di storia della scienza,* **1** (1976); Aage G. Drachmann, *Ktesibios, Philon, and Heron: A Study in Ancient Pneumatics* (1948) and *The Mechanical Technology of Greek and Roman Antiquity* (1963); William Eamon, "Technology as Magic in the Late Middle Ages and the Renaissance," in *Janus,* **70** (1983); Franz M. Feldhaus, *Die Technik der Antike und des Mittelalters* (1931); Bertrand Gille, *Engineers of the Renaissance* (1966); Jean Gimpel, *The Medieval Machine* (1976); Rozelle Parker Johnson, *Compositiones variae: An Introductory Study* (Illinois Studies in Language and Literature, XXIII, no. 3) (1939); Eric W. Marsden, *Greek and Roman Artillery: Historical Development* (1969) and

Greek and Roman Artillery: Technical Treatises (1971); Mary P. Merrifield, *Original Treatises on the Arts of Painting,* 2 vols. (1849, repr. 1967); Frank D. Prager and Gustina Scaglia, *Brunelleschi: Studies of His Technology and Inventions* (1970) and *Mariano Taccola and His Book De ingeneis* (1972); Ladislao Reti, ed., *The Unknown Leonardo* (1974); Erla Rodakiewicz, "The *Editio Princeps* of Roberto Valturio's *De re militari* in Relation to the Dresden and Munich Manuscripts," in *Maso Finiguerra,* 5 (1940); Daniel V. Thompson, *The Materials and Techniques of Medieval Painting* (1956); Lynn White, jr., *Medieval Technology and Social Change* (1962) and *Medieval Religion and Technology: Collected Essays* (1978).

WILLIAM EAMON

[See also **Alfonso X of Castile; Bells; Benedictine Rule; Benedictines; Bronze and Brass; Brunelleschi, Filippo; Cannon; Catapults; Clocks and Reckoning of Time; Enamel; Glass, Western European; Guido da Vigevano; Guilds and Métiers; Hugh of St. Victor; Literacy, Western European; Metalwork; Parchment; Peter Peregrinus of Maricourt; Richard of Wallingford; Theophilus; Translations and Translators, Western European; Villard de Honnecourt; Warfare, Western European.**]

TECHNOLOGY, WESTERN. Since this *Dictionary* contains specialized articles on different sorts of technology, the task of the present essay is not to review in detail the total accomplishment of Western medieval engineers and technicians. It is to examine the distinctive qualities of medieval technology, sketch its general patterns of change, and discuss the more plausible explanations for the dynamism in innovation that laid the foundations for the industrialization and global imperialism of the centuries separating us from the Middle Ages.

MEDIEVAL TECHNOLOGY AND MEDIEVAL SCIENCE

Medieval technology was in no way based on prior scientific discoveries. It was entirely empirical. Modern assertions that Gothic architects were influenced by the twelfth-century translation of Euclid in six Latin versions have been refuted. The daringly novel structures of that age were produced by skilled craftsmen who were not concerned with theory. Today we find it hard to believe that the invention of eyeglasses about 1285 in lower Tuscany had nothing to do with the fact that contemporary Western scientists studying optics were making discoveries—for instance, about the refraction of light in rainbows—that went considerably beyond those of the Greeks and Arabs on whose works they were building. To be sure, Friar Roger Bacon in 1267 remarked that a lens could help the elderly to read, and Bernard of Gordonio, who taught from 1285 to 1307 in the medical school at Montpellier, said the same thing. The indifference of optical scientists, however, to practical applications of their learning is shown by the fact that no scientist undertook to explain how eyeglasses help to remedy a physical defect until the appearance of Francesco Maurolico's *De conspiculis,* written in 1554 but not published until 1611.

The invention of eyeglasses was a by-product not of science but of a still-unexplained thirteenth-century alteration in religious piety that demanded, for the first time, the visual experience of consecrated hosts in transparent monstrances and of relics of saints in transparent reliquaries. The clearest substance available for making such containers was rock crystal, but it was costly and hard to shape. To meet the demands of a new market, Italian glassmakers developed a very clear glass, and found inexpensive ways to cut and polish it. Presumably, glass cutters occasionally made lenses for optical scientists. When, about 1285, an unknown genius balanced on the nose two lenses set in a wire frame, another large market was opened. By 1300 convex lenses for spectacles to help presbyopics were being produced in quantity at Venice. By 1450, Florentines were marketing concave-lensed eyeglasses for astigmatics. If scientists had been adequately interested in the skills of craftsmen, the invention of the telescope might not have been delayed until 1609.

The idea that systematic scientific research can advance technology was first clearly stated in 1450 by Cardinal Nicholas of Cusa in Book IV of his *Idiota de mente,* but he himself did nothing concrete to realize it. The great Jewish medical astrologer Abraham Zacuto, who had studied at Salamanca, fled in 1492 to the protection of King John II of Portugal when all Jews were expelled from Spain, and in 1497 he prepared tables of solar declination to help Vasco da Gama's navigation during the latter's voyage around Africa to India and back (1497–1499). Sea captains, however, had an old tradition of empirical dead reckoning, and it appears that science-influenced navigational methods were not widely used until the later eighteenth century. Following Nicholas of Cusa's lead, Sir Francis Bacon (*d.* 1626) passionately preached the importance of applying science to meet human needs, but he too did not descend to the specific. Robert Boyle (*d.* 1691), while primarily a theoretician, had a strong empirical bent, and did as much as anyone to transmute alchemy into chemistry. In the eighteenth century a consciously scientific industrial chemistry began to appear. Our present axiom that technological advance comes primarily from applications of prior scientific findings, however, did not become dominant in the Occident until about 1850. That Western medieval technicians were able to produce a vivid new style of technology without benefit of formal science should increase our respect both for their ingenuity and for empiricism as a mode of action.

THE WESTERN MEDIEVAL INVENTION OF INVENTION

One of the few correct historical clichés tells us that the invention of invention was the most important invention in the human past. In the Hellenistic-Roman era there was a brief but notable increase of tempo in specific areas of engineering. We have no evidence, however, that anyone of that time envisaged invention as a total project for meeting human needs. Indeed, the Roman invention of, and then abandonment of, the very useful and economical application of flattened arches to bridges shows an ominous indifference to engineering creativity.

The emergence and consolidation in northern Europe of new items (the heavy wheeled plow; two-field rotation of crops with the strip system of cultivation; the close meshing of cereal production with herding; then the more intensive three-field rotation; the efficient new horse harness; the nailed horseshoe; the widespread replacement of oxen by horses for plowing and hauling; the whiffletree and the large farm wagon) into an unprecedented and highly productive system of agriculture extended from the early sixth century into the early twelfth. That Charlemagne (*d.* 814) rejoiced at the way this process was already enriching his empire is shown by his effort to rename the Roman months to fit the new schedule of plowing, haying, and harvesting that was spreading in his time. By the early ninth century the idea was springing up in Europe that technological change is beneficent, and that to encourage it is virtuous. The Utrecht Psalter, illuminated near Rheims between 820 and 830, contains a picture showing a small band of the godly, led by the Psalmist himself, guarded by an angel and blessed by the hand of God emerging from a cloud, preparing for battle against a larger troop of the unrighteous. In each camp a large sword is being sharpened. The wicked are using a big, flat, stationary whetstone. The righteous employ the first rotary whetstone known anywhere, and it is turned by the first crank depicted outside China. The monk who drew that picture was saying unambiguously that technological advance is an expression of God's love for his children.

The detailed manuscript plan of the abbey of St. Gall in Switzerland (*ca.* 820) proves that the Benedictines were much interested in technical improvement. It shows us the first known non-industrial chimneys, with flues set in walls and with manteled fireplaces. Compared with the Roman hypocaust or the Celtic-Germanic central fireplace, this was a flexible method of heating, and one economical of fuel. The plan also marks an epochal departure in the use of waterpower. With one transient exception, the Romans had employed it only for grinding grain. Now, on the plan of St. Gall, close to the flour mills, we find hydraulic trip-hammers for making the mash for beer. The hammers are operated by cams set in the rotating horizontal axle of a vertical waterwheel. This marks a great advance in machine design because it enabled engineers to guide natural forces not only in circular but now also in reciprocating motions. Since, as has been noted, at almost that same moment the crank, the other basic device for relating these two sorts of motion, appeared in Europe, we must assume that an increasing number of Western craftsmen of that generation were thinking in very original ways about machine design.

We have no reason to believe that monks were the major inventors of the early Middle Ages, although many of them worked with their hands and some were obviously interested in such matters. Since monks did much of the writing in that period, the emergence of technological novelties in monastic contexts may simply indicate the state of the surviving records. Whatever their origin, engines like the beer-mash mill of the plan of St. Gall increasingly were applied to fulling cloth, washing laundry, preparing hides for tanning, crushing ore, pumping the bellows of furnaces, operating the hammers of forges, sawing logs into lumber, and many other processes. The cam had been known to Hellenistic mechanics, but they seem not to have applied it to manufacturing. From the early ninth century on, medieval craftsmen steadily elaborated powered machinery involving cam and crank to serve an always widening spectrum of useful purposes. In this development there has been no interruption from the reign of Louis the Pious (814–840) to our own time.

Nevertheless, inventions in the early Middle Ages, and from then until after 1200, would seem to have been largely ad hoc. The invention of invention, involving not only wide-ranging thought about technical improvements that are needed but also intercommunicating groups of technicians striving to produce them, is datable to about the middle of the thirteenth century in Europe. Invention as a movement has flourished in the West ever since then.

About 1150 the Indian mathematician and astronomer Bhāskarā described two gravitational perpetual-motion machines. By 1200 the idea of perpetual motion, and one of Bhāskarā's designs, is found in Islam. By about 1235, in Villard de Honnecourt's sketchbook, we find two originally Arabic suggestions for such machines. In 1269 Peter Peregrinus of Maricourt proposed in his *Epistola de magnete* a perpetually operating clock motored by magnetism. Both Villard and Peter noted that many of their contemporaries were trying to invent such engines. There is no indication that in either India or Islam the idea of perpetual motion incited efforts toward practical application. In the Occident, however, it helped to spread the notion that nature is filled with energies waiting to be exploited by mankind. As a result, Westerners made great—if futile—efforts to diversify the motors of *perpetua mobilia.* Medieval physics provided no basis for ridiculing this enthusiasm, and the fairly recent invention of the horizontal-axle windmill (in the 1180's) on the flatlands of eastern England, where the wind blew almost constantly, doubtless encouraged such attempts.

In 1269 Friar Roger Bacon, who probably was a friend of Peter Peregrinus of Maricourt, pondered the general problem of transportation and confidently prophesied an age of automobiles (self-moving wagons), submarines, and flying machines. Arrow wounds were a common medical problem, and about 1267 Bishop Theodoric of Cervia tells us in his treatise on surgery that, to extract arrows "every day some new instrument and method is invented by the skill and imagination of a physician." Water clocks were not entirely satisfactory as time measurers. In 1271 Robertus Anglicus, writing about plans for a weight-driven clock, admitted that the problem of an escapement had not been entirely conquered, but he was confident that soon it would be. At almost that same time, at the court of Alfonso el Sabio, Rabbi Isaac ben Sid of Toledo not only described new sorts of water clocks that he considered to be better than the earlier kinds but also depicted, as a prime novelty, a weight-driven clock with a mercury brake. Before 1313 someone invented the sandglass, which was chiefly useful on shipboard, where neither water clocks nor weight-driven clocks would work because of the constant movement of the ships. But technicians experimented from the 1260's until close to 1330 before the true mechanical clock was invented. The intensity and diversity of the quest are shown by the fact that almost simultaneously inventors reached two related solutions: the verge and the wheel escapements.

The invention of invention was first codified in a sermon preached at S. Maria Novella in Florence on 26 February 1306 by a well-known Dominican, Giordano of Pisa. The topic of the sermon was supposedly repentance, but it quickly turned into a eulogy praising the contemporary expansion of technology. "Not all the arts," said the preacher, "have been found; we shall never see an end of finding them. Every day one could discover a new art . . . they are being found all the time." Then, like any good orator, he offered an exemplum that we have noted above. "It is not twenty years since there was discovered the art of making spectacles which help you to see well, and which is one of the best and most necessary in the world. And that is such a short time ago that a new art, which never before existed, was invented. . . . I myself saw the man who discovered and practiced it, and I talked with him."

By the early fourteenth century, Europe had arrived at a technological attitude toward problem-solving that since then has remained characteristic of Western culture.

THE SAVING OF TIME, LABOR, AND MATERIAL

Frankish monks were commanded by St. Benedict's Rule to labor systematically with their hands as a way of praising God: "Work is worship." One of their distinctive ways of working was to copy manuscripts. During the four decades from 780 to 820, primarily in abbeys located in the core of Charlemagne's empire, the lands between the Loire and the Rhine, the monks developed a new form of writing, the Caroline minuscule, which was one of the greatest advances in the history of communication. (This book is printed in it.) It saved the scribe's labor because the letters were simple; it

Machines from the sketchbook of Villard de Honnecourt, mid 13th century. Clockwise from bottom left: lectern eagle with moving head; device to make a statue point toward the sun; self-propelled saw; "a crossbow that cannot miss"; engine for raising weights. Paris, Bibliothèque Nationale, MS fr. 19093. FOTO MARBURG/ART RESOURCE

Post-mill showing the wooden body of the mill and the long pole for turning the whole mill to face the wind. Early-14th-century Italian miniature. London, British Library, MS Royal 10.E.IV., fol. 70. COURTESY OF THE TRUSTEES OF THE BRITISH LIBRARY

saved parchment because they were compact. Part of this latter economy was wisely spent by leaving spaces between words and by elaborating punctuation to clarify meaning. This saved the reader's time and energy. Until then, most solitary reading had been reading aloud to avoid the phonic confusions inherent in unspaced script. The Caroline minuscule reflects the same frugality, efficiency, and compassion for those who labor that we find in the plan of St. Gall's innovations in heating methods and beer making, and in the ongoing Frankish agricultural revolution that was so notably improving productivity per peasant by developing a more capital-intensive, as compared with the earlier labor-intensive, style of farming.

The spread of powered machinery in industry obviously involved a similar growth of the capital component in production compared with that of labor. The capital for new industrial mills came from nobles, clergy, and prosperous burghers. Such investors normally were able to require the common people, for a fee, to use their technologically superior facilities to grind grain, full cloth, and the like. So long as agricultural advance gave the lower classes a generally rising standard of living, such arrangements seemed to meet the needs of most people. By the early fourteenth century, however, overpopulation, underemployment, the slackening of agricultural innovation, and irregularities of climate leading to crop failures brought hard times for the workers. To the impoverished, saving labor has no merit if it adds to their costs. For example, the great abbot of St. Albans, Richard of Wallingford—himself the inventor of the first mechanical clock—was faced about 1330 by a rebellion of the town of St. Albans against the compulsory use

Timekeeping devices of the 15th century. At the left is a 24-hour clock with a single hand. On table are a spring-driven clock, a quadrant, and a sundial. Miniature from the *Horologium sapientiae* of Heinrich Suso. BRUSSELS, BIBLIOTHÈQUE ROYAL ALBERT, MS IV.III, FOL. 13v

of the abbey's grain mills. He reacted by confiscating all hand querns within his jurisdiction. This episode, and others like it, should not be interpreted as a sign of popular opposition to technological advance. The people were objecting to the abbot's exactions, not to water-powered mills, with which they had had many centuries of experience.

Indeed, Western medieval society was not structured to permit rejection of a useful technical novelty. In the cities, craftsmen were normally organized into guilds according to their specialties. The prosperity of members of a guild depended largely on their ability to produce goods of widely acceptable quality at prices competitive with similar products of other cities. Every innovation had to be scrutinized carefully in terms of its cost efficiency and its effect on quality. When the spinning wheel reached Europe from China in the later thirteenth century, there was no doubt about the spectacular way in which it reduced the labor cost of thread. But what about the strength of wheel-spun yarn compared with that twisted by the hand spindle? For the durability of a textile, the long warp threads are more important than those of the weft. About 1280 a guild regulation at Speyer (repeated in 1298) permitted wheel-spun thread for the weft only. At Abbeville in 1288 caution was greater: wheel-spun yarn was prohibited. Within a few years, however, the cloth industry of Europe learned that the new wheel could produce entirely satisfactory thread, and its saving of labor costs compelled universal adoption.

There seems to have been no successful blocking of any labor-saving device in Europe until the middle of the sixteenth century. In 1534 an Italian, Matteo del Nassaro, constructed a mill on piles over the Seine at Paris, to polish precious stones. In 1552 this mill was purchased by the royal mint, on orders of King Henry II, to house and operate new water-powered machines recently designed and built at Augsburg to produce coins. In 1559 Henry II died, and in the following confusion the guild of coiners persuaded the advisers of the youthful King Francis II to restrict the new power machines to the making of medals. Thenceforth, until 1645, French coinage was minted in the traditional way, by manual striking. Obviously, if the coiners had been dealing with a competitive market rather than with a brutally enforced royal monopoly of coinage, their efforts to destroy innovation would not have succeeded.

The same urge to save labor (which is often best seen as saving time) and increase productivity pervades the history of medieval shipbuilding. Roman square-rigged vessels could tack into a contrary wind only at blunt angles, which delayed the voyage. Fore-and-aft rigs capable of tacking at sharp angles, especially the lateen sail, seem to have originated in the western Mediterranean. In the first century B.C. small lateen-rigged boats sailed not only about the harbor of Ostia but also among the Aegean islands, where the goal of the trip was constantly in sight and the helmsman could compensate for the leeward drift involved in tacking. The economical routes for large Roman ships making long voyages often took them out of sight of landmarks, and thus the lateen apparently was not considered appropriate for them. For reasons that are not clear, this attitude changed by the middle of the sixth century, when two large ships equipped with lateen sails appeared in the harbor of Marseilles. From then on, the lateen rig became normal for Mediterranean merchant ships. This must have contributed considerably to the speed of travel and the efficiency of commerce.

Another great improvement was the invention of the sternpost rudder, which replaced the old lateral rudder in the North and Baltic seas during the thirteenth century, and in the fourteenth spread to the Mediterranean. It was stronger than the lateral rudder and less likely to break in heavy seas.

The most notable change in medieval ship construction was the shift from the skin-first to the skeleton-first sequence in building the hull. Whether in the Baltic or in the Mediterranean, in ancient times hulls were built up with laborious care by attaching each plank by rivets, or mortises and tenons, to the plank below it. When the hull was entirely shaped, ribs and other internal supports were sculptured and inserted into the outer shell. Roman and early medieval shipbuilding was almost like cabinetwork, and even in the Roman slave economy its cost must have been great. Setting up the hull's frame, nailing the planks to it, and then caulking the cracks to prevent leakage provides an equally seaworthy vessel more quickly and at considerably less expense in labor. We do not yet know with certainty when or where the change of method occurred. The earliest present evidence of a ship completely built in the skeleton-first sequence is a freighter—probably Byzantine but with a largely Islamic cargo—wrecked in 1024 or shortly thereafter on the coast of Anatolia near Rhodes. By the later eleventh century the new method is seen in a boat a little over thirty-four feet (10.5 m) long excavated in the delta of the Po. With cheaper construction costs, more ships could be built for the same investment of capital, and the financial impact of loss by shipwreck or piracy was reduced. Since a swift and fairly steady increase in seaborne commerce and the size of fleets occurred in the western Mediterranean, and particularly in Italian maritime cities, from the later tenth century into the fourteenth, it is probable that eventually new evidence provided by underwater archaeology will push the invention of skeleton-first construction back into the tenth century at least.

In the last decade of the twelfth century the introduction of the magnetic compass into Europe from China provided another great economy for salt-water traders. In Roman times, for fear of storms, the season for all but emergency voyaging extended only from late May until early September. During the early Middle Ages, despite the increased average speed of ships made possible by the lateen sail's capacity for coping with adverse winds, the same limitations were normally observed, because in the off-season clouds often obscured the North Star and made navigation uncertain. After the 1190's, the compass identified the position of Polaris in any weather. Before the thirteenth century, a ship could sail from Italy or Catalonia to the Levant and return only once a year. Thanks chiefly to the compass, during the later Middle Ages two such round trips were feasible annually. This made possible the doubling of profit on capital invested in a ship; it provided better employment for mariners; and it quickened the tempo of commerce. For the same reason Italian merchants began on a regular basis to cut their costs for overland transport of goods to and from northern European markets by means of yearly voyages of large fleets past Gibraltar to the ports of England and the Netherlands.

The medieval European passion for saving labor, time, and material is seen likewise in structural engineering. In the Latin-speaking parts of the late Roman Empire and the early Middle Ages, large buildings, such as churches, normally had beamed ceilings. As Christianity penetrated the northern forests of Europe, great and richly endowed cathedrals and abbeys began to rise in areas closer to the Arctic zone than had ever before witnessed the development of cultures so complex and so able to construct buildings of this magnitude. During no small part of the year in northern Europe there was relatively little sunlight, and, compared with the Mediterranean region, light took on a special significance and symbolic value. As the clergy prospered, liturgies became more elaborate. On major festivals the altars of churches were immersed in a sea of candles and lamps, their light joining the ascending waves of incense and song in God's praise. Sometimes a candle would be knocked over, the fire would spread to altar textiles, tapestries, and choir stalls, and sparks would rise to ignite the tinder-dry beams of the roof. In a few minutes the whole structure would be a ruin. Toward the year 1000 the chief problem of northern architects was how to build fireproof churches.

The solution was obvious, but not easy to pay for. Wooden ceilings were replaced by barrel vaulting protecting the beams that held up the outer roof. This vaulting, however, had to be a light shell of masonry, otherwise its lateral thrust would require huge external buttresses. All quarrying and stonecutting was done by hand, and unless suitable stone was available nearby, the transportation of materials would be costly. A thin vault, however, unless it was very lofty, would be calcined and crumbled by the rising heat of a considerable fire at floor level. The solution was to use not round but pointed arches and vaults that tipped the thrust of the vaulting at a downward angle so that it could be sustained by lighter, and therefore cheaper, walls and buttresses. But pointed arches did not originate in northern Europe, having earlier been used in Mycenaean Greece, in India, and later in the Muslim world. Their use reached medieval Europe through Islam.

The first pointed arches and vaults thus far firmly dated in a Latin church were those built in 1071 as part of a porch on the facade of the church of the great Benedictine abbey of Monte Cassino, the shrine of St. Benedict. Their purpose was ornamental rather than structural. In 1080 the abbot of Cluny, already planning a vast new church for his own monastery, visited Monte Cassino. Presumably some engineer in his retinue saw that those pointed arches would help solve both structural and budgetary problems of the projected edifice in Burgundy. The new Cluny (known as Cluny III) was begun in 1088 and effectively finished in 1130, when the church was dedicated. Semicircular arches were retained where they were not a source of structural strain, but at critical points Cluny III had 196 ogival arches, with more in the high vaults. Even while construction was in progress, word of this daring change in masonry design spread through the Benedictine network. Probably, when the new monastic cathedral at Durham was begun in 1093, its architect was already planning its ogival features. In 1130 Abbot Suger of St. Denis visited Cluny. In 1135 he commenced, and in 1144 he finished, at St. Denis what is usually regarded as the first true "Gothic" church. From the beginning of the new Cluny in 1088 to the beginning of the new St. Denis was a span of forty-seven years. (The only comparable change in building methods to occur more recently was construction with steel girders. This started in the 1850's, and the fully realized skyscraper was achieved in the 1890's. Medieval innovation was not necessarily slow.)

During the rest of the Middle Ages, architects became increasingly skillful in reducing the mass of masonry needed to enclose a given interior space. The process culminated at St. Ouen in Rouen and in the cathedral of Palma, Majorca, in the fourteenth and fifteenth centuries. By concentrating thrusts and weights upon a few points, walls were deprived of their carrying function and became windscreens. Windows grew larger, especially in northern latitudes, where light was valued. In Roman times and the early Middle Ages, glass was costly, largely because the alkali to make it was imported from Egypt. In the tenth century Europeans found that local beech ashes could be substituted, and presumably the price of glass declined notably. It is no accident that the first formula for making the new kind of glass is found in a handbook for monastic craftsmen written by Theophilus, a German Benedictine, in the later 1120's.

The major churches of the Middle Ages were the first immense masonry monuments in history to be built by free—indeed, by unionized (members of guilds)—workers rather than by slaves or conscripted peasants. Whether Gothic architecture is more aesthetically satisfying than Romanesque, or than the almost brutal massiveness of Roman architecture, is a debate that cannot be resolved. It is clear, however, that the ogival way of building was more compassionate to labor than its predecessors. It was a moral achievement as well as an engineering triumph.

Structural developments were matched in spirit by the contemporary and continuing effort to apply waterpower—and, from the 1180's, windpower as well—to tasks once dependent entirely upon human muscle. From about 1136 we have two independently written descriptions of St. Bernard's abbey of Clairvaux, both from the quills of visiting Cistercian monks. One, himself an abbot, delightedly offers a picture of water-operated machines for milling, blacksmithing, fulling, tanning, and other industrial processes in the monastic workshops. The other rejoices in the same engines, but is particularly attracted by a device for automatically sifting the flour produced by the grain mill. He makes a little monkish joke, saying that the fulling mill has dispensed the fullers from the penance for their sins, and he ends by thanking God for these gracious machines that relieve the drudgery of both man and beast. In trying to explain the distinctive qualities of medieval technology, the ethical perceptions of that period cannot be overlooked.

TECHNOLOGICAL RAMIFICATION: THE EXAMPLE OF THE CROSSBOW

The eleventh century saw a notable shift in one area of Christian ethics. It can serve our effort to understand the interplay of engineering with the rest of contemporary culture, and it can also provide a nontechnological standpoint for seeing the radiation of one technological novelty into other kinds of technology.

During the first thousand years of Christian history, the clergy of the Latin West (in contrast with the Greek clergy after Constantine's conversion) had generally insisted that a soldier who kills an enemy in battle, even in what he regards as a good cause, must do penance for murder. But after 1000 the *Reconquista* in Spain developed into a holy war that soon received papal sanction by grants of indulgences to those who fought the Muslims. In 1086, at Burgo de Osma in north-central Castile, a splendid manuscript of Beatus' *Commentary on the Apocalypse* (fol. 85v) was illuminated with unprecedented vigor and iconographic imagination by a cleric named Martin. In illustrating the vision of the Four Horsemen (Apoc. 6:2), Martin adopted the fairly common exegesis that the First Horseman, riding a white horse (as high medieval churchmen tended to do) and armed with a bow, was none other than Christ himself, going forth "conquering and to conquer" the pagan Roman Empire. Martin's Christ, however, is not carrying a traditional bow. This illumination is the first preserved picture of a murderous new kind of crossbow.

A decade later, when the first wave of crusaders reached Constantinople, the observant Princess Anna Komnena looked upon this strange weapon as a demonic Frankish novelty "absolutely unknown to the Byzantines." The ancient Romans had used crossbows, but their model seems to have been ineffective in warfare; they used it mostly for hunting birds. In the early Middle Ages it became a rarity west of Iran.

The power of a crossbow depends chiefly on the level of the trigger's capacity to maintain tension in the bowstring. Perhaps as early as the eighth century, craftsmen in the West began to develop a better trigger: a notched circular nut pivoting horizontally in the bow's stock. Five stages in its evolution have been identified, but not dated. The process was obviously completed by the late eleventh century.

The Four Horsemen of the Apocalypse. Illumination by Martin in the Beatus *Commentary* of Burgo de Osma (fol. 85v). HIRMER ARCHIVE

Like the Byzantines, the Muslims regarded the new crossbow as a horrible Frankish device, and in the major languages of South India it is called the *parangi* or "Frankish" bow. It usually shot not arrows but square-headed bolts that made terrible wounds. At Hastings, William the Conqueror had crossbowmen in his army as well as conventional archers. In the Bayeux Tapestry, however, only the latter are shown. Perhaps William was ashamed of using such weapons to achieve victory. He was sensitive to the traditional Latin ecclesiastical condemnation of warfare. He founded Battle Abbey, on the hill of Senlac, to provide prayers for the souls of all slain there, whether Anglo-Saxon or Norman, and "in penance for the shedding of blood," as the abbey's chronicle tells us. A generation later the

Norman nobility of England thought of Battle Abbey simply as a monument to celebrate the triumph that had put them into dominion over England.

In 1139 the Second Lateran Council banned the crossbow except in combat against infidels. Ever since then, in the Occident, Christians have been confident that their foes were, at the least, crypto-infidels. The ban did not work.

During the twelfth and thirteenth centuries no major changes appeared in crossbows. They were made of wood or horn, or a combination of both, and they were spanned by fairly simple devices that enabled the archer to use the strength of his back, as well as of both arms and both knees, in drawing the bowstring to the catch in the trigger. In 1316, however a basic mutation emerged. A list of items belonging to a very great lady, Countess Mahaut of Artois, who, as we know from other sources, was interested in gadgets, mentions "a gilded steel crossbow." Its appearance means that by the early fourteenth century, European metallurgists could produce a steel with the qualities of a spring.

Obviously, the spanning of a steel crossbow demanded the marshaling and storing of much greater force than when the bow was made of organic materials. An extraordinary range of new spanning implements began to appear, consisting of ratchets, cranked gears, endless screws, levers, and pulleys, in many variations and combinations. The metal parts of these appliances had to be composed of steel or very hard iron, since the pressures involved in drawing a steel bow would have deformed and jammed any part made of softer metal. Makers of crossbows had to become expert in shaping intractable metal into complex forms and calibrating them precisely so that they would move easily in relation to each other in the process of spanning.

The development of such skills, which were fundamental to the always-increasing mechanization of Western engineering, has usually been credited to the late medieval instrument makers and clockmakers. A clock constructed of brass or bronze, however, like Giovanni de' Dondi's relatively small mechanical miracle built between 1348 and 1364, cannot stand the wear of constant motion. Richard of Wallingford, who invented the weight-driven mechanical clock in the late 1320's, understood this problem. He was the son of a blacksmith and—to judge by a contemporary picture of him—practiced his father's art even after he was elected abbot of St. Albans. He built his great clock of iron, and the basic mechanisms of all the monumental clocks that survive from the Middle Ages are likewise made of iron.

In trying to understand Europe's passion for, and success in producing, intricate and durable machinery, we should surely give the clockmakers much credit. Nevertheless, we must recognize that when mechanical clocks were invented, crossbow makers had been struggling for at least a decade with the related problems of producing implements to span steel crossbows. Moreover, there were doubtless more crossbow makers than clockmakers in fourteenth-century Europe. The probable interaction between these two groups has not yet been studied, it seems. In 1389 the city council of Dubrovnik in Dalmatia imported a clockmaker from Lecce in Apulia to construct a large chiming clock for their city hall. The contract provided that the builder would train a successor to care for the clock. That successor was already in the employ of Dubrovnik, making crossbows for the city's arsenal. He died in 1405, and his post as curator of the city clock was taken over by another maker of crossbows. Clearly the city fathers of Dubrovnik saw a relation between clocks and crossbows that has eluded historians of engineering.

The most curious connection between clocks and crossbows, however, emerges in the early fifteenth century. In 1405 Conrad Kyeser of Eichstätt, who had served the king of Bohemia as a medical astrologer, died, leaving a treatise on military engineering, *Bellifortis,* which, although unfinished, had great influence in northern Europe during the next 150 years. One of his most remarkable illustrations shows a crossbow spanner that combines pulleys with a cranked conical spindle. Around this spindle a cord, connected with the center of the bowstring, is wound spirally. As the spindle is rotated, the force drawing the bowstring increases according to the diameter of the spindle. Within thirty years clockmakers, excited by the possibilities inherent in the new metallurgy, were developing portable and miniaturized clocks powered by coiled steel springs. Their problem was to equalize the flow of force from the spring, as it unwound, through the clock's mechanism. For a second time in the history of horology, two different escapements were found, almost simultaneously. One was the stackfreed. The other was Conrad Kyeser's conical spindle, called by clockmakers the fusee. Fusees are still used in some extremely accurate chronometers employed to navigate ships and airplanes.

The most common form of spring used in wagons, railway cars, automobiles, and the landing gear of airplanes in the early twentieth century was likewise a by-product of the steel crossbow. Ever since the tenth century Europeans had been trying to devise a suspension system for the bodies of coaches that would make speedy travel over rutted and potholed roads endurable. The favorite early modern solution was suggested in 1615–1616 by a learned Dalmatian bishop, Faustus Verantius, who proposed that between the axles and the body of a coach bent bars of iron be placed that would absorb the shocks by opening and closing "like the bow of a crossbow." In Italian today the common name for a wagon spring is *balestra* (crossbow).

The craftsmen who made weapons were closely connected with those who made armor. Throughout the Middle Ages weapons improved, battle became more violent, and armor was constantly changing to meet the new exigencies of warfare. The advanced metallurgical skills that made possible the appearance of steel crossbows by 1316, and then the intricate spanners of closely correlated moving parts made of hard metal, likewise led to a great alteration in armor design to counter the terrible force of the crossbow bolt. By the fifteenth century, armor for the upper class had become a complete carapace of splendid steel carefully tailored to fit the purchaser. Only the armpits, the seat, and the inside of the thighs were not covered. Yet every steel plate was so carefully articulated with those around it that—as modern experiments with extant specimens have shown—no movement of the body was inhibited. The armor's weight was not excessive for a trained man, and the thickness of the plates was carefully gauged and tapered to offer the greatest resistance to blows where experience showed it was most needed.

The lance, sword, battle-ax, and mace were all feared. The greatest peril, however, was the crossbow bolt. The proof is that, on many surviving suits of costly armor from the end of the Middle Ages, on the left side of the breastplate, precisely over the heart, one finds a small dent made by a crossbow bolt, shot by a bow of standard strength from a standard distance. That dent proved to the noble customer that he was getting his money's worth. The best armorers were so proud of their products that they often decorated the dent with a nimbus of etched ornament. The skills developed by clockmakers and crossbow makers, as well as by the armorers who met the challenge of the bolts from the new steel crossbows after 1316, were essential elements in the evolution of modern sophisticated machinery.

The foregoing sketch is not a history of the Western crossbow, but rather of the crossbow's interplay with other elements of European technology and culture. It offers in some detail an illustration of the general fact that medieval European engineering, unlike that of other earlier and contemporary cultures, did not consist of isolated and almost random improvements. By contrast, from at least the early ninth century it was a remarkably coherent movement, in which innovations in one craft were not infrequently transferred to another. We have seen above that, by the middle of the thirteenth century, Western technicians were conceiving their multiple projects as interrelated, and were talking to each other about inventions that should be made. By 1450 the history of post-Roman engineering novelties began to be written when Giovanni Tortelli, a humanist at the papal court, composed an essay listing inventions that he believed—sometimes incorrectly—had been made since antiquity. Tortelli's work was published seventeen times in the fifteenth century and provided the foundation for Polydore Vergil's more famous *De inventoribus rerum* (1499), which is usually regarded as the beginning of the modern historiography of engineering.

MEDIEVAL EUROPE'S TECHNOLOGY SEEN IN THE FRAMEWORK OF EURASIA

One cannot understand the Middle Ages in Europe unless one recognizes that in curious ways what much of Asia called Frankistan was then integral to a garland of very different and creative cultures extending from the Moluccas and Japan on the east to Greenland, Ireland, and Morocco on the west. The perils of travel prevented all but a few Europeans from penetrating to the further reaches of Asia until the later thirteenth century. Nevertheless, in 883 King Alfred sent a delegation of Anglo-Saxons bearing gifts to the tomb of St. Thomas the Apostle near Madras; and when it returned to England, its leader, Sighelm, was rewarded by consecration as bishop of Sherborne. Moreover, about 973 a Jewish ambassador from the ruler of Muslim Spain visited Mainz and recorded his amazement at the variety and quantity of Indonesian spices in its market, "brought," as he said, "from one end of the world to the other." Goods got through, passing from hand to hand, even when individuals found such distances unfeasible.

If merchandise could move freely throughout Eurasia, so also could technological ideas and objects. The fiddle bow appeared first in Java in the late eighth century, and, having migrated through India and Islam to Christian northern Spain by 980, it swiftly became an important part of European musical instrumentation. Following the same route, the Malay blowgun arrived in Italy by 1425 at the latest. In Italian it was called the *cerbottana,* derived from the Arabic *zabaṭāna* but ultimately from the Malay *sumpitan.* In Europe the blowgun was used chiefly to shoot birds with small pellets. This utilization of air pressure led, by 1474 at Nuremberg, to bellows specially designed to transfer wine from one keg to another. These, in turn, are the ancestors of modern devices for loading and unloading not only liquids but also particulate commodities like grain and cement.

Several European medieval borrowings from the more distant parts of Asia have been mentioned earlier in this article. The list may be lengthened: in agriculture, rice, cotton, sugar, the silkworm, and the water buffalo; in transport, the stirrup, two forms of efficient horse harness, and perhaps the wheelbarrow; in manufacturing, the horizontal loom, paper, and perhaps printing; in music, the transverse flute and the two-ended drum; in mechanics, the paternoster pump and the vertical-axle windmill; in warfare, gunpowder, rockets (but not, it appears, the cannon), and the trebuchet.

The present state of scholarship does not permit us to track all of these east-to-west diffusions as precisely as we would wish by date and place. Nevertheless, to offer one example, several scholars, working independently, recently have enabled us to trace the path of the trebuchet with some accuracy. The earliest form of the trebuchet appeared in China by the third century B.C. at the latest. It consisted of a long beam pivoting on a frame; at one end of the beam was a sling carrying the missile, and at the other end were ropes on which men pulled downward simultaneously at a signal, thus raising the sling end of the beam and hurling the missile. Since Chinese armies frequently penetrated Central Asia, it is not surprising that this form of traction trebuchet was known to the Byzantines by 587, when a Byzantine prisoner purchased his life by showing the Avars how to construct one. In 597 an Avar army besieging Thessaloniki used such trebuchets in considerable numbers. In Islam traction trebuchets were used at the siege of Mecca in 683. West of the Avars, the Merovingians continued to use Greco-Roman torsion artillery, but this was not effective when the frequent rains of northern Europe wet the twisted skeins of hair or sinews that stored the power in such engines. Traction trebuchets were invulnerable to moisture, and in 885/886 the Franks used them to defend Paris against besieging Norsemen.

This sort of artillery continued to be used in Europe in its original Chinese form until the later twelfth century, when, probably first in Europe, a great counterweight replaced the men pulling ropes. This change much increased the potential power and accuracy of trebuchets. The new type of trebuchet was quickly spread eastward into Islam. In Europe, although cannon appeared at Florence in 1326 and in England in 1327, the counterweight trebuchet continued in declining use until the invention of corned gunpowder in the 1420's rendered the cannon clearly superior. Cannon appeared in China in 1332, a time when many Italians were there; gunpowder artillery reached not only Islam but also India and eventually Japan not from China but, rather, from Europe.

In discussing cultural diffusions over as long a period as the Middle Ages and as vast an area as Eurasia, the possibility of duplicate inventions looms. The more we learn, however, the less frequent duplications appear to have been. The crank is as simple, and as important in the history of machine design, as the wheel. But, like the wheel, it has no utility in itself: it can travel only as part of a more complex device. The crank first appeared in the second or first century B.C. in China as a means of turning a rotary fan for winnowing chaff from hulled rice. This machine did not reach Europe until the eighteenth century, when it was brought by Jesuits from China to Transylvania, and by Swedish merchants from China to Scandinavia. As has already been mentioned, the first evidence of a crank in Europe is found in a drawing of about 830 made in northern France. Here the crank is turning the first known rotary whetstone. Rotary whetstones were not introduced into China until the nineteenth century. The second European application of the crank, datable in the tenth century, was to the hurdygurdy. Hurdygurdies were unknown in traditional China. We must therefore conclude that the crank was invented twice, and that China in this instance was nearly 1,000 years ahead of Europe.

The perceptive medieval Muslims, who were

geographically located centrally in Eurasia, and who therefore were best placed to judge the qualities of each of its cultures, had a proverb that "Allah has made three marvels: the brain of the Greek, the hand of the Chinese, and the tongue of the Arab." The number and importance of Western medieval technological borrowings from China confirm the second of these judgments for the greater part of the Middle Ages. By about 1350, however, European engineering creativity had surpassed that of East Asia and was surging onward. The uniquely Western invention of invention in the thirteenth century involved a self-conscious and very broad search for engineering problems that needed solving. A perpetual, and often collaborative, tinkering pervaded Europe. After the 1180's, when the horizontal-axle windmill was invented, no new harnessable natural force was found until the late eighteenth century, when James Watt's tinkering produced a steam engine of wide applicability. Yet the European tinkers of the later Middle Ages in each generation continued to produce new wonders and to polish new kinds of technical skills.

No such coherent and persistent technological movement has been identified even in China, much less in India or Islam. All three of these cultures were sophisticated and innovative in many ways, but their interest in the advance of engineering was less vivid than what we observe in the medieval West.

Islam offers a particularly puzzling case. At times it eagerly adopted a technological novelty. In 751, Muslims defeated a Chinese army at Samarkand. Some of the prisoners had been papermakers in their homeland. Thanks to their skills, the manufacturing of paper spread swiftly throughout Islam. The Byzantines were using paper manufactured by Muslims as early as the tenth century (although the oldest surviving examples of paper in Constantinople date from the mid eleventh century). The Byzantines seem not to have ever made any paper for themselves; they bought what they needed from Muslim merchants. The Muslims never mechanized the pulping of rags to make paper, but the first Western paper manufacturers—at Fabriano in the Apennines, by 1276—were using for that purpose hammers operated by cams on the axle of a waterwheel: the device that is first noted on the plan of St. Gall about 820. The saving of labor costs through mechanization quickly enabled Italian papermakers to undersell the Muslims and drive them out of the Byzantine market.

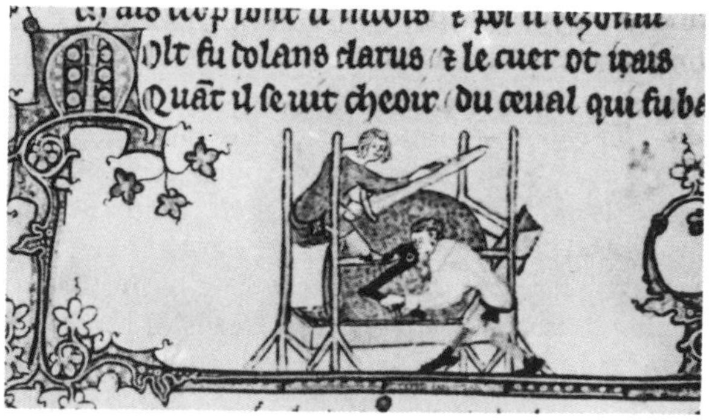

Crank turning a rotary whetstone. Miniature from a 14th-century copy of the *Roman d'Alexandre* in the Bibliothèque Nationale. SNARK INTERNATIONAL/ART RESOURCE

The world's first operating windmills appeared in Muslim southern Afghanistan in the early tenth century, revolving on vertical axles. This form of windmill reached China in the late thirteenth century and Italy in the early fifteenth century, but it never spread out of Afghanistan to other parts of Islam. The European horizontal axle windmill, independently invented (as we have already noted) in the 1180's on the mechanical analogy of the Vitruvian watermill, was taken to Syria in 1192 by German crusaders. When, in 1271, the greatest of crusader castles, the Krak des Chevaliers, was surrendered by the retreating Christian forces, a Western-style windmill was standing on one of its bastions. Since most of the Islamic countries are arid but windy, windmills were better adapted to the environment than were watermills. They were known to Muslims but not adopted by them.

Johannes Gutenberg's invention of printing by means of movable metal type cast in molds was taken to the Turkish empire in 1492 by Jews expelled from Spain. Soon their printing in Hebrew was followed by Syriac printing in the Maronite Christian community of Syria, and by printing under Turkish rule both in Armenian and in Greek. There was no printing in the major Islamic languages—Arabic, Persian, and Turkish—until the early nineteenth century. The usual explanation is the great prestige of calligraphy in Islam; but every civilization using manuscripts admires beauty in them, most notably the Chinese, even though they originated the idea of printing in ink on paper. The prolonged spurning of printing by Muslims must be understood in relation to their comparable indifference to power machinery, notably windmills. This attitude is so unintelligible to Westerners, who are unconsciously steeped in their own distinctive medieval traditions, that they tend to assume that Islam then was a moribund culture. The Alhambra, the Houghton manuscript of the *Shāhnāma,* the mosque of Suleiman the Magnificent, or the high quality of pure science in medieval Islam should dispel any such ethnocentric illusion. Medieval Muslims, like the Byzantines, were far less interested in technology as a means of producing useful goods than as a means of producing wonder and pleasure. In this they continued the tradition of the Alexandrian engineers and artists of antiquity. The most important Arabic treatise on machine design, Ibn al-Razzāz al-Jazarī^c's *Kitāb fī ma^črifat al-ḥiyal al-handasīya* (Book of knowledge of ingenious mechanical devices), written during 1205–1206, has no utilitarian intent—even his elaborate water clocks are primarily vehicles for the display of wonderful automata—unless machines that produce surprise and delight can be considered useful.

In traditional Tibet, technology's focus was the mechanization of perpetual prayer to achieve liberation from reincarnation. Travelers, as they walked, constantly twirled hand-held prayer cylinders filled with written sutras; to get the cylinder over the rotational "dead spot," a small metal ball was attached by a chain to the outer edge of the cylinder. Streams turned small waterwheels with cylinders on their vertical axles praying for the souls of those who had placed them there. Everywhere little vertical-axle windmills similarly turned prayer cylinders without ceasing. In the big felt tents of Tibetan nomads, a small turbine was placed in the smoke hole at the top of the tent, and sutras were turned by the force of rising hot air.

The two most original items in this series of devices were the ball-and-chain governor and the hot-air turbine. Following the Black Death of 1347–1350 in Europe, the dearth of servants led to a revival of slavery, especially in Italy. Turkic and Mongol merchants harvested young people throughout Central Asia and sold them in the Genoese ports on the north shore of the Black Sea. Presumably these "Tartar slaves" served to diffuse to Italy some elements in the simple technology of their homelands. By the 1480's the famous Sienese engineer Francesco di Giorgio was using ball-and-chain governors to smooth out the rotation of mills involving compound cranks and connecting rods. Not long afterward, Leonardo da Vinci sketched a device that entranced Montaigne in the next century. A metal turbine placed in a chimney was connected by gearing to a spit on the hearth. When the fire burned hot, the roast turned rapidly; as the fire died down, the rotation slowed. If a robot is defined as a machine that, without human intervention, adjusts the way it performs its task according to changes in its environment, this was the first robot. Tibetan technology aided the achievement of salvation; European medieval technology sought efficiency in production, largely by the saving of labor, time, and material. Almost everything that the medieval West borrowed from the East was in some way modified or elaborated to serve its own occidental values.

WESTERN MEDIEVAL TECHNOLOGY AND WESTERN CHRISTIAN VALUES

People put their brains, imagination, energy, and capital into what they value most. The major civilizations have differed, and continue to differ, considerably in their general character, in their priorities, and consequently in their highest achievements. From 800 at the latest, Western Europe has put great and increasing value upon technological development. By 1500, cities like Milan and Augsburg were far advanced in an industrial activity of which the world's more recent industrialization is the direct outgrowth.

In the history of technology there is no defensible frontier between the Middle Ages and "modern times." By 1500, Europe had engineering equipment that enabled Westerners not only to open the global sea-lanes but also to sustain connections with the most distant parts of the world, exploring, trading, looting, conquering, and colonizing. As late as 1400, it would seem to modern eyes that the Chinese had a better chance than the Europeans of being the world openers; but for internal political reasons they suddenly withdrew from the seas, and it was the Europeans who made Earth functionally round. The eagerness for far adventure and the level of brutal aggression with which Westerners attacked the other peoples of the world cannot be explained by the high level of European technology in 1500. Nevertheless, that technology was an indispensable enabling condition of what Europeans accomplished globally. If one is to understand world history, one must try to grasp why the Western Middle Ages came to value technological progress so highly.

The great caesura in the history of the Western world came with the conversion of the Roman Empire to Christianity. Viewed historically, rather than metahistorically, Christianity is an amazingly succeessful Jewish heresy. Its victory in the fourth century marked the ideological semitization of the Mediterranean, and eventually of northern Europe as well. Obviously, as Hellenistic Alexandria and pre-Ming China show, striking advances in engineering have occurred quite apart from Christian influences. Nevertheless, it appears that in the specific historical situation of medieval Western Europe, Christian views provided a fertile soil for the vigorous growth of technology, in three basic ways.

First, the Hebrew-Christian faith centers on a Creator God who is totally outside his creation. By the time of Jesus, Judaism had eliminated all spirit from the physical objects of nature. There were, indeed, angels and demons recently borrowed from Persian Zoroastrianism, but these were bodiless and unattached creatures, very different from the genii that in Greco-Roman paganism had inhabited every physical object. In animistic societies, like those of antiquity, if one kills an animal, one placates its spirit; one negotiates with a tree before felling it. Christians have always felt free to do what they wish with other natural objects, without considering their concerns. The technologist's approach to materials and forces was simplified and made more direct by the new religion. Christianity is ruthlessly anthropocentric; paganism was not.

Connected with this despiritualization of nature was the belief that God created the world for mankind's use and instruction, and for no other purpose. Man has been given absolute dominion over all other creatures. Two other, and more kindly, views of the man-nature relationship can be found in the Jewish Scriptures, but neither seems to have had much influence on Western Christian thinking about the exploitation of nature.

Second, in the Judeo-Christian tradition, time is part of God's creation. Pagan time was cyclical, repetitive, as Hindu time continues to be. Christian time is unrepeatable and unidirectional. God has placed us as individual souls in this stream of time, in which every moment is unique. Time is the most evanescent of natural resources. If we waste an instant, it is lost to us forever. By using time well to serve God and our neighbors, we achieve our final reward in Abraham's bosom. It follows that every new means of speeding travel or production, or of increasing the output of a worker in a given time, has a spiritual implication. Saving time and labor helps to save souls, as the Benedictines and Cistercians have told us by their actions.

Third, in the most intensely religious parts of their communities, first Judaism and then Christianity fostered a sense of the spiritual importance of manual labor, which was in great contrast to the contemptuous Greco-Roman attitude. Under Roman rule, the rabbis often worked with their hands. St. Paul, who had studied for the rabbinate, was a tentmaker who, on his missionary journeys, occasionally supported himself by his craft. When Christian monasticism arose in the third century, it strongly affirmed the rabbinical teaching that personal physical labor is essential to the religious life. When monasteries grew corrupt, monks tended to abandon manual labor, but every reform movement stressed work as a religious duty and privilege.

In the early twelfth century, new groups of regular canons attempted to propagate the monastic ideal of labor among the devout laity. The effort was not successful until, a hundred years later, St. Francis created his Third Order of laymen, who did not retire from the world but who stayed with their families, their work, and their communities. It was with these tertiaries that the vision of the potential sanctity of lay life was first seen by any large number of people. This began a spiritual revolution that spread particularly in northern Europe, and at last gave birth to late medieval and Protestant Puritanism and to its "work ethic." Technological development on a grand scale demands an influential group in society that works hard with its hands and believes passionately in what it is doing. Since the victory of Christianity over paganism, the Occident has never lacked such groups.

CONCLUSION

The expulsion of spirit from the objects of nature, the conviction that mankind, by God's will, exercises a rightful rule over all of nature, the idea that time is a unique resource to be conserved and utilized to man's advantage, and the belief—never universal, but sufficiently widespread to be socially operative—that labor is virtuous are Judeo-Christian alterations of contrary Greco-Roman views that do much to explain the remarkable contrast between the technological style of antiquity and that of the Western Middle Ages and more recent times. The technology of Frankistan became amazingly innovative largely because it was so closely integrated with a specific and dominant faith, Latin or Roman Christianity.

Two Western technological achievements, the pipe organ and the mechanical clock, perhaps best demonstrated the uniqueness of Western medieval civilization compared with those of the East, even with Eastern Christendom. Byzantium was as devoutly Christian as was Latin Christendom, yet the Christian East, with rare exceptions, was little interested in technological innovation or change. Eastern churches tolerated no instruments in their liturgies, but from the ninth century on, the pipe organ, the most mechanically intricate of all instruments of music, came to dominate the liturgies of the West. No clocks of any sort were permitted in or on Eastern churches. To place them there would contaminate eternity with time. In complete contrast, the first mechanical clock was invented by a Benedictine abbot, and within a few decades great astronomical clocks, decorated with religious automata that moved at the striking of the hours, had been built as part of many Latin churches to show the delighted laity, by visual means, the orderliness and magnificence of God's cosmos as a frame for the Christian history of salvation.

It is a commonplace among church historians that Eastern and Western Christians have been nourished by the same religion, but have taken it in quite different flavors. The East considers sin to be primarily wrong thinking; the remedy is contemplation leading to right thinking (ortho-doxy). The West believes that sin is primarily wrong action, to be cured by repentance resulting in right action. The goal of the East is illumination; that of the West is virtue. One stresses the mind, the other the will. A religion of activism is a religion for engineers, and that was the sort of religion that dominated the Western Middle Ages and most of what we call "modern times." The deeper question of underlying, and probably unconscious, contrasting preferences that shaped Christianity into two such different historical entities has not been resolved.

BIBLIOGRAPHY

Until the late twentieth century the history of technology was neglected by scholars; for that reason, everything published on it, including this article, must be read with caution.

Bibliographies include Eugene S. Ferguson, *Bibliography of the History of Technology* (1968); and "Current Bibliography in the History of Technology," published annually in *Technology and Culture* (1964–). Magda Whitrow, ed., *Isis Cumulative Bibliography 1913–65*, III, *Subjects* (1976), 521–603, lists topical studies not confined to one period; items specifically medieval appear in IV, *Periods*. See also Gray C. Boyce, *Literature of Medieval History, 1930–1975*, 5 vols. (1981), esp. 957–969.

Studies include Alistair C. Crombie, *Augustine to Galileo* (1953), esp. 143–211, rev. repr. as *Medieval and Early Modern Science*, 2 vols. (1959); Franz M. Feldhaus, *Die Technik der Antike und des Mittelalters* (1931); Umberto Forti, *Storia della tecnica dal medioevo al rinascimento* (1957); Bertrand Gille, "The Medieval Age of the West (Fifth Century to 1350)," in Maurice Daumas, ed., *A History of Technology and Invention*, Eileen B. Hennessy, trans. (1969), I, and "The Fifteenth and Sixteenth Centuries in the Western World," *ibid.*, II; Jean Gimpel, *The Medieval Machine* (1977); Joseph Needham *et al.*, *Science and Civilisation in China* (1954–); William B. Parsons, *Engineers and Engineering in the Renaissance* (1939); Charles Singer *et al.*, eds., *A History of Technology*, II (1956) and III (1957); Lynn White, jr., *Medieval Technology and Social Change* (1962, repr. 1963) and *Medieval Religion and Technology: Collected Essays* (1978).

LYNN WHITE, JR.

[See also **Agriculture and Nutrition; Alfonso X of Castile; Animals, Draft; Arch; Arms and Armor; Bacon, Roger; Benedictines; Bow and Arrow/Crossbow; Cannon; Clocks and Reckoning of Time; Compass, Magnetic; Dondi, Giovanni de'; Francis of Assisi, St.; Glass, Western European; Gothic Architecture; Heating; Literacy, Western European; Mills; Monte Cassino; Nicholas of Cusa; Optics, Islamic; Optics, Western European; Paper, Introduction of; Peter Peregrinus of Maricourt; Printing, Origins of; Richard of Wallingford; Romanesque Architecture; St. Denis, Abbey Church; Ships and Shipbuilding, Mediterranean; Ships and Shipbuilding, Northern Europe; Suger, Abbot of St. Denis; Textile Technology; Vault; Villard de Honnecourt; Warfare, Western European.**]

TEGLIACCI, NICCOLÒ DI SER SOZZO (*d.* 1363), Sienese painter and illuminator, active from the 1330's or 1340's. The signed miniature of the Assumption in the Caleffo dell'Assuntà (Siena, Archivio di Stato, Capitoli 2), the key work for identifying Niccolò's style, displays firm yet delicate figures and refined color, and reflects the influence of Simone Martini and Pietro and Ambrogio Lorenzetti.

BIBLIOGRAPHY

Bruce Cole, *Sienese Painting* (1980), 188–191, 229; Cristina De Benedictis, "I corali di San Gimignano I: Le miniature di Niccolò Tegliacci," in *Paragone*, 27 (1976), 103–120; Millard Meiss, *Painting in Florence and Siena*

Assumption of the Virgin. Miniature by Niccolò di Ser Sozzo Tegliacci, 1336 or late 1340's, in the Caleffo dell'Assuntà (Siena, Archivio di Stato, Capitoli 2). ALINARI/ART RESOURCE

After the Black Death (1951), 169; Gordon Moran and Sonia Fineschi, "Niccolò di Ser Sozzo-Tegliacci or di Stefano? (Some Unpublished Documents Relating to the Problems of Luca di Tommè and Niccolò di Ser Sozzo)," in *Paragone,* 27 (1976).

MICHAEL JACOFF

[See also **Barna da Siena; Gothic Art: Painting; Lorenzetti, Ambrogio; Lorenzetti, Pietro; Siena.**]

TEKOR. The Armenian church of Tekor (known as St. Sargis) near Ani, one of the most important monuments of Armenian architecture, is attributed to the fifth century on the basis of its architecture and an inscription, considered the earliest in Armenia, by a contemporary prince, Sahak Kamsarakan. Destroyed in 1935, Tekor was originally a basilica, possibly a pagan structure. A stone dome was added in the late fifth century together with a horseshoe-shaped apse and three porticoes, making Tekor one of the earliest domed churches to be constructed in Armenia. A later inscription states that the queen of Ani, Katranidē, renovated the church in 1008.

BIBLIOGRAPHY

Architettura medievale armena: Roma, Palazzo Venezia, 10–30 giugno 1968 (1968); Sirarpie Der Nersessian, *The Armenians* (1969) and *Armenian Art,* Sheila Bourne and Angela O'Shea, trans. (1977, 1978); Varaztad Harouthiounian and Morous S. Hasrathian, *Monuments of Armenia* (1975), 36; A. Khatchatrian, *L'ar-*

chitecture arménienne du IV au VI siècle (1971); Richard Krautheimer, *Early Christian and Byzantine Architecture* (1965, repr. 1967); Josef Strzygowski, *Die Baukunst der Armenier und Europa,* I (1918); Charles Texier, *Description de l'Arménie, de la Perse, de la Mésopotamie,* I (1842), 120–121; N. and M. Thierry, "Notes sur des monuments arméniens en Turquie (1964)," in *Revue des études arméniennes,* n.s. 2 (1965), 171; T^c^oros T^c^oramanyan, *Nyut^c^er haykakan čartarapetut^c^yan patmut^c^yan,* 2 vols. (1942–1948).

LUCY DER MANUELIAN

[See also **Armenian Art.**]

TEMPERA PAINTING, the primary form of panel painting involving the use of pigments mixed with an egg-yolk binder. Fast-drying tempera paint was best suited to a methodical, deliberate working method in which the image was well planned before the painting was begun. Its nonviscous property helped shape the detailed, linear style that characterizes medieval panel painting.

BIBLIOGRAPHY

Cennino Cennini, *Il libero dell'arte,* ed. and trans. by Daniel V. Thompson, Jr., as *The Craftsman's Handbook* (1933, repr. 1954); Bruce Cole, *The Renaissance Artist at Work* (1983).

ADELEHEID M. GEALT

[See also **Cennini, Cennino; Dugento Art; Gothic Art: Painting; Panel Painting; Trecento Art.**]

TEMPLARS. See **Chivalry, Orders of.**

TEMPLON SCREEN. See **Screen, Chancel.**

TENOR. Deriving its name from the Latin *tenere* ("to hold"), the tenor of a medieval polyphonic composition holds the plainsong; that is, its melody is based on an ecclesiastical chant. Since it refers to the function of the melody in the structure of the piece, to support the upper parts, the tenor has nothing to do with the male voice, and the part could be sung in any range, even by boys or nuns, provided the other parts were moved correspondingly. In compositions of the fourteenth and fifteenth centuries, the plainsong was sometimes in one of the upper parts or, in secular pieces, was absent altogether. In such pieces, a lower supporting part was still called the tenor, although its basis was no longer in plainsong. By the late fifteenth century, the tenor was the next-to-lowest part in a four- or five-part piece, thus aligning itself with the normal high range of the male voice.

ANDREW HUGHES

[See also **Ars Antiqua; Ars Nova; Contratenor.**]

TENSO (tenson), a poetic form in troubadour and trouvère literature from the twelfth and thirteenth centuries. The tenso is presented as a debate between two or more individuals—usually two poets mentioned by name—often on the subject of appropriate conduct in love. The fourteenth-century poetic theorist Guilhem Molinier, in *Las leys d'amors* (1328, rev. 1337), distinguishes between the tenso and the partimen or *jeu-parti,* stating that the participants in the former argue from conviction and those in the latter for the sake of argument only. The distinction is blurred in practice, however, and the two forms may be regarded as identical.

In structure, the tenso usually presents the participants' opinions in alternating stanzas. The composition of stanzas is variable with respect to line length, number of lines, and meter. The tone is often jocular, with the participants jibing at each other and criticizing personal qualities as well as opinions. In a few cases it is not certain whether the poem was actually written by two authors, or whether it is the work of a single poet presenting several viewpoints by assigning them to different speakers.

BIBLIOGRAPHY

Pierre Bec, *La lyrique française au moyen âge (XIIe–XIIIe siècles),* 2 vols. (1977–1978); Paul Zumthor, *Langue et techniques poétiques à l'époque romane (XIe–XIIIe siècles)* (1963).

MARCIA J. EPSTEIN

[See also **Partimen; Provençal Literature; Troubadour, Trouvère.**]

TENTHS. See **Tithes.**

TENURE OF LAND, ISLAMIC. In Islamic theory, all property, whether movable or immovable, belongs to God, on the grounds that he created everything in heaven and earth. "Does not," says the Koran (10:56) "what is in heaven and what is in the earth belong to God?" Since property was created for the benefit of mankind (Koran 2:29, 31:19, 45:12), it follows that although God is ultimately the owner, men have been granted the right of possession. But it is not clear from the Koran whether God has granted the right of possession to men collectively, without the intention of distribution among them, or has left to men the mode of distribution. With regard to land, the latter assumption seems to have prevailed. All the principles and rules governing land tenure that have been dealt with in Islamic law were drawn essentially from the legislation laid down by the prophet Muḥammad (*sunna* of the Prophet, often called Traditions) and the opinion of jurists, within the general framework of the Koran.

Following his migration in 622 to Medina, first capital of the Islamic state, the Prophet began to deal, among other things, with problems relating to land and taxation. Concerning immovable property there had already existed in some parts of Arabia before Islam a land tax called *ᶜushr* (tithe), which was a tribute paid in kind or cash to God or to rulers. The term *ᶜushr* is not used in the Koran, but there is an implied reference to it as a tax (6:141) consistent with the revelations that God created (and therefore is the owner of) all property, and that men, who cultivate it, are possessors. Men, therefore, must "pay the due thereof on the day of its harvest" (6:142). The Prophet, in accordance with this revelation, laid down the *sunna* confirming an existing practice that a tenth (*ᶜushr*) should be paid on all lands irrigated by rain or running streams and half a tenth on lands artificially irrigated. *ᶜUshr* became the term used in Islamic law in reference to lands possessed by believers before Islam began to expand outside Arabia. Although it was taken for granted that God is ultimately the owner of all property, the subtle distinction between ownership and possession was nominal, and the latter concept was for all practical purposes equated with ownership.

After the expansion of Islam by conquest outside Arabia in the seventh century, vast territories in Southwest Asia and North Africa passed under Islamic rule. The status of lands taken by force (*ᶜanwatan*) from the enemy was naturally not the same as that of lands that surrendered peacefully (*fayᵓ*). Moreover, some of the owners of lands that were surrendered, whether in response to force or by peaceful arrangements, adopted Islam, while others, who retained their religion, preferred to pay a tribute, called *jizya* (poll tax), in return for the protection granted to them. All these new situations raised legal questions for the Muslim authorities that called for quick answers. At the outset, lands acquired by peaceful arrangements (*fayᵓ*) were divided and treated as *ᶜushr* lands, on the grounds that they had passed into the possession of Muslims; likewise, all land whose owners became converts was considered *ᶜushr* land, provided the cultivator had improved it by a well or irrigation channels.

Lands owned or cultivated by those who held to their own religious beliefs (Christians, Jews, Zoroastrians) that passed under Muslim rule, whether by force or by peaceful arrangements, were considered, however, to be in a different category and paid a special land tax. The caliph ᶜUmar I (*r.* 634–644) decreed that these lands were not to be divided among warriors as spoils of war, like other property, but were to be considered state lands, and their occupants were to be allowed to exercise control over them virtually as possessors, provided a tax called *kharāj,* estimated on the value of the produce of the land, was paid to the state either in kind or in cash. This kind of land is called *kharāj* land. The legal rules governing *kharāj* land, which the jurists worked out and which became part of Islamic law, were based on the early decrees of ᶜUmar, his instructions to the commanders in the field, and the treaties and other arrangements made with the people of the occupied territories.

Non-Muslims living in Islamic lands, called dhimmis (protected people), were required to pay the *jizya* in accordance with Islamic law (Koran, 9:29). Under the Prophet, the practice was to pay an annual tribute based on a rough estimate of the number of each religious community and paid collectively, not individually, as the treaties concluded between the Prophet and the Christians of Najrān about 631 and others demonstrated. The *jizya,* as an annual tribute, was continued for a while after the Prophet. The *kharāj* paid to the state, an innovation introduced by ᶜUmar I, was a form of land tax, and the *jizya* was included in it if the occupants were non-Muslims. For this reason, *jizya* and *kharāj* were at the outset used interchangeably. These terms, however—*kharāj* as land tax and *jizya* as poll tax—became clearly distinct in usage when, under ᶜUmar II (*r.* 717–720), a decree was issued requiring payment of the *jizya* both by the individual dhimmi not engaged in the cultivation of land—and therefore not required to pay the *kharāj*—and by the individual dhimmi who cultivated the land and was bound to pay the *kharāj*. Moreover, a Muslim who bought *kharāj* land from a dhimmi was required to pay the *kharāj*, even though the land passed from an unbeliever to a believer, because the *kharāj* tax was on land that belonged to the state, not on the head of the possessor (although the early practice had been to treat all lands owned by believers as *ᶜushr* lands). The Christians of the tribe of Banū Taghlib, who refused to pay the *jizya* because they viewed it as a sign of degradation, were allowed instead to pay a double *ᶜushr,* although this exaction was dropped when they became converts.

The estimate of the extent of the *kharāj* and the amount due varied from province to province, and the jurists provided their estimate on the basis of existing practice and custom in each province and on the method of evaluation of the school of law to which they belonged. A case in point was the Sawād—the southern lands of Iraq. Abū Ḥanīfa, founder of the school bearing his name, and his disciples (Abū Yūsuf, Shaybānī, and others) maintained that all the Sawād had become *kharāj* land because it was taken by conquest. Land taxable as such consisted of all the land that had access to water and was cultivable, regardless of whether it was actually cultivated or not.

The *kharāj* was estimated to be one *qafīz* (a measure of grain) and one dirham (a silver unit, the Greek drachma) on each *jarīb* (a measure of land equivalent to 1,592 square meters or 17,135 square feet) per year, regardless of whether its farmer raised one crop a year or more. If the land was sown to rice, sesame, or vegetables, and the crops were completely destroyed by hail, fire, flood, or like causes, no tax should be paid for that year (but a tax must be paid if part of the crop survived). No tax was to be paid on date palms or other fruit trees unless the land was fully planted with trees under which no other crops could be cultivated, in which case the tax per *jarīb* would be ten dirhams. For every *jarīb* of grapevines ten dirhams must be paid, and for every *jarīb* of lucerne, five dirhams. If the crop was blighted, no tax was due. If land was in part salinated and uncultivable, this part would not be subject to *kharāj*; but if it could be reclaimed and cultivated, the *kharāj* would be due. If the farmer was unable to cultivate *kharāj* land or neglected or abandoned it, the imam had the right to take it from him and give it to another who was prepared to cultivate it.

The Sawād became the model for conquered territories elsewhere, although in Syria and Egypt the governors relaxed the rules about payment in cases where the land was less productive than in the Sawād. Moreover, in situations where certain parts of the territory were not taken by force but by peaceful surrender of its people (for instance, parts of the delta of Egypt, except Alexandria), the land was divided among believers and considered a tithe land.

A third category of land is *mawāt* (dead land), which either is in the state of nature or has been deserted and no longer can be cultivated. The jurists were in agreement that such land would come into the possession of the person able to reclaim it and bring it under cultivation by digging a well or a channel that could bring water for its cultivation in accordance with a *ḥadīth* of the Prophet: "Dead land belongs to him who revives it, and no trespasser has a right." (According to another version, the Prophet said, "He who revives dead land, not belonging to anyone before him, acquires it, and a trespasser has no right.")

Since in theory all lands belong to God, the person who reclaims land that is in the state of nature or that has fallen into disuse and is not claimed by anyone else has legitimate possession of it, provided he obtains the permission of the state to revive it, according to some jurists. But most jurists insisted that permission of the authorities was not necessary. However, since registration of the land in official records was necessary, the state must be notified of the reclaimed land. Perhaps for this reason, al-Shāfiᶜī, founder of the school of law bearing his name, held that the state must be informed of the action as a matter of courtesy. With regard to taxation, dead lands brought into cultivation by Muslims fell under the *ᶜushr* category. The possessor of dead land had to pay the tithe if the land was irrigated by rain or running water; if it was irrigated by a well or a channel constructed for bringing the water to the land, only half of the tithe was due.

Apart from lands acquired by purchase or lease from the state, the imam had the power to grant land to any believer who had rendered service to the state or the community, or to men who had an ancient right to it. Such lands were called *qaṭāʾiʿ* (fiefs) and fell into the category of *ʿushr* for the purpose of taxation.

Land bequeathed for charitable purposes (*waqf,* pious foundation) was subject to no change of status. No tax on *waqf* land was due; but if the income from such land was assigned partly to charity and partly to the heirs of the deceased, the latter had to pay the tax on the income.

The medieval concepts of land tenure remained valid in theory under Ottoman rule, though practice varied considerably between the European and Asiatic provinces. In the Arab countries, taxes on land were paid in accordance with Islamic law and lands were considered at least in theory as belonging to the state (or God). It was on the basis of this theory that Pasha Muḥammad ʿAlī, viceroy of Egypt (1805–1849), claimed control over agricultural lands and paid farmers as possessors, not as owners, of their lands. In all other Ottoman Asiatic provinces, most cultivable lands, including unclaimed and uncultivated lands, were considered *mīrī* lands. At the outset, taxes were collected by tax farmers who gradually acquired rights of possession, but later taxes were collected by regular officials.

After the *tanẓīmāt* decrees, which gradually replaced the traditional Islamic taxation system, possessors of land became owners, and the *jizya,* paid by non-Muslims, was abolished. Modern codes of laws regulating landholdings and taxes were enacted by the successor states that came into existence following the dissolution of the Ottoman Empire after World War I.

BIBLIOGRAPHY

Sources. Listed in accordance with the order of each writer's period and authority are Qudāma ibn Jaʿfar, *Kitāb al-kharāj wa sināʿat al-kitāba, al-Zabīdī,* ed. (1981); Yaḥya ibn Ādam, *Kitāb al-kharāj,* Theodore W. Juynboll, ed. (1896, repr. 1928); Abū Yūsuf, *Kitāb al-kharāj* (1844)—an English translation of these works may be found in Aharon Ben Shemesh, trans., *Taxation in Islam,* 3 vols. (1958–1969); Muḥammad ibn al-Ḥasan al-Shaybānī, "Kitāb al-siyar" (part of *Kitab al-Aṣl*), Majid Khadduri, trans., in *Islamic Law of Nations* (1966), chaps. 10–11; Abū al-Ḥasan ʿAlī ibn Muḥammad ibn Ḥabīb al-Mawārdī, *Kitāb al-aḥkām al-sulṭānīya,* Maximilian Enger, ed. (1853, repr. 1909); Abū ʿUbayd al-Qāsim ibn Sallām, *Kitāb al-amwāl,* Muḥammad Hāmid al-Fiqqī, ed. (1934).

Studies. Nicolas P. Aghnides, *Mohammedan Theories of Finance* (1916, repr. 1969); Daniel C. Dennett, *Conversion and the Poll Tax in Early Islam* (1950); Majid Khadduri, *War and Peace in the Law of Islam* (1955, repr. 1979), chap. 17; Frede Løkkegaard, *Islamic Taxation in the Classic Period* (1950); A. N. Poliak, "Classification of Lands in the Islamic Law and Its Technical Terms," in *American Journal of Semitic Languages and Literatures,* 57 (1940).

MAJID KHADDURI

[See also **Agriculture and Nutrition: The Islamic World; Islamic Administration; Poll Tax, Islamic; Taxation, Islamic; Waqf.**]

TENURE OF LAND, SLAVIC. When the Slavs settled on the east European plain, they evidently brought with them strong bonds of kinship and relatively weak notions of land ownership. The *Russian Primary Chronicle* describes the early history of the Slavs in this way: "Each lived with his own clan, separately, in their own places, [and] each had his own clan." While there are few written sources with which to reconstruct the earliest history of the Slavs, later medieval legal texts underline the importance of patrilineal kinship to the Slavs, and simultaneously make almost no mention of land ownership. It would appear, therefore, that until relatively late in the Middle Ages the Slavs held land in common and possessed only rights of usufruct. As the codes make clear, among the medieval Slavs movables had far greater significance than did immovable property.

The oldest extant Slavic codes make scant reference to landed property. The *Russkaya pravda,* for example, which came to exert great influence over the legal codes of Poland, Lithuania, and other societies on the east European plain, makes no mention whatever of land boundaries or landed property in its oldest, short redaction. The expanded redaction, compiled in the twelfth century, includes among a host of articles defending rights to movables only two articles regarding boundary trees and other border markers. Whose borders these are the law does not say.

The medieval Bulgarian code, the *Zakon sudnyi ljudem,* devoted the bulk of its articles to matters of Christian practice. However, when describing property transactions, the code, like the *Russkaya pravda,* concentrates nearly all its attention on movables—livestock, slaves, weapons, and the like. Only in one article of the oldest redaction does the law mention landed property, and even then the code protects only forests.

The Vinodol Statute, which originated late in the thirteenth century, makes frequent reference to the theft of movables, but no direct reference whatever to land ownership. Instead, in repeating the common Slavic preference for male heirs, it neglects to mention land among heritable property.

Stefan Dušan's Code suggests that in fourteenth-century Serbia boundaries of landed property were still difficult to distinguish. Villages were obliged to present witnesses who, like their coevals in Muscovy, walked off the limits that separated one village's holdings from another's. Likewise, damaging crops on someone's land was punishable, but in none of this did the code specify individual land tenure; except for the king's land grants made to servitors, only village lands were mentioned.

In other words, by the end of the fourteenth century, Slavic society had not yet developed a sense of individual land tenure. Where the laws mention landed property, it is clear that the compilers have in mind some form of communal or joint, rather than individual, proprietorship. As Dušan's Code and other, later texts demonstrate, limited individual proprietary rights emerged only in tandem with the growth of royal power.

Among the medieval Slavs joint families or other communal kin associations controlled landed property. The sources are extremely laconic, unfortunately, so it is difficult to describe these associations precisely. Furthermore, over time there were some changes in the composition of these groups. In spite of the difficulties, however, some common characteristics are discernible.

Everywhere among the Slavs patriliny prevailed. The opening sections of the *Russkaya pravda,* for example, indicate that patrilineal kinship defined social status in medieval Rus. Homicides were to be avenged only by agnates of the deceased; should they elect not to retaliate against the homicide, they were designated the rightful recipients of compensation. Likewise, the later inheritance provisions of the *Russkaya pravda* demonstrate a pronounced preference for males, and unless specified otherwise by the testator, legacies were to be divided evenly among surviving sons. Daughters could inherit only in the absence of male heirs. Therefore, when land devolved upon the sons of a man who died intestate, as must often have happened in the medieval period, some form of joint household emerged in which brothers shared the rights of tenure, the fruits of their agricultural labors, and the obligation of marrying off and dowering their sisters.

The extant South Slavic medieval codes reproduce the *Russkaya pravda*'s perspective on patriliny. The thirteenth-century Korčula Codex, for example, specifies male heritability and permits females to inherit only in the absence of surviving brothers, sons, or sons' sons. The Code of Stefan Dušan also confirms Serbian patriliny: "If a lord have children, or if he have no children, and die, and upon his death the patrimonial estate remains vacant, wherever there be found someone of his clan up to the third cousin, that one shall have his patrimonial estate." The fifteenth-century Poljica Statute, while demonstrating the changes that time brought to South Slavic society, nevertheless maintains the Slavic preference for males and joint households based upon patriliny.

> While brothers or others who participate in a division still do no separate, then they hold everything in common: both the good and the bad, the profits and the losses, and the debts, both those to whom they are indebted as well as those who are indebted to them. Everything is held in common so long as they do not separate; but when they separate, then each receives his share.

The Poljica Statute, therefore, does assert legal protection for landownership. Indeed, the law specifically protected a man's right to disinherit unruly, disobedient sons, and went so far as to specify differences between movable and immovable property, directly mentioning among the latter "land or house." At the same time, however, the Poljica Statute, a relatively late compilation of Slavic law, retains the emphasis upon patriliny among the South Slavs, whose male ancestors had held these lands in common.

Daughters, then, were commonly viewed as expendable, and when dowered off generally took no land with them, even after the Slavs began the practice of willing landed property to their sons. All the medieval Slavic codes refused to admit daughters to heritability unless no male collaterals or descendants survived. Instead, daughters were to receive a dowry—from their brothers if the parents had died before the girls married. Evidently the dowries generally did not include landed property, at least not until later in the Middle Ages. While much remains to be studied with respect to dowries, it would appear that even in times of great demographic crisis the South Slavs refused to dower their daughters and sisters with land.

Slavic society, then, did not develop individual tenure rights to land until the end of the Middle Ages. The great mass of Slavs, members of large patrilineal kin associations who worked the land communally, counted only movables among their private possessions. The land belonged to them all. Only with the arrival of powerful princes and kings who wished to retain, and therefore reward, their followers did Slavic law come to recognize individual land tenure.

BIBLIOGRAPHY

Sources. "The Code of Stephan Dušan, Tsar and Autocrat of the Serbs and Greeks," Malcolm Burr, trans., in *Slavonic and East European Review,* **28** (1949–1950); Venelin Ganev, *Zakon soudnyi liud'm* (1959); Boris D. Grekov, *Politsa* (1951) and *Die altkroatische Republik Poljica* (1961); V. V. Jagić, "Sakon Vinodol'skii," in *Pamiatniki drevnei pis'mennosti,* **54** (1880); *Medieval Russian Laws,* George Vernadsky, trans. (1947, repr. 1965); *Pamiatniki russkogo prava,* 8 vols. (1952–1963); Vladimir T. Pashuto and Irina V. Shtal', *Korchula* (1976); *Pravda Russkaia,* B. D. Grekov, ed., 3 vols. (1940–1963); *Zakonik tsara Stefana Dushana,* Mekhmed Begović, ed., 2 vols. (1975–1981); *Zakon sudnyi liudem, kratkoi redaktsii,* M. N. Tikhomirov, ed. (1961); *Zakon sudnyj ljudem (Court Law for the People),* Horace W. Dewey and Ann M. Kleimola, eds. and trans. (1977).

Studies. Marija Gimbutas, *The Slavs* (1971); Ivan I. Liapushkin, *Slaviane vostochnoi Evropy nakanune obrazovaniia drevnerusskogo gosudarstva* (1968); Lubor Niederle, *Manuel de l'antiquité slave,* 2 vols. (1923–1926); Wojciech Wasiutyński, "Origins of the Polish Law, Tenth to Fifteenth Centuries," in Wenceslas J. Wagner, ed., *Polish Law Throughout the Ages* (1970).

DANIEL KAISER

[See also **Agriculture and Nutrition, Slavic World; Bulgaria; Eclogue; Law, Russian (Muscovite); Lithuania; Muscovy, Rise of; Poland; Primary Chronicle, Russian; Serbia; Slavs.**]

TENURE OF LAND, WESTERN EUROPEAN.

"Land tenure" is a modern term. In a narrow, literal sense it denotes the legal rights and obligations of persons with regard to the acquisition, retention, exploitation, and transfer of specific portions of terrain and its products. Most historians and social scientists use "land tenure" in a more general sense to refer to the complex relationships among categories of individuals and groups concerning land, water, and their respective products ("agrarian organization" is a common synonym). The broader usage recognizes that understanding the place of landholding in a historical situation requires more than just the technical vocabulary of law. This article introduces certain concepts useful for comparative historical discussion of land tenure and then describes conditions of tenure as part of changing rural institutions in what came to be Latin Christian Europe between about 500 and about 1500.

Medieval Europeans thought and spoke about land tenure in local and regional vernacular dialects and wrote in Latin, so their tenurial vocabulary was inconsistent. The same arrangement in two villages a day's walk from each other might have totally different names; the same word a few hundred years or miles apart might denote sharply different conditions. Modern students must comprehend medieval terms but also need analytical concepts to classify and compare tenurial conditions. The accompanying chart indicates some of the more important variables for land tenure. Most medieval agrarian regimes can be described in terms shown there.

In the chart dichotomous variables are shown as opposing pairs, and continuous variables are connected by broken lines between conceptual limits. The left column lists variables in the condition of tenure itself. Rights to land may have full security under law or be somehow insecure to the extreme of being nonexistent, just a revocable permission given by another. Even secure rights may have a fixed term less than perpetuity. Claims to land and/or its product may belong to a collectivity or to an individual. One may own land or derive rights as a tenant from the superior rights of the owner. Owner or tenant may reside on the land or manage it as an absentee. Rights to land may be vested in public authority or private legal persons. Besides questions of title, a private holder may possess land with full freedom or with constraints set by recognized custom or by a formal agreement with another. The holder of a conditional tenure may or may not be able to sell, give, pledge, or will it, in whole or in part, to another. On any of these criteria conventional practice may not coincide with legal prescription.

Other patterns (the right side of the chart) affect how tenure shapes landholding. Units of possession may differ from those of actual resource use. With respect to size of holdings or operations, "large" and "small" are relative to the situation being described; a useful benchmark is to remember that in medieval European grain farming, a peasant household needed in the range of eight to twenty hectares (twenty to fifty acres) to support itself. A holding may form one piece or, at the other extreme, many tiny parcels. In fact or in law, a holder may make no special payments by virtue of his tenure or may pay another party for the land and its products. Such payments (rent, tithe, land tax, and so forth) may be defined in nominal terms or relative to quantities produced; they may be in money, goods, services, or some mix of these. The relative importance of labor dues compared with produce and/or cash is often a central issue in medieval agrarian history.

Tenurial variables like those on the chart never fully specify the key structures in agrarian relations and rural life. Whether defined narrowly or broadly, land tenure interacts with patterns of cultivation, with personal status, and with institutions in the larger society surrounding the rural community. The millennium of the Middle Ages and the different lands of Latin Christendom had no single pattern of medieval land tenure; there were no necessary associations among tenurial variables; there were no unambiguous links between specific tenurial features and given levels of peasant well-being; there were no uniformly shared historical tendencies. There were, however, common trends and frequent associations of tenurial features into what might be called agrarian regimes. Records from the early Middle Ages tell best about the

Tenurial Variables in Agrarian Organization

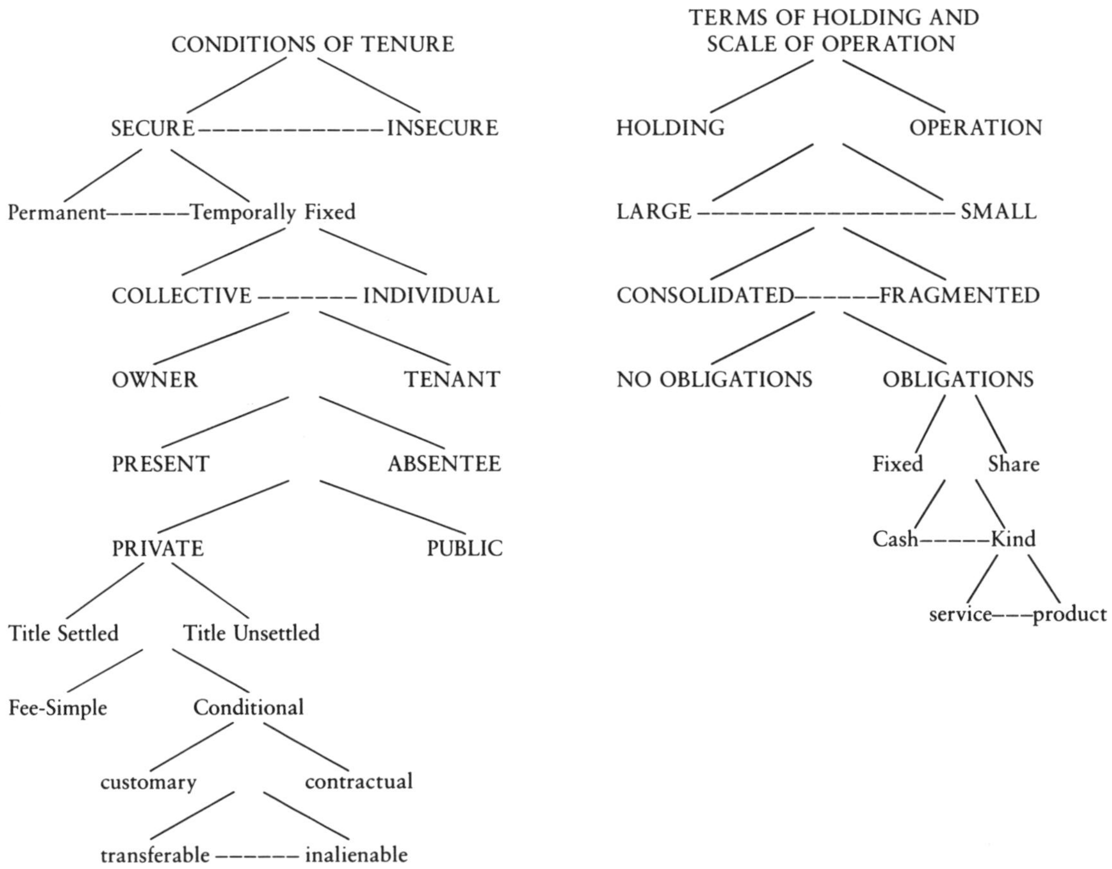

SOURCE: Adapted from Elias H. Tuma, *Twenty-six Centuries of Agrarian Reform: A Comparative Analysis* (1965).

diffusion of dependent tenant farming and certain major variations in this principal Western tenurial institution. From the twelfth century on, increasing evidence allows recognition of differences among the agrarian regimes of European regions. Against a common background of lord-peasant relations, the histories of medieval land tenures form a regional rural mosaic.

SIXTH THROUGH NINTH CENTURIES

Tenurial institutions characteristic of the early medieval West were formed from the conjunction of three trends during the merger of formerly separate Roman and Germanic societies. Great absentee owners took over much of the land of Europe, many tenant cultivators became less than wholly free, and estate holders organized institutions to exploit the resources of small tenant farms in the operation of their own large farms. The sparse records typical of this period tell more about conditions at its beginning and end than about the specific course of intervening movements.

Agricultural land in late Roman Western Europe was owned by peasant farmers and by absentees in differing regional proportions. The law called *ius Quiritium* gave all such owners full private property rights; they owed the taxes that provided most state revenues, but otherwise each could work, retain, or transfer land as he desired and inheritance laws allowed.

Independent peasant proprietors declined sharply in number during late Roman and early medieval times. Their farms, smaller than those of many tenants, were subject to division among the farmer's heirs. They bore heavy fiscal burdens, especially in the land tax (*annona*), but had little say in how local elites assessed it. Any agricultural misfortune or outbreak of violence could force a peasant to seek loans, to carry heavy debts, to suffer foreclosure from a well-off creditor, or to surrender his land in return for protection from a well-placed patron. On what had been his own property, the farmer or his heirs might become a tenant. Late-fourth-century witnesses distinguished between villages of small resident proprietors and those on land owned by an absentee.

Absentee owners included the state, municipalities, churches, senatorial aristocrats, and a broad spectrum of private city-dwellers. Some estates, especially those of senatorial dynasties, covered hundreds of square kilometers; others, then diminishing in importance, were only a few parcels owned by urban craftsmen. Both large and small estates usually consisted of scattered parcels and farms of varying size. The basic unit of ownership, the fundus, identified a stable collection of such holdings that retained its name for generations, though in practice it was not necessarily indivisible. Large owners grouped nearby fundi into management units called *massae*. Absentees rarely involved themselves directly in the day-to-day operation of their properties and, with the decline since the second century of large farms (latifundia) worked by gangs of slaves, habitually leased their land to contractors or peasant tenants called coloni.

Earlier Roman coloni enjoyed full personal freedom. The normal lease contract (lustrum) fixed the rent for a five-year term. When it expired, the colonus could leave the farm or, by mutual tacit agreement with the owner, remain with successive annual occupancies. Other coloni enjoyed emphyteutic tenure for the lifetimes of one or more persons or, on crown lands, perpetuity. These longer leases were, with the consent of the landowner, transferable by sale or inheritance.

Late Roman and early medieval state policies and landowner power debased agricultural tenants, transforming their tenurial conditions and personal status. To secure revenues for the army, late-third- and fourth-century emperors had all cultivators registered as taxpayers and bound to the land from which they would pay. Tenants became the responsibility of their landowners, who were to collect the *annona* with the rent but could not raise rents, expel the tenants, or sell the land without them. Not only were sitting tenants immobilized, but their heirs were equally compelled to remain and work their natal soil. Legal action against the landowner was prohibited and rental obligations, increasingly in kind or even in labor service, were set by the *lex saltus* or "decree of the domain" on which they lived. Such "bound coloni" were described in a late-fourth-century edict as "slaves of the land to which they were born." Thus the term "colonus" came to denote not the tenant's personal freedom but his servitude.

While the position of formerly free Roman farmers declined, that of slaves moved upward toward it. Because the gangs of agricultural slaves once used on some Roman estates did not reproduce themselves and replacement costs soared, landowners had stopped running their own farms and set up the remaining slaves with small holdings to cultivate and support a family. These *servi casati* (hutted slaves) were still chattels, turning over their produce to their owner and doing his bidding. Their tenure was wholly at the owner's will. But stability and slave reproduction were the owner's aim, and for the sake of their production the late Roman state also intervened. Laws prohibited removal of registered *servi casati* from agricultural employment or their sale apart from the land they worked. In de facto possession of land and with the right to acquire property of their own (peculium), such slaves had become unfree tenant farmers. Even if manumitted, they and their heirs retained obligations to the former owner.

The Germanic peoples, the other major contributors to early medieval society, had their own traditions of individual and family ownership of land. They usually distinguished between ancestral property and acquests, permitting rather free disposal of the acquests but giving to male heirs a precedence over equivalent females for the ancestral property. Heirs often voluntarily kept their patrimony in joint ownership, and neighboring owners probably claimed preference over strangers when land was alienated. But the early Germans and their successors who entered the Roman world during the fifth and sixth centuries did not practice collective, communal, or clan ownership of land. In this they differed from the Celtic peoples along the western Roman frontiers, among whom land belonged to a four-generation male kin group (Old Irish: *derbfine*).

Barbarian society before and during the migrations had less unequal distribution of land ownership than did Roman, in part because wide uncultivated tracts in Germany remained without ownership rights. Archaeological and rare written evidence suggests less subdivision and scatter of fields among Germanic landholders than on the Roman side of the frontier. Most landowners among the Germans were free peasant farmers; those with larger properties put them out to dependents, slave or free, as family farms. Opportunities to do this increased with the takeover of Roman territories.

Thus, at the time of the migrations, expanding absentee ownership and declining tenant status among both Romans and barbarians were antecedents for development of a new tenurial regime. When these trends reached some quantitative threshold, we can speak of dependent agriculture, the principal parameter of most medieval land tenure. By around 800, wherever texts make visible the land of western Europe, one central fact framed the lives of most peasants: They were tenants on the land of another, a much wealthier and more powerful social superior, their lord. (The German term *Grundherrschaft* literally denotes "land" and "lordship." Dependent agriculture was spreading at the expense of owner-operators from the fourth century into at least the eleventh on the western continent and even longer elsewhere. The ninth century constitutes a benchmark, not as a turning point or a time of stability, but because the rich documentation of the Carolingian and middle Anglo-Saxon periods illuminates it far more clearly.

The view from the ninth century reveals large estates in most settled areas of Europe. By exploiting the misfortunes of the poor, the favor of princes, or private force, the powerful had during early medieval times much extended their control over land. Some they owned outright (allod), more they held from a royal concession, whether revocable (precarium) or more secure, even hereditary (benefice). The greatest royal churches, for instance, had amassed thousands of hectares, though rarely as much as late Roman senators or in a single territorial unit. In northern Gaul and parts of Lombardy, the ninth-century elite commonly possessed numbers of whole villages close to one another and at times several such clusters. Further south and east, parcels and rights were normally more scattered, although in Germany the ninth-century trend was toward greater consolidation by landords.

The ways great absentees chose to manage their estates shaped and specified tenurial conditions for their tenants. The rights by which a lord held the land seem to have been less decisive than spatial relationships among his holdings. Where these were dispersed and with few large consolidated blocks, the owner could exercise only loose control, taking from tenants only various payments in cash or kind for their personal subjection and their use of the land. A piece the lord could supervise might have a few fed slaves to work a home farm or kitchen. But a lord with some hundreds of hectares or dozens of tenant farms close together could actively manage these resources. Whether the consolidated block had once been a Roman fundus or the farms of peasant proprietors now become coloni, the lord could treat land and people as a great coordinated unit, a single estate called a manor or villa. In Gaul, northern and central Italy, and southern England, villae were the most powerful economic institutions of the eighth and ninth centuries and, in the poor and localized economy of early medieval Europe, the only real concentrations of productive resources and wealth.

Manors might be managed only for efficient collection of dues from resident tenants, but lords tried to maximize their utility. Probably in the early seventh century, churchmen in northern Gaul began to organize their villae into what came to be considered the classic form. They divided the land into two parts, one kept for direct exploitation on the lord's account (*mansus indominicatus,* reserve, demesne, home farm) and the other parceled out to peasant tenants. Where it existed, this bipartite villa deeply affected peasant rights to land, for it established their holdings and conditions of tenure.

Closely associated in space and time with estates organized into villae was a standard unit of tenant landholding called a *mansus* (early German: *huba*; English: hide). The Latin word derives from the verb *manere* (to remain), so it has some connotation of "secured" or "settled," but the central idea so expressed was "the land of one family." Its seventh-century appearance thus marks elite recognition that family farming units had become the norm among the post-Roman Western peasantry. The *mansus* reflected a division of tenant land into normative family subsistence farms, each provided with a farmstead, parcels of arable commensurate with productive capacity, and access to necessary nonarable resources. This did not make *manses* uniform in area, however. Regional differences arose from the natural fertility or intractability of the soil and, it seems, from larger or smaller family structures.

At the local level of each villa, moreover, *manses* formed a complex economic and juridical hierarchy. In villages of western Francia this normally at least distinguished larger "free" *manses* from smaller "servile" ones; Germany and Burgundy knew intermediate *manses lidiles* as well. Such distinctions of tenurial status (and consequent obligations) may once have corresponded to the personal status of the tenants, but by the early ninth century the tenant's legal position did not always accord with that of his land. Nor did whole *manses* last that long as actual units of possession. In the 810's, for instance, Abbot Irminon found on the estates of St. Germain-des-Prés many tenant families inhabiting half or even quarter *manses.* Just as the initial decisions to establish standard tenurial units are obscure, so are the motives for dividing them, whether the result of a lord's order, population growth, sale of peasant land, or division of an inheritance.

To speak of inheriting a *mansus* is a matter of fact, not law, for the tenants, servile or free, held only at the will of their lord under whatever he accepted as local custom or practice. Since, however, only the presence of tenants made the land remunerative to the lord, compulsion to remain in hereditary succession and to pay for that privilege was more likely than arbitrary expulsion of competent heirs. Lordly control over peasant mobility made much of Carolingian Europe a patchwork of densely settled village groupings separated by broad uninhabited expanses. Such control may have weakened with the decay of Carolingian authority, when more expansion of settlement began to occur without lordly direction and when more sale or exchange of tenant land is evident.

So the peasant's rights to the *mansus* had no status in public law, but his use of this resource was the source of his obligations to the lord. Not atypical of tenants throughout regions with villae, half-free ceorls of Hurstbourne Priors, Hampshire, about 900 owed the church of Winchester from each hide forty pence, six measures of beer, three sesters of wheat, all the labor to work three acres of arable, three pounds of barley, mowing of half an acre, the splitting of a stack of wood, sixteen poles for fencing, two ewes with two lambs and the shearing of these, "and work as they are bidden every week but three." The typical organization of the manor commonly made labor services a condition of tenure.

On early bipartite villae in seventh-century Gaul, unfree workers kept by the landowner still covered most of the labor needs of his demesne farm, for tenant labor services were then limited, often defined only as a fixed amount of land to be worked (the later lot-corvée). What would become the traditional corvée, labor obligations defined in days per week if not left unlimited, as at Hurstbourne, developed in eighth-century Neustria and Austrasia, where lords exercised some royal authority and where expansion of arable on the reserve required more labor. Thus the Carolingian villa, especially in the region between the middle Loire and the Rhine, treated all peasant tenures as economic satellites of the demesne: tenant *manses* supported labor to work the *mansus indominicatus,* a large grain farm. These classic manorial arrangements were also found in the Lombard plain during the eighth and ninth centuries and in pre-Viking England.

Villae did not dominate tenurial relations everywhere in the early medieval West. Estate owners in Gaul south of the Loire kept slaves to work their farms; those who tried tenant corvées soon abandoned them for hired laborers. In Aquitaine estates lacked the size and consolidation to establish dependent *manses*. Much property in Lombardy was too fragmented for any complex estate organization; by about 900 many demesne farms had already passed from direct management to leases for the lifetime of one or more persons. Further south in Italy, large consolidated holdings in the mountains served pastoral purposes, while highly fragmented holdings in the arable plains continued to be rented for payments in cash or in kind. East of the Rhine in Germany, classic manorial organization was a ninth-century introduction, long incomplete because most estates comprised isolated parcels and rights scattered over large and discontinuous areas. Here individual nuclei of lordship rights might have constituted a bipartite villa, but more distant properties and tenants yielded only a few dues. At this time genuine villae and labor rents had barely penetrated across the Pyrenees into Catalonia, but not further west into León and Galicia. In the absence of villae even dependent peasants had less of their lives directly structured by the demands of their lords.

Dependent agriculture engulfed less of early medieval rural life than it does of the extant written record. Free, landowning peasants survived but were of little interest to those who wrote the records lords wanted kept. In those, peasant allods appear only when their holders give them up—which they seem to have been able to do throughout this period. Peasant ownership under public law was always at risk, not only from the hazards of agriculture, political insecurity, and equal hereditary division, but also from the costs of public obligations incurred by free men.

NINTH THROUGH TWELFTH CENTURIES

Between late Carolingian times and the end of the twelfth century, rural Europe was dominated by large absentee landholders on whose properties lived dependent peasant farmers. Improved tenurial conditions came slowly to Western European peasants, and they endured greater nontenurial (seigneurial) exploitation. Opportunities and gains were piecemeal.

The many local varieties of early medieval peasant status groups and tenurial obligations greatly diminished by the end of the tenth century. Country people were more often considered an undifferentiated mass of villeins (*villani, rustici, manentes*). This evaporation of the old forms of servile and of free status came largely from the imposition of seigneurial authority (the private exercise of public power and jurisdiction) over all within a territory. Even free proprietors were hard pressed to defend their independence against a local potentate who asserted the right to judge and command them. Seigneurial lords gained ever more of their incomes from using their ban (power of command) to enforce lucrative monopolies (*banalités*) and impose arbitrary taxes (taille, *Bede*) irrespective of tenurial or personal status. No wonder later lawyers saw in such general peasant subjection to a superior's will grounds for the servitude of villeins.

Managerial and spatial units of Carolingian agriculture slowly disintegrated. Competitive struggles within the elite during the late ninth and tenth centuries, new conditional lordly tenures, and then the rise of new military groups dismembered many villae into several separate and smaller lordships; though some such properties were subsequently reconstituted, the average estate unit likely did not regain its earlier size. The *mansus,* in many places in the ninth century already endangered as the standard unit of peasant tenure, broke up under the pressure of population growth and institutional change. In Normandy a new kind of unit, the *charruée,* which measured land by the plow used to work it, was the norm by the eleventh century. A century later half- and quarter-*manses* still typified the Île-de-France and much of central Germany, but in Swabia, Alsace, Lorraine, and Flanders no standard unit survived and rents rested on individual parcels. English royal tax assessments used the hide (120 acres, on average), which lasted into the thirteenth century before yielding to the virgate (one-fourth hide) or bovate (one-eighth hide). Even where normative tenurial units remained, their progressive shrinking reflected greater human numbers and agricultural productivity.

Population and production growth in tenth- through twelfth-century Europe enabled some peasants to improve their condition by creating new arable on lands formerly unworked. At the simplest local level, farmers who squatted on little plots they carved from woodlands evaded many of the controls lords exercised over older villages. Scattered settlers were hard to manage for labor services, so the lord might be satisfied with money payments. More formal arrangements enter the documentary record when those who controlled empty land realized they could get more from it if farmers had incentives to take on the work. French and Catalan agreements called *complant* or *medium plantum* provided for five years of rent-free possession and then equal division of the new arable between the original owner and the *plantador,* who received a hereditary tenancy or even an allod. Most German or French migrants (*hospites*) were offered locally customary forms of hereditary free leaseholds or rental tenures. Along the advancing and insecure Spanish frontier, those willing to take up empty land held it by right of *aprisio* as freehold subjects of the king. In the tenth century they formed a zone of small peasant proprietors along much of the Duero Valley and in parts of Catalonia. Dutch and Flemish migrants went to northwestern Germany in the eleventh century, and others to the eastern Alps, for tenurial privileges and more self-government. By the twelfth century lords of long-settled territories found they had to compete or lose their peasants. This need coincided with older and gradual changes in the ways they managed their estates.

By the eleventh and twelfth centuries, classic manorial organizations in many areas had become unstable. Socioeconomic changes and redistribution of lordships within the elite, plus renewed opportunities for market exchange in the more dynamic parts of the West, gave impetus for innovation. In 1100 most lordships still contained demesne lands from which forced labor from peasant farmers yielded the lord needed revenues. But to run a demesne farm cost administrative time and effort, tied up capital, required continual dealing with often recalcitrant peasant laborers, and produced only local agricultural goods. Under less constrained conditions than those of the eighth or ninth century, other uses of land could be contemplated. Attempting these modified in several ways the old pattern of a manor with demesne farm, dependent tenant farms, and labor services.

A lord might lease the entire demesne on a fixed term to a large tenant who could manage all the resources directly. In France and parts of Germany, demesne leases were occasional in the early twelfth century and common by its end, sometimes being given for a share of the product (*bail à part des fruits*), more commonly going for a fixed annual payment (*bail à ferme*). This "farming" of whole manors was also used on some twelfth-century English monastic estates. Early leases given for life could conceal or inadvertently cause alienation of the property; later leaseholds normally had terms of three to twenty years. But lessees of large farms still faced the same labor problems as did owners. They might continue to coerce work from peasant subjects, they might rely on permanent staff (the *familia* or *servi quotidiani*), or they might hire village smallholders for daily wages. Escape from the exigencies of demesne agriculture came only by partitioning the large farm among settled or newly established tenants. Either choice raised rental incomes and lowered administrative costs. While few demesne farms had wholly disappeared by 1200, many were whittled away and still more had become leasehold farms worked by paid permanent or seasonal hands.

Decisions of eleventh- and twelfth-century estate owners about demesne lands affected labor obligations of tenants, setting three broad regional patterns. South of the Loire and the Alps, services had always been light and of little value to landowners. For those remaining, they quickly substituted cash payments. Further north on the Continent, obligations remained heavy around 1100 and even, in parts of Germany, increased. But many northern French, Low Countries, and German lords were learning it was easier to tap peasant resources and savings with their seigneurial powers and cheaper to employ day laborers than reluctant peasants. So they commuted to added rents the unwanted services, first general week-works (*opera*) and later lots-corvées and other specific tasks. This trend, which eliminated piecemeal those incidents of tenure that jurists used to define serfdom and which pushed tenurial relations toward the mere exchange of cash for land, became widespread by 1200. It had already reached logical extremes with the charters of franchise or of liberties issued for a price by twelfth-century lords. For example, the charter issued to Lorris (1108/1137), later copied and adapted for dozens of central French villages, codified and limited a wide variety of customary obligations. The result was legal freedom for the community and its members. Comparable exchanges of cash for liberty were called *Handfeste* in the German Rhineland. Elsewhere, German lords confirmed *Weistümer,* solemn declarations by the peasant communities of the customs by which they agreed to live. These did not grant legal freedom but did fix tenurial arrangements and personal rights. Through commutations, franchises, and *Weistümer,* stay-at-home peasants obtained for cash much of what migrants got for pioneering on new and privileged land.

Tenurial conditions had a third distinctive history in England. Except for the free sokemen holding for money rents in Danish settlement areas of the northeast and the peculiar free tenures of Kent, most late Anglo-Saxon and post-Conquest peasants held by what the Normans called "villein tenure," here defined as unfree and at the lord's will. Twelfth-century labor obligations were high. Free men might owe only specified plowing (boonworks, *precarie*), but villein tenements normally had weekworks (*opera*) three days in seven and more at seasonal peaks. Because English monarchs retained lucrative powers of command over people, the elite had to rely more on revenues from land and kept jealous control over it. Even lords with no immediate use for tenant labor permitted only ad hoc redemption for cash, so as not to impede their right to take it when they wished. Lawyers emphasized the arbitrary control lords wielded over peasant obligations and peasant use of land. In practice, however, needs of lords and peasants alike made local customs encourage continuity of tenure, hereditary succession, and even de facto sales—for which mercies the lords took payment (heriot, mortmain). Institutional peculiarities made English peasant tenures move hesitantly in directions well established elsewhere.

Synergy among rural social change, arable expansion, and innovative estate management promoted new tenurial norms in much of Western Europe: more and more peasant farmers were working the land of others as free tenants for rent. Tenures, called *censalis, hostise, censaux, en vilainage,* or *unter Erbzinsrecht,* owed a payment fixed by agreement between owner and tenants, whether by orally accepted custom or written contract, and whether the tenants acted collectively or as individuals. Individual written contracts became common in France only after 1200.

Rental tenants enjoyed greater security and more rights to convey holdings by inheritance, gift, or sale. Early agreements limited possession to the lives of two or three named individuals, but even landowners might hope that full perpetuity would encourage continuous occupancy and capital improvements. By the early twelfth century de facto hereditary transfer was common on many German estates and a more explicit *accensement à toujours* was well known in both the Île-de-France and the Mâconnais. For additional payments or higher rents, lords might convert such expectations to permanent and legally defensible hereditary rights, almost always with a token payment ("relief," "best beast") at the time of actual transfer. Critical for future evolution of regional agrarian regimes were the rules of inheritance each recognized: impartibility promoted the continuity of a few large farming units; partibility broke farms into constituent parcels. In most of France and southwestern Germany, the latter custom helped make distinct and separately held parcels the normal mode of landholding; working farms had temporary social and economic unity but not the permanent identity of the old *manses*.

Like effects might come when living tenants gained rights of alienation. These were more slowly won, for lords and kinfolk alike resisted the idea that a holder might sell the whole farm or pieces thereof to an outsider. As late as 1150 tenancy agreements by Parisian lords characteristically forbade sale or subdivision, and de facto arrangements in Germany limited such transactions to members of the village community; but by century's end most landowners willingly entertained offers from prospective buyers and sellers of payments to have these rules waived. Soon full rights of a tenant to sell were the custom, though almost always with an obligatory entry fine (*lods et ventes, Laudamien*) to the lord. This recognizance of his superior ownership right (*domaine éminent*) some customs made nominal and symbolic; others, a hefty and arbitrary share in the sale price. In the south of France the lord's consent signified waiver of his own preemption right (*retrait féodale*). Almost everywhere prospective heirs of the tenant persisted in asserting their own (kinsmen's) right (*retrait lignager*). The broad new tenant rights over the holding the lawyers called *domaine utile* or even, though erroneously, *proprietas.* The latter term rightly applied only to surviving true allods and to lands, like some in Tyrol, for which peasants bought with a one-time payment to the former owner complete freedom of possession under the territorial ruler (*Erbrecht*).

Rental tenants paid the landowner a predetermined annual rent (*census, cens, Zins*). Before the twelfth century rents were often fixed in kind, but thereafter progressively converted into coin. Original money rents accurately reflected the productive capacity and resale value of the land, but rising prices made them ever more nominal. Local peasant communities effectively resisted lords who tried to adjust their customary fixed rents upward. Another kind of rental tenancy, *tenure à champart* (*terrage, tâche, tasque, pressage*), kept up with inflation by making the rent a fixed proportion of the harvest, normally about 10 percent on northern French arable and 25 percent or more in the south or on vineyards. Probably devised for newly cleared land, *tenure à champart* did not involve capital goods provided by the landowner. More and more connected to tenure of the land itself were other obligations owed by twelfth-century and later peasant farmers: the tithe to the church, the taille or *Bede* to the seigneur, and specific payments in lieu of some *banalités*. The importance of these increased as inflation eroded rent values.

If many twelfth-century peasants were on the way to greater tenurial freedom vis-à-vis their landlords, they also felt countervailing constraints from their own communities. Earlier medieval peasants had often worked cooperatively with neighbors and kin, but the family farm was little subject to external control over farming practice. By the twelfth century, however, growing village communities in much of the West so pressed against their local resource base that customary regulation of land use gradually became a norm. In England, northern France, and the Rhineland the first clear evidence of villagers collectively determining crop rotations, harvest regulations, and common pasture on the stubble and fallow appears at this time. Some village communities also began to obtain collective tenure in nonarable resources.

The general evolution of land tenure in much of tenth- through twelfth-century Western Europe came from a real but limited and indirect influence of market relationships on agriculture. Market exchange had more immediate and thoroughgoing effects where commercial and urban development was precocious, as in northern and central Italy. Here the characteristic scatter of estate properties had given little incentive to create or retain classic manorial structures, so that even in the ninth century labor services were often small and leasehold tenure not uncommon. By the tenth century most villae were decaying, more rents were assessed and paid in cash, and labor services were virtually gone. Landowners who wanted more income granted uncultivated tracts to free tenants as *libelli,* long, fixed-term contractual tenancies, often alienable, and owing a fixed rent. Demesne lands, too, went out on lease, whether the traditional emphyteusis, the precaria, or the *libellus*. All this meant a relative separation of peasant activities from the concern of the landowner that culminated in owners freeing their servile tenants in order to gain direct control over lands once used to lodge them. At about the same time communes asserted political control over the countryside, which deprived landowners of seigneurial authority and compelled them to gain their livelihoods from urban activities or their lands. Forms of leasehold tenure became the norm. Owners not constrained by long leases at uneconomic rents aimed to shorten the terms by which they let out their land and to impose commercial values on it. Economic, rather than traditional, leases appeared by the end of the twelfth century on lands worked by free cultivators near the burgeoning towns of Flanders, which arose almost as early as in Italy.

Conversely, a relative lag in tenurial conditions marked those areas of the Continent newly added during the tenth and eleventh centuries to the cultural community of Western Christendom. In Viking and post-Viking Scandinavia, most land was held by free farmers in hereditary ownership (*bóndi* on *odal* land). They deferred to wealthier community leaders, who also put out land to free or slave tenants. All free men owed military service to the king, though by the twelfth century this obligation was becoming a land tax. In east-central Europe free peasant agriculturalists of early medieval Slavic and Hungarian tribal groupings slipped into dependency with the tenth- and eleventh-century creation of rudimentary state structures. Mid-twelfth-century rural populations included many groups defined by the specific services they owed to state officials and/or private landowning magnates. Few were then construed as free. The Spanish frontier against Islam advanced from the Duero to the Tagus and the lower Ebro in the eleventh and twelfth centuries, sometimes, as along the Catalan coast, promoted by privileged tenures for new settlers and elsewhere organized into large estates for churchmen, magnates, and military orders. Muslim landowners and sharecroppers often became tenants of new Christian possessors. In the Western kingdoms, settlers commonly received revocable rental tenements called *prestimonia.* Only where monarchs created urban-centered municipal districts under their own authority were free landowning farmers and pastoralists the norm.

THE LATER MIDDLE AGES

By the late twelfth century the regional character of rural cultures in Western Christendom was fully established. Tenurial conditions in the last three centuries of the Middle Ages are understandable less as deviations around a norm and more as a complex of interrelated regional developments. Lords and peasants in different antecedent institutional environments responded to long-term economic trends, notably the late phases of high medieval expansion and then the depopulations and crises of the fourteenth and early fifteenth centuries.

In the French-speaking lands from the Loire Valley and Burgundy north, movements of agricultural expansion and commutation culminated in the thirteenth century by spreading to the properties of lesser lords. Traditional manorial regimes continued slowly to erode, especially by reduction of direct operation of demesne farms in favor of leases to cultivators. High demand for such leases from the growing population, and the hazard of fixed returns at a time of rising prices, encouraged landowners to shorten terms of leases from life to six, nine, twelve, or twenty-four years and, even in the north, to take shares in the crop rather than fixed money payments. Inflation also weakened the relative value of those seigneurial charges which had been commuted to cash. Peasant farmers often worked parcels belonging to several different owners, normally as customary rental tenancies (*censive, hostise,* or *en vilainage*). Until the mid 1300's hereditary subdivision in an expanding population shrank the size of such peasant holdings and forced those with lands that provided less than the minimum for subsistence to take low-paying wage work on larger farms.

Famine, epidemic, and war in the fourteenth century sharply reversed rural conditions in northern France, dealing a near-fatal blow to the seigneurial economy and giving advantages to those peasants who survived. In a depopulated countryside land was cheap and human labor dear. When most attempts in France to reimpose servile obligations failed, high labor costs accelerated lords' withdrawal from direct exploitation. They leased entire demesnes at long terms and fixed rates, and carved others into new rental tenancies, thus putting a piecemeal end to most classic manorial arrangements. At the same time, abandoned farms and devalued coinages reduced returns from rent rolls and *banalités.* Formal improvements in tenures now helped peasants less than did the ease with which they could find better opportunities. By inheritance from the many who died, survivors gained marginally larger farms; they even refused tenures too heavily burdened with services. Some obtained operational control over more land by long-term leases of former demesnes. Dynasties of these *fermiers* appeared around Cambrai by the 1420's. When conditions improved, such people were well placed to gain more.

The rural reconstruction that began a new wave of economic expansion after 1450 built upon tenurial trends established during the crisis. To attract newcomers willing to restore production on land abandoned by customary tenants, lords assembled larger peasant holdings and let them out as fully free hereditary tenures owing a perpetual money rent and seigneurial dues. Some absentees returned to direct management of their reserves. Most, however, leased small and eccentric parcels to tenants wishing to round off their own holdings and consolidated the main body of their demesne lands into large, self-contained farms of thirty or more hectares (seventy-five or more acres). Called *ferme* in the Paris basin and *cense* in Artois and the Cambrésis, these were put out on lease to well-capitalized and skilled farm operators. A *fermier* owed traditional dues, minor services, and a low symbolic entry fine, but mainly a large fixed rent in kind or, more often, cash. *Ferme* leases ran for about ten years. By 1500, then, many rural areas in the north of France had established a distinctive differentiation between a few large peasant *fermiers* (*coqs du village,* village aristocracy) and a much greater number of smallholders, only the most fortunate of whom could support their families from their lands alone.

Other tenurial patterns developed south of Burgundy and the Loire. Average peasant holdings were smaller than in the north, though often including bits of allodial land (some from long use of the *complant* contract). This region, too, passed from a high man-land ratio around 1300 to much lower population densities in the late fifteenth century, but more general poverty hampered emergence of a well-off peasant elite. Fifteenth-century conditions in Auvergne, Languedoc, and the Pyrenees encouraged formation of extended family households (*frérèches*) whose joint tenure of loose, medium-sized holdings covered farm labor needs without external costs. Special tenurial arrangements for local conditions especially favored the *métayage* (in Provence, *facherie*) sharecropping contract. Around Toulouse, fifteenth-century lords made from their reserves unitary farms called *bordes,* at ten to thirty hectares (twenty-five to seventy-five acres) somewhat bigger than traditional village holdings. These they put out with a complex local variant of *métayage:* the lessee contributed half to two-thirds of production costs, including all labor, and retained half the produce from the fields and 70 to 80 percent from the vineyards; livestock was the subject of a separate contract. Leases of *bordes* were short-term and neither hereditary nor partible. In Poitou sharecropping tenure was used to remodel the countryside after 1450. Seigneurs bought out customary tenants and reorganized the land into coherent *métairies,* each with a farmstead and acreage appropriate for use by a single family with the necessary stock and capital. The tenant paid half of all produce and had no rights to woodland or waters.

Movement of the manorial economy in the Low Countries resembled that of neighboring French regions, but tenurial regimes were more influenced by urban and commercial development in the south and by reclamation of marshlands in the north. Most Flemish abbeys had by the twelfth century put their granges out to perpetual lease, though in the thirteenth century they tried, where possible, to use leases for a specific term (six to twelve years) instead. Villein tenures early came through commutation and fixing of low hereditary rents to resemble those held by free peasants or *hospites;* many thirteenth-century tenants then used single quitclaim payments to gain full ownership rights. But both landlords and the dense rural population of Flanders were so impoverished in the fourteenth century that much land passed from both to wealthy townspeople. Peasant farms remained very small (two to three hectares, or five to seven acres around late-fourteenth-century Ghent), and Flanders became known for intense peasant self-exploitation and nonagricultural by-employment. Unlike some lords elsewhere, Flemish landowners continued in the fourteenth and fifteenth centuries to offer emancipations for a fee; the last serf disappeared from this region by the sixteenth century. Landowners did, however, try to take more dues in kind and, where the death of hereditary tenant lineages gave them the opportunity, shifted perpetual tenures to leaseholds of four to six years. Much of Holland was settled by draining and colonizing vast peat bogs between the eleventh and the fourteenth centuries. Pioneers received free tenures in full ownership; Dutch lords exercised only seigneurial authority over them.

Into much of western Germany, where German dialects were spoken and the Carolingians had ruled (except for Thuringia and Bavaria), manorial organization had penetrated only slowly eastward. Its decay likewise was tardy and partial. Some areas had rural institutions affected by important expansions of settlement. Many regions were much depopulated during the later Middle Ages, but political fragmentation meant some lords had the power to stop peasants from taking advantage of their own scarcity. Thus tenurial conditions developed kaleidoscopic variety.

The westernmost areas along the middle Rhine most resembled lands further west in their once nearly complete organization as villae and, by 1200, the advancing breakup of these. Peasant tenants gained hereditary rights and fixed rents; some even achieved full ownership. On the third or more of the land that remained in the lords' hands throughout the later Middle Ages, leasehold tenure predominated. But in this region the old organizations of permanent farm servants, the *familiae* of unfree *Laten*, rarely were wholly abandoned and emancipated. Housed without land, they became laborers and *Leibeigene* (serfs), still less than fully free, though their former duties were now mostly converted to dues. Where surviving demesne farms made labor of value to landowners, the latter used their judicial powers to draft youths from *Laten* and customary tenant families to serve as farmhands (*Gesindezwangsdienst*).

Further east, across the Rhine, two central areas exhibit how different neighboring conditions could be. Peasants in Hesse had major tenurial disadvantages: traditional servitude lasted well into the fourteenth century and then became *Leibeigenschaft* (personal subjection) to the territorial ruler, who was also the largest landowner; servile (*Leibrecht*) and arbitrary (*Lassrecht*) tenures gave no hereditary security; obligations were fixed only toward the end of the Middle Ages. In Franconia, however, free settlement with good tenures on royal land influenced older properties as well; by the fourteenth century traditional serfdom was gone. Small demesne farms remained common through the later Middle Ages, but labor services lapsed. Most Franconian peasants held hereditary rental tenancies (*Erbzinsrecht*) even if in the important ecclesiastical territories in the fifteenth century they became personal *Leibeigene* of their rulers.

The north and the south of western Germany developed other contrasts. In both Lower Saxony and the region from Alsace to the Bavarian border, the twelfth- and thirteenth-century decay of villae left large former demesne farms (*Meierhöfe, Dinghöfe*) in the hands of heirs to manorial officials as relatively consolidated blocks amid smaller tenant farms. Fixed-term leases gradually became hereditary. In Saxony late medieval territorial rulers defined and limited the obligations of *Meierrecht* and enforced rules of impartible inheritance so as to protect these important taxpayers. The region became one of a few large peasant farms that, with surviving landlord farms of comparable size, hired labor from neighboring smallholders. In the southwest, partible inheritance practices fragmented customary tenancies and *Dinghöfe* alike; absentee holders further split many of the latter into parcels leased to peasant operators. Thus the predominantly small farms there came to owe, from lands of whatever legal origin, comparable money rents, while the few labor services exacted went not to landowners but to holders of public high-justice rights. From the late fourteenth century, however, the latter used these claims to establish the personal *Leibeigenschaft* of their subjects, more a matter of political subjection and economic obligation than of land tenure.

Among regions with much manorial agriculture, England was in the thirteenth century distinctive for its significant departure from trends elsewhere. Beginning around 1200, English lords took advantage of favorable prices for agricultural produce and their authority over villein tenants to reinvigorate direct exploitation and halt or retract commutation. They let demesne leases lapse, enforced labor services, and, as heavy peasant populations competed for land, raised fines for entry to customary tenures. This heyday of "high farming" lasted a century and more. Weakening grain prices before the Black Death began to reverse the trend; high labor costs thereafter put to landlord farming in England the same definitive end they did elsewhere. Long leases and grants of demesnes to political henchmen, then division into rental tenancies, left little arable in lords' hands. They often retained good pasture for sheep, but by the end of the fifteenth century in England, as elsewhere, the very large grain farms that had for nearly a millennium dominated the agrarian institutions of northwestern Europe were extinct.

English villein tenure was wholly unfree in 1300, but a general movement toward commutation was under way by mid century. Rarely did this involve explicit grants or changes in the formal basis of tenure, for it remained customary. Needing to hold and attract tenants in a time of demographic decline and less concerned to extract labor from them, English lords bargained away their claims in agreements with individuals. The terms were recorded in the manor court roll, so that customary tenure came to be called "copyhold." On most manors the copyhold tenant came to pay only customarily fixed entry fines and annual cash rents for land held for the lives of several named persons, if not hereditarily, unless he chose to exercise his rights to sublet or alienate it and to depart the manor. By the 1450's English common-law courts, which had always refused jurisdiction over villein tenures, were treating copyholds as free.

Rural land tenure in peninsular and peripheral regions of Western Christendom evolved during the thirteenth through sixteenth centuries in ways other than those of the continental and English northwest. During the Reconquest most Spanish and Portuguese farm operators achieved reasonably firm rights to their holdings. In the 1200's free peasant proprietors with obligations to the king alone dominated lands between the Duero and Tagus, much of Valencia, Majorca, and parts of Algarve and Andalusia. Subsequently their independence weakened as the royal domain passed to favored magnates; many became tenants of large absentee owners and *hombres de behetría,* commended freemen subject to their lords. Tenant farming had long been the norm in northern Portugal, Galicia, northern Castile, Aragon, and Catalonia, though the availability of alternatives on the frontier bettered conditions in those regions during the twelfth and thirteenth centuries. When the late-thirteenth-century halt of the Reconquest removed this outlet, lords quashed the right of their tenants to leave freely. Guarantees of mobility in late-thirteenth-century Castilian laws were abrogated in the next generation. Catalan legislation of 1283 bound tenants to the land as *payeses de remensa* (redemption peasants), permitted to depart only after paying a fee set by the landlord. Against this and other "evil customs" Catalan peasants agitated and rebelled from the late fourteenth century on, finally achieving de facto freedom in 1462 and formal abolition in 1486, both from monarchs then in conflict with the landowners. The mass of the rural population on the southern and central plateau and in Andalusia never possessed land. On the vast estates of magnates and military orders, peasants with their own plow teams might be alloted parcels on annual contracts for payments in kind, but most country people worked for an annual, monthly, or daily cash wage.

Rural institutions in southern Italy and Sicily bore some similarity to those of southern Spain. Noble *latifondi* covered large areas devoted both to pastoral and to arable farming. On the latter, peasants normally worked for wages, though in parts of Sicily seasonal tenancies were not rare. *Paraspolari* worked a designated parcel of the lord's land, using the lord's seed and capital equipment, for a portion of the harvest. Other tenants paid rents in kind, services, or shares. Servile burdens were not unknown: fifteenth-century *angararii* had no right to leave their holdings.

Late medieval tenurial developments in the economically advanced parts of Italy north of Rome still are not well understood, in part because it is difficult to synthesize the great variety revealed by local studies. By the late twelfth and thirteenth centuries customary tenancies everywhere paid fairly low rents and were seen as perpetual and alienable. Many achieved quasi-proprietary status. An active land market accentuated historic fragmentation of holdings at all levels. But countermovements are also visible throughout the later Middle Ages. From the thirteenth century, at least, landownership was slowly restructured as both traditional large *signori* and peasant proprietors sold out for cash to city people and new nobles, whose estates of middling size were, at times, more consolidated. Landowners who could extinguish customary tenurial claims organized from the welter of small, separately held parcels larger and more coherent family farms (*poderi* in Tuscany, Emilia, and Umbria; *cascine* in Lombardy). These they put out as leaseholds, either *afitto* (for long-term fixed rents) or as *mezzadria*. Sharecropping was known in earlier medieval Italy, but in the north it spread rapidly from the twelfth century under the specific form of the *mezzadria*. Around Siena in 1316 one-third of all properties and more than three-fourths of leaseholds had this contractual character. Though variations were common, in a typical *mezzadria* the landowner contributed the land and much working capital for half of the returns. These leases ran for as few as one or two seasons, during which the tenant had strict obligations for performance of work and maintenance. So long as he was in debt to the landowner, he could not vacate the holding. *Mezzadria* remained the single most common peasant tenure in late medieval and postmedieval Italy.

Rural depopulation in late medieval Italy hastened replacement of customary with commercial leasehold tenures. Some urban authorities took effective measures against peasant mobility to ensure a continued supply of tenants and laborers. The latter worked on large estate farms leased whole for short terms to peasant or urban entrepreneurs (*fittabili, mercanti di compagna*). Sharper inequality of wealth among country people was reflected in legislative distinctions like that drawn in fifteenth-century Emilia among *bubulci* (cattlemen or cultivators), *bracentes* (laborers), and *familiares apactoati* (farmhands).

Tenurial developments in central continental Europe first followed, then diverged from, trends further west. Interior regions of Germany formed zones of transition. Thuringia and Upper Saxony in the center, and the Bavarian and Austrian lands of the southeast, in the twelfth and thirteenth centuries had old manorial settlements and tracts of recently colonized land. In the former territories institutional arrangements were perfected in the mid twelfth century that were used to promote settlement by free migrants still further east. Under such influences personal servitude vanished by the end of the thirteenth century. Thuringian and Saxon peasants lived in strong village communities and paid firmly fixed dues from either hereditary rental tenancies or what were thought of by jurists as "encumbered property" (*zinsbelastete Eigentum*). By the fifteenth century, however, some of these people had such small holdings that they made much of their living from wage work, and most of them owed labor services about one day a week. These they performed on the farms of their landlords, who also usually had judicial authority over the tenants.

The slow wasting away of villae in the southeastern German-speaking lands followed, from the twelfth through the fifteenth century, a now familiar process. It left extensive lordly reserves and, in the hands of *Meier*, the privileged holdings of well-endowed manorial stewards. Peasants in areas of new settlement had tenurial and personal freedom; in fourteenth- and fifteenth-century Tyrol the annually revocable *Freistift* (free lease) gave way to more secure hereditary rental tenure. In most of Bavaria, however, landownership and judicial authority were united and tenures were the weak *Freistift* or *Leibrecht* (servile customary tenure). Lords with like advantages in fifteenth-century Austria started to enlarge their demesne farms, either using land abandoned by tenants or expelling those with insecure rights. They sought to revoke freedoms dating back to the medieval clearances and to reimpose labor services. By century's end, lords in much of the southeast were combining rental incomes and large-scale direct control over rural production and marketing to form what modern scholars call *Wirtschaftsherrschaft* (economic lordship).

The pattern of delayed but extensive free settlement and development, followed by a strong shift at the close of the Middle Ages to lord-dominated, large-scale agriculture, is clear across all of east-central Europe, from Pomerania and Prussia in the north to Hungary in the south. During the later twelfth century, Czech and Polish rulers encouraged development of unfarmed areas by granting to *hospites* secure tenures and judicial privileges; Hungarian kings followed suit somewhat later. Meanwhile, in the trans-Elbe territories of Brandenburg, Mecklenburg, and Pomerania, both German conquerors and germanizing indigenous rulers found especially suited to their improvement plans the arrangements for new settlement recently worked out along the Elbe. As these techniques were spread eastward and proved as useful for reforming existing lordships as for establishing new ones, they came collectively to be called "German law" (*ius Theutonicum*). Put simply, a landowner made an oral agreement with a settlement entrepreneur (*locator*), who undertook to establish a village with either migrants or indigenous unfree peasants. The *locator* arranged to endow each tenant with arable and other resources in the village lands and to collect from each an annual rental payment, fixed in kind and/or in money and assessed uniformly on arable acreage. This he in turn paid to the lord. Peasants and tenures were free, governed by recognized customary law in a village court chaired by a hereditary village headman (*Schulze, scultetus, soltys*), normally the *locator* himself. The *Schulz* received for his services a hereditary rent-free holding larger than that of other peasants. Few German-law tenants owed labor services; all had fully hereditary and alienable rights. The German law and local customs modeled on it founded new villages and reformed old ones all across east-central Europe: more than a fifth of the villages in Great Poland had it by 1369. Landowners traded their claims to peasant services for much larger money incomes from better-populated estates. Direct exploitation farms shrank in size and used wage labor. Peasants gained freedom and security of tenure. Thus the trend from the late twelfth into the fourteenth century followed Western precedents, though many participants were indigenes.

Free and secure peasant tenure did not survive the fifteenth century in east-central Europe. Peasant well-being and peasant numbers suffered from crop failures, epidemics, and wars, while landowners found fixed or falling returns from their rental lands ever less adequate for their climbing expenses. Rising noble influence in the east-central European states made possible strong countermeasures. One was to stop peasants from leaving their holdings: legal curbs, then bans, on tenants departing were enacted from the mid fifteenth century on. Another was to expand production of marketable agricultural surpluses from land in the lords' hands, old demesne farms, deserted rental lands, or even those of tenants deemed, in a 1423 Polish statute, "useless and recalcitrant." When labor shortages threatened to drive up wage rates, even with limits on peasant movement, compulsory labor (*robot*) was introduced, sometimes in lieu of rents the impoverished could not otherwise pay. Peasant tenants in parts of Poland owed one day in seven in the early 1400's, and three a century later. Legal protection from village courts was circumvented when the lord's own bailiffs replaced hereditary *Schulzen*. All these measures were confirmed and enforced by late-fifteenth-century laws imposing landlord jurisdiction on all peasants without appeal to royal courts. When the Bohemian Constitution of 1500 called all non-nobles "destined to servitude" and legislation imposing serfdom followed elsewhere within a few decades, these formalized a tenurial revolution that, during the fifteenth century, turned east-central Europe onto a path wholly different from that of the West.

Less severely impaired was the tenurial position of late medieval Scandinavian cultivators. In the thirteenth century free peasant proprietors and tenants (*landbo, leilending, colonus*) had fiscal obligations to the crown, though these were changing from military service to payment of tax. Peasant freeholds likely covered as much as half the arable.

Tenants paid their landlords entry fees (*staedja, gipt*) and annual rents (*landgille, avrad*) in a mixture of grain and coin for renewable leasehold tenures running from a year in Denmark to six or eight years in parts of Sweden. The Scandinavian countryside suffered impoverishment and depopulation during the fourteenth and fifteenth centuries. Owners of rental land saw their incomes fall and responded by curbing the rights of their tenants. In Denmark an exit fee (*forlov*) was introduced, followed by *vornedskab,* a requirement that tenants remain in their native village and take up empty farms. Fifteenth-century Swedish laws forbade departure before expiry of the lease and permitted some labor services. Taxes posed the main threat to landowning peasants. Nobles and the church had gained exemption for their own farms and then the right to take taxes from the farms of their tenants; peasant proprietors owed the same payment to the crown and thus came to be thought of as "royal peasants." When financially weakened, they might prefer to sell their land and enter into tenancy, thus depriving the king of their taxes. To protect these fiscal resources, monarchs legislated preemptive rights for kinsmen, prohibited sales to the tax-exempt, and even, as in Sweden in 1396, nullified all sales from the previous generation. Still, from the fourteenth century on, land in peasant ownership shrank continually.

Land tenure in Celtic societies on the northwestern edge of medieval Europe maintained distinctive features despite external influences. In traditional patron-client relationships, landowners of high status and free peasants exchanged enjoyment of land for renders of the food it produced. Bondsmen worked the chief's holding. Stricter definitions of property rights tended to come via England, whether slowly, as in Wales, or more abruptly, as in Scotland in the century after David I (1124–1153) or during the Anglo-Norman invasion of Ireland from the 1160's. The lordship structures thus diffused were something more than traditional paternalism; by the later thirteenth century, rural relationships in Wales and southern Scotland resembled those of neighboring English counties. Anglo-Norman conquerors reduced Irish peasants to agricultural serfs (*betagh*) and offered the free "burgage tenure" of English towns to induce Englishmen to settle on Irish land. Free Irish communities held to their old customs and, as the Anglo-Norman tide turned after 1300, absorbed many Anglo-Irish into norms of indigenous brehon law.

In Scotland personal servitude disappeared by the early fourteenth century, but in many areas labor services and rents in kind remained central to landlord-tenant relations. The end of serfdom also meant the end of the peasant's hereditary link with the land. Fourteenth-century tenants held by several different rights. A "tack" was a one-to-five-year lease, slowly shifting to a life tenure during and after the fifteenth century. Tenure "at will" was more precarious, really just year-to-year. Most Scots agriculturalists were "kindly tenants," a term with unstable and local meanings but generally implying some expectancy of unimpeded occupancy and the right to pass it on to an heir. Better than these and analogous to good tenures common elsewhere was the feu, a perpetual lease at fixed annual rent. Feuing occurred on some church lands as early as the twelfth century, but it spread rapidly only at the end of the fifteenth, when lords hoped more security would promote higher productivity and higher rents. The effect was blunted when feus went to overtenants or tacksmen who profited by subletting to cultivators on short terms. Older patriarchal arrangements survived in the Highlands, where the typical clansman held by temporary tack, though kindly (unhindered occupation, with the right to pass it to an heir) and with a right called *duthchas* suggesting customary inheritance. Only the northern islands contained peasant freeholds, *odal* tenures after the practice of Norse settlers, which survived beyond 1500.

BIBLIOGRAPHY

Jerome Blum, "The Rise of Serfdom in Eastern Europe," in *American Historical Review,* **62** (1957); *Cambridge Economic History of Europe,* I, *The Agrarian Life of the Middle Ages,* Michael M. Postan, ed., 2nd ed. (1966); Francis L. Carsten, *The Origins of Prussia* (1954); Robert A. Dodgshon, *Land and Society in Early Scotland* (1981); Georges Duby, *Rural Economy and Country Life in the Medieval West,* Cynthia Postan, trans. (1968), *The Early Growth of the European Economy,* Howard B. Clarke, trans. (1974), and, as editor, *Histoire de la France rurale,* I–II (1975); H. P. R. Finberg, ed., *The Agrarian History of England and Wales,* I, pt. 2, *A.D. 43–1042* (1972); Guy Fourquin, *Lordship and Feudalism in the Middle Ages* (1976); Walter Goffart, *Caput and Colonate* (1974); J. N. Hillgarth, *The Spanish Kingdoms, 1250–1516,* 2 vols. (1976–1978); J. A. van Houtte, *An Economic History of the Low Countries, 800–1800* (1977); Arnold H. M. Jones, *The Later Roman Empire, 284–602,* II (1964); Robert Latouche, *The Birth of Western Economy: Economic Aspects of the*

Dark Ages, E. M. Wilkinson, trans. (1961, 2nd ed. 1967); Archibald R. Lewis, *The Development of Southern French and Catalan Society, 718–1050* (1965); Friedrich Lütge, *Geschichte der deutschen Agrarverfassung vom frühen Mittelalter bis zum 19. Jahrhundert* (1963); László Makkai, "Neo-Serfdom: Its Origin and Nature in East Central Europe," in *Slavic Review,* **34** (1975); Edward Miller and John Hatcher, *Medieval England—Rural Society and Economic Change 1086–1348* (1978); Alexander C. Murray, *Germanic Kinship Structure: Studies in Law and Society in Antiquity and the Early Middle Ages* (1983); Joseph F. O'Callaghan, *A History of Medieval Spain* (1975); Michael M. Postan, *The Medieval Economy and Society: An Economic History of Britain in the Middle Ages* (1972); Norman J. G. Pounds, *An Economic History of Medieval Europe* (1974); B. H. Slicher van Bath, *The Agrarian History of Western Europe, A.D. 500–1850,* Olive Ordish, trans. (1963, repr. 1966); Chris Wickham, *Early Medieval Italy: Central Power and Local Society, 400–1000* (1981).

RICHARD C. HOFFMANN

[See also **Agriculture and Nutrition; Allod; Ban, Banalités; Barbarians, Invasions of; Benefice, Ecclesiastical; Benefice, Lay; Burgage Tenure; Class Structure, Western; Colonus; Copyhold; Corvée; Family; Feudalism; Fief; Grain Crops, Western European; Heriot; Hide; Inheritance, Western European; Law; Mortmain; Peasants' Rebellion; Serfs and Serfdom; Slavery, Slave Trade; Taille, Tallage; Taxation; Tithes; Tools, Agricultural; Villages; Virgate.**]

TEREM. The *terem,* in Russian medieval domestic architecture, usually refers to the upper-story abode of women. But the most famous *terem* is the Palace of the Tsar in the Moscow Kremlin, sometimes called the Terem Palace, built largely in the seventeenth century. It is noted for its rooms of state and private apartments.

BIBLIOGRAPHY

Kathleen Berton, *Moscow: An Architectural History* (1977), 76–78.

ANN E. FARKAS

TERMINISM is the approach to logic that determines the truth or falsity of statements by the way in which terms are used in propositions. Although the label "terminists" (*terministae*) came into use only in the fifteenth century, the approach had its roots in the late-twelfth- and early-thirteenth-century treatises on the properties of terms (*de proprietatibus terminorum*). These treatises concerned signification, supposition, syncategorematic terms, relation, appellation, restriction, and distribution. They supplemented Aristotle's examination of predication, the categories, syllogisms, argumentation, demonstration, and fallacies. By the mid thirteenth century the various aspects of terminist logic, sometimes referred to by modern scholars as the *logica modernorum,* were brought together in textbooks by William of Sherwood (Shyreswood), Peter of Spain, and Lambert of Auxerre. Other treatises in terminist logic were gradually added in the thirteenth and early fourteenth centuries—specifically, treatises on sophisms (logical problems whose difficulty lay in the use of terms in propositions), insolubles (self-contradictory propositions), consequences (logical inference), and obligations (rules of argumentation and inference when, in debate, one was "obliged" to argue within the framework of certain given presuppositions).

In the fourteenth century the study of the function of terms in propositions came to dominate logic, first at Oxford, then at Paris, and eventually at centers of study in Germany and northern Italy. Throughout that century terminist logic was compatible—but not synonymous—with nominalism. William of Ockham's *Summa logicae* (1320–1324), which adopted a nominalist approach to universals, and Walter Burley's *De puritate artis logicae* (later redaction *ca.* 1326–1328), based on realist presuppositions, were both organized around the fundamental importance of the meaning of terms in propositions. Similarly the logical works of Jean Buridan, Albert of Saxony, Marsilius of Inghen, Pierre d'Ailly, and John Gerson were terminist.

By the opening years of the fifteenth century the supporters of terminism were opposing themselves to those who, through the revival of the thought of Thomas Aquinas and Albert the Great, were limiting logic to the writings of and commentaries on Aristotle. In addition to the latter group's adherence to the logic of the ancients (*logica antiquorum*), they determined the truth or falsity of propositions according to those things to which the propositions refer. In this way terminism gradually came to be associated with nominalism, which refused to consider abstract concepts or grammatical structures to be actually existing entities. Those of nominalist persuasion became the principal defenders of terminist logic. By contrast, the realists became the defenders of a logic based on things rather than terms and rejected the treatises on the properties of terms in the name of a more faithful adherence to the logical works of Aristotle.

BIBLIOGRAPHY
Étienne Gilson, *History of Christian Philosophy in the Middle Ages* (1955); William C. Kneale and Martha Kneale, *The Development of Logic* (1962), chap. 4; Alfonso Maierù, *Terminologia logica della tarda scolastica* (1972).

WILLIAM J. COURTENAY

[See also **Ailly, Pierre d'; Albert of Saxony; Aristotle in the Middle Ages; Buridan, Jean; Burley, Walter; Dialectic; Gerson, John; Logic, Islamic; Nominalism; Ockham, William of; Peter of Spain; Philosophy and Theology, Western European.**]

TERRA SIGILLATA, Roman tableware of a glossy red clay ceramic, richly decorated with relief designs of masks, garlands, mythological figures, and so forth. The name derives from the seals used to stamp pieces with the name of the artisan. Also known as *aretina,* most of this ware was made in Arezzo and exported. Imitations were produced in northern Europe, France, and Spain.

BIBLIOGRAPHY
Hans Dragendorff, *Terra Sigillata* (1895).

MARY GRIZZARD

TESSERA (probably from Greek *tessares,* four), a small, usually roughly cubic piece of stone, glass (from the first century B.C. on), or, less commonly, terracotta or mother-of-pearl set in mortar to form a mosaic. Glass tesserae, produced by sandwiching metallic leaf between a sheet of transparent glass and a thin glass sealer to protect the metal, provide the widest range of colors, including gold and silver. Glass tesserae were cut from larger sheets and therefore have dull and, along the fresh cuts, glossy sides, a condition exploited by better mosaicists.

Divinities and initiates on a processional barge. Fragment of a *terra sigillata* dish from Roman Egypt, 1st–3rd centuries. NEW YORK, THE METROPOLITAN MUSEUM OF ART, GIFT OF J. PIERPONT MORGAN, 1917 (17.194.2039)

The glass cubes were expensive and difficult to produce; hence, old mosaics were sometimes dismantled and the glass cubes reused. Such recycling, apparent from the dulled and sometimes pitted surfaces of the cubes that resulted when the old tesserae were heated to burn off any mortar adhering to them, occurred both in Byzantium and, characteristically, Carolingian Rome.

LESLIE BRUBAKER

[See also **Mosaic and Mosaic Making.**]

TETRACONCH. A conch is a semicircular apse or large niche surmounted by a half dome. A tetraconch is a building whose plan consists of four conchs disposed around a central space; a triconch plan has three conchs, and so on. In use mainly from the late fifth to the seventh century, the type appeared first in the West (Milan) and somewhat later in the East (Syria, Armenia).

BIBLIOGRAPHY
Richard Krautheimer, *Early Christian and Byzantine Architecture,* 3rd ed. (1979).

GREGORY WHITTINGTON

[See also **Apse; Early Christian and Byzantine Architecture.** Illustrations at **Aštarak; Gelard.**]

TETRAMORPH (from the Greek *tetra,* "four," and *morph,* "shape"), the union into a single figure of the four symbols of the Evangelists, based on the figure in Ezekiel's vision (Ezek. 1:10), in contrast to the four separate figures as described in the Apocalypse (Rev. 4:7). Examples in medieval book illumination include a tetramorph preceding St. Jerome's prologue to the Gospels in the eighth-century Trier Gospels (Dombibliothek, 61/134 fol. 5v). Matthew's symbol, the man, has the appendages of the ox (Luke's symbol), the lion (Mark's symbol), and the eagle (John's symbol).

BIBLIOGRAPHY

Ormonde Maddock Dalton, *Byzantine Art and Archaeology* (1911, repr. 1961), 676; Carl Nordenfalk, *Celtic and Anglo-Saxon Painting: Book Illumination in the British Isles, 600–800* (1977), 93.

JENNIFER E. JONES

[See also **Cherub (with illustrations); Early Christian Art; Evangelist Symbols.**]

TEUTONIC KNIGHTS. See **Chivalry, Orders of.**

TEXTBOOKS. The medieval textbook is largely a product of the institutionalization of the university and its curriculum in the thirteenth century. Instruction in the universities consisted primarily of commenting upon texts according to the Scholastic or dialectical method of question and answer. Because teachers based the determination of philosophical and theological premises on authoritative works, and the student successfully attained the degree only by mastering the writings on which the master lectured, there resulted formal lists of required reading for each discipline and faculty. Furthermore, the introduction into the Latin West of the majority of the known writings of Aristotle not only provided the logical framework for Scholasticism but also presented the university with an increasing number of treatises to use as textbooks. As the university became more and more defined and organized during the course of the thirteenth century, a standard curriculum with mandatory texts came into existence. It lasted, with only minor changes, until the end of the Middle Ages.

Aristotle had a place in the arts course of the twelfth century. Since the ninth century the West had known Boethius' translations of Aristotle's logical works, the *Categoriae* and *De interpretatione.* These two treatises formed the basis for the new school of theology at Paris that used the dialectical form of reasoning made fashionable by Peter Abelard and others. John of Salisbury (*ca.* 1125–1180), in his *Metalogicon,* a particularly good source for our knowledge of twelfth-century education, discussed and lamented the increasing influence of dialectic and philosophy. He clearly emphasized the need for familiarity with the writers of ancient Rome and for the traditional disciplines of the trivium (grammar, logic, and rhetoric) and the quadrivium (arithmetic, geometry, astronomy, and music). These subjects provided the foundation for the education of a free man (hence the term "seven liberal arts").

Students had few works to study during the early Middle Ages. For grammar there was Donatus' *Ars minor* (fourth century), an elementary text, and his *Ars grammatica,* of which only the third book, the *Barbarismus,* continued to be read throughout the medieval period. Also for grammar there was Priscian's *Institutio grammatica* (sixth century), frequently referred to as the "two Priscians," with the first sixteen books on the parts of speech, known as the *Priscianus maior,* and the two books on syntax, the *Priscianus minor.* Supplementing these grammars were reading books with selections of prose and poetry from the Latin classics. Rhetorical studies consisted of the works of Quintilian and Cicero, particularly the *Topica* and the *De oratore.* Aristotle's *Organon,* known in its entirety by the mid twelfth century, was used for logical studies. The *Organon* included the "old logic" (*Categoriae* and *De interpretatione*) and the "new logic" (*Analytica priora,* which covered the study of the syllogism; *Analytica posteriora,* on the analysis of proof; the *Sophisticae elenchi,* on common fallacies; and the *Topica,* on probable premises).

In the quadrivium such books as the incomplete *Timaeus* of Plato, on the nature of the universe, and Boethius' works on music (*De institutione musica*) and arithmetic (*De institutione arithmetica*) were studied.

Through the first half of the twelfth century, grammar and literature still dominated the liberal arts. By the second half of the century, however, logic, spurred on by the increasing number of translations of Aristotle's works and the introduction of the Scholastic method, began its ascent and prevailed in the arts curriculum until the end of the Middle Ages.

ARISTOTLE IN THE WEST

The introduction of Aristotle into the university drastically changed the curriculum, and we can consider this phenomenon as one of the great watersheds of Western intellectual history. Spain in the twelfth century produced the earliest translations from Arabic versions of the Greek originals; only later did translators work directly from Greek copies imported from the East. By 1230 the greater part of Aristotle's work had been discovered, and by the end of the thirteenth century almost the entire corpus of his writings had entered the university.

In twelfth-century Spain the patronage of Archbishop Raymond of Toledo and Michael of Tarrazona accomplished many translations of works on astrology, astronomy, and mathematics. The principal twelfth-century translators from the Arabic were Adelard of Bath, Plato of Tivoli, Robert of Chester, Hermann of Carinthia, Domingo Gundisalvo, Rudolph of Bruges, Gerard of Cremona, Hugh of Santalla, and the Jewish scholars Petrus Alfonsi and John of Seville. Michael Scot, Alfred of Sareshel, and Herman the German carried on this work into the early thirteenth century.

The tricultural milieu of Sicily generated the translations from the original Greek. Chief among the translators were Henry of Aristippus, Eugene the Emir, James of Venice, Burgundio of Pisa, and Moses of Bergamo.

By the early thirteenth century, the known works of Aristotle included the complete *Organon,* with the old and new logics; the natural philosophy works: the *Physica* (on motion, time, and space), *De generatione, De caelo* (theories of the universe), *Meteorica, De anima, Parva naturalia* (includes *De sensu et sensato, De somno et vigilia, De memoria et reminiscentia, De longitudine et brevitate vitae*), *Metaphysica vetustissima;* and the moral and practical philosophy treatises: the *Ethica vetus* (*Nicomachean Ethics*), *Rhetorica,* and *Poetica.* When William of Moerbeke translated the *Politica* and treatises on animals in the second half of the thirteenth century, Aristotle's corpus was almost complete. In addition, and very important for Western thought, many of the Neoplatonic and Arabic commentaries and other works were translated and transmitted as Aristotle's intellectual baggage. Included were Porphyry's *Isagoge,* al-Kindī's *De intellectu,* Ibn Gabirol's *Fons vitae,* and Ibn Sīnā's *Sufficientia.* These works would have far-reaching consequences. For instance, Ibn Rushd's commentary on Aristotle's *De anima* contained his theory of the single intellect, an idea that led to the great condemnation of philosophical propositions at Paris in 1277. These Greek and Arabic writings, with commentaries by the great Western Scholastics, formed the basis of intellectual life and the curriculum in the Western universities until the end of the Middle Ages.

TEXTBOOKS IN THE ARTS

The University of Paris provided the curricular model for texts in the liberal arts. A series of statutes dating from 1215 to 1452 gives a clear picture of the incorporation of required textbooks into the curriculum.

The cardinal legate, Robert of Courson, drew up the first rule of studies for the university in 1215. In grammar the statute decreed the study of at least one of the "two Priscians." The old and new dialectic of Aristotle (the *Organon* in its entirety) was prescribed for logic. Rhetorical studies consisted solely of the *Barbarismus* of Donatus. The texts in philosophy were the first four books of Aristotle's *Ethica vetus* and the fourth book of the *Topica.* Although the statute mentioned works in arithmetic, geometry, music, and astronomy, it listed no specific titles. The recently translated *Metaphysica* and the other works on natural philosophy of Aristotle were specifically forbidden, as were the pantheistic writings of David of Dinant and Amaury of Spain (previously condemned in 1210). Pope Gregory IX renewed the prohibition of the natural philosophy texts in 1231 but also decreed that the same books should be examined and purged of errors.

The church forbade Aristotle's writings on nature, tinged with Arabic commentary, primarily because the ideas propounded, such as the eternity of the world, the immortality of the soul, the unity of the intellect, and the impassive Prime Mover, were antithetical to accepted Christian dogma. However, by the mid thirteenth century, the books proscribed in 1215 and 1231 were very much a part of the arts curriculum. The force of the Aristotelian wave was too strong to hold back for long.

A manuscript dating between 1230 and 1245 and discovered in Barcelona in the twentieth century contains a guide to the arts courses in Paris and lists the natural philosophy works of Aristotle. In

TEXTBOOKS

1252 the statutes of the English-German Nation at Paris for the determination in arts added to the texts listed in 1215 Gilbert de la Porrée's *Sex principia,* a commentary on Aristotle's *Categoriae;* the *Divisiones* of Boethius; and the *De anima* of Aristotle, the first official example of one of the natural philosophy texts in the arts curriculum.

The university regulations of 1255 provide clear evidence of Aristotle's domination of the arts faculty by the mid thirteenth century. In addition to the Aristotelian logical works and the *Ethica vetus,* the decree required the master of arts to lecture on the *Physica, Metaphysica, De anima, De animalibus, De caelo et mundo, Meteorica, De generatione, De sensu et sensato, De somno et vigilia, De memoria et reminiscentia, De morte et vita,* and the spurious *De plantis.* Also required were a pseudo-Aristotelian and very skeptical work drawn from Plotinus and Proclus, the *Liber de causis,* and Qusṭa ibn Lūqā's *De differentia spiritus et animae.* Priscian's *De accentu* was added to these works.

The papal legates Giles de Montaigu and John de Blandy promulgated the next set of regulations over a century later, in 1366. This legatine reform document divided the texts required among the stages of a student's career. A bachelor of arts studied grammar, logic, and philosophy. The only difference from the earlier texts is that for grammar, instead of the two Priscians, the student read the *Graecismus* of Evrard of Béthune and Alexander de Villa Dei's *Doctrinale puerorum,* a grammar in verse. The bachelor also read, as before, the *Organon,* the *Topica,* and the *De anima.* The license required reading the *Physica,* the *De generatione et corruptione,* the *De caelo et mundo,* the *Metaphysica,* the *Parva naturalia,* and unspecified mathematical works. To be admitted to the master of arts after obtaining the license to teach, the student learned the *Ethica* and the first three books of the *Meteorica.*

Cardinal d'Estouteville's 1452 reform of the university made practically no change in the curriculum except for an added emphasis on verse-making.

The other universities of Europe used similar required texts for courses leading to degrees. For instance, the earliest official Oxford university regulations, those of 1431, prescribed for grammar the *Priscianus maior* or *minor;* for rhetoric Aristotle's *Rhetorica,* or book IV of Boethius' *Topica,* Cicero's *Nova rhetorica,* Ovid's *Metamorphoses,* or Vergil; for logic the *De interpretatione, Topica,* or *Priora analytica;* for astronomy a choice of Aristotle's *Physica, De caelo, De proprietatibus elementorum, Meteorica, De vegetabilibus et plantis, De anima, De animalibus,* or one of the small works; for moral philosophy the *Ethica, Economica,* or *Politica;* and for metaphysics the *Metaphysica.*

TEXTBOOKS IN THEOLOGY

The University of Paris again provided the curricular model for the course of studies in theology. Early in the twelfth century the city supplanted other centers of learning in theology and remained preeminent in the discipline until the end of the Middle Ages.

The degree in theology took much longer to attain than the one in the arts. Robert of Courson's statutes of 1215 decreed that a master in theology should be at least thirty-five years old and have studied for a minimum of eight years beyond the six years necessary for the arts degree. Thus, the theology course lasted for fourteen years. The reform of 1366 lengthened the time to sixteen years, and in 1452 Cardinal d'Estouteville shortened it to fifteen. At Oxford the ordeal was only a bit shorter.

Theology was the queen of the sciences in the medieval university. On the authority of the church fathers (Ambrose, Augustine, Jerome, and Pope Gregory the Great), the liberal arts were merely handmaidens to prepare one for scriptural study. The theological degree required a master of arts or exemption from it, and a greater age and maturity. The prestige of the school at Paris and the limited number of chairs in the discipline generated more competition and higher quality in the faculty. The greatest intellectual activity came out of theological study, which attracted the greatest minds and purest thinkers in the Middle Ages. Theology could also bring great fame and high honors in the church and in the university. The list of masters in theology at Paris reads like an honor role of medieval genius: Albertus Magnus, Alexander of Hales, Thomas Aquinas, Bonaventure, John Duns Scotus, William of Ockham, and many others.

Throughout the medieval period the most important book for the study of theology was, of course, the Bible. Scriptural analysis was the basis for the university curriculum in theology. The other text used throughout the Middle Ages was the *Liber sententiarum* (*ca.* 1152) of Peter Lombard, an Italian scholar at Paris who later became archbishop of that city. Peter divided the *Sentences* into four books: the first treats God, the Trinity, providence, predestination, and evil; the second book concentrates on the Creation, the angels and devils, the fall of Adam, supernatural grace, and sin; the third book discusses questions on the Incarnation, the redemption of man, the virtues, and the Ten Commandments; the fourth and final book covers sacraments, death, judgment, heaven, and hell.

Peter compiled a great mass of material from the church fathers and other ecclesiastical authorities on these subjects. Using the style of biblical exegesis developed in the cathedral schools of Laon and Paris, he employed the Scholastic method of question and answer in an attempt to reconcile numerous varying viewpoints and arguments.

The Bible and the *Sentences* were read for the first ten years of the theological course. In addition, in the thirteenth century the reading of numerous commentaries on the Bible and *Sentences* became necessary for success in examinations. For example, William of Auxerre's *Summa aurea,* Philip the Chancellor's *De bono,* and Bonaventure's *Commentarii in qualtuor libros sententiarum* aided the student in understanding the theological issues of the day. Also, the great summaries or collections of questions and answers on theological points, the summae, of which Thomas Aquinas' *Summa theologiae* was the greatest, provided material on every facet covered in the *Sentences,* the Bible, and the writings of the church fathers. Other writings or lectures written down by student *reportators*—the expositions, *postillae,* and free debates on any subject, the *quodlibeta*—became part of the corpus of student aids in theology but never reached the status of standard texts.

TEXTBOOKS IN LAW

As Paris provided the curricular model for the liberal arts and theology, so Bologna provided the model for the study of civil and canon law. Pope Honorius III prevented potential competition when he proscribed the teaching of civil law at Paris in 1219.

In the sixth century Emperor Justinian had the basic texts for civil law assembled from Roman sources. Roman legists compiled praetors' edicts, magistrates' decisions, decrees of emperors, and the writings of scholars such as the second- and third-century jurists Papinian, Gaius, Ulpian, Paulus, and Modestinus into four books: an elementary legal manual, the *Institutes;* fifty volumes of legal interpretations in the *Digest* or *Pandects,* known in the Middle Ages as the *Digestum vetus,* the *Infortiatum,* and the *Digestum novum;* twelve volumes of imperial statutes in the *Code* (*Codex,* books I–IX, and *Tres libri codicis,* books X–XII); and new statutes, collected in the *Novellae* or *Authentica.* The whole compilation was called the *Corpus iuris civilis.*

Until the great legal scholar Irnerius rediscovered the *Digest* in the eleventh century, apparently only the *Code* and the *Institutes* were known through much of the early Middle Ages. The *Corpus* became the textbook for civil law throughout the remainder of the medieval period, and the commentaries on it, or summae, using the dialectical method, became auxiliary texts necessary for the attainment of the law degree.

The writings, lectures, disputations, and explanations or glosses of Irnerius (*d. ca.* 1130) and his students, known as the Four Doctors (Bulgarus, Martinus Gosia, Hugo de Porta Ravennate, and Jacobus de Porta Ravennate), provided the earliest accompanying texts. Later scholars, such as Johannes Bassianus, Azo, and Placentinus, succeeded Irnerius and the Four Doctors. The greatest commentary on the *Corpus* was the work of Accursius (*d. ca.* 1263), who compiled a collection of more than 96,000 glosses. Accursius' work became the standard gloss (*glossa ordinaria*) until the end of the Middle Ages.

For canon law, the *Decretum* by Gratian became the basic textbook in the medieval period. About 1140 he collected and arranged by the question-and-answer method all the previous conciliar laws and decrees of the church in some 3,900 canons. Because many of the canons were contradictory, he went about reconciling the texts according to the rules of logic; hence the original title, the *Concordantia discordantium canonum.*

In the thirteenth and fourteenth centuries authorities added other texts to Gratian's work. Of particular importance were the *Decretales* of Pope Gregory IX in 1234; the *Constitutiones Clementinae* of Pope Clement V in 1317; and the later papal laws, the *Extravagantes.*

In addition to the set text, legal scholars produced a considerable body of commentaries or glosses on the *Decretum.* The universities increasingly accepted these glosses as supplementary texts. Chief among the canon-law glossators who contributed to the *Glossa ordinariae* were Rufinus (1157–1159), Huguccio (*ca.* 1191), and especially Hostiensis (Henry of Susa; *d.* 1271), who produced the

Lectura in quinque libros Decretalium and the comprehensive *Summa aurea*.

TEXTBOOKS IN MEDICINE

The primary medical schools in the Middle Ages were at Salerno and Montpellier. The writings of the Greeks Hippocrates and Galen provided the basic texts for the study of medicine. The work of Hippocrates (*ca.* 460–*ca.* 370 B.C.) included such treatises as *On Anatomy, On the Nature of the Bones, On the Humors,* the attributed *On the Child of Seven Months, On Fractures, On Fistulas, On Wounds of the Head,* and many others. Galen (129/130–199/200) was the second great authority in the schools. He wrote numerous expositions—well over 400—on just about every branch of medical theory and anatomy. At least eighty authentic ones have been transmitted to the West.

In the eleventh century the Salerno scholar Constantine the African translated medical works from Arabic into Latin, and these translations led to a collection of texts of Hippocrates, Galen, and others into the standard compilation known as the *Ars medicinae*. Besides the works of Hippocrates and Galen, the *Ars medicinae* included the *De urinis* of Theophilus; al-Jezzar's *Viaticum;* Isaac Israeli's *Books of Isaac* (*Urines, Fevers,* and *Diets*); Nicholas of Salerno's *Antidotarium* (*Pharmacopeia*); Giles of Corbeil's versified *De urinis;* and the *Opus pantegni* (*Theoretica* and *Practica*) of Haly Abbas (ᶜAlī ibn al-ᶜAbbās).

In the thirteenth century Theodoric of Lucca's works on the use of narcotics and the formation of pus were added to the standard corpus, as was Guido Lanfranchi's surgical text, the *Chirurgia magna* (1296). The fourteenth-century surgeon Guy de Chauliac produced an important treatise on surgery, also titled *Chirurgia magna,* that was influential in the later Middle Ages.

In general, it required approximately eight to nine years of study to earn the medical degree. In 1309 Pope Clement V's regulations for the University of Montpellier listed the following texts: Galen's *De complexionibus, De malicia complexionis diverse, De simplici medicina, De morbo et accidente, De crisi et criticis diebus, De ingenio sanitatis, Tegni,* and *Antidotarium;* Hippocrates' *Liber amphorismi* and *De prognosticis;* Johannicius' *De regimine acutorum;* Isaac Israeli's *Liber febrium;* and the works of Ibn Sīnā, Abū Bakr al-Rāzī, and Constantine the African.

In 1340 the books mentioned for lectures included Ibn Sīnā's *Primus canonis* and *Quartus canonis;* Galen's *De morbo et accidente, De differentiis febrium, De crisi et criticis diebus, De malicia complexionis diverse, De simplicibus medicinis, De complexionibus, Liber deiuvamentis membrorum, De interioribus, De ingenio sanitatis, Ad glauconem,* and *Tegni;* Hippocrates' *Liber amphorismi, De regimine acutorum,* and *De prognosticis;* Bartholomaeus Anglicus' *De regimine sanitatis* and *De virtutibus naturalibus;* and Isaac Israeli's *Liber febrium* and *De dietis universalibus*.

By 1395 the medical works of Ibn Rushd (the *Colliget*) had joined Ibn Sīnā's *Canon* in the curriculum, and they were studied with all the Scholastic rigor used in the arts, law, and theology. In the medieval university, medical training was primarily theoretical, consisting of reading and lecturing on textbooks, although regulations did require varying periods of clinical experience to prepare practicing physicians.

THE REGULATION AND PRODUCTION OF TEXTBOOKS

By the early thirteenth century the need for standard texts led many universities, most notably Paris, Oxford, and Bologna, to regulate the production and selling of books. The stationer (*stationarius,* sometimes called the *librarius* or *venditor librorum*) combined the roles of publisher, bookseller, and lending librarian. Most important, however, he served the vital function of preparing and lending the official copy, or exemplar, of a text the university used.

Under close supervision of the university, the stationer employed the scribes, illuminators, and binders who prepared the exemplar. In 1264 a statute of the University of Padua mentioned the importance of the exemplar when it stated that a university would not exist without it.

The exemplar was usually divided into sections of four to six folios, or eight to twelve pages each, called *peciae*. Six university masters (the number varied according to the university) examined the *peciae* for accuracy. After the approval of the entire exemplar, the title was added to the official list of texts that a bookseller could lend. Each *pecia* had a set price, and the list stated the number of *peciae* that constituted an exemplar. A scholar could rent *peciae* individually. After returning a *pecia* he could rent another. Thus, at one time several people were copying the same text, and the system thus satisfied popular demand. This process of producing texts gives a good indication of why there are so many variants of medieval works and the variety of textual problems involved in their study.

The universities also regulated parchment dealers, inspecting and pricing their wares before sale.

Stationers had to take an oath to be faithful and obedient to the university, and in return the university often accorded them the same privileges and exemptions the masters and scholars received.

The *pecia* system of textbook production changed the format of books in use for centuries, and we can probably consider it the first "paperback revolution" in the West. Because the student and scholar had to carry the book around with him, it had to be smaller and more portable.

Besides causing a format change, the system necessitated a new style of handwriting. Scribes had to produce texts quickly and efficiently; therefore they used even and standard strokes. Parisian Gothic textual script, with its regular lines, became the script of the textbook trade. In addition, to achieve rapid copying, the copyists abandoned the reed pen and adopted the feathered quill, which offered greater ease of control.

Ornamentation of books diminished. Almost all extant *pecia* copies have blank initials. Also, scribes abbreviated more and more words, using a form of shorthand for almost all texts.

With the standardized textbook in the university, the book became a commodity of the marketplace, a premium being placed on the rapid and cost-effective production of multiple copies. The next step was the printing press. And when printing with movable type finally came to Europe, the university's regulation of text preparation formed the basis for its claim to control the printing of books.

BIBLIOGRAPHY

The following works discuss the development of various university curricula and reading requirements: John W. Baldwin, *The Scholastic Culture of the Middle Ages, 1000–1300* (1971); Leonard Boyle, "The Curriculum of the Faculty of Canon Law at Oxford in the First Half of the Fourteenth Century," in *Oxford Studies Presented to Daniel Callus* (1964); Lowrie J. Daly, *The Medieval University, 1200–1400* (1961); Charles Homer Haskins, *The Rise of Universities* (1923, repr. 1940, 1957, 1976), and *Studies in the History of Mediaeval Science* (1960); Gordon Leff, *Paris and Oxford Universities in the Thirteenth and Fourteenth Centuries* (1968); Jacques Le Goff, *Les intellectuels au moyen âge* (1957); Louis J. Paetow, *The Arts Course at the Mediaeval Universities with Special Reference to Grammar and Rhetoric* (1910); Hastings Rashdall, *The Universities of Europe in the Middle Ages,* F. M. Powicke and A. B. Emden, eds., new ed., 3 vols. (1936); Beryl Smalley, *The Study of the Bible in the Middle Ages* (1964); Fernand van Steenberghen, *La philosophie au XIIIe siècle* (1966).

Documents relating to textbooks can be found in Heinrich Denifle and Émile Chatelain, eds., *Chartularium universitatis Parisiensis,* 4 vols. (1889–1897); Strickland Gibson, *Statuta antiqua universitatis Oxoniensis* (1931); Arthur O. Norton, *Readings in the History of Education: Medieval Universities* (1909, repr. 1971); Lynn Thorndike, *University Records and Life in the Middle Ages* (1944, repr. 1949).

The following works treat the production and regulation of textbooks: Jean Destrez, *La pecia dans les manuscrits universitaires du XIIIe et du XIVe siècle* (1935); Pearl Kibre, *Scholarly Privileges in the Middle Ages* (1962); Graham Pollard, "The *Pecia* System in the Medieval Universities," in Malcolm B. Parkes and Andrew G. Watson, eds., *Medieval Scribes, Manuscripts, and Libraries: Essays Presented to N. R. Ker* (1978).

LARRY E. SULLIVAN

[See also **Aristotle in the Middle Ages; Corpus Iuris Civilis; Decretists; Dialectic; Gloss; Grammar; Law, Schools of; Literacy, Western European; Manuscript Books, Production of; Medicine, History of; Medicine, Schools of; Pecia; Quadrivium; Rhetoric, Western European; Theology, Schools of; Trivium; Universities; Writing Implements, Western European;** and individual authors and universities.]

TEXTILE TECHNOLOGY underwent changes in the Middle Ages, particularly from the eleventh to the thirteenth century, that were almost as revolutionary for the medieval European economy as those of the eighteenth-century Industrial Revolution in cotton textiles were for the modern. (In fact, the textile industries collectively were the most important manufacturing industry in terms of employment, value of output, and contributions to international trade in much of Europe during the twelfth to nineteenth centuries.) This discussion of textile technology will be limited to those for woven fabrics in medieval Western Europe, with primary attention given to wool-based cloths in their major production centers of Italy, northern France, the Low Countries, and England.

The word "textile" comes from Latin *texere,* "to weave"; and because weaving is so central to this topic, that process must be clearly defined at the outset: the insertion of transverse threads or yarns known as wefts at right angles between alternate longitudinal yarns, the loom's foundation yarns, known as warps. The treatment of these warp and weft yarns differed throughout most processes of cloth-making (as did the technology of the production processes themselves) according to the type of wool-based fabric being manufactured, whether woolens, worsteds, or serges.

The essential distinctions between woolens and worsteds began with their particular wools: the differences in the length, fineness, and shape of their fibers. Medieval woolens were composed in both warp and weft of relatively fine, curly, scaly, short-stapled wools that provided relatively weak yarns, with the finest and softest reserved for wefts. Consequently cloths woven from such yarns had to undergo a subsequent treatment known as fulling (involving compression and felting) to obtain the necessary strength, cohesion, and density. They then were shorn to give the cloths the proper smooth finish and texture, especially in the more luxurious varieties. In general, woolens were the heavier, more costly, luxury-oriented cloths, though many were cheap. True worsteds, on the other hand, were generally much lighter, coarser, cheaper cloths composed of longer, tougher, straight-fibered, more tightly twisted wools. But medieval worsted wools were not as long-stapled as those that came to be produced in Stuart England by selective breeding and sheep management. Nevertheless, even worsteds had sufficient strength and cohesion in warp and weft yarns when woven to make the fulling and shearing processes largely unnecessary (though some were lightly shorn). The coarseness and lack of felting properties in their yarns made them generally unsuited to the finishing processes for woolens. Worsteds, therefore, were most visibly distinguished from woolens by their variously patterned weaves, which in most medieval woolens (except striped cloths) were generally obliterated by the fulling and finishing processes. A third, bastard variety of cloth, under a variety of local names (serge, *saye, saye drappeé, baye*), was woven from worsted warps and woolen wefts, which usually required some fulling and shearing. Fustians were a related fourth variety, containing a linen warp and a woolen or cotton weft.

WOOL PREPARATION

A very wide variety of wools, making possible an equally broad spectrum of manufactured cloths, was to be found in medieval Europe. The finest short-stapled wools came from England, especially the Welsh Marches (Herfordshire, Shropshire), the Cotswolds, and Lincolnshire. These wools remained unsurpassed in fineness until the later fifteenth century, when they began to be challenged by merino wools from Spain, whose quality was so improved by the seventeenth century that they had succeeded in outclassing all but prime Herfordshire wools. For the best-quality luxury woolens, West European draperies used selected wools only from mature sheep raised in these regions—never lamb's wool. For cheaper woolens, worsteds, and mixed worsted-woolen fabrics, however, they used both sheep's and lamb's wool secured from other parts of the British Isles (especially Scotland), the Low Countries, northern Germany, France (especially Burgundy), Italy, and North Africa.

Wools were obtained either from live sheep, the preferred source for reasons of both economy and quality, or from slaughtered sheep, whose fleece was called "woolfell." The wool from live sheep was removed as a single fleece by shearing, and medieval shears appear to be virtually identical to the Roman: two sharp iron or steel blades, about 6 inches (15 cm) long, joined by a U-shaped spring. Since the fleece usually contained so many different wools, the first task after separating them from the fleece was to sort and select them according to staple lengths and qualities.

The wools were then subjected to the cleansing processes. First they were scoured with wooden rakes in a large wooden trough or tub containing hot alkaline water, lye, and/or stale urine (the ammonia content of urine served as a detergent). The natural greases, dirt, and other foreign matter thereby removed constituted from 15 to 25 percent of the wools' weight. The wools were then rinsed in cold water, usually in a running stream: short-fibered wools in sieve baskets, long wools in containers with crook-fitted poles for twisting and squeezing the fibers. The wools were then spread out on wooden boards or hung on hurdles to dry in the sun. When fully dried, the wools were placed over a table or bench composed of narrow slats and beaten or "broken" with willow branches, sticks, or rocks. This process served a triple purpose: to remove any remaining foreign matter; to separate fibers entangled or matted by cleansing and drying (and also by wool dyeing); and to complete wool separation and sorting.

Those fine, curly wools that were destined to serve as both warp and weft yarns in the manufacture of true woolens and as weft alone for serges were then heavily greased or oiled. Such lubrication was absolutely necessary to soften and protect these fine wools from any damage resulting from friction or entanglement in the ensuing production processes of combing, carding, spinning, warping, and weaving.

The long, straight-fibered, and much coarser wools used in the worsted or *sayetterie* industry did not require such extensive greasing—or scouring (thus retaining some of their natural lubrication). In the Low Countries, the terms "greased" and "dry" were in fact used to distinguish the two chief branches of the cloth industry: *draperie ointe* and *draperie sèche* (Middle Dutch: *gesmoutte* and *droge lakenindustrie*).

COMBING

The final stage in preparing wools for spinning into yarn was either combing or carding. Combing is the much more ancient of the two processes and was originally used for all wools, long- and short-fibered, warp and weft. In the medieval Flemish cloth industry, two types of combs were used: the larger one for woolens (with twenty-one teeth in three rows) and the smaller for *sayettes.* The teeth were finely tapered spikes of steel or iron, which were rooted in horn and inserted through a wooden board with a long wooden handle, forming a T-shape. The wool combs were generally heated over a charcoal fire, so that the warm teeth would soften the greased wool fibers and facilitate their passage through the comb. Invariably, wool combs were used in pairs, upper and lower. The back of the lower comb was placed on the comber's knee with the teeth positioned upward to receive the wools; short-stapled fine wools were frequently greased or oiled once more at this point. In later medieval draperies, this lower comb, much enlarged, was usually fixed securely to a solid wooden post. The upper comb, teeth facing downward, was then drawn across the teeth of the lower comb several times until all the wool was transferred to this second comb. After removal from the teeth, the wool was then attached to a wooden stake or stick and then combed several times again and partially twisted to form a "roving" of parallel fibers, about a meter or yard long, ready to be spun.

CARDING

The technique of carding was introduced into the woolen industries as a rival method of preparing fine, curly, short-stapled, greased wools for spinning wefts. Ideally suited to the very short-stapled cotton fibers, carding may first have been used in the newly emerging cotton industries of northern Italy and Barcelona during the late eleventh or twelfth centuries and was probably introduced there from the cotton industries of Muslim Spain and Sicily. The earliest documented references are for Apulia, in southern Italy, in the mid eleventh century; and in Portugal, in the twelfth century (Malanima). The instrument itself, the card, resembled a veritable wire brush. It was a rectangular wooden board, about 10 inches by 5 to 6 inches (25 cm × 12–15 cm) with an underside covered in leather, through which were inserted hundreds of fine, short, sharp hooks or wires bent toward the handle, fitted on the longer side. Like the combs the cards were always used in pairs, with the hooks working in opposite directions. The wool was placed on the teeth of the upward-facing lower card; the other card was then drawn or brushed against the former several times, until the wool was fully transferred and thereby carded. Just as in later medieval combing, the lower card was commonly much enlarged and fixed to a rigid post and hence was known as a stock card, to differentiate it from a hand card. The first objective of carding, as in combing, was to disentangle and align the wool fibers. But carding had certain advantages over combing; the former technique made possible the separating and multiplying of the strands without removing the short fibers. Indeed, carding was far better suited than combing for short fibers, which naturally curled around the base of the comb's teeth. While combing had a second objective of forcing the wool fibers to run in a parallel formation, carding instead encouraged the short, curly, and scaly or serrated fibers to protrude and become crisscrossed, in order to promote their natural attributes of interlacing or felting—whose great importance will be discussed subsequently under "Fulling." The result was a spongy, soft, air-filled cylinder of fibers known as a "sliver." Finally, carding provided the best means of blending together a variety of wools, particularly variously dyed wools, and thus to permit the spinning of yarns with a mélange of colors. Combing, on the other hand, remained the superior method of preparing long-stapled wools; the much straighter and coarser fibers of these wools had few felting properties and required parallel formation to give proper twist and necessary strength to the spun yarns. Thus, combing continued to prevail in the worsted and *sayetterie* industries into modern times; but for many medieval woolen draperies, combing also remained the preferred, often mandatory, method for short-fibered wools.

Despite its important advantages in preparing such wools, in terms of both labor productivity and quality control, carding did not succeed in displacing combing completely in European woolen manufacturing until early modern times. Whether or not carding, in the words of de Poerck, "was born in an atmosphere of suspicion," it certainly encountered strong opposition in many West European draperies. In some European towns, carding came to be totally banned: Paris, 1273; Lier, 1332; Valenciennes, 1358; Ghent, 1350; Douai, 1352; Leiden, 1363; Mechelen, 1364; Brussels, 1365 and 1372. Some towns, however, did relent to permit carding, if only grudgingly, in those cheap-line draperies producing for local or regional consumption: Tournai (1365), Brussels (1375), and Douai (1390). But in other draperies—in Italy, France, and the Low Countries—carding was forbidden only for the preparation of the warps, and thus was permitted explicitly or implicitly for the wefts: Florence, 1317; St. Omer, 1350; Troyes, 1359 (explicitly, 1377); Ypres, before 1363. Such a dichotomy between the two yarns is reflected in medieval European linguistics. For in Italian, French, and Flemish (Dutch), the words for carded and combed wools are the same as those for weft and warp, respectively: *lana, trame,* and *wevel* (for carded weft); and *stame, estain,* and *waerp* (for combed warp).

Why carding was banned outright or so rigorously restricted for so long in so many places is a mystery, but one whose solution may be revealed by the name of the instrument itself. The term "card" (Middle French: *cardon;* Middle Dutch: *caerde*) was derived from the Latin *carduus* (*-i,* m.), a thistle; and originally it meant, and indeed continued to mean as well, an important textile instrument of the fullers and finishers, the teasel, *Dipsacus fullonum.* A prickly plant of the thistle family, the teasel was used to raise the nap, the protruding hairy fibers of fulled, felted cloth. Certainly regulatory authorities everywhere, guilds and town government alike, strictly forbade the use of metal cards in fulling and finishing, on the quite understandable grounds that they would damage the woven cloth. Perhaps, therefore, some draperies also banned metal cards for wool preparation (carding) for fear that they would similarly damage wool fibers; or for fear that, if permitted in wool preparation, they would then surreptitiously be used for cloth finishing as well. A more likely explanation, especially for those draperies concerned about quality control in international competition, was the fear that carding would facilitate the blending of cheap, inferior wools with the good. But these reasons would still not explain why other quality-conscious draperies, competing in the same markets, banned carding only for the preparation of warp yarns. The reasons for this more limited ban perhaps should be sought in the different methods for spinning warp and weft yarns in medieval Europe: carding may not have permitted warps to be spun with sufficient twist (and thus strength) to prevent breakage when stretched and pulled on the loom.

Even so, restrictions on carding were neither universal nor immutable. None can be found documented, for example, in medieval England, where carding was officially recognized by statute in 1464. Brussels, which had forbidden carding except in the petty draperies, altered its drapery regulations in 1467 to permit the use of wools "either combed or carded," as the individual draper saw fit, in its best luxury-quality woolen broadcloths, even its scarlets, so long as those wools continued to be "good English Staple wools" (the fine Welsh March, Cotswolds, and Lincolnshire wools sold at the Calais Staple). From 1435 the neighboring town of Mechelen was describing its best-quality woolens as *gecaerde lakenen,* which undoubtedly meant cloths made wholly from carded wools. Nevertheless, many West European draperies continued to use combed warps for their woolen cloths well into the sixteenth century: for example, at Florence, Leiden, Armentières, and Ghent, and even some in England (Mann, Lowe).

BOWING

Also known as *arçonnage,* bowing was an alternative or ancillary technique for the preparation of short-fibered wools that may have entered medieval Western Europe before carding, possibly via the Muslim cotton industries. A cotton bow was used in Norman Sicily and Apulia as early as the twelfth century. But it may also have been introduced from Eastern European felt-hat making, especially fur hats, for which an almost identical bow had long been essential in felting. Bowing, though far from being practiced anywhere as widely as carding in medieval Western Europe, was never subjected to similar prohibitions or restrictions. The bow itself, the *arc,* was a long elastic, arched framework of wood whose center was suspended by a cord from the ceiling and whose two ends were connected by a tautly stretched string or catgut cord. The bowstring was set in the middle of a pile of cotton or short-stapled wool (or fur) and was struck by a mallet to produce vibrations that forced a separation of the fibers. In general the results were similar to those from carding, in particular promoting the fibers' felting properties. Bowing (instead of carding) is still widely practiced today with a virtually identical instrument in felt and hat making.

Woman carrying a distaff while feeding chickens. 13th-century miniature from the Lutrell Psalter, British Library MS Add. 42130, fol. 166. COURTESY OF THE TRUSTEES OF THE BRITISH LIBRARY

SPINNING

Spinning is the art of converting the combed and/or carded fibers into long threads or yarns, for both warp and weft, by a three-part process that became fully continuous only in the fifteenth century: (1) drafting or drawing out the fibers from the mass of previously prepared wool (the roving or sliver); (2) twisting the drafted fibers to make them cling together and so form one continuous yarn; and (3) winding the spun yarn onto a spindle or bobbin.

Hand spinning. The original process was simply hand spinning: drafting and twisting with thumb and forefinger. From very ancient times, however, hand spinning had been facilitated by using a spindle or distaff. The original instrument was a narrow stick or rod, about 12 inches (30 cm) long, whose dual purpose was to hold the mass of raw fibers, usually wound in slivers onto its forked or cleft upper end, and to contain the spun yarn, wound around the lower end. This distaff was held high in the spinner's left hand, while the right thumb and forefinger drew out and then twisted the wool or other fibers. A much more advanced (though still ancient) instrument was the drop spindle or spindle whorl. In this device the spindle itself was rod-shaped, separated from the distaff, narrowed at both ends (to about 1 cm), and then inserted or threaded through a disk-shaped whorl, fitting securely at the thicker lower-middle end of the spindle. The whorl, made of stone, clay, shell, bone, or wood, served as a flywheel to make the spindle drop vertically and rotate rapidly in one direction. These spindles and their attached whorls—descriptively called the "rock" in medieval Europe—differed in dimension and weight according to the type of fiber being spun and the degree of twist required. The larger spindles with heavier weights (stone or clay whorls) were used for such coarse and strong fibers as linen (flax) and worsted wools, which also had to be tightly twisted, especially for the warp yarns; conversely, the lighter spindles with small whorls (wood) were used in spinning wools for true woolens and cottons.

In using this implement, the spinner first wound the mass of prepared fibers onto a long, separate distaff (whose base was often hooked into her girdle or waistband). To the upper end of the spindle, which could be hooked or notched, she attached a lead yarn made from fibers drawn from the bottom of the roving and twisted in the same direction that the spindle was to be rotated for spinning. A clockwise rotation (from left to right) produced Z-twist, which was used for hemp, worsted warps and wefts, and combed woolen warps; a counterclockwise rotation produced S-twist, used for linen yarns, cotton yarns, and woolen wefts. In Roman and early medieval Western Europe, however, virtually all woolen yarns, both warp and weft, were given a Z-twist, while an S-twist was utilized in the Eastern Roman provinces (where linen had long predominated).

With the lead yarn so attached, the spinner then grasped the top of the spindle with thumb and forefinger, gave it a quick twist, and let the spindle drop vertically, drawing out more fiber from the distaff with her right hand while using her left to control the twist. When the spindle hit the floor, the spinner picked it up and wound the spun yarn onto its bottom end, serving as a bobbin. The yarn could

Women spinning and carding wool. 13th-century miniature from the Lutrell Psalter, British Library MS Add. 42130, fol. 193. COURTESY OF THE TRUSTEES OF THE BRITISH LIBRARY

be very strong, yet very thin and quite even. The degree both of fineness (amount of stretch) and of twist in the yarn was thus determined by the weight of the spindle whorl, the extent of its drop, and the speed of its rotation, while the yarn's uniformity depended on the spinner's manual dexterity. Sometimes, in spinning very fine, delicate woolen wefts, or cotton yarns (for which the distaff was often omitted), the spindle was rotated with its bottom end supported by a dish to obviate the danger of yarn breakage from a rapid drop.

The spinning wheel. This method of spinning remained virtually unchanged in the West from the ancient Greek era to the later twelfth or thirteenth century, when the European textile industries made one of their greatest technological advances: the adoption of the spinning wheel, which involved quite simply the mechanization of the spindle whorl. The spindle itself was mounted horizontally between two short slotted uprights, with bearings, to serve as an axle; but the spindle tip protruded freely through and well beyond the upright to receive the fibers. The former whorl-disk, placed at the spindle's center, was grooved as a pulley to receive a continuous driving band or cord from the wheel. If that band was crossed before encircling the whorl, in figure-eight fashion ("closed band"), an S-twist yarn was produced; if it was uncrossed ("open band"), then a Z-twist resulted. The driving wheel, which was also attached by an axle to uprights on the same floorboard, came in two forms: the Small wheel, used especially for cotton spinning, and the Great (or Indian) wheel, used for wool. One turn of the wheel produced many revolutions of the spindle, in what Lynn White has called "the first instance of the belt transmission of power." Thus, a Great wheel with a 45-inch diameter and a 1.25-inch pulley could achieve a 36:1 gain, so that 100 revolutions per minute (rpm) by the wheel could produce 3,600 rpm in the spindle-pulley. The replacement of the spindle by the wheel permitted labor productivity in spinning wool to increase more than threefold—from an average output of about 120 yards (110 m) with the spindle to one of about 383 yards (350 m) of yarn per hour with the wheel.

The basic principles of spinning did not greatly differ, however, with the new machine. The spinner first took a small amount of twisted, carded fiber from the sliver on the distaff and attached it to the spindle tip. With her right hand, she then rotated the wheel (and thus the spindle) clockwise while her left hand slowly drew the distaff away from the spindle tip at a forty-five-degree angle. The rapid rotation and the resulting tension attenuated and drafted the fibers while making them spiral up to the spindle tip and then slip off, so that with each revolution one twist was inserted into the length of the new yarn. The higher the angle (90 degrees), the tighter the twist. When the spinner had drawn the distaff and the newly spun yarn out to the full length of her left arm, she reversed the wheel for a few turns to wind off the last few turns; then, by slowly resuming the original rotation, while holding the yarn at ninety degrees, she transferred and wound the new yarn onto the spindle shaft near the upright, or onto the "cop" of previously spun yarn. Placing the last of the new yarn onto the spindle tip, she repeated the cycle. Note that, as with the traditional spindle whorl, spinning (drafting and twisting) and winding-on remained intermittent, separate processes.

This spinning wheel is oriental in origin and appears to be quite ancient, but those origins are much disputed. Some argue that it first developed in the Indian cotton industry, dating it variously from 500 B.C. to A.D. 750, while others ascribe its origins to the Chinese silk industry (from about the third century A.D.), as will be discussed below under "Reeling." Whatever its true origins, the spinning wheel arrived very late in Western Europe, most likely again via the Muslim cotton industries. Its first documented European use was indeed evidently in spinning cotton wefts (according to Walter Endrei and Maureen Mazzaoui), in the twelfth-century Italian fustian industry; but it was not used for the linen warps.

Documentary evidence on its use in the woolen industry does not appear until the next century, again first in Italy, in the form of outright prohibitions or bans on at least their use in spinning warps: in Venice, 1224; Bologna, 1256; Paris, 1268; Speyer, 1280; Abbeville, 1288; Siena, 1292; Valencia, 1298; Douai, 1305. Such bans, limited or total, multiplied with the spread of the spinning wheel in the fourteenth century and remained in force generally until the later fifteenth or sixteenth century. Significantly, bans on warp-spinning by the wheel are generally contained in those same ordinances that prohibited carding warp wools. Thus together, more often implicitly than explicitly, these ordinances did permit the wheel for spinning carded woolen wefts (but in Leiden, only from 1527). The object of these bans was not, therefore, to protect the hand spinners from technological unemployment, but to ensure proper quality control, particularly in the manufacture of luxury-grade woolens.

In this respect, in comparison with the traditional drop-spindle, the spinning wheel was clearly inferior, producing yarns that were too weak, too uneven, with insufficient twist, and with "too many knots" (*Livre des mestiers,* Bruges, 1349), to serve properly as warps stretched on the loom. Those defects resulted chiefly from the wheel's great speed, but also from the spinner's inability to control the drafting and twist with her right hand, which was occupied in turning the wheel. Such defects did not really matter with weft yarns, so that the spinning wheel, with its obvious superiority in productivity, quickly gained supremacy in European weft spinning for both wool and cotton. As the Bruges *Livre des mestiers* also notes, wheel-spun yarns cost much less than "rock"-spun yarns. The wheel was, furthermore, less likely to break very fine carded wools than was the unsupported drop-spindle, and it may also have been better suited to carded than to combed wool, while conversely the drop-spindle was certainly better suited to the latter. Furthermore, this particular spinning wheel was not generally (if ever) used for any other combed fibers, whether worsted, flax, or hemp.

To recapitulate for the late medieval woolen industries, in Italy, France, the Rhineland, or the Low Countries (and possibly England), typical luxury-grade cloths were composed of combed warps spun on the drop spindle, usually with a Z-twist, and of carded wefts spun on the wheel with an S-twist.

Nevertheless, in the early modern era many luxury-grade woolens in Western Europe did come to be composed throughout of wheel-spun carded wools, both warp and weft, but possibly spun by a different wheel. The first and best-documented evidence of such a change comes almost simultaneously, in 1467, in ordinances issued for the Brabantine woolen draperies of Brussels and Louvain. Both revoked long-standing bans to permit (though not require) the use of the wheel in spinning woolen warps. No change in quality or product type is indicated by either, and the Brussels ordinance is in fact the same one discussed earlier that permitted the use of carded warps in making the best-quality traditional luxury cloths from fine English wools.

We may speculate that these very significant changes were connected to the development of a new and greatly improved spinning wheel, known misleadingly as the Saxony wheel. Its invention had once been attributed to Meister Johann Jürgen of Brunswick, Lower Saxony, about 1530; but subsequently earlier drawings of this machine have been found in *Das mittelalterliches Hausbuch* of Waldburg-Wolfegg (near Lake Constance), dated about 1480; and in Leonardo da Vinci's *Codice Atlantico* of about 1490. Furthermore, the special features in these drawings appear to have been the result of considerable evolution; and undoubtedly this spinning machine, or earlier prototypes, had first been employed many years earlier. Possibly this machine was invented in Italy, during the early fifteenth century.

The radically new device on this Saxony wheel was the flyer with two arms, U-shaped, which, along with a separate bobbin, permitted the simultaneous drafting, twisting, and winding-on of the yarns. The flyer was fixed securely on the center of the spindle axle between the two uprights (maidens), with its back to the left of the drive-pulley (whorl) and with one arm above and the other below the spindle to rotate directly with it. The bobbin was fitted loosely on the spindle between the two arms of the flyer, with its own driving pulley of much smaller diameter, to rotate separately from and more rapidly than the spindle and flyer. A continuous driving belt (appearing to be two belts) was looped twice over the small driving wheel (originally hand-powered), once over the spindle's pulley, and then once over the bobbin's pulley. The roving or sliver of fibers was placed on a distaff attached to the frame's left side. The lead yarn, drawn from the distaff, was fed through the spindle's front end, through the opening of its hollow shaft, outside the left upright, then out through a hole in the side of the shaft underneath the flyer arms, and over hooks (hecks) on the flyer, which guided the yarn onto the bobbin. The spindle's rotation drafted the fibers, while the flyer imparted one twist per revolution to the yarn, which was then wound directly onto the more rapidly revolving bobbin, all in one continuous movement. Subsequent improvements added a "tensioner," a wooden screw in the stock or base that moved the flyer-spindle mechanism away from or closer to the wheel in order to adjust the tension on the driving band; and a foot treadle, with crank and axle, to power the driving wheel. Both hands of the now-seated spinner were thus fully liberated to guide the fibers into the spindle orifice, to adjust the tension on the driving band, the hooks on the flyer, and the speed of the bobbin, thereby governing the yarn's degree of twist and uniformity of fineness. Finally (and perhaps subsequently), the spindle pulley was given two grooves for the driving band: the deeper one for spinning warps; the shallow one, for wefts. For Z-twist yarns, the wheel was turned clockwise; for S-twist, counterclockwise, with the same drive band.

This spinning machine, therefore, with its smooth, continuous action, seems to have offered the requisite conditions for spinning fine carded wools (as well as combed wools) with sufficient evenness or homogeneity, strength, durability, and freedom from knots to serve as warps in woolen cloths. Abbott Payson Usher contends that the Saxony wheel not only produced yarns of much higher quality than did the old Great wheel, but also doubled the spinner's productivity. According to Endrei, furthermore, output from the Saxony wheel was 500 to 600 percent greater than that from the traditional drop spindle in wool spinning, though only 200 percent greater in flax spinning. Some historians have argued, however, that while the linen industry rapidly adopted the Saxony wheel, the woolen industry did not; but its use in the latter is certainly indicated by several early sixteenth-century Flemish paintings and engravings, one showing wool cards and teasel frames along with the new wheel. Nevertheless, both the drop spindle and older Great wheel long continued to be used in European woolen draperies; and the view advanced here that the Saxony wheel, or some variant, was responsible for the grudging acceptance of wheel-spun carded warps remains only a hypothesis. With or without the new wheel, spinning evidently remained by far the most costly stage in the cloth manufacturing process. The sixteenth-century account books of the Medici's woolen firm in Florence show that spinning accounted for 47 percent of pre-finishing costs, compared to 20 percent for wool preparation, 28 percent for weaving, and 5 percent for fulling and tentering.

Reeling and winding. The final stages of spinning, necessary for the preliminary stage of weaving, are reeling and winding the two yarns. Reeling evolved out of the process of removing the spun yarn from the spindle: unwinding it by hand and rewinding it into balls or skeins. From ancient Greek times, that was facilitated by using a cross-reel, a rectangular frame whose four corners were joined diagonally by two crossed pieces of wood. The cross-reel subsequently evolved into a rotary drum-reel with a crank-operated axle. The reeler was thus able to unwind the yarn directly from the spindle onto this drum to form an easily removable skein; by knowing the yarn's length and counting the rotations, she could also grade its fineness.

The reel came into use in the Western European woolen industries about the same time as did the spinning wheel. Its origins may well have been Chinese, in view of its obvious similarity with the spoke-reel in the ancient Chinese silk industry. Since that reel in turn evolved into the belt-driven spool winder for twisting and winding-on silk yarns, many historians believe that the reel was ultimately the ancestor of the spinning wheel.

Reeling was followed by winding, the transfer of the reeled warp and weft yarns by the spinning wheel itself or by a similar bobbin winder onto bobbins in preparation for weaving; in the case of warps, they formed conical balls known as "cops." The weft skeins were placed on freely rotating cone-shaped swifts, from which their yarns were rewound onto bobbins that were then inserted into weaving shuttles.

WEAVING

Warping. Weaving began with warping, the preparation of the warp yarns, which changed considerably from the early to later Middle Ages. In its final form, the yarns from the cops on a dozen bobbins, rotating on pegs attached to posts (spool racks), were unwound and passed together through a single hole in a hand-held board or paddle to be grouped more tightly together. That group of yarns was then wound onto a series of wooden pegs on the warping board, an upright frame, often formed by two posts planted in the ground. Beginning with the top left peg the warper wound the yarns on the lower pegs from side to side in zigzag fashion until she reached the last peg at the bottom right; then she wound the yarns around the same pegs back to the first, where the warps, now measured for the proper length on the horizontal loom, were cut and tied, and then removed and wound into skeins.

Warp-weighted loom. In ancient, Greco-Roman, and early medieval times, however, weaving did not utilize a warping board, because the looms were then entirely different. The most prevalent was the "warp-weighted loom," so named because the warps, tied to an upper crossbar, were vertically stretched taut by weights of stone, pottery, bone, or marble tied to their bottom ends. The framework of this vertical loom, which rested against a wall or supporting post at approximately a seventy-degree angle, consisted of two wooden parallel uprights about three yards high; at the top the uprights were joined by a revolving crossbar about two yards long, which served as both the warp beam and the cloth beam. The warps were stitched onto this beam, which, when rotated, rolled up the cloth as it was woven. Toward the bottom of the two uprights was a fixed crossbar known as the shed rod, fundamental for the weaving itself, in that it divided the warps.

Bundles of vertical warp ends were weighted about 4 inches (10 cm) apart and divided into two sets. The odd-numbered ends, which were movable, were placed behind (below) this fixed shed rod; the even-numbered ends, which remained stationary,

Vertical warp-weighted loom as shown in an 11th-century MS of Hrabanus Maurus' *De universo* (Monte Cassino MS 132). Reproduced from Marta Hoffmann, *The Warp-weighted Loom.* © 1974 THE NORWEGIAN RESEARCH COUNCIL FOR SCIENCE AND THE HUMANITIES

were set in front (above). The opening thereby created between them, known as the natural shed, allowed the first passage of the weft yarn. A second (alternating) opening for the wefts, known as the countershed, was produced by another movable crossbar called the heddle rod, which rested on projecting brackets about halfway up the uprights (at the weavers' breast level). The rear set of warps was "knitted" to this rod by the heddles themselves: threads or linen cords, with looped ends (leashes) through which passed the individual rear warps. Initially resting at the junction of the upright and the brackets, the heddle rod was then lifted up and placed on the fork ends of the brackets, thereby bringing the attached rear warps in front of the upper warps, locking the first weft in a permanent binding, while creating the countershed, or opening, for the second passage of the weft. All of the warps were kept evenly spaced across each shed by other cords fitted with loops (chains) and tied to the uprights.

The weft yarn, attached to a stick, was inserted first through the natural shed of warps and passed by hand from the weaver on one side of the loom to the weaver on the other; each weaver operated one end of the heddle rod(s) while passing the weft back through the countershed. After five or so weft insertions (picks), those wefts were beaten up through the warps into the fell of the cloth and put firmly in place. The most commonly used weft-beating tool in ancient Europe was the weaving sword: a long flat blade (about 20 in. or 50 cm) of wood, iron, or bone fitted with handles. In less common use was the pin beater: a cigar-shaped piece of bone about 4 inches (10 cm) long, polished, and sometimes sharpened at both ends; a third tool was the "weaving comb," from 4 to 8 inches (10–20 cm) long, also made of bone and notched to contain ten short teeth, to fit between the warps.

The type of weave just described is known as plain, tabby, or linen. It involves two sheds (natural and counter) with each weft passing under and over single warps, forming a "regular binding"—the uniform interlacing of single warps and single wefts at right angles. It was used for all linens, indeed all bast-fiber yarns, and it accounts for about 60 percent of late Roman and early medieval textile finds, according to J. P. Wild. A less common variant in this era was the basket or canvas weave, in which two wefts were together woven under and over two warps in succession.

Increasingly popular from very late Roman through early medieval times, especially in worsteds, were the various twill weaves, by which a single weft passed over two (or more) warps and under one or more warps. That uneven alternation between weft and warp produced "interruptions" in the weave or shifts of the binding-points, as the underpass of the weft in the alternate rows was moved one warp thread to the right or left, thus forming diagonal patterns. Such weaves required more sheds and a corresponding increase in the heddle rods to create them. The most common of these weaves was the 2/2 (two over two) plain twill, using four sheds (three heddle rods), in which each weft passed over two warps and then under two, with a regular diagonal. Much more striking patterns, the most complex produced by the warp-weighted loom, were the related 2/2 broken warp, chevron (herringbone), and lozenge twills. In the first, the diagonals formed by the binding points were asymmetrical, "broken" at regular intervals; in the chevron, the direction of the diagonals was reversed (by reversing the order of lifting the heddle rods) over either groups of ends (warp-chevrons) or groups of picks (weft-chevrons); in the lozenge twills, the diagonals were reversed to form diamond or lozenge shapes by a combination of warp-chevron and weft-chevron twills. Such twill weaves are particularly prominent in the early medieval (*ca.* 800–1000) textile finds from Birka and elsewhere in Scandinavia, the majority of which are unfulled worsteds with Z-spun twists for both warp and weft, and a warp-weft ratio of at least two to one; they were evidently products of warp-weighted looms.

That was not, however, the only form of weaving in early medieval Europe. Another was tablet weaving, using square plates of bronze or bone with holes in the four corners for passage of the warps, one end of which were tied to a post and the other to the weaver's waist. These tablets were often used in a series, hand-held like a pack of cards. The sheds for the wefts were changed by turning the tablets backward or forward, while at the same time twisting the warps into cords, which were held together by the wefts. Tablet weaving was in fact particularly important for producing starting borders on the warp-weighted loom to provide an especially strong anchor for the warps.

The true alternative to the warp-weighted loom was the Roman two-beam vertical loom, an ancient instrument of Eastern origin, probably introduced into Europe from Egypt in the first century (when it was described by Seneca). This loom stood about 2.2 yards (2 m) high and was freestanding, resting on floor blocks. The warps were similarly attached to the upper beam, wound over a shed rod and then (from the back) around a rotating lower beam, which thus replaced the warp weights and became the cloth beam to wind up the woven fabric. Consequently, the seated weaver beat the weft down, rather than up, into the fell of the cloth, usually with comb-beaters. This loom became and long remained particularly important for tapestry weaving, which may have been introduced into Roman Europe about the same time; but for other textiles, it did not supplant the warp-weighted loom, in part because the warps lacked flexibility and the sheds were necessarily very narrow.

Horizontal treadle loom. Certainly, in northern Europe, the warp-weighted loom remained predominant until about the eleventh or twelfth century, when one of the most important technological changes in European textile manufacturing occurred: the spread of the horizontal treadle loom. It was first described in an eleventh-century talmudic commentary by Rashi of Troyes (Rabbi Solomon

Horizontal loom with two men weaving and a woman warping below. From a 19th-century copy of the Ypres Kuerboek. Reproduced from Jean Gimpel, *The Medieval Machine*. © 1976 HOLT, RINEHART & WINSTON.

ben Isaac, *ca.* 1040–1105) as a new loom "by which men weave with their feet." Like so many textile implements, its origins were undoubtedly oriental, and probably Chinese. Silk weaving in China had utilized an evidently similar horizontal loom from at least the first century. Horizontal looms had also been commonly utilized in Roman Syria and Egypt, though none with foot treadles has been documented before the sixth century. How and why this loom was introduced into Europe remains a mystery, though possibly again Muslim influences were responsible.

The original European version of the horizontal loom had a narrow, boxlike construction with a raised seat in front for the weaver. The warps were stretched tight horizontally from the warp beam in the rear to the cloth beam in the front; both beams consisted of rollers on ratchets rotated by a lever. Instead of the shed and heddle rods, this loom utilized heddle harnesses suspended from pulleys hooked to the upper crossbeam of the loom (or to the ceiling) and operated by the foot-powered treadles underneath the front of the loom. The harness itself was an iron or wooden rod to which were attached the numerous heddles, similar to those in earlier looms: cords through whose looped ends passed the individual, alternate warps. Each weaving shed had its own heddle harness, pulley, and treadle: thus, two sets of each for plain weave, three for 1/2 or 2/1 twills, and four for the 2/2 twills.

Finally, completing this horizontal loom were the actual weaving instruments: the sley (laysword) and reed. These were suspended from the upper crossbeam (or ceiling) and placed between the heddles and the front of the loom and then joined together. The sley's movable frame contained a grooved wooden channel for the passage of the shuttle, itself first introduced with the new loom. The shuttle encased the weft, wound on a spool, which unraveled and passed through a hole in the side of the shuttle as it moved along the sley. Attached to the front of the sley, and parallel to the shuttle channel, was the reed, beater, or wool comb, which was constructed to the desired width of the cloth with the requisite number of warps. Thus, each cloth type had its own specific reed. It consisted essentially of two narrow horizontal strips of wood (laths) joined together by a multitude of evenly spaced, thin, vertical wire teeth. The individual warps or groups of warps were passed between these teeth, which thus kept them equidistant and parallel during weaving, ensuring the proper width of the cloth much more efficiently than had the chain of the warp-weighted loom. The reed was enclosed in a heavy wooden frame known as the batten, which served to beat up the weft.

The final warping, weaving, and "beating-up" processes for a two-shed plain weave may now be briefly illustrated. After the warps had been wound on the warping-board pegs, measured, and rewound into skeins, they were sized in a glue bath (made from boiled flour or boiled animal skins) to strengthen and protect them from friction in the ensuing weaving processes. The sized warps were then mounted and fully wound onto the loom's (removable) warp beam. Several yards of free warp ends were next inserted individually through the loops of the heddles (the even-numbered ends for the first harness, the odd-numbered for the second), then through the teeth of the reed (which was then reattached to the laysword), and finally were tautly stretched and tied onto the cloth beam. Afterward, the weaver depressed the left foot treadle, thereby raising the right treadle and the right heddle harness, opening the natural shed (even-numbered warps) for the first interlacing. He then slung the weft-bearing shuttle through the grooved sley with his right hand, grasping it at the other side with his left, and pulled it through the shed, thus unwinding and inserting the weft; with the first pick so inserted, he then pulled the sley with reed and batten to the front of the loom, beating the weft up into the fell of the cloth. Next, he depressed the right foot treadle, thereby raising the left treadle and left harness, completing and "locking" the first interlacing or binding while opening the countershed (odd-numbered warps) for the second passage of the shuttle. Repeating the steps just described, the weaver periodically thereafter used the levers on the two beams to feed out more warps and wind up the woven cloth.

This horizontal loom provided a number of significant advantages over the older, vertical looms, especially the warp-weighted. First, its treadle-operated heddle harnesses permitted the much easier creation and control of the weaving sheds for all types of cloth. In particular, three-shed or odd-numbered weaves—for 2/1 and 1/2 twills—were far easier to produce, since the vertical looms, with their fixed shed rods, naturally divided the warps evenly into two groups (thus for 1/1 or 2/2 weaves). Secondly, by fully winding the warps on the rear beam and separately winding the woven fabric, the new loom could produce cloths of far longer lengths, typically 30 yards (27.5 m) or more. Cloths woven on the vertical, warp-weighted loom were effectively limited in length to the loom's height (about 3 to 5 yards, or 2.7 m to 4.6 m) or not much more. Thirdly, the warps were stretched much more tautly on the new loom, with even tension, and the wefts were beaten up much more uniformly and fully than was possible with the warp-weighted loom. Fourthly and consequently, in the view of several historians, this new loom was responsible for creating the true woolen cloth in the form so popular from the twelfth to eighteenth centuries: a cloth with proportionally much more weft than warp, which was then felted (fulled) and shorn. But it is far from certain that the warp-weighted loom had produced only worsted- or serge-type fabrics, though any woolens would certainly have been very loosely woven. Fifthly, and more indisputably, the horizontal loom permitted a considerable increase in productivity. By the late Middle Ages, according to Endrei, weavers could insert up to 425 yards (390 m) of weft per hour on this loom, compared to about 130 yards (120 m) on the warp-weighted loom, a more than threefold increase. Some of these productivity gains undoubtedly resulted, however, from improvements in the loom design.

Broadloom. The chief limitation of the original horizontal loom was that it was too narrow, limiting the cloth width to the arm stretch of the single weaver, while the warp-weighted looms, utilizing two weavers (one on each side) had long been producing cloths of 2 yards (1.8 m) or more in width. For this reason, along with various reasons that typically inhibited the acceptance of technological innovations in the medieval era, the new loom did not displace the old for perhaps two centuries, until the development of the horizontal broadloom, which Endrei had contended was a Flemish innovation of the mid thirteenth century. While that view or dating has been widely adopted, there is no documentary foundation for it; and Endrei himself eventually retreated, suggesting an earlier, if unknown, origin.

The broadloom, designed to weave cloths from 2 to 3 yards (1.8 m to 2.7 m) in width, was simply a doubled version of the former: with two weavers, seated side by side, each operating his own set of treadles, pulleys, and heddle harnesses, but manipulating together the single shuttle and the mechanism that included the sley, reed, and batten. The first weaver slung the shuttle along the sley with his right hand toward the outstretched left hand of his partner, who repeated these movements in reverse, in a constant rhythm, without alternating arms, thus permitting a much more rapid weft insertion per unit of width.

If the resulting increase in productivity was no doubt impressive, as was the improvement in quality, we should place those gains in proper perspective by noting that, in late medieval Flanders, weaving a standard broadcloth of 32 yards by 2.75 yards (42 ells by 3.5 ells—30 m by 2.5 m), containing 84 pounds of wool (36 lb warp and 48 lb weft) typically required about twelve days. At the same time, twelve or more days' labor was expended in wool beating, carding, combing, and spinning yarns for the same cloth, involving in total the labor of twenty-six to thirty persons. With about 240 working days a year, annual output averaged about twenty such broadcloths per loom, or ten cloths per weaver. Productivity evidently did not increase further before the Industrial Revolution. According to an English parliamentary commission report on the 1780's, two men and a boy weaving a superfine broadcloth of 34 yards (31 m), with 70 pounds of wool, required 364 man-hours (or 14.5 days); another 888 man-hours were spent in wool preparation, spinning, reeling, and warping.

Finally, if the broadloom did displace the warp-weighted loom in most parts of Europe (except northern Scandinavia and Iceland), it did not oust the narrow, single-weaver horizontal loom, which retained two advantages: it cost much less to build, operate, and maintain; and it allowed the skilled weaver to work unimpeded by potentially careless or delinquent partners. The single loom continued to be used well into modern times for weaving smaller, less densely woven, cheaper woolens and most worsteds.

FULLING

Following weaving, fulling is the process that completed the actual manufacture of woolen and some serge cloths and prepared them for the finishing processes of nap raising, shearing, and, in some circumstances, dyeing. For reasons mentioned earlier, fulling was generally unnecessary for true worsted textiles (apart from washing); nor for similar reasons was it applied to linen, cotton, or silk fabrics. For woolens and semiwoolens (serges), this process involved the following stages: (1) scouring and washing, (2) burling, (3) fulling itself, (4) final washing, (5) preliminary napping and shearing, and (6) tentering. Because all woolen cloths were woven from wools containing grease, and usually warp sizing as well, those impurities obviously had to be removed. The principal scouring, cleansing, and bleaching agent employed was called "fuller's earth" or *floridin,* a claylike substance containing hydrous aluminum silicates. Many fullers also used various other (generally prohibited) scouring additives: wine dregs, lime, and urine. The use of urine in particular was especially widespread, for the uric acid improved the bleaching efficiency of fuller's earth and promoted shrinkage, while the ammonia content combined with the grease to form a cleansing soap. All of these scouring agents also made the wools more receptive to the mordant or dye fixer (usually alum) in subsequent cloth dyeing. The cloth was then immersed in an emulsion of warm water and fuller's earth (with other chemicals) in a large wooden or stoneware vat, and thoroughly scrubbed, especially by foot treading. After the cloth had been thoroughly scoured and then rinsed out in running cold water, it was subjected to burling, the removal of any knots and other defects that arose from weaving and from scouring.

Fulling itself then followed: the cloth was placed in the fulling vat, immersed again in hot water, sometimes with a mixture of oat flour (*grummel*), and trod upon and pummeled to remove wrinkles and untwist the fibers. It was briefly removed, given a butter or lard application, then restored to the fuller's vat with more hot water and much soap for more thorough trampling and pummeling. Finally, the cloth was scoured, washed, and again rinsed to remove that grease. The combination of heat, pressure, pummeling, water, soap, and other chemicals compressed the warp and weft yarns tightly together and forced all the loose, scaly fiber ends to interlace, contract, and mat together. That compression, shrinkage, thickening, and felting gave the cloth far greater strength and durability, homogeneity, density, and thus weight per square unit of area. Woolens normally underwent a shrinkage of about 30 percent in length, 35 to 40 percent in width, and up to 60 percent in surface area (for example, Bruges *bellaert,* of 1460: from 84.3 to 36.8 square yards, or 70.4 to 30.7 sq m).

The process just described was traditional foot fulling sometimes supplemented by hand fulling with clubs, especially for smaller cloths. For standard-sized luxury quality woolens (about 21 yards or 19.2 m by 1.8 yards or 1.6 m finished) in late medieval Flemish draperies, such fulling required the labor of two full-time journeymen and the supervision of the master fuller for three to five days, depending on the cloth type and the season. That meant a maximum annual output (240 days) of twenty-four to forty woolen cloths per journeyman fuller, on average a higher output than that for weavers. Cheaper and smaller woolens required perhaps two days' fulling; and most serge-type fabrics, only a day's fulling (about nine to ten hours)—more for scouring and cleansing than for

Drapers' market in Bologna. 15th-century miniature in the Museo Civico, Bologna. ALINARI / ART RESOURCE

any compression and felting. Virtually all major draperies in the Low Countries retained this ancient method up to the sixteenth century or later; but in many other parts of Europe, from England to Italy, foot fulling had much earlier given way to a mechanized form: the fulling mill, which can be documented from the tenth century, first in Italy (Abruzzo, 962; Parma, 973; Verona, 985), and then in northern Europe, from the eleventh century (at Argentan, Normandy, 1086).

Fulling was the first industrial manufacturing process to be truly mechanized (by waterpower); it was the only cloth-production process to be so mechanized before the fifteenth century, when gig mills for nap raising were first introduced, and the only important stage before the Industrial Revolution. The structures involved, particularly in later medieval fulling mills or "fulling stocks," could be quite large, requiring a significant capital investment: a two-story building to whose outer wall was attached a large wooden waterwheel, either undershot or overshot, often with a millpond (to which the water was diverted from a river, for storage) and millrace. With either, using a camshaft, the waterwheel rotated a drum with wooden tappets on each side that alternately lifted two large, heavy oak trip-hammers and then released them at the top to drop with great force on the cloth in the fulling trough below. In early modern English mills, with a typical shaft rotation of thirteen rpm, each hammerhead pounded the cloth up to forty times a minute. With just one attendant, these mills required about twenty hours to scour and full a standard-sized good-quality woolen cloth, and as few as nine for lesser-quality cloths.

Estimates of the productivity gains and cost savings achieved by substituting mill fulling for foot fulling vary enormously. The most extreme are those of Schmoller and Endrei, who have postulated thirty-five- to fiftyfold gains (savings up to 98 percent), which seem grossly excessive. At the other extreme, a fuller's tariff for Aire-sur-Lys (Artois) in 1359, pricing both mill and foot fulling per cloth, offered only a 25 percent saving by the former; but those prices may conceal a large economic rent for the fulling-mill owner. For sixteenth-century Brabant, Raymond Van Uytven has estimated a 70 percent saving by mill fulling (a 3.3 fold productivity gain). Support for that estimate may be found by comparing the relative costs of foot fulling at Leuven and Leiden in the 1430's with those of mill fulling at Florence in the 1550's: the former accounted for 22.5 percent of pre-finishing manufacturing costs, compared to 5.1 percent of such costs at Florence (for equivalent woolens), representing a 77 percent advantage for the latter.

Waterpowered fulling spread through many of the European textile-producing centers during the twelfth and thirteenth centuries, but perhaps even more so in some regions during the fourteenth and fifteenth centuries when it was favored by changes in relative costs. Depopulation in particular raised the real cost of labor, while cheapening the cost of land sites and capital for fulling mills; and agrarian recession, especially marked in grain farming, encouraged the conversion of many waterpowered grain mills to fulling mills.

Major geographical exceptions in the late Middle Ages were the Low Countries and Normandy. Contrary to some authorities (notably E. M. Carus-Wilson), the Low Countries had in fact long used waterpower for many agricultural and industrial purposes, including even mechanical fulling in several districts during the thirteenth century; but the shift to fulling mills was generally abandoned in the fourteenth. The increased power of textile guilds in urban governments during that century fails to provide an adequate explanation, because the fullers were economically and politically subordinate to their employers, the weaver-drapers, whose guilds succeeded in excluding the fullers from many town governments in their chronic wage disputes.

The real explanation may lie in the fact that most Low Countries draperies had also abandoned export-oriented production of cheap woolens and serges during that century to concentrate much more on high-priced luxury woolens. They found that, while they still retained many comparative advantages in the luxury field, the production of cheap textiles became uneconomic because of a steep rise in the relative costs of transporting and marketing them across war-torn Europe. These urban draperies, faced moreover with declining markets and stronger international competition in the late Middle Ages, refused to risk their product reputation—their chief advantage—by engaging in mechanical fulling. Certainly the contemporary documentation reflects the strongly held view that waterpowered mechanical fulling was quite injurious to the quality of luxury woolens. For that very stated reason also, several Norman draperies (Rouen, Louviers, St. Lô, Torigini) either similarly abandoned mill fulling or refused to permit it (except for very cheap cloths sold locally) during the fourteenth and fifteenth centuries. In general, such factors may also explain resistance in the Low Countries draperies to technological innovations in carding and spinning, a resistance that was in fact much more marked in the fourteenth than in the thirteenth century.

Only in the sixteenth century, with a renewed emphasis on the export-oriented production of cheap textiles in the Low Countries, was there a renewed shift to fulling mills in that region by both rural and urban draperies. New fulling mills were also established in Normandy from the late fifteenth century.

The final stages of fulling, both in foot- and waterpowered forms, also commenced the finishing processes. Indeed, the fulled cloth was first subjected to a preliminary raising and shearing by the fuller himself, using fuller's teasels, while the cloth was still wet, to raise all the loose fibers, its "nap," and then to cut them off with shears. That was known as wet shearing to distinguish it from the much more major tasks undertaken by the professional shearers; and it was often performed while the cloth was hung to dry on the tentering frame.

TENTERING

Tentering, the drying and stretching of a fulled cloth upon a tentering frame, was designed to eliminate any wrinkles, creases, or other defects that occurred as a result of fulling; to restore some of the loss in surface area (up to 50 percent); and, above all, to ensure that the cloth, while drying, maintained a uniform width and length throughout and a uniform surface area for subsequent finishing. The frame, adjustable to the various cloth sizes, consisted of a wooden platform supporting a succession of equally spaced wooden uprights or poles, which were joined at their tops by a fixed crossbar, and along their slotted lower portions by a moveable crossbar. A rotating post, the *boem* or *templet,* turned by a hand-winch, was installed at the far end of this framework. The fixed upright at one end, the templet at the other, and the two crossbars were all fitted with tenterhooks. The wet cloth, placed lengthwise, was first attached at one end to the hooks on the fixed upright and then at its other end to the templet, which was then turned to stretch the cloth along its length. The cloth was then attached along its sides (selvages, lists) to the hooks on the upper and lower crossbars, and was stretched across its width by forcing the lower bar down to the bottom slots. Tentering frames were sometimes located inside heated buildings; but more generally and more economically they were placed outdoors to dry the cloth in the sun and wind. The process took from two days in the summer to four in the winter.

RAISING

Also known as napping, raising—alternating with shearing—commenced the ensuing finishing processes. Both raising and shearing were usually conducted several times, beginning with the wet cloth hung on the tentering frame (if the fuller had not already subjected it to wet shearing). The required teasels were set tightly inside a rectangular

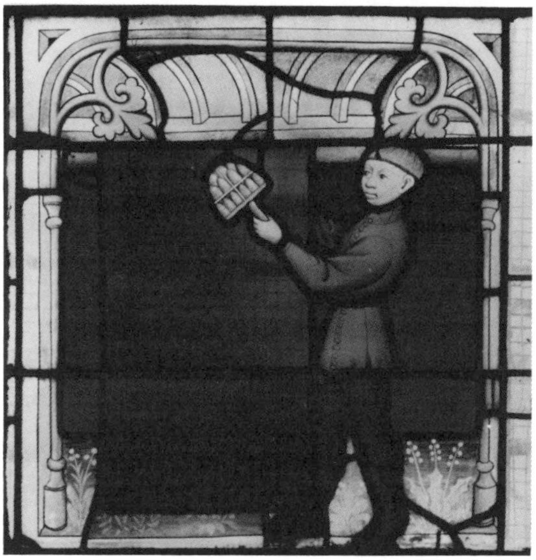

Raising cloth (*left*) before shearing or cropping (*right*). From the stained glass clothiers' window at Semur-en-Auxois, *ca.* 1460. © SONIA HALLIDAY PHOTOGRAPHS

wooden frame with a long handle, and the tool itself was often simply called a "handle." A handle with rough or hard teasels was used for initial raising and one with softer teasels was employed for subsequent raising. While raising the nap on a wet cloth was sometimes performed by drawing or pulling the teasels over its face, raising on a dried, tentered cloth was always done by pushing the handle from the bottom to the top of the cloth. This was a most laborious and tedious task; the initial raising on a good-quality dry woolen might take up to eight hours. In fifteenth-century England, raising was mechanized by the waterpowered gig mill, often constructed as part of a fulling mill. With this machine, teasels set into a rotating cylinder by wooden frames were drawn across the face of a moving cloth placed on a revolving belt. Such mechanical raising was strongly resisted in many draperies, and they were frequently banned by parliament. The chief concern may have been quality control, but another was surely technological unemployment. For a 1640 parliamentary report, commenting on the illegal spread of gig mills, stated that one mill with two men and a boy could perform the raising traditionally done by eighteen men and six boys (a 9:1 gain). Similar gig mills can also be found in seventeenth-century Italy.

SHEARING

Shearing describes the process of clipping, cutting, or cropping the raised nap as close as possible to the weave, thus completing the effects of fulling, felting, and raising in eliminating any visible weave patterns in true woolens. More importantly, repeated raising and shearing also made the cloth surface completely uniform and smooth, often as smooth as silk, and allowed most dyes (subsequently applied) to achieve their maximum brilliance. The shears employed in medieval finishing, little changed from Roman times, were similar to those for wool shearing, though much larger. The razor-sharp steel blades, about 18 inches (45 cm) long, branched out from the U-shaped steel bowspring, serving also as a handle usually much longer than the blades. The lower blade was weighted with lead to set it firmly into the cloth's surface. The table on which the cloth was placed for shearing had a padded, slanted top, and small hooks along its two ends for securing one section of the cloth. The shearman then placed his shears along the cloth edge at the upper end of the table; opening and shutting the upper blade by his left hand, while using the right hand and his body to position the shears, he allowed them to slide by their own weight gently down the slope of the cloth as they cropped the nap. The extent of the cut was determined by both the weight of the shears and the amount of table padding. That portion of the cloth now shorn was then unhooked, and the adjacent portion was next fixed to the table for shearing.

Both wet and dry shearing, and their associated raisings, were each performed several times; the latter method was usually conducted many more times, the exact number varying according to the type and quality of the woolen. In between wet and dry shearing, or before the final shearing, the shorn woolen was often sent to be "dyed in the piece"; it was then subjected to further tentering and a final shrinkage, often by steaming and ironing, before further (or final) raising and shearing. The final nap raisings and shearings were done lightly and finely, to avoid damaging the dyed fibers but to give them more sheen. Finally, the finished cloth was pressed in a manner unchanged from Roman times: usually without any heat, in a wooden vise, using wooden pressing blocks and two sets of screws rotated by levers, forcing the top plate onto the lower. In the early modern era, pressing was improved by the process known as calendering: running the cloth through rollers, which were mechanically powered from the seventeenth century. The pressed cloths were then folded and packaged for delivery to market, or to the merchants or other clients who had commissioned the finishing.

DYEING

Although the process of dyeing has been discussed elsewhere in this Dictionary, some technological details should be added here. Dyeing could take place in the wool, in the yarn, and/or in the piece (before, during, or after shearing). Many cloths woven from woad-dyed wools were re-dyed in the piece with red or yellow dyes to produce various colors for which woad served as the base: sanguine, brown, purple, mulberry, perse, gray, black, and green. While wools and yarns were obviously dyed in various colors, to produce striped and medley cloths, woad was certainly preferred for wool dyeing because it did not require a mordant to be fixed to the wool fibers; mordants such as alum, among others, made it more difficult to work with the wools.

The technology of dyeing, of woad dyeing in the following example, evidently changed little during the Middle Ages. Water, containing bran and grated madder, was heated in copper boilers, with a wood- or coal-burning brick furnace; once boiled, the water was removed from the heat to allow the bran impurities to precipitate out of the solution. The resulting clear, purified *eau sure* was then decanted, poured via wooden troughs into the wooden or stoneware vats. Potash (potassium hydroxide) was added to the woad to make it water-soluble; both were immersed in the *eau sure* and mashed together by wooden rakes. The vat was then sealed with an airtight lid to promote fermentation, free from oxidation. When the dye solution was ready, after about three days, the wool, yarn, or cloth was moistened, then plunged into the vat, stirred thoroughly with wooden forks, and passed through wringers. Finally the wool or cloth was hung on wooden ladders to drip-dry; and with exposure to air, the oxidation changed the colorless leucodye, absorbed by the fibers, into a fast blue.

Mordant dyeing was usually conducted in a totally different establishment by different dyers. In such dyeing, the alum and frequently also tartar were added with the wool or cloth to the water, which was boiled for several hours to allow the alum to dissolve, adhere to the fibers, and cleanse them. Then, for standard red dyeing, the madder was added and the solution was reboiled. The mordant permitted the permanent chemical union of the wool fibers with the alizarin, obtained from the madder by hydrolysis and fermentation in alkaline water, thereby producing a fast color. Although some new natural dyestuffs were added in the early modern era, dyeing technology remained basically unchanged until the synthesis of aniline dyes in the 1850's.

CONCLUSION

The technology of the other processes of cloth production and finishing remained basically unaltered until the Industrial Revolution. The textile technology of the early modern era differed from the medieval only in the improvement and spread of the Saxony spinning wheel, and of fulling and gig mills, and the adoption of waterpowered calendaring machines. None of these changes can compare in their impact on textiles with the medieval innovations in carding, spinning weaving, and fulling; and none fundamentally altered the nature of textile manufacturing in the early modern era, which remained highly labor-intensive.

BIBLIOGRAPHY

Patricia Baines, *Spinning Wheels, Spinners, and Spinning* (1978); A. R. Bridbury, *Medieval English Clothmaking: An Economic Survey* (1982); Dorothy Burnham, *Warp and Weft: A Dictionary of Textile Terms* (1981); Claude Carrère, *Barcelone: Centre économique à l'époque des difficultés, 1380–1462* (1967); Eleanora M. Carus-Wilson, "An Industrial Revolution of the Thirteenth Century" and "The English Cloth Industry in the Late Twelfth and Early Thirteenth Centuries," in her

Medieval Merchant Venturers: Collected Studies (1954), "The Woollen Industry," in M. M. Postan and E. E. Rich, eds., *The Cambridge Economic History of Europe,* II: *Trade and Industry in the Middle Ages* (1952), "Wiltshire: The Woollen Industry Before 1550," in Elizabeth Crittall and R. D. Pugh, eds., *A History of Wiltshire* (1959), and "Haberget: A Medieval Textile Conundrum," in *Medieval Archaeology,* **13** (1969); Patrick Chorley, "The Cloth Exports of Flanders and Northern France During the Thirteenth Century: A Luxury Trade?" in *Economic History Review,* **40** (1987); Donald C. Coleman, "An Innovation and Its Diffusion: The New Draperies," *Economic History Review,* **22** (1969); Émile Coornaert, *Un centre industriel d'autrefois: La draperie-sayetterie d'Hondschoote, XIVe–XVIIIe siècles* (1930) and "Draperies rurales, draperies urbaines: L'evolution de l'industrie flamande au moyen âge et au XVIe siècle," in *Revue belge de philologie et d'histoire,* **28** (1950); Raymond De Roover, "A Florentine Firm of Cloth Manufacturers: Management and Organization of a Sixteenth-century Business," in *Speculum,* **16** (1941); Alain Derville, "Les draperies flamandes et artésiennes vers 1250–1350," in *Revue du Nord,* **54** (1972); M. J. Dickenson, "Fulling in the West Riding Woollen Cloth Industry, 1689–1770," in *Textile History,* **10** (1979); J. F. Drinkwater, "The Wool Textile Industry of Gallia Belgica and the Secundini of Igel: Questions and Hypotheses," in *Textile History,* **13** (1982); Walter Endrei, *L'évolution des techniques du filage et du tissage du moyen âge à la révolution industrielle* (1968), and "Changements dans la productivité de l'industrie lainière au moyen âge," in *Annales: Economies, Sociétés, Civilisations,* **26** (1971); Georges Espinas, *La draperie dans la Flandre française au moyen âge,* 2 vols. (1923), and, with Henri Pirenne, eds. *Recueil de documents relatifs à l'histoire de l'industrie drapière en Flandre,* pt. 1: *Des origines à l'époque bourguignonne,* 4 vols. (1906–1924); Félicien Favresse, *Études sur les métiers bruxellois au moyen âge* (1961); Robert J. Forbes, *Studies in Ancient Technology,* IV, 2nd rev. ed. (1964); Agnes Geijer, *A History of Textile Art* (1979); A. Rupert Hall and N. C. Russell, "What About the Fulling Mill?" in *History of Technology,* **6** (1981); Negley B. Harte and Kenneth G. Ponting, eds., *Cloth and Clothing in Medieval Europe: Essays in Memory of Professor E. M. Carus-Wilson* (1983); A. E. Haynes, "Twill Weaving on the Warp Weighted Loom: Some Technical Considerations," in *Textile History,* **6** (1975); Herbert Heaton, *The Yorkshire Woollen and Worsted Industries: From the Earliest Times up to the Industrial Revolution,* 2nd ed. (1965); Marta Hoffmann, *The Warp-weighted Loom: Studies in the History and Technology of an Ancient Implement* (1974); Hidetoshi Hoshino, *L'arte della lana in Firenze nel basso medioevo: Il commercio della lana e il mercato dei panni fiorentini nei secoli XIII–XV* (1980); J. Geraint Jenkins, ed., *The Wool Textile Industry in Great Britain* (1972); Henri Laurent, *Un grand commerce d'exportation au moyen âge: La draperie des Pays-Bas en France et dans les pays mediterranéens, XIIe–XVe siècle* (1935); Hugo Lemon, "The Development of Hand Spinning Wheels," in *Textile History,* **1** (1968–1970); Ephraim Lipson, *The History of the Woollen and Worsted Industries* (1921) and *A Short History of Wool and Its Manufacture, Mainly in England* (1953); T. H. Lloyd, "Some Costs of Cloth Manufacturing in Thirteenth-century England," in *Textile History,* **1** (1968–1970); Norman Lowe, *The Lancashire Textile Industry in the Sixteenth Century* (1972); Paolo Malanima, "The First European Textile Machine," in *Textile History,* **17** (1986); Marian Malowist, "Les changements dans la structure de la production et du commerce du drap au cours du XIVe et du XVe siècle," in his *Croissance et regression en Europe, XIVe–XVIIe siècles: Recueil d'articles* (1972); Sara Mariotti, ed., *Produttività e tecnologie nei secoli XII–XVII* (1981); Maureen F. Mazzaoui, *The Italian Cotton Industry in the Later Middle Ages, 1100–1600* (1981); Federigo Melis, *Aspetti della vita economica medievale: Studi nell'Archivo Datini di Prato,* I (1962); Edward Miller, "The Fortunes of the English Textile Industry in the Thirteenth Century," in *Economic History Review,* **18** (1965); Adam Nahlik, "Les techniques de l'industrie textile en Europe orientale, du Xe au XVe siècle," in *Annales: E.S.C.,* **26** (1971); William Partridge, *A Practical Treatise on Dying of Woollen, Cotton, and Skein Silk with the Manufacture of Broadcloth and Cassimere* (1823), reissued with introduction and technical notes by Julia DeLacy Mann and Kenneth G. Ponting (1973); R. Patterson, "Spinning and Weaving," in Charles Singer *et al.,* eds., *A History of Technology,* II: *The Mediterranean Civilizations and the Middle Ages, c. 700 B.C. to c. 1500 A.D.* (1956), 191–220; Guy de Poerck, *La draperie médiévale en Flandre et en Artois: Technique et terminologie,* 3 vols. (1951); Kenneth G. Ponting, *The Woollen Industry of South-west England* (1971), "Sculpture and Paintings of the Textile Processes at Leiden," in *Textile History,* **5** (1974), and *Beginners' Guide to Weaving* (1982); Nicolaas Posthumus, *De geschiedenis van de leidsche lakenindustrie,* 3 vols. (1908–1939); George D. Ramsay, *The Wiltshire Woollen Industry in the Sixteenth and Seventeenth Centuries* (1943, 2nd ed. 1965); Michael L. Ryder, "The Origin of Spinning," in *Textile History,* **1** (1968–1970); Johan-Henri de Sagher *et al.,* eds., *Recueil de documents relatifs à l'histoire de l'industrie drapière en Flandre,* pt. 2: *Le sudouest de la Flandre depuis l'époque bourguignonne,* 3 vols. (1951–1966); E. Kilburn Scott, "Early Cloth Fulling and Its Machinery," in *The Newcomen Society Transactions,* **12** (1931–1932); Marco Spallanzani, ed., *Produzione, commercio, e consumo dei panni di lana, nei secoli XII–XVIII* (1976); Abbott Payson Usher, *A History of Mechanical Inventions,* (1929; rev. ed. 1954); Herman Van der Wee, "Structural Changes and Specialization in the Industry of the Southern Netherlands, 1100–1600," in *Economic History Review,* **28** (1975); Maurice Van Haeck, *Histoire de la sayetterie à Lille,* 2 vols. (1910); Raymond Van Uytven, "The Fulling Mill: Dynamic of the Revolution in Industrial Attitudes," in *Acta Historiae Neerlandicae,* **5** (1971); Hans Van Werveke, "Industrial Growth in the Middle Ages: The Cloth Industry in Flanders," in *Economic History Review,* **6** (1954); Lynn White, jr., *Medieval Technology and Social Change* (1962); J. P. Wild, *Textile Manufacture in the Northern Roman Provinces* (1970); M. G. Willemsen, "La technique et l'organisation de la draperie à Bruges, à Gand, et à Malines, au milieu du XVIe siècle," in *Annales de l'Académie Royale d'Archéologie de Belgique,* **68** (1920); Andrew Woodger, "The Eclipse of the Burel Weaver: Some Technological Developments in the Thirteenth Century," in *Textile History,* **12** (1981).

JOHN H. MUNRO

[See also **Costume; Cotton; Dyes and Dyeing; Fairs; Hemp; Linen; Scarlet; Silk; Tapestry, Art of; Technology; Trade; Wool.**]

TEXTILE WORKERS. Medieval textile workers led such varied lives that generalizations are futile and detailed analyses impractical. In connection, therefore, with the companion essay on textile technology, this one will also focus chiefly on northern wool workers from the eleventh century. In the following centuries, such workers experienced four major and related status changes: a much more formalized division of industrial labor, as textiles became a major component in expanding international trade; a gender change in occupations that reflected ensuing changes in both commercial and industrial technology; the organization of the four major crafts (weaving, fulling, dyeing, and finishing) into guilds; and finally, in some major textile towns, chronic industrial strife as these crafts fought for more economic power, first against the cloth merchants or drapers and then against each other.

Through the earlier medieval era, textile-making of all varieties—linens, woolens, worsteds, serges, fustians, and various other mixed fabrics—had undoubtedly been chiefly a rural domestic or family-based craft with little if any formal division of labor, except perhaps in the workshops of religious orders and aristocratic estates, the latter called *gynaecia.* As that term indicates, almost everywhere the actual cloth-manufacturing processes—wool preparation, combing, spinning, and weaving—were done chiefly by women. Any required cloth finishing (unnecessary for most worsteds, linens, and fustians) was undertaken by both men and women.

While textile production of this type based on local resources and local consumption can be found throughout most parts of later medieval Europe, certain regions developed urban industries (with rural appendages) that were highly dependent upon international trade for both raw materials and markets. The first region to gain prominence for its export-oriented textile industries was northern France, especially Artois and Flanders, followed by Normandy, principalities in the imperial Low Countries (Brabant, Hainaut, Holland), England, southern France, northern Italy, and Catalonia. The history of these industries exemplifies Adam Smith's famous dictum that the extent of the market determines the division of labor. No household could itself produce an entire cloth at a price and level of quality that would sell in competitive foreign markets. Such low-cost efficiency and high quality could be achieved only if textile workers each specialized in one specific task: as woolsorters and beaters, combers, carders, warp and weft spinners, reelers, warpers, weavers, fullers, tenterers, burlers, raisers (nappers), shearers, and dyers. Many of these artisans also utilized specialized assistants for subsidiary tasks. Nor could any individual household or other small production unit efficiently acquire the necessary raw materials or market the finished products itself; for these purposes, textile producers necessarily became dependent upon wool and cloth merchants in particular.

Those who traded internationally in wool, dyestuffs, or finished cloths could justifiably be called merchant capitalists, particularly because they had to command considerable capital, especially working capital, to engage in long-distance journeys of many months and to hold large inventories. Many such merchants also extended credit to textile producers to acquire customers and trading goods. Some historians have further contended that, particularly in thirteenth-century Flanders, such merchants had imposed a form of industrial capitalism on the textile crafts, exploiting an "industrial proletariat."

Such a claim is, however, a great exaggeration, insofar as it is based largely upon the legal records of the singular Jean Boinebroke of Douai (*d.* 1286). Principally a wool merchant and secondarily a cloth merchant, he was also a landowner with a sheep farm and many urban properties. He served several terms as alderman (*échevin*) in the town government. He usually sold wool (especially costly English wools) on credit to weaver-drapers, who sometimes pledged their looms, homes, and more frequently their woven cloths as security. Some cloth-makers also rented their houses from him. But most of the industrial workers hired directly by Boinebroke were those typically required for the wool trade: sorters, beaters, washers, and wool dyers. The very few other artisans that he employed directly in cloth-making worked on his own tentering frames. Even during the zenith of the Flemish cloth industry, in the late thirteenth century, when its wool and cloth trades were still dominated by domestic merchants, merchant-draper capitalists like Boinebroke were atypical; and even Boinebroke did not oversee the central processes of cloth-making.

In the export-oriented woolen crafts of later medieval Western Europe, the actual industrial entrepreneur was commonly the small weaver-draper, who typically operated by a "putting out" or domestic system, which was very small-scale and highly labor-intensive with much more capital invested in materials than tools. In France and the Low Countries, he was called the *drapier*; in Italy, the *lanaiuoli*; in England, the clothier. He (or she) first purchased the wools, which were sorted, beaten, washed, and greased by either his own employees or those of the wool merchant in his own shop, and such wools were then "put out" to combers and carders; in Florence the *lanaiuoli* often subcontracted this "putting out" to *stamaiuoli* (yarn dealers). The warp and weft wools were then collected and put out to the distaff- and wheel-spinners, respectively. These workers, who were all paid piecework wages, were almost all female, and most worked with their own tools in their own homes, which were often rural, primarily agricultural households. Only rarely would they work directly in the draper's home or workshop with his own equipment.

The draper then collected the spun warp and weft yarns for delivery to his warpers and winders, chiefly female employees, who did work in the draper's home or workshop: the former to set up warps for the loom and the latter to insert weft in the shuttles. Even the draper who was also a master weaver commonly employed other weavers, usually journeymen and apprentice weavers (again for piecework wages) to work other looms in his establishment and at least one to assist on his own horizontal broadloom. Neither weaving nor draping was necessarily a full-time occupation: many of these artisans, whether urban or rural, earned supplementary income from farming or other crafts and trades.

The development of the horizontal loom, and especially the broadloom, also accompanied the most significant gender change in the medieval woolen textile industry. For in the earlier Middle Ages, when the vertical warp-weighted loom predominated, weavers were almost exclusively female. But with the advent of the horizontal loom from about the mid eleventh century, and especially with the spread of the broadloom from the thirteenth century, weavers became predominantly, though never exclusively, male. The reasons for that gender change may lie with the technical requirements of the horizontal loom (especially the broadloom) in working the foot treadles and throwing the shuttle. Or, perhaps more likely, male dominance may have resulted from structural changes imposed on this industry as it became export-oriented, using the new technology, and then guild-organized. If female weavers were uncommon in this industry, they were somewhat more numerous among the class of drapers, frequently (if not always) as their husbands' partners and then as widows carrying on their husbands' businesses.

The final group of artisans employed by the drapers were the fullers, who worked in their own establishments, urban or rural (especially for water-powered fulling mills), requiring some capital investment. In the Low Countries, traditional foot fulling of luxury-grade woolens was typically undertaken by one male master and two journeymen (apart from tentering and burling, which were often female tasks), and one master might operate up to four fulling vats in the same fashion. They were paid a combination piecework and daily wage by the draper: so much per broadcloth fulled within three days (or four, as specified). A Flemish fuller processed about thirty to thirty-five broadcloths a year (*ca.* 1400), while the average weaver produced only twenty broadcloths or less annually; thus the Flemish cloth industry employed fewer fullers than weavers (in a 6:10 ratio, approximately).

In this purely industrial process of cloth manufacturing, the one group of artisans who did not earn wages were the master weaver-drapers. Their income was instead profit: the difference between their labor, raw materials (principally wool), and other production costs, and the price received from selling the woven, fulled cloth to various cloth finishers (*upzetters*) or cloth merchants, domestic or foreign—increasingly the latter in the Low Countries from the early fourteenth century. Most drapers, even those controlling several looms, had very small profit margins and thus very modest incomes. Those few who became wealthy did so primarily by becoming merchant-drapers: engaging in the wool, cloth, finishing, or dyestuffs trades (despite urban legislation forbidding such cumulative practices, as in late medieval Flanders and England).

Those engaged in the finishing crafts (as masters) also enjoyed generally greater incomes and social status than did ordinary weavers or weaver-drapers. Dyers and shearers in fact performed more purely commercial than industrial functions, usually at the behest of cloth merchants, who were more cognizant than ordinary drapers of shifts in consumer fashion, of changing demands for style, cut, and color of cloths. They were fully professional craftsmen, earning stipulated fees, each working for a variety of clients—domestic and foreign merchants, cloth brokers, *upzetters,* and even some local drapers. Since they themselves had to purchase raw materials and tools and hire assistants, their income must also be considered a form of profit, though evidently with a much larger profit margin than that enjoyed by most weaver-drapers. In late medieval Florence, however, the dyers if not the finishers lost their professional independence, becoming little more than employees of the *lanaiuoli,* whose guild, the Arte della Lana, itself set the dyeing fees with government approval.

During the later Middle Ages, especially in northwestern Europe, these last four groups of urban artisans—weavers, fullers, dyers, and shearers—organized themselves into formal male-dominated craft guilds, whose experiences varied greatly. In Flanders, for example, formal, legal textile guilds developed much later than in English or French towns; but ultimately, after violent struggles, they gained far greater economic and political power there than elsewhere. Industrial strife in French, Flemish, and Brabantine towns began from the 1240's, when the weavers' and fullers' crafts, led by the industrial drapers and masters, rebelled against the wool and cloth merchants' guilds, which dominated both their town governments and the cloth industry, arbitrarily regulating it through urban legislation.

In Flanders, this industrial strife, with ensuing rebellions between 1274 and 1275 and in 1280, culminated in a veritable revolution during the Anglo-French wars between 1294 and 1303, which directly involved Flanders as a French fief and the chief market for English wool, embargoed by war. Much earlier, from 1274 to 1275, in response to social unrest and petitions from the cloth crafts, still excluded from urban administration, the counts of Flanders had attempted to curb the powers of the town oligarchies, the "patriciates," who in turn quickly secured protection from the French kings and their Parlement de Paris, thereby acquiring the sobriquet of *Leliaerts* (men of the fleurs-de-lis).

Philip IV (1285–1314) went even further by installing royal bailiffs and "guardians" in the Flemish towns, imposing economic ordinances on Flanders, conspiring with neighboring princes (Hainaut, Holland) against his overmighty Flemish vassal, and finally, in 1296, by having Parlement declare Flanders forfeit to the crown. The next year, the desperate Count Guy de Dampierre (1278–1305) allied himself with Edward I of England, thereby restoring the vital wool trade. He also abolished the *Leliaert* governments of Ghent and Douai (1296–1297) and permitted his supporters, who were known as *Clauwaerts* (men of the lion's claw—the count's emblem), especially urban craft guildsmen, to persecute the *Leliaerts.* Philip IV responded with an invasion of Flanders, which his armies finally conquered in May 1300, after Edward had deserted the Flemish. Chafing under French military occupation and the oppressive rule of the *Leliaerts,* the *Clauwaerts,* led by Bruges guildsmen and then by the imprisoned count's sons, revolted in 1301–1302. Incredibly, their infantry army, chiefly guild militia, defeated the pride of the French cavalry at the Battle of Courtrai in July 1302 and proceeded to oust and despoil the *Leliaerts.*

Although the Flemish lost crucial battles in 1304 and had to cede the Walloon towns (Douai, Lille) to France, the final peace of 1320 guaranteed Flanders' de facto independence and new urban constitutions, which gave the textile and other craft guilds a permanent majority share of the aldermanic seats in the Flemish town governments (Ghent, Bruges, Ypres). The former *Leliaert* "patriciate" families, now called the *poorterie,* with some nouveau riche adherents, were not excluded, however, even though their economic power had been gravely weakened by the loss of their international wool and cloth trades to foreign merchants. Sometimes the *poorterie* allied with the "small guilds" (to which some of them belonged) to reassert power in the town governments. Thus the two leading cloth guilds, the weavers and fullers, were only rarely able to dominate these governments; for instead of joining forces, more frequently throughout much of the fourteenth century they fought each other for urban supremacy.

In fact, the dominant feature of labor history in the later medieval Low Countries, when their cloth industry suffered severely from increasing competition in depressed and contracted foreign markets, was industrial guild strife. Particularly in times of coinage debasement and inflation, the fullers' guild went on strike, bargaining for higher wages. With their profit margins so squeezed, the weavers' guilds sought fuller control of their urban governments to oust the fullers and to repress their wage demands. To be sure, more than just these industrial guild conflicts were involved in Flanders' three most famous urban rebellions and civil wars—from 1323 to 1328, 1338 to 1349, and from 1379 to 1385—but they certainly figured strongly in the latter two. Strikes and other industrial violence in Flanders and Holland can also be documented in many of the years between 1355 and 1478.

It must be stressed that the fullers were the sole group of artisans directly employed by the weaver-drapers (or merchant-drapers in Holland) who also had the power to bargain for wages through guild organization. The other, subsidiary wool workers, so many of them part-time female rural labor, lacked such protection and thus were entirely at the mercy of the drapers, accepting the proffered wages without recorded protest. Although the dyers and shearers earned fees that were also set by urban legislation, their guilds usually succeeded in determining those fees, which were of lesser concern to Flanders' industrial drapers, at least, especially after cloth exports fell under the control of Italian and Hanseatic merchants.

In the Mediterranean south, the closest counterparts to this industrial struggle were the Florentine revolts of the fourteenth century, directed against the Arte della Lana, a leader of the seven-member Arti Maggiori, which then dominated the Florentine government. In 1324 and more severely in 1338 the Arte della Lana prohibited any organization by any employees or subordinate artisans (*sottoposti*) of the *lanaiuoli* on pain of *divieto*: expulsion from the cloth trades. The first challenge came during the brief military rule of the duke of Athens, Walter de Brienne (1342–1343). Seeking more popular support, and responding to complaints of cloth dyers and soapmakers against the Arte della Lana, in particular its payment practices, de Brienne authorized the formation of their own guild, the Arti di Tintori e Saponai. But when de Brienne was overthrown in August 1343, the new regime, while giving the traditional Arti Medie and Arti Minori (the fourteen lesser guilds) more power in the government, immediately abolished the new dyers' guild. Shortly thereafter, in May 1345, after a group of wool carders and combers agitated for their own guild and higher pay, the new regime arrested and then hanged its leader, Ciuto Brandini—despite or because of a strike in his defense. The next strike, by cloth dyers demanding higher wages during the famine of August 1368, was also crushed when the Arte della Lana imposed the dreaded *divieto*.

The most famous of all the Florentine revolts was that of the Ciompi, which began at the end of the ruinous "War of the Eight Saints" against the papacy and during a severe economic depression. In June 1378, the populace attacked adherents of the pro-papal Parte Guelfa and installed a new revolutionary government. The next month, when promised reforms were not effected, a mob of industrial artisans and workers, chiefly from the cloth industry, attacked the Palazzo, demanding their own separate guild with full participation in the Florentine government. Their leader, Michele di Lando, a wool carder, became leader of the revolutionary government. By early August it had created not one but three new textile guilds, with separate representation in the government: the Arte dei Tintori (the dyers' guild, but also including carders, fullers, and weavers); the Arte dei Farsettai (the shirtmakers' guild, but including shearers); and the Arte dei Popolo Minuto (the Ciompi, by far the largest, with wool beaters and dressers, combers, spinners, and journeymen and apprentices in weaving and fulling). Dissatisfied with the pace of reforms, the Popolo Minuto leaders formed a revolutionary committee to demand greater power in the government, which responded by attacking, routing, and thoroughly crushing the Ciompi. The Arte dei Popolo Minuto was immediately abolished. The other two new guilds, which had sided with the government, were temporarily spared this fate of extinction, but only until the next communal political and economic crisis, in 1382, when the seven Arti Maggiori regained control of the reorganized twenty-one-guild government. Thereafter, the Arte della Lana encountered no further challenges to its dominance from its subordinate artisans.

Elsewhere, subsidiary textile workers did not have much better luck in establishing legal guilds, with the major exception of fifteenth-century Cologne, whose weaver-draper guild had been a leader in the 1396 revolt that established a new corporate government. The three new textile guilds were, furthermore, exclusively female: the yarn makers, the gold-thread spinners, and (from 1437) the silk makers. But these guilds lacked any political power and were in fact controlled by males, who were frequently the merchant-husbands of these artisans. The formation and subsequent activities of these guilds certainly involved no industrial strikes or rebellions.

While various other rebellions of textile workers can also be documented, their reputation for violence, if not totally undeserved, has certainly been exaggerated. The vast majority in medieval Europe were peaceful citizens; textile artisans were not directly responsible for most of the major revolts and, with the possible exception of the Ciompi revolt in 1378, they were not oppressed industrial proletarians. It should be remembered that most of them were unorganized, powerless females, working in and confined largely to their own homes. As Martha C. Howell has cogently argued, men dominated "high status" crafts in market-oriented industries such as weaving, fulling, dyeing, and shearing because they had so much greater freedom to engage in various essential activities that necessarily took place outside the home and family: some purely industrial, but also commercial, political, and military functions. In the leading textile towns some of the most important functions were those involved with guild and urban government offices, from which women were excluded, for a variety of other reasons as well, in the patriarchal society of late medieval Europe.

BIBLIOGRAPHY

In addition to the works cited in the bibliography for "Textile Technology," see the following: Thomas W. Blomquist, "The Drapers of Lucca and the Marketing of Cloth in the Mid-thirteenth Century," in David Herlihy, Robert S. Lopez, and V. Slessarev, eds., *Economy, Society, and Government in Medieval Italy* (1969); Frances Consitt, *The London Weavers' Company,* I (1933); Renée Doehaerd, *L'expansion économique belge au moyen âge* (1946); Georges Doudelez, "La révolution communale de 1280 à Ypres," in *Revue des questions historiques,* **132–133** (1938–1939); Robert S. DuPlessis and Martha C. Howell, "Reconsidering the Early Modern Urban Economy: The Cases of Leiden and Lille," in *Past and Present,* **94** (1982); Georges Espinas, *Les origines du capitalisme,* I, *Sire Jehan Boinebroke, patricien et drapier douaisien* (1933); Martha C. Howell, *Women, Production, and Patriarchy in Late Medieval Cities* (1986); Jean Lestocquoy, *Aux origines de la bourgeoisie: Les Villes de Flandre et d'Italie sous le gouvernement des patriciens, XIe–XVe siècles* (1952); John Munro, "Industrial Protectionism in Medieval Flanders: Urban or National?" in David Herlihy, Harry A. Miskimin, and A. L. Udovitch, eds., *The Medieval City* (1977), and "Monetary Contraction and Industrial Change in the Late-medieval Low Countries, 1335–1500," in Nicholas J. Mayhew, ed., *Coinage in the Low Countries (880–1500): The Third Oxford Symposium on Coinage and Monetary History* (1979); David M. Nicholas, *Town and Countryside: Social, Economic, and Political Tensions in Fourteenth-century Flanders* (1971) and "Economic Reorientation and Social Change in Fourteenth-century Flanders," in *Past and Present,* **70** (1976); Henri Nowé, *La bataille des éperons d'or* (1945); Henri Pirenne, *Belgian Democracy,* J. V. Saunders, trans. (1915), republished as *Early Democracies in the Low Countries: Urban Society and Political Conflict in the Middle Ages and the Renaissance* (1963); Georges Renard, *Histoire du travail à Florence,* 2 vols. (1913); Niccolò Rodolico, "The Struggle for the Right of Association in Fourteenth-century Florence," in *History,* n.s. 7 (1922); Ferdinand Schevill, *Medieval and Renaissance Florence,* 2 vols. (1936); Margret Wensky, "Women's Guilds in Cologne in the Later Middle Ages," in *The Journal of European Economic History,* **11** (1982); Hans van Werveke, *Jacques van Artevelde* (1943), *Gand: Esquisse d'histoire sociale* (1946), *De koopman-ondernemer en de ondernemer in de Vlaamsche lakennijverheid van de middeleeuwen* (1946), and "Esquisse d'une histoire de la draperie," in his *Miscellanea Mediaevalia* (1968).

JOHN H. MUNRO

[See also **Bruges; Class Structure, Western; Florence; Guilds and Métiers; Textile Technology; Wool.**]

TEXTILES, ISLAMIC. Textiles were exceptionally important in the art and economy of Islam from the beginning. Their role has been compared to that of steel in the modern industrial economy, and it has been estimated that in the Middle Ages textile manufacture and trade may have occupied a majority of the working population. This preeminence can be partly explained by the variety of uses to

Portion of a *ṭirāz* band. Linen cloth with inscription embroidered in tan silk, Egyptian, 10th century. NEW YORK, THE METROPOLITAN MUSEUM OF ART, GIFT OF GEORGE D. PRATT, 1931 (31.106.33)

which textiles were put in the Near East and along the Mediterranean shores. Aside from clothing, they also constituted the bulk of household furnishings. Nomad women, of course, wove tent bands, saddlebags, cradles, and other appurtenances of their mobile lives, but even in the urban centers and in the palaces furnishings consisted mainly of carpets, covers, curtains, and hangings of various kinds. Instead of chairs, people sat on cushions and leaned against bolsters, all covered with cloth whose quality and richness reflected their owners' means. Textiles played an important political role as well; aside from lavish diplomatic gifts, it was customary to reward high officials and other favorites, both at regular intervals and on special occasions, with "robes of honor" (*khil^{c}a*), turbans, and other garments woven in the rulers' own establishments and often richly decorated with embroidery and gold. It was also the caliphs' prerogative—and after 1250 that of the Mamluk sultans—to provide each year the new *kiswa,* the richly ornamented cloth that veiled the Kaaba at Mecca.

The full array of textile fibers was available in the Islamic world. Wool and linen were produced in quantity from Iran to Spain, and additional supplies of the latter were imported from Byzantium. Cotton, native to India but already cultivated as far west as Mesopotamia in the Sasanian period, was probably first produced on a large scale in the Mediterranean after the Muslim conquest; it became particularly identified with Syria and Palestine. The cultivation of silkworms had reached Persia during the time of the Sasanians and northern Syria by the sixth century, but again it was under the unified Islamic empire that this technology spread around the Mediterranean basin.

The Umayyad rulers (661–750) and their successors borrowed from the Persian and Byzantine emperors the practice of maintaining palace weaving establishments; indeed, they may actually have taken over the Byzantine imperial factory in Alexandria, which was largely manned by Copts. It was in these *dūr al-ṭirāz,* so called because *ṭirāz,* or inscription, bands were embroidered there, that most textiles for princely use were produced. In addition, private workshops specializing in particular types of textile work flourished in nearly every Islamic city and region. Trade was active both within the Islamic world and with Byzantium and Western Europe.

Although texts reveal the scope and magnitude of this activity, most of the textiles and fragments preserved in museums cannot yet be definitively assigned to specific centers. Only a few large groups of textiles from the first five Islamic centuries can be clearly identified and described. Perhaps the largest consists of simple *ṭirāz* bands, primarily from the Egyptian delta and Mesopotamia; usually they are embroidered in silk on fine glazed cotton, *mulḥam* (a combination of cotton and silk), or linen, occasionally combined with other kinds of decoration. The earliest dated example, a linen turban fragment in the Museum of Islamic Art, Cairo (no. 10846), was made for Samwīl ibn Mūsā in 707. There are important collections of *ṭirāz* textiles in the Metropolitan Museum of Art, New York; Museum of Fine Arts, Boston; Textile Museum, Washington, D.C.; Royal Ontario Museum, Toronto; Museum of Islamic Art, Cairo; and many European museums. This type of inscription band began to die out at the end of the eleventh century.

A second group represents a continuation into the Islamic period of designs belonging to Coptic and Byzantine Egypt. These textiles, primarily associated with Upper Egypt and the Faiyūm, were woven in silk, wool, or wool combined with linen and, especially at first, were characterized by bold colors among which a deep blue-green or tomato red predominated. The designs frequently consist of multiple bands, each composed of series of small elements: palmettes, abstract plant forms, running animals, and even human figures. A preference for multiple bands of small component elements, especially the running animals, persisted in Egypt through the Fatimid period (909–1171), though the colors eventually became more varied and subtle, the techniques and materials more diverse.

As for Mesopotamia, though it was the site of the caliphal capital through most of the Middle Ages, relatively few preserved pieces can be ascribed to its workshops with certainty. Aside from some *ṭirāz* bands from the first group, the most distinctive are the gold-embroidered silks and *mulḥams* attributed to Baghdad on the basis of inscriptions, technique, and richness of decoration. An important small group of such pieces is in the Museum of Fine Arts, Boston. Despite the small number of surviving examples, however, the prestige of Baghdad can be gauged from its impact on other centers. Iraqi textiles were reaching Spain in the tenth century and were much admired there; so great was their reputation that a famous silk, also in the Museum of Fine Arts, though manufactured in Spain in the eleventh or early twelfth century, was falsely inscribed "made in the city of Baghdad." Closer to the source, Mesopotamian embroideries had a demonstrable influence on the style of some stone relief carvings on the Kharpūt gate (909–910) at Āmid (modern Diyarbakir) in the northernmost reaches of Mesopotamia. Even one important woven silk made for a patron from Khorāsān, the famous elephant silk of al-Qāʾid Abū Manṣūr

Textile fragment of silk and metal thread showing monocephalic eagle and medallion frame. From the reliquary of S. Librada in the cathedral of Sigüenza, 12th century. NEW YORK, THE METROPOLITAN MUSEUM OF ART, FUNDS FROM VARIOUS DONORS, 1958 (58.85.2)

Bikhtakīn (*d.* 961), now in the Louvre, reveals close connections in the style of its animal drawing with the same embroideries.

This silk was found in a reliquary from the small abbey church of St. Josse near Calais. Indeed, scholars owe to the European practice of wrapping holy relics in precious imported silks—often the fragmentary remains of worn-out clerical vestments—much of their present knowledge of medieval Islamic weaving. Particularly noteworthy is a group of seventh- and eighth-century silks from the region of Bukhara, first identified by means of a Soghdian inscription in India ink on the back of a piece in the collegiate church of Notre Dame at Huy in Belgium. With its rows of medallions enclosing symmetrically paired animals flanking stylized trees or plants, this silk is closely linked to at least eleven others in various European and American collections. Many are known to have been preserved in church reliquaries, but two were found in the library at the Buddhist site of Ch'ien-fo-tung in eastern Turkestan. This so-called "Zandanī-jī group" takes its name from the small weaving town of Zandana, near Bukhara, where it is thought to have originated.

Spain, Syria, and the Iranian province of Fārs are among other regions known from textual sources to have supported flourishing textile industries in the early Islamic centuries, but it has not yet proved possible to assign large and clearly defined groups to any of them.

The surviving medieval textiles from the twelfth century and later, though probably proportionately much greater in number than those from earlier periods, have received little systematic scholarly attention, with the exception of the rich output of the Spanish peninsula. Although Spain had produced textiles from the beginning of the Islamic period—the most famous early example is the so-called "veil of Hishām" in the Real Academia de la Historia, Madrid—it is best known for a splendid group of diasper-weave silks produced under the Almoravids (1056–1147) and their Almohad successors (1130–1269). One of these silks, the largest piece of which is preserved in the parish church of San Martín at Quintanaortuña near Burgos, is inscribed to the Almoravid Caliph ᶜAlī (*r.* 1106–1142). The group as a whole is distinguished by hieratic designs in medallion frames: confronted animals flanking stylized plant forms, as on the Baghdad forgery mentioned earlier; monocephalic or bicephalic "eagles" (frequently grasping prey), as on a textile from the reliquary of Santa Librada in the cathedral of Sigüenza; or human figures between pairs of animals, as on the famous "lion strangler" silk found in the tomb of Bishop Bernard of Calvó at Vich. Another noteworthy group of Spanish silks is woven with repeated scenes of drinkers and entertainers.

A collection of silk textiles that appeared on the market in the late 1920's and 1930's was said to have been discovered in a tomb near Rayy in north-central Iran. Its authenticity is, however, still a matter of heated debate. No other textiles can be assigned with certainty to twelfth- or thirteenth-century Iran. There are, however, a few silks that include among their background motifs large multipetaled palmettes on scrolling stems; these palmette scrolls can be closely paralleled on contemporary Iranian ceramics and in Koran illuminations and thus probably justify an Iranian attribution.

In the thirteenth century Anatolia emerged as a prominent Islamic weaving region. It is from western Anatolia that the earliest surviving Islamic pile carpets are known, and the same area continued to produce a rich variety of carpets for many centuries. These carpets were much sought after in Europe, and the basic chronology of types and styles in fact depends on representations in European paintings.

Egypt continued as a major textile producer through the fourteenth century. The multiple-band designs so long popular there persisted into the Mamluk period, though with bolder and more monumental inscriptions and animal bands that, though less frequent, were more naturalistic in style. More innovative were silks reflecting Mamluk appreciation of Chinese motifs (particularly the distinctive large lotus blossom), an influence equally visible in the other decorative arts of the period. A series of such silks woven in the time of the sultan al-Malik al-Nāṣir Muḥammad (*r.* 1293–1340, with interruptions) and his contemporaries the Rasulid sultans of Yemen exemplify this group; many of them exhibit large, flame-shaped blossoms containing sultanic inscriptions. Outside courtly circles a new type of embroidery appeared, probably in the thirteenth century; it is characterized by cursive inscriptions, interlaced grids, S-curves, and half-palmettes stylized in wedge shapes. One example has been excavated at Quṣeir al-Qadīm on the Red Sea, which has yielded valuable information on utilitarian textiles of Upper Egypt in the early Mamluk period.

As for Mongol Iran, information is still based almost entirely on the depiction of textiles in manuscript miniatures of the fourteenth century. They, too, are remarkable for the frequency of Chinese elements in both costume and pattern. In fourteenth-century Islamic Spain, on the other hand, vegetal, as well as figural, motifs gave way almost entirely to geometrical interlaces and radial star designs comparable to those on the ceramic revetments of the Alhambra in Granada.

BIBLIOGRAPHY

Esin Atil, "Textiles and Rugs," in *Renaissance of Islam: Art of the Mamluks* (1981), 223–228; John Beckwith, "Coptic Textiles," in *CIBA Review,* **12** (1959); Nancy P. Britton, *A Study of Some Early Islamic Textiles in the Museum of Fine Arts, Boston* (1938); Florence E. Day, "The Inscription of the Boston 'Baghdad' Silk: A Note on Method in Epigraphy," in *Ars orientalis,* **1** (1954); *The Encyclopaedia of Islam,* "Ṭirāz," 1st ed., IV

(1934), and "Ḥarīr," 2nd ed., III (1971); C. Enlart, "Un tissu persan du Xe siècle découvert à Saint-Josse (Pas-de-Calais)," in *Monuments et mémoires publiés par l'Académie des Inscriptions et Belles-Lettres,* **24** (1920); Kurt Erdmann, "Turkish Carpets," in *Seven Hundred Years of Oriental Carpets,* Hanna Erdmann, ed., May H. Beattie and Hildegard Herzog, trans. (1970), 41–60; S. D. Goitein, *A Mediterranean Society,* I (1967), esp. 101–108; Hassan M. El-Hawary, "Un tissu abbaside de Perse," in *Bulletin de l'Institut d'Égypte,* **16** (1933–1934); Ernst Kühnel, "La tradition copte dans les tissus musulmans," in *Bulletin de la Société d'Archéologie Copte,* **4** (1938); Ernst Kühnel and Louisa Bellinger, *Catalogue of Dated Tiraz Fabrics* (1952); Carl J. Lamm, *Cotton in Medieval Textiles of the Near East* (1937); Maurice Lombard, *Les textiles dans le monde musulman du VIIe au XIIe siècle* (1978); Muhammad A. Marzouk, *History of Textile Industry in Alexandria, 331 B.C.–1517 A.D.* (1955); Florence L. May, *Silk Textiles of Spain: Eighth to Fifteenth Century* (1957); R. B. Serjeant, *Islamic Textiles* (1972); Dorothy G. Shepherd and W. B. Henning, "Zandanījī Identified?" in *Aus der Welt der islamischen Kunst,* Richard Ettinghausen, ed. (1959), 15–40; Donald S. Whitcomb and Janet H. Johnson, eds., *Quseir al-Qadim 1978* (1979), chaps. 5 and 7.

For the controversy about the Rayy silk textiles, see Gaston Wiet, *Soieries persanes* (1948), Florence E. Day's review of same with reply by Wiet and counterreply by Day in *Ars islamica,* **15–16** (1951), 231–250; the entire issues of *Bulletin de liaison du Centre International d'Étude des Textiles Anciens,* **37** (1973) and **39–40** (1974); and Patricia L. Fiske, ed., *Irene Emery Roundtable on Museum Textiles, 1974 Proceedings: Archaeological Textiles* (1975), 175–204.

ESTELLE WHELAN

[See also **Bedestan; Coptic Art; Costume, Islamic; Dībāj; Khil^c^a; Kiswa; Mulḥam; Rugs and Carpets; Silk; Ṭirāz Stuffs; Trade, Islamic.**]